FORD MOTORS

1950
4th edition

At mid-century, advertising entered a golden age of meeting pent-up consumer demand for virtually every category of product.

DANSKIN

1966
5th edition

Advertising coped with a changing society and produced some of its most creative advertising.

It's the real thing. Coke.
Wouldn't an ice cold Coke taste good right now?

COCA-COLA

1973
6th edition

Advertising felt the full effects of television as print ads adapted their messages to an audience of viewers rather than readers.

McDONALDS

1979
7th edition

Enlightened advertisers began the first small steps in recognizing the emergence of a diversified society with recognition of women and minorities.

Kleppner's

Advertising
Procedure

THIRTEENTH EDITION

Kleppner's
Advertising Procedure

THIRTEENTH EDITION

J. Thomas Russell
UNIVERSITY OF GEORGIA

W. Ronald Lane
UNIVERSITY OF GEORGIA

PRENTICE HALL, Englewood Cliffs, New Jersey 07632

Library of Congress Cataloging-in-Publication Data
Russell, Thomas, 1941–
    Kleppner's advertising procedure / J. Thomas Russell, W. Ronald
Lane.—13th ed.
       p. cm.—(The Prentice Hall series in marketing)
  Includes bibliographical references and index.
  ISBN 0-13-348830-6
  1. Advertising.   I. Lane, W. Ronald, 1940–   II. Kleppner,
Otto, 1899– Advertising procedure. III. Title. IV. Series.
HF5823.K45 1995
659.1—dc20   94-25208
                                          CIP

Project Manager: Cathleen Profitko
Acquisitions Editor: David Borkowsky
Editor-in-Chief: Jim Boyd
Director of Production/Manufacturing: Joanne Jay
Managing Editor: Joyce Turner
Manufacturing Buyer: Vincent Scelta
Design Director: Patricia Wosczyk
Interior Design: BB&K Design
Cover Design: BB&K Design
Copy Editor: Brenda Melissaratos
Proofreader: Florrie Gadson, Marielle Reiter
Assistant Editor: Melissa Steffens
Editorial Assistant: Theresa Festa
Production Assistant: Florrie Gadson
Cover: Hunter Freeman Studio/San Francisco. Courtesy of AT&T Culver Pictures, Inc. Courtesy of Coca Cola.

© 1996, 1993, 1990, 1988, 1986, 1983, 1979, 1973, 1966, 1950, 1941, 1933, 1925
by Prentice-Hall, Inc.
A Simon & Schuster Company
Englewood Cliffs, New Jersey 07632

Printed in the United States of America

10 9 8 7 6 5 4 3 2 1

ISBN 0-13-348830-6

Prentice-Hall International (UK) Limited, *London*
Prentice-Hall of Australia Pty. Limited, *Sydney*
Prentice-Hall Canada, Inc., *Toronto*
Prentice-Hall Hispanoamericana, S.A., *Mexico*
Prentice-Hall of India Private Limited, *New Delhi*
Prentice-Hall of Japan, Inc., *Tokyo*
Simon & Schuster Asia Pte. Ltd., *Singapore*
Editora Prentice-Hall do Brasil, Ltda., *Rio de Janeiro*

Brief
Contents

Contents

Preface

The thirteenth edition of *Kleppner's Advertising Procedure* is a combination of its traditional strengths with significant new material to introduce students to the exciting changes in marketing, advertising, and media. Change is the key element in modern advertising, and instructors and students will find a number of changes in the current text. As has been the case in the past 12 editions of the book, the authors seek to emphasize the important concepts of advertising and promotion and discuss these in an environment that places these functions in a matrix of the total business function.

The current text presents advertising in a context of marketing communication and integrated marketing. As we move into the twentieth century, students must be conversant with all forms of promotion. They must be flexible enough to adapt to all forms of communication that are likely to persuade the diverse and fragmented audiences to whom they will sell their products and services. Several examples of products categories and individual companies are carried across a number of chapters so that students can study the manner in which the same products are sold through a number of media and with different creative approaches.

Despite a more integrated approach to marketing communications, the major emphasis of the text continues to the practice and philosophy of advertising. The text is not a marketing book but rather an advertising book that places the advertising function with a marketing framework. The authors seek to show how the advertising function must be coordinated with all other aspects of marketing communications.

The thirteenth edition also offers a global perspective to the advertising function. Recent changes in agency ownership, the growing importance of multinational advertising, and the cultural and ethnic nature of the U.S. market are all discussed throughout the text. It is rare that companies selling any product or service, even those sold exclusively in the United States, can be successful without some international perspective. Some of the major marketing disasters of recent years have been caused by an ignorance and sensitivity to the cultures and customs of other groups within our society or in other countries.

Advertising is one of the most apparent and, to many, controversial business functions. Advertisers are increasingly coming to realize that their messages have effects far beyond the intended selling messages. For example, the manner in which minorities and women are portrayed in advertisements and commercials can offer realistic pictures of how these groups function in society or, conversely, can be a means of negatively stereotyping these people. By the same token, many nonprofit and public opinion advocacy groups are using advertising as an effective and efficient means of exposing their messages to the general public.

Students must understand both the intended and unintended messages conveyed by advertising. In a diverse society where consumers are very aware of the power, for good and evil, of advertising, it is imperative that advertisers perceive the totality of their messages.

The thirteenth edition also explores the exciting new world of new media and the current and future impact that these technologies will have on advertising. In the near future, technology will provide speedier and more personal communication. It also will provide the public with the availability of two-way communication much more under the control of the audience. The transition from one-way to two-way communication offers a number of challenges and opportunities to advertisers. The text seeks to put these emerging media in a context of how they will affect advertising as well as which ones are truly practical in the coming years.

As in past years the text is designed for those students who plan careers in advertising, for those who seek an introduction to the field as a supplement to other majors and even for those wanting to become more educated consumers. Regardless of the career goals of those reading the text, the overview of advertising seeks to define its function as an integral part of our everyday lives.

The text is divided into six parts with a total of 26 chapters. The first section begins with a historical overview of the foundations of selling and exchange of goods up to the present. Chapter 2 offers a brief description of the various functions of advertising at all levels. The authors seek to delineate the flexibility of advertising to solve a host of marketing communication problems as well as outline the manner in which advertising complements other forms of promotion.

Part 2 discusses the foundations of research and audience analysis so imperative to successful advertising. Chapter 3 introduces the concept of the produt life cycle and the strategies needed to keep products vital in a changing marketplace. Chapter Four addresses the problems of identifying prime prospects and developing plans to reach these groups most effectively.

Part 3 emphasizes the organization of the advertising function from both the agency and the client perspectives. As the advertising function grows more complex, management of the function has changed dramatically. In Chapters 5 and 6 the process of planning and executing advertising is discussed. In addition, the various skills needed to carry out sophisticated advertising is discussed.

In Part 4 we begin our discussion of the various media formats that carry promotional messages to audiences. In recent years the cost and diversity of media have increasingly required significant expertise of media executives. New technology being introduced each year will make this area even more interesting and demanding in the future.

In Chapter 7 we introduced the general topic of media planning and a comparative overview of the major media categories. This chapter is followed by seven chapters that discuss in detail the role of the individual media in carrying out the advertising communications function. The media planner must be well versed in marketing, careful and proficient in statistics, and able to interpret research data. This section emphasizes the fact that there are no superior or inferior media. Rather, different communication vehicles are more suitable for solving certain types of problems. The media planner must be able to judge objectively all media and promotional vehicles to select the combination that will best serve the specific needs of a particular marketing problems.

In Part 5 we begin our discussion of the creative function. While advertising is largely identified with the finished advertisements and commercials we see everyday, creative ideas are usually the result of research that offers insight into consumer production selection, and media preferences. Chapters 15–24 seek to outline the many steps of planning, research, and production necessary to bring the rough idea to fruition as a finished ad. Contrary to popular opinion, great advertising is rarely the result of spontaneous ideas but rather the fruit of long hours of hard work and study.

This edition concludes with a discussion of some of the specialized areas of advertising. Chapter 24 discusses the special problems inherent in advertising on a multinational stage. Chapter 25 outlines the many regulatory and legal pitfalls facing advertising in a litigious society. Finally, Chapter 26 brings into focus the ethical and economic foundations of advertising.

The thirteenth edition of *Kleppner's Advertising Procedure* seeks to brings students the latest information concerning the existing field of advertising. At the same time, it recognizes that advertising is both an art and a science. The authors hope that we have offered you insights into the profession and at the same time conveyed our sense of anticipation and enthusiasm over this everchanging but never dull business.

J. Thomas Russell
W. Ronald Lane

Supplements

Completely revised, expanded, and fully integrate, this new comprehensive ancillary package is available upon adoption of KLEPPNER'S ADVERTISING PROCEDURE, 13/E

Instructor's Resource Manual with Video Guide

Complete with chapter overview, learning objectives, a detailed lecture outline, answers to all end-of-chapter questions, class projects and exercises, and additional readings, this guide provides an invaluable teaching tool. The lecture outline provides a concise overview of each chapter and thoroughly integrates all key lecture components, including all three video libraries (ABC News, EFFIE, and New York Festivals) and the color transparencies. Each chapter offers at least three projects or exercises at various levels of difficulty, plus a special "Humor in Advertising" section with additional class projects.

Test Item File

Includes multiple-choice, true/false, and essay questions. The test bank is designed to reflect Kleppner's practical approach through realistic questions and an applications-oriented approach. In addition, the test bank incorporates questions based on the extensive video material available with the thirteenth edition.

3.5" IBM Test Manager

This powerful computerized testing package, available for DOS-based computers allows instructors to create their own personalized exams using questions from the Test Item File. It offers full mouse support, complete question editing, random test generation, graphics and printing capabilities. Toll free technical support is offered to all users, and the Test Manager is free upon adoption.

ABC News Video Library

Our ABC News/Prentice Hall Video Library contains timely and relevant video segments from acclaimed ABC News programs, such as Nightline, World News Tonight, and Business World, available for the college market exclusively through Prentice Hall. Designed specifically to complement the text, this library is an excellent tool for bringing students into contact with the world outside the classroom. Fully supported by integrated teaching notes in the Instructor's Resource Manual.

EFFIE Video Library

This video features some of the award-winning campaigns from EFFIE, the only advertising honor awarded on the basis of objective marketing results. Since 1969, the New York chapter of the American Marketing Association has been awarding the EFFIE to advertisers and their agencies. The EFFIE competition recognizes the highest achievement in advertising: superior results in meeting sales objectives. All text video case clips are fully supported by integrated teaching notes in the Instructor's Resource Manual.

New York Festivals Video Library

In conjunction with the New York Festivals International Advertising Awards, Prentice Hall offers you and your students a comprehensive bank of award-winning international advertisements that will enhance your in-class discussions and add unparalleled "real world" relevance to your lectures. These video clips are available exclusively from Prentice Hall. All clips are supported by teaching notes in a separate New York Festivals Video Guide. In addition, segments are referenced in the lecture outlines within the Instructor's Resource Manual for easy lecture integration.

Color Transparencies

50 full-color transparencies highlight key concepts for presentation and offer additional advertisements for class discussion and analysis. Each transparency is accompanied by a full page of teaching notes that includes relevant key terms and discussion points from the chapters as well as additional material from supplementary sources. All acetates and lecture notes are available on Powerpoint 4.0. The disk is designed to allow you to present the transparencies to your class electronically. The Color Transparencies are also available in slide format.

New York Times/Prentice Hall "Themes of the Times" Program for Advertising

Prentice Hall and The New York Times, one of the world's top news publications, join to expand your students' knowledge beyond the walls of the classroom. Upon adoption, professors and students receive a specialized "mini-newspaper" containing a broad spectrum of carefully chosen articles that focus on events and issues in the world of advertising as well as on some of the news-making marketing professionals of the 1990s. To ensure complete timeliness, this supplement is updated twice a year.

Acknowledgements

This 13th edition of *Kleppner's Advertising Procedure,* like its predecessors, depends on the expertise and cooperation of numerous companies, advertising agencies, trade associations, and individuals. The authors are most appreciative of the time and advice offered by dozens of experts in the various fields of advertising, marketing, and promotion. While the authors are solely responsible for the content of the text, we are sincerely indebted to the following people who have provided wise counsel in so many areas.

Joe Anson	Anson-Stoner
Lisa Barber	Cole Henderson Drake, Inc.
Amy Barkema	Alternative Postal Delivery, Inc.
Connie Barry	Shelter Advertising Association
Tanya Baugus	Promotional Products Association International
John Beeze	(sic) Advertising
Sheri Bevil	Folks, Inc.
Erin Boyd	Fitzgerald & Company
Craig Briggs	McCann-Erickson Atlanta
Edyie Brooks	Healthtext, Inc.
Mona R. Brooks	University of New Orleans
Tammy Carney	Direct American Marketing, Inc.
Ralph Casado	Promotion Solutions, Inc.
Marion Cofer	Magazine Publishers of America
Cathy Coffey	Cox Enterprises, Inc.
Frank Compton	Sawyer Riley Compton, Inc.
Tom Cordner	Team One Advertising
Alan Cronk	Star Watch
Bruce Danielson	John H. Harland Co.
Sande Deitch	Miles, Inc.
Rick Devlin	Radio Network Association
Jim Drawbridge	Nabisco Brands, Inc.
Tim Duncan	Advertiser Syndicated Television Association
Karen Elliott	Folks, Inc.
Vincent J. Fazio	Cabletelevision Advertising Bureau, Inc.
Charlie Fedak	Conocraft
Randy Fluharty	Biltmore Company
Michael Fowler	Brookdale Community College
Jeff Francis	Keep America Beautiful, Inc.
Angelica French	Outdoor Advertising Association of America
Susan Frost	The Morrison Agency
Bob Green	Bob Green Production
Debra Goldstein	Council of Better Business Bureaus, Inc.
Jeff Goodby	Goodby, Silverstein & Partners
Pola B. Gupta	University of Northern Iowa
Pam Guthrie	Price/McNabb, Inc.
Ron Huey	The Martin Agency
Leigh Kain	Leigh Kain Advertising & Design
Tom Kane	Anson, Stoner, Inc.

Karen Kcenehan	Semco, Henschel-Steinau, Inc.
Paul Kessinger	Actmedia, Inc.
Steve Knipe	NewsRadio WGST
Alfred S. Larkin, Jr.	*The Boston Globe*
J. D. MacKay	Radio Advertising Bureau
Skip McKinstry	Oklahoma City Ad Club
Fred Moench	Lowe's Companies
James Mountjoy	Loeffler Ketchum Mountjoy, Inc.
Gary Mueller	Birdsall Voss & Kloppenburg
Jamie Nichols-Hernandez	Cramer-Krasselt
Nancy Osborn	NAA Foundation
Philip Payne	Doe-Anderson Advertising Agency
Bernard H. Petrina	Executive Management Renewal Programs
Jim Pollak	Pollak Levitt Chaiet Advertising, Inc.
Tracy Poltie	International Advertising Association
Terence Poltrack	*Presstime*/NAA
Herman Ramsey	WGNX-TV
Michael Reinemer	Claritas, Inc.
Richard Riley	Sawyer Riley Compton, Inc.
Tom Robinson	Robinson & Associates
Kim Rowland	Kim Rowland Creative
Ken Sammon	Traffic Audit Bureau
Earl C. Sawin	KHYPE
Phil Sawyer	Roper Starch Worldwide, Inc.
Gene Sekeres	Youngstown State University
Ron & Sara Sharbo	Sharbo & Co.
Paul Silverman	Mullen Advertising
Mark Simonton	J. Walter Thompson
Tommy V. Smith	University of Southern Mississippi
Ron Strauss	Gordon Baily & Associates
Theckla Sterrett	Sterrett Dymond Advertising, Inc.
Nunciata A. Sullivan	Spencer Products, Inc.
Tom Swinson	Longwater, Inc.
Mike Trost	Publishers Express
Paula A. Veale	The Advertising Council
Andrea Wagenaar	Campbell Mithun Esty
Ron Waggener	Waggener & Associates, Inc.
Francis Wee	Saatchi & Saatchi Advertising
Lonnie Willard	Nabisco Foods Group
C. Donald Williams	C. Donald William Advertising, Inc.
Maria Zimmann	Nielson Media Research
Curt Zimmerman	The Zimmerman Agency
Bill Kurynetz	POPAI

A book such as this could never be produced without the assistance of many people at Prentice-Hall, Inc., especially our Editor, David Borkowsky and Assistant Editor, Melissa Steffens. As you would expect with so many ads and exhibits, there has to be a very special production person expertly putting all the pieces together. We were very fortunate to have such a jewel in Cathleen Profitko, Production Editor.

The Authors would also like to take this opportunity to thank Ruhanna Neal, Clara Stewart, and Donna LeBlond of the University of Georgia's College of Journalism staff for their invaluable help in the preparation of the manuscript.

About the
Authors

OTTO KLEPPNER
(1899–1982)

A graduate of New York University, Otto Kleppner started out in advertising as a copywriter. After several such jobs, he became advertising manager at Prentice-Hall, where he began to think that he, too, "could write a book." Some years later, he also thought that he could run his own advertising agency, and both ideas materialized eminently. His highly successful agency handled advertising for leading accounts (Dewar's Scotch Whisky, I. W. Harper Bourbon and other Schenley brands, Saab Cars, Doubleday Book Clubs, and others). His book became a bible for advertising students and his writings have been published in eight languages.

Active in the American Association of Advertising Agencies, Mr. Kleppner served as a director, a member of the Control Committee, chairman of the Committee of Government, Public and Educator Relations, and a governor of the New York Council. He was awarded the Nichols Cup (now the Crain Cup) for distinguished service to the teaching of advertising.

J. THOMAS RUSSELL

Thomas Russell is Professor of Advertising and Dean of the College of Journalism and Mass Communication at the University of Georgia. Tom received his Ph.D. in communications from the University of Illinois and has taught and conducted research in a number of areas of advertising and marketing. He was formerly editor of the Journal of Advertising and is the author of numerous articles and research papers in both academic and trade publications.

In addition to his academic endeavors, Tom has worked as a retail copywriter as well as principal in his own advertising agency. Russell is a member of a number of academic and professional organizations including the American Academy of Advertising, American Advertising Federation, and the Arthur W. Page Society. He has also served as a judge and faculty member for the Institute of Advanced Advertising Studies sponsored by the American Association of Advertising Agencies.

W. RONALD LANE

Ron has worked in most aspects of advertising. He began in advertising and promotion for a drug manufacturer. Ron has worked in creative and account services for clients including Coca-Cola, National Broiler Council, Minute-Maid, and Callaway Gardens Country Store.

He is a professor of advertising at the University of Georgia and has served as advertising manager of the Journal of Advertising. He was coordinator of the Institute of Advanced Advertising Studies sponsored by the American Association of Advertising Agencies for six years. He is also a partner in SLRS Communications, Inc., an advertising-marketing agency.

Currently, Ron is a member of the American Advertising Federation's (AAF) Academic Division, Executive Committee. He has been the AAF Academic Division Chair. Served as member of the AAF Board of Directors, Council of Governors, and Executive Committee. He has been a member of the Board of Directors of the American Advertising Foundation. He's been an ADDY Awards judge numerous times and has been a member of the Advertising Age Creative Workshop faculty. He is a member of the Atlanta Advertising Club, American Academy of Advertising, American Marketing Association, and the ACEJMC Accrediting Council.

PART
I
The Place of Advertising

SEE, HEAR AND FEEL THE DIFFERENCE

"IT'S GOT 'LET'S GO' STARTS AND CAT'S PAW STOPS"

To understand advertising,

it is necessary to know something of its colorful history and the fundamentals of both the art and the science of this complex field. While modern advertising is largely a product of this century, communication has been a part of the selling process almost as long as goods have been exchanged from one person to another. The advent of technology and research has made the advertising process increasingly sophisticated in recent decades. However, the goals of advertising have not changed since the clay tablets of ancient Babylonia or the tavern signs in medieval England. In Chapter 1 we trace the 7,000-year-long development of advertising.

Advertising is not a single technique, but rather it is adapted to the needs of a host of products, companies, and marketing strategies. In Chapter 2 we examine the versatility of advertising and its uses and misuses as it attempts to solve a host of marketing communication problems and, through a number of creative approaches, bring products to a sometimes indifferent public.

Background

1

of Today's Advertising

CHAPTER OBJECTIVES

The history of advertising is closely related to the economic development of the United States. After reading this chapter you will understand:

- **The development of product promotion**
- **Advertising and the American industrial revolution**
- **The emergence of responsible advertising**
- **Advertising growth during the post-World War II era**
- **Advertising and global marketing and communication**

The exchange of goods and the need to identify both the source of these goods and those who made them **have been** well-established functions since prehistoric times. **However,** modern advertising has its roots as a vital part of a sophisticated economic system in the United States of the late nineteenth and early twentieth centuries. **As we will discuss in this chapter,** the first movement toward a formal advertising industry can be found in the advertising space sellers and newspaper directories of the 1870s.

4

Advertisements of the period promoted local goods and outlets and were closer to the simple product notices and postings of the seventeenth century than to the modern advertising we see today. The shift from these rudimentary product notices to sophisticated advertising resulted from "the development of national markets for the branded, standardized products of large-scale manufacturers. Striking innovations in technology and corporate organization resulted in mass production; selling quantities of goods so produced to millions of consumers often required intensive advertising."[1]

The convergence of the availability of branded products, the ability to provide national distribution, and a growing middle class as a market for these products had evolved sufficiently by 1920 to support the creation of an advertising industry that demonstrated most of the basic functions found among modern agencies and corporate advertising departments today.

The two elements missing in much of the advertising industry of the early years of this century were (1) an ethical framework for judging promotional messages and (2) research to measure the success of these messages. Despite efforts as early as 1890 to ensure honest advertising, it would be many years before the industry adopted effective means of self-regulation.

Likewise, the pioneering work of early advertising researchers such as Claude Hopkins would not gain widespread acceptance until the latter half of this century. "Several agencies boasted of . . . research into consumer attitudes in the late 1920s, but their crude, slapdash methods made these 'surveys' of questionable value in providing accurate feedback. One agency reported that it could obtain quick, inexpensive results . . . by having all members of the staff send questionnaires to their friends."[2] Generally, the advertisers of the period thought that an intuitive "feel" for the consumer was quite sufficient to produce effective advertising. However, research did exist in the many mail-order ads of the day that could measure results by returns of coupons. However, pretesting of advertising was largely unknown.

Let's begin our survey of this exciting business enterprise by examining the history of advertising, which we will divide into three broad periods:

1. *The premarketing era.* From the start of product exchange in prehistoric times to the middle of the eighteenth century, buyers and sellers communicated in very primitive ways. For most of this period "media" such as clay tables, town criers, and tavern signs were the best way to communicate a product or service. Only in the latter decades of the period did primitive printing appear.

2. *The mass communication era.* From the 1700s to the early decades of this century, advertisers were increasingly able to reach large segments of the population, first with faster presses and later through broadcast media.

3. *The research era.* During the past 50 years advertisers have methodically improved the techniques of identifying and reaching narrowly targeted audiences with messages prepared specifically for each group or individual (in the case of direct mail). Modern communication technology has aided in this quest for the perfect advertising campaign.

Premarketing Era

The period from prehistoric times to the 18th century. During this time, buyers and sellers communicated in very primitive ways.

The Mass Communication Era

From the 1700s to the early decades of this century, advertisers were able to reach large segments of the population through the mass media.

The Research Era

In recent years advertisers increasingly have been able to identify narrowly defined audience segments through sophisticated research methods.

---

[1]Daniel Pope, *The Making of Modern Advertising* (New York: Basic Books, 1946), p. 5.
[2]Roland Marchand, *Advertising the American Dream* (Berkeley: University of California Press, 1985), p. 76.

In its evolution as a marketing power, advertising has become a major economic and social force. Advertising practitioners have come under close public scrutiny, and they find themselves working within a complex legal and regulatory framework. Perhaps the most important change in twentieth-century advertising is the sense of social responsibility of advertisers. Many advertising practices that were almost routine a century ago are universally condemned by the industry today. Advertisers realize that public trust is the key to successful advertising. Throughout the remainder of this chapter we will discuss the forces that have shaped contemporary advertising.

BEGINNINGS

The urge to advertise seems to be a part of human nature, evidenced since ancient times. Of the 5,000-year recorded history of advertising right up to our present television satellite age, the part that is most significant begins when the United States emerged as a great manufacturing nation about 100 years ago. The early history of advertising, however, is far too fascinating to pass by without a glance.

It is not surprising that the people who gave the world the Tower of Babel also left the earliest known evidence of advertising. A Babylonian clay tablet of about 3000 B.C. bears inscriptions for an ointment dealer, a scribe, and a shoemaker. Papyri exhumed from the ruins of Thebes show that the ancient Egyptians had a better medium on which to write their messages. (Alas, the announcements preserved in papyrus offer rewards for the return of runaway slaves.) The Greeks were among those who relied on town criers to chant the arrival of ships with cargoes of wines, spices, and metals. Often a crier was accompanied by a musician who kept him in the right key. Town criers later became the earliest medium for public announcements in many European countries, and they continued to be used for centuries. (At this point, we must digress to tell about a promotion idea used by innkeepers in France around A.D. 1100 to tout their fine wines: They would have the town crier blow a horn, gather a group—and offer samples!)

Roman merchants, too, had a sense of advertising. The ruins of Pompeii contain signs in stone or terra-cotta, advertising what the shops were selling: a row of hams for a butcher shop (Exhibit 1.1), a cow for a dairy, a boot for a shoemaker. The Pompeiians also knew the art of telling their story to the public by means of painted wall signs like this one (tourism was indeed one of advertising's earliest subjects):

- **Traveler**
- **Going from here to the twelfth tower**
- **There Sarinus keeps a tavern**

- **This is to request you to enter**
- **Farewell**

Outdoor advertising has proved to be one of the most enduring forms of advertising. It survived the decline of the Roman empire to become the decorative art of European inns in the seventeenth and eighteenth centuries. That was still an age of widespread illiteracy, so inns vied with one another in creating attractive signs that all could recognize. This accounts for the charming names of old inns, especially in England—such as the Three Squirrels, the Man in the Moon, the Hole in the Wall (Exhibit 1.2). In 1614, England passed a law, probably the earliest on advertising, that prohibited signs from

One of the oldest signs known. It identified a butcher shop in Pompeii.

extending more than eight feet out from a building. (Longer signs pulled down too many house fronts.) Another law required signs to be high enough to give clearance to an armored man on horseback. In 1740, the first printed outdoor poster (referred to as a "hoarding") appeared in London.

ORIGINS OF NEWSPAPER ADVERTISING

Johann Gutenberg

Began the era of mass communication in 1438 with the invention of movable type.

The next most enduring advertising medium, the newspaper, was the offspring of Johann Gutenberg's invention of printing from movable type (about 1438), which, of course, changed communication methods for the whole world. About 40 years after the invention, William Caxton of London printed the first ad in English—a handbill of the rules for the guidance of the clergy at Easter. This was tacked up on church doors. (It became the first printed outdoor ad in English.) But the printed newspaper was a long time coming. It really emerged from the newsletters, handwritten by professional writers, for nobles and others who wanted to be kept up to date on the news, especially of the court and important events—very much in the spirit of today's Washington newsletters.

The first ad in any language to be printed in a disseminated sheet appeared in a German news pamphlet in about 1525. And what do you think this ad was for? A book extolling the virtues of a mysterious drug. (The Food and Drug Administration did not exist in those days.) But news pamphlets did not come out regularly; one published in 1591 contained news of the previous three years. It was from such beginnings, however, that the printed newspaper emerged. The first printed English newspaper came out in 1622, the *Weekly Newes of London*. The first ad in an English newspaper appeared in 1625.

Siquis—Tack-Up Advertisements

Siquis

Handwritten posters in sixteenth- and seventeenth-century England—forerunners of modern advertising.

The forerunner of our present want ads bore the strange name of *siquis*. The clergy were apparently the first to make use of the written word for the purpose of bringing together the forces of supply and demand. A candidate seeking a clerical position would post a notice setting forth his qualifications, while someone having an appointment to make would post a notice specifying the requirements. These early "want ads" were usually in Latin and began *si quis* ("if anybody"): hence the name siquis. The name continued, although soon these notices covered a variety of subjects, including lost-and-found objects, runaway apprentices, and so on.[3]

Advertising in the English newspapers continued to feature similar personal and local announcements. The British have, in fact, shown so much interest in classified ads that until a few years ago the *London Times* filled its first page with classified advertising.

---

[3]George Burton Hotchkiss, *An Outline of Advertising* (New York: Macmillan, 1957), p. 10.

EXHIBIT

1.2

· · · · · · · · · · · · · · · · ·

Signs outside seven-
teenth-century inns.

Hog in Armour

Three Squirrels

King's Porter and Dwarf

Harrow and Doublet

The Ape

Hole in the Wall
"A Guide for Malt Worms"

Barley Mow

Bull and Mouth

Man in the Moon

Goose and Gridiron

Advertising Comes to America

The Pilgrims arrived on American shores before the *Weekly Newes of London* was first published, so they had had little chance to learn about newspapers. But later colonists acquainted them with the idea, and the first American newspaper to carry ads appeared in 1704, the *Boston Newsletter* (note the newsletter identification). It printed an ad offering a reward for the capture of a thief and the return of several sorts of men's apparel—more akin to the ad offering a reward for returned slaves written on Egyptian papyrus thousands of years before than to the advertising printed in the United States today. By the time the United States was formed, the colonies had 30 newspapers. Their advertising, like that of the English newspapers of the time, consisted mostly of ads we would describe today as classified and local.

THREE MOMENTOUS DECADES: 1870–1900

Neither those ads nor all the ads that appeared from ancient Egyptian days until the American industrial revolution explain the development of advertising in the United States. The history of advertising in the United States is unique because advertising took hold just as the country was entering its era of greatest growth: Population was soaring, factories were springing up, railroads were opening the West. Advertising grew with the country and helped establish its marketing system. The United States entered the nineteenth century as an agricultural country, following European marketing traditions, and ended the century as a great industrial nation, creating its own patterns of distribution. A new age of advertising had begun.

We pick up the story in about 1870, when this era of transition was crystallizing. Among the major developments, transportation, population growth, invention, and manufacturing ranked high.

Transportation

Here was a country 3,000 miles wide. It had sweeping stretches of rich farmland. It had minerals and forests. It had factories within reach of the coal mines. It had a growing population. But its long-distanced transportation was chiefly by rivers and canals.

Railroads today are fighting for survival, but 100 years ago they changed a sprawling continent into a land of spectacular economic growth. In 1865, there were 35,000 miles of railroad trackage in the United States. By 1900, this trackage was 190,000 miles. Three railroad lines crossed the Mississippi and ran from the Atlantic to the Pacific. Feeder lines and networks spread across the face of the land. Where railroads went, people went. No longer limited to the waterways, they established farms, settlements, and cities across the continent. The goods of the North and East could be exchanged for the farm and extractive products of the South and West. Never before had a country revealed such extensive and varied resources. Never since has so vast a market without a trade or language barrier been opened. This was an exciting prospect to manufacturers.

People

In 1870, the population of the United States was 38 million. By 1900, it had doubled. In no other period of American history has the population grown so fast. This growth, which included those recently freed from slavery, meant an expanding labor force in the fields, factories, and mines; it also meant a new consumer market. About 30 percent of the new population were immigrants. But all the settlers before them had been immigrants or descendants of immigrants who had had the courage to pull up stakes and venture to the New World, a land far away and strange to them, in search of a new and better life. The result was a people who were mobile, both in their readiness to move their homes and in their aspirations to move upward in lifestyle.

Inventions and Production

The end of the nineteenth century was marked by many notable inventions and advances in the manufacture of goods. Among these were the development of the electric motor and of alternating-current power transmission, which relieved factories of the need to locate next to waterpower sources, thus opening the hinterland to development and growth. The internal combustion engine was perfected in this period; the automobile age was soon to follow.

It was the age of fast communications; telephone (Exhibit 1.3), telegraph, typewriter, Mergenthaler linotype, high-speed presses—all increased the ability of people to communicate with one another.

In 1860, there were 7,600 patent applications filed in Washington. By 1870, this number had more than doubled to 19,000; by 1900, it had more than doubled again, to 42,000.

Mergenthaler Linotype
Ottmar Mergenthaler invented the linotype, which replaced hand-set type by automatically setting and distributing metal type.

EXHIBIT 1.3

The first telephone ad (1877).

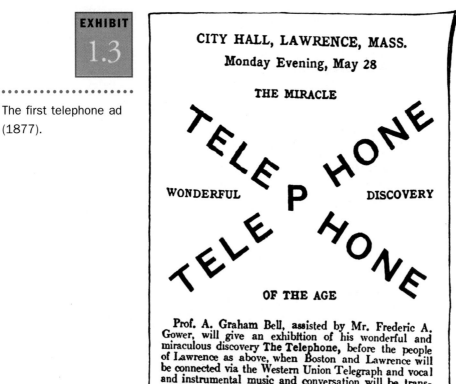

CITY HALL, LAWRENCE, MASS.
Monday Evening, May 28

THE MIRACLE

TELEPHONE
TELEPHONE

WONDERFUL DISCOVERY

OF THE AGE

Prof. A. Graham Bell, assisted by Mr. Frederic A. Gower, will give an exhibition of his wonderful and miraculous discovery The Telephone, before the people of Lawrence as above, when Boston and Lawrence will be connected via the Western Union Telegraph and vocal and instrumental music and conversation will be transmitted a distance of 27 miles and received by the audience in the City Hall.
Prof. Bell will give an explanatory lecture with this marvellous exhibition.

Cards of Admission, 35 cents
Reserved Seats, 50 cents
Sale of seats at Stratton's will open at 9 o'clock.

Steel production has traditionally served as an index of industrial activity. Twenty *thousand* tons of steel were produced in 1867, but 10 *million* tons were produced in 1900. There is also a direct correlation between the power consumption of a country and its standard of living. By 1870, only 3 million horsepower was available; by 1900, this capacity had risen to 10 million. More current means more goods being manufactured; it also means that more people are using it for their own household needs. Both types of use form a good economic index.

The phonograph and the motion-picture camera, invented at the turn of the century, enhanced the American lifestyle.

The Columbian Exhibition in Chicago in 1893 was attended by millions, who returned home to tell their friends breathlessly about the new products they had seen.

Media

Newspapers. Since colonial times, newspapers had been popular in the United States. In the 1830s, the penny newspaper came out. In 1846, Richard Hoe patented the first rotary printing press, and in 1871, he invented the Hoe web press, which prints both sides of a continuous roll of paper and delivers folded sheets. By the end of the nineteenth century, about 10,000 papers were being published, with an estimated combined circulation of 10 million. Ninety percent of them were weeklies (most of the rest dailies) published in the county seat and contained farm and local news. By 1900, 20 of the largest cities had their own papers, some with as many as 16 pages. Newspapers were the largest class of media during this period.

To save on the cost of paper, many editors (who were also the publishers) bought sheets already printed on one side with world news, items of general interest to farmers, and ads. They would then print the other side with local news and any ads they could obtain (forerunners of today's color insert). Or else they would insert such pages in their own four-page papers, offering an eight-page paper to their readers.

Religious Publications. Religious publications today represent a small part of the total media picture; but for a few decades after the Civil War, religious publications were the most influential medium. They were the forerunners of magazines. The post–Civil War period was a time of great religious revival, marking also the beginning of the temperance movement. Church groups issued their own publications, many with circulations of no more than 1,000; the biggest ran to 400,000. But the combined circulation of the 400 religious publications was estimated at about 5 million.

Religious publications had great influence among their readers, a fact that patent-medicine advertisers recognized to such an extent that 75 percent of all religious-publication advertising was for patent medicines. (Many of the temperance papers carried advertisements for preparations that proved to be 40 percent alcohol. Today we call that 80 proof whiskey.)

Magazines. Most of what were called magazines before the 1870s, including Ben Franklin's effort in 1741, lasted less than six months—and for good reason: They consisted mostly of extracts of books and pamphlets, essays, verse, and communications of dubious value. Magazines as we know them today were really born in the last three decades of the nineteenth century, at a time when many factors were in their favor. The rate of illiteracy in the country had been cut almost in half, from 20 percent in 1870 to a little over 10 percent in 1900. In 1875, railroads began carrying mail, including magazines, across the country. In 1879, Congress established the low second-class postal rate for publications, a subject of controversy to this day, but a boon to magazines even then. The Hoe high-speed rotary press began replacing the much slower flatbed press, speeding the printing of magazines. The halftone method of reproducing photographs as well as color artwork was invented in 1876, making magazines more enticing to the public. (*Godey's Lady's Book*, a popular fashion book of the age, had previously employed 150 women to hand-tint all of its illustrations.)

Literary magazines intended for the upper middle class now appeared—*Harper's Monthly, Atlantic Monthly, Century*—but their publishers did not view advertising kindly at first. Even when, at the turn of the century, Fletcher Harper condescended to "desecrate literature with the announcements of tradespeople," he placed all the advertising in the back of his magazine.

Inspired by the success of popular magazines in England, a new breed of publishers came forth in the 1890s to produce magazines of entertainment, fiction, and advice, forerunners of today's women's and general magazines. Magazines brought the works of Rudyard Kipling, H.G. Wells, Mark Twain, and Sir Arthur Conan Doyle to families across the face of the land. By 1902, *Munsey's* had a circulation of 600,000; *Cosmopolitan,* 700,000; *Delineator,* 960,000. The *Ladies' Home Journal* hit the million mark—a great feat for the age. The ten-cent magazine had arrived.

The amount of advertising that magazines carried was comparable to modern magazine advertising. *Harper's* published 75 pages of advertising per issue; *Cosmopolitan,* 103 pages; *McClure's,* 120 pages. Today a typical issue of the *Ladies' Home Journal* has 100 pages of advertising; *Reader's Digest,* 75; *Better Homes & Gardens,* 125. Magazines made possible the nationwide sale of products; they brought into being nationwide advertising.

Patent-Medicine Advertising

Patent-medicine advertisers had been around for a long time, and by the 1870s, they were the largest category of advertisers. After the Civil War, millions of men returned to their homes, North and South, many of them weak from wounds and exposure. The only kind of medical aid available to most of them was a bottle of patent medicine. As a result, patent-medicine advertising dominated the media toward the end of the nineteenth century, its fraudulent claims giving all advertising a bad name (Exhibit 1.4).

National Advertising Emerges

Meanwhile, legitimate manufacturers saw a new world of opportunity opening before them in the growth of the country. They saw the market for consumer products spreading. Railroads could now transport their merchandise to all cities between the Atlantic and Pacific coasts. The idea of packaging their own products carrying they own trademarks was enticing, particularly to grocery manufacturers: it allowed them to build their businesses on their reputations with the consumer instead of being subject to the caprices and

pressures of jobbers, who had previously been their sole distributors. Magazines provided the missing link in marketing—magazine advertising easily spread the word about manufacturers' products all over the country; Quaker Oats cereal was among the first to go this marketing route, followed soon by many others (Exhibit 1.5).

This was the development of national advertising, as we call it today, in its broadest sense, meaning the advertising by a producer of his or her trademarked product whether or not it has attained national distribution.

Mass Production Appears

The words *chauffeur, limousine,* and *sedan* remind us that some of the earliest motor cars were made and publicized in France. In the United States, as in France, they were virtually handmade at first. But in 1913, Henry Ford decided that the way to build cars at low cost was to make them of standardized parts and bring the pieces to the worker on an assembly-line belt.

EXHIBIT

1.5

Leaders in national advertising in the 1890s. (Reproduced from Presbrey, *History and Development of Advertising*, p. 361.)

LEADERS IN NATIONAL ADVERTISING IN 1890'S

A. P. W. Paper
Adams Tutti Frutti Gum
Æolian Company
American Express Traveler's Cheques
Armour Beef Extract
Autoharp
Baker's Cocoa
Battle Ax Plug Tobacco
Beardsley's Shredded Codfish
Beeman's Pepsin Gum
Bent's Crown Piano
Burlington Railroad
Burnett's Extracts
California Fig Syrup
Caligraph Typewriter
Castoria
A. B. Chase Piano
Chicago Great Western
Chicago, Milwaukee & St. Paul Railroad
Chicago Great Western Railway
Chocolat-Menier
Chickering Piano
Columbia Bicycles
Cleveland Baking Powder
Cottolene Shortening
Cook's Tours
Crown Pianos
Crescent Bicycles
Devoe & Raynolds Artist's Materials
Cuticura Soap
Derby Desks
De Long Hook and Eye
Diamond Dyes
Dixon's Graphite Paint
Dixon's Pencils
W. L. Douglas Shoes
Edison Mimeograph
Earl & Wilson Collars
Elgin Watches
Edison Phonograph
Everett Piano
Epps's Cocoa
Estey Organ
Fall River Line
Felt & Tarrant Comptometer
Ferry's Seeds
Fisher Piano
Fowler Bicycles
Franco American Soup
Garland Stoves
Gold Dust

Gold Dust Washing Powder
Gorham's Silver
Gramophone
Great Northern Railroad
H-O Breakfast Food
Hamburg American Line
Hammond Typewriter
Hartford Bicycle
Hartshorn's Shade Rollers
Heinz's Baked Beans
Peter Henderson & Co.
Hires' Root Beer
Hoffman House Cigars
Huyler's Chocolates
Hunyadi Janos
Ingersoll Watches
Ives & Pond Piano
Ivory Soap
Jaeger Underwear
Kirk's American Family Soap
Kodak
Liebeg's Extract of Beef
Lipton's Teas
Lowney's Chocolates
Lundborg's Perfumes
James McCutcheon Linens
Dr. Lyon's Toothpowder
Mason & Hamlin Piano
Mellin's Food
Mennen's Talcum Powder
Michigan Central Railroad
Monarch Bicycles
J. L. Mott Indoor Plumbing
Munsing Underwear
Murphy Varnish Company
New England Mincemeat
New York Central Railroad
North German Lloyd
Old Dominion Line
Oneita Knitted Goods
Packer's Tar Soap
Pearline Soap Powder
Peartltop Lamp Chimneys
Pears' Soap
Alfred Peats Wall Paper
Pettijohn's Breakfast Food
Pittsburgh Stogies
Pond's Extract
Postum Cereal
Prudential Insurance Co.
Quaker Oats

He introduced to the world a mass-production technique and brought the price of a Ford down to $265 by 1925 (when a Hudson automobile cost $1,695 and the average weekly wage was $20). But in a free society, mass production is predicated upon mass selling, another name for advertising. Mass production makes possible countless products at a cost the mass of people can pay and about which they learn through advertising. America was quick to use both.

The Advertising Agency

We have been speaking of the various media and their advertising. The media got much of that advertising through the advertising agency, which started with people selling advertising space on a percentage basis for out-of-town newspapers. Later they also planned, prepared, and placed the ads and rendered further services. The story of the advertising agency is deeply rooted in the growth of American industry and advertising. Later in the book we devote a whole chapter (Chapter 5) to the American agency, from its beginning to its latest patterns of operation. Until then, we need keep in mind only that the advertising agency has always been an active force in developing the use of advertising.

AMERICA ENTERS THE TWENTIETH CENTURY

The moral atmosphere of business as it developed after the Civil War reflected laissez-faire policy at its extreme. High government officials were corrupted by the railroads; the public was swindled by flagrant stock market manipulations; embalmed beef was shipped to soldiers in the Spanish-American War. Advertising contributed to the immorality of business, with its patent-medicine ads offering to cure all the real and imagined human ailments. There was a "pleasing medicine to cure cancer," another to cure cholera. No promise of a quick cure was too wild, no falsehood too monstrous.

The Pure Food and Drug Act (1906)

As early as 1865, the *New York Herald-Tribune* had a touch of conscience and eliminated "certain classes" of medical advertising, those that used "repellent" words. In 1892, the *Ladies' Home Journal* was the first magazine to ban *all* medical advertising. The *Ladies' Home Journal* also came out with a blast by Mark Sullivan, revealing that codeine was being used in cold preparations and that a teething syrup had morphine as its base. Public outrage reached Congress, which in 1906 passed the Pure Food and Drug Act, the first federal law to protect the health of the public and the first to control advertising.

The Federal Trade Commission Act (1914)

Federal Trade Commission (FTC)
The agency of the federal government empowered to prevent unfair competition and to prevent fraudulent, misleading, or deceptive advertising in interstate commerce.

In addition to passing laws protecting the public from unscrupulous business, Congress passed the Federal Trade Commission Act, protecting one business-owner from the unscrupulous behavior of another. The law said, in effect, "Unfair methods of doing business are hereby declared illegal." John D. Rockefeller, founder of the Standard Oil Company, got together with some other oilmen in the early days of his operation and worked out a deal with the railroads over which they shipped their oil. They arranged not only to get a secret rebate on the oil they shipped, but also to get a rebate on all the oil their *competitors* shipped. Result: They were able to undersell their competitors and drive them out of business. What was considered smart business in those days would be a violation of the antitrust laws today.

In time, the Federal Trade Commission (FTC) extended its province to protecting the public against misleading and deceptive advertising—as all who are responsible for advertising today are very much aware. Of this period of exposure and reform, the historian James Truslow Adams said, "America for the first time was taking stock of the morality of everyday life."

Yet, despite these praiseworthy efforts at self-regulation and many others in the years that followed, as well as general acceptance, the advertising industry was and continues to be the target of criticism for its social effects. Chapter 26 in this book answers such criticism, and it has been placed at the end of the book so that in judging the criticisms you will have had the benefit of the advertising background that the intervening chapters provide.

ADVERTISING COMES OF AGE

Better Business Bureau

An organization, launched by advertisers and now with wide business support, to protect the public against deceptive advertising and fraudulent business methods. Works widely at local levels. Also identified with the National Advertising Review board.

In about 1905, there emerged a class of advertising executives who recognized that their future lay in advertising legitimate products and in earning the confidence of the public in advertising. They gathered with like-minded peers in their communities to form advertising clubs.

These clubs subsequently became the Associated Advertising Clubs of the World (now the American Advertising Federation). In 1911, they launched a campaign to promote truth in advertising. In 1916, they formed vigilance committees that developed into today's Council of Better Business Bureaus, which continues to deal with many problems of unfair and deceptive business practices. In 1971, the bureaus became a part of the National Advertising Review Council, an all-industry effort at curbing misleading advertising. The main constituency of the American Advertising Federation continues to be the local advertising clubs. On its board are also officers of the other advertising associations.

In 1910, the Association of National Advertising Managers was born. It is now known as the Association of National Advertisers (ANA) and has about 500 members, including the foremost advertisers. Its purpose is to improve the effectiveness of advertising from the viewpoint of the advertiser. In 1917, the American Association of Advertising Agencies was formed to improve the effectiveness of advertising and of the advertising agency operation. Over 75 percent of all national advertising today is placed by its members, both large and small.

In 1911, *Printers' Ink*, the leading advertising trade paper for many years, prepared a model statute for state regulation of advertising, designed to "punish untrue, deceptive or misleading advertising." The *Printers' Ink* Model Statute has been adopted in its original or modified form by a number of states, where it is still operative.

Audit Bureau of Circulations (ABC)

The organization sponsored by publishers, agencies, and advertisers for securing accurate circulation statements.

Up to 1914, many publishers were carefree in their claims to circulation. Advertisers had no way of verifying what they got for their money. However, in that year, a group of advertisers, agencies, and publishers established an independent auditing organization, the Audit Bureau of Circulations (ABC), which conducts its own audits and issues its own reports of circulation. Most major publications belong to the ABC, and an ABC circulation statement is highly regarded in media circles. The ABC reports of circulation are fully accredited in most areas. (Today, similar auditing organizations are operating in 25 countries throughout the world.)

In June 1916, President Woodrow Wilson, addressing the Associated Advertising Clubs of the World convention in Philadelphia, was the first president to give public recognition to the importance of advertising. Advertising had come of age!

Advertising in World War I

World War I marked the first time that advertising was used as an instrument of direct social action. Advertising agencies turned from selling consumer goods to arousing patriotic sentiment, selling government bonds, encouraging conservation, and promoting a number of other war-related activities. One of the largest agencies of the era, N.W. Ayer & Sons, prepared and placed ads for the first three Liberty Loan drives and donated much of its commission to the drive.[4]

Soon these efforts by individual agencies were coordinated by the Division of Advertising of the Committee of Public Information, a World War I government propaganda office. This wartime experience convinced people that advertising could be a useful tool in communicating ideas as well as in selling products.

The 1920s

The 1920s began with a minidepression and ended with a crash. When the war ended, makers of army trucks were able to convert quickly to commercial trucks. Firestone spent $2 million advertising "Ship by Truck." With the industry profiting by the good roads that had been built, truck production jumped from 92,000 in 1916 to 322,000 in 1920. Door-to-door delivery from manufacturer to retailer spurred the growth of chain stores, which led, in turn, to supermarkets and self-service stores.

The passenger car business boomed, too, and new products appeared in profusion: electric refrigerators, washing machines, electric shavers, and, most incredible of all, the radio. Installment selling made hard goods available to all. And all the products needed advertising.

Federal Communications Commission (FCC)

The federal authority empowered to license radio and TV stations and to assign wavelengths to stations "in the public interest."

Radio Arrives. Station KDKA of Pittsburgh was on the air broadcasting the Harding–Cox election returns in November 1920, some months before its license to operate had cleared. Many other stations soon began broadcasting. There were experimental networks over telephone lines as early as 1922. The first presidential address to be broadcast (by six stations) was the message to Congress by President Coolidge in 1923. The National Broadcasting Company (NBC) started its network broadcasting in 1926 with six stations and had its first coast-to-coast football broadcast in 1927. That was the year, too, that the Columbia Broadcasting System (CBS) was founded and the Federal Radio Commission (now the Federal Communications Commission, FCC) was created.

Making radio sets proved to be a boon to industry (Exhibit 1.6). According to Irving Settel:

> Radio created one of the most extraordinary new product demands in the history of the United States. From all over the country, orders for

---

[4]Ralph M. Hower, *The History of an Advertising Agency* (Cambridge, Mass.: Harvard University Press, 1949), p. 180.

EXHIBIT
1.6

....

The earliest radio sets.
The Aeriola Junior had
heavy use in the early
1920s. Rural listeners,
particularly, turned to
their sets for farm information, weather re-
ports, and even church
services.

(Source: Irving Settel, A Pictoral History of Radio *[New York: Grosset & Dunlap, 1967] © Irving Settel, 1967.)*

radio receiving sets poured into the offices of manufacturers. Said *Radio Broadcast Magazine* in its first issue, May 1922:

"The rate of increase in the number of people who spend at least a part of their evening listening in is almost incomprehensible. . . . It seems quite likely that before the market for receiving apparatus becomes approximately saturated, there will be at least five million receiving sets in this country."[5]

Business boomed in the mid-1920s—and so did advertising. The December 7, 1929, issue of *The Saturday Evening Post* is historic. It was the last issue

---

[5]Irving Settel, *A Pictorial History of Radio* (New York: Citadel, 1960), p. 41.

whose advertising had been prepared before the stock market crash of October 1929. The magazine was 268 pages thick. It carried 154 pages of advertising. The price: five cents a copy. Never again would *The Saturday Evening Post* attain that record. It was the end of an era.

The 1930s Depression

The stock market crash had a shattering effect on our entire economy: Millions of people were thrown out of work; business failures were widespread; banks were closing all over the country (there were no insured deposits in those days). There was no Social Security, no food stamps, no unemployment insurance. Who had ever heard of pensions for blue-collar workers? There were bread lines, long ones; and well-dressed men on street corners were selling apples off the tops of boxes for five cents (Exhibit 1.7). The Southwest was having its worst windstorms, which carried off the topsoil and killed livestock and crops. Farmers abandoned their farms, packed their families and furniture into old pickup trucks, and headed west. (John Steinbeck wrote his *Grapes of Wrath* around this experience.) The government finally launched the Works Progress Administration (WPA) for putting people to work on public-service projects, but the bread lines continued to be long.

Out of that catastrophe came three developments that affect advertising to this day:

1. Radio emerged as a major advertising medium. In March 1933, President Franklin D. Roosevelt made the first inaugural address ever to be broadcast by radio, giving heart and hope to a frightened people. His line "We have nothing to fear except fear itself," spoken to the largest audience that had ever at one time heard the voice of one man, became historic. In one broadcast, radio showed its power to move a nation. Radio had arrived as a major national advertising medium. It quickly became part of the life of America. The 1930s began with 612 stations and 12 million sets and ended with 814 stations and 51 million sets.

2. The Robinson-Patman Act (1936) was passed to help protect the small merchant from the unfair competition of the big store with its huge buying power. This law is still operative today.

Wheeler-Lea Amendments
Broadened the scope of the FTC to include consumer advertising.

3. Congress passed the Wheeler-Lea Act (1938), giving the FTC more direct and sweeping powers over advertising, and the Federal Food, Drug and Cosmetic Act (1938), giving the administration authority over the labeling and packaging of these products. These laws, which we discuss in Chapter 25, are a pervasive consideration in advertising today and a forerunner of the government's increasing interest in advertising.

Advertising during World War II

With World War II, industry turned to the production of war goods. Because all civilian material was severely rationed, many firms curtailed their advertising. Others felt that though they were out of merchandise, they were not out of business, and they wanted to keep the public's goodwill, so they applied their advertising efforts to rendering public service. The Goodyear Tire & Rubber Company's advice on how to take care of tires in days of product shortages was akin to ads that were to appear in 1974 and 1975 during the Arab oil embargo.

SPECIAL	PRICES TODAY	PRICES A YEAR AGO	CHANGE IN PRICE
POTATOES MAINES 100 lb. bag / PRINCE EDWARD ISLES 90 lb. bag	$2.35	3.17	—82¢
PEACHES CALIFORNIA	2 lge. cans 25¢	2 for 46¢	—21¢
UNEEDA BAKERS MACAROON SANDWICH	3 pkgs. 25¢	NEW PRODUCT	. . . .
STRING BEANS STANDARD QUALITY	3 No. 2 cans 28¢	3 for 30¢	— 2¢
TOMATOES STANDARD QUALITY	3 No. 2 cans 20¢	3 for 30¢	—10¢
AUNT JEMIMA **PANCAKE FLOUR**	2 pkgs. 25¢	2 for 30¢	— 5¢
AUNT JEMIMA **BUCKWHEAT FLOUR**	2 pkgs. 25¢	2 for 34¢	— 9¢
DEL MONTE **FRUIT SALAD**	lge. can 29¢	41¢	—12¢
MILK WHITEHOUSE BRAND	3 tall cans 22¢	3 for 23¢	— 1¢
CATSUP BLUE LABEL	sm. bot. 13¢	15¢	— 2¢
CATSUP BLUE LABEL	lge. bot. 19¢	23¢	— 4¢
ORANGE JUICE	2 15¢	2 for 20¢	— 5¢

	PRICES TODAY	A YEAR AGO	CHANGE IN PRICE
Red Circle Coffee . . . . lb.	29¢	39¢	—10¢
Eight O'Clock Coffee . . . . lb.	25¢	35¢	—10¢
Bokar Coffee . . . . lb. tin	35¢	45¢	—10¢
Grandmother's Bread . . . . 20 ounce loaf	7¢	8¢	— 1¢
Jack Frost Sugar . . . . 5 lb. cotton sack	25¢	29¢	— 4¢
Pure Lard . . . . lb.	15¢	17¢	— 2¢
Nucoa . . . . lb.	23¢	25¢	— 2¢
Salt . . . . 4 lb. sack	8¢	10¢	— 2¢
Pea Beans . . . . lb. package	10¢	17¢	— 7¢
Lima Beans . . . . lb. package	17¢	23¢	— 6¢
Sunnyfield Flour . . . . 24½ lb. sack	75¢	89¢	—14¢
Sunsweet Prunes . . . . 2 lb. package	15¢	29¢	—14¢
Puffed Wheat . . . . package	12¢	13¢	— 1¢
Puffed Rice . . . . package	14¢	15¢	— 1¢

FRESH MEATS & FOWL AT A&P MARKETS

	PRICES TODAY	A YEAR AGO	CHANGE IN PRICE
PORK LOINS HALF OR WHOLE . . . . . . lb.	25¢	31¢	— 6¢
Prime Ribs of Beef (CUT FROM FIRST 6 RIBS) . . . . lb.	35¢	41¢	— 6¢
Sirloin Steak . . . . lb.	49¢	55¢	— 6¢
Loin Lamb Chops . . . . lb.	35¢	51¢	—16¢
Roasting Chickens (3½ to 4 lbs.) . . . lb.	39¢	42¢	— 3¢

The War Advertising Council

Throughout history, propaganda has played a vital role in the conduct of war. However, until the War Advertising Council was founded in 1942, there had never been such a concerted effort to build morale and communicate the necessity of civilian sacrifice as that demonstrated by the American advertising industry and the War Advertising Council.

In January 1942, just four weeks after the bombing of Pearl Harbor, the War Advertising Council was founded as an adjunct of the Federal Office of War Information. The mission of the organization was to work with the government to help mobilize the nation for victory (see Exhibit 1.8). By coincidence, the industry had just virtually invented the idea of public service advertising, to help in good causes and by so doing, to try to improve the public standing of business.

By the end of the war, the War Advertising Council could report that advertisers and the media had contributed an estimated $1 billion worth of space and time for war-related messages. The results were significant: More than 800 million war bonds totaling $35 billion were sold. Fifty million Victory Gardens were planted. Millions of pounds of rubber, tin, steel, and waste fats were salvaged. Over 60,000 nurses joined the Cadet Nurse Corps, and the Women's Army Corps recruiting increased 400 percent in one year of advertising.

The effort of the War Advertising Council was so successful that, before he died, President Franklin Roosevelt urged that the council be continued to promote peacetime projects. In 1945, the organization was renamed the Ad-

EXHIBIT

1.8

World War II ushered in an era of public-service advertising.

(Courtesy: The Advertising Council.)

vertising Council and, as we will discuss in Chapter 26, continues to promote a number of social causes.[6]

Advertising from 1950 to 1975: The Word Was Growth

This period is marked by the evolution of television from a novelty to a social institution. As millions of viewers gave up playing bridge, going to the movies, and even social conversation to tune in to Milton Berle, *The $64,000 Question*, and numerous westerns of the era, advertising dollars soon followed.

By the 1960s, videotape, color programming, and better production made television the major medium for national advertisers and forever changed both magazines and network radio as advertising media. Television also altered both sports and politics.

In its insatiable appetite for programming, television brought thousands of hours of sports into the living room. It was responsible for creating sports leagues such as the old American Football League and allowed even mediocre players to become millionaires. But perhaps television of the period had its greatest impact on politics.

As television's popularity continued to grow, it soon became apparent to political advertisers that the same formulas used so successfully in selling soap might be adapted to selling candidates. Rosser Reeves is generally credited with introducing the television spot to American politics during the 1960 election campaign of Dwight Eisenhower. In a series of one-minute spots, Reeves converted the reserved, rather stiff and awkward candidate into the personable "Man from Abilene." For better or worse, politics would never be the same again.

The Figures Also Said Growth.   Between 1950 and 1973,[7] the population of the United States increased by 38 percent, while disposable personal income increased by 327 percent. New housing starts went up by 47 percent, energy consumption by 121 percent, college enrollments by 136 percent, automobile registrations by 151 percent, telephones in use by 221 percent, number of outboard motors sold by 242 percent, retail sales by 250 percent, families owning two or more cars by 300 percent, frozen-food production by 655 percent, number of airline passengers by 963 percent, homes with dishwashers by 1.043 percent, and homes with room air-conditioners by 3,662 percent.

Advertising not only contributed to the growth but was part of it, rising from an expenditure of $5,780 million in 1950 to $28,320 million in 1975—a growth of 490 percent. There were many developments in advertising during this time:

■ **In 1956, the Department of Justice ruled that advertising agencies could negotiate fees with clients rather than adhere to the then-required 15 percent commission on all media placed. This encouraged the growth of specialized companies, such as independent media-buying services, creative-only agencies, and in-house agencies owned by advertisers.**

---

[6]Information in this section was provided by the Advertising Council.
[7]We select 1973 as the last full year before the high inflation brought on by the oil embargo of 1974.

- The voice of the consumer became more powerful.

- Congress passed an act limiting outdoor advertising alongside interstate highways. Cigarette advertising was banned from television.

- The FTC introduced corrective advertising by those who had made false or misleading claims. Comparison advertising (mentioning competitors by name) was deemed an acceptable form of advertising.

- The magazine-publishing world saw the disappearance of the old dinosaurs—*The Saturday Evening Post, Collier's*, and *Women's Home Companion*. There was no vacuum at the newsstand, however, for there was an immediate upsurge in magazines devoted to special interests.

- Newspapers felt the effect of the shift of metropolitan populations to the suburbs. Freestanding inserts became an important part of newspaper billings.

- Radio took a dive when television came along. The story of how it came out of that drastic decline is a good example of turning disadvantages into advantages.

- Direct-response advertising soared from $900 million in 1950 to $8 billion in 1980, reflecting the growth of direct marketing.

- The two biggest developments to emerge were television and electronic data processing. Television has changed America's life as well as the world of advertising. Data-processing systems have brought before the eyes of management a wealth of organized information. This, together with the syndicated research services, has revolutionized the entire marketing process and the advertising-media operation.

Advertising in the Fragmented 1980s

As we have seen in this chapter, advertising is rarely a stable business. It changes with business conditions, technology, and the social and cultural times. In some cases, it has a role in causing these changes; in others, it simply follows. The 1980s were a period of significant change in American society, and certainly advertising was affected by many of these changes.

Let's briefly discuss some of the major developments during this period:

1. *New technology.* Changes in technology and diversification of the communication system had profound effects on advertising during this period. Cable television, home video recorders, a proliferation of specialized magazines, the success of direct mail and home shopping techniques, and the growth of sales promotion changed the practice of advertising in fundamental ways. The advertising practitioners of today are much more likely than their predecessors to be marketing generalists, competent in evaluating research and understanding the psychology of consumer behavior.

Audience fragmentation

The segmenting of mass-media audiences into smaller groups because of diversity of media outlets.

2. *Audience fragmentation.* The 1980s may have marked the end of the traditional mass market. Advertisers no longer identified markets by households or size, but rather by demographics and number of heavy users of specific products. Television, which at one time offered three channels, now offered fifty; newspapers, rather than appealing to a single homogeneous readership, were positioned more as cafeterias where readers choose only

what they want to read; and the VCR and home computers began to let the audience control the media.

3. *Consolidation.* Paradoxically, as the media and audience proliferated, ownership of brands, ad agencies, and media was consolidated among a few giant companies. Firms such as Procter & Gamble, American Home Products, and Philip Morris provided corporate umbrellas for dozens, even hundreds, of separate brands. With their billion-dollar-plus budgets, they held tremendous control over the advertising agencies vying for their accounts. Like their clients, ad agencies also merged into so-called mega-agencies designed to offer greater service to these giant conglomerates. Often as not, these agency mergers led to as many headaches as benefits, starting with unmanageable client conflicts. Finally, the media were increasingly under the control of fewer and fewer communication companies. The Turner empire of cable networks, Time Warner's ownership of a bewildering array of media, and Gannett's interest in everything from newspapers to outdoor to TV production were only a few examples of the changing media landscape during the 1980s.

4. *Credit.* Perhaps the greatest long-term legacy of the 1980s was the buy now, pay later mentality that pervaded every facet of American life from the federal government to the individual household budget. The leveraged buyouts of corporate America and the overuse of consumer credit created an atmosphere in which living within one's income was an illusion. By 1990, when companies and consumers began the slow process of paying for the excesses of the past decade, advertising was often the first victim of any cutbacks. Media saw advertising revenues fall; advertising was harder to sell even with deep discounts; merchants began to deal with a reluctant consumer more interested in deals than fancy advertising; and some of the most famous names in American business faced serious trouble, if not outright bankruptcy.

Advertising and the Twenty-first Century

The technology of the past decade has set the stage for yet another new era of advertising and communication. It is difficult to determine exactly what the next decade will bring, but one thing is certain: It will be marked by much greater consumer involvement and control and to some degree a move toward two-way communication.

On-line services
Refers to computer-accessed data bases and information services for business and home use.

Millions of Americans already use their VCRs to control when they will watch previously broadcast programs, or they circumvent broadcasters altogether with rental movies. A number of cable systems offer movies on demand, interactive game shows, and other consumer services. The on-going mergers between cable, telephone companies, and program services are an indication of the fact that these major corporations think interactivity is the wave of the future.

As we will discuss in detail in Chapter 8, a number of on-line services such as Prodigy are already reaching several million American households. On-line computer links as well as TV shopping networks are offering the first glimpse at the future of interactive communication where consumers never have to leave their living rooms to conduct their business and be entertained. Some people predict that even institutions such as the postal service will be made obsolete early in the next century.

The so-called electronic superhighway offers the prospect of easy two-way access between buyers and sellers. It also makes inexpensive, readily available worldwide communication a reality. The global village, first suggested by Marshall McLuhan some thirty years ago, is fast becoming a technical reality. However, some observers question the more optimistic predictions of those who see an interactive world at our doorstep.

Too often the proponents of the on-line revolution emphasize their technical capability and largely overlook the importance of public acceptance. One critic points out a number of factors that must be successfully addressed before the electronic superhighway is any more than a toy for a small group of high-tech wizards. Among the most important of these issues are the following:[8]

1. *What if nobody wants to play.* A large portion of the population, even those with computers and technical know-how, remain reluctant to use the new technology. Some are wary of privacy concerns, and some don't trust the new technology to replace face-to-face encounters with retailers, bankers, etc.

2. *It isn't easy.* Despite the improvements in making the technology more user-friendly, it remains more technical than most consumers wish.

3. *It isn't cheap.* At some point, many services will be greatly reduced in price as more consumers use them. In addition, when a certain level of penetration is reached, more advertisers will be willing to underwrite at least a portion of the cost of reaching consumers with a variety of services. However, in the near future, the cost of many on-line services are beyond the ability or willingness of consumers.

4. *People change their habits slowly.* We can trace the adoption of everything from microwave ovens to facsimile (fax) machines, and the one constant is a relatively slow period of adoption. The difference between most innovations and on-line services is that very high levels of acceptance are necessary to make them profitable and useful to the average consumer for daily activities. Changing consumer habits may be the real challenge for the future of these new media.

Regardless of the obstacles to fuller usage of on-line services and our inability to predict their exact form and timing of general public acceptance, it is clear that within a relatively few years they will have major implications for both advertising and mass communication. It is obvious that advertisers can no longer count on a captive audience for their messages. The explosion of media alternatives has created sophisticated consumers with a multitude of choices that they are all too willing to use.

If there is one aspect of future advertising that is certain, it is that the cost of reaching potential buyers will continue to increase. Clients' demand for efficiency in the advertising function will continue to cause profit squeezes on agencies. Already we are seeing sometimes acrimonious negotiations between agencies and their clients over methods of compensation. Likewise, agencies are demanding concessions on media advertising rates. Many advertising executives on both the agency and corporate side wonder if the same

---

[8]Denise Caruso, "Ahead of Ourselves," *Wall Street Journal,* November 15, 1993, p. R27.

level of advertising can be sustained as in past years in the face of these spiraling costs.

SUMMARY

As we write this text, the history of advertising is being written. In the mass-communication field, the next decade will bring fundamental changes not seen since the advent of high-speed presses and the introduction of broadcasting. In this edition, we have tried to explain the current practice of advertising while offering insights and suggestions for this fast-changing field. In a real sense, the readers of this text, the future advertising practitioners, will write the history of the industry. They will face a number of challenges unique to their generation. With these challenges will come opportunities, responsibilities, and rewards that advertisers of earlier periods could not have imagined.

Questions

1. Discuss the three broad periods of advertising.
2. How did the railroad contribute to the growth of national brands and media?
3. How did the Federal Trade Commission Act differ from other consumer protection laws of the period?
4. What is the importance of the *Printer's Ink* Model Statute?
5. What was the purpose of the War Advertising Council?
6. Discuss the term *audience fragmentation.*
7. What role did the *Ladies' Home Journal* play in passage of the Pure Food and Drug Act?

Roles of Advertising

CHAPTER OBJECTIVES

Advertising can be used for a number of marketing communication problems. It is found in a wide assortment of formats, creative strategies, and media placements. After reading this chapter you will understand:

- Advertising as a marketing communication tool
- Advertising and the marketing mix
- The importance of strong brand identification
- Variances in the use of advertising
- Advertising as both consumer and trade communication
- Advertising of ideas and nonprofit organizations

As we will see in this chapter, advertising is used for a number of purposes by industrial giants, nonprofit organizations, and the smallest retail establishments. Modern advertising is undergoing a significant change from earlier years. "In the most fundamental transformation of commerce since the invention of the assembly line, **information technology** is driving businesses away from their one-size-fits all struggle for mass brand recognition. . . . The explosive growth of interactive technology will make dialogues with individual consumers more and more possible in the future."[1]

Advertising achieves its greatest success when it is used to solve narrowly defined *communication issues*. When advertising is used to solve marketing problems, it often fails. The American Marketing Association defines marketing as "the process of planning and executing the conception, pricing, promotion, and distribution of ideas, goods, and services to create exchanges that satisfy individual and organizational objectives."[2] It is clear from this definition that marketing encompasses many functions that are beyond the scope of advertising or any other communication tool.

Understanding specific consumer problems is often more important than the actual execution of an advertising campaign. A mediocre advertising message properly directed has more chance of success than the most professionally developed campaign aimed at the wrong prospects or using inappropriate appeals.

To understand advertising, you must have a perspective of the overall marketing and marketing communication problems of a firm. Properly executed, the advertising plan will flow directly from the marketing plan. Too often advertisers confuse marketing goals and advertising goals and are then disappointed when advertising fails to solve these more general issues, which may have nothing to do with communication.

Let's first look at the components of a marketing plan:[3]

1. *Overall goal of the plan.* Usually, the goal is expressed in financial terms such as expected sales revenues at the end of the first year and percentage increases over previous years.

2. *Marketing objectives.* Here the objectives and rationale of the plan are stated. For example, we may want to show a significant increase in market share relative to specific competitors.

3. *Marketing strategy.* Here we outline the steps to achieve our goals and objectives. We might suggest a greater investment in advertising or promotion or a switch from television to magazines. The strategy is a broadstroke and doesn't outline the execution of the strategy.

4. *Situational analysis.* This analysis is a thorough statement of the product and all the pertinent data available concerning sales trends, competitive environment, and industry trends.

5. *Problems and opportunities.* At this point, we try to outline the major problems facing the brand along with any opportunities that are available. For example, a major manufacturer of lawn tools found that it was losing sales because its major competitors had signed exclusive contracts with major retail chains. However, the company soon found that their were numerous opportunities to sell through local independent retailers who did not have access to several brands.

---

[1]Don Peppers and Martha Rogers, "The New Marketing Paradigm: One to One," *American Advertising,* Winter 1993–94, p. 20.

[2]*Marketing Definitions: A Glossary of Marketing Terms* (Chicago: American Marketing Association, Committee on Definitions, 1985).

[3]Adapted from David W. Schropher, *What Every Account Executive Should Know About a Marketing Plan* (New York: American Association of Advertising Agencies, 1990).

6. *Financial plan.* The financial plan is an outline of the expected profit or loss that will be experienced over various time frames.

7. *Research.* Sometimes the marketing plan suggests that research is needed to answer questions for which there is no information available.

Only after a marketing plan has been developed can we move ahead to begin our advertising program. As we mentioned previously, the advertising plan should flow easily and directly from the marketing plan. A typical advertising plan would include the following elements:

1. *Goals.* State the advertising objective(s) in terms of the marketing goals and objectives. There is a discipline in making yourself relate and justify the advertising objectives in marketing terms.

2. *Market.* Companies rarely advertise to everyone. Instead, they define a limited number of groups (for example, women aged 18–35) and direct their marketing efforts to those customers. These customers are called target markets. As part of the marketing plan, advertisers define the target market in terms of potential sales and, if possible, the percentage of product usage by the various subcategories of the total market. The market should also be identified on the basis of demographic, geographic, and behavioral factors.

3. *Budget.* The budget should be justified along with any changes from previous years.

4. *Value added.* How will advertising enhance the product and differentiate it from other products.

This general overview of the advertising plan is followed by more detailed creative and media plans. These will be discussed in later chapters.

It should be emphasized that the advertisements and commercials we see every day are the result of a long and complex planning process. However, marketing and advertising goals are not the same and should not be confused with each other. Marketing objectives are predominantly sales oriented. They outline the end result of the total marketing program. For example, a marketing objective would be to increase market share from 20 percent of industry sales to 25 percent in three years.

Advertising goals are designed to accomplish the marketing communication part of the total marketing goal. Again, assuming a marketing goal of increased market share, the advertising objective may be to increase brand awareness among our target audience from 50 to 75 percent in the same three-year period.

Note that we have stated our advertising objective in specific terms. At the same time, we should have in mind a method of measuring whether or not our goal was achieved. Advertising, like every part of the marketing plan, should ultimately be judged on its contribution to profits. Exhibit 2.1 shows a typical process of advertising and marketing communication.

Obviously, most advertising is seeking to create or maintain brand preference. The first step is to make potential customers aware of a brand's existence. Awareness can be created by a number of methods from direct salespersons

---

Advertising goals

The communication objectives designed to accomplish certain tasks within the total marketing program.

Advertising objectives

Those specific outcomes that are to be accomplished through advertising.

Preference

When all marketing conditions are equal, a consumer will choose a preferred brand over another.

EXHIBIT

2.1

Creating Product Awareness, Preference, and Share of Market

(Source: "How to Improve Profitability through Advertising," Cahners Publishing Co.)

to trade shows to promotion. However, advertising remains the least expensive and most readily available tool for creating awareness for most brands.

Once our target audience is aware of our product, we move to the crucial step of preference. Preference for a brand does not guarantee its purchase. It may be priced too high for some consumers who would otherwise buy it, not be available in their area, or not be stocked by the stores in which they shop. However, in the normal situation, brand preference is an excellent indicator of sales.

The next step beyond preference is increasing share of market. A product's market share is the percentage of sales accounted for by each brand in a product category. For example, Pampers diapers account for approximately 26 percent of the total disposable-diaper market. Advertising can play a number of roles in maintaining or increasing market share. Advertising can play a role in reinforcing past purchase decisions, attempt to get current users of a brand to purchase more units, or introduce product improvements or special promotions that add to share levels.

Basically, the product begins to stand on its own at this stage. For example, no amount of advertising will overcome a bad experience with a poorly de-

EXHIBIT

2.2

Advertising that creates
brand awareness.

(Courtesy: Actmedia, Inc.)

signed or overpriced product. While advertising plays many roles, gaining initial usage of a product is among its most important. Advertising is much less of a factor in achieving return purchases.

The final stage of our marketing process is profitability. Increasing market share is only important if it is done profitably. Any marketing plan must include a provision for profits. While on the surface this statement seems apparent, it is often the case that companies, in their quest for higher gross sales and market share, lose sight of profitability. Advertising contributes to profits by reaching consumers with creative messages designed to gain brand awareness and identify specific product attributes (see Exhibits 2.2 and 2.3). Indeed, the fact that advertisers spend some $140 billion annually on advertising is ample evidence of its effectiveness.

Once we have completed our planning and have clearly identified both advertising and marketing goals, we can begin the job of integrating advertising into the total marketing program.

ADVERTISING, THE MARKETING MIX, AND INTEGRATED MARKETING

Marketing mix

Combination of marketing functions, including advertising, used to sell a product.

As we have discussed in the previous section, advertising functions within a marketing framework. Marketing consists of four primary elements: product, price, distribution, and communication. Advertising's primary role is concerned with building brand awareness and preference—both communication functions. However, successful advertising also depends on sound management decisions in the other three areas of the "marketing mix" for its success.[4] Poor product quality, pricing higher than comparable brands, or inad-

EXHIBIT
2.3

The purpose of some advertising is to highlight a single product attribute.

(Courtesy: Actmedia, Inc.)

---

[4]*Marketing Mix* is a term coined in the early 1930s by Professor Neil H. Borden of the Harvard Business School to include in the marketing process such factors as distribution, advertising, personal selling, and pricing.

equate retail distribution will doom even the finest advertising campaign to failure.

Advertising is only one of several marketing communication options available to a company. To understand the complex relationships among advertising and other marketing communications, we need to briefly review the following four elements:

1. *Personal selling.* Personal communication is the most effective means of persuading someone. However, it is also the most expensive and impractical as a means of mass selling. Personal selling is most often used as a follow-up to mass communication to close the sale or develop a long-term relationship that will eventually result in a sale.

2. *Sales promotion.* Sales promotion is an extra incentive for a customer to make an immediate purchase. Sales promotion may consist of a special sale price, a cents-off coupon, or a chance to win a trip in a sweepstakes. Ideally advertising builds long-term brand loyalty, while sales promotion acts as a short-term boost to sales. To be effective, sales promotion should be used infrequently to introduce new products and provide a short-term boost to established ones. When overused, sales promotion may achieve short-term sales at the expense of long-term profitability by creating an atmosphere of price cutting and deals. Coupons and automobile rebates are often cited as examples of sales promotion techniques that have been used to the point that consumers either wait until the next round of price cutting or purchase only products offering them.

Public relations
Communication with various internal and external publics to create an image for a product or corporation.

3. *Public relations.* According to the Public Relations Society of America, "Public relations helps an organization and its publics adapt mutually to each other." It is one of the most familiar forms of business communication. One of the most common categories of public relations communication is publicity. It differs from advertising in that the advertiser directly pays for exposure of the message, controls in what medium and how often it will appear, and dictates exactly the message. The public relations communicator can influence all these elements but has no direct control over them. The most used public relations technique is the press release, in which a company asks media to place its stories in news columns or on broadcast programs.

4. *Advertising.* Advertising is a message paid for by an identified sponsor and delivered through some medium of mass communication. Advertising is persuasive communication. It is not neutral; it is not unbiased; it says; "I am going to sell you a product or an idea."

Integrated marketing
The joint planning, execution, and coordination of all areas of marketing communication.

Not too long ago, these elements of marketing communication were regarded as discrete functions. Separate departments within companies handled each one, and an executive in one area was not necessarily expected to have expertise in another. In the past decade, a major change affected the way marketing communication is viewed. Increasingly, we see the term *integrated marketing communication.* This integrated perspective seeks to use all forms of marketing communication in an organized manner. Rather than one competing with another, the marketing communicator is expected to determine what part of the communication function can best be handled by advertising, public relations, etc.

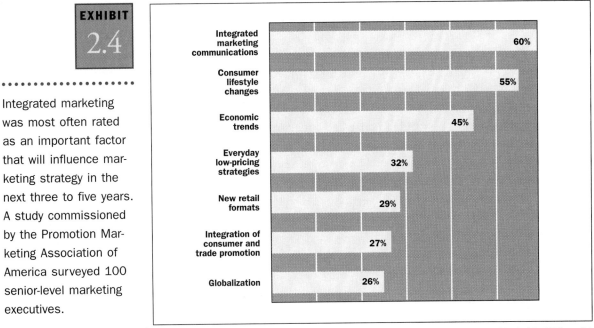

EXHIBIT 2.4

Integrated marketing was most often rated as an important factor that will influence marketing strategy in the next three to five years. A study commissioned by the Promotion Marketing Association of America surveyed 100 senior-level marketing executives.

Integrated marketing communications	60%
Consumer lifestyle changes	55%
Economic trends	45%
Everyday low-pricing strategies	32%
New retail formats	29%
Integration of consumer and trade promotion	27%
Globalization	26%

(Source: Advertising Age, March 22, 1993, p. 3.)

In one study, marketing executives indicated that integrated marketing was likely to be the most important factor influencing marketing over the next few years (see Exhibit 2.4). As one marketer pointed out, "Integrated marketing is not an option. I don't agree with those who say it's time you got on the integrated marketing bandwagon. All marketing is integrated in the mind of the consumer. Your only choice is how your message is integrated."[5]

This integrated view of marketing communication is dramatically changing the way we view advertising and also the expectations that clients have of their advertising agencies. Some argue that we must redefine advertising and, more importantly, the way we are currently doing business. For some time, sales promotion and advertising have been viewed as, if not the same, coming from the same roots. Now we are seeing public relations increasingly added to the central focus of companies' marketing communication programs. Note in the John H. Harland Company case how public relations is treated as a primary part of its media strategy.

As we mentioned earlier, in considering public relations you must balance the low cost and credibility of a "news" story against the loss of control of the message. Free exposure carries risk. It may be downright expensive if a reporter leaves with a negative impression of a product. In addition, there is the problem of measuring the results of public relations, especially in the short run. Some national clipping services count mentions of a company or its products. However, counting and placing a value on these mentions are much different.[6]

This trend toward integrated marketing communications is not limited to traditional avenues of promotion. For example, Hal Riney & Partners, long

---

[5]Scott Hume, "Integrated Marketing: Who's in Charge Here?" *Advertising Age,* March 22, 1993, p. 52.
[6]Lindsay Chappell, "PR Makes Impressions, Sales," *Advertising Age,* March 22, 1993, p. S-18.

recognized as one of the best creative agencies in the country, also has been a leader in integrated communications. Among the projects that Riney has worked on were a seven-minute tape for Alamo Rental Car customers to watch at the rental counter, a new package for Stroh Brewery, and the annual report for Mirage Resorts.[7]

The move toward marketing integration is a function of three factors:

1. Intense and increasing competition

2. Rapidly changing demographics

3. An explosion of new media choices

This environment means that agencies must be able to respond quickly to fast-changing consumer tastes. In order to do so, "Agencies must help clients

---

[7]Alice Z. Cuneo and Raymond Seratin, "With Saturn, Riney Rings Up a Winner," *Advertising Age*, April 14, 1993, p. 2.

Case History

JOHN H. HARLAND COMPANY: Major League Baseball Checks

MARKETING SITUATION

Two key areas in the financial industry today are account retention and profitability. As direct-mail check companies have a greater impact on the checking business, financial institutions must compete by providing a more diverse product offering to retain accounts and generate revenues. To assist financial institutions in this endeavor and to set its company apart from other check printers, Harland developed a special product targeted to fans of Major League Baseball. In 1992, Harland entered into an exclusive licensing agreement with MLB to become the first check printer to offer logos of big-league teams on a check. Baseball has a wide demographic appeal and is America's number one spectator sport. Through this exclusive national licensing agreement, Harland was able to provide a product that satisfied a demand from financial institution customers and consumers.

CAMPAIGN OBJECTIVES

The objective was to create a checking product that would appeal to financial institutions and the check-writing public. Existing customers and prospects would view the product as a method of retaining accounts and boosting revenue. Check-writers would see the product as a special, one-of-a-

kind item that appealed to their baseball interests. The product was also packaged with several value-added extras, such as a free matching vinyl cover and autograph/quiz book, to enhance the end user's perception. In addition to providing the product to Harland's existing customers, an important component of this introduction was to entice nonusers of Harland products to carry Baseball Checks. Harland sales reps used Baseball Checks as a way to get their foot in the door of nonusers, with hopes of later making the institutions full-time Harland customers. The unique nature of this product was critical to achieve this objective.

TARGET AUDIENCE

There are two audiences for Harland's Baseball Checks—consumers and financial institutions. One is the ultimate end user of the product, and the other sells it. The check-writing public is comprised of male and female adults age 18 and over. Seventy-five percent of baseball fans are between the ages of 18 and 49 (prime check-writing years are 21–55). Nearly half of all MLB fans are women, and women write more than 70 percent of the checks in this country. More than half of all baseball fans are in the "white-collar" sector, where check writing is prevalent. The financial institution audience, comprised of commercial banks, savings and loans, and credit unions, is responsible for selling Harland's Baseball Checks to these end users. Harland's sales force was the vehicle used to roll out this product in institutions across the country. They provided product samples, marketing support materials, and promotional ideas.

CREATIVE STRATEGY

This strategy involved communicating to Harland sales representatives and financial institution customers and prospects. Harland reps received the introductory "Babe Ruth" mailer to pique interest, along with the "Starting Line Up" kit to provide detailed information on the program. At the financial institution level, point-of-sale materials included a catalog page, lobby easel (with a "take-one" version), sales sheets, stickers, and buttons. A 3″ × 6″ insert was also produced for use in check orders and for the "take-one" easel. As part of the introduction, Harland reps offered suggestions to their customers/prospects on product rollout promotions (see accompanying sheet in "Lineup" kit).

MEDIA STRATEGY

Two versions of a new product release was drafted, along with a propped 8″ × 10″ black-and-white photograph. These were sent to dailies in Harland's plant cities, as well as major weeklies in Harland markets. Through publicity, Harland hoped to create demand for the product as consumers read articles in their local papers and called or visited their institutions for more information. In addition, Harland placed black-and-white test ads in the daily papers of eight major league team cities. These ads contained a coupon valid for $1 off an order of Baseball Checks when presented at their financial institution. Ads were also placed in two team-oriented tabloid publications in local markets.

OTHER MARKETING PROGRAMS

To provide an incentive for Harland reps and financial institution reps to sell Baseball Checks, Harland created a contest to send two lucky winners to the 1992 World Series in Toronto. Customers had to sell nine orders of Baseball Checks to complete an entry form, and these entry forms were sent to Harland for tallying. Harland randomly drew the names of a financial institution winner. A Harland sales rep winner was also chosen in a separate procedure. In addition, Harland reps worked closely with MLB team marketing directors to provide support materials that promoted the checks at local ballparks and to season ticket holders and other fans.

EVIDENCE OF RESULTS

Results of the Major League Baseball check program can be discussed on various levels. From a customer awareness perspective, Harland reps were quite successful in generating excitement among financial institutions. Existing customers were thrilled to have a unique, exclusive product to offer, and nonusers were interested enough to permit some Harland reps to set up the check program in their branches.

In some cases, this led to contracting Harland as a primary supplier (one of the program's original objectives).

From a sales perspective, Harland's MLB checks sold more than 55,000 orders from their introductions in May 1992 to year end. At a suggested price of $14.95 retail, the checks generated in excess of $800,000 in gross revenues. Baseball Checks are part of Harland's MasterPieces product line, one of two lines the company markets. (The other is called Lifestyles.) Of the nine checks in Master-Pieces, Baseball ranked either first, second, or third in sales throughout the year. It fell to third in the fall, after the season had ended. Sales of Atlanta Braves checks represented 42 percent of all Baseball Check orders, far outselling other teams.

The newspaper and tabloid ads experienced a fair return, and once again the Braves dominated the responses. In fact, coupons from the *Atlanta Journal/Constitution* represented 83 percent of all coupons redeemed in the promotion. We regard the modest overall results to the fact that the ad—even though it ran in the sports section—was not targeted specifically to baseball fans exclusively.

On the other hand, the publicity campaign was a resounding success, generating at least eighty-three print mentions. According to published circulation reports, this translates into at least 9.1 million impressions. Of these clips, 49 percent used the accompanying photo. In addition, there was also pick-up on radio broadcasts in some local markets and in various financial trade publications.

The last litmus test came from Major League Baseball itself, which would be the ultimate judge of the program's success and would use 1992 results to determine if the licensing agreement would be extended in the future. MLB was duly impressed and has since granted Harland a two-year extension for 1993–94.

develop compelling advertising concepts that will serve as launching pads for the broad range of other marketing tools available. That list includes packaging, in-store promotions, direct-mail, direct response, product 800 numbers, data base marketing, coupon redemption programs, cable programming—to name a few."[8]

Obviously, agencies cannot operate in this new world of integrated marketing without significant adjustments. One approach to integration is to create separate units within agencies to handle clients needs beyond traditional advertising. For example DDB Needham formed a unit called DDB Needham Worldwide Marketing. This unit will service clients' in areas such as sales promotion and product sampling as well as advertising.[9]

As integration of the various promotional functions becomes more typical, it is clear that more than ever the advertising person of the future will be required to make decisions about the role that both advertising and other promotional tools will play in any particular campaign. This assessment will include an evaluation of marketing goals and strategies, identification of prime prospects, product characteristics, and the budget available for communication.

The emphasis in this chapter is on the diversity of the advertising function and how advertising must complement other areas of marketing objectives. In later chapters we will discuss in more detail the complementary aspects of the many marketing communication tools available to the advertiser.

ADVERTISING AS AN INSTITUTION

Advertising is more than just a means of disseminating product information. It is a primary communications tool of our economic system. Advertising is also used to promote charitable causes, political ideas, and social and economic development (see Exhibit 2.5). Aside from its diverse role as a persuasive communication tool, it is also part of the everyday culture of virtually every American. It is estimated that the average person sees or hears as many as 1,200 ads and commercials each day. Advertising is part of our social, cultural, and business environment. It mirrors this environment as well as bringing about subtle changes in the mores and behavior of the public who uses it. It is no wonder that advertising is one of the most scrutinized of all business enterprises.

Today, advertisers are closely examined not only by the audiences they intend to reach, but by society in general. Advertisers must reach a targeted group of prospective buyers with a relevant, interesting message that will move them toward a purchase decision. At the same time, advertisers realize that they are operating in a sensitive environment where every misstep is scrutinized by a variety of legal, regulatory, and public policy groups. Each of these groups has different standards and expectations for advertising. To meet these diverse and often contradictory standards is a major challenge of contemporary advertising.

---

[8]Timm Crull, "Nestle to Agencies: 'Shake Mindset,'" *Advertising Age,* May 3, 1993, p. 26.
[9]"Two Big Agencies Start Special Units," *New York Times,* June 7, 1993, p. C7.

EXHIBIT
2.5

Various government agencies are frequent users of advertising.

(Courtesy: Economic Development Partnership of Alabama.)

Advertising's role as an institution has been studied for most of this century by both critics and proponents of advertising. These perspectives about the roles of advertising generally fall into one of the three following categories.

What Advertising Does for People. One of the important things that advertising does is give consumers higher-quality products. "Product differentiation as reflected in brands makes it possible for the consumer to identify the manufacturer. Thus, it becomes vital to establish and to maintain high standards of quality which the buyer then associates with the brand. In fact, it often is necessary to improve the quality in order to differentiate it from competitive products."[10] Advertising is a necessary ingredient in the complex economic system that allows consumers the wide array of choice and availability of products they currently enjoy (see Exhibit 2.6).

What Advertising Does for Business. Without advertising, businesses would not be able to bring new products to the attention of enough consumers fast

---

[10]Jules Backman, "Advertising and Competition," in Otto Kleppner and Irving Settel, *Exploring Advertising* (Englewood Cliffs, N.J.: Prentice Hall, 1970), p. 37.

This year black suede dances out of the dark with shimmering gold straps. You'll find them at Kinney for about thirty-seven dollars. That's right, Kinney. The reason we didn't put a big Kinney logo on this ad is because there are some people who still don't think of Kinney as a place to buy fashionable leather shoes. Hey, fashion is where you find it.

(Courtesy: Arnold Fortuna Lawner & Cabot Inc., Advertising—Kinney Shoes)

EXHIBIT 2.6

· · · · · · · · · · · · · · · · · ·

Advertising introduces consumers to new products and eases entry into the marketplace for sellers.

enough to make the enormous cost of creating, developing, manufacturing and distributing these products a rational business decision. In a mass-market economy, companies are limited in the ways they can inform prospects of new products and services. In addition to creating new markets, advertising is also instrumental in revitalizing old markets and maintaining and defending markets for established brands.

What Advertising Does for Society. Advertising has both intended and unintended results. Obviously, the intended result of most advertising is to contribute to the profitable sale of products. However, "Advertisements do more than inform or persuade. They eloquently translate feelings and opinions. Through advertising and the media we receive an enormous amount of *silent* information: how to act in relation to people, property and ourselves. And that information is a barometer, attuned to social change."[11] It is the awareness of advertising's role in social change that results in various groups examining ads and commercials to make sure they are portrayed in a favorable and realistic manner. In recent years, the advertising industry has become significantly more sensitive to its social role.

In addition to their role as a social barometer, advertising revenues support a diverse and independent press system protected from government and special interest control. As a key communication link in the marketing process it is also a major stimulant to vigorous economic growth and stability.

---

[11]Ronald Berman, "Advertising and Social Change," *Advertising Age,* April 30, 1980, p. 18.

ADVERTISING TO DIVERSE CUSTOMER INTERESTS

Advertising is a form of mass communication and as such reaches numerous people simultaneously. When designing an advertisement or an advertising campaign, firms must consider the many publics that will be reached with advertising and take into account the perception that advertising will have on each. Often an advertising campaign is intended to carry out several functions at once.

Some of the groups that must be considered even in advertising primarily intended for consumers are the following:

1. *The distribution channel.* With the growth of huge national retailers such as Walmart and Kmart, national advertisers must demonstrate to retailers that they are offering brands with high consumer demand and ones they are willing to support with significant advertising dollars.

2. *Employees.* A company's product advertising is a means of instilling pride and loyalty in its employees. Sometimes this is done overtly by mentioning the quality workmanship that goes into a product. More often, the message is less overt but nevertheless an important function of advertising.

3. *Customers.* Current customers can be encouraged to use more of a product, not consider a competitor, and have previous purchase of the product reinforced as a good decision.

4. *Potential customers.* As we discussed earlier, one of the primary objectives of advertising is to create awareness among those who are unfamiliar with a brand. Obviously, a person who doesn't know about a brand will not buy it. For most products, advertising provides the lifeblood for continued success by encouraging prospects to become customers.

5. *Stockholders.* Most large national companies are publicly held and depend on stockholders as a major source of operating revenue. Studies have shown that high brand awareness and positive reputation for a company are contributing factors to keeping stock prices higher than they might otherwise be. Stockholders are a major reason why companies such as airplane manufacturers advertise in consumer and business magazines.

6. *The community at large.* Many companies operate local plants throughout the country. Advertising is often used to influence public opinion so that when the inevitable disputes about local tax assessment, excessive noise, or zoning ordinances arise, the company is viewed as a generally good neighbor.

Advertising is only one of the many marketing communication tools available to a company. We must start by determining whether, and in what proportion, advertising can profitably be used. At this point, our marketing situation analysis will tell us if the marketing conditions are conducive to the use of advertising, alone, or more likely in concert with other marketing communication tools.

Manufacturers, even those marketing similar products, demonstrate markedly different approaches to advertising. For example, the Isuzu Trooper is selling more than simple transportation (see Exhibit 2.7). The Trooper advertisement will not appeal to the majority of drivers or new-car and truck prospects. However, the copy and illustration are designed to single out those drivers who are interested in a vehicle built for rough roads and off-the-beaten-path driving.

The Trooper advertisement, like all successful advertising, is built around a specific marketing plan. This advertisement was not created in a vacuum. Rather, the message is intended to carry out the specific marketing goals and objectives of the firm. Advertising must be viewed as unique to each brand and product category. The Trooper strategy would not work for every competing brand.

Even with the most meticulous planning, advertising success is not guaranteed. If advertising could wield the influence ascribed to it by both critics and proponents, we would not have seen some of the marketing failures of the past decade. When a product is introduced without a clear consumer benefit or differentiation from competing brands, even the most creative advertising usually fails.

Advertising in the 1990s and beyond will be in a stage of transition in terms of both broad strategy and tactics of execution. However, the one assurance is that it will increasingly be consumer-oriented. The advertising practitioner will be constantly seeking to find the subtle dynamics of brand preference to differentiate one product from its many competitors.

(Courtesy: Goodby, Berlin & Silverstein—Isuzu Trooper)

Brand Name

Brand name

The part of a trademark that is words, not pictures; a trademark word.

In the earliest days of product exchange, branded goods did not exist. Rather, people purchased commodities such as flour, salt, and sugar from barrels. Brands were introduced to assure quality and later to differentiate one seller's goods from another. Modern advertising is only possible because of the use of brand names. Brands allow a consumer to buy a product with the assurance of consistency from one purchase to another. Without brand identification, advertising could serve only a limited function in promoting generic goods. When a brand name becomes associated with a quality product, it is a great asset to a firm.

Brand names have become so important that dollar values have been assigned to the intangible value that companies enjoy from their established brands. Exhibit 2.8 shows some of the values assigned to brands by *Financial World* magazine.

It is obvious why companies go to such great lengths to further enhance and protect their brands. Once established, a popular brand provides future sales at lower promotion costs to a company and at the same time makes it more difficult for competing brands to enter the marketplace.

Today, major national brands face competitive pressure from generic store brands and price-cutting promotion from second-tier brands putting the value of a brand into question. However, even with the greater difficulty of establishing and maintaining a brand, the rewards for success are enormous. It is also clear that advertising must play a primary role in communicating continuing brand perception. As one advertising executive concluded, "Advertisers and agencies need to counter consumer apathy and media fragmentation by focusing on the brand's character or personality, building an emotional bond between the brand and its consumers."[12] Exhibit 2.9 demonstrates one company's experience with the way in which brand awareness and advertising interacted.

Basically, there are three corporate strategies used in nurturing brands. Each of these strategies is a function of overall corporate philosophy, the type of products offered for sale, and the consumer markets with which the corporation deals. However, each of these approaches has a significant influence on the advertising approach and the company's investment in advertising.

EXHIBIT 2.8

Dollar Values of Selected Brands

Coca-Cola	$24.4 Billion
Budweiser Beer	10.2 Billion
Nescafe Instant Coffee	8.5 Billion
Kellogg Cereals	8.4 Billion
Campbell Soups	3.9 Billion

Source: Tom Walker, "Intangible Assets Can Be Worth Real Money to Company," Atlanta Journal and Constitution, August 12, 1992, p. B4.

---

[12]Julie Liesse, "Endangered Species: Brands," *Advertising Age*, October 29, 1992, p. 52.

EXHIBIT
2.9

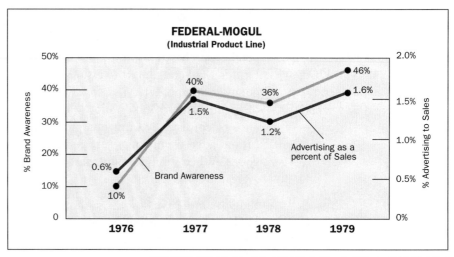

Brand awareness rises
and falls according to
the level of advertising
expenditures measured
as a percentage of
sales.

(Courtesy: Cahners Advertising Research Report, Cahners Publishing Co.)

1. *Corporate branding.* Companies such as IBM, Kodak, and Fisher-Price devote most of their advertising to establishing a corporate brand. They take the position that the corporate name, as a guarantee of quality, is more important then individual product brands.

2. *Combination of corporate and product brand promotions.* Some companies devote advertising to promoting both the corporate name as well as products sold under separate brand names. Often this strategy evolves as a company diversifies from a core business established under a corporate brand name. For example, when Levi Strauss wanted to reach an older target market, it introduced Dockers to differentiate this line from the younger line of Levi Strauss clothes. Sara Lee has adopted a similar strategy for its Hanes underwear, L'Eggs pantyhose, and Coach luggage, since none of these products is a good fit with the frozen food line that originally established the company.

3. *The product comes first.* The final corporate strategy is one where the average consumer does not identify any of a company's brands with the corporate name. Procter & Gamble is the best-known company in this category. One reason for the P&G strategy is that it sells multiple brands in the same category. It would be difficult to establish an overall corporate identity when Pampers and Luvs, both Procter & Gamble brands, are competing with each other for market share.[13]

Regardless of the brand strategy used by a firm, it is clear that advertising must play a major role in sustaining the importance and awareness of a brand. As we continue our discussion of the roles of advertising and the conditions under which advertising is most successful, remember that it all begins with the brand.

A GOOD PRODUCT THAT MEETS A PERCEIVED NEED

If the necessary ingredient for advertising is the brand, then the key to continued successful advertising is a good product. No amount of advertising will persuade consumers to buy a bad product a second time. Movie pro-

---

[13]Allan J. Magrath, "A Brand by Any Other Name," *Sales & Marketing Management,* June 1993, p. 26.

ducers learned years ago that their worst films should be introduced simultaneously in as many theaters as possible to keep word of mouth to a minimum. The strategy rarely works with bad movies and is even less likely to work with bad products.

Successful product advertising is most likely when the item meets a consumer need, is offered at a fair price, is of good quality, and is one for which there is no better substitute—obviously, a tall order! More often, a seller finds a situation in which product differentiation in an industry is minimal and advertising must contrast one product to another. In this sense, advertising is only one of a number of techniques in the sales process. As we saw in Exhibit 2.1, advertising is most important at the initial stages of building awareness and product preference with consumers. Note in Exhibit 2.10 how the advertisement for JBL Audio concentrates on the quality of the product and its brand name with very little copy.

Beyond making a quality product, a company has to keep in touch with its market. A well-built product for which there are no customers is of little value to a company. Sometimes companies are tempted to expand into areas where they have technical expertise but where there is no market, or the company has so little knowledge of the market that it is unable to deal with existing competitors.

For example, Yamaha has long been recognized as a world leader in the manufacture of fine pianos and electronic organs. Since the company's artisans were experts in bending and laminating woods for piano cabinets, Yamaha decided to apply this expertise to skis, tennis rackets, and furniture. Critics charged that the company was more interested in product techniques and

Advertising can be effective with a short message and interesting visuals.

EXHIBIT 2.10

TOM CAMP PERFORMING LIVE WITH CRACKER ON HIGHWAY 101.

JBL
Concert sound
for your car.

(Courtesy: Livingston/Keyes—JBL Audio)

quality than ultimately selling their products. Today, the company is focusing on a balanced view of production and marketing and looking to expanding into top-of-the-line musical instruments, a market it fully understands.[14]

Unfortunately, even the most focused and marketing-oriented company cannot guarantee success for all its products. The estimates for new-product failures run as high as 90 percent. Behind each of these failures is a company that took a wrong turn. Sometimes the error was made at the very beginning by overestimating consumer demand; sometimes a good product idea is wrecked by inferior quality or service; sometimes an indifferent or untrained sales staff is the culprit; and sometimes unrealistic or poorly executed advertising must take the blame.

Regardless of the reason for the failure of a particular product, some marketing mistake almost always plays a role. The concept of matching product quality with consumer demand is one that is fundamental to advertising and marketing. As we continue our discussion, keep in mind that it is consumer *perception* of a product that ultimately determines its success. Perception is largely based on experience with the product, but advertising can play a major role in differentiating a *good* product from its competitors.

Advertisers must realize that consumer demand is not created simply by product characteristics and the function of a product. Rather, it encompasses a host of product benefits of a qualitative or psychological nature. Consumption is determined by a complex environment in which the consumer lives and works. For example, a survey found that 36 percent of children 6–17 years old prepare meals for themselves, a 200 percent increase in less than ten years.[15] Obviously, this information is important in developing both products and advertising for a market that was virtually nonexistent only a few years ago.

We must be careful to define a "good" product in terms of consumers. In the 1990s, companies will have to adhere to environmental standards in manufacturing and packaging, take care in using animals to test certain product, and promote their products in a responsible manner. It is no longer satisfactory to simply make a product that lasts. Advertising functions in a complex and frustrating environment where all aspects of a consumer's life must be considered in manufacturing and marketing products.

Sales, Revenues, and Profit Potential

As we have discussed earlier, advertising is rarely the sole contributor to sales. Even in the case of direct response or direct-mail advertising, customers usually have some prior product experience, or talk to someone else who does, before making a purchase. In addition, it is important that we continue to link the notion of sales, revenues, and, most importantly, *profit* with advertising.

The primary justification for advertising is its contribution to overall profits. This contribution can take a number of forms. In some cases, it may create

[14]Brenton R. Schlender, "The Perils of Losing Focus," *Fortune,* May 17, 1993, p. 100.
[15]Gary Levin, "Youth Monitor Data Show Kids Are Savvy Shoppers," *Advertising Age,* June 14, 1993, p. 30.

a favorable corporate image, it may complement short-term sales promotion, or it may introduce new products or improved features for old ones. However, in almost every case, advertising's role is relatively long term. Even in the case of retail advertising, its exact role is hard to measure.

Regardless of the specific function a particular ad is assigned, it usually works in concert with other promotional elements and always within a broader marketing concept. In the current environment of high costs and cutbacks by many firms, it is more incumbent than ever that advertisers be able to justify what they do in terms of their contributions to the bottom line.

The pressure to justify the advertising function has led to calls for more accountability. Since each company's advertising has unique objectives, it is difficult to judge advertising in a general way. However, increasingly advertisers are focusing on the role of advertising in *maintaining* sales and market share as a major goal. This view of advertising will not show up as *increased* profits, but "the sales [and profits] results produced by advertising mature products are most likely to take the form of a defense against competitors' inroads."[16] It is difficult to measure the value of advertising against sales not lost versus sales gained. However, the overall contributions to profitability are just as great from one contribution as the other.

Advertising tends to contribute most to sales and profits during the introduction and growth phase of a product. As advertising, promotion, and other forms of marketing communication become more intertwined, the difficulty of measuring the contribution to profits of any one factor becomes more complex. Despite the difficulty of evaluating advertising on a long-term basis, its role must be determined for established products over extended periods. It is not only a mistake to measure a communications tool such as advertising solely against short-term sales, but it shows an ignorance of the fundamental purposes of most advertising.

Finally, don't fall into the trap of viewing sales and revenues as substitutes for profits. A quick review of the past decade would show that some of the largest companies in America (in terms of sales volume) experienced the largest financial losses. It doesn't take a genius to devise a marketing program that will result in greater sales, if profits are not considered.

Product Timing

Product timing

The correct gauging of market demand that assures successful product introduction.

Comedians say that timing is everything. In advertising it isn't everything, but success is often as much a matter of good timing as a good product. Timing is a consideration both for product introduction and advertising. For example, many products have failed, only to see the same product succeed a few years later. By the same token, products that come into a market late often find it unprofitable to compete with established competitors.

Good timing, to paraphrase an advertising slogan, is being only slightly ahead of your time. Product innovations that capture a new trend or previously un-

---

[16]Anthony F. McGann, "Comment on 'Speculation on the Future of Advertising Research,'" *Journal of Advertising,* September 1992, p. 83.

tapped need are almost always a guaranteed success. For more than a decade, companies have been trying to introduce interactive technology that will allow consumers to bank, make airline reservations, buy stocks, and conduct a number of other tasks from a home computer. To date, these efforts have met with only limited success. However, the next generation of computer-comfortable and computer-literate customers might make these efforts wildly profitable.

At one time, car phones were considered a luxury item for business tycoons. Today, the sight of a telephone antenna is taken for granted, and the annual increase in car phones has reached double-digit growth. On the other hand, a manufacturer wanting to crack the microwave market would find a saturated market with little hope for entry by a new brand.

Today, companies are banking on changing consumer tastes to propel the next group of product winners. Companies marketing clear soft drinks, frozen yogurt, and salsa are hoping their products have staying power rather than being passing fads. The new success stories of the future have yet to be determined. However, it is clear that innovative companies willing to take significant financial risk will probably be those that reap the greatest rewards. Successful firms will be those that are able to anticipate consumer demand and come into the marketplace with the right product at the right time.

Another aspect of timing is the placement of advertising. Advertisers must be able to anticipate the best time to advertise in order to reach consumers in the most receptive mood. For example, watch companies generally spend 90 percent of their budgets during spring graduation time and during the Christmas season, and children's clothing manufacturers are big advertisers during the late summer/back-to-school season. It is rare for any product category to have consistent sales throughout the year. Advertisers must be tuned into consumer buying patterns and advertise accordingly.

Product Differentiation

Product differentiation
Unique product attributes that set off one brand from another.

The marketplace is not stagnant. Product improvement to meet the challenge of new competitors is a requirement for most companies if they are to survive. The number of new and reformulated products introduced each year is staggering. "Marketers are banking on new products more than ever for future growth. New products will account for 31 percent of profits over the next five years, compared with 22 percent over the past five years. New products will also account for 37 percent of total sales growth, compared with 28 percent in the earlier period."[17]

Advertising's role in promoting product differentiation is to convey these improvements in a manner that makes product differential meaningful to consumers. The key element in successful product differentiation is consumer perception. If consumers *perceive* a product as differentiated from its competitors, then it is.

Some product differentiation is so apparent and so beneficial to consumers that advertising's only role is to make consumers aware of its existence. For

---

[17]Booz, Allen, & Hamilton, Inc., as reported in "What Every Account Executive Should Know about Managing the Risks and Costs of New-Product Advertising," (American Association of Advertising Agencies, 1989).

example, when AquaFresh Flex toothbrushes were introduced, the company could barely keep up with demand. The advantage of the flexible neck that helps prevent gum damage was obvious. However, it is extremely rare when such differentiation exists, and when it does, it is even rarer that a brand has a unique advantage for very long. In any case, when these fortunate circumstances exist advertising has a relatively easy task of simply communicating to those consumers who demonstrate demand for the product and the particular differentiation.

A second type of differentiation is one in which the advantage over other brands is real but not obvious to consumers. For example, Mentadent was introduced to compete with Arm & Hammer baking soda toothpaste. The primary difference between the two brands is that Mentadent had hydrogen peroxide to whiten teeth. Advertising was needed to tell consumers about these ingredients, and initial sales figures indicated that it was done successfully. Another "hidden" differentiation that was advertised with great success was Kellogg's Low-Fat Granola. Sales of the product marked it as one of the major stories of 1992, and sales continue to increase.

Another type of product differentiation is where advertising must explain why a product feature is important and should be of interest to consumers. It is in these cases that advertising has a major role and garners the greatest share of criticism. A product feature currently being promoted across a number of product categories is "clear." Led by Crystal Pepsi, manufacturers have introduced Tab Clear, clear Ivory, Crystal Fresh (clear) Lavoris mouthwash, clear Ban deodorant, and a dozen or more other clear products.

Advertising is faced with a twofold task. One is how to convince consumers that a colorless product is necessarily better than others. More importantly, the advertising message must not do any harm to the core brand. For example, if Crystal Pepsi is a better product, then why buy traditional colored Pepsi? Again, the key is consumer perception *and* segmentation. Advertising must attempt to create a new niche in the marketplace without simply moving customers from one brand of the company to another. This type of internal brand switching would be unprofitable and in the long term would perhaps be detrimental to both the old and the new brands.

Successful advertising must communicate a message that makes one product stand apart from another. Much of the criticism of modern advertising is that it tries to make obscure and inconsequential product differences important. There is no question that some advertising offers little information to the consumer. However, the best and most successful products can demonstrate an obvious difference from their competitors and whose advertising effectively conveys these differences.

Price

Value

The subjective worth that a consumer places on a product.

It has long been an axiom of advertising that a strong brand reputation insulated a product against price competition. However, in recent years even the strongest brands have found that consumers have a growing interest in price and the perceived value they receive for their money. In 1993, Philip Morris stunned the marketing world with its severe price cutting of its Marl-

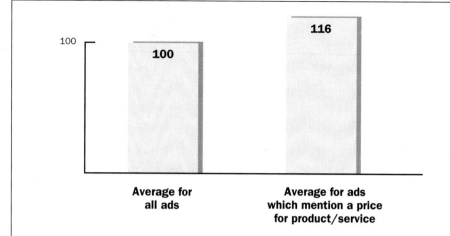

(Courtesy: Cahners Advertising Research Report, Cahners Publishing Co.)

EXHIBIT 2.11

Advertisements which mention a price for a product/service receive 16 percent higher "Remember Seeing" scores.

boro brand cigarettes to counter competitive pressure from generic and other low-cost brands.

The economic uncertainty of the past several years has made consumers more price conscious and willing to experiment with low-cost alternative brands. Consumers also expect companies and their advertising to reflect a price and value environment. One study indicated that 64 percent of respondents thought that price was a primary consideration in brand selection. This was an increase of 13 percent since 1989.[18] Consumer expectation for price information is also reflected in advertising awareness. Exhibit 2.11 shows that advertisements mentioning the price of a product score 16 percent higher in awareness than those without price information.

Price is much more than a mechanism for selling products. In the current value-conscious environment, it is a strategic marketing tool. For example, in the summer of 1993, Procter & Gamble announced sweeping price reductions of several of its leading brands of cleaning products and detergents including Tide, Cheer, and Ivory Snow. A primary goal of the price-cutting program was to reduce promotional spending for such things as coupons and instead offer everyday low pricing. The strategy was also intended to compete with smaller brands and store brands on a price basis.[19]

Price-oriented advertising and marketing are most familiar at the retail level. Chain retailers such as Walmart have built their business philosophy around low prices. Many retailers offer customers shelf comparisons against either suggested retail price or, in some cases, comparisons against competing retailers by name. The recent success of Kmart and Walmart is ample demonstration of the current appeal of a price strategy.

In spite of the importance of low price in current marketing, it would be a mistake to suggest that low price is the only strategy to success. A number of successful companies have found that financially profitable niches can be found for higher-priced products if consumers perceive that the quality of

---

[18]Gary Levin, "'Price' Rises as Factor for Consumers," *Advertising Age,* November 8, 1993, p. 37.
[19]"Procter & Gamble to Reduce Prices as Part of Program to Cut Expenses," *Atlanta Journal,* July 14, 1993, p. E5.

the product is worth the higher price. For example, let's review some advertising headlines and slogans that appeal to price and value in different ways:

You shouldn't have to sacrifice everything you own to own a car that has everything.   *(Honda Civic)*

Buick Ultra. Even the Lease is Comfortable.

Eagle Vision. Not Intended for the General Public.

Our competitors are so confident of their products, they guarantee them to last a third as long as ours.   *(Compaq)*

The New Satellite 486 Cuts the Price of Admission to All These Features.   *(Toshiba)*

It is clear that each of these advertisers has made different decisions on how important price is in its marketing strategy. Obviously, Toshiba is competing on a price basis, with lower cost being the major sales point. Compaq, as one of the industry leaders, seeks to position itself on the basis of quality and longer service protection. Eagle Vision readily admits that the car is not for everyone, but the message is clear that those in the market for the Vision are special.

Price will not necessarily determine whether or not a product will be profitable. However, the price of a product will determine in large measure the advertising strategy that should be used in selling it. Will price be emphasized? Will the product be sold primarily through discount stores? Will it be sold as an upscale brand emphasizing quality? These considerations will be determined by the company's basic marketing strategy. It is up to the advertising to properly convey the price/quality message to the intended audience.

One important function of advertising is to create a positive gap between the price of a product and the value the average consumer ascribes to the product. The greater this "value gap," the more insulated the product is from competitive inroads into its market. Since price can be so easily matched, it is not a particularly safe means of establishing a long-term, competitive advantage.

VARIATIONS IN THE IMPORTANCE OF ADVERTISING

As we have discussed earlier, advertising is increasingly being considered as part of integrated marketing communications. As companies look for communication synergism from the various elements of marketing communication, we inevitably see a great diversity in the various marketing communication plans. Companies with similar products use advertising in vastly different ways, and companies that have used certain sales techniques for years are looking for alternative communication mixes.

Avon Products, known throughout its history for its door-to-door sales representatives, has greatly diversified its approaches to selling its line of cosmetics. For example, in 1993 Avon tripled its advertising budget, heavily promoted an 800 number for direct catalog sales, and produced television infomercials featuring actress Linda Gray. In addition, Avon has opened some retail distribution centers.

The determining factors that move a company or product category to a particular communication option are both diverse and complex. However, four major factors seem to play the most important role in deciding to what degree to use advertising:

1. *Volume of sales.* In almost every case, as sales increase, the percentage of dollars spent on advertising decreases. This decrease is largely a matter of economies of scale—that is, regardless of a company's sales figures, there are only so many prospects to be reached with advertising. After sales reach a certain level, the ad budget may continue to rise, but at a slower rate.

2. *Competitive environment and profit margin.* The strength of competition will usually mandate a relatively high advertising budget. Companies facing intense competitive pressure are often forced to increase their advertising significantly. Both beer and soft drinks are in markets with great competition and high profit margins. Yet soft drink makers spend almost 60 percent more as a percentage of sales than beer. Why? Because beer companies, for social and political reasons, choose to invest a greater percentage of their promotional dollars in event marketing (stock car races, rock concerts, etc.) than soft drink companies, which are welcome sponsors in any medium.

3. *Overall management philosophy of advertising.* Obviously, the determining factor in the use of advertising is the management decision to use advertising versus some other promotional tools. For example, it was reported by the Radio Advertising Bureau that Domino's Pizza was "promotion driven and hooked on television because they need to see the cheese bubble."

4. *New product introductions.* The greater the number of new products introduced and the higher the percentage of total revenues from new products, the greater the advertising budget. New-product introductions are extremely expensive and usually require heavy advertising support. As we discussed earlier, without initial product awareness, it is impossible for a product to achieve market penetration. Advertising is almost always the most efficient means of achieving awareness.

We now move on to the next big step—to see how advertising fits into the marketing process.

THE PLACE OF ADVERTISING IN THE MARKETING PROCESS

As we have seen, the link among marketing, advertising, and other forms of promotion has never been greater. In fact, it has been suggested that the continuing blurring of lines among marketing and various forms of marketing communications will soon require a new definition of advertising. Increasingly, agencies are being asked to handle in-store promotion, package design, direct mail, and, in some cases, cooperating in developing the overall marketing plan for a company including product development.

For most of this century, agencies were judged by their creative advertising. The "hot" agency of any particular year was the agency that was known for its creative product. Agencies vied with one another to win the most awards and get the most mentions for their advertising. In most cases, these creative efforts were also effective selling tools. However, occasionally clients wondered if their agencies were creating great art or literature rather than pragmatic sales messages.

In the current environment, this detachment between advertising and marketing is rarely tolerated. For instance, VF Corporation developed a strategy for its Lee and Wrangler jeans that targets two distinct markets. The Lee Easy Rider brand is promoted to casual jeans wearers. The Wrangler brand is aimed at rugged consumers with a western flair. Wrangler is a longtime sponsor of the rodeo circuit. While VF is satisfied with its agency's advertising, it sees its success as a function of clever branding strategy. As Mackey McDonald, group vice president in charge of both Wrangler and Lee says, "Our sales are not dependent on good creative. Positioning the brand and understanding how the consumer perceives it is the most critical step."[20]

The VF Corporation's view of advertising's role in the marketing mix is not an isolated case. Companies realize that the great advertising campaign will seldom spell success for a product. This view in no way denigrates the importance of outstanding creative advertising. What it does is put advertising in a proper perspective as a partner in the marketing process.

One of the advertising campaigns that will be cited for years to come is the introduction of Saturn by Hal Riney & Partners. The agency's image-building advertising featuring "the friendliest car company in America" was credited with one of the best automobile rollouts in history. However, the campaign was coordinated with a marketing strategy that offered no-haggle pricing, elimination of confusing rebates, and a focus on customer service that went beyond anything an American car company had ever done.[21] Without a product and marketing plan that delivered what the advertising promised, there would have been no Saturn success story.

In the remainder of this chapter we will examine some of the specific ways in which advertising functions in various industries and stages of the marketing channel. While you are most familiar with consumer advertising, it is only one of a number of categories that are used to bring products to market. Effective advertising must be successful on two levels: (1) communication and (2) carrying out marketing goals. Unfortunately, it is often the case that you have successful communication on one level (a humorous ad that everyone remembers but can't identify the brand) without accomplishing marketing goals.

Perhaps the easiest way to evaluate advertising's role in the marketing process is according to the *directness* of the intended communication effect and the anticipated *time* over which that effect is supposed to operate. In other words, how much of the total selling job should be accomplished by advertising, and over what time frame should the job be accomplished?

Advertising designed to produce an immediate response in the form of the purchase of a product is called direct-action, short-term advertising. Most retail advertising falls into this category. An ad that runs in the newspaper this morning should sell some jeans this afternoon. Advertising used as a direct sales tool, but designed to operate over a longer time frame, is called direct-action, long-term advertising. This advertising category is used with high-priced ticket items (washers and automobiles) where the purchase decision is a result of many factors and the purchase cycle is relatively long.

---

[20]Jeanne Whalen, "Lee/Wrangler," *Advertising Age,* July 5, 1993, p. S-13.
[21]"Party On, Wayne," *Advertising Age,* December 21, 1992, p. 12.

Another category of advertising includes advertisements that are used as an indirect sales tool. Such indirect advertising is intended to affect the sales of a product only over the long term, usually by promoting general attributes of the manufacturer rather than specific product characteristics. Included in this category are most institutional or public relations advertising. The exception would be remedial public relations advertising designed to overcome some negative publicity concerning product safety, labor problems, etc.

Regardless of its category, advertising should move a product or service through the various levels of the marketing channel. The objectives and execution of advertising will change from level to level. The intended target audience will result in markedly different advertising strategies. In the following section we will examine advertising to the consumer and to business.

Advertising to the Consumer

National Advertising. The term *national advertising* has a special nongeographic meaning in advertising: It refers to advertising by the owner of a trademarked product (brand) or service sold through different distributors or stores, wherever they may be. It does not mean that the product is necessarily sold nationwide.

Traditionally, national advertising has been the most general in terms of product information. Items such as price, retail availability, and even service and installation are often omitted from national advertising. Instead, national advertising often identifies a specific target audience and creates an image for the product.

While this general approach remains the norm, national advertisers are starting to take more regional (in a few cases even local) approaches to their advertising. As national advertisers are able to identify more narrowly and reach specific market segments, we will see more regionalized advertising. When this occurs, national advertisers will be able to provide more information of interest to each segment, and national advertising executions will begin to approach local advertising in terms of content. However, in the short term, national advertising will continue to emphasize brand introductions of new products and greater brand loyalty for established products.

Retail (Local) Advertising. Usually retail advertising combines aspects of hard-sell messages with institutional advertising. On the one hand, retailers must compete in one of the most competitive business arenas to move large volumes of merchandise. At the same time, their advertising must convey the image of the type of store and people with which the consumer would like to do business.

To accomplish these dual tasks, retailers often include price information, service and return policies, location of their stores, and hours of operation—information that the national advertiser cannot provide. Often, retail advertisements will include a number of products in a single advertisement showing the range of merchandise available. Retail advertisements are often designed to feature sale merchandise that will build store traffic, with the hope that customers will buy other full-priced items once they are in the stores. Retail advertising is the unglamorous workhorse of the advertising industry.

End-Product Advertising. What do products such as Intel, Lycra, Teflon, and NutraSweet have in common? They are rarely purchased direct by consumers. Instead, they are bought as an ingredient in other products. The promoting of such products is called end-product advertising (or *branded-ingredient advertising*). End-product advertising is most commonly used by manufacturers of ingredients used in consumer products. Successful end-product advertising builds a consumer demand for an ingredient that will help in the sale of a product. The knowledge that such a consumer demand exists will move companies to use these ingredients in their consumer products.

A number of companies have adopted aggressive end-product advertising campaigns. Longtime brands such as Teflon (manufactured by DuPont), Scotchgard (manufactured by 3M Company), and the "Intel Inside" campaign for Intel's computer chips have all created consumer awareness. One of the great end-product success stories is NutraSweet, which has adopted an end-product strategy since its 1983 introduction. In less than a decade NutraSweet was being used in more than 3,000 products. In addition, many of the companies using NutraSweet were promoting the product as part of their brand differentiation, further increasing consumer awareness.[22]

Building demand through end-product advertising is not easy. You must have a recognized ingredient that both manufacturers and consumers recognize and believe will improve a product. In addition, these ingredients are often not obvious in the product, and therefore extensive advertising is required to make consumers aware of their advantages. End-product advertising is a variant of the more traditional national advertising that asks the consumer to buy a product by name. End-product advertising is an extremely small part of total advertising but can be important to those companies that can successfully use it.

Direct-Response Advertising. Direct marketing and direct-response advertising are not new. Ben Franklin is credited with the first direct-sales catalog, published in 1744 to sell scientific and academic books. The modern era of direct selling was ushered in with the publication of the Montgomery Ward catalog in 1872. Throughout the next century, direct selling was a popular method of reaching many consumers, especially those in rural areas without access to retail stores.

Today, direct marketing is used by most of the leading national companies as part of their sales strategy. The need for targeted selling to clearly defined audiences is tailor made for direct response marketing. Technological advances such as 800-numbers, "plus the introduction of the computer and the development of computerized databases, have all directly contributed to the growth and expansion of direct marketing. At the same time these advancements have enhanced the ease and convenience of buying direct for the consumer."[23]

Some form of direct response is becoming common in traditional advertising. Often companies offer 800-numbers not only to sell a product, but to allow customers to obtain information about local retailers who sell a product and more detailed information about the item. In addition, cable TV shopping channels and videocassettes give consumers the opportunity to see merchandise "live" before ordering it from their living rooms. The future holds great promise for various forms of interactive media that will provide even more innovative ways of communicating with prospects.

---

[22]Nancy Arnott, "NutraSweet Inside," *Sales & Marketing Management,* February 1994, p. 81.
[23]"Direct Marketing: An American Success Story" (Direct Marketing Association, 1993), p. 7.

Advertising to Business and Professions

The average person doesn't see a very important portion of advertising, because it is aimed at store buyers, doctors, architects, and others who consume goods at some point in the marketing channel short of the ultimate buyer. This type of advertising is done in addition to advertising products to consumers for their personal use. Advertising to business takes several different forms.

Trade advertising
Advertising directed to the wholesale or retail merchants or sales agencies through whom the product is sold.

Trade Advertising. Before consumers have an opportunity to purchase a product, it must be available in retail stores. Manufacturers use trade advertising to promote their products to wholesalers and retailers. Trade advertising tends to emphasize the profitability to retailers and the consumer demand that will create high turnover of the product for the retailer. In addition, trade advertising also promotes products and services that retailers need to operate their business. Advertising for shelving, cleaning services, and cash registers are also part of retail promotion.

Trade advertising can accomplish several goals:

1. *Initial trial of a product.* Manufacturers are interested in increasing the number of retail outlets that carry their brands. Trade advertising can create brand recognition for follow-up by personal salespersons or offer coupons and 800-numbers for retailers to get more information.

2. *Increase trade support.* Manufacturers compete for shelf space and dealer support with countless other brands. For example, the typical grocery store stocks over 6,000 different items. Trade advertising can encourage retailers to give prominent position to products, use a manufacturer's point-of-purchase material, or take advantage of dealer incentives offered by a company.

3. *Announce consumer promotions.* Many trade advertisements offer a schedule of future consumer promotions. Manufacturers want to let dealers know that they are supporting retailers with their own advertising and encourage dealers to coordinate local promotions with national advertising efforts.

There are approximately 9,000 trade publications—several for virtually every category of retail business. The average consumer has probably not heard of most of these publications, but trade journals such as *Progressive Grocer* and *Drug Topics* play an important role in the advertising plans of most national advertisers.

Industrial advertising
Addressed to manufacturers who buy machinery, equipment, raw materials, and components needed to produce the goods they sell.

Industrial Advertising. A manufacturer is a buyer of machinery, equipment, raw materials, and components used in producing the goods it sells. Companies selling to manufacturers most often address their advertising to them in appropriate industry publications, direct mail, telemarketing, and personal selling. This method is quite unlike consumer advertising and is referred to as *industrial advertising*.

Industrial advertising is directed at a very specialized and relatively small audience. The target audience of most industrial advertising is composed of few buyers with each responsible for relatively large purchases. Industrial advertisements are written for experts, often containing product specifications and details that would be understood only by professionals in a particular manufacturing segment.

Industrial advertising rarely seeks to sell a product directly. The purchase of industrial equipment is usually a complex process that includes a number of decision makers. Note in the accompanying case for Dickerson Vision Tech-

Case History

DICKERSON VISION TECHNOLOGIES, INC.:
"What's Wrong With This Picture?"

MARKETING SITUATION

At this time, the market for a product such as LabelCheck is $912.5 million worldwide with $479 million accounted for in North America. With the growing industrial concern for quality control and production/loss management, the market continues to expand rapidly.

Most companies in this field market their products in high-tech/technical magazines and newspapers, with very little direct-mail activity.

The problem faced by Dickerson Vision Technologies (a fairly new company) was the lack of awareness of its product and its company by a large portion of the market. The opportunity was to create a promotion to make the target audience aware of the company and the unique LabelCheck application.

CAMPAIGN OBJECTIVES

1. To obtain a base of names in the industries for which the product is uniquely suited
2. To create a promotion in which the target audience would be interested in participating
3. To raise awareness of LabelCheck software and its capabilities
4. To create a unique promotional campaign that creates a positive image of Dickerson Vision Technologies

TARGET AUDIENCE

The target audience included engineers, quality-control managers, and executives in charge of purchasing items for quality control/product inspection—in other words, anyone in an industrial situation where label application is an important function.

CREATIVE STRATEGY

Since they usually receive dry, industrial/technical information, Dickerson created a direct-mail promotion to involve and interest its target audience. The promotion concept was a contest where readers had to look at a photograph of bottles to find the bottle label with the error. They then mailed in their guess on the enclosed contest response card. If they found the error, their name went into a drawing for a Hewlett-Packard Palmtop PC—an appealing prize to the audience. The "What's Wrong with This Picture?" concept focused on the capabilities of the LabelCheck product, a system that can find defective, incorrect or missing labels on products as they move down the line—an important quality-control issue with our audience. The format for the promotion was also unique for the market—a miniposter (with BRC) rolled up and mailed in a bright yellow mailing tube. Dickerson felt it was something its target audience couldn't ignore and would want to open.

MEDIA STRATEGY

Direct mail was selected as the medium for the promotional campaign because of its ability to zero in on exactly the kind of customer Dickerson wanted to reach. Dickerson Vision rented a list of 8,000 names from Penton Publishing, including names/addresses of engineers, quality-control managers, and industrial purchasing executives in companies located in Texas and all states east of the Mississippi. It then added an additional 1,000 names from its company mailing list for a total mailing of 9,000 pieces.

OTHER MARKETING PROGRAMS

Of the 2,200 contest responses, 250 wanted additional information immediately on Dickerson Vision and the LabelCheck application. Of these names, 210 were farmed out to our manufacturing representatives who contacted them personally with more information. The remaining 40 received an information package directly from Dickerson Vision.

EVIDENCE OF RESULTS

Nine thousand direct-mail pieces were mailed out, and Dickerson Vision received 2,200 reply-card responses back . . . for a total response rate of 24 percent! Of these responses, 250 requested immediate information about the product and applications.

The large number of responses showed the market for Dickerson's product to be targeted correctly. It also provided Dickerson Vision with a strong base of names for sales calls and future promotions/mailings.

The piece also created a positive image for Dickerson Vision Technologies. At trade shows and follow-up sales calls by DVT reps, the promotion and DVT name are recognized. In addition, several of the contest response cards included remarks about the creativeness of the campaign and other positive feedback about the mailing.

(Courtesy: Kim Rowland Creative.)

---

nologies's LabelCheck system how the advertising was used to gain awareness of the product and follow-up from the company and sales representatives.

Professional Advertising. Professional advertising is similar in intent to other types of trade advertising. That is, it is directed toward people who are not the actual users of a product but who influence the usage of ultimate consumers. The primary difference between professional advertising and other trade advertising is the degree of control exercised by professionals over the purchase decision of their clients.

Whereas a grocery store encourages consumer purchases of certain goods by the brands it stocks, people can go to another store with more variety, lower prices, or better-quality merchandise. On the other hand, a person will rarely change doctors because a physician doesn't prescribe a certain brand of drugs, change banks because the bank orders checks for its customers from a particular printer, or choose an architect based on how designs are reproduced. Consequently, professionals often make the final purchase decisions for their customers. In the case of professional products and services, customers are probably not aware of how professional advisers decide on the various brands they recommend.

Corporate (or Institutional) Advertising. Traditionally, institutional advertising has been viewed as a promotional technique intended to improve or maintain a corporate image, apart from selling the benefits of any single product. While institutional advertising remains a long-term image-building technique, in recent years it has taken on a decided sales orientation in terms of audience reached and intent of communication.

A review of corporate advertising indicates that the purpose of such advertising changes with the business climate. "Over the past five decades, corporate advertising experienced a number of shifts in emphasis. Initially, goodwill and portraying a positive image were the primary objectives. As political and economic

Professional advertising

Directed at those in professions such as medicine, law, or architecture, who are in a position to recommend the use of a particular product or service to their clients.

Institutional advertising

What an organization does when it speaks of its work, views, and problems as a whole in order to gain public goodwill and support rather than to sell a specific product. Sometimes called *public-relations advertising.*

changes influenced American business and industry, corporate advertising extended itself to issue/advocacy presentations. Currently, much of corporate advertising serves as a support function to promote the company's products."[24]

Like any advertising, corporate advertising reaches an identified target audience with a specific objective. Among the groups most often targeted for corporate advertising are ultimate customers, stockholders, the financial community, government leaders, and employees. Frequently cited objectives of corporate advertising are the following:

- **To establish a public identity**
- **To overcome negative attitudes toward a company**
- **To explain a company's diverse mission**
- **To boost corporate identity and image**
- **To overcome a negative industrywide image**
- **To persuade target audiences for later sales**
- **To promote and relate a company to some worthwhile project**

These are only a few examples of possible corporate advertising objectives. The competitive environment of recent years has brought about dramatic changes in corporate advertising. Note how the Hoechst Celanese Corporation combines elements of end-product and corporate advertising in a beautifully executed advertisement that grabs the reader's attention (see Exhibit 2.12).

Nonproduct Advertising

Idea Advertising. We are living in a period of conflicting ideas and special-interest groups. It is understandable that the same advertising techniques that are used to solve marketing problems and sell products and services would be used to sway public opinion. As we saw in Chapter 1, advertising propaganda is not a new phenomenon. What is new is the number of groups using advertising and the sophistication of the communication techniques being employed. Gun control, abortion, animal rights, and environmental issues are only a few of the topics that have used mass advertising in recent years.

Idea advertising is often controversial. Apart from the emotionalism of many of the topics being espoused, there are those critics who think that advertising messages are too short and superficial to debate many of these issues fully. Proponents counter that advertising is the only practical way to get their message before a mass audience. They point out that idea advertising may be the most practical means of these groups using their First Amendment privileges. Regardless of one's position on idea advertising, the increasing ability of media to narrowly target audiences, by ideas as well as product preference, will make this type of advertising more prevalent in the future.

Service Advertising. We are becoming a nation of specialists, and more and more Americans are seeking advice and services for everything from financial planning to child care. Exhibit 2.13 is an example of an advertisement offering health-oriented services for drug- and alcohol-dependent workers. On a broader scale, a complex society needs various financial, insurance, and medical services. The advertising of these services is much more difficult than

Idea (nonproduct) advertising

Advertising used to promote an idea or cause rather than to sell a product or service.

Service advertising

Advertising that promotes a service rather than a product.

---

[24]David W. Schumann, Jan M. Hathcote, and Susan West, "Corporate Advertising in America: A Review of Published Studies on Use, Measurement, and Effectiveness," *Journal of Advertising,* September 1991, p. 37.

Andy Carson of Jackson Hole Mountain Guides sound asleep at 5,100 ft. on the face of Mt. Wilson, Red Rock Canyon, Nevada

You May Not Know Us, But We Help The North Face Satisfy Their Off-The-Wall Customers.

When The North Face, America's premier outdoor gear company, wanted to make a sleeping bag that could protect even their most high-minded customers, they turned to Hoechst Celanese. Always up to a challenge, Hoechst created Polarguard®, a remarkable insulating fiber that allows a sleeping bag weighing next to nothing to keep a body warm and dry down to 30 degrees below zero.

It's no wonder companies all over the world trust Hoechst Celanese for solutions and a never-say-never attitude. For whether it's creating the fabrics that keep you warm, the medicines that keep you well, or ways to protect the earth we share, at Hoechst Celanese, we take all our responsibilities very seriously. And with a partner like that, what company wouldn't rest comfortably?

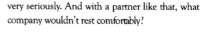

Hoechst Celanese   Hoechst

The Name Behind The Names You Know

The North Face name is a registered trademark of The North Face. The Hoechst name and logo are registered trademarks of Hoechst AG. Polarguard is a registered trademark of Hoechst Celanese Corporation for continuous filament polyester fiberfill.

An advertisement from the April 16, 1992 issue of FORTUNE

(Courtesy: Hoechst Celanese.)

most product advertising, since what is being sold is essentially the expertise of a company.

Since services are basically people enterprises, service advertising almost always has a strong institutional component. Often, service companies keep the same slogan, theme, or identifying mark over long periods of time to increase consumer awareness. Since service industries are so similar (and often legally regulated), it is difficult to develop a distinct differentiation among competitors. Banks and insurance companies have a particularly difficult time in establishing an effective identity.

Fundamentals of good advertising are the same regardless of whether a product or service is being promoted. However, many marketing experts point

(Courtesy: (sic) Advertising)

out that differences between the two categories require some care in the manner in which service messages are handled. Some basic principles of service advertising include the following:

1. *Feature tangibles.* Since service advertising cannot feature a product in use, the service should be personalized in some way. For example, service ads often use testimonials. Service messages should show the benefits of the service such as an on-time plane trip that results in closing a deal or a contented older couple as a result of good investment advice by their broker.

2. *Feature employees.* Since the value of a service largely depends on the quality of a firm's employees, it is important to make them feel an important part of the service. Often, service ads feature real employees in their ads. This approach has the advantage of personalizing the service to customers and building employee morale.

3. *Stress quality.* Since services cannot be measured as products in terms of quality control, ads should feature consistency and high levels of services. Hospitals use terms such as *caring, professional,* and *convenience* in their advertising.

SUMMARY

This chapter has shown the diversity of the communication goals that advertising is asked to accomplish. Within this diversity, we see two major areas of commonality for all successful advertising. First, it must be based on an understanding of the marketing goals and objectives. Second, advertising must develop a creative execution that will gain initial attention *and* reach prospects with a problem-solving message.

Advertising is only one of a number of possible sales tools. Advertising most often fails when it is asked to accomplish inappropriate tasks. The advertising practitioners of the future will actually be marketing communicators. They will first determine if advertising is the most effective tool in their commu-

Miles Inc., one of America's largest corporations, is a research-based company with businesses in chemicals, health care, and image technologies. As a company dependent on technology, Miles is concerned about the lack of scientific knowledge among students and the population at large.

In order to address the problem, Miles launched a multifaceted community initiative. The communications goal was to create awareness—both inside and outside the company—of Miles as a corporation that is concerned about the issue of science literacy and that believes it has the responsibility to give of its own resources to the communities in which it operates. In Pittsburgh, the company's headquarters, it is working to develop a model curriculum through a pilot program in two area school districts. Teachers in the system will work with a Miles scientist and faculty members from Duquesne University and the Carnegie Science Center.

The company sponsored a series of corporate advertisements to keep the issue before the public, as well as to enlist support from educators and other businesses. Miles president and chief executive officer, Hedge H. Wehmeier, explained the importance of the program to Miles, "One is workforce-preparedness. Miles depends on a scientifically literate workforce to compete. Further, the improvement of local school systems helps to create a better quality of life

for our employees, our children, and our communities." In the future, Miles hopes to extend the pilot program into all school districts in Allegheny County, Pennsylvania, and other Miles business locations.

Kids have a natural interest in science. How can we keep it alive?

Before science becomes a subject in school, it's a way of life. Before it's a textbook, it's an experience. A fascination. So why do so many kids turn away from something they like so well?

By third grade, half of our children are already turned off to science. And 83 percent of our college graduates lack even a basic knowledge of the subject. Those are minds we can't afford to lose.

As a research-based company with businesses in chemicals, health care and imaging technologies, Miles feels an important responsibility. That's why we're working with scientists, teachers and students, trying to make science just as captivating in the classroom as it was in the backyard.

As we see it, it's not a question of creating interest. But simply capturing the spark that was there all along.

nications arsenal; then, and only then, will they set about to plan and execute advertising plans. Regardless of the specific role of advertising, the key to its success is developing an interesting message that will reach potential customers in an appropriate editorial environment at the proper time.

The specific reasons why a company chooses to advertise at a particular level is often difficult to determine. However, there are a number of situations that usually dictate a higher proportion of advertising to sales than might otherwise be the case:

1. *To introduce a new product or service.* To enter the marketplace against established competition, extra weight is needed.

2. *To counter competition.* We all know of "price wars" or "Can you top this?" promotional challenges. Some industries have far more competition than others, especially when nobody is a real leader in the field.

3. *To maintain a leadership position.* Everyone else is anxious to unseat the champion. That's why many of America's leading brands, such as McDonald's, Campbell Soup, Kodak, and Coca-Cola, are consistently the largest advertisers in their categories. They must maintain their brand leadership.

4. *To emphasize price.* It takes more ad budget to drive home one's price statement because of competition. Among all competitive pressures, price is probably the most promotable.

5. *To keep up with a fast-growing industry.* In fields like video, computers, sports drinks, and athletic shoes it is vital to spend more on advertising to prevent others from growing faster than you.[25]

Planning is the foundation for successful advertising. During the remainder of the text we will discuss the techniques of advertising against a backdrop of marketing, research, and planning.

Questions
1. How is the overall goal of a marketing plan usually stated?
2. What is the value-added component of the marketing plan?
3. What is the first step in creating brand preference, and how does advertising play a role?
4. What is marketing communications?
5. What is meant by the term *brand equity*?
6. What is the role of consumer perception in product success?
7. What are some of the factors that will determine the role of advertising?
8. What is end-product advertising?
9. What is the difference between trade and industrial advertising?
10. What are some of the prime means of making service advertising interesting and distinct?

---

[25]From "Retail Ad Budget Guide" (Radio Advertising Bureau, 1993).

MARKETING SITUATION

The Detroit Zoo was faced with falling attendance (−11 percent) and engaged W.B. Doner & Company to develop a marketing plan to reverse the situation. Low attendance was attributed to a number of factors:

1. Inclement weather and a weak economy
2. A decrease in state funding of $1.1 million resulting in a reduction in maintenance, repairs, and exhibit improvements
3. Declining memberships as a result of the economy

To offset this marketing situation, the zoo decided to develop a four-acre site and build a dinosaur exhibit that would include 22 life-sized robotic dinosaurs. The exhibit built on the popularity of dinosaurs among children and the summer release of the movie *Jurassic Park*.

CAMPAIGN OBJECTIVES

The marketing strategy for the Detroit Zoo included the following:

1. To increase gate attendance at the zoo by 20 percent
2. To increase earned revenue for the zoo that would help offset state budget cuts
3. To produce a net profit for the dinosaur exhibit
4. To increase zoo memberships
5. To help the zoo build partnerships with the private sector to generate contributions and increase operating revenue

TARGET AUDIENCE

Research showed that women aged 25–54 were the prime decision makers when it comes to weekend activities for the family. The secondary decision makers were men aged 25–54, since research showed that single fathers as well as those in dual-parent households often brought children to the zoo.

150 Million Years Before The Pistons, These Were The Bad Boys.

D'NOSAURIA
AT THE DETROIT ZOO

CREATIVE STRATEGY

The dinosaur exhibit needed a name and positioning that would reflect the educational value that the Detroit Zoo provides in all exhibits for its visitors. It was determined that the Latin term for dinosaur, *dinosauria* ("a terrible lizard") would be used for the entire advertising campaign. The campaign team researched the size, height, weight, etc., of dinosaurs so they could easily be compared to modern-day symbols and objectives and communicate the fun and educational aspects of the exhibit.

OTHER COMMUNICATION PROGRAMS

The exhibit was introduced at a press conference and through releases to the media.

MEDIA STRATEGY

Due to the limited budget and the civic nature of the zoo, the agency negotiated free time and space for zoo promotions. Reach and frequency were maximized to the 25- to 54-year-old target market through a multimedia schedule that included television, radio, and magazines. In addition, outdoor signs at the Detroit airport and various arenas and stadiums in the area were used.

EVIDENCE OF RESULTS

The Dinosauria campaign exceeded all the original objectives for the Detroit Zoo.

1. Attendance at the zoo rose more than 33 percent over the previous year. It marked the first time in more than 30 years that zoo attendance passed the one million mark (1.2 million visitors).
2. Earned revenue from parking fees, concession sales, and admissions was up significantly.
3. The Dinosauria exhibit earned a net profit that was placed in an endowment for future exhibits.
4. Detroit Zoo membership increased 37 percent to an all-time high of 24,000.
5. The zoo built 44 new relationships with corporations whose contributions of money, time, materials, and talent were donated to the development of the Dinosauria exhibit.
6. The press conference generated nearly 30 local, regional, and national news stories for Dinosauria.

Video Case

MARKETING SITUATION

The box office success or failure of *The Nutcracker* determines the financial health of the Atlanta Ballet. It accounts for 25 percent of annual revenues and 50 percent of annual ticket sales. During this Christmas season there was substantial competition from the International Rotary performing *The Nutcracker* at the historic Fox Theatre in Atlanta (which seats about 5,000). The Atlanta Ballet performs at the Civic Center, a larger, less intimate environment. The Atlanta Ballet's performance was not new; it used the same costumes, arrangements, and dancers from previous performances.

CAMPAIGN OBJECTIVES

The objectives for this public service/nonprofit campaign was to increase sales by 10 percent to $880,000.

TARGET AUDIENCE

The campaign targeted women aged 35–55, with and without children, household income of $75,000 plus, college graduate, and not a regular attendee of the ballet. They were interested in area entertainment events like Holiday on Ice, the circus, etc.

CREATIVE STRATEGY

The aim was to communicate that the holidays are not complete without experiencing the one-hundredth anniversary performance of *The Nutcracker* by the Atlanta Ballet. The performance was designed to sell the event as entertainment, not ballet. This positioning was key in reaching and motivating a nonballet attendee to come to *The Nutcracker* by the Atlanta Ballet.

INTEGRATED PROGRAMS

In addition to advertising, there was a coordinated public relations, direct mail, and co-op promotions with Revco Drugs, and special appearances of *Nutcracker* characters at area malls.

MEDIA STRATEGY

Taushe Martin Lansdorf, the Atlanta Ballet advertising agency, had to be innovative because of the limited budget. First, it maximized sponsor contributions. The Atlanta Journal & Constitution was a sponsor that traded over $500,000 worth of ad placement for use of its logo on all promotional materials. The contribution allowed the agency to direct most all of the media budget to television. The media mix included television, newspaper, consumer magazine, direct mail, and cinema slides.

EVIDENCE OF RESULTS

This campaign generated sales of $980,000, an increase of $180,000, and generated an attendance of 44,028, the second largest in the history of the Atlanta Ballet's *Nutcracker*. These strong sales represented a 22 percent increase over the previous year, while the projected increase was only 10 percent.

Planning and Advertising

Good ads don't

just happen. In general, the essence of successful advertising is the planning that takes place at the beginning of the process. Proper planning gives an advertiser the ability to better understand and reach prime prospects with the right message placed in the proper media environment. It is rare that a great campaign is simply the result of simple intuition. Most great advertising comes from hard work and research.

Rarely can good advertising sell consumers bad products. The product's quality, its competition, and its stage of development will affect the role of its advertising campaign. Consumers are very perceptive about the products they buy. Chapter 3 discusses the strategic development of advertising from introduction, through maturity to the probable decline of the product it sells using the concept of the advertising spiral. The chapter also examines the importance of brands, brand equity, and the integration of all of an advertiser's marketing communications.

Advertisers must understand who and where their prospects are when they develop successful ad plans. In Chapter 4, we move from the product to the consumer as we examine target markets. We learn that to be successful means to be able to zero in on narrow groups of people with specific messages. This means exploring the specific niche a product may occupy in the marketplace. Product success hinges on an advertiser's ability to target the right group effectively. Later, we'll use targeting information to help create the right message and make the appropriate media buys.

The **Advertising**
Spiral and Brand
Planning

CHAPTER OBJECTIVES

One of the critical aspects of advertising decision making is developing a strategy. It has been said that strategy is everything. After reading this chapter you will understand:

- **Relationship of the advertising spiral**
- **Advertising spiral as a management tool**
- **Behavior and brand's assets**
- **Brands and integrated marketing**
- **Brand equity**

The understanding, nurturing, and protecting of the investment in brands has become a very hot topic in the 1990s and will continue to be on the minds of marketing communication people through the end of this century. **Many marketers** have been guilty of neglecting their brands in favor of short-termed profit solutions—extensive couponing, pricing discounts, and so on—which weakened their product's value among consumers. As a result, there has been a lot of focus ways to integrate marketing communications, build brand equity, and other strategic efforts in the product development and marketing objectives—*the strategic plan*—process prior to creating ads. In this chapter we will examine several aspects important to creating the strategic plan and the advertising implications. Despite many marketing practices being challenged today, one of the constants is the need to have a clear understanding of the product and consumer wants and needs when making strategic advertising decisions.

The developmental stage a product is in determines the advertising message. As products pass through a number of stages—from introduction to dominance to ultimate demise—the manner in which advertising presents the product to consumers depends largely upon the degree of acceptance the product has earned with consumers. The degree of acceptance can be identified as the product passes through its life cycle. It is this degree of acceptance that determines the *advertising stage* of the product.

This life-cycle model discussed in this chapter consists of three primary stages (Exhibit 3.1):

- **Pioneering stage**
- **Competitive stage**
- **Retentive stage**

We'll discuss the nature and extent of each stage.

PIONEERING STAGE

People don't always run to buy a revolutionary new product. For one thing, it may never have occurred to consumers that they need or want the product and as a result don't feel compelled to buy it. Until people appreciate the fact that they need it, a product is in the pioneering stage.

Advertising used in the pioneering stage introduces an idea that makes previous conceptions appear antiquated. It must show that methods once accepted as the only ones possible have been approved and that the limitations long tolerated as *normal* are now overcome. It is hard to believe, but consumers didn't rush out to buy the first deodorants. Many who were concerned with body odor simply used baking soda under the arms. So we can't take for granted the fact that consumers will change their habits. The advertising

Pioneering stage

The advertising stage of a product in which the need for such product is not recognized and must be established or in which the need has been established but the success of a commodity in filling those requirements has to be established. *See* Competitive stage, Retentive stage.

EXHIBIT

3.1

Primary stages of the life-cycle model.

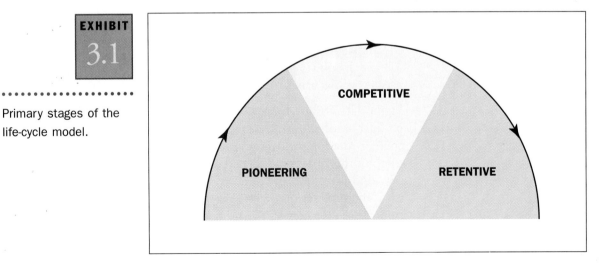

EXHIBIT

3.2

Original Egg Beaters was a "frozen" egg substitute. Exhibit 3.2 promotes using the product instead of eggs in making omelettes and Exhibit 3.3 touts using the product in the making of French Toast.

(Courtesy: Fleischmann's Division of Nabisco Foods.)

in this stage must do more than simply present a product—it must implant a new custom, change habits, develop new usage, or cultivate new standards of living. In short, advertising in the pioneering stage of a product's life cycle must educate the consumer to the new product or service.

Original Egg Beaters, a frozen egg alternative made from real eggs but without the yolk, was introduced in 1973. The company had to convince consumers that Egg Beaters was an egg alternative. It was no easy task to change egg eaters into Egg Beater customers, but it did and has since controlled the market. The market was consumers concerned about high cholesterol and fat of real eggs—eggs represent 36 percent of dietary cholesterol for the average consumer. Egg Beaters tried to expand the market in the early 1990s with an ad campaign built around When *the recipe calls for eggs* theme (see Exhibit 3.2 and Exhibit 3.3). These ads try to sell Egg Beaters as the things to use because you're using *the healthiest part of real eggs. No cholesterol. No fat.*

In the late 1980s, Interplak introduced a revolutionary new home dental product—an automatic instrument that removed plaque using two rows of counter-rotating oscillating brushes. It cleaned better than manual or electric toothbrushes. This product had to convince consumers that it was better than any kind of toothbrush—electric or otherwise. This was no easy problem, since the product originally cost about $100 at introduction. Interplak introduced consumers to the product with an ad that said: "Announcing the most dramatic development in home dental care since the invention of the toothbrush" (see Exhibit 3.4).

(Courtesy: Fleischmann's Division of Nabisco Foods.)

The copy started, "Since early man invented the first toothbrush, the technique for using it has remained just as primitive. So primitive that even today, 9 out of 10 Americans end up with some form of gum disease. The problem, historically, has been how to remove plaque . . . ." The copy used three headings to bring consumers into the details: "The INTERPLAK instrument cleans teeth virtually plaque-free"; "How the INTERPLAK instrument cleans circles around ordinary brushing"; and "Dental professionals approve."

The purpose of the pioneering stage of a product's life cycle, reduced to its simplest term, is:

■ **To educate consumers about the new product or service.**

■ **To show that a person has a need that was unknown before and that the advertised product fulfilled that need.**

■ **To show that a product now exists actually capable of meeting a need that had already been recognized but that could not have been fulfilled before. Pioneering advertising generally stresses what the product can do, offer, or provide that could not have been done, offered, or provided by any product before.**

A true pioneering product offers more than a minor improvement. It is important for the advertiser to remember what determines the stage of the advertising is consumer perception of the product. In the pioneering stage, the consumer is trying to answer the question *What is the product for?* It does not really matter what the manufacturer thinks. Does the consumer think the im-

(Courtesy: Bausch & Lomb Oral Care Division.)

proved changes in the product are significant? Or is this really a better way of doing things?

The ad copy for many pioneering products contains references to the progress of time. Some variation of "Now you can do this" or "At last you can do that" is often found in the copy, as well as what is actually new. The copy will emphasize the generic aspect of the product category in an attempt to educate or inform the consumer.

The pioneering Interplak ads suggested, "Plaque is the real villain in oral hygiene. If not removed daily, its bacterial film can lead to early gum disease and tooth decay. But clinical studies have shown that manual brushing removes only some of the plaque buildup . . . ."

Consumer acceptance and understanding may take a long period of time—a few months or a number of years or never. The original idea behind Snapple was to create an all-natural juice drinks line to be sold primarily in health-food stores. It was introduced in 1972, and today it is a juice, soda, and iced-tea company. It didn't become a national beverage company until 1992. The idea of natural beverages, which is common today, wasn't an overnight success with the masses of beverage consumers. The concept of the fax machine was originated some fifty-plus years ago. Today a large part of the population would love to own a fax machine—and may as prices continue to fall.

As with today's fax machines, manufacturers may produce a product that does something many consumers instantly desire—a VCR, a cellular phone, a lap-top computer, or a home computer. For these products, advertising will not exhort consumers to raise their standards of acceptance, but rather will aim at convincing them that they can now accomplish something they couldn't before through the use of the new product. For instance, they can keep their personal finances or recipes on a home computer, or fax granny a message while she's at work. The cellular phone industry told business women that not only could the cellular phone keep them in touch with their clients but also the world, especially as a security device—especially if they had car trouble or were threatened in some way. Take the acceptance of computers in the home: In 1992 about 16 percent of the households had a home computer, but it is predicted that by the year 2010 that number may reach as high as 52 percent; among households with children under 18 years of age it may reach over 60 percent. Obviously, the concept of a computer in the home isn't a real hard sell. The deterrent to growth, and what may continue to be a factor, is the cost to households. Many people want a home computer, but are delaying because of cost or are waiting for newer technology.

Usually during the introduction of a new product, heavy advertising and promotional expenses are required to create awareness and acquaint the target with the product's benefits. The manufacture to expand must gain new distribution, generate consumer trial, and increase geographic markets. At this stage, the product in the pioneering stage is not usually profitable. In other words, there can be a number of factors involved in the acceptance and purchase.

When Procter & Gamble decided to introduce a new pain reliever called Aleve containing naproxen, it created a new category in a very mature analgesic market. If we look at the categories, manufacturers first had aspirin (that is, Bayer) to fight pain; then came aspirin compounds (Anacin, BC tablets, etc.), then acetaminophen (Tylenol), then ibuprofen (Advil, Nuprin), and now naproxen (see Exhibit 3.5). Where will the customers come from? Bayer users? Tylenol users? Across the analgesic spectrum? Will they create new pain reliever users or share from other category users? Aleve's advertis-

EXHIBIT

3.5

· · · · · · · · · · · · · · · · · · ·

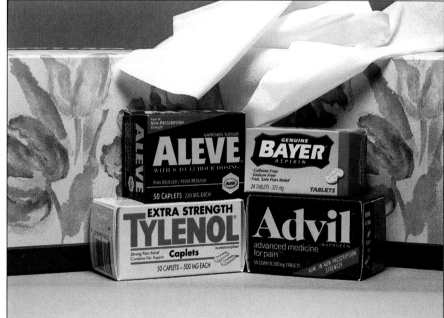

ing support for the introduction was projected at about $50 million—no small amount. As you can see, pioneering advertisers incur heavy expenses in the process of educating the public about the advantages of a new type of product. If the advertiser has some success with the new idea, one or more competitors will quickly jump into the market and try to grab a share from the pioneer.

Usually the main advantage of being a pioneer is that you become the leader with a substantial head start over others. So a pioneering effort can secure customers before the competition can get started. Then the trick is to hold onto your share.

THE COMPETITIVE STAGE

When a pioneering product becomes accepted by consumers and they have a desire for it, there is going to be competition. The consumer now knows what the product is and how it can be used. At this point, the main question the consumer asks is *Which brand shall I buy?* When this happens, the product has entered the competitive stage and the advertising for it is referred to as *competitive advertising*. (Note that this is a restrictive meaning of the term, not to be confused with the looser meaning that all ads are competitive with one another.)

Competitive stage

The advertising stage a product reaches when its general usefulness is recognized but its superiority over similar brands has to be established in order to gain preference. (*Compare* Pioneering stage; Retentive stage.)

In the short term, the pioneer usually has an advantage of leadership that can give dominance in the market. Snapple was the dominant leader in the ready-to-drink iced-tea market, but Pepsi and Coke quickly became aggressive with their versions of ready-to-drink iced tea to get a piece of the pie. In the rotisserie chicken market there were many local or regional fast food outlets selling the product. However, in 1993 Kentucky Fried Chicken (KFC) unleashed its Colonel's Rotisserie Gold chicken nationwide to the tune of about $55 million in advertising. The next year America's Favorite Chickens, the parent of Popeye's Famous Fried Chicken & Biscuits and Church's Chicken, launched new products aimed at KFC, along with new efforts from Boston Chicken—in short, competition. Generally, in the early competitive stage, the combined impact of many competitors, each spending to gain a substantial market position, creates significant growth for the whole product category. In the ready-to-drink iced-tea market, the combined advertising of Snapple's, Coke's, and Pepsi's versions created additional consumer interest and sales in that category. If the pioneer can maintain market share during this initial period of a competitor's growth, it can more than make up for the earlier expense associated with its pioneering efforts.

Vermont American says, "It took a different breed of engineer to create a different breed of carbide" (see Exhibit 3.6). And Healthtex tells how its clothes are made to withstand children's toughness (Exhibit 3.7).

Among the many everyday products in the competitive stage are deodorants, soaps, toothpaste, cars, detergents, headache remedies, shaving creams, shampoos, televisions, VCRs, cat food, computers, and packaged foods. The *purpose* of the competitive stage advertising is to communicate the product's position or differentiate it to the consumer; the advertising features the differential of the product.

Vermont American tries to differentiate their people and product in an unusual way.

IT TOOK A DIFFERENT BREED OF ENGINEER
TO CREATE A DIFFERENT BREED OF CARBIDE.

DYANITE. A TOUGHER BREED OF CARBIDE.

(Courtesy: Vermont American.)

A lighting fixture company ad said:

When you purchase a light fixture elsewhere, they box it for you.

When you purchase a light fixture at Progressive Lighting, we hang it for you.

Here are some competitive automotive headlines:

You're looking at the reason a lot of our competitors don't build wagons anymore. (Ford Taurus)

You can't buy a more impressive car for less. (Toyota Corolla)

Healthtex takes an interesting approach to speak to consumers about its products durability.

This typical 5-year-old will now demonstrate the durability of our new Playwear Denims.

(Courtesy: Healthtex and The Martin Agency.)

Enough room to keep backseat drivers comfortably out of earshot. (Lexus)

Dual Air Bags. $11,435 Think of the impact.   *(Geo Prizm)*

The Parklane with traction control. When it comes to safety, we're not spinning our wheels.   *(Buick Parklane)*

These heads don't tell you or educate you as to the advantages of automobiles; that is taken for granted. Instead, each headline and copy that follows set out to tell you why you should select that particular brand of automobile.

THE RETENTIVE STAGE

Products reaching maturity and wide-scale acceptance enter the retentive, or reminder, stage of advertising.

When a product is accepted and used by consumers, there may not be a need for competitive advertising. At this point, everybody knows about this product and likes or dislikes it . . . why advertise? Over the years, many manufacturers of successful products have stopped advertising and seen the public quickly forget about them. Therefore, most astute advertisers try to retain their customers by keeping the brand name before them. This is called *reminder advertising*—it simply reminds consumers the brand exists. This kind of advertising is usually highly visual or name advertising, meaning the ad gives little reason to buy the product. Most reminder ads look like posters— they have a dominant illustration of the product and a few words. Generally, there is little or no body copy because there is no need to give consumers this kind of information.

Very few advertisers reach the point where they can consider their product entirely in the reminder stage. There are usually other products in the pioneering and competitive stages challenging their leadership position. In fact, if your product is truly all alone in the retentive stage, that may be cause for alarm. It may mean the product category is in decline, and the competition sees little future in challenging you for consumers.

The advertiser's goal in the retentive stage is to maintain market share and ward off consumer trial of other products. Products in the retentive stage do not necessarily cut back on their advertising expenditures, but they adopt marketing and promotional strategies different from those used in the pioneering and competitive stages. When a brand is used by a large portion of the market, its advertising is intended to keep present customers and increase the total market, on the assumption that the most prominent brand will get the largest share of the increase.

Generally, products in the retentive stage are at their most profitable levels because developmental costs have been amortized, distribution channels established, and sales contacts made. The development of advertising and promotion may often be routine at this stage. Obviously, companies like to maintain their products in the retentive stage as long as possible.

THE ADVERTISING SPIRAL

The advertising spiral (Exhibit 3.8) is an expanded version of the advertising stages of products. It provides a point of reference for determining which stage or stages a product has reached at a given time in a given market and

Retentive stage

The third advertising stage of a product, reached when its general usefulness is widely known, its individual qualities are thoroughly appreciated, and it is satisfied to retain its patronage merely on the strength of its past reputation. *See* Pioneering state, competitive stage.

EXHIBIT

3.8

· ·

The advertising spiral.

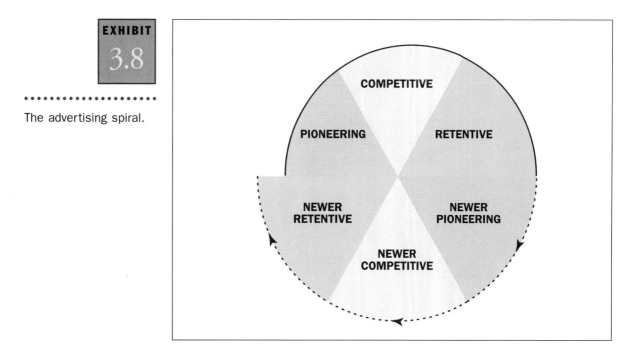

what the thrust of the advertising message should be. This can be important information for deciding on strategy and giving the creative team a clear perspective on what information they need to communicate to prospects. In many respects, the advertising spiral parallels the life cycle of the product (Exhibit 3.1), except that it shows what has to be done at each stage and where the product can go when it reaches a high level of success.

COMPARISON OF STAGES

There are fewer products in the pioneering stage than in the competitive stage. The development of new types of products or categories does not take place frequently. Most advertising is for products in the competitive stage. As we have pointed out, such advertising often introduces a new product features that is in the pioneering stage and gets the spotlight for a period of time.

In using the advertising spiral, we deal with one group of consumers at a time. The advertising depends upon an attitude of *that* group toward the product. A product in the competitive stage may have to use pioneering advertising aimed at other groups of consumers to expand its markets. Fax machines are in the competitive stage among business people, where their use is accepted, but they are largely in the pioneering stage for home use. Thus, pioneering and competitive advertising will be going on simultaneously for fax machines. Each series of ads, or each part of one ad, will be aimed at a different audience for the same product.

Products in the retentive stage usually get the least amount of advertising. This stage, however, represents a critical moment in the life cycle of a product, when important management decisions must be made. Hence it is important to create effective advertising in this stage.

Product in Competitive Stage, Improvement in Pioneering Stage. It is not unusual for a new brand to enter the competitive stage without doing any pioneering advertising. A new product entering an established product category must hit the ground running to differentiate itself from the competition. Every new brand thus enjoys whatever pioneering advertising has already been done in the product category.

Change is a continuum: As long as the operation of a competitive product does not change, the product continues to be in the competitive stage, despite any pioneering improvements. Once the principle of its operation changes, however, the product itself enters the pioneering stage. Think about the change from the needle record player to compact disc technology. When a product begins to move into more than one stage, the changes are not always easy to categorize.

Whenever a brand in the competitive stage is revitalized with a new feature seeking to differentiate it, pioneering advertising may be needed to make con-

(Courtesy: Fleischmann's Division of Nabisco Foods.)

sumers appreciate the new feature. Huggies diapers added a soft elastic band. If its advantage had not been advertised, consumers might have ignored the feature.

In 1992, Scramblers and Better'n Eggs, Healthy Choice egg, and Simply Eggs created nonfrozen egg substitutes to compete with Egg Beaters' frozen product. Egg Beaters developed a refrigerated version to go with its frozen product. Exhibit 3.9 shows the television commercial for the new product telling consumers they can find Egg Beaters either in the freezer or in the egg section of the grocer. Exhibit 3.10 shows a free-standing insert promoting both products with a coupon. Is the new Egg Beaters in the competitive stage or the pioneering? Or both?

After the Retentive Stage

The life of a product does not cease when it reaches the retentive stage. In fact, it may then be at the height of its popularity, and its manufacturer may feel it can just coast along. But a product can coast for only a short period of time before declining.

As noted earlier, the retentive stage is the most profitable one for the product. But all good things have to come to an end. A manufacturer has a choice between two strategies when the product nears the end of the retentive stage.

In the first strategy, the manufacturer determines that the product has outlived its effective market life and should be allowed to die. In most cases, the product is not immediately pulled from the market. Rather, the manufacturer simply quits advertising it and withdraws other types of support. During this period, the product gradually loses market share but remains profitable because expenses have been sharply curtailed. This strategy is the one

EXHIBIT
3.10

. . . .

Egg Beaters uses a free-standing insert promoting a coupon for both products in the dairy section and in the freezer section.

(Courtesy: Fleischmann's Division of Nabisco Foods.)

EXHIBIT

3.11

· · · · · · · · · · · · · · · · · · ·

A typical product life-cycle model.

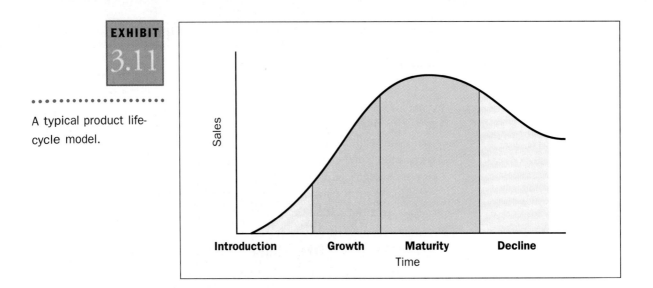

typically presented in textbook descriptions of the product life cycle, but not necessarily the one that corresponds to actual product development.

The problem with the model in (Exhibit 3.11) is that it portrays an inevitable decline in the product life cycle, whereas most long-term products go through a number of cycles of varying peaks and duration before they are finally taken off the market. The advertising spiral depicted in Exhibit 3.8 shows these cycles. The advertising spiral, the second strategy available to the manufacturer of a product nearing the end of the retentive stage, does not accept the fact that a product must decline. Instead, it seeks to expand the market into a newer pioneering stage.

Brand managers at General Mills work very hard to prove that their brands are not washed up: Hamburger Helper, introduced over two decades ago, is having record sales; Betty Crocker, the 70-plus-year-old dessert mix, has increased its business; the volume of Kix cereal, a 60-year-old brand, has risen significantly since 1981; Cheerios is up 74 percent versus industry growth of 28 percent. CEO of General Mills Atwater's advice is, "Do not believe in the product life cycle. Innovate constantly. Take risks. Do not live and die on consumer research. Reward everyone for his or her ideas."[1]

The three basic stages of the spiral shown in the top half of Exhibit 3.8 (pioneering, competitive, and retentive) are straightforward and easy to understand. However, the stages in the bottom half (newer pioneering, newer competitive, and newer retentive) are trickier. In order to continue to market an established product successfully and profitable, creative marketing is necessary.

The newer pioneering stage attempts to get more people to use the product. Basically, there are two ways to enter this new stage. The first is by product modification. This can be minor, such as adding a new ingredient to a detergent or a deodorant to a bar of soap, or—in the other direction—taking caffeine or sodium out of a soft drink or fat out of a food product. Alternatively, it may entail a complete overhaul of a product such as a radical model change for an automobile. In some cases, advertising alone may be enough to get consumers to look at the product in a new light.

---

[1]Patricia Sellers, "A Boring Brand Can Be Beautiful," *Fortune,* November 18, 1991, pp. 169–179.

Advertisers cannot afford to rely simply on old customers, because they die off, are lured away by the competition, or change their lifestyles. Smart advertisers will initiate a change in direction of their advertising when their product is enjoying great success. They will show new ways of using the product and give reasons for using it more often. For instance, if you are a successful soup company and your customers are eating your canned soup with every meal, you have reached a saturation point. How can you increase sales? Simply by encouraging people to use soup in new ways. You create recipe advertising—showing new food dishes, casseroles—requiring several cans of your product. You now have your customers eating your soup as soup, along with casseroles made from your soup. Of course, this means more sales and a new way of thinking about soup. That's exactly what Egg Beaters did once Fleischmann's got consumers to switch from eggs to Egg Beaters for breakfast. Exhibit 3.12 tries to get cooks to use Egg Beaters in recipes for chocolate cookies and (Exhibit 3.13) meatloaf—not just for breakfast.

New Pioneering Stage and Beyond

A product entering the new pioneering stage is actually in different stages in different markets. Longtime consumers will perceive the product as in the competitive or retentive stage. New consumers will perceive it as being a pioneer. For instance, the personal computer is in the competitive stage (over 150 PC manufacturers were at a recent computer show) for most large and many medium-sized businesses, but in the pioneering stage for small busi-

EXHIBIT 3.12

Egg Beaters is trying to expand the market by getting consumers to change their habits–using Egg Beaters instead of eggs in recipes.

(Courtesy: Fleischmann's Division of Nabisco Foods.)

EXHIBIT

3.13

When the recipe calls for eggs is the message to consumers. If it is successful Egg Beaters will have significantly changed habits and expanded the use of the product.

(Courtesy: Fleischmann's Division of Nabisco Foods.)

nesses and home users. Hence the dual nature of computer advertising. Some advertising focuses on a number of users and the sophistication of the computer, assigning that the firm has already bought a computer system. Other computer ads are clearly trying to sell the value of having a computer. We will soon see computers becoming pioneers in other markets. Think about the opportunities for expanding the market for desktop publishing as prices fall on hardware and software becomes easier to use. At this point the advertising spiral will have entered still another cycle (Exhibit 3.14), which we will call the *newest pioneering stage,* where the focus is on getting more people to use this type of product.

The product in this stage is faced with new problems and opportunities. Can you convince segments of the market not using your product that they should? Obviously you have to understand why they were not interested in the product earlier. Creature marketing and a flexible product help this process.

Nike, Jell-O, Pepsi-Cola, Mountain Dew, Budweiser, Miller High Life, and Gillette are a few of the brands that reached the retentive stage and began to look for ways to move beyond it. When Gillette introduced its Sensor razor for men in 1990, it was such a success that demand exceeded supply. The company wanted to move beyond this success and seek new markets, so it looked to take that success to the women's shaving market by introducing the woman's Sensor. The woman's version used the same technology with the exception of a different head, a different-color handle, and moisturizers added to the lubricating strips. All of the above companies moved into new pio-

EXHIBIT

3.14

....

The expanded advertising spiral.

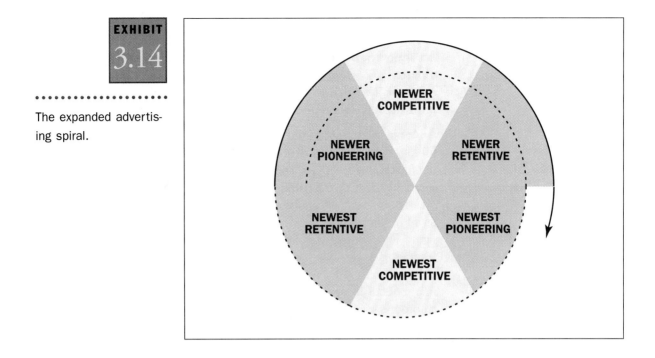

neering with product innovations. Hence products such as Diet Coke, Cherry Coke, Diet Pepsi, Diet Dr. Pepper, Diet Mountain Dew, Miller Genuine Draft, Bud Light, and Michelob Dry were born. New pioneering can be the result of reworking the original product or a line extension—with a new formula and name—that is related to the original version of the product. Does the Egg Beaters' dairy section product belong in this stage? Again, consumer attitude decides.

It doesn't always translate into brand share. Royal Crown Cola has been an industry innovator—first with national distribution of soft drinks in cans (1954), a low-calorie diet cola (1962), a caffeine-free diet cola (1980), and a sodium-free diet cola (1983).[2] Royal Crown had the innovation but didn't effectively manage its advertising against the larger companies—Coca-Cola and Pepsi—and, of course, communicate with consumers.

The advertising focus in *newer pioneering* must be on getting consumers to understand what the product is about. Michelob's research found that consumers had absolutely no idea what *dry* meant when it came to beer. The same is true for ice in relationship to beer brands. Advertising in the newer competitive stage aims at getting more people to buy the brand. Interplak had additional competition from new types of plaque fighters: the Ultra Sonex toothbrush, with high-frequency sound waves to remove plaque; Optiva's Sonicare, with vibrating head at 31,000 strokes per minute; and oral irrigator products such as Oral-B Plaque Center. The newer retentive stage relies on existing prestige to keep customers. Diet Pepsi and Diet Coke are looking for ways to enter the newer pioneering stage. If Pepsi discovered that its product would remove warts, it might consider this new market potential and create appropriate advertising. Of course, this is an extreme example, but it illustrates how the spiral can continue (see Exhibit 3.14).

---

[2]"Royal Crown Plotting a Comeback with New Owners' Financial Support," *Atlanta Journal and Constitution,* March 6, 1994, p. C8.

Moving through these stages—newer pioneering, newer competitive, newer retentive—is not easy. It requires the manufacturer to develop either product innovations or advertising positioning strategies that make the product different in consumers' eyes. Also, as we move to the newer stages of the spiral, there are usually fewer prospects for the product. Therefore, a company must become more efficient at targeting smaller groups of prospects.

As Apple introduced faster, more powerful Macs to businesses and desktop publishing, these products were not pioneering in the same sense that a new product introduced by a new company would be, as Apple had established itself as a leader in desktop publishing and portable computers. The introduction of their PowerBook changed the landscape of the notebook computer market in a matter of months despite getting a late start in the category. As a product manager said, "The Competition keeps changing. The challenge is to build enough *equity* in the PowerBook name so that when people think of notebooks, they think of PowerBook."[3] Then came Apple's PowerPC, which Apple's advertising touted in a series of informative reports about how the revolutionary RISC-based microprocessor will allow users to run both PC's MS-DOS programs on the Mac.

THE ADVERTISING SPIRAL AS A MANAGEMENT DECISION TOOL

A product may try to hold on to its consumers in one competitive area while it seeks new markets with pioneering advertising aimed at other groups. We must remember that products do not move through each stage at the same speed. In some instances, a product may go quickly from one stage in one cycle to a newer stage in another cycle. This change may also be a matter of corporate strategy. A company may believe it can obtain a greater share of business at less cost by utilizing pioneering advertising that promotes new uses for the product. It is possible that the same results could be obtained by continuing to battle at a small profit margin in a highly competitive market. A retentive advertiser may suddenly find its market slipping and plunge into a new competitive war, without any new pioneering work. Like a compass, the spiral indicates direction; it does not dictate management decisions.

Before attempting to create new ideas for advertising a product the advertiser should use the spiral to answer the following questions:

- **In which stage is the product?**

- **Should we use pioneering advertising to attract new users to this type of product?**

- **Should we work harder at competitive advertising to obtain a larger share of existing market?**

- **What portion of our advertising should be pioneering, what portion competitive?**

- **Are we simply coasting in the retentive stage? If so, should we be more aggressive?**

So far in this chapter, we have shown how the life cycle of a product or brand may be affected by many conditions. If the brand is to continue to be mar-

---

[3]"Playing to Win," *Sales & Marketing Management,* August 1993, p. 39.

keted, its advertising stage must be identified before its advertising goals can be set. Next we examine how to expand on what we have learned to develop a strategic plan for a brand.

BUILDING STRONG BRANDS AND EQUITY

David Martin believes each product, service, or company with a recognized brand name stands for something slightly different from anything else in the same product category. If the difference is desirable, and is known and understood by consumers, the brand will be the category leader. Today more than ever before the perception of a quality difference is essential for survival in the marketplace.[4]

The Origin of Brands

In the mid-1880s, there were no brands and little quality control by manufacturers. Wholesalers held power over both manufacturers and retailers. Manufacturers had to offer the best deals to wholesalers in order to get their product distributed. This created a squeeze on profits. As a result of this profit squeeze, some manufacturers decided to differentiate their products from the competition. They gave their products names, obtained patents to protect their exclusivity, and used advertising to take the news about them to customers, over the heads of the wholesalers and retailers. Thus, the concept of branding was born. Among the brands still viable today are Levi's (1873), Maxwell House Coffee (1873), Budweiser (1876), Ivory (1879), Coca-Cola (1886), Campbell Soup (1893), and Hershey's chocolate (1900).[5] In 1923, a study showed that brands with "mental dominance" with consumers included Ivory (soaps), Gold Medal (flour), Coca-Cola (soft drinks), B.V.D. (underwear), Kellogg's Cornflakes (breakfast food), Ford (automobiles), Del Monte (canned fruit), and Goodyear (tires).[6]

Brands in Trouble

Stores have been overrun with brands looking for niches as well as a flood of discount brands. The competition for shelf space has made marketing efforts fierce. Many brands with a 40-, 50-, 60-year history have lost their prominence. There are many reasons: The company was sold, used a different focus, or new competitors reduce its market share. Companies like Procter & Gamble have killed off weak products like White Cloud bathroom tissue and Solo liquid detergent, brands in restructuring their priorities and resources. Clive Chajet, of Lippincott & Marguilies, a New York marketing firm and corporate identity, says, "companies are being forced to fish or cut bait. A major cause of the accelerated death rate is the U.P.C."—the Universal Product Code that is scanned at the checkout counter. In today's competitive environment, even large manufacturers are having difficulty providing advertising and marketing resources for dynamic and weak brands.[7] As a result, many consumers' old friends are or have been in trouble—Ajax and Fab detergents; Pepsodent toothpaste; Lux and Cashmere Bouquet soaps; Schlitz, Carling

---

[4]David Martin, *Romancing the Brand* (New York: Amacon, 1989), p. xiv.
[5]Norman Berry, "Revitalizing Brands," *Viewpoint*, July–August 1987, p. 18.
[6]Martin, *Romancing the Brand*, p. xiv.
[7]Stuart Elliott, "The Famous Brands on Death Row," *New York Times*, November 7, 1993, p. 3-1.

Black Label, Rheingold, and Pabst Blue Ribbon beers. Many old friends of consumers will die in the life cycle of brands—from introduction to dominance to decline or replacement. Yet brands, at least some, can defy this rule.

Understanding the Inner Brand

Many well-known, mature brands in trouble—lost share, plateaued, or worse—can be successfully restaged (remember, new pioneering). Despite mature brands carrying some baggage, they also have been around and probably mean something to a lot of people. Do your homework and find the inner brand— *"that tangible asset that no other brand owns."* Look at all those things that built the brand: its most important product promises, its package graphics and logo, its history, its founder or inventor, the company, its most famous advertising themes and campaigns.

The inner brand can be color, as National Car Rental decided with its new "Green Means Go" relaunch. It can even be a brand's technology, as "instant" is with Polaroid. With mature brands, chances are consumers remember something very specific: 7 UP, consumers think "Uncola." Citibank means consumers think "never sleeps." The Avis agency recognized the inner brand and kept a variation of their familiar theme, "Avis. Working harder than ever." Another major advertiser, Burger King, after dropping the successful "flame-broiled" theme for many years decided to return to "flame-broiled" as the brand's positioning. Brett Shevack of Partners and Shevack says, "After often spending hundreds of millions of dollars establishing an image, it's amazing how many smart marketers and smart agencies ditch the past and start over. This casual disregard for the inner brand is not only irresponsible, it's foolish."[8]

No, not every failing mature brand can be saved. And as indicated, many companies are deciding on where to put their resources older faltering brands or new ones or more successful older brands. Marketers doing their homework and keeping what works may keep a brand profitable.

Everyone agrees that brands haven't been managed as carefully as they should. The concern for short-term profits has driven marketers to discounting, couponing, and other promotions that can devalue a brand's equity and position.

Elements of a Brand

Brands with a carefully constructed strategy offering consumers a consistent ad message and a regularly updated product will lead their industries and provide excellent returns for the advertiser, a higher return on investment, higher shares market, and higher quality perceptions among consumers and according to D'Arcy, Masius Benton & Bowles study.

Because brands are the most valuable assets a marketer has, we need to understand what they are all about. The product is *not* the brand. A product is manufactured, a brand is created. A product may change over time, but the brand remains. A brand exists only in and through communication. The communication of the brand proclaims its singular and durable identity, its territory as a brand is therefore not sufficient for a brand to promote a motivating quality of the product for another product can always equal or copy

---

[8]Brett Shevack, "Unlocking the Inner Brand a Key to Marketing the Mature Product," *BrandWeek,* June 27, 1994, p. 20.

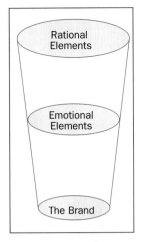

EXHIBIT

3.15

....

The basic elements of a brand.

it. The brand must be distinct from its competition. In fact, it is the competition that helps form the brand identity. A brand is a memory bank carrying all its history, which constitutes accumulated capital. The brand must continue to build new communications; assert its presence, but in doing so *it must consistently maintain its identity.*

At any point in time a brand is made up of two types of elements (see Exhibit 3.15). The *rational* elements (thinking) stem predominantly from "what" brand is doing, telling, showing. They:

■ **Embody the content and theme of the brand's communications, its proposition and promise**

■ **Speak more to the left or rational side of the brain[9]**

■ **Are the most visible part of the brand, the easiest part to articulate and measure**

The *emotional elements* (feeling) stem mainly from "how" the brand is expressing, telling, showing, or promising itself. They:

■ **Set the brand's style, tone, character, mode, mood of execution**

■ **Speak more to the right or intuitive-nonverbal side of the brain**

■ **Are less visible and therefore more difficult to express directly and measure**

In evaluating a brand, it is important to understand both the rational and the emotional elements that define it. We can decide to act directly on either group of elements, and the implications of each decision are very different.

Behavior and Brand Assets

There's been a growing trend in this decade among marketers to be more interested in brands as assets and building and preserving those assets. One of the Brand Managers' most important goal is protecting the brand's good name. To succeed, they must answer three questions: Who buys the brand, what do they want from it, and why do they keep coming back? According to the Roper Organization, many people buy familiar brands even if they believe the product has no actual advantage. Just half of Americans think that a specific brand of mayonnaise is different from or better than others and worth paying more for. However, 62 percent know what brand of mayonnaise they want when they walk into the store. Another 22 percent look around for the best price on a well-known brand. *Brand behavior is complex.* Not everyone is brand-conscious, and not all brand conscious people are truly brand driven.[10]

In supermarkets, 81 of the top 100 best-selling items are national brands; 14 of the remaining 19 store-brand items are in the dairy case. In drugstores, 92

---

[9]The brain is divided into two hemispheres: the left and the right brain. The left brain is the rational side. It reads images, is logical, and deals with math, verbal, and memory functions. It is the conservative side of the brain. The right brain is intuitive. It scans images, controls the creative process, and thinks nonverbally. It is the emotional side of the brain.

   People obviously use both sides of their brain, but it is not unusual for one side to be dominant. The following occupations are supposed to attract left-brain individuals: accounting, the law, research, engineering, medicine. Right-brain individuals are more likely to take up art, photography, music, acting, etc. and other occupations that require intuitive thinking.

[10]Diane Crispell and Kathleen Brandenburg, "What's in a Brand?" *American Demographics,* May 1993, pp. 26–28.

EXHIBIT

3.16

Verbatim builds brand image by positioning its product as the best defense against data loss.

(Courtesy: Verbatim and Loeffler Ketchum Mountjoy.)

of the 100 best-selling items are national brands. With mass merchandisers, 87 of the 100 best-selling items are national brands.[11] Even the majority of private-label products aren't the generics of days past. The correct term is *store brands.* Wal-Mart, for example, designs a package, gives the product an identity, and promotes it, just the same as Coke or Pepsi.

Researchers attempt to rank brands in a number of ways. One study of brand ranking was done by Total Research Corporation *on Best Brands* in terms of quality: Disney World/Disneyland ranked first, followed by: Kodak photographic film, Hallmark greeting cards, United Parcel Service, Fisher-Price toys, Levi's jeans, Mercedes-Benz. Their *Mega-Brands* survey determined that the first step in building loyalty to a brand is to make sure consumers are familiar with it. The leaders were Campbell Soup, Hallmark greeting cards, United Parcel Service, Hershey's, McDonald's, Sears, Kmart, etc. Verbatim tapes, optical, and floppy disks (Exhibit 3.16) establishes the brand as *your best defense against data loss.*

Consumers and Brands

Research tells us that people's past experiences with a brand is consistently the most important factor in their future choice. Despite all the press about quality, *past experiences* followed by *price, quality,* and *recommendations from other people* lead the reasons people buy a brand. These factors haven't significantly changed over the past two decades; however, price has become more important. Yes, psychological motivations are important, but a brand's most powerful advantage is rooted in the human tendency to form habits and stick to routines. Most people will buy the same brand over and over again if it continues to satisfy their needs. Advertisers have to overcome or change habits as indicated in the discussion of advertising stages.

Marketers need to be aware that as consumers' needs change, their purchase behavior also may change. It is not unusual for needs to change when peo-

---

[11]C. Manly Molpus, "Brands Follow New Shopping Patterns," *Advertising Age,* February 14, 1994, p. 22.

ple's lives change. For example, a couple may trade in their sports car for a van when they have a child. A recently divorced parent may be forced to change buying patterns due to less income. Interestingly, 40 percent of the people who move to a new address change their toothpaste. Yes, we need to understand consumers and their relationship to brands.

Brands and Integrated Communication

In the past, many marketing functions were created and managed independently in most organizations—advertising, promotion, packaging, direct marketing, public relations, events, etc. The economic pressures facing companies in the 1990s have created the need to manage these activities more efficiently and to ensure they all reinforce each other. The result has been what is labeled *integrated communications.*

Integrated communications refers to all the messages directed to a consumer on behalf of the brand: media advertising, promotion, public relations, direct response, events, packaging, etc. Each message must be integrated or dovetailed in order to support all other messages or impressions about the brand. If this process is successful, it will build a brand's equity by communicating the same brand message to consumers. Let's look at other definitions.[12]

> The AAAA's working definition of integrated communications: "A concept of marketing communications planning that recognized the added value of a comprehensive plan that evaluates the strategic roles of a variety of communications disciplines and combines these disciplines to provide clarity, consistency, and maximum communication impact."

> Ernan Roman's definition of "integrated direct marketing": the "art and science of managing a diverse marketing media as a cohesive whole. These interrelationships are catalysts for response. The resulting media synergy generates response rates higher than could be achieved by individual media efforts."

> Maxi Marketing', (by Stan Rapp and Tom Collins) definition of the new direction in advertising: "one-to-one" marketing. Examples of customer database applications are provided that maximize "lifetime consumer value."

This database capability marketers have today makes the process of integrating easier than in the past. There are those who say integration has been around for 20 years, but it wasn't as an important issue as it is today. (We'll be discussing aspects of integrated communication throughout this text, and its organization in Chapters 5 and 6.)

All during the 1980s too many marketers were milking their brands or looking for short-term profits instead of protecting and nurturing their brands. In the 1990s, brand building has become fashionable as marketers realize the brand is their most important asset. Because integrated programs and brand building are so important, we will discuss a system integrated communications that build brand equity. Lintas:Worldwide developed a strategic planning process to integrate all the communication disciplines. Its process is

Brand equity

The value of how such people as consumers, distributors, and salespeople think and feel about a brand relative to its competition over a period of time.

---

[12]Neil M. Brown, *Marketing News,* March 19, 1993, p. 4.

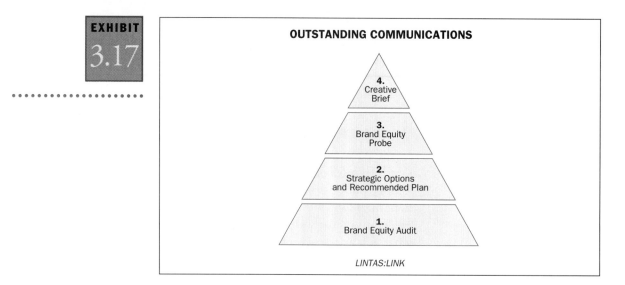

EXHIBIT

3.17

called Lintas:Link. It helps to synergize communications to build strong brand equity for existing and new products. The most important factor in determining the actual value of a brand is its equity in the market—how consumers (end users and others such as employees, salespeople, and distributors) think and feel about a brand (Exhibit 3.17).

LINTAS:LINK STRATEGIC PLANNING PROCESS FOR INTEGRATED MARKETING COMMUNICATIONS

There are four successive steps in the Link process designed to help the user be innovative and anticipatory in understanding the market, the market environment, the consumer, and thus the marketer's options for dealing with all of these:

- **Brand equity audit**

- **Strategic options and recommendation plan**

- **Brand equity probe**

- **Creative brief**

Let's take a look at each of these steps that help understand the brand.

Brand Equity Audit

The initial step is to identify the present equity of our brand and the factors that have a significant impact on it so that we can develop the most effective communication strategy for the future. The brand equity audit is not a market analysis. We are interested only in evaluating how consumers think and feel about our brand versus the competition. The brand equity audit is divided into four areas.

Market Context. We begin by examining the existing situation from two angles: the market and the consumer. What we are looking for are clues and factors that positively or negatively affect brand equity. The sole purpose is to set the scene. Here are some examples of the type of questions we may be asking: What is our market and whom do we compete with? What other brands/product categories? What makes the market tick? How is the market structured? Is it segmented? How? What segment are we in? What is the status of store and generic brands? Are products highly differentiated? What kind of person buys products in this category? In the mind of these consumers, what drives the market or holds it back (needs, obstacles, etc.)? What are the key motivators? Do consumers perceive the brands as very much alike or different? Is the product bought on impulse? How interested are consumers in the product? Do they tend to be brand loyal?

These questions should help us understand the status and role of brands in that given market. For example, when the share of generics and store brands is abnormally high, that may well be an indication that the different brands present in the market are not doing their job. Or when the market is made up of a limited number of brands, the consumer will probably be more brand sensitive than if the market is split up into innumerable brands.

We must look at the market from varying angles—and select only the relevant ones—so that we can set the scene for understanding and building brand equity.

Brand Equity Indicators. Once we understand the market context, we go on to examine current brand equity—how strong or weak consumer bias is toward our brand, relative to other brands. Here we must be selective and shrewd, picking out those indicators that will provide maximum insight. The following is a list of indicators often used.

- **Brand awarenesss—top-of-mind is best**

- **Market share, price elasticity, share of voice, and the like**

- **Brand sensitivity—the relative importance of brand to other factors involved in the purchase, such as price, pack size, model**

- **Assumed leadership—consumers' perception of leadership of the brand**

- **Consistency of the brand's communication over time**

- **Image attribute ratings, or ranking attributes**

- **Distribution, pricing, product quality, and product innovation**

- **Brand loyalty—the strength of a brand lies in the proportion of its customers who buy it as a brand rather than just as a product**

Once the key indicators have been identified, they are used for future tracking purposes.

Brand Equity Description. Now that we understand the market in which our brand operates and have a clear indication of the strength or weakness of our brand equity, we move to the most difficult and important area in the brand equity audit—identifying and describing the consumer thoughts and feelings that result in the strong or weak bias consumers have toward our brand relative to other brands. This personal relationship between the consumer and the brand provides the most meaningful description of brand equity.

To achieve this description of brand equity, we need to carry out our analysis from two viewpoints:

- **We need to review all the available research to get as close a feeling as possible on how consumers view the brand and how they feel about it.**

Brand loyalty
Degree to which a consumer purchases a certain brand without considering alternatives.

- **We must analyze in depth our brand's and its competitors' communications over a period of time. It is from these communications that most of the consumers' feelings and opinions about the brand are derived.**

A brand equity description for the Golf GTI automobile might look like this:

EMOTIONAL ELEMENTS	RATIONAL ELEMENTS
My little sports car	inexpensive
Sets me free	High gas mileage
It makes me feel/look good	Retains value
Simple	Durable

EMOTIONAL ELEMENTS	RATIONAL ELEMENTS
It's there when I want it	Dependable
I'm in control	Handles well
	Easy to park—small

Competitive Strategies and Tactics.   This area of the audit is designed to provide a clear summary of the current communication strategies and tactics of our brand and of key competitors. It should include an analysis of current advertising and other communications in relation to brand equity. Is the strategy designed to reinforce current brand equity or to change it? Who is the target audience? Are there different target audiences? What are the theme and executional approach? How are the marketing funds being spent (consumer pull versus trade push, advertising, promotions, direct marketing, etc.)? An assessment of problems/opportunities is also in order here.

Strategic Options and Recommended Plan

Brand Positioning
Consumers' perceptions of specific brands relative to the various brands of goods or services currently available to them.

This step in the Lintas:Link strategic planning process draws on the conclusion from the brand equity audit to develop a viable recommended plan. The strategic options include:

- *Communication objectives:* **What is the primary goal the message aims to achieve?**

- *Audience:* **Whom are we speaking to?**

- *Source of business:* **Where are customers to come from—brand(s) or product categories?**

- *Brand positioning and benefits:* **How are we to position the brand, and what are the benefits that will build brand equity?**

- *Marketing mix:* **What is the recommended mix of advertising, public relations, promotion, direct response, and so on?**

- *Rationale:* **How does the recommended strategy relate to, and what effect is it expected to have on, brand equity?**

Alternate plans can be developed by changing the content of any of the major options.

Brand Equity Probe

The probe is the proprietary, qualitative research step in the Lintas:Link process. It is exploratory and task oriented. Here we need to determine which element(s) of brand equity must be created, altered, or reinforced in order to achieve our recommended strategy, and how far we can stretch each of these components without risking the brand's credibility. In other words, what are the boundaries we should not cross?

Example: Our brand is seen as too technical and aloof. How far can we take it to make it more friendly?

If not enough information is available from previous research to complete this step, we may need to do the brand equity probe right at the start of the Link process. If sufficient information is available, simply summarize the results here.

The probe results in a revised list of rational and emotional elements that describe *how we want consumers to think and feel about our brand in the future.*

In the mid-1990s, Burger King probed consumers to help them get back to basics. Their chief executive said, "We've focused in on what consumers are looking for. The consumer today wants true value. If you can deliver that, you can win market share." Burger King found that value is more than low price. Consumers said it's not a great value if it's not a great burger. The end result was a new campaign and direction: *Get your burger's worth.* Burger Kings' back-to-basics emphasis generated sales growth after starting this new direction with a 13 percent increase in sales. During the same period McDonald's growth was 4 percent, and competitor Wendy's was 5.6 percent.[13]

Creative Brief

The audit process ends with the creative brief for all communication variables. In this step, we synthesize the first Link steps into an action plan for the development of all communications for the brand: advertising, direct marketing, promotion, public relations, and so on. Strategies for reaching the target audience, the desired *equity* or rational emotional elements considered ideal, and lastly the *creative tone* the campaign should assume. Ad tonality is what happens when strategy is translated into execution. The strategy might call for a light-hearted comparison with the competition. The creatives must then come up with a communication that compares in a humorous way. Of course, people's interpretation of what is funny varies.

The creative brief consists of three elements:

- **Strategy**
- **Desired brand equity**
- **Creative guidelines**

Strategy. This is a one-page statement that clearly defines what audience we are talking to; how they think, feel, and behave; what communication is intended to achieve; and the promise that will create a bond (link) between the consumers and the brand. The strategy consists of:

- *Key observation:* **The most important market/consumer factor that dictates the strategy**
- *Communication objective:* **The primary goal the advertising aims to achieve**
- *Consumer insight:* **The consumer "hot button" our communication will trigger**

---

[13]Stuart Elliott, "Burger King Mounts a Populist Campaign to Get Back to Basics," *New York Times,* September 1, 1994, p. C-5.

EXHIBIT

3.18

· · · · · · · · · · · · · · · ·

You need to fill in one
idea in each box in the
creative brief.

```
┌─────────────────────────────────────────────────────┐
│                    LINTAS: LINK                       │
│  CLIENT: _____  BRAND: _____  Date: _____    │
│  4-CREATIVE BRIEF                                      │
│  4.1-STRATEGY                                          │
│  ┌─────────────────────────────────────────────────┐ │
│  │ KEY OBSERVATION                                   │ │
│  └─────────────────────────────────────────────────┘ │
│  ┌────────────────────────┐┌─────────────────────────┐│
│  │ COMMUNICATION OBJECTIVE ││ CONSUMER INSIGHT        ││
│  │                         ││                         ││
│  └────────────────────────┘└─────────────────────────┘│
│  ┌─────────────────────────────────────────────────┐ │
│  │ PROMISE                                           │ │
│  │                                                   │ │
│  └─────────────────────────────────────────────────┘ │
│  ┌────────────────────────┐┌─────────────────────────┐│
│  │ SUPPORT                 ││ AUDIENCE                ││
│  │                         ││                         ││
│  └────────────────────────┘└─────────────────────────┘│
│  MANDATORIES:                                         │
│  ════════════════════════════════════════════════    │
│  Account:      Research Planning:      Creative:      │
└─────────────────────────────────────────────────────┘
```

- ■ *Promise:* The link between the consumer and the brand: what the brand should stand for in the consumer's mind

- ■ *Support:* The reason the brand gives the consumer permission to believe

- ■ *Audience:* Whom are we speaking to? How do they think and feel about the brand?

The key to writing the strategy is to have one idea per element (or box in Exhibit 3.18.)

"Mandatories" are actually optional and should only be used when compulsory constraints exist—for example, if there is a specific legal requirement or corporate policy that impacts the direction of the strategy.

Desired Brand Equity. This is the list of rational and emotional components that describes how we want consumers to think and feel about the brand in the future. The *desired* brand equity is compared to the *current* brand equity to show clearly, side by side, the changes the communication program is intended to create (Exhibit 3.19). Changes in brand equity, especially in the emotional elements, come very slowly. We would expect the differences between current and desired brand equity to be subtle—or, if substantial, to take a long time to be achieved.

Creative Guidelines. This part of the creative brief is written in close cooperation with the creative director on the brand and is based on insights gained from the brand equity probe as well as on judgment and experience. The creative guidelines are a simple list of do's and don'ts giving the creative team clear direction about the attitude, approach, and tonality the advertising should take in order to create the desired brand equity.

EXHIBIT

3.19

∙∙∙∙∙∙∙∙∙∙∙∙∙∙∙∙∙∙∙∙∙

The desired brand equity is compared to current brand equity, showing changes the communications program is intended to create. This information is part of the creative brief, along with creative guidelines for all communications.

LINTAS: LINK

CLIENT: _____ BRAND: _____ Date: _____

CURRENT BRAND EQUITY

EMOTIONAL ELEMENTS	RATIONAL ELEMENTS

DESIRED BRAND EQUITY

EMOTIONAL ELEMENTS	RATIONAL ELEMENTS

ALL COMMUNICATIONS

SHOULD	SHOULD NOT

Other Brand Factors

Master Brands. Some markers try to turn mere brands into master brands that compete across product segments. For instance, the Colgate name in the oral-care category is on toothpaste, toothbrushes, and mouthwash. In competition with Colgate, Oral-B has tried to develop master branding initiatives using its name in oral rinses, toothpaste, toothbrushes, and plaque remover brushes. Chesebrough-Pond's has developed a number of body-care products under the Vaseline Intensive Care umbrella. At the root of this activity is a push to leverage brand equity and build brand synergies.

Megabrands dominate their category through marketing an extended line of products built around an established brand. Each product in the extended line develops a distinct subidentity.

Global Brands. The world is the marketplace requiring marketers to assess how to compete on a global basis. Brands like Coca-Cola, Kodak, Gillette, and Pepsi have established themselves around the world many years ago, but most U.S. companies have only recently picked up the challenge. U.S. companies have been far less global in their vision than from countries that must export—for example, Japan and European countries. Michael Perry, chairman of Unilever (the world's largest advertiser outside the United States), says, "As a rule, product concepts must be driven by consumers, not imposed by marketers." Unilever never started out to create an international brand. Each one of your consumers is a very local person who lives in a very specific location, shops in a very specific number of stores, and chooses your brand or your competitor's brand against a very specific background of perception of what those brands are, related to one another. *Every successful international brand starts by being a successful local brand . . . reproduced many times.*

In global advertising you have to be conscious of local attitudes and economics. AmEx Travel Related Services retired chairman says, "Eighty percent of the emotional element of our brand is the same around the world."[14] American Express Company's global advertising looks at the brand's core values—places you want to go, people you want to be. All global ads follows a basic formula—with distinctive local details that set them apart from cookie-cutter testimonials. Merchants discuss their business philosophies, then talk about the card. A number of marketers believe you should run the same ads around the globe to create a consistent brand image versus ads developed to reflect the local culture. American Express localizes its international ad efforts.

Global brand equity can be problematic where food is concerned because tastes are an expression of culture. Unilever does not attempt to cross borders with basic foods, such as soup, citing examples like extreme cultural disparities between French and Dutch concepts of pea soup. Of course, U.S. fast food chains McDonald's and Pizza Hut have demonstrated that an eating experience can be branded in such a way that regional differences can be transcended. In advertising Lipton tea, the company is faced with such problems as the British prefer it very hot and diluted with milk, Americans like it iced, and Middle East consumers drink it very sweet. Developing global brand equity can be a major challenge.

Financial World's brand value report ranked Coca-Cola the world's most valuable brand, followed by Marlboro, Nescafe, Kodak, Microsoft, Budweiser, Kellogg's, Motorola, Gillette, and Bacardi.[15] *Financial World's* valuations are based on branded products' worldwide sales, profitability, and growth potential minus costs such as plants, equipment, and taxes.

Virtual Brands. Just as the dawn of television created modern brand advertising, today's new interactive media tools augur the arrival of the post modern brand reformation. The explosion of media alternatives will redefine the brand concept and transform the nature of consumption. New media will be capable of understanding a consumer's existing product context and social circumstances before a message is delivered. Once the new media have learned what individual customers have and want in their lives, advertisers can customize benefits for more persuasive personal selling. The virtual brand will be like a chameleon, looking and acting differently to different people while satisfying, servicing and shaping individuals more intensely.[16]

Yes, branding can be a complex process. There are a lot of factors to consider. Protecting and promoting brands in the future will be more complex despite larger databases full of market and consumer information.

---

[14]"Don't Leave Home without It. Wherever You Live,": *Business Week,* February 21, 1994, p. 76.
[15]Keith J. Kelly, "Coca-Cola Shows That Top-Brand Fizz," *Advertising Age,* July 11, 1994, p. 3.
[16]Andrew Susman, "New Media and Brand Reformation," *Advertising Age,* August 8, 1994, p. 18.

SUMMARY

Products pass through a number of stages, from introduction to ultimate demise, known as the *product life cycle*. Advertising plays a different role in each stage of product development. Until consumers appreciate the fact that they need a product, that product is in the pioneering stage. In the competitive stage, an advertiser tries to differentiate its product from that of the competition. Once consumers know about products and use them, they may become part of the retentive stage, which uses reminder advertising.

The age of a product has little to do with what stage it is in at any given time. Rather, consumer attitude or perception determines which stage a product is in. As consumer perception changes, moving the product from one stage to another, the advertising message should change. It is very possible for the advertising to be in more than one stage at a time. Creative marketing may propel a product through the new pioneering, new competitive, and new retentive stages. And it is even possible for the cycle to continue into the newest pioneering, newest competitive, and newest retentive stages. As products age, so do their users, which is why no product can survive without constantly attracting new consumers. Long-term success depends on keeping current customers while constantly creating new ones.

There were no brands in the mid-1880s. When manufacturers wanted people to know who manufactured their products, they differentiated and named them; thus, brands were born.

Brands are among the most valuable assets a company owns. The product is not a brand. A product is manufactured; a brand is created and is made up of both rational and emotional elements.

Integrated marketed communications recognizes the added value of a comprehensive plan that evaluates the strategic roles of a variety of communication disciplines (including advertising promotion, direct marketing, events, design, public relations, etc.) and combines these disciplines to provide clarity, consistency, and maximum communication impact.

Brand equity is the value of how consumers, distributors, and salespeople think and feel about a brand relative to its competition over a period of time. In other words, a product like Coca-Cola has built brand equity for decades among consumers. Lintas:Link is an example of strategic planning (integrated marketing) that involves the brand equity audit, strategic options and recommendations plan, brand equity probe, and the creative brief.

Questions
1. Briefly discuss each of the three primary stages in the advertising spiral.
2. What is the essence of the advertising message in each stage of the spiral?
3. Which stage of the advertising spiral would normally be the most profitable for the manufacturer?
4. How does the advertising spiral differ from the traditional product life-cycle model?
5. What is brand equity?
6. What are the four segments of Lintas: Link?
7. What is the integrated communications?

Target Marketing

CHAPTER 4

CHAPTER OBJECTIVES

Marketers need to determine who their prime prospects are. They need to understand changes taking place in society and their impact on their business. After reading this chapter you will understand:

- **Defining prime prospects**
- **Trends to watch**
- **New marketing concept and targeting**
- **Planning the advertising**
- **Niche marketing and positioning**
- **Beyond demographics: psychographics**

Who is going to buy our product? Who are we going to aim our advertising and or promotion? Has our target market changed? Is it going to be profitable? What was our rationale for selecting this target? Yes, a lot of questions. The brand equity audit seeks to answer a number of questions and examine the existing state of the brand in the context of markets and consumers. There are an **increasing number** of information sources to help a marketer plan integrated marketing programs for its brands. It's a new day in marketing.

The nature of strategic planning has changed because we're in the process of a marketing revolution—the marketing environment that made brand marketing so successful in the past has and is changing. Part of this revolution is the availability of new techniques and data never before available in planning integrated marketing decisions. It has a lot of names: database marketing, relationship marketing, one-to-one marketing. This new marketing is aimed at the individual and not the mass market. In this chapter we'll discuss the marketing terminology and concepts that help advertisers use all the data.

Advertisers have always needed to answer basic questions relating to targets. Who are the best prospects for becoming users of the brand or increasing their usage of the brand? How many are there? Where do they live and shop? How do they think and act? What is their lifestyle? Are they male or female? Are significant numbers members of a specific group—Hispanic, black, Asian, babyboomers, Xer's, singles, and so on? What about geographic differences? Education? Income? Are their enough to make a profit? Have we examined all the possibilities?

As you consider these questions, you must determine which answers are critical to your decision making. Do you need more information to reach your prospects successfully? Do you understand their problems? Have you thought about what you want people to think and feel about your brand as a result of being exposed to your advertising?

DEFINING PRIME PROSPECTS

Target marketing

Identifying and communicating with groups of prime prospects.

One of the keys to success is defining the prime prospect so that you do not waste time and money advertising your product to people unlikely to buy it, or that you can't make a profit by attracting. This search for the best prospects among all consumers is called *target marketing.*

The process of finding prime prospects can be very complex because there are numerous ways of looking at consumers, many different kinds of information to consider, and a constant changing consumer environment.

The Yamaha golf cart ad is obviously designed for a segment of the golfing market (Exhibit 4.1), but is it aimed at every golfer? Who are they? Where are they? Does income matter? How about age? Gender? How often do they play?

The 1990 census data gave advertisers and marketers information that wasn't available previously, for example, the government's *Topologically Integrated Geographic Encoding and Referencing* system known as Tiger. This coding of the country's natural, political, and statistical boundaries includes every street, road, and subdivision. Tiger provides the data for computer maps to plan sales territories and pinpoint direct marketing prospects. This information can be linked to a number of relevant characteristics such as age, income, and race. Custom research companies using these data has developed software for marketers to access geodemographic databases—for example, Survey Sampling, Inc.'s, ClickUSA.

TRENDS TO WATCH
Population

Let's look at some changes in population and the implications on advertising planning. By the year 2020, California will remain by far the most populous

Last round of the season.

Fairbanks, Alaska.

The northernmost place you can play the game.

Up here, it's either Yamaha or dogsleds.

YAMAHA USA
The Extra Mile.

SOMETIMES, AT FAIRBANKS GOLF & COUNTRY CLUB, THE GOLFING SEASON ONLY LASTS THREE MONTHS. But, for a golf car, it's three months of pure hell. From June, when the sun shines on golfers 22 hours a day, all the way through August, when snows begin to dust the greens.

It's more than the average golf car can take. Which is why the Fairbanks Golf & Country Club wouldn't use anything but a Yamaha. After all, only

Yamaha cars incorporate so many components made especially to stand up to the unique demands of your golf course. Like a Yamaha-designed engine on gas models and an electronic speed control designed and manufactured by Yamaha for electric models. Which may be why only Yamaha cars – both gas and electric – need as little as 1/4 the maintenance time of our biggest competitors.

So, you're thinking, why does your course

need a golf car as rugged as the Alaskan interior? Maybe because, with golf cars this reliable, you wouldn't need backup cars in your fleet. Or maybe because they could save you incredible amounts of time, money and aggravation. But the best reason of all is that only Yamaha cars are designed and built to go the extra mile – and keep you out of the cold.

For the name of your nearest Yamaha dealer, call 1-800-843-3354, extension 61.

©1993 Yamaha USA Golf Car Group, 1000 Highway 14 East, Newnan, Georgia 30265, 404-254-4150. *Based on on manufacturers' recommended preventive maintenance and average usage of 250 18-hole rounds per year per car.

(Courtesy: Sawyer Riley Compton, Inc.)

EXHIBIT
4.1

. . . .

Yamaha targets golfers that want to ride.

state with a projected population of some 47.9 million people, but both Texas (25.6 million) and Florida (with 19.4 million), will move ahead of New York (19.1 million people), which will drop to the fourth most populous state. California, like New York, will lose more residents to other states than it will gain from in-migration from other states (see Exhibit 4.2). However, the flow of immigrants—mostly Hispanics and Asians—will boost the growth rate above 50 percent by 2020.

The fastest-growing market in the U.S. is the group 50 years and older. The mature consumers represent 31 percent of the U.S. population by the year 2020, according to the U.S. Census Bureau, up from 21 percent in 1990.

Income

Another variable that may influence target market is income. In 1995, 8.0 percent of all U.S. households earned between $50,000 and $74,000 and account for 17.8 percent of the country's total income. The importance of income may vary significantly according to product category—it means little in selling soft drinks but it is very important in selling real estate and luxury automobiles. Another way of looking at targets might be in terms of spending, not just income. The Bureau of Labor Statistics' Consumer Expenditure (CE) Survey produces annual estimates of household spending on hundreds of items, cross-tabulated by demographic characteristics. As with most data, you need to use these data wisely. Many marketers ignore low-income households because of low spending levels. But remember the late Sam Walton became the richest man in America by serving low-income shoppers.

EXHIBIT 4.2

Predicted Population Projections

State 2020 Rank	1993 Rank	2020 Population	1993–2020 Increase
1. California	1	47,900,000	52.7%
2. Texas	3	25,600,000	42.3
3. Florida	4	19,400,000	41.7
4. New York	2	19,100,000	5.3
5. Illinois	6	13,200,000	12.9
6. Pennsylvania	5	12,600,000	5.0
7. Ohio	7	11,900,000	7.1
8. Michigan	8	10,400,000	9.4
9. Georgia	11	9,400,000	37.2
10. New Jersey	9	9,100,000	15.6

(Source: U.S. Census Bureau.)

Minority Changes

Market Segment Research, the U.S. Bureau of Census, WSL Marketing, and the Urban Institute indicate significant changes in minorities adapting the social and economic habits of mainstream America. In the past, immigrants adopted the prevailing culture, but now minorities are no longer assimilating in that way. Instead, they are holding on to their culture and changing American culture in the process. Marketers should be careful not to make generalizations about minorities as a group. Marketing to minorities will offer major challenges because of the tremendous diversity among Hispanics, Asian-Americans, and blacks. Consider these differences: 58 percent of blacks reported that they preferred to buy products made in the United States; only 25 percent of the Asian-Americans agreed. Research indicates there is wide diversity within each of the group's subsegments. For example, Hispanics are known to be heavy consumers of beans; however, Mexicans eat refried beans, Puerto Ricans eat red beans, and Cubans eat black beans.

Marketers must be careful to do their homework in advertising to these groups. Blacks and Hispanics are particularly concerned about seeing positive images of minorities in advertising, avoiding stereotypical images that might alienate the minority. For example, all blacks walking into fast-food restaurants don't carry boom boxes and dance. Most just walk in and order. Let's take a quick look at some targeting considerations.

African Americans

Blacks represent about 13 percent of the U.S. population, consisting of 30 million. Over 1.6 million blacks have incomes of $50,000 or more. Despite a high concentration of single-parent households, over half of black households are married-couple families. The majority (76 percent) said they choose a store based on quality and not price. They are somewhat brand-loyal. About 57 percent of food, beverage and household product purchases are for the same brand and don't switch just because a brand is on sale.

Asian Americans

This group is the fastest-growing minority in the nation, doubling in size during the 1980s, reaching 7.3 million, and representing 3.3 percent of the population. The group is projected to reach 6 percent of the population by 2010. Most retain their native language no matter the country of origin, and 35 percent reported speaking it exclusively. Most Asian-Americans prefer to watch or listen to television or radio programs in their native language. Yet younger Asian-Americans had a higher preference for English-language programs. When selecting a store, 66 percent said they look for quality over price. WSL Marketing found that Asian women shopped close to home, and when they found a store or brand they liked, they were most loyal of any ethnic group.[1] When buying food, beverage, and household products they are not particularly brand loyal. When we examine subgroup differences, the Chinese are more apt to buy an item on sale than Koreans or Japanese.

Hispanics

The 22.3 million Hispanics are predicted to outnumber blacks in this country by about the year 2010. In general, they identify strongly with their culture and country of origin. Some 97 percent of respondents to the Market Segment study said they speak Spanish, and 51 percent speak it exclusively. They watched 14 hours of Spanish-language television, listened to 11 hours of Spanish-language radio, and spent 3.5 hours reading Spanish-language publications. Seventy-two percent indicated quality over price when choosing a store. They are somewhat brand-loyal when buying food, beverage, or household items. They have the lowest rate of home ownership of the three minorities and, on average, had the largest number of children, and other adults, living at home.[2]

It is logical for people of different ethnic backgrounds and family histories to have different preferences for products, stores, and services. Marketers and advertisers need to understand the needs and concerns of groups they are interested in reaching.

Most Hispanics in this country have come from Mexico, Puerto Rico, and Cuba. Marketers have begun to pay attention to the differences brought from the country of origin. Hispanics from other Latin American nations and cultures are less well understood, but they constitute one-quarter of an estimated $170 billion consumer market in this country.

The 1990 census provides marketers with information on 12 nations of Hispanic origin—Mexico, Puerto Rico, Cuba, El Salvador, the Dominican Republic, Colombia, Guatemala, Nicaragua, Ecuador, Peru, Honduras, and Panama—as well as *other* Central American and *other* South American countries. These data provide the first opportunity to advertisers to understand where these specific Hispanic groups live. These migration patterns can be very important to marketing and advertising decisions. Take, for example, the fact that initially most Hispanic immigrants settled in New York or Los Angeles. Many today have chosen Miami, Washington, D.C., and San Francisco instead of New York or Los Angeles. Despite the fact that 18 percent of all Hispanics live in Los Angeles and 12 percent live in New York, Chicago has the country's second largest Puerto Rican population, and the third largest Guatemalan and Ecuadorian populations. To communicate with any group,

---

[1]Cyndee Miller, "Study: Shopping Patterns Vary Widely among Minorities," *Marketing News,* January 18, 1993, p. 11.
[2]Cyndee Miller, "Researcher Says U.S. Is More of a Bowl Than a Pot" *Marketing News,* May 10, 1993, p. 6.

EXHIBIT
4.3

The growth of family
versus non-family
households from
1985–2000.

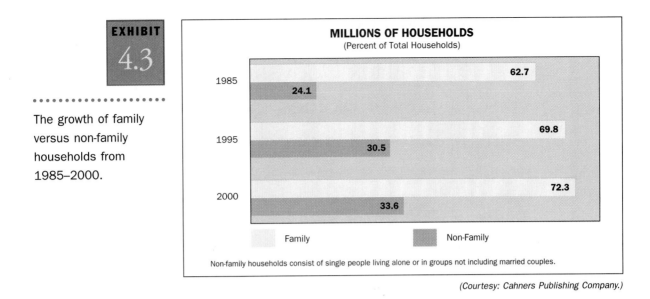

MILLIONS OF HOUSEHOLDS
(Percent of Total Households)

1985	62.7	24.1
1995	69.8	30.5
2000	72.3	33.6

Family   Non-Family

Non-family households consist of single people living alone or in groups not including married couples.

(Courtesy: Cahners Publishing Company.)

understanding is a key. A specific problem for marketers trying to reach Hispanics is that many are not interested in participating as full-fledged consumers—owning a home or car. For example, most Brazilians are in New York only to save money for the return to Brazil. Avianca, the airline of Colombia, focuses its U.S. advertising on Colombians—some 86,000 in New York City. It runs ads primarily on Spanish-language television, radio, and newspapers. In its media selection it is not interested in high ratings for all Hispanics, but specifically is interested in Colombians. Advertisers may need to look beyond the general Hispanic label.[3]

Living Patterns

Changes in living arrangements offer advertisers a number of targeting considerations: *Singles* (persons living alone or with nonrelatives) have increased significantly over the past 20 years in both numbers of households and income gains. Exhibit 4.3 illustrates family and nonfamily household growth (nonfamily households consist of single people living alone or in groups not including married couples.) *Single-parent families,* the census tells us, account for about 10 percent of all households. *Mature couples,* age 65 and over without children living in home, have seen an increase in income due in part to higher pensions and retirement incomes. *Childless young couples* have experienced an increase in income partly because of the high incidence of working wives. Numbers for *dual-earner married couples with children* have remained fairly constant over the years with income improvements. *Married couples* continue to be among the highest income group. Healthtex is obviously targeting people with children—single-parent families or married couples with children or both (Exhibit 4.4). *Empty nesters,* married couples aged 45–64 with no children in the household account for about 13 percent of households yet are the highest income group. Married, dual-earners, and empty nesters account for only about 32 percent of households and about 50 percent of income.

[3]Morton Winsberg, "Specific Hispanics," *American Demographics,* February 1994, pp. 44–53.

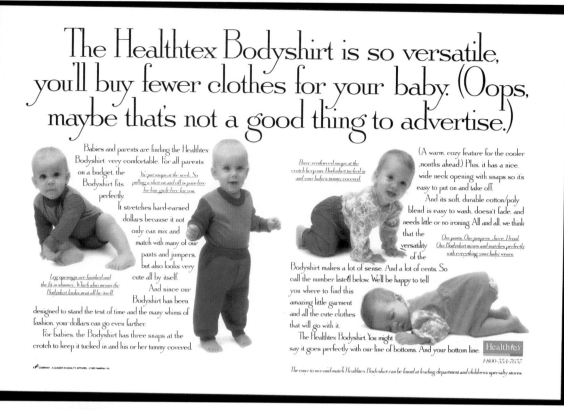

(Courtesy: Healthtex™.)

NEW MARKETING CONCEPT AND TARGETING

Marketing segmentation is an extension of the *marketing concept,* defined by Kotler and Armstrong, that achieving organizational goals depends on determining the needs and wants of target markets and delivering the desired satisfactions more effectively and efficiently than competitors. This idea has been stated as "find a need and fill it" or "make what you can sell instead of trying to sell what you can make."

Frederick E. Webster, Jr., however says, the old marketing concept—the management philosophy first articulated in the 1950s—is a relic of an earlier period of economic history. Most of its assumptions are no longer appropriate in the competitive global markets of the 1990s. Today the world is moving rapidly toward a pattern of economic activity based on long-term relationships and partnerships among economic actors in the loose coalitional frameworks of *network* organizations. The concept of *customer value* is at the heart of the new marketing concept and must be the central element of all business strategy.

Under the old marketing concept the objective was to make a sale. Under the new marketing concept, the objective is to develop a customer relationship, in which the sale is only the beginning. Under both the old and new, market segmentation, marketing targeting, and positioning are *essential* requirements for effective strategic planning. In the new marketing concept the focus is sharpened by adding the idea of the value proposition.[4]

[4]Frederick E. Webster, Jr., "Defining the New Marketing Concept," *Marketing Management* 2, no. 4, pp 23–31.

Marketing's job under the new marketing concept is to provide information to decision makers throughout the organization and develop total marketing programs—including products, prices, distribution, and communications—that respond to changing customer needs and preferences. Under the new marketing concept, companies will not have a central marketing department to review and approve all activities involving the company's product offering and relationships with customers. Market-driven companies will understand how customer needs and company capabilities converge to form the customer's definition of value.

The new marketing concept is more than a philosophy; it's a way of doing business. It includes customer orientation, market intelligence, distinctive competencies, value delivery, market targeting and the value proposition, customer-defined total quality management, profitability rather than sales volume, relationship management, continuous improvement, and a customer-focused organizational structure.[5]

What Is a Product?

A product may be defined as a bundle of ingredients put together for sale as something useful to a consumer. You don't go into a store to buy cetylpyridimium chloride, purified water, SD alcohol 38-f (9.9 percent), sorbitol, sodium bicarbonate, Poloxamer 407, polysorbate 80, sodium saccharin, domiphen bromide. Many, however, do go into a store and buy Scope with baking soda. Scope is more than a physical object. It represents a bundle of satisfactions—clean breath, clean taste, relief of dryness, self-esteem—that are considered more or less important by each consumer. Egg Beaters is a product for a specialized market (Exhibit 4.5).

It is necessary to remember that different people have different ideas about what satisfactions are important. Products are often designed with satisfactions to match the interests of a particular group of consumers. We are judged in large measure by our physical possessions—think of your attitude toward BMWs, Jags, cellular phones, and so on. The products that we purchase say something about us and group us with people who seek similar satisfactions from life and products. As we match people and benefits, we create product loyalty that insulates us against competitive attacks.

It is difficult for a new product to find a place in the market against established competition. Its manufacturer must be selective in defining the most profitable market segments because the cost of introducing a new product can be expensive.

How can a new-product advertiser estimate the chances of getting a heavy user of another brand to try the new brand? One technique is to define market segments according to their brand loyalty and preference for national over private brands. Studies of package goods brand loyalty found six segments:

1. *National-brand loyal.* Members of this segment buy primarily a single national brand at its regular price.

2. *National-brand deal.* This segment is similar to the national-brand-loyal segment, except hat most of its purchases are made on deal (that is, the

---

[5]Frederick E. Webster, Jr., "Executing the New Marketing Concept." *Marketing Management*, 3, no. 1, 9–16.

EXHIBIT
4.5

No Cholesterol. Fat Free. Egg Beaters is obviously different from eggs. It appeals to people who must be concerned with fat and cholesterol and those concerned with health in general. Their market is not the masses.

(Courtesy: Fleischmann's Division of Nabisco Foods.)

consumer is loyal only to national brands but chooses the least expensive one). To buy the preferred national brand on deal, the consumer engages in considerable store switching.

3. *Private-label loyal.* Households in this segment primarily buy the private label offered by the store in which they shop (for example, Eckerds, A&P, and other store brands.)

4. *Private-label deal.* This segment shops at many stores and buys the private label of each store, usually on deal.

5. *National-brand switcher.* Members of this segment tend not to buy private labels. Instead, they switch regularly among the various national brands on the market.

6. *Private-label switcher.* This segment is similar to the private-label deal segment, except that the members are not very deal-prone and purchase the private labels at their regular price.[6]

Price, product distribution, and promotion also affect the share of market coming from each competing brand. However, a new national brand would

---

[6]Robert C. Blattberg, Thomas Buesing, and Subrata K. Sen, "Segmentation Strategies for New National Brands," *Journal of Marketing,* Fall 1980. p. 60 (Courtesy: Journal of Marketing, a publication of the American Marketing Association.)

expect to gain most of its initial sales from segments 2 and 5, while segments 1 and 3 would normally be poor prospects to try a new brand.

What Is a Market?

Market

A group of people who can be identified by some common characteristic, interest, or problem; use a certain product to advantage; afford to buy it; and be reached through some medium.

For our purposes, a *market* can be defined as a group of people who can be identified by some common characteristic, interest, or problem; could use our product to advantage; can afford to buy it; and can be reached through some medium. Examples of potential markets are computer owners, golfers, mothers with young children, newly marrieds, physicians, weight watchers, stamp collectors, football fans, indoor sports fans, do-it-yourselfers, runners and tourists.

Majority fallacy is a term applied to the assumption, once frequently made, that every product should be aimed at, and acceptable to, a majority of all consumers. Alfred Kuehn and Ralph Day have described how successive brands all aimed at a majority of consumers in a given market will tend to have rather similar characteristics and will neglect an opportunity to serve consumer minorities. They use chocolate-cake mixes as an example: Good-sized minorities would prefer a light chocolate cake or very dark chocolate cake to a medium chocolate cake, which is the majority's choice. So although several initial entrants into the field would do best to market a medium chocolate mix to appeal to the broadest group of consumers, later entrants might gain a larger market share by supplying the minorities with their preference.[7]

What Is Competition?

Have you ever wandered into a drug or grocery chain and looked at the toothpaste choices? There were probably a lot of choices. Or the analgesic section looking for a pain killer? You find many brands competing for your attention: Bayer, Tylenol, Advil, Excedrin, Aleve, Panadol, Anacin, Asprin Free Anacin, Empirin, Vanquish, Cope, Bufferin, Motrin IB, Goody's, BC, Excedrin IB, Nuprin, and the list goes on. Why does one consumer choose one brand and another consumer something else? How do you even get on the shelf to compete? Very important questions to the makers of these products. Examining these products we find that each is in a subcategory: Bayer, Tylenol, Aleve, and Nuprin are each in different analgesic categories—aspirin, acetaminophen, naproxen, ibuprofen. Advil and Nuprin are each in the same subcategory. Does that mean they only compete with themselves? The answer generally is no. If consumers are looking only for the benefits of an ibuprofen product then the answer is yes. Advil, Motrin, Excedrin Ib, Nuprin would all compete. The point is that advertisers and marketers need to try and find the answer as to which products in what categories compete for the consumer's attention and dollar. It may sound confusing because you don't know the category, but the seasoned marketer for these products knows its category and the products and the reasons people buy.

The marketers must answer a number of questions: Who are our competitors? What brands? What other product categories? Are there many brands

---

[7] Alfred A. Kuehn and Ralph A. Day, "Strategy of Product Quality," Harvard Business Review, November–December 1962, pp 100 ff.

or only a few? Which are strong? Which are vulnerable? What impact, if any, do store brands and generics have? Are there any strong, long-established brands, or is the market volatile? In this context, how would you define the competition for Mountain Dew? Is it Sprite? 7-Up? Mellow Yellow? All Sport? Colas? Iced tea? Again, the answer could be any or all of these. A major purpose of target marketing is to position a brand effectively within a product category (soft drinks) or subcategory (lemon-lime soft drinks).

Traditionally, a marketing strategy for a brand should seek to demonstrate how that product meets the needs of a particular consumer group. Your brand will gain value in a particular consumer segment by more exactly meeting its needs. Your ability to accomplish this will enhance the chances of your brand's success against a more generally positioned brand, which may not fully satisfy any single consumer segment. Products are normally competitive within a segment rather than across several groups. Shampoos, for example, are manufactured to meet a wide range of preferences—for clean hair; for manageable hair; for permed hair; for oily, dry, and regular hair. In Chapter 3, we illustrated how new brands must appeal to different segments of the general market according to their brand preferences and loyalty.

While most advertising emphasizes direct brand competition (7-UP versus Sprite or Colgate versus Crest), competition more broadly includes all the forces that inhibit the sale of the product. Thus, competition may be products outside your product's class as well as products in the same subclass as yours.

PLANNING THE ADVERTISING
Market Segmentation

Market segmentation
The division of an entire market of consumers into groups whose similarity makes them a market for products serving their special needs.

"One size does not fit all." Gannett Newspaper Division vice president of marketing is describing the premise behind segmentation marketing. "It's about maximizing your potential in the marketplace by targeting your product to certain segments of the population with similar behaviors," such as people of the same age, gender, ethnic background or lifestyle. From a communication standpoint, it is more difficult than you may think. "You must understand each segment's cultural nuances and choose the right message, so you don't stereotype the service or product you're selling as one designed for only them."

"Sometimes when you talk to everybody, you end up talking to nobody," says Coca-Cola Nestle Refreshments director of marketing JoAnn Miller of the effort to specifically target 18-to 29-year-olds for their *Plunge In* ad campaign, which reflected a shift to a more active lifestyle image for Nestle canned iced tea.[8]

Several years ago Uptown cigarettes and Power Master malt liquor were introduced to targeting African-Americans. The campaign backfired. Many blacks got angry because they felt stereotyped as socially irresponsible because of the health risks involved with smoking and drinking. These are examples of doing the right thing the wrong way. The companies identified a segment but came up with the wrong ideas for marketing them. The ads for these

---

[8]Coca-Cola Nestle Refreshments, *AdWeek,* March 21, 1994, p. 13.

(Courtesy: Sawyer Riley Compton)

products used people from the target they were selling, but the *ingroup bias* theory didn't work. It's not just about including people from certain groups in ads, but how they're portrayed.[9]

There are a number of factors to be considered in planning advertising to take advantage of market segmentation. The first step is to determine the variable to use for dividing a market. In addition to demographics, the major means of market segmentation are geographic, product user, and life style segmentation. Pro Balanced is obviously selling to dog owners, but the copy sells the fact that the product *is made fresh right here in the Southeast* (Exhibit 4.6).

Geographic Segmentation. This oldest form of segmentation, designating customers by geographic area, dates back to earlier days when distribution was the primary concern of manufacturers. Today geomarketing is of particular importance to media planners in deciding on national, regional, and local ad campaigns. It is only recently that geomarketing has been elevated to

---

[9]Mary Hardie, "On Target Segmentation Marketing Latest Technique," *Gannetteer,* July–August 1994, pp. 8–9.

a marketing discipline the way demographics was in the 1950s and psychographics in the 1970s. In this instance, consumers haven't changed, but marketers' awareness of regional and global marketing has. Geodemographical marketing is just another way of segmenting the market for companies in search of growth.

There has been a "data explosion" on local markets. Some of the information comes from an abundant number of research services for use on merchandising and buying decisions. Many retail companies such as Harris Teeter, a supermarket chain based in Charlotte, North Carolina, practice micromarketing—treating each individual store as its own market and trading area. Often this approach translates into different ads for different markets. When thinking about geographic segmentation, advertisers have a number of categories to explore:

- **Census tract data**
- **ZIP codes**
- **County**
- **Metropolitan statistical areas (MSAs)**
- **Area of dominant influence (ADI)**
- **State**
- **Census region**
- **Total United States**

For example, some automobile manufacturers use this kind of segmentation information to decide which cars to promote in which markets. Mercedes-Benz of North America set up a field force of 50 marketing managers to work with dealers on local ad and promotional programs. Each manager reports to one of the six sales regions in the country. Their agency provides assistance with selection of tactical advertising consistent with brand strategy, and does custom work for individual markets.

Companies that lack national distribution may consider geographic segmentation. Pro Balanced dog food is distributed basically in the South but has to compete against national brands to survive. There are many local or regional brands that must be successful in their geographic areas to survive. Budwine and Cheerwine are cherry cola–like soft drinks that are strong in their home area but would have problems in areas where their history and tradition weren't known. In these examples, geographic segmentation is a distribution strategy rather than a promotional one.

It is not unusual for national companies to divide their advertising and marketing efforts into regional units in order to respond better to the competition. McDonald's uses a major advertising agency to handle its national advertising and numerous (generally smaller) agencies to handle franchise and regional efforts supplementing the national effort. This gives McDonald's the ability to react to the marketplace by cities, regions, or individual stores.

Product-user segmentation

Identifying consumers by the amount of product usage.

Product-User Segmentation. User segmentation is a strategy based on the amount and/or consumption patterns of a brand or category. The advertiser is interested in product usage rather than consumer characteristics. As a practical matter, most user segmentation methods are combined with demographic or lifestyle consumer identification. Here the advertiser is interested in market segments that have the highest sales potential. Typically, a market segment is first divided into all users and then subdivided into heavy, medium, and light users:

The Frequency of Weekly Use of Fast Foods

	Adults	Men	Women
Heavy (4 plus visits)	11.4%	14.8%	8.3%
Medium (1–3 visits)	44.9	46.5	43.3
Light (Less than weekly)	22.8	20.6	24.8

The definition of usage varies with the product category. For example, heavy fast-food users may be defined as four or more times per week, luxury restaurants users once a week, and seafood restaurants once a week. As you can see, product user segmentation can get quite complex, but this kind of data allow marketers to use a rifle instead of a shotgun.

Lifestyle segmentation
Identifying consumers by combining several demographics and lifestyles.

Lifestyle Segmentation.   Lifestyle segmentation makes the assumption that if you live a certain way, so do your neighbors, and therefore any smart marketer would want to target clusters filled with these clones. Lifestyle clusters are more accurate characterizations of people than any single variable would be.

Each research company has its own terminology for the various clusters it identifies. For example, SRI developed a system called VALS that classifies people according to their values and lifestyles. Some advertisers had problems applying the clusters to their problems, and SRI refined the research as VALS 2, which puts less emphasis on values and more on the psychological underpinnings of behavior (see Chapter 15 for a description of VALS 2). The new version divides people into three groups (people who are principle-oriented, status-oriented, or action-oriented) and subdivides these into eight segments. Researchers Kevin Clancy and Robert Shulman argue that "off-the shelf segmentation studies cannot be as good as customized segmentation done with a specific product or service in mind. VALS will help break up the world into pieces, but the pieces may or may not have any relevance for any one brand.[10]" Another example is the Upper Deck survey, available from Mediamark Research, with its clusters of affluent investors whose incomes are in the top 10 percent.

A widely used approach to determining lifestyle characteristics is to identify consumers' activities, interests, and opinions (AIO). Typical AIO measures are the following:

- **Activities, leisure time, preferences, community involvement, and preferences for social events**

- **Interests, family orientation, sports interest, and media usage**

- **Opinions, political preferences and views on various social issues**

---

[10]Kevin J. Clancy and Robert S. Shulman, *The Marketing Revolution* (New York: HarperBusiness; 1991), p. 63.

Looking at the table below, you can see that consumers A and B are identically demographically, but an advertiser would detect important differences by examining their lifestyles.

	Demographic Profile	Lifestyle Profile
Consumer A	Age: 38; sex: male; race: white; occupation: managerial; income: $40,000; married, two children	Republican, President of Rotary Club, Member Board of Directors, Little League Baseball, Member of the Town and Gown Theater, and the Rolling Hills Sports Car Club
Consumer B	Age: 38; sex: male; race: white; occupation: managerial; income: $40,000; married, two children	Politically independent, President of the Carlton Coin and Stamp Club, and Executive Secretary of the Woodland Preservation Society

Benefits and Attitude Segmentation.   Not everyone wants the same thing from a product. You don't just have a single toothpaste, because some people are interested in taste or fresh breath, or whiteness of their teeth, or decay prevention, or tartar control for gums, or value, etc. The basis here is to cluster people into groups based upon what they want in a product.

Segmentation Risks. Although segmentation is very important to successful advertising, it isn't without risks. One problem is that once the outer limits of the niche is reached, sales growth will be limited unless the company can expand beyond its niche. As the market became saturated, Reebok had to enter other shoe markets to keep growing. By too narrowly defining your market—that is, by excessive segmenting—you can become inefficient in media buying, creating different ads, and obtaining alternative distribution channels.

Niche marketing can serve at least two purposes. It can gain a product entry into a larger market by attacking a small part of it not being served by the competition. It can also cater to latent needs that existing products do not adequately satisfy.

Niche marketing

Λ combination of product and target market strategy. It is a flanking strategy that focuses on niches or comparatively narrow windows of opportunity within a broad product market or industry. Its guiding principle is to pit your strength against their weakness.

Niche Marketing

Companies seek to find a niche or niches for their products in today's marketplace. Niche marketing is not another buzzword for marketing segmentation, says Alvin Achenbaum.[11] It is essentially a flanking strategy, the essence of which is to engage competitors in those product markets where they are weak or, preferably, have little or no presence. The guiding principle of niche marketing is to pit your strength against the competitor's weakness. No-frill motels did not exist for many years, but they were logical means of competing against other motel segments. Red Roof Inn opened its motel with an ad claiming "Sleep Cheap" and positioned itself to value consumers not wanting to pay high prices for a place to sleep. Later it even made fun of hotels placing a chocolate mint on your pillow for an extra $30 or $40. Today, Holiday Inn has moved into that niche with its own no-frills Holiday Inn Express.

---

[11] Alvin Achenbaum, "Understanding Niche Marketing," *AdWeek*, December 1, 1986, p. 62.

The demand for anti-aging cosmetic products is creating a lucrative niche in skin care. Census projections indicate that by the year 2000, women aged 35 to 54 will outnumber those aged 18 to 34 by 10 million, increasing the demand for cosmetic skin care products.

In the very turbulent airline market, Southwest Airlines has shown that niche marketing can be very profitable. With careful control of costs, astute selection of short-haul routes, inexpensive fares, and no-frills service, it became a thorn in the side of the major air carriers. Its advertising hammered home its policy of low fares for all seats on all flights against its competitors' many restrictions surrounding their low fares.

Ethnic niches
Specifically targeting marketing efforts toward narrow ethnic groups or subgroups. For instance, Hispanic: Puerto Ricans, Cubans, Mexicans, etc.; blacks, Asians, and so on.

Ethnic Niches. The major growth segments in the United States for the future are in the minority population as indicated earlier in this chapter. In 1991 Maybelline introduced Shades of You, a complete cosmetic line for African American women, and within two years it captured a 31 percent share of the ethnic-cosmetic market.

Folgers coffee has used integrated messages across multiple marketing platforms, such as advertising, sampling, and event promotion to reach the Hispanic market. A recent campaign used the theme, "Despiertan lo mejor en ti" ("Wake up the best in you") using Telemundo sponsorship and shelf-talkers in retail outlets. Hispanic ad agencies have plenty of experience in integrating campaigns, but bringing these to national scale is a big challenge, since the Hispanic market has lacked the depth and effectiveness of the general market's communications infrastructure. For example, public relations is not well developed because of the lack of publicity outlets, like print vehicles. A Los Angeles agency head indicates there is more information on the Hispanic segment almost daily. "Every week I get more information about FSI [free-standing inserts], direct marketing, and promotion opportunities in the Hispanic segment . . . but sometimes you have to improvise to reach consumers."[12]

Despite targeting African Americans for a number of years, in 1994 Cadillac tested several programs specifically aimed at reclaiming its share lost to import buyers. It had been successful in accomplishing this goal with the general market, but black boomers remained aloof. Cadillac launched a campaign with two-page color print ads showing black employees talking about the cars, television spots with a similar approach, a direct marketing piece inviting test drives, and a donation to one of three black charities. The basic message was not significantly different from that used with the mass market. Research indicated that blacks were slightly more safety oriented. People buying a luxury car want to know the same things: How safe is it? How reliable is it? How durable is it?[13]

Many marketers think their general-market advertising efforts are effective in reaching ethnic groups; some marketing researchers argue that generic efforts miss the mark. Black people are not dark-skinned white people, says a Burrell Communications Group head. Blacks are significantly different in terms of approach and history. There is a significant difference in behavior, and that manifests itself all the way to the marketplace.[14]

---

[12]Junu Bryan Kim, "Market Forces Integrated Messages," *Advertising Age*, January 24, 1994, p. S-2.
[13]Cyndee Miller, "Cadillac Promo Targets African-Americans," *Marketing News*, May 23, 1994, p. 12.
[14]Christie Fisher, "Ethnics Gain Market Clout," *Advertising Age*, August 5, 1991, p. 3.

Research companies such as Yankelovich Clancy Shulman indicate that demographic changes are taking marketers to a multiethnic, multilingual future.

It should be noted that while segmentation is extremely important to successful advertising, it is not without risks. One problem is that once the upper limits of the niche are reached, sales growth will be limited unless the company can expand beyond its niche. Reebok International's niche was the aerobic shoe segment. As that market became saturated, Reebok had to enter other shoe markets to keep growing. By too narrowly defining your market—that is, by excessively segmenting—you can become inefficient in buying media, creating different ads, and obtaining alternative distribution channels. Stanback headache powders have been unable to crack the California market despite several attempts because the headache powder appeals to a peculiar southern proclivity to self-medicate.

Positioning

Positioning

Segmenting a market by creating a product to meet the needs of a select group or by using a distinctive advertising appeal to meet the needs of a specialized group, without making changes in the physical product.

Positioning is another term for fitting the product into the lifestyle of the buyer. It refers to segmenting a market by either or both of two ways: (1) creating a product to meet the needs of a specialized group, and (2) identifying and advertising a feature of an existing product that meets the needs of a specialized group.

Estrovite vitamins recognized a potential problem among women on birth control pills and created a product positioned to fulfill that need. Its headline read, "Your birth control pills could be robbing you of essential vitamins and minerals." The copy explained why.

It is possible for some products to successfully hold different positions at the same time. Arm & Hammer baking soda has been positioned as a deodorizer for refrigerators, an antacid, a freezer deodorizer, and a bath skin cleaner without losing its original market as a cooking ingredient.

Positioning is what you do to the mind of the consumer. Specifically, you position the product in the mind of the prospect. The concept is giving a product a meaning that distinguishes it from other products. This must be in harmony with the lifestyle and values discussed earlier. Positioning must be planned with a target in mind. It is necessary to understand what motivates people to buy in the product category—what explains their behavior. It is also necessary to understand the degree to which the product satisfies the target's needs.[15] One automobile may be positioned as a sports car, another is positioned as a luxury sports car, another as the safest family car, and still another as a high-performance vehicle.

You might try to get the following reactions from consumers to a new line of frozen entries that are low in calories, sodium, and fat, and have larger servings than the competition's. Before seeing your advertising, the consumer thinks:

> I like the convenience and taste of today's frozen foods but I don't usually get enough of the main course to eat. I would like to try a brand that gives me plenty to eat but is still light and healthy—and, most important it's got to taste great.

---

[15]Clancy and Shulman, *The Marketing Revolution,* pp. 84–87.

After being exposed to your advertising, the consumer thinks:

> I may buy Judi's Frozen Food entrees. They taste great and I get plenty to eat, but they are still low enough in calories so I don't feel I'm overeating. They're better for me because they have less sodium and fat than others. And there is enough variety so that I can eat the foods I like without getting bored by the same old thing.

Creating a Product for Selected Markets

One of the ways that marketers attract a focused consumer group is through variations on a conventional product. A new variation looks for a group with needs not fully met by existing products. In addition, marketers of products in the retentive stage may see variations as a means of rejuvenating a product whose sales have gone flat.

St. Joseph's chewable aspirin positioned the orange-flavored pain reliever exclusively for adult sufferers of heart-condition. The aspirin that consumers normally take contains 325 milligrams; however, for patients having suffered an initial heart attack doctors have been recommending a daily therapy of 81 milligrams or more. St. Joseph's 81-milligram tablet will allow more flexible dosage. St. Joseph's chewable children's aspirin had been a leader for years.

Positioning to Expand Brand Share

Positioning—or, more accurately, repositioning—can be an effective method of increasing brand share when a company already has a high percentage of the market for a type of product. Let's assume our company, Acme Widgets, has 80 percent of the widget market. Two strategies that the company might adopt are shown in the following tables.

Strategy I: Traditional Brand Promotion (No Brand Repositioning)

1993 Brand Share, %		1994 Advertising	1995 Brand Share, %	
A,	10		A,	9.9
B,	5	$10 million spent	B,	5.0
C,	5	against brands	C,	5.0
Acme,	80	A, B, and C	Acme,	80.1
Total	100			100.0

Strategy II: Acme Widgets' Brand Repositioning

1993 Brand Share, %		1994 Advertising	1995 Brand Share, % Primary market:	
A,	10	$6 million spent	A,	10
B,	5	to keep present	B,	5
C,	5	market share	C,	5
Acme,	80		Acme,	80
Total	100			100

(cont.)

		Alternative market:	
$4 million spent to promote repositioned Acme Widget to new market		Other brands and brands already in market, A, B, C, Acme	85 5 10
Total			100

In Strategy I, Acme, by engaging in direct brand competition, has increased its market share very slightly. However, it is extremely doubtful that further sales can be profitably taken from the competition. Increased advertising expenditures to make inroads into brands A, B, and C will probably cost proportionally more than the revenues realized.

The repositioning strategy depicted in Strategy II has allowed Acme to keep its overwhelming share. At the same time, by spending 40 percent ($4 million of its $10 million advertising allowance) of its budget to position the company in a new market, Acme gained 10 percent of this formerly untapped market segment rather than the 0.1 percent of the primary market it achieved with the first strategy. In this example, no physical changes were made in the product—only different appeals were used. This is the basis for positioning by choice of appeal.

How to Approach a Positioning Problem

As you would expect, not all products lend themselves to the type of positioning discussed here. The advertiser must be careful not to damage current product image by changing appeals and prematurely expanding into new markets. Jack Trout and Al Ries, who have spoken and written about positioning for several decades, say that the advertiser who is thinking about positioning should ask the following questions:[16]

> What position, if any, do we already own in the prospect's mind?
> What position do want to own?
> What companies must be outgunned if we are to establish that position?
> Do we have enough marketing money to occupy and hold that position?
> Do we have the guts to stick with one consistent positioning concept?
> Does our creative approach match our positioning strategy?

David Aaker says the most used positioning strategy is to associate an object with a product attribute or characteristic. Developing such associations is effective because when the attribute is meaningful, the association can directly translate into reasons to buy the brand. Crest toothpaste became the leader by building a strong association with cavity control in part created by an endorsement of the American Dental Association. BMW has talked about performance with its tag line: "The Ultimate Driving Machine"; Mercedes, "The Ultimate Engineered Car"; Hyundai, "Cars that make sense." The positioning problem is usually finding an attribute important to a major segment and not already claimed by a competitor.[17]

---

[16]Jack Trout and Al Ries, *The Positioning Era* (New York: Ries Cappiello Colwell 1973), pp. 38–41.
[17]David A. Aaker, *Managing Brand Equity* (New York: Free Press, 1991), pp. 114–115.

The following are positioning examples:

Dove is positioned as a moisturizing beauty bar.
Cheer is the detergent for all temperatures.
Surf liquid detergent removes dirt and odors with half the liquid.
Spray 'n Wash is the tough stain remover for laundry.
Lever 2000 is the deodorant soap that's better for your skin.
Saturn is a different kind of company, a different kind of car.
Milk-Bone dog biscuits clean teeth and freshen breath.
Wrangler is the western original.
Advil is the advanced medicine for pain.
Mitsubishi is the new thinking in automobiles.

It is amazing how marketers frequently alter a brand's positioning for *the sake of change*. This is especially unfortunate for those brands that are firmly entrenched and successful because their reason for being is widely accepted. Witness "Good to the last drop" and "Pepperidge Farm remembers" and "Two mints in one," etc. These campaigns were revised long after they were discontinued because they truly represented the consumer end benefit and character of the brand.[18]

Profile of the Market

Market profile

A demographic and psychographic description of the people or the households of a product's market. It may also include economic and retailing information about a territory.

Up to this point, we have discussed market segments. Now we examine the overall market for a product. First, we determine the overall usage of the product type. This is usually defined in terms of dollars, sales, number of units sold, or percentage of households that use such a product. Then we determine if the category is growing, stagnant, or declining. We compare our share of the market to the competition (see Exhibit 4.7). Next we ask what the share trends have been over the past several years. Finally, we want to know the chief product advantage featured by each brand.

Friskies dry cat food brand (13.1 percent) share was worth $97 million and Kozy Kittens (3.9 percent) share netted about $29 million in sales. In adult cold remedies we find that private labels combine for a 12.3 percent share, followed by Vicks Nyquil with a 12.2 percent share and Sudafed with a 7.8 percent share. The tenth best selling cold remedy, Drixoral, has a 3.1 percent share of the market. Obviously there are a lot of cold remedies that have very small shares, yet many are able to make nice profits. A marketer of a leader

EXHIBIT 4.7

Every Share Point May be Worth Millions of Dollars in Sales

Dry Cat Food Brand Share (%)		Dry Dog Food Brand Share (%)	
Friskies	13.1%	Pedigree	32.4%
Purina Cat Chow	10.3	Alpo	17.3
Meow Mix	8.6	Mighty Dog	9.2
Private Label	5.9	Skippy	6.6
Chef's Blend	5.9	Cycle	6.1
Purina Deli-Cat	4.7	Reward	3.0
Kozy Kitten	3.9	King Kuts	1.9

(*Source:* Advertising Age, *April 25, 1994, p. 42.*)

---

[18]Lewis Brosowsky, "Ad Themes That Last," *Advertising Age,* February 28, 1994, p. 26.

and a marketer with a very small share will probably approach advertising in very different ways.

It is important for the advertiser to know not only the characteristics of the product's market, but also similar information about media alternatives. Most major newspapers, magazines, and broadcast media provide demographic and product-user data for numerous product categories. Database marketing is giving the marketer an abundance of information upon which to base integrated promotional decisions.

Profile of the Buyer

Earlier in this chapter we highlighted ethnic groups (Hispanics, blacks, Asians) that were largely ignored by advertisers in the past but whose increasing numbers demand attention in today's marketplace. The Xers, boomers, teenagers, college students, and the 50-plus markets all are studies by smart advertisers to understand their potential for specific products and services. As indicated, these groups of consumers are not necessarily easy to understand or reach with effective integrated programs. Not all boomers act the same, and all Xers don't respond to messages in the same manner. Advertisers have to look at demographics and lifestyle, for starters, to understand any market.

Demography is the study of vital economic and sociological statistics about people. In advertising, demographic reports refer to those facts relevant to a person's use of a product. Below (Exhibit 4.8) is a snippet of average weekly regular and diet soft drink demographics.

The selected soft drink demographics probably offer few surprises to you. However, be sure to examine the male/female differences in regular and diet; age 18–24 and older consumers; and compare regional differences for starters. You can begin to understand how demographic differences could be an important factor in advertising strategy and expenditures decisions.

Now let's look at another group: 50-Plus.

EXHIBIT 4.8

Selected Demographics of Regular/Diet Soft Drink
Average Weekly Consumption for Specific Types

	Regular		Diet	
	COLA	OTHER	COLA	OTHER
Total 18+	60.3%	43.3%	42.2%	29.2%
Sex: Male	65.5	46.1	38.6	27.8
Female	55.5	40.5	45.6	30.4
Age: 18–24	72.5	50.4	32.7	24.4
25–34	67.6	48.8	42.5	30.1
35–44	62.6	45.1	45.2	29.3
65+	46.3	34.5	41.2	29.2
Region: Northeast	59.8	45.3	37.6	27.7
Midwest	56.6	42.6	46.8	31.6
South	65.0	42.2	41.8	26.9
West	57.2	43.4	42.2	31.5
Race: White	58.9	41.1	43.5	29.1
Black	69.3	55.4	35.7	27.2

(Source: Radio Advertising Bureau.)

Reaching the 50-Plus Market

In 1990, there were 63.5 million people over the age of 50 in the United States. By 2000, with baby boomers joining the fray, that figure jumps to 76.4 million. These mature consumers are not only the wealthiest; they're also living longer and thinking younger. An Ogilvy & Mather study indicated that they are basically satisfied with their lot in life. They are independent, in control of their lives, have discretionary incomes, appreciate a bargain, and are not as uptight about life as younger age groups. To reach this growing market, advertisers are starting to create advertising that goes beyond traditional stereotypes. Hill, Holiday, Connors, Cosmopolos advertising was asked by the Bank of Boston to communicate a one-to-one relationship and be considered approachable and friendly. Their research found that most advertising to this group was very condescending and a key to the whole campaign was the fact that over-50s consider themselves 15 years younger than society perceives them to be.[19] One of the print ads headline read, "To sign up for this account you must undergo a long, complicated and often confusing process. Life." Accompanying art showed a woman in different life stages with the body copy: "You've been through bell bottoms, Moon landings. Pet rocks. Wars. Peace. Diapers. Disco. Mortgages. Reunions. And your surprise 50th birthday party. Which all means you're an official, experienced member of something called life."

Goodby, Berlin & Silverstein created a campaign for Unum Corporation, a company specializing in disability and long-term-care insurance. Its advertising treats the subject with humor and directness and stands out in a category traditionally filled with gray *insurance-speak*. Exhibit 4.9 body copy says, "Something wonderful is happening. We're all getting older. And living longer. Consider that for the first time ever, the fastest-growing segment of the population is over 90 years old." Research indicated that respondents show an

EXHIBIT 4.9

This insurance ad treats the subject with directness and humor.

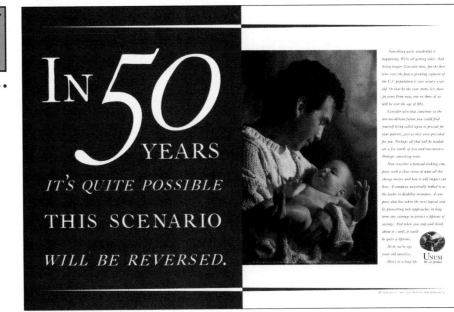

(Courtesy: Unum Corporation)

---

[19]Ann Cooper, "50–Plus: A Lighter Touch for the Gray Market," *AdWeek,* July 10, 1993, pp. 38–44.

overwhelming attraction to the ad. Readers are initially drawn in by the feeling invoked by the graphics, photo, and artwork. One of the creative team says the purpose was to take the positive side and stay off the gloom and doom side. Living longer and getting older are good, we're living healthier lives, and we all want to be around longer.

This market wants to be portrayed as active, healthy, vibrant, attractive, and intelligent. The old stereotype ads "Help, I've fallen and I can't get up" message won't cut it in. The 50-plus market will become more significant when the baby-boom generation arrives at that age—the boomers said it was okay to be middle age. Within the next 10 years the 50-plus will pass on to baby boomers some 10 trillion in inheritances and with that kind of assets *it will be hip to be 50-plus.* As with any market group—be it Hispanic, Generation X, or the 50-plus—marketers must understand what makes the group tick in order to create effective programs and messages.

Heavy Users

Take any product category and you'll find that a small percentage of users are responsible for a disproportionately large share of sales. The principle of heavy usage is sometimes referred to as the 80/20 rule—that is, 80 percent of the units sold are purchased by only 20 percent of the consumers. Of course, the exact figure varies with each product and product category, but the 80/20 rule is representative of most product sales. Heavy users are identified not only by who they are, but also by when they buy and where they are located.

In the following table, for example, we find that the heavy users of brand X are women aged 55 and older. In addition, the most effective selling is done from January to June in the east Central and Pacific regions. Obviously, heavy users are an important part of the market; however, they are also the group most advertisers are trying to target, and therefore the competition can be fierce and expensive. Some advertisers find that aiming for a less lucrative segment—medium or light users—may be more reasonable expectations.

Users of Brand X

1. Target Audience: Current Consumers

Women	Pop., %	Consumption, %	Index (100 = national average)
18–24	17.5	5.0	29
25–34	21.9	10.1	46
35–54	30.1	24.0	80
55+	30.5	61.0	200
Total	100.0	100.0	

2. Geography: Current Sales

Area	Pop., %	Consumption, %	Index
Northeast	24	22	92
East Central	15	18	120
West Central	17	16	94
South	27	24	89
Pacific	17	20	118
	100	100	

(cont.)

3. Seasonality

Period	Jan.–Mar.	Apr.–Jun.	Jul.–Sept.	Oct.–Nov.
Consumption, %	30	36	20	14
Index	120	144	80	56

A marketer cannot just assume the best prospects are 18- to 49-year-old women, heavy users, or people similar to current customers. Instead, marketers need to study its target audience in great depth. In defining your market, then, you must determine who the heavy users are and identify their similarities, which would define your marketing goal (see Exhibit 4.10).

EXHIBIT 4.10

. . . .

The 4As recommended standard segments for demographic characteristics in surveys of consumer media audiences.

BEYOND DEMOGRAPHICS: PSYCHOGRAPHICS

Driving on a highway past modest-sized backyards of middle-class homes, one is struck first by their similarity. But a harder look is more illuminating, for behind the similarities lie differences that reflect the interests, personalities, and family situations of those who live in such homes. One backyard has been transformed into a carefully manicured garden. Another includes some shrubs and bushes, but most of the yard serves as a relaxation area, with outdoor barbecue equipment and the like. A third yard is almost entirely a

Characteristic	Data to be Gathered and Reported (If Possible, to be Directly Accessible)	
	Minimum Basic Data to be Reported	**Additional Data—Highly Valued**
I. Persons Characteristics		
A. Household Relationship	Principle Wage Earner in HH (defines HH head) Principle Shopper in HH (defines homemaker) Spouse Child Other Relative Partner/Roommate Other Non-Relative	
B. Age	Under 6 6–11 12–15 16–20 18–20 16 or older 18 or older 18–24 25–34 35–44 45–49 50–54 55–64 65–74 75 or older	2–5 6–8 35–49 25–49
C. Sex	Male Female	

(cont.)

Characteristic	Minimum Basic Data to be Reported	Additional Data—Highly Valued
D. Education	Last Grade Attended: Grade School or Less (Grade 1–8) Some High School Graduated High School Some College (at least 1 year) Graduated College . . . . If currently attending school . . . . Full-Time Student Part-Time Student	any postgraduate work —(If pertinent to study)— Live home Live away —Live in student housing —Live off campus
E. Marital Status	Married . . . . Widowed Divorced or Separated Single (never married) Parent Pregnant 'Living together'	Spouse Present Spouse Absent Spouse working Engaged
F. Religion—Political		Protestant ⎫ ⎡ Active (Practicing) Catholic ⎟ ⎣ Inactive (Non-Practicing) Jewish ⎟ Other ⎟ None ⎭ Political—Conservative —Liberal —Moderate
G. Race	White Black Other	
H. Principle Language Spoken At home	English Spanish Other	
H1. Other Languages Spoken At home	English Spanish Other	
I. Individual Employment Income	Under $10,000 $10,000–14,999 $15,000–19,999 $20,000–24,999 $25,000–29,999 $30,000–39,999 $40,000–49,999 $50,000–74,999 $75,000 and over	$75,000–99,000 $100,000 and over IEI Income by Quintile as Determined by the Survey Ziptiles. Other Income

IEI by Quintile
Income Interval

Quintile	% Adults	Low	High	Median Income
1	20	—	10,156	6,391
2	20	10,757	19,999	13,959
3	20	20,000	29,999	24,953
4	20	30,000	43,243	34,967
5	20	43,244	—	60,150

Characteristic	Minimum Basic Data to be Reported	Additional Data—Highly Valued
D. Presence/Age of Children In Household	No Children Under 18 Youngest Child 6–17 Youngest Child Under 6	Youngest Child 12–17 Youngest Child 6–11 Youngest Child 2–5 Youngest Child Under 2
E. Household Type		Family Members Only Non-Family Members Only Both Family and Non-Family Members
F. Household Size	1 Member 2 Members 3 Members 4 Members	Number of Adults (Persons 18 and Over) Male/Female HH Female Only HH Male Only HH
G. Number of Children Under 18 In Household	None One More Than One	Number of Children 6–17 Number of Children Under 6 Number of Children by Household Size
H. Household Income	See I., Individual Employment Income	$ 75,000–99,999 $100,000 and over Household Income by Quintile as Determiined by Survey Ziptiles
I. Other Household Characteristics		Numbers of Adults Employed Full Time
J. Home Ownership	Own Home —Private Ownership —Cooperative Ownership —Condominium Rent Home	Residence Five Years Prior to Survey —Lived in Same House/Home —Lived in Different House/Home —In Same Country —In Different Country —In Same State —In Different State
K. Type Housing Unit	Single Family Home Multiple Family Home Apartment Mobile Home or Trailer	

Note: The recommended minimum and additional data standards apply to generalized surveys. Those surveys done to more specific purposes—e.g. particular geographic sections of the country, affluent markets, publications directed towards a specific target, etc.—may choose to collapse or expand characteristic segments as appropriate to their context.

American Association of Advertising Agencies.

....

Psychographics

A description of a market based on factors such as attitudes, opinions, interests, perceptions, and lifestyles of consumers comprising that market. See Demographic characteristics.

....

playground, with swings, trapezes, and slides. A swimming pool occupies almost all the space in another yard. A tennis court occupies yet another. Still another has simply been allowed to go to seed and is overgrown and untended by its obviously indoor-oriented owners.

Despite the neighborhood being of similar homes, age, and value, it doesn't mean the people are all the same. The homes may look alike, but the people have differences. If you want to advertise to this neighborhood, you would be speaking to people with different interests, different tastes. There may be a big difference in the nature and extent of purchases between any two groups of buyers who have the same demographic characteristics. The attempt to explain the significance of such differences has led to an inquiry beyond demographics into psychographics.

Emanual Demby, president of Demby & Associates and considered one of the founders of psychographics, has described psychographics as:

> The use of psychological, sociological, and anthropological factors, such as benefits desired (from the behavior being studied), self-concept, and lifestyle (or serving style) to determine how the market is segmented by the propensity of groups within the market—and their reasons—to take a particular decision about a product, person, ideology, or otherwise hold an attitude or use a medium. Demographics and socioeconomics are also used as a constant check to see if psychographic marketing segmentation improves on other forms of segmentation, including user/nonuser groupings.[20]

As previously stated, Detroit automakers found in the mid-1990s they had lost a large segment of the black consumer to the imports. As a result, marketing efforts tried to appeal to blacks more efficiently than before. As a Chrysler spokesperson indicated, micromarketing is becoming the industry standard. It leads to all kinds of different special interest groups, whether ethnically based, lifestyle-based, demographically based, or geographically based. Cadillac had a similar problem with young affluents in the early 1990s; they considered Cadillac an older person's car. Cadillac designed the 1992 Seville and Eldorado for this group and advertised focusing on upscale lifestyle images featuring professional-looking people in their 30s talking about why they had stayed away from domestic luxury cars.

Psychographics—studying lifestyles—sharpens the search for prospects beyond the demographic data. It has been said that lifestyle information gives the soul of the person. Good creative people can devise copy that appeals to this segment or segments' lifestyle interest. Exhibit 4.11 illustrates how lifestyle can help differentiate the product or services—"As original as the people who stay here . . . a refuge from everything ordinary"—clearly positions BelAge Hotel. The media are then selected, and advertising is directed to that special target group or groups. Put very simply, lifestyle information gives the soul of a person; demographics alone gives only a skeleton and not a whole person.

Target Audience: Beyond Demographics

This travel advertiser's target audience illustrates demographics alone doesn't help this advertiser; lifestyle and geography are also important. This target profile is based upon national research and the organization's own research that define those people most likely to visit the area.

Research indicates that the basic demographic guideline for the consumer target is households with a combined household income of $35,000-plus. Households with less than $35,000 simply do not have the discretionary income necessary for vacation travel.

The other qualifiers in defining a consumer target audience are lifestyle and geography:

■ **Primary vacation travelers.** Vacation travelers who take a one-week plus vacation during the primary season (summer).

---

[20]Emmanual H. Demby, "Psychographics Revisited: The Birth of a Technique," *Marketing News,* January 2, 1989, p. 21.

EXHIBIT

4.11

BelAge Hotel positions itself as a refuge from everything ordinary. This lifestyle approach is different from typical hotel ads.

(Courtesy: The Zimmerman Agency and BelAge Hotel.)

- ■ ***Weekend travelers.*** Those people living in states within close proximity who can be attracted during the fall, winter, and spring seasons.

- ■ ***Mature market (50+).*** Those having both the discretionary income and available time to travel.

- ■ ***Business travelers.*** Those travelers coming to our area on business who can be encouraged to either extend their stay for pleasure travel purposes or to bring their spouse/family along.

- ■ ***International travelers.*** Canada provides an enormous influx of visitors. Also, the increasing number of international flights to and from the area provide increasing opportunities.

What is the target for the North Carolina tourism ad in Exhibit 4.12?

Psychographic Research

Today there is much more refined information available. Agency research information includes syndicated research from outside sources, client's research, and the agency's own.

Syndicated research services specialize in different types of information on what types of products people buy and which brands, who buys them and their demographic and psychographic distinctions, a comparison of heavy and

In the Great Smoky Mountains of North Carolina, an ancient sanctuary waits for you, its thick columns soaring 150 feet into the sky. It is called the Joyce Kilmer Memorial Forest, the only vast stand of virgin hardwood trees remaining in the Eastern United States.

vistas the Cherokees once did. Still other trails will lead you to crystal clear waterfalls and whitewater streams with old Indian names like Nantahala, Hiwassee and Cullasaja. Of course, when you're ready to be transported back to the present, the Blue Ridge

IN MANY OF THE WORLD'S GREAT PLACES, YOU'LL FIND AWE-INSPIRING CATHEDRALS. THIS IS OURS.

Walk a while among these towering 400-year-old hemlocks and yellow poplars, and you get the feeling you've taken a journey back deep into the past. Back to a time when man and nature more peacefully coexisted. But then, that's the feeling you get whatever path you take in those quiet hills and coves. There are places along the Appalachian Trail, for example, where you can stand on a mile-high peak and gaze across the same unspoiled

Parkway and gently winding back roads beckon, with new surprises waiting for you around every bend. Regardless of where you NORTH CAROLINA travel in our state, from our mist-covered mountains to the windswept barrier islands that lie just off our coast, you'll discover places that can lift your spirit and restore your soul. And you'll discover something else: Very few of them were designed or built by man.

(Courtesy: Loeffler Ketchum Mountjoy.)

EXHIBIT
4.12

. . . .

Tourism ads appeal to different segments of the population. What is the target audience for this ad?

light users, how people react to products and to ads, and people's styles of buying and what media reach them.

Lifestyle research categories are numerous. Here is a sampling of data categories available to advertisers and their agencies to help them select the target market.

■ **CREDIT CARD USAGE**
    Travel/Entertainment (approx 16% of U.S. households)
    Gas/Department Stores (35%)
■ **GOOD LIFE ACTIVITIES**
    Attend cultural/Arts events (16.7%)
    Fine arts/Antiques (10.4%)
    Foreign Travel (13.2%)
    Gourmet cooking/Fine foods (17.2%)
■ **HIGH TECH**
    Photography (22.3%)
    Science/New technology (8.8%)
■ **OUTDOOR**
    Bowling (16%)
    Golf (18%)
    Racquetball (7.2%)
    Tennis frequently (7.2%)

Lowe's (Exhibit 4.13) sells all kinds of hardware and items for the home, but this ad is selling the Weed Eater GatorVac to make yard work easier.

(Courtesy: Lowe's as seen in Southern Living.*)*

Advertisers can also order customized data from these research services. Here are a few examples:

MRI National Study. Contains a study of 20,000+ adults age 18-plus every year since 1979. Data include demographics, media usage, product consumption/purchase, activities, and lifestyles.

ClusterPlus. This is a segmentation system that classifies every neighborhood into lifestyle categories. ClusterPlus is linked to the Residential Master file, which includes the names, addresses, and demographic characteristics of 90 percent of U.S. households.

BrandTab. Contains the entire Mediamark consumer database, along with formats for brand management. The database includes demographic, lifestyle, and usage data for more than 450 product categories and almost 6,000 brands.

Upper-Deck Report on the Affluent Market. This annual study of affluent population as represented by the top 10 percent of national household income. Includes five demographic/lifestyle classifications.

Teenmark. Annual survey of persons aged 12–19. Data include estimates of demographics, media usage, product consumption, brand volume, household purchase influence, activities, and lifestyles of teenagers.

MRI Business-to-Business. Annual study of business purchase decision makers measuring 36 products and service categories by business-related media, demographics, and spending.

PRIZM. Claritas LP's system classifies neighborhood geography, including census block groups, postal carrier routes, and zip codes, into some 40 basic lifestyle clusters.

NuStats Hispanic InfoSource. Hispanic American study of consumer product consumption, media usage, and language preference.

Test Marketing

All the research available cannot replace market testing as the ultimate guide to predicting successful advertising and marketing. Manufacturers rarely introduce a new product without doing some prior test marketing. This kind of testing helps determine whether or not consumers will really purchase a product or react to specific advertising and promotional activities. For instance, when Campbell-Taggart wanted to know if the average American youngster would eat high-fiber, high-iron bread—if it looked like regular white bread—the company tested Iron Kids bread.

Saatchi & Saatchi's top performing test markets in the early 1990s included Minneapolis–St. Paul, Denver, Portland (Oregon), Columbus (Ohio), Kansas City, Atlanta, Syracuse, Houston, and Pittsburgh: "You can't say one place represents everything because there are so many different lifestyles," says Ira Weinblatt, a Saatchi senior vice president. Some cities are historically popular for test marketing. The Midwest has been because, geographically, it was the heartland of America. Each test market represents a kind of microcosm of America. To make Saatchi & Saatchi's list:

■ **A city's demographics must fall within 20 percent of the national average.**

■ **The city should be somewhat isolated.**

■ **Local media should be relatively inexpensive.**

■ **Citizens should not be extremely loyal to any particular brand.**

■ **Supermarkets should be impartial enough to give new products good display on their shelves.**[21]

Milwaukee ranks twelfth on the Saatchi & Saatchi list of test market cities. The Milwaukee papers off marketers the flexibility to split production runs two or four ways, testing up to four ads at a time, and to experiment with run-of-paper color or free-standing inserts. Typically, researchers examine purchases for a number of weeks before the ads run, during the period of test, and afterward.

Procter & Gamble recently started testing Fit Produce Rinse, a product designed to clean fruits and vegetables, in Colorado and Wyoming supermarkets and mass-merchandising outlets with print and television ads touting "Good. Clean. Fit." A year prior to P&G's testing of Fit Produce Rinse, Uncle Bob's Fruit & Vegetable Wash and Garden Fresh Fruit & Vegetable Wash tested horribly. The perils of introducing a product nationally without test marketing include results like new Coke—failure. And failure can be ex-

---

[21]Jeffry Scott, *Atlanta Journal,* July 2, 1991, p. 13.

tremely expensive. RJR lost an estimated $40 million on its Real cigarettes in the late 1970s when it made the mistake of thinking that smokers cared if a cigarette had all-natural ingredients. They did not. Most marketers are not willing to take that risk without some type of testing.

SUMMARY

Identifying current and prospective users of a product will often mean the difference between success and failure. The targeting of advertising to these prospects in an efficient media plan with appropriate creative is critical.

In this chapter we've concentrated on fundamentals such as: Defining prospects. What is the market? Competition? Positioning? Numerous methods of examining segmentation and other important considerations in planning integrated marketing programs have been discussed. You must understand the changes that are taking place in society and within markets—population, lifestyle, usage, income. Research can be the key to successful target marketing. It is important to understand the role of research in identifying prime marketing segments. Product research helps meet the needs of these segments. Advertising research allows us to devise effective messages to reach the target. Also, we need to be familiar with the multitude of research services available to supply needed information for planning.

Advertisements are increasingly used as a rifle instead of a shotgun approach. In the media section, we learn how it is becoming easier to tailor messages through a variety of special-interest media vehicles.

Demographic characteristics are taking a lesser role than lifestyle characteristics because we know not everyone in any demographic category reacts and lives the same way. Advertisers realize that purchase behavior is the result of a number of complex psychological and sociological factors that cannot be explained by a superficial list of age, sex, income, or occupational characteristics.

We need to be aware of the implications of the changes taking place in society. If advertisers have a better understanding of such market segments as Hispanics, blacks, Asians, 50+, Generation X, boomers, then better communications can be developed to research these segments. We need to know more than simply numbers and location. We need to understand consumer lifestyles, identities, and motivations.

Questions
1. What is target marketing?
2. What is a product?
3. How do Kotler and Armstrong define the marketing concept?
4. What is positioning?
5. What do we mean by the phrase repositioning a product?
6. What is the 80/20 rule as it relates to target marketing?
7. What is the importance of income and population data for advertisers?

MARKETING SITUATION

The flea and tick product market accounts for $200 million in annual sales. The market is highly fragmented with a number of competing products and brands. Consumers express general dissatisfaction with most products in the category and are highly skeptical of new-product claims. Dipping by a veterinarian has become the gold standard for effectiveness, with flea and tick collars the standard for convenience.

Exspot was developed by Pitman-Moore as a concentrated product that kills fleas and ticks for up to four weeks with a single easy application. However, it was being sold only to veterinarians, who comprise only 25 percent of the potential market.

To take advantage of the potential in the consumer market, the product was renamed Defend with a marketing mission to capture a dominant share of the upper-priced flea and tick treatment category.

CAMPAIGN OBJECTIVES

The primary campaign objectives of the Defend campaign were:

1. To achieve 25 percent awareness nationwide
2. To achieve 55 percent target awareness among the target audience in high-potential markets
3. To achieve 5 percent trial nationwide
4. To build awareness of core values of superior efficacy and convenience to support a premium price position
5. To achieve 30 percent distribution penetration of veterinary clinics and pet stores in the first year
6. To establish Defend as a master brand to support later line extensions

TARGET AUDIENCE

The primary demographic market for Defend is female dog owners who are 25 to 54 years old, married with children living at home, employed with household income of at least $30,000, and reside in suburban or rural counties in single-family dwellings that they own. Geographically, fleas and ticks are a problem nationwide with the most severe infestations occurring in the hot, humid areas of the South. Psychologically, the target market is made up of those dog owners who are emotionally attached to their pets.

You Can Dip Your Dog For Fleas And Ticks. Or You Can Use A Squirt Of New Defend.

It Works Like Nothing Else.

CREATIVE STRATEGY

The creative strategy was to position Defend as the brand of professional-quality products that delivers the most relief. It was critical that advertising communicated the uniqueness of Defend, since research showed that most dog owners perceived treatments other than dips to be ineffective, and to justify Defend's premium cost.

The campaign used a snorkeling dog icon to present Defend as credible and to overcome the distaste of dipping in a light-hearted manner.

MEDIA STRATEGY

To achieve national reach with limited funding, four-color advertisements were scheduled in women's service magazines, shelter, and lifestyle publications. Regional editions were used in the South. Spot television was used in primary markets with an average of 900 to 1,000 ratings points scheduled against the target market. Four-color print ads in the major veterinary and pet store publications and direct mail were used to support the product. Since Defend (Exspot) was already established among veterinarians, the product was sampled through these offices. Free offers, point-of-purchase and media press releases were used to encourage usage and to heighten public awareness of the product.

EVIDENCE OF RESULTS

Among the primary brand awareness objectives achieved in the first four months were:

1. Awareness increased 25.5 percent nationwide and 46.4 percent in high-potential markets. A significant number of consumers perceived Defend as more effective than competitors as well as more convenient.
2. The campaign successfully established Defend as a good value despite its higher price.
3. The distribution objective of 30 percent was exceeded.
4. The company was able to successfully introduce line extensions under the Defend master brand.

MARKETING SITUATION

Louisville, Kentucky, was added as the thirty-fifth city in the Southwest Airlines system. Southwest has had the reputation as being a very profitable airline and has enjoyed success in new city introductions, including Chicago, Cleveland, and Columbus, Ohio. The strategy employed in these introductions was to promote SWA's low-fare position backed by a strong, factual, *credibility* message, to familiarize consumers with the airline.

Louisville required *a special introductory effort in addition to* this proven *credibility* package. Key factors that indicated this was needed were:

1. The market was *below* average for plane travel. Driving greater distances was common due to the high price of air travel.
2. Most air travel from Louisville was to non-SWA markets (only 283 people per day flew to Southwest's markets versus the 1,600-seat capacity SWA would have).
3. Louisville has a slower-paced lifestyle than other recent SWA cities (Chicago, Cleveland)—people enjoyed their city and didn't seem to *get up and go* as much.

Competitive Market Shares. United Airlines, 47 percent; American Airlines, 27 percent; TWA, 13 percent; Delta, 9 percent; and Northwest, 1 percent.

CAMPAIGN OBJECTIVES

Southwest Airlines set the following campaign objectives:
1. To create awareness that SWA was entering the market
2. To gain trial among competitive fliers
3. Change consumer behavior: from driving to flying, from staying at home to going somewhere

TARGET AUDIENCE

The campaign was directed at a broader target audience than usual for Southwest. There was a need to fill what appeared to be a great excess capacity of seats versus the apparent available market. Therefore, the target consisted of three consumer groups.

Business Travelers. Tend to be primarily males, aged 25–54, most likely managerial, sales, or entreprenuer. They could usually be flying or driving to business destinations.

Leisure Travelers. Adults aged 25–65, primarily includes families with children and senior citizens (both groups are most interested in saving money).

Stay-at-Homes. Demographically, this could include anyone. The key is mindset, that is, these are people who enjoy quieter lifestyles.

CREATIVE STRATEGY

The advertising communicated the strategy that Southwest Airlines *makes travel affordable,* and fun. These key messages were conveyed through fare-oriented copy, which in some cases made direct comparisons of SWA fares to the higher costs of driving or flying other airlines. Herb Kelleher, the CEO of SWA, was used to drive home the point in radio. The fun aspect was brought in by communicating the different destinations available on Southwest, and by giving the consumer ideas for quick trips, such as dinner in Kansas City. The bold headline approach ("Get Out of Town") was intended to grab people's attention and make the consumer think about traveling somewhere soon.

This strategy was designed to motivate the target to travel by offering low fares and a reason to go somewhere.

EVIDENCE OF RESULTS

The Louisville introduction was a huge success for Southwest. Early indicators of this success were the advanced bookings (bookings made prior to the start of service), which exceeded 30,000. Awareness of Southwest was high and positive as portrayed in taped *on-the-street* interviews conducted by Cramer-Krasselt prior to the service start date.

Southwest Airlines carried more local passengers flying out of Louisville to its three nonstop destinations in the five and a half weeks after introduction than all other Louisville carriers combined.

The total number of passengers flying out of Louisville before and after SWA introduction increased dramatically. The market for flying was expanded by approximately 46 percent after Southwest's entry.

Managing the Advertising

In studying advertising,

we must always remember that advertising is more than creating ads. It is a business. It is a process. It has a structure. It has organization. And it must be managed. Despite being very obvious, these things can get lost in the excitement of creating ads. But to be successful, the business of advertising must use many of the same sound business practices used by other fields. At the same time, the advertising business is different.

Chapter 5 concentrates on the advertising agency, its structure and its people. Agencies *are* basically people. It has been said that the assets of the agency go down the elevator at the end of the day. It is a people-driven business. Today it is a complex business, one which is extremely competitive. There are agencies finding their special advertising niches—among them consumer, global, pharmaceutical, business-to-business, Hispanic, and financial, to name a few. Each agency must serve a select few clients, satisfying their marketing and advertising needs. Advertising is, after all, a service business.

Chapter 6 looks at the management of advertising from the clients' or advertisers' perspective. Clients may or may not find the need to use an agency. If they do, they expect the agency to be a partner in the development of advertising and, in some cases, integrated marketing programs to help make the company more competitive in the marketplace. Often, what makes the relationship work is the personal chemistry among all the players, along with the agency's ability to deliver communications that accomplish goals and impact bottom lines of profit.

The **Advertising Agency, Media Services,** and **Other Services**

CHAPTER OBJECTIVES

The advertising agency has been the core of national and international advertising development. The agency role and relationships are changing. After reading this chapter you will understand:

- ■ **The agency**
- ■ **How agencies developed**
- ■ **The full-service agency**
- ■ **The reengineering of the agency**
- ■ **Global advertising agencies**
- ■ **Other advertising services**

As you've read, the 1990s is a period where every business is being reinvented. The advertising business is no exception. Today's agencies are reengineering themselves to become more receptive to clients' needs; are concerned with building brand equity, interactive media, **integrated communications,** globalization; and are becoming more responsive to the new consumer. Agencies of today are significantly different from those of the past.

As Bill Ludwig, executive vice president, creative director of Lintas Campbell Ewald says, "Individual roles are changing. Within the organization, agency or client, there's more of a team approach to developing and marketing the product. Make no mistake about it, its not business as usual—not in our business. Roles and relationships are changing."

Once upon a time, agency names stood for an advertising philosophy and a distinct personality—like branded products. Today the names change overnight before they have a chance to be branded, as mergers and affiliations take place as they try to position themselves to be more competitive in a global environment. In the past, Benton & Bowles touted "It isn't creative unless it sells." D'Arcy, MacManius & Masius emphasized the importance of understanding consumer behavior with its belief dynamics. But today they are merged with no clear image or personality other than being a strong packaged-goods agency. The personalities and philosophies of the past—Bill Bernbach, David Ogilvy, Leo Burnett, and Rosser Reeves—are only part of advertising history. Today the philosophies are emerging with the changes taking place in business and communications. The old guard is gone or merged, and emerging leaders are making their imprint on the industry—in unlikely places as Minneapolis, Raleigh, Richmond, Portland, to name a few—instead of the more traditional ad centers of New York, Chicago, and Los Angeles. And make no mistake, these new agencies do have philosophies. Because they're basically young, they don't have a history of brand equity. Due to the mergers and startups of new agencies, it is difficult to keep up with agencies' names, much less have a clear understanding of the agency culture. The agency remains in transition. However, despite all the changes, advertising agencies continue to be the most significant companies in the development of advertising and marketing in the world.

THE AGENCY

The definition of an advertising agency, as defined by the American Association of Advertising Agencies (A.A.A.A., or the 4As), is an independent business, composed of creative and business people who develop, prepare, and place advertising in advertising media for sellers seeking to find customers for their goods or services. The Martin Agency created Exhibit 5.1 for Healthtex to appeal to mothers.

According to the U.S. Census, there are over 10,000 agencies in operation in this country. The *Standard Directory of Advertising Agencies* (also known as the *Agency Red Book*) lists 8,700 agency profiles—including full-service agencies, house agencies, media buying services, sales promotion agencies, and public relations firms. The *Adweek Agency Directory* lists over 4,300 agencies and media buying services. There are about 2,000 agencies listed in the *New York Yellow Pages* alone. Unfortunately, there isn't a single directory that lists every agency throughout the country. The majority of agencies are small one- to ten-person shops (we'll talk about size and services later in this chapter). Longwater Advertising (Exhibit 5.2) is a small agency that develops exceptional print ads for specialized client needs.

EXHIBIT

5.1

(Courtesy: Healthtex™ and The Martin Agency.)

HOW AGENCIES DEVELOPED

Before we discuss present-day agencies further let us take a look at how advertising agencies got started and how they developed into large worldwide organizations that play such a prominent role in the marketing and advertising process.

The Early Age (Colonial Times to 1917)

It is not generally known that the first Americans to act as advertising agents were colonial postmasters:

> In many localities advertisements for Colonial papers might be left at the post offices. In some instances, the local post office would accept advertising copy for publications in papers in other places; it did so with the permission of the postal authorities. . . . William Bradford, publisher of the first Colonial weekly in New York, made an arrangement with Richard Nichols, postmaster in 1727, whereby the latter accepted advertisements for the New York Gazette at regular rates.[1]

Space Salesmen. Volney B. Palmer is the first person known to have worked on a commission basis. In the 1840s, he solicited ads for newspapers that had difficulty getting out-of-town advertising. Palmer contacted publishers and offered to get them business for a 50 percent commission, but he often set-

---

[1]James Melvin Lee. *History of American Journalism,* rev. ed. (Boston: Houghton Mifflin, 1933), p. 74.

(Courtesy: MOL and Longwater Advertising.)

tled for less. There was no such thing as a rate card or a fixed price for space or commission in those days. A first demand for $500 by the papers might be reduced, before the bargain was struck, to $50. (Today we call that negotiation.) Palmer opened offices in Philadelphia, New York, and Boston. Soon there were more agents, offering various deals.

Space Wholesalers. During the 1850s in Philadelphia, George P. Rowell bought large blocks of space for cash (most welcome) from publishers at very low rates, less agents' commissions. He would sell the space in small "squares"—one-column wide—at his own retail rate. Rowell next contracted with 100 newspapers to buy one column of space a month and sold the space in his total list at a fixed rate per line for the whole list: "An inch of space a month in one hundred papers for one hundred dollars." Selling by list became widespread. Each wholesaler's list was his private stock in trade. (This was the original media package deal.)

The First Rate Directory. In 1869 Rowell shocked the advertising world by publishing a directory of newspapers with their card rates and his own estimates of their circulation. Other agents accused him of giving away their trade secrets; publishers howled too because his estimates of circulation were lower than their claims. Nevertheless, Rowell persisted in offering advertisers an estimate of space costs based on those published rates for whatever markets they wanted. This was the beginning of the media estimate.

The Agency Becomes a Creative Center. In the early 1870s, Charles Austin Bates, a writer, began writing ads and selling his services to whoever wanted them, whether advertisers or agents. Among his employees were Earnest Elmo Calkins and Ralph Holden, who in the 1890s founded their own agency, famous for 50 years under the name of Calkins and Holden. These men did more than write ads. They brought together planning, copy, and art, showing the way to combine all three into effective advertising. Not only was their agency one of the most successful for half a century, but the influence of their work helped establish the advertising agency as the creative center for advertising ideas. Many of the names on the list of firms advertising in 1890 (see Chapter 1) are still familiar today; their longevity can be attributed to the effectiveness of that generation of agency people who developed the new power of advertising agency services. The business had changed from one of salesmen's going out to sell advertising space to one of agencies that created the plan, the ideas, the copy, and the artwork, produced the plates, and then placed the advertising in publications from which they received a commission.

To this day, the unique contribution to business for which agencies are most respected is their ability to create effective ads.

Agency-Client Relationship Established. In 1875, Francis Ayer established N.W. Ayer & Son (one of the larger advertising agencies today). Ayer proposed to bill advertisers for what he actually paid the publishers (that is, the rate paid the publisher less the commission), adding a fixed charge in lieu of a commission. In exchange, advertisers would agree to place all their advertising through Ayer's agents. This innovation established the relationship of advertisers as clients of agencies rather than as customers who might give their business to various salespeople, never knowing whether they were paying the best price.

The Curtis No-Rebating Rule. In 1891, the Curtis Publishing Company announced that it would pay commissions to agencies only if they agreed to collect the full price from advertisers, a rule later adopted by the Magazine Publishers of America. This was the forerunner of no-rebating agreements, which were an important part of the agency business for over 50 years. (Agency commissions, however, ranged from 10 to 25 percent in both magazines and newspapers.)

Standard Commissions for Recognized Agencies Established. In 1917, newspaper publishers, through their associations, set 15 percent as the standard agency commission, a percentage that remains in effect for all media to this day (except local advertising, for which the media deal directly with the stores and pay no commission). The commission would be granted, however, only to agencies that the publishers' associations "recognized." One of the important conditions for recognition was an agency's agreement to charge the client the full rate (no rebating). Other criteria for recognition were that the agency must have business to place, must have shown competence in handling advertising, and must be financially sound. These three conditions are still in effect. Anyone may claim to be an agency, but only agencies that are recognized are allowed to charge a commission.

Today's agencies still receive commissions from the media for space they buy for clients. However, artwork and the cost of production are generally billed by the agency to the advertiser, plus a service charge—usually 17.65 percent of the net, which is equivalent to 15 percent of the gross. By preagreement, a charge is made for other services.

The American Association of Advertising Agencies. The most important agency association is the American Association of Advertising Agencies established in 1917. This organization has continuously acted as a great force in improving the standards of agency business and advertising practice. Its members, large and small, place over 80 percent of all national advertising today.

The No–Rebate Age (1918–56)

We summarize the events of this era that left their mark on today's agency world.

Radio. One of the main events of 1925 was the notorious Scopes trial, and the main advent was radio. They did a lot for each other. Radio dramatized evolution-on-trial in Tennessee; it brought the issue of teaching scientific evolution home to Americans and it brought people closer to their radios. Tuning in to radio soon became a major part of American life, especially during the Great Depression and World War II. Radio established itself as a prime news vehicle. It also gave advertising a vital new medium and helped pull agencies through those troubled years. A number of agencies handled the entire production of a radio program as well as its commercials. By 1942, agencies were billing more for radio ($188 million) than they were for newspaper ($144 million) advertising. The radio boom lasted until television came along.

Television. Television became popular after 1952, when nationwide network broadcasts began. Between 1950 and 1956, television was the fastest-growing medium. It became the major medium for many agencies. National advertisers spent more on television than they did on any other medium. TV expenditures grew from $171 million in 1950 to $1,225 million in 1956.

Electronic Data Processing. The computer entered advertising through the accounting department. By 1956, it was already changing the lives of the media department, the marketing department, and the research department—all having grown in competence with the increasing number of syndicated research services. Agencies prided themselves on their research knowledge and were spending hundreds of thousands of dollars for research every year to service their clients better.

Business was good, and American consumers were attaining a better standard of living than they had ever enjoyed before. The period from 1950 to 1956 proved to be the beginning of the biggest boom advertising ever had. Total expenditures jumped from $4.5 billion in 1950 to $9.9 billion. Over 60 percent of this spending was national advertising placed by advertising agencies. And the agency business was good, too.

The Age of Negotiation (1956–90)

Consent Decrees. In 1956, a change occurred in the advertiser-agency relationship. The U.S. Department of Justice held that the no-rebating provision between media associations and agencies limited the ability to negotiate between buyer and seller and therefore was in restraint of trade and a violation of antitrust laws. Consent decrees to stop no-rebating provisions were entered into by all media associations on behalf of their members.

Although the Justice Department's ruling in no way affected the 15 percent that commission agencies were accustomed to getting from the media, it opened the way to review the total compensation an agency should receive for its services, with the 15 percent commission a basic part of the negotiations. Later we look at the effects this has had on the agency-client relationship.

The Reengineering Age (1990–Present)

Integrated Services. The 1990s has been about agencies reevaluating how they operate. Integrated services has been a buzzword relating to efforts to coordinate a client's entire marketing mix, including public relations, promotion, direct marketing, package design, and so on. Some agencies have expanded their communication services to clients by expanding departments or buying or creating subsidiary companies that enable them to offer sales promotion, public relations, direct marketing, logo and packaging design, and even TV programming. One of the reasons is financial—clients have been moving dollars from advertising to promotion, and clients want their communications integrated. Agencies are trying to change to supply those needs. The concept, similar to Lintas:Link discussed in Chapter 3, involves coordinating all marketing communication efforts to the same objective, not developing them independently.

Interactive Communications. As cable, computers, satellite communication, video technologies, and the like become global, agencies have to learn how to use this technology for their clients. This involves understanding the hard-

EXHIBIT
5.3

This page from their agency information tells about their services.

Sterrett-Tucker Agency

Full-Service Agency Capabilities

✔ Marketing and Media Planning

✔ Research and Analysis

✔ Advertising Campaigns—Local, Regional, National

✔ Creative Concepting/Copywriting

✔ Logo/Corporate Identity Development

✔ Graphic Design and Production

✔ Radio and Television Production

✔ Direct Marketing Programs

✔ Media Placement

✔ Public Relations/Special Event Planning

(Courtesy: Sterrett-Tucker Agency.)

ware of how interactive services are delivered, the message development that will be different from traditional advertising, and understanding the interactive consumer. The future will be different.

THE FULL-SERVICE AGENCY

The concept of the full-service agency is changing. In the traditional sense, it is an agency offering all the services necessary to handle the total advertising function. Exhibit 5.3 illustrates services offered by a medium sized agency. As indicated above, this may mean offering promotion, public relations, etc., and other services needed by clients. Lintas' integrated multiservice process of "one advertiser, one voice," carries the product's message through a variety of disciplines—advertising, sales promotion, direct marketing, and so forth—with a tight strategic marketing focus so that the brand image is reinforced every time the consumer is exposed to a communication. Most major agencies have subsidiaries or divisions that offer a range of specific services. Exhibit 5.4 is an example of an ad aimed at businesses and not consumers.

Despite the fact that there isn't a universal approach, let's take a look at the functions that full-service agencies perform. When a new account or a new product is assigned to a full-service agency, work will generally proceed along the following lines:

What Is the Marketing Problem?   The marketing problem entails gathering and analyzing all the information necessary to market the product or service. Who are the prime prospects? Where are they? What are their demographic and psychographic characteristics? How does the product fit into their lifestyle? How do they regard this type of product? This particular brand? Competitive products? What one benefit do consumers seek from such a product? In what distinctive way can the product solve the prime prospects' problem? What media will best reach your market?

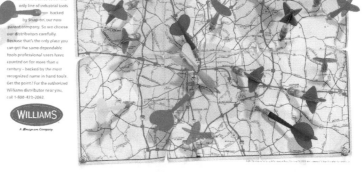

Sawyer Riley Compton specializes in business-to-business advertising. Here they tell about Williams distributors industrial tools.

(Courtesy: Williams and Sawyer Riley Compton.)

The Strategy. Using the answers to these questions, you formulate a strategy that positions the product in relation to the prime-prospect customer and emphasizes the attribute that will appeal to the prime prospect.

The Creative Response. Once the overall strategy is determined, you decide on the creative strategy, write copy, and prepare rough layouts and storyboards.

The Media Plan. Next you define media strategy, checking objectives to ensure that they parallel your marketing objectives. Then you select media and prepare schedules with costs.

The Total Plan. You present roughs of the copy, layout, and production costs, along with media schedules and costs—all leading to total cost.

When the total plan is approved, you proceed with the production of ads, issue media orders, and ship plates and prints to media or tapes and films, as required.

Notify Trade of Forthcoming Campaign. You inform dealers of the campaign details early enough so that they can get ready to take advantage of the ad campaign.

Billing and Payments. When ads are run, you take care of billing to client and payment of bills to media and production vendors. As an example of the billing procedure, let us say that through your agency an advertiser has ordered an ad in *Leisure-Time* magazine for one page costing $2,000. When the ad appears, the bill your agency gets from the publisher will read something like this:

1 page, October *Leisure-Time* magazine	**$2,000**
Agency commission @ 15% (cash discount omitted for convenience)	**300**
Balance due	**$1,700**

Your agency will then bill the advertiser for $2,000, retain the $300 as its compensation, and pay the publisher $1,700.

The agency commission applies only to the cost of space or time. In addition, as mentioned earlier, your agency will send the advertiser a bill for production costs for such items as:

- **Finished artwork**
- **Typography**
- **Photography**
- **Retouching**
- **Reproduction prints**
- **Recording studios**
- **Broadcast production**

These items are billed at actual costs plus a service charge, usually 17.65 percent (which is equivalent to 15 percent of the net).

THE TRADITIONAL AGENCY ORGANIZATION

First, we'll examine the traditional approach to full-service agency structure, and then we'll look at the reengineering of this process.

Advertising agencies come in all sizes and shapes. The largest employ hundreds of people and bill thousands of millions of dollars every year. The smallest are one- or two-person operations (usually a creative person and an account manager). As they grow, they generally must add to their organizational structure to handle all the functions of a full-service agency.

All agencies do not structure themselves in exactly the same manner. For discussion purposes, we have chosen a typical organizational structure under the command of major executives: the vice presidents of (1) the creative department, (2) account services, (3) marketing services, and (4) management and finance (Exhibit 5.5). We discuss briefly how each department is organized.

Creative Department

As the head of the creative department, the creative director is responsible for the effectiveness of all advertising produced by the agency. The success of the agency depends on this department. The creative director sets the creative philosophy of the agency and its artistic standards and generates a stimulating environment that inspires the best people to seek work there.

At first, all writers and artists will work right under one creative director; but as the business grows, various creative directors will take over the writing and art activities of different brands. A traffic department will be set up to keep the work flowing on schedule.

EXHIBIT 5.5

....

Organization of a typical full-service agency.

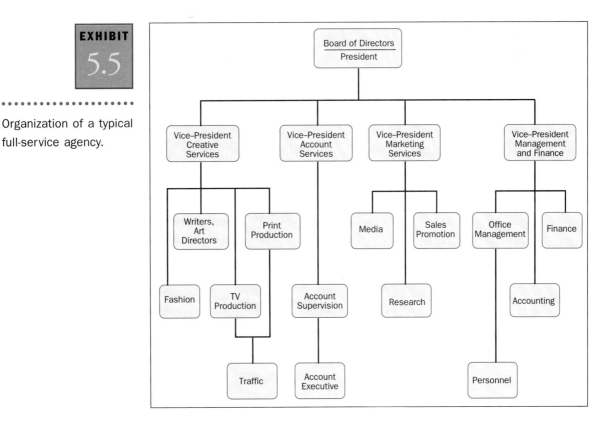

The print production director and the TV manager also report to the creative director, who is ultimately responsible for the finished product—ads and commercials.

Account Services

The vice president in charge of account services is responsible for the relationship between the agency and the client and is indeed a person of two worlds: the client's business and advertising. This vice president must be knowledgeable about the client's business, profit goals, marketing problems, and advertising objectives. He or she is responsible for helping to formulate the basic advertising strategy recommended by the agency, for seeing that the proposed advertising prepared by the agency is on target, and for presenting the total proposal—media schedules, budget, and rough ads or storyboards—to the client for approval. Then comes the task of making sure that the agency produces the work to the client's satisfaction.

As the business grows and takes on many clients, an account supervisor will appoint account executives to serve as the individual contacts with the various accounts. Account executives must be skillful at both communications and follow-up. Their biggest contribution is keeping the agency ahead of its client's needs. But the account supervisor will continue the overall review of account handling, maintaining contacts with a counterpart at the client's office (Exhibit 5.6).

Marketing Services

The vice president in charge of marketing services is responsible for media planning and buying, for research, and for sales promotion. The marketing

EXHIBIT 5.6

....

Typical team responsibilities. In some agencies, the account planner works directly with creative to provide research and consumer viewpoints.

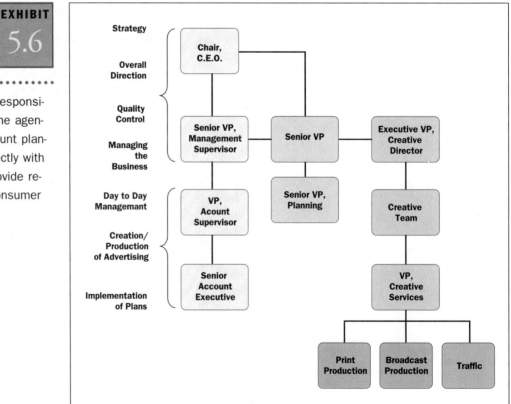

vice president will appoint a media director, who is responsible for the philosophy and planning of the use of media, for the selection of specific media, and for buying space and time. As the agency grows, there will be a staff of media buyers, grouped according to media (print, TV, or radio), accounts, or territory. The media staff will include an estimating department and an ordering department, as well as a department to handle residual payments due performers. The media head may use independent media services, especially in the purchase of TV and radio time.

The research director will help define marketing and copy goals. Agencies usually use outside research organizations for field work, but in some agencies, research and media planning are coordinated under one person. The division of work among the executives may vary with the agency.

The sales-promotion director takes care of premiums, coupons, and other dealer aids and promotions.

Management and Finance

Like all businesses, an advertising agency needs an administrative head to take charge of financial and accounting control, office management, and personnel (including trainees).

THE REENGINEERING OF THE AGENCY

During the past decade a number of attempts have been made to reengineer the agency. At this point in time, there isn't a standard structure brought about by reengineering or even a desire by most agencies to radically restructure. Some of the efforts have been successful, and others have been questionable. However, the driving force behind any reengineering is the desire to meet the wants and needs of clients cheaper, faster, and better. Lou Schultz, Lintas Worldwide Media guru, puts it this way, "There has been a great deal of talk about reengineering the agencies. I wonder if much of it represents an attitude of 'get moving' without having the foggiest idea about where they should be heading."[2]

Jay Chaiet, a pioneer in agency reengineering says, "We believe the hierarchical structure [of the traditional agency], if not obsolete at present, is on its way. The traditional pyramid is about personal power and focuses on how to run a business. Therefore most decisions are about the organization's needs, concentrating on fiscal and administrative issues. An agency is a service organization whose sole existence depends on satisfying client needs."[3]

What Does Reengineering Do?

It attempts to put the top management of agencies directly in touch with clients instead of playing administrators. In traditional agencies, senior managers spend 15 to 20 percent of their time on client business. In reengineered agencies, they spend about 60 percent of their time in the trenches working on client business. Middle managers in reengineered agencies act as coaches, team leaders, and quality control managers. One of the significant changes

---

[2]Lou Schultz, "Re-engineering Media—Another Buzzword or a Necessity?" Speech delivered to Adcraft Club of Detroit, October 8, 1993.
[3]Jeff Weiner, "Anious Ranks," *Agency*, Spring 1994, p. 42.

is that creative, account managers, media planners must work together as a *team*—a team of people working together to rapidly solve problems. Chiat/Day calls its units *team architecture,* and another agency, Kallir Phillip Ross, calls them *business service teams.* Most reengineers say teams consist of 8 to 12 people; although, Sawyer Riley Compton uses teams, called *account circles,* of about 20. Most agencies' structure is somewhat similar to traditional structure. It is how business works that is different. People don't do their thing in isolation; they approach problem solving together. It is thought that the team concept helps younger people because it allows them to work side by side with their mentors.[4] Changing technology also plays an important part in most restructuring efforts. The linking of teams and clients electronically and the reduction of the time and cost of producing advertising are part of the effort to use technology effectively.

MARC advertising is handling the same amount of work with 20 percent less staff since reengineering because it has eliminated so many steps and clerical procedures. It also added senior creative and media people as a result of savings. In some restructured agencies, some functions—media buying, accounting, creative services, research—are kept intact as departments and serve all teams. As stated, there isn't a reengineered single structure.

As with any new management trend, traditional agencies will copy and modify those reengineering structures that have been successful to meet their specific needs. There is little doubt that the agency structure in the future will not be a copy of today's.

What's Different in Reengineering?

There isn't necessarily a major shift in the organizational chart in terms of job function. However, there is a significant shift in how that job function relates to others in the process. For example, under the traditional structure an account person may meet regularly with creative people to discuss strategy and ad copy or with media people to review scheduling, or with the public relations person. In some cases, there might be a meeting where specific players in the process meet to discuss a problem or progress. In most reengineered operations, the key people on the team meet on a regular basis so that everyone knows what is going on in every aspect of the account. At Sawyer Riley Compton the account circle meets every Monday morning to review the week's work—and meets again when necessary. This means the sales promotion person knows about the public relations work, and the art director knows about the media planning. If necessary, the client participates in the review. Exhibit 5.7 shows the players on a typical account circle team. One of the pluses in this process is that everyone on the team—senior or junior staffer—understands every function in the process and how their work relates to everyone else's work. In theory, a client could call anyone on the team to get an answer.

GLOBAL AGENCIES AND GLOBAL MARKETS

Major clients have demanded global sophistication from their advertising agencies. Major agencies have been global in nature for decades to service

---

[4]Thomas Forbes, "Re-engineering the Advertising Agency," *Agency,* Spring 1994, pp. 34–42.

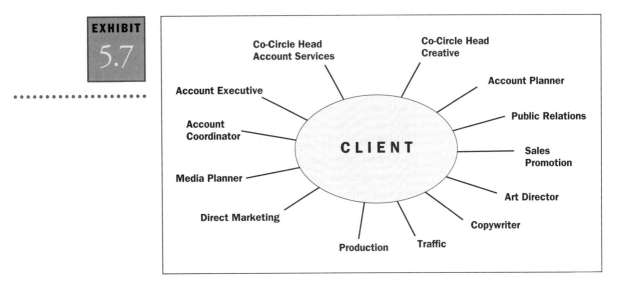

their clients' international needs. For example, Leo Burnett was a latecomer in comparison to other major U.S. agencies in establishing itself in the international arena. It began to develop a major international presence in the early 1970s and now has offices in over 50 countries. Today, the demands on marketers to survive in a global economy place pressures on large and medium-sized agencies to become global partners. Many small to medium shops that don't have the resources for international offices have made affiliations with agencies or independent agency networks throughout the world to service clients and give advice. If agencies don't have the resources to help clients engage in international marketing, then the client is likely to turn to agencies that do have the resources and knowledge, or the client may seek a local agency in the country where it is doing business. In Chapter 24, we deal extensively with international operations (Exhibit 5.8 is an international ad by a global company).

DeBeers is a global company selling wedding bands. This ad was created by J. Walter Thompson, Japan.

(Courtesy: DEBEERS & New York Festival International Advertising Awards.)

The leading international advertising centers ranked in terms of local advertising billings are New York and Tokyo—fighting neck and neck for world leadership. These two advertising giants are followed by London, Paris, Chicago, and Los Angeles. Almost every country has an advertising agency center. For U.S. agencies, setting up a foreign office can be very complex. Each country is a different market, with its own language, buying habits, ways of living, mores, business methods, marketing traditions, and laws. So instead of trying to organize new agencies with American personnel, most American agencies purchase a majority or minority interest in a successful foreign agency. They usually have a top management person as head of an overseas office. Key members of the international offices meet regularly for intensive seminars on philosophy and operation of the agency, and to share success stories. Remember, good marketing ideas can come from anyplace. The United States doesn't have a lock on great ideas.

Global advertising always promised marketers the opportunity for one-world execution that can save money on production, and give the marketer global brand equity. Remember, the Unilever quote in Chapter 3, " . . . every international brand starts out as a successful local brand . . . reproduced many times." Being a global advertiser with one global campaign sounds easy. But it is not. Despite being a global advertiser for decades, it was only in 1992 that Coca-Cola launched its first global advertising campaign—*all the ads being similar in each country.* In 1994, it was reported that Chanel No. 5 was having problems with its global campaign because it was taking a manufacturer approach instead of a consumer approach. Ashish Banerjee, former international account person with McCann-Erickson and J. Walter Thompson, says that, unless a brand and its advertising are presented in relevant and meaningful ways in the context of these local environments, consumers couldn't care less. As many experienced multinational marketers like Unilever, Gillette, and Nestlé know that for any given brand its advertising, eliciting the same response from consumers across borders matters much more than running the same advertising across borders. That may mean using the same brand concept or advertising concept and similar executional format across borders—but the executions need to be customized to local markets so the consumers can relate to and empathize with the advertising.[5] Simply translating American ads into foreign languages has proved dangerous. Frank Perdue's Spanish translation of "It takes a tough man to make a tender chicken," actually said, "It takes a sexually excited man to make a chick affectionate."

It is only logical that multinational clients want their agencies to know how to develop great advertising campaigns that can run across all the principal markets of the world. As the chairperson of Leo Burnett International said, "As the world gets smaller, there needs to be brand consistency so people don't get confused as they move from market [country] to market."[6] The result of this need is pressure on U.S. agencies to produce, place, and research global advertising. The following table lists a sampling of Lintas Worldwide's offices that enable them to service marketers across the globe.

---

[5]Ashish Banerjee, "Global Campaigns Don't Work; Multinationals Do," *Advertising Age,* April 18, 1994, 9.23.
[6]"Coke Seeks Ad Formula with Global Appeal," *Atlanta Journal and Constitution,* November 18, 1991, p. A5.

Lintas Worldwide

Sampling of Domestic and International Office/Affiliates

United States	Africa	Asia	Europe	Latin America	Canada
Los Angeles	Abidjan	Tokyo	Oslo	Buenos Aires	Toronto
Warren, MI	Dubai	Sydney	Vienna	Caracus	
New York	Bryanston	Shanghai	Brussels	Santiago	
	Nairobi	Hong Kong	Budapest	Bogota	
	Harare	Bombay	Copenhagen	Mexico City	
	Winhock	Seoul	Paris	Sau Paulo	
		Singapore	Amsterdam		
		Taipei	Stockholm		
		Bangkok	London		
		Auckland	Istanbul		

COMPETING ACCOUNTS

The client-agency relationship is a professional one. Much of the information exchanged between client and agency is confidential. This may include plans for new products or new marketing strategies. Therefore, the client generally will not approve of an agency's handling companies or products in direct competition. Sometimes agencies will handle accounts for the same type of product if they do not compete directly—for example, banks that do not compete in the same markets may be handled by the same agency. Many client-agency conflicts result from mergers in which one merger partner handles an account for a product that competes with a product being handled by the other merger partner. When agencies consider merging, the first question is, "Will any of our accounts conflict?" Currently, a number of the large national agencies run their local offices independently in the hope that clients will not view the same type of account in another office as a conflict. Competing accounts also present a problem in dealing with outside creative services and are conceivably an inhibiting factor.

THE AGENCY OF RECORD

Large advertisers employ a number of agencies to handle the advertising of their various divisions and products. To coordinate the total media buy and the programming of products in a network buy, the advertiser will appoint one agency as the agency of record. This agency will make the corporate media contracts under which the other agencies will issue their orders, keep a record of all the advertising placed, and transmit management's decisions on the allotment of time and space in a schedule. For this service, the other agencies pay a small part of their commissions (usually 15 percent of their 15 percent) to the agency of record.

AGENCY NETWORKS

In general, the agency networks are composed primarily of small- and medium-sized agencies that have a working agreement to help with information gathering or sharing. In the 1920s, Lynn Ellis, an advertising management consultant, saw that middle-sized agencies with no branch offices had difficulty in dealing with the regional problems of their clients. He organized such agencies (one agency in each main advertising center) into an agency network so that they could help one another cope with problems in their respective areas and could exchange ideas, experiences, and facilities. Today there are a number of agency networks operating throughout the country.

Do not confuse associations like the American Association of Advertising Agencies with agency networks. Members of the 4As are in direct competition with one another—there may be dozens of 4A agencies in the same city.

THE MEGA-AGENCY

Saatchi & Saatchi PLC, London, began one of the most significant changes in the advertising business by systematically expanding from a small agency in 1986 to a mega-agency network with capitalized billings of over $13.5 billion in two years. It became the world's largest advertising organization for a brief period of time. Today, the world's leading advertising organizations include WWP Group (London), Interpublic Group (New York), Omnicom Group (New York), Dentsu (Tokyo), Saatchi & Saatchi (London/New York). These, and the other mega-advertising organizations, own many advertising agencies throughout the world. For example, Interpublic owns Lintas:Worldwide, the Martin Agency, McCann-Erickson, etc., each in competition with one another.

Mega-agencies offer several advantages to their clients. Among the most important are a greater reservoir of talent; an ability to shift portions of accounts from one agency to another without going through the time-consuming, and often confusing, agency review (Coca-Cola has switched assignments for its brands between Interpublic's McCann-Erickson and Lintas:Worldwide), and

EXHIBIT 5.9

· · · · · · · · · · · · · · · · · · ·

Agencies may create collateral material—brochures, folders, sales pieces—for clients. However, many clients will produce these materials internally or have freelance art studios handle them. Exhibit 5.9 is a collateral piece produced by Leigh Kain Advertising & Design.

(Courtesy: Leigh Kain Advertising & Design.)

superior clout in negotiating with the media. There are also some disadvantages for clients dealing with a mega-agency, the most important of which is conflicts with competing accounts.

Smaller agencies claim that the mega-agency is quite impersonal and not as creative in advertising clients' products. The fact is that all agencies—large and small—are composed of small units or teams that work on an assigned account or group of accounts. The ability of the team and its dedication to creative and professional excellence are dictated by the talent and innovative abilities of individuals, not the size of the company they work for. Many medium and smaller agencies are in fact traveling the merger road themselves in order to become more competitive.

The size and structure of an agency will attract or repel clients, depending on what level and quality of services they are seeking. Some large corporations have been critical of agency mergers and mega-agencies. Yet, in truth, the advertising business is following business in general in attempting to diversify, economize, and become more efficient and profitable.

OTHER ADVERTISING SERVICES

New services are continually springing up in competition with advertising agencies. Each new service is designed to serve clients' needs a little differently. This competition has impacted agency structure and operations.

Talent/Production Agencies Creating Creative

There is a new breed of organizations that combine a range of talents to produce creative for both agencies and clients. The most famous is Creative Artists Agency. Creative Artists Agency (CAA), a production/talent agency involving entertainment stars, writers, directors, etc., made inroads with Coca-Cola in working as a partner with Coke's advertising agencies or independently to develop advertising concepts and commercials. As a result, CAA usurped McCann-Erickson Worldwide's creative stronghold on the Coca-Cola Classic account. Previously, McCann-Erickson was totally responsible for developing Coca-Cola Classic's creative as most advertising agencies do for their clients. A number of other talent agencies have tried to work agreements with other marketers and their advertising agencies to provide creative and talent services. Some in the advertising industry believe such talent agency relationships can add another dimension to the advertising agency/client resources. Others feel clients and agencies can seek the same kind of talent as needed without having to create formal long-term working relationships.

Peter Sealey, the former Coca-Cola global marketing director who managed the introduction of diet Coke, believes that changes in the way advertising is to be created are forthcoming. He believes that during the 1980s the relative effectiveness of advertising was severely hindered because the quality of the creative product didn't keep pace. At Coke, he was responsible for the 1993 Coke-guzzling polar bears created by both Coke's agency and Creative Artists Agency. CAA replaced much of the agency's responsibility in creative development—a rather radical departure. "What we attempted to do with CAA was go outside the four walls of an ad agency and go into some of the finest creative resources in the world . . . " As Sealey points out, the motion picture studio of today identifies options on the entertainment horizon and basically goes into the creative community and says, "Okay, we want summer movies or adventure films." And they look at scripts and available directors from the freelance creative community. It occurred to Sealey that Coke could do the same thing with advertising. He contends that the agency of 1990 is like the motion picture studio of the 1940s or 1950s; therefore, we should make the advertising agency of the mid-1990s like today's motion picture studio.[7]

Independent Creative Services

Some advertisers seek top creative talent on a freelance, per-job basis. Many creative people do freelance work in their off hours. Some make it a full-time job and open their own *creative shop* or *creative boutique.*

Butler, Shine & Stern (Sausalito, California) opened in mid-1993 and attracted interest with no media department, no researchers, and no account people except the president. Its formation was based upon the hiring of Coca-Cola of CAA to create and produce most of its commercials. John Butler says, " . . . if a marketer like Coke was going off and finding a nontraditional way of communicating with America, who's to say other companies can't."[8] A year after opening, it had business equal to $13 million in billings and was planning to add a strategic planner. This creative boutique or agency hybrid believes in researching its concepts and really understanding the market and the target, and is moving a little closer to a traditional agency structure.

Á La Carte Agency

Today, many agencies offer for a fee just part of their total services that advertisers want. The à la carte arrangement is used mostly for creative services and for media planning and placement.

In-House Agency

When advertisers found that all the services an agency could offer were purchasable on a piecemeal fee basis, they began setting up their own internal agencies, referred to as *in-house agencies.* Exhibit 5.10 is an example of an ad created by an in-house agency for Lowe's.

The in-house agency can employ a creative service to originate advertising for a fee or markup. It can buy the space or time or employ a media-buying service to buy time or space and place the ads. As a rule, the in-house agency is an administrative center that gathers and directs varying outside services for its operation and has a minimum staff. Folks, Inc., an Atlanta restaurant management company that owns several restaurant concepts, has a two-person in-house agency. It has a regular creative partner who executes Folks' ideas and production. Almost all the concepts, creative ideas, and copy are developed in-house, although, the creative partner often has input. It buys all print media in-house and sometimes uses an independent media service to buy radio and television for all its advertising. It also develops all store marketing, public relations, and promotion.

In-house agency
An arrangement whereby the advertiser handles the total agency function by buying individually, on a fee basis, the needed services (for example, creative, media services, and placement) under the direction of an assigned advertising director.

---

[7]"Doin' the Real-Time Thing," *Marketing Management,* 3, no. 1 (1994): pp. 4–7.
[8]Gary Levin, "Butler Makes Mark with Quirky Humor," *Advertising Age,* June 20, 1994, pp. 16–17.

EXHIBIT

5.10

Lowe's House Agency developed this striking ad.

"Color Guard"

There's a color out there to symbolize almost everything. Red, green, and "take your chances" yellow on stop lights. Blue ribbons for winners. And a few new ones. Purple, teal, or royal blue on a work glove means trouble for anything even resembling a prickly rose bush.

Wells Lamont® Work Gloves For Women are designed to fit a woman's hand. From durable goatskin work gloves, to stretchable jersey gloves with reinforced tips, Wells Lamont® has a colorful glove for any use. For the complete selection of Wells Lamont® Work Gloves For Women, come to Lowe's.

WELLS LAMONT

LOWE'S®
Helping Add Value To Your Home®

(Courtesy: Lowe's and Wells Lamont and Southern Living.*)*

Saving money is not the only, or even the chief, reason some firms use an in-house agency. For industrial companies that have highly technical products that constantly undergo technological changes and advances, it may well be more efficient to have in-house technical people prepare the ads. This saves endless briefings that would be necessary if outside industrial writers were used. But the companies place their ads through an agency of their choice, at a negotiated commission.

Rolodex Agency

An agency run by several advertising specialists, usually account and/or creative people, that has no basic staff is called a *rolodex agency*. It hires specialists—in marketing, media planning, creative strategy, writing, whatever—who work on a project basis. The concept is similar to hiring freelance creative people to execute ads, except that the experts are hired as needed. The rolodex agency claims to be able to give advertisers expertise that small full-service agencies cannot match.

Media-Buying Services

There has been significant growth of independent media services outside traditional advertising agencies in recent years. These services developed with the rapid growth of television in the 1960s and pressure on agency media directors for the best deal. They handle such tasks as media planning and buying. These services promote themselves as specialists in that the media are their business, their only business. By one estimate, outside media services will handle media buys representing 10 to 12 percent of all domestic advertising billings by the year 2000.[9]

Agency media directors have been under great pressure to make the most effective use of their budgets by planning, placing, and negotiating the best deal for a media schedule. Negotiations have become such an art that many agency media directors have left their agency to form media-buying services. For example, Richard Kostyra, former executive vice president and U.S. director of media services, left to form Media First International. Obviously, agency media people don't like this trend. John O'Toole of the American Association of Advertising Agencies says, media services contribute to the very dangerous trend of commoditization, buying advertising by the pound. The input from creative, from account planners, from everybody else, should be contributing to the media, so that the media program is based on more than what the computer tells you.

In-House Services. A few large advertisers have taken the media-buying function in-house so they will have more control over the buying operation.

However, this doesn't appear to be a trend. It is more likely that advertisers will keep a seasoned media consultant on staff to ride herd on their agency or media service's performance.

Agency Media Groups. It is fairly common in Europe for agencies to jointly buy media through a combined media-buying group. The combined efforts give the agencies more media-buying clout resulting in media savings for their clients. If this concept is to be successful, it must overcome client conflicts from within the participating agencies.

FORMS OF AGENCY COMPENSATION

Historically agency compensation has been fairly standardized since the 1930s. An agency received a commission from the media for advertising placed by the agency. The commission would cover the agency's copywriting and account service charges. This method of compensation hasn't been satisfactory during recent years due to the changing nature of business. The straight 15 percent remains; but in some instances, there are fixed commissions less than 15 percent (some large advertisers have negotiated a rate closer to 12 percent), sliding scales based upon client expenditures, flat-fee arrangements agreed upon by clients and agency, performance-based systems, and labor-based fee-plus-profit arrangements. In other words, compensation arrangements now take many forms. Despite this change, there are only two basic forms of advertising agency compensation: *commissions* and *fees*.

■ *Media commissions.* The traditional 15 percent commission remains a form of agency income, especially for modestly budgeted accounts. Clients and agency may agree to a relationship in which the rate is fixed at less than 15 percent. This generally applies to large budget accounts—the larger the budget, the lower the rate for the agency. With a sliding-scale commission agreement, the agency receives a fixed commission based upon a certain expenditure. After that level of spending, the commission is reduced (there

[9]Stuart Elliott, "A Tug-of-War between Traditional Agencies and New Media Services," *New York Times,* January 21, 1993, p. C18.

may be a 14 percent commission for the first $20 million spent by the client and a 7 percent commission on the next $15 million.) The combinations are endless.

- **Production commissions or markups.** As indicated earlier, agencies subcontract production work (all outside purchases such as type, photography, illustrators) and charge the client the cost plus a commission—17.5 percent is the norm.

- **Fee arrangements.** At times the 15 percent commission is not enough for agencies to make a fair profit. For example, it may cost an agency more to serve a small client than a large one. The agency and client may negotiate a fee arrangement. In some cases it is a commission plus a fee. There are a number of options: A *cost-based* fee includes the agency's cost for servicing the account plus a mark-up, a *cost-plus* fee covers the agency cost and a fixed profit; a *fixed* fee is an agreed-upon payment based on the type of work being done (for example, copywriting at hourly fixed rates, artwork charges based on the salary of the involved personnel); a *sliding* fee is based on a number of agreed-upon parameters. Again, there are many possibilities based on agency and client needs.

- **Performance fee.** A predetermined performance goal may determine the compensation fee. For example, ad recall scores, unit sales, or market share may determine the level of compensation. If the agency meets the goals, compensation may be at the 15 percent level; if it exceeds them, a bonus could give the agency a 20 percent level; if it fails to meet the goals, compensation could be much less than 15 percent.

Most agencies aim for a 20 percent profit on each account to cover personnel and overhead costs plus a profit. The president of Campbell-Mithun-Esty says, "There's a broad acceptance among clients that it's in their best interest that their account be profitable for their agency. The smarter client understands that's what gets it the best people on their account. That's what gets it the best service."[10]

Stan Beals, an advertising management consultant, suggests the key flaw of compensation based on the price of traditional media is the lack of a consistent relationship between income generated and the cost of providing services required by the clients. This will continue to be a problem as new media techniques are developed. He suggests that agencies align their compensation with their roles as salespeople, not buyers of media, and to link agency profit goals to agreed-upon performance standards.[11] The typical agency profit target is 16 percent to 20 percent profit on each account to cover personnel and overhead costs plus a profit.

OTHER SERVICES

Barter

Barter
Acquisition of broadcast time by an advertiser or an agency in exchange for operating capital or merchandise. No cash is involved.

One way for an advertiser or agency to buy media below the rate card price, especially in radio or television, is barter. For example, a barter company, Media Store, placed all the radio time for Lufthansa Airlines involving a six-year

---

[10]Terrence Poltrack, "Pay Dirt," *Agency,* July/August 1991, pp. 20–25.
[11]Stan Beals, "Fresh Approaches to Agency Compensation," *Advertising Age,* August 29, 1994, p. 20.

lease for Manhattan ticket office. The airline had too many ticket offices, and the original lease was extremely high per square foot. So the Media Store took over the lease on barter and sublet it. It then paid Lufthansa with radio time for the regular schedules it runs.

According to the International Reciprocal Trade Association, in 1993, $7.01 billion in goods and services were traded compared to $4.35 billion in 1988—of that figure about 45 percent was in media. These figures represent a fast-growing trend toward more barter, particularly through three-way alliances among barter companies, advertisers, and their ad agencies.[12]

Some barter houses become virtually brokers or wholesalers of time. They build inventories of time accumulated in various barter deals. These inventories, known as *time banks,* are made available to advertisers or agencies seeking to stretch their TV or radio dollars.

Barter has its drawbacks, of course. Often the weaker stations in a market use it the most. Some stations will not accept barter business from advertisers already on the air in the market. Much of the time is poor time (even though it is still good value at the low rate paid). Nevertheless, barter is used by many well-known advertisers.

Agencies also use barter on behalf of their clients: The agency goes to the station and offers a syndicated show free. All the station must do is retain three or four minutes in the first half-hour for the agency's clients. The station is then free to sell three or four minutes of commercials on its own to other advertisers. The advantage to the advertiser of *trade-out* shows, as they are often called, is not only a possible saving in TV costs but, more important, control over the quality of the environment in which the commercial appears. Competitive commercials or overcrowding of spots can be managed.

Research Services

The advertiser, the agency, or an independent research firm can conduct any needed original research. Large agencies may have substantial in-house research departments. On the other hand, many smaller agencies offer little in-house research staffing, although many agencies have moved to add account planners. The account planner's responsibility is to be well versed in data and information about the consumer and conduct any needed research. Generally, the planner will manage the research function by using outside firms specializing in research services.

In addition to the syndicated research previously discussed, which regularly reports the latest findings on buyers of a product—who and where they are, how they live and buy, and what media they read, watch, and listen to. These research companies offer many custom-made research reports to advertisers and their agencies, answering their questions about their own products and advertising. Studies cover such subjects as advertising effectiveness, advertising testing, customer satisfaction, concept and product testing, premium or package design testing, image and positioning, brand equity measurement, market segmentation, strategic research, media preferences, purchasing patterns, and similar problems affecting product and advertising decisions.

[12]Sandra Pesmen, "Ad Agencies Face Barter Boom," *Advertising Age,* June 13, 1994, p. 62.

154   PART THREE   *Managing the Advertising*

A fascinating variety of techniques is available to gather such information, including consumer field surveys (using personal or telephone interviews or self-administered questionnaires), focus groups, consumer panels, continuous tracking studies, cable testing of commercials, image studies, electronic questionnaires, opinion surveys, shopping center intercepts, and media-mix tests. Regardless of the technique used in collecting data for a research report, its real value lies in the creative interpretation and use made of its findings.

WORLDWIDE TRENDS

Major trends that will affect the advertising business and agency and change the marketing process by the end of the decade as seen by Lou Schultz, Lintas, include the following:[13]

1. *The idea of crossing boundaries or from a client perspective—resource mobility.* Multi-national clients recognize that there is a new world market and world culture which impacts their decisions. And creative trends are developed in far-off places like Africa and imported to Europe or the United States. The point is that clients are moving their basic advertising resources and building their plans from whatever base offers them the *best value.* It doesn't matter where they find solutions.

2. *The decline of the American premium.* There was once a time that marketers viewed the U.S. as the gold standard—we had the goods, services and marketing expertise. Today, clients are partnering with non-U.S. (local) companies and developing advertising ideas—creative and media—that can be exported back to the U.S. In Europe, traditional agencies have virtually abandoned the full service media department concept. Many U.S. agencies are unbundling their media services.

3. *Segment-of-one marketing trend.* The worldwide trend is away from mass marketing, toward selectivity. Slowly companies are beginning to believe in the single consumer and are developing an information mentality in the marketing process. In an attempt to better understand the consumer, companies will more aggressively move toward a database planning system.

4. *Consolidation of groups.* People still want to belong to Image Tribes—to be identified with a particular group or style or cultural phenomenon. Marketers have looked at traditional and biological definitions of groups like Generation X or the Thirteenth Gen and the Baby Busters. In the future we may have to change our definition of what constitutes a generation. Could the pace of change and information cause attitudinal generations versus biological ones? As marketers we have to think of the consolidation of groups in smaller bites than the typical 18 to 34 or generation A label. Niche marketing means more tightly focused creative and media messages.

5. *The development of new partnerships or media alliances.* Media and clients are working directly together in ways that were unprecedented a few years ago. These partnerships are between media and the clients and not the agency.

---

[13]Lou Schultz, speech delivered to the Adcraft Club of Detroit, October 8, 1993.

AGENCY OF THE FUTURE

"The agency of the future will arrive in the future, and any talk about it today is basically nonsense," says BBDO's Allen Rosenshine. He also says that the biggest operational and professional challenge for BBDO is how to transfer the things they do very well, which is create long-term, long-standing, brand-building advertising campaigns, to whatever new technologies will bring. The creative will have to adapt itself.[14]

Despite Rosenshine's point of view, here's a brief look from a collection of senior agency executives' views:

- **Agencies must retrain their people to be communication planners. The lines between sales promotion, advertising, and merchandising are blurring and with a full-service network concept they will ultimately disappear.**

- **Traditional agencies will evolve into a noncompartmentalized series of communication teams, where the team leader will be someone trained as a communication planner. This person will probably emanate from the current media or creative departments.**

- **The agency will focus on the creation and execution of communications.**

- **Agencies will need to be lean and productive.**

- **Agencies will need to brand themselves. As a result, agency philosophies will be more clearly understood by clients.**

- **There will be increasing demand for more effective global advertising strategy that can effectively cross borders.**

- **Agencies will be on the cutting edge of interactive media. The new media will change how advertisers and agencies build brand equity with individual consumers.**

SUMMARY

An advertising agency is an independent business composed of creative and business people who develop, prepare, and place advertising for clients.

Today's agencies are reengineering themselves to become more receptive to client needs. Roles of personnel and structure is changing in many agencies as they experiment with means of being more efficient and responsive.

Full-service agencies offer all the services necessary to handle the total advertising function for clients. In today's integrated agency this may include promotion, public relations, direct response, etc. services in addition to traditional media advertising. The agency develops a plan revolving around *What is the marketing problem?* Develops a strategy, a creative response, a media plan, a total plan as well as billing the client and payment to media involved. Agencies are usually organized into four divisions: account services, marketing services, creative services, and management and finance. There is a trend towards more of a team approach to developing and marketing products.

---

[14]Alison Fahey, "Who Says the Traditional Madison Avenue Mega-Agency Is Headed for Extinction?" *AdWeek,* March 21, 1994, p. 12.

Regardless of the way agencies are organized they face the problem of being linked to the profitability of their clients. On the one hand, it is reasonable to reward agencies on their successful campaigns. However, it is rare that success or failure rests solely with the advertising. Seldom will great advertising save a poor product. However, performance based fees set up by many clients often create an unrealistic causal relationship between advertising and sales.

There are other types of advertising services besides the traditional advertising agency: Creative Artist Agency (CAA) is an example of a new creative direction for developing ads; in-house agencies, à la carte agencies, media buying services, etc.

The agency of the future or creative organizations will have to deal with marketing problems beyond advertising tactics. It will have to have an understanding of international communications and be organized to support clients throughout the world. Finally, compensation will be more and more based on the success of the client and the profitability of the goods and services.

Questions

1. Briefly discuss the beginnings of the modern advertising agency.
2. Discuss the Age of Negotiation and the effects of the 1956 consent decree between the major agencies and the Justice Department.
3. Compare and contrast the full-service agency and the mega-agency.
4. Briefly discuss the organizational units of a full-service agency.
5. What are the two basic ways in which major agencies conduct global advertising?
6. Discuss fee arrangements versus commissions as methods of agency compensation.
7. Discuss integrated marketing services as the term is used in full-service agencies.
8. What is the difference between an in-house agency and a Rolodex agency?

The Advertiser's
Marketing/Advertising
Operation

CHAPTER 6

CHAPTER OBJECTIVES

Advertising and marketing operations are going through changes in concept and operations as a result of the restructuring by companies and corporations. Yet many goals and functions remain essentially the same. Here we learn about some of the fundamentals. After reading this chapter you will understand:

- **The marketing-services system**
- **Integrated marketing brand management**
- **How advertising budgets are set**
- **The changing marketing environment**
- **Agency/client relationships**

The 1980s and 1990s have brought all kinds of pressures to corporations. It hasn't been unusual to read about a 5,000 to 20,000 reduction in workforce by company after company. Mergers and partnerships, both domestic and foreign, have been common. The same kind of pressures have affected **marketing and advertising** departments. Marketers have struggled with price wars, recession, and the growing strength of private labels. It seems no company—successful or not—has been untouched by these pressures to be more competitive. Companies have restructured and reorganized divisions and departments. Obviously, when a restructuring takes place there will be changes in how they manage or handle marketing and advertising. For example, Lever Brothers' personal wash (soap) and homecare (dish liquids and detergents) operations became one business unit, and its fabric business (laundry additives) another.

Companies have also been evaluating their integrated marketing services, which have changed some organizational structures. Everyone wants to be more efficient and competitive. Or for some companies it is simply a case of survival. The advertising and marketing departments control the dollars and decide on the need for an advertising agency or in some case agencies for different products. At times they may hire an agency to handle only creative or to place the ads in the media. They may choose to use freelancers or creative boutiques or to use a media buying service or combine their media buying strength for all their products with one agency. They may decide to staff an in-house agency to develop its ads as discussed in the last chapter. It is their ballgame. They call the shots.

The size of the advertising and marketing staffs may vary significantly from organization to organization. It may have a large department controlling all marketing activities, or it may have limited personnel in marketing, or it may rely on operation managers or the president to make the marketing decisions. Before we complicate the process of integrated marketing structure, let's examine the typical structure.

MARKETING-SERVICES SYSTEM

With increased structured and organization changes in business, the results are being felt in the advertising and marketing function. The advertising department structure—the traditional system—worked well for most companies. Exhibit 6.1 illustrates this organizational structure.

However, as companies like Procter & Gamble grew with a number of brands, this structure needed to change to solve its marketing problems. The result

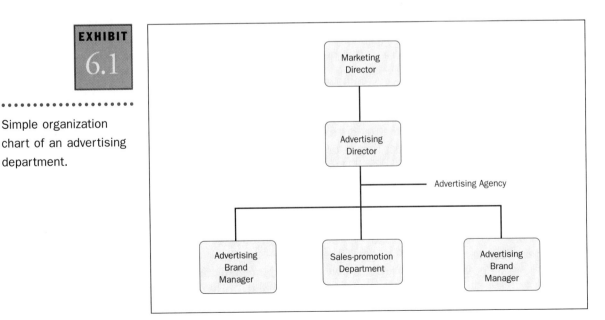

EXHIBIT 6.1

Simple organization chart of an advertising department.

was a new organizational concept called the *marketing-services system.* This concept has been widely adopted, especially in the package goods field, and by a number of service-oriented companies.

Under this concept, developed in 1931, each brand manager is, in essence, president of his or her own corporation-within-the corporation. The brand manager is charged with developing, manufacturing, marketing, promoting, integrating, and selling the brand.

The marketing-services system has two parts. One is the marketing activity, which begins with the product manager assigned to different brands. The other part of the structure is a structure of marketing services, which represents all the technical talent involved in implementing a marketing plan, including creative services, promotion services, media services, advertising controls, and marketing research services. All of these services are available to the product manager, as is the help from the advertising agency assigned to that manager's brand. The product manager can bring together the agency personnel and his or her counterpart in the marketing-services division, giving the company the benefit of the best thinking of both groups—internal and external. Each group has a group product manager who supervises the individual product managers (Exhibit 6.2).

The *product manager* is responsible for planning strategy and objectives, obtaining relevant brand information, budget and controls, getting agency recommendations, and is the primary liaison between the marketing department and all other departments. The product manager's plans must be approved by the group product manager, who then submits the plans for approval of the vice president for marketing and finally to the executive vice president.

The advertising department is a branch of the marketing-services division. The vice president for advertising, responsible for the review and evaluation of brands media plans, attends all creative presentations to act as an adviser and consultant on all aspects of advertising. The vice president for advertising reports to the senior vice president, director of marketing.

Under this system, the advertising does not all come through one huge funnel, with one person in charge of all brands. The advantage to the corporation is that each brand gets the full marketing attention of its own group, while all brands get the full benefit of all the company's special marketing services and the accumulated corporate wisdom. The more important the decision, the higher up the ladder it goes for final approval.

Large companies with many categories of products, like Procter & Gamble or Lever Brothers, may have another layer of management called the *category manager.* All disciplines—research, manufacturing, engineering, sales, advertising, etc., report to the category manager. The category manager follows the product line he or she is in charge of and decides how to coordinate each brand in that line. The category manager decides how to position brands in each category—the category manager for laundry products decides how to position and advertise Tide and Cheer detergents to avoid conflicts and overlap (Exhibit 6.3).

INTEGRATED MARKETING BRAND MANAGEMENT

Previously, we discussed integrated marketing or one voice marketing from the agency perspective. There has been debate about whether or not agencies can effectively implement this concept because of their structure. One of the ma-

---

Product manager

In package goods, the person responsible for the profitability of a product (brand) or product line, including advertising decisions. Also called a brand manager.

Category manager

A relatively new corporate position. This manager is responsible for all aspects of the brands in a specific product category for a company including research, manufacturing, sales, and advertising. Each product's advertising manager reports to the category manager. Example: Procter & Gamble's Tide and Cheer detergent report to a single Category Manager.

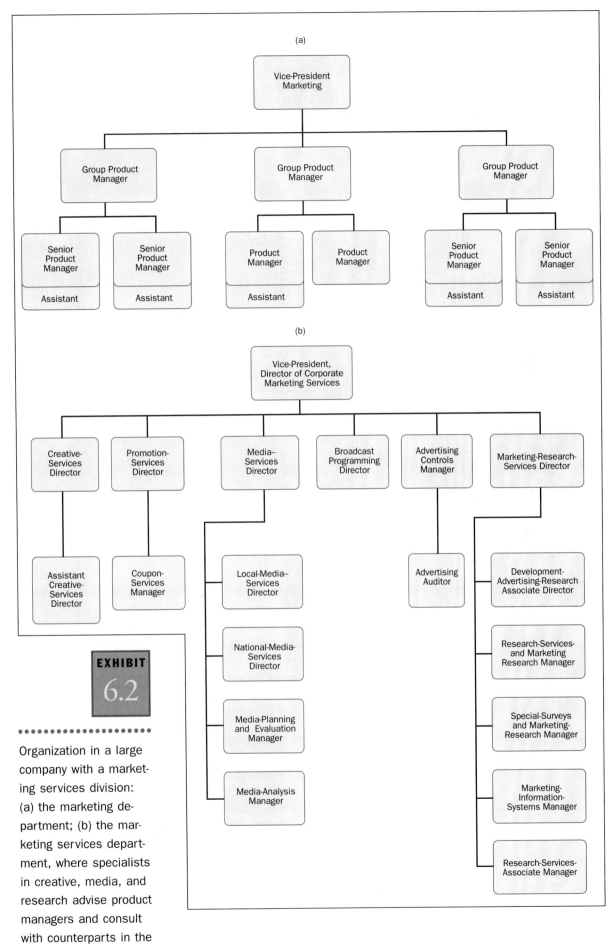

(a)

Vice-President
Marketing

Group Product
Manager

Group Product
Manager

Group Product
Manager

Senior
Product
Manager

Assistant

Senior
Product
Manager

Assistant

Product
Manager

Assistant

Product
Manager

Senior
Product
Manager

Assistant

Senior
Product
Manager

Assistant

(b)

Vice-President,
Director of Corporate
Marketing Services

Creative-
Services
Director

Promotion-
Services
Director

Media–
Services
Director

Broadcast
Programming
Director

Advertising
Controls
Manager

Marketing-Research-
Services Director

Assistant
Creative-
Services
Director

Coupon-
Services
Manager

Local-Media–
Services
Director

National-Media-
Services
Director

Media-Planning
and Evaluation
Manager

Media-Analysis
Manager

Advertising
Auditor

Development-
Advertising-Research
Associate Director

Research-Services-
and Marketing
Research Manager

Special-Surveys
and Marketing-
Research Manager

Marketing-
Information-
Systems Manager

Research-Services-
Associate Manager

EXHIBIT

6.2

Organization in a large company with a marketing services division: (a) the marketing department; (b) the marketing services department, where specialists in creative, media, and research advise product managers and consult with counterparts in the agency.

EXHIBIT

6.3

. . . .

The category manager is responsible for all aspects of the brands in his or her category. Each product's advertising manager reports to the category manager.

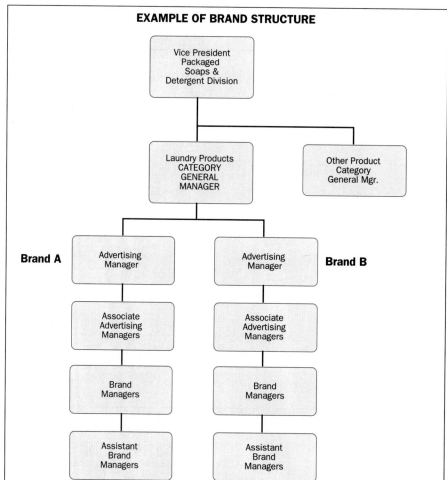

jor problems is that agencies are set up as separate profit centers, which results in competition among their own units for a strong bottom-line showing.

An NPD Group study of marketing executives indicated that integration of advertising, promotion, public relations, and all other forms of marketing communications is the most important factor influencing how strategies will be set in the next three to five years. Larry Light, the former chairman of the international division of Backer Spielvogel Bates Worldwide says, "The reason integrated marketing is important is consumers integrate your messages whether you like it or not. The messages cannot be kept separate. All marketing is integrated in the mind of consumers. Your only choice is how that message is integrated."[1]

An *Advertising Age* survey found major disagreement between agencies and advertisers in terms of whether or not integration should be managed inside the corporation or by the agency; 82.9 percent of marketers say integration is their responsibility in terms of setting strategy for and coordination of integration, 63 percent of agencies said that's their domain.[2] Advertisers feel they can put in place, or already have in place, ad agencies, public relation firms, promotion agencies, direct-marketing companies, and design firms—all outside communication specialists needed to accomplish its integrated goals.

---

[1]Scott Hume, "Integrated Marketing: Who's in Charge Here?" *Advertising Age,* March 23, 1993, p. 3.
[2]Adrienne Ward Fawcett, "Marketers Convinced: Its Time Has Arrived," *Advertising Age,* November 8, 1993, p. S-1.

Integrated Functions

Integrated marketing communications (IMC) can function in the marketing services system if there is management of this process between all the departments involved—advertising, sales promotion, public relations, and other existing departments. Radical organizational changes don't seem to work well with regard to implementation. Many organizations have found that integrated functions become evolutionary. However, there are marketers that feel this kind of management isn't practical because of the resistance to change by managers is just too great. Don Schultz, author of *Integrated Marketing Communications* and president of Agora Inc., suggests reengineering the communications function and structure within the company is sometimes necessary. He suggests the following functions:

- **Start with the customer or prospect and work back toward the brand or organization. That's the outside-in approach. Most organizations are structured to deliver inside-out communications, which allows the budget cycle to dictate when communications can be delivered.**

- **Good communications requires knowledge of customers and prospects. Without specific customer information, the marketing organization will continue to send out the wrong message and information to the wrong people at the wrong time at an exorbitant cost. A database is critical to carry out the IMC communication task.**

- **Brand contacts, all the ways the customer comes in contact with the organization, are the proper way to think about communications programs. This goes beyond traditional media. It includes managing the impact and influence of packaging, employees, in-store displays, sales literature, and even the design of the product so that the brand clearly or concisely communicates with the right person, at the right time, in the right way, with the right message or incentive through the right delivery channel.**

There are three forms of adaptation to integrated marketing within corporate structures:[3]

Marcon manager

In integrated marketing communication organizations adapting the business-to-business structure where all the communication activities is centralized under one person or office.

Marcon Manager. This method is adapting a business-to-business organizational structure called marcon management. It centralizes all the communication activities under one person or office (see Exhibit 6.4). Under this structure all communication is centralized. Product managers request communication programs for their products through a marcon manager. The manager develops the strategy and then directs the communication programs either internally or externally.

Restructured Brand Management Approach. This structure reduces the layers previously involved in the process. All sales and marketing activities for the brand, category, or the organization are reduced to three groups, all reporting to the CEO, and all are on the same organizational level. They include marketing services/communications (MSC), marketing operations, and sales. Marketing operations is responsible for developing and delivering the product to the MSC, which works with sales to develop and implement all sales and marketing programs (including advertising).

---

[3]Don E. Schultz, "Managers Still Face Substantial IMC Questions," *Marketing News,* September 27, 1993, p. 10.

EXHIBIT
6.4

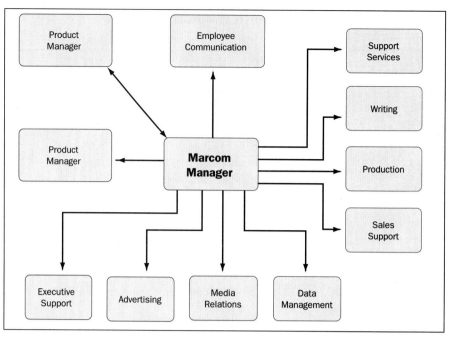

Communications Manager. This structure names a communication manager who is responsible for approving or coordinating all communications programs for the entire organization. The various brands develop their own communication programs as they have traditionally done. These plans go to the communications manager, who is responsible for coordinating, consolidating, and integrating the programs, messages, and media for the organization (see Exhibit 6.5).

EXHIBIT
6.5

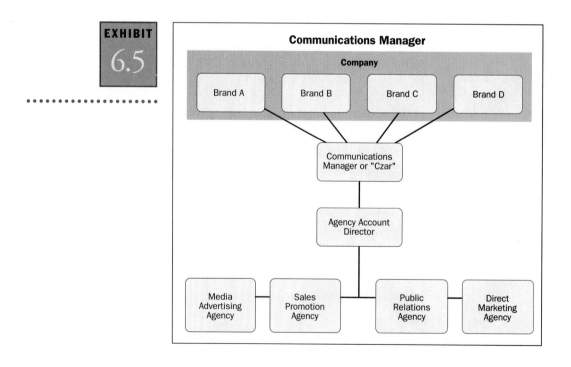

CORPORATE RESTRUCTURING

In the business press we've seen heads discussing Quaker Oats, Coca-Cola, Campbell Soup, Taco Bell, Amoco, Texaco, Pepsi-Cola, etc., restructuring and consolidating their marketing organizations in various ways. For example, in field marketing at Taco Bell, which has been a trendsetter in the fast food business with its value menu, extended the responsibility of their surviving field supervisors from 6 units to at least 20 units. Their duties shifted from command-and-control to consultative-and-supportive in an effort to streamline and become more efficient at decision making. As part of the business restructuring, Taco Bell consolidated its accounting operations with other PepsiCo divisions.[4]

Also, Quaker Oats, whose seven out of eight product lines have been outpacing category performance (cold cereals were up 14 percent, granola bars up 24 percent, rice cakes up 36 percent, Rice-a-Roni noodles up 14 percent, and Gatorade up in double digits) announced a mid-1990s restructuring despite good growth. Quaker told employees that if doing something does not provide a competitive advantage and does not represent a clear cost savings compared to using an outside specialist service, then the role or function was outsourced. As a result, Quaker folded its in-house 800-line promotions, package design, media buying services divisions as part of its restructuring.[5] An analyst stated that this is Quaker's movement beyond cost savings and into its pursuit of brand building so it could focus on spreading its equity across product lines and in new channels of distribution. Five major divisions were to be restructured with changes in job descriptions. It is fair to say that marketing and related advertising organizational structures have been and are in flux.

SETTING THE BUDGET

Advertising is supposed to accomplish some objective. It is a business decision. The three ads in Exhibits 6.6, 6.7, and 6.8 are for three totally different kinds of advertisers, each with a different reason for being. What is it the ad or campaign is supposed to accomplish? Launch a new product? Increase a brand's awareness level? Neutralize the competition's advertising? A key question is how much money is it going to take to accomplish the objective. Even if we've been successful with the product, do we know whether we're spending too much on advertising, or not enough? Despite all the technology available to help us to determine how much should be spent, the final decision is a judgment call by corporate management. The person responsible for the budget decision varies across companies and according to objectives. In general, a Gallagher Report says that the vice president of marketing and the vice president of advertising are the people most responsible for setting the ad budget (see Exhibit 6.9). Two-thirds of advertising budgets are submitted for approval in September or October; almost 80 percent are approved between September and November. As you might expect for such an important decision, most presidents or chief operating officers strongly influence the approval process.

---

[4]Richard Martin, "Taco Bell Revamps, End HQ Move Threat," *Nation's Restaurant News,* July 11, 1994, p. 3.
[5]John McManus, "Quaker Matric Management Models for Turbulent Future," *Brandweek,* May 23, 1994, p. 16.

This newspaper ad
touts a new change.

As seen below, Verba-
tim tries to warn com-
puter disk users the
dangers of using
ordinary data disks.

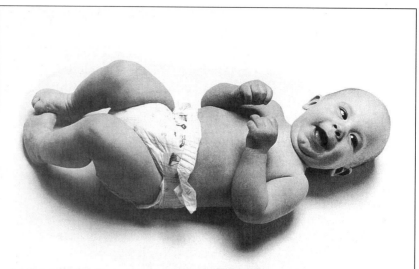

(Courtesy: Tallahassee Democrat—The Zimmerman Agency.)

(Courtesy: Verbatim and Loeffler Ketchum Mountjoy Inc.)

Georgia's Ports for Georgia's People

*T*oday in Sandersville, Stephanie Cullens loaded 200 tons of kaolin clay destined for Japan. In Atlanta, Lee Archibald got his stuffed bunnies from Indonesia just in time for Brittany Martin's birthday. The next time William Murkerson sees the linerboard he ran today, it'll be cardboard boxes full of bananas from Costa Rica.

Is international trade big business in Georgia? Just ask one of the hundreds of thousands of Georgians who feel the impact of this $7 billion industry every day.

Where are they? At a textile mill in Columbus, or at a gift shop in Valdosta. Looming carpet in Dalton, or producing electronics in Norcross. And they all pour their hard-earned pay back into the local economy.

As the globe shrinks, more and more Georgians depend on international trade for their livelihood. So, we must continually enhance our deepwater ports in Savannah and Brunswick to keep our economic lifeblood flowing.

Georgia's ports for Georgia's people— our gateway to the world.

For additional information contact Tom Moore, Director of Public Affairs, Georgia Ports Authority, P.O. Box 2406, Savannah, Georgia 31402. Or call toll-free 1-800-841-1107.

GEORGIA PORTS AUTHORITY

(Courtesy: Georgia Ports Authority.)

Budgets are usually drawn up using one of four approaches:

Percentage of Sales

This method simply means the advertising budget is based upon a percentage of the company's sales. For instance, a family restaurant chain might budget 5 percent of its sales for advertising. Companies using this method to determine their advertising budget will not spend beyond their means because the ad budget will increase only when sales increase. If sales decrease, so will their advertising; however, if competitive pressures are severe, they may have to maintain or increase the budget to retain market share, even though there is no prospect of increased profit. This method can actually reverse the assumed cause-and-effect relationship between advertising and sales. That is, since the budgeting is either based on the previous year's sales—usually with some percentage of increase added—or next year's anticipated sales, then it can be said that sales are causing the advertising rather than advertising causing the sales.

A Gallagher Report indicates that about 9 percent of companies surveyed used this method of budgeting.[6] Roughly 35 percent use a percentage of anticipated sales, and another 9 percent calculate a medium between last year's actual sales and anticipated sales for the coming year (Exhibit 6.10). In either method, a change in sales changes the amount of advertising expenditure.

---

[6]26th Gallagher Report Consumer Advertising Survey.

EXHIBIT 6.9

Who Prepares Clients' Ad Budgets[a]

VP/Marketing	63.2%
VP/Advertising	31.6
Ad manager	22.2
Brand manager	16.3
Ad agency	21.7
Sales promotion	5.6

Who Approves Clients' Ad Budgets[a]

President or CEO	68.5%
VP/Marketing	37.3
Executive VP	20.9
Division manager	17.2
VP/Advertising	14.4
Treasurer or controller	8.6

[a]Totals more than 100% due to multiple responses.

(Source: 26th Gallagher Report Consumer Advertising Survey.)

Payout Plan

The payout plan looks at advertising as an investment rather than an expenditure. It recognizes that it may take several years before the company can recover startup costs and begin taking profits.

This method of budget strategy is more complex. Basically, the advertiser spends at a level that will be acceptable at some future date. The payout plan is normally used for new products that require high advertising expenditures (relative to low initial sales) in order to establish themselves in the marketplace. Whatever the specific payout method used, the underlying principle is that present advertising budgets are based on future sales. Of course, the advertiser who overestimates future sales runs the risk of accumulating major debt.

The following tables are examples of typical payout plans. Let's go briefly through the payout plan for a new fast-food operation. In the first year of operation, the company spends the entire gross profits ($15,274,000) on advertising. In addition, the company invested $10,300,000 in store development, for a first-year operating loss.

EXHIBIT 6.10

How Do Clients Calculate Ad Budgets?

34.8% take a percentage of anticipated sales.

30.4% combine needed tasks with percent of anticipated sales.

13.0% outline needed tasks and fund them.

13.0% sit arbitrary amounts based on general fiscal outlook.

8.7% take a percentage of the previous year's sales.

8.6% calculate a medium between last year's actual and next year's anticipated sales.

(Source: 26th Gallagher Report Consumer Advertising Survey.)

In the second year, the company again invested gross profits ($18,122,000) in advertising and carried over the $10,300,000 debt from the first year. By the third year, sales had increased to the point where advertising as a percentage of gross sales had dropped to 13 percent, or $46,312,000, leaving a profit of $35,625,000. After covering the first-year debt of $10,300,000, the payout was $25,325,000.

If the company had demanded a 10 percent profit in the first year (0.10 × $84,854,000 = $8,485,400), it would have had to curtail advertising drastically, reduce corporate store investment, or do some combination of both. In that case the company would have made a profit the first year but risked future profits and perhaps its own long-term survival.

Fast-Food Payout Plan

Systemwide Payout (Fiscal Years 1, 2, 3)

		Year 1		Year 2		Year 3
Sales		$84,854,000		$218,737,000		$356,248,000
Food Cost	34%	28,850,000	34%	74,371,000	34%	121,124,000
Paper Cost	5%	4,245,000	5%	10,937,000	5%	17,812,000
Labor	22%	18,668,000	20%	43,747,000	20%	71,250,000
Overhead	21%	17,819,000	19%	41,560,000	18%	64,125,000
Total Op. Exp.	82%	69,580,000	78%	170,615,000	77%	274,511,000
Gross Profit	18%	15,274,000	22%	48,122,000	25%	81,937,000
Advertising/Promo		*$ 15,274,000*		*$ 48,122,000*	*13%*	*$ 46,312,000*
Store Profit		0		0	10%	35,625,000
Corp. Invest.		10,300,000		0		0
Corp. Profit		(10,300,000)		0		35,625,000
Cumulative		(10,300,000)		(10,300,000)		25,625,000

Package Goods Product Payout Plan

Investment Introduction—36-Month Payout

	Year 1	Year 2	Year 3	3-Year Total	Year 4
Size of Market (MM Cases)	8	10	11		12
Share Goal:					
Average	12½%	25%	30%		30%
Year End	20	30	30		30
Consumer Movement (MM Cases)	1.0	2.5	3.3	6.8	3.6
Pipeline (MM Cases)	.3	.2	.1	.6	—
Total Shipments (MM Cases)	1.3	2.7	3.4	7.4	3.6
Factory Income (@ $9)	$11.7	$24.3	$30.6	$66.6	$32.4
Less Costs (@ $5)	6.5	13.5	17.0	37.0	18.0
Available P/A (@ $4)	$ 5.2	$10.8	$13.6	$29.6	$14.4
Spending (Normal $2)	$12.8	$10.0	$ 6.8	$29.6	$ 7.2
Advertising	10.5	8.5	5.4	24.4	5.7
Promotion	2.3	1.5	1.4	5.2	1.5
Profit (Loss):					
Annual	($ 7.6)	$ 0.8	$ 6.8	—	$ 7.2
Cumulative	($ 7.6)	($ 6.8)	—	—	$ 7.2

Competitive Budgeting

Another approach to budgeting is to base it on the competitive spending environment. In competitive budgeting, the level of spending relates to percent of sales and other factors, whether the advertiser is on the offensive or defensive, media strategies chosen (for example, desire to dominate a medium); or answers to such questions as "Is it a new brand or an existing one?" The problem here is that competition dictates the spending allocation (and the competing companies may have different marketing objectives.)

The Task Method

The task method of budgeting is possibly the most difficult to implement, but it may also be the most logical budgeting method from a logical standpoint. The method calls for marketing and advertising managers to determine what task or objective the advertising will fulfill over the budgetary period and then calls for a determination of how much money will be needed to complete the task. Under this method, the company sets a specific sales target for a given time to attain a given goal. Then it decides to spend whatever money is necessary to meet that quota. The task method might be called the "let's spend all we can afford" approach, especially when launching a new product. Many big businesses today started that way. Many businesses that are not here today did too.

The approach can be complex. It involves several important considerations: brand loyalty factors, geographic factors, product penetration. Advertisers who use this method need accurate, reliable research; experience; and models for setting goals and measuring results.

The task method is used most widely in a highly competitive environment. Budgets are under constant scrutiny in relation to sales and usually are formally reviewed every quarter. Moreover, they are subject to cancellation at any time (except for noncancelable commitments) because sales have not met a minimum quota, money is being shifted to a more promising brand, or management wants to hold back money to make a better showing on its next quarterly statement.

No one approach to budgeting is always best for all companies.

THE CHANGING MARKETING ENVIRONMENT

The changes that have taken place over the past few years in advertiser organizations have not been a result of business cycles. Marketers are in an irreversible restructuring in the way businesses operate, one that may require a major rethinking of the agency/client relationship in the late 1990s and beyond. Some of the factors driving the change at companies include:[7]

- **Fragmented consumer target.** Consumer groups are more fragmented than ever before by demographics, age, ethnicity, family type, geographic location, and media usage.

- **Parity performance.** The importance of value, convenience and service in influencing preference is increasing, and the impact of low-priced, satisfactorily performing private brands is growing.

---

[7]Robert M. Viney, "Solving the Agency-Client Mismatch," *Advertising Age,* May 24, 1993, p. 20.

- **Cost control.** Marketers must remain price competitive and must develop new strategies for offsetting internal cost increases.

- **Erosion of advertising effectiveness.** Advertisers have settled for advertising that doesn't present a compelling basis for consumer preference and fails to effectively reinforce relevant brand equity in other marketing activities.

- **Strengthened retailer influence.** Retailers are equipped with detailed data on consumer purchase behavior, which gives them leverage against marketers.

The Nation's Mood

Nations, like people, go through mood swings. Over the past 15 years, Roper research says there have been three distinct national moods, each lasting about five years. The United States is now beginning a new period. These emerging social, economic, and political environments in which business will operate to the end of this century are significant departures in the way people look at their lives—and the brands they buy, the services they use, the work that they do, and the major issues that concern them. Among the trends:[8]

- **Moderation.** Americans are seeking greater balance in nearly all aspects of their lives. A new sense of moderation and realism is changing people's perspectives and choices as they seek a satisfying lifestyle that is not too exhausting. Perhaps most importantly, the public's approach to the traditional work ethic has fundamentally changed: Work has lost ground as a basic priority, while leisure has gained. In the quest for more family time, almost half of working parents have considered cutting back on, or even quitting, their jobs. The Popular goal: balance.

- **Time control.** In a growing number of upscale and even luxury markets, consumers are placing ever higher premiums on their time and seeking more control over how it is used. They are segmenting their time, allocating it more efficiently, and looking for more ways to stretch their leisure hours. This desire for greater time control created a culture of convenience that drove product and service innovations throughout the 1980s and early 1990s. As such innovations proliferate, consumers simply have come to *expect* time-saving features in products and services.

- **Tactical consumerism.** Price cuts, private labels, generous promotions, and the "deep discounted" retail landscape came of age in the 1980s, and the recent recession only heightened their appeal. The result is a new breed of shopper who regularly expects and gets high quality without a high price. When choosing among brands, more people than at any time in the past 20 years now say a *reasonable* price is their top purchase criteria, rivaling even quality. In the late 1990s, expect consumers to look increasingly to middle-range and lower-priced products. Premium-priced brands will suffer the most in this climate. Manufacturers must establish both a clear and justifiable reason for higher prices—and even that may not be enough to satisfy this new breed of consumer. Without some distinct, clearly superior benefit—considerable timesavings, uniqueness, better craftsmanship producing tangible consumer benefits, stress relief, or whatever—paying more money usually seems pointless to them.

[8]"25 Major Trends Shaping the Future of American Business," *The Public Pulse* 5, no. 5 (1994).

EXHIBIT

6.11

· · · · · · · · · · · · · · · · · · ·

An ad that demands
attention.

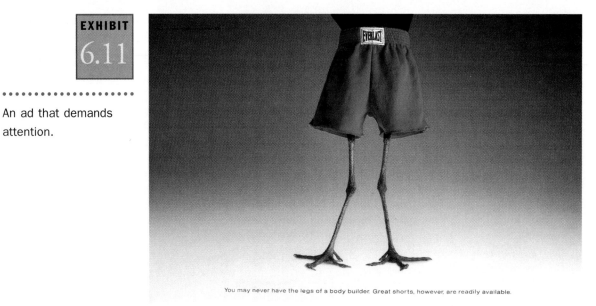

You may never have the legs of a body builder. Great shorts, however, are readily available.

(Courtesy: Goldsmith & Jeffrey and Everlast.)

■ *Eye-catching information.* Americans praise most types of advertising for their information value, but they are becoming more discriminating about the ads they choose to view. Ad messages need to be more memorable and attractive to the eye, without detracting from useful consumer information. Visual recall is half the challenge (see Exhibit 6.11). Corporate and product logos need to be strong and eye-catching. Creative efforts should turn increasingly to dramatic staging, exciting images, and bold graphics. In print, copy should strive to be more inviting to the eye and easier to read. Creating strong images which also draw the eye to informational text emphasizing product benefits is the goal.

■ *Backlash against Elites.* The 1990s are witnessing a new backlash against elites. But the nature of the backlash is different. Public trust—not wealth—is the issue. It is characterized by one simple rule: It's not how much money you have, but how you made it. Most Americans did not benefit from the "opulent eighties," but they are still clinging to material aspirations themselves. They resent elites who seem to have profited at the public's expense; they still aspire to wealth. They generally accept athletes and entertainment personalities being millionaires because they make money based upon their own talents.

■ *Personal responsibility.* As disenchantment with the nation's elites grows, people are increasingly looking inward for the solutions to the country's problems. There is a growing evidence of an emerging ethos of personal responsibility among Americans.

■ *Environment movement matures.* In keeping with the growing sense of personal responsibility, individuals are admitting to their own shortcomings with respect to environmental protection. They realize that business is no longer solely responsible for environmental degradation. They also expect business to respond in kind. The best opportunity for business may be advertising and communications that encourage and help individuals to take action, while reaping the benefits of national leadership.

■ **The family.** Despite overwhelmingly pessimistic rhetoric, the evidence suggests the future vitality of the American family. This change is partly due to the fact that the baby-boom generation is in its family-forming years. The nature of the modern family is different from the traditional family. First, most families will have both parents working. Second, the average size of the family will be smaller. Third, the number of nontraditional family structure—single parents, step-families, unmarried couples with children, grandparents with children, etc.—will continue to rise. (see Exhibit 6.12).

■ **Shift in women's priorities.** After more than a decade of being drawn into the workplace, a majority of women say they would rather stay home to care for a house and family than be employed. However, this shift does not mean there will be a mass exodus of women from the workplace. The reality is that most working women say they simply cannot give up their job. This desire will help fuel the growing call for employee benefits that help women balance the demands of work and home life—homework, flexible scheduling, job-sharing, and on-site day care, among others. While the average working woman has grown disillusioned with the workplace, increasing numbers of female executives and professionals report being satisfied with their working situation, and have become more resolute about their choice to remain in the workplace.

■ **Generation X.** Reaching the 46 million consumers aged 18 to 29 requires understanding where this group has been and where they expect to go in the future. So far, this group's experience is quite different from the baby boomer. The boomers came of age in an expanding economy during a time when the social fabric was under siege. This combination gave birth to

(Courtesy: Healthtex™.)

cynicism, even indignation, leading many boomers to adopt nontraditional or anti-establishment identities. The circumstances have been reversed for Generation X. Their economic horizons have been limited by a sluggish job market, and the high cost of real estate, higher education, and health insurance. Their expectations grew faster than the group's ability to realize their dreams, and this has led to a huge meltdown. Just one in five say they have a very good chance of achieving the proverbial good life—compared to twice as many boomers at the same age who expected to achieve it. To communicate with Generation X, an advertiser must understand the level of frustration that comes from wanting so much more than they have or can easily attain. Whether or not members of this group become the first generation to do less well than their parents, they expect less prosperity. Living for today becomes a way of life when long-term goals appear out of reach.

MANAGING BRANDS
Efficient Consumer Response

In 1993, the grocery industry launched its efficient consumer response (ECR) initiative designed to make the industry more efficient. This initiative includes using technology in purchasing, distribution, promotion, reducing inventories, and other aspects of the business including marketing. It is another attempt by business to prepare for the future by eliminating the inefficient parts of the system of selling grocery products by changing the approach to creating, selling, and distributing those products. In the process, ECR is forcing marketers and retailers to rethink new products, pricing, in-store merchandising, and the division of dollars between trade promotion and consumer marketing.

Slotting Allowances

Every square foot of a supermarket costs money and needs to pay for itself by moving products and brands quickly. There is only so much shelf space for the category manager to obtain from grocers. Since grocers control the space, many charge *slotting allowances* for shelf space (Exhibit 6.13). This admission fee, which comes primarily from the marketer's trade promotion funds, ensures space for a period of about three to six months. Supermarkets use the slotting allowance to pay for slow-moving products, administrative overhead for placing a new product into their system, including warehouse space, computer input, communications to individual stores about the product's availability, and the redesign of shelf space. The frozen food section has only a finite amount of space and almost always demands slotting allowances for that space.

EXHIBIT
6.13

· ·

Retailer Control

There is no doubt about the control of shelf space and entry into supermarkets, discounters, and mass-merchandise stores today. The marketer is at the mercy of the retailer. As a result, category managers must learn the following:[9]

■ **Marketplace leverage is at the local level. As consumers' taste, needs, and wants continue to expand and fragment, leverage can be achieved only by de-**

[9]Spencer Hapoienu, "Supermarketing's New Frontier," *Advertising Age,* April 14, 1988, p. 18.

livering relevant products, services, messages, and promotions to consumers as individuals.

- Building brand equity among retailers should become as important as building brands among consumers.

- Marketing decisions must shift to the sales level. Manufacturers' marketing and promotion programs must eventually become store-specific to succeed.

- Information is the most important asset you have. Only the first company to use information wins. As brand building moves from national media to the supermarket shelf, marketing and merchandising executions must be adapted to the needs of each consumer market and store franchise.

Experimentation and Risk

Marketers are forced to find the right formula and be innovative in marketing new products today. Old marketing rules don't necessarily work in today's environment. Normally, products with the same name are the same product, right? Wrong. Pepsi Max, a mid-calorie soft drink, was introduced in the mid-1990s in Canada. At the same time, a sugarfree Pepsi Max was available throughout Europe and scheduled to be marketed in Latin America and Asia. Same name, same package, different products, different objectives: The sugar-free Pepsi Max was developed for global markets aimed at consumers who have notoriously shunned diet drinks. The initial thrust was aimed at 20 countries, and it was predicted that the product wouldn't enter the U.S. market because it competed with the established Diet Pepsi. At the same time, Pepsi studied the acceptance of its Canadian version of Pepsi Max before deciding whether or not the product would be introduced in the United States. "We want to make sure there's a reason for being and we won't do anything unless we're convinced that mid-calories says something people care about," said Craig Weatherup, president of Pepsi-Cola North American, referring to Canada as a "big test market." Market research indicated that roughly a third of Canadians switch back and forth between regular and diet soft drinks. The advertising in Canada focused on "All the taste of Pepsi with 1/3 less calories.[10]"

Diet drinks have had a rough go outside the United States, accounting for less than 5 percent of beverage sales. Specifically, diet drinks present image problems for European men. Pepsi figured a one-calorie product with the mouth-feel of regular cola would appeal to consumers looking for strong flavor but no diet aftertaste. TV ads feature rock climbers and sky divers. Initially, Pepsi Max drew a 1.2 percent share of supermarket cola sales, while diet Coke lost 0.4 percent share.

Bill Borders, president of Borders, Perrin & Norrander, says, "risk taking is the lifeblood of an agency." However, a former director of creative at Pepsi-Cola says, "The problem with most clients is that they are not willing to join the agency in the risk. Through the years Pepsi-Cola has told BBDO to take the risk. If you miss, we understand that not everything is going to be a home run. But it could be a single. Occasionally, we have burned the film knowing that we tried and it just didn't work.[11]" Unfortunately, most

---

[10]Karen Benezra, "Double Entendre: The Life and The Life of Pepsi Max," *BrandWeek,* April 18, 1994, p. 40.
[11]Joe Mandese, "How Far Is Too Far?" *Agency,* May/June 1991, p. 39.

clients can't find the courage to join Pepsi in taking chances or risk cutting-edge advertising.

AGENCY/CLIENT RELATIONSHIPS

It has been said that agency-client relationships are much like interpersonal relationships: If you don't like each other, you move apart. If you like each other, you gravitate toward each other and great stuff gets produced. The agency should be trusted as an employee—it's in business with the client. The relationship between the agency and the client is a partnership.

A study conducted by the North American Advertising Agency Network suggests that agency professionalism, strategic planning, and cost-efficiency beat leading-edge creative and integrated communications capabilities when marketers select an advertising agency. The study suggests that some clients were willing to accept mediocre work delivered on time and on budget. Other factors revealed that integrated communications capabilities, agency experience on a similar account, and longevity of client relationships was more important than account rosters with big-name or blue-chip clients.[12] Agencies have always prided themselves on selling the creative product; however, many people feel today's agencies are not producing the strongest creative product.

Why do clients hire agencies? Tom Patty, executive vice president of Chiat/Day says, "In essence, clients hire ad agencies because they believe they can help them persuade customers *to do* or *think something*." Clients select an agency based on the agency's ability to be persuasive. The real task is to become a persuasion partner.[13]

When advertisers develop a new product or become disenchanted with their existing advertising, they will conduct advertising reviews in which their current agency and others can compete for the account. This review process may take several months. The advertiser will evaluate which agencies it wants to participate in the review. Keep in mind that there are agencies that specialize in certain types of accounts. For example, Leo Burnett and Lintas are considered giant consumer agencies; Longwater specializes in shipping and transportation; Baxter, Gurian & Mazzi in health care; Sawyer Riley Compton in business-to-business (see Exhibit 6.14 an example of an animal health ad); Casanova Pendrill Publicidad in the Hispanic market; Ogilvy & Mather Direct in direct response; and Burrell Advertising in the African American market. All of the mentioned agencies may have other expertise to sell clients, so advertisers would evaluate their needs and seek agencies to match those needs.

SELECTING AN AGENCY

Choosing an agency can be a complicated matter. Do you need a full-service agency, one with integrated services, with strong media departments, or do you need a specialized agency? After deciding whether you want a large, medium, or small; specialized, full-service, domestic, or global, the following points may help you in evaluating specific agencies.

---

[12]Melanie Wells, "Many Clients Prize Agency Efficiency over Creativity," *Advertising Age,* May 16, 1994, p. 28.
[13]Tom Patty, "Clients Today Need Partners in Persuasion, Not Agencies," *Advertising Age,* January 24, 1994, p. 26.

(Courtesy: Sawyer Riley Compton.)

1. Determine what types of service you need from an agency, and then list them in order of their importance to you. For instance: (a) marketing expertise in strategy, planning, and execution; (b) creative performance in TV, print, radio, or outdoor; (c) media knowledge and clout; (d) sales-promotion and or trade relations help; (e) public relations and corporate- or image-building ability; (f) market research strength; (g) fashion or beauty sense; (h) agency size; (i) location in relation to your office. Your special needs will dictate others.

2. Establish a five-point scale to rate each agency's attributes. A typical five-point scale would be: (1) outstanding, (2) very good, (3) good, (4) satisfactory, (5) unsatisfactory. Of course, you should give different values or weights to the more important agency attributes.

3. Check published sources, and select a group of agencies that seem to fit your requirements. Use your own knowledge or the knowledge of your industry peers to find agencies responsible for successful campaigns or products that have most impressed you. Published sources include the annual issue of. *Advertising Age,* which lists agencies and their accounts by agency size, and the "Red Book" *(Standard Advertising Register),* which lists agencies and accounts both alphabetically and geographically. In case of further doubt, write to the American Association of Advertising Agencies, 666 Third Avenue, New York, NY 10017, for a roster of members.

4. Check whether there are any apparent conflicts with accounts already at the agency. When agencies consider a new account, that is the first question they ask (along with the amount of the potential billings).

5. Now start preliminary discussions with the agencies that rate best on your initial evaluation. This can be started with a letter asking if they are interested or a phone call to set up an appointment for them to visit you or for you to visit the agency. Start at the top. Call the president or the operating head of the agency or office in your area, who will appoint someone to follow up on the opportunity you are offering.

6. Reduce your original list of potential agencies after the first contact. A manageable number is usually no more than three.

7. Now again prepare an evaluation list for rating the agencies on the same five-point scale. This list will be a lot more specific. It should cover personnel. Who will supervise your account, and how will the account be staffed? Who are the creative people who will work on your business? Similarly, who will service your needs in media, production (TV) research, and sales promotion, and how will they do it? What is the agency's track record in getting and holding on to business and in keeping personnel teams together? What is the agency's record with media, with payments? Make sure again to assign a weighted value to each service aspect. If TV is most important to you and public relations aid least, be sure to reflect this in your evaluation.

8. Discuss financial arrangements. Will your account be a straight 15 percent commission account, a fee account, or a combination of both? What services will the commission or fee cover, and what additional charges will the agency demand? How will new-product work be handled from both a financial and an organizational point of view? What peripheral service does the agency offer, and for how much?

9. Do you feel comfortable with them?

10. If your company is an international one, can the agency handle all of your nondomestic business, and if so, how will they do it?

APPRAISING NATIONAL ADVERTISING

The big questions that national advertising and marketing management must answer are: How well is our advertising working? How well is our investment paying off? How do you measure national advertising, whose results cannot be traced as easily as those of direct-response advertising?

Advertising goals
The communication objectives designed to accomplish certain tasks within the total marketing program.

Advertising Goals versus Marketing Goals

The answer is not simple. Much of the discussion on the subject centers around a report Russell H. Colley prepared for the Association of National Advertisers.[14] The thesis of this study is that it is virtually impossible to measure the results of advertising unless and until the specific results sought by advertising have been defined. When asked exactly what their advertising is

---

[14]Russell H. Colley, *Defining Advertising Goals for Measured Advertising Effectiveness* (New York: Association of National Advertisers, 1961).

supposed to do, most companies have a ready answer: Increase their dollar sales or increase their share of the market. However, these are not advertising goals, Colley holds; they are total marketing goals.

....

Marketing goals

The overall objectives that a company wishes to accomplish through its marketing program.

....

National advertising alone cannot accomplish this task. It should be used as part of the total marketing effort. The first step in appraising the results of advertising, therefore, is to define specifically what the company expects to accomplish through advertising. The Colley report defines an advertising goal as "a specific communications task, to be accomplished among a defined audience to a given degree in a given period of time."

As an example, the report cites the case of a branded detergent. The marketing goal is to increase market share from 10 to 15 percent, and the advertising goal is set as increasing, among the 50 million housewives who own automatic washers, the number who identify brand X as a low-sudsing detergent that gets clothes clean. This represents a specific communications task that can be performed by advertising, independent of other marketing forces.

The Colley report speaks of a marketing-communication spectrum ranging from unawareness of the product to comprehension to conviction to action. According to this view, the way to appraise advertising is through its effectiveness in the communication spectrum, leading to sales.

Researchers disagree on whether the effectiveness of national advertising— or, for that matter, of any advertising—should be judged by a communication yardstick rather than by sales. As a matter of fact, in Chapter 15 we discuss whether an ad's effectiveness should be measured by some research testing score.

Appraising the Campaign Before It Is Run

There are those who believe that the time to appraise a campaign is before it is run. They would do this by testing idea options in different markets—a familiar practice, of course, with one big drawback; It tips off the competition to what you are planning to do, and they will try to beat you to it in other markets, especially if the campaign involves a new product or is based on a promotion.

The Company/Agency Research Conflict

Ideally, a company and its agency should have no conflict about the goals of advertising. However, conflicts do arise, often over the different priorities given creative and marketing values by agencies and companies. These different priorities are reflected in the way advertising is evaluated by client and agency.

Twenty-one of the largest advertising agencies jointly examined the question of advertising evaluation and copy testing. The PACT (Position Advertising Copy Testing) report discusses their findings.[15] Two major aspects of the report should be noted:

1. The PACT study recognized that advertising's contribution to overall marketing objectives should be the focus of any copy test. The copy test for a

---

[15]PACT-Positioning Advertising Copy Testing. The *PACT* Agencies Report, 1982, p. 6.

specific ad should consider the advertisement's potential for achieving its stated objectives. Among these objectives might be:

- **Reinforcing current perceptions**
- **Encouraging trial of a product or service**
- **Encouraging new uses of a product or service**
- **Providing greater saliency for a brand or company name**
- **Changing perceptions and imagery**
- **Announcing new features and benefits**

2. The PACT report viewed advertising as performing on three levels:

- **Reception (Did the advertising get through?)**
- **Comprehension (Was the advertising understood?)**
- **Response (Did the consumer accept the proposition?)**

The PACT report offers a starting point from which specific measures of advertising can be designed.

The PACT report did not solve the copy-testing dilemma nor the inherent conflict between agency and client. However, it did address the general problem and offered some basic principles for further discussion. For us, it also demonstrates the complex marriage that exists between a company and its advertising agency.

SUMMARY

The marketing services system has two parts: one managed by the brand manager who is assigned to a brand, and marketing services—which is comprised of the technical talent involved in implementing the marketing plan, including creative services, promotion services, media services, advertising controls, and marketing research.

As companies consider implementing integrated marketing communications into their firms, there are three basic structures available: a centralized communication function under a marcon manager, a restructured brand manager approach, and a communications manager who is responsible for approving and coordinating all communication programs.

Budgets are set in various ways using the task method, the payout plan, competitive budgeting, and the most commonly used percent-of-sales method. Some of the factors driving change in the way companies are doing business include fragmented consumer target, parity performance, cost control, erosion of advertising effectiveness, and strengthened retailer influence.

Efficient consumer response (ECR) is forcing marketers and retailers to rethink new products, pricing, in-store merchandising and trade promotions, and consumer marketing.

Evaluation of national advertising begins with a definition of what you want the advertising to accomplish. Advertising goals are not the same as marketing goals; advertising is a specific communication task. The PACT report addressed the question of what constitutes good advertising.

The marketing environment continues to change as well as the mood of the nation. Some of the areas of concern include moderation, tactical consumerism, personal responsibility, the family, shift in women's priorities, backlash against elites, the growing evidence of people looking inward for solutions, and the gaining importance of personal responsibility.

Questions

1. What is a category manager?
2. What is a marcon manager?
3. What is a payout plan?
4. What is the value of a brand extension?
5. What is happening to the advertising budget as a percentage of the overall marketing budget?
6. Who in the corporation prepares most of the advbertising budgets?
7. In what month are most advertising budgets approved?
8. In the marketing-services system, to whom does the advertising director report?

MARKETING SITUATION

The telephone is a necessity, but thousands of Hispanic households in Texas didn't have telephone service. The market has a penetration of 90 percent versus 78 percent for Hispanics. Southwestern Bell wanted to determine if it could profitably increase phone service among Hispanics. San Antonio was chosen as a test market because about 42,000 Hispanic households there were without telephone service.

CAMPAIGN OBJECTIVES

The objectives were to motivate people lacking residential phone service to call the Southwestern Bell Telephone Spanish-language Customer Service Representatives, therefore, increasing the access line penetration rate with targeted Hispanics in San Antonio. A sales goal of 1,500 *new connects* was targeted.

TARGET AUDIENCE

The primary target was nonsubscribing Hispanic adults aged 18–55, primarily Spanish-speaking females. The secondary target was bilingual females. Household income was less than $18,000 per year.

Sí puede tener servicio telefónico básico por sólo $17 al mes incluyendo impuestos.

• La instalación es menos de $55.
• Le atenderemos en español.
• ¡Llame a SWBT al 1-800-559-0050 y ordene su servicio hoy!

Southwestern Bell
Telephone

CREATIVE STRATEGY

The strategy was to use Spanish-language mass media to convince Spanish customers that (1) telephone service is *necessary* to communicate with your world, (2) phone service from Southwestern Bell is affordable, (3) the company speaks Spanish, and (4) Southwestern Bell is ready to take your call. The tone of the advertising was designed inviting, and informative.

Positioning Statement: "At Southwestern Bell Telephone, we speak your language (Spanish)." It also implies that *we understand your needs*.

Key Messages:
* Telephone service is necessary in everyday life
* Telephone service helps you communicate with your world
* Southwestern Bell speaks your language
* Call us now

INTEGRATED PROGRAMS

Southwestern Bell launched programs to assist advertising: It had a Spanish Language Media Reception; it obtained time on radio and TV talk shows to communicate the importance of telephone service; the company identified 100 leaders to be informed about the test; public relations was instituted featuring a drop-out prevention program; it produced talks in community centers, and produced a bilingual video highlighting community relations projects; point-of-purchase was used in payment agencies at grocery stores; and key events and fiestas promoted information on basic telephone service.

MEDIA STRATEGY

Media included television, radio, outdoor, and newspapers. Television maximized *reach potential* by purchasing top-rated programs during heavy weeks and implementing road blocks, and maximize *frequency of message* potential by negotiating bonus-weight and augmenting paid advertising with PSA schedules. It stretched the advertising through merchandising and promotions. Radio was purchased with formats that effectively impact on the target, and negotiate media promotions and merchandising with each.

A nine-month outdoor campaign was scheduled utilizing a 50-showing in "D" and "E" wealth ratings in Hispanic dominant zip codes and the newspaper plan scheduled ad placement to coincide with mid-month pay periods.

EVIDENCE OF RESULTS

This test campaign produced more than 1,700 Hispanic subscribers and enhanced the image of Southwestern Bell as a company with a responsible attitude toward Hispanics.

Many new subscribers asked for information about other services. The new sign-ups resulted in more than $2 million in gross revenue.

The advertised Spanish 800 phone number generated more than 10,000 calls. Post-test research conducted by Strategy Research Corporation resulted in a 200 percent increase in Hispanics' positive perceptions of Southwestern Bell Telephone.

Southwestern Bell Telephone moved to implement similar marketing in major Hispanic population centers in Texas.

Video Case

BLUE CROSS AND BLUE SHIELD FEDERAL EMPLOYEE PROGRAM

MARKETING SITUATION

The political and media attention on health care brought Blue Cross's health insurance to the forefront of everyone's consciousness. Blue Cross and Blue Shield Federal Employee Program (BCBS FEP) addressed this emerging trend by implementing a preferred provider network, offering savings to federal employees when they used participating providers.

Federal employees select their insurance carrier once a year during a six-week period called Open Season. The competitive area consists of over 340 insurance carriers whose benefit structure and premiums, as well as advertising, are regulated by the federal government. BCBS challenge was to differentiate its new product, positioning it as an alternative to fee-for-service carriers and HMOs and still remain in the federal guidelines.

Its goal was to position BCBS FEP as a *best of both worlds* option—offering the freedom of choice associated with fee-for-service plans and low costs associated with HMOs.

CAMPAIGN OBJECTIVES

Blue Cross and Blue Shield set the following objectives:
1. To achieve a goal of 40,000 new contracts
2. To introduce and establish awareness of the new Preferred Provider Program
3. To maintain/increase retention rate by reassuring current subscribers of quality and dependability of coverage
4. To increase market share
5. To effectively reach key prospects–young actives
6. To establish product differentiation against HMOs

TARGET AUDIENCE

The target is all active and retired federal employees, with the primary target being nonenrolled, active federal employees. It is also important in this campaign to reassure current subscribers of the quality of their coverage.

The audience is predominantly male, married, with children under 18 years old. Nearly half are college educated,

Federal Employees Say:

"Better Than Ever."

"Good Deal."

"You Still Give Me Choices."

"More Ways To Save."

BlueCross BlueShield
FEDERAL EMPLOYEE PROGRAM
Standard Option

with a median household income of $42,900. The median age is 42, and Open Season decision making is done predominantly by the female.

The primary target of young actives is shopping for a health plan that promotes healthy lifestyles and covers preventive services with low costs.

CREATIVE STRATEGY

BCBS wanted an advertising campaign that conveyed the excitement of the product and relayed the message "The Blue Cross and Blue Shield Option now provides coverage that also helps you to plan for your health care costs."

The campaign concept was "everyone's talking about our new program." The BCBS program had a word-of-mouth feeling. It was designed to come across as conversational.

BCBS wanted the advertising to feel personal. The colorful collage approach helps the advertising out among other ads.

MEDIA STRATEGY

The media plan stimulated phone responses, generate/increase awareness, and increased subscriber's buying decisions. The first medium utilized was direct mail (33 percent) because the audience could be easily identified, and tailor the messages to address specific needs.

The following objectives were used for other media: target geographic areas with the greatest potential for acquisition, maximize the reach to federal employees, and provide frequency in key areas. Shared mail was used (15 percent) because BCBS could identify federal employees by zip codes. Newspaper inserts were utilized (40 percent) because of their wide reach and low cost, and were selected based on their MSA index of federal employees.

After coverage was ensured, the remaining budget was used to increase reach and frequency through newspaper ads (2 percent), radio (2 percent), out-of-home (2 percent), and television (5 percent). National publications provided additional support (1 percent).

PART

IV

Media

In recent years, the media function of advertising has taken on a significantly greater role in the process of developing advertising campaigns. The proliferation of media, especially the advent of new cable outlets, requires better-trained media planners and more sophisticated research tools to reach prime prospects successfully. In addition, the great cost of using the media has dramatically increased both the budgets for media schedules and the risk of mistakes.

Not only have the number of media increased, but the way in which media are being used by the audience is changing dramatically. The audience is fragmented in a manner that presents both problems and opportunities to the media planner. On the one hand, it is now becoming easier to identify and reach narrow segments of the audience. However, as advertisers are required to use more media vehicles to reach this fragmented audience, the cost of reaching prospects has risen dramatically. In addition, we are on the threshold of a new generation of media where the audience will control to a great extent the advertising that reaches them. In a few years, two-way communication systems that operate on an interactive basis with the audience may be common in most households.

Clearly, media personnel must be experts in a number of areas. Not only are they required to have a first-hand knowledge of the basic characteristics of the various media. More importantly, they must know how media interact with each other and the audience to create a synergistic effect where the whole is greater than the parts. The media planner must also be well-versed in the fundamentals of marketing, research, and the techniques of mass communication. Clearly, the need for professionally trained media planners has never been greater.

Basic

7

Media

Strategy

CHAPTER OBJECTIVES

Advertisers depend on proper media selection to reach prime prospects with their messages. After reading this chapter you will understand:

- New technology and increased media options
- Media planning and research in the media function
- Unique characteristics of each of the media
- The distinct components of the media plan
- Coordination between creative components and media
- Balance between media effectiveness and efficiency

As we will see throughout this section, technology is changing the fundamental relationships among media, audiences and advertisers. Media processes are combining in a manner in which distinctions between print and electronic media are not as apparent as in prior years. **For example,** is the delivery of newspaper content over a computer still a "print" medium? Likewise, are text messages available through television still "broadcast" signals?

The new interactive media will demand that consumers carry a higher share of editorial costs. In return, consumers can expect a number of media options, many unavailable today:

1. *Choice.* Increasing channel capacity via compression and digitization will allow viewers to "shop" for programs on their own schedules in the same way they do in a book or video store.

2. *Timeliness.* With choice has come the opportunity to give customers what they want when they want it. Multimedia will deliver the top 50 movies in real time and retrieve information from massive databases to consumers over new cable and satellite networks.

3. *Convenience.* Customers will be able to buy most merchandise easily and pay for it without leaving their living rooms.

4. *Quality.* Choice will increase the importance of quality as a differentiating factor as viewers pay premium prices for premium material.

5. *Control.* Increasingly, the world of multimedia will be controlled by the consumer. Consumers will largely decide both the timing of content and the content itself.[1]

In recent years, the responsibility for media planning has increased significantly. With total expenditures for advertising currently at the $140 billion mark, most of which will go to media time and space, it is not surprising that advertisers are giving increasing attention to the media planning function. In addition, media planners often are being asked to coordinate media plans with other forms of marketing communication, especially sales promotion. Consequently, it is necessary for the contemporary media planner to be an expert in all forms of marketing communications, not just traditional media.

The media function also is made more difficult by the proliferation of media choices and the dawn of the age of multimedia. Not that many years ago, the media planner could expect to build an advertising schedule from among three networks, a relatively few widely circulated national magazines, and, on the occasions when a client demanded it, a local media buy of the leading radio station or newspaper in the top markets. Today, the media buyer faces the daunting task of dealing with more than 50 cable networks, 9,000 radio stations, numerous suburban newspapers, and new technology that promises to create more media vehicles faster than we can catalog them.

You will recall from Chapter 5 that advertising media is bought by both agencies and independent media buyers. Since the basic function of media buying is similar in each type of organization, we will devote the majority of our discussion in this chapter to the agency media department. However, we should not overlook the growing importance of independent media buying firms as a competitor to full-service agencies.

The media departments of most large agencies are divided into three areas: media planning, media research, and media buying. An examination of each of these departments and their functions can give us a good idea of how the media function is carried out in contemporary advertising practice.

---

[1] Janice Hughes, "The Changing Multimedia Landscape," *Media Studies Journal,* Winter 1994, pp. 55–56.

MEDIA PLANNING

Media planners must coordinate the overall media strategy for a campaign. In order to accomplish this task, planners must have a systematic approach to the following components of the advertising campaign. The key to successful advertising is targeting all aspects of the plan:

- *Advertisers must target their media.* **They don't run commercials for denture cream on** *Beverly Hills 90210,* **and they don't run ads for acne cream during reruns of Doris Day movies.**

- *Advertisers target the season.* **They sell oatmeal during the winter and lemonade during the summer, garden supplies in the spring and sweaters in the fall.**

- *Advertisers target their message.* **Merrill Lynch found that its ads for investments showing a herd of cattle was unsuitable when selling to investors. The common denominator among investors was individualism. Now, Merrill Lynch has adopted the theme "a breed apart."[2]**

The media plan considers the overall marketing objectives of the client, the basic advertising goals to accomplish marketing objectives, the creative strategy and how the media will interact with the basic themes of the campaign, and the budget available to accomplish the designated tasks. However, the key to the development and execution of specific media buys is a targeted approach to every aspect of the plan.

The media planner must be involved with the total advertising and marketing program, not just the buying and placing of media. The interrelation between medium and message is important in all communications. However, nowhere it is more vital than in advertising. The medium must not only reach the correct target audience, but must create an environment that relates positively to the product. The popularity of narrowly defined magazines such as *Golf Digest* is due in large measure to their ability to create a relationship between advertising and editorial.

The growing responsibility of media planners has seen some significant changes in their responsibilities. The most apparent change is the placement of more hands-on responsibility on senior media managers and the elimination of the appearance that junior media buyers are making big decisions. These changes were largely in response to client complaints that agency media departments had grown top heavy with senior planners increasingly removed from the day-to-day media buying process.

"This [criticism] hit home several years ago when stories began circulating about young media planners—barely out of college—who were making virtually unsupervised media spending decisions for millions of advertising dollars."[3] These changes also were a tacit acknowledgment that independent media buying services were creating competition for agencies by concentrating solely on the media function.

---

[2]Rodman A. Sims, "Advertising Has Mass Appeal, but It's Not Mass Marketing," *Marketing News,* August 30, 1993, p. 4.

[3]Joe Mandese, "Media Departments Streamline, Put Senior Execs on Firing Line," *Advertising Age,* July 20, 1992, p. S-2.

MEDIA RESEARCH

Media research serves two primary functions. First, it provides both primary and secondary information about audience characteristics, which allow buyers to most efficiently develop a schedule. Second, it meets the growing demands of clients for advertising-accountability. As clients have become more sophisticated, media planners have had to justify their schedules and the results obtained by the media advertising they place.

This client demand for objective measurement of media has not only placed more importance on the research function, but also has changed the way media plans are developed by agencies for their clients. Some of the key trends that this era of media accountability has created are the following:

1. Marketers are seeking measurable results for every marketing communication dollar they spend.

2. Marketers are seeking direct consumer contacts through direct mail, telemarketing, etc. The demand for more direct response media changes the schedules for many advertisers and requires the planner to have extensive knowledge of new media vehicles.

3. Marketers recognize that most people "reached" by traditional marketing communications programs will not be influenced by them, and that they must consider this in measuring effectiveness. Marketers are demanding evidence of customer contacts (either sales or viable leads) rather than advertising exposure.

4. Finally, marketers are finding that demand-based advertising totally changes the rules of the game. Soon consumers will have information on products and services available at anytime from home computers and shop-at-home TV networks.[4]

The media researcher's primary function is to support both media planners and buyers by providing information on which they can make their decisions. Another role of the media researcher is to keep the agency and clients aware of changes and trends relating to media. The research department of most agencies is very small, with the director acting as a coordinator and much of the actual research done on a contract basis with private firms or through secondary syndicated research services.

Some advertising executives believe that the deemphasis of agency research is a mistake and that a strong research department can be a major differentiation among agencies in gaining new business. "Increasingly, agencies that have strong research departments are reaping rewards with clients. BBDO and Leo Burnett USA . . . have traditionally been among the strongest agency performers and, not coincidentally, have maintained the strongest research departments."[5] Research may become a major competitive weapon in full-service agencies' battle with independent media buying services.

---

[4]Ron Kaatz, "One for Good Measure," *Mediaweek*, May 24, 1993, p. 12.
[5]Pat Sloan and Julie Liesse, "New Agency Weapon to Win Clients: Research," *Advertising Age*, August 30, 1993, p. 3.

MEDIA BUYING

Media buyers

Media buyers execute and monitor the media schedule developed by media planners.

In most media departments media buyers make up the largest group and often are divided into national and local teams for broadcast buys. The function of the buyer is twofold: (1) to negotiate the most cost-efficient media schedules for their clients and (2) to monitor the buys as they run and develop post-analyses, comparing actual delivery against the original plan.

The job of the media planner is becoming increasingly complex as the number of media alternatives increase. The proliferation of media vehicles during the 1980s will accelerate into the next century. This dramatic change in the media landscape will be accompanied by social and demographic trends that will further change media decisions of both planners and clients. Exhibit 7.1 shows some major demographic changes during the past 15 years.

The media function is in a period of transition that will focus on three major areas: media diversity, media negotiation, and unbundling of media services.

Media Diversity

Media planners

Media planners are responsible for the overall strategy of the media component of an advertising campaign.

As we mentioned in an earlier section, the advertising media options of the 1990s are far different from those of only a few years ago (see Exhibit 7.2). This diversity not only makes the job of analyzing the numerous media vehicles more difficult, but also creates a problem of reaching a mass audience with fragmented media. For those large advertisers who need to reach a critical mass of consumers, it is becoming more and more expensive to do so as the audience for each medium decreases.

Media plan

The complete analysis and execution of the media component of a campaign.

Media planners find that creative media buying is mandatory if client needs are to be met. For example, at one time media planners determined the general type of media (for example, women's magazines, soap operas, newspaper fashion sections, etc.) that would reach a specified audience and then chose the vehicles that provided the most cost efficient reach. Today, media planning is much more complex, since even the highest-rated show or largest-circulation magazine will rarely reach all a company's prospects.

In order to overcome the lack of a "critical mass" medium, media planners have had to implement new tactics for developing a media plan to reach large audi-

EXHIBIT

7.1

The consumer of today is better educated, has more real disposable income, and is typically in a smaller family.

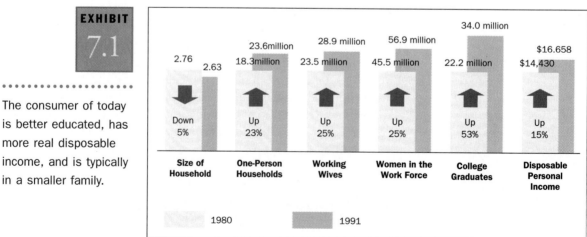

					34.0 million
2.76	23.6million	28.9 million	56.9 million	22.2 million	$16.658
2.63	18.3million	23.5 million	45.5 million		$14,430
Down 5%	Up 23%	Up 25%	Up 25%	Up 53%	Up 15%
Size of Household	One-Person Households	Working Wives	Women in the Work Force	College Graduates	Disposable Personal Income

1980   1991

(Courtesy: Cahners Publishing Company.)

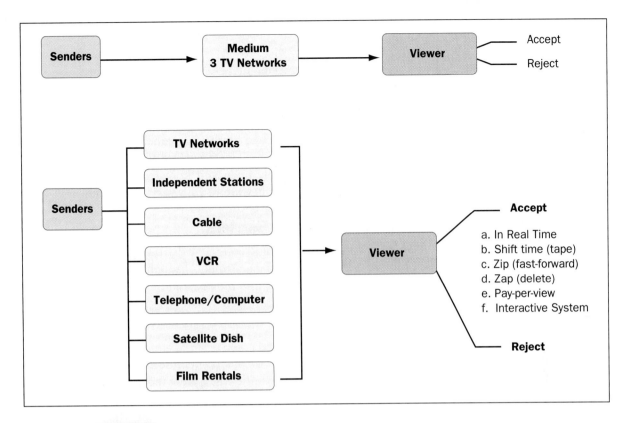

ences. For example, an advertiser might buy a prime-time spot to run simultaneously on CBS, NBC, and WGN. This technique is called *road blocking.*

The term was originally used by advertisers who wanted to advertise on all three major networks for a special event such as the introduction of a new car model. It effectively "road-blocked" any viewer regardless of what network they were watching. With the increase in channel availability, full road blocking is no longer practical, but the term now refers to simultaneously running a commercial on several stations at the same time. Road blocking is only one technique that points out that media planners must use all the tools in their arsenal to meet the expectations of clients.[6]

Media Negotiation

Advertising time and space are not normally bought on a fixed price basis. Rather, media buyers negotiate with the media for a variety of concessions. Traditionally, newspapers are the least likely to offer price concessions (called coming off the card), while negotiation is a common practice in television and radio. The propensity of broadcasters to negotiate should not be surprising. Since they are dealing with a perishable commodity—time—they must be willing to make a deal or lose potential revenue permanently.

As the media faced a tough economy and greater competition for the advertising dollar during the 1980s, there were more and more deals made with advertisers. In particular, consumer magazines began to negotiate their rates, an unheard of practice in earlier years. However, the astute media look beyond price as a negotiating tool. While price continues to be the most pop-

---

[6]Bill Sternberg, "A Theory of Critical Mass," *Mediaweek,* May 10, 1993, p. 12.

ular and obvious subject for negotiation, some media prefer to deal in other areas.

For example, a magazine might be willing to offer a large advertiser a back cover at regular page cost, or a newspaper might guarantee prominent placement in a popular section such as sports. More and more deals are being offered on a merchandising basis where a magazine advertiser will be offered space in a newsletter sponsored by the magazine, or in point-of-purchase displays paid for by the medium. The merchandising arrangements require that media buyers are even more open and knowledgeable of all forms of marketing communications if they are to fully service their clients.

Unbundling of Media Services

Perhaps the most interesting trend in media buying is the dramatic changes in full-service agency media departments brought about by competition from independent buying services and the demand by clients for greater economies. As we discussed earlier, many agencies are assigning senior executives to the buying function, in part as a reaction to competition from independent media buying services.

The long-term significance of this competition between agencies and independents is the trend toward offering agency media assistance to clients apart from the other services of the agency. The term *unbundling* means that the media department is separated (unbundled) from the other services of the agency and is allowed to operate as an independent contractor. Some agency executives predict that the media function will be "outsourced" rather than continuing as part of full-service, integrated agencies.[7]

The advantages of this approach is that otherwise underutilized resources in the media department can be devoted to special media projects and media-only clients. It also allows the media department to develop more expertise than it might have if it served only full-service clients. A larger and more professional media staff would presumably serve both full-service and unbundled clients better.

On the other hand, there are major negative aspects to the stand-alone media department. First, many large advertisers such as Procter & Gamble and Phillip Morris have shown zero tolerance for any client conflicts. Since one of the selling points of an unbundled department would be expertise in specialized areas such as package goods, these client conflicts would be inevitable if the department were profitable.[8]

A second, more pragmatic problem, of the unbundled media department is the entrepreneurial spirit needed to make such a department a success. "The media director and senior staff of a department probably represent talented media strategists and negotiators, but most likely none of them have ever been trained in the fine art of selling."[9]

It is clear that media planners and the media function in both agencies and among independents will continue to undergo significant changes in coming years. Regardless of the specific nature of these changes, the media profes-

---

[7]Joe Mandese, "Agencies Find Media Clout in Outside Services," *Advertising Age,* March 14, 1994, p. 3.
[8]Richard Brunelli, "The Brave New World of Agency Media," *Mediaweek,* March 8, 1993, p. 19.
[9]Ed Ronk, "Time to Change or Die," *Mediaweek,* April 5, 1993, p. 16.

sional must have a range of skills including marketing, research, and both an analytical and creative approach to problem solving.

MEDIA CHARACTERISTICS

As we indicated earlier, media planners must be experts in the marketing plans, advertising goals, and creative strategy of their clients. However, the primary task of the media planner is to determine those vehicles that will best communicate the message of the advertiser at the most efficient cost. Media planners must keep up with basic media characteristics, latest trends in each of the media, as well as new technology that may have long-range effects on advertising media. To set the stage for our examination of basic media strategy, it will be helpful to briefly outline their major characteristics. To begin, let's examine the advertising support given each of the media in the following table.

Estimated Advertising Expenditures in Major Media, 1994

	$(billions)	Percent of Total
Newspapers	32.9	23.2
Television	32.7	22.9
Direct mail	27.3	19.1
Radio	9.2	6.5
Consumer magazines	8.1	5.6
Business and farm magazines	3.5	2.5
Outdoor	1.1	0.8
Other	27.4	19.2

The double-digit increases experienced in media expenditures during the 1980s are over. In fact, media increases in the 3 to 6 percent range are a welcome change from the recession years of 1990–92. However, the competition among traditional media, coupled with the inroads of new and emerging technology, promises to make the next decade one of significant upheaval for the media, agencies, and their clients. The starting point for developing a media plan is the analysis of the media's strengths and weaknesses and how these characteristics fit a particular advertiser's strategy.

Newspapers

Newspapers, long the major recipient of advertising dollars, are primarily a local medium with less than 15 percent of revenues coming from national advertisers. For the past decade, newspapers have faced declining advertising shares as new competitors have taken ad dollars and many retailers have cut advertising budgets or moved to direct mail.

Pros:

1. Newspapers have wide exposure especially to an upscale audience of 35 and older adults.

2. Newspaper advertising is extremely flexible with opportunities for color, large and small space ads, timely insertion schedules, coupons, and some selectivity through special sections and targeted editions.

3. Newspapers are timely and reach their audiences at the convenience of the reader and maintain high credibility as an advertising medium.

Cons:

1. Many newspapers have 60 percent advertising content. This high ratio of advertising, combined with average reading time of less than 30 minutes, means few ads are read.

2. Overall newspaper circulation has fallen far behind population and household growth. In some cases, it is difficult to reach certain target markets. In particular, teen and young adults do not demonstrate high newspaper readership.

3. Advertising costs have risen much more sharply than circulation in recent years.

4. Newspapers face growing competition from television as a primary source of news.

Television

Television reaches every demographic category and achieves creative impact with both color and motion. Many advertising executives predict that television will soon pass newspapers as the primary source of total advertising dollars, a distinction television has long held among national advertisers. For example, the top 100 national advertisers place almost 40 percent of their budgets in television with over 20 percent in network alone (see Exhibit 7.3). If cigarettes and liquor were not excluded from television, the figure would be even higher.

Pros:

1. Television is an extremely creative and flexible medium. Virtually any product message can be adapted to television.

2. Despite recent cost increases, it remains extremely cost efficient for large advertisers needing to reach a mass audience. By utilizing selected cable

EXHIBIT 7.3

. . . .

Television is the dominant medium among national advertisers.

National Ad Spending by Media

| | 100 Leading National Advertisers | | | | |
| | Advertising Expenditures | | | Media as % of Total | |
Category	1992	1991	% chg	1992	1991
Consumer magazine	$3,154.2	$2,782.9	13.3	8.7	8.1
Sunday magazines	367.8	304.1	21.0	1.0	0.9
Local newspapers	2,476.2	2,463.2	0.5	6.8	7.2
National newspapers	243.2	213.8	13.7	0.7	0.6
Outdoor	209.9	263.7	−20.4	0.6	0.8
Network TV	7,881.7	7,546.5	4.4	21.8	22.0
Spot TV	4,002.0	3,786.7	5.7	11.1	11.0
Syndicated TV	926.5	913.3	1.4	2.6	2.7
Cable TV networks	934.4	709.3	31.7	2.6	2.1
Network radio	315.5	314.2	0.4	0.9	0.9
Spot radio	340.4	389.0	−12.5	0.9	1.1
Measured media	20,851.8	19,686.8	5.9	57.6	57.4
Estimated unmeasured	15,340.4	14,593.3	5.1	42.4	42.6
Total	36,192.2	34,280.1	5.6	100.0	100.0

Notes: Dollars are in millions. Sources: Measured media for the 100 Leaders and all advertisers from CMR.

(Source: Advertising Age, September 29, 1993, p. 64.)

outlets and local broadcast stations, advertisers are able to provide a local or regional component to their national television schedules.

3. Television offers advertisers prestige lacking in most other media.

Cons:

1. The TV message is perishable and easily forgotten without expensive repetition.

2. The TV audience is fragmented with alternatives such as cable, independent stations, VCRs, etc., vying for limited viewing time. The potential of 500-channel systems combined with interactive technology makes fragmentation even more of a problem in the future.

3. The advent of the 15-second commercial has led to more and shorter messages, which contribute to confusing commercial clutter.

Radio

Radio is a personal medium that takes advantage of its many stations and formats to direct advertising to extremely well defined audience segments. Radio has high weekly coverage and station loyalty by the audience; still it maintains the lowest costs of all major media.

Pros:

1. With the exception of direct response, radio can more selectively target narrow audience segments, many of whom are not heavy users of other media. For example, teenagers are particularly heavy users of radio.

2. Radio is a mobile medium going with listeners into the marketplace and giving advertisers proximity to the sale.

3. Radio, with its relatively low production costs and immediacy, can react quickly to changing market conditions.

Cons:

1. Without a visual component, radio often lacks the impact of other media. Also, many listeners use radio as "background" rather than pay full attention to the programming.

2. The low average audience of most radio stations requires high frequency to achieve acceptable reach and frequency.

3. Adequate audience research is not always available, especially in the important drive-time and out-of-home listener categories. Many small-market stations have no audience research available.

Direct Response

Direct-response advertising can reach virtually any demographic, product-user, or even lifestyle segment with extreme accuracy. It is a medium particularly attuned to the target marketing philosophy of the 1990s and has shown significant growth in the past decade.

Pros:

1. Direct response has the ability to target even the most narrowly defined audiences.

2. Direct response can provide instant feedback to an advertising message using virtually any medium as well as telemarketing, coupons, etc.

3. Direct response offers research opportunities for measuring advertising effectiveness unavailable in most other media.

Cons:

1. High cost per inquiry is a major problem with many forms of direct response. Expenses for printing, production, and personnel have all increased significantly in recent years.

2. Prospect lists must be constantly updated at considerable expense to the advertiser.

3. Direct response, especially direct mail and telemarketing, has an image problem among many consumers and lacks the credibility of other major media.

Magazines

Magazines offer advertisers a number of specialized titles as well as geographic and demographic editions to reach narrowly defined audience segments.

Pros:

1. Like radio, the number and range of specialized magazines provide advertisers with an opportunity for narrowly targeted audiences. Magazines can effectively use messages that reach these audiences with creative themes (see Exhibit 7.4).

2. Magazines provide a prestige, quality environment for advertisers.

EXHIBIT

7.4

Magazine advertising reaches narrowly targeted audiences with specific messages.

(Courtesy: DFSD Bozell, Ltd.)

3. Magazine advertising has a long life and is often passed along to several readers. Business publications are especially useful as reference tools and are routinely passed along and kept for long periods of time.

Cons:

1. In recent years, magazine audience growth has not kept up with increases in advertising rates.

2. Most magazines have relatively long advertising deadlines, reducing flexibility and the ability of advertisers to react to fast-changing market conditions.

3. Despite the obvious advantages of magazine specialization, it means that a single magazine rarely reaches the majority of a market segment. Therefore, several magazines must be used, or alternative media must supplement the magazine schedule.

Outdoor

Outdoor advertising is a visual medium intended for brand name reinforcement. It also can be effective in introducing new products and brands. From the familiar highway billboard to the one-of-a-kind spectacular, outdoor is impossible to ignore (see Exhibit 7.5).

(Courtesy: Arnell Group.)

Pros:

1. Outdoor can reach most of the population in a market with high frequency at a very low cost per exposure.

2. It is an excellent means of supplementing other media advertising for product introduction or building brand name recognition.

3. With the use of color and lighting, outdoor is a medium that is highly visible.

4. The outdoor industry has diversified the product categories using the medium in an attempt to lose its image as a "beer-and-cigarette" medium.

Cons:

1. Outdoor is rarely able to communicate detailed sales messages. Copy is usually limited to 7 to 10 words.

2. The effectiveness of outdoor is extremely difficult to measure.

3. Outdoor has been attacked in many communities as a visual pollutant that has made it the topic of some controversy and legal restrictions. Some state and local legislation bans the medium altogether. This negative image may discourage some advertisers from using the medium.

THE COMPONENTS OF THE MEDIA PLAN

A thorough knowledge of the characteristics of the various advertising media is somewhat like knowing the vocabulary to a language without the grammar. Like a vocabulary, media characteristics don't allow you to put the pieces together into a meaningful whole. A media plan is made up of many elements in addition to a descriptive analysis of the various media. While there is no standard format, the following elements are found in most national plans:

■ **Description of the target audience**

■ **Communication requirements and creative elements**

■ **Geography—where is the product distributed?**

■ **Efficiency/effectiveness balance—shall we emphasize reach, frequency, or continuity?**

■ **Pressure of competition**

■ **Budget**

The Target Audience

Target audience
That group that composes the present and potential prospects for a product or service.

One of the fundamental jobs of the media planner is to identify the prime prospects of a product or service, and the media that will most economically and efficiently reach them. Media buying is undergoing fundamental changes as new technology and sophisticated consumers require major modifications in media planning. These changes encompass a number of factors, but four important means of reaching consumers are emerging.[10]

---

[10]Patricia Sellers, "The Best Way to Reach Your Buyers," *Fortune,* Autumn/Winter 1993, p. 15.

1. *Narrowly define your market.* Narrowcast instead of broadcast by fine-tuning your advertising to tightly specific groups of consumers. A Coca-Cola Classic campaign used two dozen ads in many styles and moods for 20 different TV networks. They included quick-cutting commercials for the MTV generation, heart-tuggers for *Murder She Wrote,* and one entitled *Spaceship* for teenage boys.

2. *Take advantage of captive consumers at live events.* John Hancock invests $1.5 million as primary sponsor of the Boston Marathon, where its name is shown throughout the race on everything from results boards to runners' numbers.

3. *Think innovatively about traditional media such as newspapers, magazines, and radio, which are demonstrating major changes.* Many newspapers are already providing telephone and computer access. Advertisers must be prepared for the challenge of greater audience control of the media.

4. *Use the new media to sell directly to customers by combining advertising and selling.* In selected markets, Time Warner offers coupons and direct selling pieces to consumers through TV-top printers. Customers can see a commercial, ask for more information, and, in some cases, receive a discount on their next cable bill from the company sending the information.

In the future, agency researchers must develop more sophisticated tools to get a clear picture of consumers and the ways in which they interact with media and advertising messages. Audience profiles are constantly changing, and advertisers must track these fluctuations.

The emphasis on narrowly defined markets requires that media plans maximize delivery of prospects as opposed to people or households. Although techniques differ from agency to agency, all agencies tend to use some variation of the *weighted* or *demographic* cost per thousand (CPM). Let's look at an example of the weighted CPM.

Cost per thousand (CPM)

A method of comparing the cost for media of different circulations. Also weighted or demographic cost per thousand calculates the CPM using only that portion of a medium's audience falling into a prime-prospect category.

The CPM is a means of comparing media costs among vehicles with different circulations. The formula is stated:

$$\text{CPM} = \frac{\text{ad cost} \times 1000}{\text{circulation}}$$

McCall's has a circulation of 5 million and a four-color page rate of $60,800. Therefore:

$$\text{CPM} = \frac{(\$60,800 \times 1,000)}{5,000,000} = \$12.16$$

Now, assume that we are only interested in reaching women with children under two years old. We find that 600,000 *McCall's* readers are in this category. Therefore:

$$\text{Demographic CPM} = \frac{(60,800 \times 1,000)}{600,000} = \$101.33$$

The demographic CPM simply adjusts the circulation to include only that part of the audience of interest to a particular advertiser. In recent years, advertising research has developed extremely sophisticated techniques for identifying prospects. Most of these new techniques recognize that proper identification of prospects demands the use of several variables.

To return to our *McCall's* example, we realize that all women with children under two years of age are not alike. They differ in terms of education, income, housing, geography, and lifestyle. Obviously, these differences must be considered.

You will recall that in Chapter 4 we discussed a number of different means of identifying target markets. In the weighted CPM example above, a media planner can substitute any number of lifestyle, product-user, or psychographic data for the demographic category we used in the *McCall's* example. It is important to note that CPM figures are important only as comparisons with those of other media. *McCall's* CPM of $12.16 is of interest only to the extent that it might be compared to *Redbook,* with a CPM of $16.33, or *Self,* with $18.44.

One of the newest innovations in target marketing is so-called *place-based* media planning. The concept of place-based media is to design methods of reaching a mobile population in out-of-home environments that will most likely attach potential prospects. "With home TV viewership declining, advertisers are getting out of the house and hitting consumers with messages in airplanes, airports, train stations, doctors' offices, retail outlets, college campuses, health clubs and even public restrooms."[11]

The ingenuity of these media pioneers is limited only by the tolerance of the public and their ability to sell advertisers on the idea. There will be as many misses as hits. For example, Ted Turner's airport Flight Channel met with public enthusiasm, while his grocery-store-based Checkout Channel got a yawn from both consumers and advertisers.

Place-based media are simply another example of the problem facing advertisers in reaching an elusive, mobile, and fragmented audience. In addition to the logistical nightmares presented by some of the these media formats, the problem of audience measurement creates other barriers to widespread advertiser acceptance. As we will see in later chapters, even established media such as radio and outdoor face major research methodology problems. However, compared to elevator signs and grocery cart TV these problems are simple. The key to place-based media is that they try to reach prospects as close to the purchase decision as possible. The potential rewards of a successful place-based system is so great that we will no doubt see more attempts in the coming years.

Claritas' Potential Rating Index by Zip Code

PRIZM (Potential Rating Index by ZIP Market)
A method of audience segmentation developed by the Claritas Corporation.

One of the most innovative methods of segmenting markets on a multiple-variable basis is the Potential Rating Index by Zip Code (PRIZM) system developed by the Claritas Corporation. PRIZM divides the population into 15 social groups (see Exhibit 7.6) and further subdivides these large segments into 62 subcategories (see Exhibit 7.7). The primary variables for determining these social groups are urbanization and social class.

The PRIZM categories are arranged in descending order of affluence from the "Blue Blood Estates," who reside in the Elite Suburb social group to "Hard

---

[11]John P. Cortez, "Media Pioneers Try to Control On-the-Go Consumers," *Advertising Age,* August 17, 1992, p. 25.

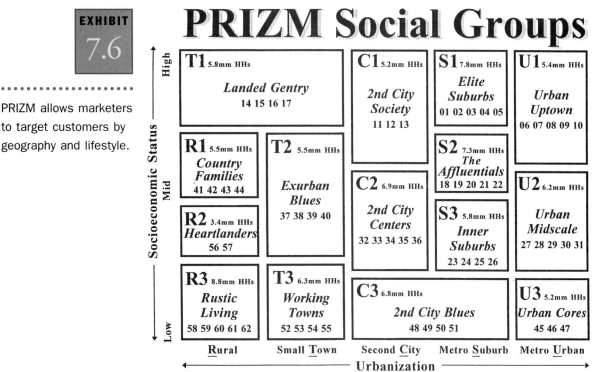

PRIZM Social Groups

PRIZM allows marketers to target customers by geography and lifestyle.

Socioeconomic Status

High · Mid · Low

T1 5.8mm HHs
Landed Gentry
14 15 16 17

C1 5.2mm HHs
2nd City Society
11 12 13

S1 7.8mm HHs
Elite Suburbs
01 02 03 04 05

U1 5.4mm HHs
Urban Uptown
06 07 08 09 10

R1 5.5mm HHs
Country Families
41 42 43 44

T2 5.5mm HHs
Exurban Blues
37 38 39 40

S2 7.3mm HHs
The Affluentials
18 19 20 21 22

U2 6.2mm HHs
Urban Midscale
27 28 29 30 31

R2 3.4mm HHs
Heartlanders
56 57

C2 6.9mm HHs
2nd City Centers
32 33 34 35 36

S3 5.8mm HHs
Inner Suburbs
23 24 25 26

R3 8.8mm HHs
Rustic Living
58 59 60 61 62

T3 6.3mm HHs
Working Towns
52 53 54 55

C3 6.8mm HHs
2nd City Blues
48 49 50 51

U3 5.2mm HHs
Urban Cores
45 46 47

Rural · Small Town · Second City · Metro Suburb · Metro Urban

Urbanization

Copyright 1994, Claritas Inc.

Scrabble," whose residents live in the most rural and lowest social class areas of the country. The value of PRIZM groups is that these general categories can be matched with those products and media that members of the groups are most likely to use. For example, inhabitants of the "Elite Suburbs" are likely to drive luxury cars and be among the heaviest readers of magazines. By identifying these groups geographically, companies can develop efficient marketing and advertising plans without the waste circulation of a less-targeted campaign.

In the future, the computer and more sophisticated research methodology will make even more finely tuned audience identification possible. In fact, we may be approaching a time when audience segmentation techniques will be able to target prospects more precisely than media vehicles will be able to practically or efficiently reach them. Even the most thoroughly researched media plan will reach some nonbuyers. The job of the media planner is to keep waste circulation to a minimum while achieving maximum cost efficiencies. A media schedule with zero nonprospects would not only be theoretically impossible to achieve, but prohibitively expensive.

Communication Requirements and Creative Elements

When we use the word *creativity* in an advertising context, we usually do not think about the media function. However, the effective media planner must consider the creative goals, the message themes, and the actual creative execution in developing a media plan. Because of the high cost of time and space, there is a tendency to become so concerned with media cost analyses that we forget that effective advertising must communicate to our listeners and readers.

Communications component (media plan)

That portion of the media plan that considers the effectiveness of message delivery as contrasted to the efficiency of audience delivery.

EXHIBIT
7.7

PRIZM by Claritas
Demographic Reference Chart

Race/Ethnicity
W-White, B-Black, A-Asian
H-Hispanic, F-Foreign Born
■ Prevalent • Above Avg

PREDOMINANT CHARACTERISTICS

Grp	Clstr	Nickname	Income Level	Family Type	Age	Education	Occup	Housing	W	B	A	H	F
S1	01	Blue Blood Estates	Elite	Family	35-54	College	Exec	Single	■		•		•
	02	Cashmere & Country Clubs	Wealthy	Family	35-54	College	Exec	Single	■		•		•
	03	Executive Suites	Affluent	Couples	25-34	College	WC/Exec	Single	■		•		•
	04	Pools & Patios	Affluent	Couples	55-64	College	Exec	Single	■		•		•
	05	Kids & Cul-de-Sacs	Affluent	Family	35-54	College	WC/Exec	Single	•		•		•
U1	06	Urban Gold Coast	Affluent	Singles	35-54	College	Exec	Hi-Rise	■		•		•
	07	Money & Brains	Affluent	Couples	55-64	College	Exec	Single	■		•		•
	08	Young Literati	Upper Mid	Sgl/Cpl	25-34	College	Exec	Hi-Rise	•		•		•
	09	American Dreams	Upper Mid	Family	35-54	College	WC	Single		•	•	•	•
	10	Bohemian Mix	Middle	Singles	< 24	College	WC	Hi-Rise	•	•	•	•	•
C1	11	Second City Elite	Affluent	Couples	35-64	College	WC/Exec	Single	■		•		
	12	Upward Bound	Upper Mid	Family	25-54	College	WC/Exec	Single	■		•		
	13	Gray Power	Middle	Sgl/Cpl	65+	College	WC	Single	■				
T1	14	Country Squires	Wealthy	Fam/Cpl	35-64	College	Exec	Single	■				
	15	God's Country	Affluent	Family	35-54	College	WC	Single	■				
	16	Big Fish Small Pond	Upper Mid	Family	35-54	HS/College	WC	Single	■				
	17	Greenbelt Families	Upper Mid	Family	25-54	HS/College	WC	Single	■				
S2	18	Young Influentials	Upper Mid	Sgl/Cpl	< 35	College	WC/Exec	Multi	•		•		•
	19	New Empty Nests	Upper Mid	Couples	35-64	College	WC/Exec	Single	■		•		
	20	Boomers & Babies	Upper Mid	Family	25-54	College	WC/Exec	Single	•		•		•
	21	Suburban Sprawl	Middle	Fam/Cpl	< 35	College	WC	Mixed	•	•	•	•	•
	22	Blue-Chip Blues	Middle	Family	35-54	HS/College	WC/BC	Single	■				
S3	23	Upstarts & Seniors	Middle	Cpl/Sgl	Mix	College	WC/Exec	Multi	■		•		•
	24	New Beginnings	Middle	Sgl/Cpl	< 35	College	WC/Exec	Multi		•	•	•	•
	25	Mobility Blues	Middle	Fam/Cpl	< 35	HS/College	BC/Serv	Mixed		•	•	■	•
	26	Gray Collars	Middle	Couples	> 55	HS	BC/Serv	Single		•	•	•	
U2	27	Urban Achievers	Middle	Cpl/Sgl	Mix	College	WC/Exec	Hi-Rise	■		•	•	•
	28	Big City Blend	Middle	Family	35-54	HS	WC/BC	Single		•	•	■	•
	29	Old Yankee Rows	Middle	Couples	55+	HS	WC	Single	•		•	•	■
	30	Middle America	Middle	Fam/Cpl	35-54	HS/College	WC/Serv	Multi		■			•
	31	Latino America	Middle	Family	25-34	< HS	BC/Serv	Multi				■	•
C2	32	Middleburg Managers	Middle	Couples	> 55	College	WC/Exec	Single	■		•		
	33	Boomtown Singles	Middle	Sgl/Cpl	< 34	College	WC/Exec	Multi	■		•		
	34	Starter Families	Middle	Family	25-34	HS	BC	Mixed	•			•	
	35	Sunset City Blues	Lower Mid	Couples	> 55	HS	BC/Serv	Single	•				
	36	Towns & Gowns	Lower Mid	Singles	< 35	College	WC/Serv	Hi-Rise	•		•		•
T2	37	New Homesteaders	Middle	Family	35-54	College	WC	Single	■				
	38	Middle America	Middle	Family	25-44	HS	BC	Single	■				
	39	Red, White & Blue-Collar	Middle	Family	35-64	HS	BC	Single	■				
	40	Military Quarters	Lower Mid	Family	25-54	College	WC/Serv	Multi		•	•		

PRIZM by Claritas
Demographic Reference Chart

Race/Ethnicity
W-White, B-Black, A-Asian
H-Hispanic, F-Foreign Born
■ Prevalent • Above Avg

PREDOMINANT CHARACTERISTICS

Grp	Clstr	Nickname	Income Level	Family Type	Age	Education	Occup	Housing	W	B	A	H	F
R1	41	Big Sky Families	Upper Mid	Family	35-44	HS/College	BC/Farm	Single	■				
	42	New Ecotopia	Middle	Fam/Cpl	35-54	College	WC/BC	Single	■				
	43	River City, USA	Middle	Family	35-64	HS	BC/Farm	Single	■				
	44	Shotguns & Pickups	Middle	Family	35-64	HS	BC/Farm	Single	■				
U3	45	Single City Blues	Lower Mid	Singles	Mix	Mix	WC/Serv	Multi		•	•	•	•
	46	Hispanic Mix	Poor	Family	< 35	< HS	BC	Hi-Rise		•	•	■	•
	47	Inner Cities	Poor	Sgl/Fam	Mix	< HS	BC/Serv	Multi		■		•	•
C3	48	Smalltown Downtown	Lower Mid	Sgl/Fam	< 35	HS/College	BC/Serv	Multi	•	•		•	
	49	Hometown Retired	Lower Mid	Sgl/Cpl	65+	< HS	Service	Mixed	■				
	50	Family Scramble	Lower Mid	Family	< 35	< HS	BC	Mixed		•		■	•
	51	Southside City	Poor	Sgl/Fam	Mix	< HS	BC/Serv	Multi		■			
T3	52	Golden Ponds	Lower Mid	Couples	65+	HS	BC/Serv	Single	■				
	53	Rural Industria	Lower Mid	Family	< 35	HS	BC	Single	■			•	
	54	Norma Rae-Ville	Poor	Sgl/Fam	Mix	< HS	BC/Serv	Single		■			
	55	Mines & Mills	Poor	Sgl/Cpl	55+	< HS	BC/Serv	Single	■				
R2	56	Agri-Business	Middle	Family	35+	HS	Farm	Single	■			•	
	57	Grain Belt	Lower Mid	Family	55+	HS	Farm	Single	■			•	
R3	58	Blue Highways	Lower Mid	Family	35-54	HS	BC/Farm	Single	■				
	59	Rustic Elders	Lower Mid	Couples	55+	HS	BC/Serv	Single	■				
	60	Back Country Folks	Lower Mid	Couples	35+	HS	BC/Farm	Single	■				
	61	Scrub Pine Flats	Poor	Family	35+	< HS	BC/Farm	Single		■			
	62	Hard Scrabble	Poor	Family	35+	< HS	BC/Farm	Single	■				

Income Level / **Avg Annual HH Income**

Income Level	Avg Annual HH Income
Elite/Wealthy	$65,000 and over
Affluent	$50,000 - $64,500
Upper Mid	$37,000 - $49,500
Middle	$28,000 - $36,500
Lower Mid	$20,000 - $27,500
Poor	under $20,000

Education

< HS	Grade School
HS	High School / Technical School
HS/College	High School / Some College
College	College Graduates

Family Type

Family	Married Couples w/Children or, Single Parents w/Children
Couples	Married Couples (few children)
Singles	Singles / Unmarried Couples
Fam/Cpl	Mix of Married Couples with/without Children
Sgl/Cpl	Mix of Married Couples and Singles

Occupation

Exec	Executive, managerial & professionals (teachers, doctors, etc.)
WC	Other White-Collar (technical, sales, admin/clerical support)
BC	Blue-Collar (assembly, trades & repair, operators, laborers, etc.)
WC/BC	Mix of White-Collar & Upper-Level Blue Collar
Service	Service (hospitality, food prep, protective & health services, etc)
WC/Serv	Mix of Other White-Collar & Service
BC/Serv	Mix of Blue-Collar & Service
Farm	Farming, Mining & Ranching (farm operators, forestry, etc.)
BC/Farm	Mix of Blue-Collar and Farming

It is extremely important for the media planner to distinguish simple exposure to advertising from advertising communication. In the past, a major criticism of the advertising process was that media and creative functions were not coordinated closely enough. The result, according to critics, was advertising that did not fully utilize the communicative strengths of the various media vehicles. Fortunately, the separation between the creative and media functions seems to have diminished in recent years. Among major advertising agencies there seems to be a heightened sensitivity that creative/media cooperation is necessary for effective advertising.

Among the primary communication considerations that should be considered by the media planner are the following:

1. *Creative predispositions of the audience.* For example, teens are predisposed to radio in a different way than print.

2. *Qualitative environment for the message. Golf* magazine reaches readers who are in the proper frame of mind for ads for golf balls and golf clubs.

3. *The synergistic effect.* Advertisers seek a combination of media that results in a communicative effect that is greater than the sum of each medium. For example, outdoor is used by automobile manufacturers to gain brand recognition; magazines for detailed product information; newspapers for dealer location and price; and television for demonstration and image. The net effect is greater than any single medium used alone.

4. *The creative approach.* Does the need for long copy or quality reproduction require print, even if other media might be more cost-efficient (see Exhibit 7.8)?

Roadblocking
Simultaneously airing the same commercial on a number of stations.

EXHIBIT
7.8

An example of a message which is ideal for print format.

(Courtesy: Columbia Sportswear.)

EXHIBIT

7.9

Changing Messages

New media's messages will be more intimate, playful, and individualistic. (selected themes for advertisers)

	Mass Media	New Media
Form of audience	Crowd	Individual
Status of source	Dominant	Slightly submissive
Claim of message	"Listen to me"	"Want to play?"
Implied relationship	Solidarity Authority	Intimacy
Impact of message	Emotional arousal Imagery associations Memorization	Information Formed relationship Increased attention
Structure of message	Standardized Stereotyped Generalized	Variable Personalized Specific
Goal of message	Purchase	Further interaction

(*Source:* American Demographics, *Jan. 1994.*)

New media will have a profound effect on future advertising messages.

In the future, new, interactive media will require even closer coordination between media placement and the communication environment with consumers. "The feeling and tone of advertising will change from a distant, status-driven relationship to an intimate, playful adventure. In many cases, advertising and entertainment will merge to become 'infotainment.' Traditional advertising often communicates information through a dramatic image such as a character, scene, or story. New media advertising might mix image and copy in a conversational way by addressing the audience as a member of the user community."[12] Exhibit 7.9 shows the manner in which messages will change in an interactive media climate.

It is important to remember that although creative considerations must be considered, they will rarely dictate the media buy. Factors such as cost-effectiveness and media usage by prime prospects will almost always be paramount in determining media plans. However, for the media planner to ignore the campaign, creative strategy would be extremely shortsighted.

Geography—Where Is the Product Distributed?

Brand Development Index (BDI)

A method of allocating advertising budgets to those geographic areas that have the greatest sales potential.

Geography is an important consideration for the media planning process. Obviously, those areas with the greatest population also offer the highest potential for sales of most products (see Exhibit 7.10). However, the media planner must also relate population to prospects for a particular product and allocate the budget to different areas in the most efficient manner. One method of relating sales, advertising budgets, and geography is the brand development index (BDI). An example of the BDI is shown in the following table.

---

[12]Bruce MacEvoy, "Change Leaders and the New Media," *American Demographics,* January 1994, p. 45.

Computing the Brand Development Index

ACME Appliance has a media budget of $2 million and sells in 20 markets. The media planner wants to allocate the budget in the 20 markets according to the sales potential of each market

Market	Population (%)	ACME Sales (%)	Budget by Population (000)	BDI (Sales/ Population)	Budget by BDI
1	8	12	$ 160	150	$ 240,000
2	12	8	240	67	160,800
3	6	6	120	100	120,000
etc.					
20	100%	100%	$2,000	—	$2,000,000

Example: Market 2, based on its population, should have an advertising allocation of $240,000 (0.12 × $2,000,000). However, the sales potential of market 2 is only 67 percent as great as its population would indicate (sales/population or 8/12). Therefore, the media planner reduces the allocation to market 2 to $160,800 ($240,000 × 0.67) and reallocates funds to markets with greater potential such as market 1.

In recent years, regional differences in consumption have required many firms to develop a secondary localized media plan to supplement their national media schedule. Studies indicate that more than 60 percent of national advertisers indicate that their media plans are becoming more localized. Furthermore, local cable television is the most popular media choice for this localization, followed by regional editions of national magazines.

The move toward localization is a result of advertising needing to present a local advertising message in different markets. This message localization is especially needed to promote differential local pricing strategies and regional tastes, to meet local competition, and to target specific audience segments.[13]

Reaching regional and local audiences by national advertisers will become even more important in the future. As we examine the various advertising media in the coming chapters, note the ways in which virtually all media are attempting to meet advertiser demands for localization. As advertisers increasingly become able to more narrowly define their prospects, the burden will be even greater for media to deliver both demographic and geographic subcategories of their total circulation.

The Efficiency/Effectiveness Balance: Should Reach, Frequency, or Continuity Be Emphasized?

At this stage, the media planner is moving into the specific tactics of the media schedule. The first step is consideration of audience reach, frequency, and continuity. *Reach* refers to the total number of people to whom you deliver a message: *frequency* refers to the number of times it is delivered within a given period (usually figured on a weekly basis for ease in schedule planning); and *continuity* refers to the length of time a schedule runs. Only the biggest advertisers can emphasize all three factors at once, and even they seek to spread their money most efficiently.

Reach, frequency, and continuity must be balanced against the demands of a fixed budget. However, the media planner must also consider the balance be-

---

Reach

The total audience a medium actually covers.

Frequency

(1) The number of waves per second that a transmitter radiates, measured in kilohertz (kHz) and megahertz (MHz). The FCC assigns to each TV and radio station the frequency on which it may operate, to prevent interference with other stations. (2) Of media exposure the number of times an individual or household is exposed to a medium within a given period of time. (3) In statistics the number of times each element appears in each step of a distribution scale.

---

[13]Junu Bryan Kim, "Many Media Plans Becoming More of a Local Attraction," *Advertising Age*, July 20, 1992, p. S-24.

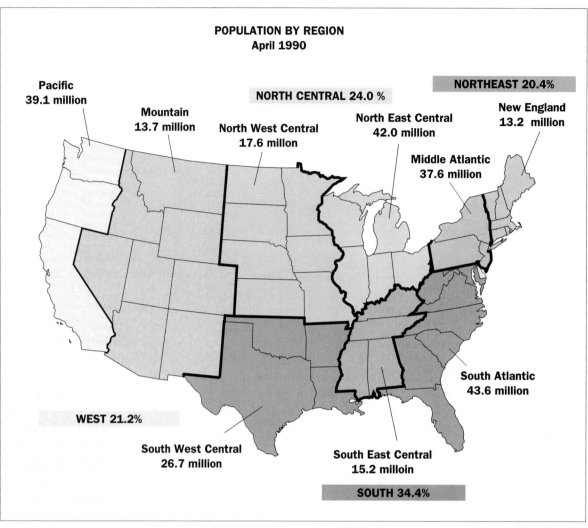

POPULATION BY REGION
April 1990

Pacific
39.1 million

Mountain
13.7 million

North West Central
17.6 millon

NORTH CENTRAL 24.0 %

North East Central
42.0 million

NORTHEAST 20.4%

New England
13.2 million

Middle Atlantic
37.6 million

WEST 21.2%

South West Central
26.7 million

South East Central
15.2 milloin

South Atlantic
43.6 million

SOUTH 34.4%

(Courtesy: Cahners Publishing Company.)

EXHIBIT

7.10

· · · · · · · · · · · · · · · · · · · ·

The South is the most heavily populated region, with 34.4% of the total U.S. population. The Northeast, with a population representing 20.4% of the total, is now the smallest.

· · · · · · · · · · · · · · · · · · · ·

Continuity

A TV or radio script. Also refers to the length of time given media schedule runs.

· · · · · · · · · · · · · · · · · · · ·

tween the least expensive media (efficiency) and those most able to communicate the message and reach the best prospects (effectiveness). Exhibit 7.11 shows the relationship among the three elements in some typical media strategies.

In reality, the media planner's primary considerations are reach and frequency. Normally, the budget is predetermined and the planner functions within fairly strict guidelines as to the continuity of the campaign. In other words, the media planner rarely has the option of reducing a year-long campaign to six months in order to fulfill reach or frequency goals.

Most media planners start with frequency as the first building block. A determination is made as to the minimum exposures required to make an impact on the prospect during some buying cycle. We might look at the reach/frequency question in terms of total exposures that can be purchased with our ad budget.

Let's say our budget will purchase 2 million exposures. These exposures can be bought in a number of ways as long as they total 2 million. However, each time we increase the number of exposures per prospect, we reduce the number of prospects we can reach:

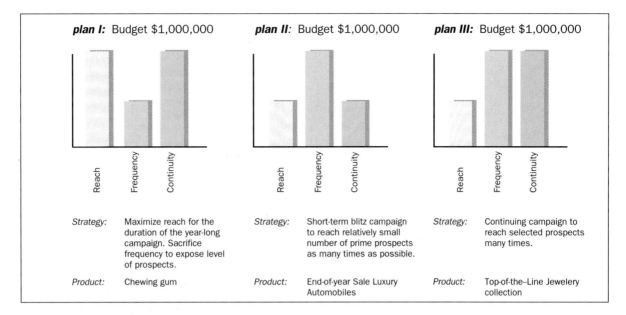

plan I: Budget $1,000,000	*plan II*: Budget $1,000,000	*plan III*: Budget $1,000,000
Strategy: Maximize reach for the duration of the year-long campaign. Sacrifice frequency to expose level of prospects.	*Strategy:* Short-term blitz campaign to reach relatively small number of prime prospects as many times as possible.	*Strategy:* Continuing campaign to reach selected prospects many times.
Product: Chewing gum	*Product:* End-of-year Sale Luxury Automobiles	*Product:* Top-of-the–Line Jewelery collection

EXHIBIT 7.11

. . . .

Reach, frequency, and continuity relationships with a fixed budget.

5 exposures × 400,000 prospects = 2,000,000

10 exposures × 200,000 prospects = 2,000,000

2 exposures × 1,000,000 prospects = 2,000,000

As you can see, if we decide to increase the number of exposures per prospect, we risk failing to reach other prospects at all. Yet we must be careful to break the communications barrier, or else our ad message will be totally ineffective.

The decision to emphasize reach or frequency in the communication strategy will most definitely influence the media tactics. Detailed below is a comparison of some general tactics of reach and frequency strategies.[14]

Reach Tactics	Frequency Tactics
Primetime television	Late night television
Large-circulation magazines	Specialty magazines
Commercial roadblocks	Limited networks/stations
Multiple networks/stations	Limited media elements
Multiple media elements	Cable television
Newspapers	Promotional sponsorships

. . . .

Effective reach

The percentage of an audience that is exposed to a certain number of messages or has achieved a specific level of awareness.

. . . .

In recent years, planners have been concerned with the effectiveness of advertising as contrasted to simply generating exposure figures. Increasingly, media planners are concerned with the "quality of exposure," that is, the degree to which the message is understood and remembered (sometimes referred to as *effective communication*). In order to measure communication versus exposures, media planners have adopted the term *effective* reach and *effective* frequency.

With modern computers it is relatively easy to estimate the effective reach and/or frequency for a particular schedule. However, it is much more difficult to determine at what point a media schedule has effectively communi-

---

[14]Allen Brivic, *What Every Account Executive Should Know About Media* (New York: American Association of Advertising Agencies, 1989), p. 14.

cated a message to a satisfactory number of prospects. Nevertheless, it is incumbent on the media planner to estimate the number of exposures needed to move a prospect toward a sale and at the same time not overspend by continuing to deliver exposures to a consumer who has already made a purchase decision. At one time, advertisers viewed three exposures as the optimum level for effective frequency. However, any rule of thumb is probably dangerous given the multitude of different marketing conditions that advertising must address. For example, movie advertising for a new release might require a frequency level of 24–36 in a 10-day period to accommodate the short "sales" period of movies.[15]

You will recall that in Chapter 2 we discussed the emerging concept of integrated marketing where all forms of marketing communications are developed in a systematic manner to complement each other. Many marketing executives view added frequency as a primary benefit of integrated marketing. "One of the most obvious benefits of integrated marketing is increased frequency. If you reach your target audience with advertising, direct marketing, public relations—with every form of communications available—you're increasing frequency. That softens the ground so when your promotion comes along, it can do its job."[16]

To this point we have considered reach and frequency from a very elementary, single-medium perspective. Of course, media schedules are not comprised of a single medium. Instead, large national advertisers may use dozens or even hundreds of discrete media vehicles in a campaign. The problem of reach must be dealt with on the basis of audience overlap and duplication. A concept called *random reach* is sometimes used to estimate the combined reach of two different media if the reach of each medium is known.[17]

Let's look at a simple example of the random reach estimation.

Assume that we have developed a media plan where the reach of our TV schedule is 70 percent and the reach of our newspaper schedule is 50 percent. Now we want to find the combined reach of both media by taking into account the duplicated audience between the two media.

$$\text{Random reach} = \text{TV reach} + \text{newp reach} - (\text{TV reach} \times \text{newp reach})$$
$$= .70 + .50 - (.70 \times .50)$$
$$= 1.20 - .35$$
$$\text{Random reach} = .85$$

If a third medium is added to the plan, we can apply the formula a second time, using the random reach (.85) for the combination of television and newspapers, and the third medium becomes medium two. For example, let's assume we add radio as a third medium with a reach of .20. The random reach is now .88. The random reach is calculated as follows:

$$\text{Random reach} = .85 + .20 - (.85 \times .20)$$
$$= 1.05 - .17$$
$$= .88$$

[15]Jack Myers, "More Is Indeed Better," *Mediaweek,* September 6, 1993, p. 18.
[16]Michael Wikes, "Ask the Experts," *Sales and Marketing Strategies & News,* July/August 1993, p. 62.
[17]*Guide to Media Research* (New York: American Association of Advertising Agencies, 1987), p. 25.

THE MEDIA SCHEDULE

Media schedule

The detailed plan or calendar showing when ads and commercials will be distributed and in what media vehicles they will appear.

The media schedule is the calendar or blueprint of the advertising plan. The schedule must offer in specific detail exactly what media will be bought, when they will be purchased, and how much time or space will be used for each advertisement or commercial. For example, if we decide to purchase *Sports Illustrated,* will we use four-color or black-and-white insertions? Will we place a full-page or half-page advertisement? Will we use the entire circulation of the publication or one of the numerous geographic editions offered? Which of the 52 issues will we buy?

Remember that we must make similar decisions for each of the media vehicles that we purchase. For a national advertiser, a media schedule might encompass dozens or even hundreds of stations, networks, magazines, and out-of-home opportunities. In addition, many of these buys must be negotiated and availabilities determined. As we will discuss in Chapter 8, just because you want to buy a spot on *Roseanne,* or *Home Improvement,* doesn't mean that they will be available. It is not unusual for a media buying group to spend several days on a single network buy.

The development of the media schedule and the media buys themselves must be done in terms of the overall advertising and marketing goals of the client. The experienced media planner will combine reach and frequency goals with the buying pattern most conducive to reaching the maximum prospects. It might be instructive to review some of the most used scheduling patterns.

Flighting

Flight

The length of time a broadcaster's campaign runs. Can be days, weeks, or months—but does not refer to a year. A flighting schedule alternates periods of activity with periods of inactivity.

One of the most used advertising scheduling techniques is flighting (also known as pulsing). Flighting consists of relatively short bursts of advertising followed by periods of total or relative inactivity. For example, Taster's Choice coffee runs a segment of its continuing drama and then backs off before another flight begins with the next segment. The idea is to build audience awareness for your product so that brand awareness carries over these periods of inactivity. Done correctly, the advertiser achieves the same brand awareness at a greatly reduced cost compared to a steady advertising schedule.

The concept is obviously appealing to advertisers who rarely think they have enough funds to reach all their prospects with a consistent advertising program. The problem facing the advertiser is that available research on flighting cannot precisely predict the awareness levels needed to achieve any particular flighting strategy. One thing is certain: The advertiser must guard against significant erosion of brand awareness during breaks between flights. Exhibit 7.12 demonstrates the ideal outcome of a properly executed flighting strategy compared to a steady schedule when both use the same advertising budget.

In the steady schedule, audience awareness peaks fairly quickly (after about 20 weeks) and afterward shows little if any increase. The flighting schedule grows much more slowly, but because of budget savings is able to reach more prospects and therefore actually achieve higher levels of brand awareness. As we cautioned earlier, an advertiser must be careful to consider the communication component of the media plan. Some media planners think that a flighting plan may sacrifice depth of communication even though minimal awareness may be achieved.

EXHIBIT

7.12

Steady versus flighting media schedules.

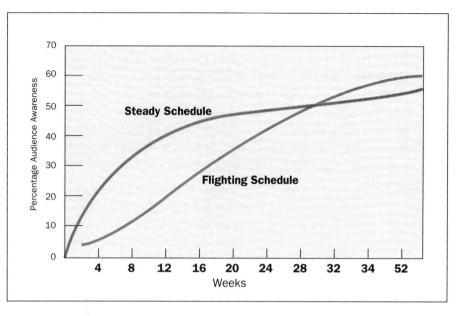

Regardless of the flighting schedule used, the following factors should be considered:

1. *Competitive spending.* How does your plan coincide with primary competition? Are you vulnerable to competition between flights?

2. *Timing of flights.* Does the schedule go contrary to any seasonal features found in the product-purchase cycle?

3. *Advertising decay.* Are you spending enough in peak periods to remain visible between flights?

4. *Secondary media.* Should secondary or trade media be used between flights to maintain minimal visibility?

THE PRESSURE OF COMPETITION

Advertising has never functioned in a more competitive environment. The media planner must not only develop an effective campaign for a product, but must do so in a way that distinguishes the product from others. Keeping a wary eye on the competition should not be construed as working from a defensive mentality or only reacting to what other advertisers are doing. It does mean that you should take a practical stance in determining what your marketing and advertising plan can reasonably accomplish.

One of the factors determining the level of awareness of your advertising is the degree with which consumers are satisfied with the alternative brands they are currently using. Remember, the consumers who are aware of your brand but who have never used it are probably satisfied with the product they are currently buying. Both the creative and media plans will have to work hard to give these consumers a reason to switch. In fact, we may have to recognize that some market segments cannot be captured regardless of the quality of our advertising. In such a case, brand switching would be an inappropriate strategy, and we instead might target another market segment with new advertising appeals, positioned products, or both.

Case History

BONITA BAY PROPERTIES
CREATIVE COMFORTS:
An Example of a Multimedia Schedule

MARKETING SITUATION

Bonita Bay is a 2,400-acre, upscale residential community located on Florida's west coast in Bonita Springs. It is a private residential country club community with residential options of single-family homes, homesites, condominiums, and villas in 24 neighborhoods. Home prices range from $130,000 to more than $1 million. Bonita Bay is primarily a second-home community with over 80 percent of its homes purchased as second homes.

Competition in the area includes seven communities with similar product, price, and style opportunities. All compete for the same affluent second-home buyer. While Bonita Bay's offering far exceeds its competitors' amenities, the development is priced competitively and is ranked fourth among the seven competitors in price.

Bonita Bay's communication positioning had been very lifestyle and amenity oriented. Its competitors used a similar positioning (lifestyle and amenity orientation) as well as

similar media. Bonita Bay's challenge was to break through the clutter to increase qualified traffic and sales.

Although Bonita Bay had enjoyed sales growth since 1988, its outlook for 1991 and 1992 was not as encouraging. By the fall of 1991, Bonita Bay was facing a 20 percent decrease in annual unit sales as well as a 20 percent decrease in sales revenue as compared to 1990. The Florida housing market was static and overcrowded. While Bonita Bay's target market was upscale, it appeared to be affected by the recessionary climate and decreased consumer confidence. It was at that time that Cole Henderson Drake was selected to redefine the personality and the creative message of the property.

CAMPAIGN OBJECTIVES

For the calendar year 1992, extremely high goals were set based on the enthusiasm and certainty that a better way to market Bonita Bay had been discovered (through the research):

1. Increase sales revenue by 60 percent to $58,760,000.
2. Increase units sold (combination of homesites, single-family homes, condos, and villas) by 31 percent to 208.
3. Based on the more tightly focused creative message, generate traffic that was much more qualified (as measured by the ratio between number of visitor registrations and sales revenue).

TARGET AUDIENCE

Consumers *Demographically:* Local: Adults age 45+; household income of $150,000+; married; current homeowners; active business professionals or retired; possibly family with children present in home; living in Naples, Ft. Myers, or Bonita Springs. Midwest or Northeast: adults age 45+; household income of $150,000+; married; current homeowners; active business professionals, retired or in the process of retiring.

Consumers *Psychographically:* Active, country club lifestyle important, as well as a planned community. Those purchasing a primary residence are possibly looking for a "move up" in residence.

CREATIVE STRATEGY

1. *Communicate that Bonita Bay provides a naturally beautiful setting in which to live.* Focus groups consisting of property owners were conducted to gain insight into the

LIVE WITH ALL
THE CREATURE COMFORTS
AT BONITA BAY.

psyche of the current Bonita Bay resident and to provide information to help conduct benefit testing with potential prospects. A key finding was that the decision to purchase was based on multiple influences and multiple benefits. These benefits were tested with two focus groups. As a result of this research, it was discovered that the groups rejected the amenity-rich advertising so prevalent with Bonita Bay's competition and instead voted for a more sensitive and unusual approach built around a need to protect what attracted each of them to Florida in the first place—the naturally beautiful environment and the resulting lifestyle that environment has enabled them to enjoy. Bonita Bay's environmental sensitivity and natural beauty evolved as the key "reason for being." This was consistent with consumer trends and implied superiority over the competition.

2. *Differentiate Bonita Bay from competitive communities that stress amenities.* As mentioned, the research found that Bonita Bay's environmental sensitivity and natural beauty is the strategic distinction versus the competition. This distinction was used to reposition Bonita Bay and was the focus of all communications.

MEDIA STRATEGY

A broad target audience dictated a mix of media, that is, newspaper, magazine, radio, television, and outdoor. The emphasis was on the local market because these prospects were predisposed to the benefits of the area due to the choice of location for vacationing, second home, or currently being a resident. A media mix was used heavily during first quarter, the "high season" in south Florida, when prospects were vacationing in the area (Bonita Bay is not registered to solicit real estate outside of Florida and therefore cannot advertise outside the state). A media mix was used to a lesser extent during the fourth quarter to reach the prospects arriving in the area for the holidays.

Newspaper comprised 47 percent of the media budget, as prospects rely on the real estate section when looking for property. Television totaled 21 percent of the budget in order to create high reach and frequency necessary to increase awareness.

OTHER MARKETING PROGRAMS

Bonita Bay developed a coordinated package of sales materials for prospects which provided specific information on the property while reinforcing the nature theme.

Direct Mail: The sales force utilized visitor registrations input into Bonita Bay's database to send follow-up letters and newsletters at regular intervals to its prospects. This kept the property "top of mind" with its prospects.

Direct Response: A toll-free 800 number was utilized in all communications to facilitate response.

Public Relations: An ongoing public relations program was utilized. An average of four press releases were issued each month resulting in an average of 29 articles/mentions per month.

Realtor Program: To encourage broker participation, a "Gold Key" program was developed for the realtors. It allowed them to register with the property and receive a membership card. Membership gives realtors access to the property as well as dining privileges for the realtor and his client.

EVIDENCE OF RESULTS

1. 1992 sales revenue increased by 90 percent to $69,927,325 (achieving 119 percent of their goal).
2. 1992 unit sales increased by 48 percent to 264 units (achieving 127 percent of their goal).
3. The traffic at Bonita Bay became much more qualified as evidenced by the 90 percent *increase* in sales revenue coupled with a 28.7 percent *decrease* in visitor registrations.

(Courtesy: Cole Henderson Drake, Inc.)

A competitive analysis also must consider the various media alternatives and how they are reacting to their own competitive situation. Earlier we discussed the importance of negotiation in the buying process. Competition among media, both inter- and intramedia, will determine in large measure how receptive they are to making price concessions to advertisers. As we mentioned earlier, magazines were forced to make deals with advertisers in the 1980s largely due to a weak economy and a large number of competing titles.

Media buyers must be aware of this competitive pressure on media in general and particularly among those media vehicles that are being considered for a specific schedule. The knowledgeable buyer can significantly stretch a limited budget by astute negotiation based on prevailing media competition.

The key point is that advertisers should undertake a thorough and candid appraisal of all aspects of the competitive situation. In doing so, a media buyer becomes an integral member of the campaign team.

THE BUDGET

If there is any advertising axiom, it is that no budget is ever large enough to accomplish the task. With the spiraling cost of media over the past several years, media planners view the budget with a growing sense of frustration. In addition, media planners are constantly caught between large media (especially the major TV networks) demanding higher and higher advertising rates and clients demanding more efficiency for their advertising dollars. Since the media budget is by far the largest segment of the advertising allocation, it is the media planner who is expected to make the greatest cost savings.

Advertisers and their agencies have reacted to this cost squeeze by instituting more stringent cost controls and accountability for their advertising dollars. In addition to these stricter controls on media costs, we will see advertisers looking for alternative methods of promotion and advertising in the future. Already, consumer sales promotion (sweepstakes, coupons, price-off sales, etc.) is taking a larger share of total promotional dollars. Advertisers also are using media such as cable and first-run syndicated programming to circumvent the high cost of network television. As the media continue to fragment, we will probably see even more experimentation with nontraditional media vehicles, many that did not exist only a few years ago.

If there is any encouraging sign for advertisers, it is that the increases in media costs of past years seem to have moderated. Instead of double-digit increases, media costs are being held to levels more in line with the overall Consumer Price Index. In response to these increases, advertisers are more specifically defining their prospects to cut down on waste circulation and are negotiating more aggressively with media salespeople. With the proliferation of media options and new technology, it is doubtful that we will see significant increases in advertising costs in the near future. However, the fragmentation of media and audiences is driving up the CPM levels to a point that it is costing more and more to reach selected target audiences.

THE CROSS-MEDIA CONCEPT

We cannot leave the topic of advertising media without mention of the concept of cross-media buying. The growth of huge media conglomerates spawned the appealing idea that advertisers should be rewarded for buying a number of media vehicles from the same organization. In other words, an advertiser who agrees to place advertising in magazines, TV stations, and cable outlets all owned by the same company would qualify for special discounts. In addition to financial savings, advertisers also would be able to place advertising in a number of media outlets with one insertion order and one bill.

Multimedia or cross-media opportunities within and outside companies, and between separate print broadcast and other media outlets, are now offered by a growing number of media suppliers. Concerned with the downturn in ad-

Synergistic effect

In media buying, combining a number of complementary media that create adverting awareness greater than the sum of each.

Consumer Price Index

Comparative index that charts what an urban family pays for a select group of goods including housing and transportation.

Cross-media buys

Several media or vehicles usually owned by a single company and sold as a package usually at a discounted price.

vertising spending, they have responded by joining forces. This is to the advantage of advertisers and marketers for whom these packages offer a greater range of options, thereby allowing the media buyer to develop more creative strategies aimed at maximizing overall marketing efficiency.[18]

An example of a major cross-media deal was the introduction of Nissan's Altima. Nissan agreed to budget $50 million to buy commercial time on the ABC TV network, the eight ABC-owned TV stations, three ABC radio networks, nine ABC-owned radio stations, and the Lifetime cable TV network. In return for the media buy, Nissan was given free promotion announcements on both television and radio stations and an unprecedented cast commercial by actors on the *Roseanne* series.[19]

Two of the earliest cross-media programs were Time Inc.'s Max Plan and Gannett Corporation's Gannettwork. The Max Plan offered corporate discounts to advertisers, increasing their share of advertising in Time Inc. publications including *People, Sports Illustrated,* and *Time.* Gannettwork was a more extensive program that included all Gannett-owned media, including TV and radio stations, outdoor, newspapers, as well as direct marketing.

The concept was appealing to both advertisers and media. As one Gannett executive summed up the plan, "Instead of shopping the media one by one, we offer advertisers a way to one-stop shop all of them and add ideas and solutions to help them achieve their marketing goals."[20]

Despite a number of large media companies jumping into the cross-media concept, the results have been mixed at best. In fact, Time has discontinued the Max Plan. For one thing, many agencies and clients see the idea as one that is to the advantage of the media more than the client. Clients regarded some cross-media plans as limiting their options. There was a temptation for a media buyer to buy such a plan even though some of the media vehicles in a cross-media package might not be ideal.

As one advertiser commented on the demise of Max Plan, "the Max Plan had become outdated in a market where negotiated ad rates are the norm and advertisers press for custom-designed marketing packages."[21] While we will continue to see various types of cross-media packages, media companies have learned that these will be successful only when they can deliver tightly targeted audiences that meet the product usage profiles of advertisers. Advertisers are not interested in engaging in a system that is perceived as largely a means of solving the media's advertising sales problems.

SUMMARY

The complexity and proliferation of new technology, target marketing techniques, and the sheer number of media options have fundamentally changed the advertising media function in recent years. With CPM levels continuing to climb, clients are demanding more and more expertise and accountability from media planners. Demands for advertising efficiency and cost controls

[18]"Multi-Media\Cross Media Opportunities," in *Marketers Guide to Media* (New York: *Adweek,* 1992), p. 89.
[19]Cleveland Horton and Joe Mandese, "Nissan Joins ABC to Roll Out Altima," *Advertising Age,* October 5, 1992, p. 3.
[20]Mary Hardie, "Cross-Media Concept Showing Results," *Gannetteer,* July–August 1992, p. 14.
[21]Scott Donaton, "Time Inc. Sinks Max Plan for Ad Discounts," *Advertising Age,* June 21, 1993, p. 10.

are increasingly the responsibility of media planners and buyers. With as much as 90 percent of the typical advertising budget allocated to the purchase of time and space, this pressure on media departments will only grow.

A number of factors in the media business have already occurred or are beginning to emerge in the 1990s that call for more intuitive and creative media planning than ever before. For example:

1. *The number of media outlets continue to grow, but non-traditional media activity is also accelerating sharply.* For example, videocassette advertising is becoming more popular, signage on ski slopes is available, and in-store advertising is increasing.

2. *The TV viewing audience is becoming more splintered, with cable and VCR penetration increasing.* Consumers don't watch less television, but they watch it differently. The dramatic drop in network shares during the past decade is but one example.

3. *Market segmentation is increasing with greater emphasis on regional and local media.*

4. *There is improved data-available, enabling the planner to better target prospects demographically, geographically, and, in some cases, psychographically.*

5. *Increasing dollars are being spent on promotion relative to advertising.* The lines between media planning, buying, and promotion are beginning to blur on a broad basis.[22]

> The effects of all of these changes on the roles of media planners and buyers are several. Clients' increased demands for the lowest media pricing available has elevated the buying function somewhat, with buyers becoming more involved in strategic decisions than before. Cost-cutting, however, is leading more and more media departments to bring print buying within the realm of the media planner or to centralize all buying operations at a single U.S. location. Meanwhile, the growth of cross-media deals and integrated marketing have increased the complexity and challenge of media planning. Some believe that the media function will have to be completely restructured.[23]

Accompanying the increasing complexity of the media function will be a greater financial risk to the advertiser. Agencies will be asked to justify their media plans in more detail than ever before. In the following chapters, we will examine each of the media available to the media planner as well as some promotional techniques associated with advertising. As you will see, the nature of the media function will require a media planner who is well versed in quantitative skills, marketing strategy, and, of course, all aspects of advertising.

---

[22]Jay B. Schoenfeld, "Beyond the Numbers," *Journal of Media Planning,* Spring 1991, p. 25.
[23]Helen Katz and Peter B. Turk, "The Winds of Change: The Outlook for Media in the 1990s and Beyond," *Journal of Media Planning,* Spring 1992, p. 48.

Questions

1. Why has the media function become more important in recent years?
2. In what significant ways has the responsibility of media planners changed during the past decade?
3. What is meant by the fragmented audience?
4. What is meant by the term *road blocking?*
5. Many large agencies are "unbundling" their services. Explain.
6. Why is direct response growing at its current rate?
7. What is the starting point for a successful media plan?
8. What is meant by place-based media?
9. What is meant by media synergism?
10. What is meant by *effective* frequency?
11. What is cross-media buying?

Using
Television

CHAPTER OBJECTIVES

Television is the leading advertising medium among national advertisers. In recent years, it has become a tremendously diversified vehicle. After reading this chapter you will understand:

- **High exposure levels of various population segments**
- **Television rating services**
- **Various segments of the television industry**
- **The importance of cable and syndication to advertisers**
- **The VCR and television viewing**

Despite being a significant part of the everyday lives of millions of Americans, television is very much in transition. Technology has overwhelmed its ability to provide programming for the hundreds of hours available each week, and the fragmentation of the audience has resulted in unprofitable ratings levels for many outlets. **In many respects,** television is moving from a mass medium to a niche medium with characteristics common to radio and magazines.

Since in 1960 the
T.V. has becomes part of a family

The level of network dominance enjoyed in its early years is now part of TV history. The viewer, through VCRs and multiple program alternatives, is increasingly taking control of the medium. There are opportunities for specialized programming that would have no chance of airing on one of the big three networks. The inevitable introduction of two-way TV communication will speed up the process of viewer control dramatically.

Marketing to both advertisers and viewers will become more of a consideration in the TV industry. Television will follow the lead of newspapers and radio in showing advertisers how the medium can function as part of a unified media mix. TV marketing will also reach out to local and regional advertisers to compete with other local media for additional advertising dollars. Predictions are that television will emerge from the current turmoil as an even stronger force in advertising. It will have a broader base of different advertisers, and the fragmented audience offers advertisers tremendous opportunities to reach narrowly defined prospects.

TELEVISION AS AN ADVERTISING MEDIUM
Advantages

The primary advantage of television as an advertising medium is that it reaches virtually *everyone.* With 98 percent of American households having a TV set and 33 percent owning three or more sets, television is both a mass and, increasingly, a segmented medium. Despite recent declines, average audience levels among network affiliates is still over 70 percent of total viewers. On the other hand, specialty cable networks, local independent stations, and cable system outlets provide advertisers with specialized alternatives that appeal to a variety of viewers. Exhibit 8.1 shows the diversity of broadcast vehicles and the audience watching each one.

With the average household viewing time approaching seven hours a day, television is a medium that few advertisers can fail to use. From General Motors, Procter & Gamble, and Philip Morris with their million-dollar-a-day TV advertising budgets to a local restaurant spending a few dollars a week on the local cable outlet, television is a valuable marketing tool for selling virtually any product or service.

In addition to its high household penetration, television offers a creative flexibility not found in any other medium. With its combination of sight, sound, color, and motion, television is equally adept at communicating humorous, serious, realistic, or tongue-in-cheek commercials. Television is a 24-hour medium to reach viewers of every lifestyle, from housewives to third-shift workers. Television also offers a number of advertising formats from the 15-second announcement to the 30-minute program-length commercial.

In addition to the quantitative features of television, such as ratings, it also provides qualitative advantages to advertisers. For example, research shows that most people think their most credible source of information comes from TV news. From an advertising perspective, surveys indicate that television has the most positive image of all media. A study by Bruskin Associates indicated that television compared to other media is:

- **Most authoritative**
- **Most influential**[1]
- **Most exciting**

EXHIBIT 8.1

Television is close to a universal medium in American households.

GENERAL TRENDS
Growth in TV Ownership

Nielsen has been measuring television since 1950. but the '90s have brought a whole new era to the television industry. The aveage American television household has the capability to access more than 30 channels. Cable penetration topped 60 percent, 77% of all homes own a VCR and over 85% have remote control capabilities.

31%
1 TV Set

36%
2 TV Sets

33%
3+ TV Sets

33% of TV households in 1993 own three or more sets.

Growth in TV ownership

% of Total Households:	1950	1960	1970	1980	1990	1993
TV Households	10	87	96	98	98	98
Multi-Set		12	35	50	65	69
1 set			65	49	35	31
2 sets			29	36	41	36
3+ sets			6	15	24	33
Cable						
- Total Cable			7	20	56	61
- Basic					27	33
- Pay					29	28
VCR					66	77
Remote Control					77	87

Remote control ownership in 1993 reached 87%

(Courtesy: Media Nielsen Research.)

---

[1]"Media Comparisons," a report of the Television Bureau of Advertising, p. 10.

It is obvious from this research that advertisers gain a qualitative edge with their association with the medium. The general credibility of television, combined with the increasing specialization of programming formats, will provide advertisers with an excellent environment to reach viewers with narrowly targeted messages.

While television will face a number of challenges in the coming years, there is no question that it will remain the major advertising medium for national advertising and provide significant competition for newspapers and other media for local advertising dollars.

Limitations

Cost. In the past several years, TV rate increases have moderated compared to the double-digit spiral of the 1980s. However, television remains an expensive medium. TV costs must be considered from three perspectives:

1. *Network television advertising.* Network audiences continue to decline slightly after a decade of significant slippage. However, network advertising still delivers a huge audience, especially for top-rated shows. Network television is a medium for heavy hitters. Fewer than 700 companies use network television, and the top 10 network advertisers account for almost one-third of all network billings. Unless an advertiser is willing to invest millions of dollars, network advertising is probably not a viable option.

2. *Local and cable advertising.* The proliferation of nonnetwork options has made television a practical alternative for many advertisers formerly shut out of the medium. However, many (most) of these options draw very small audiences. On a CPM basis, advertisers using independent stations, local cable outlets, and many cable networks are paying a premium for the viewers they reach. In some cases, audience selectivity partially offsets this high CPM. In other cases, advertisers simply are lured by the glamour of television without realistically figuring its cost.

3. *Production costs.* The total cost of TV advertising must consider both time and production expenses. High-quality TV commercials routinely cost from $100,000 to as much as $300,000 for a 30-second message. Costs of local commercials are much less, but they often suffer from unfavorable viewer comparisons with network quality spots.

Clutter. Clutter is defined as any nonprogram material carried during or between shows. Commercials account for approximately 80 percent of this material, with the other time devoted to public service announcements and program promotional spots. Prime-time network television has the lowest clutter with other dayparts showing significantly higher levels. Local station clutter is higher still. In recent years, the four networks have averaged 13 minutes of nonprogram material per hour during prime time, with almost 10 minutes devoted to commercials. The Fox Network leads all networks in nonprogram material.

Daytime is the culprit when it comes to clutter. Over 18 minutes (33 percent) of the daytime network schedule is filled with nonprogram material. Early morning and late night have approximately 16 minutes of clutter.[2] Lo-

Cable television

TV signals that are carried to households by cable. Programs originate with cable operators through high antennas, satellite disks, or operator-initiated programming.

Fragmentation

In advertising a term that refers to the increasing selectivity of media vehicles and the segmenting of the audience that results.

Clutter

Refers to a proliferation of commercials (in a medium) that reduces the impact of any single message.

---

[2]Jeff Jensen, "Prime-Time Clutter Falls Slightly," *Advertising Age,* March 8, 1993, p. 33.

cal stations routinely have over 20 minutes of clutter, especially during late night.

As expected, studies show that clutter is an annoyance to viewers. More importantly, advertisers are concerned that the effectiveness of their messages are diluted by too much nonprogram material and too many commercials within a short viewing period. Advertisers are torn by conflicting research on the effects of commercial clutter. On the one hand, studies indicate that a 30-second commercial is 72 percent as effective as a 60-second message, and a 15-second spot is 52 percent as effective as a 60.[3] These data and accompanying cost constraints have moved advertisers to adopt the 30-second commercial as the standard unit as opposed to the 60-second message, which was prevalent prior to the 1970s.

Yet other research indicates that increased commercials result in overall negative attitudes toward TV advertising.[4] Reinforcing this finding was another study that indicated that despite a steady bombardment of advertising messages, 67 percent of adults reported that they could not remember *one* advertisement from the past 24 hours.[5] The study further indicated that clutter might be a primary contributing factor to the indifference of the public to all advertising messages. Clutter, caused by the continuing demand for high-rated time periods, is a dilemma that has no short-term solution.

Marketing TV Advertising

Prior to the proliferation of cable networks, superstations, independent stations, and local cable access, TV salespeople did not sell time; they simply took orders. However, the competition for advertising dollars and advertisers' concerns with rising costs of commercial time have ushered in a environment that requires television to be marketed to advertisers. In addition, each category of television is sold almost like a separate medium. For example, there are separate associations that represent cable, network, and local television to advertisers.

One of the most significant effects of this new competitive environment is the way that television is sold in concert with other media. In the Simmons Beautyrest case, note how the advertising theme used the TV commercial as the focus of its print promotion to provide an integrated campaign for Beautyrest.. In recent years, the TV industry increasingly has adopted a more realistic approach to selling the medium by encouraging a complementary approach to all media. The Television Advertising Bureau (TvB) was a leader in adopting a synergistic approach to advertising.

As the audience of all media become increasingly fragmented, advertisers have come to realize that no single medium will reach all the potential prospects and buyers of their products. Some consumers are heavy users of televison, while other may read magazines as their primary "window on the world." Still other media are directed toward certain ethnic, age, or vocational segments. Farm radio, Spanish-language newspapers, and Saturday morning TV

---

[3] *TV Dimensions* study reported in "TV Commercial Length," publication of the Television Advertising Bureau.

[4] Sang Hoon Kim, "The Effectiveness of 15-Second TV Commercials: An Experimental Study," in *Proceedings of the 1990 Conference of the American Academy of Advertising*, p. RC-9, 1990.

[5] Adrienne Ward Fawcett, "Even Ad Pros Hate Ad Clutter," *Advertising Age*, February 8, 1993, p. 33.

cartoons all have their place in the media plans of many advertisers. No longer do advertisers seek the *best* medium; rather the search is for the combination of media that most efficiently reaches prime prospects.

As a result of the advent of target marketing, television is being promoted in terms of "media synergism." Basically, synergism promotes the use of a variety of media that work together to accomplish more than each can do alone. The TvB offers the following example of synergism:

> It is very difficult for a prospective customer to make a decision about which Yellow Pages advertiser to use among the page after page of businesses with whom the prospective customer has no previous knowledge. But if that customer has seen the Yellow Pages advertisers on television, the customer will choose that company with which he or she is most familiar.

As advertisers become more sophisticated in the use of media, we will see more reasonable approaches to the selling of time and space. It is rare that a single medium can effectively reach all the prospects of any company or brand. The marketing of television will continue to reflect this reality in the future.

THE RATING-POINT SYSTEM

Rating point (TV)

(1) The percentage of TV households in a market a TV station reaches with a program. The percentage varies with the time of day. A station may have a 10 rating between 6:00 and 6:30 P.M., and a 20 rating between 9:00 and 9:30.

TV advertisers evaluate the medium according to the delivery of certain target audiences. In the case of networks and large affiliates, advertisers tend to look for exposure to fairly broad audience segments such as women aged 18 to 49. Cable networks and some independent stations are evaluated by their ability to deliver more narrowly defined audiences that are both smaller in size and more expensive to reach on a CPM basis but have less waste circulation.

The basic measure of television is the rating. The rating, expressed as a percentage of some population (usually TV households), gives the advertiser a measure of coverage based on the potential of the market. The rating is usually calculated as follows:

$$\text{Rating} = \text{program audience/total TV households}$$

When ratings are expressed as percentages of individuals, the same formula is used, but the population is some target segment rather than households. For example, if we are interested only in 18- to 34-year-old males, the formula would be:

$$\text{Rating} = \text{18--34 males viewing program/total 18--34 males in population}$$

A household rating of 12 for a program means that 12 percent of all households in a particular area tuned their sets in to that station. Prime-time network programs usually achieve a rating of between 9 and 25, with the average being around 15.

As we discuss later in this chapter, TV advertising is rarely bought on a program-by-program basis. Instead, advertisers schedule a package of spots that are placed in a number of programs and dayparts. The weight of a schedule is measured in terms of the total ratings for all commercial spots bought (the gross rating points, or GRPs).

Let's look at a typical TV buy:

Vehicle	Rating	Cost	Spots	GRPs
All My Children	8.6	$15,950	25	215.0
General Hospital	8.7	15,950	25	217.5
Guiding Light	7.4	15,950	19	140.6
One Life to Live	7.4	15,950	14	103.6
Total GRPs				676.7

Reach = 99.9.
Frequency = 6.77.

Gross rating points (GRP)

Each rating point represents 1 percent of the universe being measured for the market. In TV it is 1 percent of the households having TV sets in that area.

GRPs were calculated by multiplying the insertions times the rating. In the case of *All My Children,* the rating was 8.6 × 25 (the number of insertions) = 215 GRPs.

Advertisers also use GRPs as the basis for examining the relationship between reach and frequency. These relationships can be expressed mathematically:

$$R \times F = GRP$$
$$\frac{GRP}{R} = F \text{ and } \frac{GRP}{F} = R$$

where R = reach and F = frequency.

To use these relationships, you must know (or be able to estimate) the unduplicated audience. In the TV schedule in Exhibit 8.2, we estimate that we have reached virtually the entire target market (reach = 99.9 percent) and that the average number of times we reached each person in the audience was 6.77. We can check the formulas using the solutions previously calculated:

$$R \times F = GRP \text{ or } 99.9 \times 6.77 = 676$$
$$\frac{GRP}{R} = R \text{ or } \frac{676}{6.77} = 99.9$$
$$\frac{GRP}{R} = F \text{ or } \frac{676}{99.9} = 6.77$$

One of the principal merits of the GRP system is that it provides a common base that proportionately accommodates markets of all sizes. One GRP in New York has exactly the same relative weight as one GRP in Salt Lake City. GRPs cannot be compared from one market to another unless the markets are of identical size. However, the cost of TV commercial time varies by city size. Here is an idea of the use of GRPs in two markets. Los Angeles and Boston:

TV Homes	TV Homes (THOUSANDS)	Avg. Cost per Spot	Avg. Prime Time Rating
Los Angeles	4,241	$2,800	18
Boston	1,930	2,200	18

The advertiser has to decide how much weight (how many GRPs) to place in his or her markets and for how long a period. This is a matter of experience and of watching what the competition is doing. Suppose the advertiser selects 100 to 150 per week as the GRP figure (considered a good working base). Within this figure, the advertiser has great discretion in each market.

Case History

MARKETING SITUATION

Four manufacturers account for over 60 percent wholesale share of market. Simmons is number 2. Industry sales have been relatively flat and very much in the commodity phase. There's no significant industry product variation except for the Simmons Beautyrest pocketed coil technology.

Bedding dealers have not supported "institutional" brand TV advertising via funds from their co-op accounts because they haven't seen manufacturers' brand spots (or campaigns) as being effective for their needs. As a result, manufacturers (including Simmons) have ended up paying 100 percent of the cost to run dealer-tagged versions of their brand TV.

Opportunity: By replacing the costly 100 percent reimbursement rate with a 50 percent dealer/50 percent Simmons co-op ratio, significant dollars could be freed up to increase the Simmons brand budget. This kind of funding increase could go a long way in helping build unit and dollar sales.

To make this happen would require the creation of a dramatically different brand advertising campaign. It would have to excite dealers enough to get them to run the dealer-tagged version of brand TV at the 50/50 ratio.

CAMPAIGN OBJECTIVES

1. Increase unit sales of Beautyrest mattresses (including box springs) by +10 percent for 1992 versus 1991.
2. Attain this unit increase by getting existing and new Beautyrest dealers involved with the new campaign and financially supporting the dealer version of the new brand TV spot.

    Shift the burden from Simmons funding of dealer-tagged, brand TV at a 100 percent level to funding from dealers' co-op accounts at a 50/50 ratio.
3. Achieve a significant level of dealer participation at the 50/50 funding ratio. The goal was set at 66 percent of dealers who tagged and aired brand TV spots in 1991 when Simmons had paid 100 percent of all associated costs.

    Generate a brand advertising budget increase for 1993 at +300 percent versus the 1992 budget level.

TARGET AUDIENCE

Consumers: Adults age 25–54 female skew at 60 percent, HHI +30.0M

Dealers: Management/owners, buyers, sales managers, and retail floor reps of sleep shops, department stores, mass merchandisers, and furniture stores
Geography: National

CREATIVE STRATEGY

Positioning: Beautyrest provides a whole new level of comfort and support over any other mattress.

Benefit: Beautyrest supports you better so you sleep better and thus, you feel and perform better.

Support: Beautyrest's totally unique construction technology utilizes independent pocketed coils that support every inch of your body like no other mattress can.

The campaign focused on the shared experience of a problem—tired at day's end—to a solution—energized by a Beautyrest for the next day, thus, "Nothing makes your day like a Beautyrest night."

"Energize" was sold in to dealers under the banner of "How to Energize Your Sales." While Simmons had its own

DEALER IMPRINT

(Courtesy: Pllack Levitt Chalet Advertising-Simmons.)

set of pure brand materials, dealers received versions that could be customized for retail use but still supported the brand story.

Television was the primary vehicle of Simmons and dealer choice. Dealers received a spot with :07 for tagging versus the traditional :03 or :04 tag areas.

MEDIA STRATEGY

Direct-mail video invitations encouraged dealers to see the new campaign at trade shows.

The campaign was introduced via network television around the 1992 Winter Olympics to tighten dealer awareness, excitement, and interest.

A fighting approach was employed, two weeks on/off/on/etc., to reach the infrequent bedding customer who's in the market once, for only two to three weeks, every 10.8 years.

Postcards detailing media programming were sent regularly to select dealers for their tie-in benefit.

Direct mail, circulars, newspaper, and TV were scheduled Thursday–Sunday prior to and during key shopping days. Brand TV ran during sleep-related dayparts (AM/PM news, late prime, late night).

Coordinated with public relations agency to appeal to trade, relevant consumer print and broadcast editorial opportunities.

OTHER MARKETING PROGRAMS

1. Campaign-themed collateral—circulars, direct mail, statement stuffers, ad slicks, consumer brochures, corner streamers, tent cards, postcards, hang tags, billboards, mobiles, posters, display systems, radio scripts.
2. Strategic marketing assistance incentives—offered at trade shows for new account sign-ups.
3. Key dealer seminars—targeted large influential dealers for initial sell-in. Smaller dealers would emulate them to avoid a competitive disadvantage.

4. "Energize Your Life" national consumer sales events/promotions.
5. Public relations trade and consumer programs.

EVIDENCE OF RESULTS

The campaign objectives have been achieved with outstanding results:

1. Beautyrest 1992 units increased +14 percent (vs. the +10 percent objective) while industry units increased only +4.9 percent.
2. The shift in dealer reimbursement from a 100 percent to a 50/50 ratio was achieved with exceptional success. Over 72 percent of 1991 participating TV dealers (vs. objective of 66 percent) funded "Energize" TV from their co-op accounts a 50/50 ratio.
3. Over 5 percent of these dealers supported "Energize" TV above and beyond co-op allowances by paying for incremental flights at 100 percent dealer expense.
4. The successful co-op shift allowed Simmons to free up additional brand TV dollars for 1993, increasing its brand budget by +931 percent.
5. Contributing to sales results, Simmons new-dealer account sign-ups increased +210 percent in 1992 versus 1991.
6. Simmons and the Beautyrest brand received more free trade and consumer press in 1992 than in the previous two years combined. Clippings from the trade press focused on Simmons' aggressiveness in generating dealer enthusiasm, participation, and sales results from the new campaign.
7. The TV spot was acclaimed by dealers and the trade press.

Sources: Simmons Company, Ketchum Public Relations, and International Sleep Products Association

(Courtesy: Pollak Levitt Chaiet Advertising, Inc.)

How shall the time be allocated: Put it all on one station? Divide it among all the stations? Use what yardstick to decide? The answers depend on whether the goal is reach or frequency.

Look again at the hypothetical pricing structure in the above table.

If we buy three prime-time spots in these markets, we would expect to receive 54 GRPs (3 spots × 18 average rating). However, it would be a serious mistake to equate a 54 GRP buy in Los Angeles with the same level in Boston. In Los Angeles, 54 GRPs would deliver 2,290,140 household impressions (0.54 × 4,241,000 HH, or households) at a cost of $8,400 (3 spots × 2,800 per spot). On the other hand, a 54 GRP buy in Boston would deliver

1,042,200 households impressions at a cost of $6,600. In order to estimate buys, advertisers often use the cost per rating point (CPP) calculation:

$$CPP = \frac{\text{cost of schedule}}{GRPs}$$

In this case:

Boston: $CPP = \dfrac{\$6,600}{54} = \$122.22$

Los Angeles: $CPP = \dfrac{\$8,400}{54} = \$155.55$

If we make the mistake of comparing GRPs from markets of different sizes, it would appear that a rating point costs 27 percent more in Los Angeles than in Boston. However, a rating point represents 42,410 households (1 percent of 4,241,000) in Los Angeles versus only 19,300 in Boston. The advertiser is actually getting 219 percent more households for 27 percent higher cost in Los Angeles. So Boston is hardly a bargain.

In addition to the problem of intermarket comparisons, the GRP has other limitations. It does not tell us the number of *prospects* for the product who are being reached by a program. Still, the GRP concept does provide a unified dimension for making scheduling judgments.

It must also be remembered that GRPs alone cannot tell how effectively a broadcast schedule is performing. If an advertiser's target audience is women aged 18 to 49, for example, 5 GRPs will often deliver more women in that group than 10 GRPs will. This, as you would expect, is a function of where the GRPs are scheduled. Five GRPs during a Sunday night movie will almost always deliver many times more women aged18–49 than will 10 GRPs scheduled on a Saturday morning.

Depending on the scheduling of commercials and the advertising objectives of the advertiser, television can deliver high levels of either reach or frequency. As we saw earlier, it is possible to achieve the same GRP with markedly different levels of reach and frequency. According to the TvB, the level of reach and/or frequency used by an advertiser depends on a number of factors:

- **A new product will normally require relatively high television frequency to build awareness.**

- **Likewise, a new campaign for an existing product, will normally emphasize frequency at the outset, and then move into a "reminder" mode as the campaign becomes established.**

- **High brand loyalty normally allows an advertiser to have lower frequency while increasing reach to bring in new customers.**

- **Products facing stiff competition or high levels of competing advertising will use higher levels of frequency.**

SHARE OF AUDIENCE

Although the rating is the basic audience-measurement statistic for TV, another measure, the *share of audience* (or simply, *share*), is often used to determine the success of a show. The share is defined as the percentage of households using television that are watching a particular show. It is used by advertisers to determine how a show is doing against its direct competition.

Let's assume that the *Today Show* has 5,000 households watching it in a market with 50,000 households. In this case we know that the rating for the *Today Show* would be 10.

$$\text{Rating} = \frac{\textit{Today} \text{ viewers}}{\text{total TV households}} \times 100 = \frac{5,000}{50,000} \times 100 = 10$$

The share calculates the percentage of households using television (HUT) that are tuned to the program. Let's assume that of the 50,000 households, 25,000 are watching television. In this case, the share for the *Today Show* would be 20:

$$\text{Share} = \frac{\textit{Today} \text{ viewers}}{\text{HUT}} \times 100 = \frac{5,000}{25,000} \times 100 = 20$$

It is understood that both the ratings and share of audience are expressed as percentages (hence the factor of 100 in the equations). Therefore, we do not use decimal points to refer to the measures in the example as "10 percent" and "20 percent." Instead, we say that the rating is 10 and the share is 20.

THE MANY FACES OF TELEVISION

As we noted earlier, television is not a homogeneous medium. It serves vastly different advertisers, reaches a variety of audiences, and accomplishes a diversity of promotional objectives. The various segments of the television industry use different technology and terminology, have different buying patterns, and, in some cases, feature different advertising executions. The one constant in all forms of television is that in recent years it has begun to appeal to more defined audience segments, and this targeting of both programming and advertising will become more apparent in the future. Already, television is exhibiting the characteristics of an individual-user medium with the majority of viewers being alone during most dayparts. The concept of buying TV households is quickly being replaced by demographic buys where the quality of the audience is as important as its size.

To some users, television is a constant companion, to others it is an occasional diversion or only a source of news, and to many it is basically a conduit for their favorite video game. In this section, we will examine the many aspects of this extremely complex medium that occupies so much of our time and advertisers' dollars.

Network Television

Network

(1) Interconnecting stations for the simultaneous transmission of TV or radio broadcasts. (2) Any group of media sold as a single unit.

In a simpler time, a *TV network* was defined as two or more stations broadcasting a program originating from a single source. Currently, the Federal Communications Commission defines a network as a program service with 15 or more hours of prime-time programming. Clearly, the changing face of television has muddied the definition of a network.

One executive defined a TV network as "a group of TV outlets of any description (cable, broadcast) that run the same programs at the same time." The problem with this definition is that many shows such as *Nightline* and *Latenight with David Letterman* are delayed at different times. A more contemporary definition by another executive is "a group of broadcast stations in most of the country that carry the same program—not necessarily at the same time." Under this definition, what is *NYPD Blue* which is carried on 50 non-ABC affiliates in markets where the ABC station refused to carry the show?[6]

In the case of cable networks, which we will discuss in a later section, this definition has to be altered slightly, since they do not broadcast in the strictest sense of the word. In addition, there are a number of regional or special-event networks that exist only to broadcast a particular program. These networks exist for only one program they are sometimes referred to as *ad hoc networks*. Virtually every Saturday in the fall and winter a number of football and basketball games will be shown over a select group of stations. In addition, minor bowl games are broadcast over ad hoc networks.

Another example of a special network is the annual Jerry Lewis telethon for muscular dystrophy. The telethon network is made up of both network affiliates and independent stations that sign up as part of this special network and don't come together again until the next Labor Day. At the end of the broadcast their "affiliation" comes to an end.

Despite the problem coming up with a universally agreed upon definition of a network, to most viewers a network is one of the big three: CBS, NBC, and ABC. Since 1986, these three have been joined by the upstart Fox network. Given little chance for survival when it was launched, Fox has combined irreverent, youth-oriented programming with aggressive marketing to become a major player in network television. If there was any doubt that Fox is a significant factor in network television, the appropriation of NFL football in 1994, which had been broadcast by CBS, removed any questions. In fact, largely based on its success in acquiring rights to pro football, a number of major network affiliates have switched to Fox. CBS was particularly hard hit, losing a number of large market affiliates to Fox.

The success of Fox has moved other companies such as Paramount to explore the possibilities of yet other networks. However, many of these "networks" will provide limited programming and limited national coverage compared to existing networks. Many observers see these arrangements as intended more to control syndicated programming such as Paramount's *Star Trek* series than serious attempts to establish traditional networks.

The problems of the networks have been well documented in recent years. However, their critics have in many cases overstated their difficulties. Networks expect to maintain a combined 60 share and moderate rate increases of 5 to 7 percent during the next several years. However, for advertisers, a relatively flat ratings picture and higher rates have resulted in substantial increases in CPMs during the past two decades. According to Television Bureau of Advertising figures, CPM household costs rose from $1.98 in 1965 to $8.37 in 1993, an increase of 423 percent.

A major factor working to the advantage of network television is the maturing of cable. For a number of years, cable has gained both audiences and advertisers on the basis of its novelty appeal. However, after more than a decade,

---

[6]Tim Duncan, "What Exactly Is a Network Today?" *Advertising Age,* February 14, 1993, p. 22.

viewers are demanding programming that at least approaches network quality. Continuous reruns of off-network shows and old movies will no longer satisfy cable viewers, and networks are taking advantage of the growing dissatisfaction with cable alternatives.

Howard Stringer, ex-president of CBS/Broadcast Group, summed up his network's response to the growing diversity of TV programming:

> Those maestros of the monopoly, the cable operators and their high priests of hardware, promise the viewer's moving finger a positive plethora of programming, an Aladdin's cave of interactive pleasure. But, consider the following surprising observations. A noted psychologist, George A. Miller, conducted a series of famous experiments in the 1950s. In these experiments he demonstrated that when we are confronted with a large number of options, we tend to reduce those options to the number that we can deal with effectively. He found that number to be "seven, plus or minus two." Today the average television viewer has 35 channels to choose from. Guess how many of those channels the average viewer watches with any degree of regularity. Yes, the number is seven. And it was seven back in 1985 when the selection was limited to 25 channels.[7]

Clearly, predictions of the demise of the major networks is premature. They continue to set the television standard for news, entertainment, and advertising. As one television executive observed, "Find one independent station that would not trade places with a network affiliate in that market and I'll talk to you about the demise of the networks."

Organization of the Networks

....

Compensation

The payment of clearance fees by a TV network to local stations carrying its shows.

....

The networks are essentially brokers between program suppliers (mainly, major studios and independent producers) and local stations. The networks contract with program supplies to provide programs, which they then offer to local station affiliates. The networks sell advertising to offset their costs of buying shows and pay a fee (called *compensation*) to local stations to carry their programming.

Each of the networks has approximately 220 affiliates. When a station carries a network program this is called *clearance* because the local station clears the time for network programming. It is extremely important for a network to have as high a clearance rate as possible to offer advertisers total national coverage. Most network programs have 95–100 percent clearance. Shows that fail to achieve clearances in the high 90s are probably headed for cancellation.

A major battle is currently being fought over compensation. During the past decade, the networks have cut back significantly on the fees that they pay their affiliates. Network executives have even suggested that compensation be eliminated in the largest markets. Faced with the danger of lower compensation, local stations have retaliated with their own threat to refuse to clear the weaker shows in a network's schedule or consider affiliation with another network. Compensation is a continuing source of tension between the networks and their affiliates. Given the addition of the Fox network and the potential

---

[7]Howard Stringer, "Television Looks at Its Future," address to CBS affiliates, May 26, 1993.

of new ones coming on the scene, there is every reason to believe local stations may gain greater leverage in the future with networks over the issue of compensation.

Buying Network Time. As we have seen, network television advertising is concentrated among a relatively few advertisers and advertising agencies. These advertisers spend millions of dollars, and the rules of the game are well defined between networks sales departments and agency media buyers. These rules of network buying center on three basic elements:

1. *Negotiation.* Unlike most other media, there are no rate cards for network TV advertising. Instead, agencies determine what level of cost per rating point they will pay, and networks arrive at the bargaining table with some gross dollar figure in mind for their upcoming schedule. Each knows that there will be some give and take, and generally these experienced negotiators know the parameters within which the final deal will be made. However, a difference of a few dollars per rating point has great significance when an agency is buying hundreds of commercials.

2. *Scatter plans.* While most viewers assume that advertisers sponsor particular shows, this is rarely the case. Instead, the networks offer an inventory of programs broken out by predicted household ratings and, more importantly, by ratings against some demographic audience segment. Advertisers are equally concerned with overall ratings as the ability of shows to reach the prospects for their products.

In the early days of television, advertisers not only sole-sponsored shows, but often produced them and bought time from the networks for the total program package. With the rising costs of television, advertisers found that sole sponsorship drastically reduced the number of shows (and audience reach) in which they could advertise. Therefore, they gave back the programming function to the networks a long time ago and now buy commercials across a number of programs, which increases their flexibility in achieving both reach and frequency.

Agencies want to place their clients' commercials in the most popular shows that conform to predetermined demographic profiles. The more advertiser demand for these spots, the tougher the negotiating stance of the networks. For example, beer and automotive companies prefer to buy commercials on football and other sports programs. Consequently, *Monday Night Football* commands a higher commercial cost than its ratings would otherwise indicate.

3. *Availabilities.* The final piece in the network advertising buying puzzle is availability of time (called *avails*). Commercial time is limited, especially on highly rated shows or those with high-demand audience niches. One of the major negotiating tasks of the networks is to spread out the choice spots in the scatter plans of their largest and most important advertisers. The problem is that there are more potential advertisers than there are premium spots. Therefore, we should not assume that just because a particular advertiser wants to buy a spot on *Roseanne* that it will be available.

In addition, the availability of such a show to an advertiser will depend as much on the company's total advertising investment on that network as the price it is willing to pay. Scatter plans allow the networks to negotiate

---

Scatter plan (TV)

The use of announcements, over a variety of network programs and stations, to reach as many people as possible in a market.

---

with agencies to place commercials across their entire schedule, with the understanding that each advertiser will have to accept some lower-rated (but demographically acceptable) spots in order to obtain some "jewels."

Up-Front Buys. Traditionally, the network buying season was divided into two distinct periods. The first was the *up-front* buying session followed by quarterly scatter buying sessions.[8] The up-front buying period takes place in late spring or early summer right after the networks announce their fall schedules. The up-front buying season usually involves the largest network advertisers and offers them several advantages:

- **They have a better selection of highly rated shows. If an advertiser waits for the later scatter period, most of the commercial time on top-rated shows will be gone.**

- **Networks will offer rating guarantees during the up-front period, a practice rarely offered for scatter buys.**

- **Prices may be lower (on a CPP basis) during the up-front period, but in exchange advertisers must lock in long-term commitments for the following season.**

Primarily due to the recession of the early 1990s and the proliferation of TV options, the up-front market has lost some of its prominence. With advertisers cutting budgets and seeking more flexibility for the money they spent, there were fewer firms willing to make the long-term guarantees demanded by up-front buys. The soft economy required networks to offer ratings guarantees during the scatter market as well as lower prices. "When the Big Three controlled more than 90 percent of the television audience, advertisers risked getting shut out of network, for which there was no suitable replacement media. The networks now hold about a 60 percent share of the audience; advertisers can now reach TV audiences with cable, syndication, spot and non-wired networks."[9]

With the combination of an economic downturn and increasing media choices, advertisers can obtain most of the advantages of an up-front buy without long-term commitments. The dramatic change in the up-front market is shown in Exhibit 8.3, which indicates that in a three-year period the number of advertisers viewing it as "very important" dropped from 59.5 to 38 percent.

There are separate up-front periods for daytime, children's programming, cable networks, etc. However, in terms of dollars invested and importance to the industry, it is prime time that drives the up-front market. In fact, except for special cases, such as toymakers, most of these up-front buys are delayed until prime-time buys are made.

Make-Goods. As the name implies, make-goods are concessions to advertisers for a failure to achieve some guaranteed ratings. Make-goods are normally offered on the basis of total GRPs for an advertiser's total TV advertising schedule. That is, when the advertiser fails to achieve a certain agreed-upon cost per point, the make-good provisions are initiated. At one time, make-goods were part of most advertising negotiations—they were al-

---

[8]The term *scatter plan* has two definitions. The first refers to buying a group of spots across a number of programs. The second refers to those spots that are still available after the up-front buying season is completed.
[9]"A Midsummer Night's Lull," *Adweek,* June 7, 1993, p. 11.

EXHIBIT

8.3

•••••••••••••••••••

Up-front buys are not as important in the diversified TV industry of the 1990s.

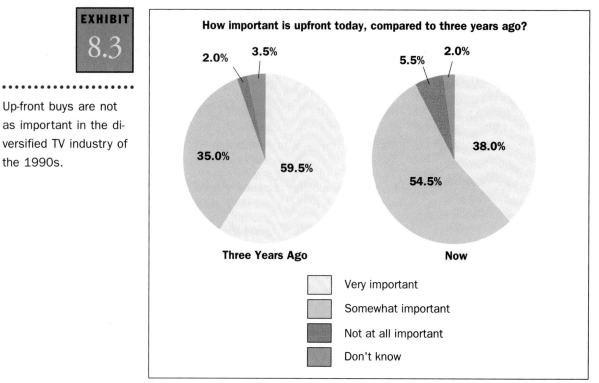

How important is upfront today, compared to three years ago?

Three Years Ago: 2.0%, 3.5%, 35.0%, 59.5%

Now: 5.5%, 2.0%, 54.5%, 38.0%

- Very important
- Somewhat important
- Not at all important
- Don't know

(Source: Advertising Age, *May 24, 1993, p. S-8.)*

ways part of the up-front market. Make-goods usually take the form of future commercials to make up for a shortfall in ratings. Refunds are virtually never given as part of a make-good plan.

It has only been in the past several years that make-goods have become a major point of contention between networks and agencies. Prior to that time, the networks were so dominant that it was rare for an advertiser to qualify for a make-good. Each network could reasonably expect to get a 25–35 share of the total prime-time schedule. Consequently, a make-good was a relatively risk fee incentive for agencies and their clients.

The new competitive environment has changed the make-good situation dramatically. With some network shows achieving sub-10 ratings, the make-good has become a major negotiating point with agencies and a high-risk endeavor for networks. For example, several of the major cable networks failed to meet their rating guarantees during the spring of 1993. Make-goods were so numerous that they used up a significant inventory of time during the next three months. In fact, the USA network gave all its commercial inventory on the U.S. Open Golf Championship as bonus time to advertisers.[10]

Spot Television

When national advertisers buy local stations the practice is known as *spot* television or *spot buys*. The term comes from the fact that advertisers are spotting their advertising in certain markets as contrasted to the blanket cover-

••••••••••••••••••••••••

Spot TV

Purchase of time from a local station, in contrast to purchasing from a network.

••••••••••••••••••••••••

---

[10]Michael Burgi, "Make-Goods Eat 3rd QTR Inventory," *Mediaweek,* August 2, 1993, p. 18.

age offered by network schedules. The primary disadvantages of spot television are that it requires a great deal more planning and paperwork than network, since each market must be bought on a one-to-one basis and it is more costly on a CPM basis.

Most spot advertising is placed through station representatives called *reps*. The rep is paid a commission by the station based on the time sold. The commission is negotiable, but it may range from 5 percent for large stations to 10 percent for smaller ones. The good sales rep is both a salesperson and a marketing specialist for advertisers. The rep must be able to show a national advertiser how a schedule on WAWS-TV in Jacksonville or KDKA-TV in Pittsburgh will meet a national company's advertising objectives.

Rep firms may have 100 or more station clients on a noncompetitive basis. Reps go to agencies and advertisers and attempt to convince them that their clients and the markets in which these stations broadcast have important prospects for specific brands. To make the purchase of spot buys more efficient, a rep will allow advertisers to buy all or any number of stations that it represents. Since the idea is to provide one order and one invoice, it is similar to a network buy. However, the stations sold through a rep are not linked in any way other than being a client of a particular rep; these station groups are called *nonwired networks*. The commercials bought on a nonwired network, unlike a real network, are not broadcast at the same time. The unwired concept is simply a means of providing buying efficiency for spot advertisers.

Why Buy Spot?

There are two types of spot advertisers. The first are those that use spot exclusively. The second category is advertisers who use spot advertising as a complement to their network buys. Spot advertising offers a number of advantages for national advertisers. Among the primary reasons for entering the spot advertising market are the following:

1. *Uneven product distribution or inadequate budgets for network.* Many products have distribution patterns that are so irregular that network coverage would create unacceptable waste circulation. By the same token, many national companies simply lack the funds to purchase adequate time on a national TV basis. However, by judicially buying in markets where they have strong sales or sales potential, they can compete in selected areas.

2. *Geographic targeting.* Few brands, even those with strong national distribution, have consistent sales patterns in every market. Spot offers a method of building local TV weight in those markets with the greatest potential while still taking advantage of the lower CPMs of network for national exposure. Exhibit 8.4 shows how combining spot and network television takes advantage of the sales potential of an advertiser's best markets while providing adequate exposure to all markets through network advertising.

3. *Local identity.* By using spot advertising, a national advertiser can more closely identify with the local market and its retailers. In addition, different markets have unique viewing habits that network cannot deal with easily. For example, spot advertising can buy strong local news shows and other locally produced programming that fit the demographics of prime prospects in that market. Spot also offers opportunities for local coopera-

EXHIBIT

8.4

· · · · · · · · · · · · · · · · · · ·

Spot television buys are
an important supple-
ment for many national
advertisers.

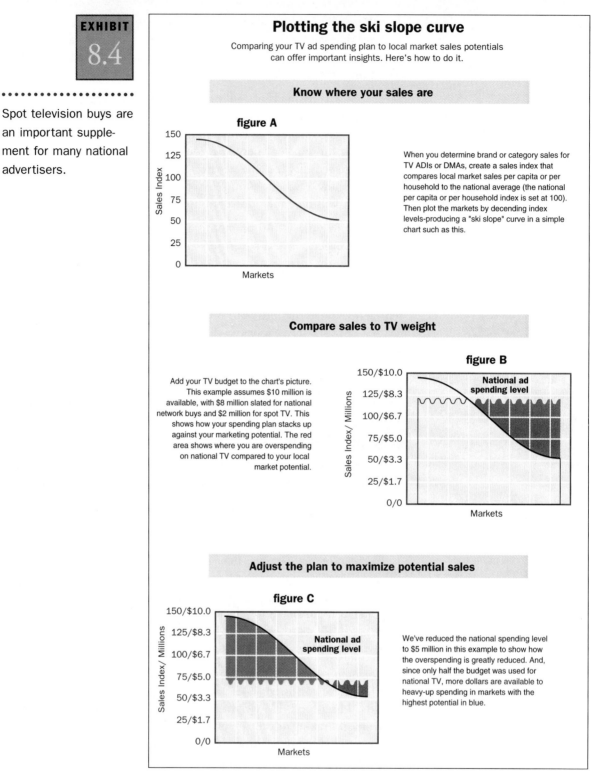

Plotting the ski slope curve

Comparing your TV ad spending plan to local market sales potentials
can offer important insights. Here's how to do it.

Know where your sales are

figure A

When you determine brand or category sales for
TV ADIs or DMAs, create a sales index that
compares local market sales per capita or per
household to the national average (the national
per capita or per household index is set at 100).
Then plot the markets by decending index
levels-producing a "ski slope" curve in a simple
chart such as this.

Compare sales to TV weight

Add your TV budget to the chart's picture.
This example assumes $10 million is
available, with $8 million slated for national
network buys and $2 million for spot TV. This
shows how your spending plan stacks up
against your marketing potential. The red
area shows where you are overspending
on national TV compared to your local
market potential.

figure B

National ad
spending level

Adjust the plan to maximize potential sales

figure C

National ad
spending level

We've reduced the national spending level
to $5 million in this example to show how
the overspending is greatly reduced. And,
since only half the budget was used for
national TV, more dollars are available to
heavy-up spending in markets with the
highest potential in blue.

(Source: "The Power of SPOT TV," Advertising Age, September 23, 1992, p. T-6.)

tive promotions with retailers, which would be impossible in network. Finally, spot buys can be made on independent stations that are not network
affiliated, but might have special strengths such as sports programming.

4. *Flexibility.* Unlike network advertising, where commitments are made several weeks or months in advance, spot buys allow an advertiser to react

immediately to changing market conditions. Assuming commercials are ready, an advertiser can be on air in as little as 48 hours.

Defining the TV Coverage Area

Before the advent of television, companies generally established sales and advertising territories by state boundaries and arbitrary geographic areas within them. However, TV transmissions go in many directions for varying distances; they are no respecter of maps. In order to coordinate sales territories with TV planning for advertising rating companies and advertisers have established three levels of signal coverage:

1. *Total survey area.* The largest area over which a station's coverage extends.

2. *Designated market area.*[11] A term used by the A.C. Nielsen Company to identify those counties in which home market stations receive a preponderance of viewers.

3. *Metro rating area.* Corresponds to the standard metropolitan area served by a station.

Local TV stations also provide advertisers with signal coverage maps to show the *potential* audience reach of the station (see Exhibit 8.5). The signal coverage designations have become less important in recent years as cable has greatly extended the area over which a TV station can be viewed.

Local TV Advertising

TV advertising is increasingly purchased by local advertisers. Businesses as diverse as record stores and banks place advertising on local stations. However, a significant portion of the more than $8 billion invested in local television is placed by local franchise outlets of national companies. For example, Pepsico (owner of Kentucky Fried Chicken, Pizza Hut, and Taco Bell) and McDonald's are the two largest local advertisers.

Local TV advertising expenditures are slightly ahead of spot and could challenge network revenues by the end of the decade. Advertisers spend more than $18 billion on spot and local television combined, approximately 50 percent more than the amount invested in network. The growth in local station advertising is indicative of three factors:

- **The effective marketing promotions by local stations and the TV industry to show how television can effectively be used by local retail outlets.**

- **The increased number of local TV outlets has created a competitive environment that has kept prices down, bringing the medium within the budget of more local advertisers.**

- **The trend by national marketers to move to local strategies. In many cases, this trend has been reflected by greater advertising allowances and control of budgets by local or regional advertisers.**

Local TV advertising is an important source of revenue for most stations. A decade ago, most network affiliates paid little attention to their local accounts.

---

[11]The Arbitron Company used a similar designation known as *area of dominance influence.* Even though Arbitron no longer conducts TV ratings, the term is still used by many advertisers.

EXHIBIT

8.5

The power of a local station's broadcast signal has been greatly extended by the growth of cable.

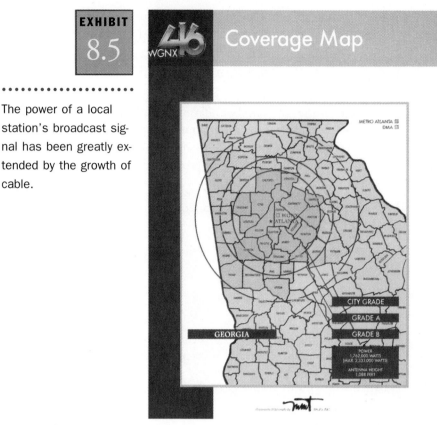

(Courtesy: WGNX-TV, Atlanta, GA.)

Profitability was assured from network compensation and national spot accounts. However, strong independent stations in many markets showed that aggressive selling could substantially increase local advertising (see Exhibit 8.6). Soon, affiliates were creating local advertising departments, promoting television as a viable local medium, and playing catch-up with their independent counterparts.

Local TV stations also realized that they could not expect to garner the majority of local retail advertising dollars and adopted the familiar stance of selling television as a *complement* to other local media. It is much easier to convince local advertisers to convert 5 percent of their budgets to television than 95 percent. Once stations were successful in getting retailers to give television a try, it was much easier to compete for more dollars and approach other retailers.

Buying and Scheduling Spot and Local TV Time.   Because advertisers have shifted more of their budgets to local markets, media buyers must be familiar with the specifics of buying spot and local TV time.

The TV Day.   Spot and local TV advertising are often purchased by daypart rather than by specific program. Each daypart varies by audience size and demographic profile. Media planners must be familiar with the audience makeup of various dayparts. Some typical daypart designations are:

1. Morning: 7:00–9:00 A.M. Monday through Friday

2. Daytime: 9:00 A.M.–4:30 P.M. Monday through Friday

EXHIBIT

8.6

**1992 Scarborough Consumer, Media, & Retail Report
Monday–Friday Late News Index**

Local TV stations routinely provide audience research to advertisers.

	WGNX	WAGA	WSB	WXIA
	NEWS AT TEN	EYEWITNESS NEWS	ACTION NEWS	11 ALIVE
Household Income:				
$100,000k+	147	58	63	105
$75–99,999k	126	79	78	80
$50,000k+	131	73	95	90
$30,000k+	111	97	93	89
College graduate or more	113	90	114	62
Home Owner	102	95	93	102
Value of Home:				
$250,000 or more	107	94	95	122
$100,000 or more	123	97	85	110
$50,000 or less	88	101	73	97
Employed	111	107	98	81
Unemployed	76	84	104	141
Chief Wage Earner	113	102	110	90
Profession:				
White Collar	113	115	111	92
Exec/Admins/Managerial	135	93	132	91
Professional Specialty	130	72	102	79
Technicians/Related Support	154	225	141	116
Sales	93	164	91	100
Administrative Support/Clerical	75	121	99	94
Blue Collar	108	92	70	56
Service	85	120	80	94
Precision production/Repair	123	105	46	44
Laborers, Farming & Other	31	74	42	38

(Courtesy: WGNX-TV, Atlanta, GA.)

3. Early fringe: 4:30–7:30 P.M. Monday through Friday

4. Prime time access: 7:30–8:00 P.M. Monday through Saturday

5. Prime time: 8:00–11:00 P.M. Monday through Saturday and 7:00–11:00 P.M. Sunday

6. Late news: 11–11:30 P.M. Monday through Friday

7. Late fringe: 11:30 P.M.–1:00 A.M. Monday through Friday

Preemption Rate. A considerable proportion of spot TV advertising time is sold on a preemptible (lower-rate) basis, whereby the advertiser gives the station the right to sell a time slot to another advertiser that may pay a better rate for it or that has a package deal for which that particular spot is needed. Although some stations offer only two choices, nonpreemptible and preemptible advertising, others allow advertisers to choose between two kinds of preemptible rates. When the station has the right to sell a spot to another advertiser any time up until the time of the telecast, the rate is called the *immediately preemptible* (IP) rate (the lowest rate). When the station can preempt only if it gives the original advertiser two weeks' notice, the rate is designated *preemptible with two weeks' notice* and is sold at a higher rate. The highest rate is charged for a nonpreemptible time slot, the two-week preemptible rate is the next highest, and the immediately preemptible rate is the lowest.

The following table is a quotation from a rate card.

Rate-Card Excerpt

	I	II	III
Tues., 8–9 A.M.	$135	$125	$115

The three columns show the preemption rates: column I, the nonpreemptible rate; column II, the rate for preemption on two weeks' notice; and column III, the rate for preemption without notice. Observe how the rate goes down.

SPECIAL FEATURES.   News telecasts, weather reports, sports news and commentary, stock market reports, and similar programming are called *special features*. Time in connection with special features is sold at a premium price.

RUN OF SCHEDULE (ROS).   An advertiser can earn a lower rate by permitting a station to run commercials at its convenience whenever time is available rather than in a specified position. (This is comparable to ROP in printed advertising; see Chapter 10.)

PACKAGE RATES.   Every station sets up its own assortment of time slots at different periods of the day, which it sells as a package. The station creates its own name for such packages and charges less for them than for the same slots sold individually. The package rate is one of the elements in negotiation for time.

PRODUCT PROTECTION.   Every advertiser wants to keep the advertising of competitive products as far away from its commercials as possible. This brings up the question of what protection against competition an ad will get. Although some stations say that they will try to keep competing commercials 5 to 10 minutes apart, most say that although they will do everything possible to separate competing ads, they guarantee only that they will not run them back to back.

SCHEDULING SPOT AND LOCAL TIME.   *Rotation of a schedule* refers to the placement of commercials within a schedule to get the greatest possible showing. If you bought two spots a week for four weeks on a Monday-to-Friday basis, but all the spots were aired only on Monday and Tuesday, your rotation would be poor. You would miss all the people who turn to the station only on Wednesday, Thursday, or Friday. Your *horizontal rotation* should be increased. *Vertical rotation* assures there will be differences in the time at which a commercial is shown within the time bracket purchased. If you bought three spots on the *Tonight Show,* which runs from 11:30 P.M. to 12:30 A.M., but all your spots were shown at 12:15 A.M., you would be missing all the people who go to sleep earlier than that. To avoid this situation, you would schedule one spot in each half hour of the program, vertically rotating your commercial to reach the largest possible audience.

TV SYNDICATION

Syndicated TV programming is one of the fastest-growing segments of the industry and one that is very popular with both advertisers and local stations. In the past decade it has become a major advertising medium with advertising revenues of over $1.5 billion (see Exhibit 8.7). In fact, advertising increases are among the highest of any media segment.

Syndication is the sale of programs on a station-by-station basis. Stations contract with a program supplier such as Paramount for *Entertainment Tonight* or Multimedia for *Rush Limbaugh*. In the case of popular programs such as *Cheers*, which have previously run on one of the networks, fees in large markets may be over $100,000 per episode for multiple showings. Syndicators contract individually with the more than 1,000 commercial stations in over 200 markets to sell their shows. In effect, syndication allows program producers to sell programming directly to stations rather than to networks. However, with recent changes in FCC regulations, networks can participate in the ownership of their shows and thus profit from syndication of their programs.

Obviously, each syndicated show is sold on an exclusive basis in each market. Syndication cuts across all types of programming and includes such diverse shows as the tabloid *A Current Affair*, the adult-oriented *Love Connection*, the popular *Teenage Mutant Ninja Turtles*, and the long time staple of syndication, talk shows such as Phil Donahue and Oprah Winfrey.

There are two basic types of syndicated programs. The first is *off-network*, consisting of shows that have been on a major network and are now offered for syndication. Many long-running shows such as *Cheers* and *Home Improvement* enter the syndication market before they are removed from the network schedule. The second type of syndication is called *first-run* and is comprised of shows produced for syndication. *Wheel of Fortune* is an example of first-run syndication.

Syndication is not new, just its popularity and profitability. Syndication began when producers sold their canceled network shows to stations for inex-

EXHIBIT 8.7

Syndicated TV advertising has demonstrated steady growth in recent years.

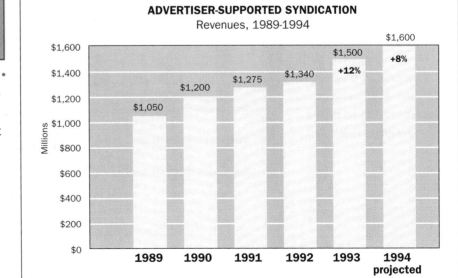

(Courtesy: Advertiser Syndicated Television Association.)

pensive "fillers" during late afternoons or other time periods not programmed by the networks. During the early days of syndication, no one thought that it was anything but a method of picking up a few extra dollars for a program that had completed its network run.

Today, syndication is a major part of the advertising schedules of many advertisers. While syndication has been the primary program source for late-night and children's television, syndicators have now begun to compete with the major networks in prime time. In some cases, programs such as *Star Trek: Deep Space Nine* have attracted network affiliates that have substituted these shows for network programming.[12] Advertisers are finding that combining network and syndicated programming offers higher levels of reach at cost efficiencies unavailable with either used alone (see Exhibit 8.8).

The current popularity of syndication is a result of a number of factors, some dating back almost 20 years:

1. *The Primetime Access Rule.* In 1971, the FCC limited the amount of time local network affiliates could broadcast network-supplied programs during prime time. This limitation was intended to provide prime-time access to program suppliers other than the networks and diversify programming at the local station level.

Under the rule, the FCC also forbid large market affiliates from using off-network syndicated reruns. Since most local stations could not afford to produce local programming during this access period, it opened a market for first-run syndication. With the expansion of broadcast and cable outlets since 1971, the program diversity sought by the rule has been achieved. Consequently, the FCC agreed to allow the prime-time rule to expire. A relaxation of the rule would, of course, greatly enhance the financial value of off-network shows.[13]

2. *Local news became a profit center as stations increasingly looked to news as a profitable and relatively inexpensive source of programming.* During the past

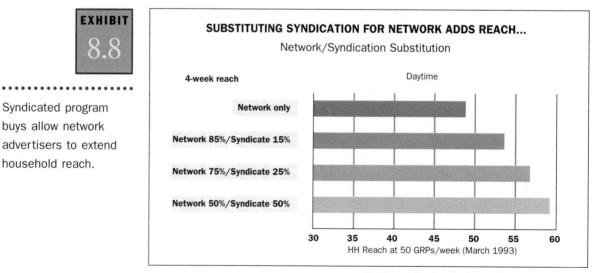

(Courtesy: Advertiser Syndicated Television Association.)

---

[12]Joe Mandese, "Power Surge," *Advertising Age,* March 8, 1993, p. S-1.
[13]Michael Freeman, "The Escalating War over PTAR," *Mediaweek,* March 14, 1994, p. 18.

decade, the local news period has become a major battleground for stations as they fight for advertising dollars. Since major market stations were limited by the FCC from showing reruns in prime time, but not in other dayparts, they competed to buy the highest-rated syndicated shows as lead-ins to news. Whereas off-network shows once sold for less than $10,000 per episode, the most popular reruns were commanding $500,000 or more *per episode.*[14]

3. *The increasing number of outlets for syndicated programming.* The resulting increase in demand has created a sellers market for syndicators. For example, USA network paid $350,000 per episode for reruns of *Major Dad,* and *L.A. Law* reportedly cost the Lifetime network $300,000. Although these cable network buys are not syndication, they effectively remove inventory from the syndication market and drive up the prices of remaining programs.

4. *Affiliates use syndication as leverage with networks.* The first-run syndication market has benefited by the continuing squabble over network compensation. As we discussed earlier, as the average ratings for network shows declined, they began to reduce compensation to affiliates. Affiliates retaliated by threatening to preempt network shows and replace them with first-run syndication. Today, syndicators produce some of the most popular shows on television.

5. *Profitability of syndication to stations.* Related to the affiliate/network dispute, are the economics of television. In the typical network show, stations are allowed to sell one minute of commercial time. In a syndicated show, the station can sell from 6 to 12 minutes of commercials depending on how the program was obtained by the station. Consequently, a syndicated program does not have to generate huge ratings to be a financial success for a station.

Since local stations can find syndication profitable and the demand for new syndicated programming continues to grow, there is every reason to believe that syndication will be a major advertising vehicle in the next decade. If anything, syndication will be an even stronger competitor to the traditional networks, and the relationship between syndicators and stations may become more formal.

Ad hoc network
Television networks consisting of affiliates that come together only for a special program such as a sporting event.

Because popular syndicated shows often have virtually 100 percent national audience coverage, they are sometimes referred to as *ad hoc* networks. However, unlike the four broadcast networks, syndicated shows are usually shown on different nights, with a variety of advertisers buying spots on the local stations that carry the programs. Some syndication executives are exploring the advantages of entering into long-term relationships with stations to guarantee future programming as opposed to selling shows on an individual basis.

Buying Syndicated Television

Syndicated advertising is very different from network television. There are three categories of syndicated television: cash, barter, and a combination of cash and barter.

---

[14]Generally, the per-episode price allows a station 7 to 10 reruns.

1. *Cash.* The simplest form of syndication is where a station simply buys a program from a producer and is then responsible for selling all the commercial time within the program to either spot or local advertisers. A cash syndicated show will offer 12–15 minutes of commercial time to be sold by the local station.

2. *Barter.* Barter syndication consists of the syndicator providing a show with presold national spots and approximately one minute of commercial time available for the station to sell. One of the longest-running barter shows is *Wild Kingdom* sponsored by Mutual of Omaha Insurance Company. The advantage to the station is that there is no out-of-pocket expense to obtain the program. Barter became especially popular during the late 1980s, when stations were short of cash. National advertisers like barter, since it gives them more program options at lower CPMs than they would pay for network shows. The disadvantage for national advertisers is that they have little control over when the show is broadcast in each local market.

3. *Cash/Barter.* In recent years, the most popular form of syndication has been a combination of cash and barter. Here, the program is offered with some presold spots as well as making time available to be sold by the local station. The program is offered to stations at a price much lower than the same program would command on a cash basis alone.

Special Syndicated Networks. We are seeing more and more special programming distributed on syndicated networks. A syndicated network program will run at the same time on all the stations that carry it. Therefore, except for the fact that the "affiliates" of the network are together only for a single show, it has all the characteristics of a network.

This concept was originally used for holiday specials. However, it is quite common to see movies and other programming packaged as a continuing series. Universal's *Action Pack* is an example of a group of movies that appear during prime time on independent stations. It is very difficult to get individual stations to agree to broadcast a syndicated program at a particular time. Therefore, instances of such shows are relatively infrequent. In addition, the growth of program opportunities through cable and independent stations has resulted in fewer syndicated networks than in the past.

Stripping and Checkerboarding. Most local stations schedule syndicated shows on a five-night-a-week basis. That is, they will run *Jeopardy* or *Inside Edition* Monday through Friday in the same time slot. This practice is called *stripping,* since the show is stripped across a time period. By contrast, *checkerboarding* is where a different show will be used each day during the time period.

Checkerboarding is seldom used, since the cost of five different programs is much more expensive than using the same show. Stations also find that it is very difficult to obtain five shows that will provide consistent ratings. Since most syndication is used as a lead-in either for early news or prime time, stations don't want huge ratings differences from one program to another. Occasionally, stations will use checkerboarding as a method of testing several program alternatives before settling on a strip format.

CABLE TELEVISION

From its humble beginnings as a method of importing broadcast signals into rural areas, cable television has become a major sector of the industry. In-

Barter syndication

Station obtains a program at no charge. The program has presold national commercials and time is available for local station spots.

Checkerboarding

When a station runs a different syndicated show in the same time slot each day.

Cable networks

Networks available only to cable subscribers. They are transmitted via satellite to local cable operators for redistribution either as part of basic service or at an extra cost charged to subscribers.

creasingly, cable is included in the advertising schedules of both local and national advertisers. Currently, there are approximately 11,000 local cable *systems* serving more than 60 million households. Approximately 65 percent of households have cable, and it is projected to rise to 76 percent by the year 2000. Cable homes spend an average of 18 hours a week watching basic cable programming, a 69 percent increase in six years. More than 95 percent of cable homes receive at least 30 channels. Cable also reaches an upscale market compared to other major media vehicles (see Exhibit 8.9).

Total audience investment in cable television is almost $23 billion. Whereas broadcast stations and networks receive 100 percent of their revenues from advertising, cable has a diversity of income sources:

- **Basic cable fees**   **61 percent**
- **Pay cable fees**   **22 percent**
- **Cable advertising**   **17 percent**

The majority of the $3.9 billion invested in cable advertising are placed in cable networks (see Exhibit 8.10). Among these cable networks, the bulk of revenues are concentrated in a relatively few services. Although there are approximately 80 cable networks, the top 10 account for more than 65 percent of total advertising revenues. In a recent ratings period, only five cable networks carried all of the top 20 rated shows.

EXHIBIT 8.9

Cable offers advertisers the opportunity to reach young, educated and affluent households which also exhibit high levels of employment.

Viewers to Basic Cable Programming are Upscale

Household Income	Total U.S.	Cable* Network	Prime-time TV	Radio	News-paper	Maga-zine
$75,000+	100	126	95	108	116	112
$40,000–$75,000	100	117	99	108	110	109
$20,000–$40,000	100	98	101	99	99	101
Under $20,000	100	72	102	89	83	85
Education						
College Graduate	100	113	97	106	114	111
Attended College	100	112	97	106	107	111
HS Graduate	100	103	102	102	103	101
Not HS Graduate	100	73	102	86	77	78
Occupation						
Executive/Managerial/ Administrative	100	121	98	109	112	111
Professional	100	110	96	111	113	113
Employed Full-Time	100	107	98	108	104	104
Not Employed	100	88	103	87	93	92
Household Size						
3+ persons	100	107	99	105	100	104
2	100	98	102	94	102	98
1	100	75	100	92	94	88
Age						
18–49	100	103	98	109	99	105
25–54	100	103	99	107	101	103
55+	100	91	104	79	101	88

*Any viewing past week

(Courtesy: Cable Television Advertising Bureau, 1993 Cable TV Facts, p. 45.)

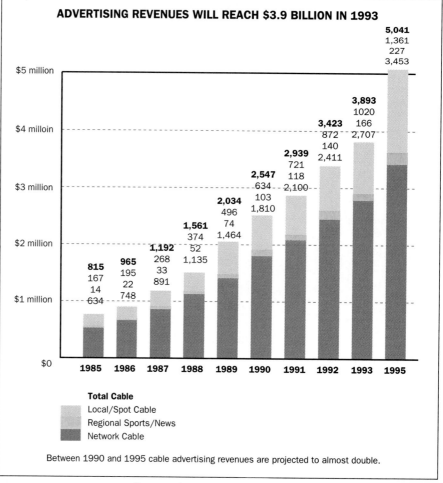

ADVERTISING REVENUES WILL REACH $3.9 BILLION IN 1993

Year	Total Cable	Local/Spot Cable	Regional Sports/News	Network Cable
1985	815	167	14	634
1986	965	195	22	748
1987	1,192	268	33	891
1988	1,561	374	52	1,135
1989	2,034	496	74	1,464
1990	2,547	634	103	1,810
1991	2,939	721	118	2,100
1992	3,423	872	140	2,411
1993	3,893	1020	166	2,707
1995	5,041	1,361	227	3,453

Total Cable
Local/Spot Cable
Regional Sports/News
Network Cable

Between 1990 and 1995 cable advertising revenues are projected to almost double.

(Courtesy: Cable Television Advertising Bureau, 1993 Cable TV Facts, p. 8.)

Making up for relatively low ratings, cable is able to offer niche programming for many advertisers. Specialized programming can reach narrowly targeted audiences and combine an identified audience with a program environment especially designed for specific buying habits. Advertisers are able to buy commercials on the TV Food network, the younger targeted ESPN 2. In the near future, advertisers will be offered a number of channels based on popular magazines such as *Car & Driver, Better Homes & Gardens,* and *Glamour.*[15]

In addition to the relatively low ratings per network, national advertisers find it difficult to get national coverage with cable. The four biggest cable networks (ESPN, CNN, USA, and TBS) each have household penetration of approximately 60 million households. In other words, at their maximum, the largest cable systems can offer an advertiser only 65 percent of the coverage of the three major networks.

Buying Cable

In recent years, much has been written about cable television's encroachment on network ratings. In the aggregate, there is no question that cable has con-

---

[15]Kathy Haley, "Marketers Tune in to Cable's Appeal," *Cable '94* (supplement to *Advertising Age*), February 28, 1994, p. C-3.

tributed to significant audience erosion in network television. However, it is important to note that the erosion in network audiences is created by dozens of cable networks as well as stronger independent stations (some carried by cable such as TBS and WGN). During one ratings period, only four cable networks (ESPN, USA, TNT, and TNN) had average ratings over *1* (see Exhibit 8.11). By contrast, late-night network programs such as Jay Leno's *Tonight Show* will average a 4 or 5 rating, and even "about-to-be-canceled" network prime-time shows will achieve a 6–8 rating. Buying cable requires a broad mix of cable networks to achieve suitable levels of reach and frequency against selected target markets.

Historically, television has been considered by advertisers to be part of the mass media. However, as cable becomes more established, advertisers are having to adjust to the medium as both a mass and niche vehicle. Many advertisers are comparing cable to radio as a medium to reach narrowly defined audiences, but one that requires numerous spots on several networks to achieve adequate levels of reach or frequency. In fact, radio stations often promote to advertisers a combination of specific radio formats and niche cable as a method of extending reach. Cable also reinforces media synergism that is becoming an integral part of selling many media.

The diversity of contemporary television has fundamentally changed the way both programming and advertising will be developed in the future. One industry executive summed up the future of television:

> I believe that the future of television will parallel what has happened in publishing. Today there are over 1,000 specialized magazines aimed at special interest markets. Hundreds of regional newspapers have grown up over the past decades. Books appear almost instantly, addressing very recent happenings, almost on an ad hoc basis. We see the same trends in the cable business. People who normally do not like television will subscribe to a class movie channel or the Arts & Entertainment channel. Sports programming is becoming more niche oriented with regional networks and specialized fare. . . . We can expect this trend to continue. Future offerings may cater to camera buffs, audiophiles, and the specialized needs of minorities and ethnic groups.[16]

Most TV executives predict that cable will reach its saturation household penetration of approximately 80 percent by the turn of the century. Already, over 85 percent of households have access to cable. The problem facing the cable industry is basically one of programming. As one broadcast executive cynically noted, "by the year 2000 we will be able to get 'Leave it to Beaver' reruns any time day or night."

The challenge for cable is that viewers and advertisers are increasingly asking for the same quality of programs that they get from networks. The typical cable network is in an impossible position being asked to provide network quality with radio ratings. Whether or not the cable industry can convince advertisers that lower costs, but highly specialized programming is a worthwhile investment, is a question that will determine the success of the industry.

Clearly, a steady diet of off-network reruns is not a formula for success. At a time when one group within the cable TV industry is touting its 500-

---

[16]Richard R. Green, "Future Challenges for Cable Television," *Lectures in Cable Television*, Pennsylvania State University, October 18, 1990.

EXHIBIT

8.11

· · · · · · · · · · · · · · · · · · ·

Cable networks, rating are far behind those of the four major broadcast networks.

Viewing Alternatives

Cable Networks

Viewership to National Cable Networks Primetime*

Cable Networks	Cable Networks Coverage Area Rating %	Share	Total U.S. Rating %
Pay Cable			
Cinemax	4.7	7	0.4
Home Box Office	7.5	12	1.6
Showtime	4.7	7	0.5
Ad-Supported			
Arts &Entertainment	0.9	1	0.5
Black Entertainment TV	0.5	1	0.2
The Cartoon Network	1.1	2	0.1
CNBC	0.2		0.1
Cable News Network	0.9	1	0.6
Comedy Central	0.4	1	0.1
Coutry Music Television	0.4	1	0.1
The Discovery Channel	0.9	1	0.6
E! Entertainment TV	0.2		0.6
ESPN-Total Sports Network	1.5	3	1.0
The Family Channel	0.9	1	0.5
Headline News	0.3	1	0.2
Lifetime Television	**	**	**
MTV: Music Television	0.6	1	0.4
Nickelodeon/Nick-at-Nite	1.1	2	0.7
Nostalgia Television	0.1		
Preview Guide Channel	0.3		0.1
TBS-Superstation	2.2	4	1.4
The Learning Channel	0.3	1	0.1
TNN: The Nashville Network	1.0	2	0.6
Turner Network Television	1.9	3	1.2
The Weather Channel	0.2		0.1
USA Network	2.3	4	1.5
VH1	0.3		0.1
WGN Cable	1.0	2	0.4

Note: Data may represent primary feed for each cable network within its respective universe.
Cable Network Coverage Area Rating %= Average audience in percent of homes able to recieve an individual cable network/superstation.
Total U.S. Rating %= Average audience in percent of total U.S. households.
* Monday-Sunday 8-11 P.M.
** Network does not telecast for the full duration of this daypart.
  Below minimum reporting standards.

(Courtesy: Nielsen Media Research.)

channel future, another is wondering where the programming is coming from to fill the 50-channel present now. Meanwhile, the broadcast networks are more than satisfied to sell advertisers their 15–20 audience shares.

THE VIDEOCASSETTE RECORDER

We have discussed the continuing fragmentation of the broadcast audience. Contributing to this reality is the growth of the VCR market. The VCR is a media phenomenon. Few media forms have grown as fast as the VCR. For example:

	VCR Households (millions)	% Penetration (U.S. TV households)
1980	1.9	2.5
1990	55.8	66.0
2000	76.0	90.0

There are two types of VCR viewing: prerecorded tapes and time-shift recording from on-air programming. By far the greatest amount of time is spent watching prerecorded programming, usually rental movies. Blockbuster Video and other local and national chains have created a multi-billion-dollar business from America's insatiable demand for movies. In addition to rental movies, millions of tapes are sold each year, including movies and various self-help programs. Purchased tapes constitute about 25 percent of the total prerecorded market.

Of course, each hour spent watching these prerecorded tapes is time not available for regular television. Of particular concern to both broadcasters and advertisers is the demographic makeup of heavy VCR users. For example, young, affluent adults, prime prospects for many TV advertisers, are the most likely to rent videotapes. This audience is then unavailable for exposure to traditional broadcast and cable outlets and their advertisers.

The second type of videocassette audience are those viewing previously recorded programming from on-air sources. This practice is called *time-shift* viewing, since the audience watches the program at a time other than when it was originally broadcast. Most recording of programs is done during daytime hours, and almost 60 percent of all recording is of network affiliate programming (see Exhibit 8.12).

Time-shift viewing

Recording programs on a VCR for viewing at a later time.

Time-shift viewing presents two problems for advertisers. First, over half of the programs recorded off the air are never watched. Viewers have every intention of looking at the show at some later time, but never get around to it or accidentally record over it.

Another problem is that time-shift viewers do not exhibit the same audience characteristics as original viewers. One study indicated that original viewers of *L.A. Law* were 33 percent women, aged 35–54. The time-shift audience showed 75 percent fit that demographic profile.[17] Finally, the viewers who prerecord the show have the ability to fast-forward through commercials.

---

[17]Jonathan Sims, "VCR Viewing Patterns: An Electronic and Passive Investigation," *Journal of Advertising Research,* March/April 1989, pp. 11–17.

According to the Nielsen national sample, 77% of all U.S. television households own a VCR. Daytime is the most recorded daypart, followed by primetime. When recording, the majority of homes (61%) have the TV set in the off position, 26% have the set on and tuned to the same channel, and 13% have the set on and tuned to a different channel.

Network shows are the most popular programs recorded. During July, 59% of all shows recorded were network programs (ABC, CBS, NBC, FOX), 20% were cable programs, 10% were programs on independent stations, 7% were pay cable programs and 4% were PBS programs.

36% of all recording is done during daytime.

VCR Usage, July 1992

When is recording done?

	Prime-time	Day-time	Late Night	Early Morning	Fringe	Weekend Day	Other	Total
1992	26%	36%	8%	3%	7%	7%	13%	100%

How is recording done?

	With TV set off	TV on Different Channel	TV on Same Channel	
1992	61%	13%	26%	100%

What do VCR households record?

	Network Affiliates*	Independent	Public	Pay Service	Cable Origin	
1992	59%	10%	4%	7%	20%	100%

Source: Nielsen Media Research, VCR Annual Tracking Report 1991–92
Note: Primetime = Monday–Saturday 8–11 p.m.. Sunday 7–11 p.m.: Daytime = Monday–Friday 10 a.m.–4:30 p.m.:
Latenight = Monday–Sunday 11 p.m.–1 a.m.: Early Morning = Monday–Friday 6–10 a.m.: Fringe = Monday–Friday 4:30–8 p.m.:
Weekend Day = Saturday 1–8 p.m.. Sunday 1–7 p.m.: Other = Saturday/Sunday 6 a.m.–1 p.m.. Monday–Sunday 1 a.m.–6 a.m.
*ABC, CBS, NBC, FOX

(Courtesy: Nielsen Media Research.)

EXHIBIT

8.12

· · · · · · · · · · · · · · · · · ·

The VCR has become an important viewing alternative in many households.

Therefore, the viewers of prerecorded programs are different from regular viewers, and they are unlikely to watch commercials—a less than great option for advertisers buying the show.

Advertiser Participation in Videocassettes

Advertisers obviously want to reach the VCR audience. Beginning in 1987 with a Diet Pepsi ad on the video release of *Top Gun,* the era of advertising on major theatrical video releases began. Since then, a number of movie videos have included commercials. Coca-Cola *(Batman),* Nestlé *(Dirty Dancing),* and Chrysler *(Platoon)* all followed Pepsi's lead in placing video commercials. When we speak of commercials, we are not including promos for future movies, which are routinely included in most videos.

Most companies simply use versions of their TV commercials in the tapes. However, several advertisers have created commercials especially to tie in with video movies. For example, John Cleese, a star of *A Fish Called Wanda,* was featured in a Schweppes commercial accompanying the tape of the movie.

EXHIBIT

8.13

Criteria Used in Judging the Merits of Videocassette Advertising

Videocassette advertising like most advertising must deliver a targeted audience segment to be of value.

Criteria	Respondents Who Have Used It	
	N	(%)
Big theatrical hit	5	(26.3%)
Association with lead actor(s)	1	(5.3%)
Association with movie character(s)	1	(5.3%)
Potential audience size	10	(52.6%)
Demographic compatibility	15	(78.9%)
Product placement in the movie	4	(21.1%)
Good fit between brand's personality and movie's theme	14	(73.9%)

Source: Journal of Media Planning

The *Top Gun* tape commercial carried out the fighter pilot theme of the movie, but did not feature any of the actors from the film.

Many marketing executives regard video advertising as a form of sales promotion rather than traditional advertising. In that regard, a number of video advertisers have developed joint promotions with the movies in which they advertised. For example, Procter & Gamble heavily promoted its participation with *All Dogs Go to Heaven* with $5 rebates on bottles of Downy fabric softener for purchase of the tape.[18]

Depending on the theatrical success of a movie, video advertising can command fees of as much as $400,000. Consequently, it is important that advertisers develop clear objectives for their video advertising. Just as the demographics, audience size, and qualitative association with TV programs are considered by advertisers, likewise similar concerns are part of the planning of a video campaign. Exhibit 8.13 shows that the three most important criteria in placing a video commercial are:

■ **Demographic compatibility**

■ **Fit between a brand's personality and movie theme**

■ **Potential audience size**[19]

One of the concerns with video advertising is the attitudes of audiences toward these messages. Obviously, exposure to an audience predisposed to dislike a promotional message is hardly the format that advertisers seek. Research has found that more than half of viewers think that videocassette advertising is intrusive, and some are offended by it.[20]

In some respects, the attitudes of viewers toward video advertising are mirrored by those of consumers for a number of "new" advertising vehicles. For instance, studies have shown that consumers are undecided or hostile toward shopping-cart advertising, mall advertising, and movie-theater commercial

---

[18]Wayne Friedman, "Tape Delay," *Inside Media,* June 27, 1990, p. 43.
[19]Wei-Na Lee, "The Potential of Advertising on Pre-Recorded Videocassettes in the 1990's: A Survey of Top U.S. Advertising Agencies," *Journal of Media Planning,* Spring 1992, p. 31.
[20]Wei-Na Lee and Helen Katz, "New Media, New Messages: An Initial Inquiry into Audience Reactions to Advertising on Videocassettes," *Journal of Advertising Research,* January/February 1993, p. 82.

messages. Whether these attitudes will become more positive with familiarity is still to be determined.

A much less expensive method of reaching the video market is the use of the video movie box to carry an advertising message. In addition to its low cost, this type of advertising has several other advantages. It is unobtrusive, with most consumers indicating few negative attitudes toward these ads. In some cases, the ads offer coupons for later rental or other merchandise available in the store. The ads have high audience recall and reach a relatively narrow audience of movie renters. Obviously, movie-box advertising does not have the impact of a full-length commercial. However, the fact that advertisers are using these ads points up the necessity of reaching the lucrative video market.

SYNDICATED RATING SERVICES

Commercial television only exists because of continuing revenues from advertisers. As we have mentioned earlier, more than half of all national advertising is spent in television. Advertisers make this investment because television delivers a huge audience of demographically defined viewers. The bond between the TV industry and these advertisers is the major rating services that provide audience data on a continuing basis.

In recent years, the problems of accurately accounting for this fragmented audience have become more and more difficult. At the same time, as audiences for each TV outlet decrease, the magnitude of any error increases as a percentage of the total viewing audience. For example, a one-rating-point error for a program with a 20 rating is 5 percent; the same error for a program with a five rating is 20 percent. Since advertising rates are directly determined by ratings, these errors are a cause for considerable concern among advertisers.

Committee on Nationwide Television Audience Measurement

Committee on Nationwide Television Audience Measurement (CONTAM)

Industry-wide organization to improve the accuracy and reliability of television ratings.

The Committee on Nationwide Television Audience Measurement (CONTAM) was established in 1963 as a joint effort by the three networks and the National Association of Broadcasters (NAB). Its purpose was to improve the accuracy and reliability of ratings research. Currently, CONTAM is working to provide an accurate and reliable reflection of a TV audience that is constantly changing. In pointing out the importance of these changes, one TV executive concluded, "the growth in remote control penetration is truly astounding. We also know something about the pervasiveness of VCRs, TV stereo sound and picture-in-picture. Better than one in ten households enjoys the use of a small set. Moreover, in one out of two homes the TV set has invaded the bedroom. And in just about one million homes, the television has even barged into the bathroom."[21]

TV technology that was unknown two decades ago is now a reality. This reality is creating tremendous methodological problems for rating services. For example, how do you count viewers watching a picture-in-picture screen? Do you double-count them (certainly unfair to competing shows)? Do you half them? Do you give more weight to the picture on the larger portion of the screen?

---

[21]Nicholas P. Schiavone, "Where CONTAM Finds Progress," *Feedback,* Winter 1993, p. 2.

Another technological ratings nightmare is measuring the time-shift viewers discussed earlier. With great difficulty, we are able to measure the recording and the replaying of prerecorded programs. However, one prediction is that by the end of the decade, 60 percent of households will own VCRs that can be programmed to eliminate all commercials.[22] Again, the rating services can barely deal with one innovation before being faced with another, even more formidable one.

Out-of-Home Ratings

One area of particular controversy is the measurement of out-of-home viewers. The networks contend that there is a growing segment of viewers who regularly watch television in nontraditional (and largely unrated) environments. These sites include bars, hotels, the workplace, prisons, and college campuses. Broadcasters contend that this audience would have a significant impact on ratings if it were measured.

Preliminary studies indicate that certain shows would benefit greatly from regular measurement of this audience. For example, it is estimated that 12 percent of women aged 18–49 watching *Another World* are out of home. Likewise, 16 percent of men aged 18–24 viewing college football are in this category.[23] Obviously, with these numbers, networks are pushing strongly to have them included in future ratings.

Advertisers are resisting the attempt to combine this out-of-home audience in regular syndicated ratings. They are concerned that the current rating techniques also make it impossible to gather accurate numbers from this transient group. They also are very leery about the quality of this audience. "From the advertiser's point of view, there's a feeling that if a commercial runs in a bar with a few hundred patrons, they're not necessarily watching the commercial, so is it really an impression that should count?"[24]

The Rating Services

When the Arbitron Rating Company dropped its local TV measuring service in January 1994, it left only the A.C. Nielsen Company as a major supplier of syndicated TV ratings. Network ratings are provided through the Nielsen Television Index (NTI) and local market ratings through the Nielsen Station Index (NSI). Nielsen produces numerous individual reports—some on a 24-hour basis for network prime-time programming (see Exhibit 8.14).

The TV industry was understandably concerned by the prospect of a single ratings supplier. In 1994, the three major networks, leading cable networks as well as advertisers and syndicators, announced that they would develop an experimental ratings laboratory called System for Measuring and Reporting Television (SMART). The intent is to develop new ratings methodologies to track the diverse audiences of television. Some TV executives speculated that it might evolve into competition to Nielsen.[25]

---

[22]Joe Mandese, "Video Technology Foils Measurement," *Advertising Age,* March 9, 1992, p. 30.
[23]Elizabeth Kolbert, "Networks Press Nielsen to Count the Barflies, Too," *New York Times,* March 15, 1993, p. C-1.
[24]Joe Mandese, "What People Watch Away from Home," *Advertising Age,* March 29, 1993, p. 35.
[25]Michael Freeman, "Big 4 Call Ratings Powwow," *Mediaweek,* April 4, 1994, p. 8.

INTRODUCTION
The Services of Nielsen Media Research

Nielsen Television Index—NTI©

Established in 1950, NTI provides continuous audience estimates for all national broadcast network television programs. In 1987, this service began collecting data on nationwide television viewing on a daily basis through the Nielsen People Meter.

Nielsen Station Index—NSI©

Established in 1954, NSI provides local market television audience measurment. This service provides continuous metered market overnight measurement in 30 major markets and diary measurement in more than 200 Designated Market Areas (DMAs) in the country.

Nielsen Homevideo Index©—NHI

NHI was established in 1980 and provides a measurement of cable, pay cable, VCRs, video discs and other new television technologies. The data are collected through the use of the Nielsen People Meters, set-tuning meters and paper diaries.

Nielsen Syndication Service—NSS

Formed in 1985 to meet the needs of the rapidly growing program syndication segment of the television industry, NSS markets reports and services on both a local and national level.

Nielsen New Media Services—NMS

Renamed New Media Services in 1991, this unit was born out of the Special Research and New Business Development groups which were a part of Nielsen since 1980. New Media Services provides custom research and startup services for new syndicated products, both national and local. This includes measurement performance of non-traditional research such as place-based and out-of-home media.

Nielsen Hispanic Television Index—NHTI

Started in November 1992, NHTI is the first metered national Hispanic audience measurement. Based on a sample of 800 Hispanic households across the U.S., it uses the same methodology—the Nielsen People Meter—as other national television.

Nielsen Hispanic Station Index—NHSI

Based on a sample of 200 Hispanic households in the Los Angeles DMA, this local Hispanic audience measurement service, launched in September 1992, utilizes the Nielsen People Meter to gather audience data.

1954 NSI Established		1980 NHI Established			1992 NHTI Established
1950 NTI Established		1980 Special Research/ New Business Development Established	1985 NSS Established	1991 NMS Established	1992 NHSI Established

(Courtesy: Nielsen Media Research.)

EXHIBIT 8.14

· · · · · · · · · · · · · · · · · ·

As television has become a more complex medium, rating services have provided more reports to reach a diverse audience.

Rating Methodologies

As audience researchers grapple with the growing problems of measuring the fragmented audience for television, they constantly review and refine their research methodologies. The methods used to measure the TV audience continue to evolve as new technology becomes available. Rating methods have gone through several phases over the years:

1. *The telephone.* The first rating service, the Cooperative Analyses of Broadcasting (CAB), began in 1930. Arch Crossley used the telephone recall method to determine listening behavior during the previous 24 hours. Telephone research is still used for special research projects, but not on a regular basis for syndicated TV ratings.

2. *The diary.* The diary method requires that all persons in a household keep a record or their viewing habits. For many years, the diary has been the mainstay for TV ratings. It is still used for smaller market local ratings. However, the multichannel television of the 1990s cannot be adequately

measured by research methods of the 1950s. It is clear that the diary, as a primary source of research data, is being phased out.

3. *The household meter.* The next development in the quest to provide better ratings information was the metered household. Since 1950 when Nielsen introduced the Nielsen Storage Instantaneous Audimeter (referred to as either SIA or simply Audimeter), metered audience measurement has been the principal method of obtaining national ratings. The meters give an accurate profile of the programs the TV set is tuned to. However, they do not measure who, if anyone, is watching and are significantly more expensive than diaries.

4. *People meters.* A new era in TV ratings was initiated in 1987 when Nielsen introduced the so-called people meter. It attempted to overcome the problems of both diaries and set meters. Ideally, people meters combine the accuracy of set meters with the diary's ability to gather demographic information, for it not only records what is being watched, but by whom. When the people meter expanded to its present sample of 4,000 households in 1988, the major beneficiaries were the cable networks. The smaller, but more homogeneous audiences of these networks could now be sold to advertisers with some certainty as to what they were buying.

People Meters—the Next Generation

The Passive People Meter. A problem with the people meter is that viewers have to remember to program them as they begin watching. Much like the diary, there is nothing wrong with the methodology except human nature. The rating services are testing the so-called passive people meter. One technique would have a meter programmed through a sensor in the TV set that is unique to each member of the household. When that person comes into the room where a TV set is turned on, the sensor will automatically begin to record that person's viewing. One problem is that a person may be in a room with the television tuned in, but not watching, yet be recorded as a member of the audience. However, the method still overcomes major shortcomings of both the diary and people meter.

The Pocket People Meter. A method that many think is more practical than the sensor-activated passive people meter is the portable people meter that an individual would carry and record any viewing during a rating period. The questions about the pocket people meter center on the willingness of people to carry them and also the concerns about out-of-home viewing discussed earlier.

The practical application of the passive and pocket people meters is in the future. They do demonstrate the problems of measuring a mobile, segmented audience in the current TV environment. It is imperative that the TV industry deliver credible ratings to advertisers in exchange for their multi-billion-dollar advertising investments.

Qualitative Ratings

The foundation of TV audience measures is the number of people (or demographic segments) viewing a particular program. However, the traditional rating measures offer no insight into audience involvement or degree of preference for particular TV shows or personalities. These measures can be ex-

---

People meter

Device that measures TV set usage by individuals rather than by households.

Passive meters

Unobtrusive device that measures individual viewing habits through sensors keyed to household members.

TvQ

A service of Marketing Evaluations that measures the popularity (opinion of audience rather than size of audience) of shows and personalities.

---

tremely important in determining factors such as deciding whether or not to use a person in a testimonial commercial or looking at trends to see if a once-popular show is "wearing out."

The best-known qualitative research service is Marketing Evaluations, which compiles a number of "popularity" surveys called "Q" reports. The most familiar of these are the TvQ and Performer Q.

Let's assume that a TV show, *Big Bob Monday Night Circus,* is familiar to 50 percent of the population, and 30 percent of the people rank it as one of their favorite shows. The Q score would be calculated as follows:

$$Q = \frac{FAV}{FAM}, \text{ or } \frac{30}{50} = 60$$

Q ratings will not take the place of traditional audience ratings. However, they can provide evidence of which personalities and programs might benefit from more promotion or a change to a higher-profile time slot. For example, after six episodes, only 33 percent of respondents indicated they were familiar with *Dr. Quinn, Medicine Woman.* However, among those viewers familiar with the show, it achieved the highest Q rating of any program in prime time.[26] With this information, CBS immediately began a major promotion to introduce more people to the show.

It is important to note that a Q score is not a substitute for minimum ratings. For example, in the fall of 1992, one of the most liked shows on NBC was *Out All Night.* However, despite promotional support from the network, dismal ratings led to an early cancellation.

THE FRAGMENTED AUDIENCE AND THE ELECTRONIC HIGHWAY

The fax machine was available for almost 40 years before businesses took advantage of it. Now it is rare that a business card does not carry a fax number, and fax machines are as common as computers and telephones in offices throughout the world. The supporters of interactive television and home-delivered information services point to the fax as an example of how demand and custom must catch up with technology. However, once society adopts a technology, its success is assured.

Today, companies are betting billions of dollars that they can guess what consumers may eventually want from this new electronic medium. While there is disagreement about the services that should be provided, everyone agrees that the key to this electronic revolution is *interactivity*—the ability of viewers to talk back to their TV sets and/or communicate through computer networks. Various forms of interactive systems have been introduced over the past 20 years.

Currently, the largest system is Prodigy, established by Sears Roebuck and IBM with approximately 1.5 million subscribers. Other interactive services include H&R Block's CompuServe, General Electric's Genie, and America Online. Users of these services can communicate electronically with other members, conduct banking transactions, reserve airline tickets, order from on-line catalogs, and play electronic games.

---

[26]Joe Mandese, "'Dr. Quinn' Could Cure CBS' Blues on Saturday" *Advertising Age,* February 15, 1993, p. 3.

To date, these services have not gained widespread acceptance, with fewer than 2 percent of households subscribing. The problem is not technology but marketing. What do consumers want? Most observers agree that the key to on-line services is television. Television will add a dimension of immediacy and credibility to computer communication. As we will discuss in Chapter 13, the rapid growth of shop-at-home television networks offers a glimpse at the possibilities of such a service.

Interactive television will provide opportunities for on-demand entertainment, education, and information. It also holds great potential for marketing and promotion. "Interactive TV will create opportunities for advertisers and consumer product marketers. In fact, advertisers can be expected to help finance the offerings of interactive services in return for reaching clearly defined target markets. For example, viewers will have the ability to press a button on their television remote control or interactive device in order to receive more information about a ski parka, or travel options to a mountain resort."[27]

The new age of television and related information systems is often referred to as the *electronic superhighway,* a road over which we will buy, sell, laugh, and be informed. The electronic highway will not only change the way we use television and other media, but according to its most optimistic proponents, it will change the way we live and work. In fact, many executives in the communications industry think that business applications, from telecommuting to home banking, will be the first general uses of the technology. However, to make any such system economically viable, it must appeal to the general public.

Whether the electronic highway ultimately becomes a reality depends of two factors—*compatible technology* and *consumer demand.* Everyone agrees that the electronic highway will be a billion-dollar gamble for companies that want to participate. However, there are expected to be plenty of players on this road. As one telecommunications executive points out, "The marketplace is not the $20-billion-a-year cable market or the $12-billion-a-year movie rental market. It is into the hundreds of billions of dollars. It's for work force training, medical services, and shopping. It's the ability to see real estate before traveling there. It's videoconferencing and using multimedia. It's transmitting recipes. It's endless."[28]

The major problem with making the investment in this new TV technology is that no one is sure exactly which options consumers want and what price they will be willing to pay for them. These are related, but separate issues. For example, will this new system be supported by advertising or viewer fees or, as is most likely, some combination of both?

In either case, there must be a certain number of users to make the system profitable to providers and advertisers. For all our talk of segmented marketing, advertisers must have exposure to some minimum audience size. As one advertising executive observed, "Although new networks might corner a certain niche audience, their audiences still must have a critical mass. I don't know what the penetration level is, but there's a [minimum] line that networks must cross for us [advertising agencies] to recommend it to a client."[29]

---

[27]Britton Manasco, "The Age of Interactive Television," *Response TV,* October/November 1992, p. 27.
[28]Andrew Kupfer, "The Race to Rewire America," *Fortune,* April 19, 1993, p. 56.
[29]Junu Bryan Kim, "Step Aside for the 500-Channel Elephant," *Advertising Age,* April 19, 1993, p. S-2.

As exciting as the prospects of the future electronic highway may be, it is still the value of the information that will determine if it is ultimately successful. "It might help to keep things in perspective if you remember that all of this technology, as imaginative as it might be, is only a delivery system. A delivery system is only as good as the merchandise it is delivering. Let me assure you that a lousy movie is still a lousy movie whether you see it in a theater or watch it on a fiber optic cable system."[30]

While the promise of the future is interesting, for the next few years TV advertisers will deal with a less complex, but nevertheless changing environment. For the remainder of this decade advertisers face the challenges and opportunities associated with TV, keeping in mind that significant and often unpredictable changes are closer than most of us believe.

SUMMARY

"From where we stand today, we can't be sure that ad-supported TV programming will have a future in the world being created—a world of video-on-demand, pay-per-view and subscription television."[31] These words of Paul Artz, chairman and chief executive officer of Procter & Gamble, offer insight into the uncertain future of the medium. We are quickly moving from television as a medium of entertainment, information, and advertising to an indispensable electronic helpmate. In a number of markets, telecommunication providers are establishing revolutionary interactive systems that allow viewers to pay bills, make airline reservations, receive pay-per-view programming on demand, and even play computer games with other viewers.

How long it will be before these systems are generally available and what their final form will take are still very much in question. However, programmers, advertisers, and the general public will all be dealing with a dramatically changed TV medium in the not-too-distant future.

The widespread use of fiber optics and digital technology will create a TV medium marked by three major characteristics:[32]

1. *The opportunity to program 500 different channels to every household.* With the use of file servers and other sophisticated computer technology, these channels will be programmed on a networked basis with all of them plugged in together to create an infinite number of options.

2. *This new technology will usher in an age of interactive television.* Viewing will no longer be passive. Television will create an instant two-way pipeline for entertainment, news, and business. TV executives will get immediate feedback. We may see a day when viewers "vote" on the ending of a TV movie or the next play in a football game.

3. *The combination of fiber optics and interactive systems will create an environment of even more specialized programming than what is available today.* We already have comedy, legal, cartoon, and sports channels. In addition, channels featuring military history, baseball, golf, romance, and the fine

[30]D. Claeys Bahrenburg, "Assuring a Prosperous Future for Magazines," speech delivered at the Pierre Hotel, New York City, October 25, 1993.
[31]"P&G's Artz: TV Advertising in Danger," *Advertising Age,* May 23, 1994, p. 24.
[32]Blan Holman, "New Age Television," *American Advertising,* Summer 1993, p. 10.

arts are being planned. Not only will this new medium change viewing habits, but it will be a dramatically different advertising vehicle. Instead of a mass medium, television will become a video magazine rack with specialized programming for every taste and a targeted audience segment for every advertiser and brand.

Television is entering a period of *narrowcasting*. While the three major networks continue to be the dominant source of programming for most viewers, an erosion of network shares will continue into the next century. This erosion will be brought about by niche services that appeal to fewer viewers than the networks can profitably reach. Already the first move toward interactive television can be seen in the home-shopping networks, where viewers call in, comment about merchandise, and place orders.

Among the primary problems facing both advertisers and programmers are the proliferation of channels and a relatively stable audience. The available pool of viewers makes it impossible for the total audience to increase significantly in the future. However, TV channels will continue to grow with the obvious consequence—fewer viewers per channel and increasing costs of reaching them. Like magazines before them, TV advertisers will be forced to become more efficient by seeking specialized programs with little waste circulation. The days of television as a truly "mass medium" are numbered.

Questions

1. What is meant by the electronic superhighway?
2. How has television contributed to the fragmented audience?
3. What is the major ramification of the fragmented audience to TV advertisers?
4. What is meant by the term *clutter?*
5. Contrast ratings and share of audiences.
6. What is clearance in television terminology?
7. What is the difference between upfront and scatter buys?
8. Contrast checkerboard and strip syndication.
9. What is barter syndication?
10. How does the Q rating differ from traditional household ratings?

Using Radio

CHAPTER OBJECTIVES

Radio is the most fragmented of all major media. It offers a multitude of formats to serve virtually any audience segment or advertiser. After reading this chapter you will understand:

■ Radio's transition from a mass to selective medium

■ Radio's out-of-home characteristics and low cost

■ The lack of visual element in radio

■ Dominance of FM

■ The rating system in radio

Radio has undergone dramatic changes in the past 30 years. At one time radio was the premier mass medium for both audiences and advertisers. From 1926, when the first network, the National Broadcasting Company, was formed to the mid-1950s, radio was the most prestigious of the national media. **During those golden years** of radio the family gathered around the living room radio set and was entertained by Jack Benny, Fred Allen, and Bob Hope, while news personalities such as Edward R. Murrow enlightened them. All of this programming was brought to the audience by the major advertisers of the day.

However, the future of radio during the period was not bright. A number of factors, many beyond the control of the radio industry, were coming on the horizon to make radical changes in radio.

> Despite its prestigious status for over four decades, radio's popularity began to slip after the war. Advertisers had fewer dollars to spend in the post-war economy, leaving network programming departments with less extravagant budgets. But most important in radio's slump was the advent of radio's electronic offspring, television, in the late 1940s. Television was introduced officially to the American public when, on camera, FDR opened the New York World's Fair. Spectators were delighted by the new device. Despite distribution difficulties during World War II, media critics prophesied that TV would quickly overtake its electronic predecessor, radio; some even predicted that radio would become a forgotten medium within a decade. Soon it seemed the gloomy forecast might be correct; by 1950, more than 4 million television sets had replaced the console radio's honored place in American living rooms.[1]

Radio's harshest critics of the period underestimated the public demand and the management creativity of radio executives. Without dismissing the rough times that radio has had over the past 20 years, the medium is anything but forgotten. Radio is in many ways a medium tailor-made for the target marketing of the 1990s. Radio, in the aggregate, can deliver huge audiences, but with over 9,000 stations and dozens of programming formats, it is ideal to reach narrowly segmented prospect categories. Radio also is an excellent medium for reaching audiences such as teenagers, who are light users of other media.

Radio can fit into a media schedule as either a primary medium or a secondary vehicle, depending on the demographics of the target audience. In addition, radio's portability makes it the preferred medium for out-of-home audiences both in cars and in the workplace. Its portability also allows advertisers to reach audiences while they are in the marketplace. Only point-of-purchase is able to reach prospects closer to the time of purchase. Finally, radio is inexpensive, both on a CPM basis and from a production standpoint. While many TV commercials cost more than $100,000, the cost of the typical radio commercial is very inexpensive. In fact, some local stations will produce commercials at no cost to an advertiser.

....

Radio Advertising Bureau (RAB)

Association to promote the use of radio as an advertising medium.

....

While statistics alone do not tell the complete story of radio, they are impressive. With over 550 million radio sets in use, there is virtually no American who doesn't have ready access to a set. Radio is a constant companion for entertainment, information, and advertising. Exhibit 9.1 demonstrates the pervasiveness of the medium in our lives.

The value of radio as an advertising medium is evident from the wide variety of advertisers who use the medium on a regular basis. While radio has the reputation of being primarily a local medium, approximately 30 national advertisers spent over $10 million dollars in radio in 1993. More significant

---

[1]Marilyn J. Matelski, "Resilient Radio," *Media Studies Journal*, Summer 1993, p. 10.

EXHIBIT
9.1

· · · · · · · · · · · · · · · · · ·

Radio Statistics

Adults reached weekly by radio	79%
Adults with radio sets at work	61%
Average radios per household	5.6
Average daily radio listenership	3.17
Cars with radio	95%
Teenagers with portable radios	33.5%

(Compiled from statistics provided by the Radio Advertising Bureau.)

than the dollars, is the eclectic composition of these advertisers. Advertisers as diverse as General Motors, Sears, Roebuck & Co., Delta Airlines, and PepsiCo make substantial investments in the media. As we will see in this chapter, radio's success as an advertising medium is a result of the medium matching the marketing goals of advertisers in a way that other media find difficult to duplicate.

FEATURES AND ADVANTAGES OF RADIO

"In some ways, radio listeners act more like magazine subscribers than television viewers. They tend to listen habitually, at predictable times, to stations with narrowly targeted formats. They are loyal, identifiable, and cheaper to reach than are TV audiences . . . demographics can accurately predict the match between a person and his or her radio station. The demographic profiles are highly consistent."[2]

Radio offers a variety of features to advertisers. Many of the medium's characteristics have been given greater weight in recent years as advertisers have moved to a more targeted and localized strategy. In this section we will discuss some of the primary advantages of the medium from an advertiser's perspective.

A Personal Medium

Radio is the most personal of all the mass media. It is the closest thing to one-to-one communication. Most radio programming is especially designed to reach narrow audience segments, which brings a synergism between programming and advertising. The personal nature of radio combined with its mobility make it a constant companion to a majority of the population. Local radio stations also are part of the communities they serve. Virtually every major radio station engages in some public service activity each year (see Exhibit 9.2).

One of radio's major advantages is its ability to reach people in the workplace. It is estimated that more than 50 percent of workers listen to radio on the job. Radio is particularly adept at reaching the elusive working woman. It is estimated that over 60 percent of women have access to radio in the workplace. Almost 80 percent of all women listen to radio from 10 A.M. to 3 P.M., a daypart other media find increasingly difficult to reach women.

Broadly Selective

Radio has the unique ability to deliver both high levels of reach and frequency as well as narrowly targeted market segments. For example, on a weekly ba-

---

[2]Rebecca Piirto, "Why Radio Thrives," *American Demographics*, May 1994, p. 43.

EXHIBIT

9.2

· · · · · · · · · · · · · · · · · · ·

Local radio is an
important link to the
community.

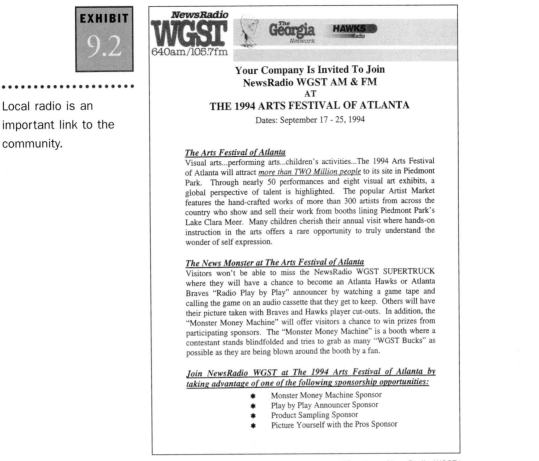

NewsRadio
WGST
640am/105.7fm

The Georgia Network   HAWKS Radio

Your Company Is Invited To Join
NewsRadio WGST AM & FM
AT
THE 1994 ARTS FESTIVAL OF ATLANTA
Dates: September 17 - 25, 1994

The Arts Festival of Atlanta
Visual arts...performing arts...children's activities...The 1994 Arts Festival
of Atlanta will attract _more than TWO Million people_ to its site in Piedmont
Park. Through nearly 50 performances and eight visual art exhibits, a
global perspective of talent is highlighted. The popular Artist Market
features the hand-crafted works of more than 300 artists from across the
country who show and sell their work from booths lining Piedmont Park's
Lake Clara Meer. Many children cherish their annual visit where hands-on
instruction in the arts offers a rare opportunity to truly understand the
wonder of self expression.

The News Monster at The Arts Festival of Atlanta
Visitors won't be able to miss the NewsRadio WGST SUPERTRUCK
where they will have a chance to become an Atlanta Hawks or Atlanta
Braves "Radio Play by Play" announcer by watching a game tape and
calling the game on an audio cassette that they get to keep. Others will have
their picture taken with Braves and Hawks player cut-outs. In addition, the
"Monster Money Machine" will offer visitors a chance to win prizes from
participating sponsors. The "Monster Money Machine" is a booth where a
contestant stands blindfolded and tries to grab as many "WGST Bucks" as
possible as they are being blown around the booth by a fan.

Join NewsRadio WGST at The 1994 Arts Festival of Atlanta by
taking advantage of one of the following sponsorship opportunities:
  ✽ Monster Money Machine Sponsor
  ✽ Play by Play Announcer Sponsor
  ✽ Product Sampling Sponsor
  ✽ Picture Yourself with the Pros Sponsor

(Courtesy: NewsRadio WGST.)

sis, radio reaches 98.8 percent of young adults aged 18–34, 95.5 percent of
African Americans, and 95.6 percent of Hispanics. In fact, there is virtually
no audience segment that cannot be successfully and economically reached
with radio.

Reaching an audience segment and providing a medium that is an integral
part of a marketing program are not necessarily one in the same. You will recall that in Chapter 7 we mentioned that specific prospect categories favor
certain media and that these same prospects are likely to demonstrate particular purchasing behavior. This finding makes radio an ideal medium for
many marketing situations. In some sense, each programming category,
whether it's country, classical, all-talk, or rhythm & blues, can be treated as
a distinct medium for marketing purposes. From a marketing perspective,
magazines are becoming more like radio with a number of specialized titles
designed to reach relatively small audiences (that is, women, sports, hobby,
news, etc.).

Because of the relatively low cost of creative production, advertisers are able
to adapt commercials to the various stations they buy, a strategy that would
normally be prohibitively expensive in television. Coca-Cola has long been a
pioneer in developing commercials for the diverse radio-station formats that
it buys. Many radio advertisers, in order to provide an even closer association between commercials and formats, elect to have local station talent announce their commercials rather than having them preproduced. (We will
discuss the creative approaches to radio in more detail in Chapter 20.)

Radio as a Complement to Other Media

Radio is often used as an inexpensive medium to extend the reach and frequency of primary vehicles in an advertising schedule. For many advertisers, radio serves as a means of reaching prospects who are not regular users of other media. Recently, Visa followed up its summer TV campaign with a heavy schedule of radio spots. A Visa advertising executive explained, "Radio allowed us to expand the number of merchants we use, it reaches light TV viewers, and obviously it's less expensive [than television]."[3]

Low CPM

As we discussed earlier, advertisers demand that media reach specific target audiences, but they are also giving much more attention to cost efficiencies. For more than a decade, radio has offered advertisers the most efficient media on a cost-per-thousand basis. Not only are the CPM levels for radio low, but the rate of increases has been significantly below those of other media during the past decade. As demonstrated in Exhibit 9.3, radio CPM increases have been approximately half of all media increases, and, with the exception of outdoor, radio is the only medium with rate increases lower than the Consumer Price Index.

Because of the number of radio stations and resulting competition for advertising dollars, future increases in radio will remain moderate. Most advertising executives expect radio costs to increase at an annual rate of approximately three percent or about the rate of inflation. Radio has such a huge

EXHIBIT

9.3

••••••••••••••••••••

Radio is cost-effective compared to all other media.

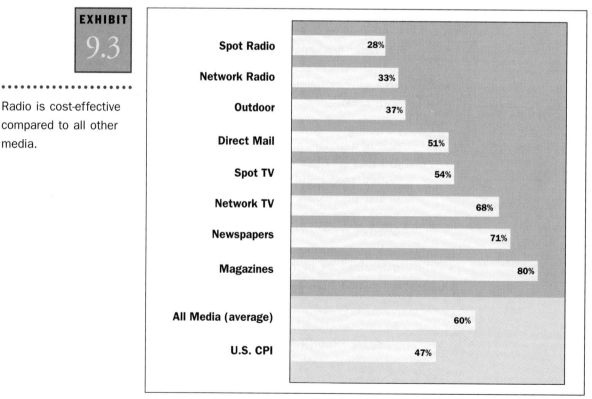

Spot Radio	28%
Network Radio	33%
Outdoor	37%
Direct Mail	51%
Spot TV	54%
Network TV	68%
Newspapers	71%
Magazines	80%
All Media (average)	60%
U.S. CPI	47%

(Courtesy: Radio Advertising Bureau.)

[3]Terry Lefton, "Visa Will Hike Spending 25%; Radio Budget Gets a Big Boost," *Mediaweek*, August 16, 1993, p. 2.

inventory of time that it is difficult for any but the strongest stations or networks to demand significantly higher rates from advertisers. There is nothing on the horizon that indicates any change in that situation.

It would be a mistake to leave the impression that CPM levels can be directly compared among all media. For example, the CPM figures for radio must be considered in light of the frequency needed for effective reach and communicative impact. The CPM level for a single, perishable radio spot cannot be compared directly to that of a magazine ad, which can be read and reread at a person's convenience.

Proximity to Purchase

An advertising medium should only be judged on the basis of its contribution to the marketing communication process. That is, how does it carry out the specific advertising and marketing goals of the advertiser? As we have already discussed, radio can play a major role as either the primary or secondary medium in a schedule. In addition, radio has the ability to reach potential customers at close proximity to purchase.

"The closer a selling message can get to the cash register, the better its chance of actually influencing the purchase. Surveys show that consumers spend more time with radio than any other medium during key shopping hours."[4] The Radio Advertising Bureau (RAB) research indicates that consumers are two to five times more likely to use radio within 30 minutes of purchase compared to any other medium (see Exhibit 9.4). This close proximity to sale is one of radio's primary strengths.

EXHIBIT

9.4

• • • • • • • • • • • • • • • • • • • •

Radio is an important influence on shopping behavior.

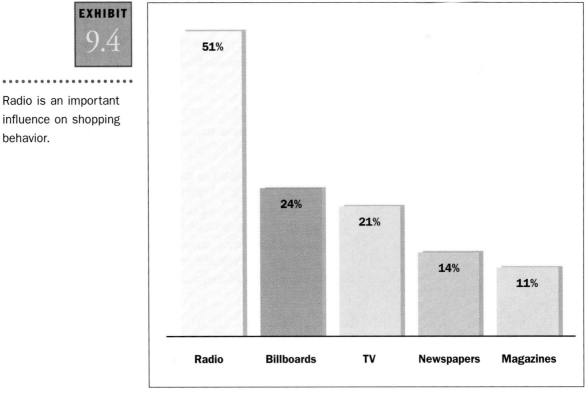

(Courtesy: Radio Advertising Bureau.)

---

[4]"Why Radio," publication of the Radio Advertising Bureau.

EXHIBIT 9.5

Upscale Consumers Tune in to Car Radio

Percent Reached Weekly by In-Car Radio (Mon.–Sun., 24 Hours.)

	Adults 18–	Men 18–	Women 18–
Professional/Managerial	91.4%	92.1%	90.6%
College Graduates	87.8%	89.8%	85.5%
Household Income $50,000+	89.3%	92.4%	85.7%
Professional/Managerial/ Household Income $50,000+	94.2%	94.6%	93.8%
College Graduates/ Household Incomes $50,000+	92.4%	93.7%	90.7%

(Courtesy: Radio Advertising Bureau.)

Despite the strength of radio as a sales tool, the myth continues that the medium is not suitable for upscale audiences. Instead, many advertisers continue to regard radio as a medium for teenagers and rock n' roll enthusiasts. In fact, radio can be an excellent medium to reach affluent prospects. Research shows that higher income and education audience segments are just as likely to listen to radio as any other demographic category. Through the careful placement of radio commercials, the medium can be an excellent means of economically reaching the prime upscale market (see Exhibit 9.5).

Radio Creativity and Flexibility

Unlike other out-of-home messages, radio commercials are not static but can be changed almost immediately to reflect different market conditions or new competition. The personal nature of radio, combined with its flexibility and creativity, makes it a powerful medium for all types of advertisers and product categories (see Exhibit 9.6). One of radio's greatest strengths is its flexibility. Copy changes can be made very quickly. When marketing conditions suddenly change, you can react instantly with radio. The short lead time in production and copy changes is an enormous benefit to advertisers who may need last-minute adjustments to their sales messages.[5]

The ability to anticipate or react to changing conditions cannot be underestimated. For example, when the Indianapolis 500 ends on Memorial Day afternoon, radio commercials touting tire and oil companies begin running that evening. The simplicity of radio can be a major advantage in making tactical marketing decisions. Radio's sense of immediacy and flexibility, all at a cost within the budget of even the smallest advertiser, has made it an important part of the strategy of many advertisers.

LIMITATIONS AND CHALLENGES OF RADIO

Radio, like all advertising media, has both advantages and disadvantages and is not an ideal medium for every objective. As we discussed in the last section, radio has a number of characteristics that make it an ideal vehicle for numerous advertisers as either a primary or secondary medium. In this sec-

---

[5]"Why Radio," publication of the Radio Advertising Bureau.

EXHIBIT
9.6

....

Radio reaches buyers
of all types of products.

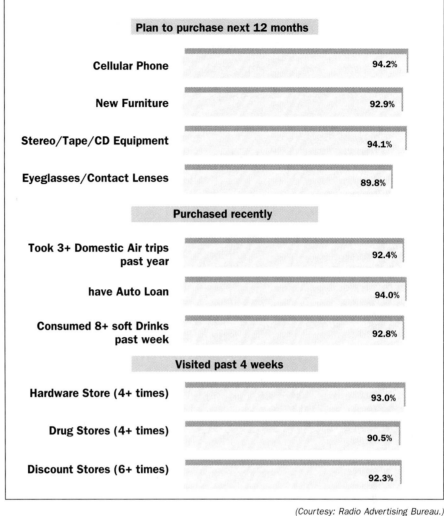

AVERAGE WEEKLY RADIO REACH AMONG ADULTS 18+ WHO...

Plan to purchase next 12 months

Cellular Phone	94.2%
New Furniture	92.9%
Stereo/Tape/CD Equipment	94.1%
Eyeglasses/Contact Lenses	89.8%

Purchased recently

Took 3+ Domestic Air trips past year	92.4%
have Auto Loan	94.0%
Consumed 8+ soft Drinks past week	92.8%

Visited past 4 weeks

Hardware Store (4+ times)	93.0%
Drug Stores (4+ times)	90.5%
Discount Stores (6+ times)	92.3%

(Courtesy: Radio Advertising Bureau.)

tion, we will examine some of the major disadvantages that must be considered before using radio.

Audience Fragmentation

You will recall that radio offers a wide variety of stations and programming formats that allow advertisers to find virtually any marketing niche. Some advertisers and agencies are beginning to question whether or not radio is oversegmented to the point that it is impossible to deal with all the options. To put the situation in perspective, there are more than twice as many radio stations as TV stations, consumer magazines, and daily newspapers combined!

The critics of radio charge that segmentation may have been carried too far. Especially for product categories with broad appeal, it makes life more complicated. On the other hand, there are media buyers who "not only say that fragmentation isn't bad, but it's natural. Media buyers should be grateful for it, because the more precise the target audience, the better the fit with a brand's target demographics."[6]

---

[6]Victoria Kahn, "Fragmentation!" *Adweek*, May 3, 1993, p. 18.

Regardless of media buyers' view of radio's fragmentation, it is clear that the number of stations and program options present special problems for advertisers. First, since radio spots are relatively inexpensive, agencies earn a lower per-spot commission than if they were placing the same number of advertising insertions in other media. Second, the audience research available in radio, especially in measuring out-of-home listeners, is often difficult to evaluate and compare to that of other media. Consequently, the agency media planner may have to work harder for less profit. Sometimes it is the path of least resistance simply to exclude radio as a major part of a client's media plan.

Lack of a Visual Element

Imagery transfer research

A technique that measures the ability of radio listeners to correctly describe the primary visual elements of related television commercials.

Although the logistical problems of buying radio can be countered, a more fundamental problem is radio's lack of a visual element. In this age of self-service retailing and competitive brand promotions, package identification is critical for many advertisers. The radio industry has developed creative techniques to partially overcome this visual shortcoming. Sound effects; jingles; short, choppy copy; and vivid descriptions attempt to create a mental picture. A major research study by Statistical Research, Inc. (SRI) demonstrated that listeners are effectively able to develop "mental pictures" as a result of radio commercials. Using *imagery transfer research*, SRI showed that a majority of listeners correctly described the prime visual element of TV commercials when listening to radio commercials for the same products. Many listeners also *created* correct product images even when they had not appeared in TV commercials.

The implications of imagery transfer research are extremely important for a number of reasons:

1. Radio's ability to evoke visual images based on what a listener has seen on television makes it a highly efficient method for reinforcing a TV campaign.

2. Imagery transfer offers opportunities for advertisers to extend their TV campaigns with radio so that their advertising can be exposed over a longer period of time for roughly the same budget.

3. Radio can be used to fill seasonal gaps, such as summer, when TV viewing is low and radio listening is stable.

4. Advertisers who use a flighting strategy for television might maintain consumer awareness between flights with a radio schedule.

5. SRI data show that younger listeners are more likely to transfer images successfully. This finding is important, since most radio formats tend to skew toward younger age groups.

While the lack of a visual element is an obvious disadvantage to radio, the SRI study shows that listeners do invoke mental images already established in television. This research only reinforces the value of radio as a cost-efficient complement to other media and shows that radio can provide a visual impact for multimedia campaigns.

Low Cost

As we noted earlier, the CPM and rate increases for radio have been the lowest among the major media in recent years. While an advantage to the advertiser purchasing time on the medium, this does not bode well for the fu-

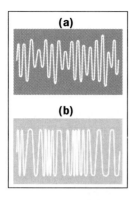

(a)

(b)

In amplitude modulation (a) waves vary in height (amplitude): frequency is constant. Frequency modulation (b) varies the frequency but keeps the height constant. These drawings, however, are not made to scale, which would reveal that width is the significant difference between AM and FM. The FM wave is 20 times wider than the AM wave. This fact helps to explain how FM captures its fine tones.

ture financial health of the industry. With the radio advertising dollar and listening audience being continually divided among more and more stations, all but the strongest stations in each market see the potential for even greater financial trouble ahead.

Difficulty of Obtaining Research Data

In a later section of this chapter, we will discuss the primary means of collecting radio audience data. However, we should mention that the difficulty of gathering reliable research information is a problem for the industry. With the number of stations, lack of distinctive programming for accurate recall of listening behavior, high percentages of out-of-home audience, and relatively small ratings for any given station or daypart, radio represents a major challenge for researchers attempting to gather accurate audience data.

TECHNICAL ASPECTS OF RADIO

The Signal

The electrical impulses that are broadcast by radio are called the *signal*. If a certain station has a good signal in a given territory, its programs and commercials come over clearly in that area.

Frequency

All signals are transmitted by electromagnetic waves, sometimes called *radio waves*. These waves differ from one another in frequency (the number of waves that pass a given point in a given period of time). Frequencies for AM stations are measured in Kilohertz, or KHz, and FM stations frequencies are measured in Megahertz, or MHz. The FCC has assigned the following frequencies to all radio stations: AM = 540 to 1700 KHz; FM = 88.1 to 107.9 MHz.

Amplitude

All electromagnetic waves have height, spoken of as *amplitude*, whose range resembles the difference between an ocean wave and a ripple in a pond, and speed, measured by the frequency with which a succession of waves passes a given point per minute. If, for example, a radio station operates on a frequency of 1,580 KHz, this means that 1,580,000 of its waves pass a given point per second.

On the basis of these two dimensions—amplitude and frequency—two separate systems have been developed for carrying radio waves. The first system carries the variations in a sound wave by corresponding variations in its amplitude; the frequency remains constant. This is the principle of amplitude modulation (AM) (Exhibit 9.7a). The second system carries the variation in a sound wave by corresponding variations in its frequency; the amplitude remains constant. This is the principle of frequency modulation (FM) (Exhibit 9.7b).

The technical structure of AM and FM radio has created, in effect, two distinct media, each offering different values to the listener and the advertiser. AM signals carry farther but are susceptible to interference. FM has a fine tonal quality, but its signal distances are limited. A particular station's quality of reception is determined by atmospheric conditions and station power (broadcast frequency).

SELLING RADIO COMMERCIAL TIME

Radio is very much a local medium. Unlike television, network radio remains a very minor advertising vehicle in terms of total advertising expenditures. In the foreseeable future, the relationship between national spot, network, and local radio advertising is anticipated to remain fairly constant. Exhibit 9.8 shows the total estimated expenditures over the next several years with a comparison to 1991 spending levels.

It is obvious that radio must be positioned to both local and national advertisers as a local medium. The biggest mistake radio salespeople can make in attempting to sell an advertiser is to assume they are selling time. Radio commercial time is simply the unit of sale. What is being sold is an audience that is in the market for a specific product and can provide profits to a company more efficiently than if the company does not use radio.

The astute radio salesperson must combine the target audience of the advertiser with the likely audience for a specific brand and then find the particular station that will combine the two. Exhibit 9.9 demonstrates the way in which radio reaches buyers of various products. However, an advertiser is only marginally interested in the way radio as a medium delivers a particular audience. Advertisers do not buy an entire medium; they buy a single network or station or group of stations.

A radio salesperson must be able to show how the station's audience constitutes a potential market for any advertiser's good or services. Once this relationship is shown, the next step is to address the question of competitive efficiency. In other words, can we deliver this market segment better than competing media? Often the question is not an either/or proposition, which brings us to a common error of selling radio time, that is, presenting an unreasonable media schedule to a client.

Even though radio offers a great deal of promise to many advertisers, it is unlikely that any but the smallest firms are going to use radio as their exclusive advertising medium. You will recall that one of the major strengths of radio is its ability to function as a secondary medium in a schedule. Consequently, advertisers must be presented with a reasonable alternative to their current advertising strategy, not a 180-degree departure.

In order to sell radio as a complement to an advertiser's primary schedule, the media salesperson must know both the advertising goals of the firm and have a thorough knowledge of the competitive strengths of other media. The radio salesperson walks a tightrope between selling as a complement to other media and selling against other media.

Another problem radio faces in getting additional advertising dollars is the reluctance of some national agencies to treat it as a full partner in clients' me-

EXHIBIT 9.8

Radio Advertising Revenues (in millions)

	Local	Spot	Network
1991	$6,375	$1,580	$495
1996	8,650 (+35.7)	2,195 (+44%)	655 (+32.3%)

(Source: The Veronis, Suhler & Associates Communications Industry Forecast, June 1992, pp. 89, 92.)

EXHIBIT

9.9

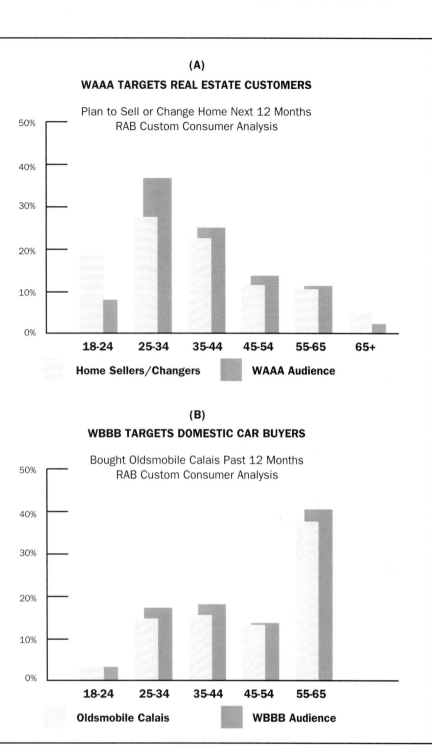

(Source: Radio Advertising Bureau)

dia schedules. As we discussed earlier, this problem is in part a result of the complexity of determining the stations and networks most appropriate for a specific brand. This "step-sister" mentality of agencies toward radio extend to both media and creative. In too many cases, is routinely assigned to the most junior media buyers and creative directors.

One radio executive urged advertising agencies "to take a fresh look at radio as a major advertising opportunity and to act now to capitalize on it. Either start thinking of radio as an integral part of your creative [and media] department, or contract it out to people who know what they're doing."[7]

Radio advertising faces challenges both from within the industry and from other media as it competes for advertising dollars, First, it must compete with selective media, especially those such as Yellow Pages and direct response, which also reach targeted audiences. Of equal concern is competition from other radio stations in a particular market. Whereas a typical city usually has one major daily newspaper, a few suburban weeklies, three network affiliates, a couple of independent TV stations, and perhaps two out-of-home media companies, there may be 30 or more radio stations in the metropolitan area. While radio advertising, like television, is made up of network, local, and spot advertising, the similarity ends there.

Although local radio advertising is the largest category of radio revenues, both network and spot advertising are important to most stations. In the next sections we will discuss these categories of radio advertising.

Network Radio

Network radio has very little in common with its TV counterpart. Even with the inroads of cable television and independent stations, the four major TV networks control the majority of viewers and dominant national advertising. In the case of network radio, it has revenues of less than $500 million, or about 6 percent of total radio revenues of more than $9 billion. But it is not just the relatively low revenues that separate network radio from TV networks.

There are currently more than 40 radio networks. However, defining a network is not always easy. "Network radio is essentially a program service. The networks provide only a small part of total programming. For many stations, a radio network provides short segments, such as news, inserted into locally originated programs. In other cases, stations obtain virtually all of their programming from radio networks. The strength of radio networks depends ultimately on the strength of the stations that carry network programming."[8]

Despite the fact that radio networks do not match the prestige, audiences, or advertising revenues of their TV counterparts, they are still a vital program source for many stations. Major radio networks provide a number of services, many featuring national personalities. For example, ABC Radio Networks offer ABC Prime featuring personalities from ABC news including Sam Donaldson, Hugh Downs, Barbara Walters, and Peter Jennings. Likewise, ABC Platinum, targeting 25- to 54-year-olds, and ABC Galaxy, programming to smaller market stations, bring news and entertainment features that few local stations could afford. Altogether, ABC offers over 80 hours of program services each week. Other leading radio networks are CBS, and Infinity Broadcasting, which, together with ABC, reach approximately 80 percent of total network radio audiences.

Unlike TV stations, a single radio station may belong to several radio networks simultaneously. For example, a station might get sports reports from

---

[7]James Conlan, "Clients Like Radio, but Agencies Seem Reluctant to Embrace It," *Advertising Age*, June 14, 1993, p. 20.
[8]*The Veronis Suhler & Associates Communications Industry Forecast*, June 1992, p. 90.

one network, personality profiles and news from another, and entertainment fare from yet another. Whereas in television local stations sell advertising time on the basis of the strength of the network programming, in radio the networks must depend on local ratings to garner national advertising support.

Another major difference between TV and radio networks is that while TV networks dominant the media schedules of most national advertisers, network radio is a secondary medium to virtually every advertiser who uses it. For example Sears, Roebuck & Co. has been the consistent leader in network radio advertising during the past several years. However, the radio budget for Sears accounts is less than 4 percent of the company's total advertising expenditure. This pattern is consistent with almost all radio network advertisers.

The fact that radio networks exist at all is a surprise to many people who saw their plight in the wake of television's introduction. By the 1960s, most radio networks had ceased regular programming and provided only limited hourly newscasts and occasional informational services. Network clearance fees accounted for less and less station revenue, and, in fact, network time was often bartered in exchange for station clearances. By the early 1970s, the growth of stations created a competitive atmosphere that demanded unique program identification and quality that many local stations could not afford. To address the problem, syndication companies were formed to provide quality programming that would be impractical for all but the largest market stations.

While this "new" network era in radio began in the 1970s, it was the coming of satellite technology in 1981 that opened the full potential of network radio. The satellite downlink, now inexpensive enough for even the smallest station, can provide local stations with anything from a single program to a 24-hour schedule of music, news, or all-talk formats.

Despite the many differences with television, radio networks do offer some of the same advantages as television. For example, an advertiser prepares one insertion order for multiple stations, pays one invoice, and is guaranteed uniform production quality for the commercials on all stations. Radio networks also provide economical reach and, like all radio, are able to target special audience segments who may be light users of other media.

While still representing a small portion of total national advertising budgets, radio has grown on a percentage basis at a faster rate than most media in recent years. National advertisers find that they can generate high levels of reach against target audiences at a fraction of the cost of television. For example, a spot on a popular network radio show may cost as little as $3,200 compared to the $325,000 advertisers pay for a top-rated TV program such as *Home Improvement*.

The emergence of satellite networks offers a number of advantages for their local station affiliates:

1. Stations are guaranteed quality programming based on the latest audience research for a particular format.

2. Radio networks bring celebrities to the medium that local stations could not afford.

3. Even the smallest stations can obtain national advertising dollars as part of a network. Stations that would not be considered by national advertis-

ers as part of a local spot buy may now be included in a network radio schedule.

4. The cost efficiencies of sharing programming with several hundred other affiliates keeps both personnel and programming costs to a minimum.

Network radio will never return to its former status as a primary medium for national advertisers. However, as a source of program services, with its ability to target narrow audience segments, it will continue to play an important role for a number of national advertisers. Exhibit 9.10 shows how the addition of network radio to a network TV schedule can extend both reach and frequency against two primary target markets.

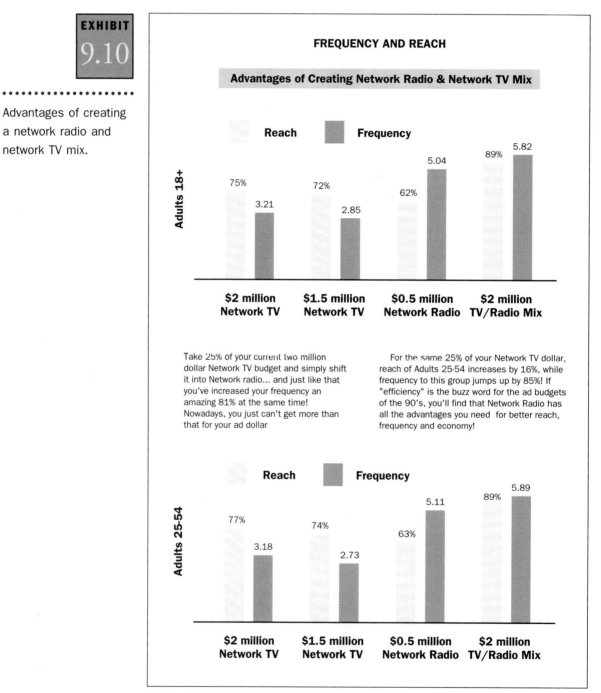

(Courtesy: Radio Network Association.)

Spot Radio

You will recall from our discussion in Chapter 8, spot broadcast is the buying of local stations by national advertisers. As in the case with television, spot radio can be used as a supplement to network radio or as a primary medium. For example, AT&T spends over $25 million on network radio and adds exposure in some major markets with $10 million in spot radio. This strategy is in sharp contrast to Southland's expenditure of $15 million on spot and nothing in network for its 7-11 stores. Regardless of the relative expenditures between spot and network radio by an advertiser, spot radio is almost always used as a secondary medium by national advertisers.

National advertisers use spot radio to reach specific demographic segments. Slightly over 50 percent of all spot radio dollars are spent to reach the 25–54 age group, followed by 18–49 age group (16.9 percent), and 18–34 age group (6.5 percent). No other age category accounts for over 6 percent of buys.[9] Radio marketing executives predict that spot radio will grow at a faster rate than either local or network during the coming years.

The significance of these data is that they show how spot radio is perceived by national advertisers. It is clear that national advertisers use spot just as they use local and network radio. That is, they reach small demographic niches such as Hispanic, farm, or older audiences as well as add weight to those audiences that constitute the best potential for sales and profits.

Nonwired networks
Groups of radio and TV stations whose advertising is sold simultaneously by station representatives.

As we discussed in Chapter 8, most spot broadcast purchases are made through reps. In principle, radio reps serve the same function as those in television. The best reps are those who serve as marketing consultants for their client stations. They work with agencies to match target audiences with the appropriate stations in their client list. Sometimes this is done on a market-by-market basis. In other cases, buys are made through nonwired networks in the same manner as TV nonwired networks, which we discussed in the previous chapter. In fact, radio reps initiated the unwired network, which has been adopted by TV. In both radio and television these "networks" offer advertisers the ability to buy many markets with one insertion order and one bill. This greatly simplifies the media planner's job and helps to increase spot buying, especially among smaller stations.

AM versus FM as an Advertising Medium

The growth of FM radio audiences and advertising revenues during the past 20 years is the most important trend in the industry in recent years. In many respects, the development of FM resulted in the revitalization of radio as a medium. In 1960, there were only 815 commercial FM stations, or 19 percent of total stations. Currently, there are almost 5,000 FM stations, or about half of total commercial radio stations. However, the number of stations does not begin to tell the story of FM as an advertising medium.

Over the past 20 years, there has been a steady loss of AM audiences to FM. Today, FM radio's share of audience is approaching 80 percent of the total radio listenership. Obviously, advertising dollars follow audiences. However, in recent years many AM stations have benefited from the popularity of na-

---

[9]*Radio Business Report Source Guide and Directory*, 1993, p. 213.

tional radio talk shows hosted by personalities such as Rush Limbaugh, Paul Harvey, and G. Gordon Liddy. For example, Limbaugh is carried by over 500 stations with a weekly audience of 19 million listeners.[10]

Despite some growth in AM popularity, FM will continue to be the dominant radio sector. There are several reasons for the emergence of FM:

1. In 1972 the FCC ruled that joint owners of both AM and FM stations in the same market had to program different formats. This ruling opened the way for FM as a separate medium.

2. The sound quality of FM is markedly better than AM. Since music formats dominate radio, FM steadily gained audience share at the expense of AM.

3. The decline in the cost of FM sets coincided with the popularity of the medium. Twenty years ago, radio sets with an FM band were much more expensive than AM-only sets. Also few cars were equipped with FM radio. Currently, 88 percent of car radios are AM/FM and it is difficult to find a radio set without both AM and FM capability.

4. As radio audiences turned to FM for the most popular music formats, AM was left with news, talk, and specialty formats such as religion. With the exception of some popular talk shows, AM formats often do not appeal to those market segments most desired by advertisers. Therefore, the switch to FM by audiences was quickly followed by an increase in advertising dollars.

It is clear that FM will continue to be the dominant radio medium as AM stations search for a niche to ensure their survival. We can expect AM stations to be popular with an older audience and concentrate on information, talk, news, and some specialized music formats such as nostalgia and easy listening that appeal to these listeners. AM stations are also attempting to develop more creative programming to this older audience. For example, some stations offer financial, health, and other specialized programming that appeals to the majority of the upscale segment of the "talk-radio" audience.

Time Classifications—Dayparts

The broadcast day is divided into time periods called dayparts as follows:

Drive time (radio)

A term used to designate the time of day when people are going to, or coming from, work. Usually 6 A.M. to 10 A.M. and 3 P.M. to 7 P.M., but this varies from one community to another. The most costly time on the rate card.

Daypart	Characteristics
6 A.M.–10 A.M.	Drive time, breakfast audience, interested chiefly in news
10 A.M.–3 P.M.	Daytime, programs characteristic of station, talk, music, or all-news
3 P.M.–7 P.M.	Afternoon, drive time; radio primetime and same as morning drive time
7 P.M.–12 A.M.	News, music, talk shows
12 A.M.–6 A.M.	Music, talk shows

Weekends are regarded as a separate time classification. Most radio spot time is sold in 60-second units. The cost varies with the daypart.

The size of radio audiences varies widely from daypart to daypart. The peak listening period is from 7 A.M. to 10 A.M., with an average of 31 to 24.5 per-

---

[10]Andrea Adelson, "Advertising," *New York Times*, December 28, 1993, p. C16.

cent of the audience tuning in during subsequent quarter hours. TV viewing, of course, peaks between 8 and 10 P.M., with average quarter-hour audiences in the 50 percent range. Radio also differs from television in seasonality of audience levels. Radio listening is remarkably stable throughout the year, whereas TV audiences fluctuate as much as 25 percent from fall to summer.

TYPES OF PROGRAMMING

Radio is not a medium of programming in a traditional sense. Instead, radio stations appeal to audiences with general formats. Unlike television, where viewers tune to a certain program for a half-hour or hour and then move to another station for another show, radio audiences tend to demonstrate loyalty to a station because of the *type* of music, sports, or information it carries on a regular basis.

Currently, the most popular radio format is country with over 2,000 stations, followed by adult contemporary with some 1,300 stations. At the other extreme, six stations broadcast at least 20 hours per week of polka music, and two stations broadcast Japanese-language programming. While every station would like to be the leader in a popular format, radio executives know that it is extremely difficult for more than one or two stations in a market to be financially successful in any particular format. Why would an advertiser buy the third- or fourth-rated country station?

Consequently, second- and third-tier stations are constantly searching for niche formats that will allow them to be the leader among some audience segment that is of value to advertisers. There are currently 13 formats that have at least 1 percent of the total radio listening audience (see Exhibit 9.11). Other formats such as classical or jazz depend on an upscale audience that is difficult for advertisers to reach in other media. However, with as many as 30 stations in a large-market listening area, selling formats is not only cut-throat, but often a little silly. For instance, stations without impressive total numbers may resort to calling themselves the number-one station in a particular daypart (for example, midnight–6 A.M.) or developing subcategories of a format to differentiate themselves from other stations (easy listening country).

The bottom line for a successful radio station is the same as most commercial media. That is, stations must deliver a homogeneous audience that represents a major target segment for some group of advertisers. Without such an audience, no amount of selling or research data are going to convince an advertiser to invest in a station. Radio stations are continually fine-tuning their formats to differentiate themselves from competing stations to maximize advertising revenues. However, those stations that are constantly changing or tinkering with their formats are virtually always the weaker stations in a market.

Occasionally, these format changes result in lightning striking, and a station moves dramatically ahead in ratings. More often, it is seen by advertisers as smoke and mirrors with little value to anybody. One factor that works in the favor of stations trying to make changes to enhance their audiences is the relatively low ratings achieved by radio stations.

Radio should be considered a quasi–mass medium. Despite its generally high-aggregate audiences, the number of people listening to any particular station

EXHIBIT
9.11

Radio offers a multitude of formats for both listeners and advertisers.

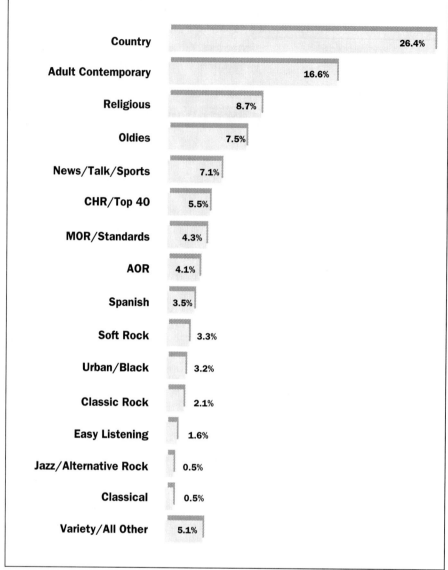

Format	Percentage
Country	26.4%
Adult Contemporary	16.6%
Religious	8.7%
Oldies	7.5%
News/Talk/Sports	7.1%
CHR/Top 40	5.5%
MOR/Standards	4.3%
AOR	4.1%
Spanish	3.5%
Soft Rock	3.3%
Urban/Black	3.2%
Classic Rock	2.1%
Easy Listening	1.6%
Jazz/Alternative Rock	0.5%
Classical	0.5%
Variety/All Other	5.1%

(Courtesy: Radio Advertising Bureau.)

at a given time is very small. Even the top stations in a market will be lucky to achieve ratings of 8 or 10, and a rating of 1 to 3 is more common. Consequently, an audience increase that would be insignificant in other media, might make a major difference in the financial health of a radio station. For example, a change of 1 rating point for a station with an average rating of 3 is an increase of 33 percent.

RADIO RATINGS SERVICES

Because of the number of stations, the diversity of formats, and the relatively small per-station listenership, radio ratings are much more difficult to obtain than those for television. For one thing, radio listeners (unlike TV viewers) do not have the advantage of regularly scheduled programs by which to recall their listening habits. Therefore, recall of listening behavior is very difficult. Added to the lack of specific programming is the fact that radio is increasingly an out-of-home medium. It is impossible to measure listenership in cars and impractical to contact survey respondents in the workplace. Consequently, a large portion of the radio audience is missed, miscounted, or dependent on recall to give their responses.

Arbitron Ratings Company

Syndicated radio and TV ratings company. Dominant in local radio ratings.

Local radio station ratings are obtained largely through the Arbitron Ratings Company. However, in recent months a service known as AccuRatings has initiated a telephone-based rating service that measures listeners who say they listen to a particular station the most.

Depending on the long-term success of AccuRatings, the basic tool for gaining radio ratings information is Arbitron's self-administered diary. Despite their widespread use, there are two primary problems with diary methodology. The first drawback is not the methodology, but human nature. Diaries can be put aside and either not returned or filled in all at once, creating a recall problem.

The diary is also a less-than-adequate means of measuring the increasing out-of-home audience. We discussed the same problem in connection with TV ratings in the previous chapter. However, except for a few categories of shows such as sports and late night, the out-of-home TV audience remains relatively small. In radio, the out-of-home audience is large and growing. It is estimated that only 45 percent of the total radio audience listen at home. Obviously, out-of-home listeners are neither inclined nor able to fill out diaries.

As we discussed in Chapter 8, the portable people meter is an attempt to gain more accurate ratings. While the major application will probably be in television, the device also can be used for radio ratings. It is the size of a pager and picks up an inaudible code in the audio of station broadcasts. At the end of the survey period, the data would be sent by modem to a central computer. While the system is not due for introduction for a few years, it promises to provide accurate ratings without the current problems of diaries.

Radio All Dimension Audience Research (RADAR)

Service of Statistical Research, Inc., major source of network radio ratings.

Because of the local nature of radio, station ratings are much more critical to most advertisers than those for networks. However, as we have discussed earlier, network radio is an important medium to a number of advertisers. The major source of radio network ratings is RADAR, a service of Statistical Research, Inc. Exhibit 9.12 is an example of one of the RADAR reports. Data used in RADAR reports are collected through telephone recall interviews. RADAR measurements are based on information gathered over a 48-week period. Data on radio listening for a one-week period are obtained by daily telephone interviews.

RATE CLASSIFICATIONS

Every station establishes its own classifications and publishes them on its rate card. The negotiated cost of time depends on those classifications, which are typically the following:

- **Drive time.** The most desired and costly time on radio, it varies by the community and usually has the highest ratings.

- **Run-of-station (ROS).** The station has a choice of moving the commercial at will, wherever it is most convenient. Preemptible ROS is the least costly time on the rate card.

- **Special features.** Time adjacent to weather signals, news reports, time signals, traffic, or stock market reports usually carries a premium charge.

	Total Pers 12+	Total Adults 18+	Men Total	Men 18–49	Men 25–54	Men 25+	Men 35+	Women Total	Women 18–49	Women 25–54	Women 25+	Women 35+	Teens 12–17
Full 24 Hour Day													
Average Quarter Hour	25075	22680	10551	7936	6354	8353	5242	12129	8166	6806	10012	7313	2395
Average 1 Day Cume	153746	135433	65606	47073	38816	53156	35813	69827	46984	38807	57587	40948	18313
7 Day Weekly Cume	184581	163575	78554	54927	45977	64650	44374	85021	55741	46827	71081	50923	21006
6.00 AM to 12.00 M													
Average Quarter Hour	31055	28095	13025	9743	7845	10356	6508	15070	10176	8512	12463	9081	2960
Average 1 Day Cume	151500	133358	64525	46300	38117	52240	35193	68833	46313	38310	56820	40438	18142
7 Day Weekly Cume	184280	163274	78328	54848	45868	64433	44182	84946	55715	46801	71006	50861	21006
6.00 AM to 10.00 AM													
Average Quarter Hour	38969	36281	16531	11648	10229	13984	9236	19750	12494	11291	17234	12986	2688
Average 1 Day Cume	106871	95899	46571	32620	28430	39059	26680	49328	32395	28057	41891	30477	10972
7 Day Weekly Cume	168896	149491	72185	50845	42995	59752	40833	77306	51665	43301	64287	45744	19405
10.00 AM to 3.00 PM													
Average Quarter Hour	36524	34021	15576	11675	9475	12517	7719	18445	12549	10576	15307	10948	2503
Average 1 Day Cume	86804	78265	36543	26822	21408	29062	18728	41722	28737	23382	33961	24050	8539
7 Day Weekly Cume	163471	144987	68420	48907	40161	55460	37297	76567	51534	42772	63189	44731	18484
3.00 PM to 7.00 PM													
Average Quarter Hour	31966	28433	13486	10455	8330	10551	6533	14947	10562	8627	12059	8585	3533
Average 1 Day Cume	87087	76302	37879	29075	23882	30210	19193	38423	27843	22678	30945	21053	10785
7 Day Weekly Cume	160000	140102	67810	49485	40959	55005	36541	72292	50823	41799	59060	40611	19898
7.00 PM to 12.00 M													
Average Quarter Hour	18527	15350	7302	5717	3921	5140	3099	8048	5641	4134	6124	4485	3177
Average 1 Day Cume	61272	50568	24734	19358	14029	17979	11316	24834	18425	13949	19932	13944	10704
7 Day Weekly Cume	133060	113868	55627	42666	33627	43365	27981	58241	42366	33395	46105	31091	19192
12.00 M to 6.00 AM													
Average Quarter Hour	7133	6433	3126	2512	1878	2341	1441	3307	2137	1687	2661	2009	700
Average 1 Day Cume	35348	31807	15649	11931	9466	12241	7894	16158	11069	9123	13139	9744	3541
7 Day Weekly Cume	83458	72696	36416	28531	21541	27521	17648	36280	26303	20056	28006	19589	10762

(Courtesy: Statistical Research Inc.)

EXHIBIT
9.12

· · · · · · · · · · · · · · · · · ·

As seen above, national advertisers need network audience figures.

Package Plans

Most spot time is sold in terms of a weekly package plan, usually called *total audience plans,* or TAP. A station offers a special flat rate for a number of time slots divided in different proportions over the broadcast day. A typical TAP plan distributes time equally through the broadcast day.

An advertiser can buy the total plan or parts of it. In all instances, there is a quantity- or dollar-discount plan, depending upon the total number of spots run during a given period of time:

Number of Times[a]	8	12	20	32	40
1 minute, $	110	100	92	86	79
30 seconds, $	88	80	74	69	63

[a] Per week $\left(\frac{1}{4} \text{ A.M.}, \frac{1}{4} \text{ P.M.}, \frac{1}{4} \text{ housewife}, \frac{1}{4} \text{ night}\right)$.

Negotiations

In buying spot radio time, as in buying spot TV time, negotiation is the rule rather than the exception. The successful media planner is a hard, but reasonable bargainer. There is no formula to determine what radio spots should cost; therefore, negotiation is critical to cost efficiency for the advertiser. Radio advertising is basically worth whatever the advertiser will pay. As we have seen, the number of stations, formats, and purchase plans make buying radio extremely complex. Regardless of whether you enter media negotiations as a buyer or a seller, several points are key to an efficient buy:

1. *Do your homework.* The media buyer should know the demand for various dayparts and the general pricing policies of each station in a market. The salesperson should know the marketing strategy of advertisers, budgets available for radio, and the media mix of the advertisers with which he or she is dealing.

2. *Be fair.* Advertising sales depend on mutual respect between buyer and seller. The media buyer often looks to the media salesperson as a source of information beyond the buy at hand. The seller who takes advantage of this relationship by offering spots that do not fulfill the advertiser's goals is making short-term gains at the risk of future loss of sales.

3. *Know your counterpart.* The astute negotiator knows not only the rating numbers, but also the personalities of those with whom he or she deals and what techniques work with them.

4. *Do not be greedy.* The best negotiator knows when to close the deal. There is a fine line between being a tough negotiator and losing a sale by keeping the price unrealistically high or losing a spot by refusing to pay a reasonable rate.

Obviously, negotiation is something that can be learned only by doing. This is why most of the top broadcast salespeople and media buyers started in small markets or as media research assistants in agencies and worked up slowly to larger markets and greater agency buying responsibility.

BUYING RADIO

Before radio salespeople can convince clients to buy the medium, they must put themselves in the place of individual clients to determine how radio will accomplish their marketing and advertising goals. The successful salesperson must approach the sale from the client's point of view. At one time, radio held a unique role in the media schedule of most advertisers. Generally, radio accomplished one of three functions for an advertiser:

1. *It supplemented other media to add weight to a schedule.* It is particularly valuable for special sales or to react to unanticipated marketing conditions.

2. *Radio was valuable as a niche medium.* As we have seen, radio often reaches market segments that are not heavy users of other media. For example, for many teenagers radio is the primary medium, while print is very ineffective.

3. *For a few retailers, especially smaller stores or those with narrowly segmented clientele, it was their only medium.*

Today, advertisers continue to use radio for each of these marketing and advertising objectives. However, the radio salesperson finds that the medium landscape is full of new competitors, each claiming to accomplish many of the same tasks as radio. The localized strategy adopted by many national advertisers, discussed in Chapter 7, led media such as television to see the advantages of competing for local dollars as well as selling added local weight to national advertisers.

At one time, radio competed only with newspapers for local dollars. Today, radio finds Yellow Pages, local cable outlets, broadcast stations, outdoor, direct mail, free shoppers and specialty books for real estate, automobiles, etc.—all trying to get a share of the local advertising dollar. All of these competitors have a visual element that radio lacks. It has never been more important for radio to develop creative strategies to overcome this major disadvantage.

The radio salesperson must become a marketing consultant, a partner with the client in showing how radio can solve specific advertising problems. A central element in successful radio sales "is an understanding of other media—not merely to identify and take advantage of a competitor's weak spots, but to be able to speak from an informed, objective point of view about the strengths and weaknesses of all media, and to work with the client in developing the most productive marketing plan."[11]

It is clear that clients buy radio as part of an overall media strategy. Radio, or for that matter any medium, is rarely purchased on an individual basis. The client and the media salesperson must view the media plan as a synergistic one in which each medium complements the others. Unless radio can create a value to other media, it is unlikely it will be part of a media schedule. Fortunately, radio offers unique characteristics that will allow it to be considered for at least a secondary role in the advertising plans of virtually all advertisers.

USING RADIO RATINGS

You will recall that we defined both TV ratings and share of audience in the previous chapter. Radio also uses ratings and shares and calculates them in the same way. However, the audiences and programming of radio mandate that ratings be used in a way much different from the way ratings are used in television. In this section, we will discuss some uses of ratings that are unique to radio.

Among the primary differences between the use of ratings in television and radio are the following:

1. Radio advertisers are interested in broad formats rather than programs or more narrowly defined television scatter plans.

2. Radio ratings tend to measure audience accumulation over relatively long periods of time or several dayparts. Most TV ratings are for individual programs.

3. The audiences for individual radio stations are much smaller than television, making radio ratings less reliable.

4. Since most radio stations reach only a small segment of the market at a given time, there is a need for much higher levels of advertising frequency compared to other media. Consequently, it is extremely difficult to track

---

[11]Radio Advertising Bureau, "Competitive Media Fact Book," 1990.

accurate ratings information for national radio plans that include a large number of stations.

Let's begin our discussion by examining several definitions used in radio ratings analyses.

Geographical Patterns of Radio Ratings

Radio audience ratings use two geographic boundaries to report audiences: Metro Survey Area (MSA) and Total Survey Area (TSA). Typically the majority of a station's audience comes from within the MSA.

Metro Survey Area. An MSA always includes a city or cities whose population is specified as that of the central city together with the county (or counties) in which it is located.

Total Survey Area. The TSA is a geographic area that encompasses the MSA and certain counties located outside the MSA, but meets certain listening criteria.

Definitions of the Radio Audience

The basic audience measures for television are the ratings and share of audience for a particular show. Some media planners mistakenly buy radio and television on the same basis without considering major differences between the two media. In radio, audience estimates are usually given by either Average Quarter-Hour (AQH) audiences or the cumulative or unduplicated audience (Cume) listening to a station over several quarter-hours or dayparts.

Average quarter-hour estimates (AQHE)

Manner in which radio ratings are presented. Estimates include average number of people listening, rating, and metro share of audience.

1. Average Quarter-Hour Estimates (AQHE)

   a. Average Quarter-Hour Persons

   The AQH persons are the estimated number of people listening to a station for at least 5 minutes during a 15-minute period.

   b. Average Quarter-Hour Rating

   Here we calculate the AQH persons as a percentage of the population being measured:

   $$\frac{\text{AQH persons}}{\text{population}} \times 100 = \text{AQH rating}$$

   c. Average Quarter-Hour Share

   Here we are interested in determining what portion of the average radio audience is listening to our station:

   $$\frac{\text{AQH persons to a station}}{\text{AQH persons to all station}} \times 100 = \text{Share}$$

2. Cume Estimates

   Cume estimates are used to determine the number or percentage of different people who listen to a station during several quarter-hours or dayparts.

   a. Cume persons

   The number of *different* people who tuned to a radio station for at least five minutes.

Lower GRPs May Give Equal or Greater Reach

STATION	# OF SPOTS	AQH RTG.	CUME	GRPS	REACH	FREQUENCY
WCCC	12	1.8	130,300	87.0	11.7	7.5
WDDD	12	1.5	159,600	72.8	13.4	5.4

Station "D" delivers 16% less GRPs but delivers 15% more reach than station "C"

(Courtesy: Radio Advertising Bureau.)

Media buyers must carefully analyze all data from radio rating sources to measure efficiency.

b. Cume rating

The percentage of different people listening to a station during several quarter-hours or dayparts.

$$\frac{\text{Cume persons}}{\text{Population}} \times 100 = \text{Cume rating}$$

Let's look at a typical station's audience and calculate these formulas.

Station XYYY, Monday–Friday, 10 A.M. –3 P.M., Adults age 12+

AQH persons = 20,000
Cume persons = 60,000
MSA population = 500,000
MSA AQH persons = 200,000

For station XYYY:

The AQH rating = 4 (20,000/500,000)[12]
The Cume rating = 12 (60,000/500,000)
The AQH share = 10 (20,000/200,000)

3. Using our XYYY example, we can also calculate the following:

a. Gross Impressions (GI) = AQH persons $\times$ number of commercials

If we buy six commercials on XYYY, we have purchased 120,000 impressions (20,000 AQH persons $\times$ 6 spots).

Remember these are *impressions,* not people.

b. Gross Rating Points = AQH rating $\times$ number of commercials

Again, six commercials would deliver 24 GRPs (4 AQH rating $\times$ 6 spots).

c. Listeners per dollar (LPD) = AQH persons/spot cost

If a spot of XYYY costs $500, then the LPD is 40 (20,000 AQH persons/$500).

The media planner must be able to manipulate the various radio data to develop a plan most suited to any particular client. Although the computer makes these manipulations quickly, it does not substitute for a basic understanding of the process. The same budget, and even the same number of spots, used in different dayparts and across multiple stations delivers vastly different results. Exhibit 9.13 shows how as few as 12 spots bought on two stations in the same market result in major differences in cume, reach, and frequency.

---

[12]It is understood that decimals are not used in reporting ratings and share figures.

The Radio Buy

To this point, we have examined the stations, formats, and costs of the radio stations in the markets we wish to consider. We have evaluated radio as a medium, and the available stations in light of other media alternatives, our marketing strategy (both quantitative and qualitative factors), and advertising requirements such as compensating for the medium's lack of a visual element. It is now time to actually schedule the radio spots for our campaign.

Scheduling for Radio. The first step in buying a radio schedule is to rank the stations in each market against the previously defined target market for your product. In the past, stations would be ranked according to standard demographic data. Let's assume that we are selling luxury cars and we know that our target market is men aged 35–64. Using Arbitron ratings, we rank the following stations against this group of prospects:

Market Population = 445,900
Monday–Friday, 6–10 A.M.
Men 35–64

Station	AQH (00)	Avg. Rating	Market Rank
WXXX	252	5.5	1
WAAA	211	4.6	2
WYYY	190	4.1	3
WZZZ	129	2.8	4

Remember, the media planner of the 1980s has much more powerful marketing tools than were available in previous decades. As you will recall from Chapter 7, the use of lifestyle data such as PRIZM allow us to identify market segments more narrowly. Let's assume that our prime prospects for luxury cars are in the Blue Blood and Pools and Patios categories. Our computer model now ranks our stations on the basis of cluster ratings rather than demographic ratings, with the following results:

Station	Demographics Average			Cluster Ratings		
	AQH (00)	Rating	Rate	AQH (00)	Avg. Rating	Rate
WXXX	252	5.5	1	101	2.2	2
WAAA	211	4.6	2	96	2.1	3
WYYY	190	4.1	3	109	2.4	1
WZZZ	129	2.8	4	88	1.9	4

By using lifestyle measures, we are able to identify those stations that best reach more narrowly targeted markets of upscale men. The next step is the actual scheduling of the spots on each station. Computer technology and statistical estimates make these calculations fairly routine.

Intermedia Scheduling in a Market. Because radio listeners are often light users of other media, radio is an excellent means of extending both reach and frequency of an advertising schedule. As already discussed, radio is most often used as a supplemental medium. The media planner is frequently asked to schedule radio in combination with other media in a manner that yields the best results per dollar.

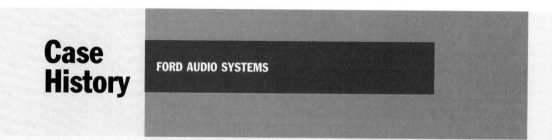

EXHIBIT 9.14		Full-Page Ad Reach × Freq. = GRPs	$\frac{1}{2}$ Page + Station A Reach × Freq. GRPs
	Top 10 Markets	18 × 1.0 = 18	29 × 2.3 = 66
	Markets 26–50	20 × 1.0 = 20	30 × 2.5 = 75
	Markets 101–150	11 × 1.0 = 11	32 × 3.6 = 115
	Markets 151–200	20 × 2.0 = 40	31 × 2.2 = 68
	Markets 201–250	28 × 1.0 = 28	63 × 3.3 = 208

Newspaper/radio mix comparisons by market size (adults 18+.)

A single selected market was used for purposes of comparison from each of the above groups. (AM/FM combination shown as one station.)

(Sources: Arbitron, Metro Area, Spring 1984.)

(Courtesy: Radio Advertising Bureau.)

For several years now, the RAB has studied the role of radio combined with other advertising media. As Exhibit 9.14 shows, radio in combination with newspapers is much more effective than either medium alone.

Case History

FORD AUDIO SYSTEMS

RADIO HELPED BOOST FORD JBL AUDIO INSTALLATION RATES 250% IN JUST FOUR YEARS

Don Duncan, Manager of Planning & Marketing for the Electronics Division of the Ford Motor Co., recalls the unsettling conclusion reached in 1980: research showed that consumers were not interested in purchasing their automotive sound systems from Ford. In fact, it appeared they'd rather buy car stereos from just about anyone else. Ford responded by dramatically improving the quality and flexibility of its sound systems to better suit customer needs. The introduction of Ford's Premium Sound System in the early '80s signaled the start of a new era of Ford Audio quality, but the real breakthrough came in 1985 with the development of the Ford JBL Audio System. "We'd really come full circle, but we needed to let the rest of the world in on all the great changes," says Duncan.

SOLUTION

Duncan teamed up with ad agency Wells Rich Greene BDDP to develop an advertising campaign to raise awareness of the new quality of Ford sound systems. "Advertising car radios on Radio really made sense to us, especially during drive time." Duncan says.

The first Ford Audio Radio campaign aired in ten markets. A mix of station formats, including News/Talk, Classical Music and Jazz, was used to reach Ford's best prospects, defined as adults 35–60. In 1988, Ford reinforced its Radio schedule with the addition of network Radio.

"At least 75% of our ad budget goes into Radio each year." says Duncan, "supplemented with some print ads in specialty magazines."

From the beginning, a humorous approach was used to highlight the superior quality of Ford sound systems. Dick Orkin's Radio Ranch, one of Radio's most awarded creative boutiques, currently creates the entertaining commercials associated with Ford Audio.

RESULTS

Since Ford entered into Radio advertising full force in 1988, installation rates on its Ford JBL Audio System have skyrocketed 250%

"We're really pleased with Radio. Not only have Ford JBL installation rates accelerated dramatically, but the Ford JBL Audio System was even cited by *Fortune* magazine as best in its class—and I'm positive that recognition was influenced by the awareness we built through our Radio advertising." says Duncan.

As a result, Ford has chosen Radio to launch the introduction of its new voice-activated cellular phones, available in its Lincolns and Ford Crown Victoria models.

The media planner must be able to manipulate the various radio data to develop a plan most suited to any particular client. While the computer makes these manipulations quickly, it doesn't substitute for a basic understanding of the process. The same budget, and even the same number of spots, used in different dayparts and across multiple stations can deliver vastly different levels of cumes, reach, and frequency.

SUMMARY

Radio offers a significant advantage to advertisers seeking to reach specific target segments. Radio provides numerous stations programming in dozens of popular formats. Radio commercial time is inexpensive and has demonstrated the lowest CPM increases of all media during the past decade. Given the advertising demand for narrowly defined audience segments, it would appear that radio should be a major consideration in virtually every media plan.

The reality is that radio is considered a minor player by most national and even large retail advertisers. Except in rare cases, radio is a secondary medium in most media plans. The industry has acknowledged criticisms of advertisers and has addressed many issues raised by advertisers in an attempt to bring more dollars into the medium.

One of the major problems facing radio is its lack of a visual element in this day of self-service retailing and the need to establish brand identity by national advertisers. In addition, many advertisers have the perception that radio often fails to utilize its creative capability. "According to numerous radio executives, there is little doubt that this perception has kept some national advertisers from using radio. When radio executives from different companies make joint sales pitches to national advertisers, the first objection to the medium is usually the limitations of radio creative."[13] Exhibit 9.15 shows the creative manner in which radio can provide effective sales messages.

The radio industry has created the Radio Mercury Awards, which recognize the most creative efforts in radio advertising. Clearly, the industry is moving to improve both the perception and the fact of utilizing the medium in a more creative manner.

A second difficulty in bringing more major advertising into the medium is the problem of solving the complex audience research problems. With the growing out-of-home audience, the industry knows that the diary method is no longer suitable to provide the type of data demanded by advertisers. Arbitron is experimenting with a portable people meter to measure all forms of listenership. When the technology will be practical or whether advertisers will support these efforts remains to be seen.

With all its problems, radio can still compete with any medium in delivering a narrowly targeted audience. Technological advances and decreases in the cost of satellite time and equipment have made it easier, cheaper, and less risky to launch national syndicated shows. Shows such as Rush Limbaugh demonstrate that properly packaged, syndicated radio can deliver significant advertising impact to advertisers on both a local and national basis.

---

[13]Peter Viles, "Industry Faces Its Advertising Drawbacks," *Broadcasting & Cable*, May 31, 1993, p. 25.

EXHIBIT

9.15

Radio commercials overcome the lack of a visual element with numerous attention-getting devices.

"Playin' In The Dirt"

A spade and a bucket
and a little tin hoe
It was fun back then
but you never know
You might meet a memory
of a childhood friend
If you come and play in the dirt again

CHORUS
It's funny how sunny
Pike's Nurseries
Can make me
We'll grow us
a memory. . .
Come play in the dirt again

VERSE 2
Planting make believe gardens
as a barefoot kid
doing just like your mama
and your daddy did
Taught you what the fun
and what the work was worth
and how to love our Mother Earth

(SIMULTANEOUSLY)

CHORUS
And if you loved what playing
in the dirt felt like
The fun that you felt can be
found at Pike's
So for dirty little knees
And a big, big grin
Come play in the dirt again. . .

KID'S CHORUS
It's funny how sunny
My garden
Can make me
We'll grow us
A memory

CHORUS
So for dirty little knees
And a big, big grin
Come play in the dirt again. . .

©1994 Pike Family Nurseries, Inc. All Rights Reserved.

(Courtesy: Scharbo & Co.)

Many radio executives see the popularity of national radio syndication as creating a renaissance for radio as it attracts new listeners, advertisers, and attention to the medium. As Gordon Hastings, president of the Katz Radio Group, observed, "For too long, . . . radio has been looked upon as a niche medium, and only as a target demographic medium. As radio creates new national stars, the story of radio as a big-reach medium becomes heard and talked about among advertisers as well as key advertising agency people. I really believe it helps create a better image of a healthy, strong, big reach medium."[14]

There is an irony that radio, once the major national medium, may be returning to its roots for current success. Obviously, national syndication alone cannot propel radio back into the media spotlight. However, this new-found success coupled with radio's inherent strengths as a vehicle to deliver narrowly targeted audiences bode well for the future.

---

[14]Peter Viles, "Talk Explodes in National Syndication," *Broadcasting & Cable*, May 17, 1993, p. 34.

As one leading communications scholar said, "With the country's changing social and cultural makeup, radio's role—as always—is adapting to reflect the changing tastes and needs of consumers. As a reflective, reactive medium, radio's proven ability to adapt to the needs of the society and the marketplace, and to react quickly to events, places it at the forefront of media as we approach a new century. In the 1990s, radio confronts the same challenges—social, economic, technological—as the rest of the country. But its immediacy, local identity and portability give it an edge on competing media."[15]

Questions

1. What has been the major contributing factor to the lack of rate increases in radio during the past decade?
2. What is the major disadvantage of radio for most advertisers?
3. What are the primary advantages of radio to advertisers?
4. How is radio used by most national advertisers?
5. What is the role of radio networks?
6. Who are the listeners of AM radio? What do they listen to?
7. Where do most advertisers obtain radio audience information?
8. Define the following: Drivetime, Run-of-station, and Total audience plans.

---

[15]Eric Rhoads, "Looking Back at Radio's Future," Summer 1993, p. 20.

Using
Newspapers

10

CHAPTER OBJECTIVES

Newspapers are the largest source of advertising revenue. They are a major local medium for retailers, national franchises, and host of other advertisers. After reading this chapter you will understand:

- **Newspaper readership trends**
- **Newspaper marketing techniques**
- **Options available to advertisers**
- **National/local character of newspapers**
- **Significance of weeklies and ethnic publications**

Newspaper advertising has partially recovered from the dismal recession years of the early 1990s. However, the industry will be hard-pressed to maintain its position as the leading advertising medium as various forms of television continue to amass advertising dollars. **In an attempt to achieve** greater efficiencies, newspapers have moved into a period of consolidation much as we have seen in other areas of U.S. business. Currently, there are approximately 1,560 daily newspapers, a decrease of almost 200 in the past two decades. Many publishers have found it much more profitable to publish a single newspaper in a market rather than offer both morning and evening editions.

These mergers are just the most obvious manifestation of the industry's drive for cost cutting. In the past decade, the newspaper industry has recognized the problems facing the business. The Newspaper Association of America (NAA) has developed an industrywide effort to address the future of newspapers.

The primary problems can be summarized as eroding readership and growing advertising competition. More specifically, the newspaper industry must confront the following challenges to remain the dominant advertising medium:

1. *Readership.* In 1993, total daily newspaper circulation fell below 60 million for the first time in 30 years. This marked a loss of more than 3 million in circulation in seven years. Of particular concern is the lack of newspaper readership among young adults, which may indicate a worrisome trend for the future. According to the NAA, only half of adults aged 18–24 read a daily newspaper, compared to 61 percent of all adults.

2. *Audience fragmentation.* Newspapers are no longer the primary source of news, entertainment, and advertising for many Americans. Newspapers must increasingly market the medium to readers who have found a number of other outlets that compete for their leisure time.

3. *Advertising share.* Newspapers have traditionally been the major advertising medium for local retailers. With the exception of radio, throughout most of this century newspapers have faced little serious competition for local advertising dollars. That situation has changed dramatically. Metropolitan growth moved away from the central city, making suburban newspapers and free shoppers major competitors for retail advertising dollars. Likewise, preprinted inserts and direct mail have either cut newspapers' profits or allowed large retailers to move out of the medium altogether. Both radio and television have mounted major efforts to encourage retailers to move into the broadcast media. Cable channels and independent TV stations offer extremely competitive spot costs, making it possible for even small retailers to experiment with television. Exhibit 10.1 demonstrates the wide array of media that vie for the local advertising dollar.

4. *Targeting consumers.* Advertisers require more efficiency and less waste circulation. Targeted media are the result—special-interest magazines, geographic editions of newspapers and magazines, and narrowcasting on cable television offer advertisers the ability to reach niche prospects.

5. *Bypassing traditional media.* Increasingly, advertisers are bypassing traditional media advertising. These advertisers are opting for mail, telephone, point-of-purchase coupons, and other direct links to selected consumers. The process of bypassing media is best represented by direct mail and direct marketing and is the greatest long-term threat to newspaper advertising revenues.

The newspaper still commands huge daily readership and is extremely profitable. However, it is obvious that long-term trends will continue to erode the basic foundation of newspaper readership and advertising. In order to

	Of Those Who Use Medium
	AVERAGE %
Daily Newspapers	43%
Radio	27%
Weekly Newspapers	26%
Billboards or Outdoor	23%
Broadcast Television	23%
Direct Mail	19%
Magazines	17%
Cable Television	16%
Shoppers/Coupon Books	12%
Yellow Pages/Phone Directories	5%
OTHER	14%

Average Number of Media Used = 5 per advertiser
Sample Size = 190

(James M. Cox, Jr. Institute for Newspaper Management Studies)

meet the challenge of keeping the newspaper viable into the next century, the NAA has developed four possible strategies to compete in this new environment.[1] While each of these strategies carries risk, they all recognize that newspapers must change to compete effectively in the future.

Strategy 1. The Mass Appeal. This strategy advocates the fewest fundamental changes in the industry. It seeks to maintain traditional mass-market volumes and share through modest price increases and product refinements. Under this plan, newspapers will not rush to compete for narrowly defined media audiences but will keep their positions as the dominant mass medium.

Strategy 2. The Class Appeal. This strategy advocates an increase in subscription rates and focuses on the top one-third of the market. This approach would provide advertisers with a more homogeneous group of readers and give the newspaper a balanced revenue stream between advertising and circulation. Following this strategy also would provide an affluent readership base but might be too small or expensive for traditional retail advertising clients.

Strategy 3. The Individual Appeal. This strategy attempts to develop a number of new products that will appeal to a segmented audience. For example, a newspaper might offer special-interest tabloids, demographically targeted lifestyle sections, real estate, and automotive publications. Some of these products would be included in the newspaper and sustained by advertising; others would be bought separately and be heavily reader supported. Newspapers would compete with other media, but with the advantage of a large consumer database that would include both demographic and lifestyle information to create and market these new products. This approach would also greatly expand the financial base of newspapers by creating a number of revenue sources beyond the newspaper itself.

Strategy 4. The Direct Appeal. This strategy takes the individual-appeal approach one step further and competes on a one-to-one basis with direct-mar-

---

[1]Newspaper Association of America, "Mastering Your Market," 1993, p. 1.

keting vehicles. It is an "if you can't beat 'em, join 'em tactic." This strategy calls for significant new investment for laying a full-service direct-marketing business onto the core newspapers. Some 150 newspapers offer fax and computer editions, interactive telephone information, and other direct services. This strategy may be confined to the largest markets, where there are sufficient numbers of people and advertisers to support the investment.

As we move into the next century, we will probably see parts or all of these strategies adopted by various newspapers. However, it is clear the newspaper is undergoing fundamental changes where the status quo may be a guaranteed formula for failure. Newspapers will continue to demonstrate the consolidation and cost cutting witnessed in many industries. In this chapter, we will discuss the many changes occurring in the newspaper business. While these innovations involve a number of procedures, they have in common an emphasis on marketing. Newspapers must market themselves to both readers and advertisers with an aggressiveness and creativity that was unnecessary in the past. The fact that the industry is moving to do so bodes well for its future.

THE NATIONAL NEWSPAPER

For many years, publishers have searched for the formula for a profitable national newspaper. Certain specialized newspapers such as the *Wall Street Journal* have achieved this status with a narrowly defined audience of people interested in financial news. In addition, a few elite newspapers such as the *New York Times*, the *Washington Post*, and the *Los Angeles Times*, have achieved some level of national distribution but are written for local readers.

In 1982, *USA Today* was founded by the Gannett Corporation and remains the most widely distributed and successful general-interest newspaper in history. The goal has not been without its financial risk, and, indeed, few corporations would have had either the resources or management support to invest in such an endeavor. It is estimated that before the publication had its first profitable year in 1993, it had lost over $750 million. This loss was not the result of a lack of readers. The paper averages over 2 million daily circulation with readership in excess of 6.5 million.[2]

The major problem with a national newspaper is the start-up costs. Printing plants must be established around the country, distribution channels started, and coordination of a national news staff demand a high initial investment. *USA Today* was fortunate that it could use Gannett newspaper facilities throughout the nation and defray much of the costs associated with a stand-alone national paper. In fact, *USA Today* has become an international newspaper with printing plants in London, Hong Kong, and Switzerland and circulation in approximately 100 countries.

Despite its popularity with readers, *USA Today* continues to cope with advertiser resistance to the publication. A national newspaper is a hybrid vehicle for most advertisers. Unlike other newspapers, national papers are unlikely to gain advertising from grocery stores, department stores, and other traditional local product categories. Instead, *USA Today* depends on national automotive, computer companies, and financial services for much of its revenue.

---

[2]Mary Hardie, "10 Years of USA Today," *Gannetteer,* September 1992, p. 12.

USA Today more closely resembles a national medium than a typical newspaper. For example, the publication offers a "broadcast pricing structure" for large advertisers. The plan works much like up-front network TV buys. The advertiser contracts for an extended schedule with specific dates and placements. In return, the paper gives greater discounts, but the advertiser has little cancellation flexibility. This pricing plan is more familiar to magazine advertising than the fast-paced world of newspapers. However, the advertising practices of *USA Today* are more in tune with the national advertisers that are most likely to purchase space in the publication.

The popularity and influence of *USA Today* are evident in the design of other newspapers. In the past decade, newspapers throughout the world have added color, maps and charts, and the short-story format that appeals to the TV generation and drives newspaper purists crazy. The *USA Today* style and format also have created profitable spinoffs, most notably *USA Today Baseball Weekly*, which takes advantage of the popular sports section of the core newspaper.

After a long struggle, it appears that *USA Today* has turned the corner on profitability. It has taken a long time for the advertising community to embrace the notion of a national paper. Now that the medium is a part of the plans of many advertisers, its future seems secure.

MARKETING THE NEWSPAPER

Newspapers, facing unprecedented competition for both readers and advertisers, have increasingly adopted marketing research and a consumer orientation to stay ahead of competing media. Publishers realize that readers no longer regard the newspaper as a single publication. Instead, they are likely to read only those sections of particular interest to them (see Exhibit 10.2). This "cafeteria" approach to newspaper readership has obvious ramifications for placement of advertising.

In order to deal with the segmentation within their readership, newspapers have taken a number of steps during the past decade to identify their customers, advertisers, and preferences of both. This process starts with marketing research. Most newspapers conduct at least one readership or market survey each year. Large newspapers often conduct several annual studies of their markets.

EXHIBIT
10.2

. . . .

The number of people who say they generally read every page of their daily newspaper has been declining since 1983's 65%. Readership of specific sections hasn't been growing either, with the biggest declines since 1989 coming in the classifieds and food sections.

Read all about it? Not really

	1989	1990	1991	1992
Generally read every page	61%	58%	56%	54%
Read some pages or sections	39	42	44	46
Business/finance	76	73	74	71
Classified	76	73	72	70
Comics	75	74	74	72
Editorial	79	78	76	74
Entertainment (movies, theater, etc.)	81	78	80	76
Food or cooking	77	74	75	70
General news	93	93	91	92
Home (furnishings, gardening, etc.)	75	73	72	71
Sports	79	77	75	74
TV, radio listings	76	74	74	71

(Source: Christy Fisher, "Newspaper Readers get Choosier," Advertising Age, July 26, 1993, p. 22.)

Several factors have become apparent as a result of these studies. The key to their future success is going to be determined by how well newspapers can react to the information they have gained about their readers and advertisers. Let's examine some of the primary findings of various newspaper marketing studies.

American Society of Newspaper Editors (ASNE)

An organization primarily concerned with matters of editorial content and readership of newspapers.

1. *There is no single newspaper audience.* Newspapers must identify their audiences by topical interest, media preference, and demographic and lifestyle categories, and then relate this information to the development of the newspaper. For example, a study by the American Society of Newspaper Editors (ASNE) divided the newspaper audience into four categories: loyal, at-risk (of dropping the paper), potential, and poor prospects. The study found that these four groups had widely different views of the importance of the newspaper and used the medium in vastly different ways. At-risk readers wanted "use-papers" offering practical help with their everyday problems, while potential readers wanted to expand their general knowledge. The ultimate conclusion was that newspapers might have to move to a medium tailored to different readership groups.[3]

2. *Newspapers must develop new products and strategies to keep advertisers.* As we discussed earlier, direct mail has become a major competitor to newspapers by offering advertisers the ability to reach target audiences within a more general market. Newspapers must develop means of reaching nonsubscribers, occasional readers, and other special readership niches at a cost that is competitive with other media.

3. *Newspapers must incorporate design changes to meet contemporary audience preferences.* Color, improved writing and editing, and shorter stories will all contribute to gaining marginal readers.

4. *Make the newspaper user-friendly.* The Associated Press recommends that newspapers emphasize packaging newspapers in a manner that allows readers to more selectively use the medium. In the future, newspapers must devote as much attention to presentation as information. For example, use more lists, pull-out quotes, summary paragraphs, and graphics to highlight information. Newspapers must also make their publications relevant to the everyday concerns of their readers. This approach not only builds readership, but offers an excellent advertising tie-in with editorial matter. For instance, financial services might want to be associated with family budgeting features.

5. *Newspaper readership research should be closely related to advertisers.* Newspaper audience information should be packaged and made available to advertisers to let them relate the characteristics of a market with the audience for a specific newspaper (see Exhibit 10.3). Not only does the information help advertisers but it is viewed as a value-added, instilling goodwill toward the publication. One such newspaper-supported study found that mall shoppers go to an average of three stores, down from five in the past. Using this information, the newspaper went to smaller mall retailers showing them that they could not depend on traffic from large department stores and had to increase their advertising budgets to gain "specific-purpose" shoppers.[4]

---

[3]"Keys to Our Survival," American Society of Newspaper Editors," 1990, p. 17.
[4]Mary Hardie, "Market Surveys Help Newspapers Pinpoint Customers," *Gannetteer,* July/August 1993, p. 16.

how do ajc readers compare with the atlanta market?

Audience composition measures how well a newspaper's audience reflects the market. As noted here, it also shows how the daily Atlanta Journal-Constitution overperforms among upscale demographic groups such as college-educated Atlantans.

how educated is the atlanta market?

Part High School 26%
High School Graduate 11%
Part College/Tech. School 24%
Post Grad. Work/Degree 12%
College Graduate 26%

how educated are our daily readers?

Part High School 6%
High School Graduate 20%
Part College/Tech. School 25%
Post Grad. Work/Degree 17%
College Graduate 32%

the atlanta journal-constitution is an educated choice

Within the metro area, the Journal-Constitution's readership strength comes from better-educated, higher-income, professionally-employed adults.

how do you read this chart?

Following the highlighted line, the chart reads as follows:

In metro Atlanta, 642,277 adults or 29% of the market are in professional/managerial occupations. On an average weekday, 380,466 or 34% of the daily newspaper readers belong to this group.

The Journal-Constitution reaches 57% of Atlanta's professional/managerial adults on an average weekday, and 76% on Sunday.

| | atlanta adults | % of market | average issue atlanta journal-constitution readers | | | | | |
			daily readers	% of readers	% of reach	sunday readers	% of readers	% of reach
Total Adults	2,207,137	100%	1,125,640	100%	51%	1,478,782	100%	67%
gender								
Male	1,039,562	47.1	599,966	53.3	55.9	699,464	47.3	67.6
Female	1,167,575	52.9	525,674	46.7	43.6	779,318	52.7	67.1
household income								
Under $20,000	291,342	13.2	100,182	8.9	33.4	121,260	8.2	42.4
$20,000-29,999	361,970	16.4	137,328	12.2	36.6	209,987	14.2	58.2
$30,000-34,999	147,878	6.7	61,910	5.5	41.1	93,163	6.3	63.8
$35,000-49,999	547,370	24.8	290,415	25.8	51.5	387,441	26.2	71.1
$50,000-74,999	538,541	24.4	317,430	28.2	57.0	409,623	27.7	76.2
$75,000-99,999	194,228	8.8	124,946	11.1	61.7	153,793	10.4	78.7
$100,000 or more	125,807	5.7	92,302	8.2	71.8	103,515	7.0	83.4
age								
18-24	286,928	13.0	118,192	10.5	39.7	165,624	11.2	57.7
25-34	600,341	27.2	291,541	25.9	47.1	421,453	28.5	70.5
35-44	549,577	24.9	291,541	25.9	51.3	306,314	26.8	72.3
45-54	335,485	15.2	181,228	16.1	52.3	220,339	14.9	66.1
55-64	203,057	9.2	108,061	9.6	51.4	124,218	8.4	61.3
65 and over	211,865	9.6	124,946	11.1	57.3	137,527	9.3	65.6
ethnicity								
White	1,644,317	74.5	861,115	76.5	50.8	1,129,789	76.4	69.1
Black	489,984	22.2	229,631	20.4	45.5	300,193	20.3	61.7
education								
Part High School or less	242,785	11.0	64,161	5.7	25.3	93,163	6.3	38.6
High School Graduate	576,063	26.1	221,751	19.7	37.2	340,120	23.0	59.2
Part College/Tech. School	531,920	24.1	283,661	25.2	51.6	368,217	24.9	69.5
College Graduate	576,063	26.1	360,205	32.0	60.4	449,550	30.4	78.3
Post Graduate Work/Degree	264,856	12.0	193,610	17.2	70.7	221,817	15.0	84.0
occupation								
Professional/Manager	642,277	29.1	380,466	33.8	57.4	486,519	32.9	75.9
Technical/Sales	269,271	12.2	139,579	12.4	50.4	190,763	12.9	71.5
Administrative/Clerical	238,371	10.8	111,438	9.9	45.2	165,624	11.2	69.7
Blue-Collar/Service	443,635	20.1	186,856	16.6	40.8	243,999	16.5	55.2
Retired	342,106	15.5	175,600	15.6	49.9	209,987	14.2	61.9
marital status								
Married	1,260,275	57.1	665,253	59.1	51.1	879,875	59.5	70.2
Single (never married)	573,856	26.0	280,284	24.9	47.4	375,611	25.4	65.9
Divorced/Widowed/Sep.	359,763	16.3	174,474	15.5	46.6	212,945	14.4	59.1
home ownership								
Own	1,447,882	65.6	763,184	67.8	51.0	987,826	66.8	68.5
Rent	710,696	32.2	341,069	30.3	46.5	456,944	30.9	64.7
type of dwelling								
Single Family Unit	1,551,617	70.3	810,461	72.0	50.6	1,060,287	71.7	68.7
Condo/Townhouse	125,807	5.7	73,167	6.5	55.9	87,248	5.9	69.7
Apartment	377,420	17.1	191,359	17.0	49.1	258,787	17.5	68.6
Duplex/Mobile Home/Other	139,050	6.3	45,026	4.0	32.3	65,066	4.4	46.6
children in household								
None	1,266,897	57.4	687,766	61.1	52.6	853,257	57.7	67.8
One Child	408,320	18.5	194,736	17.3	46.0	273,575	18.5	67.1
Two Children	359,763	16.3	163,218	14.5	43.9	241,041	16.3	67.1
Three or more	161,121	7.3	74,292	6.6	45.2	104,894	7.1	64.8

Source: Atlanta Consumer Market Study, 1992

(Courtesy: Cox Enterprises, Inc.—The Atlanta Journal/The Atlanta Constitution.)

EXHIBIT 10.3

Newspapers often conduct market research as a competitive tool for their advertising clients.

The contemporary newspaper offers unique advantages to both readers and advertisers. However, since newspapers dominated the local market for so long, they did not develop a marketing mentality. Unfortunately, the industry is now playing catch-up with its more aggressive media competitors. In the next sections, we will discuss how newspaper publishers are successfully selling the medium to both readers and advertisers.

Marketing to Readers

Newspapers are faced with the problem of shifting from a strategy of mass marketing to one of a more customized approach to identify and sell their audiences. As we discussed in an earlier section, one of the four strategies being examined by the newspaper industry is to keep a mass-appeal focus. Most industry experts think that although this approach might work for a short time and in smaller markets, it is not one that holds long-term potential for a healthy newspaper industry.

Most observers agree that the growing diversity of newspaper readership will force publishers to adopt unique techniques to reach specific audience segments. Newspapers not only must attract new readers but maintain their present audience. Publishers are particularly concerned about bringing in younger readers, most of whom are not presently heavy newspaper users. Newspaper publishers fear that once media habits are established and exclude newspapers, it will be very difficult to reach these people as older adults. Newspaper reading habits are formed by about age 30 and tend to change very little after that. Research indicates several reading segments and differences in their reading preferences:[5]

1. *All readers.* Interest in "news as entertainment" is falling. Interest in "news you can use" is rising. Fewer people want newspapers to amuse them or give them fodder for conversations. Instead, they want practical help with their everyday lives.

2. *Children.* Children begin to develop the newspaper reading habit at home once they see their own names or photos in the paper. Appearing in the paper gives them a sense of their own importance, and a sense of connection between their own lives and events described in the paper. Newspapers have added special sections on individual grammar schools, "kid" pages within sports sections, and other features to appeal specifically to children.

3. *Teenagers.* Two-thirds of teenagers read at least one daily newspaper a week. The challenge is to turn occasional readers into regular readers. Teenagers will read traditional content if it is easy to find, concisely presented, and made relevant to their lives. They do not want separate content written by adults for teenagers. Studies show that teens love new technology and are among the heaviest users of newspaper information services that use telephone, fax, or computers.

4. *Young adults.* Young adults represent the prime market for newspapers. Unfortunately, they prefer magazines and books three to one over newspapers. Newspapers must demonstrate that they provide content that is unavailable from other sources. Young adults are very career oriented and want to see topics dealing with jobs, career management, leisure activities, luxury goods, and personal relationships.

5. *Women.* Women below the age of 35 exhibit 7–9 percentage points lower newspaper readership than men. Yet the female market is a prime segment for advertisers, and newspapers should be an excellent medium for reaching working women. In addition, women read more than men, but they prefer magazines and books. This gap is not surprising given the fact that newspapers devote twice as much space to topics of special interest to men than women. Research shows topics of interest to women include parenting, family relationships, friendships, work relationships, food, health, ethics, values, and religion. Women want to see themselves in the publications they read. They want to read about women like themselves, facing the same challenges, demands on their time, and multiple roles.

Even a cursory review of the various readership segments emphasizes the need for the newspaper to provide a variety of material that is suited to only one target audience. Newspapers can meet this problem in one of two ways:

- **They can make their publications more diverse but organized in such a way that readers can easily choose content according to their interests.**

- **Or they can remain a general, mass-market publication but develop other products such as special-topic tabloids and electronic communication systems to reach niche markets.**

---

[5]"Scripps Howard Editors Newsletter," April, 1993, p. 1.

We will probably see a combination of both approaches continue into the next century, but with a recognition that marketing the newspaper is a major priority. "The newspaper companies . . . share a common desire to reach elusive demographic categories and ensure their place in a world where news may no longer be delivered primarily through print."[6] In a diverse, multicultural society, appealing to readers is more difficult than it was in earlier times when our population was much more homogeneous.

Marketing to Advertisers

Newspapers are one of the greatest bargains available to consumers. For as little as 25 cents, readers can be informed, entertained, and persuaded by a host of national and local writers and advertisers. There is something in the newspapers for every age, sex, and income category. However, the finances of the modern newspaper is dependent in large measure on advertising (see Exhibit 10.4).

The marketing task for newspapers is a twofold enterprise: (1) to deliver the audience and (2) to compete for advertisers. The newspaper industry must convince advertisers that it represents the best local medium and should constitute an important element in national advertising strategy. To accomplish these goals means that newspapers must retain the local retailers that have traditionally comprised the bulk of newspaper revenues and bring in national

<table>
<tr>
<td>

EXHIBIT

10.4

. . . .

Newspapers and their readers both benefit from the financial support of advertising.

</td>
<td>

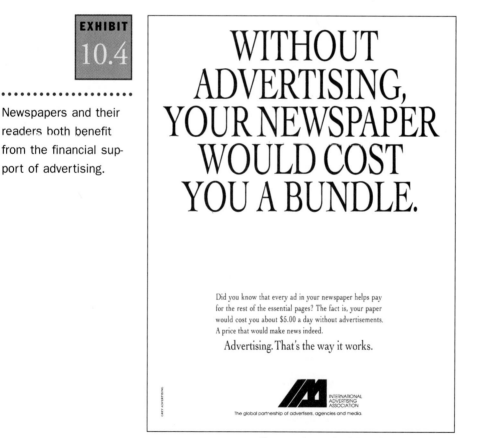

</td>
</tr>
</table>

(Courtesy: International Advertising Association.)

[6]Hanna Liebman, "Newspapers: Making Strange Bedfellows," *Mediaweek,* January 31, 1994, p. 22.

advertisers that have not used newspapers to any great extent. In the current media climate neither job will be easy.

The NAA has identified a number of problems in marketing newspapers to advertisers:

1. *New local media competition.* Direct mail, radio, local cable, and broadcast TV advertising have all cut into the newspaper's position in local advertising.

2. *Declining revenues from major products such as food and automotive.* Grocery stores and chain retailers are increasingly using direct mail and automobile dealers, and regional associations are investing more dollars in television. The combination has put a severe profit squeeze on many newspapers.

3. *Centralization of regional marketing decisions.* More and more local advertising and marketing decision making is being moved to regional and national headquarters. Decisions makers at these levels often come from national advertising backgrounds. They look to targeted promotional and advertising vehicles, often overlooking local strengths of newspapers.

4. *Gaining consideration from agency media planners for national buys.* As newspapers confront the competitive situation on the local level, they have attempted to increase national advertising dollars. However, they find that many media buyers are not newspaper readers themselves and are likely to recommend other media with which they are more familiar.

Listing the problems faced by newspapers is the easy part; doing something about them is much more difficult. The first step newspapers have taken to address these problems is to develop a consumer-oriented perspective. Rather than attempting to sell an array of services to advertising clients, newspapers are developing a *relationship marketing* attitude where advertising services are client driven.[7] Ideally, newspaper ad staffs are working with their clients as partners to solve problems rather than operating on a salesperson/customer basis.

Newspapers are also developing a number of strategies and products to bring new advertisers into the medium. These new tactics encompass a host of elements including some as sophisticated as electronic communication and others as simple as promotional tie-ins between the newspaper and advertisers.

Another concern of newspapers is that they are widely regarded as stodgy and uncreative. Many newspapers are working with agencies to enhance advertising creativity. For example, newspapers are encouraging advertisers to use more color, and, at the same time, they are improving the production quality of the newspaper so that color ads can be shown to their best advantage. The Pizza Hut advertisement (see Exhibit 10.5) is an excellent example of this new approach to newspaper advertising.

Newspapers are also approaching major agency media buyers on a personal basis to demonstrate the utility of newspaper advertising in national media schedules. Many of the complaints of media buyers center on the difficulty of buying local newspapers on a market-by-market basis. This is a particular

Relationship marketing
A strategy that develops marketing plans from a consumer perspective.

EXHIBIT
10.5

Many newspapers now provide advertisers with high quality color.

(Courtesy: Anson-Stoner, Inc.)

[7]Pam Janis, "Advertising Strategies, 'ADvance,'" *Gannetteer,* July/August 1992, p. 4.

problem for media buyers who are accustomed to the relative ease of buying national broadcast and magazine media. In a later section, we will discuss some of the steps being taken by newspapers to make the buying process more efficient.

Despite the difficult competitive environment in which newspapers must operate, they will remain a major advertising medium for both local and national advertisers. However, newspapers will change. Their survival in the long run depends on their ability to react to market conditions as they are delineated by readers and advertisers. It appears that newspapers are well prepared to meet this challenge into the next century.

ZONING, TOTAL MARKET COVERAGE, AND NEWSPAPER NETWORKS

Zoning

Newspaper practice of offering advertisers partial coverage of a market, often accomplished with weekly inserts distributed to certain sections of that market.

Marketing the newspaper to advertisers involves far more than simply selling its attributes. In the contemporary advertising environment, newspapers must offer services that meet the demands of their advertising clients and prevent any further erosion of advertising dollars to competing media. As we have discussed in earlier sections, newspapers serve a wide variety of advertisers whose needs cover an array of requirements. Marketing newspapers involves developing delivery systems that match the needs of both readers and advertisers. A single edition of a newspaper is not suitable for the advertising objectives of all its advertisers nor the reading preferences of all its readers. In recent years, newspapers have begun to offer a number of services that recognize the diverse needs of their advertising and reading audiences.

Zoned Editions

Many advertisers do not want to advertise in the full distribution area of a newspaper. Exhibit 10.6 shows the various zoned editions offered by *The Atlanta Journal and Constitution*. Small retailers draw customers from a limited trade area within a larger metropolitan region, and full-circulation coverage brings unacceptable waste circulation. National advertisers may also identify some sections of a city as being more valuable than others and prefer zoned coverage. Most large newspapers meet this demand for zoned editions by providing separate inserts with news and advertising about a particular suburb or neighborhood.

In the past, many newspapers devoted limited resources to these editions. They were very weak editorially and were viewed primarily as advertising vehicles. Readers saw little value in these editions, and they resulted in few new subscribers. Likewise, advertisers did not want to be associated with an inferior editorial product. Despite its growing use, successful zoning cannot prosper as a device only for advertisers. Readership is the key to successful zoned editions. This means a commitment of editorial staff to make the zoned editions more than fluff pieces to carry advertising. Today, newspapers are making significant investments in their zoned editions, and, in many cities, publishers have been rewarded with significant readership and advertising increases.

Simple geographic zoning is not enough to meet the demands of many advertisers. Some national advertisers are interested in penetration by ZIP codes

EXHIBIT
10.6

Newspapers increasingly offer different options to advertisers.

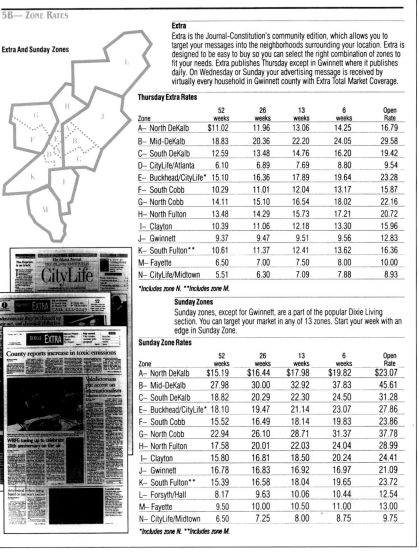

5B— ZONE RATES

Extra And Sunday Zones

Extra

Extra is the Journal-Constitution's community edition, which allows you to target your messages into the neighborhoods surrounding your location. Extra is designed to be easy to buy so you can select the right combination of zones to fit your needs. Extra publishes Thursday except in Gwinnett where it publishes daily. On Wednesday or Sunday your advertising message is received by virtually every household in Gwinnett county with Extra Total Market Coverage.

Thursday Extra Rates

Zone	52 weeks	26 weeks	13 weeks	6 weeks	Open Rate
A– North DeKalb	$11.02	11.96	13.06	14.25	16.79
B– Mid-DeKalb	18.83	20.36	22.20	24.05	29.58
C– South DeKalb	12.59	13.48	14.76	16.20	19.42
D– CityLife/Atlanta	6.10	6.89	7.69	8.80	9.54
E– Buckhead/CityLife*	15.10	16.36	17.89	19.64	23.28
F– South Cobb	10.29	11.01	12.04	13.17	15.87
G– North Cobb	14.11	15.10	16.54	18.02	22.16
H– North Fulton	13.48	14.29	15.73	17.21	20.72
I– Clayton	10.39	11.06	12.18	13.30	15.96
J– Gwinnett	9.37	9.47	9.51	9.56	12.83
K– South Fulton**	10.61	11.37	12.41	13.62	16.36
M– Fayette	6.50	7.00	7.50	8.00	10.00
N– CityLife/Midtown	5.51	6.30	7.09	7.88	8.93

*Includes zone N. **Includes zone M.

Sunday Zones

Sunday zones, except for Gwinnett, are a part of the popular Dixie Living section. You can target your market in any of 13 zones. Start your week with an edge in Sunday Zone.

Sunday Zone Rates

Zone	52 weeks	26 weeks	13 weeks	6 weeks	Open Rate
A– North DeKalb	$15.19	$16.44	$17.98	$19.82	$23.07
B– Mid-DeKalb	27.98	30.00	32.92	37.83	45.61
C– South DeKalb	18.82	20.29	22.30	24.50	31.28
E– Buckhead/CityLife*	18.10	19.47	21.14	23.07	27.86
F– South Cobb	15.52	16.49	18.14	19.83	23.86
G– North Cobb	22.94	26.10	28.71	31.37	37.78
H– North Fulton	17.58	20.01	22.03	24.04	28.99
I– Clayton	15.80	16.81	18.50	20.24	24.41
J– Gwinnett	16.78	16.83	16.92	16.97	21.09
K– South Fulton**	15.39	16.58	18.04	19.65	23.72
L– Forsyth/Hall	8.17	9.63	10.06	10.44	12.54
M– Fayette	9.50	10.00	10.50	11.00	13.00
N– CityLife/Midtown	6.50	7.25	8.00	8.75	9.75

*Includes zone N. **Includes zone M.

(Courtesy: The Atlanta Journal / The Atlanta Constitution)

within a metropolitan area. In order to compete with direct mailers that can easily pinpoint these ZIP codes, newspapers have developed even more finely tuned products than the current zoned editions. Exhibit 10.7 shows the ZIP code distribution available to advertisers in Atlanta. Note that the newspaper also allows advertisers to zone their preprinted inserts through the Zones Area Preprint (ZAP) program. A question raised by some critics is whether a paper can "overzone" to the point that it loses its identity as *the* mass medium in the market.

Total Market Coverage

While some advertisers are interested in a narrowly defined group of readers, others want total penetration of a market. Since no newspaper has complete coverage of its market (in some major markets it may be as low as 30 percent), other means must be used to augment regular circulation and achieve

Total market coverage (TMC)

Where newspapers augment their circulation with direct mail or shoppers to deliver all households in a market.

EXHIBIT

10.7

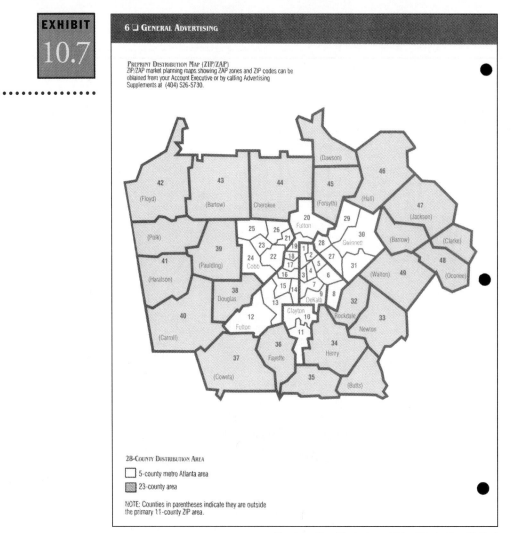

6 ❑ GENERAL ADVERTISING

PREPRINT DISTRIBUTION MAP (ZIP/ZAP)
ZIP/ZAP market planning maps showing ZAP zones and ZIP codes can be obtained from your Account Executive or by calling Advertising Supplements at (404) 526-5730.

28-COUNTY DISTRIBUTION AREA

☐ 5-county metro Atlanta area

▨ 23-county area

NOTE: Counties in parentheses indicate they are outside the primary 11-county ZIP area.

(Courtesy: The Atlanta Journal/The Atlanta Constitution)

total market coverage (TMC). Total market coverage may be accomplished in a number of ways:

■ **Weekly delivery of a nonsubscriber supplement carrying mostly advertisements**

■ **Using direct mail to nonsubscribers**

■ **Delivering the newspaper free to all households once a week**

Most newspapers that offer TMC programs provide a free weekly edition to nonsubscribers. By combining the regular daily paper with the TMC product, advertisers can reach virtually 100 percent of the households in a market. Most TMC products are made up of stories reprinted from the previous week's editions. However, it is very difficult to gain the interest of a non-newspaper-reading audience segment with a rehash of old news. On the other hand, newspapers find it cost prohibitive to produce a separate edition for their TMC editions.

In recent years, a number of syndicated TMC newspapers have been published. These newspapers emphasize features and entertainment. By spreading the cost of the publications across a number of markets, they can be produced at a price and quality unavailable in a single city. In 1988, *Express*

Line was introduced as the first syndicated TMC newspaper. It has since been joined by *US/Express, CoverStory, Headlines,* and *Star Watch* (see Exhibit 10.8). These papers are distributed on a weekly basis and have circulations of a million or more readers.

Newspaper Networks

One of the major problems faced by newspapers attempting to increase national advertising is the perception that newspapers are very difficult to buy. Agency media buyers are accustomed to making network TV buys where 200 markets are bought with one order and one bill. Many buyers have traditionally been reluctant to take the trouble to deal with individual newspapers and have excluded newspapers from their media schedules. To overcome this problem and gain national advertising dollars, many newspapers have entered into cooperative programs with other newspapers to offer package deals to national advertisers. Currently, there are approximately 250 networks. They

EXHIBIT

10.8

....

TMC products reach nonreaders of newspapers.

(Courtesy: Starwatch)

vary from those with as few as eight papers within a single state to national networks such as Newspapers First offering newspapers in such markets as Los Angeles and Miami.

As we will see in our discussion of other media, virtually every medium is now offering some form of network buying. The unwired network concept was first developed by radio station reps and has quickly spread to other media. In periods of economic downturn, when the advertising medium can afford to make it difficult for advertisers to purchase time and space.

Newspaper networks are much more than several papers offering space to advertisers on a joint basis. Many advertisers want to use preprinted inserts so the distribution of these pieces must be coordinated among the network papers. Also some advertisers will demand that a newspaper network provides TMC capability in each market. Since newspapers solve their TMC problem in a number of different ways, this also adds to the complexity of newspaper networks.

Advertisers are not interested in the problems newspapers face in developing their networks; they are only interested in results. Unfortunately, newspapers were late to develop formal networks, and there is still a lack of national coordination for such buys. The NAA is currently moving to develop standard procedures that should make newspaper network buying easier in the future.

CATEGORIES OF NEWSPAPER ADVERTISING

Newspaper advertising revenue comes from a number of sources, but like almost all media these revenues constitute the majority of financial support for the medium. Circulation accounts for approximately 25 percent of total newspaper revenues, with over 70 percent coming from subscriptions. Of the more than $32 billion spent in newspaper advertising, approximately half comes from local retail advertisers.

Newspaper advertising is composed of several categories and subcategories. The two major types of newspaper advertising are display and classified. Within the display category there are local (also called retail) and national advertisers. The breakout of these categories according to advertising expenditures are:

Classified advertising

Found in columns so labeled, published in sections of a newspaper or magazine set aside for certain classes of goods or services—for example, Help Wanted, Positions Wanted, Houses for Sale, Cars for Sale. The ads are limited in size and generally are without illustration.

	Dollars (billions)	Percentage
Classified	11.2	35
Local	16.8	52
National	4.1	13

(Source: "Scripps Howard General Managers Newsletter.")

Classified Advertising

Classified advertising, the common "want ads," has for years been the most profitable source of revenue for newspapers. Newspapers had this lucrative source of profits to themselves, with most classified advertising coming in with little or no selling by the newspaper and with very low production costs.

Classified advertising is very concentrated in a few categories. Automotive ads account for 43 percent of all classifieds, followed by employment and real estate with 18 percent each. In fact, classified advertising is considered an excellent barometer of the nation's economic health. In particular, economists watch the employment notices to see the ratio of "help wanted" to "positions sought" advertisements.

Newspapers also carry advertisements with illustrations in the classified section. These are known as *classified display* advertisements and are normally run in the automotive and real estate sections. All fall under the heading of classified advertising, which has its own rate card and usually operates as a separate department.

Newspapers are facing growing competition for the classified market. For example, a service called Vehicle Information Network provides a toll-free number where prospective buyers can call for listings of certain types of vehicles and get a mail or fax listing of used cars or trucks for sale in their area. Sure-Find Classified by Telephone is a similar service offering real estate information by phone. In addition, home computer services such as America Online and local cable companies have extensive listings of classified information.[8]

Newspapers are not sitting by and allowing these attacks on their classified franchise to go unchallenged. Major newspapers throughout the country are establishing telephone, fax, and computer classified databases that can be reached 24 hours a day. Newspapers are also redesigning their classified sections, adding color, photographs, and more locator maps and grids.[9]

Newspapers have no intention of conceding the classified fight to their competitors, and they have several advantages in the battle. First, people associate classified advertising with newspapers and will have to be convinced to go to another source. Second, newspapers are challenging these new competitors by adding new classified services. For example, several major newspapers have started ClassiFacts, a national database for employment, real estate, and automotive classified ads that ran in the past Sunday paper. Third, newspapers have huge cash flows from classified to invest in marketing to prospective classified customers. Fourth, newspapers have the largest databases of classified products for sale.

With the potential revenues involved and the relative ease of selling and producing classified ads, many advertising executives predict that classified advertising will be one of the first major battlefields for the electronic highway of the future. However, for now the traditional newspaper classified sections will be the primary source of these notices for most customers. Moreover, newspapers are well positioned to maintain their dominance in this category, albeit with greater competition and expenses than has been the case in the past.

Display Advertising

With the possible exception of legal advertising and public notices, most nonclassified newspaper advertising is display advertising, which has two categories: local and national.

Local Advertising. For years, local advertising has been the primary revenue source for daily newspapers. Local advertising refers to all nonclassified advertising placed by local businesses, organizations, and individuals. A list of the leading newspaper advertisers demonstrates the importance of retail ad-

---

[8]Christy Fisher, "Newspaper Call to Arms in Fight over Classified," *Advertising Age,* April 26, 1993, p. S-1.
[9]Laura Dalton, "Classifieds," *Gannetteer,* February 1992.

vertising. Circuit City, Sears, Macy's, Dillard's, and Montgomery Ward all spend more than $100 million in the medium. In fact, there is only one non-retailer among the top 10 newspaper advertisers.[10]

There is every expectation that newspapers will continue to be the dominant local advertising medium. However, the share of advertising dollars will be reduced by the many options now available to retail advertisers. A major source of this competition is the result of other media increasing their local news coverage to appeal to local audiences and advertisers. As one financial analyst report commented, "We expect newspaper publishers to encounter increasing competition from other media in the morning. Television stations are looking to expand local news programming in the morning, a number of radio stations are switching to all-news formats, and news programming on cable television is expanding."[11]

Direct mail represents the other major competitor for local advertising dollars. As we discussed earlier, newspapers realize that they must offer advertisers more narrowly targeted audience segments to compete with direct mail. Although steps are being taken to counter the threat of direct mail, it remains to be seen if the newspaper industry can effectively develop services that meet the growing challenge of direct mailers.

One way in which newspapers have tried to accommodate local advertisers is by making the buying process simpler. In 1993, the NAA introduced the Standard Advertising Invoice (SAI), which standardizes the local advertising invoice and statement. The form consolidates 29 elements into a single form and makes it especially efficient for retailers that purchase space in more than one newspaper.

A major characteristic of retail newspaper advertising is its emphasis on price competition. Compared to other media, local newspaper advertising is much more likely to emphasize short-term sales. It features price, place, and product with few advertising frills. Most local newspaper advertising attempts to create immediate results that the retailer can see within 24 hours.

National Advertising. One of the continuing problems of the newspaper industry is how to bring more national advertising dollars to the medium. As the competition heats up at the local level, newspapers have tried to offset these losses in advertising share with increased national dollars. However, national newspapers' expenditures remain relatively small compared to other media.

For the past several years, the newspaper industry has discussed the problem of increasing national advertising dollars and has developed various plans to address the problem. National advertisers and their agencies remain largely unconvinced that newspapers will take the necessary steps to make it a major medium for most national advertisers.

While there are a number of points of disagreement between national advertising and newspapers, most can be categorized under one of three headings.

1. *The local versus national rate differentiation.* The major area of contention between national advertisers and newspapers is the so-called local/national

....

Rate differential

The controversial practice of newspapers charging significantly higher rates to national advertisers as compared to local accounts.

....

---

[10]"Advertising Facts & Figures," *Advertising Age,* April 26, 1993, p. S-14.
[11] *The Veronis, Suhler & Associates Communications Industry Forecast,* June 1992, p. 170.

rate differentiation. Most newspapers charge a substantial premium to national advertisers. In the most recent figures released by the American Association of Advertising Agencies, national advertisers were charged an average of almost 75 percent more than local advertisers for the same space. On some large papers, this differential is close to 100 percent.

Newspapers defend the difference on the basis that they must pay an agency commission for national advertising, and many of these advertisers are only occasional users of their papers unlike retailers with whom they enjoy continuing support. However, many agency planners "cite the outrageous rate differentials, alongside the complexity of the national buy, as major impediments. It is implicit that newspapers would get greater consideration and probably a great deal more use (one share point is tantamount to about $1 billion), if they came to the table with newly structured rates."[12]

National advertisers not only complain about the rate structure of newspapers but think that it is made even worse by a lack of consistent discounts similar to those offered in other media. National newspaper advertising is among the most expensive media in terms of cost per thousand. National advertisers cite the fact that many newspapers charge a premium for national advertising and then compound the problem by denying discounts similar to those offered retail clients for comparable buys.

Some newspaper executives see that the competition for newspaper ad dollars is creating the first signs of rate negotiation. Already there seems to be an openness on the part of some papers to consider differentiating rates among different advertisers. Observers view this trend as the first step toward an era of newspaper rate negotiation as a common practice.[13]

2. *Standardization.* National advertisers not only want lower prices but a national network that will provide standard discounts, rates, and positions to place advertising with a one-order/one-bill approach. There are many newspaper networks, but no single source comparable to broadcast. The NAA is currently working with advertisers to develop such a system. However, it appears that with the present state of newspaper advertising rates, it will take some time for a national plan to become a reality.

One of the most important steps toward standardization was the introduction in 1981 of the Standard Advertising Unit (SAU) system (see Exhibit 10.9 and 10.10). The SAU allows national advertisers to purchase space in virtually every major U.S. newspaper and prepare one advertisement that will be accepted by each of them. The SAU shows that standardization in at least some areas will work and perhaps offers some optimist for future developments toward a more acceptable process of buying national advertising.

3. *The image of newspapers toward national advertisers.* Even more difficult to overcome than the price and standardization problems is the perception by many agencies and national advertisers that newspapers are not interested in dealing with them on an equitable basis. Many advertisers claim that newspapers have had a take-it-or-leave-it attitude toward national advertising for so long that it is very difficult for them to change.

---

[12]Hanna Liebman, "The Last Stand," *Mediaweek,* April 26, 1993, p. 32.
[13]"Just Follow the Bouncing Rate Card," *Mediaweek,* March 28, 1994, p. 30.

Suggested SAU® Nomenclature

Depth in inches	1 Column Width (2¹⁄₁₆″)	2 Columns Width (4¼″)	3 Columns Width (6⁷⁄₁₆″)	4 Columns Width (8⅝″)	5 Columns Width (10¹³⁄₁₆″)	6 Columns Width (13″)	13 Columns** Width (26¾″)
1	1 × 1						
1.5	1 × 1.5						
2	1 × 2	2 × 2					
3	1 × 3	2 × 3					
3.5	1 × 3.5	2 × 3.5					
5.25	1 × 5.25	2 × 5.25	3 × 5.25	4 × 5.25			
7	1 × 7	2 × 7	3 × 7	4 × 7	5 × 7	6 × 7	
10.5	1 × 10.5	2 × 10.5	3 × 10.5	4 × 10.5	5 × 10.5	6 × 10.5	13 × 10.5
13	1 × 13	2 × 13	3 × 13	4 × 13	5 × 13		
14	1 × 14	2 × 14	3 × 14	4 × 14	5 × 14	6 × 14	13 × 14
15.75	1 × 15.75	2 × 15.75	3 × 15.75	4 × 15.75	5 × 15.75		
18	1 × 18	2 × 18	3 × 18	4 × 18	5 × 18	6 × 18	13 × 18
FD*	1 × FD*	2 × FD*	3 × FD*	4 × FD*	5 × FD*	6 × FD*	13 × FD*

*FD (Full Depth) can be 21″ or deeper. Depths for each broadsheet newspaper are indicated in the Standard Rate and Data Service. All broadsheet newspapers can accept 21″ ads, and may float them if their depth is greater than 21″

** Double truck sizes
The N size, measuring 9⅜″ by 14″, represents the full page size for short cut-off tabloids such as the New York Daily News and Newsday.

Going, going,

Soon 1984 will be gone. And even sooner all the 1984 model Hondas will be gone. Too good. Including this Accord LX 4-Door Sedan. So if you're thinking of buying a 1984 Honda, you'd better hurry. Get going, going...and go to your Southern California Honda Dealer™ Today.

Southern California Honda Dealers.

The base ad—to dealer segment—is described in SAU® nomenclature as a 6 × 14: six columns wide by 14 inches deep; 84 column inches. Local variables such as dealer names can be added to a base ad in ¼″ ad-wide increments.

Measurement: Column inches replace agate lines

Ads are sized in columns and inches instead of agate lines. All ordering, measuring and billing is done in column inches. An ad 1 column wide by 1 inch deep (the smallest available) is described as a 1×1 (one by one) and is measured and billed as 1 column inch. An ad 2 columns wide by 3 inches deep is described as a 2×3 (two by three), and is measured and billed as 6 column inches. A horizontal half-page is described as a 6×10.5 (six by ten-and-a-half), and measured and billed as 63 column inches. And so on.

Special ¼-inch increments for variables such as dealer listings

Space for dealer listings, theater names and similar needs may be added to SAU® sizes in ¼-inch increments for the full width of the ad. Thus, a 3×7 ad with ¾-inch added at the bottom for theater listings would be described as a 3×7.75 (three by seven and three-quarters) and is measured and billed as 23.25 column inches:

Base ad: 3 × 7.00 =	21.00 column inches
Listings: 3 × .75 =	2.25 column inches
Total ad: 3 × 7.75 =	23.25 column inches

An ad in one of the 56 standard sizes of the Standard Advertising Unit (SAU®) System—shown in reduction on the SAU® Grid at right—will fit virtually every broadsheet newspaper in the United States; 33 will fit tabloids.

(Source: Guide to Quality Newspaper Reproduction, *a joint publication of the American Newspaper Publishers Association and Newspaper Advertising Bureau.*)

EXHIBIT 10.9

The Expanded ⸺SAU⸺ Standard Advertising Unit System

Depth in Inches

	1 COL. 2-1/16"	2 COL. 4-1/4"	3 COL. 6-7/16"	4 COL. 8-5/8"	5 COL. 10-13/16"	6 COL. 13"
FD*	1xFD*	2xFD*	3xFD*	4xFD*	5xFD*	6xFD*
18"	1x18	2x18	3x18	4x18	5x18	6x18
15.75"	1x15.75	2x15.75	3x15.75	4x15.75	5x15.75	
14"	1x14	2x14	3x14	4x14	N 5x14	6x14
13"	1x13	2x13	3x13	4x13	5x13	
10.5"	1x10.5	2x10.5	3x10.5	4x10.5	5x10.5	6x10.5
7"	1x7	2x7	3x7	4x7	5x7	6x7
5.25"	1x5.25	2x5.25	3x5.25	4x5.25		
3.5"	1x3.5	2x3.5				
3"	1x3	2x3				
2"	1x2	2x2				
1.5"	1x1.5					
1"	1x1					

13"

1 Column 2-1/16"
2 Columns 4-1/4"
3 Columns 6-7/16"
4 Columns 8-5/8"
5 Columns 10-13/16"
6 Columns 13"

Double Truck 26-3/4"
(There are four suggested double truck sizes:)

13xFD* 13x18
13x14 13x10.5

*FD (Full Depth) can be 21" or deeper. Depths for each broadsheet newspaper are indicated in the Standard Rate and Data Service. All broadsheet newspapers can accept 21" ads, and may float them if their depth is greater than 21".

Tabloids: Size 5 x 14 is a full page tabloid for long cut-off papers. Mid cut-off papers can handle this size with minimal reduction. The N size, measuring 9¾ x 14, represents the full page size for tabloids such as the New York Daily News and News day, and other short cut-off newspapers. The five 13 inch deep sizes are for tabloids printed on 55 inch wide presses such as the Philadelphia News. See individual SRDS listings for tabloid sections of broadsheet newspapers.

Printed in U.S.A. 11/83

(Source: Guide to Quality Newspaper Reproduction, *a joint publication of the American Newspaper Publishers Association and Newspaper Advertising Bureau.*)

A NAA study of senior agency media planners indicated that they rated newspapers last when considering their media schedules. "They complained about the medium's complex and expensive rates, lack of guaranteed positioning and the difficulty in making multimarket buys. They also said newspaper sales reps were 'order takers' who did not understand creative use of the medium or their own markets and readers."[14]

Obviously, newspapers must overcome a number of obstacles if they are to significantly increase their national advertising share. Yet, given the tight retail market and the potential for growth in the national sector, newspapers are compelled to settle many of the long-standing rifts with potential national clients. An effective system of national newspaper advertising will take time. However, it is encouraging that both advertisers and newspapers are addressing their problems. The ultimate catalyst to finding solutions to the national advertising dilemma will probably be the mutual self-interest of both groups.

Cooperative Advertising

Cooperative advertising

Joint promotion of a national advertiser (manufacturer) and local retail outlet on behalf of the manufacturer's product on sale in the retail store.

One of the historical outgrowths of the newspaper local/national rate differential was the development of a relationship between national advertisers and their retail distributors called *cooperative (co-op)* advertising. We will discuss cooperative advertising more fully in Chapter 14 with other sales promotion techniques, but it is such an important part of newspaper advertising that we need to mention it here.

Co-op advertising is placed by a local advertiser but paid for, all or in part, by a national advertiser. The national manufacturer usually provides the ad, allowing space for the retailer's logo. The original reason for the development of co-op advertising was that it allowed national advertisers to place ads at the local rate.

Today, co-op is a huge source of advertising funds. It is estimated that approximately $18 billion dollars are available for co-op in virtually all media including television, radio, outdoor, and direct mail. Co-op also is a source of building goodwill with distributors and retailers and exercising some creative control over local advertising as well as saving money.

Since national advertisers pay anywhere from 50 to 100 percent of the cost of locally placed co-op, it extends the budgets of local advertisers as it saves money for national firms. It is ironic that a system that was developed largely to circumvent the national/local newspaper rate differential is strongly supported by the newspaper industry. Since newspapers receive over half of all co-op dollars placed, their sales staffs are extremely aggressive in helping retail accounts find and use co-op money.

The Rate Structure

The local advertiser, dealing with one or two newspapers, has a fairly easy job buying newspaper space. The rate structure and discounts for any one newspaper are usually straightforward. However, as we have seen, the national ad-

---

[14]Christy Fisher, "Newspaper Group Sets New Plan," *Advertising Age,* June 28, 1993, p. 43.

vertiser has a much more difficult time. An advertiser buying space in a number of newspapers confronts an unlimited set of options and price structures, including discounts, premium charges for color, special sections, preferred positions, and zoned editions. In the following discussion, we look at some of the primary options and rate decisions that an advertiser must make.

Discounts. Newspapers are divided into two categories: those with a uniform *flat rate* that offers no discounts, and those with an *open rate* that provides some discount structure. The open rate also refers to the highest rate against which all discounts are applied. The most common discounts are based on *frequency* or *bulk* purchases of space. A bulk discount means there is a sliding scale so that the advertiser is charged proportionally less as more advertising is purchased. A frequency discount usually requires some unit or pattern of purchase in addition to total amount of space. Examples of each discount are shown below:

<table>
<tr><td colspan="2">Frequency
Within 52-Week Contract Period
Full-Page Contract</td><td colspan="2">Bulk
Within 52-Week Contract Period</td></tr>
<tr><td>Open Rate</td><td>$2.50/Column Inch</td><td></td><td></td></tr>
<tr><td>10 insertions</td><td>2.20</td><td>500 column inches</td><td>2.40</td></tr>
<tr><td>15 insertions</td><td>2.20</td><td>1,500 column inches</td><td>2.30</td></tr>
<tr><td>20 insertions</td><td>2.10</td><td>3,000 column inches</td><td>2.20</td></tr>
<tr><td>30 insertions</td><td>2.00</td><td>5,000 column inches</td><td>2.10</td></tr>
<tr><td>40 insertions</td><td>1.90</td><td>10,000 column inches</td><td>2.00</td></tr>
<tr><td>50 insertions</td><td>1.80</td><td>15,000 column inches</td><td>1.90</td></tr>
</table>

ROP and Preferred-Position Rates. The basic rates quoted by a newspaper entitle the ad to a run-of-paper (abbreviated ROP) position anywhere in the paper that the publisher chooses to place it, although the paper will be mindful of the advertiser's request and interest in getting a good position. An advertiser may buy a choice position by paying a higher, preferred-position rate, which is similar to paying for a box seat in a stadium instead of general admission. A cigar advertiser, for example, may elect to pay a preferred-position rate to ensure getting on the sports page. A cosmetic advertiser may buy a preferred position on the women's page. There are also preferred positions on individual pages. An advertiser may pay for the top of a column or the top of a column next to news reading matter (called *full position*).

Each newspaper specifies its preferred-position rates; there is no consistency in this practice. Preferred-position rates are not as common as they once were. Now many papers simply attempt to accommodate advertisers that request a position, such as "Above fold urgently requested."

Combination Rates. A number of combinations are available to advertisers. What they all have in common is the advantage of greatly reduced rates for purchasing several papers as a group. The most frequently seen combination rate occurs when the same publisher issues both a morning and an evening paper. By buying both papers, the advertiser can pay as little as one-third to one-half for the second paper. This type of combination may involve as few as two papers in a single metropolitan market or many papers bought on a

Flat rate

A uniform charge for space in a medium, without regard to the amount of space used or the frequency of insertion. When flat rates do not prevail, *time discounts* or *quantity discounts* are offered.

Open rate

In print, the highest advertising rate at which all discounts are placed. It is also called Basic rate, Transient rate, or One-time rate.

national basis. In either case, the advertiser has to deal with only one group and pays a single bill.

The Rate Card

The newspaper rate card is fast becoming the last champion of rate consistency. As we mentioned in the broadcast chapters, most stations and networks don't even publish formal rate cards, since rates are determined by negotiated scatter plans that are unique to each advertiser. During the 1980s, magazines also began to negotiate their rates with individual advertisers. However, newspapers are the most likely medium to maintain rate integrity by offering all advertisers the same rates and discounts.

Of course, newspapers have a major advantage over their broadcast counterparts in maintaining rates. As one advertising executive points out, "The nature of broadcasting puts more pressure on its salespeople . . . broadcast time, unlike newspaper space, is a use-or-lose proposition. Even if no advertising is sold, the broadcast outlet still has the expense of putting on a show. By contrast, newspaper managers can adjust the size of their product and hence their costs by simply printing fewer or more pages as advertising dictates.[15]

However, despite the fact that most publishers adhere to their rate cards, newspapers have changed their pricing structure in the face of new competitive pressure. Some of the ways that newspapers have developed more rate flexibility include the following:

- **New, more flexible rates.** Many newspapers offer a number of rate cards for different categories of advertisers. For example, package goods, travel, business, and retail stores may all qualify for different rates. Some critics charge that newspapers offering an array of different rates are not only making the buying process unnecessarily complex but still maintaining a type of discrimination from one group of advertisers to another that has the same intent as individual rate negotiation.

- **Value-added programs.** Many newspapers, while refusing to directly negotiate rates, are willing to make other types of merchandising concessions. These programs may include sharing of detailed audience research and providing free creative or copy assistance to advertisers.

- **Pick-up rates.** An advertiser that agrees to rerun an ad will receive a lower rate. This encourages return business and passes along some of the savings that the newspaper enjoys from not having to produce a new ad.

Because of the tradition of the newspaper rate card, it is unlikely that we will see the type of rate negotiation that has become so prevalent in other media. However, newspapers recognize that they will have to meet the competition of other media. Consequently, we will see even more creative value-added programs offered by newspapers in the future.

Comparing Newspaper Advertising Costs

National advertisers, many of whom consider hundreds of newspapers in a single media plan, want to make cost comparisons among their potential newspaper buys. For many years, the standard measure for comparing the

---

[15]Walt Potter, Newspapers Deal with Pressure on Rate Cards," *Presstime*, March 1992, p. 7.

cost of newspaper space was the milline rate.[16] The milline rate has been replaced in recent years by the CPM comparison we discussed earlier.

Using the CPM for newspaper rate comparisons has two advantages:

1. It reflects the move to page and fractional-page space buys. Media planners are much more comfortable using the SAU than line or column-inch space buys.

2. Comparisons among media are more easily calculated using a standard benchmark such as the CPM. Although qualitative differences among newspapers and other media must still be considered, the CPM does offer a consistent means of comparison:

Newspaper	Open-Rate Page Cost	Circulation	CPM
A	$5,400	165,000	$32.72
B	3,300	116,000	28.45

Example: $\dfrac{\$5,400 \times 1000}{165,000} = \$32.72$

The Space Contract, the Short Rate

Short rate

The balance advertisers have to pay if they estimated that they would run more ads in a year than they did and entered a contract to pay at a favorable rate. The short rate is figured at the end of the year or sooner if advertisers fall behind schedule. It is calculated at a higher rate for the fewer insertions.

If a paper has a flat rate, obviously there is no problem with calculating costs—all space is billed at the same price regardless of how much is used. However, space contracts in open-rate papers must have flexibility to allow advertisers to use more or less space than they originally contracted for. Normally, an advertiser will sign a *space contract* estimating the amount of space to be used during the next 12 months. Such a space contract is not a guarantee of the amount of space an advertiser will run, but rather an agreement on the rate the advertiser will finally pay for any space run during the year in question.

The space contract involves two steps: First, advertisers estimate the amount of space they think they will run and agree with the newspaper on how to handle any rate adjustments needed at the end of the year; they are then billed during the year at the selected rate. Second, at the end of the year, the total linage is added, and if advertisers ran the amount of space they had estimated, no adjustment is necessary; but if they failed to run enough space to earn that rate, they have to pay at the higher rate charged for the number of lines they actually ran. That amount is called the *short rate*.

The Newsplan contract outlines the arrangement as follows:

Advertiser will be billed monthly at applicable contract rate for entire contract year. At end of contract year advertiser will be refunded if a lower rate is earned or rebilled at a higher applicable rate if contract is not fulfilled.

---

[16]The milline rate is a hypothetical figure that measures what it would cost per agate line to reach a million circulation of a paper, based on the actual line rate and circulation. The formula is:

$$\text{Milline} = \frac{1,000,000 \times \text{rate per line}}{\text{circulation}}$$

(There are 14 agate lines per column inch.)

As an example, let's assume that a national advertiser plans to run advertising in a paper whose rates are as follows:

- **Open rate, $5.00 per column inch**
- **1,000 column inches, $4.50/column inch**
- **5,000 column inches, $4.00/column inch**
- **10,000 column inches, $3.50/column inch**

The advertiser expects to run at least 5,000 column inches and signs the contract at the $4.00 (5,000 column-inch) rate (subject to end-of-year adjustment). At the end of 12 months, however, only 4,100 column inches have been run; therefore, the bill at the end of the contract year is as follows:

Earned rate: 4,100 column inches @ $4.50 per column inch = $18,450
Paid rate: 4,100 column inches @ $4.00 per column inch = 16,400
                                              Short rate due = $ 2,050

or

Column inches run × difference in earned and billed rates
                    = 4,100 column inches × 0.50
                    = $2,050

If the space purchased had qualified for the 10,000 column-inch rate ($3.50), the advertiser would have received a *rebate* of $5,000. The calculation then would be:

Paid rate: 10,000 column inches @ $4.00 per column inch = $40,000
Earned rate: 10,000 column inches @ $3.50 per column inch = $35,000
                                                 Rebate due = $ 5,000

Newspapers will credit a rebate against future advertising rather than actually paying the advertiser. Some papers charge the full rate and allow credit for a better rate when earned.

CIRCULATION ANALYSIS
The Audit Bureau of Circulations

Until the founding of the Audit Bureau of Circulations (ABC) in 1914, advertisers had little reliable information about newspaper circulation. Since its establishment, the mission of the ABC has been to standardize, verify, and disseminate circulation information for the benefit of its members.[17]

The organization serves advertisers, agencies, and publishers. It is a self-regulating and self-supporting cooperative body. Revenues for the ABC come from annual dues paid by all members and auditing fees paid by publishers.

The verification process involves three reports: two publisher's statements and the ABC audit. The publisher's statements are issued for six-month periods ending March 31 and September 30. The ABC audit is conducted annually for 12-month periods ending either March 31 or September 30. Advertisers can also get summary information in reports called FAS-FAX, which are available more quickly than the full reports. Exhibits 10.11 and 10.12 are a por-

---

[17] *Academic Casebook,* Audit Bureau of Circulations.

Audit Bureau of Circulations

AUDIT REPORT:

THE TRIBUNE (Evening)
Anytown (Red County), Illinois

TOTAL AVERAGE PAID CIRCULATION FOR 12 MONTHS ENDED SEPTEMBER 30, 19--:

	Evening
1A. TOTAL AVERAGE PAID CIRCULATION (BY INDIVIDUALS AND FOR DESIGNATED RECIPIENTS):	41,315

1B. TOTAL AVERAGE PAID CIRCULATION (BY INDIVIDUALS AND FOR DESIGNATED RECIPIENTS) BY ZONES:
(See Par. 1E for description of area)

CITY ZONE

	Population	Occupied Households
1980 Census:	80,109	29,143
#12-31-87 Estimate:	80,500	30,000

Carrier Delivery office collect system, See Pars. 11(b) & (c).....	1,875
Carriers not filing lists with publisher.......................	18,649
Single Copy Sales....................................	2,168
Mail Subscriptions	47
School-Single Copy/Subscriptions, See Par. 11(d)	50
Employee Copies, See Par. 11(e)	100
Group (Subscriptions by Businesses for Designated Employees), See Par. 11(f)	50
TOTAL CITY ZONE	22,939

RETAIL TRADING ZONE

	Population	Occupied Households
1980 Census:	268,491	75,140
#12-31-87 Estimate	272,000	79,000

Carriers not filing lists with publisher	15,138
Single Copy Sales....................................	1,549
Mail Subscriptions	908
School-Single Copy/Subscriptions, See Par. 11(d)	25
Employee Copies, See Par. 11(e)	25
Group (Subscriptions by Businesses for Designated Employees), See Par. 11(f)	50
TOTAL RETAIL TRADING ZONE	17,695
TOTAL CITY & RETAIL TRADING ZONES	40,634

	Population	Occupied Households
1980 Census:	348,600	104,283
#12-31-87 Estimate:	352,500	109,000

ALL OTHER

Single Copy Sales & Carriers not filing lists with publisher	256
Mail Subscriptions	375
School-Single Copy/Subscriptions, See Par. 11(d)	20
Employee Copies, See Par. 11(e)	20
Group (Subscriptions by Businesses for Designated Employees), See Par. 11(f)	10
TOTAL ALL OTHER	681
TOTAL PAID CIRCULATION (BY INDIVIDUALS AND FOR DESIGNATED RECIPIENTS)	41,315

1C. THIRD PARTY (BULK) SALES:

Airlines — Available for passengers	1,000
Hotels, Motels — Available for guests	500
Restaurants — Available for patrons	500
Businesses — Available for employees.....................	50
Other	600
TOTAL THIRD PARTY (BULK) SALES....................	2,650

#S&MM Estimate. See Par. 11(a).

ABC reports provide valuable information concerning the distribution patterns of newspapers and type of purchase. (Courtesy: Audit Bureau of Circulations.)

EXHIBIT 10.11

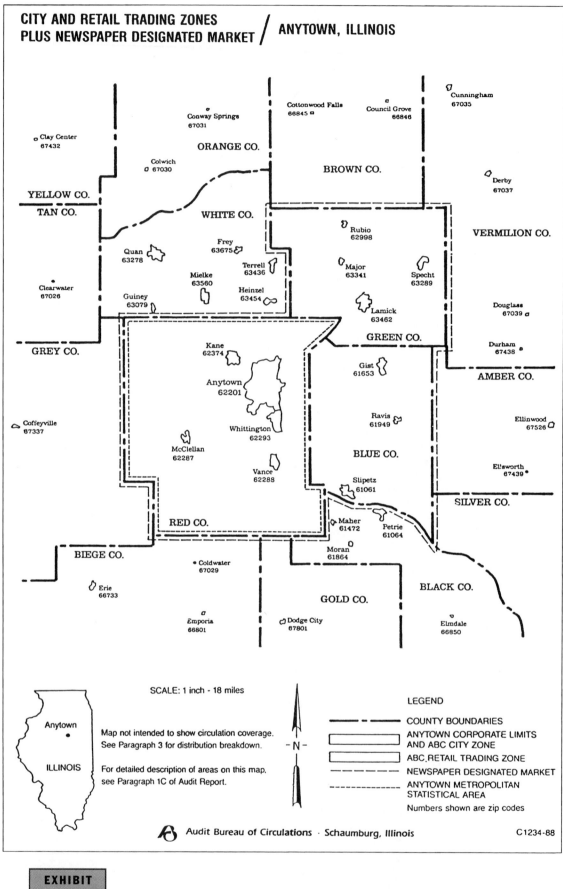

CITY AND RETAIL TRADING ZONES PLUS NEWSPAPER DESIGNATED MARKET / ANYTOWN, ILLINOIS

SCALE: 1 inch - 18 miles

Map not intended to show circulation coverage. See Paragraph 3 for distribution breakdown.

For detailed description of areas on this map, see Paragraph 1C of Audit Report.

- N -

LEGEND

COUNTY BOUNDARIES
ANYTOWN CORPORATE LIMITS AND ABC CITY ZONE
ABC RETAIL TRADING ZONE
NEWSPAPER DESIGNATED MARKET
ANYTOWN METROPOLITAN STATISTICAL AREA

Numbers shown are zip codes

Audit Bureau of Circulations · Schaumburg, Illinois   C1234-88

EXHIBIT
10.12

tion of an ABC audit report. It should be noted that the information in ABC reports is constantly changing in response to subscribers' needs.

The report includes the following primary information:

1. Total paid circulation.

2. Amount of circulation in the city zone, retail trading zone, and all other areas. (*Note:* The city zone is a market made up of the city of publication and contiguous built-up areas similar in character to the central city. The retail trading zone is a market area outside the city zone whose residents regularly trade with merchants doing business within the city zone.)

3. The number of papers sold at newsstands.

The ABC reports have nothing to do with a newspaper's rates. They deal with circulation statistics only. Publishers have always been glad to supply demographic data on their readers, but the ABC now has its own division for gathering demographic data for many of the markets in the United States. All data are computerized and quickly available.

TECHNOLOGY AND THE FUTURE OF NEWSPAPERS

Advertisers are not in the business of creating new media. They're in the business of selling soap.—Martin Nisenholtz, Ogilvy & Mather.

Without information, all the superhighways in the world are useless.—Vicki Vance, Apple Computer.[18]

In some respects, these two quotes summarize the current relationship among advertisers, newspapers, and their audiences. For a number of years, engineers, computer analysts, and assorted technocrats have told us that the world of the electronic newspaper is here and will become a common sight in every home any day now. However, for at least 20 years, the promise of the electronic newspaper has failed to meet these lofty predictions.

While there are numerous reasons why household penetration of the various delivery options has been limited, the primary reason is that customers have been resistant to adopt technology that offers few advantages they do not already have from traditional media and other services. How many readers are interested in a computer service that will provide baseball scores 24 hours a day when they are readily available from free broadcast and print media? Likewise, will we pay to bank, make airline reservations, or find out the latest stock quotations from on-line technology when the same services are readily available, many as near as the telephone? The key to the success of in-home information services is their ability to provide *information* that is not obtainable from other sources. To this point, they have not convinced a majority of users that they can provide such services.

By the same token, the media have to understand that advertisers don't care how they reach their audiences—so long as *prospects* are reached as economically as possible. In this sense, they are not partners with the media in paying to develop new technology. Newspapers have the responsibility of delivering an audience that advertisers think is more valuable than those provided by

---

[18]"Quotes from All Over," *Presstime,* July 1993, p. 56.

competing media. The technology used to reach this audience is not the problem of the advertiser.

One of the largest examples of an alternative newspaper delivery system involves a joint agreement between the Prodigy on-line system and a consortium of newspapers led by Cox Newspapers. Prodigy's approximately 1.5 million subscribers can obtain constantly updated news and information provided by the newspapers. Readers have access to the information included in these newspapers as well as stories that were deleted because of space limitations. This material, while too specialized for the general newspaper, can be stored easily in a computer database. The service will also provide an electronic bulletin board so that users can communicate with one another as well as editors at the newspapers.

Many observers think that newspapers are smart to get into the alternative delivery services as early as possible. Even though these services reach relatively few readers, they tend to go to an extremely upscale and educated audience. More importantly, many experts think that the current generation of teens and younger children are so computer literate that they will prefer the same electronic delivery systems currently resisted by their parents.

NEWSPAPER-DISTRIBUTED MAGAZINE SUPPLEMENTS
Sunday Supplements

Thirty years ago, the Sunday supplement was a vital part of virtually every major newspaper. These supplements usually emphasized home and garden, the local restaurant and entertainment scene, and features. However, in the past several years these locally produced supplements were replaced by syndicated publications. Today, there are only 32 local supplements for the 800-plus Sunday newspapers.

While the Sunday supplements have witnessed the same consolidation as the media in general, they have never been more popular in terms of circulation or advertising revenue. Total weekly circulation is approximately 73 million, with advertising revenues approaching $1 billion. The Sunday supplement field is dominated by two publications: *Parade* magazine and *USA Weekend.*[19]

Parade, distributed in 345 newspapers, is the largest of the supplements in terms of circulation (37 million) and advertising revenue ($450 million). *USA Weekend* is distributed in 383 newspapers, but with circulation of 17 million it is most prevalent among small and medium-sized Sunday newspapers. Total advertising revenues are $171 million.

All but two locally produced Sunday supplements can be bought as a package through the Sunday Magazine Network (SMN). An advertiser may buy all or any number of these supplements. The 28 members of SMN have a combined circulation of over 16 million, with total revenues of almost $100 million. One advantage cited for the SMN package is that these individually edited magazines provide local features as contrasted to the nationally syndicated *Parade* and *USA Weekend.* However, some advertisers like the guaranteed consistency of production and placement offered by the national publications.

---

[19]Russell Shaw, "And on the 7th Day," *Mediaweek,* April 26, 1993, p. 35.

The two remaining Sunday supplements are the *New York Times Magazine* and the *Los Angeles Times* magazine, both with circulations of over 1.5 million. Even these magazines have seen some loss of advertising support in recent years. For example, the prestigious *Times* magazine underwent a complete redesign in the fall of 1993 to make the publication more appealing to both advertisers and readers.

With the exception of a few large markets, most newspapers find that it is not cost-efficient to produce their own Sunday supplements, and there is probably going to be a further consolidation among the members of SMN. However, it is clear that the features, entertainment news, and opportunities for advertisers to buy Sunday newspaper circulation in a magazine format will make the supplement a continuing part of our Sunday reading ritual.

Before leaving our discussion of national supplements, we should mention one other that is directed to a Hispanic audience, *Vista.* It is an English-language monthly publication distributed in some 25 newspapers in metropolitan areas with large Hispanic populations. Since its start in 1985, it has shown remarkable growth in an extremely competitive market. With projections for significant increases in the Hispanic population, *Vista* has a secure future.

Special Sections

At one time, the Sunday magazine was the only supplement offered by the typical newspaper. However, in recent years newspapers have begun to produce a number of editorial products to reach both readers and nonreaders. Sometimes these are presented as weekly or monthly tabloids within the daily newspaper. For example, the *Tampa Tribune* publishes *Apartment Plus,* an every other week real estate book that is carried in the *Tribune,* but also is available in racks to compete with other real estate magazines. The paper also offers *Upscale Tampa* to newspapers distributed in high-income ZIP codes and in grocery stores in those areas.

In addition to editorial products distributed in the paper and provided free through racks, many newspapers are putting out separate publications as additional profit centers. Some of these publications are advertiser-supported, while others are supported by both ads and circulation fees. Publications such as the *Miami Herald's South Florida Golf* and the *Charlotte Observer's Community Pride,* a magazine for African American families with incomes of at least $25,000, provide a means of reaching both nonreaders and nonadvertisers of the core newspaper.[20] In addition, these publications use excess press time and other facilities of the newspaper that keep their overhead low.

THE AFRICAN AMERICAN AND HISPANIC PRESS

At one time, many major metropolitan newspapers did not print birth, wedding, or funeral notices for African Americans. Unfortunately, most news of the black community was also largely ignored. In this environment, it was understandable that a number of newspapers were directed specifically at African American readers. In fact, the black press has a distinguished history since the early nineteenth century.

---

[20]"Newspaper Augmentation," *Knight-Ridder News,* Summer 1993, p. 15.

The black press was at its height during the 1960s, with almost 300 papers and total circulation of 4 million. These newspapers were sources of news, political agitation, and advertising. They contributed to much of the social progress made during this period. One of their significant legacies was passage of the Voting Rights Act and other civil rights legislation during the term of President Lyndon Johnson.

Ironically, the black press has suffered financially as opportunities have opened to African American citizens. The majority press, led by liberal columnists such as Ralph McGill of the *Atlanta Constitution,* began to incorporate coverage of black readers into their papers. As time went on, it was less important to have separate newspapers to cover news for black readers.

Today, there are only three daily newspapers directed primarily to African American readers: the *Atlanta Daily World,* the *Chicago Daily Defender,* and the *New York Daily Challenge.* In addition, there are a number of smaller black newspapers published on a weekly or biweekly basis. During the past two decades, most black-oriented newspapers have lost both circulation and advertising revenue.

Advertisers, particularly major national companies, have shifted significant dollars into television, radio, and magazines with high African American audiences. For example, *Soul Train, Jet, Black Enterprise,* and *Essence* have all enjoyed notable support from corporations seeking to reach the lucrative African American market.

In the future, it appears that the black press will continue to struggle. Research indicates that African American adults prefer television and magazines to newspapers, and black teenagers, like their white counterparts, overwhelmingly use radio as their medium of preference. In one sense, the current troubles of the black press are a tribute to the job it did in bringing fairness and equity to the African American community in the past.

The Hispanic press is enjoying major growth in a number of cities. Nationally, there are 330 newspapers (176 Spanish language, 117 bilingual, and 37 English language) that target Hispanic readers, and more than 400 magazines, journals, and newsletters are published for Hispanic readers.[21] Approximately one-fourth are published in Southern California.

Increasingly, these newspapers are being published by mainstream newspaper companies. For example, *El Nuevo Tiempo* by the New York Times Company and, one of the largest, *Nuestro Tiempo* with a circulation of 450,000, by the Los Angeles Times Company. Nine percent of the U.S. population is Spanish speaking, and it is growing at a faster rate than the total population.

Testifying to the strength of the Hispanic community is the continuing growth of the Hispanic press. Since 1993, 26 Spanish-language newspapers were started. Many of these newspapers have done well with national advertisers. Some, such as Coca-Cola, are heavy investors in the Spanish-language press even though they normally place very little newspaper advertising.[22]

---

[21]Margaret G. Carter, "Latin Lessons," *Presstime,* May 1994, p. 40.
[22]Hanna Liebman, "Newspapers Hablan Espanol," *Mediaweek,* August 16, 1993, p. 10.

While the Spanish-language press is the largest category of foreign-language newspapers, there are also newspapers available in over 20 foreign languages including Albanian, Croatian, and Finnish.

WEEKLY NEWSPAPERS

Weekly newspapers fall into a number of categories: suburban papers covering events within some portion of a larger metropolitan area, traditional rural weeklies providing local coverage, specialty weeklies covering politics or the arts, and free shoppers with little editorial matter. During the past 30 years the number of weeklies has decreased approximately 10 percent from more than 8,000 papers to fewer than 7,500. However, during the same period, the average circulation of weeklies has grown dramatically, reflecting the move from a basically rural to suburban medium. According to the National Newspaper Association, average circulation has tripled in the past three decades:

Average Weekly Circulation	
Year	Circulation per Paper
1960	2,566
1970	3,660
1980	5,324
1992	7,629

The number of weeklies has declined slightly for the past decade and now numbers slightly more than 7,400 newspapers, almost five times the number of dailies. However, the complexion of the weekly industry has changed dramatically in the period since World War II. The 1980s saw a dramatic increase in the number of weeklies that are free to readers and a decline in those charging a circulation fee.

Weekly growth will be concentrated in suburban and urban areas for the remainder of the 1990s. Weeklies will occupy a separate niche for small retailers that cannot afford major dailies or that have a limited distribution area. These weeklies are rarely considered by large metro retailers or national advertisers. Consequently, there is little direct competition for either readers or advertisers between weeklies and dailies. The weekly battlefield is largely between traditional small-town, paid-circulation papers and free circulation publications that have moved into many of these communities.

SUMMARY

For all their problems and challenges, the daily newspaper remains the predominant advertising medium. However, the future of newspapers is one of transition and changing methods of doing business. The newspaper industry must find ways to reach nonreaders and occasional readers. The fact that many young adults do not read the newspaper with any regularity is an especially acute problem for the industry. Studies indicate that young readers who do not get in the habit of newspaper reading rarely become readers later in life. At the same time, newspapers must continue to experiment with alternative methods of reaching audiences to prepare for the electronic super-highway of the future.

Given the growing competition for local advertising budgets, newspapers must develop ways of accommodating national advertisers if they are to significantly increase expenditures from advertising agencies. Newspapers must standardize all aspects of the buying and placing of ads. The NAA's attempts to build a national newspaper network are the latest hope for a move in this direction.

However, no amount of standardization will outweigh the perception by national advertisers that newspapers are unfairly priced. The huge local/national rate differentials are the primary impediment to increased national investment. In addition, newspapers must be prepared to offer national discounts and value-added programs on an equal basis with their retail clients.

Compounding the continuing difficulty of increasing national dollars is the defection of many local advertisers to other media. The newspaper no longer has a stranglehold on the local advertising dollar. Today's retailer can choose from a media menu of everything from direct mail to cable television. The loss of readers and the growing competition come at a time when publishing costs and accompanying advertising rate increases are continuing to increase CPMs to unacceptable levels for some advertisers.

In spite of these problems, it would be wrong to suggest that newspapers will not continue to be a viable medium in the future. However, newspapers will increasingly be forced to devote time and money to marketing themselves to readers and advertisers. This marketing orientation will mean new formats and designs, including color. It will also mean that the newspaper will have to appeal to specific audiences with editorial matter directed especially to them. Some editors worry that newspapers in the future will be edited according to readership surveys.

In terms of advertisers, newspapers must diversify the categories of products and services that use the paper. They can no longer depend solely on retail stores to provide the majority of their advertising. Total market coverage must be offered on an easy-to-buy basis for both local and national advertisers. We will continue to see consolidation of information companies where newspapers, cable and broadcast television, city magazines, direct-mail firms, and virtually all other media will be owned by single firms, Advertisers increasingly will be sold on a cross-media basis, with newspapers being part of an overall communication package for advertisers.

Questions

1. What are some of the factors that have eroded the local newspaper advertising base?
2. What has been the major hurdle *USA Today* faced in becoming an effective national newspaper?
3. Many newspapers are offering "value-added" merchandising to advertisers. Explain.
4. What does the term *relationship marketing* mean in newspaper advertising?
5. Contrast zoned editions and total market coverage programs.

6. What are the three major categories of newspaper advertising, and how much advertising revenue does each account for?
7. What are the two major problems in newspapers gaining national advertising?
8. In what area have newspapers been most successful in achieving standardization?
9. What is the difference between the short rate and rebate?
10. What are the primary advantages of newspaper magazine supplements?

11

Using Magazines

CHAPTER OBJECTIVES

The success of magazines, like their radio counterparts, depends on reaching narrowly defined audiences who have common interests. Both consumer and trade publications must be selective in the way they tailor their audiences. After reading this chapter you will understand:

- **The evolution of magazines from a mass to class medium**
- **Cost and selectivity considerations**
- **Magazine options available to advertisers**
- **Paid and controlled circulation**
- **Differences between business and consumer magazines**

Despite some recent optimism, these are not the best of times for consumer magazines. Although most publishers have experienced increased revenues, the combination of hefty increases in postage costs, dealer fees for newsstand sales, and a generally soft advertising market among prime product categories have eroded publishers' profits. **Magazines have had** to reposition themselves in the face of new competition, a fickle reading audience, and, most of all, the marketing needs of national advertisers.

Consumer magazines do not represent a single unified medium with common strengths and weaknesses. Instead, there are simultaneously successes and failures among different categories of publications. For example, although magazine advertising pages have shown little growth in a number of years, some publishers have demonstrated significant increases in both advertising revenues and advertising pages during the same period. "Last year the magazine industry got its first intoxicating whiff of an economic recovery. Publishers Information Bureau figures show a 1.6 percent increase in consumer magazine ad pages and an 8.3 percent increase in ad revenues after two decades of decline. Many titles—mostly in service-oriented categories such as health, personal finance and parenting—broke out of the pack with gains of 20 percent and more."[1] Throughout this chapter, we need to keep in mind that general statements about consumer magazines invariably encounter a number of exceptions.

In order to understand the contemporary consumer magazine industry, we have to examine two primary characteristics: selectivity and cost.

SELECTIVITY

The consumer magazine industry can be described as "survival of the discriminating." Virtually without exception, the successful titles are those that offer both readers and advertisers a narrowly focused editorial product in an environment suited to selling specific product categories. Not only are these publications targeted to identified audience segments, but their high-interest readers are usually willing to pay a premium for the magazines, thus increasing publishers' profits.

A list of recent magazine success stories includes publications as disparate as *Martha Stewart's Living, Worth, Snow Country, Golf for Women,* and *Backpacker.* The only thing these publications have in common is that they appeal to a specific reader category. Without even having read any of these publications, we could probably come up with an extremely accurate list of their top advertising categories and reader profiles.

Although selectivity is one of the keys to contemporary magazine success, audience and editorial selectivity is actually rooted in the historical development of magazines.

The Evolution of the Modern Magazine

The magazines of the mid-nineteenth century were targeted to audiences of special interests, sold at a high cost, and carried little advertising. Most magazines were literary, political, or religious in content and depended on readers or special-interest groups to provide most of their financial support.

In the latter years of the nineteenth century a rising middle class, mass production, and national transportation combined to provide the opportunity for nationally distributed branded goods. The opportunities offered by national brands could only be exploited with the efficiencies of mass promotion. During the 1890s a trio of publishers provided the beginnings for the ad-supported, mass-circulation magazine. Frank Munsey *(Munsey's),* S. S. Mc-

---

[1]Stephen Barr, "Survival of the Fittest," *Adweek,* March 1, 1993, p. 9.

Clure *(McClure's)*, and Edward Bok's *Ladies Home Journal* brought low-cost magazines to an enthusiastic public.

Until the advent of radio in the 1920s, magazines remained the only national advertising medium. With the introduction of radio, they had to share the national advertising dollar. Still, magazines were the only *visual* medium available to national manufacturers. However, when television became a national medium in the 1950s, people's reading habits became viewing habits, and national magazines had to change to survive.

Magazines found themselves in a difficult situation. As a mass medium they could not compete with television's low CPMs. On the other hand, the mass magazines of the 1950s such as *Life* were not selective enough to reach narrowly defined target audiences demanded by many advertisers. Clearly, after more than 50 years of unchallenged success as a mass medium, magazines had to make some radical changes. In the future, only those magazines with a clear editorial focus will survive.

It is extremely difficult for general magazines to be successful. With few exceptions, the large-circulation, mass-appeal magazine is a dinosaur in this age of target marketing. In fact, we are now seeing a process of subcategorization, similar to that found in radio. For example, *Family Life* is positioned as a magazine for families with children beyond the infant stage. The publication is for children aged 3 to 12 years of age, or "past diapers and colic." An ad for the magazine says, "As your kids start to grow up, baby magazines begin to feel two sizes too small."[2] Exhibit 11.1 shows the new magazine titles introduced in recent years. Each of these publications thinks it has found an untapped market. Unfortunately, if history repeats itself, only 20 percent will survive.

COSTS

Rarely do magazine publishers meet that cost control is not a major topic of conversation. While magazines have successfully addressed the need for selectivity, they have found the problem of rising costs much more difficult to solve. Paper, printing, and distribution account for approximately 36 percent of a typical magazine's expenses. Attesting to the competitive environment of magazines, another 32 percent of total revenues is spent in gaining and maintaining readers. In contrast to these expense items, only 11 percent of expenses is allocated to the editorial product.

The profit squeeze felt by many magazines is attributed in part to the concentration of advertising categories. According to the Magazine Publishers of America (MPA), the top five categories of magazine advertising account for 46 percent of total advertising revenues. The top 10 categories account for 73.5 percent of the total for all magazines. A significant decline in advertising budgets among one of these bellwether categories, such as automotive or apparel, has an immediate effect on the entire industry.[3]

Not only do magazine advertisers concentrate in a relatively few product categories, but they also tend to be the same companies that are heavy users of

---

[2]Stuart Elliott, "Advertising," *New York Times,* June 14, 1993, p. C 7.
[3]"Top Advertising Categories," *Mediaweek,* February 28, 1994, M.Q. p. 23.

EXHIBIT

11.1

Statistics: New Magazines by Category 1987–93

	1987	1988	1989	1990	1991	1992	1993
Arts & Antiques	0	5	1	5	6	9	13
Astroloty	0	0	0	3	1	0	0
Automotive	32	29	26	22	19	17	24
Aviation	6	4	0	1	2	4	8
Boating & Yachting	7	0	5	1	2	3	3
Brides & Bridal	0	5	0	1	3	8	7
Business & Finance	12	12	8	11	5	3	13
Camping	0	0	0	0	0	0	0
Children's	5	11	5	12	7	15	17
Collectibles	0	0	3	13	11	11	18
Comics	11	6	7	5	14	21	17
Computers	14	25	22	9	17	18	31
Crafts, Games & Hobbies	15	15	24	21	32	35	33
Dogs & Pets	0	4	3	0	1	5	4
Dressmaking & Needlework	11	15	30	17	17	12	17
Electronics	13	6	8	8	7	7	4
Epicurean	19	9	22	15	14	23	30
Fishing & Hunting	11	14	12	8	18	15	10
Gardening	1	3	4	3	4	4	9
Gay & Lesbian	8	14	11	10	22	17	11
Health	7	11	12	24	7	15	18
Home Service	17	24	32	28	19	20	45
Humor	0	0	0	0	0	0	4
Lifestyle & Service	25	40	55	56	40	60	34
Literary	4	8	4	6	7	14	18
Media Personalities	38	10	4	41	34	33	22
Men's	3	0	0	4	0	4	7
Metropolitan, Regional & State	8	31	58	27	26	26	18
Military & Naval	16	10	23	18	26	12	8
Motorcycle	5	4	7	3	0	7	16
Music	23	23	29	21	19	32	41
Mystery & Adventure	7	6	2	4	5	16	13
Newspaper Magazines	4	6	3	0	0	0	0
Photography	3	4	2	3	3	1	1
Political	2	5	0	1	2	4	8
Puzzles	33	4	19	12	19	15	14
Religion	7	5	2	3	2	3	2
Science & Technology	0	2	0	2	2	2	5
Sex	28	46	73	62	66	97	95
Sports	38	43	36	42	41	40	84
Travel	10	6	11	8	7	10	20
Video & Movies	6	10	14	5	8	12	20
Women's	5	4	9	6	3	8	3
Women's Fashion & Beauty	20	18	14	13	9	4	15
Youth	11	12	6	5	5	12	9
Total	485	509	608	557	553	679	789

(Source: Magazine Publishers of America 1994–1995 Magazine Handbook.)

television. Since television is the dominant medium for national advertisers, when budgets are cut by these advertisers, magazines go first. Even when magazines have convinced advertisers to continue advertising, advertisers have required publishers to cut ad rates or offer other expensive merchandising programs that have reduced profits. There is little question that magazine publishers will be forced to economize even further in coming years.

A major problem for publishers is continuing postal increases. Since 1990, second-class mailing costs have increased more than 20 percent. At the same time, magazine distributors are demanding higher fees to carry magazines, thus cutting off newsstand sales as a less costly alternative to mailing. Some major publishers have turned to independent delivery systems such as Publishers Express to deliver their magazines (see Exhibit 11.2). However, independent companies can provide service only in areas with significant circulation density.

On the plus side, printing and paper costs have not risen significantly in recent years. Furthermore, many magazines are experimenting with desktop publishing systems designed to save on typesetting and design. Finally, publishers are optimistic that an improving economy will bring advertisers back. However, it is certain that the number of magazines and publishing houses will be reduced by the end of this decade.

In response to a weak advertising environment and rising costs, magazines have dramatically increased the cost of both subscriptions and newsstand sales to readers. Historically, magazine profits depended heavily on advertising revenue. Up until 1950, magazines were sold at a very low price. At that time, the basic revenue formula for magazines was to sell publications as cheaply as possible, build up a large audience base, and then sell this audience to advertisers at a premium. It was not uncommon for major mass-circulation publications to cost 10–25 cents at the newsstand, and even less by subscription. As recently as 1970, advertising accounted for 65 percent of total magazine revenues. However, 1985 marked a milestone in magazine financing, when the percentage of magazine revenues from readers passed that of advertisers.

Currently, advertising accounts for approximately 47 percent of total revenues, with readers contributing the remaining 53 percent. The primary contributor to this increase has been single-copy prices, which increased 80 percent during the 1980s. The shift to greater revenues from magazine readers was greeted enthusiastically by advertisers. Obviously, as consumers contributed a higher share of revenues, magazine advertising rates rose less rapidly. Advertisers also welcomed the change, since by paying a higher price, readers indicated a greater commitment to a publication, both to its advertising and editorial content. In moving toward a higher level of reader financing, magazines have taken the position that they will emphasize *profitability* of circulation rather than size.

EXHIBIT 11.2

The USPS is the only organization allowed to place mail inside or on mailboxes. Private deliveries can be hung in plastic bags on the doorknob or put into newspaper tubes.

(Courtesy: Publishers Express.)

MEDIA COMPETITION AND MEDIA IMPERATIVES (COMPARATIVES)

Media imperatives

Based on research by Simmons Media Studies, showed the importance of using both TV and magazines for full market coverage.

One of the elements that characterizes magazine marketing and makes it markedly different from most other media is the degree of intramedia competition. While television, magazines' major competitor for national advertising dollars, continues to market itself by outlining its strengths relative to other media, magazine marketing strategy is largely a matter of pitting one publication against another.

Of course, competition exists in all media and, to a degree, it is healthy. However, "over many years, magazine-versus-magazine competition has helped undermine the value of many of the tools the industry depends on for its prosperity . . . when one magazine after another questions the veracity of competitors' . . . research . . . these figures become questionable for all magazines. After all, what makes your statistics any more accurate than your competitors'?"[4] This fierce in-fighting has diverted the focus of the magazine industry away from the real competition, which is television.

Publishers are aware of the long-term damage done to their industry and are taking steps to correct the situation. Working with the MPA, individual magazines have supported a number of research projects to sell the value of magazine advertising. One of the most effective approaches is to show that certain audiences can be reached effectively only by magazines.

This study divides the U.S. population into five groups or quintiles, according to their degree of magazine usage. These groups are called magazine *Imperatives,* or *Comparatives,* because it is essential that magazines be used in a significant way to reach the heavy users of magazines (who are also light users of television). There are other groups that are TV comparatives, that is, heavy viewers (and light magazine users), who can only be reached using television.

The importance of this research to magazines is that it shows an inverse relationship between heavy TV viewers and heavy magazine readers. Consequently, large national advertisers cannot reach a mass audience by using only television. In addition, the magazine comparative audience represents much better prospects for a number of product categories than television. For example, Exhibit 11.3 shows that heavy magazine readers (comparatives) have a much higher level of financial activity than heavy users of television. Heavy users of magazines are 57 percent more likely than the general population to carry the American Express Gold Card, while heavy TV users are 46 percent less likely to own the card than the average American.

Magazine executives applaud this type of research. It not only positions magazines favorably in relation to television, but it also shows magazines in general in a positive light. It does not remove the problems of magazine-against-magazine competition, but it is a beneficial first step in that direction.

CROSS-MEDIA BUYS

As we have noted in previous chapters, advertising media are evaluated as part of the total marketing communication mix. Taking their cue from radio and cable television, magazines are selling themselves as part of a synergistic ap-

---

[4]Bruce Sheiman, "We Have Met the Enemy . . . ," *Folio,* April 1, 1993, p. 33.

EXHIBIT 11.3

Financial Profile Index

	Media Comparatives	
	Magazine	TV
Regular checking account	107	93
Interest-bearing checking account	113	90
Savings account	112	87
Individual retirement account	121	76
Purchased/sold U.S. Savings Bonds	132	67
Purchased/sold stock	134	74
$100,000 + homeowners insurance	126	73
$50,000 + life insurance	134	65
Credit cards:		
American Express Green	122	65
American Express Gold	157	54
Discover	118	78
Master Card	119	76
Master Card Gold	131	77
VISA	120	74
VISA Gold	126	77

Note: 100 = U.S Average

(Source: "The Magazine Handbook," A publication of the Magazine Publishers of America.)

Cross-media buys
Several media or vehicles within one medium package themselves to be sold to advertisers to gain a synergistic communication effect and efficiencies in purchasing time or space.

proach to an overall media plan. Today we are seeing more and more magazine advertising sold as part of a buying concept known as cross-media buys.

The most common cross-media buys are those put together by multimedia companies that offer special advertising programs and discounts that involve a number of their properties. For example, major media conglomerates such as the Gannett Company (which owns *USA Today, USA Weekend,* and TV stations such as WXIA in Atlanta and KUSA in Denver), numerous newspapers, and outdoor companies, customize ad packages from among their media holdings. An advertiser may get a special discount by buying television, magazines, and outdoor from the same corporation. This type of cross-media buy is relatively straightforward.

Magazine publishers have been prime movers in developing cross-media vehicles that take advantage of the equity of their publications. Often, these magazine-initiated cross-media projects involve supplementing magazine content with some form of video. This approach is not new. In 1931, *Time* magazine produced a radio series called "The March of Time," which featured enactments of current news stories. Likewise, since the 1960s National Geographic TV documentaries have been among the most popular shows of their kind.

In recent years, demands from advertisers and a fragmented magazine audience have increasingly moved publishers to explore cross-media vehicles. An executive with Time Telepictures Television sees many opportunities to convert magazine content into television. "We've been charged with creating a new entity whose primary mission is to take the journalistic assets of all 25 [Time Warner] magazines into television . . . we are looking at everything from conventional syndication, selling product [programs] to networks, cable and even video cassettes."[5]

[5]James McBride, "Magazines in Motion," *Mediaweek,* February 1, 1993, p. 23.

Cross-media projects not only meet advertiser demands but create a huge profit center for publishers. They also introduce and promote the publication to an audience of TV viewers, many of whom are probably not regular readers (note our earlier discussion of media imperatives). Some typical examples of such cross-media productions are *Rolling Stone's* coproduction of "Rolling Stone 25: Presented by MTV," *Field & Stream's* video shorts on ESPN, *Better Homes & Gardens'* "Preparing Your Home to Sell" video, and "The Cosmopolitan Work-Out Series," a video that sold more than 2 million copies.

Cross-media selling fits in perfectly with the current emphasis on the media mix and segmented audience identification. By using an established magazine, an advertiser is guaranteed high name recognition and credibility with that portion of a publication's audience who are interested in some activity or topic. There is little question that the cross-media market will become a normal extension of the business of virtually every major publisher.

An indirect benefit of cross-media selling is that it further emphasizes the media synergism gained through a combination of magazines and television. By developing these broadcast spinoffs of success magazines, there is a recognition of the need to use the two media in a complementary fashion. In the long term, the appreciation of the need for a more intermedia approach to media planning may be a greater benefit to the magazine industry than the short-term profits made from these projects.

MAGAZINES AS AN ADVERTISING MEDIUM: ADVANTAGES AND DISADVANTAGES

As we discussed in Chapter 7, one of the primary functions of a media planner is to determine how a medium or individual vehicle will enhance the advertising objectives of a particular company. It requires an experienced planner to sort through the numerous titles, formats, rates, and editorial viewpoints of the hundreds of consumer magazines available to advertisers. In this section we will examine the primary considerations that determine whether or not magazines in general, or a particular title, will be included in a media plan.

1. *Audience selectivity.* As we noted earlier, the audience niche reached by a publication is normally the starting point for evaluating a magazine. Successful magazines tend to appeal to relatively audience segments, especially compared to the general magazines of the 1950s such as *Life, Look,* and *The Saturday Evening Post.* However, today even the largest-circulation publications have an identifiable editorial focus. *Sports Illustrated, TV Guide,* and *Modern Maturity* all reach millions of readers but concentrate on relatively few topics.

   The closest publications to the general-circulation magazines of the past are *Reader's Digest* and the newspaper-distributed supplements *USA Weekend* and *Parade.* However, it is apparent that the typical consumer magazine reaches a particular demographic or lifestyle category. The combination of clearly defined demographics and compatible editorial environment make magazines important to many advertisers, either as the primary building block of a media schedule or as a valuable supplement to other media.

2. *Exposure to a company's primary target audiences.* Magazines can reach narrowly defined audience segments, especially among high-income households. There is no question that magazines represent the most efficient means of reaching a significant segment of affluent prospects. Furthermore, the majority of this audience are not heavy users of other media. Therefore, when the marketing objective is to reach affluent customers, magazines will almost always play a central role in the advertising plan.

For more and more national advertisers, the decision is not one of deciding *between* magazines and television, but rather how best to use them as complementary media. A study commissioned by the MPA found the following:

■ **The combination of print and television produces greater communication of brand attributes than print alone or television alone.**

■ **The selection of a brand versus its competitor increases more when print and television are used in conjunction with each other than when television or magazines are used separately.**

■ **It is evident that advertisers must plan their creative strategies and executions to strengthen and enhance the communication objectives for both media. The complementary advantages of combining magazines and television are greatly reinforced when creative strategies are complementary for both media.[6]**

3. *Long life and creative options.* A TV commercial is over in 30 seconds, we whiz by a highway billboard so quickly that only a fleeting glance is possible, and the average newspaper is in the recycling bin before we leave for work. In this disposable media world, magazines stand alone as a tangible vehicle. Magazines are often used as reference sources. Articles are clipped, back issues are filed, and readers may go back to a favorite magazine numerous times before finally discarding it. Advertisers potentially benefit from each of these exposures.

Magazines also offer advertisers a wide range of flexible formats such as double-page spreads, bright colors, even product sampling. Magazines are particularly suited to long copy. Discussions of detailed product attributes for automobiles and appliances as well as advertising for financial services all lend themselves to magazines.

Partial run editions

When magazines offer less than their entire circulation to advertisers. Partial runs include demographic, geographic, and split-run editions.

4. *Availability of demographic and geographic editions.* In Chapter 11 we discussed newspaper zoning as a reaction to advertiser demand for selected segments of a publication's circulation. On a national scale, magazine demographic and geographic editions meet the same demands of large advertisers. It is very rare that a national magazine does not offer some type of regional or demographic breakout of its total circulation. These special editions are called *partial runs* and are so common and important to magazine advertising that they will be discussed separately in a later section of this chapter.

---

[6]"The Research Study: The Advertising Impact of Magazines in Conjunction with Television," *The MPA Research Newsletter, no. 65,* Magazine Publishers of America.

5. *Qualitative factors.* Advertisers buy magazines based on their ability to deliver a particular audience at a reasonable cost. However, more than any other medium, magazines depend on less easily measured, qualitative factors for their success. Among the major qualitative criteria that advertisers traditionally look for in magazines are the following:

CREDIBILITY. Many consumer magazines are considered the leading authority in their field. Car owners look to *Road & Track,* hunters to *Sports Afield,* stockholders to *Fortune,* and gardeners to *Southern Living* as sources of reliable information. As we discussed earlier, it is this position of magazines as authoritative sources that has led to so many cross-media spinoffs into other media. Sometimes the relationship between media credibility and advertising is direct. For example, the Good Housekeeping Seal has been used by *Good Housekeeping* magazine for more than 50 years as a method of endorsing products that are advertised in the publication. In other cases, the connection is less obvious but nevertheless an important part of the qualitative selling environment of magazine advertising.

COMPATIBLE EDITORIAL ENVIRONMENT. When a person picks up *Golf Digest, Money, Glamour,* or *PC Computing,* there is little doubt about their interests. These same readers also watch prime-time television, listen to the radio on the way home from work, and see numerous billboards each day. However, it is difficult to anticipate what they are thinking about at these moments. On the other hand, specialized magazines can practically guarantee a synergism between reader and editorial content.

READER INVOLVEMENT. The average reading time for a consumer magazine is 52 minutes. More importantly, the more highly educated a reader, the more thoroughly he or she reads a magazine. Studies by the MPA show that readers with a college degree are exposed to the average magazine page more frequently and also are more likely to see the advertisements. Reader involvement is related to the credibility and editorial relationship that readers develop with their favorite magazines. While not easy to quantify, these factors play a role in determining in which medium advertisers will invest their dollars.

Advertising planners have for some years looked for a method of integrating qualitative analyses into the largely quantitative media planning process. Exhibit 11.4 shows the results of a qualitative measurement developed by Total Research, Inc. The technique matches personality types with the media for which they have high or low affinity. For example, the "Youthful Irreverents" are sexy and rebellious. As we would expect they have high affinity for MTV and little time for *Ladies' Home Journal.*

Despite the recent attention given to qualitative characteristics, we should not assume that they will replace traditional magazine buying guidelines. Regardless of the qualitative nature of a publication, prime prospects must be delivered at a competitive cost. Media planners will continue to judge magazines on a cost-efficiency basis using criteria such as CPMs, and reach and frequency. The ultimate evaluation of magazines, as with any medium, is whether they can deliver the right audience, at the right price, and in the right environment.

Despite the many advantages that magazines offer advertisers, there are several problems that must be considered before buying magazine advertising.

		Affinity for . . .		Little Affinity for . . .
UPSCALE SOPHISTICATES	Cerebral and Elitist	Wall Street Journal Arts & Entertainment Masterpiece Theatre	Ordinary Life and Mass-Appeal Celebrities	Rescue 911 People America's Funniest Home Videos
PRACTICAL TRADITIONALISTS	Wholesome and Pragmatic	Family Channel Rescue 911 Popular Mechanics	Vulgar and Stylish	Roseanne MTV Vogue
STYLE AND FAMILY	Fashion and Family-Oriented	Vogue Oprah Nickelodeon	Scientific and Masculine	Star Trek Field and Stream Smithsonian
YOUTHFUL IRREVERENTS	Sexy and Rebelliuos	MTV Married with Children Penthouse	Educational and Family-Oriented	Masterpiece Theatre Ladies' Home Journal PBS
NON-MACHO HUMANISTS	Mature and Qualitative	Murphy Brown Northern Exposure Ladies Home Journal	Athletic and Hard-Factual	NFL Football National Enquirer Popular Mechanics
DRAMATIC FANTASISTS	Sensational and Indulgent	National Enquirer General Hospital Home Shopping Net.	Realistic and Positive	Time/Life Disney Channel CNN
FACTUAL MATERIALISTS	Quantitative and Educational	U.S. News House & Garden Fortune	Humorous and Family-Centered	Nickelodeon Roseanne Family Channel

(Source: Mediaweek.)

EXHIBIT 11.4

1. *High cost.* Magazines tend to be among the most expensive media on a CPM basis. It is not unusual for specialized magazines to have CPM levels of over $100 compared to $10–$20 for even relatively low rated TV shows. Of course, magazines point out that these high costs are tempered by very selective audiences. While this may be the case, advertisers find that many magazines are too expensive to use as anything but a niche supplement in their media schedule.

2. *Long closing dates.* Unlike the spontaneity of radio and newspapers, magazines require a long lead time between when advertising material must be submitted and when the ad will run. For example, a magazine advertisement may run 8 to 10 weeks after an advertiser submits it. This long lead time makes it difficult for advertisers to react to current marketing conditions either in scheduling space or developing competitive copy. The long closing dates are one reason why most magazine copy is very general.

Many magazines have one date for space reservations and a later date for when material must be submitted. Normally, the space contract is non-cancellable. For example, *Family Circle* requires that space be reserved two months prior to publication and material sent six weeks before publication. On the other hand, *Reader's Digest* requires that material be submitted with the order. For the January *Digest*, advertising material must reach the publisher by November 1. In the case of partial-run advertising, it must be submitted approximately two weeks earlier than full-run advertising.

Fast close

Some magazines offer short-notice ad deadlines such as a premium cost.

Many magazines have sought to overcome the competitive disadvantage of long closing dates by providing *fast-close advertising*. As the name implies, fast-close allows advertisers to submit ads much closer to publication date than standard closing dates allow. At one time, fast-close was very expensive, carrying a significant premium compared to other advertising. However, competitive pressure has forced many publications to offer fast-close at little or no extra expense.

The use of computer technology and satellite transmission has allowed magazines to offer major advertisers fast-close services that would have been impossible a few years ago. For example, *Business Week* permits a limited number of advertisers to place ads one week before publication instead of the normal five weeks. Likewise, *Sports Illustrated* can send material via satellite to its eight printing plants, allowing the magazine to take an ad on Monday for an issue distributed on Wednesday.[7]

Ad banking

Practice of some magazines of clustering ads at the front and back of their publications.

3. *Ad banking.* While not an inherent disadvantage of all magazines, ad banking is a practice that some advertisers do not like. Ad banking is the practice of publications such as *National Geographic* to cluster (or bank) all the advertisements toward the front and back of the publication. Advertisers fear that banking creates advertising clutter and makes it less likely that their advertising will gain high readership. Some advertisers exclude such publications from their media schedules.

In the remaining sections of this chapter we will examine some specific features and techniques involved in buying advertising in magazines.

FEATURES OF MAGAZINE ADVERTISING
Partial-Run Magazine Editions

When an advertiser buys the entire circulation of a magazine, it is known as buying the *full-run* edition. As we mentioned earlier, the demand for even more selective audience delineation, has required magazines to provide advertisers with special audience segments within their total circulation. These less-than-full-run buys are called *partial-runs*. Among the more common partial-run editions are:

1. *Demographic editions.* Major magazines routinely offer advertisers those ZIP codes with the highest average income. Advertisements can limit their ads to subscribers in those areas.

2. *Vocational editions.* A magazine may identify professionals or executives among its readers and allow advertisers to purchase a partial-run directed only at these readers.

3. *The oldest, and still most available, form of partial-run is the geographic edition.* Depending on the publication, a magazine may offer a combination of city, state, or regional editions. One advantage of geographic editions is that they can be used for both subscription and newsstand sales, whereas both demographic and vocational editions are confined to subscribers. It is extremely common for even relatively small circulation magazines to offer some form of partial-run advertising. In the case of the circulation gi-

---

[7]Junu Bryan Kim, "Plan for a Year, but Execute from Month to Month," *Advertising Age,* October 11, 1993, p. S-14.

ants such as *Time* or *Reader's Digest,* advertisers may have over 100 combinations of geographic or demographic editions to choose from. These options do not count the many international editions offered by a number of major publications.

Split-Run Editions

A special form of the partial-run edition is the split-run. Whereas most partial-run editions are intended to meet special marketing requirements of advertisers, split-run editions are used by both advertisers and publishers for testing purposes. The simplest form of split-run test is where an advertiser buys a regional edition (a full-run is usually not bought because of the expense) and runs different advertisements in every other issue.

Each advertisement is the same size and runs in the same position in the publication. The only difference is the item being tested. It may be a different headline, illustration, product benefit, even price. A coupon is normally included, and the advertiser can then determine which version of the advertisement drew the highest response. This split-run technique is called an A/B split. Half of the audience gets version A and half version B. As the competition for readers has grown, so has the use of split-run tests by magazines themselves. Magazines sometimes experiment with different covers for the same issue. For example, *Men's Health* used different logos on the same issue, *Worth* magazine used different logos and different pictures on the same issue, and in the most radical experiment, *Decorating Remodeling* magazine was retitled on some newsstands as *American Homestyle.* For a Christmas issue, *Good Housekeeping* not only tested different covers, but three different combinations of price and cover.[8]

Partial-run and split-run editions offer a number of benefits to advertisers (and in some cases publishers):

1. Geographic editions allow advertisers to offer products only in areas where they are sold. For example, snow tires can be promoted in one area, regular tires in another.

2. Partial-runs can localize advertising and support dealers or special offers from one region to another. As advertisers increasingly adopt local and regional strategies, the partial-run advantages will become even more apparent.

3. Split-run advertising allows advertisers to test various elements of a campaign in a realistic environment before embarking on a national rollout.

4. Regional editions allow national advertisers to develop closer ties with their retailers by listing regional outlets. This strategy also provides helpful information to consumers for products that lack widespread distribution.

According to the MPA, over 250 magazines currently offer some form of geographic/demographic editions. In addition, approximately 100 magazines have split-run editions available to advertisers. As technology improves and advertiser demands for these options increase, we will see more and more publications move to offer advertisers these services.

---

[8]"Samir Husni's Double Vision," *Folio,* April 15, 1993, p. 40.

Partial-run editions also have some disadvantages that make them less than ideal for all advertising situations:

1. CPM levels are usually much more expensive than full-run advertising in the same publication, and close dates can be as much as a month earlier than other advertising.

2. In the case of demographic editions, the lack of newsstand distribution for these advertisements can be a major disadvantage if single-copy sales are significant for the publication.

3. Some publications bank their partial-run advertising in a special section set aside for such material. There also may be special restrictions placed on partial-run advertising. For example, such advertising often must be full-page, and only four-color will be accepted by some publications.

Selective Binding

Selective binding
Binding different material directed to various reader segments in a single issue of a magazine.

A special form of partial-run editions is selective binding. The concept of selective binding is essentially the same as that of partial-run advertising. However, the term is usually used to refer to different editorial material or large advertising sections that are placed in less than the full-run of a publication. Using computer technology and sophisticated printing techniques, advertisers and publishers can develop advertising and editorial material specifically for one group or even individual readers.

Selective binding first gained popularity among major farm publications. Articles and advertisements were published only in editions delivered to farmers who raised certain types of crops or livestock. In recent years, selective binding has been offered to advertisers by consumer magazines on a limited basis.

Selective binding is most useful when there are significant subcategories of larger target markets. For example, the older affluent market of people over age 50, with household incomes of $50,000+ is a special target segment ignored by most mainstream media. Yet these "older affluents" are an important market for many advertisers, since they tend to have the highest levels of disposable income of any major demographic group.

In order to reach this group, Cadillac Motor Division worked with a number of business publications to place selective bound inserts in ZIP codes with affluent retiree demographics. Selective binding is an example of a technology that, in order for it to be successful, must be advertiser driven. That is, advertisers must be convinced that it offers enough value to justify the additional expense. Many advertising executives think that the practical applications of selective binding is more apparent for business and farm publications than for consumer magazines where there are a number of selective publications. Like interactive television, selective binding is a technology that is readily available, but where widespread demand by either advertisers or consumers is not yet apparent.

Obviously, the widespread use of selective binding has major implications for direct mail. If the technique becomes generally available, advertisers could combine the individual characteristics of direct mail with the credible environment of the magazine. Just as importantly, selective binding costs the advertiser about double what a normal magazine ad costs, but direct-mail CPMs generally run five times that of consumer magazines. Like most partial-run techniques, a major drawback of selective binding is that it can be used only for subscribers.

Since selective binding adopts some of the techniques of direct response, it also raises the same questions of readers' concerns with invasion of privacy. If subscribers are targeted by anything more than name and address, they may regard selective binding as inappropriate, with negative ramifications to both the advertiser and magazine. Still, the idea that each reader can have a custom-made magazine, including both editorial and advertising material of specific interest to that individual, is an intriguing concept.

City Magazines

Magazines directed to readers within a particular city are not a new idea. *Town Topics* was published in New York City in the late nineteenth century, but most observers credit *San Diego* magazine, first published in the 1940s, as the forerunner of the modern city magazine. Today, there are approximately 100 city magazines that vary in circulation from *New York* with 435,000 readers to *Columbia* (South Carolina) with 5,000 subscribers.

These publications have in common a homogeneous, upscale readership and an editorial mission directed to the local community. Among the most reported topics in these magazines are business, education, health, crime, and the environment.[9]

The financial health of city magazines tends to be cyclical. During the economic downturn of the early 1990s, many city magazines experienced significant decreases in advertising pages. A soft economy tends to be seen first in areas such as retailing and automobile sales, two prime categories of city magazine advertising.

Despite recent woes of city magazines, they remain an important medium to a number of advertisers and product categories. Advertisers find these publications ideal to reach an affluent, urban audience. In fact, readership studies show that city magazines appeal to a significantly higher education and income group than any but the most selective national publications.

City publications are in some ways a hybrid between small-circulation specialty publications and the partial-run editions of national magazines. They have an advantage over both in reaching upscale local audiences with editorial and advertising content specifically directed to their interests.

Psychographics
A description of a market based on factors such as attitudes, opinions, interests, perceptions, and lifestyles of consumers comprising that market. *See Demographic characteristics.*

Magazines and Psychographic Research

As mentioned earlier, magazines cannot effectively compete with other media on a cost basis, since advertisers can readily find less expensive media. However, magazines offer an environment that projects a style of living to both advertisers and readers. Advertisers are interested in the demographics of the audience, but they are also interested in how the audience thinks of themselves when they read a particular publication. The *Playboy* man and the *Cosmopolitan* woman are as much a matter of readers' perception as reality.

---

[9]Ernest Hynds, "Today's Diverse City Magazines Have Many Roles, Much Potential," Association for Education in Journalism and Mass Communication convention paper, 1993, p. 25.

In Chapter 7 we discussed the PRIZM system of categorizing people by their lifestyle characteristics. Increasingly, magazines use psychographic and lifestyle research to sell advertisers on the qualitative aspects of their audiences. Take a moment to review the various PRIZM categories in Exhibit 7.7 and try to match these audiences with the primary readers of some major magazines. Unlike many other media, magazines offer advertisers relatively high levels of audience involvement. Consequently, magazine advertisers are more apt to use understated creative approaches as contrasted to the hard-sell advertising found in so many other media.

MAGAZINE ELEMENTS
Sizes

The page size of a magazine is the type area, not the size of the actual page. For convenience, the size of most magazines is characterized as *standard size* (about 8 by 10 inches, like *Time*) or *small* (about $4\frac{3}{8}$ by $6\frac{1}{2}$ inches, like *Reader's Digest*). When you are ready to order printing plates, you must get the exact sizes from the publisher's latest rate card because sizes may change.

Position and Space-Buying Designations

Space in magazines is generally sold in terms of full pages and fractions thereof (half-pages or quarter-pages, three columns or one column; see Exhibit 11.5).

EXHIBIT
11.5

....

Various ways of using magazine space.

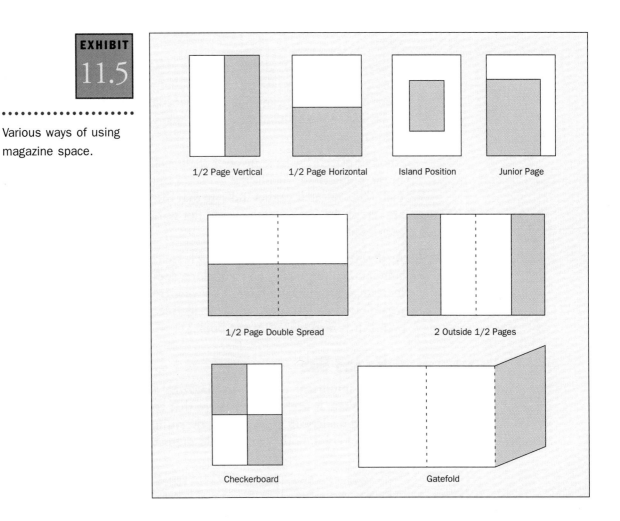

1/2 Page Vertical   1/2 Page Horizontal   Island Position   Junior Page

1/2 Page Double Spread   2 Outside 1/2 Pages

Checkerboard   Gatefold

The small ads in the shopping pages of many magazines are generally sold by the line. Most magazines are flexible about allowing one page or double-page ads to be broken up into separate units. Advertisers are constantly trying to gain an advantage over their competitors' messages. For many years, magazine advertisers have conducted research to determine the best position for an advertisement. Traditionally, advertisers have regarded right-hand pages at the front of the book, preferably near related editorial matter, as the ideal ad placement. "FFRHPOE" or "far forward, right-hand page opposite editorial" is routinely stamped on many insertion orders delivered to magazines.

Publishers, faced with growing placement requests, are in an impossible situation trying to accommodate too many advertisers in too few spaces. Publishers are particularly frustrated, since most research shows that when cost is factored in, position tends to add little to the efficiency of most advertising. The positions that demonstrate the highest readership levels are the covers. The front cover of a magazine is called the *first cover*. This is seldom, if ever, sold in American consumer magazines (although it is sold in business publications). The inside of the front cover is called the *second cover,* the inside of the back cover is the *third cover,* and the back cover the *fourth cover.* Normally, advertisers pay a premium for a cover position.

Studies show that the second cover achieves almost 30 percent more attention than an inside page; the third cover, 22 percent; and the fourth cover 22 percent.[10] Although cover positions almost always result in higher readership, they also cost significantly more than inside pages. Therefore, the cover CPM may be higher than inside pages even with their increased attention scores.

A second concern of advertisers is the effect on readership of left- or right-hand page placement. Research shows that right-hand versus left-hand placement plays no significant role in readership. In spite of the lack of evidence of benefits of right-hand placement, many advertisers persist in requesting (demanding) it.

Another placement issue involves the benefits of placing advertising forward in the publication. Again, the evidence suggests that the difference is minimal. Most research studies indicate that the advantages of forward placement are very slight and certainly would not warrant paying a premium to achieve such positioning.

As the MPA points out, and research seems overwhelmingly to support the contention, "In general, position alone does not affect readership of an ad or increase awareness for a brand. A strong creative execution will perform well regardless of its placement in the magazine. A 'bad ad' will not perform well even if it is in the front of the book.[11]"

Color and Size

Another important element in magazine advertising is color. Unlike positioning, there is irrefutable evidence that color significantly increases the interest and readership of magazine advertising. Depending on the specific size and use of color, both elements add dramatically to the value of advertising.

---

[10]"The Magazine Handbook, 1992–1993," Magazine Publishers of America, p. 24.
[11]"The Magazine Handbook, 1992–1993," A publication of the Magazine Publishers of America, p. 23.

Magazine advertising benefits from the use of both color and large size.

(Courtesy: CME KHBB Advertising and Andersen Windows.)

The Andersen Windows advertisement (Exhibit 11.6) benefits from both size and color in demonstrating the detailed features of the product. Of course, as in the case of cover advertising, adding color and/or increasing size also adds significantly to the cost of advertising. However, it appears that in many cases the increase in cost is more than offset by additional readership.

As advertising space increases, the size of the audience does not grow proportionately (nor does the cost). For example, Exhibit 11.7 demonstrates that compared to fractional-page ads, a one-page advertisement will increase the number of readers by 67 percent (from 24 to 40 percent). However, a two-page spread increases readership by only 38 percent (from 40 to 55 percent). The reason, of course, is that a large number of prospects will see the full-

As the size of the advertisement increases, the readership score also increases.

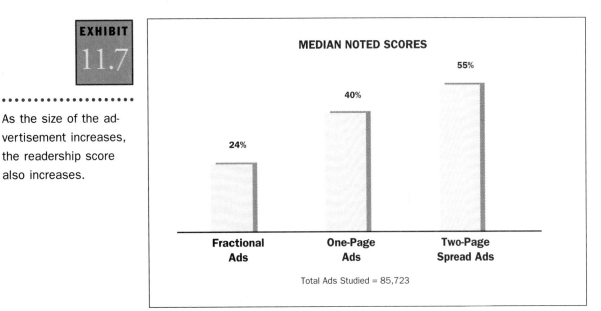

(Courtesy: Cahners Publishing Company.)

Magazines allow advertisers the luxury of long copy.

EXACTLY HOW SMOOTH

IS THE RIDE IN A STARSHIP?

THIS AD WAS WRITTEN IN ONE.

(Courtesy: Beechcraft and Team One Advertising.)

page advertisement. There are not enough interested readers left to continue to increase readership at the same rate.

Although audience exposures are not proportionate to increases in magazine ad size, larger space allows more creative flexibility. Advertising objectives that require long copy can be much more effectively presented in a larger space. For example, the advertisement for the Beechcraft Starship (see Exhibit 11.8) has extremely long copy relative to most magazine advertisements. However, the two-page spread gives it an openness that invites prospects to read the copy.

Color is another element with a proven capability to increase readership. However, most studies indicate that adding two-color is of limited value, and added readership will not offset increased costs. In most circumstances, if you are contemplating using color, you should probably invest in four-color advertising. As we see in Exhibit 11.9, two-color advertising adds little to readership, while four-color increases it almost 40 percent.

It is also important to remember that averages do not hold for any particular circumstance. For example, MPA research shows that two-page spreads add virtually nothing to the readership of floor covering, wine, or tanning lotion advertising. On the other hand, import cars, travelers checks, and major appliances increased readership by as much as 50 percent with two-page spreads. These findings point out again that the specific objectives and creative approach must be considered in designing magazine advertising.

Bleed Pages

Bleed

Printed matter that runs over the edges of an outdoor board or of a page, leaving no margin.

Magazine advertising is able to use a number of formats and designs unavailable or impractical in other media. A common technique is bleed advertising, in which the ad runs all the way to the edge of the page. Bleed ads

EXHIBIT

11.9

....

4-color ads receive 39%
higher readership
scores than black and
white ads.

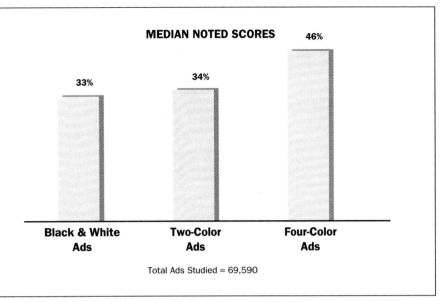

MEDIAN NOTED SCORES

33%   34%   46%

Black & White   Two-Color   Four-Color
Ads   Ads   Ads

Total Ads Studied = 69,590

(Courtesy: Cahners Publishing Company.)

are used to gain attention and use all the space available. Without a border, the advertisement does not have the appearance of being confined to a particular space. Typically, bleed advertising will be seen by 10 to 15 percent more readers than nonbleed advertising.

In the competitive marketplace for magazine advertising, a number of publications make no charge for bleed advertising. Instead, they offer it free as a value-added inducement for advertisers. When a charge is made for bleed advertisements, it is typically 15 percent of the normal four-color rate. Large advertisers will often negotiate with publishers over bleed rates; the cost of bleed may be reduced as advertising commitments to the publication increases. For example, when Buick began final media planning for its 1994 models, it put publishers on notice that extra charges for bleed advertising would not be viewed favorably and that publishers who eliminated bleed charges could expect greater advertising allocations for their magazines.[12]

Inserts and Multiple-Page Units

Multiple-page advertising covers a broad spectrum of insertions. The most common form of multipage advertising are facing, two-page spreads. The advertising for All Star Sports (see Exhibit 11.10) is an example of such an advertisement. A spread increases impact to the message and eliminates any competition for the consumer's attention. Some spreads come off the front cover and are normally either two or three pages. These advertisements are known as *gatefolds.*

More elaborate forms of multipage advertisements consist of bound-in booklets. Advertisers often use these booklets as both multipage advertisements as well as point-of-purchase collateral material for dealers. Traditionally, the ma-

---

[12]Richard Brunelli, "GM's Buick Is Blasting the Bleed Charge in Negotiations with Publishers for 1994," *Mediaweek,* September 6, 1993, p. 3.

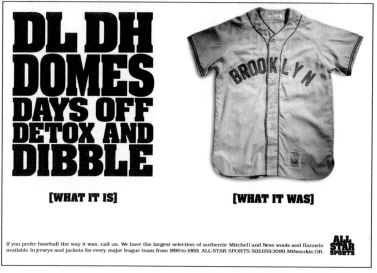

(Courtesy: Birdsall Voss and Kloppenburg.)

jor users of multiple-page units have been automobile manufacturers, computer companies, and suppliers of financial services. A less frequently used form of multiple-page advertising is to run ads in separate parts of the same issue. This approach, when it is used, is most often found in business publications.

Cost is a major consideration when planning inserts. The expense of an insert will reduce the number of media vehicles that can be included in a media schedule. Since an advertiser is putting a disproportionate share of advertising into one or a few vehicles, the likely result is a reduction in reach and frequency compared to a more traditional media plan.

Cost is a primary consideration in using multiple-page advertisements, but especially in considering inserts. There is no question that inserts gain readership, but their use cannot be justified solely on a cost basis, in the absence of a specific marketing objective. The cost of an insert will vary with the publication, but it is common for inserts to cost double the regular four-color rate. In addition, the advertiser is also responsible for the cost of design, printing, and paper. In some cases, a magazine may pass on extra postage costs if the insert is very large or printed on heavy paper. As we have discussed earlier, it is almost impossible for the increase in audience awareness to match the added cost of advertising. Therefore, the CPM of an insert is also significantly higher than for the magazine as a whole.

Finally, one of the problems with the growing use of multiple-page advertising is that it has lost much of its novelty to consumers. When a reader can turn to practically any consumer magazine and find numerous examples of such advertising, the ads come to be taken for granted, even by serious prospects. It is important to consider the qualitative environment of the publication before budgeting a multiple-page advertisement. It is equally important to work closely with the creative team to make sure that such expensive space is going to be fully utilized with a meaningful message. The most effective multiple-page units are for advertisers with an interesting product, a new story to tell, and a relatively select group of prospects.

HOW SPACE IS SOLD
Advertising Rates, Negotiation, and Merchandising

Buying full-run magazine advertising was at one time the easiest function for the media planner. Clients usually bought full-page advertisements, circulations were audited, discounts for frequent usage were obtainable from straightforward rate cards, and rates were consistent for every advertiser that qualified for available discounts. In addition, most advertisers would buy only a few, high-circulation publications.

However, magazine advertising began to experience a downturn in advertising revenues during the 1980s. The number of new titles coming on the market made the situation even worse as more magazines competed for shrinking advertising dollars. As the advertising market diminished, magazines began to negotiate with individual advertisers for special rates. This practice of one-to-one negotiation is called *going-off-the-card*. Prior to the 1980s, it was regarded as a last-ditch effort for failing magazines to survive. It also was generally viewed as an unethical practice, since one advertiser might pay more than another using the same space.

It is generally conceded that the women's service magazines were the first to begin general advertising negotiation, but it soon spread to a number of other categories. As we entered the 1990s, negotiation had become a common practice among numerous magazines. Many advertisers regarded the rate card as simply a point to start negotiation, and magazines were caught in another profit squeeze as they negotiated with more and more advertisers for lower and lower advertising rates.

Today, many publishers are desperately trying to reverse the widespread discounting. However, once started, going-off-the-card is a difficult cycle to break. Agencies are trying to get the lowest possible rates for their clients, and they have no incentive to cooperate with publishers to stop rate negotiation. In this environment, publishers find it very difficult to convince advertisers that they should not negotiate rates.

Basically, publishers have adopted a two-pronged approach to the problem. First, they are raising their rates to a level that accepts negotiation as a fact of life. In other words, instead of raising rates 4 percent, a magazine will raise rates 8 percent with the hope that they can negotiate for the 4. This does nothing to change the industry mindset that magazines are really worth less than they are asking. In addition, it assumes that experienced media planners don't know what is happening and won't negotiate away the entire 8 percent increase.

A more workable and practical solution adopted by magazines involves a second strategy of looking beyond only advertising rates and offering advertisers an array of services in exchange for their advertising placement.[13]

While magazine rate negotiation will never go away completely, many publishers have begun to offer advertisers other types of incentives rather than reducing basic advertising rates. These incentives are collectively known as *value-added*, or *merchandising, programs*. That is, publishers offer extra value to the advertiser in exchange for advertising in their publications.

---

[13]Lorne Manly, "Rate Card Recovery," *Folio*, April 15, 1993, p. 39.

These value-added programs can take many forms, but the key element is that they must differentiate a magazine from its competing publications. Among the more common forms of merchandising are the following:

- **_Premium positions, including covers, and bleed ads at no extra cost._** Many magazine publishers resist this form of merchandising, arguing that it is nothing more than another form of rate cutting.

- **_Bonus pages through credits and remnant space._** Again, unless this strategy involves a discount offered to all advertisers, then it simply reduces revenues with no long-term value-added bonus.

- **_Special editions or new sections to enhance the publication._** For example, *Child* magazine instituted 15 editions with special editorial material appropriate to the ages of the child in the subscriber family. Likewise, *U.S. News & World Report* expanded its personal finance reporting to offer a value-added relative to other news magazines.

- **_Special research projects offering more information about readers of a publication._** The publisher of *Crafts 'N Things* and other craft publications conducted research concerning reader involvement and advertising believability and made these data available to advertisers free of charge.

- **_Merchandising services to clients of advertisers._** For example, advertisers in *Crain's Chicago Business* can request free copies of the publication sent to nonsubscribing clients. The magazine then follows up to see if it can gain these clients as subscribers.

These are only a few of the value-added programs that are currently used. The key to successful merchandising programs is that they truly differentiate a publication from its competitors and provide a perceived value to advertisers. At the same time, magazines must realize merchandising cannot overcome the shortcomings of a weak advertising vehicle. As one advertising executive points out, "[U]sually the publications with the best editorial, the most loyal readership and the strongest circulation don't provide as much [merchandising services] as the weaker one. A No. 3 book cannot be turned into a category leader just because it gives away free pages provides expensive promotions."[14]

Despite the advantages of value-added programs, these programs are not inexpensive. In some respects publishers may have substituted one form of profit reduction for another. Whether a publisher decreases profits by cutting ad rates or by increasing merchandising expenditures, the end result may be the same. Exhibit 11.11 shows some of the common services offered by consumer magazines. It is clear that advertisers have come to expect at least some of the services as part of doing business with magazines.

Another problem with value-added programs is how to evaluate them as part of a media schedule. While media planners may be able to place a cost value on a particular merchandising program, they will unlikely be able to determine how this program improves the utility of the advertising for their clients or differentiates one publication from another.

[14]Gene Willhoft, "Is 'Added Value' Valuable?" *Advertising Age*, March 1, 1993, p. 18.

**EXHIBIT
11.11**

Ad-sales promotion is the service most common to our respondents, though it is far less likely to be offered by consumer magazines (74 percent offer it), than trade magazines, where more than 90 percent perform this function.

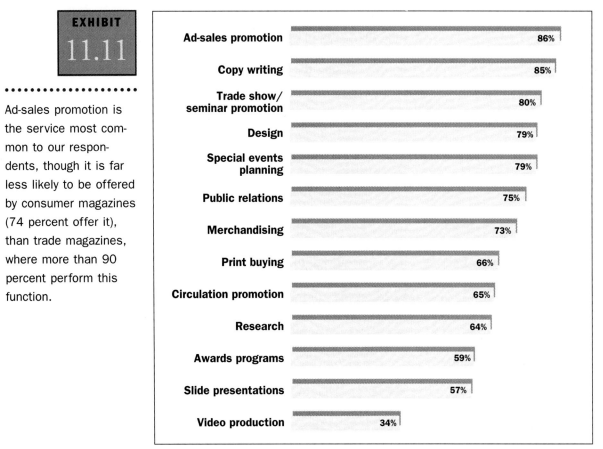

Ad-sales promotion	86%
Copy writing	85%
Trade show/ seminar promotion	80%
Design	79%
Special events planning	79%
Public relations	75%
Merchandising	73%
Print buying	66%
Circulation promotion	65%
Research	64%
Awards programs	59%
Slide presentations	57%
Video production	34%

(Source: FOLIO: *Cowles Business Media.)*

In the remaining pages of this section we will outline the basics of buying magazine space. However, remember that these steps represent only the starting point for a magazine buy. The experienced media buyer will always probe the market to come up with additional efficiencies for a client.

Magazine Rate Structure

In the examples that follow, we will assume the advertiser is making a full-run magazine buy. That is, the entire circulation of the publication is being purchased. An advertiser buying a partial-run edition will consider a number of other options. A typical rate card for a weekly publication might look like this:

		Living World Bulletin Color Rates (4-color)		
Space	1 ti	6 ti	12 ti	26 ti
1 page	32,800	29,750	28,150	26,675
2/3 page	24,210	22,950	21,740	20,630
1/2 page	22,880	18,430	20,615	19,510
1/4 page	11,800	11,050	10,550	9,860

An advertiser buying this publication will pay $32,800 for a one-time, four-color, full-page insert. The advertiser who buys at least 26 inserts in the publication will pay only $26,675 per ad for the same space.

Before placing a magazine on its advertising schedule, the advertiser will compute the cost efficiency of that publication against others being considered. Let's assume that *Living World Bulletin (LWB)* has an average circulation of 660,132. Using the CPM formula discussed earlier, we can calculate the efficiency of the publication as follows:

$$\text{CPM} = \frac{\text{cost/page}}{\text{circulation (000)}} = \frac{\$32,800}{660} = \$49.69$$

Discounts

Frequency and Volume Discounts. The one-time, full-page rate of a publication is referred to as its *basic,* or *open, rate.* In the case of *LWB,* its open rate is $32,800. All discounts are computed from that rate. Most publications present their discounts on a per-page basis in which rates vary according to frequency of insertion during a 12-month period, as we have done here. However, some publications use either *frequency* or *volume discounts* based on the number of pages run. For instance:

Frequency, Pages	Discount, %
13 or more	7
26 or more	12
39 or more	16
52 or more	20

In a similar fashion, the volume discount gives a larger percentage discount based on the total dollar volume spent for advertising during a year. The volume discount is convenient for advertisers that are combining a number of insertions of different space units or that are using a number of partial-run insertions. A volume discount might be offered as follows:

Volume, $	Discount, %
83,000 or more	8
125,000 or more	11
180,000 or more	17
260,000 or more	20

Other Discounts. Publishers are always alert to giving special rates to large advertisers and to other advertisers they are eager to attract. Among different magazines, we find various special discounts: mail-order discount, travel discount, trade-book discount. Blanketing all of these is a corporate, or total-dollar, discount. This overall discount (above all the others earned) is based on the total dollars spent by all of the corporation's divisions in a year.

There is obviously no such thing as a standard trade discount or standard use of terms. It pays to ask a lot of questions when buying space.

Remnant Space. A number of publishers, especially those with geographic or demographic editions, find themselves with extra space in some editions when they are ready to go to press. Rather than run an empty space, the publisher will often offer this remnant space at a big discount. For direct-response

---

Frequency discounts

Discounts based on total time or space bought, usually within a year. Also called *bulk discounts.*

Remnant space

Unsold advertising space in geographic or demographic editions. It is offered to advertisers at a significant discount.

---

advertisers, whose ads are not part of a continuing campaign but stand on their own, remnant space is an especially good buy. Of course, material for the ad must be ready for instant insertion.

The Magazine Short Rate

As we have seen, most magazine discounts are based on the amount of space bought within a year. However, the publisher normally requires that payment be made within 30 days of billing. Therefore, an advertiser and a publisher sign a space contract at the beginning of the year and agree to make adjustments at the end of the year if the space usage estimates are incorrect. If the advertiser uses less space than estimated, the publisher adjusts using a higher-than-contracted rate. If more space is used, the publisher adjusts using a lower rate.

Let's look at a typical short rate, using the rate card for *Living World Bulletin.*

> Acme Widgets contracted with *LWB* to run eight pages of advertising during the coming year. At the end of the year, Acme had only run five pages. Therefore, it was short the rate for which it had contracted and an adjustment has to be made, as follows:

$$\text{Ran 5 times. Paid the 6-time rate of } \$29,750 \text{ per page} = (5 \times 29,750)$$
$$\$148,750$$

$$\text{Earned only the 1-time rate of } \$32,800 \text{ per page} = (5 \times 32,800)$$
$$\$164,000$$

$$\text{Short rate due } (\$164,000 - 148,750) = \$15,250$$

Some publishers charge the top (basic) rate throughout the year but state in the contract, "Rate credit when earned." If the advertiser earns a better rate, the publisher gives a refund. If the publisher sees that an advertiser is not running sufficient pages during the year to earn the low rate on which the contract was based, the publisher sends a bill at the short rate for space already used and bills further ads at the higher rate earned. Failure to keep short rates in mind when you are reducing your original schedule can lead to unwelcome surprises.

Placing the Order

Placing magazine advertising is a two-step process. The first step is the *space contract,* which tells the magazine the total number of pages that an advertiser will use during the coming year. It enables the publisher and advertiser to establish a rate level for billing and is considered a binding contract. However, the space contract does not deal with the specific issues in which the advertising will run, but it allows both parties to agree on the cost of future advertising.

The second step is the *space order* (also called an insertion order). The space order commits the advertiser to a particular issue and is usually accompanied by production materials for the ad. Exhibit 11.12 shows an example of the 4A publication order blank. Note that the form can include both the space contract and insertion order, depending on which box is checked. In fact, an advertiser can also use the form to cancel or change ad requirements, if such changes are permitted by the magazine.

EXHIBIT
11.12

An example of a space contract and insertion order.

Order Blank For Publications   (MEMBER OF A.A.A.A.)

NAME OF AGENCY
Address

☐ If checked here this is a SPACE CONTRACT   ORDER NO. _____
                                                    Date _____
☐ If checked here this is a SPACE ORDER (INSERTION ORDER)   Advertiser _____
                                                    Product _____

☐ If checked here this is CANCELLATION   Contract Year _____
   or change of: _____   Discount Level _____

To the publisher of: Edition: (specify) National _____
                                                                Regional _____

                                                    *Subject to conditions stated above and on back hereof

ISSUE DATE   SPACE   COLOR/BLEED   FREQUENCY   RATE

Position   Less agency commission   on gross
                                                              Cash discount   on net
Additional Instructions:
                                                    Mail all invoices to:
Copy instructions & material ☐ to follow   ☐ herewith

Address all other correspondence to:

                                                    (Authorized Signature)

PLEASE FILL IN AND RETURN THIS ACKNOWLEDGMENT TO AGENCY
(NAME AND ADDRESS OF AGENCY)   ORDER NO. _____

This acknowledges that your order dated _____ covering advertising for _____
was received on (date) _____ and instructions thereon thoroughly understood.

American Association of Advertising Agencies, Inc.   PUBLICATION _____
            Copyright 1973   PER _____

(Courtesy: American Association of Advertising Agencies.)

Magazine Dates

There are three sets of dates to be aware of in planning and buying magazine space:

1. *Cover date:* the date appearing on the cover

2. *On-sale date:* the date on which the magazine is issued (the January issue of a magazine may come out on December 5, which is important to know if you are planning a Christmas ad)

3. *Closing date:* the date when the print or plates needed to print the ad must be in the publisher's hands in order to make a particular issue

Dates are figured from the cover date and are expressed in terms of "days or weeks preceding," as in the following example:

New Yorker

- Published weekly, dated Monday
- Issued Wednesday preceding
- Closes 25th of 3rd month preceding

Magazine Networks

As magazines have become more specialized and selective in their ability to reach audience segments, advertisers increasingly need to buy more titles to achieve reach and frequency goals. Another consequence of smaller circulations among magazines is that CPM levels have increased. Many large national advertisers have complained about both the difficulty of buying numerous magazines and the higher CPMs. In order to accommodate these advertisers, a number of publishers have established magazine networks. The magazine network is similar in intent to a broadcast network; that is, several publications can be bought simultaneously with one insertion order, one bill, and, often, significant savings compared to buying the same magazines individually.

Currently, there are more than 100 magazine networks representing dozens of different titles. The network concept allows several magazines to compete for advertisers by offering lower CPMs and delivering a larger audience than any single publication. Networks must be carefully tailored to reach a particular audience segment with little waste circulation. Otherwise, the network provides advertisers with nothing more than a general-circulation magazine with all the pitfalls we previously discussed.

While there are a number of magazine networks, they generally fall into two categories:

1. *Single-publisher networks.* Here a network is offered by a single publisher that owns several magazines of interest to a particular audience segment such as sports enthusiasts. Publisher networks are the most common and make up the majority of such buys. For example, the Peterson Publishing Company offers the Peterson Magazine Network. Among the titles in the network are *Hot Rod, Motor Trend, Sport,* and 11 others. In order to participate in the network, advertisers must buy six pages in at least three titles during the year.

2. *Independent networks.* The second type of magazine network is made up of different publishers that edit magazines with similar audience appeals. These networks are usually offered by a rep firm that contracts individually with each publisher and then sells advertising in the group. The concept is similar to the space wholesaling that George Rowell began in the 1850s and that we discussed in Chapter 5. Media Networks, the largest independent network firm, offers a number of networks. For example, the Media Network All-Star Network consists of *Golf, Newsweek, Time,* and five other publications with upscale male readership. To qualify, an advertiser must place 12 insertions annually in any combination of the eight publications.

Magazine networks are not confined to major national publishers. A number of regional and city publications have joined together to offer network buys. For example, the Florida Advertising Network consists of city magazines from Jacksonville, Orlando, the Miami area, and Tampa Bay. The magazine network concept is ideal for publications to offer advertisers a larger audience and a lower cost than any one magazine could provide and, at the same time, maintain a targeted audience.

MAGAZINE CIRCULATION

As with any medium, accurate readership measurement of a magazine is extremely important to advertisers. Media planners don't buy magazines, TV spots, or outdoor signs; they buy people. More specifically, they buy certain groups of people who are presently or prospectively customers for their products. Publishers have two distinct methods of determining their audiences.

Paid Circulation and the Rate Base

The first, most objective method of audience measurement, is paid circulation. Most major consumer magazines have their circulation audited by an outside company. As is done in other media, magazine rates are based on the circulation that a publisher promises to deliver to advertisers, referred to as the *guaranteed circulation*. Since the guaranteed circulation is the number of readers advertisers purchase, it is also known as the *rate base*. A magazine does not necessarily offer a rate base to advertisers. In fact, 40 percent of audited publications do not make a specific guaranteed circulation claim.[15] These publishers provide advertisers with accurate circulation for past issues, but they don't take any risk for circulation shortfalls in the future. In the volatile world of magazine advertising, many smaller magazines do not want to deal with the financial problems involved with a short-term drop in audience. A few large-circulation publications do not offer a guaranteed circulation, but this is unusual.

It is important that we not confuse an unaudited publication with one that does not offer a rate base. A rate base is an additional inducement to assure advertisers that they will obtain a certain level of audience if they buy space in a publication or be compensated for a failure to meet the magazine's guarantee. An audit, on the other hand, guarantees that over some period of time (usually a year or six months) the publication has achieved some circulation level. An audit makes no promises for future circulation.

Readership

In magazine terminology "readership" usually combines paid circulation (subscribers and newsstand purchasers) with pass-along readers. In other words, a magazine with an audited circulation of 1 million might have 1.5 million readers. Readership is usually provided by syndicated services and includes both total audience and demographic and lifestyle categories.

Many advertisers and even magazine publishers are concerned about the use of readership as a substitute for paid circulation. Historically, the use of readership is rooted in the magazine's industry competition with television. Until the 1950s, paid circulation was the only magazine readership that counted. Then "along came TV and TV audience 'measurements.' How could magazines, with their modest circulations, hope to compete with television's multi-million-viewer audiences? Everyone knew, of course, that while only one person might order and pay for a magazine, other people read it. There was a

---

[15]"Capell's Circulation Report," May 3, 1993, p. 1.

pass-along factor. The next step seemed natural enough: Just measure the pass-along readership, then magazine numbers might look better in competition with TV numbers."[16]

It would seem that total readership, accurately measured, would be a reasonable approach to measuring magazine audiences. The problem arises from studies that indicate that paid subscribers and pass-along readers of consumer magazines are different in very fundamental ways. "Subscribers and [total] readers are like the proverbial apples and oranges: They can't be compared. Proof of this incomparability comes from taking a look at the differences between subscribers and readers for the same magazine. Almost always, subscribers are more affluent. And this makes sense: Those who paid for the magazine have more money than those who are content to read a pass-along copy."[17]

Between those advertisers who see no value in readership and those who view it as equal to paid circulation, there is probably a middle ground. As in most marketing and advertising questions, the real answer is determined by the specific objectives of the publication and its readers. However, regardless of the value that one places on readership, most acknowledge that it is different from paid circulation. Exhibit 11.13 shows the views of advertisers and agencies toward circulation and total readership measures.

MEASURING MAGAZINE AUDIENCES

We now turn to the issue of how publishers verify the circulation and readership of their magazines. Advertisers will normally not purchase a magazine unless its publisher can provide independent verification of the magazine's readership. In magazine terminology, the term *readership* has two distinct meanings. One refers to the time spent with a publication (see Exhibit 11.14). The other, and the one we will discuss here, includes all readers of a magazine as contrasted to only those who buy a publication.

The Audit Bureau of Circulations

The Audit Bureau of Circulations (ABC) is the largest of several auditing organizations that verify magazine circulation. The ABC provides two basic services: the Publisher's Statement, which report six-month periods ending June 30 and December 31; and the ABC Audit, which annually audits the data provided in the Publisher's Statements. The ABC reports total circulation, as well as circulation figures by state, by county size, and per issue during each six-month period. The ABC reports also state the manner in which circulation was obtained—for example, by subscription, newsstand sales—and any discounts or premiums provided to subscribers. Exhibit 11.15 is a sample of the ABC Publisher's Statement.

The ABC reports are very matter-of-fact documents that deal only with primary readers. They do not offer information about product usage, demographic characteristics of readers, or pass-along readership. These issues are left to another group of companies known as syndicated readership services.

[16]James A. Autry, "Syndicated Research Is No Match for Rate Base," *Folio*, May 1, 1993, p. 60.
[17]Bruce Sheiman, "Management," *Folio*, May 18, 1993, p. 32.

EXHIBIT
11.13

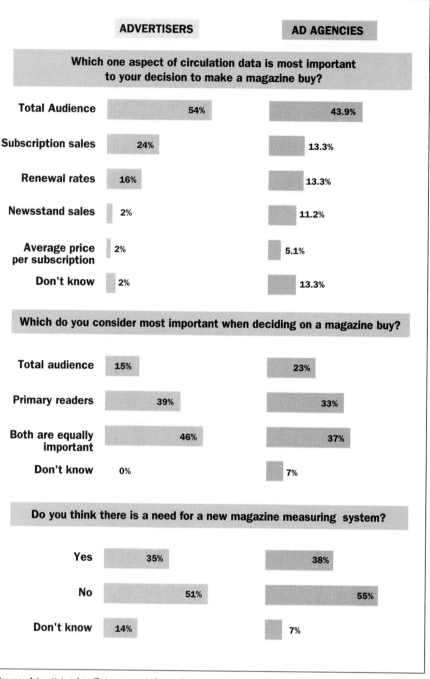

(Source: Advertising Age/Beta research Group From: Lisa & Fred, "Dissatisfied with audience measurement, some execs seek change," Advertising Age, October 11, 1993, p. 5–22.)

Syndicated Magazine Readership Research

**Simmons Market
Research Bureau, Inc.
(SMRB)**

Firm that provides audience data for several media. Best known for magazine research.

Advertisers are, of course, interested in the primary readers of magazines. But they are also interested in who these readers are and what they buy, as well as pass-along readers who are given the publications. Currently, there are two principal sources of syndicated magazine readership research: Simmons Market Research Bureau, Inc. (SMRB), and Mediamark Research, Inc. (MRI).

Both services use similar methodology. They first select a sample of approximately 20,000 household and elicit media usage, demographic information, and product purchase information. Respondents are then asked how recently

EXHIBIT
11.14

Readership of special-
ized business maga-
zines averages 1 hour
and 27 minutes per
week.

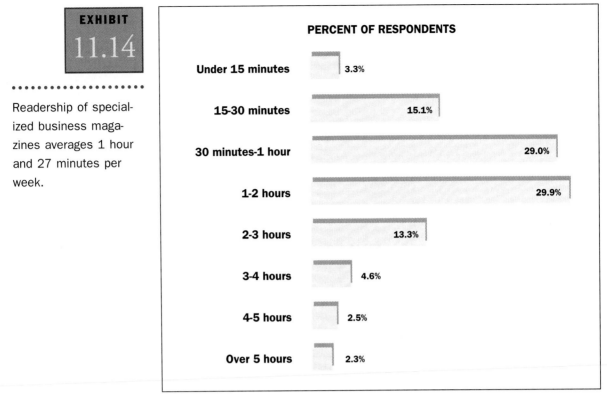

PERCENT OF RESPONDENTS

Under 15 minutes	3.3%
15-30 minutes	15.1%
30 minutes-1 hour	29.0%
1-2 hours	29.9%
2-3 hours	13.3%
3-4 hours	4.6%
4-5 hours	2.5%
Over 5 hours	2.3%

(Courtesy: Cahners Publishing Company.)

they read a particular publication. This technique is called the *recent reading method*.

The recent reading method provides only estimates of actual readership. However, it is rare for a magazine schedule to fail to mention either SMRB or MRI as part of a media presentation.

CONSUMER MAGAZINES—SUMMING UP

Despite the fact that magazines face a number of challenges in the coming years, they are well positioned as an important marketing tool. Magazines can play a role as either the primary medium for a national advertiser or as a niche medium to reach an "imperative" segment. Magazines will continue to be a major source of news, information, and entertainment for millions of prime prospects. In this era of target marketing, magazines fulfill a vital function in reaching narrowly defined audiences in an environment that is conducive to selling products and ideas.

Increasingly, advertisers realize that qualitative factors are as important as cost efficiencies in judging the value of an advertising medium. There is no medium that provides the combination of selective audiences, targeted advertising, and editorial involvement to the degree provided by consumer magazines. Another primary benefit of consumer magazines is their ability to appeal to upscale audiences. Magazines rank as the favorite medium among most high-income, highly educated audience segments. This appeal to upscale prospects make the higher cost of magazines a profitable investment in the marketing communication programs of most companies.

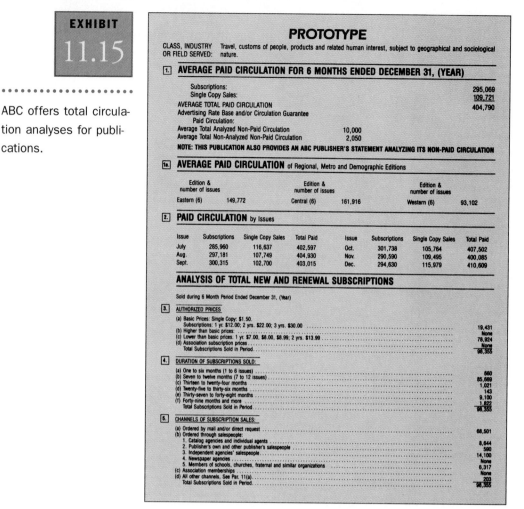

EXHIBIT 11.15

ABC offers total circulation analyses for publications.

(Courtesy: Audit Bureau of Circulations.)

THE BUSINESS PRESS AND BUSINESS-TO-BUSINESS ADVERTISING

Business-to-business advertising

Advertising that promotes goods through trade and industrial journals that are used in the manufacturing, distributing, or marketing of goods to the public.

As a marketing communications tool, the only major similarity between the business press and consumer magazines is their format. In terms of diversity, specialization of content, industry economics, and their competitive environment, the differences between business and consumer magazines are significant. Prospects for business advertisers are fewer and more concentrated, they tend to be experts concerning the products they purchase, and audience selectivity is much more important than CPMs or reach figures so important in consumer media.

The level of communication with a business audience differs significantly from consumer media. Exhibit 11.16 shows the involvement of business publication readers with the medium. The business press is a medium of reference and commerce, whereas consumer magazines are vehicles of entertainment, news, and leisure reading. Consumer magazines are, relative to mass media, an extremely targeted communication tool. However, there are approximately 850 consumer magazines compared to approximately 4,500 business publications. Health care alone accounts for over 750 titles.

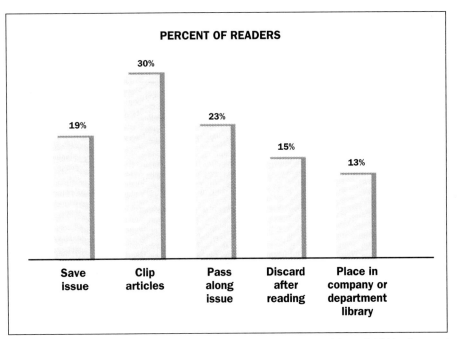

PERCENT OF READERS

19%	30%	23%	15%	13%
Save issue	Clip articles	Pass along issue	Discard after reading	Place in company or department library

(Courtesy: Cahners Publishing Company.)

Business publications are second only to radio in terms of different media vehicles. Even more than other advertising media, they are at the mercy of the industries they serve. In the early 1990s, downturns in banking, finance, building and construction, and electronics led to sharp decreases in spending in publications related to these industries. In the recession year of 1991, overall expenditures for business publications was down. However, a rebounding economy during the mid-1990s provided slow improvement for most major business magazines.

However, as we will see in this chapter, business publications face not only a weak economic recovery, but greater competition from other media and promotional vehicles for business-to-business advertising dollars. During the past decade, the share of business-to-business advertising devoted to trade publications has declined. Business-to-business advertisers have begun to allocate their dollars to a number of promotional techniques in addition to advertising. The diversity of marketing communications witnessed in consumer marketing is even more apparent in the business-to-business sector. Because the cost of individual media is much lower than consumer vehicles, business-to-business advertisers are more willing to break from traditional media patterns to reach target prospects more effectively.

In this section we will examine the business-to-business sector and view the differences and similarities with consumer advertising. We will begin by discussing some major techniques and goals of business-to-business advertisers.

Characteristics of the Business Press

Audiences. The relationship between readers and their business publications is much different from that of typical consumer magazines. Remember, the readers of a trade publication are reading as part of their business. The utility of the magazine will be determined by how well it improves their ability to do their jobs, market their products, or improve their profits. Consequently, business magazines must develop a depth of understanding of their readers that is typically not required in the consumer press.

Business publications need to develop a problem-solving partnership with their readers. For successful business publications and the advertisers using them, this relationship involves three steps:

1. *Identify the special problems and opportunities faced by readers and their industry.* For example, what are the primary competitors, what are the short- and long-term trends in the industry, and what social, legal, or technical elements are likely to play a role in the success or failure of companies within the industry?

2. *Identify specific solutions to the primary problems facing readers of the publication.* Both editorial and advertising in business publications present detailed material and technical, industry-oriented information to their readers. In Exhibit 11.17, Mitsui O.S.K. Lines outlines the specific benefits that its services can provide to transpacific shippers.

3. *Business magazines must create a long-term profitable relationship by treating their audiences as clients rather than just readers.* Remember that the success of the industry covered by a particular business magazine is usually reflected in the success of the publication.

EXHIBIT
11.17

••••••••••••••••••••

Business advertising must make product benefits specific.

Sometimes three ships can open a whole new world.

ALLIGATOR COLUMBUS

ALLIGATOR DISCOVERY

ALLIGATOR AMERICA

An all-water route to the East. It had been a dream for so long it was considered impossible. But one man saw the *impossible* as *possible,* and dared to risk everything on it.

In the process, he discovered much more than a new trade route—he discovered a new world.

Five hundred years later, Mitsui O.S.K. Lines is proud to salute Christopher Columbus as a man of vision and a kindred spirit. Some of that same spirit lives on in MOL's three newest additions to our trans-Pacific fleet, the Alligators *Columbus, Discovery,* and *America.*

These new vessels will expand Mitsui's already impressive service profile by providing a total transportation package that will meet the needs of even the most critical trans-Pacific shipments. We're also adding three larger Alligator vessels to our Pacific Northwest Service, giving shippers more choices than ever before.

As Columbus realized, intrepid action *can* make a difference. If you believe something is possible, sometimes the best way to prove it is simply to go out and do it. Columbus staked his reputation on that. So do we.

In saluting the achievement of Columbus, we suggest that you call your nearest MOL representative for more information about our trans-Pacific services. You may just discover a whole new world of shipping of your own.

 **MOL**

(Courtesy: Misui OSK Lines and Longwater Advertising Inc.)

EXHIBIT

11.18

What Percentage of Business Marketing Budgets is Spent on Specialized Business Magazine Advertising?

	% of Business Marketing Budgets			
Allocated for:	1991	1989	1988	1987
Specialized Business Magazine Advertising	23%	23%	22%	21%
Trade Shows	18%	18%	16%	16%
Promotion/Market Support	9%	10%	12%	12%
Dealer/Distributor Materials	11%	9%	9%	9%
Telemarketing/Telecommunications	7%	6%	9%	9%
Direct Mail	12%	12%	9%	8%
General Magazine Advertising	5%	6%	7%	8%
Publicity/Public Relations	5%	7%	7%	7%
Market Research	4%	4%	5%	5%
Directories	5%	5%	3%	4%
Other	1%	2%	1%	1%

For additional copies, write CARR Reports, Cahners Publishing Co., 275 Washington St. Newton, MA 02158 (617-964-3030, ext. 2120) or contact your sales representative.

(Courtesy: Cahners Advertising Research Report.)

Competition. At one time, the business press had a virtual monopoly on business-to-business advertising. Today, business publications still occupy the primary role in the advertising plans of most business-to-business advertisers (see Exhibit 11.18). However, the number of advertising options for these companies has grown substantially in recent years.

The major growth area in business promotion in recent years is various forms of direct response. One reason for the increase in direct-marketing activities is the demand for proven results in a soft economy. Advertisers "these days are into accountability in a major way, and one thing the direct-marketing people are good at is tracking results. . . . [i]n the business-to-business sector, [direct marketing] is even more valuable and viable than the consumer sector because the market is so much more identifiable."[18]

As Exhibit 11.19 vividly demonstrates, business magazine publishers are going to have to adopt the marketing mix concept of their consumer counterparts. As one business-to-business executive said, "In the heated competition for your clients' marketing dollars, you must relate the benefits of advertising in your magazine to the other options that your clients may be considering. . . . For example, a direct-mail program dropped into a market that is aware of your client's company and its products through magazine advertising will probably have a higher response rate than the same direct-mail effort dropped in a virgin market."[19] The Siemens Energy case is an example of the synergy between business publications and direct mail.

This view of marketing synergism extends beyond tradition media found in the consumer sector. A number of companies are using *fax-on-demand* programs to keep in touch with their customers. For example, Du Pont initiated

---

[18]Gary Levin, "Want Accountability? Then Go Direct," *Advertising Age,* October 26, 1992, p. B-8.
[19]Helen Berman, "Pulling Plums Out of the Pie," *Folio,* April 1, 1993, p. 41.

EXHIBIT
11.19

. . . .

Specialized business
and professional publi-
cations were rated as
the most useful source
for information about
products and services.

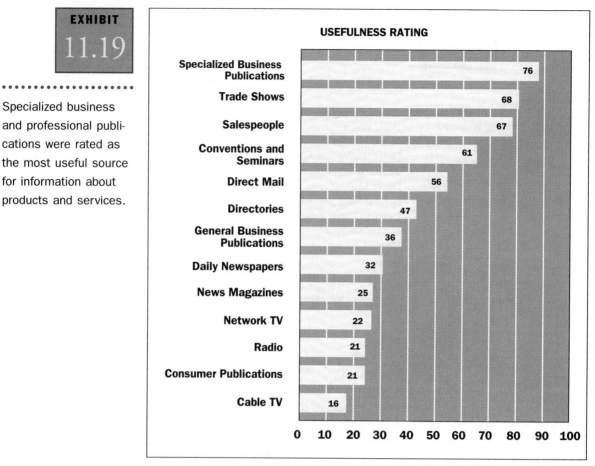

USEFULNESS RATING

Source	Rating
Specialized Business Publications	76
Trade Shows	68
Salespeople	67
Conventions and Seminars	61
Direct Mail	56
Directories	47
General Business Publications	36
Daily Newspapers	32
News Magazines	25
Network TV	22
Radio	21
Consumer Publications	21
Cable TV	16

(Courtesy: Cahners Publishing Company.)

PolyFax to keep in touch with users of its polymer chemicals. Customers can call an 800-number to get technical information or have questions answered through the fax service. It allows readers to get immediate response from advertising and other promotions. It is also an excellent means of building sales leads for follow up by salespeople.

Because of the relatively small prospect pool for most business products, business-to-business marketing allows the use of innovative technology and experimentation that would be cost-prohibitive in consumer advertising. On the other hand, given the high dollar value of a typical business-to-business sale, the constraints of CPMs found in the consumer sector are rarely a factor in business marketing.

Business Publication Expansion of Services

As the number of business-to-business advertisements and promotional competitors have grown in recent years, business magazines have not ignored the trend. In fact, major business magazines have developed their own vehicles for reaching audiences apart from their core magazine business. These ancillary promotional services discourage competitors from coming into the marketplace as well as providing new profit centers, especially important for magazines directed to industries with shrinking advertising revenues.

Case History

MARKETING SITUATION

Siemens Energy & Automation, Inc., after a series of mergers and acquisitions, contained elements of Gould I-T-E, Allis Chalmers, Siemens Allis, and other assorted corporate and brand identities. The company sells a broad line of electrical and electronic products to a multitude of specifiers and buyers in three different markets: construction, industrial, and utility.

As a result of the series of acquisitions, the company's identity among consumers had become confused in terms of products and position. This was confirmed in focus-group research conducted by Gordon Bailey & Associates. There was confusion among Siemens Energy & Automation and other Siemens USA companies. Surveys showed that among those who were familiar with Siemens Energy & Automation, there was a lack of knowledge about what products the company sold. Secondary research revealed that Siemens had low awareness in most product categories in which they competed.

CAMPAIGN OBJECTIVES

Management's challenge to Gordon Bailey & Associates was to create a communications program to the industrial market that would help Siemens:

1. Establish a credible position
2. Increase low levels of product awareness

TARGET AUDIENCE

Part of the challenge included communicating this program to a diverse audience of "influencers" that included top management, engineering management in the process control and MRO, systems consultants, and distributors, with special emphasis on selected Standard Industrial Classifications. These SICs were "heavy user" and "heavy potential" prospect SICs.

The challenge was to also communicate this formation internally at Siemens so that employees across the company's divisions engaged in marketing, sales, and distribution would all be aware of the company's theme.

CREATIVE STRATEGY

To communicate Siemens product offerings and capabilities in a credible manner, it was decided that the campaign would use "real products, real problems, real customers, and real solutions."

The positioning strategy built on what research said that customers and potential buyers in Siemens end-user markets already knew about Siemens: "A German company known for excellent engineering." Themes on quality, service, innovation, size, global reach, etc., would be consistent with what was already in people's minds.

In addition, Siemens Energy & Automation had made great strides in upgrading manufacturing facilities, computer capabilities, etc.

Gordon Bailey & Associates worked with the top marketing officers in the company to create a theme that they believed in. The result: "Technology that serves the customer."

(Courtesy: Gordon Bailey & Associates, Inc.)

Siemens tested the theme in focus groups and found that this position was believable and credible among Siemens customers and prospects. In addition, the theme also sent a strong, positive message to Siemens' own employees about the technology that was being employed internally, in manufacturing, distribution, computer systems, etc., to allow the employees to serve the customer.

Siemens had the sales and marketing organization suggest end-user applications that supported the idea of technology that serves the customer. Siemens then did an ad campaign that built on these success stories.

MEDIA STRATEGY

A three-tier target audience media strategy was developed. Tier I was comprised of top management at key SIC companies. This tier was reached by an ad campaign in magazines, such as *Industry Week.* Gordon Bailey & Associates also used targeted direct-mail pieces, using three-dimensional premiums, such as a book on the life and times of Leonardo da Vinci, along with a letter from the president of Siemens Energy & Automation to his counterpart.

Tier II was comprised of functional disciplines (process and manufacturing engineering, MRO, consultants, systems integrators). This audience was reached with ads placed in trade magazines designed to reach them, such as Plant Engineering, Consulting Specifying Engineer, Control Engineering, etc. These ads acted as an "umbrella" for other ads placed by the company's individual product groups. In addition to the ads, Siemens also had a three-dimensional direct-mail piece specially designed to appeal to engineers. The direct-mail piece featured a "starscope" and talked about competing in the new-world economy by expanding

your vision. A brochure in the mailer explained that "Siemens is rolling out new technologies, and a whole new advertising campaign."

Tier III was aimed at internal audiences and consisted of direct mailings of a brochure that contained the ad campaign and a description of how Siemens Energy & Automation was organized by product group. Plus, this pocket piece brochure was used by the sales force as a handy way to let prospects know quickly about Siemens' products and capabilities.

OTHER MARKETING PROGRAMS

Critical to the excellent results achieved by this program was the research program used to pretest the ad campaign. Since the greatest budget commitment was to the trade media campaign, Gordon Bailey & Associates put the campaign through a process that is used to pretest print advertising called the "GBA Gauntlet."

Buyers and specifiers of Siemens products are recruited for these focus groups. Two types of groups are held, one for top management, and another for engineering management.

The objective of the research is to confirm that the intended communication in an ad is in fact, what is received by the target audience.

Another element of the marketing program critical to the overall program's success was the series of meetings held around the country, at all the product group locations, to explain the program, why it was being done, what was involved, and how individuals with the organization could support the program and ensure its success. A written summary of the program was provided to all attenders.

The sales force was reached around the country via a videotape that had an introduction by the vice president of sales, and contained a recording of the program's presentation to the executive committee of the company, along with all supporting information, and research. The tape explained how each individual salesperson could best use the program's elements, and adapt them to their sales routine.

(Courtesy: Gordon Bailey & Associates, Inc.)

EVIDENCE OF RESULTS

LEADS: Response to the Tier I direct mail program was in double digits, and was in the form of personal letters from presidents of key target companies writing to the president of Siemens Energy & Automation thanking him for the direct-mail piece.

The trade media campaign has generated hundreds of leads to date.

READERSHIP: During the campaign's first year, it ran in eight issues of *Industry Week*, Option II magazine that were measured for readership by Starch INRA Hooper.

Out of these eight issues, the campaign's ads scored first for "associated" seven times. The eighth time it scored second for "associated." On an indexed basis, the ads averaged 70 percent higher "associated" scores than the issue average. Some of the ads had indexes of greater than 200 percent—which means that they more than doubled the scores of the issues' average ad.

BRAND PREFERENCE: 1Pre' and 1Post' benchmark studies for brand preference in several key Siemens product categories were done among the readers of the trade magazines used by Siemens Energy & Automation for this campaign. A total of more than 2,400 questionnaires were returned with a response rate in excess of 20 percent. Following are product segments measured, and the change in unaided, top-of-mind awareness:

Product Segment Name	Percent Increase in Awareness
Motor controls	45
Contractors, solid state	41
Adjustable speed drives, A.C.	38
AC motors, 1–500 H.P.	10
Switches	20
Medium voltage switchgear	11
Busways	5
Relays	25
Circuit breakers	71
Electrical distribution systems	25

The theme "Technology that serves the customer" has been embraced by the organization, and is now the rallying cry for all kinds of quality-based decisions. To decide if a product should be at a trade show, the marketing manager asks: Does this product support "Technology that serves the customers"?

(Courtesy: Gordon Bailey & Associates, Inc.)

Entry into these ancillary services is usually more successful for established magazines than for independent companies. The magazine provides credibility and high visibility with prospective users that would be lacking without the association of the publication. Many business magazine publishers want to be less dependent on advertising from their publications, to add to their overall profitability, and to spread their revenue stream across a number of avenues. "Toward that end, publishers are exploring and developing such franchise extensions as spin off titles, international editions, TV shows, home videos, books, branded merchandise, special newsstand issues, . . . newsletters, audiocassettes, subscriber membership clubs, seminars."[20]

Another innovative approach to reaching a business or specialized consumer audiences is self-published magazines produced by marketers. Some of these publications carry no advertising, some carry only ads for the company publishing the magazines, and a few carry outside ads for noncompeting firms.

While these self-published magazines represent competition for established business publications, they are also another source of income for business publishers. Most companies contract with a business or custom publishers to produce their magazines. Therefore, producing a competing publication can actually be another source of profit. Exhibit 11.20 lists some major self-published magazines.

Regardless of the specific promotional activity, these activities offer a number of advantages to a publisher. First, they utilize the publisher's knowledge of a particular industry to help clients develop a coordinated promotional

---

[20]Scott Donaton, "Venturing Out to Build Broad Bonds with Audience," *Advertising Age,* March 9, 1993, p. S-8.

EXHIBIT

11.20

....

Company-Sponsored
Specialty Publications

Company-Sponsored Specialty Publications

Publication (Company)	Readership	Annual Frequency
Profit (IBM)	200,000	6
Via Fedex (Federal Express)	330,000	4
Style (Sony)	500,000	2

(Source: Kerry Rottengerger-Murtha, Sales & Marketing Management, July 1993, p. 77.)

and advertising campaign. Second, they gain revenue from companies that do not use advertising as a business-to-business marketing tool. Finally, they increase a magazine's credibility by demonstrating far-reaching expertise in a number of promotional areas. In the future, we will see publishers developing a variety of information services and promotional techniques in addition to their basic magazines.

Types of Business-to-Business Publications

Despite the wide array of business publications, they can generally be placed in one of four categories:

- **Distributive trades (trade)**
- **Manufacturers and builders (industrial)**
- **Top officers of other corporations (management)**
- **Physicians, dentists, architects, and other professional people (professional)**

Trade paper

A business publication directed to those who buy products for resale (wholesalers, jobbers, retailers).

Trade Papers. Because most nationally advertised products depend upon dealers for their sales, we discuss advertising in trade papers first. Usually, this advertising is prepared by the agency that handles the consumer advertising, and in any new campaign both are prepared at the same time. The term *trade papers* is applied particularly to business publications directed at those who buy products for resale, such as wholesalers, jobbers, and retailers. Typical trade papers are *American Druggist, Supermarket News, Chain Store Age, Hardware Retailer, Modern Tire Dealer, Women's Wear Daily,* and *Home Furnishings.*

Almost every business engaged in distributing goods has a trade paper to discuss its problems. Trade papers are a great medium for reporting merchandising news about the products, packaging, prices, deals, and promotions of the manufacturers that cater to the particular industry. The chain-store field alone has more than 20 such publications. Druggists have a choice of over 30, and more than 60 different publications are issued for grocers. There are many localized journals, such as *Texas Food Merchant, Michigan Beverage News, Southern Hardware, California Apparel News,* and *Illinois Building News.*

Industrial Advertising. As we move into the world where a company in one industry sells its materials, machinery, tools, parts, and equipment to another company for use in making a product or conducting operations, we are in an altogether different ballpark—the industrial-marketing arena.

Case History

MARKETING SITUATION

Floor covering in the retail industry is a $1 billion business annually. Most retail floor coverings are hard surfaces (hardwood, marble, or tile) or broadloom, all of which have design limitations and can be costly to update and replace. Although modular floor covering—or carpet tile—is a small segment of the retail floor covering industry (2 percent), it is gaining acceptance due to its design flexibility and long-term cost-savings potential. Furthermore, no single floor covering manufacturer has taken leadership of the retail floor covering industry.

In 1990, Heuga USA positioned itself as the only manufacturer and supplier of modular flooring systems specifically designed for the retail environment. With a wide array of carpet tile products, Heuga USA gained a 50 percent market share of the $15 million retail carpet tile business by the end of 1991. This growth, however, was a result of purchases by retailers already using or predisposed to the carpet tile concept. In order to experience further growth, Heuga USA needed to expand the retail modular flooring category.

CAMPAIGN OBJECTIVES

As the only manufacturer of modular flooring dedicated solely to the retail industry, Heuga USA's marketing objective was to build awareness of and predisposition for the modular flooring category. In order to measure this growth, Heuga USA set three major sales and marketing objectives:

1. Increase the number of its *new* accounts by 10 percent over 1991
2. Increase gross sales revenues by 10 percent over 1991

3. Increase the number of media-generated inquiries by 10 percent over 1991

TARGET AUDIENCE

The target audience was primarily the flooring system purchase decision maker, such as facility managers in national chains with multiple locations, who are unaware of modular flooring and that Heuga provides modular flooring products designed specifically for retail. Primary research conducted in February 1992 also indicated that interior designs are an important gatekeeper to this segment.

CREATIVE STRATEGY

The creative strategy was to define and build awareness of the retail modular flooring category. A full-page, four-color ad was developed targeted to both end users *and* designers. As such, it featured elements familiar to both: floor plans and planning materials. The colors and tones were selected specifically to break out the clutter of the retail supplier ads with which Heuga's ads compete. The headline "You Spend Too Much Time Coming Up with a Floor Plan That Works to Put Down a Flooring System That Doesn't" focus on both target audiences' mindset: They put a lot of effort into an effective floor plan but often use what they are familiar with to cover the floor. Although not a direct response ad, a toll-free number was also included to capture inquiries and convert them into sales leads.

(Courtesy: Fitzgerald & Company.)

(continued)

MEDIA STRATEGY

To segment Heuga as the leading retail flooring supplier, the top four retail design and trade publications were utilized: *Chain Store Age, Visual Merchandising and Store Design, Display & Design Ideas,* and *Retail Store Image.* Heuga avoided major commercial design and trade publications in order to position itself as the leader in the *retail* category.

A secondary objective was to stretch the limited media dollars as much as possible. Following extensive media negotiations, Heuga secured an eight-page advertorial in *Retail Store Image* allowing it the space to relate the complete modular flooring store and the benefits of Heuga. Case studies of successful Heuga installations were also included to lend credibility and to demonstrate Heuga's commitment to the retail category.

OTHER MARKETING PROGRAMS

To support the advertising, a collateral and sampling program was also employed by the sales force. Developed prior to the ad, the graphic elements of these pieces differed to be more applicable in presentation situations:

1. *"Gameboard":* This piece was designed to aid the sales force in demonstrating the design and replacement capabilities of modular flooring. It features a grid in which miniature tiles are used to copy the design and traffic-flow challenges retailers and designers face. A "leave-behind" brochure also accompanied this piece.

2. *Corporate brochure:* This brochure was utilized by the sales force in initial presentations to introduce Heuga USA and to explain the modular flooring category. It was also used as a fulfillment piece.

3. *"Design Logic Kit":* A final leg to the program was the "Design Logic Kit" in which a salesperson could demonstrate the design flexibility of carpet tile. By changing only 20 percent of the floor, retailers can totally update their store for a new look, or replace worn areas. This piece was also accompanied by a leave-behind brochure.

In addition to the collateral program, Heuga USA instigated an extensive public relations campaign in 1992. The four trade publications were targeted along with other top retail and design publications. Eight major editorial placements in six trade publications were secured. The public relations effort was also enhanced by a quarterly newsletter distributed to existing and potential accounts.

Heuga also sponsored, in conjunction with *Retail Store Image,* a half-day seminar on retail floor covering. The seminar, open to top designers and end users, further extended Heuga's leadership position in the retail category.

EVIDENCE OF RESULTS

Despite the 1992 economic downturn in the retail industry and the subsequent challenges it presented, Heuga USA experienced a strong year:

1. Replacement orders from *existing* accounts were flat. However, the number of *new* accounts Heuga secured was up 20 percent (10 percent over goal) as 12 new accounts selected Heuga's modular flooring.

2. Heuga USA's gross sales increased by 20 percent—doubling the goal of 10 percent. Heuga USA exceeded its gross sales goal by generating awareness of and credibility in modular flooring. In 1992, Heuga retained a 50 percent share of $20 million category versus a $15 million industry in 1991.

3. Heuga also increased its media-generated inquiries by 18 percent from 128 per issue in 1991 to 150 per issue in 1992. Furthermore, as Heuga's marketing efforts created a demand for the category, the overall quality of the inquiries increased generating more potential sales leads.

(Courtesy: Fitzgerald & Company)

There are fewer customers in this arena than in the consumer market, and they can be more easily identified. The amount of money involved in a sale may be large—hundreds of thousands of dollars, perhaps even millions—and nothing is bought on impulse. Many knowledgeable executives with technical skills often share in the buying decision. The sales representative has to have a high degree of professional competence to deal with the industrial market, in which personal selling is the biggest factor in making a sale. Advertising is only a collateral aid used to pave the way for or support the salesperson; hence, it receives a smaller share of the marketplace budget.

Advertising addressed to people responsible for buying goods needed to make products is called *industrial advertising.* It is designed to reach purchasing agents, plant managers, engineers, controllers, and others who have a voice in spending the firm's money.

....

Industrial advertising

Addressed to manufacturers who buy machinery, equipment, raw materials, and the components needed to produce goods they sell.

....

Management Publications. The most difficult group for a publication to reach is managers. After all, even the largest companies have only a relatively few decision makers. When these decision makers are widely dispersed across a number of industries and job descriptions, publications find they must be extremely creative to reach them.

The management category is one that straddles a gray area between consumer and business-to-business publications. Magazines such as *Business Week, Fortune,* and *Nation's Business* have characteristics that would place them in either the business or the consumer category. Even magazines such as *Time* have at least some of their partial-run editions listed in the *Business Publications SRDS.*

Professional Publications. The Standard Rate and Data Service, in its special business publication edition, includes journals addressed to physicians, surgeons, dentists, lawyers, architects, and other professionals who depend upon these publications to keep abreast of their professions. The editorial content of such journals ranges from reportage about new technical developments to discussions on how to meet client or patient problems better and how to conduct offices more efficiently and profitably. Professional people often recommend or specify the products their patients or clients should order. Therefore, much advertising of a high technical caliber is addressed to them.

Some Special Features of Business Publication Advertising

Business publications exhibit several differences from consumer magazines. This section briefly discusses the more important ones.

Pass-Along Readership. In Exhibit 11.16, readers indicated that almost one-quarter of all business publications are read on a pass-along basis. As we discussed earlier in this chapter, such readership among consumer magazines is generally regarded as inferior to paid circulation. However, one of the notable differences between business and consumer publications is the way advertisers view pass-along readership. The typical consumer medium has a relatively short life and low pass-along readership. Occasionally, a recipe will be clipped or a magazine will be passed on to a neighbor, but consumer magazines are largely read for pleasure and tossed aside. In any case, advertisers view pass-along readership of consumer magazines as vastly inferior to primary readership.

Business publication advertisers, in contrast, view pass-along readership as quite valuable. For one thing, readers don't normally browse through *Electronic Design* or *Concrete Construction;* they pay close attention to copy. For another, some business publications limit their circulation in a way that forces pass-along readership.

Controlled Circulation. Magazines are sometimes distributed free to selective readers. Free circulation is known as *controlled circulation.* Controlled circulation publications are delivered to a carefully selected list of people who are influential in making purchase decisions for their industry. Controlled circulation makes sense when you are dealing with an easily defined audience of decision makers. To some media planners, the logic of controlled circulation is little different from that of direct mail except that the ad is delivered in an editorial environment. Despite the fact that controlled circulation is widely used in the trade press, it is not universally embraced. In the past, most research has indicated that a high percentage of both clients and media directors prefer the reader commitment inherent in paid circulation.

The number of controlled publications in the business field plays a major role in their share of advertising-to-circulation revenues compared to consumer magazines. As we mentioned in our discussion of consumer magazines, approximately 47 percent of total revenues come from circulation. By contrast, business publications receive approximately 75 percent of total revenues from advertising and this figure has risen some 7 percent in the past decade (see Exhibit 11.21). This dependency on advertising is another reason why business publications suffer so much during economic downturns.

Vertical and Horizontal Publications. Industrial publications are usually considered either *horizontal* or *vertical*. A vertical publication is one that covers an entire industry. An example is *Baking Industry,* which contains information concerning product quality, marketing, plant efficiency, and packaging.

Horizontal publications are edited for people who are engaged in a single function that cuts across many industries. An example is *Purchasing Magazine,* which is circulated to purchasing managers. It discusses trends and forecasts applicable to all industries.

Standard Industrial Classification System. One thing that greatly facilitates the industrial marketing process is the Standard Industrial Classification System, a numbering system established by the U.S. government. SIC classifies more than 4 million manufacturing firms in 10 major categories, further subdivided into more specific groups. The code numbering system operates as follows: All major business activities (agriculture, forestry, and fisheries; mining; construction; manufacturing; transportation; communication and public utilities; wholesale; retail; finance, insurance, and real estate; services; government) are given a two-digit code. A third and a fourth digit are assigned to identify more specific activities within each major business category, in much the same way that the Dewey decimal system works. For example:

25   Manufacturers of furniture and fixtures

252   Manufacturers of office furniture

EXHIBIT 11.21

Total Spending on Business Magazines, 1986–1996 ($ millions)[a]

Year	Advertising	Circulation	Total	Adv./Cir. Ratio
1986	$3,200	$1,360	$4,560	70.1
1991	4,055	1,500	5,555	72.9
1996	5,625	1,860	7,485	75.1

(*Source:* The Veronis, Suhler & Associates Communications Industry Forecast, *June 1992, p. 233.*)

2521   Manufacturers of wood office furniture

2522   Manufacturers of metal office furniture

Most industrial publications provide a breakdown of their audiences by SIC code. Exhibit 11.22 shows a distribution of the two-digit code across a number of industries.

Circulation Audits. The leading trade and industrial publications belong to the Business Publications Audit of Circulation (BPA), which audits approximately 1,000 business publications (Exhibit 11.23). BPA's audits pay particular attention to the qualifications of people on the controlled list and when they last indicated they wanted the publication.

The Audit Bureau of Circulation performs essentially the same function for over 200 paid-circulation publications, although its main effort is in the consumer field. Some publications have both ABC and BPA audits, but many, especially the smaller ones, do not offer any circulation-audit report at all.

A third auditing group is the Verified Audit Circulation Company (VAC). It tends to audit more specialized publications.

Circulation-audit reports provide the business advertiser with information and statistics to use in selecting the best publications for carrying a product's advertising.

EXHIBIT

11.22

. . . .

The SIC code is a major means of analyzing industrial magazine circulation.

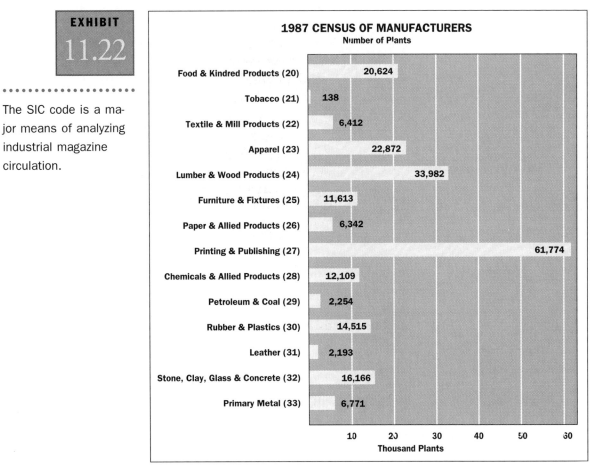

(Courtesy: Cahners Publishing Company.)

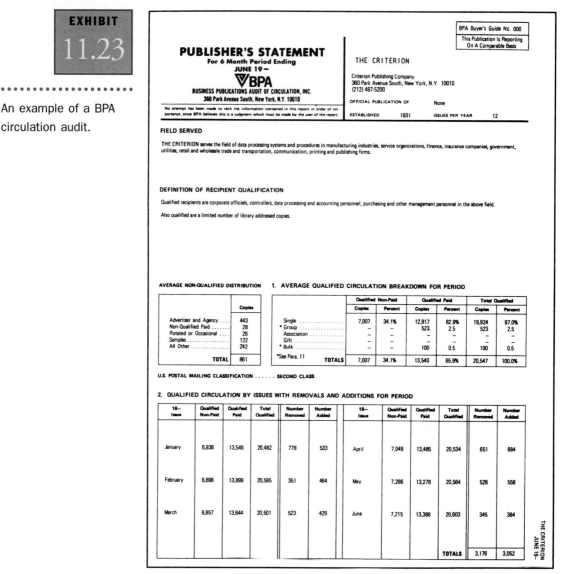

<table>
<tr><td colspan="3">

BPA Buyer's Guide No. 000

This Publication Is Reporting
On A Comparable Basis

</td></tr>
</table>

PUBLISHER'S STATEMENT
For 6 Month Period Ending
JUNE 19—
▽BPA
BUSINESS PUBLICATIONS AUDIT OF CIRCULATION, INC.
360 Park Avenue South, New York, N.Y. 10010

No attempt has been made to rank the information contained in this report in order of importance, since BPA believes this is a judgment which must be made by the user of the report.

THE CRITERION

Criterion Publishing Company
360 Park Avenue South, New York, N.Y. 10010
(212) 487-5200

OFFICIAL PUBLICATION OF   None

ESTABLISHED   1931   ISSUES PER YEAR   12

FIELD SERVED

THE CRITERION serves the field of data processing systems and procedures in manufacturing industries, service organizations, finance, insurance companies, government, utilities, retail and wholesale trade and transportation, communication, printing and publishing firms.

DEFINITION OF RECIPIENT QUALIFICATION

Qualified recipients are corporate officials, controllers, data processing and accounting personnel, purchasing and other management personnel in the above field.

Also qualified are a limited number of library addressed copies.

AVERAGE NON-QUALIFIED DISTRIBUTION

	Copies
Advertiser and Agency	443
Non-Qualified Paid	28
Rotated or Occasional	26
Samples	122
All Other	242
TOTAL	**861**

1. AVERAGE QUALIFIED CIRCULATION BREAKDOWN FOR PERIOD

	Qualified Non-Paid		Qualified Paid		Total Qualified	
	Copies	Percent	Copies	Percent	Copies	Percent
Single	7,007	34.1%	12,917	62.9%	19,924	97.0%
* Group	–	–	523	2.5	523	2.5
Association	–	–	–	–	–	–
Gift	–	–	–	–	–	–
* Bulk	–	–	100	0.5	100	0.5
*See Para. 11 **TOTALS**	7,007	34.1%	13,540	65.9%	20,547	100.0%

U.S. POSTAL MAILING CLASSIFICATION . . . . . . SECOND CLASS

2. QUALIFIED CIRCULATION BY ISSUES WITH REMOVALS AND ADDITIONS FOR PERIOD

19— Issue	Qualified Non-Paid	Qualified Paid	Total Qualified	Number Removed	Number Added	19— Issue	Qualified Non-Paid	Qualified Paid	Total Qualified	Number Removed	Number Added
January	6,936	13,546	20,482	778	533	April	7,049	13,485	20,534	651	684
February	6,696	13,899	20,595	351	464	May	7,286	13,278	20,564	528	558
March	6,857	13,644	20,501	523	429	June	7,215	13,388	20,603	345	384
						TOTALS				3,176	3,052

THE CRITERION
JUNE 19—

(Courtesy: Business Publications Audit of Circulation Report.)

Agribusiness Advertising

Advertising products to the agribusiness community uses many of the same techniques demonstrated by other sectors of business marketing. However, agribusiness promotional techniques are even more specialized than those of traditional business-to-business marketing. The relatively small agribusiness population makes sophisticated information readily available. Agribusiness advertising can target audiences and deliver a message that solves specific problems of the farm industry (see Exhibit 11.24).

The business of farming has been hit hard during recent years with an uncertain farm economy, high prices for feed and other supplies, and the ravages of the great midwestern flood of 1993. These factors have combined to make it very difficult for farm magazines and agribusiness advertising in general. A continuing consolidation of farms has reduced the number of farmers and companies involved in agribusiness. This trend toward consolidation has been reflected in the farm press by lower circulation and fewer advertising dollars.

(Courtesy: Sawyer Riley Compton.)

Farm publications are engaged in the same competitive environment faced by business publications. As the number of farms and major agribusiness suppliers has decreased in recent years, the number and diversity of media competing for advertising dollars in the sector have grown dramatically. In order to meet this situation, farm publications have utilized many of the techniques of the business press in expanding their approach to their audiences. For example, these magazines have accumulated sophisticated databases to develop subscriber list rentals, do their own direct mail to nonsubscribers, and publish special catalogs and other material. Like the business press, farm magazines will probably see more revenue coming from nonpublishing sources as they become more successful in promoting these ventures.

The Organization of the Farm Press

Farm magazines are classified as general farm magazines, regional farm magazines, and vocational farm magazines. These classifications overlap, however, because a number of the larger magazines have geographic and demographic editions.

General Farm Magazines. The three major publications in the category and their circulations are *Farm Journal* (775,000), *Successful Farming* (500,000), and *Progressive Farmer* (450,000). In recent years, each of these publications has experienced moderate circulation decreases reflecting the consolidation of the farming industry. The general farm publications are designed to address all aspects of farm life, but with a clear emphasis on business. For instance, the SRDS Publisher's Editorial Profile for *Successful Farming* reads as follows:

> *Successful Farming* editorial is designed as management guidance for business farmers and their families. Articles are written as practical help in making those decisions which directly affect the profitability of the business, and the welfare of the family. Editors seek their information from those in the forefront of farm change, and much editorial is case history reporting of successful innovation. There are also monthly reports on developments in government, finance, equipment, etc. Editorial is 100% business of farming and farm family management.

Regional Farm Magazines. A number of farm publications are directed to farmers in a particular region. These publications tend to be general in nature, but they contain little of the family-oriented topics found in the large-circulation farm magazines. They address issues of crops, livestock, and government farm policy unique to a particular region. Among the publications in this category are the *Prairie Farmer,* the majority of whose readers live in Indiana and Illinois; the *Oregon Farmer-Stockman;* and the *Nebraska Farmer.*

Vocational Farm Magazines. The last category of farm publications comprises those devoted to certain types of farming or livestock raising. Typical of these publications are *Soybean Digest, The Dairyman, American Fruit Grower,* and *Tobacco.* Many of the vocational magazines combine elements of both regional and vocational publications—for instance, *The Kansas Stockman* and *Missouri Pork Producer.*

Whatever a farmer's interests may be, a number of publications are edited to cater to them. Many farm homes take several publications.

SUMMARY

In many respects magazines reflect the challenges and opportunities faced by advertising in the 1990s. Magazines are an ideal medium for reaching the target audience segments that advertisers seek, in an environment suited to the mood of that audience. Magazines also provide audience involvement to a degree impossible in most of other media. Finally, in this era of working women and busy schedules, readers can use magazines at their convenience. With the ability of computers to track demographic and lifestyle segments and new technology to reach them through partial-run editions, magazines can compete with both broad and narrowly defined media.

On the negative side, magazines are faced by rising costs of postage, printing, and marketing as well as a number of new competitors for the advertising dollars that will only grow as technology makes even more impressive strides in the future. Clearly, magazines cannot afford to compete on a price basis with other media, especially television. Quality, credibility, believability, and audience selectivity are the elements for selling magazines to both readers and advertisers.

The future success of magazines will be linked to advertisers' perceptions of the medium as an upscale vehicle with high audience involvement. Virtually every study points up the advantages that magazines have over other media in terms of advertising attentiveness. These attention levels are reinforced by the high regard in which readers hold the medium. Statistics from Magazine Publishers of America show that magazine readers are better educated, have a higher income, and are more socially and politically active than the general population. With publishers' increasing ability to identify and reach these audiences, magazines should be a solid player in future advertising plans for most national advertisers.

Questions

1. The two major concerns of the magazine industry are costs and selectivity. Explain.
2. What is meant by the term *magazine imperative?*
3. What are some qualitative features of importance to magazine advertisers?
4. Contrast full-run and partial-run magazine editions.
5. What is selective binding?
6. What is the role of negotiation in setting magazine advertising rates?
7. Contrast circulation and readership in magazines.
8. What are the major competitors for business magazines?
9. What has been a primary method for business magazines to extend their services and increase profits?
10. What are vertical and horizontal publications?

Out-of-Home Advertising

CHAPTER 12

CHAPTER OBJECTIVES

Outdoor advertising is oldest form of promotion, dating to prehistoric times. In recent years, a vast array of out-of-home media have joined traditional outdoor posters to reach an increasingly mobile population. After reading this chapter you will understand:

- **Outdoor as a supplement to other media**
- **Standardized posters are the minority of out-of-home ads**
- **The image of outdoor advertising**
- **Formats of out-of-home and transit**
- **Measurement of the outdoor audience**

Outdoor is the oldest form of promotion. Evidence of outdoor messages can be found in pre-historic carvings on bronze and stone tablets in the Middle East. **In Egypt,** outdoor was a popular means of posting public notices as well as sales messages. These were placed on well-traveled roads and are the forerunner of the modern highway billboard. **Painted advertising dates at least to Pompeii,** where elaborately decorated walls promoted local businesses.

In this country, outdoor "broadsides" announced the Boston Tea Party and reported the Boston Massacre. Andrew Jackson's presidential campaign used posters, and the circus has long been associated with the colorful posters that announced its coming in every small town in America.

The modern era of outdoor advertising was introduced when the automobile created a mobile society. In addition to a mobile population, outdoor bene-fited from new printing techniques and a growing advertising industry that was always looking for effective means of reaching prospective customers. During this period, the industry adopted standardized signs; formed the fore-runner of its national trade association, the Outdoor Advertising Association of America (OAAA); established what is now the Traffic Audit Bureau for Media Measurement (TAB) to authenticate audience data; and initiated a na-tional marketing organization, OAAA Marketing.[1]

The traditional outdoor billboard, while still the economic foundation of the industry, has been augmented by an endless number of out-of-home adver-tising devices. In fact, the term *out-of-home* advertising has replaced the more familiar outdoor advertising in recent years. Today, outdoor normally has a more narrow meaning, referring only to highway posters and large signs. The change is more than just a difference in terminology. It reflects the diversity of the industry and its marketing strategy. As we will see in this chapter, out-of-home advertisers are using a number of different media, more narrowly pinpointing and identifying their target markets, and appealing to a broader spectrum of advertisers than in previous years.

As we will see throughout this chapter, the out-of-home medium comprises a number of advertising vehicles with a common marketing objective. That is, all out-of-home advertising seeks to reach consumers who are in the mar-ketplace, many with the intention to purchase. It does so with a colorful, spectacular message that is difficult to ignore. The two primary categories of out-of-home advertising are outdoor and transit.

OUT-OF-HOME ADVERTISING

Out-of-home advertising is a relatively small medium with expenditures of approximately $1.5 billion. However, the diversification of out-of-home media has made it difficult to categorize the various options, much less to keep track of their revenues. For instance, out-of-home encompasses a host of media from posters and transit to bus shelters, one-of-a-kind spectaculars, computer painting, and laser lightshows. For simplicity, we will confine most of our discussion in this section to standardized outdoor posters.

THE OUTDOOR INDUSTRY: AN OVERVIEW

Outdoor advertising is normally a secondary medium, especially for national advertisers. However, a number of local and national advertisers use outdoor as their primary advertising vehicle. In the past, the industry has been de-pendent to a great degree on tobacco and alcoholic beverage advertising for its revenues. While these two product categories still account for almost 25

---

[1]Unless otherwise noted, material for this section was provided by the Outdoor Advertising Association of America.

EXHIBIT

12.1

Outdoor combines size and color to achieve interest and brand awareness.

(Courtesy: Outdoor Advertising Association of America.)

percent of total expenditures, the outdoor industry has been successful in diversifying its advertising.

In 1993, retail replaced tobacco as the largest category of outdoor. Retailer spending in outdoor totals 23 percent of all expenditures in the medium. This shift of advertising dollars is significant because many outdoor executives think it will bring in many advertisers that formerly did not want to be associated with an advertising vehicle dominated by tobacco and alcohol. These newcomers to outdoor invest in the medium for a number of reasons. "Advancements in outdoor imaging, color and the timely printing of boards have contributed to an influx of new advertisers such as cosmetics companies and fashion designers.[2]

In addition, outdoor can generate tremendous reach and frequency levels at a fraction of the cost of traditional media. The growth of outdoor also reflects the need to reach a population on the move. According to the U.S. Department of Transportation, 90.8 percent of households have at least one vehicle and drive an average of 41.4 miles a day. In fact, almost 95 percent of all travel miles are by car or truck.

The OAAA has been successful in promoting the benefits of outdoor with a campaign designed to reach advertisers and agencies. The organization placed some 6,500 posters and bulletins in 252 metropolitan markets. The campaign theme "Outdoor. It's Not a Medium, It's a Large" featured products not usually seen in outdoor advertising (see Exhibit 12.1) in order to change the industry's image as that of a medium for general advertising.

Despite the recent success of outdoor, the industry continues to be hurt by criticism from various public interest and environmental groups. These critics charge that outdoor advertising is both a blight on the landscape and, by

[2]Riccardo A. David, "New Advertisers Limit Outdoor Loss," *Advertising Age,* March 15, 1993, p. 6.

targeting inner city populations for alcohol and tobacco advertising, unethical. While much of the criticism is probably unfair, some major advertisers are reluctant to get involved in what they regard as a controversial medium.

These criticisms should not detract from a generally positive future for outdoor. Perhaps the greatest long-term benefit for outdoor is the increasing fragmentation of virtually every other medium. Some advertising executives note that outdoor may soon be the last mass-market medium. Mass-market advertisers such as McDonald's benefit from the low CPMs that more than make up for any loss of targeting prospects.

Like other advertising media, outdoor is most successful when it is used in accordance with narrowly defined marketing objectives. In most cases, these objectives encompass one of the following advertising strategies:

- **Companies are introducing a new product and want immediate brand name recognition to complement other forms of advertising.**

- **Firms are marketing established, well-known, and recognized brands and want to provide reminder advertising to consumers in the marketplace.**

Advantages and Disadvantages of Outdoor Advertising

Outdoor is a dominant medium that combines high levels of reach and frequency, a colorful presentation of products, and low CPM costs, while reaching an audience already in the marketplace. Outdoor is one of the last opportunities to reach consumers prior to purchase. In this regard, it combines the best features of radio and point-of-purchase.

With its size, outdoor also is well suited to enhance the effectiveness of other advertising media. It can function as an economical supplement to a media plan or stand alone as a primary medium. Outdoor is also able to deliver dramatic messages for various nonprofit organizations (see Exhibit 12.2). Before we discuss the many features of outdoor advertising, let's take a minute to examine some of the advantages and disadvantages of outdoor. The major advantages of outdoor are the following:

1. *Audience delivery.* Outdoor maximizes both reach and frequency. During a 30-day period, a moderate outdoor campaign reaches more than 75 per-

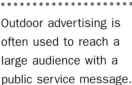

EXHITBIT
12.2

Outdoor advertising is often used to reach a large audience with a public service message.

(Courtesy: Eight-Sheet Outdoor Advertising Association.)

cent of the adults in a market at least 15 times. No other medium can provide that level of exposure.

2. *Continuity.* Outdoor provides 24-hour coverage. Whereas other media can be ignored or their exposure is dependent on the habits of the audience, outdoor can't be turned off, fast-forwarded, put aside, or left unopened. The outdoor message is always working to increase purchases and profits (see Exhibit 12.3).

3. *Cost efficiency.* From a cost standpoint, outdoor is the most efficient of all mass media. Outdoor costs seven times less than television, three times less than newspapers, and half as much as radio.

4. *Complement to other media.* A relatively small budget allocation to outdoor will result in substantial increases in audience delivery. For example, outdoor combined with television significantly increases frequency while decreasing the cost per rating point.

The major disadvantages of outdoor are the following:

1. *Creative limitations and low attention levels.* Since exposure to outdoor is both involuntary and brief, there is little depth of exposure, even among a product's most loyal customers. It is estimated that most signs are seen for less than 10 seconds by the average audience member. In addition, the average outdoor "copy" is 7 to 10 words.

2. *Little audience selectivity.* For the most part, the medium offers little selectivity among demographic groups and is more a shotgun than a rifle. However, national, regional, and local advertisers can tailor their messages to reach specific audiences by pinpointing certain neighborhoods or specific streets such as roads that lead to stadiums or ballparks.

3. *Availability problems.* In some communities, demand for certain premium outdoor sites means some advertisers cannot be served with their first choice in locations.

Despite these disadvantages, properly executed outdoor advertising can be an inexpensive method of gaining immediate product visibility.

EXHIBIT
12.3

....

Outdoor is the medium that can't be ignored.

(Courtesy: Eight-Sheet Outdoor Advertising Association.)

The Image of Outdoor

As we have seen, a major advantage of outdoor advertising is that it is a big, intrusive medium that can't be ignored. While this may be a characteristic with great charm for the advertising community, it is a source of significant criticism among environmentalists and other public activists. They have long lobbied Congress, state legislatures, and city councils to ban or severely restrict the outdoor industry. The industry is continually frustrated by the fact that many of the examples of irresponsible outdoor signs are not part of the regulated, standardized medium. Instead, they are often on-premise signs that, ironically, are often specifically excluded from legislation against outdoor in order to protect local merchants.

Highway Beautification Act of 1965

Federal law that controls outdoor signs in noncommercial, nonindustrial areas.

Federal control of outdoor advertising began in earnest with the Highway Beautification Act of 1965 (known as the Lady Bird Bill after Mrs. Lyndon Johnson, who actively supported the legislation). The act restricts the placement of outdoor signs along interstate highways and provides stiff penalties for states that fail to control signs within 660 feet of interstate roads. Since passage of the legislation, the number of signs has been reduced from 1.2 million to less than 400,000. Those that remain are concentrated in commercially zoned areas.

Today, the degree of outdoor control varies tremendously from one locale to another. The most extreme cases are the outright bans in Alaska, Hawaii, Maine, and Vermont. However, during recent years hundreds of local communities have enacted laws limiting or eliminating outdoor posters. In many cases, these state and local laws provided for a phase-out period, many of which are coming due. Throughout the country, outdoor companies are filing suits against various restrictions. The suits tend to take one of two approaches:

1. *It is a violation of free speech to limit outdoor advertising.* Most legal scholars predict that this stance has little chance of success. As we will discuss in Chapter 25, the Supreme Court has consistently ruled that commercial speech lacks the First Amendment protection of other forms of discourse.

2. *Outdoor companies must be reimbursed for loss of property.* Whether or not local government must compensate outdoor companies has not been settled by the courts. However, many attorneys think that there is precedent for requiring such payment by local governments. Everyone agrees that few cities will move ahead with such restrictions if taxpayer funds would be required for compensation.

Exclusionary zones (outdoor)

Industry code of conduct that prohibits the advertising of products within 500 feet of churches, schools, or hospitals of any products that cannot be used legally by children.

Regardless of the final ruling on these issues, the outdoor industry would like to avoid further public controversy. The industry has moved on a number of fronts to improve its image and create positive public relations in the communities it serves. One step to counteract negative publicity toward the industry has been the enactment of a voluntary Code of Advertising Practice by the OAAA.

As part of this code, outdoor companies are asked to limit in a market the number of billboards that carry messages about products that cannot be sold to minors. Specifically, the code asks that member companies "establish exclusionary zones which prohibit advertisements of all products illegal for sale to minors which are either intended to be read from, or within 500 feet of,

EXHIBIT

12.4

· · · · · · · · · · · · · · · · · · ·

The international children's symbol was adopted by the OAAA to mark billboards that are "off-limits" to alcohol and tobacco ads.

(Courtesy: Outdoor Advertising Association of America and the Institute of Outdoor Advertising.)

established places of worship, primary and secondary schools and hospitals." Furthermore, such "off-limit" boards will carry a decal featuring the symbol of a child (see Exhibit 12.4).

Outdoor companies also are engaging in public service campaigns within their communities. Throughout the country outdoor companies are supporting advertising for homeless shelters, anti-drug-abuse programs, help lines for battered women, and environmental campaigns (see Exhibit 12.5). Outdoor advertising is slowly educating the public to the fact that the standardized outdoor medium is an enlightened corporate citizen. However, outdoor must continue to overcome public misconceptions and simultaneously work to bring new advertisers into the medium, all at a time of increased competition for advertising dollars.

EXHIBIT

12.5

· · · · · · · · · · · · · · · · · · ·

Outdoor advertising provides unique, eye-catching visuals.

(Courtesy: Cramer/Krasselt and Salt River Project.)

The Outdoor Advertising Plan

National advertisers rarely use outdoor as their primary medium. Consequently, it is extremely important to plan the outdoor portion of the total advertising campaign in a manner that will assure maximum efficiency and support to other advertising and promotional vehicles. Planning and execution of outdoor follow many of the basic rules of advertising in other media. However, there are a number of unique features of outdoor that an advertiser and its agency must consider. Let's summarize the basic steps in developing an outdoor advertising campaign:

1. As with any advertising situation, we must start with the role that we expect outdoor to play in the overall marketing and advertising strategy. Most outdoor advertising is used as either an introduction of a new product or event (such as a sale) or as a reminder to keep consumers continually aware of a brand. With its headline format, outdoor is rarely suited to offer a complete sales message (see Exhibit 12.6).

2. Once the outdoor objectives are clearly defined, we are ready to move to the planning of the schedule. The first step in planning the campaign is to identify the target audience and the markets in which outdoor will be used. A number of sources exist to provide outdoor audience demographics and exposure. Among the most important are the following:

- **_Traffic Audit Bureau for Media Measurement._** TAB is a an independent, nonprofit organization that provides circulation verification for the out-of-home industry. TAB not only measures outdoor audiences but establishes standards for visibility of outdoor signs.

- **_Simmons Market Research Bureau._** The Simmons Market Research Bureau (SMRB) is a national consumer study conducted annually with over 19,000 respondents. SMRB data provide analyses of target audiences, media usage habits, and outdoor delivery for 750 consumer products and services.

- **_Telmar._** The Telmar system is used by most major advertisers and agencies. Telmar provides media cost comparisons and media mix analyses to assist in the media planning function.

- **_Leading National Advertisers._** Leading National Advertisers (LNA) provides advertising revenue data for all product types, brands, and markets for both

Traffic Audit Bureau for Media Measurement (TAB)

An organization designed to investigate how many people pass and may see a given outdoor sign, to establish a method of evaluating traffic measuring a market.

EXHIBIT 12.6

Outdoor is primarily a "headline" medium with short copy and strong visuals.

(Courtesy: Eight-Sheet Outdoor Advertising Association.)

painted bulletins and poster panels. LNA is the source for competitive spending data necessary to make strategic marketing decisions.

- **The Harris Donovan Model for Outdoor Planning.** One of the newest tools for planning outdoor media is the Harris Donovan Model. Available for personal computers, the Harris Donovan Model measures the potential audience exposed to an outdoor campaign. The model combines cost and audience information in order to determine if specific campaign objectives have been met with a particular outdoor campaign.

- **Buyer's Guide to Outdoor Advertising.** This volume provides cost information for outdoor advertising in all markets where it is available.

3. The next step in the outdoor campaign is contacting the local outdoor company to make arrangements for production and posting of signs. The basic business unit of the outdoor industry is the local outdoor company known as a *plant*. Its stock in trade are the locations it has leased or bought under local zoning regulations permitting the erection of signs. Having acquired a location, the plant builds a structure at its own expense, sells the advertising space on it (technically, leases the space), posts or paints the advertiser's message, and is responsible for maintaining the board and the ad in good condition during the life of the advertiser's contract. As we will discuss later in this chapter, most major market outdoor plants are part of large national outdoor companies that allow an advertiser to place outdoor advertising in a number of cities without going through individual offices.

4. Post-buy inspection (riding the boards). After the posters are up, an in-market check of poster locations should be made. This inspection determines if proper locations were used and that the signs were posted or painted properly.

The fact that national outdoor is not a primary medium should not suggest that fundamental principles of advertising planning do not apply. In some respects, planning in outdoor is even more complex than in other media. As a supplement to other media, planners must make certain that the characteristics and objectives of outdoor mesh properly with those of more dominant media. The complementary nature of outdoor is an overriding concern in most outdoor schedules. The planner must be certain that outdoor can, in fact, reinforce the media schedule in a cost-efficient manner.

FORMS OF OUTDOOR ADVERTISING

As we mentioned at the outset of this chapter, outdoor is only one of several categories of out-of-home advertising. However, in terms of revenues, public familiarity, and long-term usage, the two basic forms of out-of-home are posters and painted bulletins (see Exhibit 12.7). In both vehicles, the message is designed by the advertising agency. The design is then reproduced on paper and posted on panels. The larger painted bulletins are prepared by outdoor company artists either in a studio or on site.

Poster Panels

The most common type of poster is really two posters in one. Bleed and 30-sheet posters, which use the same frame, constitute the typical highway billboard with which we are so familiar. These posters are available in some 9,000

Harris Donovan Model (outdoor)

Computerized system of measuring the audience exposed to an outdoor showing.

Plant operator

In outdoor advertising the local company who arranges to lease, erect, and maintain the outdoor sign and to sell the advertising space on it.

Riding the boards

Inspecting an outdoor showing after posting.

Poster panel

A standard surface on which outdoor posters are placed. The posting surface is of sheet metal. An ornamental molding of standard green forms the frame. The standard poster panel is 12 feet high and 25 feet long (outside dimensions).

EXHIBIT

12.7

. . . .

Posters and bulletins make up the standardized outdoor industry.

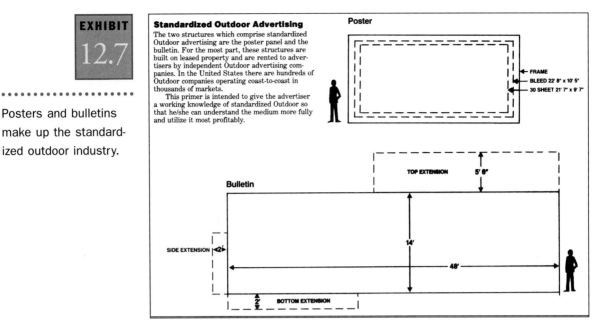

Standardized Outdoor Advertising

The two structures which comprise standardized Outdoor advertising are the poster panel and the bulletin. For the most part, these structures are built on leased property and are rented to advertisers by independent Outdoor advertising companies. In the United States there are hundreds of Outdoor companies operating coast-to-coast in thousands of markets.

This primer is intended to give the advertiser a working knowledge of standardized Outdoor so that he/she can understand the medium more fully and utilize it most profitably.

(Courtesy: Institute of Outdoor Advertising.)

communities. Poster buys can be made for a single location or total national coverage.

The standard poster panel measures 12 feet by 25 feet. The bleed poster either prints to the edge of the frame or uses blanking paper matching the background of the poster. The term *bleed* is, of course, borrowed from the bleed magazine ad, which has no border. The term *sheet* originated in the days when presses were much smaller and it took many sheets to cover a poster panel. Today, presses can print much larger sheets, but the old space designations are still used.

. . . .

Illuminated posters

75 to 80% of all outdoor posters are illuminated for 24-hour exposure.

. . . .

Poster displays are sold on the basis of *illuminated* and *nonilluminated* panels. Normally, poster contracts are for 30 days, with discounts for longer periods. Those panels in locations with high traffic volume are normally illuminated for 24-hour exposure. A typical poster showing will consist of 70–80 percent illuminated posters. When buying an outdoor showing, the advertiser is given the number of displays, the number that are illuminated and nonilluminated, the monthly and per-panel cost, and total circulation or exposure.

The Eight-Sheet Poster[3]

. . . .

Eight-sheet poster

Outdoor poster used in urban areas, about one-fourth the size of the standard 30-sheet poster. Also called *junior poster.*

. . . .

One of the fastest-growing types of outdoor advertising is the eight-sheet poster. Eight-sheet posters measure 5 feet by 11 feet, about one-sixth the size of 30-sheet posters (see Exhibit 12.8). The posters, sometimes called *junior posters,* were originally developed to provide small, local businesses with affordable outdoor advertising, but when the Eight-Sheet Outdoor Advertising Association established a standard poster size, it enabled national and regional advertisers to use the medium throughout the country. Research shows that these small displays, placed low and close to the street deliver dramatic ad-

---

[3]Unless otherwise noted, material in this section is provided by the Eight-Sheet Outdoor Advertising Association, Inc.

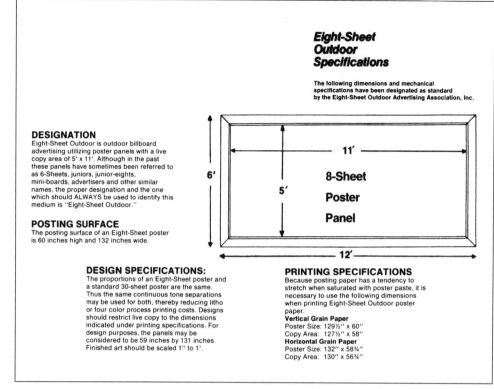

DESIGNATION
Eight-Sheet Outdoor is outdoor billboard advertising utilizing poster panels with a live copy area of 5' x 11'. Although in the past these panels have sometimes been referred to as 6-Sheets, juniors, junior-eights, mini-boards, advertisers and other similar names, the proper designation and the one which should ALWAYS be used to identify this medium is "Eight-Sheet Outdoor."

POSTING SURFACE
The posting surface of an Eight-Sheet poster is 60 inches high and 132 inches wide.

Eight-Sheet Outdoor Specifications

The following dimensions and mechanical specifications have been designated as standard by the Eight-Sheet Outdoor Advertising Association, Inc.

DESIGN SPECIFICATIONS:
The proportions of an Eight-Sheet poster and a standard 30-sheet poster are the same. Thus the same continuous tone separations may be used for both, thereby reducing litho or four color process printing costs. Designs should restrict live copy to the dimensions indicated under printing specifications. For design purposes, the panels may be considered to be 59 inches by 131 inches. Finished art should be scaled 1" to 1'.

PRINTING SPECIFICATIONS
Because posting paper has a tendency to stretch when saturated with poster paste, it is necessary to use the following dimensions when printing Eight-Sheet Outdoor poster paper.
Vertical Grain Paper
Poster Size: 129½" x 60"
Copy Area: 127½" x 58"
Horizontal Grain Paper
Poster Size: 132" x 58¾"
Copy Area: 130" x 56¾"

(Courtesy: Eight-Sheet Outdoor Advertising Association.)

vertising visibility and impact at a reasonable cost. Exhibit 12.9 demonstrates how eight-sheet posters compare to the 30-sheet poster.

Since most small businesses generate 90 percent of their sales from customers who live within a three-mile radius, eight-sheet posters are an ideal way to deliver targeted advertising messages in these well-defined trade areas while avoiding paying for costly waste circulation (see Exhibit 12.10). One of the strengths of eight-sheet posters is that they often conform to local zoning regulations that exclude larger boards.

Another advantage of eight-sheet posters is their cost efficiency. In Washington, D.C., an eight-sheet poster costs as little as $135. A 12-month campaign offering full coverage of the Washington market costs less than $40,000 per

Comparative Summary

	8-SHEETS	30-SHEETS
Visibility	30%	37%
Brand Awareness	80%	73%
Readership	29%	29%
Re-Examination	1.3	1.5
Recall	Equal	Equal
Male Vs Female	Equal	Equal
Effective Circulation	88%	100%
Cost (Average)	25%	100%
Cost-Effectiveness (Average)	3X	1X

(Courtesy: Eight-Sheet Outdoor Advertising Association.)

(Courtesy: United Advertisers and Leisure Curl.)

month, less than one-tenth the cost of the same level of TV commercial exposure. As you can see from Exhibit 12.9, eight-sheet is able to generate extremely high levels of impressions. CPM levels for eight-sheet posters are less than $1 and are clearly the best bargain among all major media.

Eight-sheet posters are handled by special poster plants, but frequently appear concurrently with 30-sheet showings in a market. The Eight-Sheet Outdoor Advertising Association (ESOAA) was founded to promote the interests of the eight-sheet poster medium. Currently they are available in some 2,500 markets.

Painted Bulletins

Painted bulletins are the largest and most prominent type of outdoor advertising. Painted bulletins are of two types: *permanent* and the more popular *rotary*. The permanent bulletin remains at a fixed location and can vary in size, since it is never moved. The rotary bulletin is a standardized sign that is three times larger (14 feet by 48 feet) than the standard poster and provides greater impact than traditional posters. It can be moved from site to site to ensure maximum coverage of a market over a period of months. Both types of bulletins are located at choice sites along heavily traveled thoroughfares. They are almost always illuminated.

Rotary bulletins (outdoor)

Movable painted bulletins that are moved from one fixed location to another one in the market at regular intervals. The locations are viewed and approved in advance by the advertiser.

Bulletins are approximately four times more expensive than posters. In recent years, the basic bulletin has been augmented with special embellishments, such as cutouts, free-standing letters, special lighting effects, fiber optics, and inflatables. Painted bulletins contracts are usually for a minimum of one year; however, short-term contracts are available at a higher monthly rate.

The rotary bulletin gives the advertiser the advantages of the greater impact of the painted bulletin along with more coverage and penetration than a single site could deliver. The rotary bulletin can be moved every 30, 60, or 90 days, so that during a 12-month period consumers throughout the market will have seen the advertiser's message.

Spectaculars

Spectacular

An outdoor sign built to order, designed to be conspicuous for its location, size, lights, motion, or action. The costliest form of outdoor advertising.

As the name implies, outdoor spectaculars are large, usually unique displays designed for maximum attention in high traffic areas. They may consist of special lighting or other types of ingenious material and innovations. In some cases they utilize a building as the canvas for the message. The cost of spectaculars is very expensive and both production and space rentals are normally negotiated on a one-time basis. However, the minimum contract period for most spectaculars is usually a year.

In the near future, we may see the combination of outdoor and video as a standard feature of outdoor. Regardless of what new technology comes to outdoor, it is obvious that the static, paper poster soon may be history.

"In the future, . . . outdoor advertising companies may be able to change the image, the text—a billboard's whole look—with the push of a computer button because billboards across the country may be connected via satellite. For example, a fast-food chain could advertise breakfast goodies for the morning crowd, and later, lunch/evening meals by changing images and copy in a matter of seconds. Technology for billboards to function as video screens exists today . . . but at this time costs don't justify its use as a mass-market tool."[4]

THE ELEMENTS OF OUTDOOR

Once the objectives of an outdoor advertising plan have been established, the media planner begins the job of executing the campaign. The outdoor campaign combines three elements: designing, buying, and verifying. In this section, we will examine the basic guidelines that will ensure that your outdoor messages have the greatest chance of achieving the desired marketing objectives.

Designing

Designing an outdoor display is among the most difficult tasks for a creative team. Creating a picture and a few words to be seen by fast-moving traffic at distances ranging up to 500 is hard enough. To do so in a manner that moves customers to buy a product adds a dimension not found in other media. However, outdoor is one of the most enjoyable media to work with from a creative standpoint. Its size and color allow maximize creativity without the constraints of other advertising vehicles.

Copy. Outdoor only allows a headline, usually no more than seven words. Unlike copy in traditional media, there is no theme development and copy amplification. Conciseness is not only a virtue; it is a necessity. Advertisers have learned to work with these constraints to make outdoor among the most creative contemporary advertising (see Exhibit 12.11).

Color. Color is one of the primary advantages of outdoor. However, color must be chosen carefully to create easy readability. Outdoor designers use those colors that create high contrast in both *hue* (red, green, etc.) and *value* (a measure of lightness or darkness). For example, Exhibit 12.12 demonstrates 18 combinations of colors with 1 being the most visible and 18 the least visible.

Type. Typefaces in outdoor should be simple, clear, and easy to read. Some of the basic rules of outdoor type and lettering include the following:

- **The use of capitals should be kept to a minimum.**

- **Considerable care should be given to spacing between letters and between words.**

---

[4]Laura Dalton, "Outdoor Meets the Electronic Age," *Gannetteer,* October 1993, p. 16.

EXHIBIT
12.11

Outdoor can be an
effective medium for
local retailers.

- **Whatever typeface is selected, the ultrabold or ultrathin version should be avoided.**

- **A simpler typeface is better for outdoor.**

Exhibit 12.13 demonstrates each of these guidelines with the preferred version on the right.

In a major study sponsored by Gannett Outdoor and the University of Alberta, researchers found that effective outdoor followed a number of guidelines. Among the most important were the following: The greater the clarity of the type, the higher the recall; the more intriguing or humorous the message the higher the recall; and, perhaps most importantly, out-of-home messages with fewer concepts have more impact.[5]

EXHIBIT
12.12

Some color combinations are much more effective than others for outdoor advertising.

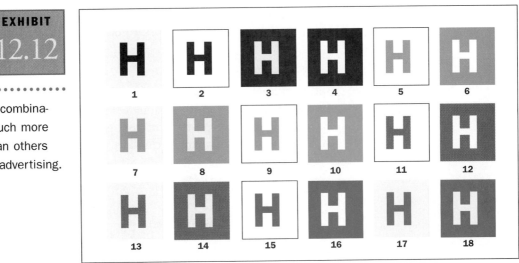

[5]Riccardo A. Davis, "Outdoor Ad Creativity Is Focus of Gannett Study," *Advertising Age,* October 18, 1993, p. 12.

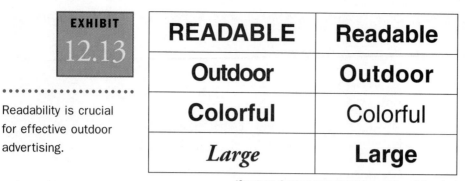
EXHIBIT 12.13

Readability is crucial for effective outdoor advertising.

Showing

Outdoor posters are bought by groups, referred to as *showings.* The size of a showing is referred to as a 100-GRP showing or a 75- or 50-GRP showing, depending on the gross rating points of the individual boards selected.

Buying Outdoor

Both the methods and terminology used in buying outdoor advertising are different in a number of ways from those used in other media. Poster advertising is purchased on the basis of *gross rating points* (GRPs) or *showings.* You will recall from our earlier discussion of television, that one GRP is equal to 1 percent of the population. Showings normally are bought in units of 50 or 100 and measure the *duplicated* audience reached by a poster *allotment.* An allotment is the number of posters in a market. A 50 showing in a market means that we will have daily exposures to our outdoor messages equal to 50 percent of the adult population of the market.

The audience for an outdoor showing is called the *daily effective circulation* (DEC) and is calculated by using the following formula:

Let us assume the 24-hour traffic count = 36,000

For nonilluminated posters, the traffic count is multiplied by .45; therefore, .45 × 36,000 = 16,200 adult DEC

For illuminated posters the traffic count is multiplied by .64; therefore, .65 × 36,000 = 23,040

Let's examine a market and work through these calculations:

Market: Metropolis
Population: 800,000
Audience level purchased: 50 GRPs (showing)
Allotment: 26 posters (20 illuminated; 6 nonilluminated)
Explanation: Our 26-poster allotment generated a DEC of 400,000. We calculate this by the following formula:

$$\text{GRP showing} = \frac{\text{daily effective circulation}}{\text{market population}}$$

$$50 \text{ GRP showing} = \frac{400,000}{800,000}$$

You may not compare GRP levels in markets of different size, except as a measure of advertising weight and intensity. For example, a 50 GRP might require an allotment of 50 or 100 posters in a larger market. By the same token, in a market of 2 million population, a 50 GRP buy would generate a

DEC of 1 million, not 400,000. One final difference in buying outdoor compared to other media is that the agency commission in outdoor is *16.67* percent rather than the standard 15 percent.

Verifying

You will remember that any outdoor campaign should be reviewed for the suitability of poster locations. In addition, this process of "riding the boards" is crucial to make sure that the proper number of posters are up, the correct proportion of illuminated and nonilluminated posters have been used, and the posters are properly maintained with no flags or tears in the paper. This process is similar to the submission of tearsheets in print advertising or verification forms in broadcast.

While local advertisers can handle their own verification, this process is impractical for a national advertiser. Many national advertisers hire audit firms that specialize in outdoor advertising to conduct an audit of the outdoor showing in each market. Verification assures the advertiser that the posting was done properly and according to agreed-upon specifications. When there is some discrepancy, an audit allows the advertiser to obtain make-goods from the plant operator.

Outdoor Networks

For many years, national outdoor was considered among the most difficult media to buy. Not only was the terminology and units of sale unique to the medium, but a national advertiser had to deal with a multitude of local plants to complete a schedule. However, during the 1980s outdoor moved aggressively to make buying space easier. Two related factors converged to allow media planners to buy outdoor in much the same way they purchase other advertising vehicles: (1) consolidation of ownership within the industry and (2) the growth of outdoor networks.

During the past decade, local, independent outdoor plants have been purchased by national outdoor companies. These national companies began to offer easy access to the markets they served and special discounts to advertisers using a number of their plants.

This consolidation was a great improvement for agencies and advertisers wanting to buy outdoor on a national basis. However, advertisers were faced with the problem that many markets were not covered by a particular national outdoor company. Consequently, advertisers still had to "fill in" their schedules by buying markets on an individual basis. The outdoor network allows advertisers to buy virtually every market, not just those where a single company owns a plant.

These networks are either cooperative efforts of plant operators or independent companies such as the rep firms we discussed in earlier media chapters. For example, Outdoor Network, USA was formed by Gannett to link its owned plants with plants in markets that it does not serve. The intent of the outdoor network is similar to the unwired radio networks and magazine networks that we discussed in earlier chapters.

MEASURING OUTDOOR

A major problem for outdoor advertising is providing accurate audience measurement. Trying to determine audience estimates for a mobile population is extremely demanding. Witness the difficulty experienced by both radio and television in gathering ratings information. Outdoor faces the problem that national advertisers increasingly demand better data. However, since these advertisers generally place a small portion of their total advertising budget in outdoor, advertisers are unwilling to support the expenditure of significant dollars in outdoor audience research.

Despite these problems, the outdoor industry has made progress in providing sophisticated research and standardized policies to advertisers. There are three areas where outdoor is coming more in line with other media's ability to provide audience measurement and delivery data:

1. *Computer-based systems that relate traffic counts to census data in selected neighborhoods.* This information allows advertisers to place outdoor signs in a manner that targets demographic audience segments within a larger market.

2. *Standardized location criteria for poster locations.* The TAB has developed a *Performance Reporting and Auditing System* (PRAS), which allows advertisers to judge each poster location against all others. The PRAS not only provides traffic counts at each poster location but also factors in variables such as visibility, competing signs at that location, illumination, and type of street where the poster is located.

3. *Guaranteed rating points for advertisers.* As the outdoor industry seeks to encourage more advertising from package goods and retail advertisers, it must adopt similar practices to other media. The industry must first offer credible audience data and then market these data just as print media promote their audited circulation and broadcast media their ratings.[6]

In one of the more unusual examples of guaranteeing outdoor advertising performance, Gateway Outdoor Advertising provided free billboard and bus space to Cybergenics Quick Trim weight loss systems. The advertising rate was based on the number of sales generated to a toll-free number listed in the ads. The president of Gateway explained that the company wanted to "show the effectiveness of the medium—build a partnership, go outside the traditional role and bridge a relationship with the company."[7]

Trends in Outdoor Advertising

The future of outdoor advertising looks much brighter than it did only a few years ago. There are a number of positive trends that bode well for outdoor as a growing media into the next century:

■ ***The lowest costs of any advertising medium.*** Regardless of the method of comparison with other media, outdoor provides audience delivery at bargain prices. The CPM for outdoor is the lowest of any print or broadcast medium, cost increases during the past decade have been minimal, and both reach and frequency levels are unsurpassed by other advertising vehicles.

---

[6]Riccardo A. Davis, "OAAA Mulls New Use for Its Auditing Service Data," *Advertising Age,* May 24, 1993, p. 38.

[7]Riccardo A. Davis, "Gateway Ties Payment of Outdoor Ads to Sales," *Advertising Age,* May 3, 1993, p. 16.

- **Diversification of the types of advertisers using the medium.** While tobacco and alcohol remain major clients for outdoor, the influx of retail, automotive, and package-goods advertisers in recent years has been encouraging.

- **Strong creativity.** The future offers the prospect of computerized displays, satellite transmission to outdoor displays, and the use of fiber optics. When these systems are in place, advertisers will be able to create a limitless array of creative messages and do so with an immediacy that will allow them to react to any changes in market conditions.

- **Improved research data.** Outdoor is providing much improved audience information and providing demographic and geographic data allowing advertisers to pinpoint audiences in a manner never before possible.

- **Meeting the public relations challenge.** Outdoor must continue to improve its public image as well as market the medium to advertisers. Finally, the industry needs to find areas of accommodation with environmentalists and other critics. Outdoor must also get the message out to the general public that it is a responsible member of the community. For example, it is doubtful the public realizes that the number of outdoor signs have decreased in the past two decades or the nuances of conforming versus nonconforming signs.

TRANSIT ADVERTISING

Transit advertising encompasses a number of formats and distinctly different advertising vehicles. Among the major forms of transit advertising are the following:

- **Bus exteriors (see Exhibit 12.14)**

- **Taxi exteriors**

- **Bus and commuter rail interiors**

- **Commuter station posters**

- **Miscellaneous displays such as terminal clocks and air terminal posters**

EXHIBIT
12.14

. . . .

Transit advertising is an efficient means of reaching a mobile population, especially in urban areas.

(Courtesy: Schwartz & Kaplan Advertising, Coral Gables, FL.)

C. Donald Williams Advertising, Inc.

SUITE 200   342 SOUTH SALINA ST.   SYRACUSE, NY 13202
CALL COLLECT (315) 422-2213

SPECIFICATIONS
Bus Advertising Displays

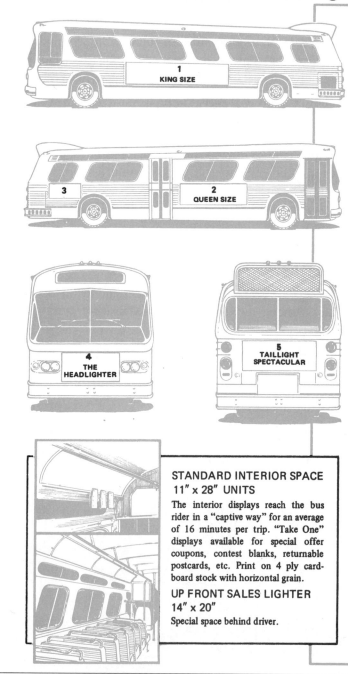

1 KING SIZE

30" x 144"
Street Side or Curb Side of Bus

The largest poster on the bus—a moving billboard at eye level—carrying its sales message daily to people downtown, in plants or offices, in suburbs or shopping centers.

2 QUEEN SIZE

30" x 88"
Curb Side of Bus

The Queen is located on the curb side of the bus between the entrance and exit doors. The Queen reaches people on the move whether walking, riding or boarding a bus. Sometimes used in conjunction with Kings to cover both sides of the street.

3 TRAVELING DISPLAY

21" x 44"
Curb Side or Street Side of Bus

The Traveling Display is our baby billboard used when high frequency and high reach is the priority but budget is tight. Can be used in conjunction with Fronts and Rears for outstanding results.

4 THE HEADLIGHTER

21" x 40"
Front of Bus

The front display is called the Headlighter. Visible in any kind of weather, the Headlighter reaches pedestrians, bus riders and drivers or passengers of other vehicles.

5 TAILLIGHT SPECTACULAR

21" x 70"
Rear of Bus

The rear spectacular offers high visibility and readability. Especially high impact and readership from auto drivers and passengers who follow immediately behind the bus. Highest exposure at traffic lights and intersections.

STANDARD INTERIOR SPACE
11" x 28" UNITS

The interior displays reach the bus rider in a "captive way" for an average of 16 minutes per trip. "Take One" displays available for special offer coupons, contest blanks, returnable postcards, etc. Print on 4 ply cardboard stock with horizontal grain.

UP FRONT SALES LIGHTER
14" x 20"

Special space behind driver.

(Courtesy: C. Donald Williams Advertising Inc.)

EXHIBIT
12.15

Transit advertising offers
a number of options.

390

Exhibit 12.15 offers a summary of several of the primary forms of interior and exterior bus displays. The king-sized posters dominate bus advertising space and are the most used format for both national and local transit advertisers (see Exhibit 12.16).

Transit provides a number of advantages to advertisers and, although still a small medium by total advertising standards, has grown at a significant rate in the past several years. Estimated revenues for transit are approximately $300 million. The popularity of transit advertising are due to a number of factors:

1. *Transit prices have low overall cost and CPM levels.* Transit prices are even lower than traditional outdoor, less than $1 CPM in many markets.

2. *Transit reaches prospects in the marketplace and is attracting an increasingly upscale audience as public transportation becomes more popular in many cities.* In the case of interior signs, advertisers are reaching a captive audience of riders who average almost 20 minutes per trip. The nature of the transit audience allows somewhat longer messages than outdoor signs.

3. *Creative opportunities are increasing.* The New York City subway system recently approved a plan to install lighted station posters that were purchased by major national advertisers such as The Gap and Calvin Klein.[8]

4. The repetitive nature of the transit audience quickly builds high levels of frequency over relatively short periods.

Transit advertising provides a low-cost option for reaching a mobile, urban audience. With the likelihood that mass transit will be more popular in the coming years, the growth of transit advertising is assured. Added to its ability to reach this audience is the fact that municipal governments are seeking

EXHIBIT 12.16

Transit advertising provides exposure throughout a market.

(Courtesy: C. Donald Williams Advertising Inc.)

[8]Hanna Liebman, "New Subway Posters Light Up the Tunnels to Attract Upscale Ads," *Mediaweek*, February 8, 1993, p. 4.

new sources of revenue and transit advertising rental space is one that is readily available.

SHELTER ADVERTISING

With traditional out-of-home media facing falling revenues and legal restrictions, shelter advertising is a major growth area. Shelter advertising is normally used as a complementary medium to outdoor posters. It has the advantage of being able to be used in areas where zoning regulations ban outdoor. In addition, shelter messages reach not only bus riders but vehicular traffic. In fact, as much as 90 percent of the total shelter audience is vehicular. Shelter advertising has grown to 26,000 panels in the United States.

According to Connie Barry, president of the Shelter Advertising Association, shelter advertising has three major advantages:

1. *It is an extremely inexpensive medium.* CPM levels are among the lowest of any advertising medium. It also is similar to other out-of-home media in that it generates high reach and frequency in a short time. Rates are available from the Shelter Advertising Association's *Buyers Guide.* (Exhibit 12.17)

2. *Advertisers can use shelter advertising to target specific markets.* For example, a packaged good may use shelters in front of supermarkets or jeanswear on the college campus.

3. *Shelter advertising is illuminated for 24-hour reach and provides maximum exposure and awareness.* With 4 × 6 signs, shelter advertising provides stopping power for both pedestrian and vehicular traffic. Unlike other media, it rarely suffers from clutter from other competing messages. Exhibit 12.18 shows some examples of outstanding shelter advertising.

As we mentioned earlier in this chapter, the out-of-home medium has been king for several years to diversify its advertising categories. Shelter advertising has been successful in doing this. One of the major categories is fashion and apparel. Advertisers such as Bugle Boy, Levi's, and Esprit have been major buyers of the medium. The success of shelter advertising may benefit other forms of out-of-home as advertisers consider these media based on their shelter experience.

Shelter advertising is one of the fastest-growing segments of transit advertising. Shelters provide a copy area that is 46 by 67 inches that is backlit for maximum visibility.

It is obvious that shelter advertising, although accounting for a small portion of all advertising revenues, will continue to grow at a faster rate than overall advertising expenditures. As new product categories come into the medium, we may even see larger increases in the shelter sector. Finally, rather than facing the regulatory problems of outdoor, the revenues generated by shelter posters are often shared with municipal transit companies, making the medium a revenue producer to many cities facing tight budgets.

SUMMARY

As advertisers continue to search for affordable alternatives to traditional media, out-of-home is sure to increase in terms of total advertising revenues. Out-of-home media serve as reminders and introductions to products as well

TRANSTOP
1994 RATE CARD

Cost is per panel per month

Quantity	1 Month	3 Months	6 Months	12 Months
5–19	$405	$390	$375	$360
20–39	$390	$375	$360	$345
40+	$375	$360	$345	$325

Agency Commissionable at 15%. Production included rates available on request.

TERMS
Bills are rendered monthly and payable on receipt. No cash discounts. Contracts may only be canceled on sixty (60) days written notice.

ROTATION AND ILLUMINATION
Posters are rotated every 30 days to cover additional audiences every month. All facings are backlit to give the advertiser 24 hour visibility.

AUDITED CIRCULATION DATA
Average Daily Effective Circulation: 11,580 impressions per panel (Based on Adults 18+)
Audited by Traffic Audit Bureau for Media Measurement (TAB) - April, 1991
Based on the Average DEC of 11,580, the number of panels per showing are:

Gross Rating Points/ Showings	Number of Illuminated Panels		
	Minneapolis	St. Paul	Twin Cities
100	68	30	98
75	51	23	74
50	34	15	49
25	17	8	25

PRODUCTION
Dimensions
      Overall poster size: 47-1/2" wide × 68-3/4" high
      Live copy area: 46" × 67"
Recommended printing stocks are opaline or any paper stock which can be backlit.
Cost of production not included in rates. Production estimates and sources for production available on request. Recommended overage of 10% of panels purchased per month. Vertical format is proportional to a magazine ad.

SHIPPING
Posters must be received at least
10 days prior to the posting date.

Ship to: Transtop, Suite 820
      One Appletree Square
      Minneapolis, MN 55425

Number of Shelter Panels:
Minneapolis - 400
St. Paul - 200
Posting Dates:
Minneapolis - 1st of the Month
St. Paul - 15th of the Month

TAB MEMBER. "Ask if it's audited."

EXHIBIT

12.17

· · · · · · · · · · · · · · · · · · · ·

Transit advertising is among the most inexpensive means of reaching a mass audience.

as increase brand awareness. They do so in a largely unobtrusive manner that allows consumers to be exposed on a continual basis. Out-of-home increasingly encompasses a number of creative options to meet the needs of any advertiser (see Exhibit 12.19).

One of the major advantages of out-of-home is the growing standardization across the industry. In past years, outdoor and major transit systems offered standard signage, but many types of displays were unique to each market with little appeal to national advertisers. The out-of-home industry has taken giant steps to solve this situation (see Exhibit 12.20) and no doubt will reap the benefits in the future.

(Courtesy: Shelter Advertising Association)

Shelter Advertising is
an effective sales tool
for an urban audience.

EXHIBIT

12.19

· · · · · · · · · · · · · · · · · · · ·

The means of reaching the outdoor home audience are limitless.

(Courtesy: National Aerial Advertising.)

A growing phenomenon within the out-of-home industry is the consolidation of ownership among transit, shelter, and outdoor companies. Once distinct industries, more and more companies are offering full-service out-of-home advertising. For example, Gannett Outdoor owns New York Subway Advertising and the largest transit firm, TDI, now receives half its revenues from outdoor. Even Patrick Outdoor, a major outdoor plant owner, has gained the transit concession on the BART system in San Francisco.

Overall there are more than 30 types of out-of-home advertising signs. Advertisers will spend more than $3 billion in these formats in 1995. The largest category of signs is the 30-sheet poster with 200,000 signs. They are followed by 140,000, 8-sheet posters; 56,000 painted bulletins; and 24,000 transit shelter signs.[9]

If there is a problem with out-of-home, it is that it is a victim of its own success. As more and more companies begin to offer out-of-home alternatives, it becomes more difficult to control the quality of the medium. The established organizations such as the OAAA and the TAA are constantly working with their members and advertisers to ensure that the industry meets the highest standards possible. However, as we noted in the case of nonstandardized outdoor signs, it is extremely difficult to deal with nonmember companies or those that don't have the social responsibility of these major out-of-home organizations.

---

[9]"Outdoor by the Numbers," *Gannetteer,* January 1994, p. 7.

EXHIBIT

12.20

The many faces of out-of-home.

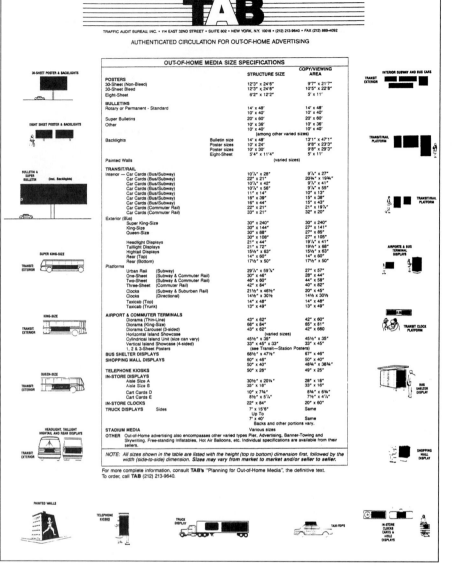

(Courtesy: Traffic Audit Bureau, Inc.)

Questions

1. Why is a diversity of product categories important to the outdoor industry?
2. Why has the term out-of-home replaced outdoor?
3. What are the primary categories of outdoor posters?
4. What is the function of the Traffic Audit Bureau for Media Measurement?
5. Why has transit advertising grown significantly in recent years?
6. What are the primary uses of outdoor for most advertisers?
7. What are the major advantages of the eight-sheet posters?
8. What are the major disadvantages of outdoor posters?

Direct-Response
and **Direct-Mail**
Advertising

CHAPTER 13

CHAPTER OBJECTIVES

Direct-response advertising is one of the fastest-growing segments of advertising and promotion. Virtually every medium, as well as direct mail, vies for customers through direct-response offers. After reading this chapter you will understand:

- **Direct marketing social factors**
- **Privacy issues and the future of direct response**
- **Computer technology and database marketing**
- **Telemarketing and home shopping**
- **Specialized techniques of direct mail**

The emergence of direct-response advertising is one of the primary changes in marketing and promotion during the past 25 years. **Only a few years ago,** direct-response advertising consisted primarily of direct mail and was regarded as a minor medium by most national firms. **Today,** many of the concepts of direct marketing and direct-response advertising are being adopted by virtually all companies.

In addition, both broadcast and print media are finding that direct response is being used by a significant percentage of their advertising clients.

DEFINITION OF TERMS IN DIRECT RESPONSE
Direct Marketing

Direct marketing is the general term that encompasses direct-response and direct-mail advertising as well as their research and support activities. The term *direct marketing* is used when sellers and/or customers deal directly with each other rather than through a retailer or medium. Direct advertising, for example, distinguishes direct-response messages from utilizing some form of mass media. In direct-mail advertising the advertiser has greater control over the communication process than traditional forms of media advertising. It is the advertiser that determines the audience, timing, and production techniques, rather than having these dictated by a medium.

The term *direct marketing* is supplanting the term *mail order* because today so much of the business uses means other than mail. Later in this chapter we will devote our attention to two of these techniques—telemarketing and broadcast direct selling.

Direct-Response Advertising

Many people confuse the terms *direct mail* and *direct response,* sometimes considering them synonymous. In fact, direct response is any advertising used in selling goods directly to consumers. The message doesn't have to come through the mail (though it often does); it can be an advertisement with a coupon in a newspaper, a telephone solicitation, or a magazine ad featuring an 800-number.

THE MODERN DIRECT-RESPONSE INDUSTRY

The growth in direct response is directly attributable to the demand among advertisers for greater accountability of their advertising and the demand for reduction in waste circulation. Among the major benefits that direct response provides are the following:

1. *It is targeted communication.* Unlike most mass media, the advertiser determines exactly who will be reached by the sales message. The copy can be tailored to the demographic, psychographic, and consumption profile of the audience. In addition, both the timing and production of advertising are totally under the control of the advertiser.

2. *Direct response is measurable.* One of the disadvantages of most traditional advertising is that the results can only be estimated. However, in many forms of direct response the results can be computed to the penny. Furthermore, the advertiser is able to measure precisely various messages and other creative alternatives.

3. *The message of direct response is personal.* In the case of direct mail, we can address our audience by name. In other cases, the direct-response medium is so targeted that we know the interests and buying behavior of the audience and can make the message relevant to their needs in a way that

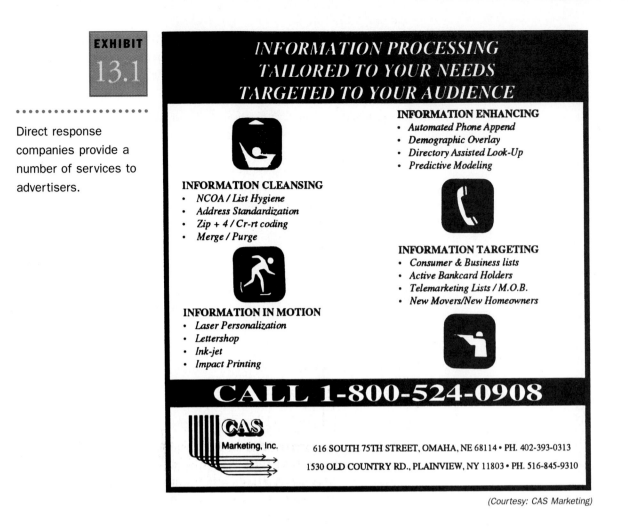

(Courtesy: CAS Marketing)

other forms of marketing communication cannot. A number of companies provide services to advertisers that allow them to greatly enhance their ability to reach a targeted audience (see Exhibit 13.1).

4. *Direct-mail advertising is personal.* In particular, direct mail allows sellers to communication one on one in a personal and private environment.

Despite these many advantages, direct response is not inexpensive. To be cost-efficient with other media, most direct-response advertising must compare the CPM of prospects rather than exposures. However, a properly executed direct-response campaign will reach a much higher percentage of prospects and produce more sales than mass advertising. Direct response is usually not appropriate for products with low profit margins, low price, low involvement, and wide retail distribution.[1]

While direct-response advertising can be both profitable and efficient in many circumstances, research has shown that it is rarely successful working alone. Just as mass advertising often must depend on public relations, sales promotion, and other marketing elements, direct response is dependent on complementary factors. One of the most important elements in direct-response

---

[1]Emily Soell, "The New Direct Marketing," in *What Every Account Executive Should Know about Direct Marketing* (American Association of Advertising Agencies, 1991), p. 10.

selling is the degree of brand equity of the product being sold. It is estimated that consumer interest is as much as 200 percent greater for an offer from a direct marketer with a strong brand compared to the same offer from a less well known direct firm.

A strong brand image is a major asset for direct marketing. Consequently, we are seeing major direct-marketing firms working to build brand equity, often through traditional media advertising. For example, both L.L. Bean and Land's End invest significant funds in magazine advertising to introduce their catalogs as well as to establish a favorable consumer image. The move to build brand images by direct marketers is based on several premises:[2]

1. *Direct marketer must develop multidimensional approaches by using equity-building strategies.*

2. *A brand must stand for something.* It is important to invest in communication that builds the image assets of a brand. A new brand will often require both image and hard-sell promotion to be successful. Remember, in most cases direct-response is requesting a purchase without the benefit of seeing the actual product in a retail setting.

3. *Position a brand away from the clutter.* Direct marketers must invest in establishing clear product differentiation. If an alternative brand can be readily purchased at a retail establishment, one of the primary benefits of direct response has been lost for most consumers.

4. *Precise targeting of consumers is not enough.* Consumers don't care how you found them. They are interested in the products and services you are offering. Direct marketers must shift energy from improving the efficiencies of their selling system to improving the effectiveness of marketing through the building of brand equity.

As we will see in this chapter, direct-response advertising takes many forms and is expected to accomplish a number of marketing objectives. In the future, we will see even more companies opting for direct marketing as a part of their total sales and communication strategy.

GROWTH OF DIRECT-RESPONSE ADVERTISING

Direct-response advertising is one of the fastest-growing methods of promotion. There are a number of factors contributing to this popularity.

Societal Factors

Our fast-paced, time-oriented society is a major reason for the growth of direct marketing. Two-income families value the convenience of direct marketing that allows them more time for enjoying their scarce leisure hours. In addition, an aging population finds out-of-home shopping inconvenient, tiring, or, in some cases, impossible. Many direct-response catalogs are directed toward either working mothers or older customers. Some people simply don't like to shop.

---

[2]Haim Oren, "The New Demands of Brand-Equity Marketing," *DM News,* February 15, 1993, p. 16.

EXHIBIT 13.2

Percentage of Shoppers Purchasing by Phone and Mail

Age	% Purchasers
18–24	12
25–34	24
35–44	23
45–54	15
55+	13

(Source: Shoppers of all Ages, Target Marketing, January, 1993, p. 52.)

It is estimated that almost 100 million Americans purchase some product or service through direct response each year. According to the Simmons Market Research Bureau, telephone and mail direct-response purchasers tend to be between 25 and 44 years old, with younger and older adults less likely to use direct response (see Exhibit 13.2).

Direct-response shopping has increased over 70 percent in the past decade, reflecting both the hectic lifestyle of the average consumer as well as the convenience of direct marketing. These days you can clothe your entire family, furnish a home, and buy just about anything through the mail. In addition, Americans "look to their mailboxes, telephones, and television sets for information on products and services from a range of businesses, such as banks and financial services, travel companies, educational organizations, publishers and more."[3]

The Image of Direct Response

Direct Market Association (DMA)

Organization to promote direct-mail and direct-response advertising.

Direct marketing has long been plagued by consumer complaints about unscrupulous sellers. While complaints about direct marketing continue to be a problem within the industry, the Council of Better Business Bureaus (BBBs) reports significant decreases in the number of complaints in recent years. Since 1986, direct-marketing complaints to the BBB have declined by almost 70 percent.[4] While there is still room for improvement, the direct-marketing industry has a number of measures to ensure that customers are not deceived or defrauded by unlawful schemes. The leading trade organization for direct-marketing, the Direct Marketing Association (DMA), has moved aggressively to initiate a number of steps for better self-regulation of the industry.

The DMA addresses a number of issues of importance to consumers. The majority of consumer complaints fall into one of three categories:

1. *Fraudulent sales offers.* Most direct-response advertisers are legitimate businesses, but like in any enterprise, there are those who use direct response for illegal activities. The DMA works with the U.S. Postal Service, the Federal Trade Commission (FTC), and other agencies to identify and prosecute criminal acts. The DMA also works with media groups to alert them to be vigilant in screening advertising for direct-response offers. DMA provides media with ad clearance tips and specific instances of frequently used

---

[3]"Direct Marketing: An American Success Story," Direct Marketing Association, 1993, p. 6.
[4]Larry Riggs, "DM Complaints Fell in 1992: BBB," *DM News,* September 13, 1993, p. 1.

illegal offers. As the DMA points out, "Readers often see the media carrying an advertisement as a source for assistance if merchandise is not received or is not satisfactory. When consumers are disappointed with the product or receive unsatisfactory treatment from the advertiser, they often blame the publication or station carrying the ad."[5]

2. *Concerns over invasion of privacy.* The introduction of the computer brought with it the ability to gather and systematically organize an infinite amount of information about consumers. From a marketing perspective this ability to identify and categorize prospects is a major benefit. However, many consumers fear that companies simply know too much about them and that the usage of the information is subject to adequate controls.

DMA has addressed this issue by encouraging list users to "be sensitive to the issue of consumer privacy and limit the combination, collection, rental, sale, exchange, and use of consumer data to only those data which are appropriate for direct marketing purposes."[6] The topic of consumer privacy has been debated for the past several years in both Congress and state legislatures. The DMA realizes that in the absence of strong industry-wide regulation, government will no doubt move to correct the problem.

3. *Consumer avoidance of unwanted solicitations.* Many people find both mail and telephone solicitations helpful and, indeed, billions of dollars worth of merchandise is sold by these methods each year. However, other consumers view direct-sales contacts as an intrusion and want to avoid them. The industry recognizes that reaching uninterested prospects is not only a public relations problem but is costly to the advertiser. Therefore, the industry supports efforts to allow consumers to eliminate unwanted sales contacts.

DMA acts as a clearinghouse for consumers who do not wish to be contacted by direct marketers. The DMA has established both a Telephone Preference Service (TPS) and a Mail Preference Service (MPS). TPS and MPS are designed to allow customers to place their names in a delete file that is send to direct marketers on a monthly basis. While the service will eliminate a number of calls or mailings, it will not eliminate local solicitations, and advertising from organizations that are not members of DMA.

One problem with the current system is that it eliminates all advertisers. However, the DMA is experimenting with a Selective Opt-Out system that will allow consumers to eliminate selected product categories in which they have no interest. In one survey, the DMA found that 33 percent of consumers who had registered with the Mail Preference Service indicated they would be willing to receive certain types of mail solicitations.[7]

Despite the problems facing the industry, direct response has made great strides in recent years. Major national advertisers are routinely using direct-response methods to reach important audience segments, and many business-to-business firms are making use of various options of direct response. In the remainder of this chapter, we will examine both the strategies and techniques currently used by companies large and small.

---

[5]"Misleading Advertisements Media Guidelines," Direct Marketing Association.
[6]"Ethical Business Practice," Direct Marketing Association, 1990, p. 13.
[7]Larry Jaffee, "DMA to Conduct Test This Summer of 'Selective Opt-Out' Program," *DM News*, June 7, 1993, p. 2.

THE SEARCH FOR ALTERNATIVE MEDIA BY ADVERTISERS

At one time direct response meant direct mail, and the users of the medium were largely confined to "occupant" mailings or offers from largely unknown companies for products of dubious value. In less than two decades, this situation has changed dramatically. As we have discussed, virtually every major corporation invests some promotional dollars in direct marketing. In fact, direct-response is one of the fastest-growing areas of advertising and promotion.

Perhaps the primary reason for this turnaround is the ability of advertisers to target their prospects in a manner that was impossible even as late as 1980. When a company is able to identify and separate prime prospects from the general population, it quickly moves from the shotgun approach of mass media to the rifle of direct response. The success of reaching narrowly defined markets has radically changed all media. As we have seen in earlier chapters, the successful magazines of the 1990s are those that deliver both niche audiences and editorial formats suitable to the interests of their audiences. Likewise, newspapers are providing various zoned editions to reach certain segments of a metropolitan population, and the major TV networks continue to see a shift of advertising dollars to cable networks competing on a "narrowcasting" basis. Radio, with its multiple formats and audience demographics, sells itself on the same rationale as direct response.

Combined with this ability of advertisers to identify audience segments is the rising cost of traditional media. Although the cost of media is not increasing as fast as in previous years, the cost increases in the past decade have been great, whether in terms of cost per thousand or time and space purchases. These increases in media prices have made direct response more competitive and have compelled increasing numbers of advertisers to consider direct response as part of their promotion plans. In addition, advertisers think that the opportunities for personal approaches through direct response more than offset the higher costs. By speaking to smaller, targeted audiences, advertisers have improved their creative approaches to utilize more fully the strengths of direct response.

Throughout the remainder of this chapter we will examine the many uses of direct response. While the ultimate objectives of direct response are similar to those of all advertising, there are many differences in techniques, terminology, and execution.

DATABASE MARKETING

Data base marketing
A process of continually updating information about individual consumers. Popular techniques with direct-response sellers.

Up to this point, we have discussed the importance of target marketing to the success of marketing and advertising. However, it is critical that we realize that a marketing segment is not a one-time snapshot but rather a constantly changing profile of core customers, potential customers, and former customers as well as those who will never be our customers (see Exhibit 13.3). Database marketing is an attempt to continually update not only where our prospects are but more importantly who they are, what they are purchasing, and, as best we can predict, what they may buy in the future.

Two primary factors have made database marketing so important. First is the cost of reaching non-prospects. Accumulating exposures through mass ad-

EXHIBIT

13.3

· · · · · · · · · · · · · · · · · ·

The U.S. population is getting older. The 0–44 age group will grow less than 3 percent by the year 2010, while the 45 and older age group will expand nearly 50 percent.

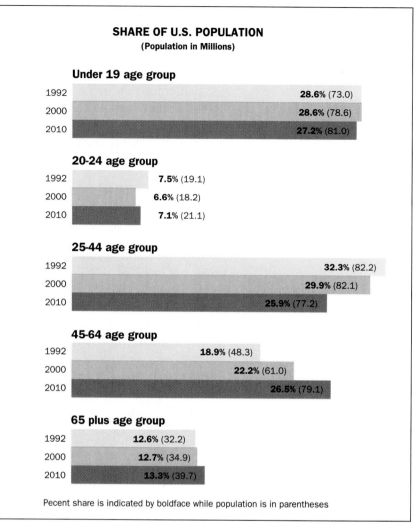

SHARE OF U.S. POPULATION
(Population in Millions)

Under 19 age group

1992	**28.6%** (73.0)
2000	**28.6%** (78.6)
2010	**27.2%** (81.0)

20-24 age group

1992	**7.5%** (19.1)
2000	**6.6%** (18.2)
2010	**7.1%** (21.1)

25-44 age group

1992	**32.3%** (82.2)
2000	**29.9%** (82.1)
2010	**25.9%** (77.2)

45-64 age group

1992	**18.9%** (48.3)
2000	**22.2%** (61.0)
2010	**26.5%** (79.1)

65 plus age group

1992	**12.6%** (32.2)
2000	**12.7%** (34.9)
2010	**13.3%** (39.7)

Pecent share is indicated by boldface while population is in parentheses

(Courtesy: Cahners Publishing Company.)

vertising with no clear idea of the potential payout for each of these exposures is no longer cost-effective. The cost of media advertising cannot be justified without an identification of the customers being reached.

Second is the need to build and maintain customer loyalty. Marketing executives refer to their continuing relationships with their customers as *tangible relationship marketing*. The key to database marketing is allowing a company to know its customers well enough to keep an ongoing positive relationship by being able to react to their changing lifestyles and product preferences.

Advertisers know that the expense of keeping a current customer is minimal compared to gaining a new one. "Failure to keep a customer carries a high price tag. Over a five-year period the cumulative profit for a five-year loyal customer is about 7.5 times the first-year profit. You can see why there is a significant migration of spending from acquisition of customers to retention and loyalty."[8]

---

[8]Kenneth Wylie, "Database Development Shows Strong Growth As Shops Gain 16.9% in U.S.," *Advertising Age*, July 12, 1993, p. S-8.

The key to successful database marketing is that it must be the central element in a firms marketing strategy. "Traditional marketing is obsolete. We have to reinvent it with the database as the basic element—not as support, but as what you drive everything off. . . . [T]he right research, the right data and access to that data are the building blocks of a profitable marketing database."[9]

Let's examine a very simple example of database marketing. The Acme Catalog Company has the following information on a customer:

Jane I. Buyer, married, 32, two children: boy 7, boy 9

Lives in an affluent ZIP code

Address:	101 Sunny Lane, Chicago—since April, 1992
	44 Olive Blvd., Miami—May 1989–March 1992
	777 Main St., St. Louis—September 1987–May 1989

Purchases from Acme:	Woman's sweater	$ 99	4/5/95
	Snow skis	133	3/25/94
	Desk set	49	12/10/93
	Dressing gown	98	12/10/93
	Perfume	124	10/4/93
	Diamond locket	566	8/3/92
	Crystal glasses	210	5/12/92

From this very simple database example, you can tell several things about the customer. Most importantly, Jane is a regular customer of Acme. She comes from an upwardly mobile household and, judging by the items she purchases, has reasonably high levels of discretionary income. From a marketing standpoint, she does not purchase children's items from Acme (is she a potential customer for these items?). Because of her purchase history, she will be on the "A" list for frequency of catalog mailings and will be contacted by special telemarketing efforts aimed at the company's best customers.

You can see from this limited example, how database marketing seeks to upgrade information continually and segment customers into subgroups. However, a thorough knowledge of our customers can be useful for numerous marketing objectives in addition to short-term sales. Database marketing is about gaining and reinforcing sales and being customer driven rather than sales driven. Once we take this customer perspective, there are several ways in which the database can be used to increase sales and profits:[10]

1. *Identify your best customers.* Consumer information should be used to rank customers in order of profitability to your current and future business.

2. *Develop new customers.* Your information about current customers allows you to gain valuable insight that will allow you to identify and develop

---

[9]"Database Marketing Demystified," *Target Marketing,* June 1993, p. 13.
[10]Rob Jackson, "Fifteen Ways to Use Your Database," *DM News,* June 14, 1993, p. 23.

plans to reach prospects. In particular, you can determine new customers who most closely resemble present customers and also identify your competition's customers to implement conversion strategies.

3. *Use creative message development.* The more you know about your customers and the primary product benefits your products offer them, the easier it is to develop creative advertising plans to reinforce their purchase behavior and influence nonusers.

4. *Use cross selling.* Many multibrand manufacturers use database marketing to sell complementary brands to current users of other products made by the company. For example, a company sends coupons for its baby powder to users of its baby diapers.

5. *Maintain customer contact.* In this era of nation retail chains, national manufacturers are increasingly losing contact with and loyalty of their best consumers. Direct contact with consumers allows national companies to have some control over their brand equity rather than being totally at the mercy of retailers. A properly maintained database allows manufacturers to have direct access to their consumers for direct advertising and, in rare cases, even direct sales outside normal retail channels.

6. *Use research.* Your database offers an identified audience for research on customer tastes, products, test marketing, media placement, distribution, communications, and other marketing-related data. Worldatabase, a service of Worldata, is one of a number of companies providing sophisticated data on various consumer segments (see Exhibit 13.4).

While the advantages of database marketing are obvious for many advertisers, it is an expensive endeavor and should be initiated only if it is right for an individual firm. Among the characteristics that must be considered before engaging in database marketing are the following:

1. Relatively frequent and/or high dollar volume of purchases by consumers

2. A diverse market where the marketing effort would benefit from segmenting it into subgroups

3. A customer list that represents opportunities for higher volume of purchases

If these three factors are not present, then it may indicate that the expense of establishing and maintaining a database is not worthwhile. However, when market characteristics are positive for such efforts, database techniques can greatly expand the profitability of a firm.

TELEMARKETING

Telemarketing
Major area of direct marketing.

One of the most important forms of direct marketing is the telephone. In less than two decades, telemarketing has moved from an infrequently used sales supplement to a key ingredient in the marketing plans of many companies. It is estimated that some 300,000 companies spend approximately $10 billion annually on in-house telemarketing operations. More than $500

(Courtesy: Worldata, Boca Raton, FL)

billion in goods or services are sold by phone each year, and 75 percent of all consumers use a toll-free number a least once a year.[11]

It is rare that a major national company does not engage in some form of telemarketing. Telemarketing is so important that 800-numbers are included on product labels to allow consumers to obtain more information or register a complaint. In addition to their use as a direct-sales tool, 800-numbers have become a familiar part of many advertisements, and research shows they aid in gaining higher consumer awareness for advertising (see Exhibit 13.5).

There are a number of techniques and definitions used in telemarketing.

· · · · · · · · · · · · · · · · · · · ·

Outbound telemarketing

A technique that involves a seller calling prospects.

· · · · · · · · · · · · · · · · · · · ·

---

[11]Kinson Southwell, *TeleProfessional,* March 1993, p. 33.

EXHIBIT 13.5

The use of toll-free numbers in advertisements contributes to higher advertisement awareness.

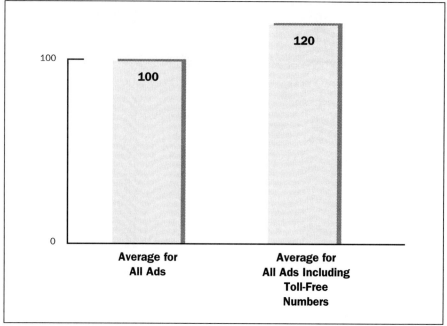

(Courtesy: Cahners Publishing Company)

Outbound and Inbound Telemarketing

There are two forms of telemarketing, outbound and inbound. *Outbound* telemarketing occurs when the seller calls prospects to make a sale, to determine interest by offering catalogs or other sales material, or to pave the way for a personal sales call. Market research is another use of outbound telemarketing.

Outbound telephone solicitations have several advantages over other techniques. Telemarketing is immediate; the offer and consumer response are practically instantaneous. In addition, telephone solicitations are flexible; sales messages can be adapted to the individual buyer as the conversation develops. Telephone offers can be tested quickly and inexpensively.

Inbound telemarketing is used with some other medium and is most often an order-taking operation. In-bound telemarketing has been made possible largely through the creation of the toll-free 800-number. Since their introduction in 1967, toll-free 800-numbers are among the most familiar forms of telemarketing. Consumers dial an estimated eight million 800-numbers each day. The 800-number is used for a variety of functions including sales calls to customers, placing orders by customers, and offering product information both before and after purchase. Some form of 800-service is a tool that most businesses cannot do without.

Upselling

A telemarketing technique designed to sell additional merchandise to callers.

Catalog sales, magazine ads that encourage customers to call for addresses of nearby retailers or more information, and product hotlines set up to give consumers help or to process their complaints are all examples of inbound telemarketing that depend on 800-numbers for their existence. However, in-bound telemarketing should not be viewed as a passive one-way process. Savvy telemarketers train their operators to use in-bound calls as a platform to sell additional merchandise. This technique is called *up-selling*.

A major innovation in in-bound telemarketing is the development of interactive voice response (IVR). IVR systems combine the technology of computers with telephones to provide a system that handles many more consumer calls at a fraction of operator exchanges. When accessing the service, callers are asked a series of questions and are given an opportunity to use their push-button phone to respond until they get the automated answer they are seeking, or in special cases a representative will come on the line. Companies using the system estimate that 90–95 percent of all calls can be handled by computer access. Furthermore, the information is available during nonbusiness hours.

The applications for IVR are infinite. Companies use the system to give consumers dealer locations for sales and service. Instead of traditional distribution of product samples or coupons, consumers can call in for requests. Such calls greatly increase the chances of reaching only serious consumers. Services such as catalog requests, sweepstakes information or entry forms, talking advertisements to augment media advertising, and other routine requests can be screened without taking up valuable staff time. Most importantly, companies are finding that consumers are attracted to the technology because of the novelty and convenience.[12]

900-Telemarketing

The 800-number represented a major breakthrough in telemarketing. The next development in telemarketing, and one that has been with much less consumer enthusiasm, is the 900-number. The 900-number requires that callers pay a fee that can vary from 50 cents to $20 or more (firms pay telephone companies approximately 30 cents per minute and then charge whatever they wish to callers). The advantage to the firm is twofold. Obviously, it covers all or part of the cost of the system. Just as importantly, it automatically self-selects serious callers who are interested in the product or information offered and are willing to pay for the service. To be successful, the 900-number has to offer some unique benefit to the consumer. People will not pay for a call unless they anticipate some immediate value.

The original promise of the 900-number, that is, to provide valuable information to consumers in exchange for a nominal fee, was quickly tainted by every imaginable charlatan and scam artist. The situation reached a point where 900 was almost interchangeable with phone sex, and legitimate companies dropped the service in droves.

Government regulators, companies wanting to use the service for appropriate business, and telephone company executives began to realize that something had to be done to clean up the industry. "Most telemedia industry players will remember 1992 as the year that 900 services crashed and burned under the strain of the economy, regulatory and legislative restraints, rampant fraud and uncollectables, and overall 900 exchange image problems. The result is a more mature, but drastically slimmed down 900 business."[13]

There are still many uses for 900-telephone service. It can provide information for everything from current stock prices, help for computer problems, and weather information at a fraction of the cost of alternatives. However, it will take years to overcome the past damage to the image of 900-services.

[12]Deserie R. Valloreo, "Thoroughly Modern Marketing," *InfoText* April, 1993, p. 41.
[13]James Ivers, "900-Services Revenues and Forecast," *InfoText,* January 1993, p. 66.

Case History

THE OBJECTIVE

Through market research, Touch-1 determined that telemarketing would be their primary sales channel for selling its long-distance products. But unlike other highly publicized telephone efforts for similar products, the emphasis for Touch-1 would be placed on an infallible (as much as possible) verification process and an incentive program based on sales revenues instead of raw numbers of sales—a "widget sale."

To achieve this, exact measurable objectives were defined:

1. To achieve production that generated a verified $30 per month in long-distance revenue per telemarketing hour.
2. To achieve an unauthorized sale rate that was less than 1 percent.

The presentation was built around the principle that Touch-1 customers would always receive a rate that, based on time of day and destination, was always equal to the lowest of AT&T, MCI, or Sprint.

THE METHODOLOGY

The TSR (telephone service representative) asks a series of questions that help define the average monthly bill of each consumer called. These questions excluded long distance charges from the monthly averages, and for a call to proceed, a monthly average of at least $15 was required.

After each sale is completed, the sales information is immediately transferred electronically to a third-party verification company that then calls the new "customer" back to verify information. Any variances in answers from the initial sales call are logged in according to the third party's figures, as they are not driven by incentives.

At day's end, tapes of all verification calls are overnighted to Touch-1, whose personnel audit or listen to every taped conversation before the customer is switched over to Touch-1 service.

THE RESULT

The program has met and surpassed its goals. The goal was $30+/month in long-distance revenue. ProMark has consistently achieved an average of $49—63 percent above target. The goal was less than 1 percent unauthorized sales. The actual rate is .104 percent—98.6 percent below the ceiling.

Touch-1 is now the fourth fastest growing residential long distance carrier in the United States.

For ProMark One, the initial 2,000-hour test has now grown to over 20,000 hours per month, on a long-term-agreement.

Only time will tell if 900-numbers ever reach the full potential held out for them at their introduction.

Automatic Dialing Systems

Automatic dialing recorded message programs (ADRMP)
Computerized telemarketing system that automatically dials random numbers in an area code.

As we saw in the case of IVR, computer technology has made a dramatic change in telemarketing, and it is a change unwelcomed in some quarters. There are two major systems of computerized telemarketing. One, called automatic dialing recorded message programs (ADRMPs), can dial hundreds of numbers a day and deliver a prerecorded sales message. The major complaints concerning ADRMP come from people with unlisted numbers and others who think indiscriminate random dialing is an invasion of privacy. These systems also tie up the line until the message is complete.

Another, more recent innovation in automatic dialing is *predictive dialing*. The predictive dialing system, like the ADRMP, automatically reaches potential customers. However, instead of delivering an impersonal sales message, a short recorded message tells the prospect what the call is about and asks that the listener remain on the line until a salesperson is available. The advantage of this system is that it combines the advantages of random computer dialing with personal contact.

Telemarketing Regulation

As is usually the case, when abuses of a system reach a certain point, government moves in to regulate both legitimate and illegal users. The exercise of governmental control was never more apparent than in the Telephone Consumer Protection Act (TCPA) enacted on December 20, 1992. The TCPA deals primarily with consumer concerns over unsolicited calls and the use of automated and prerecorded dialing systems.

Obviously, space will not permit a full discussion of the TCPA. However, we will touch on a few of the highlights of the legislation. The act applies only to commercial solicitations to *residential* telephone subscribers. Among the most important aspects of the bill are the following:

1. Calls can only be made from 8 A.M. to 9 P.M.

2. A list of persons who have previously indicated they want no telephone solicitations must be maintained.

3. Except where prior consent has been obtained, firms may not use artificial or prerecorded voice message systems to residential subscribers.

4. Autodialers cannot call emergency numbers and health-care facilities, and they must identify the source of the call at the beginning of the recording. Similar restrictions also are placed on sales messages delivered by fax.

Most charitable and tax-exempt organizations are not covered under the provisions of the bill. Likewise, companies with whom a consumer has an established relationship are not covered by most of the provisions of the act.[14]

Companies engaging in residential sales realize that the TCPA will alter the way they do business in the future. However, in March 1993 the Supreme Court added an even more chilling element to regulations on telemarketers. In a Minnesota case, the Court upheld the right of states to ban automatic dialing altogether unless prior permission was obtained. While the decision only affects Minnesota, many in the industry fear that it may open the way for state-by-state prohibitions on a number of telemarketing techniques to both consumers and businesses. At this writing, the future of telemarketing and its future growth is very much up in the air.

Television and Direct-Response Advertising

The fragmentation of TV audiences has made it an ideal medium for direct-response. With CNN appealing to news buffs, CNBC carrying numerous financial programs, Lifetime staking out a position among women, and ESPN appealing to our insatiable appetite for sports, the niche audiences that direct-response advertisers seek are available. In addition, to the segmented

---

[14]Angela Karr, "The Telephone Consumer Protection Act—How to Comply," *TeleProfessional,* June 1993, p. 12.

audiences that TV can deliver, another advantage is its ability to demonstrate the product. Television, combined with a direct-response offer, is as close to personal selling as we can get using mass media.

Television offers a number of opportunities for direct-response advertisers. However, the medium is not inexpensive and, like any direct-response vehicle, should be used only after extensive testing. It is a mistake to stereotype either your prospects or a particular TV outlet. For example, if you are selling running shoes, "ESPN would immediately come to mind as a means of reaching your target audience, but runners aren't necessarily sports nuts. Most of them prefer doing over watching. In fact, it's quite likely that CNN and Headline News would work better than ESPN. But if you're selling subscriptions to a sports magazine, ESPN may be just right."[15] In this section, we will discuss a number of elements of direct-response television.

Methods of Buying Time

Per inquiry (PI)

Advertising time or space where medium is paid on a per response received basis.

Direct-response advertising is sold both on a paid and per-inquiry (PI) basis. Unlike PI advertising in magazines, which we discussed earlier, it is very common in television. Basically, PI advertisers share their risk with a TV station or cable channel. There is no up front costs for time, but the TV outlet will divide the profits (if any) when the orders come in. On the surface, PI advertising is very beneficial, especially to companies with good products but little capital. However, PI advertising entails a number of features that are significantly different from paid TV advertising.

One of the most difficult aspects of PI is determining a fair percentage for all parties. A company considering PI advertising must estimate all the costs involved including the product itself, inbound telemarketing, fulfillment of orders, and commercial production and fees associated with getting the commercial on the air. A company contemplating PI advertising has to be fair to TV stations, or they will not carry its spots. On the other hand, if the product is a huge hit, the firm doesn't want to be locked into an agreement that provides windfall profits to stations.

PI advertising has grown so large and is so specialized that it is usually handled by companies specializing in PI sales. PI companies such as Synchronal and Media Arts not only provide all PI related services to advertisers but even lease blocks of time from cable channels to run long-form commercials for their clients.[16]

Length of Commercials

As we discussed earlier, the standard TV commercial is 30 seconds. However, direct-response advertisers are much more likely to use longer spots or even program-length messages. Remember that direct-response advertising must complete the entire sales process as well as tell consumers how to order the product, a difficult task in a 30-second spot.

The Infomercial. Long-form commercials, known as infomercials and usually lasting 30 minutes, are gaining in popularity. When the FCC lifted its

---

[15] Nancy Rieder, "Television: Today's DR Growth Medium," *DM News,* March 22, 1993, p. 47.
[16] Kathy St. Louis, "PI in the Sky," *ResponseTV,* August/September, 1992, p. 40.

12-minute-per-hour limit on commercial time, it ushered in the era of the infomercial. In 1987, an Arizona State University business professor named Claude Olney teamed with TV personality John Ritter to offer a learning course called "Where There's a Will There's an A." Some $70 million later the program is still going strong.[17] Professor Olney has been joined by a host of celebrities from Victoria Principal to Cher in pitching every imaginable health, beauty, diet, and real estate plan. Today, 90 percent of all TV outlets accept infomercials (only 20 percent on a PI basis), and major corporations such as GTE, Saturn, and Eastman Kodak regularly use them as sales tools.

Reacting to client demands, a number of advertising agencies have begun to produce infomercials. A few agencies such as D'Arcy Masius Benton & Bowles have formed separate units to handle infomercial production and placement. Clearly, agencies are reacting to clients' perceived need for long-form advertising. As one advertising executive pointed out, "Any account that needs a product explanation, something that is very demonstrable, and can capture the imagination in hardware and software would be a contender [for infomercials]."[18]

It is clear that Americans are becoming more comfortable with direct-response advertising. It is estimated that infomercial sales will top $1 billion this year. This figure accounts only for direct sales, not sales that are made at the retail level as a result of these commercials. Exhibit 13.6 shows the consumer groups most likely to watch and purchase a product as a result of an infomercial.

As large national companies increasingly use the format, we will see continued growth of infomercial selling. "The involvement of a growing number of *Fortune* 1,000 companies, national advertisers and blue-chip advertising agencies in the infomercial field is contributing to high-quality infomercial programming (production values), stronger technical sales messages and enhanced image and brand messages."[19] As is the case with most promotional techniques, the infomercial is more and more being used as a complement to other forms of advertising and marketing. With proper planning the format can serve a useful strategic role in the promotion of many product categories.

TV Shopping Networks

The logical extension of long-form infomercials is an entire TV schedule devoted to product sales. Home shopping channels are coming into their own. A number of major retailers and designers such as Saks Fifth Avenue, Calvin Klein, and Diane Von Furstenberg are using home shopping networks to sell their products to a variety of consumers.

Shopping by television is becoming more acceptable to a large group of adults. However, research conducted by Deloitte & Touche indicates that certain target segments are more likely to use television. Exhibit 13.7 shows some of the groups.

[17]David J. Jefferson and Thomas R. King, "'Infomercials' Fill Up Air Time on Cable, Aim for Prime Time," *The Wall Street Journal,* October 22, 1992, p. 1.
[18]Melanie Wells, "D'Arcy Joins Trend to Infomercials," *Advertising Age,* March 29, 1993, p. 12.
[19]Craig Evans, "Are Infomercials for Your Brand?" *Advertising Age,* January 25, 1993, p. M-6.

EXHIBIT
13.6

Here's who is watching (and buying from) infomercials

Americans are becoming more familiar with half-hour program-length advertising. In new research commissioned by Hudson Street Partners, more than half the respondents said they had seen an infomercial in the past 12 months, nearly one in 10 had experience ordering infomercial products by 800-number and nearly two in 10 said they had purchased products in a store based on information from an infomercial. Percentages shown below are percentages of the total survey sample.

	Seen an infomercial in the past year?	Ever purchased anything using 800-number at the end of an infomercial?	Ever purchased anything in a store based on information provided in an infomercial?
Sex			
Male	57%	8.0%	20.0%
Female	54	9.0	19.0
Age			
18–24	70	4.0	19.0
25–34	63	9.0	19.0
35–49	58	12.0	20.0
50–64	55	10.0	26.0
65+	33	3.0	13.0
Income			
under $15,000	53	4.5	22.5
$15,000–$20,000	52	11.0	24.0
$20,000–30,000	62	8.0	21.0
$30,000–$40,000	63	9.0	25.0
$40,000+	60	11.0	16.0
Region			
Northeast	56	7.0	24.0
North Central	52	9.0	14.0
South	57	8.0	21.0
West	55	10.0	17.0
Total	55%	8.5%	19.0%

Note: Data are based on a national telephone survey commissioned by Hudson Street Partners and conducted by Bruskin/Goldring Research in August 1992. The sample was 1,005 men and women ages 18 and older.

(Source: Advertising Age, Jan. 25, 1993, p. M.3.)

Many see the real potential of home shopping in interactive systems. The most optimist proponents of shopping networks predict that they will fundamentally change retailing in the next two decades. Predictions are that by the next century, half of all retail business will be done through interactive television systems. "[C]onsumers will be able to call up menus on their TV screens and make electronic shopping trips by picking the store, the department they want to visit or the types of products or services they want to purchase—all at the touch of a button. Boxes atop TV sets will store personal

EXHIBIT
13.7

Who Shops by Television

Category	TV Shopper	General Population
Married	44%	49%
Single	27	25
Professional	13	18
Factory Worker	12	9
White	55	72
Black	20	14
Hispanic	17	8

(Source: The Atlanta Journal/The Atlanta Constitution, March 13, 1993, p. B2.)

data, enabling viewers to order merchandise, charge it to a credit card and pick a delivery option by tapping a few buttons."[20]

Videocassettes

With videocassette recorders approaching 80 percent household penetration, it is natural that advertisers would consider the videocassette as an advertising and sales option. Videocassettes have been used for some time for business-to-business advertising and product information. They are sent to customers to introduce new products, to offer product demonstrations for personal selling, and to explain and upgrade maintenance for a variety of products. The use of videocassettes continues to grow in business-to-business marketing, but in the past few years it has been introduced in consumer sales.

The use of videocassettes in the consumer sector is largely confined to narrowly defined audiences for high ticket items. Obviously, the expense of mass mailings of videocassette is prohibitive. One popular approach to the use of videocassettes is to send them on loan to prospective customers. NordicTrack, makers of home exercise equipment, sends videotapes to those calling its 800-number. The tapes can be reviewed by customers and returned, thus saving the company a great deal of money.

Videologs
Catalogs produced on video cassettes, intended for specialized audiences.

As the cost of cassette production and distribution decreases, there is no question that we will see more consumer distribution. Some advertisers are offering videocassettes as a supplement to print and broadcast advertising. Already the cost of producing and mailing catalogs is making it more practical to consider *videologs,* or catalogs produced on video cassettes, for specialty, upscale consumer products as well as for businesses.

RADIO AND DIRECT-RESPONSE

Because it lacks a visual element, radio is at an obvious disadvantage compared to other direct-response media. The product cannot be shown, no coupons can be provided, and a toll-free number cannot be flashed on a screen. However, offsetting these disadvantages is the highly segmented nature of the radio audience. This segmentation is a characteristic made to order for the highly specialized direct-response advertiser.

The popularity of AM talk-radio has moved several advertisers to explore the possibilities of radio infomercials. The infomercials would follow the 30-minute talk-show format of their TV counterparts. One of the incentives for moving into radio infomercials is their cost. A 30-minute radio infomercial can be produced for as little as $10,000 compared to more than $200,000 for many TV infomercials.

In the near future, the age of interactive media may make radio a more important direct-response vehicle. Technology is being developed that will one day make radio direct response an important aspect of the media. One company, CouponRadio, has already developed technology that will allow a listener to save direct-response information and coupons. "If you're driving 65 miles an hour, you don't stop to write down a telephone number you heard

---

[20]Scott Donaton, "Home Shopping Networks Bring Retailers on Board," *Advertising Age,* April 19, 1993, p. S-8.

on the car radio. But with CouponRadio, you can press a number and save a telephone number. For that matter, you could save an advertiser's name or location, or a coupon for a discount on their product."[21]

Radio is often used to supplement other forms of direct response. For example, publishers use radio to alert people that a sweepstakes mailing is beginning and to encourage their participation. Radio will never be a primary direct-response medium. However, radio will continue to be of great value as a secondary support medium to targeted audience segments.

Many radio stations find that per-inquiry advertising is a means of using unsold commercial spots. With the number of stations and commercial spots available, it is almost impossible for even the most prosperous station to sell all its time. Unsold inventory can be especially acute during certain months such as January. Rather than using this time for public-service announcements or station promotions, the sales manager may be willing to run per-inquiry spots at significant discounts.

MAGAZINES AND DIRECT RESPONSE

Magazine direct-response advertising differs in a number of ways from general-publication advertising. Many magazines have mail-order sections at the back of each issue; and judging by advertisers' continued use of them, we can assume that results on the whole are good. Many a small business has grown into a large one through these advertisements. In direct-response advertising, the question is not what the CPM of the magazine is but what the cost-per-order or cost-per-inquiry will be. Direct-response advertisers can calculate the cost-per-order to the fraction of a cent.

Magazines have several advantages for the direct-response advertiser:

1. *Audience selectivity.* Magazines are able to attract an audience with common interests and characteristics. More importantly, specialized publications offer an editorial environment compatible with the advertising messages they carry, ensuring that the reader is in the proper "mood" for your advertisement.

2. *Distinct magazine audiences.* Magazine readers tend to include light users of other media. Consequently, magazine direct response can reach an audience that would normally be excluded by other media vehicles.

3. *Long life.* Magazines have a long life that allows coupons to be clipped and offers responded to days or weeks after the magazine is received. The long life of magazines also makes pass-along readership possible, thereby expanding the potential audience.

4. *Size and color.* The typical magazine advertisement offers enough space to allow for coupons and detailed product information. In addition, excellent-quality reproduction presents products to their best advantage.

5. *Prestige.* Magazines offer many of the advantages of direct mail, but with added prestige to the advertiser.

Some publications will accept per-inquiry space, to run at no initial cost. The publisher is paid on a percentage-of-sales basis. Most direct-response adver-

---

[21]Joe Mandese, "Interactive puts radio at crossroads," *Advertising Age,* October 25, 1993, p. 12.

tisers expect a full-page magazine advertisement to pull from 0.05 percent to 0.20 percent of circulation—that is, from half of a response per thousand to two responses per thousand—although results can vary widely depending on the product offered.

According to Frank Vos, an authority on the subject, direct-mail results usually range from 0.7 percent to 5.0 percent of names mailed—that is, from 7 orders per 1,000 to 50 orders per 1,000. You will notice that the ratio of response per thousand between direct mail and magazine space is roughly on the order of 10:1 or 20:1. However, the same ratio applies to the CPM of the two media. Therefore, many advertisers find that their cost per order for both magazine space and direct mail is about the same.

Overall, 40 percent of adults report that they have ordered a product through magazine mail-order advertising. Females are only somewhat more likely to order than males, and the region of the country plays no part in who will order from magazines. However, as we would expect, the audience of magazine mail order, like the audience of magazines generally, is skewed toward higher-income and better-educated buyers.

The selectivity of magazine audiences also allows advertisers to be creative in reaching special audiences. Advertisers know that certain magazines will not only reach an audience of prime prospects but will do so in an environment that makes direct-response action more likely. For example, a woman's magazine may carry an advertisement with a mail-in offer for a recipe book, or a sports magazine may run an ad for a high-performance automobile with a toll-free 800-number for additional information.

CHARACTERISTICS OF SUCCESSFUL DIRECT-RESPONSE ADVERTISING

A number of factors contribute to the success of direct-response advertising. Among the most important:

1. Specific consumers who are current or potential users of a particular product or service can be targeted.

2. Copy is written in a personal, one-to-one conversational style.

3. Products offered through direct response usually are unavailable in traditional retail outlets or have some particular differentiation such as price, style, or convenience over competing brands.

The key to successful direct-response advertising is fundamentally the same as with any type of advertising or promotion. We need to start with clearly defined marketing goals and determine how direct response can accomplish its role in the total promotional plan. Unfortunately, inexperienced advertisers sometimes treat direct response as a separate and unrelated element to other promotional vehicles. In doing so, direct response loses the synergy with other promotion and may become an inefficient step-sister to the overall marketing program.

In order to take full advantage of direct-response advertising, it should be viewed as part of the total promotional plan. Too often, direct response is viewed as an impersonal order taker. Instead, direct response must take full advantage of the database opportunities that it creates. Obviously, creative and media should be coordinated to make the communication personal and one on one. More important, the direct-response advertiser needs to make provisions for a long-term relationship with consumers available through direct response.

By the same token, direct-response advertisers must anticipate some unique problems. For example, history tells us that 85 percent of responses to direct-response TV commercials will come within one hour of airing. Are there enough operators to handle this response? Is it practical to ship the product, or is it too heavy or fragile? Can consumers easily assemble and use the product? What is the anticipated rate of product returns?

Direct marketers must deal with a number of issues that rarely face traditional retailers. Direct response offers a number of exciting alternatives to traditional media advertising. However, unless direct response is used properly, it can become a time-consuming, inefficient, and tremendously costly enterprise.

DIRECT-RESPONSE OFFERS—DIRECT SALES

Direct response is characterized by flexibility in formats, media, and types of offers. The common thread in most direct response is its ability to target audiences and communicate in a personal manner. There are two major objectives in most direct-response advertising. Business-to-business advertisers tend to use direct response to generate leads, while consumer marketers more commonly view it as a final sales tool.

As the name implies, the direct sale offer is straightforward, presenting a product and asking consumers if they want to buy it. A straight sales offer may take the form of a telephone solicitation for a magazine subscription or an elaborate brochure for a cruise. Regardless of the simplicity or complexity of the offer, the intent of the promotional effort is to close a sale. Here are some examples of direct sales offers.

One-Step Purchase of Specific Product

Bounce-back circular
An enclosure in the package of a product that has been ordered by mail. It offers other products of the same company and is effective in getting more business.

The simplest examples of this type of direct-response advertising are the small ads one sees in the back of the shopping section of many magazines or in a Sunday newspaper supplement. Whoever responds to a mail-order ad will probably receive a package containing the product ordered plus one or more circulars offering other merchandise of related interest. *Bounce-back circulars,* as these are called, can produce as much as 20 to 40 percent additional sales from the same customers and often launch a one-time customer on the path to becoming a steady buyer. The key to the one-step approach is pinpointing the prime prospects, since you cannot depend on follow-ups to complete the sale. Direct-response marketers measure the effectiveness of these offers on the basis of *cost per order* (CPO). It is one of the few cases where sales can be directly attributed to advertising and is a major advantage of direct response.

Catalogs

The use of catalogs dates at least to 1498 when Aldus Manutius published his book catalog containing 15 titles. Since its humble beginnings, the catalog has become a keystone of direct-marketing. As early as 1830, New England companies were selling fishing and camping supplies by mail. By the end of the 1800s, both Sears, Roebuck & Co. and Montgomery Ward brought retail merchandise to every household in the country through their catalogs. However, it was the 1970s that marked the major growth period of catalog selling.

The early catalogs were primarily directed to low- and middle-income families outside of major cities. Today, the catalog business is increasingly directed toward an upscale audience with an interest in specialty merchandise not readily available in retail stores. The general sales catalog has just about disappeared. In 1985, after more than 100 years of operation, Montgomery Ward left the catalog business, and Sears followed suit in 1993.

Today catalog selling is a major business. Each year almost 100 million Americans—one out of every two adults—make a catalog purchase. Approximately 8,000 catalog retailers send out over 13 billion catalogs each year. It is estimated that these catalogs produce over $50 billion in sales, and they will pass $65 billion by 1996. Catalogs account for almost 25 percent of all mail-order sales.[22] In addition, catalogs account for approximately 20 percent of all third-class mail.

Obviously, catalogs provide convenience that is ideal for working families. However, the key to successful catalog selling is offering consumers products with a perceived differentiation and greater value than they can get at their local retailer. Catalogs depend on unusual products to entice consumers to buy from one catalog over another. Many catalogs highlight products that are available only from them. Others develop a line of products or a personality in much the same way as retailers.

Types of Catalogs.   Because of their inherent differences, it is difficult to categorize catalogs. However, there are four generally recognized types of catalogs in terms of the audience they reach and the products and services they sell:[23]

1. *Retail catalogs.* In recent years a number of retailers have begun to produce catalogs. In some cases, these catalogs are designed to complement in-store sales with mail and telephone orders from customers who normally do not shop in the store. In other cases, the retail catalog is intended to build store traffic by announcing special sales or merchandise.

2. *Full-line merchandise catalogs.* The full-line catalog is by far the smallest category of catalogs. These catalogs offer a wide range of merchandise that appeals to a number of different consumers. With the demise of both Montgomery Ward and Sears as catalog companies, there is some doubt as to whether this category can survive.

3. *Business-to-business catalogs.* One of the major growth areas in recent years has been business-to-business catalogs. As the cost of personal selling has increased, businesses have looked for more cost-efficient means to reach their smaller customers or those in isolated geographic areas. The catalog offers a continuing means of contact with these customers and keeps them

---

[22]Tom Walker, "Busy, Choosy, Late? Holiday Catalogs Fill Shoppers' Needs," *Atlanta Journal,* November 11, 1992, p. C1.

[23]Bob Stone, *Successful Direct Marketing Methods* (Lincolnwood, IL: National Textbook Company, 1987), p. 297.

profitable to the company. In one study, business-to-business catalogs ranked with media advertising as the most effective means of gaining new customers (see Exhibit 13.8).

4. *Consumer specialty catalogs.* By far the largest category of catalogs are specialty books directed to consumers. These catalogs offer every imaginable product and service, many that are available only from a particular catalog company. In addition, some of these companies offer as many as 20 different books directed to special consumer groups with specialized merchandise.

The Future of the Catalog. In some respects, catalogs are becoming victims of their own success. As more and more specialty catalogs are printed, the average revenue per book tends to decrease, but the overhead for printing and mailing continues to rise. Consequently, many catalog sellers are looking for more efficient means of reaching their audiences. For example, Toys 'R' Us distributed its 1993 Christmas catalog to 50 million readers by including it in some 300 Sunday newspapers. The 72-page catalog represented the first time a national undertaking of this type had been tried by a cataloger. The catalog distribution was supported by extensive TV and radio advertising.

As some catalogers look for more creative means of distribution, other direct mailers see TV shopping as representing a real threat to traditional catalog selling. Television offers consumers the opportunity to see merchandise and place an immediate order. However, the average consumer with limited time cannot afford to spend all day in front of the TV set hoping that a particular product will be offered. In addition, studies show that consumers have an inherent trust in their favorite catalog, which may be missing in TV sales.

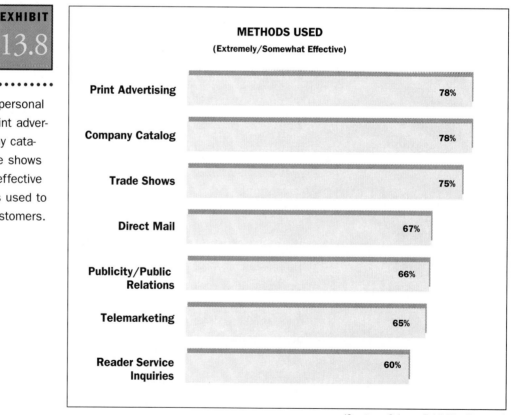

EXHIBIT 13.8

. . . .

In addition to personal sales calls, print advertising, company catalogs, and trade shows are the most effective sales methods used to attract new customers.

METHODS USED
(Extremely/Somewhat Effective)

Method	%
Print Advertising	78%
Company Catalog	78%
Trade Shows	75%
Direct Mail	67%
Publicity/Public Relations	66%
Telemarketing	65%
Reader Service Inquiries	60%

(Courtesy: Cahners Publishing Company)

Studies indicate that women are six times more likely to shop from a catalog than via television. Adults over 50 years old are nine times more likely to prefer catalogs. Overall, more than 50 percent of adults indicated they would not order anything from television.[24] There is no question that TV shopping will become more sophisticated and popular in the future. However, it is going to be some time before it represents a major challenge to traditional catalog selling.

Another approach to catalog selling currently being tried by a few companies is computerized formats. To date, these applications are practical only for specialized business-to-business selling. Two of the most popular types of automated presentations are electronic catalogs and desktop presentations. The electronic catalog can be sent to customers in the same manner as a regular catalog, but it is on computer diskettes. The customer reviews the information and places an order. In other cases, the electronic catalog is sent prior to a personal sales call to allow the sales person to focus only on items of interest to the prospect.

The desktop multimedia presentation is designed as an aid to personal salespeople. These systems provide an in-office product demonstration. One of the advantages of both desktop presentations and electronic catalogs is that they are not static systems. They can provide programs that allow viewers to get selected information tailored to their needs as opposed to a film or videotape.

These systems heighten viewer interest and involvement with the product. They are also cost-efficient over time even though initial start-up costs for production may be very expensive. Aside from technical and monetary benefits, these systems are also environmentally sound, curbing the use of paper and other expendable items.[25]

Clearly, it will be some time before interactive TV selling and various forms of electronic catalogs become readily available to the general public. However, in the next decade we will see the introduction of a number of computer-based home shopping systems. While the risks of investing in these systems is substantial, those entrepreneurs who successfully tap the consumer market will realize significant profits.

Negative Options Direct Response

Negative-option direct response

Technique used by record and book clubs whereby a customer receives merchandise unless the seller is notified not to send it.

The negative option technique provides consumers with a subscription relationship for the purchase of future merchandise. The Book-of-the-Month Club is credited with introducing this method of "one-package-a-month" selling. Today we see records, compact disks, as well as miniature cars, porcelain figurines, and a host of other merchandise offered on a negative option basis. The idea is that the buyer must notify the company in order *not* to have an item sent.

The consumer appeal of negative options is that companies make the initial offer ridiculously inexpensive in order to encourage consumers to sign up. For example, the Columbia Home Video Club offers six movies for 29 cents each with an obligation by the buyer to buy six more at full price. The ad-

---

[24]Nick Holland, "Will Television Shopping Kill Catalogs?" *DM News,* June 28, 1993, p. 31.
[25]Thayer C. Taylor, "Fight Mail Costs with Your PC," *Sales & Marketing Management,* March 1993, p. 16.

vantage to sellers is that once customers join the plan, the company is guaranteed a customer for some period of time. Consequently, sales costs are virtually nonexistent for continuing customers.

Fulfillment

Fulfillment firm
Company that handles the couponing process including receiving, verification and payment. It also handles contests and sweepstake responses.

The product inventory is selected, the colorful and well-written catalog is printed, the mailing list is fine-tuned for prospects-only, the timing of the mailing has been tested to the day. All you have to do is wait for the orders and profits to start pouring in. Well, not quite. Who is making sure that the merchandise is sent out properly packed and any errors corrected quickly and cordially? This is the job of the fulfillment operation.

Complaints about order fulfillment have become such a problem that the FTC has adopted special guidelines concerning the prompt shipping of merchandise. It is known as the "30-Day Rule." Among its major provisions are stipulations that "merchants (a) ship goods within 30 days of order placement; (b) specify in ads and promotional material that merchandise will be shipped in a given length of time; (c) notify the consumer of a new shipping date when orders can't be sent in that time frame and offer the option of canceling for a full refund."[26]

Too many companies offer prompt product fulfillment on orders but are totally deficient in handling returned merchandise or complaints. Not only should refunds and adjustments be made promptly, but you should try to find out reasons for consumer dissatisfaction and make every effort to keep the person as a customer. For example, acknowledgments should be sent when returned merchandise has been received and the account is being credited. In addition, acknowledgments should apologize for any inconvenience to the customer. A competent return department can be one of a company's most valued functions.

At one time, the fulfillment function was regarded as a shipping service and one that, sometimes grudgingly, handled complaints. Today, fulfillment operations are total customer service departments that include a multitude of services. Because of the complexity of the fulfillment process, many smaller companies contract out the fulfillment function. Independent fulfillment houses are most commonly used for one-time promotions such as a sweepstakes or premium offers. These type of fulfillment operations are discussed in Chapter 14.

DIRECT-RESPONSE OFFERS—LEAD GETTING

A second objective of many direct-response offers is identification of prospects for later contact. Companies that sell very expensive merchandise, especially business-to-business items, are often dealing with a very small universe of potential buyers. The sales force of these companies depends on solid leads from a number of sources.

The first step in successful lead-getting campaigns is to remember that they are not the same as one-step direct response. The key is to put yourself in the place of the personal salespersons who will close the deal. What information

---

[26]Arthur Winston, "Revisions to the FTC 30-Day Rule," *DM News,* March 22, 1993, p. 22.

do they need to know about the prospect, and how can your lead-getting program ensure you are separating prospects from browsers? A good lead-getting campaign involves the sales force as a support group to the marketing effort.

The sales force needs to be trained so that they can properly follow up on leads. In order to do this, salespeople have to know what information prospects received and what the sales force needs to do to complete the sale. Some keys to build leads are the following:

1. *Emphasize the offer, not creative elements, and keep copy short.* You are trying to get the consumer interested enough to follow up, not provide all the information needed to make a purchase decision.

2. *Include only the most important product benefits.* Pick the most provocative benefit and encourage customers to obtain more information.

3. *Keep copy short and highlight the benefit.* The lead-getting campaign should be viewed as a teaser to get prospects to go to the next step. The more you tell them, the less likely they think they need to inquire for more information.

4. *Assume the reader doesn't care about you or your product.* They want to know what's in it for them. How will your product solve their problems?

5. *Appeal to everyone and miss them all.* Remember, follow-ups are expensive for your company and frustrating for your sales force when they don't result in sales. Make sure you gain the interest of solid prospects.[27]

Because of the expense of personal selling, some companies actually resort to a three-step process. Instead of going directly to a personal sales call when they get a response, companies may choose instead to send more detailed literature or even a product sample. The key is to generate leads from your most profitable customers. You will recall earlier we discussed the cost-per-order as a major way of measuring the success of straight sales direct response. In two-step operations, we often see the term *cost per lead* (CPL). The CPL measure recognizes that two-step direct response is intended to generate prospects only, not final sales.

Business-to-Business Direct Marketing

The majority of the users of lead-getting direct response are business-to-business sellers. The target marketing characteristics of direct-response are ideal for business-to-business marketing. Among the most important features of business-to-business marketing are the following:

1. *A relatively small market.* Compared to the typical consumer market, the number of businesses in any industry is quite small. For example, in the industrial sector it is common for less than five firms to account for 80 percent or more of total sales.

2. *Concentrated buying decisions.* The number of purchasing decision makers on the business side is very small compared to consumer marketing. It is practical to spend a great deal of money to reach each of these decision makers and still keep the total promotional budget at a reasonable level.

---

[27]Robert Hacker, "Making Lead Generation Work!," *Target Marketing,* June, 1993, p. 8.

3. *High average per-purchase expenditures.* Business-to-business advertisers are playing for big stakes. Whereas a consumer may buy a $3,000 personal computer, a purchasing agent may buy a multi-million-dollar computer system. Factors such as CPMs, so important in consumer promotions, have little relevance to business marketers.

4. *Flexibility.* Business-to-business direct response must be flexible and adapt to the needs of different industries or even individuals in a way that consumer advertising does not.

Another factor in the growth of the business-to-business advertising segment of direct response is the cost of personal selling. The cost of a typical sales call is now close to $300, and these costs have risen sharply in recent years (see Exhibit 13.9). Increasingly, we are going to see personal selling confined to larger customers, leaving a major role for both direct-response and traditional business-to-business advertising.

DIRECT-MAIL ADVERTISING

Direct-mail advertising is only one of a number of direct-response techniques. However, because of its widespread use and the special opportunities it offers advertisers, we consider it in a separate section. Direct mail is sometimes used by a company as its primary promotional tool, and on rare occasions, its only advertising vehicle. However, it is much more common to employ

EXHIBIT

13.9

● ● ● ● ● ● ● ● ● ● ● ● ● ● ● ● ●

The cost of a personal sales call ranges from $330.46 in the South to $261.65 in the Midwest.

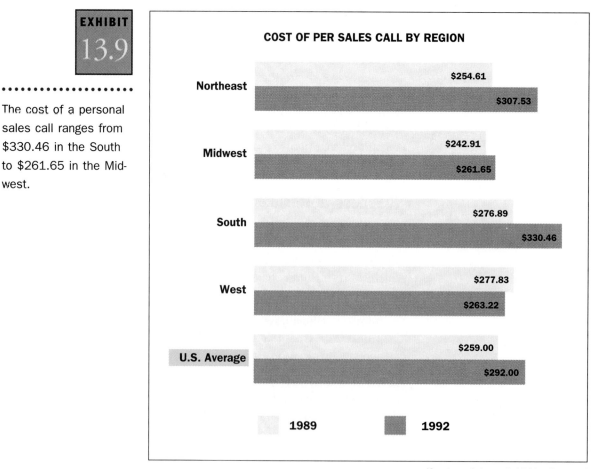

COST OF PER SALES CALL BY REGION

Region	1989	1992
Northeast	$254.61	$307.53
Midwest	$242.91	$261.65
South	$276.89	$330.46
West	$277.83	$263.22
U.S. Average	$259.00	$292.00

(Courtesy: Cahners Publishing Company)

Yes—nearly 3/4 of business professionals buy business related products/services through direct mail every year.

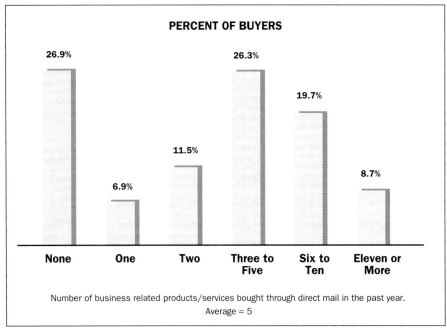

PERCENT OF BUYERS

26.9% | 6.9% | 11.5% | 26.3% | 19.7% | 8.7%

None | One | Two | Three to Five | Six to Ten | Eleven or More

Number of business related products/services bought through direct mail in the past year.
Average = 5

(Courtesy: Cahners Publishing Company)

direct mail as part of a diversified marketing communication program. In this role, it must complement traditional media advertising as well as overall marketing objectives.

Companies contemplating using direct mail should be clear about their goals and objectives, as with any other advertising or promotion. There are numerous uses of direct mail:

1. *Lead generation.* Personal salespersons can be made much more efficient by following up on leads generated by direct mail rather than making "cold calls."

2. *Mail order.* As discussed earlier in this chapter, direct mail is a primary method of selling goods directly to consumers. Exhibit 13.10 shows that over 70 percent of businesses buy products through direct mail, with an average of five purchases annually.

3. *Loyalty programs.* To most companies, keeping present customers is a major goal. Direct mail can build relationships, reward loyalty, and generate referrals.

4. *Database building.* Direct mail can provide secondary objectives such as building your mailing list or adding marketing information to existing databases.

5. *Dealer support.* Offering direct mailings to local retailers can build dealer loyalty and increase support for your products.[28]

Characteristics of Direct Mail

Direct mail is the oldest form of direct-response advertising and is second only to telemarketing in terms of sales produced. It has many unique advantages as a marketing tool. However, it also faces a number of challenges

Message management
Utilizes database information to offer different message to various consumer categories.

---

[28]Edward Nash, "Turn It On!" *Sales & Marketing Management,* October 1993, p. 66.

- **Customers who have recently ordered or who order frequently**

- **Buyers of similar products**

- **Volume buyers**

- **People who have shown interest in related products, especially when purchased by mail**

- **People who have a demographic interest in a product such as young married couples for insurance**

- **Those who are known to have replied to direct mail (hence the value of response lists)**

The second area of researching prospects is to identify the specific audience for *your* mailing. Here we want to pretest a list before undertaking a general mailing or, in some cases, even before engaging in a formal test. "The goal of list pretesting is to reduce the number and size of unsuccessful list tests before those lists are ever mailed. Any pretesting method seeks to rank the 'promise' of potential test lists, allowing mailers to assess their performance prior to testing them."[30] It is almost unheard of for a major direct-mail advertiser to use a list that has not been tested. Certainly, brokers and compilers expect this and will work with advertisers to develop testing procedures for a client.

The Message.   One of the great advantages of direct-response advertising is that you can test everything on a small, but meaningful, scale before proceeding to a general mailing. Testing is relatively simple in direct mail. You may want to test which of two prices or appeals or different formats are better. In the same manner as split-run print advertising, every other name on a list is sent mailing A; the other half is sent mailing B. All order cards have a code or key number by which replies are identified and tabulated.

However, to get meaningful differences, you must use a statistically reliable sample. Many list companies will provide a sample of their total list for testing purposes. You must also receive enough responses to show clearly which is the better ad. If mailing piece A produces 14 orders while mailing piece B produces 12, the test result is meaningless. In order to make the test bed, or mailing, large enough, you have to have some idea of the percentage of response to expect. This will vary enormously by medium and by offer. In addition, you must make sure that the names chosen for a direct-mail test are a fair sample of the total list

Timing.   Timing is a critical element in the success of a direct-mail campaign. December is the most popular month for direct mailings with 21 percent of all mail solicitations, followed by November with 18 percent. However, individual companies know that various months are best for their specific products and services. For example, fund-raisers find that November is their best month with 19 percent of all mailings, second is October with 11 percent, and February at 10 percent. Fund-raisers have found a 33 percent difference between their best and worst months in terms of revenues received.[31]

[30]Paul Taybi and Judy Frankel, "List Pretesting," *Direct,* April 10, 1990, p. 35.
[31]Judith Waldrop, "'Tis the Mail Season," *American Demographics,* December 1993, p. 4.

Once we have determined the most appropriate seasonal variations for mailing, we next must time the mailing for the exact (or close to exact) day we want prospects to get our message. For example, most mailings avoid the first day of the month when most households receive their bills. Friday may be a good day for receiving mail about leisure activities, yard furniture, and gardening when customers have the weekend ahead of them for recreational and hobby pursuits. The point is that each advertiser must consider special factors. As one direct mailer said when asked the three most important reasons for his success, "Test, test, and test."

THE MAILING LIST

Without an up-to-date and properly maintained mailing list, successful direct-mail advertising is impossible. Direct mail is the only medium where the advertiser determines the circulation. Modern computer techniques and access to various databases make it possible to build extremely selective mailing lists. Exhibit 13.13 is a promotion for the rental of a list of teachers from which even more selective lists can be drawn. The cost of a list will vary between $25 and $125 per 1,000 names, depending on its selectivity. Mailing-list costs are similar to those for other circulations; the more upscale and selective the audience, the higher the CAM.

The list is the media plan of direct-mail. Just as the media buyer must carefully analyze the audiences of the various vehicles that will make up the final media schedule, the advertiser must carefully choose that list(s) that will provide the greatest number of prospects at the lowest cost. Most lists are *compiled lists;* that is, they are developed from a number of sources, and names are compiled into a single list.

Most mailing lists come from readily available information. "If you have a telephone, unless you have an unlisted number, your name and address are available to anyone with a pencil and piece of paper. Indeed, one of the largest mailing lists in existence is simply a compilation of all the telephone-owning households listed in the nation's 4,000 plus phone books. Do you own a house, land, a car, a boat? In most states your name and address are available from public records. Did you go to college? Your school's alumni directory may list your name, address, and class. If you are a doctor, lawyer, dentist,

EXHIBIT 13.13

. . . .

There is a mailing list for virtually every consumer niche.

(Courtesy: MGI Educational Network System)

engineer, or teacher, you probably belong to one or more professional societies or associations whose membership rosters show your name and address.[32]

As we will see in the remainder of this section, names and prospects are easily available. The problem for the direct-mail advertiser is developing these names into a single list and then fine-tuning it for accuracy, duplication, etc.

There are a number of organizations that are involved in the direct-mail process:

List Brokers.   Most direct mailers use the services of a list broker. The list broker is paid a commission, usually 20 percent, by the list owner each time a list is rented. The broker represents the mailer, not the list owner. "The broker, to all intents and purposes, is akin to the media department of an advertising agency or to an independent media-buying service catering to advertisers. Their job is to research, analyze and evaluate the tens of thousands of individual media [lists] available in the marketplace."[33] Obviously, the list broker is a marketing consultant, not just a source of list rentals.

List Compilers.   The list compiler is usually a broker who rents a number of lists from published sources or lists of similar prospects and combines them into a single list and then rents them to advertisers. List compilers were already established firms in the nineteenth century. For example, Charles Groves, superintendent of Michigan City schools, compiled lists of teachers by writing other school superintendents around the country. He then sold the lists to textbook publishers and other companies wanting to reach teachers.[34] Compilers tend to specialize in either consumer or business lists, although a few do both.

List Managers.   The list manager represents the *list owner* just as the broker is the agency for the mailer. The primary job of the list manager is to maximize income for the list owner by promoting the list to as many advertisers as possible. They are usually outside consultants, but some large companies have in-house list managers. Most national magazines offer their lists for rent. These lists are ideal direct-response vehicles, since most magazines appeal to a narrowly defined, specialized audience. Another benefit of magazine lists is that magazine subscribers often buy through direct-mail offers so that they are proven direct-mail prospects.

Service Bureaus.   Service bureaus provide a number of functions. One of the primary jobs of the service bureau is constantly improving lists. This function is called *list enhancement*. List enhancement includes a number of steps. One of the most important is known as *merge/purge*. Basically merge/purge systems eliminate duplicate names from a list. Such duplication is costly to the advertiser and annoying to the customer. Duplication also offsets any personal contact with the customer by portraying the message as a mass mailing—and one done with little care. Merge/purge is accomplished by computers that are so sophisticated that names are cross-checked against the same addresses and similar spellings.

List enhancement may check a number of other factors. For example, it might separate current and past customers from those who have never dealt with a

List broker

In direct-mail advertising an agent who rents the prospect lists of one advertiser to another advertiser. The broker receives a commission from the seller for this service.

List manager

Promotes client's lists to potential renters and buyers.

Merge/purge (merge & purge)

A system used to eliminate duplication by direct-response advertisers who use different mailing lists for the same mailing. Mailing lists are sent to a central merge/purge office that electronically picks out duplicate names. Saves mailing costs, especially important to firms that send out a million pieces in one mailing. Also avoids damage to the goodwill of the public.

---

[32]"How Did They Get My Name?" Direct Marketing Association.
[33]Ralph Stevens, "Let's All Get on the Same List-Rental Page," *News,* July 5, 1993, p. 39.
[34]Lewis Rashmir, "The First Compiler Was Charles Groves," *DM News,* February 15, 1993, p. 35.

IF YOU NEED TO TALK TO ALMOST A MILLION IMPULSE BUYERS WHO WANT EVERYTHING AND WANT IT NOW,

WE'VE GOT THEIR NAMES...
FRESHLY GENERATED EVERY MONTH!

More than 1 million people participated in brand new sweepstakes and contests from Direct American Marketers last month—and their names are ready to make money for you now!

All 1,000,000+ (actually, closer to 2,000,000) of these names responded to Direct American Marketers' sweeps and contest mailings, proven pullers despite the recession, in the past month alone.

Connect with these 1,000,000+ Hot Line names from Direct American Marketers—freshly generated month after month after month—through the respected companies, shown here, that manage Direct American Marketers' lists. We request that you contact our managers directly.

Action List Services, Inc.
• Award Claim Center Ride Along
• Confidential Consumer Secrets Ride Along
• DAMI Conglomerate Package Insert Program
• Guaranteed Award Recipients Ride Along
• Hit the Jackpot Package Insert Program
• Jackpotunities Package Insert Program
• National Consumer Coupons Ride Along
• The Wishline Hot Line 900# List
• Wishing Well

Database Management
• DAMI Spanish Package Insert Program
• DAMI Spanish Speaking Opportunity Seekers

List Services Corp.
• Award Claim Center
• Easy Cash Awards

M.G.T. Associates, Inc.
• Awards by Mail
• Consumer Secrets
• Consumer Secrets Mail-in Respondents
• Credit Mania
• DAMI Enhancebase
• DAMI New Movers
• Hit The Jackpot
• Jackpotunities
• Let's Make A Deal
• National Consumer Coupons
• No-Credit Mania
• Phone Mania
• Promotional 900 Database

DAMI
DIRECT AMERICAN MARKETERS, INC.
a powerful name!
IRVINE, CALIFORNIA

(Courtesy: Direct American Marketers, Inc.)

company. Each of these groups could then receive a distinctive mailing. List enhancement also provides special services for different types of advertisers. For example, if you are offering a product where you plan to extend credit, you may want to check the list against a bad debtor file.[35]

Lettershop. The lettershop is in reality a mailing house. These companies coordinate the job of mailing millions of pieces of mail. The efficiency and timeliness of the letter shop are critical to the success of the direct-mail campaign.[36]

Response Lists. As we discussed earlier, the great majority of mailing lists are compiled. However, many mailing-list houses sell or rent lists of people who have previously responded to a direct-mail offer or demonstrated some interest in doing so (see Exhibit 13.14). People on response lists are those who are prone to order by mail; therefore, these lists are more productive than compiled lists.

Generally, response lists are more expensive than compiled lists. Compiled lists are regarded as less valuable than response lists by direct mailers. The biggest drawback cited for compiled lists is that many compiled lists don't offer a previous record of direct-response purchases. Direct-response advertisers often use compiled lists as supplements to response lists. By combining response and compiled lists, a mailer can reach both previous customers and a larger pool of prospective customers.

Response lists are often obtained from previous customers of the company. These are called *house lists* and are among the most valuable commodities that a direct mailer has. From time to time, owners of house lists will use rental

---

[35]Alicia Orr, "Taking the Mystery Out of List Enhancement," *Target Marketing*, May 1993, p. 16.
[36]Adapted from Rose Harper, *Mailing List Strategies* (New York: McGraw-Hill, 1986), p. 11.

response lists from other related, but noncompeting companies. The source and number of rental lists are almost endless. Advertisers can buy lists of people who have gone on cruises, who hunt specific animals, and who have bought books on psychoanalysis in the past six months. One list offered the names of people who had ordered false teeth adhesive by mail!

List Protection. Since mailing lists are so valuable, companies go to great lengths to protect them from misuse. The most common list abuse is multimailings beyond an agreed-upon limit. For example, one direct mailer reported that a company rented his list on a one-time basis and used it 13 times.

The traditional protection for such misuse is to include a number of fictitious names so that the list owner can trace the number of mailings. This is known as *list decoying.* There are two types of decoys: "*Permanent decoys* are names that remain on your list to protect it from theft when stored at your office or your service bureau. *Temporary decoys* are names you change each time you rent or exchange your list; they help you determine responsibility if there is an unauthorized use of your list."[37]

In addition to protecting the list itself, list renters should also ask for a sample of the mailing material. Occasionally, a mailing may be in bad taste or contain a deceptive offer. However, the much greater problem is that the mailing may be too closely competitive with the list owner's products. Renting a list should provide additional profit, not additional competition!

The protection and use of mailing lists are so important that a major professional organization, the Mailing List Users and Suppliers Association, has adopted the ML/USA List and Data Usage Guidelines. These guidelines (see Exhibit 13.15) offer specific rules for ethical use of lists to both users and renters.

Other Direct-Mail Techniques

The format and execution of direct-mail campaigns can take many forms. In this section we will briefly discuss a few of the primary ones.

---

[37]Michael Sass, "The 'Whys' and 'Hows' of List Decoying," *Target Marketing,* May 1993, p. 22.

EXHIBIT

13.15

∙∙∙∙∙∙∙∙∙∙∙∙∙∙∙∙∙∙∙∙

ML/USA's List Usage
Guidelines

GUIDELINES

1. The mailer, or its service organizations, may not use the rented list data for any purpose other than the program for which the list was supplied.

2. The mailer, or its service organizations, may not reuse the rented list data for any promotional or marketing purposes.

3. The mailer, or its service organizations, may not permanently enhance house files by using names, addresses or other information, whether specific or inferred, obtained from the rented list data. Permanent enhancements include:

   (a) Adding or coding ("tagging") response information to the house files, such as:

(cont.)

EXHIBIT

13.15

• • • • • • • • • • • • • • • • • • •

(cont.)

(i) single or multi-buyer information,

(ii) frequency and recency of purchase,

(iii) monetary value of purchase,

(iv) classifying data into categories,

(v) specific list source or type.

(b) Adding or coding demographic and psychographic information, such as age, income, personal interests and behavioral traits.

(c) Adding additional family members, such as spouses or children, to the house files.

(d) Adding to the house files such address information as avenue, road or street suffixes; directionals such as north, south, east and west; alternate address, rural route numbers, post office box numbers, and apartment numbers; or any improvements, substitutions or standardizations of street names, spellings or abbreviations.

(e) Adding or upgrading zip code information to the house files.

(f) Adding first names or initials to the house files.

(g) Adding middle initial, suffix or prefix information to the house files.

4. The mailer, or its service organizations, may not retain change of address information on a rented list obtained prior to, and expressly for, a given mailing; nor may a mailer employ an "address-correction request" program on rented lists for the purposes of retaining the information derived from the program.

5. The mailer, or its service organizations, may not send the rented lists, or any copy, to other service bureaus without the express permission of the list owner or its representative.

6. The mailer, or its service organizations, may not employ any method to detect decoy names or alter or eliminate decoys.

7. The mailer, or its service organizations, may not add telephone numbers to the rented list.

8. The mailer, or its service organizations, may not manipulate merge-purge reports to give improper weight to any list.

9. After a list's authorized use, only non-mailable matchcode versions of names and addresses may be retained and only to accomplish the following:

(a) to suppress names and addresses found in the rented list data in later mailings of the same offer against the same list made by the mailer who paid for the original rental; and

(b) to compile a mailing history data base to be compared to response history data for purposes of response analysis.

All other list data must be destroyed, erased, or returned to the list owner or its representative.

(Courtesy: Stevens-Knox List Management.)

Package Inserts. For many years direct marketers have used package inserts to promote additional purchases of products sent to customers or to promote other items in their product lines. As mentioned earlier in this chapter, these bounce-back circulars are very inexpensive, since there are no additional postage costs, but more importantly they are directed at proven customers who have just made a direct-mail purchase.

Today, many direct marketers are negotiating with other companies to use inserts in their packages much as you would buy space in a magazine. These inserts are called *ride-alongs* and can be sent at a fraction of an independent mailing. Typical ride-along CPMs are in the $40–$50 range compared to $200–$300 for the simplest direct-mail piece.

Besides their low cost, inserts allow an advertiser to gain an implied endorsement from the distributing company. Also, the number of ride-along programs available offer a degree of target marketing that approaches an independent mailing. It is estimated that there are as many as 20,000 programs available to advertisers.

A number of companies use package inserts for product sampling as well as advertising notices. For example, this method of sampling guarantees a logical product tie-in with what is already being purchased. Just as importantly, it provides the sample at a fraction of the cost of mailing the sample alone.

Cooperative (Joint) Mail Advertising. With the cost of postage continuing to increase, direct mailers often attempt to share expenses through cooperative mailings. There are a number of firms such as Carol Wright that specialize in joint mailings. These mailings may include as many as 20 different advertising offers in one envelope. Each advertiser provides a coupon or other short messages, and the joint mailer handles the mailing and divides the cost among the advertisers.

Cooperative mailings have two major drawbacks. First, they are extremely impersonal, since each advertiser's message must be very short. Second, it is difficult to reach your specific customers through joint mailings with the precision you would have with your own list. The dilemma of joint mailings is that as the number of participating advertisers increases, the cost per advertiser goes down, but, likewise, the unique feature of the mailing decreases.

Statement Stuffers. Few companies miss an opportunity to include a message with your monthly statement (see Exhibit 13.16). These messages are similar to ride-alongs and have several advantages. First, they cost nothing to deliver, since the mailing expense is going to be incurred in any case. Second, they are at least seen, since people eventually get around to opening their bills. Finally, most recipients are credit qualified and have already dealt with the company before, or they would not be getting a statement. The disadvantage is that some consumers will not be in the mood for another purchase while paying for their last one.

PLANNING AND PRODUCING THE DIRECT-MAIL PIECE

The first step in planning a direct-mail piece is to study the overall marketing and advertising program. Direct marketing is not separate from the firm's other marketing efforts but an integrated part of the system. The first ques-

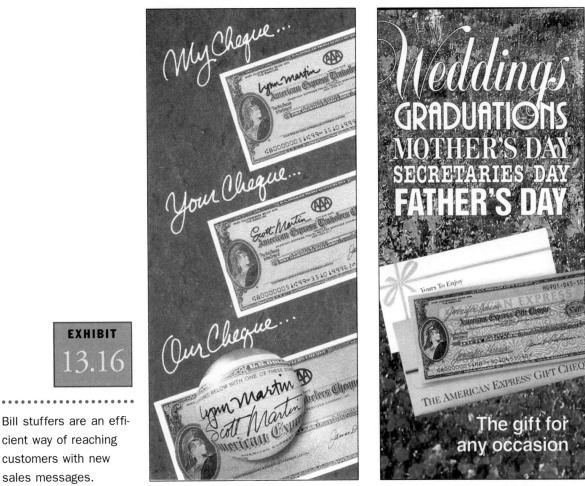

(Courtesy: Promotion Solutions.)

tion a direct marketer should ask is, "How will my direct marketing efforts
complement the total marketing program of my company?"

To answer this question you might ask yourself the following:

- **Will the direct-mail effort be supported with media advertising? Before, during, or after the mailing?**

- **Is the direct-mail message directed at present or potential customers, or both?**

- **Am I attempting a straight sale or building leads for future follow-up? If the
latter, does our sales force know about and understand the purpose of the
mailing?**

Other questions you ask will, of course, be determined by the specific marketing problem you are trying to solve. However, only after you have approached the direct-mail promotion from the perspective of your marketing
goals and objectives are you ready to begin production of your mailing piece.

The creator of direct mail has a wide latitude in format: It may be a single
card encompassing a coupon, or it may be a letter with a return card, a small
folder, a brochure, or a folded broadside with an order form and return envelope. Each format has a different function and use, depending on the cost
of the product being sold, the importance of pictures, and the nature and

length of the copy. As a rule, a warm letter, even if not personalized, should accompany any request for the order. This letter should stress the product's benefits, describe its key features and their importance, and ask for the order. No matter what kind of material is being sent, it is always possible to present it in an interesting form (within postal limitations).

What a different world direct-mail production is compared to magazine ad production! With magazine ads, the publisher is responsible for the total printing and delivery of the publication. In direct mail, the advertiser undertakes the complete burden of having all the material printed, which involves selecting the paper and the type, establishing prices, and selecting the printer. It also involves selecting a letter shop, whose functions we discuss further in a later section.

A Mail-Production Program

Perhaps the clearest way to see what is involved is to work through a schedule and touch on some of the key points.

Checking Weight and Size with Post Office. Everything begins on receipt of a layout of the mailing unit, including copy and artwork from the creative department, along with quantities and mailing dates. The first—and most important—thing to do is to check with the post office on weight and size.

Selecting the Printing Process. In Chapter 18 we discuss the three major types of printing: letterpress, offset, and gravure. For the time being, we can say that most direct-mail advertising is printed by the offset method, except very large runs, which may use rotogravure.

Selecting the Paper. Here we have to pause to become familiar with some important elements in the choice of paper, as this is not covered elsewhere in the book. The three chief categories of paper ("stocks") used in advertising are writing stocks, book stocks, and cover stocks.

Writing Stocks. This class comprises the whole range of paper meant to be written or typed on. Quality varies from ledger stock, used to keep records; to bond stock, for top-level office stationery; to utility office paper, used to keep records; to memorandum paper. If you wanted to include a letter in a mailing, you would find a paper in this class.

Book Stocks. Book stocks are the widest classification of papers used in advertising. Chief among the many variations of book stocks are the following:

- **News stock.** This is the least costly book paper, built for a short life and porous so that it can dry quickly. It takes line plates well. It is used for free-standing inserts in magazines, but it is not very good for offset.

- **Antique finish.** A soft paper with a mildly rough finish, antique finish is used for offset. Among the antique classifications are eggshell antique, a very serviceable offset paper; and text, a high-grade antique used for quality offset books, booklets, and brochures (it is often watermarked and deckle-edged or irregular).

- **Machine finish.** Most books and publications are printed on machine-finish paper. It is the workhorse of the paper family.

- **English finish.** This paper has a roughened nonglare surface. Widely accepted for direct-mail and sales-promotion printing, it is especially good for offset lithography and gravure.

- **Coated.** This is a paper given a special coat of clay and then ironed. The result is a heavier, smoother paper. Coated paper is not usually used for offset. It can take 150-screen half-tones very well for letterpress printing and is therefore frequently used in industrial catalogs, where fine, sharp reproduction is important and where there will be continuous usage over a period of time.

Cover Stocks. These are strong papers, highly resistant to rough handling. Cover stock is used not only for the covers of booklets, but also sometimes by itself in direct-mail work. Although it has many finishes and textures, it is not adaptable for half-tone printing by letterpress but reproduces tones very well in offset.

There are many other types of paper, useful for many purposes, but writing, book, and cover are the chief stocks used in advertising. The printer will submit samples of paper suitable for a given job.

Basic Weights and Sizes. Paper comes off the machine in large rolls. It is then cut into large sheets in a number of different sizes. In that way, many pages can be printed at one time. Paper is sold by 500-sheet reams, and its grade is determined by weight. To meet the problem comparing the weight of paper cut to different sizes, certain sizes have been established for each class as basic for weighing purposes:

- **For writing paper: 17 by 22 inches**

- **For book paper: 25 by 38 inches**

- **For cover stock: 20 by 26 inches**

Hence, no matter how large the sheet into which the paper has been cut may be, its weight is always given in terms of the weight of that paper when cut to its basic size. Thus, one hears a writing paper referred to as a "20-pound writing paper," a book paper referred to as a "70-pound paper," and a cover stock identified as a "100-pound cover."

Paper, which has to be selected in relation to the printing process and the plates to be used, is usually procured by the printer, after a specific choice has been made by the advertiser. In large cities, it may also be bought directly from paper jobbers. Both printers and jobbers will be glad to submit samples. Before you give the final order for paper, you should check once more with the post office for weight, shape, and size of envelope. Check the total package.

In planning direct mail, you must know basic paper sizes and plan all pieces so that they may be cut from a standard sheet size without waste. Before ordering envelopes, check with the post office to learn the latest size restrictions, which are subject to change.

Selecting the Printer. The problem in selecting a printer is, first of all, to find those printers who have the type of presses and the capacity to handle the operation that you have in mind. They may not be located near you. In any case, experience has shown that it is always best to get three estimates.

Of course, the reputation of the firm for prompt delivery is important.

Finished mechanicals with type and illustrations or photographic negatives should be made ready to turn over to the printer. Proofs should be checked carefully and returned promptly to the printer.

Selecting the Letter Shop (Mailing House).   Once all the material has been printed—including the envelope, which has to be addressed; a letter, possibly calling for a name fill-in; a folder that has to be folded; and a return card, also perhaps with the name imprinted—the whole package goes to a mailing house (also called a *letter shop*). Many letter shops are mammoth plants in which everything is done by computer. Their computerized letters not only mention the addressee's name, but also include a personal reference. The name is also printed on the return order form. Machines automatically address various units, fold all pieces that need to be folded, collate all material, and insert it in the envelope, which is sealed, arranged geographically for postal requirements, and delivered to the post office. (There is always a question of which is more wonderful: the machines with their swinging arms that do all these things, or the production director who has all the material ready in one place on time.)

Because the letter shop and the printer must work closely together, it is desirable that they be located near each other.

Production Schedule for Direct Mail

The planning and execution of a direct-mail campaign is not an overnight operation. The advertiser must work backward from the date he or she wishes the customer to receive the mailing piece to determine the necessary lead time. A reverse production timetable can be helpful in planning each step of a project (Exhibit 13.17).

SUMMARY

Direct marketing and direct-response advertising are now accepted as major components of the marketing mix. Companies have come to realize that the ability to combine personal messages with highly selective audience segments gives direct response advantages seen in few other media. The tremendous strides in computer technology combined with new technology make the future of direct response both exciting and uncertain.

Interactive television and other methods of shop-at-home are technologically feasible. However, these direct-response programs are consumer, not technology, driven. Until consumers are completely comfortable with buying through this new technology, we will continue to see most direct-response selling taking place through traditional outlets such as direct mail, catalogs, telemarketing, and traditional media offers.

The flexibility of direct response makes it practical for even smaller advertisers. In addition, the ability to test and verify direct marketing is vitally important in the current era of accountability. The ability to precisely measure many types of direct response is a major advantage to advertisers and provides the accountability increasingly demanded by companies.

Regardless of the format of future direct response, there is little question that it will continue to grow, probably at a faster rate than media advertising. Not

EXHIBIT

13.17

· · · · · · · · · · · · · · · · · · · ·

Advertisers use reverse time tables to schedule direct mail campaigns.

· · · · · · · · · · · · · · · · · ·

Reverse time table

Used in direct mail to schedule a job. The schedule starts with the date it is to reach customers and works backward to a starting date.

· · · · · · · · · · · · · · · · · ·

Description of item or Project: _____

REVERSE TIME TABLE

(The purpose of which is to work backwards to make sure enough time is allowed for proper completion.)

Final Date
Due in Hands
of Recipients _____ | This is when you expect the mailing to reach the people who are going to read it and act upon it.

Mailing
Date _____ | When you must release it to get it there on time. Avoid disappointment by allowing enough time for the P.O.

Assembly
Date _____ | All material must be in on this date to allow sufficient time for the mailing operations.

Printing
Completion
Date _____ | This could be same as ASSEMBLY DATE except where time is required for shipment to out-of-town point.

Final Artwork
Approval
Date _____ | This is the date the artwork must be ready to turn over to the printer.

Artwork
Completion
Date _____ | Although most details should have been okayed before work actually began, quite often several people must approve the finished artwork. Allow enough time for this approval.

Finished
Artwork
Assignment
Date _____ | This is the day the artist or art department gets the job. Allow at least a week. If no type has to be set, the interval can be cut short.

Consideration
and Approval
Date _____ | Allow four or five days for staff members, including legal department if necessary, to see finished copy and layout.

Copy and
Layout
Assignment
Date _____ | Allow a week or more to give the copy and layout people time to do their jobs. Give more time when you can; they will more readily come through for you when a rush job is really critical.

Starting
Date _____ | You need some time to think about the job and draw up a set of instructions.

(Source: The Direct Mail Marketing Manual, Release 4005, July 1976. Courtesy: Direct Mail/Marketing Association, Inc., New York.)

only will direct response become more important in the marketing plans of many companies, but we will see the concept of audience segmentation adopted by all media. History will probably mark the 1990s as the end of the era of mass media and mass-audience delivery. In the future, audience segmentation will be even more refined. More importantly, one-way communication will slowly give way to some form of interactive media. There is little question that direct response will play a major role in this transition.

In addition to the technological advances of direct-response advertising, societal changes also are working in its favor. For example, the two-income family, working mothers, an aging population, and less leisure time are only a few of the factors leading people to favor in-home buying. Greater demand and customer acceptability of direct response are pushing more companies to enter the field.

Perhaps the greatest challenge facing direct marketing is public skepticism. However, industry-wide efforts sponsored by the Direct Marketing Association and other organizations have made great strides in improving the industry's image. The fact that most Fortune 500 companies routinely include some form of direct marketing in their promotional plans is testimony to its growing respectability among advertisers and improved credibility among consumers. Nevertheless, the industry is aware that legislation affecting its operation is constantly being introduced and presents a threat to future growth.

Questions

1. What have been some of the major factors causing the growth of direct-response advertising?
2. What is direct marketing?
3. What steps have been taken to improve the image of direct-response advertising?
4. What role does database marketing play in direct-response advertising?
5. What is inbound telemarketing?
6. What is the key element in direct mail?
7. What is the Telephone Consumer Protection Act?
8. What is per inquiry?
9. What is the function of a list compiler?
10. What is the difference between a list broker and a list manager?

Sales Promotion

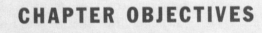

CHAPTER OBJECTIVES

Significantly more dollars are spent in all forms of sales promotion than advertising. Promotions, to both consumers and the trade, are growing faster than advertising expenditures. After reading this chapter you will understand:

- **That promotion encourages short-term sales**
- **Coordination between advertising and promotional activities**
- **Promotional formats are endless**
- **Couponing is the largest promotional activity**
- **Trade incentives versus consumer sales promotion**

A stock car, emblazoned with tire and oil company logos, wins the Daytona 500; executives receive colorful calendars from their insurance agents at Christmas; a teenager gets a **free cologne sample** when she enters a department store; and a housewife uses a cents-off coupon to purchase a detergent at her local grocery store. **What do these events have in common?** They, and numerous other incentives to buy a product, are part of the growing field of sales promotion.

Sales promotion covers an infinite array of activities to create short-term sales. In recent years, sales promotion and advertising have been increasingly used in an integrated effort to build brand loyalty and long-term sales (advertising) and create an incentive to push the consumer toward an immediate purchase (sales promotion). Despite the fact that advertising and sales promotion are being used together in an united effort to increase profitability, it is critical that we not blur the fact that advertising and sales promotion are different in terms of execution and objectives.

In modern marketing it is impossible to be successful as a client, advertising agency, marketing manager, or promotion manager, without a knowledge of the broad concepts involved in the total system of marketing communication. "Traditionally, companies marketing to the general public treated advertising funds as separate from, and more important than, promotion and direct marketing monies. In recent years, however, marketing executives in many firms have concluded that advertising should not automatically be given higher standing than other ways to reach potential customers. One explanation for their changed attitude is the belief that modern data bases ". . . allow implementation of promotion and direct marketing efforts in ways that are more precise than advertising in traditional mass media."[1]

In this chapter, we will discuss the primary types of sales promotion and how they complement media advertising. As with advertising, the opportunities for successful execution of sales promotion programs depend on an understanding of the marketing objectives of a firm or individual brand. Sales promotion failures are most often a direct result of poor planning and a lack of integration with the total marketing mix.

PROMOTION AND ADVERTISING

To begin our discussion, we need to have a clear idea of the purposes and objectives normally associated with sales promotion and advertising:[2]

Sales promotion

- **Short-term product movement**

- **Measurable, immediate results**

- **Encouraging consumers to try new products**

- **Selling undifferentiated products on price**

- **Gaining trade awareness and acceptance**

Advertising

- **Long-term image and building brand equity**

- **Cumulative effects over time**

- **Communication of product features and benefits**

- **Gaining consumer awareness and acceptance**

As you can see, advertising and promotion serve distinct, but complementary roles in achieving the objectives and goals of a marketing program. In most instances, successful sales promotion depends on strong consumer identity with a brand. In this respect, advertising "sets the table" for sales promotion to close the deal.

---

[1]Joseph Turow, "The Organizational Underpinnings of Contemporary Media Conglomerates," *Communication Research,* December 1992, p. 694.
[2]"Advertising and Sales Promotion: An Overview," Television Advertising Bureau.

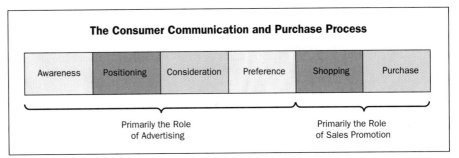

The Consumer Communication and Purchase Process

| Awareness | Positioning | Consideration | Preference | Shopping | Purchase |

Primarily the Role of Advertising

Primarily the Role of Sales Promotion

EXHIBIT 14.1

Advertising and sales promotion should function in a complementary fashion.

In order to understand the synergistic nature of sales promotion and advertising, we first have to examine the communication process at work when we make a purchase. Exhibit 14.1 shows the process from consumer awareness to ultimate purchase. As you can see, most of the sales-promotional activities occur at the end of the consumer communication cycle. However, these promotional activities must be planned in concert with the advertising so that they reinforce the advertising message at the point of purchase.

There is general agreement that both advertising and promotion should play a role in moving products through the marketplace. However, in recent years a number of marketing executives have questioned what they regard as an overdependence on sales promotion. Since most promotional activities involve some form of price reduction, consumers are encouraged to substitute discounts for brand loyalty. Once this cost versus brand perspective is instilled in consumers, it is very difficult for manufacturers to sell on any basis other than lowest cost with its accompanying damage to profitability.

The proper role of sales promotion according to most marketers is that of an *occasional* incentive for immediate purpose. Instead, product categories such as cigarettes and detergent used sales promotion to such a degree that companies such as Procter & Gamble and Philip Morris finally had to permanently lower the price of some of their major brands such as Tide detergent.

Rather than using advertising to insulate brands against competitive price cutting, these companies engaged in sales promotion to the point that they lowered the perceived value of their brands with the result being inevitable permanent price cuts. As one promotional executive declared, "[B]rands are being bargained, belittled, and battered. Instead of being brand builders we are committed to brand suicide through the self-inflicted wounds of excessive price promotion."[3]

Consumer advertising
Directed to people who will use the product themselves, in contrast to trade advertising, industrial advertising, or professional advertising.

Total promotion budgets are generally divided into three categories: consumer advertising, consumer promotion (usually referred to as either sales promotion or simply promotion), and trade promotion (known as dealer promotion or merchandising). Let's take a minute and examine the place of each in the marketing mix and the share of promotional budgets spent in these promotional categories and related promotional expenses (see Exhibit 14.2).

1. *Consumer advertising.* Traditional media advertising vehicles promote basic product attributes, location of dealers, and/or comparisons with other products. Currently, 26.9 percent of total promotional budgets are spent on advertising, the smallest share of the three categories.

---

[3]Larry Light, "At the Center of It All Is the Brand," *Advertising Age,* March 29, 1993, p. 22.

EXHIBIT

14.2

• • • • • • • • • • • • • • • •

Sales promotion uses a number of techniques and accounts for billions of dollars.

	Gross Revenues ($Millions)		
	1993	1992	% CHANGE
Premium Incentives	$19,500	$17,700	10.1%
POP Displays	16,500	15,700	5.0
Couponing	7,100*	7,000	1.4
Specialty Advertising	6,200	5,200	19.2
Promotional Licensing	4,700	4,400	6.8
Sponsored Events	3,700	3,200	15.6
Specialty Printing	2,900	2,600	11.5
Fulfillment	2,300	2,200	4.5
Telepromotions	993.4	435.0	N/A[†]
Research	778.9	728.0	6.9
Promotional Agencies	707.4	523.0	35.3
In-Store Marketing	740.0*	654.8*	13.0
Product Sampling	586.6*	175.9	N/A[††]
Total	$66.1 Billion**	$60.2 Billion	9.8%

*These gross figures contain some overlap, as coupons and samples distributed in-store are counted in each segment.

**This is the net unduplicated total after duplication in the areas of couponing and sampling is stripped out.

[†]1993 figure includes more categories of high-volume 800-number programs than were included in 1992.

[††]The 1992 figure for sampling was for outdoor sampling only.

(Courtesy: Promo Magazine *Wilton, CT.)*

2. *Consumer sales promotion.* These are sales-promotional incentives directed to the consumer. Cents-off coupons are the most common consumer promotion, but free gifts, rebates, and sweepstakes are also used frequently. Some 28.2 percent of marketing promotion is invested in consumer promotions.

3. *Trade promotions.* Trade incentives are designed to encourage a company's sales force or retail outlets to push its products more aggressively. These are the most expensive types of promotion on a per-person basis. Winning dealers or retailers may get a trip to Hawaii, a new car, or a cash bonus. Trade promotions make up approximately 44.9 percent of total promotional expenditures.

In recent years, trade promotion budgets have decreased somewhat in favor of consumer advertising and sales promotion. Manufacturers have moved more dollars into consumer-oriented programs to build brand loyalty. However, the strength of large retail chains such as Walmart and Kmart dictate a continuing high level of trade expenditures. Even with the small shift to consumer spending, the news is still not good for traditional advertising. "If, as forecast, consumer promotion spending gains an increasing share of marketing budgets, the areas likely to grow are in-store promotion, direct mail couponing, targeted coupon promotions and product sampling."[4] Most predictions see any future increases in advertising's share of total promotion budgets as minimal at best.

FORMS OF SALES PROMOTION

In the remainder of this chapter, we will discuss the primary types of sales promotion. Priority will be given to those techniques most associated with

---

[4]Scott Hume. "Trade Promotion $ Share Dips in '92," *Advertising Age,* April 5, 1993, p. 43.

advertising, especially at the consumer level. However, some attention will also be paid to trade-oriented promotions. In all cases, we need to keep in mind the complementary functions of advertising and promotion. The most frequently used forms of sales promotion are the following:

- **Point-of-purchase advertising**
- **Premium**
- **Specialty advertising**
- **Coupons**
- **Sampling**
- **Deals**
- **Event marketing**
- **Sweepstakes and contests**
- **Cooperative advertising**
- **Trade shows and exhibits**
- **Directories and Yellow Pages**
- **Trade incentives**

Sales promotion has become as routine for most product manufacturers as advertising. It is estimated that over 95 percent of firms marketing consumer products use some form of sales promotion each year.

POINT-OF-PURCHASE ADVERTISING

Point-of-purchase advertising
Displays prepared by the manufacturer for use where the product is sold.

Point-of-purchase (p-o-p) displays date to the earliest shopkeepers who probably placed a crude sign on some slow-moving merchandise. However, from its humble beginnings point-of-purchase has become one of the most prevalent and fastest-growing segments of sales promotion. P-o-p has flourished in the self-service marketing environment of the past decade. As one advertising executive pointed out, point-of-purchase is the last three feet of the marketing mix, where the customer, the product, and the dollars come together.[5] Estimated annual expenditures for p-o-p are $18 billion, and this figure has grown over 10 percent per year for the past five years.

There are a number of reasons for the recent success of p-o-p:

1. *Declining brand loyalty among consumers.* Perhaps the single most important factor in the increasing use of p-o-p is declining consumer loyalty among a number of product categories. This decline is especially noticeable among product categories most often found in grocery and drug stores, traditionally the most popular venues for p-o-p. One study indicated that 30 percent of female shoppers said they were more likely to try new or different brands than in the past.[6]

2. *Importance of impulse buying among consumers.* Related to the diminishing importance of brand loyalty is the importance of unplanned purchases. As Exhibit 14.3 indicates, over 53 percent of all supermarket purchases are made in-store. In addition, some 40 percent of drug store purchases are made on an impulse basis, and sales increase as much as 20 percent when a store has interesting displays.[7]

3. *The advantage of using p-o-p is that it is an excellent complement to other forms of promotion and advertising.* A major study of retailers found that

---

[5]Cara Chang Mutert, "Marketers Dissect the IMC Puzzle," *Sales and Marketing Strategies and News,* September/October 1993, p. 5.
[6]"How Loyal Is the New Traditionalist Shopper?" *POPAI Insider,* March 1993, p. 1.
[7]"Marketers Reach '90s Consumer via P-O-P," *Sales and Marketing Strategies & News,* July/August 1993, p. 31.

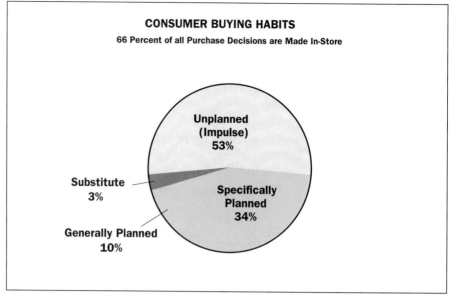

Point-of-purchase advertising plays an important role in unplanned purchases.

CONSUMER BUYING HABITS

66 Percent of all Purchase Decisions are Made In-Store

Unplanned (Impulse) 53%

Substitute 3%

Specifically Planned 34%

Generally Planned 10%

(Source: POPAI.)

all brands tested increased sales when displays were added. It also found that the increases ascribed to p-o-p, unlike most other forms of advertising and promotion, did not lessen over time. However, the same study also found that the rate of sales increases varied significantly among product categories and type of displays.[8]

Other research has found that p-o-p creates excellent synergy with advertising. It is rare that advertising does not improve the effectiveness of virtually any type of sales promotion. However, there are few combinations of advertising and sales promotion that increase sales to the degree of advertising and p-o-p. As demonstrated in Exhibit 14.4, advertising and in-store displays increase the sales produced by either p-o-p or advertising alone by approximately one-third. It is clear from these studies that store displays, like all forms of sales promotion, should be thoroughly researched and adhere to clear objectives.

The variety and creativity of displays offer a suitable means of promoting almost any product. P-o-p continues to add new in-store options. In addition, p-o-p is continually being combined with other forms of sales promotion such as sampling and in-store couponing. The p-o-p industry is also moving into electronic, interactive, and broadcast media. For example, POP Radio produces live radio format tailored to specific retailers and their customers, and a number of companies are offering shopping cart video and electronic bulletin boards.

Not only are these innovations in point-of-purchase interesting in themselves, but they point up once again that advertising, promotion, and marketing are increasingly becoming interrelated to the point that it is difficult to tell when one stops and the other begins. Rather than trying to decide in what category a technique belongs, managers are becoming more concerned with using whatever techniques work.

---

[8]From the POPAI/KMart/Procter & Gamble Study of P-O-P Effectiveness in Mass Merchandising Stores.

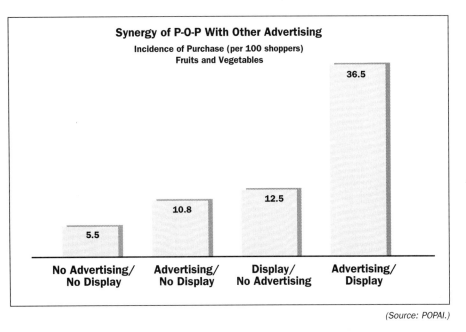

Synergy of P-O-P With Other Advertising
Incidence of Purchase (per 100 shoppers)
Fruits and Vegetables

- No Advertising/No Display: 5.5
- Advertising/No Display: 10.8
- Display/No Advertising: 12.5
- Advertising/Display: 36.5

(Source: POPAI.)

Point-of-purchase advertising is an important complement to traditional advertising.

The Future of Point-of Purchase

The techniques used in point-of-purchase will continue to proliferate. Using database technology, they will increasingly reach specific consumers, first regionally and then down to the individual store level. However, p-o-p clutter is becoming a major problem. Point-of-purchase revenue is growing five times faster than retail floor space. In the future, p-o-p will have to find promotional techniques that take into consideration the saturation of both shelf and floor space. More and more point-of-purchase displays are doubling as product shelving to overcome space limitation problems (see Exhibit 14.5). In addition, we are also seeing items such as grocery bags being used as point-of-purchase advertising. Also, more attention will be given to product packaging as a form of promotion and advertising.

Premiums

Premium
An item, other than the product itself, given to purchasers of a product as an inducement to buy. Can be free with a purchase (for example, on the package, in the package, or the container itself) or available upon proof of purchase and a payment (self-liquidating premium).

Premiums are among the oldest and most popular forms of sales promotion. Like most forms of sales promotion, premiums are designed to encourage customers to make an immediate purchase. Premiums come in an infinite number of formats and are often used in connection with other forms of advertising or promotion. A majority of premium offers are promoted through advertising. Strictly speaking many well-known forms of sales promotion are, in fact, premiums. For example, an on-pack coupon is a type of premium. Premiums are limited only by the imagination of the companies offering them. Most premiums are offered at the time of purchase. However, other premiums—known as *traffic-building premiums*—are given merely for visiting a retailer, a real estate development, or an automobile dealer.

As in the case of other sales promotion techniques, premiums should be part of a total marketing and advertising program and should be appropriate and logical for the product with which they are associated. Premiums should be selected with the same care as you would use in planning an advertising media buy. The key element in an effective premium program is whether or not

Case History

ELEPHANT/TIGER
Barnum Tower Display

Conocraft, Inc., Sussex, NJ created a display for Nabisco Brands to heighten awareness of Barnum's Animal Crackers among kids. The display had to generate higher profits, appear full at all times, and bring a newness to the Barnum animal merchandising efforts.

The display was very well received by retailers that led to a longer use for the display than the originally anticipated four weeks. The display also was attributed with stronger sales of the product over the previous year. Ten thousand of the displays were constructed.

Conocraft used die-cut corrugated board with acrylic and ultra-violet coatings. The display had a construction cost of $10 to $15 per unit.

(Courtesy: Conocraft, Inc. and Nabisco Foods)

Traffic building premium

A sales incentive to encourage customers to come to a store where a sale can be closed.

it appeals to the target audience and is logical to the product being promoted. If either of these elements is missing, the premium will probably fail.

There are a number of types of premiums. In the following discussion, we will point out the primary types of premiums, but you will note that in some cases there is overlap among these categories where a single premium may fit into more than one category.

Self-Liquidating Premiums

In this era of tight budgets, self-liquidating premiums are the most popular and the fastest-growing category. The primary advantage of self-liquidators is that they require customers to pay a portion of the cost of the merchandise. As a rule, the customer pays approximately 75 percent of the premium's cost. However, in some cases premiums actually become a major profit center for

(Courtesy: Spencer Products, Inc. Levis)

a company. For example, Marlboro cigarettes offers a catalog of "Adventure Team" merchandise that is available with payment accompanied by proof of purchase from Marlboro packs.

In rare cases, the merchandise associated with a product becomes so popular that it is offered apart from the product. In 1993, Coca-Cola began a mail-order catalog of various Coca-Cola–embossed merchandise. Earlier, the company had opened "Coke" stores selling similar products. Obviously, this merchandise is no longer a premium, but it shows the popularity that some brands (and their premiums) have achieved.

In recent years, some companies have combined premium offers based on the amount of a product purchased. For example, Ball Park hot dogs offered a free Michael Jordan lunch bag and cooler with six proof-of-purchase symbols. However, the same merchandise could be obtained for only two proof-of-purchase symbols and $6. The advantage of this type of offer is that it appeals to infrequent-users who want the merchandise and are willing to pay for it.

Self-liquidating premium

A premium offered to consumers for a fee that covers its cost plus handling.

While the popularity of self-liquidators is obvious for the firms offering them, they have to be chosen carefully if they are to be successful. Since a self-liquidating premium carries the name of the manufacturer, established brand names have a tremendous advantage in selling such merchandise. Self-liquidating premiums are most popular with children, teenagers, and young adults. Therefore, both the product and the premium must be "in" to be effective.

Direct Premiums

The second most popular type of premiums are those given to the customer at the time of purchase. The major advantage of these premiums is the immediate reward they provide for the buyer. In addition, they require no handling or mailing expenses, since the consumer collects the premium at the time of purchase. On the other hand, due to space limitations, the manufacturer is usually constrained in terms of the size of the premium. There are several types of direct premiums, including on-pack, in-pack, near-pack, and container premiums.

Collectively, these premiums are called factory-pack premiums. Historically, factory-pack premiums were the pioneers. The category is best known from the Cracker Jack toys in every box and the towels and dishes packed in detergent. Today, the factory-pack premium is often a tool for sampling new products. For example, Lubriderm Lotion provided trial sizes of Lubriderm soap in every package when it introduced its line of bar soap. This method of "premium" sampling, compared to traditional means, is very inexpensive and reaches prospects already familiar with the brand name.

Sometimes, a direct premium is so obvious that it loses its uniqueness. For example, at one time Colgate, Crest, and Aquafresh toothpaste all offered a toothbrush with the purchase of a three-pack of toothpaste. In a situation such as this, the buyer either purchases the brand he or she is most loyal to or purchases the brand with the lowest price. It can be argued that the offer made the three brands competitive, but it certainly didn't fulfill the traditional role of promotion, to offer an *extra* incentive to buy.

For the most part, direct premiums are relatively inexpensive and are often directed at children through tie-ins with cereal products. Companies offering premiums to children must be careful to make the premium safe and adhere to more stringent regulations regarding advertising and promotional messages than in adult-oriented promotion.

In addition to package goods manufacturers, magazines are one of the largest users of some form of direct premiums. Many magazines offer premiums for subscribing that relate to the editorial content of their publications. For example, *Sports Illustrated* gives a "Year in Sports" video; *Outdoor Life,* a backpack; *Traveller,* a video of national parks; and *Southern Living,* a recipe book. Since these premiums must be mailed at the time a reader subscribes, they involve an expense not entailed in other direct premiums. However, they have the other characteristics of direct premiums.

Because of the cost associated with direct premiums, some companies are moving to container premiums, which serve as both a premium and product container. It is one of the most efficient forms of sales promotion, since the premium container usually adds very little expense to what the regular product container would have cost.

Free Mail-In Premiums

Free mail-in premiums require consumers to send in a proof-of-purchase; in return, they receive a free gift. More than any other sales promotion technique, free mail-ins tend to be closely tied in with some form of advertising or other promotion.

Typically, advertisers promote their mail-in offers through point-of-purchase, direct mail and free-standing inserts, as well as traditional advertising. Ideally, customers should know about the offer before the purchase. If the buyer finds out about the free mail-in after the purchase, then it was not an incentive to buy and the money spent on the promotion was wasted. The list of free mail-in offers is endless.

Cereal products are the largest user of free direct mail-ins. The free mail-in is the most expensive type of premium offer. Manufacturers usually rely on premiums to create return purchases, since the profit on one sale will usually not cover the cost of the gift and associated administrative costs. More and more companies are moving to some limited self-liquidating program, where at least a part of the overhead is paid by the customer. Often, this is done through handling and mailing charges.

Fulfillment

As we discussed in the previous chapter, the physical work of opening, organizing, and responding to requests for merchandise is normally handled by fulfillment firms. The fulfillment function is extremely important to companies using mail-in premiums, especially in the case of self-liquidators. Fulfillment firms usually operate on a fee basis according to the number of requests. Their work is critical to the success of any mail-in promotion. Sloppy fulfillment services can virtually guarantee an unsuccessful promotion as well as long-term damage to customer goodwill.

Before contracting with a fulfillment firm, it is important to determine if it is experienced in handling the type of promotion you are planning. Fulfillment is an extension of customer service, and it is your company, not the fulfillment firm, that will be blamed if something goes wrong.

SPECIALTY ADVERTISING[9]

Specialty advertising
A gift given to a consumer to encourage a purchase.

Specialty advertising is a sales promotion technique that employs a wide array of merchandise imprinted with the advertiser's name, logo, or a short message. Advertising specialties are often confused with premiums. However, the major distinction between the two is that specialties are given free while premiums are a reward for some action by a customer, usually the purchase of a product.

Advertising specialties are used to accomplish a number of marketing objectives: thanking customers for past purchases, reinforcing established products, generating sales leads, and building morale among employees. The key to successful specialty campaigns is that there be clearly stated objectives and expected results from an identified audience segment.

Like most sales promotion, advertising specialties are most useful as a complement to other elements of the marketing mix. Specialty items can complement both mass and targeted campaigns and can be tracked to determine a cost-per-response figure. Properly executed, there should be little waste circulation, and specialty items generate high frequency levels by offering con-

[9]Unless otherwise noted, material in this section was provided by the Promotional Products Association International.

tinuing reminders to prospective customers. With 15,000 specialty items available, the medium can be used in a number of creative ways. Exhibit 14.6 shows that wearables and writing instruments are the two most popular specialty items, comprising over 36 percent of total gifts.

As is the case with all advertising and promotion vehicles, specialty does have disadvantages. There is limited space for messages, it has no natural distribution system, and unique specialty items may take up to six weeks to produce. On a CPM basis, specialty items can be an expensive means of reaching customers.

Specialty advertising is big business. Currently, companies spend more than $5 *billion* in all forms of specialty, an amount double the total for business publications and almost five times the total expenditure for outdoor advertising. Advertising specialties are so popular because recipients like them and use them as a constant reminder of some business or service. Overall, 62 percent of the population report that they received at least one specialty item in the past six months. More importantly, a high percentage of both consumer and business recipients are using specialty items and associate them with the advertisers.

Business Gifts

A special form of specialty advertising are business gifts. Although they are not truly advertising specialties, companies often work with specialty advertising firms to design and plan these gift campaigns. The most notable difference between business gifts and specialties is that business gifts normally do not carry the advertisers message, although sometimes the items will be imprinted with the logo of the firm to whom the gift is given.

EXHIBIT 14.6

. . . .

Numerous items are used for specialty advertising.

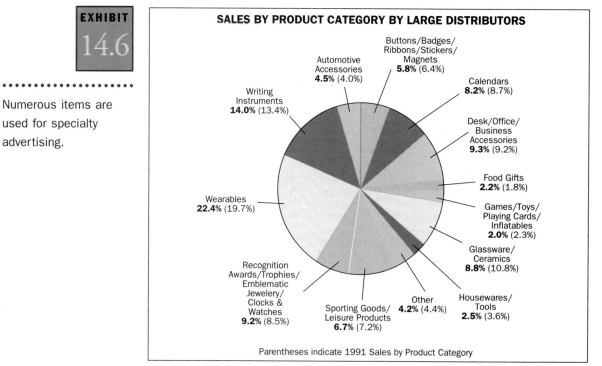

SALES BY PRODUCT CATEGORY BY LARGE DISTRIBUTORS

Buttons/Badges/Ribbons/Stickers/Magnets **5.8%** (6.4%)

Automotive Accessories **4.5%** (4.0%)

Calendars **8.2%** (8.7%)

Writing Instruments **14.0%** (13.4%)

Desk/Office/Business Accessories **9.3%** (9.2%)

Food Gifts **2.2%** (1.8%)

Games/Toys/Playing Cards/Inflatables **2.0%** (2.3%)

Wearables **22.4%** (19.7%)

Glassware/Ceramics **8.8%** (10.8%)

Recognition Awards/Trophies/Emblematic Jewelery/Clocks & Watches **9.2%** (8.5%)

Sporting Goods/Leisure Products **6.7%** (7.2%)

Other **4.2%** (4.4%)

Housewares/Tools **2.5%** (3.6%)

Parentheses indicate 1991 Sales by Product Category

(Courtesy: Promotional Products Association International.)

Most executive gifts are given to thank customers for past patronage, and more than half are given during the year-end holiday season. Executive gifts tend to be more personalized than customer specialties. In many cases, a number of different gifts will be selected, especially if more than one person in the same company will be given a gift.

Uses of Advertising Specialties

Specialty advertising is an extremely useful marketing tool. Used primarily as a supplement to other promotional and marketing plans, it can accomplish a number of objectives. Among the major strengths of specialty advertising are the following:

1. *Targetability.* Like direct mail, specialty advertising distribution is under the control of the advertiser. In fact, direct mail is a common way of distributing specialty advertising items.

2. *Long-term communication.* Unlike most other media, specialty advertising tends to stay around to be viewed again and again. There is simply no way to measure how many exposures a specialty item receives over its lifetime.

3. *Creative impact.* Because of their utility, most advertising specialties create involvement with the audience. When this involvement is combined with effective targeting, creative copy, and/or creative imprint design, the impact can be multiplied.

4. *Goodwill.* Specialty advertising is the only advertising medium that has ingratiation built in. People naturally like to receive gifts. Today, as in years past, the word *free* is one of the most powerful words in advertising.

5. *Flexibility.* Specialty advertising can be used with an unlimited number of items, formats, and marketing objectives. Specialty advertising is limited only by the imagination of the marketing professional using it.

In recent years, specialty items have become popular on a global basis. However, multinational companies find that they often must adapt gifts to the preferences of consumers in different countries. Exhibits 14.7 show how American Express offers distinct merchandise from one geographic area to another.

Organization of the Specialty Advertising Industry

Suppliers. The thousands of keychains, balloons, and pens that constitute advertising specialties are manufactured and imprinted by about 1,000 firms.

Distributors. Most specialty merchandise is sold to advertisers by distributors. Distributors contract with one supplier—or, more commonly, a number of suppliers—to provide merchandise to advertisers. There are perhaps 5,000 distributors, ranging from one-person operations to large companies with regional branch offices.

Direct houses

In specialty advertising, firms that combine the functions of supplier and distributor.

Direct Houses. Among the largest firms in the specialty industry are direct houses. A direct house combines the functions of the supplier and the distributor. It manufactures its own line of merchandise and maintains a sales force to contact advertisers.

The Advertiser. The key to the success of any specialty advertising program is the advertiser. Responsibility for the distribution, timing, and compatibil-

Case History

MELLON BANK CORPORATION:
Automated Teller Machine Processing Services

THE PROFIT FROM THE FIRST SALE PAID FOR THE ENTIRE PROGRAM

Mellon Bank Corporation, Pittsburgh, is a leading provider of Automated Teller Machine (ATM) processing services. Its objectives were tro communicate its sevices to CEOs in seven states at financial institutions with assets from $50 million to $1 billion. The niche was easily identifiable, but difficult to penetrate.

To cut through the barrage of mail received each day by the target audience, the company mailed a ceramic pig coin bank imprinted with the Mellon logo. An insert asked "Can you afford a pig in a poke when it's your job to put money in the bank?"

Follow-up calls determined a high rate of awareness and garnered an 80 percent appointment rate.

(Courtesy: Promotional Products Association International)

ity of the merchandise with the total marketing program largely rests with the advertiser. However, in recent years, distributors have been offering marketing services to advertisers rather than just selling them merchandise.

COUPONS

Coupon

Most popular type of sales-promotion technique.

Since C.W. Post issued the first coupon in 1885, good for one cent off a box of Grape Nuts Flakes, they have become the most popular form of sales promotion. It is estimated that some 300 *billion* coupons will be issued this year. Manufacturers and retailers annually distribute almost 1,500 coupons for every person in the United States. In terms of usage and popularity, coupons are without question the most familiar form of sales promotion. However, the 1990s marks a period of transition for coupons in terms of marketing strategy, methods of distribution, and future growth.

(Courtesy: Promotions Solutions, Inc.)

EXHIBIT

14.7

....

Premiums and specialty items must be suited to specific countries.

....

Everyday low pricing (EDLP)

A marketing strategy that uses permanent price reductions instead of occasional sales promotion incentives.

....

The major problem with coupons may well be that they are too popular. With 99 percent of households redeeming at least one coupon in the past year, it is clear that neither their novelty nor their ability to differentiate one product from another is a major benefit of coupons. Many marketers fear that customers view coupons as an expected price reduction and often substitute the best coupons for brand loyalty. To many, coupons represent the best example of the danger of sales promotion replacing brand equity.

Another factor with long-term implications for couponing is *everyday low pricing* (EDLP). Many package goods manufacturers have moved away from coupons and sales promotion and instituted EDLP as a marketing strategy. The reasons for this change are twofold: (1) It saves the cost of sales promotion overhead such as coupon redemption fees to retailers and other costs associated with promotions; (2) it is a move by large manufacturers to compete with smaller price-oriented companies and store brands. Clearly, EDLP has an immediate effect on couponing. For example, in the spring of 1994, General Mills announced a reduction of more than $175 million in cereal couponing. Instead of coupons, the company cut prices of its major cereal brands by an average of 11 percent. The General Mills strategy was not immediately followed by major competitors such as Kellogg, Quaker Oats, or

CUTTING THROUGH CLUTTER TO DELIVER YOUR MESSAGE

Specialty advertising is highly *accountable* in the process to reach, sell and keep customers. How an audience responds has a lot to do with how they receive your message. . .

When introduced, Perfect Balance was both a new brand and a new coffee concept, blending 50 percent each of caffeine and "decaf." To convince a narrow niche of 1,000 grocery store buyers in 15 markets to carry the product, Hills Bros. Coffee, Inc., a Nestlé company, concocted an unusual product demonstration tactic.

As illustrated on the opposite page, the firm's salespeople, carrying a colorful, custom-designed briefcase-style kit, called on food buyers. Inside was a sample jar and can of the product, along with a graphically coordinated set of imprinted advertising specialties—a napkin, coffee cups and a thermos that contained freshly brewed Perfect Balance.

After the buyer sampled and discussed the product, the salesperson presented the kit and adcentives to the buyer. Immediate orders were signed by 80 percent to 100 percent of the grocers in each of the 15 regions during a one-month introduction.

(Courtesy: Promotional Products Association International)

General Foods. However, industry executives were closely watching the move.[10]

Coupon Distribution

Despite the huge number of coupons distributed, there is surprising concentration of both product categories using coupons and types of distribution. The top five categories are the following:

---

[10]Tim Triplett, "Cereal Makers Await Reaction to General Mills' Coupon Decision," *Marketing News*, May 9, 1994, p. 1.

1. Cereals and breakfast food

2. Medications, remedies, and health aids

3. Pet food

4. Hair care

5. Household cleaners[11]

The use of coupons has shown a great deal of volatility in recent months. For example, coupons for baby food increased 150 percent in one six-month period, while during the same period coupons for film and camera supplies declined over 50 percent. A shift in promotional objectives or marketing strategy can result in major changes in the use of coupons for a product or product category.

While the method of coupon distribution has shown much greater stability, new technology might well bring significant changes. However, currently the primary means of distribution are:

1. *Free-standing inserts.* Coupons are distributed in a number of ways. However, the free-standing-insert (FSI), usually distributed by national coupon companies in Sunday newspapers, is by far the most popular format. Almost 90 percent of all coupons are distributed by FSI. The use of FSIs has grown steadily over the past decade and has reached a state of virtual saturation among most households. Despite the popularity of FSIs, their use is not without its downside.

   One of the major drawbacks is the degree of clutter associated with FSI. Not only is the typical Sunday paper full of coupon booklets, but the paper itself is so large that few readers go through every section. This clutter may well contribute to the low redemption rate, which is currently around 2.5 percent. This means that of the more than 310 billion FSI coupons distributed, less than 1 billion are redeemed. This low redemption rate can also be attributed to the untargeted distribution through newspapers.

2. *Direct-mail couponing.* Direct mail is becoming an important means of coupon distribution. Many advertisers want the precision of coupon delivery to specific market segments that they don't get from FSIs. The two largest mail distribution companies are R.R. Donnelley's Carol Wright program and Larry Tucker, Inc. While still trailing far behind FSI, direct mail is gaining popularity among manufacturers that want to reach a more narrowly defined audience than is possible with newspaper FSI.

   The same database technology, so popular in direct mail, adapts perfectly to couponing. Direct-mail coupons can combine advertising with coupon sales promotion to provide an immediate incentive for consumer purchases. Because most direct-mail coupons reach a prime prospect market, it is not unusual to see redemption rates of 8 to 10 percent.

3. *In-store couponing.* In-store promotions of all types are growing in popularity because they reach a targeted segment in the marketplace. Exhibit 14.8 shows that in-store coupons rank only behind sampling (which nor-

----

[11]Hanna Liebman, "Couponing after EDLP," *Mediaweek,* July 26, 1993, p. 18.

EXHIBIT

14.8

In-store couponing is among the most effective techniques.

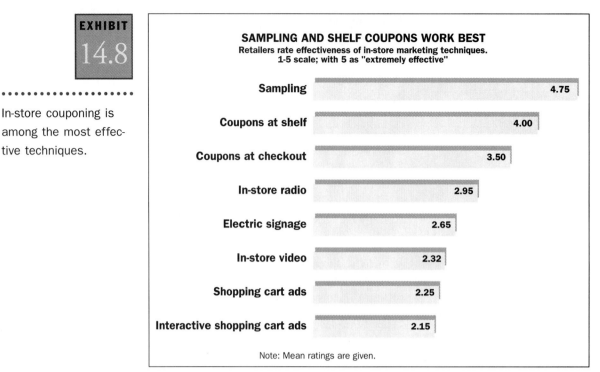

SAMPLING AND SHELF COUPONS WORK BEST
Retailers rate effectiveness of in-store marketing techniques.
1-5 scale; with 5 as "extremely effective"

Sampling	4.75
Coupons at shelf	4.00
Coupons at checkout	3.50
In-store radio	2.95
Electric signage	2.65
In-store video	2.32
Shopping cart ads	2.25
Interactive shopping cart ads	2.15

Note: Mean ratings are given.

(*Source:* Advertising Age, *May 10, 1993, p. 5–10.*)

mally is accompanied by a coupon) as a method of in-store promotions. One of the most popular methods of in-store couponing is Actmedia's Instant Coupon Machine (see Exhibit 14.9). With penetration in some 15,000 grocery and drug stores, the Instant Coupon Machine provides a coupon at point-of-purchase. The coupons may be for an immediate purchase if the objective is to gain new users or for future purchases to maintain customer loyalty. As we would expect, redemption rates are seven to nine times higher than FSI.[12]

A number of other in-store couponing methods are also used. Among the more popular are distribution of coupon books in the store or newspaper inserts in racks for store patrons. In addition, many advertisers have moved to in-pack and on-pack coupons (some with immediate redemption). The danger of on-pack coupons is that you may be reaching only customers who would have purchased the product in any case, and doing so at a reduced profit.

Coupon Redemption Fraud

When we redeem our 50-cent coupons, we give little thought to the significant investment for manufacturers offering them. Unfortunately, those interested in defrauding manufacturers through the illegal redemption of coupons are very much aware of their value. The most common type of fraud occurs when a person sends in coupons for which no product purchase has been made. There have been instances where criminals have obtained millions of coupons and sent them to manufacturers using the name of supermarkets and other retailers. In some cases, manufacturers have spent millions of dollars on redemptions for fraudulent claims.

[12]Michael Burgi, "The Next Phase in Coupons," *Mediaweek,* July 12, 1993, p. 9.

EXHIBIT
14.9

The Instant Coupon Machine significantly increases coupon redemption rates.

(Courtesy: ActMedia.)

In recent years, the U.S. Postal Service has made a number of arrests for mail fraud in connection with coupon misredemption (the mails are generally used to send coupons to fulfillment houses). Postal authorities have had some success in stopping this type of coupon fraud by publishing coupons for nonexistent products. Since no product could have been purchased, any coupon redemption request constitutes fraud. This approach has been tried a number of times and has led to the successful prosecution of many retailers and coupon thieves.

The newspaper industry is particularly concerned about the problem, since 90 percent of coupons are distributed by newspapers. Obviously, if manufacturers reduce newspaper coupon distribution because of misredemption fears, it would mean a decline in newspaper advertising. In 1981, the Audit Bureau of Circulations established the ABC Coupon Distribution Verification Service, which is basically an audit of publishers' practices concerning security and verification of distributed preprinted coupons (see Exhibit 14.10).

Continuing Use of Coupons

Coupons are more than a promotional technique, they have become an expected part of shopping for many consumers. In terms of building brand loyalty, this is an unfortunate outcome of what many marketing executives see as a reliance on a "quick-fix" solution to growing competition in many product categories. Regardless of the advisability of the current dependence on coupons, clearly they are here to stay.

In the future, we may see a more selective use of coupons with an increased utilization of in-store techniques. The sophisticated technology of database

EXHIBIT

14.10

I. Security/Storage of Preprinted Coupon Sections:

(a) Publisher's Practices:

It is the publisher's practice to verify the number of free standing coupon inserts at the time of receipt. Records are maintained of differences between the number claimed to have been shipped and the number received. Any differences noted are re-ported to the printer and advertiser. Run of press coupon sections are printed in advance of issue date and are accounted for by the publisher.

Run of press coupon sections are stored at company owned and independently owned distribution agencies. Free standing coupon inserts are stored at the publisher's mailroom. All storage areas are restricted and accessible only to qualified publishing personnel.

Free standing coupon inserts are inserted into pre-run sections at the publisher's plant. These pre-run sections and run of press coupon sections are inserted into the complete newspaper by carriers and newsdealers at various locations. All leftover pre-printed coupon material is baled with other newsprint waste and sold to a local recycling company.

(b) Auditor's Findings:

Publisher's practices were in accord with established guidelines.

II. Unsold Copies Returned to Publisher:

(a) Publisher's Practices:

It is the publisher's policy that all unsold copies of the newspaper are fully returnable from distributors and single copy sales accounts in the City Zone, Balance in Newspaper Designated Market, and Outside Newspaper Designated Market. Whole copy returns and unsold copies from newsdealers in the City Zone are brought back to the publisher's plant, where personnel make spot checks to determine that free standing coupon inserts and/or run of press coupon sections are included. Returned copies are sold to a wastepaper company for recycling.

(b) Auditor's Findings:

Publisher's practices were in accord with established guidelines.

III. Unsold Copies Not Returned to Publisher:

(a) Publisher's Practices:

It is the publisher's policy to require mastheads only for credit from dealers in the Balance in Newspaper Designated Market and Outside Newspaper Designated Market. The publisher requires these dealers to have on file a written statement attesting to the manner in which unsold copies are disposed of to render advertiser coupons unusable.

(b) Auditor's Findings:

Publisher's practices were in accord with established guidelines.

IV. Newspaper Distribution Procedure:

(a) Publisher's Practices:

Distribution of the newspaper is made through employees to single copy sales accounts, independent carriers, independent distributors, and company owned and operated agencies for home delivery and single copy sales. This practice is applicable in the City Zone, Balance in Newspaper Designated Market, and Outside Newspaper Designated Market.

The number of copies to be served to independent carriers, independent newsdealers, and independent distributors is not limited; however, it is the publisher's practice to monitor draw increases.

It is the publisher's practice not to have newsdealers for the Thursday only (coupon) issue. Sunday only newsdealers are permitted.

(b) Auditor's Findings:

Publisher's practices were in accord with established guidelines.

The records maintained by this publication pertaining to data reported for the period covered have been examined in accord with established guide-lines. Tests of records and other verification procedures considered necessary were conducted. Based on ABC's examination, the information in this report presents fairly the data verified by Bureau auditors.

(Chicago Tribune, Chicago, Illinoise October, 1985   CV#590, 591   AR#140777, 140778
RWM-KSK 01-1110-0)

(Courtesy: Audit Bureau of Circulations.)

marketing developed in direct-response advertising is being utilized in couponing. While FSI coupon distribution will continue to dominate for the foreseeable future, other in-store and direct-mail distribution methods will become more popular. One thing is clear: Many consumers have come to expect coupons, and competitive pressure will require that most package-goods manufacturers continue to provide them.

SAMPLING

Sampling
The method of introducing and promoting merchandise by distributing a miniature or full-size trial package of the product free or at a reduced price.

We have emphasized throughout the text that, regardless of the quality of the advertising and promotion, ultimately the product must sell itself. This is the philosophy behind product sampling. Sampling is the free distribution of a product to a prospect market. It virtually guarantees that consumers will give a product an initial trial. However, it is the most expensive form of sales promotion and is used to either introduce a new product or penetrate new markets with an established one.

The success of sampling is demonstrated by the fact that approximately 90 percent of national companies use sampling and currently invest 13 percent of total consumer promotional budgets in the technique. Sampling and other forms of in-store promotions have driven consumer promotional budgets past those of traditional consumer media advertising.[13]

The popularity of sampling is directly related to the ability of manufacturers to identify and reach specific target segments. "[S]ampling has become more sophisticated than just hanging miniboxes of detergent on doorknobs. Marketers are putting trial-size packages in consumers hands through targeted giveaway programs with retailers, at unexpected places like airplane and theaters as well as at special events."[14]

Examples of targeted out-of-home sampling programs include such companies as Nabisco giving Teddy Grahams to parents with children at malls, bringing Haagen-Dazs ice cream to college campuses on hot days, offering Sesame Street bandages to parents at Toys "R" Us stores, and encouraging college students to test-drive Geos at Daytona during spring break. These sampling programs are usually accompanied by coupons for future purchase. Research indicates that three times more people use a coupon received through a sampling program than coupons alone.

Another example of target market sampling is demonstrated by the use of Alternative Postal Delivery as a means of package-goods marketing.[15] Alternative Postal Delivery is a major distributor of magazines, competing with Publishers Express, which we mentioned in Chapter 11. One major manufacturer inserted a consumer questionnaire in the company's magazine packets. Alternative Postal Delivery used the questionnaires to identify consumers who used competing brands. The manufacturer was then able to include product samples and coupons in the next delivery. This "ride-along" approach combined the lower cost of a cooperative distribution, the targeting of direct mail, and the guaranteed product usage of sampling (see Exhibit 14.11).

---

[13]"Sampling Continues to Be Popular Choice," *Advertising Age*, May 16, 1994, p. 38.
[14]"Sampling Wins Over More Marketers," *Advertising Age*, July 27, 1993, p. 12.
[15]Lisa Yorgey, "Bypassing the USPS," *Target Marketing*, September 1993, p. 29.

EXHIBIT

14.11

(Courtesy: Alternative Postal Delivery.)

Alternative Postal Delivery is an important technique for many product samples.

Manufacturers are finding it increasingly necessary to balance the positive features of sampling with the need for minimal waste circulation.

EVENT MARKETING

Event marketing

A promotion sponsored in connection with some special event such as a sports contest or musical concert.

Companies will spend more than $4 billion in 1994 to buy an association with some event or charitable cause. The investment in *event marketing* covers a wide spectrum of involvement from well-known, high-visibility events such as the Virginia Slims women's tennis circuit, the various football bowl games now named for John Hancock (Sun Bowl), Mazda (Gator Bowl), USF&G (Sugar Bowl), the Ronald McDonald Houses, and, of course, the Olympics, to less well known events such as the Benson & Hedges Blues Festival and local radio station sponsorships of rock concerts. In recent years, event marketing has extended to commercial associations with stadiums and arenas. For example, Delta Airlines has purchased the name of the home of the Utah Jazz NBA basketball team now known as the Delta Center, and the home of the Colorado Rockies National League baseball team is called Coors Field.

Regardless of the event being sponsored (two-thirds are sports related), the key to event marketing is fundamentally no different from any other promotion. Among the primary reasons for investing in event marketing are the following:

■ **To increase the awareness of a company or product name**

■ **To build loyalty with a specific target audience**

- **To differentiate a product from its competitors**

- **To provide merchandising opportunities**

- **To enhance the commitment to the community or an ethnic group**

- **To impact the bottom line**

As you can see from this list, the objectives of event marketing follow those of most advertising and promotional investments. As one major user of event marketing points out, "Sponsorships are no different than a direct mail piece or an ad campaign in that you have to look at the effectiveness of any marketing you undertake."[16]

Event marketing differs from other forms of promotion in two major ways. First, it is sometimes intended to build long-term associations. In this respect, it is much like advertising. Second, the value of event marketing can be very difficult to measure. Both the immediate value, including public relations associated with the sponsorship, and the meeting of long-term goals must be considered. However, reducing these outcomes to traditional CPM or sales measures is very difficult. Nevertheless, event marketing is one of the fastest-growing sectors of promotion.

Deals

Deals are a catch-all category of promotional techniques designed to save the customer money. The most common deal is a temporary price reduction or "sale." The cents-off coupon is also a consumer deal because it lowers the price during some limited period. A deal may also involve merchandise. For example, a manufacturer may offer three bars of soap wrapped together and sold at a reduced price. Another deal possibility is attaching a package of a new member of a product family to a package of the older product at little or no extra cost—an effective way of introducing a new product.

Sometimes a deal lets the consumer save money on another product or an additional purchase of the same product. A two-for-one sale offers a free product after the consumer buys the first one. Gatorade offered a free three-pack of drink mix with the purchase of two others. Cash rebates are among the most common deals offered by manufacturers. There is hardly a time that some automobile company is not offering a rebate of several hundred dollars or reduced interest rates. In one case, an automobile dealer offered to pay off the purchaser's credit cards up to $3,000 with the purchase of a new car.

The automobile industry is an example of deals that start off as temporary incentives and become, to some buyers, an expectation. The widespread use of rebates in the automobile industry started during the Arab oil embargo of the 1970s. Dealers were stuck with large inventories of new cars and rebates used to move their stock. The promotions worked so well and were so popular with buyers that today many potential car purchasers simply wait for the next rebate plan before purchasing a car. Deals are extremely popular in building sales at the trade level. (Trade deals will be discussed later in the chapter as a type of trade incentive.)

---

[16]Gary Levin, "Sponsors Put Pressure on for Accountability," *Advertising Age,* June 21, 1993, p. S-4.

SWEEPSTAKES AND CONTESTS

The goal of sales promotion is to gain immediate sales and consumer involvement. A primary technique to accomplish both these goals are sweepstakes and contests. While the strategies of both are often similar, there are significant differences in the two types of promotions. Sweepstakes are much more popular than contests and are based solely on chance. Contests, on the other hand, must contain some element of skill, for example, writing a jingle or completing a puzzle.

Sweepstakes

Sweepstakes usually depend on some form of random drawing, but many sweepstakes use a continuity format, such as having consumers find bottle caps that spell out a word or phrase. The primary advantage of sweepstakes is that the rules are relatively simple and there is little or no judgment involved in choosing winners. In addition, it is possible to have so-called instant winners, which heightens the anticipation and consumer involvement. Fast-food chains are among the primary users of instant winners.

One problem faced by sweepstakes is that so many companies have used them over the years that they are losing some of their novelty. In addition, most consumers know that the odds of winning a significant prize are overwhelming and consequently don't bother to enter. Finally, sweepstakes promotions have lost some of their glamour in comparison to the state-run lotteries offering millions of dollars in prizes.

Another potential drawback of sweepstakes is that the product becomes secondary to the game. Many contests and sweepstakes are often entered by professional game players who have no interest in the product and will not become regular users once the contest or sweepstakes is completed. On the other hand, a major sweepstakes may generate a great deal of publicity beyond the paid advertising used to promote it. Most people are familiar with the Publishers Clearing House because of its annual sweepstakes.

Contests

As mentioned earlier, contests are not nearly as popular as sweepstakes. Advertisers conduct roughly five times as many sweepstakes as contests. Since contests call for some element of skill, there must be a plan for judging and making certain all legal requirements have been met. The typical contest is also much more expensive than a sweepstakes. When millions of entries are anticipated, even the smallest overlooked detail can be a nightmare for the contest sponsor.

Another limitation of contests is the time (and skill) required of participants. The majority of consumers are not going to devote the time necessary to complete a contest. Therefore, if the intent of the promotion is to gain maximum interest and participation, a sweepstakes will probably be better suited to the objective. On the other hand, a cleverly devised contest that complements the product and appeals to the skills of prime prospects can be extremely beneficial and more efficient than a sweepstakes.

Marketing Objectives

Sweepstakes and contests are similar in terms of many of the marketing objectives they seek to fulfill. Among the goals normally associated with contests and sweepstakes are the following:

1. *Heightening the involvement of present consumers.* Rather than passively viewing or reading an advertisement, consumers must become actively involved with the promotion in order to participate in a contest or sweepstakes. These promotions are used frequently to increase usage among present consumers.

2. *Differentiating the product from other brands.* A contest or sweepstakes can provide a change of pace from traditional advertising, especially in those product categories where brands are very similar or there is extensive competition. Note how many magazine publishers and cigarette manufacturers run contests and sweepstakes.

3. *Introducing a new product.* It is extremely difficult for new brands to gain consumer awareness. Sweepstakes and contests can create the type of consumer interest that increases buyers' perception.

4. *Increasing dealer support.* As we will discuss later, such dealer incentives as contests and sweepstakes can be very important in gaining trade support for a product. The key to a successful sweepstakes or contest is a logical tie-in between the promotion and the product. Like any promotion, sweepstakes and contests are designed to foster short-term sales. When this central objective becomes blurred, the promotion has failed.

COOPERATIVE ADVERTISING

Cooperative advertising (or *co-op*) is a category of trade promotion where national manufacturers reimburse retailers for placing local advertising promoting national brands. Co-op advertising has several purposes for both the retailer and the manufacturer:

1. *It benefits retailers by allowing them to stretch their advertising budgets.* Most co-op is offered on a 50 percent basis; that is, the national firm pays half of the local advertising costs. However, a number of co-op plans will reimburse retailers at a rate of 100 percent. In other cases, a manufacturer will place some limit on the amount of reimbursement according to a formula based on sales of the product by the retailer. As we will discuss in Chapter 25, federal law requires that regardless of the formula of reimbursement, manufacturers must treat all retailers proportionately the same.

2. *National manufacturers build goodwill with retailers, encourage local support of their brands, and, by having the retailer place the advertising, qualify for lower local rates, especially in newspapers.* Manufacturers also gain a positive association between local retailers and their products, thus enhancing the brand equity among customers of specific retailers. Many co-op advertisements are prepared by national advertisers and require only that retailers add their logo (see Exhibit 14.12).

3. *The media are among the strongest supporters of co-op.* Co-op allows current advertisers to place more advertising and at the same time brings new ad-

---

Cooperative advertising

Joint promotion of a national advertiser (manufacturer) and local retail outlet on behalf of the manufacturer's product on sale in the retail store.

EXHIBIT

14.12

Co-op advertising seeks to develop a close relationship between national advertisers and retailers.

(Courtesy: Leigh Kaln Advertising and Design.)

vertisers into the marketplace. Since co-op involves local advertising, it is not surprising that the majority of co-op dollars are spent in newspapers. However, in recent years co-op has reflected the diversity of local media. Currently over 60 percent of co-op budgets are spent in newspapers, followed by direct mail, television, and radio, each with approximately 10 percent. In the future, we will see significant dollars going into local cable co-op programs, and this will increase the share of TV co-op.

One of the surprising aspects of co-op advertising is the dollars that are available but go unspent. It is estimated that of the $20 billion allocated for co-op, as much as one-quarter may not be used. The primary reason for the failure to fully use co-op are primarily a result of a lack of knowledge on the part of retailers as to how to use co-op and an unwillingness to meet the restrictions placed on their expenditure by manufacturers.

Special Forms of Co-Op

Vendor program

Special form of co-op advertising where a retailer designs the program and approaches advertisers for support.

Vendor Programs. A special form of co-op normally used by large retailers is called vendor programs. The primary difference between vendor programs and other forms of co-op is that they are initiated by retailers. Vendor programs are custom programs designed by retailers (often in cooperation with local media). In vendor programs, manufacturers are approached by retailers to pay all or a share of the program.

For example, a department store might plan a back to school promotion. The store would then approach manufacturers of children's clothes, fall sporting goods, and school supplies and request funds to support the advertising and promotion of the event. Often vendor programs can be funded from unspent manufacturers' co-op money.

Ingredient Manufacturer Co-Op. Most co-op programs are set up between manufacturers and retailers. However, as we discussed in Chapter 2, many companies make ingredients that they sell to other manufacturers for inclusion in finished products. This is called end-product advertising and represents another opportunity for co-op. Often the ingredient manufacturer will contract with finished product manufacturers to co-op with retail outlets or even to co-op on a national basis to promote the ingredient.

Manufacturer to Wholesaler Co-Op. Occasionally, distribution in an industry is organized through a relatively few wholesale outlets, and manufacturers have little direct relationship with retailers. In this situation, it often is more practical to have co-op dollars allocated to wholesalers that then make co-op arrangements with individual retailers. Most manufacturers avoid going through wholesalers, since they lose much of the goodwill aspect engendered by direct allocation of co-op dollars by the national company.

Controlling Co-Op Dollars

Retailers are paid for advertising when they submit documentation or proof of performance. For newspaper advertisements, they show tear sheets giving the name of the newspaper, the date, and the exact ad copy as it ran. These advertisements can be matched with the newspaper invoice stating its cost. For radio and TV cooperative ads, proof of performance used to be a perennial problem until the Association of National Advertisers, the Radio Advertising Bureau, and the Television Bureau of Advertising developed an affidavit of performance (see Exhibit 14.13) that documents in detail the content, cost, and timing of commercials. The adoption of stricter controls in broadcast co-op has been a major contributing factor in the growth of co-op dollars for both radio and television.

Despite attempts to improve the process, expenditures of co-op dollars are still allocated improperly out of neglect or inexperience by retailers. In a few cases, there is evidence of outright fraud. Co-op fraud usually takes one of two forms. In the first, retailers bill manufacturers for ads that never ran, using fake invoices and tear sheets. The second type of fraud, called *double billing*, occurs when manufacturers are overcharged for the cost of advertising. Basically, retailers pay one price to the medium and bill the manufacturer for a higher price by using a phony (double) bill. It should be noted that double billing is regarded as an unethical (in some circumstances illegal) practice, and only a small minority of retailers and media engage in it.

TRADE SHOWS AND EXHIBITS

There are few industries that don't sponsor some form of trade shows and exhibits. Trade shows—from boat manufacturers to hospital suppliers—have

EXHIBIT

14.13

．．．．．．．．．．．．．．．．．．．．

An affidavit of
performance.

Use This ANA/RAB "Tear-Sheet To get retailers paid faster

ANA/RAB FORM FOR SCRIPT (IF TAPE IS USED, PREPARE SCRIPT FROM TAPE)

W___ ___ ___

ANA/RAB RADIO "TEAR-SHEET"
FORM AT BOTTOM OF SCRIPT PERMITS KNOWING
HOW MANY TIMES THIS SCRIPT RAN, AT WHAT
COST.

Client: For:

| | | Begin: | End: | Date: |

HERE'S NEWS FOR YOU HANDY HOMEOWNERS. IF YOU'D LIKE TO LEARN HOW TO
PUT UP A BEAUTIFUL NEW ARMSTRONG CEILING IN YOUR HOME, COME TO ACE
LUMBER THIS SATURDAY AT 10 A.M. ACE LUMBER IS HOLDING A HOME IMPROVE-
MENT CLINIC. IT WILL TEACH YOU EVERYTHING YOU NEED TO KNOW. YOU'LL
LEARN HOW EASY IT IS TO INSTALL ARMSTRONG CEILING TILE IN BASEMENTS,
ATTICS, OR ANY ROOM IN YOUR HOME. YOU'LL SEE HOW TO CUT AND FIT
BORDER TILES AND HOW TO DO A NEAT JOB AROUND LIGHTING FIXTURES.
YOU'LL ACTUALLY INSTALL PRACTICE CEILING TILES YOURSELF. ACE LUMBER
IS HEADQUARTERS FOR ALL THE NEW AND EXCLUSIVE ARMSTRONG CEILING
DESIGNS, SO IF YOU'RE PLANNING TO REMODEL OR REDECORATE YOUR HOME,
IT WILL PAY YOU TO ATTEND THIS CEILING CLINIC. AND THERE'S NO OBLIGA-
TION TO BUY A SINGLE THING. WRITE IT DOWN. THE PLACE IS ACE LUMPER. THE
TIME IS THIS SATURDAY AT 10 A.M.

▼ (STAMP OR PRINT THIS FORM ON THE BOTTOM OF YOUR SCRIPT PAPER)

Hand Billing Form

STATION DOCUMENTATION STATEMENT APPROVED BY THE CO-OPERATIVE ADVERTISING
COMMITTEE OF THE ASSOCIATION OF NATIONAL ADVERTISERS
This announcement was broadcast _____ times, as entered in the station's program log. The times this
announcement was broadcast were billed to this station's client on our invoice(s) number/dated
_____ at his earned rate of:
$_____ each for _____ announcements, for a total of $_____
$_____ each for _____ announcements, for a total of $_____
$_____ each for _____ announcements, for a total of $_____

Signature of station official

(Notarize above)   Typed name and title   Station

▼ (STAMP OR PRINT THIS FORM ON THE BOTTOM OF YOUR SCRIPT PAPER)

Computer Billing Form

This announcement was broadcast a total of _____ times at the dates and times coded _____ on our attached invoice(s) numbered/dated _____ as entered in the station's program log. This announcement was billed to this station's client at a total cost of $_____.

Sworn to and subscribed before me and in my
presence on this _____ day of _____ . 19 _____

Signature of station official

(Notarized above)   Typed name and title   Station call letters

For details on using this verification
document—preferred by hundreds of manufacturers—ask RAB's Co-op Department.

(Courtesy: Radio Advertising Bureau.)

become a huge business with an annual audience of 77 million visitors and expenditures of $66 billion. Trade exhibits are necessary in many industries to maintain competitive parity, but they are also a very expensive means of reaching customers.

To fully utilize the strengths of trade shows, manufacturers must do more than just show up. Successful trade-show participation demands that participants engage in extensive pre- and postplanning. Furthermore, the trade show must be part of an overall marketing plan. Exhibit 14.14 demonstrates the many details that must be considered before a trade show.

EXHIBIT 14.14

Use a Pre-Show Checklist

Cover all your bases with this pre-show checklist. Add your own items to the checklist as you see fit.

Show _____ Date_____

- ❏ Contracts signed and returned
- ❏ Distributor kits
- ❏ Budget
- ❏ Travel arrangements
- ❏ Transportation
- ❏ Lodging
- ❏ Temporary help
- ❏ Hospitality suite
- ❏ Personnel
- ❏ Target market list
- ❏ Target product list
- ❏ Theme
- ❏ Slogan
- ❏ Pre-show promotion plan
- ❏ Advertising specialties & promotion items
- ❏ Press releases
- ❏ Bulletins
- ❏ Pre-show advertising
- ❏ Show specials
- ❏ Training schedule
- ❏ Training materials
- ❏ Goals
- ❏ Objectives
- ❏ Booth
- ❏ Display
- ❏ Literature materials
- ❏ Samples
- ❏ Qualified lead form
- ❏ Exhibit transport logistics
- ❏ Carrier
- ❏ Insurance
- ❏ Security
- ❏ Tool kit
- ❏ Other _____

(Courtesy: Petrina Trace Show Training System. From Bernard H. Petrina, "Boost Your Trade Show Results," Sales and Marketing Stategies and News, January/February 1994, p. 55.)

Trade shows differ from virtually every other form of promotion. In fact, they are a hybrid between business-to-business advertising and personal selling. Trade shows offer companies a number of advantages in addition to the sale and demonstration of products:

1. They offer face-to-face contact with prescreened prospects.

2. They allow companies to maintain personal relationships with small and mid-size customers who might not be visited on a regular basis by salespeople.

3. A new company can use trade shows to create a viable customer base in a relatively short period of time.

4. Astute trade show participants use them to gain information about their products and marketing techniques to use in the future.[17]

The primary failing of most unsuccessful trade exhibits is lack of a focus and objective. "A trade show mission . . . has to mirror what the audience is looking for in educational terms. This is a lot different than Nike's emotional 'Just Do It' image/theme messages. Registrants spend upwards of $2,000 and nearly a week of their business lives just to attend a trade show. Vague emotional appeals aren't going to cut it with these people."[18]

---

[17]Edward A. Chapman, Jr., "Live and Learn," *Sales & Marketing Management,* September 1993, p. 48.

[18]Edward A. Chapman Jr., "The Autopilot Syndrome," *Sales & Marketing Management,* May 1993, p. 36.

EXHIBIT

14.15

8 out of 10 readers attend an average of 2.5 seminars and industry shows annually.

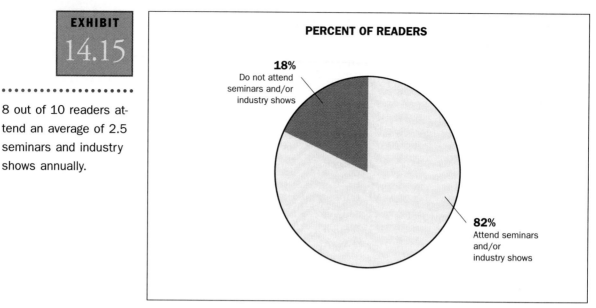

(Courtesy: Cahners Publishing Company)

Like most of the promotional techniques we have discussed in this chapter, trade shows are an important complement to media advertising. The more consumers know about your product and the higher name recognition your brand enjoys, the greater the chances that trade show participants will stop by your booth. Exhibit 14.15 shows that more than 80 percent of business publication readers also attend trade shows. This dual participation again demonstrates the synergy between advertising and most forms of promotion.

The relationship between trade shows and advertising is most apparent from the number of business publications getting into the market, both as exhibitors and sponsors. In fact, business publications are becoming primary supporters of trade shows. Trade shows provide a value-added service for advertisers that are already using a publication as well as providing a forum for solicitation of new advertisers. Shows are a source of additional profits for most publishers.

DIRECTORIES AND YELLOW PAGES

The ideal medium reaches serious prospects, in the mood to purchase, at an efficient cost. Many directories meet these requirements and are growing in popularity. It is estimated that there are more than 10,000 directories aimed at both consumers and trade buyers. Since directory advertising is available when the purchase decision is being made, there are few product categories that do not include at least some directory advertising in their marketing plans. Many retailers, particularly service businesses such as plumbers, rely on directories as their only type of promotion.

Directory advertising has many of the characteristics of the more expensive direct response media with none of their obtrusiveness. It also offers advertisers a continuing presence and high frequency without additional cost. Specialized directories are a major medium for business-to-business advertising and frequent references sources for business buyers.

Consumer Directories

At the consumer level, the most familiar directory is the telephone Yellow Pages. Since its beginning in New Haven, Connecticut, in 1878, the Yellow Pages has become a major advertising medium. Today, it is estimated that over 17 billion annual references are made to the Yellow Pages, with 60 percent of the population referring to it on a weekly basis.

Advertising expenditures in the medium are huge. Firms invest approximately $10 billion each year in the Yellow Pages, making it the fourth-largest medium in terms of revenue. The largest category of Yellow Pages advertising is for attorneys. Lawyers invest approximately $420 million each year in the Yellow Pages followed by physicians ($370 million) and insurance companies ($205 million). Overall, nine different categories invest more than $100 million annually in the Yellow Pages.[19]

The Yellow Pages is an important complement to other forms of advertising and promotion. In many cases, the medium is the last chance to reach the prospect at the time a purchase decision is being made. In fact, more than half of Yellow Pages users have not made a purchase decision when they turn to the Yellow Pages. More importantly, research shows that 84 percent of Yellow Pages references result in a contact, and more than half of those result in a sale.

The Yellow Pages is a prime example of integrated marketing in action. It is not intended to work alone. Rather than a competitor to traditional advertising media, it is *designed* to increase the effectiveness of other advertising vehicles. By combining the Yellow Pages with other advertising, the influence of both is significantly increased. Exhibit 14.16 demonstrates the way in which the Yellow Pages combines with newspapers to create a synergy that neither could provide alone. In fact, the stronger the brand equity of a product, the more likely the customer will associate the Yellow Pages listing with positive images of the product.

EXHIBIT

14.16

· ·

When we add the influence of Yellow Pages to the influence of newspapers—the combined influence is increased by 50% (from 20% to 30%).

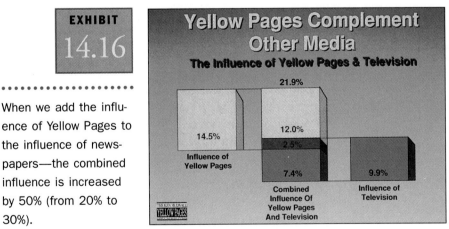

(Courtesy: KHYPE Fund.)

---

[19]"Top 20 Yellow Pages Headings of 1992," *Link,* September 1993, p. 8.

(Courtesy: KHYPE Fund.)

4 Color is available in many Yellow Pages directories.

The Yellow Pages also offers a number of creative options including four-color (see Exhibit 14.17), bleed, and white space ads. In addition, the Yellow Pages is beginning to experiment with interactive systems.

Eventually, the Yellow Pages offers some form of on-line system where entries and advertising can easily be changed and updated to reflect new addresses and telephone numbers as well as advertising information. It is this capability that will pit telephone companies against newspapers and other media competing for local advertising. There is a multi-billion-dollar reward waiting for the medium that first develops an interactive system with extensive consumer usage. In the meantime, the Yellow Pages will remain a major advertising medium, albeit one that is given much less credit than it is due.

TRADE INCENTIVES

Incentives

Sales promotion directed at wholesalers, retailers, or a company's sales force.

Trade incentives are used to increase sales by motivating those in the marketing channel to support a brand or company. Such incentives are directed at wholesalers, retailers, and a firm's internal sales staff. Companies use the same basic short-term reward system as consumer sales promotion to accomplish their objectives. However, there are a number of differences between consumer and trade promotions.

Occasionally, trade incentives are given to the retailers to then be given to customers. For example, Viasa, the Venezuelan International Airways, set up breakfast meetings with travel agents and gave attendees various information about the airline and Venezuela (see Exhibit 14.18). The information allowed these agents to be more helpful to prospective travelers.

1. *Sales promotion directed to the trade channel are called incentives.* There are two types of incentives: *dealer,* which is directed to retailers and wholesalers; and *sales,* which is directed to the company's salespeople. Almost 80 percent of incentives are offered to direct salespeople.

2. *The goals of trade incentives tend to be both long and short term.* Approximately the same number of companies cite long-range sales increases as those setting immediate sales goals as the objectives of their incentive programs. The longer horizon is a marked difference from consumer sales promotion, which is virtually always a short-term investment strategy.

EXHIBIT

14.18

Trade incentives are often provided to retailers in the form of consumer specialties and premiums.

(Courtesy: Promotion Solutions Inc.)

3. *The number of people qualifying for a sales incentive is much higher than for most consumer promotions.* For example, some 95 percent of companies offering incentives will give them to over 50 percent of those eligible. By contrast, only a very small percentage of consumers will qualify for major sales promotions such as sweepstakes prizes.

4. *The per-person value of trade incentives is much higher than consumer promotions.* In a recent survey, manufacturing companies average almost $10,000 per salesperson as an incentive for reaching incentive goals.[20]

The most common incentives to wholesalers or retailers are price reductions in the form of promotional allowances. In effect, these incentives are comparable to the cents-off promotion at the consumer level. In addition, sweepstakes, contests, and continuity promotions (some with prize catalogs) based on sales volume are all used at the trade level. Travel is also a popular incentive, where dealers are offered vacation trips in exchange for supporting a particular company's brands.

The key to successful incentive programs is to have them complement overall business strategy. The goals that the incentive program is intended to ad-

---

[20]Bob Donath, "Readers' Report: How We Use Incentives," *Sales & Marketing Management,* June 1993, p. 34.

dress should be very specific. For example, a company may use incentives to encourage its salespersons to:

- **Increase market share**

- **Introduce a new product line**

- **Extend distribution areas**

- **Open new accounts**

- **Revive inactive accounts**

- **Clear inventory before a new model year**[21]

There is no question that trade incentives can be extremely effective in increasing sales, productivity, and morale. However, regulatory agencies are increasingly questioning the ethics of some trade incentives that do not provide full disclosure to customers. For example, in a retail store consumers may seek objective information from a salesperson about one brand over another. How objective can retailers be if they are receiving significant rewards for promoting one brand over another?

To this date, there is no effective system of controlling and providing consumer disclosure for trade incentives. However, as competition in many industries grows more intense and the financial value of incentives increases, we may see both state and federal regulators take a new look at the entire system of trade incentives.

SUMMARY

The major ingredient that separates sales promotion from advertising is that it is a direct, usually short-term device to encourage sales. As in the case with advertising, sales promotion should reinforce a positive product image. Because of the higher CPMs of most sales promotion, cost-efficiency is extremely important.

Integrated marketing is a fact of life for every major advertiser. No marketing program can be successful, much less cost-effective, unless all aspects of marketing communication work together to present a consistent message to consumers. Your target audience makes no distinction regarding the communication channels through which they hear your messages. Consequently, it is essential that companies develop an understanding of the relationship between promotion and advertising. Not only must there be consistent objectives between the two, but it also is critical that promotion is used in a manner that will enhance, rather than erode, brand equity.

In addition to consumer sales promotion, companies normally use some combination of trade and retail promotions as well as advertising to carry out overall marketing objectives. There is concern in some quarters that the use of trade promotion has caused companies to move dollars away from consumer advertising and promotion and, therefore, it risks losing contact with their customers. The growth of large retail chains has caused too many national manufacturers to compete for shelf space rather than consumer loyalty.

---

[21]"Succeeding with Incentives," *Sales & Marketing Management,* September 1993, p. 113.

The consequence of this action is that they are encouraging customers to wait for the next sale or rebate or coupon offer instead of purchasing on the basis of product quality and differentiation.

Questions
1. Contrast sales promotion and advertising.
2. What is the primary disadvantage of sales promotion?
3. What is the difference between premiums and specialties?
4. What are the major advantages and disadvantages of event marketing?
5. What are the primary purposes of co-op advertising?
6. What is the primary regulation of co-op?
7. Why is point-of-purchase so important to many advertisers?

Video Case

MARKETING SITUATION

Midas competes in the "under-the-car" or exhaust brakes, and suspension segments of the automotive repair industry, a market that will perform more than 76 million repair jobs annually, but is a relatively flat area. In fact, Midas, like its major competitors, has experienced general sales declines since 1991 as a result of a poor economy, a dramatic increase in off-price competition, and well-publicized scrutiny of the auto repair business by both government and the press.

Within the category, Midas' position varies by service. For example, Midas dominates exhaust repair with a 23 percent share; Midas is the largest repairer of brakes, with an 8 percent share, but does not dominate the market; and is not a factor in suspension service except in shocks and struts with an overall 6 percent share—a weak fifth place in the market.

Consumers are confused about auto repairs. They don't know how their car works or how to figure out what is wrong. They don't know how to get their cars repaired properly or how to judge expertise of repair shops. Finally, they lack experience in determining how much repairs should cost and worry about the credibility of repair outlets.

CAMPAIGN OBJECTIVES

The Midas campaign objectives were twofold. First, reverse 10 months of retail sales declines. Second, establish Midas as the "trustworthy" auto repair facility and gain consumer support for Midas without the industry's traditional price advertising.

TARGET AUDIENCE

The primary target audience are owners of four- to eight-year-old cars in need of exhaust, brake, or suspension repair. Demographically, the target audience is predominantly male (but 42 percent of the market is female), 25–54 years old, household income above $30,000, and above-average education.

CREATIVE STRATEGY

Creative strategy was built around the theme "Midas is the only company you can trust to truly understand how you feel when something goes wrong with your car." The central strategy emphasized *trust,* since research showed that distrust of auto repair facilities was the number one concern of consumers. Furthermore, the "trust" strategy is a dramatic departure from the price advertising historically seen in the category. Price message was considered detrimental to the "trust" theme.

OTHER COMMUNICATION PROGRAMS

The "trust" theme from TV commercials was carried out in signage in all Midas shops. In addition, direct mail was used in high-index ZIP codes. Additionally, a national public relations campaign, "Project Safe Baby," was launched to encourage parents to put their children in car seats by offering a top-quality car seat at a reasonable price through Midas outlets.

MEDIA STRATEGY

Midas is the dominant advertiser in the category, accounting for $55 million (65 percent) of the $85 million spent on "under-the-car" advertising. Of Midas' total, $15 million will be spent on a national media umbrella (network/cable television, and national magazines) with the rest of the budget, or $40 million, spent locally to support 1,800 Midas shops across the country that face varying levels of competition. Most of the budget is allocated to television and radio, with secondary support provided by newspapers.

EVIDENCE OF RESULTS

The Midas campaign reversed sales declines immediately, consistently, and significantly. Compared to the previous year, sales increased for seven straight months. During, this period sales for the category continued flat except for Midas. Research indicated that consumer response was overwhelmingly positive to the campaign. Consumers viewed the campaign as believable, compelling, and evocative of the "trust" strategy.

MARKETING SITUATION

When Banana Nut Crunch was introduced it faced a chalenging marketing situation for the following reasons:

1. Banana Nut Crunch would compete in a declining and crowded segment of the cereal market. Overall, 25 brands compete for a segment share of 8.14 percent.
2. No cereal had ever succeeded with banana as a flavor or ingredient for no cereal could duplicate the taste of fresh bananas.
3. Given its relatively average advertising budget, Banana Nut Crunch faced a major challenge in competing for a place in the $8 billion cereal market.

CAMPAIGN OBJECTIVES

The objective of the campaign was to introduce Banana Nut Crunch by generating broad awareness and trial of the cereal. The goal of the campaign was to achieve a 10.4 percent trial rate and a .73 share of the first year.

TARGET AUDIENCE

The target audience was women aged 25–54 (with an emphasis on those aged 35–54) with children in households with income of $25,000+. The 25–54 age group accounted for the majority of volume of complex taste cereals. The 35-54 age group was emphasized to capitalize on the higher propensity of consumption among this age group.

CREATIVE STRATEGY

The creative strategy challenge was to develop a taste positioning for Banana Nut Crunch. This goal was achieved by creating the taste analogy—"If you like the taste of home-baked banana nut bread, you'll love Banana Nut Crunch cereal." Consumers had strong taste associations of banana nut bread and transferred these positive taste associations to the cereal.

The execution captured the feeling of home-baked goodness and timeless values by using a credible homemaker/baker spokeswoman who delivered the message in a country-kitchen setting. The execution powerfully communicated the product's "home-baked" taste.

OTHER COMMUNICATION PROGRAMS

To maximize trial and repurchase, the brand implemented consumer and retailer promotion programs. The consumer promotion utilized couponing and product sampling to encourage purchase. The retailer program generated in-store merchandising support to stimulate trial. Both promotions were coordinated with higher bursts of advertising. However, the promotional efforts were hampered by competitors' offers of higher-value coupons than Banana Nut Crunch.

MEDIA STRATEGY

The media plan followed several key strategies:

1. The first six months of media spending exceeded that of the highest-spending competitor. The next six months' spending was allocated to match the average spending levels of competitors.
2. Advertising was concentrated in bursts of two to five weeks to maximize advertising weight and break through competitive advertising clutter. These bursts were also coordinated with promotional activities to increase product awareness.
3. Prime-time and daytime television were used to achieve a mix of broad coverage and targeted delivery.
4. Magazines were used to reach the target market efficiently. They also provided an uncluttered environment, since none of the competition used print.

EVIDENCE OF RESULTS

Banana Nut Crunch was the most successful new cereal launch in 5 years. After nine months, Banana Nut Crunch achieved a .93 share, which exceeded every competitor's share and volume totals. Research indicated that advertising contributed heavily to business results.

The commercial generated a related recall score of 38 percent. The commercial beat Post commercial scores by 58 percent and generated the highest purchase interest and overall likability scores *ever* for a new Post cereal. Testing indicated that consumers thought the advertising was appetizing and compelled them to try the product.

V

Creating the Advertising

You've learned

the fundamentals of advertising planning and strategy—how to target, and how to develop sound marketing and advertising goals and media plans. It is now time to create exciting communications—especially ads. In Chapters 15 and 16 you'll learn how to determine the kind of research needed to understand and reach consumers effectively. You'll learn which kinds of appeals to use, and how to structure an ad. The process of finding the right appeal for the ads involve finding solutions for the consumers' problems. It starts with the isolation of a product attribute, which the creative team can translate into a benefit that the consumer considers to be significant.

In Chapter 17 you'll find that having the ad idea and elements is only part of the process. Preparing the ad for reproduction—the very important production process—is equally important. How can you get the final ad to look like it was meant to look? The process of taking all the ad elements and ending up with a finished ad isn't simple. The print production people need to plan and execute their jobs well if the ad is to both look good in print and remain within the production budget.

Chapters 19 and 20 examine the development and production of broadcast commercials. The creative team must understand the medium. Not only are media costs high, but broadcast production can be extremely expensive.

Integrated marketing includes package designs, logos, product names, and other corporate identity items. Chapter 21 examines these tools for building brand equity.

Chapter 22 goes beyond the mere creation of ads and commercials to study their strategy and placement. In this chapter we see the results of a complete advertising plan—the development of ad campaigns.

Research
in
Advertising

CHAPTER OBJECTIVES

Simply put, research is an informational tool. Advertisers need to know what motivates consumers in the marketplace to be successful. Advertising research can aid in the understanding of consumers and messages. After reading this chapter you will understand:

- **Account planners**
- **Anthropology, sociology, psychology, and advertising**
- **Values and life style and life-stage research**
- **The need for marketing research**
- **Research steps in advertising**
- **Types of advertising research**

Advertisers need to know what motivates consumers in the marketplace in order to be successful. They also need to know how consumers react to communications. **You can't build strong campaigns** without knowing the motivations, attitudes, and perceptions behind consumers' choices. **The failure for not** understanding the consumer may be failure for the product or service—Howard Johnson restaurants, with their orange roofs, dominated the restaurant business for about 20 years. In fact, in the mid-1960s its sales were more than McDonald's, Burger King, and Kentucky Fried Chicken combined. Where are Howard Johnson's restaurants today? If it were so easy to be successful, there wouldn't be such a high new-product failure rate, and established brands might not get into trouble. Advertisers would simply plug in the magic formulas. But there are no formulas that guarantee success.

Let's play with *your* mind for a second. Think about the items in your bathroom that you bought. Why did you buy that toothpaste? Deodorant? Shampoo? Soap? Hair spray? Why did you purchase those specific products? Was it the brand? Was it the price? Quality? Package? Do you really know? Could you explain your reasons for your preferences to a marketing researcher? Use the same thought pattern in thinking about the items you buy at the supermarket. For that matter, why do you choose the supermarket? Location? Image? Prices? Service? Fresh vegetables?

As a marketer, how do I reach you? What was the last ad that made you go out and buy something? Now sit on the other side of the desk and tell me how, as a marketer, you would use this information.

RESEARCH IS AN INFORMATIONAL TOOL

Research is and should be used to help improve an advertiser's effectiveness and profitability by staying in touch with the consumer. More specifically, much of the research is used most often in the following ways: to help identify consumers, to help look for new ideas in products or services, to help improve what is offered in products or services, to help pinpoint causes of special problems, to monitor activities, to help in communications development, and to study promotional tools. A little later we'll talk specifically about advertising research. (see Exhibit 15.1)

THE RIGHT KIND OF RESEARCH

What kind of research and how much research are always legitimate questions. And there are dangers. Former chairman of Roper Starch Worldwide's Roper division commented on a classic failure—Ford's Edsel and the misuse of research. In the case of the Edsel automobile, the research was used to make people believe something that wasn't true—not to design a product to meet consumers' tastes. Ford designed a powerful, flashy car with a horse-collar grille *before* doing any consumer research. After the car was designed, research found consumers wanted a quietly styled, conservative, American-made, Mercedes-Benz–like vehicle. Ford then tried to make consumers fit the car by marketing Edsel as a conservatively styled automobile. It generated interest, but when consumers saw the car they were disappointed.

On the other hand, Roper cited new Coke as an example of research overkill and overreliance. In several taste tests, new Coke beat Pepsi. But other studies have shown that sweeter products are often preferred initially. In-house and outside research for Coca-Cola failed because it didn't run normal usage taste tests on consumers. If Coke had given consumers a case of new Coke and came back in two or three weeks and asked them what they thought, a more accurate response would have been generated. Roper's conclusions are that people shouldn't always follow the findings of a research study, whether

DOMINOREOS

(Courtesy: Nabisco Brands Ltd., Toronto, Ontario, Canada & New York Festival International Advertising Awards.)

EXHIBIT

15.1

· · · · · · · · · · · · · · · · · · ·

What is the message consumers will take away from being exposed to this ad?

· · · · · · · · · · · · · · · · · · ·

Account planner

An outgrowth of British agency structure where a planner initiates and reviews research and participates in the creative process. In some agencies, the planner is considered a spokesperson for the consumer.

· · · · · · · · · · · · · · · · · · ·

it be a consumer products study or a political campaign. There are dangers as well as potential rewards.

STRATEGIC OR ACCOUNT PLANNERS

In the 1980s some American agencies moved toward copying the British restructuring of the research department. British agencies found clients doing much of their own research, yet the agency research function remained necessary to understand the information on consumers and the marketplace. The agencies restructured their research departments by adding *account planners,* sometimes called *strategic* or *marketing planners.* Their task was to discern not just who buys specific brands but why.

Since many marketers direct much of the needed research themselves, the agency may or may not be a partner in planning the type and direction of research studies conducted for a specific brand or company, but the agency researchers or planners are available to the account groups to help them get the needed information and may be involved in all kinds of advertising research.

Typically, a planner's role includes the following:

■ **They are well versed in data and information.**

■ **They produce insight into the consumer for other members of the team.**

■ **They help remind the team to focus on the consumer.**

The planner works with both account management and creative, covering most research functions. As you can see from the above role, the planner is more a partner to the account team than a traditional researcher—basically suppling information. The planner is considered the team's spokesperson for the consumer and an interpreter of available research. In some agencies, the account planner initiates research, reviews and redefines creative strategies, and participates in the creative process. Some agencies such as Saatchi & Saatchi use account planners only on such accounts that need such a resource.

Chiat/Day believes the planner is a means of achieving superior creative work based upon relevant strategic thinking and is based on three fundamentals:[1] Advertising must first be noticed; advertising must deeply understand, empathize with, and speak the same language as the consumer; leading edge advertising must be on the leading edge of social change.

WHAT KIND OF RESEARCH IS NEEDED?

Okay, we now better understand the research structure. Let's begin to look at the kinds of research available and some specific examples. Keep in mind that marketing has become far more complex than in the past because of the tremendous increase in new products, the high cost of shelf space, the expansion of retailer control over the distribution system, changing media habits, overload of information, and the bewildering array of communication choices.

Secondary Research
Research or data that is already gathered by someone else for another purpose.

As a general rule, no research project should be undertaken without a search of secondary research sources (that is, data already gathered by someone else for another purpose). Of course, this would include looking at any syndicated studies that were available. This is a logical part of any investigation and should be done early in the process and before collecting any primary data.

Marketing research—*upfront* research—tells us about the product, the market, the consumer, and the competition. Remember how the Lintas:Link system's brand equity probe set the stage for obtaining this kind of information. There are four basic considerations in any market research undertaking: maintaining a consumer-behavior perspective, being sure the right questions are being asked, using appropriate research techniques and controls, and presenting the research findings in a clear, comprehensible format that leads to action. After completing market research, we do advertising research—principally pretesting of ads and campaign evaluation—to get the data we need to develop and refine an advertising strategy and message. (see Exhibit 15.2.)

The behaviorial sciences—anthropology, sociology, and psychology—have had a strong influence on upfront research.

Anthropology and Advertising

Cultural anthropologists, who use direct observation to understand consumer behavior, are being used by marketers in greater numbers than ever before. Among their techniques are ethnographic studies offering an in-depth look

---

[1]Lisa Fortini-Campbell, *The Consumer Insight Workbook* (Chicago: Copy Workshop, 1992), p. 168.

"Simple Pleasures"

He has toys with names you *so you could get it on tape.* designed so you can expand
can't pronounce. You had mar- them with slides, turbo-tubes,
bles and a shiny red wagon. He Swing-N-Slide® play centers and other Swing-N-Slide® kits.
wears air-filled high tops. You are a great way to turn your yard   See a complete selection of
wore sneakers. He asked for a into a playground. From swing Swing-N-Slide® play center kits
jungle gym with a slide like you sets to climbing towers, Swing- and lumber packages at Lowe's.
had. You made him say it again N-Slide® hardware kits are

Swing·N·Slide

LOWE'S
Helping Add Value To Your Home®

"Back To Basics"

From carpool to carpool. To *simple. And if they're lucky,* flowers that attract butterflies.
office, to gym, to grocery store. *you'll share the rewards.* There are over 300 flower,
Super mom, super wife to the vegetable and herb varieties at
rescue. You're left fending for Experience true gardening Lowe's. And they're all 100%
yourself. But listen. There's a satisfaction with Ferry-Morse guaranteed to grow.
voice inside telling you to do Seeds. From old-time favorites   Get back to basics with
one thing just for you. Keep it your grandparents grew, to Ferry-Morse Seeds at Lowe's.

FERRY·MORSE SEEDS

LOWE'S
Helping Add Value To Your Home®

(Courtesy: Lowe's and Southern Living Magazine.*)*

EXHIBIT
15.2

. . . .

Will these common ex-
pressions and illustra-
tions communicate the
desired message.

at how a product or brand fits into consumers' lives. Peopletalk did an ethnographic study for a frozen-food marketer trying to determine if its brand
should expand into new categories. The participants in the study kept a diary of all meals prepared at home for a week and then videotaped them at
home preparing a meal. The results suggested that the marketer should keep
its brand focused on basic food lines.[2]

Young & Rubicam needed to find out how people viewed the U.S. Postal Service, so it sent out an anthropologist with a postal carrier. It found out that,
among other things, that letter carriers in rural areas are seen as a contact with
society and an antidote to loneliness. A new ad campaign emphasized the human-
ness of the postal service, using the theme "We deliver for you."

Anthropologists have found that certain needs and activities are common to
people the whole world over. Bodily adornment, cooking, courtship, food
taboos, gift giving, language, marriage, status, sex, and superstition are present in all societies, although each society attaches its own values and traditions to them. Because of the potential importance of this kind of research,
Saatchi & Saatchi has a network of anthropologists around the world to help

---

[2]Peg Masterson, "Brands Seek Subconscious Boost," *Advertising Age,* March 14, 1994, p. 29.

keep track of changing customs and values that may influence its clients' global advertising.

Anthropologists see the United States as a pluralistic society made up of an array of subcultures. In each subculture lives a different group of people who share its values, customs, and traditions. Think about the cultural differences among Asians, Italians, Polish people, Hispanics, and blacks as a starting point.

Some ethnic groups prefer highly spiced foods (Polish or Italian sausage) or distinctively flavored foods (Louisiana chicory-flavored coffee). Indeed, many dishes favored in certain parts of the country identify people in that area with their cultural past. Pennsylvania Dutch cookery, with its fastnachts and shoofly pie, has roots mainly in the Rhine; in Rhode Island, tourtière (meat pie) reflects the French-Canadian influence; Mexico's influence is revealed in the taco and other Mexican-style foods that took hold in California and the Southwest and have expanded across the country in the past few years.

There are regional variations in the American language, too. A sandwich made of several ingredients in a small loaf of bread is a "poor boy" in New Orleans, a "submarine" in Boston, a "hoagy" in Philadelphia, and a "grinder" in up-state New York. A soft drink in Syracuse is a "soda," and in Phoenix a "pop." In Virginia, "salad" means kale and spinach. Geomarketing permits advertisers to make use of these cultural differences in food preferences, terminology, and subgroup identities when they advertise their products.

In Chapter 4, we discussed shifting consumer values, population shifts, and other changes advertisers monitor in order to understand the consumer better. Because it sharpens our understanding of differences in cultural heritage, regional variations, rites of passage, and changing cultural roles, anthropology has significant relevance for marketing and advertising.

Although psychology and anthropology have been used in advertising for decades, current research methods are proving to be valuable tools to uncover subconscious attitudes and motivations behind brand loyalty. B/R/S Group's method lets consumers project a personality onto the brand to find out how consumers feel about the brand.

Whirlpool Brand Personality Research. Whirlpool Corporation did brand personality research to determine the personalities of its appliances. It used both focus groups and questionnaires to gather the information. It found that Whirlpool and its high-end Kitchen Aid brand were viewed as feminine by a higher percentage of respondents than other brands. In this case, feminine or masculine is not a strength or weakness but an opportunity to leverage that feeling and more clearly communicate with consumers. For example, the feminine perception may offer clues to the color or style that would most appeal to buyers. Female announcers are also used for commercial voice-overs to match the brand's personality more closely.

The Whirlpool brand was described as gentle, sensible, quiet, good-natured, flexible, modern, and creative. Personified, the brand would be a modern, family-oriented woman who lives the best of suburban life. She would be a good friend and neighbor, action oriented and successful, attractive and fashionable, but not flashy. Kitchen Aid's personality was somewhat different. Instead of a suburban mother, it was equated with a modern professional woman who is competent, aggressive, and smart, and who works hard to get the better things in life.[3] This type of information helps marketers to establish the brand concisely and forcefully in all communications, and to enhance the perceived differences for greater product differentiation.

Sociology and Advertising

Sociology examines the structure and function of organized behavioral systems. The sociologist studies groups and their influence on, and interaction with, the individual. Advertisers recognize group influence on the adoption of new ideas, media use, and consumer purchase behavior. They use sociological research to predict the probability of product purchase by various consumer groups.

Social Class and Stratification. Just about every society is clustered into classes, determined by such criteria as wealth, income, occupation, education, achievement, and seniority. We sense where we fit into this pattern. We identify with others in our class ("these are my kind of people"), and we generally conform to the standards of our class. Experienced advertisers recognize that people's aspirations usually take on the flavor of the social class immediately above their own.

Social-class structure helps explain why demographic categories sometimes fail to provide helpful information about consumers. A professional person and a factory worker may have the same income, but that doesn't mean their interests in products and services will coincide. In today's marketing environment, research has shown that no single variable, such as age, income, or sex, will accurately predict consumer purchases. We have discovered that using several variables gives a more accurate prediction of consumer behavior. Think of the differences between homemakers and working women of the same age, income, an education in food preferences for themselves and their families, usage of convenience goods, child care, and media habits.

Cohort Analysis. Using a research technique called cohort analysis, marketers can assess consumers' life-long values and preferences and develop strategies now for products they'll use later in life. Cohorts are generations of people with the same birth years and core values. According to Natalie Perkins of Trone Advertising, these values are formed between the ages of 13 and 20 by significant events and people and endure throughout one's life—for example, the Great Depression, the Korean War, McCarthyism, Vietnam, Martin Luther King, the sexual revolution, television, computers, divorced and single families, environmental crisis, the Gulf War, etc.

Generally, we study consumers using demographics, psychographics, lifestyle, and behavior. Cohort analysis combines these data and adds to the consumer profile by examining the past as well as the present. Four cohort groups exist: traditionalists, transitioners, challengers, and space-agers. Each group is unique, evolving, and maturing.

TRADITIONALISTS. In their 60s and 70s, they are enjoying retirement and leisure time and are in declining health. They are being cared for, or are

---

[3]Tim Triplett, "Brand Personality Must Be Managed or It Will Assume a Life of Its Own," *Marketing News,* May 9, 1994, p. 9.

making plans for when they will need care. Traditionalists are powerful financially and politically. Many feel guilty for no longer working and are anxious to remove financial responsibility from their children; they're determined to care for themselves as they grow older. They use wisdom and experience in making decisions.

TRANSITIONERS. In their 50s and 60s, they are caring for aging parents, enjoying prosperity and high incomes, and facing retirement. Many have empty nests and "boomerang" kids, and are in long-term or second marriages. They're brand loyal, value oriented, and don't make impulsive decisions. They value convenience and comfort, and are beginning to spend money on themselves now that their children have gone.

CHALLENGERS. In their 30s and 40s, many are in unconventional households: single parents, women working. They have high incomes and high debt and have started later than their cohorts before them to raise a family. They idolize youth but are becoming middle-aged and don't like it. Highly educated, they're concerned about retirement but are financially unable to plan for it. They are obsessed with reducing stress and guilt (note the number of self-help books). They still believe in having it all. They seek information before they buy. They are caught between reality and their black-and-white morality and have difficulty dealing with the world of gray. They are still concerned with what others think; as a result, they haven't abandoned the self-indulgent lifestyle of the 1980s.

SPACE-AGERS. This group is in their 20s, completing education, starting careers, and developing lasting relationships. They're financially unstable and have a lower standard of living since moving from their parents' home. In general, they think they have inherited an unsound system. They are skeptical. They're concerned that their future will not be as good or better than their parents'. They're economically liberal but politically conservative. This group has the *just do it* attitude, believes in unrestricted equality, and is more materialistic than it admits. Space-agers resent Challengers. They missed open *sex, drugs, and rock 'n' roll* and, instead, have been repeatedly told to say no to drugs and practice safe sex. They value products developed for them, not Challengers. Most important to marketers, they are street-smart consumers. Motivated by money for security, they look for lasting values, tangible benefits, and instant gratification. They make emotional purchases and require less information. They don't just talk action, they act.

By identifying a generation's collective hot buttons, mores and memories, we can hone messages and create persuasive icons to better attract them.[4] This kind of research can aid in developing a product marketing plan that follows the lifetime of a consumer.

Life-Stage Research. Advertisers have traditionally considered the family as the basic unit of buying behavior. Most traditional households pass through an orderly progression of stages, and each stage has special significance for buying behavior. Knowledge of the family life cycle allows a company to segment the market and the advertising appeal according to specific consumption patterns and groups. Of course, the concept of the family has significantly changed over the past decades. Yet there are still critical points in the

Family life cycle
Concept that demonstrates changing purchasing behavior as a person or a family matures.

---

[4]Natalie Perkins, "Zeroing In on Consumer Values," *Advertising Age,* March 22, 1993, p. 23.

EXHIBIT

15.3

People with children have different needs and concerns than those that do not.

lives of consumers—they leave home, get married or unmarried, bear children, raise children, and send adult children into lives of their own. As a result of these transitions in people's lives, they suddenly or gradually go from one stage of life to another (see Exhibit 15.3).

The Census Bureau tells us that over the past 20 to 30 years the nature of the traditional family life cycle has changed. For example, people are waiting longer to get married, women are postponing childbearing, the incidence of divorce has almost tripled, the proportion of single-parent households has significantly increased, and more young adults are living with their parents than in the past. As a result, some advertisers have reevaluated the way they look at the family life cycle. By examining these segments' subgroups, advertisers begin to get a clearer picture of buying behavior and lifestyles. Researchers refer to these subgroup studies as life-stage research. As with the family life cycle, life-stage research looks at the critical points in consumers' lives. Advertisers can find syndicated research services that analyze young singles, newlyweds, young couples, mature couples, and teenage households. As we approach the next century, advertisers need knowledge of the life stages to help them develop an understanding of the changes taking place so that they can develop more effective integrated marketing communications.

Psychology and Advertising

Psychology is the study of human behavior and its causes. Three psychological concepts of importance to consumer behavior are motivation, cognition, and learning. *Motivation* refers to the drives, urges, wishes, or desires that initiate the sequence of events known as "behavior." *Cognition* is the area in which all the mental phenomena (perception, memory, judging, thinking, and the rest) are grouped. *Learning* refers to those changes in behavior relative to external stimulus conditions that occur over time.[5] These three factors, working within the framework of the societal environment, create the psychological basis for consumer behavior. Advertising research is interested in cognitive elements to learn how consumers react to different stimuli, and research finds learning especially important in determining factors such as advertising frequency. However, in recent years the major application of psychology to advertising has been the attempt to understand the underlying motives that initiate consumer behavior.

A *Ladies Home Journal* (LHJ) study challenged the stereotypes about 30- to 49-year-old women. As publisher Donna Galotti says, "The baby boom woman has grown up. Her group is twice the size as Generation X." She also tends to be better educated, better paid, and more self-confident than her younger sisters. Thirty to 49-year-olds account for 51 percent of all college-educated women, 63 percent of all professional women, and 65 percent of all women with personal incomes over $30,000.[6] Responses to several questions tell advertisers how these women feel about themselves:

"There aren't many areas of life where I feel I can't cut it," 77 percent of the 30-to 49-year-olds agreed compared with 63 percent of 18-to 29-year-olds.

"I feel better about myself than I ever have," resulted in a 47 percent positive response from the older women versus 35 percent of younger women.

"I'm the kind of person who will stick with a brand if and only if it delivers everything I expect" brought agreement from 58 percent of the older women versus a 49 percent strongly agree response of 18- to 29-year-olds.

The implications from this study is that advertisers need to acknowledge the high level of self-esteem among these women, show them images they can relate to, make an effort to understand their priorities, provide them with sufficient information for them to make smart choices, and never to underestimate their intelligence: Many women in the study were appalled at how some marketers perceived them. As one woman said in a focus group, "The only product I've stuck with since I was 18 is my brand of mayonnaise."

Values and Lifestyles. The research company that popularized the lifestyle approach to psychographic segmentation developed Values and Life-Style 2 (VALS 2). SRI International's VALS 2 is designed to predict consumer behavior by profiling attitudes of American consumers. It segments respondents into eight clusters of consumers, each with distinct behavioral and decision-

Values and lifestyles system (VALS)

Developed by SRI International to cluster consumers according to several variables in order to predict consumer behavior.

---

[5]James A. Bayton, "Motivation, Cognition, Learning—Basic Factors in Consumer Behavior," *Journal Marketing,* January 1958, p. 282.
[6]"In Praise of Older Women," *Marketing Tools,* July/August 1994, pp. 25–26.

making patterns that reflect different self-orientations and available psychological and material resources (see Exhibit 15.4).

VALS 2 classifies consumers along two key dimensions: *self-orientation*—the fundamental human need to define a social self-image and create a world in

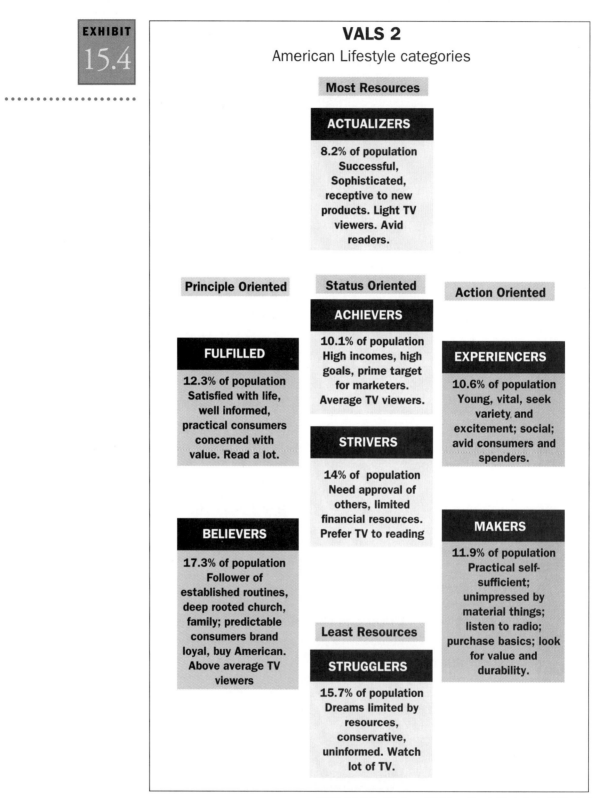

(Compiled from data from SRI International, Menlo Park, California.)

which it can thrive; and *resources*—the range of psychological and material resources available to sustain that self-concept.

This concept takes into account personal or psychological orientations such as principle, status, and action. Consumers with the *principle* orientation look inside themselves to make choices, rather than looking to physical experience or social pressure. Those with *status* orientation make choices in relation to the anticipated reactions and concerns of others in the group to which they belong or aspire to belong. *Action-oriented* consumers base their choices on consideration related to activity. They value feelings only when they result from action.

Resources, on the other hand, include both material and acquired attributes (money, position, education, etc.) and psychological qualities (inventiveness, interpersonal skills, intelligence, energy, etc.).

According to VALS 2, an individual purchases certain products and services because he or she is a specific type of person. The purchase is related to lifestyle, which in turn is a function of self-orientation and available resources. VALS 2 is a network of interconnected segments. Neighboring types have similar characteristics and can be combined in varying ways to suit particular marketing purposes. The eight lifestyle categories are:

Actualizers. These comprise about 8 percent of households but may be the most lucrative market because of their high incomes. These are successful, sophisticated, active, *take charge* people with high self-esteem. They are interested in growth and seek to develop, explore, and express themselves in a variety of ways—sometimes guided by principle and sometimes by desire to have an effect, to make a change. Image is important to them, not as evidence of their status or power, but rather as an expression of their taste, independence, and character. Actualizers are among the established and emerging leaders in business and government, yet they continue to seek challenges. They have a wide range of social and intellectual interests, are concerned about social issues, and are open to social change. They are skeptical of advertising, watch little television, but read a lot of varied publications. Their lives are characterized by richness and diversity. Their possessions and recreation reflect a cultivated taste for the finer things in life.

Principle Oriented: Fulfilled and Believers. Principle-oriented consumers seek to make their behavior consistent with their views of how the world is or should be.

Fulfilled make up about 12 percent of the households in the VALS system. They are mature, well-educated, reflective people who value order, knowledge and responsibility; they are content with their families, careers, and station in life; they tend to center their leisure activities on their home. About half of the fulfilled are 50 years and older. They have a moderate respect for the status quo, institutions of authority, and social decorum, but they are open-minded about new ideas and social change. They prefer educational and public affairs programming, and read often. Although their incomes allow them many choices, they are conservative, practical consumers; they care about functionality, value, and durability in the products they buy.

Believers constitute the largest share of U.S. households and are poorly educated with moral codes that are deeply rooted and literally interpreted. They follow established routines, organized in large part around their homes, religious organizations, families, and social organizations. As consumers, believers are predictable and conservative, favoring American products and established brands. They watch more television than the average viewer and read home, garden, and general-interest publications. Their education, income, and energy are modest but sufficient to meet their needs.

Status Oriented: Achievers and Strivers.

Status-oriented consumers have or seek a secure place in a valued social setting. They make choices to enhance their position or to facilitate their move to another, more desirable group. Strivers look to others to indicate what they should be and do; whereas achievers, who are more resourceful and active, seek recognition and self-definition through achievements at work and in their personal lives.

Strivers, who account for about 14 percent of households, are dominated by younger blue-collar workers who equate success with money. They never have enough of it and often feel that life has given them a raw deal. They seek self-definition and approval from the world around them. They are striving to find a secure place in life. Unsure of themselves and low on the social, economic, and psychological resources, strivers are deeply concerned about the opinions and approval of others. They are easily bored and impulsive. Many of them try to be stylish, in part to mask the lack of sufficient rewards from work, family, or possessions. They emulate those who own more impressive possessions, but what they wish to obtain is generally beyond their reach. They spend on clothing and carry high credit balances. Strivers prefer watching television to reading.

Action Oriented: Experiencers and Makers.

Action-oriented consumers like to affect their environment in tangible ways. Makers do so primarily at home and at work; experiencers in the wider world. Both types are intensely involved.

Experiencers are young, vital, enthusiastic, impulsive, and rebellious. They have a low median income; much of it is disposable income. Less than 20 percent have completed college, yet many continue to work on a degree. They combine an abstract disdain for conformity and authority with an outsider's awe of others' wealth, prestige, and power. They seek variety and excitement, savoring the new and off-beat and risky. They are still in the process of formulating their life values and patterns of behavior. They find an outlet in sports, outdoor recreation, and social activities. Experiencers are avid consumers and spend much more of their income on clothing, fast food, music, and video.

Makers are somewhat younger than fulfilleds; they value self-sufficiency and have the skills and income to achieve their goals. They live within the traditional context of family, practical work, and physical recreation and have little interest in what lies outside that context. Makers experience the world by working on it—building a house, raising children, canning vegetables—and have sufficient skills, income, and energy to carry out their projects. They are politically conservative, suspicious of new ideas, respectful of government authority and organized labor, but resentful of government intrusion on personal rights. They are unimpressed by others' personal possessions other than those with a practical or functional purpose (for example, tools, pickup trucks, fishing equipment).

Strugglers are the lowest-income households and account for 16 percent of U.S. households—the second largest group. Their lives are constricted. Their interests are narrow, their actions and dreams limited by their low level of resources. Chronically poor, ill educated, low skilled, without strong social bonds, aging and concerned about their health, they are often despairing and passive. Because they are so limited, they show no evidence of a strong self-orientation but are focused on meeting the urgent needs of the present moment. Their chief concerns are for security and safety. They are politically conservative and uninformed and feel powerless to influence events. They rely on organized religion for moral direction. They are cautious consumers and represent a very modest market for products and services, but they have the strongest brand loyalties of any on the VALS 2 types. They use coupons and watch for sales. Strugglers read tabloids and women's magazines and watch a lot of television.

Advertisers can use the VALS 2 typology to segment particular markets, develop marketing strategies, refine product concepts, position products and services, develop advertising and media campaigns, and guide long-range planning.

Personal Drive Analysis

BBDO has used the Personal Drive Analysis (PDA) technique to uncover a consumer's individual psychological drives—toward indulgence, ambition, or individuality—that play a role in his or her brand choices (Exhibit 15.5). It found that people are often attracted to brands because of their psychologi-

(Courtesy: Columbia Sportswear.)

Personal Drive Analysis (PDA)

A technique used to uncover a consumer's individual psychological drives.

cal reward. And it's important for marketers to identify this reward if they are to understand the equity of their brands and successfully sell their products. When the agency applied PDA to athletic shoes, Nike emerged as the brand a person would buy if motivated by such drives as status or winning. Reebok was the brand for those who desired comfort and stability. Results indicated that Reebok represents the athletic shoe you can count on; Nike represents the athlete you want to be.[7]

Marketing Environment

Companies and agencies want to accumulate as much information about their markets as possible before making crucial integrated marketing decisions. Technology has been assisting marketers to get more information faster.

Universal Product Code. Universal Product Code (UPC) information has greatly enhanced the process of tracking product sales. When the grocer scans a price into the register at checkout, that information is instantly available to the retailer. Scanner reporting systems have allowed marketers to track their performance quickly, rather than monthly or bimonthly, and at local levels. UPC information allows marketers to determine what their share of market is, if one kind of packaging sells better, and which retailers sell the most units. Cash-checking cards can be scanned into the system keeping a record of what kind of products consumers buy. This offers the retailer and manufacturer the opportunity to target promotions directly to this person who has used the product in the past. This information can contribute to any database marketing effort by the retailer.

Single-Source Data. Here retail tracking scanner data are integrated with household panel data on purchase patterns and ad exposure. The information comes from one supplier and is extracted from a single group of consumers. These data can be combined with other research sources to supply micromarketers with a wealth of information on who, what, and how. Despite these new micromarketing capabilities, research firms are far more adept at generating data than most clients are at using the information.

Databases. Marketers use sweepstakes entries, rebate information, merchandise orders, free product offers, requests for new-product information, and purchase information to build consumer databases telling them a great deal about how consumers live. This information offers many opportunities for database marketing.

Shopper Group Classifications

According to Total Research Corporation, hard-core shoppers are a minority of the population. However, all shoppers fit into seven groups based on their definitions of brand quality:

- *Intellects* **(17 percent of population) like upscale, cerebral, and technologically sophisticated brands.**

- *Relief Seekers* **(17 percent) want something that offers escape from the pressures of life.**

- *Pragmatists* **(16 percent) are simply interested in getting value for their money.**

---

[7]Cyndee Miller, "Spaghetti Sauce Preference Based on Whether You're in the Mood for Love," *Marketing News,* August 31, 1992, p. 5.

- *Actives* (15 percent) look for brands associated with a healthy, social lifestyle.

- *Conformists* (12 percent) choose the most popular brand because they want to belong to the crowd.

- *Popularity seekers* (12 percent) go for trendy brands.

- *Sentimentals* (12 percent) seek brands that emphasize comfort and good, old-fashioned flavor.

All seven groups have different opinions about the quality of specific brands. Among luxury cars, for example, intellects like the Lexus but give Cadillacs a mediocre rating. Sentimentals prefer Cadillacs and score the Lexus very low. The groups also shift over time in response to economic and social trends. Pragmatists, conformists, and actives are currently on the rise, while popularity seekers and sentimentals are declining. Relief seekers and intellects are holding steady.[8]

THE SERIES OF RESEARCH STEPS IN ADVERTISING

The term *advertising research* is broadly defined. It includes research that contributes at all four stages of the advertising process:

Advertising *Strategy* Development. It tries to answer who is the market and what do they want. What is the competition we are specifying? What communication do we want our selected market to get from our advertising? And how will we reach the persons selected as our market?

Advertising *Execution* Development. There are two kinds of research used at the execution stage of advertising. Exploratory research to stimulate the creative people and to help them know and understand the language used by consumers. Research to study proposed creative concepts, ideas, roughs, visuals, headlines, words, presenters, etc., to see whether they can do what the creative strategy expects of them.

Evaluating *Pretesting* Executions. Pretesting is the stage of advertising research where advertising ideas are tested. Partly because of the finality of much pretesting, it is the most controversial kind of advertising research.

***Campaign* Evaluation.** This is usually a tracking study to measure the performance of a campaign.

The primary goal of advertising research is to help in the process of creative development. Before we examine the research process advertisers would use in developing advertising strategy for campaigns (see Exhibit 15.6), let's get a better perspective on using research information.

Translating Information into Strategy

Jack Dempsey of McCann-Eckison says:[9] *By itself, information has no value.* It acquires value only when the strategist "takes a point of view" about what the information means—a point of view that is relevant to the marketing

---

[8]Diane Crispell and Kathleen Brandenburg, "What's in a Brand?" *American Demographics*, May 1993, pp. 26–32.

[9]Jack Dempsey, "Translating Information into Strategy," speech before the Institute of Advanced Advertising Studies, Atlanta, March 1986.

(Courtesy: Smoky Mountain Host of North Carolina.)

EXHIBIT

15.6

Pre-testing of ad ideas can answer specific questions for advertisers: which headline is most appealing, which layout attracts the most readers or which copy communicates the ad's objectives best.

and advertising issues. You have to get thoroughly involved in all the data at your disposal and, if necessary, fill in some gaps by acquiring more information. But, then, you have to step back from it. The secret of effective strategy formation lies in deciding which data are important and which are not. It is a process of organizing simplicity out of complexity, for the best strategic insights are usually the very simple ones.

Take the consumer's point of view. Ask yourself what the consumer is really buying. Is he or she really buying the product because of its functional benefits? How important are the psychological benefits? The corporate landscape is littered with examples of companies and industries that failed to appreciate what their consumers were really purchasing. Because of this, they defined their markets inappropriately and often disastrously. Begin with an analysis of how people *behave* rather than an analysis of how they feel or what they believe. You will probably get into these issues, but behavior is the foundation from which you build. And, above all, try to see the world with the consumer's eyes.

Think about the question "How many pairs of shoes do you buy in a year?" Now if you disregard such factors as style and fashion, the number of shoes bought in a year depends largely on how much walking is done, not on age, sex, or social class. These may be associated variables, but less determinant than the amount of walking the individual does. You see, information by itself has no value.

Market, Product, Competitive, and Consumer Research

This basic information is gathered and analyzed to determine the marketing strategy for a product or service, projected sales, where the business will come from, pricing and distribution factors, geographic information, and how to develop data to identify the size and nature of the product category. This kind of research includes data on competitors, sales trends, packaging, advertising expenditures, and future trends. The *situation analysis* helps to define clearly the market that the product or service competes in.

Prospect research is critical to define clearly who is expected to buy the product or service. Studies may identify users, attitudes, lifestyles, and consumption patterns—all of which identify the prime project.

The amounts and kinds of information required will vary according to the product category and marketing situation. Exhibit 15.7 outlines strategy choices indicated by different levels of brand trial and awareness. It is difficult to talk about strategy until you have information on awareness levels for each brand in the market. "Brand trial" will occur if what consumers know about the brand fits in with their needs and is sufficiently important or motivating. The relationship between a brand's level of awareness and its trials may be expressed as a ratio. A high ratio will suggest one strategy option, a low ratio another. For example, high awareness and low trial (lower left-hand box of Exhibit 15.9) clearly indicates that what people know about the brand is not sufficiently motivating or relevant, and the brand may need repositioning.

Product research can give creative teams inspiration. Research showed that Penn tennis balls needed to be more consistent in weight and bounce than the competition, giving them a highly marketable uniformity. Penn created a TV spot called the "bounce test," in which tennis balls were dropped from the Chrysler building in New York City. Each Penn tennis ball bounced to the same height and inspired the copy tag "Penn tennis balls. You've seen one, you've seen them all."

EXHIBIT 15.7

• • • • • • • • • • • • • • • • • • •

Brand trial/awareness ratios: Strategic options.

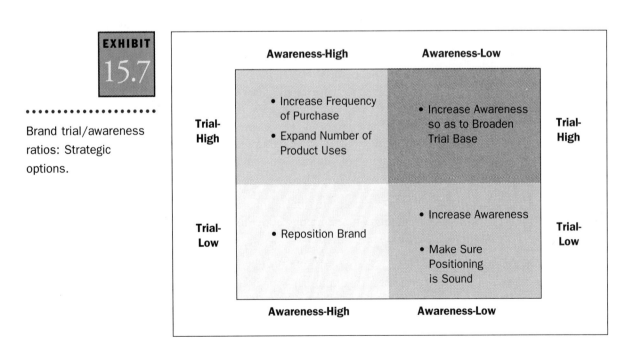

	Awareness-High	**Awareness-Low**	
Trial-High	• Increase Frequency of Purchase • Expand Number of Product Uses	• Increase Awareness so as to Broaden Trial Base	**Trial-High**
Trial-Low	• Reposition Brand	• Increase Awareness • Make Sure Positioning is Sound	**Trial-Low**
	Awareness-High	**Awareness-Low**	

Research does not always tell us what we want to hear, which can create problems if we really think an advertising idea is strong. Take the classic, "Avis. We try harder," campaign. It tested poorly in research. Consumers said the "We're number-two" concept meant Avis was second-rate. Research was against running it, but Bill Bernbach fervently believed in the idea and convinced Avis to take a chance with it. Today, the Avis campaign is considered one of the most powerful, memorable ad campaigns in history.

Advertising Strategy or Message Research

This research is used to identify the most relevant and competitive advertising sales message. It may take many forms: focus groups, brand mapping, usage studies, motivation studies, or benefit segmentation.

Focus Group Research. Focus groups have become most marketers' main method of qualitative research to find out why consumers behave as they do. The focus group offers a means of obtaining in-depth information through a discussion-group atmosphere. This process is designed to probe into the behavior and thinking of individual group members. The focus group can elicit spontaneous reactions to products or ads. A trained moderator leads a group of 8 to 12 consumers, usually prime prospects. The typical focus group interviews last one-and-a-half to two hours. The number of different group sessions will vary from advertiser to advertiser based somewhat on expense, topic being discussed, and time considerations. Most clients conduct five or six focus groups around the country. The client usually watches the interview from behind a one-way mirror so as not to disrupt the normal function of the group.

Quaker State was doing some new product testing in focus groups when it became obvious that consumers were confused by traditional motor oil labels. The marketers had invited some of the engineers to watch the focus groups from behind one-way mirrors. One of the engineers emerged from a session, stunned that no one in the group could define synthetic oil. You've got to pick smarter focus groups, he declared. A new campaign was designed so that even the oil-illiterate would recognize and focus on the product.

Focus Group Technology. Ogilvy & Mather's clients, creatives, and researchers do not have to trudge from city to city to watch focus groups. Instead, they are available to watch the nationwide action from their New York office through FocusVision Network—a company that broadcasts focus groups from a nationwide network of independently owned focus group facilities.[10] The big advantage is that consumer input is available immediately to everyone in the agency. Typically, the moderator, renting of facilities, microphones, special video setups to record the focus group, and the recruiting and paying of respondents can cost anywhere from $2,500 to $4,000 per group.

Video-conferencing links, TV monitors, remote-control cameras, and digital transmission technology allow focus group research to be accomplished over long-distance lines.

There are about 100,000 video-conferencing focus groups a year, and it is projected that number will double by the end of this decade. Advertising

---

Focus group

A qualitative research interviewing method using indepth interviews with a group rather than with an individual.

Qualitative research

This involves finding out what people say they think or feel. It is usually exploratory or diagnostic in nature.

---

[10]Cyndee Miller, "Network to Broadcast Live Focus Groups", *Marketing News,* September 3, 1990, p.10.

agencies say that video-conferencing enriches the creative process because it gives more people input. "Now we have up to 14 agency and client people watching groups, including the CEO and executive creative director. That wouldn't happen if they had to travel," says Susan Eisler, executive vice president and director of strategic planning for Lintas.[11]

FocusVision, a video-conferencing company, uses two cameras focused on the group of participants controlled by the client (agency or advertiser), who holds a remote keypad. Executives in a far-off boardroom can zoom in on faces and pan the focus group room at will. The transmission itself costs about $1,500 per session. A two-way sound system connects viewers to the boardroom, focus group room, and directly to the moderator's earpiece.

Critics of the emphasis on focus groups point to the fact that good ideas—whether a 30-second commercial or a new product or concept—often get killed prematurely because they did not do well with a focus group. The director of research services at BBDO says, "Focus groups should never be used as a replacement for quantitative research. But they can work well to determine consumer reaction to certain language in a TV commercial or in the development process for creative."[12]

Pretest Research.   There are several levels of research aimed at helping advertisers determine how well an ad will perform. Copy testing is done in two stages:

1. Rough copy research is needed to determine if the copy is effectively achieving its goals in terms of both message communication and attitude effects.

2. Finished copy research is done on the final form of the copy to evaluate how well the production process has achieved communication and attitude effects.

Pretesting is the stage of advertising research in which a complete ad or commercial is tested. It is important that the objectives of pretesting research relate back to the agreed advertising strategy. It would be wasted effort to test for some characteristic not related to the goal of the advertising.

A number of variables can be evaluated in pretesting, including the ability of the ad to attract attention, comprehension by the reader/viewer, playback of copy points (recall), persuasion—the probability that the consumer will buy the brand, attitude toward the brand, credibility, and irritation level.

Pretests should be used as guides and not as absolute predictors of winners or losers. In copy testing, a higher score for one ad over another does not guarantee a better ad. As the great creative genius Bill Bernbach once said, "Research is very important, but I think it is the beginning of the ad." And Norm Grey, JWT creative director, once commented on creative testing, "If you don't like the score an ad gets, demand another test. The only thing that's certain is that you'll get another score." These comments do not imply that creative testing is bad. They simply point to the fact that it is controversial and simply another tool for the advertiser. There have been arguments about the value of testing ads for years. In general, clients demand them and agency creatives are suspect of the process. Ed McCabe, chairman of McCabe & Company, makes a distinction between *research* and *testing:* "Without great

[11]Rebecca Piirto Heather, "Future Focus Groups," *American Demographics,* January 1994, p. 6.
[12]Sarah Stiansen, "How Focus Groups Can Go Astray," *Adweek,* Dec. 5, 1988, pp. F.K. 4–6.

research, you can't make great advertising. However, testing is the idiocy that keeps greatness from happening. Testing is a crutch the one-eyed use to beat up the blind." He points to his Hebrew National hot dog campaign in which an actor portraying Uncle Sam is brought up short by the company's insistence on exceeding federal regulations because its products are kosher and must "answer to a higher authority." The ads did not test well, and the client was reluctant to run them. After much discussion the ads ran. Some 20 years later, the ads are still running. The point is that testing can be useful, but it is not a foolproof science. If you were spending millions of dollars on a creative idea, wouldn't you do everything possible to reduce the risk—or, to put it another way, "to better guarantee" a chance for success?

Campaign Evaluation Research.   In evaluating advertising, within the total marketing effort, an advertiser should analyze the market and competitive activity and look at advertising as a campaign—not as individual ads. This information can help determine whether changes in the advertising strategy are needed to accomplish the objectives established for the campaign or to deal with a changed situation (Exhibit 15.8).

Advertisers frequently conduct tracking studies to measure trends, brand awareness, and interest in purchasing, as well as advertising factors. The research at the end of one campaign becomes part of the background research for selecting the next campaign strategy.

TESTING CREATIVE RESEARCH

Creative research takes place within the context of the preceding research stages. This kind of research aids in the development of what to say to the target audience and how to say it. Copy development research attempts to help advertisers decide how to execute approaches and elements. Copy testing is undertaken to aid them in determining whether to run the advertising in the marketplace.

In Chapter 6, PACT (Positioning Advertising Copy Testing) was discussed in the context of the agency-client relationship. Here we need to further examine the role of PACT:

1. A good copy-testing system provides measurements that are relevant to the objectives of the advertising. And, of course, different advertisements have different objectives (for example, encouraging trial of a product).

Copy testing

Measuring the effectiveness of ads.

EXHIBIT

15.8

Effectiveness measures by type of consumer response for copy research.

Response Criterion	Measurement
Cognitive (Think)	
Attention	Eye camera
Awareness	Day-after recall
Affective (Feel)	
Attitude	Persuasion
Feelings	Physiological response
Conative (Do)	
Purchase intent	Simulated shopping
Sales	Split cable/scanner

(Adapted from John Leckency. "Current Issues in the Measurement of Advertising.")

2. A primary purpose of copy testing is to help advertisers decide whether to run the advertising in the marketplace. A useful approach is to specify *action standards* before the results are in. Examples of action standards are:

- **Significantly improves perceptions of the brands as measured by _____.**

- **Achieves an attention level no lower than ____ percent as measured by _____.**

3. A good copy-testing system is based on the following model of human response to communications: the reception of a stimulus, the comprehension of the stimulus, and the response to the stimulus. In short, to succeed, an ad must have an effect.

- **On the eye and the ear—that is, it must be received *(reception)***

- **On the mind—that is, it must be understood *(comprehension)***

- **On the heart—that is, it must make an impression *(response)***

4. Experience has shown that test results often vary according to the degree of finish of the test. Thus, careful judgment should be exercised when using a less-than-finished version of a test. Sometimes what is lost is inconsequential, at other times it is critical.[13]

Forms of Testing

Each advertiser and agency uses similar but modified steps in the testing of creative research. The following are examples of this process.

Concept testing

The target audience evaluation of (alternative) creative strategy. Testing attempts to separate good and bad ideas and provide insight into factors motivating acceptance or rejection.

Concept Testing. This may be an integral part of creative planning and is undertaken for most clients as a matter of course. Creative concept testing can be defined as the target audience evaluation of (alternative) creative strategy. Specifically, concept testing attempts to separate the "good" ideas from the "bad," to indicate differing degrees of acceptance, and to provide insight into factors motivating acceptance or rejection.

There are a number of possible concept tests:

1. *Card concept test.* Creative strategies are presented to respondents in the form of a headline, followed by a paragraph of body copy, on a plain white card. Each concept is on a separate card. Some concepts cannot be tested in card form (for example, those requiring a high degree of mood, such as concepts based on humor or personalities.)

2. *Poster test.* This is similar to a card test except that small posters containing simplified illustrations and short copy are used rather than plain cards without illustrations (see Exhibit 15.9).

3. *Layout test.* A layout test involves showing a rough copy of a print ad (or artwork of a TV commercial with accompanying copy) to respondents. Layout tests are more finished than poster tests, in that they use the total copy and illustration as they will appear in the finished ad. Additionally, whereas a card or poster test measures the appeal of the basic concept, the purpose of the layout test may be to measure more subtle effects such as communication, understanding, and confusion.

---

[13]PACT—Positioning Advertising Copy Testing, *The PACT Agencies Report 1982,* pp. 6–25.

RU's Kitchen FAT FREE YOGURT

YOGURT Blended with **STRAWBERRIES**

Now you and your family can enjoy a delicious yogurt that is 100% fat free. New RU's Kitchen Fat Free Yogurt is smooth creamy yogurt with delicious fruit blended in.

RU's Fat Free Yogurt is a good source of calcium and protein, and it's rich in active yogurt cultures. It contains **no fat.**

RU's Kitchen Fat Free Yogurt comes in convenient, recyclable 8 ounce containers that store easily on your refrigerator shelf. It's perfect for breakfast, lunch, or snacks and sells for only 65 cents a cup.

RU's Kitchen Fat Free Yogurt comes in a variety of delicious fruit flavors: Strawberry, Peach, Cherry and Raspberry.

1. If this product were available in stores in your area, do you think you would buy it?

   Please remember that your feelings that you would not buy are as important to the manufacturer as your feelings that you would buy.

   Please check the box next to the statement that best describes what **you** would do. **(Check ONE Box)**

   1. ☐ Yes, I definitely would buy it
   2. ☐ Yes, I probably would buy it — **(CONTINUE)**
   3. ☐ I don't know whether or not I would buy it
   4. ☐ No, I probably would not buy it
   5. ☐ No, I definitely would not buy it — **(SKIP TO QU. 5)**

2. Assuming you liked the yogurt, about how many cups would you buy in a normal 3 month period?
   Number of Cups:_____

3. Would you use this yogurt in addition to the yogurt you currently buy or in place of the yogurt you currently buy?
   1. ☐ In addition to
   2. ☐ In place of

4. What is there about this product that would make you **want** to buy it? **(PLEASE BE SPECIFIC)**

   _____
   _____

PLEASE LOOK AT THE PICTURE SHEET AND READ ABOUT THE PRODUCT. THEN SHOW IT TO OTHER FAMILY MEMBERS. DO NOT CONTINUE UNTIL YOU AND YOUR FAMILY HAVE READ THE PICTURE SHEET.

13. **a.** On line #1 below, please list **your** name, then record your **sex** and **age**. On lines #2–6, list the names of all other members of your household living at home, and each one's **sex** and **age**. Be sure to include all adults and all children. **(Record Below Beginning On Line #1)**

    b. After looking at the picture sheet and reading the description of the product, check below whether or not you, yourself, would be interested in trying the product. **(Record Below)**

    c. Next show each family member listed the picture and description and check yes or no to indicate each individual's interest in trying the product. **(Please Read The Description To Younger Children So They Know What The Product Would Be Like)**

A. Record First Names	B. Male	Female	Age	C. Interested In Trying
1.	1 ☐	2 ☐	_____	1 ☐ Yes 2 ☐ No
2.	1 ☐	2 ☐	_____	1 ☐ Yes 2 ☐ No

EXHIBIT 15.9

...................**Test Commercials.** Generally, commercial testing on film or videotape falls into one of four categories:

1. *Animatics.* This is artwork, either cartoons or realistic drawings. Some animatics show limited movement; those that do not are usually called *video storyboards.* Animatics cost from about $1,500 to $4,000 plus artists' fees, although the simplest nonmovement video storyboard may cost as little as $750.

2. *Photomatics.* These are photographs shot in sequence on film. The photos may be stock (from a photo library) or shot on location. Photomatics cost about $10,000 to produce.

3. *Liveamatics.* This involves filming or taping live talent and is very close to the finished commercial. A liveamatic commercial test costs between $10,000 to $20,000 to produce.

4. *Ripamatics.* The commercial is made of footage from other commercials, often taken from ad agency promotion reels. Ripamatics are used many times for experimentation on visual techniques.

Finished Print Tests. This testing procedure can take many forms of measuring the finished ad as it would appear in print.

Finished Commercial Testing. TV testing techniques can generally be classified into two categories:

1. Those that attempt to evaluate a commercial's effectiveness in terms of viewers' recall of a certain aspect of the commercial

2. Those that attempt to evaluate a commercial's effectiveness in terms of what it motivates a viewer to say or do

Recent advances in production technology are helping the testing process. The more closely the test spot resembles the finished commercial, the more accurate the test results will be. Computer animation has become less expensive, and so there is more computer-generated artwork in commercial testing.

Examples of Testing Procedures

Print Testing Example. Video Storyboard Test tests television and print ads. Its ad promoting the testing of *rough print* ads says ". . . developed testing procedures which allow you to compare alternative executions without spending the time and money to finish an ad." Its procedure goes something like this: Test ads, finished or unfinished, are inserted into a 20-page magazine-in-a-folder containing both editorial and control ads. Prospects preview the magazine in one-on-one interviews in high-traffic malls. Respondents are questioned regarding unaided, aided, and related recall of the test ad. Next they are asked to focus on the test ad only and are probed for reactions. Agencies are furnished with diagnostic data to improve the ad. The ads are measured for stopping power, communication, relevance, and persuasion. They also provide likes and dislikes about the ad. All of this costs about $3,500 for each test execution per 100 respondents. Results take about 12 days.

BBDO's Emotional Testing. BBDO began using the Emotional Measurement System, a proprietary device that uses photographs of actors' faces to help consumers choose their reactions to commercials. According to BBDO, traditional copy tests have failed to measure emotional response accurately. The techniques tend to measure thoughts rather than feelings. Instead of asking consumers to choose from a list or write in their own words, the agency has devised a deck of 53 photos representing the universe of emotion. Each features one of six photos with different expressions ranging from happy/playful to disgusted/revolted. There are a total of 26 categories of emotions expressed. Here is how it works:

- **As with most copy testing, consumers are shown a single commercial or group of spots. Then they are given a questionnaire to test whether brand names and copy points are remembered.**

- **Photos are given to the participants. They are asked to sort through the photos quickly, setting aside any or all that reflect how they feel after viewing the commercial.**

- **A researcher tabulates how often a particular photo is chosen by the 150 to 600 participating consumers. In the system, the expressions are plotted on a "perceptual map" to determine whether the response is positive or negative, active or passive.**

EXHIBIT

15.11

. . . .

The labels represent
the starch scores for
this ad.

SUMMARY

Successful advertisers know who their prospects are and, to whatever extent is practical, what their needs and motives are, which result in the purchase of one brand and the rejection of another. Consumer behavior is a complex network of influences based on the psychological, sociological, and anthropological makeup of the individual.

Advertising rarely, if ever, changes these influences, but rather channels the needs and wants of consumers toward specific products and brands. Advertising is a mirror of society. The advertiser influences people by offering solutions to their needs and problems, not by creating these needs. The role of the advertiser is to act as a monitor of the changing face of society.

Marketers are concerned about what we call upfront research or market research that reflects the market, the consumer, and the competition. Such information as cohort analysis and VALS 2 can help us understand consumers'

EXHIBIT

15.12

. . . .

GET MET outdoor ad.

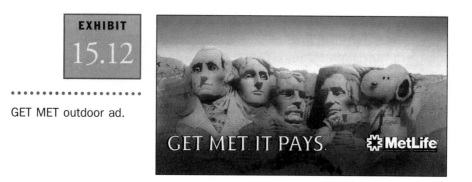

lifestyles and values in helping us develop strategies. Once this information is digested, we use it to help in the four stages of advertising development: strategy development, execution development, pretesting of executions, and campaign evaluation. We need to remember that *by itself, information has no value*. It acquires value only as we *take a point of view* about what the information means.

In creative research, there are a number of stages of testing available to the advertiser, ranging from concept testing and commercial testing techniques to finished print and commercial tests. Because of the expense of producing ads, advertisers feel compelled to evaluate concepts and ads prior to buying expensive media schedules to reach consumers.

Questions

1. What is the value of VALS 2 to the advertiser?
2. What does BIP attempt to measure?
3. How does BBDO test emotional responses in television commercials.
4. What is single-source data?
5. What is the role of the animatic commercial?
6. What is the value of product research for creatives?
7. What are some of the variables that can be evaluated in pretesting?

Creating
the Copy

CHAPTER OBJECTIVES

Great advertising copy is essential to great advertising. Understanding consumers and what appeals to them is part of the thought process needed to create great copy. After reading this chapter you will understand:

- **The nature and the use of appeals**
- **Advertising elements**
- **The structure of an advertisement**
- **Copy style**
- **Slogans**
- **The creative work plan**

The importance of good copy was heralded by Procter & Gamble's president, "I have seen through 25 years that the correlation between profitable business growth on our brands and having great copy on our brands isn't 25 percent, it's not 50 percent. It is 100 percent. **I have not seen a single** P&G brand sustain profitable volume growth for more than a couple of years without having great advertising." Lou Centlivre, formerly of Foote Cone & Belding, said: "The days are gone of left-brained reason-why messages; so insignificant and strained and boring and unbelievable they fall on deaf ears. The creative people who can get into the heart—not just the brain—and make people cry or laugh or silently say, 'Yeah, that's how I really feel'—will be the superstars of the 90s."

HOW DO WE CREATE GREAT ADVERTISING?

Ron Huey, vice president and associate creative director of the Martin Agency, says, "Simplicity is the key to great advertising. Take the single most salient feature of your product or service and communicate that in a simple, thought provoking or entertaining way. Good copy speaks to the common man. It should be smart, entertaining and conversational, not fancy or frilly. Today's best creative people are resilient. Great ideas are killed every day for sometimes stupid reasons. The best creatives accept that and come back with something even better." Huey's thoughts on advertising through the years, "The great ads from Bernbach in the 60's, Fallon McElligott in the 80's, Wieden [Wieden & Kennedy], Goodby[Goodby, Berlin & Silverstein] and the Martin Agency today, all have a common thread—The headline, visual and logo communicate the idea immediately." He also says, "Three quarters of today's best ads use humor. But it's wry humor. Not a bathroom joke or humor that's intended to shock people."[1]

THE NATURE AND USE OF APPEALS

Appeal
The motive to which an ad is directed, it is designed to stir a person toward a goal the advertiser has set.

Before we get to the nitty-gritty of creating ads, let's look at the value of using a psychological appeal in advertising. David Martin, founder of the Martin Agency, points to decades of research indicating the relative strength of motives and appeals in advertising. He believes human desires are woven into our basic nature. They do not change with lifestyles or external environmental stimuli. Consumers will always have a desire for food and drink; for rest, comfort, and security; and for a sense of social worth, independence, power, and success. Parental feelings to protect and provide are basic. Human nature is a constant. Humans are born with certain instincts: fear (self-preservation), hunger (need for food and drink), sex (love), rage (anger). People also have five senses: sight, touch, smell, hearing, and taste. The instincts and senses are often a starting point for advertising appeals.[2]

Bill Bernbach, the late creative guru of the 1960s, put it this way: "There may be changes in our society. But learning about those changes is not the answer. For you are not appealing to society. You are appealing to individuals, each with an ego, each with the dignity of his or her being, each like no one else in the world, each a separate miracle. The societal appeals are merely fashionable, current, cultural appeals which make nice garments for the real motivations that stem from the unchanging instincts, and emotions of people—from nature's indomitable programming in their genes. It is the unchanging person that is the proper study of the communicator."[3]

[1]Ron Huey, interview, September 1994.
[2]David Martin, *Romancing the Brand* (New York: Amacom, 1989), pp. 134–136.
[3]From an American Association of Advertising Agencies speech, May 17, 1980.

EXHIBIT

16.1

Wonderful human response copy. A headline that parents can relate to.

(Courtesy: Healthtex™ and The Martin Agency.)

In short, advertising motivates people by appealing to their problems, desires, and goals—and by offering a means of solving their problems, satisfying their desires, and achieving their goals. We've featured a number of Healthtex ads in preceding chapters because they are great ads and you have the opportunity to track the campaign throughout this book. Specifically, let's look at parental feelings, and also what Ron Huey said about using wry humor, in these specific Healthtex ads (see Exhibit 16.1). "Most baby bottoms stink. (And their tops aren't great, either.)" The head and the illustration work at appealing to you in a humorous way. And the body copy continues the tone, "We believe there are a lot of things that need to be changed in baby bottoms. (And we're not talking about, well, you-know-what.) For instance, wouldn't it be great if they were cuter? And better made, too?"

Selecting the Appeal

How do we go about making the decision as to which direction to go with an ad or appeal? Just about any product has a number of positive appeals that could be successfully promoted. The idea, of course, is to choose the one that is most important to the majority of our target. Because selecting the primary appeal is the key to any advertising campaign, many research techniques have been developed to find which appeal to use. In Chapter 15, we discussed some of the aspects of advertising research that help us make strategic and creative decisions. Here we specifically discuss three techniques to help us decide on appeals: concept testing, focus groups, and motivational research.

Concept Testing. Concept testing is a method to determine the best of a number of possible appeals to use in your advertising. A creative concept is defined as a simple explanation or description of the advertising idea behind the product.

A tourism association developed several appeals that might motivate prime prospects to drive two hours to the mountains from a large metro area in another state:

1. Only two hours to relaxation

2. Mountain fun in your own backyard

3. The family playground in the mountains

4. Escape to white water rafting, fishing, and the great outdoors

5. Weekend vacation planner package

Using cards with the theme statement and/or rough layouts the advertiser tries to obtain a rank order of consumer appeal of the various concepts and diagnostic data explaining why the concepts were ranked as they were.

The tourism group found that targets had not realized they were so close to these mountain areas. As a result, they had not been considered in their vacation/recreation plans.

In the case of a car rental company, a test of vacation travelers found that one benefit stood out: the lowest-priced full-size car. The second most important benefit was no hidden extras.

One drawback of concept testing is that consumers can react only to the themes presented to them. You may find that they have chosen the best of several bad concepts.

Focus Groups. In Chapter 15, we discussed the nature, cost, and typical procedure of focus group research. Here we examine the role of focus groups in selecting the primary appeal. Generally, the interviewer starts by discussing the product category, then proceeds to products within the category, and finally brings up past or current ads for a product or products. And, of course, the focus group can be used to test several new ad concepts of the appeal of print, storyboard, or more finished ad forms. The creative team watching from behind the one-way mirror has the opportunity to hear how participants perceive its products, ads, and ideas.

The leader of the group directs the conversation to determine what problems or "hang-ups" the prime prospects associate with the product. Thus, the answers are not predetermined by the advertiser or the researcher. Rather, they are direct responses to the product and the benefits and problems these prime prospects see in it. Further, because the research is done in a group, people feel less inhibited than they do in one-on-one interviews. The result is usually a good evaluation of the problems, attributes, and particular strengths and weaknesses of the product from the consumer's point of view.

One example of this type of research was conducted by the Atlanta Symphony Orchestra. Its agency interviewed two groups of prime prospects: attendees at regular-season symphony concerts and pop concert goers. The sym-

tremely important in keeping readers. As a matter of fact, the drop-off rate of readers is pretty significant during the first 50 words, but not so great between 50 and 500 words. Remember the scores of the Timberland ad in Chapter 15. Take another look at the proportion of readership between the ad elements.

The Headline

The headline is the most important part of an ad. It is the first thing read, and it should arouse the interest of the consumer so that the person wants to keep on reading and get to know more about the product being sold. If the headline does not excite the interest of the particular group of prime prospects the advertiser wants to reach, the rest of the ad will probably go unread.

Goodby, Berlin & Silverstein created an S-Works mountain bike (see Exhibit 16.3) that shows the product and communicates the idea of science and technology with an interest raising headline, "Thank God There Are People Who Stayed In The Science Club." The copy says: "While you were learning how to French kiss, they were learning how to manipulate gravity. Introducing the S-Works FSR.™ The most thought-out, dialed-in, thoroughly tested, fully suspended mountain bike there is. See your nearest physicist (or your local S-Works ™dealer) for a thorough explanation."

The structure of the ad works, if you're interested in mountain bikes, the headline gets the process started and compels you to read more.

No formula can be given for writing a good headline. However, there are several factors that should be considered in evaluating an effective headline:

- **It should use short, simple words, usually no more than 10.**

- **It should include an invitation to the prospect, primary product benefits, name of the brand, and an interest-provoking idea to gain readership of the rest of the ad.**

- **The words should be selective, appealing only to prime prospects.**

- **It should contain an action verb.**

EXHIBIT

16.3

....

A rather pointed headline that makes a statement for the brand.

(Courtesy: Goodby, Berlin, Silverstein—Specialized)

EXHIBIT

16.4

This headline speaks to
the heart of the brand
image.

(Courtesy: Bodyslimmers and Goldsmith/Jeffrey)

■ **It should give enough information so that the consumer who reads only the headline learns something about the product and its benefit.**

The Bodyslimmers headline in Exhibit 16.4 says all that needs to be communicated about the brand and the person, "While you don't necessarily dress for men, it doesn't hurt, on occasion, to see one drool like the pathetic dog that he is."

Obviously, many effective headlines violate one or more of these guidelines. However, when you write a headline that excludes any of these points, ask yourself: "Would this headline be more effective if it adhered to the guidelines?"

Many headlines fall into one of four categories:

Headlines That Present a New Benefit. The moment of peak interest in a product is when it offers a new benefit. That is why, in our innovative society, you often see headlines such as these:

The most affordable home improvement loan ever constructed.
(Texas Commerce Bank)

New GE Profile. Because you want more room for food. Not your refrigerator.
(GE Profile)

The most reliable copier ever to play the game just got better.
(Sharp copiers)

Panasonic introduces the Palm Corder with a color viewfinder, because life doesn't happen in black and white.

(Panasonic)

Get a little closer with clear protection.

(Arrid clear)

Headlines That Directly Promise an Existing Benefit. Products cannot be offering new benefits all the time, of course, so headlines often remind consumers of a product's existing features:

Big on taste. Not on fat.

(Kellogg's Low Fat Granola)

Financial Security

(Quorum)

Another day. Another chance to feel healthy.

(Evian)

The fully functional sedan with Ultra-Zesty Deluxe

(Mazda)

Curiosity-Invoking and Provocative Headlines. By invoking curiosity, an advertiser may grab attention from an otherwise disinterested audience by challenging the curiosity of the readers, thereby promoting them to read further and leading them into the key message. David Ogilvy warned against

"Old Faithful"

If you like your neighbors' garden, tell them. They deserve the praise. They've learned to be patient. They've adapted to working hard for small rewards. And they've also learned to never leave anything to chance. Swan's Soft & Supple® garden hose is the last garden hose you will ever need to buy. It's constructed to resist kinks for year round use, and the Seal Tite™ coupling offers a leakproof seal every time. Plus, it's backed by Swan's lifetime guarantee.

So for a purchase that will last a lifetime, come to Lowe's for your Swan Soft & Supple® garden hose today.

SWAN

LOWE'S
Helping Add Value To Your Home®

(Courtesy: Lowe's as seen in Southern Living.)

using heads that don't communicate the benefits in the heads, because of the large numbers of readers that don't read the body copy. It can work but the writer must be careful to build a strong relationship between the curiosity point and the brand. We've featured a number of Lowe's ads throughout the text that use a play on words (see Exhibits 16.5 and 16.6) Here are a few examples:

Why should you pay $349 for this radio?

(Bose)

Which came first, true love or TRULY LACE?

(Truly Lace)

What does the next generation want from us anyhow?

(AT&T Network System)

A thousand dollars says you can't guess how many options you get on a Toyota 4Runner.

(Toyota 4Runner)

We've just eliminated the need for willpower.

(Tostitos)

The question headline that works best is the kind that arouses curiosity so that the reader will read the body copy to find the answer. Readers do not like being tricked. They want a strong relationship between the curiosity and the product.

Selective Headlines. Readers looking through a magazine or newspaper are more likely to read an ad they think concerns them personally than one that

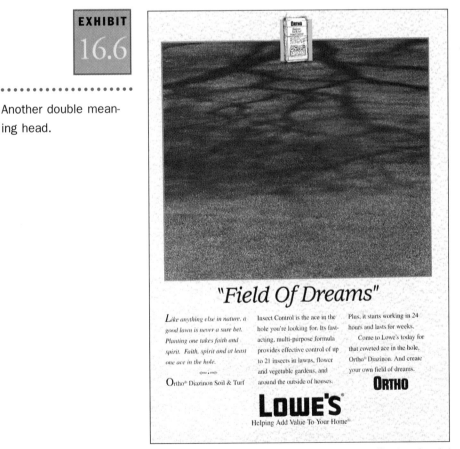

(Courtesy: Lowe's.)

talks to a broad audience. The selective headline aimed at a particular prime prospect who would be more interested in the product is often used. If the head says, "Condominium owners," and you don't own a condominium, you probably won't pay attention, and vice versa if you own a condo, you might read. Here are four such headlines:

To All Men and Women

To All Young Men and Women

To All College Men and Women

To All College Seniors

The first headline is addressed to the greatest number of readers, but it would be the least interest to any one of them. Each succeeding headline reduces the size of the audience it addresses and improves the chances of attracting that particular group. What about "All College Seniors Who Need Jobs?" You get the idea!

Besides addressing them directly, headlines can appeal to a particular group by mentioning a problem they have in common:

Oh, the sacrifices we make for our children.

(Toyota Previa)

Urinary discomfort shouldn't be a burning issue.

(AZO-Standard)

Another vital quality in headlines is specificity. Remember, consumers are more interested in the specific and not the general. Therefore, the more specific you can be in the headline, the better: "A Peppermint Peroxide Toothpaste That Will Help Kill Bacteria and Keep Tartar From Your Teeth" is better than "A Nice Tasting Toothpaste That Cleans Your Teeth."

The Subheadline. A headline must say something important to the reader. The actual number of words is not the deciding factor; long or short headlines may work well. A headline sometimes can be more than one sentence. "We know you'll like our coffee. We know you'll love the free coffee maker. We just don't know what color your kitchen is." If the message is long, it can be conveyed with a main headline (with large type) and a subheadline (with smaller type but copy larger than the body). The subhead can spell out the promise presented in the headline. It can be longer than the headline; it can invite further reading; and it serves as a transition to the opening paragraph of the copy.

Headline: What is Authentic?

Subhead: Introducing Authentic Chinos.

(Dockers Authentics)

Headline: The Greatest To Britain.

Subhead: More Nonstops To Great Britain Than Any Other U.S. Airline.
(American Airlines)

Amplification. The headline and, if used, the subheadline are followed by the body copy of the ad. It is here that you present your case for the product and explain how the promise in the headline will be fulfilled. In other words, the body copy amplifies what was hinted in the headline or sub-headline. What you say and how deep you go depend on the amount of information your prime prospect needs at this point in the buying process. A high-cost lap-top computer probably calls for more explanation than a low-cost product, such as a barbecue sauce with a new flavor. If a product has many technical advances, such as digital videorecording discs, there is probably not sufficient room to detail all the features. In this case, the objective is to create enough interest to get the prime prospect to the store for a demonstration and more information.

Amplification should emphasize those product or service features that are of primary importance but cannot be included in the headline. How different can a patio door be? Andersen tells consumers in its ad (Exhibit 16.7):

"Before A Patio Door Can Endure Father Time, It Has To Stand Up To Mother Nature. . . . It's designed to survive eight inches of rain per hour, driven by 50 mph horizontal winds, without leaking. . . . Combine that weather-tightness with our Perma-Shield® system, which protects the door from the weather, and you've got a door that repels moisture like water off a duck's back. . . . You'll save money, too, because our glass is 33% more energy efficient than ordinary double-pane glass during the heating months, and 13% better in the summer."

Proof. The body copy does amplify what the headline promised. At times the process acts to reassure the consumer that the product will perform as promised. Consumers may look for proof in an ad, and proof is particularly

Who wants to read about a patio door? Yet, this well written ad draws you into the copy and emphasizes product benefits and reasons to buy.

(Courtesy: CME KHBB Advertising and Andersen Windows, Inc.)

important for high-priced products, health, and new products with special features. Here are a few ways in which proof can be offered to the reader.

Seals of Approval.   Seals of approval from such accredited sources as *Good Housekeeping* and *Parent's* magazines, the American Dental Association, the American Medical Association, and Underwriter's Laboratories allay consumers' fears about product quality. An Ayer senior vice president of planning says that it gives a product a difference and that the seal can give a new product an edge of credibility in the market. Niagara spray starch advertises the Good Housekeeping seal.

Guarantees.   Wendy's, Arby's, and Mrs. Winner's have offered consumers money-back guarantees for trying specific products to reduce the risk for trial by consumers. Products like Silent Floor systems guarantee their floors will be free from warping or defects. Hartz Control Pet System will refund your money if you don't see an improvement in 30 days (see lifetime guarantee in Lowe's Exhibit 16.5).

Trial Offers and Samples.   BMG Music offers any eight CDs for the price of one when you try its 10-day risk-free trial. Procter & Gamble offered free Industrial Strength Spic and Span liquid samples to consumers who called an 800-number to reduce the risk and get trial.

Warranties.   James Hardie Building Products touts its 50-year warranty for its siding.

Reputation.   Copy for Woolite says, "It's recommended by the makers of more than 350 million garments."

Demonstrations.   Before-and-after demonstrations are used to show how a product works. Starch Research says showing models to demonstrate cosmetic products is powerful. Almay used Elaine Irwin in an ad shown from the neck up, making it easy to identify her facial imperfections—or lack thereof—after using Almay's line of hypo-allergenic cosmetics. Find a way to tell consumers a benefit, and you will do well; find a way to *show* them, and you will fare even better.

Testimonials.   The ability to attract attention to ads and offer a credible source has made testimonials a popular device. Testimonials should come from persons viewed by consumers as competent to make judgments on the products they are endorsing.

COPY STYLE

As with a novel or a play, good ad copy has a beginning, a middle, and an ending. And, like a good novel, the transition must be smooth from one part to another. Up to this point, we have discussed how the building blocks of copy are put together. Now we need to think about what it takes to create special attention and persuasion. It takes style—the ability to create fresh, charming, witty, human advertising that compels people to read. Remember what Ron Huey said, "Take the single most salient feature of your product or service and communicate it in a simple, thought provoking or entertaining way." See the product in a fresh way, to explore its possible effects on the reader, or to explain the product's advantages in a manner that causes the reader to view the product with a new understanding and appreciation.

Most ads end by asking or suggesting that the reader buy the product. The difference between a lively ad and a dull one lies in the approach to the message at the outset.

The lens through which a writer sees a product may be the magnifying glass of the technician, who perceives every nut and bolt and can explain why each is important; or it may be the rose-colored glasses of the romanticist, who sees how a person's life may be affected by the product. That is why we speak of approaches rather than types of ads. The chief approaches in describing a product are the factual, the imaginative, and the emotional.

Factual Approach. Here the writer deals with reality—that which actually exists. We talk about the product or service—what it is, how it is made, what it does. Focusing on the facts about the product that are most important to the reader, we explain the product's advantages.

One of the interesting things about a fact, however, is that it can be interpreted in different ways, each accurate but each launching different lines of thinking. Remember the classic example of an eight-ounce glass holding four ounces of water, of which can be said: "This glass is half full" or "This glass is half empty." As you know, both are correct and factual. The difference is in the interpretation of reality, as the Mitsui O.S.K. ad in Exhibit 16.8 illustrates. Its copy talks facts: "MOL takes a great deal of pride in catering to the needs of the world's most discriminating shippers. Salmon, shrimp, crabs, mussels and other gourmet seafood, for example, are delivered in 40′ by 40′ high-cube reefer containers so that they arrive fresh and delectable in Asian

If getting your perishable food items to and from the Far East feels too much like swimming against the current, allow us to recommend a tasty alternative: Mitsui O.S.K. Lines.

MOL takes a great deal of pride in catering to the needs of the world's most discriminating shippers. Salmon, shrimp, crabs, mussels and other gourmet seafood, for example, are delivered in 40′ and 40′ high-cube reefer containers so that they arrive fresh and delectable in Asian and American markets.

For quality and dependability, MOL is quite a catch, serving up a satisfying and perfectly prepared schedule of fixed-day, fixed-hour services. Combined with a sophisticated intermodal network and cargo tracking system, MOL brings new meaning to the term "fast food."

So give us a nibble. Call today to see how the seafood connoisseurs at Mitsui O.S.K. Lines can cater to your bottom line.

For more information on MOL's full inventory of refrigerated cargo service, call the MOLAM office nearest you: Corporate Headquarters 201/200-5200; Atlanta 404/763-0111; Chicago 312/683-7300; Long Beach 310/437-8251; Seattle 206/464-3930.

(Courtesy: Longwater, Inc.)

and American markets." Skill in presenting a fact consists in projecting it in a way that means the most to the reader.

The factual approach can be used to sell more than products or services. Facts about ideas, places—anything an ad can be written for—can be presented with a fresh point of view.

Imaginative Approach. There's nothing wrong with presenting a fact imaginatively. The art of creating copy lies in saying a familiar thing in an unexpected way. The Columbia Sportswear ad in Exhibit 16.9 says, "OLD AND UNIMPROVED." Yet the large illustration is the chairman—who we'll say isn't pictured as young—and the smaller illustration is the product, which, of course, the head is really about. A fresh approach to selling a parka.

The North Carolina Zoo could have stuck to boring presentation of facts, but it didn't (see Exhibit 16.10). It could have stuck with showing animals. It could have said we've built a zoo in a natural environment.

Jimmy John's, a submarine sandwich chain, which targets college students, uses trendy newspaper ads carrying unconventional sales pitches. Instead of using photos, logos, or other graphics, the chain promotes itself with humorous poetry. The lines are stacked in a single column, using different sizes of the same typeface to emphasize key words of copy. One ad reads:

Party
You Plan it.
You love it
It's dancin'
Romancin'
Then time to depart.
But alas!
You just met a cutie
Who says you're a beauty!
If that's your fate
It's never too late
To impress that new love
With a Jimmy John Sub
The party-goers' sub!™

Another ad reads:

No Zits
No pits
No day-old bread
No grease
No fries
Great subs instead.™

Each ad copy is followed by the restaurant's phone number, address, closing time, and Jimmy John's trademarked slogan "We'll bring 'em to ya."

The County Seat Cafe, on the other hand, integrated the same message for its baby-back ribs in its ads and in-store promotions. It used "Rack-Up A BBQ Feast!" framed with illustrations of vegetables. The copy and illustration work together to communicate in an unusual way (see Exhibit 16.11).

EXHIBIT
16.9

"OLD AND
UNIMPROVED."

····················

Columbia Sportswear
took their "old" chair-
person and made her a
mother figure; and
mother would only
make the best!

(Courtesy: Borders, Perrin & Norrander.)

Emotional Approach. Emotion can be a powerful communicator. The feelings about your product or company can be an important plus or minus.
Copy using psychological appeals to love, hate, or fear has great impact. Once
again we turn to a Healthtex ad example; not only do its ads show humor,
imagination, and humanity, but emotion—every parent can identify with the
kids in these ads (see Exhibit 16.12). Kids always evoke a degree of emotion.
Kinder-Care uses it to sell its learning centers: "The Joys of Kinder-Care" features close-ups of happy kid faces to warm the hearts of moms and dads. Often the copy will continue the emotional appeal, though at times it will take
a factual direction to inform the reader about specific features of the product

EXHIBIT
16.10

····················

Dramatic photography
and a powerful copy
idea breaks through the
clutter of ads.

When we built the North Carolina Zoo, this is what we used for a roof.

(Courtesy: Loeffler, Ketchum, Mountjoy.)

County Seat Cafe integrates their ad and instore promotion. It didn't do the obvious—using ribs—and emphasized vegetables in their background design.

(Courtesy: Folks, Inc. and Leigh Kain Advertising.)

to convince the reader of its value. On the other hand, Kodak has produced ads so emotional they bring tears to your eyes.

Research indicates emotion can create positive feelings, such as warmth, happiness, and delight, that work best for low-involvement goods. For high-involvement, higher-ticket items, such as CD players or automobiles, emotions must be unique and mesh with the brand.

Comparative advertising

Used interchangeably with the term *comparison advertising,* it directly contrasts an advertiser's product with other named or identified products.

Comparative Advertising. Comparing your product directly with one or more competitors is called comparative advertising. It is actually encouraged by the Federal Trade Commission, but it has risks. Some advertisers think it isn't smart to spend money to publicize your competition. Others think it creates a bad atmosphere for the company, which demeans all advertising. Pepsi has frequently run ads in Nation's Restaurant News featuring "Coke and Pepsi View Your Business Two Different Ways," and the copy talks about how they do business differently.

Every parent can feel a lump in their throat as they identify with their kids—Healthtex uses emotion in all of their ads.

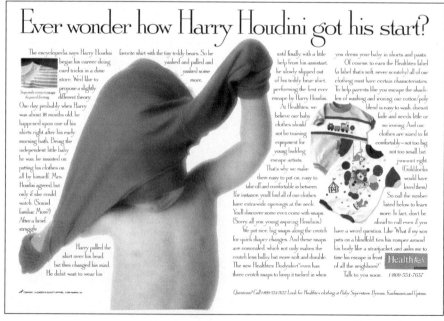

(Courtesy: Healthtex.™)

Despite each comparative ad being different, there are certain rules of thumb that can be applied: (1) The leader in the field never starts a comparative campaign. (2) The most successful comparison ads are those comparing the product with products identical in every respect except for the special differential featured in the ad. The stronger the proof that the products are identical, the better. (3) The different features should be of importance to the consumer.

Slogans

Originally derived from the Gaelic *slugh gairm,* meaning "battle cry," the word *slogan* has an appropriate background. A slogan sums up the theme for a product's benefits to deliver an easily remembered message in a few words.

There have been many very memorable slogans in advertising over the years. Yet, not all of the effective slogans are etched in every consumers mind. However, many slogans do help communicate the essence of the product position. Exhibit 16.13 is an example of a product most of us don't use on a regular basis or even think about frequently—outside insect spray—Diazinon. But the slogan helps position the product and makes it memorable, "Any bug. Any time. Any place."

Used even more often on television and radio than in print, slogans may be combined with a catchy tune to make a jingle. Slogans are broadly classified as either institutional or hard-sell.

EXHIBIT
16.13

· · · · · · · · · · · · · · · · · · · ·

"Any bug. Anytime. Anyplace," is the product's slogan telling consumers it will kill bugs.

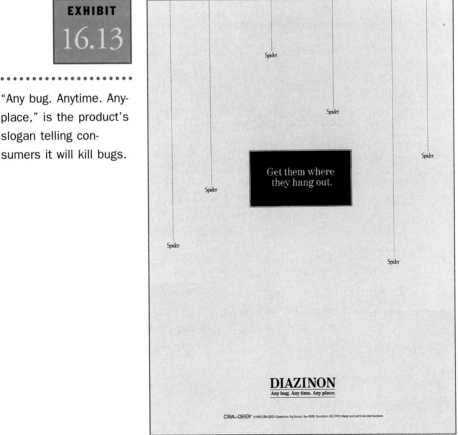

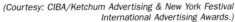

(Courtesy: CIBA/Ketchum Advertising & New York Festival International Advertising Awards.)

Institutional. Institutional slogans are created to establish a prestigious image for a company. Relying on this image to enhance their products and services, many firms insist that their slogan appear in all of their advertising and on their letterheads. An entire ad may feature the slogan. Some institutional slogans are familiar:

Showing America a New Way Home. *(Fannie Mae)*

You're in Good Hands with Allstate *(Allstate Insurance)*

The Document Company *(Xerox)*

A Tradition of Trust. *(Merrill Lynch)*

A Part of People's Lives Everywhere. *(NEC)*

Such policy slogans are changed infrequently, if at all. Stating the platform or virtues of the candidate in a few words, slogans used in political campaigns likewise fall into the institutional-slogan category. Those campaigns expire on election day (as do many of the candidate's promises).

Hard sell. These capsules of advertising change with campaigns. They epitomize the special significant features of the product or service being advertised, and their claims are strongly competitive:

Get Met. It Pays. *(MetLife)*

The Best Beer in America. *(Samuel Adams)*

It's Gotta Be Gatorade. *(Gatorade)*

A Different Kind of Company. A Different Kind of Car. *(Saturn)*

M&M's. The Milk Chocolate Melts in Your Mouth—Not In Your Hands. *(M&M's)*

Slogans are widely used to advertise groceries, drugs, beauty aids, and liquor. These are products that are bought repeatedly at a comparatively low price. They are sold in direct competition to consumers on the shelves of supermarkets, drugstores, and department stores. If a slogan can remind a shopper in one of those stores of a special feature of the product, it certainly has served its purpose. Slogans can also remind shoppers of the name of a product from a company they respect. Not all advertising needs slogans. One-shot announcements—sale ads for which price is the overriding consideration—usually do not use slogans. Creating a slogan is one of the fine arts of copywriting.

Elements of a Good Slogan. A slogan differs from most other forms of writing because it is designed to be remembered and repeated word for word to impress a brand and its message on the consumer. Ideally, the slogan should be short, clear, and easy to remember.

Boldness helps:

Advanced Medicine for Pain. *(Advil)*

Nationwide Is on Your Side. *(Nationwide Insurance)*

The Right Choice *(AT&T)*

Starch Advertising Readership Service recently put together a report that studied toiletries and cosmetic ads. Based on interviews with 25,000 magazine readers who were exposed to some 1,800 cosmetic and toiletries ads in 251 magazines over two years, it was considered the most comprehensive report on cosmetics and toiletries ever produced. What follows are principles of effective advertising that advertisers in other industries can learn from.

DEMONSTRATE THE PRODUCT BENEFIT WITH A MODEL

Starch says the key to success is to state benefits clearly. And it doesn't have to be verbal; some product categories can go beyond the verbal into the visual to show the benefits. The most powerful cosmetic ads show the results of the product, thereby allowing for a kind of on-the-spot product test.

Models are the best medium for showing off the benefits of most toiletries and cosmetics ads. That may appear to be an obvious conclusion, but many cosmetic ads don't show people at all. As Starch found, sometimes model-less ads work just fine. But the odds are with selling benefits and beauty. Consumers want to see proof that the cosmetic actually works, and rare is the man or woman who tires of looking at beauty.

Starch warns that a well-known model does not guarantee notice, but using one usually provides a good foundation for a cosmetic ad. Famous models are especially powerful in capturing readers' attention. Previous Starch studies have indicated that ads with celebrities receive more attention, especially from women, than other kinds of ads. Some of the highest Noted Starch ads feature best-known models: Paulina Porizkova for Estee Lauder and Claudia Christensen for Revlon Velvet Touch to name a few.

WITH FRAGRANCE ADS HYPE THE IMAGE

The fragrance category is highly competitive and constitutes one-quarter of all the ads studied by Starch in the cosmetic report. Fragrance ads are even more image oriented than cosmetic ads. Unlike cosmetics, the product benefits of fragrances cannot be demonstrated other than through images of people attracting attention and looking as if they smell great. Of course, you can't show they smell great, but you can suggest what happens if you do smell good. You can't make an intellectual appeal about perfume, either. Thus, perfume ads have to create a different kind of argument. The Guess parfum advertising featuring Claudia Schiffer

earned an exceptionally high Noted index of 126. Combining both sexiness and vulnerability, she captured readers' attention by looking right at you—a powerful image. The ad has nothing to do with demonstrating how good the product smells. It is a blatant use of sex as a selling tool, and it worked.

LESS IS MORE: MAKE THE LAYOUT SIMPLE AND FLOWING

The various parts of effective cosmetic ads are artfully positioned so that they fit together like the pieces of a puzzle. Color coordination of elements is a particularly useful unifying device. In contrast, less effective ads comprise elements that do not work together. For example, the copy may be scattered to too many locations. Another point: There is a lot to say about a model who *fixes* you with his or her eyes. It is easy to look away from a model when she is focused on something else off in the distance. Years of social training compel you to return the gaze of a model who's looking directly at you.

CONTRAST COLORS

The successful application of cosmetics involves knowing the art of color coordination, and such knowledge enhances the success of a cosmetic ad. Contrasting colors attract attention, but this doesn't mean an ad should necessarily have several colors. Successful ads often have just a few, with the various parts of the ad—copy, product, model—color-coordinated to create a cohesive whole.

AND A FEW MORE TIPS

Different product categories make different creative demands. Starch makes a point that some ads work better without models, since the human element tends to distract attention away from the product. Still, most product categories are better served with models because they add something that readers can relate to, and human beauty, it is no secret, attracts the eye. However, we must be reminded that beauty by itself is no guarantor of effectiveness. The model is only a vehicle for the message, not the star. It's the creative mix—or the flow—that ultimately determines an ad's drawing power. Potential consumers of almost any product implicitly demand that the advertiser clearly state what they will get from the product or service. Find a way to tell them the benefit, and you will do well; find a way to *show* them, and you will fare even *better*.

Aptness helps:

Hyatt. We've Thought of Everything.   *(Hyatt Grand)*

Trusted By More Women Than Any Other Brand.   *(Massengill)*

It is an advantage to have the name of the product in the slogan:

Delta. You'll Love the Way We Fly.   *(Delta Air Lines)*

Kroger. For Goodness Sake.   *(Kroger)*

THE CREATIVE WORK PLAN

Before most agencies start creating an ad, they develop a creative work plan to guide them in the right direction. You will recall from Chapter 3 the Lintas:Link creative brief consisting of the following elements:

- **Key observation**
- **Communication objective**
- **Consumer insight**
- **Promise**
- **Support**
- **Audience**
- **Mandatories**

The purpose of the work plan is to provide proper direction for the creative team prior to developing ideas, heads, and copy. Exhibit 16.14 shows a work plan format originally developed by Young & Rubicam that is widely used by a number of agencies and is different from the Lintas approach. Note that the work plan emphasizes factual information and research data. The creative process is not a "shot in the dark" but rather depends on knowing as much as possible about the product, the consumer, and the expected benefits. The advertising professional is able to channel objective information into a creative and attention-getting sales message. Many agencies and clients have their own format and style for specific information they think necessary for creative strategy development.

REVIEWING THE COPY

After the copy has been written, review it with these questions in mind:

- **Your copy strategy is what you say to whom and why.**
- **Does your advertising position the brand clearly?**
- **Does it tie the brand to a strong benefit?**
- **Does your advertising have a "Big Idea"?**
- **Does this idea tie into the strategy and execution?**
- **How strong is the execution of the "Big Idea"?**
- **Does your advertising promote the brand personality?**

CREATIVE WORK PLAN

PRODUCT: NEW ORLEANS

KEY FACT
Bevil Foods is a 30 year old New Orleans' based frozen food company. In 1993, Bevil Foods will introduce a new line of premium frozen entrees to be distributed nationally.

PROBLEM THE ADVERTISING MUST SOLVE
Currently there is **NO Awareness** of the New OrLEANS Product among potential consumers.

ADVERTISING OBJECTIVE
To achieve 70% awareness of the product at end of year one. To communicate the taste and low-calories-fat benefits of the product.

CREATIVE STRATEGY

PROSPECT DEFINITION
1. Women 25-54, professional/managerial, with household incomes of $25,000 plus.
2. Adults 25+ professional/managerial, with household incomes of $25,000.

   Psychographically, these people tend to be active, concerned with their health, and "on the go" a lot.

PRINCIPAL COMPETITION
Lean Cuisine, Weight Watchers, Healthy Choice.

KEY PROMISE
New OrLeans are lite entrees with the great taste of New Orleans.

REASON WHY
Less than 300 calories; low fat, great tasting, original New Orleans recipes, served in fine restaurants for 30 years.

MANDATORIES
Must use logo, calorie and fat information, and original New Orleans recipes in each ad.

■ **Is it bold and unexpected?**

■ **Does it clearly state a promise and reward the pros?**

■ **Is your advertising single-minded?**

■ **Is the ad visually arresting?**

SUMMARY

Simplicity is the key to great advertising. Good copy speaks to the common man. The great creative shops of today have a common thread running through their advertising—the headline, visual, and logo communicate the idea immediately.

Advertising motivates people by appealing to their problems, desires, and goals—and offering them a solution to their problems, satisfactions of their desires, and a means of achieving their goals.

In general, ads have a definite structure consisting of a promise of benefit in the headline (and maybe the spelling out of the promise in a subheadline), amplification of the story or facts, proof of claim, and action to take. Effective heads can be long or short, but they need to communicate the message clearly. The subheadline can expand on the promise presented in the headline, and can provide transition between the headline and the first sentence of the body copy. The body copy is where you build your case with consumers for the product and support the promise in the head or subhead. The details about the product or service are presented here, along with support for your claim.

The creative essence of copywriting is to see a product in a fresh unique way. The chief approaches used to describe products are the factual, the imaginative, and the emotional. A slogan sums up the theme for a product's benefits. It needs to be a memorable message with few words.

Slogans can be developed from several points of view; the institutional and hard-sell viewpoints are the most common.

The place to start planning an ad is the creative work plan or the creative brief. If written properly, the creative work plan will tell you what the message should be in the ad and what the ad is to accomplish. It tells you the ad's specific purpose. However, no work plan will tell you how to execute the copy—that's part of the creative process.

Questions

1. What are the advantages of using a psychological appeal in developing advertising?
2. Briefly, compare and contrast concept testing, focus groups, and motivational research.
3. What are the primary purposes of the headline? Briefly, discuss the four major categories of headlines.
4. What is the purpose of amplification and where is it found in most ads?
5. What are some of the primary ways in which an ad can offer proof for a product's advertising claims?
6. What is meant by *copy-style?*
7. What are the characteristics of an effective slogan?
8. What is the purpose of the creative workplan?

The Total Concept: Words and Visuals

CHAPTER OBJECTIVES

Ideas and ads. How does a creative team get from an idea to a finished ad? What kind of visuals are best? How do we generate fresh ideas? After reading this chapter you will understand:

- **Concepts and executional ideas**
- **Left- and right-brain ideas**
- **How a creative team works**
- **Visualizing the idea**
- **Principles of design**
- **Kinds of visuals**

The genius advertising art director George Lois once said that advertising is poison gas. It should bring tears to your eyes, and it should unhinge your nervous system. It should knock you out. He admitted that his description is probably excessive but regards it as a forgivable hyperbole because it certainly describes the powerful **possibilities** of advertising. Great advertising should have the impact of a punch in the mouth. Great advertising should ask, without asking literally, "Do you get the message?" And the viewer should answer, without literally answering, "Yeah, I got it!" Lois says all of this can be accomplished with the "Big Idea."

Concept

The combining of all elements of an ad—copy, headline, and illustrations—into a single idea.

The creative process can be broken down into four basic areas: concepts, words, pictures, and the medium or vehicle used to present them. The dictionary defines *concept* as a general notion or idea, an idea of something formed by mentally combining all its characteristics or particulars. In advertising, the total concept is a fresh way of looking at something—a novel way of talking about a product or service, a dramatic new dimension that gives the observer a new perspective. A concept is an *idea.* Many in advertising, including Lois, call it the Big Idea—*one that is expressed clearly and combines words and visuals.* The words describe what the basic idea is, and the visuals repeat what the words say or, even better, reinforce what the words say or provide a setting that makes the words more powerful.

Your creative concept must not only grab attention, it must also get across the main selling point and the brand name. How often has someone seen a compelling ad only to later say, "I don't remember the brand name or product." The Chrysler ad (see Exhibit 17.1) combines the head and visuals work to communicate a single thought.

IDEAS COME FROM THE LEFT AND RIGHT BRAIN

The left hemisphere of the brain provides reasoning, verbal skills and processes information. On the other hand, the right side provides intuition, processes information, controls the creative process, thinks nonverbally, responds to color, and is artistic. They tell us that when we dream the right side takes

EXHIBIT
17.1

Chrysler meshes visual and verbal communication.

Gentlemen, start your imaginations.

The 400 H.P. Dodge Viper. The shape of things to come from Chrysler.

CHRYSLER
All you have to do is drive one.

(Courtesy: Anson-Stoner, Inc. and New York Festivals International Advertising Awards)

Executional idea

It is a rendering in words, symbols, sounds, colors, shapes, forms, or any combination thereof, of an abstract answer to a perceived desire or need.

control. So we're talking about a left-brain person and a right-brain person working together to develop a concept. Each comes to the table with a different point of view.

Bill Backer in his book, *The Care and Feeding of Ideas*, defines a *basic idea* or concept as an abstract answer to a perceived desire or need. And an *executional idea* is a rendering in words, symbols, sounds, colors, shapes, forms, or any combination thereof, of an abstract answer to a perceived desire or need. We use *execute* in ad development. It is a schizophrenic verb. It means to complete or put into effect or to use according to a pattern—as a work of art. Of course, it also means "to put to death."

THE CREATIVE TEAM

In general, the responsibility for the visual, layout, and graphics is that of the art director. The copywriter creates the words for the ad and, maybe, the ad concept. We say maybe, because where creative teams are used it is the responsibility of the team to develop a concept. The copywriter needs to understand art direction and the art director needs to appreciate the impact of words. Together they need to have a rapport to be successful, almost a marriage of ideas. Both are concept thinkers. Both think in terms of words and pictures—after the team members arm themselves with all the information they need. When they have settled on a target audience and a creative strategy, these left- and right-brain people begin to create.

Like any creative process, the development of an ad proceeds in a systematic manner, although the process is sometimes unpredictable. Some ideas seem to fall into place quickly. Other ideas may be as difficult as giving birth to a rhinoceros. Developing any ad is a labor, and developing great ads usually is plain hard work. The creative team—the art director and copywriter—sit and bounce ideas off each other, worry together, go to lunch together, push and prod each other to find the Big Idea. It does not matter who develops a great copy line or visual idea. Their job is to find one idea that has the potential of accomplishing the advertising objectives. The most important part is that the ad reflects the creative strategy of solving the prime prospect's problem. Of course, the goal is that the end result of all this collaboration will be a Big Idea that says something dramatically in words and pictures.

THE IDEA

Strong ideas are usually simple ideas. People do not remember details as clearly as they recall concepts. Creative director Tom Monahan illustrates this with the concept of the movie *Dances with Wolves*, which might be described as follows: "It's a film about a U.S. Army officer who experiences life as a Native American, just as the Indian nations were being threatened by the white man's dominance."[1] This simple concept became a memorable film because of its execution—the direction, acting, dialogue, and cinematography. In advertising, simple concepts become great ads through the same attention to

---

[1] Tom Monahan, "Advertising Fundamentals" *Communication Arts*, March/April 1991, pp. 123–124.

detail—the words, type style, photography, and layout. A great advertising concept might survive poor execution, but the better crafted the ad, the better the chances that prospects will become customers. The idea must come alive, leap off the page, or grab your senses while you watch television. In addition, creative ideas do two other important things:

1. They make the prime prospect consider your product first.

2. They implant your brand name indelibly in the prime prospect's mind and connect it to the positive attributes of the product.

Visualizing the Idea

After the Big Idea is developed and nurtured, the creative team forms mental pictures of how the basic appeal can be translated into a selling message. It is time to execute the Big Idea. Just as a good novel has various subplots that are brought together in a creative and interesting, cohesive story line, a good ad has a well-coordinated layout that flows well to create a compelling message about the product and its benefits.[2] You might visualize a sports car as speeding on a mountain road and around hairpin curves. You might see a sedan of understated luxury in front of a country club.

These mental pictures can be shown in words or in the crudest sketches. The critical thing is to imagine the kind of mental picture that best expresses your idea. While thinking in the visual form, find the words that work with the visual for the most powerful effect. Make as many versions of the basic idea as you can. Stretch your idea to the limit. Try every possibility, but remember your end result must deliver the basic message and the brand name. Does the illustration and copy deliver the creative work plan promise?

Marketing Approach to Visualization

We know that ads are not created for the sake of creativity. Each ad is created for a specific marketing purpose. All ads for a product should conform to the same set of objectives, even though some ads may not appear to be related, and they usually use the same theme or slogan in each ad.

After digesting all of the information about the product, write a statement of the one thing you need to say about the product to the prime prospect. This is your promise or the basic theme. A family restaurant might shift to low-fat menu items and make the following promise: "We offer you all the things you like about family-style restaurants—convenience, great-tasting foods, reasonable prices—with the added benefit of fitting into your lifestyle, since you want food that is nutritious and good for you." The illustrations must reflect these marketing concepts.

The promise is a consumer benefit statement that tells the prospect what the product will do for them.

THE CREATIVE LEAP

Joseph Wallas, a creative theorist, proposed the idea that creativity was the product of four developmental stages: preparation, incubation, illumination,

---

[2]Roper Starch Worldwide, Inc., Starch Tested Copy, Vol. 5, No. 3, p. 4.

and verification or evaluation. Where does the inspiration come from? Leo Burnett, vice chairman/corporate creative director, says, "The best creative comes from an understanding of what people are thinking and feeling. Creativity is a sensitivity to human nature and the ability to communicate it." Some think brainstorming or free association is the answer to creative inspiration, but others say that very few ideas come from these techniques. The idea usually comes when you are not looking. The process is one part reason, one part heart, and one big part simple intuition, say others. So the creative leap is not necessarily the same for everyone. There may be truth to the notion that you must spend more time on the logical process, and then the emotional part gets easier. The Burnett creative team wanted to play up Kellogg's Special K's high protein. Simple enough, right? But too simple. The agency then matched the concept to other related ideas and came up with a dual focus that teamed the cereal with exercise. The result was a message that added more dimension, involvement, and appeal: "Keep the muscle, lose the fat."[3]

This process involves bridging the gap between the visualization and concrete words and pictures. As part of this process, the creative team will offer and reject numerous approaches to solving this marketing communication problem. The basic appeal will be used to write dozens of headline possibilities. As a result of these ideas, they will develop visual ideas that fit these headlines under consideration. In some cases, a headline will result from an illustration idea. The Port of Brunswick ad uses a car concept in the head and the visual, but it is logical because the port already moves 126,000 cars through its facilities. The ad is creative, yet it communicates the benefits (see Exhibit 17.2).

The Layout

The creative leap is only the first step in ad making. The ad itself has a variety of elements: headlines, illustration, copy, logotype, maybe a subheadline, several other illustrations of varying importance, a coupon—the number of components varies tremendously from ad to ad. Putting them all together in an orderly form is called making up the layout of the ad. *Layout* is another of those advertising terms that is used in two senses: It means the total appearance of the ad—its overall design, the composition of its elements; it also means the physical rendering of the design of the ad—a blueprint for production purposes. You will hear some say: "Here's the layout," while handing another person a typed or keyboarded copy and a drawing. Right now, we are talking about the layout as the overall design of the ad.

Layout Person as Editor

Although the person who creates the visual idea may be the same as the one who makes the layout, the two functions are different. The visualizer translates an idea into visual form; a layout person uses that illustration and all the other elements to make an orderly, attractive arrangement.

Before putting pencil to paper, however, the layout person—usually an art director—and the writer review all of the elements. The first task is to de-

Layout

A working drawing (may be computer developed) showing how an ad is to look. A printer's layout is a set of instructions accompanying a piece of copy showing how it is to be set up. There are also rough layouts, finished layouts, and mechanical layouts, representing various degrees of finish. The term *layout* is used, too, for the total design of an ad.

---

[3]Terrance Poltrack, "Stalking the Big Idea," *Agency*, May/June 1991, pp. 25–29.

EXHIBIT

17.2

....

This takeoff on a car
ad helps grab your at-
tention because it isn't
showing the obvious.

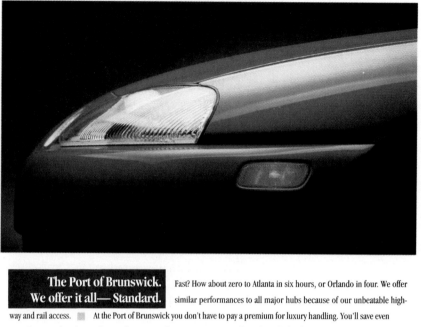

What's Fast, Affordable, Reliable & Roomy?

The Port of Brunswick. We offer it all— Standard. Fast? How about zero to Atlanta in six hours, or Orlando in four. We offer similar performances to all major hubs because of our unbeatable highway and rail access. ▪ At the Port of Brunswick you don't have to pay a premium for luxury handling. You'll save even more because of our huge volume and convenient location means we can keep those dealer destination charges to a minimum. ▲ If reliability is a major concern, the 126,000 cars we've already handled speak for themselves. Our customers keep coming back for the performance that's as predictable as it is exceptional. ▼ Top it off with spacious comfort. 125 paved acres assure improved high speed handling with no costly fender benders. ● Specify the Port of Brunswick— It handles like a dream. For additional information contact Richard Field, Director of Trade Development, Georgia Ports Authority, P.O. Box 2406, Savannah, Georgia 31402. Or call 1-800-841-1107.

▲ Port of Brunswick
▼●

(Courtesy: Longwater, Inc.)

cide what is most important. Is it the headline? The picture? The copy? How important is the package? Should the product itself be shown, and if so, should it be shown in some special environment or in use? Is this ad to tell a fast story with a picture and headline, or is it a long-copy ad in which illustration is only an incidental feature? The importance of the element determines its size and placement within the ad.

Working Hard to Get Noticed

Attracting attention. Getting noticed. High visibility. No matter how you say it, this is the primary creative objective of an ad. Today's advertising has to work very hard to get noticed. You cannot rely on strategy alone—the positioning, the product appeals, the demographic and psychographic data that tell you what wavelength the consumer is on—to sell the consumer. Obvious as it sounds, you cannot sell people until you attract their attention. Put another way, people are not going to read the ad if they do not see it. Remember, your ad is competing with all the advertising clutter and editorial matter in a publication. Unfortunately, most ads in most publications are invisible.

All the creative elements—the visual, the headline, the copy—must be strongly executed if the ad is to succeed (Exhibit 17.3). Research cannot tell us which creative techniques will work best because creative is not that scientific. Research generally tells us what has been successful, but there are no yardsticks to measure breakthrough advertising ideas. The basic guidelines for writing and designing ads are helpful, but there are not really any rules. How do you get an ad to stand out? The illustration is usually the key. Either an ad grabs people or it does not, and most often it is the illustration that gets them. Of course, many illustrations cannot tell the story alone—they require a head to complete the communication. So the headline is extremely important to keep people.

A picture is worth a thousand words, but we do not use illustrations solely to attract attention. They must have a strong relationship to the selling concept. Using a shock visual merely to gain attention is generally a mistake. If you are selling a hammer and your dominant visual is a woman in a bikini, you are using sexist imagery that has no relationship to the product. You are

EXHIBIT
17.3

. . . .

The basic appeal, illustration and head are working hard to get noticed.

(Courtesy: The Zimmerman Agency.)

EXHIBIT
17.4

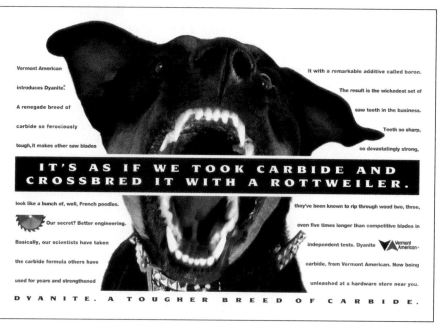

Illustration and head
are working hard to
attract the reader's
attention.

(Courtesy: Loeffler, Ketchum, Mountjoy.)

duping people: "Now that we have your attention, buy our hammer." And because most people dislike being duped, they will resent your ad—and often your product as well. Yet powerful images can demand your attention. The Vermont American ad showing an unfriendly rottweiler compels your attention (see Exhibit 17.4).

There are three basic means of attracting attention:

1. Using the visual alone

2. Using the headline alone

3. Using a combination of the visual and headline

Do not assume that because we listed the visual first that the art director is more important than the copywriter. Remember, they are a team working together on both visual and language ideas.

Basic Design Principles

There are some general principles that guide the design of advertising and promotional layouts. Some art directors may use different terminology from that used here, but the basic assumptions are the same.

The following design principles, properly employed, will attract the reader and enhance the chances of the message's being read.

Unity.   All creative advertising has a unified design. The layout must be conceived in its entirety, with all its parts (copy, art, head, logo, etc.) related to one another to give one, overall, unified effect. If the ad does not have unity, it falls apart and becomes visual confusion. Perhaps unity is the most important design principle, but they are all necessary for an effective ad.

Harmony.   Closely related to unity is the idea that all elements of the layout must be compatible. The art director achieves harmony by choosing elements that go together. This process is similar to dressing in the morning. Some items of clothing go together better than others—for example, stripes, plaids, or paisleys with solid colors. The layout needs harmonious elements to be effective; there should not be too many different type faces or sizes, illustrations, and so on.

Sequence.   The ad should be arranged in an orderly manner so it can be read from left to right and top to bottom. The sequence of elements can help direct the eye in a structural or gaze motion. Place the elements so that the eye starts where you want it to start and travels a desired path throughout the ad. "Z" and "S" arrangements are common.

Emphasis.   Emphasis is accenting or focusing on an element (or group of elements) to make it stand out. Decide whether you want to stress the illustration, the headline, the logo, or the copy. If you give all of these elements equal emphasis, your ad will end up with no emphasis at all.

Contrast.   You need differences in sizes, shapes, and tones to add sparkle so the ad will not be visually dull. Altering type to bold or italic or using extended typefaces brings attention to a word or phrase and creates contrast between type elements. Contrast makes the layout more interesting.

Balance.   By balance, we mean controlling the size, tone, weight, and position of the elements in the ad. Balanced elements look secure and natural to the eye. You test for balance by examining the relationship between the right and left halves of the ad. There are basically two forms of balance: formal and informal.

FORMAL BALANCE. A formally balanced ad has elements of equal weights, sizes, and shapes on the left and right sides of an imaginary vertical line drawn down the center of the ad. Such symmetrical ads give an impression of stability and conservatism, but at times look unimaginative. (see Exhibits 17.4 and 17.5).

INFORMAL BALANCE. The optical center of a page, measured from top to bottom, is five-eighths of the way up the page; thus, it differs from the mathematical center. (To test this, take a blank piece of paper, close your eyes, then open them, and quickly place a dot at what you think is the center of the page. The chances are that it will be above the mathematical center.) Imagine that a seesaw is balanced on the optical center. We know that a lighter weight on the seesaw can easily balance a heavier one by being farther away from the fulcrum. (The "weight" of an element in an ad may be gauged by its size, its degree of blackness, its color, or its shape.) In informal balance, objects are placed seemingly at random on the page, but in such relation to one another that the page as a whole seems in balance. This type of arrangement requires more thought than the simple bisymmetric formal balance, but the effects can be imaginative and distinctive, as illustrated by Exhibits 17.6 and 17.7.

Other Composing Elements

Color.   One of the most versatile elements of an ad is color. It can attract attention and help create a mood. Depending on the product and the advertising appeal, color can be used for a number of reasons.

1. *It is an attention-getting device.* With few exceptions, people notice a color ad more readily than one in black and white.

EXHIBIT 17.5

· · · · · · · · · · · · · · · · · · ·

This formal balance ad has basically equal weights on the left and right half of the ad.

(Courtesy: Shakespeare and Loeffler, Ketchum, Mountjoy.)

(Courtesy: The Humane Society of Utah.)

• • • • • • • • • • • • • • • • • • •

This informal layout is
highly unusual and ap-
pears not to even be
an ad.

2. *Some products can be presented realistically only in color* (see Exhibit 17.7). Household furnishings, food, many clothing and fashion accessories, and cosmetics would lose most of their appeal if advertised in black and white. Studies are done to find the best consumer color or colors. For instance, the Pantone Color Institute in the mid-1990s asked consumers to select their current and future color preferences in specific product categories. In addition, a questionnaire collected data on demographics and placed the respondents into five lifestyle categories: prudent, impulsive, pessimistic, traditional, and confident. Advertisers found that for luxury cars consumers ranked silver, blue, white, or burgundy as their choices. For economy and mid-sized, consumers preferred twilight teal for a future color.

3. *Color can highlight specific elements within an ad, but should be carefully built into the ad.* Occasionally, an advertiser will use spot color for a product in an otherwise black-and-white ad. Any color needs to be an integral part of the ad and not an afterthought. We'll discuss the technique of color production in Chapter 18 and packaging in Chapter 21.

Nuprin analgesic increased its share of the ibuprofen market by using a superficial product difference—the yellow tablet. Ads that had said research showed two Nuprins gave more headache relief than Extra Strength Tylenol did not advance its share. Grey advertising's Herb Lieberman said, "You have to convince consumers that your product is different before they will believe the product is better." The color idea happened when its group creative director emptied a whole bunch of pain relievers on his desk and found Nuprin was the only yellow tablet there. Color was a way to dramatically and graph-

Color adds appetite appeal to this promotional piece, as well as the warm and cozy feeling.

(Courtesy: County Seat Cafe.)

ically show that Nuprin was different. Thus, the yellow-tablet campaign was born, showing a black-and-white photo of hands holding two yellow tablets. And on television, only the tablets in its testimonial ads were in color. The tagline explained that Nuprin is "for your worst pain."

Color can be extremely important in everything from ad layouts, products, and packaging to the psychological messages consumers perceive.

White Space. Some layout designers become so preoccupied with the illustration that they forget that white space, or blank space, is a very significant design tool. The basic rule for using white space is to keep it to the outside of the ad. Too much white space in the middle of an ad can destroy unity by pushing the eye in several directions, confusing the reader.

Preparing the Layout

The layout is the orderly arrangement of all the copy elements in a print ad. It is basically a blueprint that the production people will follow to complete the finished ad. An ad may go through different levels of roughness as it is developed. These different types of layouts represent different stages of development of the ad:

Mechanical

A form of layout, an exact black and white copy as it will appear in printed form. Each element is pasted to an art board in precise position (or created exactly as it will appear on computer), ready for the camera.

Comprehensive

A layout accurate in size, color, scheme, and other necessary details to show how a final ad will look. For presentation only, never for reproduction.

■ *Thumbnail sketches:* miniature drawings trying out different arrangements of the layout elements. The best of these will be selected for the next step.

■ *Rough layouts:* drawings that are equivalent to the actual size of the ad. All elements are presented more clearly to simulate the way the ad is to look. The best of these will be chosen for the next step.

■ *The comprehensive, or mechanical, layout* (often just called the *comp* or the *mechanical*): all the type set and pasted in place exactly as it is to appear in the printed ad. Artwork is drawn one and a half times the actual size it will be in the ad (to be reduced by one-third for sharper reproduction) and is prepared separately; therefore, it is precisely indicated on the compre-

EXHIBIT
17.8

Words, illustrations and a string concept work to communicate to a specialized target.

(Courtesy: Longwater, Inc.)

hensive by blank boxes of the exact final size. This layout will be used not only for client approval but also for making the final print or plate.

In Exhibit 17.8 the rough layout uses markers, while the comprehensive (Exhibit 17.9), uses computer-generated type and illustration. Exhibit 17.10 is the finished color ad as it appeared in publications.

Once the basic ad for a campaign has been approved, layouts for subsequent ads usually consist of just a rough and finished layout.

Computer Design

The computer serves as a word processor and a typographer, producing heads, text, and even the development design, illustration, and finished layout. Computer software makes it easier to see alternatives to typefaces, illustration size, inexpensive layout modifications and color changes.

First, we define *computer graphics* as the ability to draw or display visual information on a video terminal. *Raster Scan Graphics* is the most common computer display. Each spot on the screen, called a *pixel*, represents a location in the computer's memory. The number of individual pixels will determine the resolution of the image—this is the difference between poor-quality computer-set type or visuals and good reproduction-quality images. The more pixels, the higher the resolution and the smoother the image. The resolution of a screen controls its clarity and sharpness.

One of the keys of computer design's growth has been the proliferation and sophistication in the software growth that tells the computer how to operate.

Pixel

The smallest element of a computer image that can be separately addressed. It is an individual picture element.

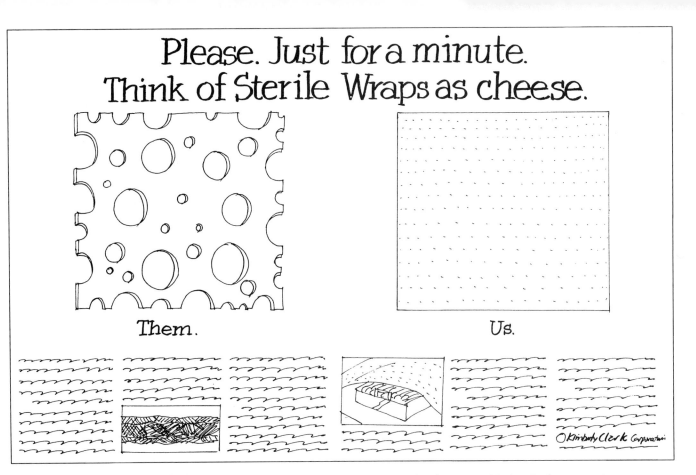

Please. Just for a minute.
Think of Sterile Wraps as cheese.

Them.

Us.

EXHIBIT 17.9

Above is an example of a rough marker layout and below is the computer comprehensive with all of the copy set in type.

Please. Just for a minute.
Think of Sterile Wraps as cheese.

Them.

Us.

True, the analogy may be dramatic. But the fact is, when it comes to preventing contamination, most sterile wraps are literally full of holes...holes that give germs direct paths for spreading infection. It's a danger to patients. And it can be a huge cost problem for your hospital.

KIMGUARD Sterile-Wrap from Kimberly-Clark reduces those risks significantly, because it doesn't have the direct paths

Multiple layers of fabric make KIMGUARD Sterile-Wrap the most effective barrier against bacteria.

that make other wraps vulnerable. KIMGUARD uses a patented 3-layer construction proven far more effective at preventing contamination. The key is it's dense inner layer with millions of micro-fibers formed into an intricate web. Steam and gas penetrate and release with ease... but not germs. In laboratory tests of dry spore filtration, KIMGUARD keeps out twice as many particles* per thousand as the closest disposable... and 27 times

more than 140-count cloth!

The inner layer is sandwiched in between 2 outer layers for added protection. This makes KIMGUARD far more durable and tear resistant than other disposables. More liquid repellent, too. And with it's excellent drapeability, KIMGUARD virtually eliminates snap back.

There's still one more critical benefit you get with KIMGUARD. Kimberly-Clark itself. And that means total commitment to quality control... the assurance of product availability... and the most responsive customer service. Any way you cut it, KIMGUARD Sterile-Wrap is by far the industry's # 1 choice. Let us show you why it should be your choice. Call our "Partners in Quality" line. 1-800-524-3577.

◯ KIMBERLY-CLARK

(Courtesy: Kimberly Clark and Pollack Levitt Chalet. Reprinted with permission of Kimberly-Clark Corporation. All rights reserved. KCC 1992.)

EXHIBIT

17.10

This is the way the ad shown in Exhibit 17.9 looks when it is finished.

Quark XPress and Aldus Pagemaker offer designers professional layout and editing software that have allowed (Macintosh and Windows) users acute text and graphic handling, and the image-creation programs like Photoshop have increased the designer's productivity. And then there is the dazzling Silicon Graphics (SGI) hardware that allows three-dimensional design graphics high-speed RIP (raster image processing) functions to go on simultaneously. The SGI machines use a UNIX-based language, which makes for faster image processing. We won't get into the specifics because the technology is changing so rapidly.

As you know, computer design and image manipulation is highly complex because you have to learn the software and that continues to be a problem with all the changes and upgrades. It is difficult for the advertising layout artist to be an expert in all of the software possibilities.

The computer allows every phase of creation and production to be developed on it, blurring the distinction between these phases of the process. We'll talk more about the meshing of computer design functions with production in Chapter 18. Here we need to get an appreciation of the role of the computer in the creative process.

Today, most agencies do some, if not all, of the layout function in-house on their own computers. However, there are independent graphic computer service houses that specialize and have the expertise to operate their expensive and highly sophisticated hardware for a reasonable fee.

In the past, the creation and production processes have been separate and distinct. Because of the advances in computer hardware and software, it is possible for one person to do both layout and production, although software expertise may continue to keep these functions specialized. Today, mastery of layout demands a knowledge of art, type, design, and also photography, computers, and electronic imaging.

The Visual

Research indicates that 98 percent of the top-scoring ads contain a photograph or illustration, proving that human beings are highly visual creatures, according to Cahners Advertising Performance Studies. In most ads the photograph or illustration takes between 25 and 63 percent of the layout space (see Exhibit 17.11).[4]

Art Directing and Photography

Art directing and photography are twin disciplines—each, in theory raises the other up a notch. Having a great photo in the wrong layout makes for bad advertising (see Exhibit 17.12). Betsy Zimmerman, art director at Goodby, Berlin & Silverstein says, "The layout's gotta come first. I'll bring a Xerox of the layout to the shoot, and we try to do Polaroids to size, so I can put the two together. The key is to shoot a million Polaroids so I can iron out all the idiosyncrasies rather than be surprised on film." It might look great as a photo, but once you put it in its environment it's totally different. Jeff Weiss of Margeotes/Fertitta & Weiss, says every ad contains two things: what you want to say and how you want to say it. What art directing can do is deliver things emotionally, not intellectually. Great art direction takes the selling idea and furthers it without your even knowing it. Take Saks, for example; their ads can't say Saks is glamorous in words—it has to *feel* glamorous and sophisticated.[5]

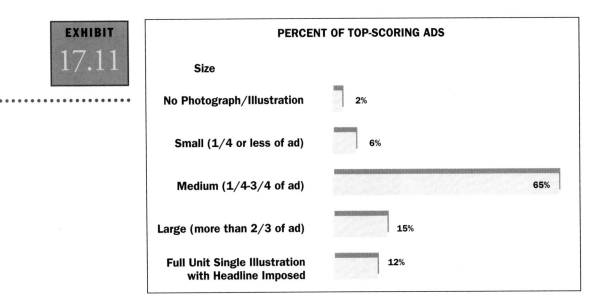

EXHIBIT 17.11

PERCENT OF TOP-SCORING ADS

Size

No Photograph/Illustration — 2%

Small (1/4 or less of ad) — 6%

Medium (1/4-3/4 of ad) — 65%

Large (more than 2/3 of ad) — 15%

Full Unit Single Illustration with Headline Imposed — 12%

[4]CARR Report, No. 118.5, p. 4.
[5]"Art Directing Photography," *Art Direction*, March 1993, pp. 42–54.

British Columbia vacations play very well for those looking for a serene getaway. This year however we've changed our tune (moderately, of course). You'll find musical events, performances and concerts everywhere, all part of our Music '91 celebration. Toe-tapping, "hey look at that" fun. You can still take in the usual sounds. A blue lake rippling from the stroke of your paddle, mountain meadows rustling with a parade of scarlet wildflowers, or the throaty gurgles of a cappuccino machine at a bay-side café. The countryside is within whistling distance of the city around these parts. For the whole score on travel here call **1-800-663-6000**. Tourism British Columbia, Parliament Buildings., Victoria, British Columbia, V8W 1X4. Now back to our regular show. **Super, Natural British Columbia**

We interrupt our normal tourism advertising to bring you a musical interlude.

(Courtesy: British Columbia & New York Festivals International Advertising Awards.)

EXHIBIT

17.12

· · · · · · · · · · · · · · · · · · · ·

Getting the right photograph is important, but is also must fit the total ad environment.

Photography can be very expensive. A photo for use in an ad may range between $700 and $10,000 depending on the photographer's reputation and the advertiser's willingness to pay.

The Artist's Medium

The tool or material used to render an illustration is called the *artist's medium,* the term *medium* being used in a different sense than it is in the phrase *advertising medium* (for example, television or magazines). The most popular artist's medium in advertising is photography. Other popular ones are pen and ink, pencil, and crayon. Perhaps a photograph will be used as the main illustration for an ad, but pen and ink will be used for the smaller, secondary illustration. The choice of the artist's medium depends on the effect desired, the paper on which the ad is to be printed, the printing process to be used, and, most important, the availability of an artist who is effective in the desired medium.

Trade Practice in Buying Commercial Art

Creating an ad usually requires two types of artistic talent: the imaginative person, who thinks up the visual idea with a copywriter or alone and makes the master layout; and an artist, who does the finished art of the illustrations. Large agencies have staff art directors and layout people to visualize and create original layouts, as well as studios and artists to handle routine work.

In the largest advertising centers, a host of free-lance artists and photographers specialize in certain fields for preparing the final art. In fact, agencies

MODEL/PERFORMING RELEASE

Advertising

SLRS COMMUNICATIONS, INC. / P.O.Box 5488 / Athens, GA. 30604 / (404) 549-2664

For value received and without further consideration, I HEREBY CONSENT that all pictures/photographs taken of me and/or recordings made of my voice or musical or video performances, may be used for advertising and trade purposes, by **SLRS** Advertising, Inc., and by advertisers SLRS Advertising, Inc., may authorize or represent, in any manner. I understand that illustrations/performances may be edited, changed or reproduced in any manner without my approval. I agree that all reproductions thereof and plates, films, and tapes shall remain the property of SLRS,Advertising, Inc., or of advertisers represented by SLRS Advertising, Inc.

WITNESS _____ SIGNED _____

SOC. SEC. No. _____

IF SUBJECT IS A MINOR UNDER LAWS OF STATE OF PERFORMANCE.

GUARDIAN _____

WITNESS _____ DATE_____

(Courtesy: SLRS Advertising, Inc.)

in some cities go to one of the major art centers to buy their graphic artwork for special assignments.

There are two important points to observe in buying artwork, especially photographs. First, you must have written permission or a legal release (Exhibit 17.13) from anyone whose picture you will use, whether you took the picture or got it from a publication or an art file. (In the case of a child's picture, you must obtain a release from the parent or guardian.) Second, you should arrange all terms in advance. A photographer may take a number of pictures, from which you select one. What will be the price if you wish to use more than one shot? What will be the price if you use the picture in several publications?

Free-lance artists' and photographers' charges vary greatly, depending on their reputation, the nature of the work, what medium the work is being used in, and whether the ad is to run locally, regionally, or nationally. An art illustration for a magazine may cost $200 if by an unknown artist and up to about $5,000 if by an established artist. A photography session may cost $200 a day for an unknown to about $2,500 for an established photographer. People charge what they think the art or photography is worth or what the client can or is willing to pay. As a result, the better the reputation of the artist or photographer, the more expensive the final product will likely be.

Other Sources of Art and Photography

Clients will not always be able to afford the money or time for original advertising art or photography. There are three basic sources of ready-made images.

Clip Art and Computer Clip Art. Ready-to-use copyright-free images are available from clip-art services. The art may be available on CD-ROM or from services printed where the illustrations are in black and white on glossy paper ready to use. All you have to do is cut it out or print it off your computer. Almost any image is available from clip-art services: families, men, women, children, business scenes, locations (farm, beach), and special events. The disadvantages to using clip art are that you have to match your idea to available images, and many of the illustrations are rather average. The advantages are the very reasonable costs and extensive choice of images. Some clip-art services offer a monthly book or computer disk (or on-line service) with a wide variety of images; others offer specialized volumes—restaurant art, supermarket art, medical art, for example. Once you purchase the clip-art service, the art is yours to use as you see fit.

Stock Photos. There are hundreds of stock photo libraries available to art directors and advertisers. Each maintains hundreds or thousands of photographs classified according to the subject, including children, animals, lifestyle situations, city landscapes, sports, and models. A photographer submits photos to the stock company, which will publish some photos in its catalog (or on a CD-ROM). The photographer pays for the space occupied by the photos. Clients then browse through the stock company's catalog to research its files for a suitable photo. The art director or advertiser then leases or contracts for use of the selected photo to use in an ad. The fee is based on the intended use of the photo. In the past, the delivered image was in the form of a transparency or chrome image. Today, the image may be marketed and delivered by means of CD-ROM. Images are scanned, stored, digitized, and reproduced on a CD-ROM.

Other companies offer a whole disc of images—averaging 336 digitized picture files—on a CD-ROM for a single purchase price. And the CD technology allows individual photographers to market their images on their own CDs. On-line capabilities have been around since 1994 featuring stock photo agencies, allowing ad agencies to select images from an on-line network from numerous stock photo sources. The agency can select images and then instantly download low-resolution *thumbnail* images for inspection. When they decide to order an image, the computer will notify the company and fees will be negotiated.

SUMMARY

We've now made the transition from thinking of ideas to making ads. We have started with the primary consumer benefit, the most important thing we can say about the product.

In advertising, the *total concept* is a fresh way of looking at something. A *concept* is an idea. A *Big Idea* is one that expresses clearly and combines words and visuals. Another way of looking at it is that a basic idea is an abstract answer to a perceived desire or need.

The creative team members (an art director and a copywriter) next develop the best approach to presenting the *executional idea*—a rendering in words, symbols, sounds, shapes, etc., of an abstract answer to a perceived desire or need. Then comes layout preparation (usually done by an art director), in which the various elements of the ad are composed into a unified whole. Creating an ad that will attract attention is one of the art director's primary concerns. When arranging the elements of an ad, the layout artist has to consider the principles of design: unity, harmony, sequence, emphasis, contrast, and balance.

Ads usually begin as thumbnail sketches. Subsequent steps are rough layout, the finished layout, and the comps. The computer simplifies this process: In computer design, the roughs are no longer rough, and the comprehensives are better because the layout and typography are exact.

In most cases, art and photography are original executions of the art director's ideas, illustrated or shot according to his or her specifications by freelance artists or photographers. When time or money is short, clip art or computer art services or stock photography may be used.

Questions
1. What is a Big Idea?
2. What is the creative team?
3. Discuss the *concepts* versus *details.*
4. What four developmental stages lead to creativity?
5. Why is unity so important in the design process?
6. What is a comp?
7. How much of a top-scoring ad's layout space is taken up by art/photography according to Cahner's research?

Print Production

18

CHAPTER OBJECTIVES

Prepress technology is rapidly changing, yet the traditional methods of print production still give the greatest quality for the money. Both the old and the new appear to have their place for the immediate future. After reading this chapter you will understand:

- **Production department**
- **Basic printing processes**
- **Mechanical and artwork**
- **Proofing**
- **New technology**

We've finally come to the end of the creative process. All the ideas have been developed; now the print production people take the copy, layout, and illustrations and create the finished ad. Every advertising and marketing person involved in ads needs to have a working knowledge of graphics basics and the production process. **The agency's** print production group performs that transformation process from the original creative concept to the client's printed communication—and may include magazines, newspapers, outdoor and transit, point-of-purchase, collateral brochures, direct response. They must have a working knowledge of all these production processes, as well as publication mechanical specifications, budgetary considerations, and quality requirements of the client. Last but not least, they must understand the time span available for the execution. All of these factors may be interrelated in a complicated manner.

These print production people are not merely technical purchasing agents who are knowledgeable and assigned to buying typesetting, printing image carriers, paper, and other graphic arts services. They are graphic arts consultants, production planners, and production liaison people, internally—with the creative, traffic, media and account management areas—and externally—with graphic arts vendors, and with the print media.

The size of a print production group will be in relation to the billing size of the agency. A very small agency may employ a single print production expert. In a vary large agency the print production staff, headed by a print production manager, may consist of a considerable number of people with very specialized expertise.

The print operations area encompasses:

ILLUSTRATION BUYERS. They are versed in various forms of photographic/illustrative techniques. They know the available talent, and make all contracts with photographers, illustrators, retouchers, photo labs, etc. in coordination with art directors (see Exhibit 18.1).

TYPOGRAPHY EXPERTS. They are trained in the creative as well as technical aspects of typography. They select, specify, mark up, and purchase all typesetting, working with the art directors. Of course, in some agencies the art director may create the final type on computer. Yet the type director may send the disk to a supplier for final output.

PRINT PRODUCERS. They coordinate all print production activities with the traffic, account management, and creative groups.

PRINTING BUYERS. They specialize in the production planning and buying of outdoor and transit advertising, newspaper and magazine inserts, as well

EXHIBIT 18.1

The production people had to take several photographs for this ad so they would reproduce as the art director envisioned and to ensure that all elements were properly produced.

(Courtesy: Andersen Windows, Inc. and CME Advertising.)

as collateral printed material from brochures to elaborately die-cut direct-mail pieces. A printing buyer's knowledge reaches into properties of paper and ink, and into the capabilities of printing, binding, and finishing equipment.

In addition to those functions already mentioned, a large production department may include estimators and proofreaders. Generally, clients require an agency to submit a production budget on work to be done. Sometimes this budget is based upon a yearly campaign, or, although estimates are on an individual job basis, for collateral material. In either case, it is important for the production department to supply accurate production cost estimates.

The production department works closely with the traffic department, which sets and monitors schedules of the operation from creative through final production.

PRODUCTION DATA

Production people need to be well versed in the technical aspects of art and type processes, printing methods, and duplicate plates, which we discuss later in the chapter. Let's look first at sources of information for print media. The production person will usually reach for the Standard Rate and Data Service (SRDS) production source—*SRDS Print Media Production Data*—which carries essential production information for major national and regional publi-

EXHIBIT

18.2

• • • • • • • • • • • • • • • • • •

Publications have specific mechanical and due date requirements advertisers must follow.

1996 Mechanical and Due Date Requirements

Mechanical Specification

All national editions are printed offset. The SWOP standards for proofing should be followed

Proofs

Black and white—10 complete proofs.

2-color and 4-color—10 complete proofs and 10 sets of progressives.

Bleed Sizes

Page 8-1/4″ × 11-1/8″

2 pages facing- 16-1/2″ × 11-1/8″

For bleed pages keep essential matter 1/2″ from top, bottom and sides of all film, and at least 11/16″ from front bleed edge on both pages of facing page spread.

Live matter in facing pages should not be closer than 1/8″ to center fold.

Publication reserves the right to crop up to 3/16″ from either side of full page film to compensate for variations in trim page size.

Columns	Column Width In Picas	Minimum Depth In Agate Lines
1	13 picas and 9 points	14
2	28 picas and 2 points	28
6	85 picas and 10 points	148

Due Dates

Issue	Color	Black & White
August 9	June 19	July 3
23	July 4	July 11
September 6	July 25	August 7
20	August 8	August 21
October 10	August 15	August 28
24	September 4	September 18
November 8	September 18	October 2
21	October 2	October 16
December 6	October 16	October 30
27	October 30	November 12

Page Makeup

All run-of-paper advertising units are measured in terms of agate lines and number of columns. The width of a single column is 13 picas and 9 points (2 9/32″). Each additional column is 14 picas and 5 points (2 3/8″)

Advertisements exceeding 270 agate lines line depth must occupy full columns (296 agate lines)

SRDS

Standard Rate and Data Service (SRDS) publishes a number of directories (including print production data) giving media and production information.

cations. The other media SRDS publications (newspapers, consumer, business, etc.) carry closing dates and basic mechanical production requirements, but not in as complete detail as the *Print Media Production Data* publication. Production people must directly contact publications that are not included in the SRDS to obtain their production requirements. Of course, each publication determines its own advertising due dates and mechanical specifications based upon printing requirements. Exhibit 18.2 shows some of the specifications for a typical publication.

PRODUCTION PLANNING AND SCHEDULING

To ensure that the creative and production work moves along with the necessary precision, a time schedule is planned at the outset. The closing date is the date or time when all material must arrive at the publication. Once this is known, the advertiser works backward along the calendar to determine when work must be begun in order to meet the date.

The following can be used as a rule of thumb in determining the length of time needed to make printing materials and revisions: for black-and-white ads, 2–3 working days, depending on the printing process; for process color ads, about 20 working days. You may need another 4 to 5 days to produce progressive proofs and obtain client approvals.

The following table is a typical time schedule for production of a color ad to be sent to several publications with a closing date of November 1:

Work	Date
In order to reach publications by closing date	November 1
Shipping date of duplicate materials	October 29
Start making duplicate materials	October 25
Final photoplatemaker's proof	October 22
Photoplatemaker's first proof available by	October 13
Material to photoplatemaker	September 28
Retouched art and mechanical ready by	September 22
Typesetting order date	September 16
Finished artwork (photograph) delivered by	September 15
Finished artwork (photography) order date	September 7
Creative work (copy and layout) approved by	September 4
Start of creative work	August 23

Now that we better understand the production environment, let's take a look at the key considerations in a number of production steps.

Computer Production

Before desktop computers, most art directors had only to design, create accurate mechanicals, and specify color breaks or other information on tissues. But many art directors working on their computers perform many production steps (see Exhibit 18.3).

Design and Production Revolution. A late 1994 survey of the graphic design community—corporate, ad agency, publishing companies, and design firms—indicated that 94 percent of the firms use the computer for creative and production. A Cahners Publishing research study in 1993 indicated com-

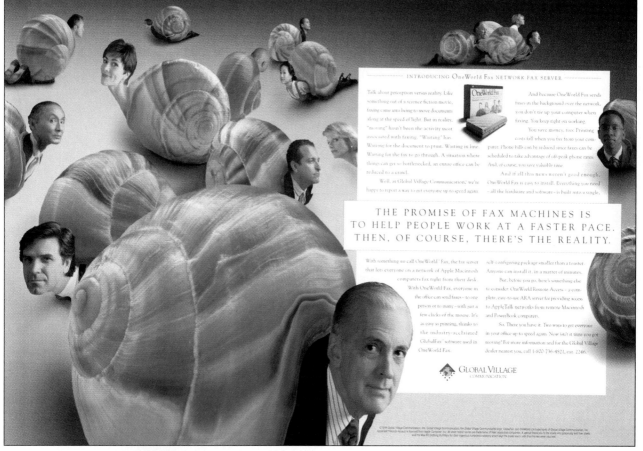

(Courtesy: Anderson Lembke.)

EXHIBIT

18.3

. . . .

The illustration was created on the computer for this OneWorld Fax ad.

. . . .

Digital artist

A computer specialist that works as an art director or with an art director depending on the agency structure.

. . . .

puter design and production at an 85 percent level. These levels of digital technology were unimaginable as recently as 1989, as the shift from traditional methods were thought then to be many years away—maybe even decades. The fact is that we're in the middle of one of the most momentous changes in design and production history.[1]

Digital Studios.   Some agencies call their computer area an image studio or digital imaging studio, where art directors work on computers to develop the visuals and layout. In some agencies (especially in small or medium-sized shops) the art director takes on part of a production person's job. They can design, typeset, do layouts, create tints, scan, separate, produce final film, and, in some cases, transmit the job directly to the press. In other words, the computer operator can create and prepare the entire job for the printer or publication. Many art production people haven't mastered the complicated process or haven't been trained to do so (see Exhibit 18.4).

FCB, San Francisco, established a Digital Imaging Studio in 1989. It now has six *digital artists* who served as part of the creative teams in a department of about 55 people. An outgrowth of having art directors use computers to create their work was that they started doing production instead of working on their next project. FCB's solution was to hire more computer-literate specialists to handle the mechanical art faster rather than have the ill-prepared

---

[1]"Computer-for-Graphic Design Use Jumps to 94%," *Graphic Design: USA*, October 1994, p. 1.

(Courtesy: Longwater Advertising, Inc.)

EXHIBIT

18.4

· · · · · · · · · · · · · · · · · · · ·

It took more than magic to create this ad on the computer incorporating illustrations and type.

art directors perform such tasks. Now, production tasks have been transferred from all its art directors. Graphics people now can use one tool at every step of design and production to develop an entire project. Yet the concept of one person being the artist, typesetter, copy editor, proofreader, color separator, filmmaker, computer expert, production guru, and so on, sounds good, but as FCB found out—it does not quite work in reality. As software gets more sophisticated, it requires an expert to produce the degree of *quality* required by advertising clients.

The future of computer production lies in both the knowledge of the people involved and the sophistication of the hardware and software to perform quicker, less expensive, quality, computer-generated design and production.

Today, most agencies use computers for producing layouts, typesetting, creating comps, and sometimes creating proofs. The sophisticated hardware and software required to equal the quality of traditional production methods have been expensive, although this is changing somewhat. As a result, most major agencies still rely heavily on traditional production methods.

As you would expect, creating layouts on the computer takes much less time than the traditional method, which might require the art director to send work outside the agency, especially for color prints, drawings, or illustrations. Lintas:Campbell-Edwald uses an expensive computer system that allows the artist to do a typical layout in one or two hours, and a simple one in 30 minutes. Saatchi & Saatchi's senior vice president for technology management says that the firm creates comps but does not do mechanicals on the computer because of its lack of speed. Many agencies create desktop comps with low-quality images (about 300 dots per inch, dpi), and then send their discs to—or go on-line with—high-tech service companies, where the images are rescanned at 3,600 dpi to create finished high-quality ads. The computer has changed how print production works, but not the intrinsic nature of intelligent design.

SELECTING THE PRINTING PROCESS

In most cases, the printing process used depends on the medium the ad is running in, not on the advertiser or the agency. However, in some areas such as sales promotion, ad inserts, direct mail, and point-of-sale, the advertiser must make the final decision regarding print production. In order to deal effectively with printers, the advertiser must have some knowledge of the basic production techniques and which is the most appropriate for the job at hand.

If the printing process is not predetermined, the first step in the production process is to decide which process is most suitable. There are three major printing processes:

- **Letterpress printing (from a raised surface)**

- **Offset lithography (from a flat surface)**

- **Rotogravure (from an etched surface)**

Each of these printing processes has certain advantages and disadvantages, but one process may be more efficient for a particular job. Once the printing process has been established, the production process has been dictated, for all production work depends on the process used.

Let's get a basic understanding of these processes.

Letterpress Printing

This isn't as popular as it once was in printing publications; however, advertisers have many uses for this printing process, and you need to know the basics. In its simplest form, think of the concept of letterpress as follows: If you have ever used a rubber ink stamp (with name, address, etc.), you've applied the principle of letterpress printing. You press the rubber stamp against an ink pad. Then, as you press the stamp against paper, the ink is transferred from the stamp to the paper, and the message is reproduced.

Letterpress

Printing from a relief, or raised, surface. The raised surface is inked and comes in direct contact with the paper, like a rubber stamp. *See* Offset, Rotogravure.

In letterpress printing, the area to be printed is raised and inked. The inked plate is pressed against the paper and the result is a printed impression (see Exhibit 18.5).

Your artwork, photographs, type, etc., must be converted to a photoengraving (a process of making the plate a raised surface) before printing can occur. The advertiser or agency must supply the photoengraving or duplicates of such plates to the newspaper, magazine, or letterpress printer. In general, this process doesn't reproduce photos as well as offset or gravure. Each of the printing processes has advantages and disadvantages that the advertising person needs to learn over time.

EXHIBIT
18.5

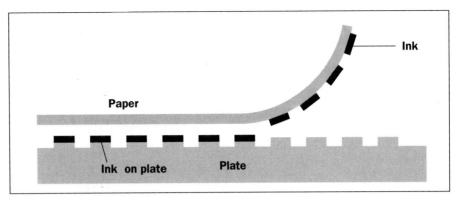

Letterpress printing. Notice the raised surface of the plate.

Offset Lithography

In its basic description, offset printing is a photochemical process based upon the principle that grease and water will not mix. In theory, offset can print anything that can be photographed. In reality, there are some things that will not print very well by offset.

Offset is a planographic (flat-surface) process using a thin, flat aluminum plate that is wrapped around a cylinder on a rotary press. The plate is coated with a continuous flow of liquid solution from dampening rollers that repel ink. The inked plate comes in contact with a rubber blanket on another cylinder. The inked impression goes from the plate to the rubber blanket. The inked blanket then transfers or offsets the inked image to the paper, which is on a delivery cylinder. The plate does not come in direct contact with the paper (Exhibit 18.6).

Because offset is a photographic process, it is very efficient and the most popular printing process in this country. It is used to reproduce books (including this text), catalogs, periodicals, direct-mail pieces, outdoor and transit posters, point-of-sale, and most newspapers.

Advertisers or their agency must supply the artwork and mechanicals or films from which offset plates can be made.

Rotogravure

The image in gravure printing is etched below the surface of the copper printing plate—the direct opposite from letterpress printing—creating tiny ink-

Lithography

A printing process by which originally an image was formed on special stone by a greasy material, the design then being transferred to the printing paper. Today the more frequently used process is *offset* lithography, in which a thin and flexible metal sheet replaces the stone. In this process the design is "offset" from the metal sheet to a rubber blanket, which then transfers the image to the printing paper.

EXHIBIT
18.6

Offset printing press plate system, showing image coming off plate, onto rubber blanket, and offsetting to paper.

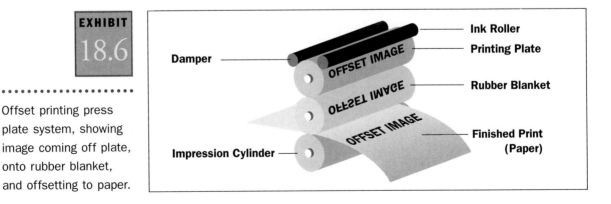

Rotogravure

The method of intaglio printing in which the impression is produced by chemically etched cylinders and run on a rotary press; useful in long runs of pictorial effects.

wells (tiny depressed printing areas made by means of a screen). The gravure plate is inked on the press and wiped so that only the tiny inkwells contain ink. The plate is then pressed against the paper, causing suction that pulls the ink out of the wells and onto the paper (see Exhibit 18.7).

Gravure is used to print all or parts of many publications, including national and local Sunday newspaper supplements, mail-order catalogs, packaging, and newspaper inserts.

The gravure plate is capable of printing millions of copies very efficiently; however, it is not economical for short-run printing. Rotogravure becomes competitive with offset when printing exceeds about 100,000 copies. When printing exceeds a million copies, gravure tends to be more efficient than offset.

Rotogravure prints excellent color quality on relatively inexpensive paper, but the prepatory costs are comparatively high, and it is expensive to make major corrections on the press.

Sheet-Fed versus Web-Fed Presses

Letterpress, offset, and gravure printing processes can all utilize sheet-fed or web-fed presses.

Sheet-fed Presses. These presses feed sheets of paper through the press one at a time. The conventional sheet-fed press prints about 6,000 to 7,000 "sheets" per hour.

Web-fed Presses. In web printing, paper is fed from a continuous roll and the printing is rapid—about 1,000 feet per minute. Most major promotional printing utilizes web-fed presses.

Screen Printing

Screen Printing

A simple printing process that uses a stencil. It is economical but is limited in reproduction quality.

Another printing process, screen printing, which is based on a different principle from letterpress, offset, and rotogravure, is especially good for short runs.

This simple process uses a stencil. The stencil of a design (art, type, photograph) can be manually or photographically produced and then placed over a (usually silk) textile or metallic-mesh screen (it actually looks like a window screen). Ink or paint is spread over the stencil and, by means of a squeegee, is pushed through the stencil and screen onto the paper (or other surface), as illustrated in Exhibit 18.8.

EXHIBIT
18.7

Rotogravure. Ink wells fill with ink.

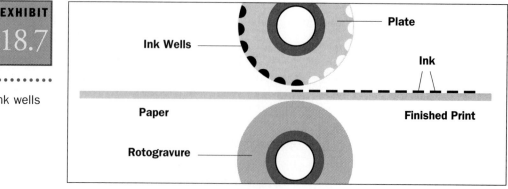

Ink Wells

Plate

Ink

Paper

Finished Print

Rotogravure

EXHIBIT

18.8

Screen printing.

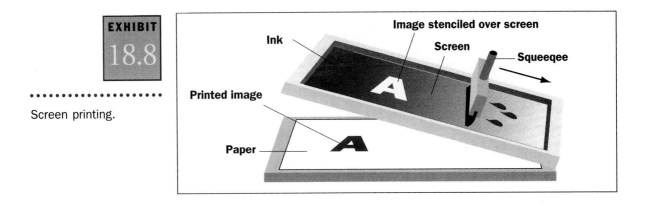

Screen printing is economical, especially for work in broad, flat colors, as in car cards, posters, and point-of-sale displays. It can be done on almost any surface: wallpaper, bricks, bottles, T-shirts, and so on. Basically, screen printing is a slow short-run process (for 1 copy to 100 or 1,000 or so copies), although sophisticated presses can print about 6,000 impressions per hour. This expanding printing process is becoming more useful to advertisers.

UNDERSTANDING TYPOGRAPHY

Typography
The art of using type effectively.

Type has always been an important part of ad design. It creates moods, enhances or retards readability, and gives your communication an image. It is more important than ever before for advertising people to understand how to use type because so much of it is being created in-house on the agency or client computer. Before the computer explosion, art directors would use specialists—typesetters/typographers—for type. Most agree that few art directors or designers have as good an understanding of type use as the typesetters/typographers. Getting type up on the screen does not mean that it is typeset effectively. We talk about this again after we learn some of the fundamentals.

The art of using type effectively is called *typography*. It entails a number of issues: choosing the typeface and size of type; deciding on the amount of space between letters, words, and lines; determining hyphenation use; and preparing type specifications for all the ad copy. Notice the differences in type styles, line length, and size in Exhibits 18.9, 18.10 and 18.11.

TYPE AND READING

The objective of text typography is to provide quick and easy communication. Display headlines are supposed to attract the reader's attention and encourage reading of the body copy. Using uppercase (all-cap) typography does not generally accomplish these objectives.

Over 95 percent of text is set in lowercase letters. Research has shown that readers are more comfortable reading lowercase letters than all caps. Studies have also proved that the varying heights of lowercase letters forming words create an outline shape that is stored in the reader's mind, which aids in recalling the words when they are seen. Words comprised of lowercase characters can be read faster than words set in all caps.

The ideal reading process occurs when the eye is able to scan across a line of copy, grasping groups of three or four words at a time, and then jump to another set of words, then another. The separate stops, or fixational pauses, take

EXHIBIT

18.9

....

"These are examples of
different typefaces,
each presenting a dif-
ferent mood or feeling."

Impact Advertising
Peignot Advertising
Playbill Advertising
Gill Sans Advertising
MACHINE ADVERTISING
Arial Advertising
Bookman Advertising
Braggadocio Advertising
CASTELLAR ADVERTISING

about one quarter of a second each. Words in lowercase letters allow this process to take place. On the other hand, words set in all caps force the reader to read individual letters and mentally combine the letters into words, and the words into phrases and sentences. The result is 10 to 25 percent slow-down in reading speed and comprehension.

There are times when all-cap headlines or subheadlines are, graphically, the right thing to use. Design may take precedence over the "rules of communi-cation," or you may not be able to convince a client or art director that low-ercase is a better idea. In these instances, words and lines should be held to a minimum. More than four or five words on a line and more than a couple of lines of all caps become difficult to read.[2]

EXHIBIT

18.10

....

The head is reverse
copy—white letters on
a dark background—
and body copy uses
italic.

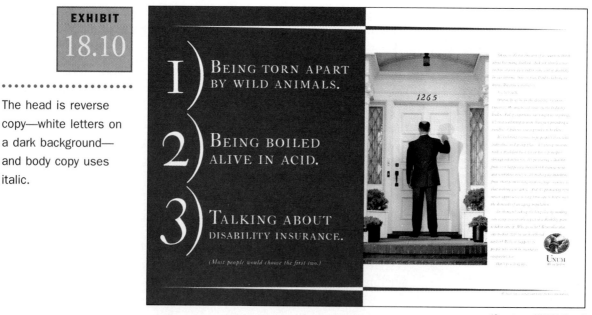

(Courtesy: UNUM Corp.)

---

[2]Allan Haley, "Using All Capitals Is a Graphic Oxymoron." *U & lc*, Fall 1991, pp. 14–15.

EXHIBIT

18.11

Lines and copy make this ad unique. The body copy is set in all caps using a flush left alignment.

YOUR BELOVED CAMPAIGN GETS KILLED

CLIENT ADDS SNIPE TO AD

CLIENT'S WIFE CHANGES BACKGROUND COLOR

ACCOUNT EXECUTIVE CUTS PRODUCTION SCHEDULE IN HALF TO IMPRESS CLIENT

GETTING SNUBBED BY MODELS DURING SHOOT

ATTENDING TRADE SHOW TO BOND WITH CLIENTS

BREATHING TOXIC MARKER FUMES

BREATHING SECOND-HAND SMOKE IN PRODUCTION MANAGER'S OFFICE

WORKING WITH EMOTIONALLY FRAGILE GRAPHIC DESIGNER

WORKING FOR CREATIVE DIRECTOR WHO THINKS HE'S GOD

WORKING FOR CREATIVE DIRECTOR WHO THINKS HE'S PYTKA

HEADHUNTER SPILLS A DECAF LATTE INTO YOUR BOOK

YOU SEND YOUR ADS TO THE LAMINATOR—HE SENDS YOU BACK CHUCK E. CHEESE PLACEMATS

REPEATED EXPOSURE TO PHRASE "THE BIG IDEA"

PULLING ALL-NIGHTERS FOR NEW BUSINESS PITCH

PULLING ALL-NIGHTERS FOR NEW BUSINESS PITCH AND LOSING

IRS SAYS $20,000 HOME ENTERTAINMENT SYSTEM WASN'T A PROFESSIONAL EXPENSE

YOUR 24 YEAR-OLD ASSISTANT BECOMES YOUR CREATIVE DIRECTOR

FACE IT, YOU'RE NOT GETTING ANY YOUNGER. SO MAYBE YOU SHOULD CALL STAN MUSILEK. MANY ART DIRECTORS FIND THAT SHOOTING WITH STAN ACTUALLY REVERSES THE AGING PROCESS BY AN AVERAGE OF TWO YEARS PER SHOOT. BUT EVEN IF YOU DON'T WANT TO SHOOT WITH STAN, CALL HIM ANYWAY AT 800-669-5330 OR 415-621-5336. HE'LL SEND YOU A FREE PORTFOLIO.

HOW OLD ARE YOU IN AD YEARS?

(Courtesy: "Stan Musilek.")

TYPEFACES

The typeface selected for a particular ad is very important. Exhibit 18.12 illustrates the major classifications of type: Text, Old Roman, Modern Roman, Sans Serif, Square Serif, and Decorative.

TYPE FONTS AND FAMILIES

A *type font* is all the lowercase and capital characters, numbers, and punctuation marks in one size and face (Exhibit 18.13). A font may be roman or italic. Roman (with a lowercase "r") type refers to the upright letter form, as distinguished from the italic form, which is oblique. Roman (capital "R") denotes a group of serified typeface styles.

Type family is the name given to two or more series of types that are variants of one design (Exhibit 18.14). Each one, however, retains the essential characteristics of the basic letter form. The series may include italic, thin, light, semibold, bold, medium, condensed, extended, outline, and so forth. Some type families have only a few of these options while others offer a number of styles. The family of type may provide a harmonious variety of typefaces for use within an ad.

Exhibit 18.15 illustrates the differences perceived by art directors and readers for type selection for body copy and headlines, according to Cahners Publishing research studies. Do not interpret these results as the best typefaces to use because these were limited studies. They do indicate similarities and differences among those choosing and those reading a typeface.

Measurement of Type

Typographers have unique units of measurement. It is essential to learn the fundamental units of measure if you are going to interact with production

Text	𝔒𝔩𝔡 𝔈𝔫𝔤𝔩𝔦𝔰𝔥
Old Roman	Garamond
ModernRoman	Century
Square Serif	Lubalin
Sans Serif	**Avant Garde**
Decorative	Ransom

Goudy Bold
abcdefghijklmnopqrstuvwxyz
ABCDEFGHIJKLMNOPQRSTU
1234567890$(&?!%.,.:;-)*   VWXYZ

Goudy Extra Bold
abcdefghijklmnopqrstuvwxyz
ABCDEFGHIJKLMNOPQRSTU
1234567890$[&?!%.,.:;-]*   VWXYZ

Goudy Black
abcdeffffiflghijklmnopqrstuvwx
ABCDEFGHIJKLMNOPQRSTU
1234567890$¢[&?!;,.] yz VWXYZ

Goudy Heavyface
abcdeffghhijkklmmnnopqrrſs
A₄ABCDEFGH₄HIJKLM₄MN₄NOP
QRSSTTUVVWWXYYZ tuvw
1234567890$¢(&!?;,.-)* xyyź

A family of type retains its basic letter form and style characteristics through all its variations. Some type families consist of only roman, italic, and bold versions. Others, like the popular Helvetica family, have many variations and different stroke thicknesses.

Helvetica Thin
Helvetica Light
Helvetica Light Italic
Helvetica
Helvetica Italic
Helvetica Italic Outline
Helvetica Regular Condensed
Helvetica Regular Extended
Helvetica Medium
Helvetica Medium Italic
Helvetica Medium Outline
Helvetica Bold
Helvetica Bold Compact Italic
Helvetica Bold Outline
Helvetica Bold Condensed
Helvetica Bold Condensed Outline
Helvetica Bold Extended
Helvetica Extrabold Condensed
Helvetica Extrabold Condensed Outline
Helvetica Extrabold Ext.
Helvetica Compressed
Helvetica Extra Compressed
Helvetica Ultra Compressed

Readers rank Helvetica first; while art directors rank Century first for body copy.

**Body Copy Typefaces Ranked
By Readers and Art Directors**

Selected Typefaces for Body Copy

Typefaces	Readers Ranking	Art Directors Ranking
Helvetica	1	2
Garamond	2	3
Melior	3	4
Century	4	1
Times Roman	5	6
Univers	6	5
Optima	7	7
Avant Garde	8	8
Caledonia	9	9
Bodoni	10	10

(Courtesy: Cahners Publishing Company.)

EXHIBIT

18.16

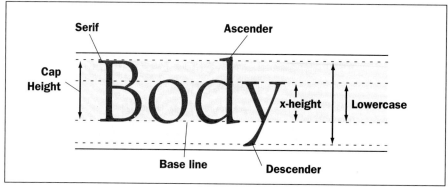

people. The *point* and *pica* are two units of measure used in print production in all English-speaking countries. The *point-system* is used to measure type sizes and to mark up copy for typesetting: length of line, space between lines, dimensions of type, and so forth. Let's take a closer look at these two units of measure.

Point.   A point is used to measure the size of type (heights of letters)—there are 72 points to an inch. You need to know instantly that 36-point type is about $\frac{1}{2}$ inch high and 18-point type is about $\frac{1}{4}$ inch high. Exhibit 18.16 illustrates the major terms used in discussing the height of type.

Type can be set from about 6 points to 120 points. Body copy is generally in the range of 6 to 14 points; most publications use type of 9, 10, or 11 points. Type sizes above 14 points are referred to as *display* or *headline type*. However, these ranges are simply labels—in many newspaper ads, the body copy is 18 points or so, and there have been ads where the headline was in the body-copy size range. Exhibit 18.17 provides a visual perspective on basic type sizes.

Points are used to measure the height of space between lines, rules and borders, as well as the height of the type.

Pica.   A pica is a linear unit of measure—12 points of space, or 6 picas to an inch. Picas are used to indicate width or depth and length of line.

Em.   An em is a square of the type size and is commonly used for indentation of copy blocks and paragraphs.

Agate Line.   Most newspapers (and some small magazines) sell advertising space in column inches or by the agate line, a measure of the depth of space. There are 14 agate lines to a column inch, regardless of the width of the column. Newspaper space is referred to by *depth* (agate lines) and *width* (number of columns): For "100 × 2," read "one hundred lines deep by two columns wide."

Line Spacing.   Also called *leading*, line spacing is the vertical space between lines of type and is measured in points. Lines are said to be set solid when no additional line spacing has been added. Leading is added to make type more readable. The rule of thumb is that leading should be no more than 20 percent of the type size. In other words, if you are using 10-point type, the maximum extra space between the lines is 2 points.

Advertising (8 point)

Advertising (10 point)

Advertising (12 point)

Advertising (14 point)

Advertising (24 point)

Advertising (36 point)

Adv (48 point)

EXHIBIT

18.17

A visual perspective on basic type sizes.

Type specifications are usually determined by art directors, print production personnel, or specialized type directors. The following factors may be involved in the decision process:

- **Type set in lowercase letters is read 13.4 percent faster than that set in all caps.**

- **Reverse copy—white or light type on a dark background—is read more slowly than black-on-white type (Exhibits 18.18, 18.19, 18.20). As a result, you should be extra careful in choosing type size and a readable typeface when a reverse is desired.**

Before the size of type can be chosen, the number of characters (letters, punctuation, and other symbols) in the copy typescript must be determined. Published tables show how many characters of various typefaces and point sizes fit into different widths. In advertising agencies, type specification might be handled by art directors, print production personnel, or specialized type directors.

TYPESETTING METHODS

Plenty of current writing about typography seems to assume (1) that all typesetting, particularly for graphic design and advertising, is now performed on desktop computers, and (2) that, while some type may still be set by trained

EXHIBIT

18.18

This Healthtex logo is reversed out of the black background.

(Courtesy: Healthtex.™)

EXHIBIT

18.19

· · · · · · · · · · · · · · · ·

This ad uses reverse type and bleeds on all four sides (the printed image goes to edge of page).

(Courtesy: The Zimmerman Agency.)

EXHIBIT

18.20

· · · · · · · · · · · · · · · ·

The headline is over-printed the illustration and the body copy is reversed out of the illustration.

(Courtesy: CECO Building Systems and Robinson & Associates, Inc.)

and experienced typesetters who have switched over to desktop, the typographer of the future is, increasingly, an art director or designer—maybe even a copywriter—for whom type is more a means to an end.

The fact is, a lot of supposedly obsolete "traditional" typesetting equipment is still hard at work, often on jobs for agencies and studios that have their own Macintoshes or IBMs, perched next to (or on top of) their old, dusty drawing boards.

Many agencies use low-end laser printers (usually 300 dpi), which is not high enough resolution for reproduction. However, it is fine for doing layout comps. In order to achieve high-resolution type, it is not unusual for the computer operator to "dump" the file into a high-quality imagesetter, often at an electronic type house or typographer. There the more sophisticated typesetter (about 3,600 dpi) prints type of reproduction quality that is camera-ready. The typographer's more expensive high-end computers and printers offer more type fonts than the agency generally has on its computer.

MECHANICAL AND ARTWORK

After the copy has been set to the proper dimensions (copy fitting) and all corrections have been made, the type may be pasted up or composed on the desktop system with the rest of the ad's material (illustrations, logos, etc.). At this point, the advertiser reviews the mechanical or computer comp. After approval by the advertiser, the mechanical is sent to the photoplatemaker.

Photoplatemaking

Making plates (and the films preceding the plates) for any printing process by camera, in color or black and white.

Typesetting is normally the first step in the production process. The second step is the preparation of the artwork for printing. This process is called *photoplatemaking* or prepress—the producing of a printing plate or other image carrier for publication printing. In offset and gravure, films are normally sent to the publication printers, from which they produce their own plates. For letterpress printing, the advertiser produces photoengravings (combining photography and chemical engravings).

The two major forms of photoengravings (letterpress) or photoplatemaking (offset and gravure) for reproduction are line and halftone plates.

Line Plates

Line drawing

A drawing made with a brush, pen, pencil, or crayon, with shading produced by variations in size and spacing of lines, not by tone.

Line Art. Artwork drawn in black ink on white paper using lines and solid black areas (only solid color with no tonal value or changes) is called *line art.* The printer uses a photographic process to get a line negative of the art (the process may vary according to the printing process). Type is an example of line art (if it is in solid form). Most artwork is drawn larger than needed for the mechanical to minimize the art's imperfections when reduced and printed. The negative is used in the appropriate printing-process plate production. Exhibit 18.21 contains examples of line art.

Linetint. You can give line art some variation in shades by breaking up the solid color with *screen tints* or *benday screens*. Exhibit 18.22 uses a screen tint to give the illusion of gray and contrast. The platemaker adds the screens during the film-stripping stage just prior to platemaking.

Line Color Plates. Artwork does not need to be in color to produce line plates, in two, three, or more flat colors. Instead, each extra color is marked on a separate tissue or acetate overlay on the base art as a guide for the

Examples of line art.
No tonal value; all lines
are solid color.

platemaker, who then makes a separate plate for each color. Line color plates provide a comparatively inexpensive method of printing in color with effective results.

A solid color (flat or match color) is printed with the actual color. The color is specified with a Pantone Matching System (PMS) color reference number, and the printer mixes an ink that is literally that color. It is like going into a paint store and choosing a color swatch and having the clerk mix the paint to match your color. The ink is applied to the paper through printing, and the specified color is obtained.

Halftones

At the end of this chapter we discuss some of the new production technology (including stochastic screening) that may eventually change the way photos (continuous art) are reproduced. At the present, the hundred-year-old technology does the job reasonably well.

If you look at photographs and watercolor or oil paintings, you recognize they are different from line art—they have tonal value. Photos have a range of tonal value between pure blacks and pure whites and are called *continuous-tone* artwork.

To reproduce the range of tones in continuous-tone art, the art (photo) must be broken up into dots, which are then called *halftones*. Exhibit 18.23 shows the reproduction of a black-and-white halftone. Remember that black ink is black ink and not shades of gray, so the production process must create an optical illusion by converting the tonal areas to different-size halftone dots on the printed paper that the eye perceives as gray. However, if you look at

Continuous tone

An unscreened photographic picture or image, on paper or film, that contains all gradations of tonal values from white to black.

MAGNOLIA'S NEW REGIONAL REHABILITATION CENTER... LETS YOU GET BACK IN STEP

YOUR FAMILY... OUR FUTURE... TOGETHER!

Accident or illness may have temporarily set you back physically. Magnolia Regional Rehabilitation Center's program will put you back in step with life.

Our team of experienced professionals in physical and occupational therapy will assist you in fulfilling your expectations of yourself. And, it's all close to home and to family -- for the support you really need.

Our new downtown location is larger, more convenient, and has longer hours than you would expect. And, we're prepared to give you "that-day" service for sports injuries, back problems, and work-related physical problems. Magnolia Regional Rehabilitation Center -- teamed with you for your future.

Magnolia
REGIONAL HEALTH CENTER

Your Family... Our Future... Together!

(Courtesy: Robinson & Associates.)

the printed halftone gray areas with a magnifying glass, you will see little black dots and not gray (Exhibit 18.24 shows a magnification). The dots are formed on the negative during the camera exposure when a screen is placed between the film and photograph (or other kinds of continuous-tone copy). As the film is exposed, light passes through the screen's 50 to 200 hairlines per square inch, and the image reaching the film is in dot form. The size of the dots will vary according to the contrast of tone in the original; this simply means that dark areas in the original photo will give one size dot, medium tones another size dot, and lighter tones still another size dot. The result is a negative with dots of varying sizes, depending on the tonal variations in the original.

It's Time To Change The Paper.

If you'd like something new when you reach for the paper, starting April 14th the Tallahassee Democrat takes on a whole new role.

(Courtesy: The Zimmerman Agency.)

After the halftone negative is made, it is placed on a metallic plate just like the line art negative and exposed to the plate. In letterpress printing, the engraving is splashed with acid that eats away the metal, leaving the dots as a raised surface. In offset printing, the dots are transferred to the smooth, flat plate photographically.

Halftone screens come in a variety of standard sizes. Each publication has its own requirement for the screen size, dictated somewhat by the printing process and paper being used. Newspapers, magazines, and promotional materials printed by offset use screens that generally range from 110 to 133 lines per square inch. In other words, a 133-line screen produces 133 dots to an inch. The more dots per inch, the greater the quality of detail reproduced from the original. The quality of the paper must also increase to accommodate the higher dot levels, which drives up paper costs.

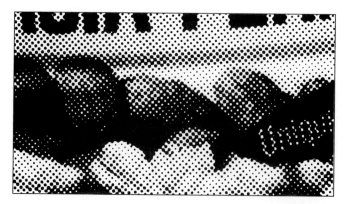

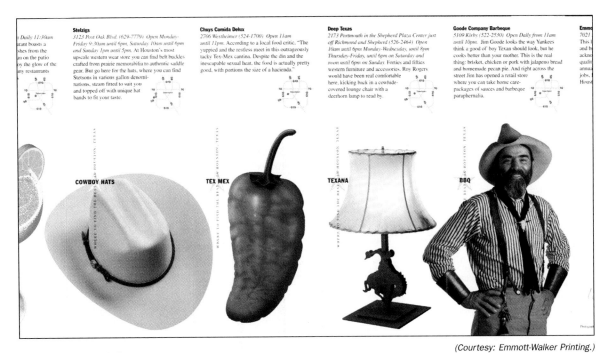

EXHIBIT

18.25

• • • • • • • • • • • • • • • • • • • •

Background has been removed from the illustrations.

• • • • • • • • • • • • • • • • • • • •

Four-color process

The process for reproducing color illustrations by a set of plates, one which prints all the yellows, another the blues, a third the reds, and the fourth the blacks (sequence variable). The plates are referred to as *process plates.*

• • • • • • • • • • • • • • • • • • • •

The Halftone Finish.   If you want to make a halftone of a photograph, the platemaker can treat the background in a number of ways; that treatment is called its *finish.* Here are a few of the techniques that can be applied to halftones:

- **Square halftone.** The halftone's background has been retained.

- **Silhouette.** The background in the photograph has been removed by the photo-platemaker (Exhibits 18.25 and 18.26).

- **Surprint.** This is a combination plate made by exposing line and halftone negatives in succession on the same plate, as illustrated in Exhibit 18.20.

- **Mortise.** An area of a halftone is cut out to permit the insertion of type or other matter (Exhibit 18.27).

Line Conversion.   A line conversion transforms a continuous-tone original into a high-contrast image of only black-and-white tones similar to line art. The conversion transfers the image into a pattern of some kind: mezzotint, wavy line, straight line, or concentric circle (Exhibit 18.28).

Two-Color Halftone Plates.   A two-color reproduction can be made from monochrome artwork in two ways. A screen tint in a second color can be printed over (or under) a black halftone. Or the artwork can be photographed twice, changing the screen angle the second time so that the dots of the second color plate fall between those of the first plate. This is called a *duotone.* It produces contrast in both colors of the one-color original halftone (see Exhibit 18.29).

Four-Color Process Printing.   Another printing system is needed when the job requires the reproduction of color photos. This system is *four-color process.* The four colors are cyan (blue), magenta (red), yellow, and black. (CMYK are the letters used to indicate these colors.) These are the least number of colors that can adequately reproduce the full spectrum of natural colors in-

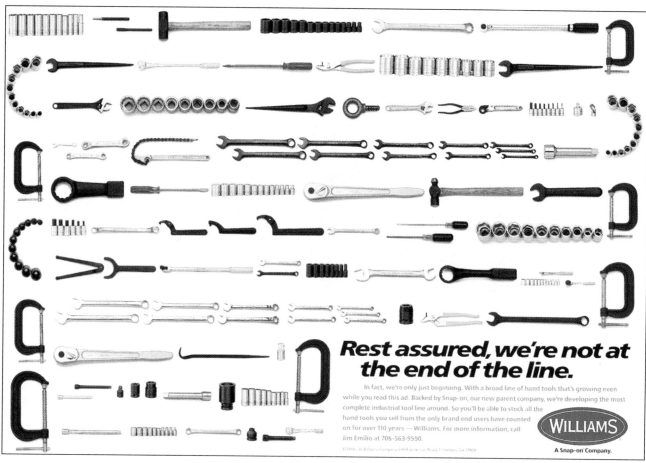

Rest assured, we're not at the end of the line.

In fact, we're only just beginning. With a broad line of hand tools that's growing even while you read this ad. Backed by Snap-on, our new parent company, we're developing the most complete industrial tool line around. So you'll be able to stock all the hand tools you sell from the only brand end users have counted on for over 110 years — Williams. For more information, call Jim Emilio at 706-563-9590.

©1994, J.H.Williams Company e908 Jones Mill Road, Kennesaw, GA 30606

WILLIAMS

A Snap-on Company.

(Courtesy: Sawyer Riley Compton, Inc.)

herent in photography. The first three—cyan, magenta, and yellow—provide the range of colors: The black provides definition and contrast in the image.

Full-color or process color requires photographic or electronic scanner separation of the color in the photographs (or other continuous-tone copy) into four negatives, one for each of the process colors. This process of preparing plates of the various colors and black is called *color separation* (see Exhibit 18.30). If you examine any of the color ads in this text (or any other publication) with a magnifying glass, you will find the halftone dots in four colors.

(Exhibit 18.31 shows examples of color printed pieces that look like fabric. Each publication is produced with four color halftone dots).

Desktop Color

Color reproduction has always been a tricky process in terms of getting the desired quality. Moving from traditional methods of making color separations to digital has simply changed the nature of the problem. Color is a tough taskmaster. There are still many steps in the process; each job is a little different technically.

In general, most large a agencies don't make their own color separations on their computers because the start-up is very expensive. Another factor is quality. The improvements taking place at traditional separation and engraving

Even as a little boy, Benson Timmons wanted to help people look their best.

Benson Timmons always wanted to be a plastic surgeon.

So he got his undergraduate degree from UNC Chapel Hill and a Doctor of Medicine Degree from East Carolina University School of Medicine. He did his residencies at the University of North Carolina Hospitals and at Duke University Medical Center.

And now he has opened a practice in Gastonia, where he is putting all his knowledge to work to help people look their best. His specialties include cosmetic surgery of the face, nose, and eyelids, skin cancer surgery, liposuction and tummy tuck, breast reduction and reconstruction, trauma reconstruction surgery and pediatric plastic surgery.

Dr. Timmons is available to perform these aesthetic and reconstructive procedures any time. And he's always available for advice and consultation, too.

Just like he's been since he was a little boy.

"Josh, has anybody ever told you about the benefits of **Rhinoplasty?"**

Southeastern
Plastic Surgery
Benson E.L. Timmons, MD
365 North New Hope Road, Suite 4
Gastonia, North Carolina 28054
704/866-4005 ~ Fax 704/866-0450

(Courtesy: Sterrett Dymond Advertising, Inc.)

The illustration is an example of a mezzotint line conversion.

UNLIKE OTHER OUTER SPACE MOVIES, OURS WAS ACTUALLY FILMED ON LOCATION.

"THE DREAM IS ALIVE" OPENING NOVEMBER 3.

(Courtesy: Loeffler Ketchum Mountjoy)

EXHIBIT 18.29

The duotone uses a black and white photo and reproduces it in two colors (with contrast in both colors).

houses have been dramatic. Companies like Scitex and Hell Graphics have brought state-of-the-art digitization and retouching to the industry. As a result, it is inefficient for most agencies to do their own color separations—if their clients' demand top-quality reproductions.

A typical procedure is for art directors to create the graphics on their computer or scan them on their color scanner. Once the layout is completed, the file is sent to a company such as Scitex, where the same graphics are scanned again on a much higher resolution scanner. The entire image is assembled, retouched, and color corrected on powerful workstations and then output as film.

Few agency art directors or production people are proficient enough with the software to produce high-quality color separations for national ads. It is a skill that is almost a full-time job in itself. However, many smaller agencies with clients who do not need top-quality color work have found their desktop color separations to be a fast, low-cost alternative.

The *Star Ledger's* color manager says, "More and more agencies are sending ads to our newspaper in a digital manner. The newspaper is having to become a service bureau [that converts disk data into the final ad]." The agency may spend $200,000 a year with a PostScript output service bureau and wants to send their ads to the paper via modem. Part of what a service bureau does is to debut PostScript files, and that's not a skill most newspapers have at this point in time.[3]

---

[3]David M. Cole, "Quality Color," *Presstime Planner,* November 1994, pp. 12–16.

There are more desktop colors than an advertiser can use. The video monitor can display more than 16 million colors; the human eye can discern about 10 million; process color printing can effectively blend about 500,000. With all the variables included, a typical printing press can reproduce 50,000 distinct solid colors. At the moment, color consistency between computer programs, output systems, etc., does not exist.

Of course, all of this sounds very complicated, and it is. Pantone offers a number of printing guides for solid colors (for example, the Pantone Color Imaging Guide shows 736 solid colors mixed and printed) and process colors (Pantone Process Color System—a three-book set available for computer use—helped advertisers' select process colors just as they do solid colors (see Exhibit 18.32) and contains over 3,000 colors) to make the job easier. It is like going into a paint store and looking at swatches of color. The Pantone Process Color System is achievable with any desktop computer running desktop design software.

Color Proofing

Achieving color reproduction that satisfies ad agencies and advertisers is one of the most critical roles of the magazine production manager. Agencies generally demand to see a proof before the job is printed.

In today's *electronic* color production, *traditional* proofing systems seem to have taken a back seat to digital color proofers, color printers, networked color copiers, and short-run color production devices.

EXHIBIT
18.30

······················

Progressive steps in four-color process printing. Four plates yellow, red, blue and black—combine to produce the desired colors and contrasts.

Yellow, red, blue, and black plates

(cont.)

Exhibit 18.30 (cont.)

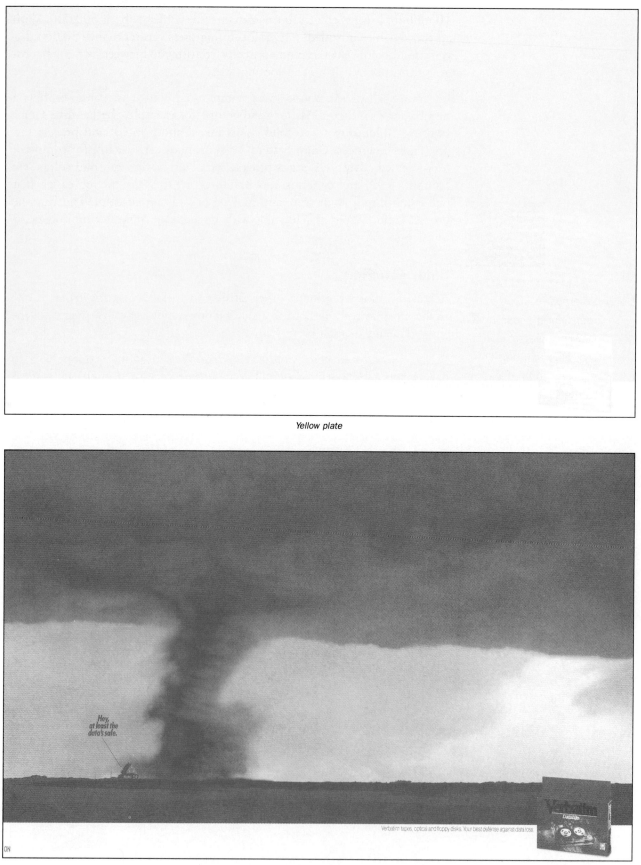

Yellow plate

Red plate

Red and yellow plates

Blue plate

(cont.)

Exhibit 18.30 (cont.)

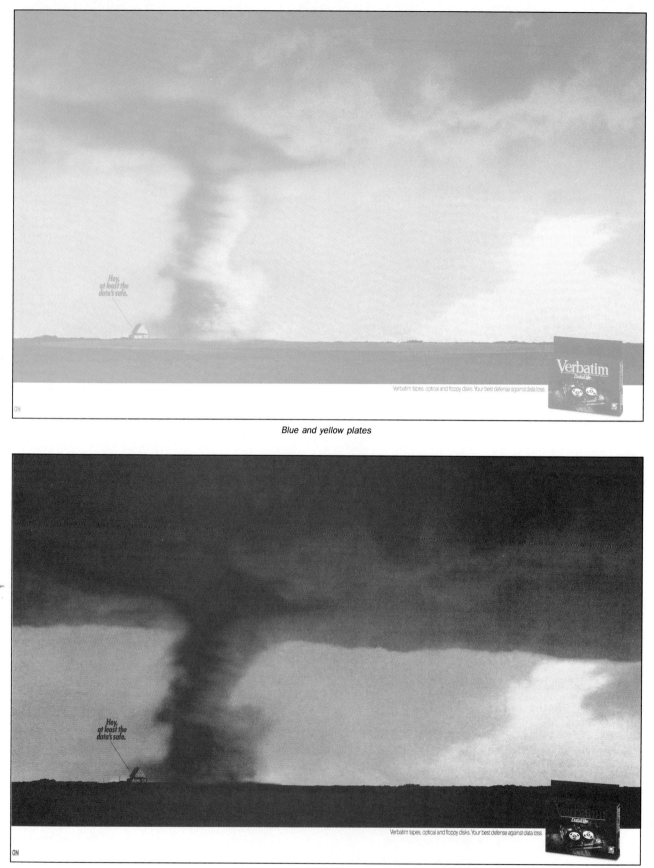

Blue and yellow plates

Blue, red and yellow plates

Black plate

(Courtesy: Verbatim, Inc.)

EXHIBIT

18.31

• • • • • • • • • • • • • • • •

Ad production people not only have to produce ads for publications but collateral material such as the Hancock Annual and Quarterly Reports.

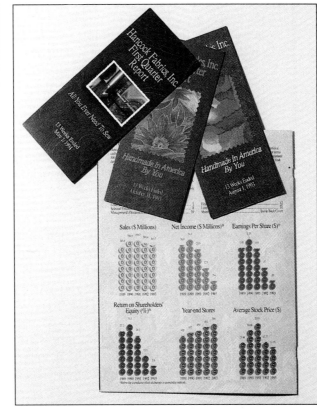

(Courtesy: Robinson & Associates.)

This is an example of using solid PMS color and screening to give the illusion of using two colors of blue. This promotional piece actually uses only blue and black.

(Courtesy: County Seat Cafe.)

For the most accurate contract proofs—those requiring the best match to jobs printed by conventional offset lithography—nothing beats a film-based laminated, or single-sheet off-press proof. An off-press proof ensures the separator that color separations have been made according to customer expectations.[4]

Press Proofs

For years, press proofs, or progressives, usually made on special proofing presses, were the standard proofs sent to agencies for checking. Prior to the development of off-press proofs, color separators used press proofs. Making a press proof involved stripping the separations on film, making plates, mounting the plates on a proof press, and printing the desired number of proofs. Press proofs are made with ink on paper—often the same paper that will be used for the job—rather than with a photographic simulation process of off-press systems. Today, they are still used by many ad agencies that are willing to pay the steep price for what they believe is the most accurate proof. In theory, press proofs provide a virtually exact representation of the final project.

PROGRESSIVE PROOFS (PROGS). These give the advertiser a separate proof for each color (red, yellow, blue, and black), as indicated in Exhibit 18.25 as well as a proof for each color combination (red and yellow, red and blue, blue and yellow)—seven printings in all. After approval by the advertiser and agency, the proofs are sent to the printer to use as a guide in duplicating the densities for each color.

OFF-PRESS PROOFS. Less expensive and faster than press proofs, and adequate in most cases, off-press proofs are the usual proof today. No plate or printing is involved. There are numerous types of off-press (prepress) proofing systems. The most popular are overlay and adhesive proofs.

---

[4]Richard M. Adams II, "Color-Proofing Systems," *Pre*, March/April 1994, pp. 55–59.

OVERLAY PROOFS. The development of overlay proofing enabled color proofs to be made from film without using a proof press. The overlay proofs consist of four exposed sheets containing the cyan (blue), magenta (red), yellow, and black process colors—overlaid on a backing sheet. The four overlays (yellow, red, blue, and black) are then stacked to produce a composite image. Because they use multiple, separate, plastic layers, overlay proofs cannot be expected to predict color accurately on press; but they are still used today for checking color break, or general color appearance and position.

3M's Color Keys are an example of overlay proofs that art directors use as guides for making adjustments on the color separations.

ADHESIVE OR TONER TRANSFER PROOF. In 1972, DuPont introduced the first off-press proofing system that closely resembled printed images, the Cromalin system. Cromalin is a laminated or single-sheet proof, one in which four (or more) layers are exposed separately and laminated together to reproduce the image of cyan, magenta, yellow, and black separations. DuPont's Cromalins use dry pigments to produce images or photosensitive adhesive polymers or pretreated carrier sheets. Cromalin is generally considered the superior adhesive process. The proofs are keyed to SWOP (Specifications for Web Offset Publications)/GAA (Gravure Association of America) guidelines, which set standards for inks, density of tones, reverses, and other technical matters. Among the highest-fidelity four-color proofs are the "match print" and the "signature proof," both very similar but from different suppliers. Campbell-Mithun-Esty says the Kodak Signature system has enabled its supplier to eliminate one or perhaps two rounds of press proofs, saving it money. These proofs can be made on the actual paper stock chosen by the agency and advertiser. Among the popular adhesive brands are the 3M Matchprint, Agfa Agafaproof, Hoechst-Celanese PressMatch, and Fuji Color-Art.

There are digital hard and soft copy systems that eliminate film to produce continuous-tone proofs. The soft proofing systems allow production and design people to call up a digitized color image and evaluate it before separations are made for an intermediate or position proof. D'Arcy Masius Benton & Bowles (St. Louis) was the first agency to employ an interactive system that allows artists to make on-screen adjustments at the agency and instantly relay the changes to the printer to be incorporated into the final proof. The interactive system gives the agency more flexibility with deadlines and saves time and money for clients.

OFFSET AND GRAVURE PHOTOPLATEMAKING

In letterpress publication printing, the advertiser or agency furnishes the plate to the publication or printer. Offset and gravure publications require film only from the advertiser because they make their own plates.

If the agency wishes to retain complete control over the preparatory steps, it usually sends the mechanical and artwork to its own supplier to be prepared for the printer. This can be an offset separation house, a gravure service company, or a company that prepares materials for all printing processes.

The preparatory work for the three major printing processes is similar. In offset and gravure, the photoplatemaker produces plates merely for proofing purposes. These plates are not sent to the publication—only the final cor-

> **Match print**
>
> A high-quality color proof used for approvals prior to printing. Similar to a Signature print.

rected films are sent, along with proof and progressive proofs (progs) pulled from these plates. As mentioned earlier, in letterpress, actual plates are sent.

MAKING DUPLICATE MATERIAL

Most print ads run in more than one publication. Frequently, advertisers have different publications on their schedules, or they need to issue reprints of their ads or send material to dealers for cooperating advertising. There are various means of producing duplicate material of magazine or newspaper ads.

Letterpress Duplicates

There are several kinds of letterpress duplicate plates because publishers may require a specific type of duplicate plate. Stereotypes are still used to duplicate ads for some newspapers. This process makes a paper or plastic mold or mat, which is sent to the paper. The paper then pours hot molten lead into the mat, converting it into a metal stereotype plate. This process is being replaced by the photopolymer plates, which are produced on photosensitive plastic. Electrotype is another duplicate plate produced from a plastic mold using a combination of metals; it is very durable and is capable of printing millions of impressions. Cronapress plates (called *Cronars*) can be made with a pressure-sensitive material capable of duplicating the original impression exactly.

Offset and Gravure Duplicates

Duplicate material for offset publication can consist of repro proofs (reproduction proofs) or 3M Scotchprints (a plasticized repro proofing material). Usually, photoprints or reproduction proofs are preferred for partial-page newspaper ads; film is often required for full-page newspaper insertions. Duplicate films can also be made from the original artwork or mechanicals. For color gravure magazines or Sunday supplements, duplicate positive films are usually supplied. For black-and-white offset or gravure ads, photographic prints are often substituted for films.

A number of newspapers use satellite transmission systems to send a facsimile of each page of the newspaper to a reception station, where it is recorded on page-size photofilm. The film is then used to make offset plates, which are placed on the presses to reproduce the newspaper in the usual way. This system permits the papers to run different regional editions utilizing the main news items from headquarters, while allowing for variations in advertising content within each regional edition. There are services that can transmit an advertiser's ad by satellite to publications with reception stations in much the same way.

Color Copier

Color copier interfaces, also known as printer controllers, link the color copier directly to a computer, turning the copier into a multifunctional workhorse. These interfaces provide such capabilities as scanning from the copier into a Mac or Windows application, print spooling and job-queue management, image editing, color proofing, and printing. BIS Strategic Decisions estimates that 60 percent or more of all color copiers sold in the United States in 1993 included digital interfaces.

JCPenney typically prints about 100 different catalogs annually with runs of up to 15 million per book. "We do page layout, text and page assembly internally," says Tim Dawson, manager of Electronic Publishing. "All of the last-stage color proofing is done on our Cannon copier which is linked to a Colorbus Cyclone." The Cyclone is a digital printer controller that runs on a Silicon Graphics workstation.

NEW PRODUCTION TECHNOLOGY

The rapid changes in technology during the past few years have been changing the prepress and printing processes. In the near future, the production managers and art directors will have many new options for handling their projects. In all cases, the new technologies are beginning to make an impact on the production and printing process as we know it. These new techniques range from color separation, color management, and proofing to printing. The following deserve to be brought to your attention:[5]

Stochastic Screening and Color Separations

Stochastic screening, or frequency modulation screening, is a process for producing incredible tone and detail that approximate photographic quality. With conventional halftone screens, the dots are spaced equally on a grid (110, 133, etc., lines per inch), and the tonal value is achieved with increasing or decreasing the size of the dots. On the other hand, stochastic screening has dots that are all the same size, that are very tiny, and whose numbers vary according to the tonal value. Used by a quality printer, the image appears to be continuous tone or photographic quality and much better than any traditional process. At this time, the companies producing this process are few: Linotype-Hell with its Diamond screening, Agfa with CristalRaster, Scitex with FULLtone, and Black Box of Chicago. Agfa and Linotype are processed from a Macintosh platform. These companies offer an advertiser the ability to produce higher-quality color separations, which in turn allow them to print sharper color ads.

HiFi Color. High-fidelity color is expanding what we know and can do with print reproduction techniques and processes. HiFi color was born out of the limitations of the conventional color printing gamut, which are only a fraction of what the human visual system can see. It is a group of emerging technologies that will expand this printed gamut and extend control by improving and increasing tone, dynamic range, detail, spatial frequency modulation, and other appearance factors of print and other visual media.

HiFi color *comprises the technologies* of stochastic, or frequency modulation screening, four-plus color process and waterless printing methods, specialty papers, films, coatings, laminates, proofing systems, color management systems, software, and hardware.

Color Management Systems (CMS). These can be as simple as a software program loaded into a computer or as complex as an array of measuring devices used to calibrate and control the color. They have been designed to solve the disparity of what you see on your computer screen and what the final

---

[5]Kurt Klein and Daniel Dejan, "New Printing Technology," *Communication Arts*, Design Annual 1993, pp. 283–290.

product looks like. The ideal, and we haven't easily gotten to this point in technology, is seeing an image on a screen and getting an exact printed image, or as it is touted "What You See Is What You Get," known as WYSIWYG. This is very important in terms of quality control and design.

Direct Digital Proofing. They are a host of new digital proofing systems on the market for production people to use. These are several distinct categories, and each has its own advantages and disadvantages. The types include thermal transfer proofing (QMS is an example), digital ink-jet proofing (such as IRIS), digital electrostatic color copiers (Canon and Kodak color copiers), thermal dye-sublimation proofers (3M Rainbow), and electrophotographic digital proofing (Kodak Approval and 3M Digital Matchprint). Most of the digital proofers are for internal or presentation use on work-in-progress, client alterations, color variations of the same design, or color corrections specified by the client.

The only digital proofs currently being accepted by printers as contract proofs are Kodak Approval, 3M Digital Matchprint, and IRIS.

Waterless Printing. This new technology is gaining popularity; however, we'll keep the explanation simple. Most offset presses use a dampening system of water to cover the plate. Remember, we said offset is based upon the fact that water and grease (ink) don't mix. In waterless printing, a silicone-coated plate is used and rejects ink in the nonimage areas. The result is spectacular detail, high-line screens, richer densities, and consistent quality throughout the press run—in short, great quality.

Other Developments. *Gamut Color,* in simplified terms, adds the primary colors of red, green, and blue (actually closer to orange, green, and purple) to the process colors (magenta, cyan, yellow, and black), giving a much wider range of hues for printing. This system may offer expanded color options and quality. *Presstek/Heidelberg GTo-DI* has created another waterless printing process. It uses no film, no stripping, no plate processing, recyclable plates, faster-make-ready, no ink/water balance problems, time saving and reduction in production costs. It has some problems though; it is basically designed to run good short-run color for jobs in the 500- to 5,000-impression range.

The computer and digitization are spawning most of this advancement in printing and production technology. The day is not far off when the printing/production industry will have a completely filmless digital process production.

The student of advertising production will have to learn these advances in the field, many of which will be both revolutionary and evolutionary, complicating the choice of system to use.

SUMMARY

All advertising people need to understand the basics of production. The production terms, concepts, and processes are not easy to learn but are essential to know.

Publications set the mechanical requirements for their publication. Advertising production people need to be familiar with sources of information pertaining to print production requirements.

There are three basic printing processes: *letterpress* (printing from a raised surface, *offset lithography* (printing from a flat surface), and *gravure* (printing from a depressed surface), In addition, *silk screen* or *screen* printing offers advertiser's additional production applications.

The form of printing affects the type of materials sent to the publication to reproduce the ad.

Today, advertisers may use new prepress digital technology or traditional means to prepare ads for production. Each has advantages and disadvantages depending on the degree of quality required. Typography concerns the style (or face) of type and the way in which copy is set. Typefaces come in styles called *families*. The size is specified in *points* (72 points to the inch). The width of typeset lines is measured in *picas* (6 picas to the inch). The depth of newspaper space is measure in lines (agate lines are 14 to the column inch, regardless of column width. The space between lines of type is called *leading* or *line spacing*.

Desktop publishing is suitable for setting some kinds of promotional material, depending largely on the capabilities of the output system. Many files must be sent to a PostScript service bureau for quality output.

The graphics and production process can be complex because what you see isn't always what really is. Continuous-tone art (a photograph) must be converted into halftone dots so that the tonal values of the original can be reproduced. Line art has no tonal value; it is drawn in black ink on white paper using lines and solid black areas.

The new digital technology is changing the production process. Copiers and computers may work together as one in producing part of the production process. Stochastic screening technology is offering higher-quality color separations; however, it is not widely available. Advances in color management systems are helping advertisers "see what you get" off the computer. Waterless printing is gaining new popularity.

Questions
1. Differentiate between letterpress and offset printing.
2. What is continuous-tone copy?
3. When do you need to make a halftone?
4. What are points and picas?
5. What are color separations?
6. What kind of color proofs do advertisers use?
7. What is line art?
8. What colors are used in process color?
9. Where do you find publication mechanical requirements?

The Television Commercial

19

CHAPTER OBJECTIVES

It is estimated that the average person spends over 1,500 hours per year watching TV programs. TV advertising is powerful and expensive. It is complicated by the fact that every viewer is a TV advertising expert. Everyone knows what he or she likes and dislikes about TV spots. This creates a challenge for advertisers. After reading this chapter you will understand:

- **Copy development**
- **Creating the commercial**
- **Producing the commercial**
- **Controlling the cost**

Take the Big Idea; blend words, visuals, motion and technology; and add the ability to create emotional reactions—this is what makes television the most powerful advertising medium.

The high cost of producing and running TV spots is a constant reminder to advertisers of the need to plan their messages very carefully. **In this chapter,** we'll touch on a whole array of techniques available to writers and producers of TV commercials and the cost factors.

COPY DEVELOPMENT AND PRODUCTION TIMETABLE

The creative process is difficult to predict in terms of the agency's ability to develop new breakthrough copy within the planned timetable and the client's reaction to the copy. The agency may love it—the client may hate it. It may take time to develop the right ideas. However, it is important to develop a reasonable timetable for copy development and production. Below is a brief look at a typical copy/development timetable sequence:

- **Copy exploratory**

- **Present ideas to client**

- **Revisions to client for approval to produce**

- **Circulate copy for clearance (legal, R&D, management)**

- **On-air clearance (network/local stations)**

- **Prebid meeting (specifications/sets)**

- **Bid review/award job**

- **Preproduction meeting**

- **Shoot**

- **Postproduction**

- **Rough cut to client for approval**

- **Revisions**

- **Final to client**

- **Ship date**

The responsibility for such a timetable is shared by the advertising agency and the client.

CREATING THE TV COMMERCIAL

The TV commercial has two basic segments: the video (the sight or visual part) and the audio (spoken words, music, or other sounds). The creation process usually starts with the video because television is generally better at showing than telling; however, the impact of the words and sounds must be considered.

Visual Techniques

It is not sufficient to develop an extremely creative dramatic script with strong sell. That great script idea has to be produced creatively on film or tape. Many great ideas have not come off because the production was not good enough. Let's take a look at some successful visual techniques.

Testimonials.   This technique can be delivered by known or unknown individuals. Viewers are fascinated with celebrities. A celebrity personality (for example, Cindy Crawford, David Robinson, Tim Allen, Michael Jordon) will grab a viewer's attention. Despite the problems of some celebrities like Tonya Harding, Shannen Doherty, Burt Reynolds, and Rush Limbaugh, advertisers continue to use the technique with enthusiasm. There's always a risk, but it's worth it because of all the attention the celebrities get and the impact they have, says a vice president for Total Research Corp.[1] Advertisers need to spend the $20,000 it takes to research a celebrity to get diagnostic information on not only the personality but whether or not the personality fits the product or service.

Spokesperson. This technique features a "presenter" who stands in front of the camera and delivers the copy directly to the viewer. The spokesperson may display and perhaps demonstrate the product. He or she may be in a set (a living room, kitchen, factory, office, or out of doors) appropriate to your product and product story, or in limbo (plain background with no set). You need to choose as a spokesperson someone who is likable and believable but not so powerful as to overwhelm the product. Remember, the product should be the hero.

Demonstration. This technique is popular for some types of products because television is the ideal medium for demonstrating to the consumer how the product works: how a bug spray kills, how to apply eye pencils in gorgeous silky colors, or how easy it is to use a microwave to cook a whole meal quickly. When making a demonstration commercial, use close shots so the viewer can see clearly what is happening. You may choose a subjective camera view (which shows a procedure as if the viewer were actually doing whatever the product does), using the camera as the viewer's eyes. Make the demonstration relevant and as involving as possible. Do not try to fool the viewer for two important reasons: (1) Your message must be believable; and (2) legally, the demonstration must correspond to actual usage—most agencies make participants in the commercial production sign affidavits signifying that the events took place as they appeared on the TV screen.

Close-Ups. Television is basically a medium of close-ups. The largest TV screen is too small for extraneous details in the scenes of a commercial. A fast-food chain may use close-ups to show hamburgers cooking the appetizing finished product ready to be consumed. With this technique, the audio is generally delivered offscreen (the voice-over costs less than a presentation by someone on the screen).

Story Line. The story-line technique is similar to making a miniature movie (with a definite beginning, middle, and end in 30 seconds), except that the narration is done offscreen. A typical scene may show a family trying to paint their large house with typical paint and brush. The camera shifts to the house next door, where a teenage female is easily spray-painting the house, the garage, and the fence in rapid fashion. During the scenes, the announcer explains the advantages of the spray painter.

Comparisons. Their soft drink has sodium. Our brand is sodium-free. Comparing one product with another can answer questions for the viewer. Usually, the comparison is against the leader in the product category. You could do a *user* lifestyle comparison between your brand and a competitive brand. In direct product comparisons, you must be prepared to prove in court that your product is significantly superior, as stated, and you must be credible in the way you make your claim, or the commercial may induce sympathy for the competitor.

---

[1]Cyndee Miller, "Celebrities Hot Despite Scandals," *Marketing News,* March 28, 1994, pp. 1–2.

Still Photographs and Artwork. Using still photographs and/or artwork, including cartoon drawings and lettering, you can structure a well-placed commercial. The required material may already exist, to be supplied at modest cost, or it can be photographed or drawn specifically for your use. Skillful use of the TV camera can give static visual material a surprising amount of movement. Zoom lenses provide an inward or outward motion, and panning the camera across the photographs or artwork can give the commercial motion (*panning* means changing the viewpoint of the camera without moving the dolly it stands on).

Slice-of-Life. It's an old dramatic technique where actors tell a story in an attempt to involve people with the brand. It is a short miniplay in which the brand is the hero. Most slice-of-life commercials open with a problem, and the brand becomes the solution.

The viewer must see the problem as real, and the reward must fit the problem. Because problem solving is a useful format in almost any commercial, slice-of-life is widely used.

Customer Interview. Most people who appear in TV commercials are professional actors, but customer interviews involve nonprofessionals. An interviewer or offscreen voice may ask a housewife, who is usually identified by name, to compare the advertised kitchen cleanser with her own brand by removing two identical spots in her sink. She finds that the advertised product does a better job.

Vignettes and Situations. Advertisers of soft drinks, beer, candy, and other widely consumed products find this technique useful in creating excitement and motivation. The commercial usually consists of a series of fast-paced scenes showing people enjoying the product as they enjoy life. The audio over these scenes is often a jingle or song with lyrics based on the situation we see and the satisfaction the product offers.

Humor. Humor has long been a popular technique with both copywriters and consumers because it makes the commercial more interesting. The danger is that the humorous aspects of the commercial will get in the way of the sell and that the viewer will remember the humor rather than the product or the benefit. The challenge is to make the humorous copy relevant to the product or benefit.

Animation (TV)

Making inanimate objects appear alive and moving by setting them before an animation camera and filming one frame at a time.

Animation. Animation consists of artists' inanimate drawings, which are photographed on motion-picture film one frame at a time and brought to life with movement as the film is projected. The most common form of animation is the cartoon. A favorite among children but popular with all ages, the cartoon is capable of creating a warm, friendly atmosphere both for the product and for the message. Animation can also he used to simplify technical product demonstrations. In a razor commercial, the actual product may be shown as it shaves a man's face, and an animated sequence may then explain how the blades of the razor remove whisker after whisker. The cost of animation depends on its style: With limited movement, few characters, and few or no backgrounds, the price can be low.

Stop Motion. When a package or other object is photographed in a series of different positions, movement can be stimulated as the single frames are projected in sequence. Stop motion is similar to artwork photographed in animation. With it, the package can "walk," "dance," and move as if it had come to life.

Rotoscope. In the rotoscope technique, animated and live-action sequences are produced separately and then optically combined. A live boy may be eating breakfast food while a cartoon animal trademark character jumps up and down on his shoulder and speaks to him.

Problem Solution. This technique has been around since the beginning of television. The purpose of many products is to solve the prime prospect's problem—a headache, poor communication, or plaque. You get the idea. The product is selling the solution. Problem-solution is similar to slice-of-life, but lacks the depth of story line or plot development.

Mood Imagery. This technique is expensive and difficult. It often combines several techniques. The main objective is to set a certain mood and image for the product you are trying to sell. An example of this technique is the GE "We bring good things to life" campaign.

Serials. This technique is the strongest response so far by the industry to zapping. The serial is commercials created in groups or campaigns; each commercial advances a story. MCI's serial campaign about a fictional publishing house, Gramercy Press, is a take-off on the technique made popular by the Taster's Choice couple. MCI developed a 12-part series of commercials, and each communicated much more information about the product than those commercials in the Taster's Choice serial. Several beer companies have also tried the serial approach, as have Pacific Bell, Ragu, and the Energizer Bunny.

The Taster's Choice serial of its romantic couple was first run in November 1990. Consumers became intrigued by the couple's romance, from their first meeting as new neighbors. The product moved from the third largest selling instant coffee to surpass Folger's and Maxwell House in less than three years after the commercials started.

Split and Bookend Spots. A variation on the serial commercial is the split spot: Two related (usually 15-second) spots run with a completely unrelated spot between them. For example, Post Grape-Nuts ran a split spot in which a woman asks a man how long the cereal stays crunchy in milk. The man does not want to find out, but she insists, and viewers are left hanging. Next is an unrelated 30-second commercial for another product. The couple then comes back and she says, "After all this time it's still crunchy."

The theory behind split and bookend commercials is that breaking out of the expected format will get your product remembered.

Infomercials. As we discussed in Chapter 8, the infomercial is a commercial that looks like a program. These commercials sell everything from woks to make-a-million-in-real-estate programs, and usually run for 30 minutes. The National Infomercial Marketing Association recommends that every infomercial begin and end with a "paid advertisement" announcement so that consumers understand what they are watching. The obvious advantage is that the advertiser has an entire program about its product.

Combination. Most commercials combine techniques. A speaker may begin and conclude the message, but there will be close-ups in between. In fact, every commercial should contain at least one or two close-ups to show package and logo. Humor is adaptable to most techniques. Animation and live action make an effective mixture in many commercials, and side-by-side comparisons may be combined with almost any other technique.

MTV Influence

Many techniques used in commercials were once unique to MTV. They have become visual rules, according to George Felton. These include hyperkinetic imagery, visual speed and sophistication; ironic, wise-guy attitudes, unexpected humor; quick, suggestive cuts rather than slow, sensible segues; narrative implications rather than whole stories; attitudes, not explanations; tightly cropped, partial images instead of whole ones; odd mixtures of live action, newsreel footage, animation, typography, film speeds film quality; and unexpected soundtrack/audio relationships to video.

Which Technique?

There have been a number of studies to help advertisers make up their minds as to what kind of commercials to run. None provide all the answers, however. Ogilvy & Mather found that people who liked a commercial were twice as likely to be persuaded by it compared to people who felt neutral toward the advertising. Perhaps the single most striking finding was the fact that commercial liking went far beyond mere entertainment. People like commercials they feel are relevant and worth remembering, which could have an impact on greater persuasion. Original or novel approaches by themselves seem to have little to do with how well a commercial is liked. Ogilvy & Mather also found that liking was a function of product category, and that a lively, energetic execution also contributed to liking, but was less important than relevance.

In other research findings, Video Storyboard Tests reinforce consumers like commercials with celebrities. In fact, consumer preference for this type of commercial has risen over the past 10 years. They find such commercials more persuasive than slice-of-life vignettes or product demonstrations. Exhibit 19.1 shows that celebrities are bested only by humor and kids as executional elements that characterize persuasive commercials. By contrast, Video Story-

Video Storyboard Persuasion Results

	Women	Men	18–34	34–49	50+
Commercials with **humor**	57	**68**	58	63	64
Commercials with **children**	**61**	44	52	56	52
Commercials with **celebrities**	39	34	**44**	34	30
Real-life situations	34	30	**39**	33	24
Brand **comparisons**	32	23	**35**	31	20
Musical commercials	**29**	18	27	23	20
Product **demonstrations**	17	**26**	19	24	21
Endorsements from experts	**17**	13	16	16	14
Hidden-camera testimonials	12	10	**14**	10	9
Company **presidents**	6	**12**	**12**	9	7

(Source: Adweek, August 15, 1994, p. 17.)

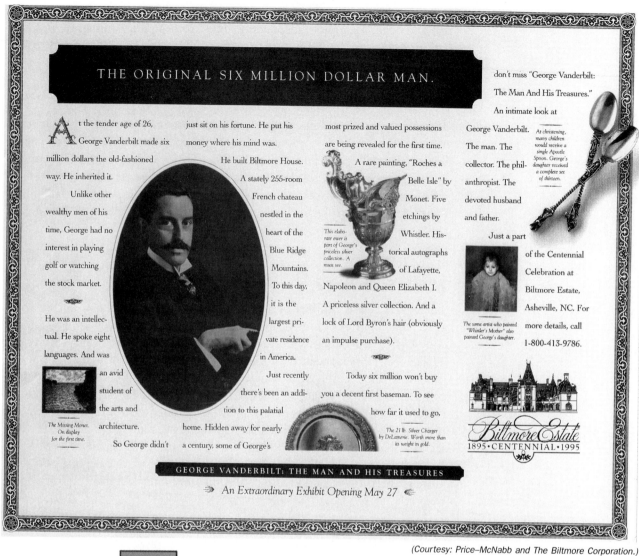

THE ORIGINAL SIX MILLION DOLLAR MAN.

At the tender age of 26, George Vanderbilt made six million dollars the old-fashioned way. He inherited it.

Unlike other wealthy men of his time, George had no interest in playing golf or watching the stock market.

He was an intellectual. He spoke eight languages. And was an avid student of the arts and architecture.

So George didn't

The Missing Monet. On display for the first time.

just sit on his fortune. He put his money where his mind was.

He built Biltmore House. A stately 255-room French chateau nestled in the heart of the Blue Ridge Mountains. To this day, it is the largest private residence in America.

Just recently there's been an addition to this palatial home. Hidden away for nearly a century, some of George's

most prized and valued possessions are being revealed for the first time.

A rare painting, "Roches a Belle Isle" by Monet. Five etchings by Whistler. Historical autographs of Lafayette, Napoleon and Queen Elizabeth I. A priceless silver collection. And a lock of Lord Byron's hair (obviously an impulse purchase).

This elaborate ewer is part of George's priceless silver collection. A must see.

Today six million won't buy you a decent first baseman. To see how far it used to go,

The 21 lb. Silver Charger by DeLamerie. Worth more than its weight in gold.

don't miss "George Vanderbilt: The Man And His Treasures." An intimate look at George Vanderbilt. The man. The collector. The philanthropist. The devoted husband and father.

Just a part of the Centennial Celebration at Biltmore Estate, Asheville, NC. For more details, call 1-800-413-9786.

The same artist who painted "Whistler's Mother" also painted George's daughter.

At christening, many children would receive a single Apostle Spoon. George's daughter received a complete set of thirteen.

Biltmore Estate
1895 · CENTENNIAL · 1995

GEORGE VANDERBILT: THE MAN AND HIS TREASURES

An Extraordinary Exhibit Opening May 27

(Courtesy: Price–McNabb and The Biltmore Corporation.)

EXHIBIT 19.2

Print and TV for Biltmore Estates have the same objectives and promise, but are different in execution.

board finds declining effectiveness for expert endorsements and company president spokespersons.[2]

Price/McNabb Advertising created a campaign for Biltmore Estate trying to get tourists to visit the new Centennial Celebration and Exhibit at the 255-room home. The copy in the print and television are similar but not the same. Exhibit 19.2 shows the print ad, and Exhibit 19.3 shows a few frames from a TV commercial.

Planning the Commercial

In planning the TV commercial, there are many considerations: cost, medium (videotape or film), casting of talent, use of music, special techniques, time, location, and the Big Idea and its relationship to the advertising and marketing objectives and, of course, to the entire campaign.

---

[2]"Why Watch a Jowly CEO When There's Cindy Crawford?" *Adweek,* August 15, 1994, p. 17.

EXHIBIT

19.3

Lets review some of the basic principles of writing the commercial script or thinking the idea through:

- **You are dealing with sight, sound, and motion. Each of these elements has its own requirements and uses. There should be a relationship between them so that the viewer perceives the desired message. Make certain that when you are demonstrating a sales feature, the audio is talking about that same feature.**

- **Your audio should be relevant to your video, but there is no need to describe what is obvious in the picture. Where possible, you should see that the words interpret the picture and advance the thought.**

- **Television generally is more effective at showing than telling; therefore, more than half of the success burden rests on the ability of the video to communicate.**

- **The number of scenes should be planned carefully. You do not want too many scenes (unless you are simply trying to give an overall impression) because this tends to confuse the viewer. Yet you do not want scenes to become static (unless planned so for a reason). Study TV commercials and time the scene changes to determine what you personally find effective. If you do this, you will discover the importance of pacing the message—if a scene is too long, you will find yourself impatiently waiting for the next one.**

- **It is important to conceive the commercial as a flowing progression so that the viewer will be able to follow it easily. You do not have time for a three-act play whose unrelated acts can be tied together at the end. A viewer who cannot follow your thought may well tune you out. The proper use of opticals or transitions can add motion and smoothness to scene transitions.**

- **Television is basically a medium of close-ups. The largest TV screen is too small for extraneous detail in the scenes of a commercial. Long shots can be effective in establishing a setting, but not for showing product features.**

- **The action of the commercial takes more time than a straight announcer's reading of copy. A good rule is to purposely time the commercial a second or** two short. Generally, the action will eat up this time, so do not just read your script. Act it out.

- You will want to consider the use of supers (words on the screen) of the basic theme so that the viewer can see, as well as hear, the important sales feature. Many times, the last scene will feature product identification and the theme line.

- If possible, show the brand name. If it is prominent, give a shot of the package; otherwise, flash its logotype. It is vital to establish brand identification.

- Generally, try to communicate one basic idea; avoid running in fringe benefits. Be certain that your words as well as your pictures emphasize your promise. State it, support it, and, if possible, demonstrate it. Repeat your basic promise near the end of the commercial; that is the story you want viewers to carry away with them.

- Read the audio aloud to catch tongue twisters.

- As in most other advertising writing, the sentences should usually be short and their structure uncomplicated. Use everyday words. It is not necessary to have something said every second. The copy should round out the thought conveyed by the picture.

- In writing your video description, describe the scene and action as completely as possible: "Open on man and wife in living room" is not enough. Indicate where each is placed, whether they are standing or sitting, and generally how the room is furnished.

Writing the Script

Writing a TV commercial is very different from writing print advertising. First, you must use simple, easy-to-pronounce, easy-to-remember words. And you must be brief. The 30-second commercial has only 28 seconds of audio. In 28 seconds, you must solve your prime prospect's problems by demonstrating your product's superiority. If the product is too big to show in use, be certain to show the logo or company name at least twice during the commercial. Think of words and pictures simultaneously. You usually divide your script paper into two columns. On the left, you describe the video action, and on the right you write the audio portion, including sound effects and music. Corresponding video and audio elements go right next to each other, panel by panel. Some agencies use specially designed sheets of paper 8 1/2 by 11 inches, with boxes down the center for rough sketches of the video portion (Exhibit 19.4). For presentations, most agencies use full size TV storyboards. Write copy in a friendly, conversational style. If you use an off-camera announcer, make certain that his or her dialogue is keyed to the scenes in your video portion. Though it is not always possible, matching the audio with the video makes a commercial cohesive and more effective. The audio—words, sound effects, or music—in a script is as important as the video portion. They must work together to bring the viewer the message. You need strong copy and sound and strong visuals. All are vital for an effective commercial.

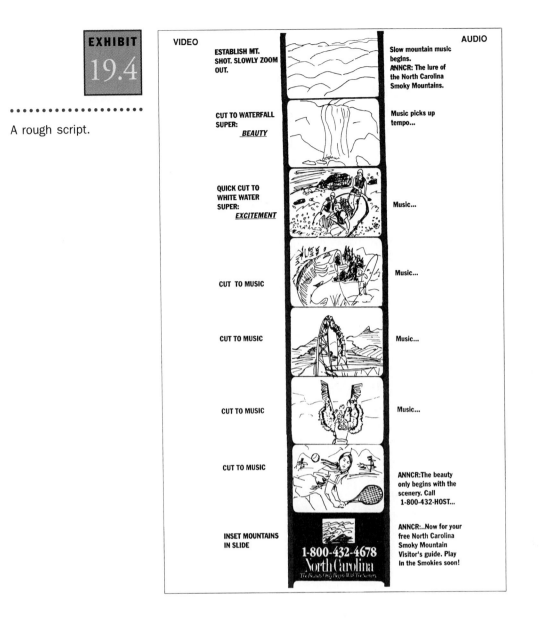

Developing the Storyboard

Once the creative art and copy team has developed a script, the next step is
to create a storyboard, which consists of a series of sketches showing key
scenes developed in the script. It is a helpful tool for discussing the concept
with other agency or client personnel, who may not know the background
or who may not be able to visualize a script accurately. Without a storyboard,
each individual may interpret the script's visuals differently.

It is extremely difficult, if not impossible, to visualize the look of a finished
commercial from the storyboard. Director Jim Edwards says, "The hardest
thing to do in directing is to make someone understand your vision before
you actually make the pictures and then it's too late. Most people [clients,
account people] are very literal minded and don't work well with their imaginations"—and that's what a storyboard is supposed to help you do. Of course,
the quality of the storyboards varies from virtual stick figures in limbo to full-

color drawings. Keep in mind that in this limited medium it is difficult to show all the details that are necessary to understand for production purposes.

Storyboards consist of two frames for each scene. The top frame represents the TV screen (visual). The bottom frame carries a description of the video (as per script) and the audio for that sequence (some storyboards carry only the audio portion). The number of sets of frames varies from commercial to commercial and is not necessarily dictated by the length of the commercial. There may be 4 to 12 or more sets of frames, depending on the nature of the commercial and the demands of the client for detail.

The ratio of width to depth on the TV screen is 4 by 3. There is no standard-size storyboard frame, although a common size is 4 by 3 inches (Exhibit 19.5 illustrates the 4:3 ratio of a TV screen).

The storyboard is a practical step between the raw script and actual production. It gives the agency, client, and production house personnel a common visual starting point for their discussion. Upon client approval, the storyboard goes into production.

Other Elements of the Commercial

Opticals. Most commercials contain more than a single scene. Optical devices or effects between scenes are necessary to provide smooth visual continuity from scene to scene. They are inserted during the final editing stage. The actual opticals may be one of the director's functions. However, these are used to aid in the transition of getting from one scene to the next scene or establishing a visual. Sometimes which technique depends on the importance of a particular scene or the detail that needs to be seen. Exhibit 19.6 illustrates some very basic optical decisions. Among the most common are the following:

CUT. One scene simply cuts into the next. It is the fastest scene change because it indicates no time lapse whatsoever. A cut is used to indicate si-

EXHIBIT
19.5

Slides of TV frame showing the 4:3 ratio of TV screen.

EXHIBIT

19.6

. . . .

Examples of camera
directions.

ECU - An Extreme Close Up shows, for example, person's lips, nose, eyes.

CU - The Close Up is a tight shot, but showing face on entire package for emphasis.

MCU - The Medium Close Up cuts to person about chest, usually showing some background.

MS - The Medium Shot shows the person from the waist up. Commonly used shot. Shows much more detail of setting or background than MCU.

LS - Long Shot. Scene shown from a distance, used to establish location.

multaneous action, to speed up action, and for variety. It keeps one scene from appearing on the screen too long.

DISSOLVE. An overlapping effect is which one scene fades out while the following scene simultaneously fades in. Dissolves are slower than cuts. There are fast dissolves and slow dissolves. Dissolves are used to indicate a short lapse of time in a given scene, or to move from one scene to another where the action is either simultaneous with the action in the first scene or occurring very soon after the preceding action.

FADE-IN. An effect in which the scene actually "fades" into vision from total black (black screen).

FADE-OUT. This is opposite of a fade-in. The scene "fades" into total black. If days, months, or years elapse between one sequence of action and the next, indicate "Fade out . . . fade in."

MATTE. Part of one scene is placed over another so that the same narrator, for example, is shown in front of different backgrounds.

SUPER. The superimposition of one scene or object over another. The title or product can be "supered" over the scene.

WIPE. The new scene "wipes" off the previous scene from top or bottom or side to side with a geometric pattern (Exhibit 19.7). A wipe is faster than a dissolve but not as fast as a cut. A wipe does not usually connote lapse of

EXHIBIT

19.7

· · · · · · · · · · · · · · · · · · · ·

Optical examples.

time as a dissolve or fade-out does. There are several types of wipes: *flip* (the entire scene turns over like the front and back of a postcard), *horizontal* (left to right or right to left), vertical (top to bottom or bottom to top), *diagonal, closing door* (in from both sides), *bombshell* (a burst into the next scene), iris (a circle that grows bigger is an *iris out*), *fan* (fans out from center screen), *circular* (sweeps around the screen—also called *clock wipe*). Wipes are most effective when a rapid succession of short or quick scenes is desired, or to separate impressionistic shots when these are grouped together to produce a montage effect.

ZOOM. A smooth, sometimes rapid move from a long shot to a close-up or from a close-up to a long shot.

Soundtrack. The audio portion of the commercial may be recorded either during the film or videotape shooting or at an earlier or later time in a recording studio. When the soundtrack is recorded during the shooting, the actual voices of the people speaking on camera are used in the commercial. If the soundtrack is recorded in advance, the film or videotape scenes can be shot to fit the copy points as they occur; or if music is part of the track, visual action can be matched to a specific beat. If shooting and editing take place before the soundtrack is recorded, the track can be tailored to synchronize with the various scenes (see sound studio in Exhibit 19.8).

Music. Music has the ability to communicate feelings and moods in a unique way. As a result, the use of music can make or break a TV commercial. In some commercials, it is every bit as important as the copy or visuals. It is often used as background to the announcer's copy or as a song or jingle that is integral to the ad.

Here are some ways you can put music to work:[3]

- **Backgrounds.** In many commercials, background music is used primarily to contribute to the mood. Appropriate music can be used to establish the setting; then it can fade and become soft in the background (Exhibit 19.10).

- **Transitions.** Music can be an effective transition device to carry viewers from one setting to another. The music may start out being sedate as the scene is peaceful. As it switches to the product being used, the music changes to rock and the tempo builds, marking the transition from place to place.

- **Movement.** Sound effects (SFX), natural sounds, and music can contribute to movement. Music that moves up the scale, or down, supports something or someone moving up or down.

- **Accents.** Music can punctuate points or actions. The "beat" of the music and visuals can match to hold viewers' attention and drive the commercial. Musical sounds—as little as a single note—can attract attention.

American music tastes are broadening, according to the National Endowment of the Arts and the Census Bureau. When people were asked to name the kind of music they liked best, country/western music ranked first by 21 percent of adults, followed by rock (14 percent), gospel/hymns (9 percent), mood/easy listening (9 percent), classical (6 percent), and jazz (5 percent).

EXHIBIT 19.8

A modern sound studio.

(Courtesy: Bob Green Productions.)

[3]"Music—How to Use It for Commercial Production." Television Bureau of Advertising, New York.

Yet one-third of adults said they liked classical and jazz artists, and that represents about 60 million people. The top five musical genres are liked by 40 to 50 percent of the adult population, or between 72 and 96 million people.

The most evident trend in America's musical tastes is a hefty increase in the popularity of blues, rhythm and blues, and soul music. Rock increased in popularity over the past 10 years, from 35 percent to 44 percent.

Whatever the tone of the music, it can help transfer drama, love, happiness, or other feelings to the viewer. It is a tool to cue the viewer's feelings. Original music can be written and scored for the commercial, or licensing of old or popular songs can be obtained, which can be very expensive. The least expensive music is stock music and is sold by stock music companies. It is cheap because it is not exclusive.

PRODUCING THE TV COMMERCIAL

The job of converting the approved storyboard is done by TV production. There are three distinct stages to this process:

■ *Preproduction* includes casting, wardrobing, designing sets or building props, finding a location or studio, and meeting with agency, client, and production house personnel.

■ *Shooting* encompasses the work of filming or videotaping all scenes in the commercial. In fact, several takes are made of each scene.

■ *Postproduction,* also known as editing, completion, or finishing, includes selecting scenes from among those shots, arranging them in the proper order, inserting transitional effects, adding titles, combining sound with picture, and delivering the finished commercial.

In charge of production is the producer, who combines the talents of coordinator, diplomat, watchdog, and businessperson. Some producers are on the staffs of large agencies or advertisers. Many work on a free-lance basis. The work of a producer is so all-embracing that the best way to describe it is to live through the entire production process. Let's do that first and pick up the details of the producer's job in the section headed "Role of the Producer."

Let's begin with the problems of shooting the spot, for which a director is appointed by the producer.

The Director's Function

TV Director

The person who casts and rehearses a commercial and is the key person in the shooting of the commercial.

The key person in the shooting, the director takes part in casting and directing the talent, directs the cameraperson in composing each picture, assumes responsibility for the setting, and puts the whole show together. A director of a regional commercial will earn about $7,500 per day, and national commercial directors average about $13,000 per commercial; however, better-known directors may demand $25,000–$35,000 per spot.

The Bidding Process

There is only one way to provide specifications for a commercial shoot when you are seeking bids from production companies, and that is in writing. There is an industry accepted form (AICP Bid and Specification Form). Information for this form is provided by the agency and client. The use of this form ensures that all production companies are provided with identical job specifications for estimating production costs. It ensures that all bids are based on the same information.

The Preproduction Process

A preproduction meeting must be held prior to every production. The agency producer is expected to chair this meeting. The following agency, client, and production company personnel usually attend:

> Agency: producer, creative team, account supervisor
> Client: brand manager or advertising manager
> Production company: director, producer, others as needed

The following points should be covered at every preproduction meeting: direction, casting, locations and/or sets, wardrobe and props, product, special requirements, final script, legal/claims contingencies, timetable update.

In addition to covering the points listed above, the creative team and the director will likely present shooting boards and the production thinking behind the commercial. The shooting boards should be used for the following purposes:

- **To determine camera angles**

- **To determine best product angles**

- **To project camera and cast movement and help determine talent status (extra vs. principal)**

- **To determine number of scenes to be shot**

- **To determine timing of each scene**

ROLE OF THE PRODUCER
Agency Producer

The producer's role begins before the approval of the storyboard. Conferring with the copywriter and/or art director, the producer becomes thoroughly familiar with every frame of the storyboard.

1. The producer prepares the "specs," or specifications—the physical production requirements of the commercial—in order to provide the production studios with the precise information they require to compute realistic bids. Every agency prepares its own estimate form. The estimate form shown in Exhibit 19.9 gives an excellent idea of the chief elements of such estimates. In addition, many advertisers request a further breakdown of the cost of items such as preproduction, shooting, crew, labor, studio, location travel and expenses, equipment, film, props and wardrobe, payroll taxes, studio makeup, direction, insurance, editing.

2. The producer contacts the studios that have been invited to submit bids based on their specialties, experience, and reputation; meets with them either separately or in one common "bid session"; and explains the storyboard and the specs in detail.

EXHIBIT

19.9

· · · · · · · · · · · · · · · · · · ·

An estimate sheet for a commercial.

BROADCAST PRODUCTION ESTIMATE

Client _____ Code _____ Job Code _____

Product _____ Code _____ Job Name _____

Media ☐ Radio   ☐ Television

WORK CODE	WORK CATEGORY	ESTIMATED COST	
A5	Pre-Production		
B2	Production		
B3	Animation		
C4	Artwork		
C6	Color Corr Prod		
D4	Record Studio		
D7	Sound Track		
E2	Talent & P + W		
E5	Tlnt Trvl & Exp		
F3	Music		
F4	Musicians (AFM)		
G2	Editorial		
G5	Vtr/Film Trnsfr		
G7	Cassettes		
G9	Prints & Tapes		
H9	Miscellaneous (Com)		
	COMM SUB-TOTAL		
S2	BBDO Trvl & Exp		
S5	Casting at BBDO		
S8	Contingency		
S9	Weather Contingency		
T3	Handling		
T6	Shipping		
T9	Miscellaneous (Non-com)		
V3	Pyrl Tax & Hndlg		
V5	NY Sales Tax		
V6	NJ Sales Tax		
	N/C SUB-TOTAL		
	COMMISSION		
	GROSS TOTAL		

ESTIMATED BY

APPROVALS

Producer _____ Date

Acct. Exec. _____ Date

Client _____ Date

DATE INPUT

INPUT BY

COMPETITIVE BIDS

1. _____ $ _____

2. _____ $ _____

3. _____ $ _____

RECOMMENDED CONTRACTOR

RECOMMENDED EDITOR

COMMERCIAL ID. No.	TITLE	LENGTH	COLOR	35mm	16mm	VTR
1.						
2.						
3.						
4.						
5.						
6.						

Further explanation of charges by work category _____

_____

_____

_____

PROD 857 5/80 REV.

(Courtesy: BBDO.)

3. The production house estimates expenses after studying specs, production timetable and storyboard. Generally, a 35 percent markup is added to the estimated out-of-pocket expenses to cover overhead and studio profit. Usually, the production company adds a 10 percent contingency fee to the bid for unforeseen problems. The bids are submitted. The producer analyzes the bids and recommends the studio to the client.

4. The producer arranges for equipment. The studio may own equipment such as cameras and lights, but more often it rents all equipment for a job. The crew is also freelance, hired by the day. Although the studio's primary job is to shoot the commercial, it can also take responsibility for editorial work. For videotape, a few studios own their own cameras and production units; others rent these facilities.

5. Working through a talent agency, the producer arranges, or has the production company arrange, auditions. Associates also attend auditions, at which they and the director make their final choices of performers. The client may also be asked to pass on the final selection.

6. The producer then participates in the preproduction meeting. At this meeting the producer, creative associates, account executive, and client, together with studio representatives and director, lay final plans for production.

7. During the shooting, the producer usually represents both the agency and the client as the communicator with the director. On the set or location, the creative people and client channel any comments and suggestions through the producer to avoid confusion.

8. It is the producer's responsibility to arrange for the recording session. Either before or after shooting and editing, he or she arranges for the soundtrack, which may call for an announcer, actors, singers, and musicians. If music is to be recorded, the producer will have had preliminary meetings with the music contractor.

9. The producer participates in the editing along with the creative team. Editing begins after viewing the dailies and selecting the best takes.

10. The producer arranges screenings for agency associates and clients to view and approve the commercials at various editing stages and after completion of the answer print.

11. Finally, the producer handles the billings and approves studio and other invoices for shooting, editing, and payment to talent.

The "Outside" Producer

This is the person representing a production company whose entire business is filmmaking. He or she is hired by the agency producer to create the TV commercial according to agency specifications.

Outside Producer
The production company person who is hired by the agency to create the commercial according to agency specifications.

Shooting

Most productions consist of the following steps:

PRELIGHT: This is simply the day (or days) used to set the lighting for specific scenes. To do this exclusively on shoot days would tie up the entire crew.

SHOOTING: This phase of the production process is the filming (or taping) of the approved scenes for the commercial. These scenes are then "screened" the next day (dailies) to ensure that the scene was captured as planned.

WRAP: This signals the completion of production. It is at this stage that most of the crew is released.

EDITING: This takes place after the shoot is completed. Scenes are screened and selected for use in the commercial. The scenes are then merged with a soundtrack, titles, and opticals to comprise a completed or finished commercial.

In shooting a commercial for their PoFolks restaurants, Folks, Inc. had to shoot part of the commercial before the store had to open. This meant careful planning with the production company so the commercial could be shot between 6:00 a.m. and 10:00 a.m. Sounds like a long time but it isn't. Exhibit 19.10 shows the production crew unloading equipment at daybreak for the location shooting for the in-store shots of the commercial. Exhibit 19.11 shows the shooting of food shots in a studio environment. Of course, the location and studio shots had to be edited into a finished commercial. Exhibit 19.12 shows video stills from the finished TV commercial.

The role of the client and account service at the shoot is one of adviser. It's really the creative's day and it's their responsibility to deliver the spot. In situations where the client needs to provide input on the set, the prime contact is the account representative or agency producer. The producer is generally the liaison between the agency and the director. This chain of command is simple and direct and eliminates confusion on the set, which is an absolute necessity when shooting.

Postproduction Process

Postproduction begins after a production company exposes the film in the camera at your "shoot." The film that comes out of the camera must be developed in a chemical bath and then printed onto a new strip of positive film called the "dailies." The editor then screens these "dailies" and selects the good takes from the day's shooting.

The editor then physically splices the takes selected from each scene together with the next to create a "rough cut," which is a rough rendition of the finished commercial. Once the editor has cut this film and the agency and client approve the cut, the editor takes the original film that was shot and developed and pulls the takes from that film that matches his selected workprint takes.

• • • • • • • • • • • • • • • • • •

The crew unloading equipment at daybreak for the location shooting at a PoFolks restaurant.

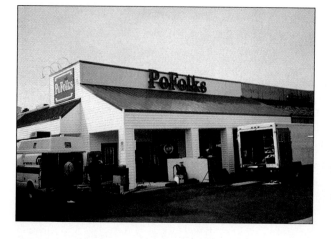

(Courtesy: Folks, Inc.)

EXHIBIT

19.11

The production crew and creative team preparing to shoot food shots in a studio where they have more control of the lighting, and view a TV monitor to see results of taping.

EXHIBIT

19.12

WHAT'S YOUR PLEASURE?
GRILLED·BAKED·FRIED

PoFolks

Today, virtually all final edits, effects, and opticals are done on videotape. The original camera film takes (35mm motion picture film) are transferred electronically to one-inch videotape. During this transfer of film to videotape, the color is corrected.

The editor then takes this material into a video edit where each take is run on videotape and the "cut-in" through "cut-out" points for each take are laid down in sequence, from the first frame of the first scene to the end frame of that scene (to match the workprint), until the entire commercial is laid down from the color-corrected videotape matter (called the "unedited tape master"). Titles and other special effects are added during this final unedited-tape-to-edited-tape session. The sound (which the editor and agency had worked on along with the picture) is then electronically relayed onto the video-edited master, and the spot is finished. Sound complicated? It is.

Postdirectors are independent contractors in the production mix. They are in their own business of cutting film and creatively supervising videotape transfers from film; supervising video edits and special effects; recording narration, sound, music, and sound effects; mixing these sounds together; relaying them onto the picture; and delivering a finished product to the agency.

Computer Postproduction Technology

The computer is, and has been, revolutionizing some aspects of print production and prepress activities and is also active in revolutionizing TV postproduction. Advances in hardware and software are continuing to change the creation and production of TV commercials. Names like Silicon Graphics, Avid, Wavefront, Flame, Quantel's Henry and Harry have been mainstays for a number of years. Terms like 3-D animation, compositing, morphing, 2D animation, nonlinear editing, live-action compositing, and real-time are common among the professionals who generate visual images and special effects. The systems used in the early 1990s to produce the video magic could cost $25,000 to $250,000. Today, Macintosh offers many of the same video effects to more producers of commercials at lower costs. As usual, when discussing computer hardware and software, each system has a plus and a minus; but the availability offers more creative and production people more options to create unique visuals and commercials. We won't attempt to define all of these options, but we'll give you a quick tour.

Computer generated imagery (CGI)
Technology allowing computer operators to create multitudes of electronic effects for TV—to squash, stretch, or squeeze objects— much more quickly than earlier tools could. It can add layers of visuals simultaneously.

It is safe to say that today's computer-generated imagery (CGI) offers creative minds great new opportunities in production and postproduction. This technology allows creative people to squash, squeeze, stretch, and morph objects in less time than ever before. Computers are turning live action into cartoon action. At production facilities, creative talents can use digital-graphics/animation-compositing systems to top four or five layers of live action with five or six layers of graphics, all simultaneously, allowing the finished visual composite to be seen as it develops. A Toronto-based software artist says, "The big issue facing artists merging live video and computer graphics is the compatibility and recreation of the real world into the digital world."[4]

---

[4]Beth Jacques, "Industry Report: Live Action Animation." *Millimeter,* April 1994, p. 84.

Let's look at a few of these electronic production tools and techniques.

Morphing. Morphing is an industry term for metamorphosing that means to transform from one object to another. For example, in a Schick shaving spot, a man's head is turned into a 3-D cube, and for Exxon a car turns into a tiger. This computer graphics technique allows its operator to move between the real world and computer graphics by electronically layering visual transitions between live action.

The cost of morphs varies, as they can range from $5,000 for a *garage* job using via PC, up to $70,000, depending on the complexity. But meticulous advance planning remains the key to a successful job. A Schick shaving heads commercial, which morphed a series of six talking shaving heads and upper torsos, required a two-day blue-screen shoot, composited over a bathroom background.[5]

Harry. The Quantel Henry/Harry on-line system is an editing device with an optical device tied to it. It allows computer composites to mix with live video. Ninety percent of Harry work can be created on a Macintosh. The Harry is faster and much more expensive, but the Mac appears to be closing the gap quickly with its Apple RISC-based PowerPC.

Flame. On the other hand, flame is an optical device with an editing device tied to it. It functions as a high-capacity, random-access, multilayer compositing system, with video editing/effects/digital-audio capacity. So you can see that you have to have the right technology for the right job. And, yes, it can be confusing to the nonproduction person in the advertising industry.

Letterbox. Letterboxing is a fairly simple process. Basically, you put up a 1.85:1 ratio mask on the screen, creating a box surrounding the visual image. It's almost like a wipe. It has been a staple of music videos for some time. At times, this technique borrows interest from the cinema. A Mazda Mania commercial parodies a feature-film trailer. It is more or less a spoof of the 1960s cinema, Cinemascope.

In-house Desktop. During the early 1990s, agencies could use their in-house Macintosh computers to interface with video composers. This made video editing, long the domain of highly trained specialists, a viable in-house option. This allowed the agency personnel to cut and paste video images just as desktop computers cut and paste print graphics. The quality isn't quite the level of the production houses' hardware/software, but it is getting closer and allows agencies to cut costs and use them for producing the storyboard, the animatic for testing, and rough cuts and then send the disc to the production company, where the spot is polished into a final commercial of broadcast quality. Those clients that do not need top-quality images can complete the entire commercial postproduction process on the system.

CONTROLLING THE COST OF COMMERCIAL PRODUCTION

The cost of producing a TV commercial is of deep concern to both the agency and the advertiser. The chief reason that money is wasted in commercials is

---

[5]Beth Jacques "The Do's and Don'ts of Mixing Animation and Live Action," *Millimeter,* April 1994, pp. 77–82.

inadequate preplanning. In production, the two major cost items are labor and equipment. Labor—the production crew, director, and performers—is hired by the day, and equipment is rented by the day. If a particular demonstration was improperly rehearsed, if a particular prop was not delivered, or if the location site was not scouted ahead of time, the shooting planned for one day may be forced into expensive overtime or into a second day. These costly mistakes can be avoided by careful planning.

Cost Relationships

Here are several areas that can have a dramatic impact on TV production costs:

Location or Studio. Is the commercial planned for studio or location? Location shoots, outside geographic zones, mean travel time and overnight accommodations for the crew, adding a minimum average cost of $7,500 per away day.

Style. By style we mean the extent of propping, wardrobe and ambiance—*fancy* or *plain*. It may mean wide camera coverage, song, and dance work, heavy set changes, or lots of cuts.

Talent. The number of principals on the storyboard is important and can be expensive. The more people on-camera in your commercials, the higher the talent residual bill. The rates for talent are based on the Screen Actors Guild (SAG) union contract. For national commercials, you can roughly estimate your talent cost per on-camera principal as .0015 of your media budget for the spot. That is, $15,000 per person per $10 million in exposure. If 20 on-camera people are involved in your spot, expect a $300,000 residual bill. That chunk of your budget may exceed the entire net cost of production. So it is important to discuss how many on-camera principals are planned for the spot and how many are absolutely necessary.

Residual

A sum paid to certain talent on a TV or radio commercial every time the commercial is run after 13 weeks, for the life of the commercial.

Residuals. Another major expense is the *residual,* or reuse fee, paid to performers—announcers, narrators, actors, and singers—in addition to their initial session fees. Under union rules, performers are paid every time the commercial is aired on the networks, the amount of the fee depending upon their scale and the number of cities involved. If a commercial is aired with great frequency, a national advertiser may end up paying more in residuals than for the production of the commercial itself. This problem is less severe for the local advertiser because local rates are cheaper than national rates. The moral is: Cast only the number of performers necessary to the commercial and not one performer more.

The use of extras presents less of a cost issue. The first 30 extras in a spot must be paid a session fee ($232/day) and are not entitled to residuals. Rates for use of extras beyond the first 30 can be negotiated.

Special Effects. If the board indicated the use of special effects or animation (either computer generated or cell), ask how the special effect will be achieved. It is not unusual for complicated computer-generated effects to cost $6,000 to $12,000 per second and more! To prevent surprises, ask questions. What may appear to be a simple execution on the surface may in fact contain extremely expensive elements. Neither the agency nor client should be satisfied until everyone understands the project. Anything short of this can result in surprise creative and expenditures.

Estimate Costs. Given the potential complexity of shooting commercials due to a wide range of factors (location, special rigs, special effects, talent, set construction), it is not uncommon to believe a relatively "simple" looking spot presented in storyboard form will be "relatively" inexpensive. This is simply not the case. Both the client and the agency must always, always require a rough cost for each spot recommended. The number provided will help put the project into focus relative to the planned media support for the commercials. Generally, it is not uncommon for clients to spend 10 percent of their planned media budget in production. As this percentage escalates, the production decision becomes more difficult, particularly in today's economic climate.

Editorial Fee Cost. There is a creative labor fee for the editor's service. This charge is for the editor's and assistant editor's time. Depending on the editor and the difficulty of the edit, a creative fee can range from $400–$500 (to supervise sound only, for example, on a single scene commercial) to over $9,000 to cut a multi-image, complex spot with special effects manipulations and music.

The Cost of Film Transfer and Videotape Conform or Edit and Finishing. This cost can range from about $1,000 for this work, including tape stock and finished materials, to $7,500 for expansive and difficult treatments.

Special Effects and Titling. This cost can range from $100 to make a title art card and include it in the edit session, to $10,000 to $30,000 for heavy design, frame-by-frame, picture manipulations.

Recording and Mixing. The cost of recording and mixing a voice-over, music, and sound effects together can range from $450 to $4,000 or more.

If you total all the above possibilities, from the combined lowest to the combined highest, the cost can be $2,136 to $67,100 to edit a 30-second commercial!

TV Cost Average

An American Association of Advertising Agencies' study indicates that the average national commercial rose to $222,000 to produce. Obviously, there is great variation in producing commercials: Interviews/testimonials averaged $249,000, animation $210,000, and tabletop/products, food averaged $111,000. These figures indicate the importance of producing a TV spot that is on target because the investment simply to get the idea on film or tape is significant.[6] Historically, location shoots take more time than studio shoots; and in 1993, for the first time, more location shoots were done than studio shoots.

Satellite Transmission of Spots

Spot TV commercials can be sent by satellite directly to TV stations. This process can save agencies and the advertiser money on tape duplication and

---

[6]Joe Mandese, "Study Shows Cost of TV Spots," *Advertising Age*, August 1, 1994, p. 32.

MARKETING SITUATION

The Orkin Exterminating Company experienced problems in gaining leads for new customers in the California region. From 1988 to 1991, new leads declined 11 percent in California compared to an increase of 16 percent in the rest of the country.

Feedback from the Orkin field sales force and available research suggested that environmental concerns regarding the use of pesticides were suppressing demand for professional pest control on the West Coast.

In the fall of 1991, new research showed that consumers interpreted Orkin's technological superiority over the competition as an indication that Orkin's service would be more environmentally responsible.

In early 1992, "The Exterminator" campaign was launched in California. This campaign, based on a cyborg character, positions Orkin as the technological leader in professional pest control because research had revealed that high technology translated to safety and effectiveness for the consumer.

CAMPAIGN OBJECTIVES

The objectives were to increase consumer lead growth patterns in California, which has been depressed since 1988. Specifically, the primary objective was to generate lead growth in California In 1992 equal to the rest of the United States, which had been growing at an average rate of 5 percent since 1988 and was projected to grow 5 percent again in 1992.

TARGET AUDIENCE

The primary target market are homeowners aged 25–54. Their homes tend to be very important to them and they invest time and money in maintaining them. They consider having bugs in their house unclean and unhealthy. They also are environmentally conscious but not extremists.

CREATIVE STRATEGY

Orkin's strategy in California was shifted entirely to the *technological leader* positioning. The hope was that the emphasis on advanced technology would prove effective in addressing environmental concerns in California and demonstrate in new customer leads.

TV and radio advertising, public relations, and point-of-sale materials all supported the *technological leader* position, whereas previous Orkin advertising in the California market supported a safety position.

MEDIA STRATEGY

Television was the primary medium in the campaign, supported by radio. Advertising weight was compressed from traditional three- and four-week flights into one-week bursts to maximize impact.

EVIDENCE OF RESULTS

The impact of The Exterminator campaign was immediate. Leads were up 75 percent over previous year levels in March, the first month of the campaign. Total year lead production was up 37 percent in California, well outdistancing the performance in the remainder of the United States (+4 percent).

This performance in 1992 not only exceeded by over nine times the goal of matching remaining U.S. performance; it came very close to bringing California's five-year trend back in line with the rest of the country.

Feedback from the Orkin field sales force has been overwhelmingly positive. The only complaint they have is that they can't get more.

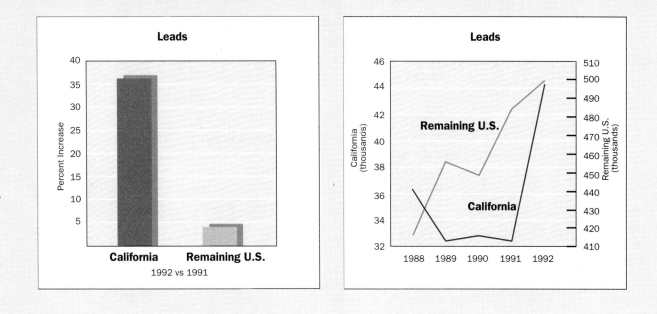

delivery costs. The ad agency delivers a one-inch master to the transmission company uplink office in most major markets, where agency traffic information is entered onto the computer and the commercial is sent by satellite to only those stations specified. Most TV stations have satellite decoders for receiving the spots. The equipment at the station records the commercial on the station's one-inch VTRs and prints hard copy of the traffic instructions for the station.

SUMMARY

Television is the most flexible and creative advertising medium because it uses sight, sound, and motion and has the ability to create emotion. The time to communicate is very short—usually 15 or 30 seconds—and creates a challenge for communicating the product story or position.

For the creator of television commercials there are numerous techniques available: testimonials, demonstrations, spokesperson, comparisons, slice-of-life, customer interviews, humor, animation, problem solution, serials, infomercials, etc. However, it isn't quite as confusing as it may appear because there have been a number of research studies conducted that help advertisers choose which kind of techniques to use.

Storyboards are usually created to help communicate the idea to the advertiser and the production company. It is important for everyone to clearly visualize the same commercial before time and money are invested in the idea.

The act of creating involves understanding production terminology terms such as dissolves, wipes, close ups or long shots help communicate the nature of a particular visual or the transition from one scene to the next. Writing and visualizing the commercial in simple easy-to-understand terms is essential to success—it is, after all, a visual medium. Because a good idea can be destroyed by bad production, producing the finished commercial is just as important as conceiving the "Big Idea." Production involves preproduction, shooting, and postproduction.

Questions

1. What is the problem-solution technique?
2. Contrast the writing of television and print copy.
3. What is a bookend commercial?
4. Who attends the pre-production meetings?
5. What is the role of the "outside" producer?

The Radio Commercial

CHAPTER OBJECTIVES

In print and television, visuals are an integral part of the communication. Radio is a different medium, one for ears alone. After reading this chapter you will understand:

- **The nature of the medium**
- **How to create from a strategy**
- **Structuring the commercial**
- **Writing the commercial**
- **Musical commercials**
- **Producing radio commercials**
- **Unions and talent**

Logic would tell you radio advertising should be easy. All you have to do is talk to someone about the product. Right? Well, maybe. Great radio advertising is very difficult. You need to be able to awaken images in the listener's mind by using sound, music, and voices. You have the opportunity to play with their imagination in what is referred to as **the theater of the mind.**

Theer of the mind

In radio, a writer paints pictures in the mind of the listener through the use of sound.

Canon Computer Systems used radio to create awareness among those people ready to buy a printer for their Canon Bubble Jet 200. The voice of Kelsey Grammar, who plays Frasier Crane on *Frasier,* was used to invite listeners to envision the superior printing quality and compact size of the product. "Now watch closely as I turn it on," he told listeners. "See how quiet the Bubble Jet 200 is? . . . the final test is to see the document it's created. Look. C'est magnifique." Grammar then invites the listener to "see the printer you saw on radio."

THE NATURE OF THE MEDIUM

In print and television, visual images can be powerful in attracting attention and full of emotion. Obviously, radio is different. There is no visual or color or boldness to attract people to the communication. Yet sound messages can be powerful. Some copywriters might even argue radio is the most visual medium. So let's look at the medium.

In Chapter 9, radio was said to offer more than other advertising media. It has the flexibility, the marketability, the promotionability, and the price to fit advertisers' needs to reach their targets—if they choose the right stations and use the right message.

There are more than 20 primary programming formats for the more than 9,000 radio stations allowing listeners and advertisers many choices, including country, hot country, adult contemporary, news/talk/sports/business, oldies, top 40 (CHR), religion, adult standards, Spanish, soft adult contemporary, rock, classic rock, urban rhythm and blues, southern gospel, contemporary Christian, easy listening, alternative rock, black gospel, urban adult contemporary, rhythm and blues oldies, variety, ethnic, classical, gospel, jazz and new age, and preteen. This makes radio a highly selective medium for the advertiser. In reflecting the ethnic multinational nature of our society, there are many foreign-language stations in many markets available to advertisers.

CREATING THE COMMERCIAL

Even though radio requires a different style of advertising, ads are developed through a thought process similar to that used in other media. You have to understand your target. As Tom Little, award-winning creative director, once said, "People don't buy products. They buy solutions to problems." Last year people bought about 350,000 1/4-inch drill bits in this country. People didn't want 1/4-inch drill bits. They wanted 1/4-inch holes. The radio creative writer has to refer back to the objectives and strategy and describe the target in both demographic and psychographic terms before beginning the creative process. The writer needs to be sure the message is going to be believed, that it says the right things to the right people, and needs to ask if the copy strengthens the brand position—the place you want to occupy in the consumer's mind. Is it credible? Do you have all the copy points that your research indicates is needed? Is it human? Is it believable communication? Do people really talk like that? Or is it simply copy lingo? These are some of the things the radio copywriter must think about when sitting down to the blank page or computer screen.

The writer for radio has the opportunity to develop an entire commercial alone (although in some agencies a creative team may work on a project). That means writing the script, picking the talent, and producing the commercial. In radio, the copywriter enjoys the freedom to create scenes in the theater of the listener's imagination by painting pictures in sound—a car starting or stopping, a phone ringing, water running, ice cubes falling into a glass, crowds roaring, a camera clicking. Remember, sound alone has an extraordinary ability to enter people's minds.

Let's look at three elements the copywriter uses to create mental pictures, memorability, and emotion: words, sound, and music.

Words

Words are the basic building blocks of effective radio commercials. They are used to describe the product, grab attention, create interest, build desire, and evoke a response from the listener. The warmth of the human voice may be all that is needed to communicate your message.

Sound

Used properly, sound can unlock the listener's imagination and create feelings. Any sound effect used should be necessary and recognizable; you should never have to explain it for the audience.

The sound has to convey a special message or purpose; it has to attract attention and complement the words. Sound can be used to underscore a point; create feelings of suspense, excitement, or anger; and invoke almost any mood you desire.

There are three basic sources of sound effects: manual, recorded, and electronic. *Manual effects* are those that are produced live, either with live subjects or with studio props; opening doors, footsteps, and blowing horns are examples. *Recorded effects* are available from records, tapes, or professional sound libraries. They offer the copywriter almost every conceivable sound— dogs barking, cats meowing, leaves blowing, thunder crashing, cars racing. *Electronic effects* are sounds that are produced electronically on special studio equipment. Any sound created by using a device that generates an electrical impulse or other electronic sound is an electrical effect.

Music

Music can be very powerful in catching the listener's attention and evoking feelings. Not for nothing has music been called the "universal language." Different kinds of music appeal to different emotions: A minor is sadder than a major key; an increased tempo creates a sense of anticipation.

Commercials are often set to music especially composed for them or adapted from a familiar song. A few bars of distinctive music played often enough may serve to identify the product instantly. Such a musical logotype usually lasts from 4 to 10 seconds. Jingles are a popular means of making a slogan memorable—think of the music for Coca-Cola, Pepsi, Chevrolet, Oldsmobile, and McDonald's over the years.

Create from Strategy

As with other ads, radio commercials are created from a written strategy. PoFolks family restaurants, basically a southern chain, had specialized in fried foods since its inception. As many people changed their eating habits away from fried foods, PoFolks lost its customer base. As a result, over time it changed its menu to include other tasty dishes, some grilled and others baked. As a matter of fact, after fried chicken, its vegetable plate was usually the number two seller. Research indicated that many potential customers didn't realize this change in menu and still perceived PoFolks as a place only to get fried meats and fried vegetables. Out of this research, Karen Elliott, of Folks, Inc. (PoFolks largest franchisee), director of marketing, wrote and developed an advertising and promotional campaign focusing on *Grilled-Baked-Fried.* The campaign communicated to consumers that grilled, baked, and fried foods were available. Exhibit 20.1 shows the basic 60-second commercial with three different tags: one featuring the grilled-baked-fried theme, another featuring its new vegetables, and a third that reminded consumers about the holiday catering.

Diet Coke ran a nationwide radio contest in more than 130 markets for a free lunch with Lucky Vanous, the hunky star of the Diet Coke Break TV commercial, who played a construction worker ogled by a group of female office workers every morning at 11:30 as he drank a Diet Coke. The contest idea came from consumers who called Coca-Cola for more information about the actor. Coca-Cola integrated the promotion further by having Mr. Vanous appear at a number of retail outlets to greet his fans.

DEVELOPING THE RADIO SCRIPT

You will find some differences in the formats used in the script examples in this chapter. This is because most agencies have their own format sheets for copywriters to use. Formats also vary according to how the script will be used: If you are going to be in the studio with the producers and talents, you can verbally explain how the script is to be read or answer any questions that come up. If, however, you are going to mail the script to DJs to be read live, you need to be certain that anyone reading it will understand exactly what you want. The guidelines shown in Exhibit 20.2 illustrate explicit script directions.

STRUCTURING THE COMMERCIAL

There are no hard-and-fast rules about the structure of a radio commercial, but most radio spots contain an introduction, or intro (the attention-getter), product benefits, and close. The following thoughts have been selected from the NAB *Guidelines for Radio Copywriting.*[1]

It is important to grab the attention of the listener in the first few seconds of the spot. The intro can take the form of a sound effect, a statement, a question, a promise, a benefit, or a number of other methods that will make the audience listen for more. Here are a few techniques to accomplish this:

---

[1]Reed Bunzel, *Guidelines for Radio Copywriting* (National Association of Broadcasters, 1982), p. 18.

EXHIBIT

20.1

· · · · · · · · · · · · · · · · · · ·

POFOLKS
GRILLED-BAKED-FRIED RADIO
:60
#FIK-009-60

MUSIC INTRO

ANNOUNCER:	What's your pleasure, Atlanta?
VOICE (1):	Pofolks' tender, juicy chicken breasts grilled over an open flame.
VOICE (2):	Aw, sometimes simple pleasures are the best. like pofolks' *baked* chicken.
VOICE (3):	Now hold on! I say stick with a tried and true favorite. Everybody knows PoFolks serves "Atlanta's best" *fried* chicken.
VOICE (1):	Grilled!
VOICE (2):	Baked!
VOICE (3):	Fried!
ANNOUNCER:	Whatever your pleasure, we've got the recipe for you. Fresh from the oven, skillet, or grill, we're cooking all your hearty, homestyle favorites with lots of choices. Grilled, baked, fried and *always* a value. Come on over and let us please you at today's PoFolks.

MUSIC OUT

ANNOUNCER:

TAG A - GBF (:04)

The choice is yours! Grilled, baked, or fried! We've got your pleasure!

TAG B - NEW VEGETABLES (:08)

Try our newest vegetables—baked squash and broccoli and rice casserole. They're made-from-scratch and served-to-please.

TAB C - HOLIDAY CATERING (:08)

If you enjoy *eating* more than *cooking* during the holidays, call 874-5555. Hearty, homestyle favorites for all your holiday occasions.

(Courtesy: PoFolks.)

■ *Expand on your intro and work it into part of the selling offer:* A sound effect can be used to grab attention and then inserted throughout the spot to build interest in the product. A comparison between the quiet purr of a SuperMo lawn mower and an old clickety-clack model, for example, can have great appeal.

■ *Describe one fundamental aspect of the product:* "A new SuperMo garden mower comes with a free lawn chair to relax in because it takes you half the time to cut your grass."

■ *Emphasize the benefits of owning the product:* "If you get your lawn mowed Saturday morning, you have time to golf all afternoon."

EXHIBIT
20.2

Example of radio form
directions.

CLIENT: Wild corporation
Length: :60
Job No. 3364

LEFT SECTION OF PAGE IS FOR INFORMATION RELATING TO VOICES, ANNOUNCER, MUSIC, SOUND, USUALLY IN CAPS.	The right section of the script consists of copy and directions. It should be typed double-spaced. Pause is indicated by dots (. . .) or double dash (— —). Underline or use CAPS for emphasis.
MUSIC:	Music is usually indicated by all caps. WILLIAM TELL OVERTURE ESTABLISH AND FADE UNDER. In some cases, music is underlined. Directions may be indicated by parentheses ( ).
VOICE #1	(LAUGHING LOUDLY) Excuse me sir . . .
OLD MAN	Yes . . . (RAISING VOICE) What do you *want?*
SFX:	SUPERMARKET NOISES, CRASHING NOISES AS SHOPPING CARTS CRASH. Sound effects indicated by SFX: (:08) BUZZER
SINGERS:	He's bright-eyed and bushy-tailed . . .
ANNCR:	This indicates announcer talking.
VO:	Voice Over.

- *Explain the selling points that deliver the desired benefits:* "The SuperMo mower comes with a grass catcher lined with disposable garbage bags to make your job easier."

- *Demonstrate the enjoyment that comes from ownership:* "The SuperMo is so much fun you won't let anyone else use it."

- *Illustrate the disadvantages of not owning the product:* "Everyone on the block owns a SuperMo except the Willetts. And you can't see their house for the grass."

Every spot should close with an invitation to act, the product theme, the solution to the problem set, or a punch line. The more effective the close, the more effective the spot. Therefore, the close should be set up powerfully, progressing logically from one step to the next. Examples of closings:

- *Provide good reasons for buying:* "Tired of paying the kid down the block twenty bucks for cutting your grass? Buy a SuperMo and cut it yourself."

- *Explain how easy it is to buy and select the product:* "Over 50 SuperMo models to choose from at over 1,500 dealers coast to coast. Call 1-800-555-MOWER for the nearest dealer."

WRITING THE COMMERCIAL

Some agencies now have a special creative director who is in charge of radio advertising. For years, the feeling has been that agencies have assigned junior talent to write radio commercials. It is now hoped that having a specific person in charge of radio will generate enthusiasm for doing great radio. Backer Spielvogel Bates has a radio creative director with the responsibility of finding new opportunities to use radio as well as pulling together agency creatives to develop radio ideas.

There are radio boutiques that have been used for years by clients and agencies to help create and produce radio commercials. Some of the most popular boutiques include Dick Orkin's Radio Ranch, Los Angeles; Chuck Blore & Don Richman, Inc., Hollywood; Bert, Barz & Co., Hollywood; and Joy Radio, New York.

Like the TV commercial, the radio commercial has as its basic ingredient the promise of a significant and distinctive benefit. Once the promise has been determined, you are ready to use your arsenal of words and sounds to communicate your product message. Here are some ways to vitalize the copy.

Simplicity.   The key to producing a good radio commercial is to build around one central idea. Avoid confusing the listener with too many copy points. Use known words, short phrases, simple sentence structure. Keep in mind that the copy needs to be conversational. Write for the *ear*, not the eye. Get in the habit of reading your copy out loud.

Clarity.   Keep the train of thought on one straight track. Avoid side issues. Delete unnecessary words. (Test: Would the commercial be hurt if the words were deleted? If not, take them out.) Write from draft to draft until your script becomes unmistakably clear and concise. At the end of the commercial, your audience should understand exactly what you've tried to say. Despite having several facts in your commercial, make sure you have the Big Idea.

Coherence.   Be certain that your message flows in logical sequence from first word to last, using smooth transitional words and phrases for easier listening.

Rapport.   Remember, as far as your listeners are concerned, you are speaking only to them. Try to use a warm, personal tone, as if you were talking to one or two people. Make frequent use of the word *you*. Address the listeners in terms they would use themselves.

Pleasantness.   It is not necessary to entertain simply for the sake of entertaining, but there is no point in being dull or obnoxious. Strike a happy medium; talk as one friend to another about the product or service.

Believability.   Every product has its good points. Tell the truth about it. Avoid overstatements and obvious exaggerations; they are quickly spotted and defeat the whole purpose of the commercial. Be straightforward; you want to convey the impression of being a trusted friend.

Interest.   Nothing makes listeners indifferent faster than a boring commercial. Products and services are not fascinating in themselves; it is the way you present them that makes them interesting. Try to give your customer some useful information as a reward for listening.

Distinctiveness.   Sound different from other commercials and set your product apart. Use every possible technique—a fresh approach, a musical phrase, a particular voice quality or sound effect—to give your commercial a distinct character.

Compulsion. Inject your commercial with a feeling of urgency. The first few seconds are critical; this is when you capture or lose the listener's attention. Direct every word toward moving the prospect closer to wanting the product. During the last 10 seconds, repeat your promise of benefit and register the name of your product. And do not forget to urge the listener to act without delay. (It is surprising how many commercials do not do this.)

David Fowler, a copywriter with the Richards Group, was writing a script for Motel 6 based upon this strategy: Let's make people feel as if they are smart to stay at Motel 6 because they do not need all the stuff that other motels charge for. The scripts were written in the language of ordinary people who use motels: truckdrivers, traveling salespeople, families on the road with their kids. Fowler had heard Tom Bodett reading an essay on National Public Radio and thought he had an interesting voice. Bodett was a carpenter and writer living in Homer, Alaska. Fowler sent Bodett some scripts because he thought his voice would appeal to the Heartland of America. Bodett agreed to do the commercials and a classic radio campaign was born. The original spots ended with "I'm Tom Bodett for Motel 6." Later spots ended with "I'm Tom Bodett for Motel 6 and we'll leave the light on for you."

Some Techniques

Basically a medium of words, radio—more than any other medium—relies heavily on the art of writing strong copy. However, just as print ads and TV commercials include pictures and graphics to add impact to the copy, radio creates mental pictures with other techniques. Radio copywriters can choose among many proven techniques to give more meaning to the copy, to help gain the attention of the busy target audience and hold that attention for the duration of the commercial. Some of these techniques parallel those used in television.

Straight Announcer. Sometimes the simplest approach works best. In this commonly used and most direct of all techniques, an announcer or personality delivers the entire script. Success depends both on the copy and on the warmth and believability of the person performing the commercial. Tom Bodett for Motel 6 was all of these things and one of the reasons the commercials were so popular. This approach works particularly well when a positive image has previously been established and a specific event is being promoted, like a sale. The Jiffy Lube spot (Exhibit 20.3) demonstrates the straight announcer technique in its "Terrible World" spot with a few "hey, no problems" thrown into the mix.

Two-Announcer. In this format, two announcers alternate sentences or groups of sentences of copy. The commercial moves at a fast pace and generates excitement. This technique gives a news flavor to the commercial.

Announcer-Actor. The listener may identify still more with the situation if the writer includes an actor's voice reading or supplementing the message delivered by the announcer. Exhibit 20.4 begins with an announcer saying, "Here's a little something entertaining from Mission Valley Center." Then a woman starts: "What she wouldn't have given for that look of elation. That wild, unabashed delight." Then the announcer closes with information about a promotion. Exhibit 20.5 begins with the announcer saying, . . . "Moms are famous for telling us what to do." Then the mom says, "Be home before dark."

EXHIBIT 20.3

· · · · · · · · · · · · · · · · · · · ·

JIFFY LUBE   GRAY KIRK/VANSANT 046
RADIO :52

JL-204-60 "TERRIBLE WORLD"

ANNCR: In a world where fast food isn't fast anymore,
          you can't get anybody on the phone,
          everything you buy breaks,
          the cable goes out constantly,
          salespeople lie,
          (hey, no problem)
          repairmen don't show up,
          stores rip you off,
          (hey, no problem)
          everything is confusing,
          the workforce is lazy,
          commercials are misleading,
          everything takes too long,
          everyplace seems dirty,
          nobody does what they're gonna do,
          (hey, no problem)
          and nobody takes responsibility for anything,

          Isn't it nice to know you can still get your car's oil changed,
          get complete 14-point service in just minutes in clean sur-
          roundings at a low price with a guarantee, by professionals
          who know what they're doing and are actually polite?

          Jiffy Lube. A job well done in minutes. There's still hope.

          (hey, no problem)

(Courtesy: Jiffy Lube.)

EXHIBIT 20.4

· · · · · · · · · · · · · · · · · · · ·

MORRIS & FELLOWS
MVC PROGRAM
:60 RADIO - :55 W/ :05 ANC. GIFT TAG
"GIVE ME A BREAK"
3-8-94

ANC.:   Here's a little something entertaining from . . . Mission
          Valley Center.

WOMAN: What she wouldn't have given for that look of elation.
          That wild, unabashed delight. Was the woman in the red
          dress newly in love? Had she found that Nirvana that al-
          ways seemed to elude most of us? Maybe the bright crim-
          son just made her look more excited. No. No, there was
          definitely more to it. She'd follow her. So . . . On they
          went past the merchants . . . Past other onlookers who
          seemed oddly untouched by the woman with the dancing
          eyes. Then they were there. At the counter. Someone slid a
          small box towards the woman. She clutched it and dashed
          off. What was in the box, I inquired? Okay, hold it. A free
          gift because the woman in red is a Mission Valley Center
          "most valuable customer"? And she visited the mall three
          times this month and got free stuff? Give me a break. And
          then give me the scoop.

ANC.:   Be an "MVC". Free gifts for just 3 visits per month.
          Chances to win $500.00 every day. "Deals of the day". A
          way cool grand prize each month for one lucky "MVC".
          Check it out at the customer service center or your fa-
          vorite store. And then get with the program. Okay?

TAG: (:05 for gift tag)

(Courtesy: Morris and Fellows.)

EXHIBIT

20.5

POFOLKS
VEGETABLES
:60 RADIO COPY
#FIK-012-VERSION B

ANNOUNCER:	Moms are famous for telling us what to do.
MOM:	Be home before dark.
ANNOUNCER:	Some things we eventually outgrow.
MOM:	Don't hit your sister!
ANNOUNCER:	But some advice is good for a lifetime.
MOM:	Eat your vegetables!
ANNOUNCER:	At PoFolks, we're cooking a bountiful crop of homestyle vegetables every day. Fresh new recipes like cornbread dressing and glazed carrots along with classics like green beans, fried okra and real mashed potatoes with gravy.
MOM:	Vegetables really make the meal and with two dozen to choose from, you can be sure PoFolks has your favorites.
ANNOUNCER:	So come on over today and make you and your Mom happy.
UNISON:	Eat your vegetables!

TAG:
1. Try our new georgia peach muffins! Sweet, homestyle goodness fresh from the oven. They're worth writing home about!
2. Call PoFolks catering for the holidays at 555-1234 cause eating's a lot more fun than cooking!

(Courtesy: PoFolks.)

Then the next line is delivered by the announcer and then the mom again. They rotate lines throughout the commercial to help hold the listener's ear.

Slice-of-Life. The most successful and creative commercials give audience members something or someone to which they can relate. Kroger supermarket featured a lady who had her photos developed at Kroger. The clerk told her she didn't have to buy any she didn't like. She was giving back a reunion photo of an old friend to get her money back, when the clerk said, "Oh your friend is pregnant." And the lady was delighted because the lady wasn't pregnant—only large. She decided to keep the photo. You've known someone who was always jealous of how friends looked or in this case happy because she looked better than her friend . . . and she had proof. This is why this technique has worked in so many instances. Overhearing bits of real-life conversation—between children, parents, lovers—makes the potential customer an active participant instead of a passive listener. One major problem in writing slice-of-life spots is that they must be done extremely well to be effective.

Jingle-Announcer. The song or jingle offers two advantages. As a song, it is a pleasant and easily remembered presentation of at least part of the copy. As a musical sound, it is the advertiser's unique property, which sets the commercial apart from every other ad on radio. Generally, an announcer is used in this flexible technique, which may be structured in countless ways. Most common is the jingle at the beginning of the commercial, followed by an-

Jingle

A commercial set to music, usually carrying the slogan or theme line of a campaign. May make a brand name and slogan more easily remembered.

nouncer copy; the commercial is concluded by a reprise of the entire jingle or its closing bars.

Sarah Scharbo, vice president and creative director of Scharbo and Company, created a commercial that was based upon music. Voice (Stuart) says, "Thank you. And now here's a little song I call 'Things I Wouldn't Pay 99 Cents for . . .' " which uses a combination of approaches centering on humor and music (see Exhibit 20.6).

Customer Interview.   The announcer may talk not with professional talent but with actual consumers who relate their favorable experience with the product or service or store. As a variation, the satisfied customer may deliver the entire commercial.

Humor.   Tastefully handled, humor may be an ingredient in almost any technique. A slice-of-life scene can have humorous overtones, and even straight

EXHIBIT

20.6

· ·

CENTRAL PARK
:60 RADIO - :06 LOCAL TAG
"THINGS I WOULDN'T PAY 99 CENTS FOR"
REVISED 3-22-94

ANNCR:	THE FOLLOWING IS BROUGHT TO YOU BY CENTRAL PARK.
MUSIC:	(STRUMMING)
STUART:	Thank you. And now here's a little song I call "Things I Wouldn't Pay 99 Cents for . . . "
LYRICS:	I'll not pay 99 cents for A wet suit made of wheat Or a knee-high umbrella Made just for my feet. I won't pay 99 cents for A pig iron basketball Or for a bag of tube socks Made for women 8 feet tall. And I'd certainly never buy A 99 cent blonde toupee That makes me look just like A walking Easter Egg display.
ANNCR:	IF YOU THINK ANYTHING WORTH HAVING IS PROBABLY A LOT MORE THAN 99 CENTS, CENTRAL PARK'S GOT A FUN FACT FOR YOU. FOR A LIMITED TIME, WHEN YOU PURCHASE A MEDIUM COKE AND LARGE FRIES, YOU'LL GET OUR FAMOUS BACON CHEESE BLASTER FOR ONLY 99 CENTS! A DELICIOUS 1/4 LB., PURE BEEF BACON CHEESEBURGER FOR ONLY 99 CENTS!
STUART:	There's no way I'd shell out My hard-earned 99 cents for A video on "How To Dance To Rap with Albert Gore."
ANNCR:	DRIVE THROUGH CENTRAL PARK TODAY . . . FOR GOOD FOOD. REAL FAST.
TAG:	:06 LOCAL ANNCR.

(Courtesy: Scharbo & Co.)

announcer copy may be written in a humorous vein. Humor is often appropriate for low-priced package products, products people buy for fun, products whose primary appeal is taste, or products or services in need of a change of pace in advertising because of strong competition. Never, however, make fun of the product or the customer or treat too lightly a situation that is not normally funny. The test of a humorous commercial is whether the customer remembers the product, not the commercial. Humor is not called for when your product has distinct advantages that can be advertised with a serious approach. You need a pool of humorous commercials to avoid wearout. In 1994, Coca-Cola created Fruitopia line of fruit drinks to compete with Snapple. The broadcast ads offered politically correct maxims in a humorous vein: "If your mouth can't say something nice—put something nice in it." "Please try Pink Lemonade Euphoria." suggested one spot. They had a series of commercials that were rotated to prevent wearout.

Combination. Radio techniques may be mixed in countless ways (for example, Exhibit 20.2). Announcer, music, voiceovers, and jingles may be used in a single commercial. To select the right technique for a particular assignment, follow the guidelines we discussed for selecting TV techniques in Chapter 19.

Copy checklist:

1. *Attract attention.* Think of how many commercials you hear that don't grab your attention. Make sure your commercial isn't one of these. Creative consultant Dan O'Day suggests that the most important part of a print ad is the headline; in a radio commercial the opening copy line is the same as a headline.

2. *Appeal to the listener's self-interest.* You have to remember that the listener doesn't care about the advertiser or commercial. The listener cares only about what the advertiser can do for him or her. Many copywriters make a mistake of writing about the advertiser instead of the listener and potential customer. You should identify a need that will be filled by the advertiser, and a consumer problem that can be solved by the product.

3. *Use word pictures.* Remember, radio is the theater of the mind, and the listener can convert the words you use into mental pictures.

4. *Don't forget to sell.* The commercial isn't made to entertain; it's one that motivates the listener to act.

5. *Avoid commercial clichés.* They are trite and empty and communicate little to the listener. Among the common clichés to avoid:

Now is the time
They won't last long
The sale you've been waiting for
Savings throughout the store

6. *Read copy aloud.* Read the copy out loud at a normal conversational pace.

7. *Time yourself.* Remember, you're reading against the clock, so don't cram too many words into the copy—a production person can't be expected to make it fit naturally.

TIMING OF COMMERCIALS

Time is the major constraint in producing a radio commercial. Most radio stations accept these maximum word lengths for live commercial scripts:

- **10 seconds, 25 words**

- **20 seconds, 45 words**

- **30 seconds, 65 words**

- **60 seconds, 125 words**

In prerecorded commercials, of course, you may use any number of words you can fit within the time limit. However, if you use more than 125 words for a 60-second commercial, the commercial will have to be read so rapidly that it may sound unnatural or even unintelligible. Remember, if you insert sound effects, that will probably cut down on the number of words you can use. If you have footsteps running for five seconds, you are going to have to cut 10 to 12 words. You need to time the musical intros and endings or sound effects because each will affect the number of words allowable. It is not unusual to go into the recording studio with a script that is a couple of seconds short because the extra time allows the talents to sound more natural. Actors need some breathing room to sound sincere.

MUSICAL COMMERCIALS

Music can be a powerful tool for getting your product remembered. As musical writer Steve Karmen has said: "People don't hum the announcer."[2]

In writing musical commercials, you have to start with an earthquake, then build to something really big. In other words, there is no room for subtlety. The thought process and strategy are different from those in regular songwriting.

There are three main elements to writing commercial music:

- *Intro:* **The beginning of the song. The tempo and lyrics may be established here.**

- *Verse:* **The middle of the song. This is where the message is developed. There may be several verses.**

- *Theme or chorus:* **May be the conclusion of the song.**

Commercial music is very flexible. You may begin with the chorus to establish your theme at the beginning, or you may repeat the theme throughout. The theme is what listeners remember. Some musical forms, such as the blues, can be thought of as both verse and chorus. A theme may serve as a musical logotype for the product, lasting about 4 to 10 seconds. Jingles are also a popular means of making a slogan memorable. PoFolks created a "down-home cookin' " jingle to communicate the good food and friendliness with the jingle in Exhibit 20.7.

---

[2]Bruce Bendinger, "The Copy Workshop Workbook" (Chicago: Bruce Bendinger Creative Communications, Inc., 1988) p. 214.

EXHIBIT

20.7

Neutral Version Final Copy	
INTRO:	Do you know. . .
1	PoFolks keeps on serving
2	All the best home cookin'!
3	The very freshest recipes
4	Goodness you can taste!
5	PoFolks loves to cook from scratch
6	Fresh to you each day
7	Feel good, Georgia. . .
8	You're at PoFolks!
	PoFolks! (Stinger)

Many commercials are composed especially for the advertiser or product. Others are simply adapted from a familiar song. A melody is in the public domain, available for use by anyone without cost, after its copyright has expired. Many old favorites and classics are in the public domain and have been used as advertising themes. That is one of their detriments: They may have been used by many others.

Popular tunes that are still protected by copyright are available only by (often costly) agreement with the copyright owner. An advertiser can also commission a composer to create an original tune, which becomes the advertiser's property and gives the product its own musical personality.

A mass marketer can position a "sound" to a specific audience. This can be done in radio relatively inexpensively compared to television. Using the same lyrics and tune, BBDO developed four different versions of the same jingle for Delta Air Lines, each aimed at a different radio format: chorus, rock, country and western, and rhythm and blues.

Pike Family Nurseries, created by Scharbo and Company uses a jingle "Playin in the Dirt," which goes like this:

1ST CHORUS

It's funny how sunny
Pike's Nurseries
Can make me
We'll grow us
a memory
Come play in the dirt again

2ND CHORUS

And if you loved what playing
in the dirt felt like
The fun that you felt can be
found at Pike's
So for dirty little knees
And a big, big grin
Come play in the dirt again . . .

So for dirty little knees
And a big, big grin
Come play in the dirt again . . .

Do you have the talent to write a jingle? Does the typical copywriter have the ability to do so? In general, the job of writing such copy is left to the music experts.

Audio Technology Changes

Over the past 10 years there has been a radical change in the way music and sound are recorded. A little over a decade ago, the world of high-fidelity multitrack recording and sync-to-picture belonged solely to record companies, postproduction houses, and commercial ventures.

In 1988, Digidesign's Sound Tools system broke this barrier by offering a CD-quality digital stereo recording environment. Using a Macintosh, musicians and sound designers could then record mono or stereo digital masters, but it was still impossible to record one track while listening to another, and there was no way to play back MIDI (musical instrument digital interface) sequences simultaneously with audio.

In 1990, OSC released Deck software to fill this void. Deck was the first Macintosh software that allowed true four-track recording and simultaneous MIDI file playback. Deck's simple interface was based on the integrated *portable studio* metaphor and required no knowledge of MIDI. It looked and functioned like a four-track cassette mixer/recorder, but it turned any Macintosh with a Digidesign NuBus card into a CD-quality production environment. It has been used extensively over the past few years to produce albums and CDs and for basic sync work. In 1993, Deck II was produced. It uses a variety of hardware systems that turn a Macintosh into a true multitrack digital audio workstation.

You can record your basic ideas digitally from the very beginning, add and edit digital audio and MIDI tracks to your composition, and synchronizes your elements to video decks or QuickTime video. You can then use the software to transfer that master digitally to a digital audio tape (DAT), you can print your stereo/master directly to time-coded DAT. Every step in the multitrack production of digital audio is in the hands of the individual.

Musicians can use it as a composition environment, and produce CDs or CD-quality demos from the original tracks. Video postproduction sound designers can use it for typical audio sweetening. MIDI studios can use it to record final audio tracks over existing MIDI tracks.

METHODS OF DELIVERY

There are three ways a radio commercial can be delivered: live, by station announcer, and prerecorded.

The Live Commercial

A live commercial is delivered in person by the studio announcer, disc jockey, newscaster, or other station personality; or perhaps by a sports reporter from another location. Though generally read from a script prepared by the advertiser, the commercial is sometimes revised to complement the announcer's style. If time allows, the revised script should be approved in advance by the advertiser. Ad-libbing (extemporizing) from a fact sheet should be discouraged because the announcer may inadvertently omit key selling phrases or, in the case of regulated products such as drugs, fail to include certain mandatory phrases.

Some commercials are delivered partly live and partly prerecorded. The prerecorded jingle, for example, can be played over and over with live-announcer copy added. Sometimes the live part (the dealer "tie-up") is left open for the tie-in ad of the local distributor.

One advantage of the live commercial is that the announcer may have a popular following and listeners tend to accept advice from someone they like. The other big advantage is cost: Station announcers usually do your commercials free of extra talent costs.

Mrs. Winner's, a regional chicken and biscuits fast-food company, introduced its skinless fried chicken in Atlanta using DJs for the key morning radio programs to read commercials live. Mrs. Winner's delivered chicken to a number of stations during the program so that the DJs could taste it prior to reading the commercial. The company got free publicity in addition to the commercials as the DJs commented during the programs about how good the product tasted. The commercials seemed more a part of the program. The company took advantage of the popularity of the local disc jockeys among its audiences to communicate the product message live.

Station Announcer

For a campaign dealing with a retail offer that will change frequently, advertisers often use a station announcer reading copy written by the agency. This is recorded at the station at no charge to the client—sometimes even with the client's musical theme in the background. This type of delivery allows for frequent changes in copy at no cost.

The Prerecorded Commercial

Advertisers undertaking a regional or national campaign will not know local announcers' capabilities. In any case, it would be impractical to write a separate script to fit each one's particular style. Commercials for these campaigns are therefore usually prerecorded. Not only does this assure advertisers that the commercial will be identical each time it is aired, but it also allows them to take advantage of myriad techniques that would be impractical in a live commercial. (Actually, in many instances, "live" commercials are recorded by the station so that they can run even when the announcer is not on duty.)

Biltmore Estates in Asheville, North Carolina, is a stately 225-room French chateau and gardens nestled in the heart of the Blue Ridge Mountains open to the public. It was built by George Vanderbilt and is the largest private residence in America. Biltmore had its centennial celebration by showing some of George's paintings and collections not seen by the public before. Price/McNabb Advertising created the following radio spot to tweak listeners' interest in visiting Biltmore Estates (see Exhibit 20.8, a prerecorded spot).

Talent and Unions

As with television, the use and payment to performers appearing in radio commercials are dictated by the AFTRA (American Federation of Television and Radio Artists) commercial contract, which was negotiated in 1994. Talent is paid a session fee when the commercial is recorded. There are other requirements for payment based upon usage, including wild spot, network, dealer, demo and copy testing, and foreign use. It is, however, another cost the advertiser must consider.

PRODUCING THE RADIO COMMERCIAL

Although there are certain broad similarities, producing radio commercials is far simpler and less costly than producing TV commercials. First, the agency or advertiser appoints a radio producer, who converts the script into a recording ready to go on the air. After preparing the cost estimate and getting budget approval, the producer selects a recording studio and a casting director, if necessary. If music is called for, the producer calls a music "house" that usually composes, arranges, and takes all steps necessary to get the finished music. If the music is not a big-budget item, the producer may call for "stock" music (prerecorded and used on a rental basis).

Stock music

Existing recorded music that may be purchased for use in a TV or radio commercial.

EXHIBIT
20.8

Date   April 12, 1994
Client   Biltmore Estate
Job Number   5675 002 94
Job Title   Locksmith Radio

(SFX): Clicking of a combination lock.

LOCKSMITH: Right 10 . . . left 16 . . . right 61. That's not it. Or was that left 10 . . . right 16 . . . left 61? No.

ANNCR: The secret vault of George Vanderbilt.

LOCKSMITH: . . . right 10 . . . left 16 . . . right 62? Huff.

ANNCR: Locked for almost a century.

LOCKSMITH: . . . left 10 . . . right 16 . . . left 63. Pfffff. (combinations continue underneath announcer)

ANNCR: Reportedly it contains a painting by Monet, a priceless silver collection.

LOCKSMITH: . . . 10 . . . 16 . . . right 6. Dang. (more and more frustrated)

ANNCR: a lock of Lord Byron's hair, and many other never before seen treasures.

LOCKSMITH: 11 . . . 16 . . .

ANNCR: Unfortunately, it also contains the combination.

LOCKSMITH: . . . left 66. Dooooh.

ANNCR: "George Vanderbilt. The Man and His Treasures." A once-in-a-lifetime exhibit. At Biltmore Estate, Asheville, North Carolina. Opening May 27.

LOCKSMITH: . . . left 16 . . . right 10 . . . left 61. Dadburnit.

ANNCR: Well, we sure hope so.

(Courtesy: Price/McNabb.)

After the cast has been selected, it rehearses in a recording studio, which can be hired by the hour. However, because most commercials are made in short "takes" that are later joined in the editing, a formal rehearsal is usually unnecessary. When the producer feels the cast is ready, the commercial is acted out and recorded on tape. Music and sound are taped separately and then mixed with the vocal tape by the sound-recording studio. In fact, by double- and triple-tracking music and singers' voices, modern recording equipment can build small sounds into big ones. However, union rules require that musicians and singers be paid extra fees when their music is mechanically added to their original recording. After the last mix, the master tape of the commercial is prepared. When final approval has been obtained, duplicates are made on 1/4-inch tape reels or audiocassettes for release to the list of stations.

Steps in Radio Production

We may summarize the steps in producing a commercial as follows:

1. An agency or advertiser appoints a producer.

2. The producer prepares cost estimates.

3. The producer selects a recording studio.

4. With the aid of the casting director, it one is needed, the producer casts the commercial.

5. If music is to be included, the producer selects a musical director and chooses the music or selects "stock" music.

6. If necessary, a rehearsal is held.

7. The studio tapes music and sound separately.

8. The studio mixes music and sound with voices.

9. The producer sees that the master tape is prepared for distribution on either tape or cassettes and shipped to stations.

You are on the air!

SUMMARY

Radio can be visual, despite its lack of visuals. It has the listener's mind to paint pictures within and is truly the theater of the mind. Words, sound effects, and music are the tools of the radio copywriter. The biggest limitation is that the radio copywriter is always working against the clock.

There have been radical changes in the way music and sound are recorded. Using a Macintosh computer, musicians and sound designers can record digital masters. So the computer and its innovative software are another creative tool—this time for broadcast. Music can be a powerful tool for getting products remembered.

When developing a commercial, it is important to keep it simple and concentrate on one main idea. Repetition of the main selling ideas is considered necessary, but the priority is to get the brand and message remembered. Some of the writing techniques and formats include straight announcer, slice-of-life, jingle-announcer, customer interview, and humor, to name a few examples.

As with television, all performers appearing in national commercials are subject to union compensation agreements.

Questions

1. Why is radio referred to as the "theater of the mind?"
2. What are the three basic sources of sound effects for radio production?
3. How do we indicate music on a radio script?
4. What type of products does "humor" seem to be a good technique for in radio?
5. What are the three main elements to writing music for commercials?

Trademarks
and
Packaging

CHAPTER 21

CHAPTER OBJECTIVES

Product names and trademarks are very important to brand equity and the marketing process. In today's market, advertising and packaging must support each other. After reading this chapter you will understand:

- What a trademark is
- Protecting the trademark
- Forms of trademarks
- General trademark rules
- The process for developing memorable names
- Packaging and marketing
- Packaging and research

Today, packaging is a very important part of the brand equity and integrated marketing equation. It has been labeled as the only truly international method of branding. **A distinctive shape** such as the Coca-Cola bottle or Johnson & Johnson's baby lotion bottle is instantly recognized anywhere. **What we are talking about** in this chapter is the power of a strong effective image—a name, a symbol, a package—to build brand equity.

There are those that believe that, in an age of 500 channels, the retail shelf will become the only true mass medium. That notion has already produced greater attention to packaging a brand banner, widespread use of contemporary colors, and more senior marketing people getting involved in packaging. It's a product of twin forces that rule most marketing decisions: time and money. Consumers have less time to shop in a leisurely manner, so marketers are seeking new methods to attract their attention. And marketers are spending more money on the message where consumers make a purchase. Strategic design firms are constantly being told that packaging has to communicate the entire brand strategy, whereas not too long ago packaging was simply a necessary evil. Herb Meyers of Gerstman+Meyers says, "Packaging and advertising have to support each other, so people are putting more work into getting their brand message across and an increasing insistence by marketers on integrated campaigns."[1]

The brand is one of the most important assets of a company, and the trademark is the brand's asset. Consider the financial investment in the name and trademark of Coca-Cola since 1886, when it was first developed. Think of the corporate and financial loss if Coca-Cola lost the exclusive right to its trademark. It is not impossible for it to lose that right. It is for that reason it goes to great lengths to protect its trademark. All companies face this threat, which we'll talk about later in this chapter.

This need to protect the investment in a brand or company name and trademark has spawned a body whole body of law. Getting legal protection is the province of the attorney; however, it begins with the creation of the trademark itself. We'll touch on some of the ground rules.

WHAT IS A TRADEMARK?

Here, and in Chapter 3, we have said that brands are among the most valuable assets a marketer has. When a product is manufactured and a brand is created, it must be distinctive from the competition.

There are several types of company and product identifications. The trademark, also called a *brand name*, is the name by which people can speak of the product. Very often a trademark will include some pictorial or design element. If it does, the combination is called a *logotype* (or simply a logo).

Specifically, a trademark is a word, design, or combination used by a company to identify its brand and to distinguish it from others, and it may be registered and protected by law. Trademark formats can include letters, numbers, slogans, geometric shapes, pictures, labels, color combinations, product and container shapes, vehicles, clothing, and even sound.

Trademarks can also be termed *service marks* when used to identify a service. In general, a trademark for goods appears on the product or its packaging, and a service mark is used in advertising to identify the services. (See Exhibit 21.1.)

The logo design is an extremely important element in the successful marketing of a product. It is difficult to sell a product until a reasonable level of name recognition is achieved among consumers. In fact, the creation of a

---

[1] Terry Lefton, "Packaging All They Can Get into What's on the Shelf," *Brandweek,* October 3, 1994, pp. 34–35.

EXHIBIT

21.1

American Express has a number of product names to promote and to protect.

Help Insure

AMERICAN EXPRESS QUALITY SERVICE

Carry the HOTLINE Card

(Courtesy: Promotion Solutions, Inc.)

logo is so important that a number of firms have been established whose primary function is the design of logos, packages, and corporate identities. Most designers attempt to forge a compatible relationship among the package design, logo, and advertising for the product. A strong logo on the package and in product advertising creates an environment of recognition.

Clearly the most successful packages combine an intriguing design scheme with a provocative logotype. What we mean is a logo that is so distinctive that if it is extracted from the package it will still project the visual personality of the product. After all, when pushing a shopping cart down a supermarket aisle, the consumer's first images will be recognizable brand names.

Trade name

A name that applies to a business as a whole, not to an individual product.

On the other hand, a *trade name* is the name under which the company does business. General Motors, for example, is the trade name of a company making automobiles whose trademark (not trade name) is Buick. The terms *trademark* and *trade name* are often confused.

If you're confused, think of yourself as a new product. Your surname is your *trade name* (Lane, Smith, Bevil, etc.). Your gender is the *product classification* (Female Lane, Female Smith, or Female Bevil, etc.) Your given name is the *brand* (Sheri Lane or Judy Smith), as it distinguishes you from other family members.

However, some personal names (as with product names) may sound the same but may have a different spelling—Sherry, Sherri, Sheri, or even Cheri (Kwik-Draw, Quick-Draw, Kwic, Kwik, Quick). Or some may simply be very familiar names—Sally, Jane, Betsy, Ann, Susan, Emily—or clearly distinctive—like Ruhanna. Yet distinctive may appear hard to read or pronounce. Companies and products have a similar problem. They want names that can easily become familiar to consumers, yet be easy to read and pronounce, and be memorable.

In order for a firm to qualify for an exclusive trademark, several requirements must be met. If these criteria are not satisfied, the trademark is not legally protected and will be lost to the firm.

The use of a design in an ad does not make it a trademark, nor does having it on a flag over the factory. The trademark must be used in connection with an actual product. It must be applied to the product itself or be on a label or container of that product. If that is not feasible, it must be affixed to the container or dispenser of the product, as on a gas pump at a service station.

The trademark must not be confusingly similar to trademarks on comparable goods. It must not be likely to cause buyers to be confused, mistaken, or deceived as to whose product they are purchasing. The trademark must be dissimilar in appearance, sound, and significance from others for similar goods. Of course, it is up to a court to decide these issues. The products involved need not be identical. Air-O was held in conflict with Arrow shirts. The marks will be held in conflict if the products are sold through the same trade channels or if the public might assume that a product made by a second company is a new product line of the first company. The product Big Boy! powder for soft drinks was held in confusion with Big Boy stick candy.

A trademark must not be deceptive—that is, it must not indicate a quality the product does not possess. For instance, the work *Lemon* soap was barred because it contained no lemon, and the word *Nylodon* for sleeping bags that contained no nylon.

Trademarks must not be merely descriptive. A baker can't say, people ask for fresh bread, so we will trademark our bread *Fresh*. When people ask for *fresh bread,* they are describing the kind of bread they want, not specifying the bread made by a particular baker. To prevent such misleading usage, the law does not protect trademarks that are merely descriptive and thus applicable to many other products.

Lindy Pen Company and Bic Pen Corporation have been in and out of court for 15 years. Lindy used the word *Auditor's* in connection with its fine point ball-point pen since 1955. In 1965, Bic started using the mark *Auditor's.* Lindy complained, and Bic stopped using it. Lindy then registered *Auditor's* in 1966. In 1979, Bic found that three other manufacturers were using the term to describe ball-point pens. So it once again used the term on their pens because it decided *Auditor's* was a commonly used term. In 1980, Lindy sued. Since then it has been through the California federal trial and appeals courts twice. Despite proving there was confusion in telephone orders over identical names, Lindy has received no damages. In fact, its argument has been weak because its trademark is a word in common usage. The courts said the mark was *merely descriptive.* The court concluded that Bic's infringement was innocent. Lindy could not prove in court that it had been damaged. The courts did prevent Bic from using the *Auditor's* mark.

Among the lessons learned: Beware if your trademark is based on a common word. It will be considered legally weak and hard to protect. Police unpermitted use of your trademark vigorously, and don't let any competitor use your mark even briefly. And, if you want to start a trademark infringement suit, don't do it unless you keep detailed records and can document lost profits accurately.[2]

Protecting a Trademark

Because a trademark is so valuable, companies go to great lengths to protect their brand names. In recent years, there have been a number of court cases involving allegations that one company has infringed on the trademark of another.

---

[2]Maxine S. Lans, "There's a Lesson for Marketers in the War of the Ballpoint Pens," *Marketing News,* October 25, 1993, p. 11.

In deciding where trademark infringement has taken place, several factors are considered by the courts:

1. The distinctiveness of the complainant's mark
2. The similarity of the marks
3. The proximity of the parties' products
4. The likelihood of the complainant's bridging the gap between noncompeting products
5. The similarity of the parties' trade channels and advertising methods
6. The quality of the alleged infringer's products
7. The sophistication of the particular customers

Advertisers sometimes believe that trademark infringement can be avoided by changing a well-known mark or by using it for a dissimilar product. They are wrong because trademark infringement is normally found when two marks are likely to cause *confusion* as to the source of products or services for which they are used. Complete identity of marks or products is not necessary.

In September 1994, Procter & Gamble sued the 124-store F & M drug chain over the chain's P&G look-alike packages. P&G said, "These look-alike products confuse people and are a disservice to our customers." One of the products, for example, cloned P&G's Pantene using the same color scheme, with a swirl symbol in a small rectangle. Many of the private-label knockoff packaging is displayed next to the brand name products in the store. P&G's move was like a warning shot to everyone with look-alike packages.[3] Of course, the burden of proof lies with P&G proving that knockoff packaging causes consumer confusion. Maxine Lans, an attorney, says, "You can't stop a competitor from bringing out a similar product, but you can prevent the consumer from buying another product by accident because it looks so much like yours."

There are some common threads running through recent legal decisions. Trademarks that are highly distinctive and well known and are part of extensive advertising campaigns are considered strong marks that deserve broad protection against unauthorized use. In all these cases, the infringing marks incorporated the dominant element of the registered marks, signaling the infringers' intent to capitalize on the long-standing reputation of the trademark owners. The best evidence in showing confusion has been consumer surveys.

Brand

A name, term, sign, design, or a unifying combination of them, intended to identify and distinguish the product or service from competing products or services.

Selecting Brand Names

A strong brand name will aid marketing objectives by helping create and support the brand image. There are several considerations in the brand name selection:[4]

■ *Name should differentiate the product from the competition.* In some product categories, there is a limit to how different brand images can be. In fragrances there has traditionally been one basic image—romance. There is great similarity among brand names—Caleche, Cacharel, Chantilly. Consider more distinctive names such as Obsession, Charlie, Passion, Safari. In

[3]Greg Erickson, "Seeing Double," *Brandweek,* October 17, 1994, pp. 30–35.
[4]Daniel L. Doden, "Selecting a Brand Name That Aids Marketing Objectives," *Advertising Age,* November 5, 1990, p. 34.

either direction, creation and support of the brand image—abstract promise rather than actual benefit—are the dominant factors in name selection.

- **Name should describe the product, if possible.** Brand names such as Post-it, Pudding Pops, and Eraser Mate are very descriptive. They communicate to consumers exactly what to expect.

- **Name should be compatible with the product.** The product should be compatible with the brand name. In other words, do not name a sleeping tablet "Awake."

- **Name should be memorable and easy to pronounce.** One-word, one-syllable brand names are often considered ideal—Fab, Tide, Dash, Bold, Surf, Coke, Tab. Even though short names may be more memorable, they may be limiting in identifying the type of product or its use.

Forms of Trademarks

Dictionary Words. Many trademarks consist of familiar dictionary words used in an arbitrary, innovative, or fanciful manner. Many common words have already been used, causing the advertiser to seek other methods to name a product: Verbatim data disks, Ivory soap, Dial soap, Whopper burgers, Glad plastic bags, Shell oil, Coach leather, Pert shampoo. This type of trademark must be used in a merely descriptive sense to describe the nature, use, or virtue of the product: Look at the work *natural* and related names: Natural Blend, Natural Brand, Natural Impressions, Natural Light, Natural Man, Natural Silk, Natural Smoothe, Natural Stretch, Natural Suede, Natural Sun, Natural Touch, Natural Woman, Natural Wonder.

The possible advantage of using dictionary words is that consumers will easily recognize them. Of course, the task is to get people to associate the word(s) with the product. Just think what the following real product names using two dictionary words are about—Healthy Choice, Skin Bracer, Budget Rent-a-Car, Drug Emporium, Wonderbra, Big Mac, Water Grabber, Action Plus.

At times, a name can be somewhat limiting. For instance, when Burger King moved into a breakfast menu, the name Burger King was a limitation because people do not think of burgers at breakfast.

Coined word

An original and arbitrary combination of syllables forming a word. Extensively used for trademarks, such as PoFolks, Mazola, Gro-Pup, Ze-rone. (Opposite of a dictionary word.)

Coined Words. When we run out of dictionary options, we sometimes make up words, such as Ticketron, Advil, Infiniti, Humana, Primerica, Kleenex, Xerox, Nynex, Unum (see Exhibit 21.2), Norelco, Exxon, Delco, Keds, Ko-dak, Mazola, ValuJet, PoFolks. Coined words are made up of a new combination of consonants and vowels. The advantage of a coined word is that it is new; it can be made phonetically pleasing, pronounceable, and short. Coined words have a good chance of being legally protectable. The challenge is to create a trademark that is distinctive. Ocean Spray took the ingredients of cranberries and apples and created the name Cranapple, which is distinctive, descriptive, and relatively easy to pronounce. There is, however, a Cranberry Apple herb tea. Is this confusing? Probably not.

The simpler coined words are one syllable. It is common to coin trademark words that have a vowel next to a hard consonant or a vowel between two hard consonants—such as Keds. This structure can be expanded—Kodak, Crisco, or Tab.

Personal Names. These may be the names of real people, such as Calvin Klein, Estee Lauder, Tommy Hilfinger, Perry Ellis, Pierre Cardin, Alexander

EXHIBIT

21.2

· · · · · · · · · · · · · · · · · · · ·

Example of a coined
word for the corporation
name.

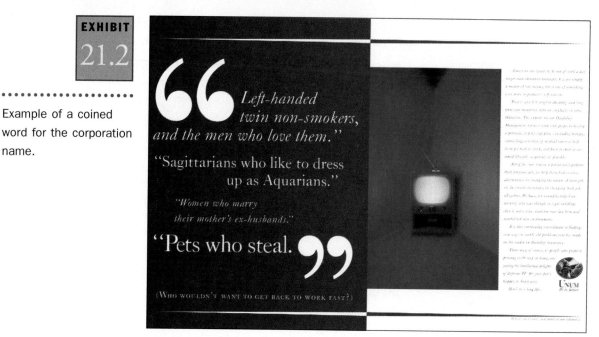

(Courtesy: UNUM)

Julian, Oscar de la Renta, Sara Lee; fictional characters, such as Betty Crocker; historical characters, such as Lincoln cars; or mythological characters, such as Ajax cleanser. A surname alone is not valuable as a new trademark; others of that name may use it. Names such as Ford automobiles, Lipton teas, Heinz foods, and Campbell's soups have been in use for so long, however, that they have acquired what the law calls a "secondary meaning"; that is, through usage the public has recognized them as representing the product of one company only. However, a new trademark has no such secondary meaning.

There are a lot of names that use Mrs.—Mrs. Fields, Mrs. Winner's, Mrs. Grimes, Mrs. Allison's, Mrs. Smith's, Mrs. Dash, Mrs. Baird's, Mrs. Butterworth's, Mrs. Lane's, Mrs. Paul's.

Foreign names have been successfully used to endow a product with an exotic quality. Of course, since we're in a global market, they are more and more common. The argument against creating foreign names may be the problem of pronunciation or remembering. However, foreign names are part of the global landscape: Toyota, Fendi, Gianfranco Ferre, Corneliani, Lubiam, Bertolucci, Giorgia Brutini, Shiseido, Gucci, Volkswagen, Fila, Ferrari, L'Aimant.

Geographic Names. A geographic name is really a place name: Nashua blankets, Utica sheets, Pittsburgh paints, Newport cigarettes. These names are old trademarks and have acquired secondary meaning. Often the word *brand* is offered after the geographic name. The law does not look with favor on giving one person or company the exclusive right to use a geographic name in connection with a new product, excluding others making similar goods in that area. However, if the name was chosen because of a fanciful connotation of a geographic setting, rather than to suggest that the product was made there, it may be eligible for protection, as with Bali bras.

Geographic names can be combined with dictionary words to create trademark names such as Maryland Club coffee and Carolina Treat barbecue sauce.

The options are many: Georgia Girl, Texas Instruments, Texas Trails, New York Woman, Florida Queen, Newport Harbor, Georgia-Pacific.

Initials and Numbers. Many fortunes and years have been spent in establishing trademarks such as IBM, RCA, GE, AC spark plugs, A&W root beer, J&B whiskey, and A.1. steak sauce (see Exhibit 21.3) Hence, these are familiar. In general, however, initials and numbers are the hardest form of trademark to remember and the easiest to confuse and imitate. How many of these are you familiar with STP, DKNY, S.O.S., AMF, M.O.M.S., S.A.V.E., A.S.A., A & P, 6-12, 666? There are also combinations of initials and numbers: (WD-40 lubricant); numbers and words (9-Lives cat food, 4 in 1, Formula 44, Formula 109, Formula 28, Formula 36, 4 Most); or dictionary words and initials (LA Gear).

Pictorial. Many advertisers use some artistic device, such as a distinctive style of lettering or a design, insignia, or picture. The combination, as we mentioned before, is called a logotype, or logo. It is important for the advertiser to make sure that any symbol or design is distinctive and will reproduce clearly when used in a small size. Tallahassee Memorial Regional Medical Center, United Arab Agencies, and Maher Terminals have distinctive symbols and designs (see Exhibits 21.4, 21.5, 21.6, and 21.7).

The Successful Trademark

Whatever the form of a specific trademark, it will only be successful if it is distinctive and complements the manufacturer's product and image. As we mentioned earlier in this chapter, the trademark cannot be considered an isolated creative unit. In most cases, it must be adaptable to a package. It must also be adaptable to many different advertising campaigns, often over a period of many years. The longer a trademark is associated with a brand, the more people recognize it and the greater its value.

EXHIBIT

21.3

· · · · · · · · · · · · · · · · · · ·

A.1. brand steak sauce is easy to remember.

(Courtesy: Actmedia)

. . . .

Tallahassee Memorial's symbol is typical of hospitals.

(Courtesy: The Zimmerman Agency.)

Trademark Law Aids United States in Global Markets

U.S. business operates on a global scale. Sweeping changes in U.S. trademark law will help American firms compete against foreign companies. Since the 1870s, trademark law has been based on use of the marks in commerce. "No trade, no trademark" was the law's basic premise. Since 1946, U.S. trademark owners have been required to submit proof of prior use when they apply to register their marks at the Patent and Trademark Office. The new law permits companies to base trademark applications on an *intent* to use the mark. This brings U.S. policy into harmony with worldwide standards.

The old policy hurt U.S. companies because almost no other nation requires use before registration. Foreign competitors could obtain trademark rights in their own country, which would automatically be valid in the United States, without using their marks anywhere. Thus, armed with a U.S.-approved trademark, a foreign company could proceed from product development to the marketplace, confident of its rights to the trademark. In contrast, a U.S. company was unable to register a trademark until it had used it. The company could spend vast sums on packaging, research, and marketing only to find the desired trademark was not available when the product was ready.

EXHIBIT

21.5

Introduces the new logo to the shipping industry. The ad explains the symbol.

Introducing the bold new symbol in shipping.

As the world's most venerable breed, the Arabian stallion has been immortalized in art and literature as the crown jewel of the equestrian kingdom. Combining a rare instinct for stamina and endurance with a matchless spirit of intelligence and loyalty, the desert steed qualifies as a true international globetrotter.

Now, United Arab Shipping Company (UASC) is proud to introduce this thoroughbred as a symbol of its new wholly-owned subsidiary, United Arab Agencies, Inc. (UAAI). UAAI will manage UASC's North American agency services, representing an array of Middle East and Southeast Asia container routes.

To see why United Arab Shipping Company has earned a reputation for quality and performance that is unmatched in the industry, call UAAI today – and harness the energetic spirit of a legendary tradition. Tel: 908-272-0050. FAX 908-272-9221.

UNITED ARAB AGENCIES, INC.

(Courtesy: Longwater, Inc.)

EXHIBIT

21.6

Shows the size of the logo in typical ads.

We know the turf.

The mystery of the Middle East has forever attracted the most adventurous minds of every generation. And those who have successfully ventured into this ancient realm have always known that it's best to go with a guide, someone who knows the territory. That's why we've formed the United Arab Agencies, Inc.–an American company created to manage United Arab Shipping Company's North American

agency services. UAAI's experienced professionals offer personalized, hands-on guidance to help you negotiate the shifting sands of this challenging region.

Like our symbol, the Arabian stallion, UAAI represents a proud and spirited tradition.

And when it comes to the Middle East trade, no one knows the turf better than we do. So please call UAAI today. Telephone: 272-0050 or FAX: 908-272-9221.

UNITED ARAB AGENCIES, INC.

(Courtesy: Longwater, Inc.)

(Courtesy: Longwater, Inc.)

The new law permits an applicant with a bona fide intent to use a mark to apply to register it, for example, on January 1, and if the registration is issued eventually—say, on October 31—to trace its rights back to the application date. A registration is issued when the application is approved by the Patent and Trademark Office and confirmed when the applicant submits proof of use within six months of approval. As many as five six-month extensions may be granted, giving the company several years to actually market a product under a particular mark. The registration period has been reduced from 20 to 10 years but may be renewed indefinitely. This 10-year term is more in keeping with international standards and allows for clearing the trademark register of "deadwood." The new law also includes prohibiting false statements in advertising about a competitor's product.[5]

Trademark Loss

Trademarks are among the most valuable assets of a company because they identify its products and services and distinguish them from those of competitors. Some companies have lost the right to their product names because they became generic terms in common usage:

Nylon	Escalator
Aspirin	Thermos

---

[5]Vincent N. Palladino, "New Trademark Law Aids U.S. in Foreign Markets," *Marketing News*, February 13, 1989, p. 7.

Lanolin	Yo Yo
Linoleum	Raisin Bran
Dry Ice	Cellophane

To protect a trademark, advertisers must use it with a generic classification so the trademark does not become the name of the product. Originally, Thermos was the trademark owned by the Aladdin Company, which introduced vacuum bottles. In time, people began asking, "What brand of thermos bottle do you carry?" The word *thermos* had come to represent all vacuum bottles, not just those made by Aladdin. The courts held that Thermos had become a descriptive word that any manufacturer of vacuum bottles could use because thermos (with a lowercase "t") was no longer the exclusive trademark of the originator.

Registration Notice

Legal departments at some companies go to great lengths to protect their valuable trademarks. Some common ways of indicating trademark registration follow.

- **The "®" symbol after the trademark as a superscript.**
  Example: Mrs. Winner's®

- **A footnote referenced by an asterisk in the text.**
  Example: McDonald's*

  * A registered trademark of McDonald's Corporation.

  or

  * Reg. U.S. Pat. Tm. Off.

  or

  Registered in the U.S. Patent and Trademark Office.

- **A *notation* of the registration in the text or as a footnote on the same page.**

- **If a trademark is repeated frequently in an ad, some firms require the registration notice only on the first use.**

Most companies require notice of unregistered but claimed words and/or symbols as their trademark, by using the "TM" symbol.

- **Example: America's Family Video Store.™**

McDonald's is very protective of its name and trademarks (see Exhibit 21.8). In its "2 for $2.00" ad, the Golden Arches has a ® registered trademark symbol. The small McDonald's also has a registered symbol at the end of "At participating McDonald's." And the ad itself is copyrighted.

General Trademark Rules

Putting a lock on the ownership of a trademark requires taking the following steps:

1. Always make sure the trademark word is capitalized or set off in distinctive type.

2. Always follow the trademark with the generic name of the product: Glad disposable trash bags, Kleenex tissues, Apple computers, Tabasco brand pepper sauce.

For a limited time only. At participating McDonald's®. © 1994 McDonald's Corp.

(Courtesy: McDonald's Corporation and Robinson & Associates, Tupelo, MS)

3. Do not speak of it in the plural, as "three Kleenexes," but, rather, "three Kleenex tissues."

4. Do not use it in a possessive form (not "Kleenex's new features," but "the new features of Kleenex tissues") or as a verb (not "Kleenex your eyeglasses," but "Wipe your eyeglasses with Kleenex tissues").

It is the advertising person's responsibility to carry out these legal strictures in the ads, although most large advertisers will have each ad checked for legal requirements including trademark protection.

HOUSE MARKS

As we mentioned earlier in this chapter, trademarks are used to identify specific products. However, many companies sell a number of products under several different trademarks. These companies often identify themselves with a house mark to denote the firm that produces these products. Kraft is a house mark, and its brand Miracle Whip is a trademark.

SERVICE MARKS, CERTIFICATION MARKS

A company that renders services, such as an insurance company, an airline, or even Weight Watchers, can protect its identification mark by registering it in Washington as a service mark. It is also possible to register certification marks, whereby a firm certifies that a user of its identifying device is doing so properly. Teflon in a material sold by DuPont to kitchenware makers for use in lining their pots and pans. Teflon is DuPont's registered trademark for its nonstick finish; Teflon II is DuPont's certification mark for Teflon-coated cookware that meets DuPont's standards. Advertisers of such products may use that mark. The Wool Bureau has a distinctive label design that it permits all manufacturers of pure-wool products to use (Exhibit 21.9). Certification marks have the same creative requirements as trademarks—most of all, that they be distinctive.

EXHIBIT 21.9

....

Certification mark.

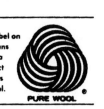

The Woolmark label on this blanket means that you're getting a quality-tested product made of the world's best . . . pure wool.

PURE WOOL

....

House mark

A primary mark of a business concern, usually used with the trademark of its products. *General Mills* is a house mark; *Betty Crocker* is a trademark; *DuPont* is a house mark; *Teflon II* is a trademark.

....

....

Service mark

A word or name used in the sale of services, to identify the services of a firm and distinguish them from those of others, for example, Hertz Drive Yourself Service, Weight Watchers Diet Course. Comparable to trademarks for products.

....

Brand Identity

The focus of brand identity previously fixated on the creation of visual identifiers. The concept was to create a distinct symbol that would be a proprietary, visual representation of a company. The difference today is that such symbols ceased to serve as the foundation of the brand-building effort, but rather as the structure by which that company conveys its personality.[6]

GE's branding strategy has a number of steps:[7]

1. *Pick a name.* In this case it's General Electric.

2. *Create a memorable trademark.* The GE monogram is recognized the world over.

3. *Make a promise.* For 60 years, GE promised better living through electricity, which became better living through technology, for the past 30 years.

4. *Effectively communicate the promise.* GE has always had highly imaginative and memorable work produced by its agencies.

5. *Be consistent.* Even as it grows and modifies its business, it carefully manages the use of its identity worldwide.

6. *Don't get bored.* GE has kept the same strategic promise for 30 years.

If you follow this basic strategy, your brand should thrive.

COMPANY AND PRODUCT NAMES
Name Changes

Corporate name changes, and, accordingly, graphic identity programs have been on the rise in the mid-1990s as reported by two separate surveys—Anspach Grossman Portugal and the Schechter Group—with increases of 25 and 34 percent in a six-month period. Among the name changes:

OLD NAME	NEW NAME
American Telephone and Telegraph	AT&T Corp.
NCR Corp.	AT&T Global Information Services
PacTel Corp.	Air Touch Communications
The Midwest Stock Exchange	Chicago Stock Exchange
Penn Central Corp.	American Premier Underwriters
CIGNA Employee Benefits Companies	CIGNA Healthcare

---

[6]Bill Burke, Sr., "Brand Identity's New Math," *Advertising Age*, April 4, 1994, p. 32.
[7]Richard A. Costello, "Focus on the Brand," *The Advertiser*, Spring 1993, pp. 11–18.

OLD NAME	NEW NAME
Grumman Corp.	Northrop Grumman Corp.
Paramount Publishing	Simon & Schuster
Illinois Power	Illinovac
Primerica	The Travelers
Computerland Corporation	Vanstar Corporation
Carter Hawley Hale	Broadway Stores
Commonwealth Edison	ComEd

According to the survey, the Schechter Group says, 56 percent of the companies continued to select names that have the potential to translate into powerful corporate brands. It also saw the trend toward using initials as alarming. It says AT&T is among the very few corporations that can successfully make the change to initials. This is because in the minds of its constituents, they own AT&T. Most companies don't have that luxury. For them, changing to initials stems from an incorrect assumption that their marketplace is aware of their shorthand moniker as they are. This is rarely the case.[8]

Another recent Schechter Group survey reported that in the 1980s companies changed their names to communicate with Wall Street, but now they are appealing to employees and customers. As a result, companies are choosing a well-known name rather than *alphabet names* that were once viewed by the financial community as a symbol of diversity.[9]

AirTouch ran a newspaper ad which stated:

> Why our new name isn't UniMobilTeleDigiComLink, Inc.

Copy read:

> There's no shortage of technical sounding names in the telecommunication business. In fact, there are 3,000 telesomethings, 7,300 commsomethings and somethingcoms, and an astonishing 10,000 cel, cells and cellulars floating around out there already.

Federal Express, the company that made *to fedex* the verb for overnight delivery, took advantage of that phenomenon with a new graphic identity. The reason for the change was to reinforce the powerful *brand equity* of the shortened name, and to strengthen the company's international presence, The new FedEx identity derives its elegance and power from its simplicity and ability to work globally, to transcend cultural and linguistic barriers. The new logo allows for consistent staging across all media and vehicles.

Global Identity

Backer Spielvogel Bates, a worldwide agency of $5.2 billion, changed its name in the mid-1990s to Bates Worldwide to strengthen the agency's global identity. Despite being a global company, Bates didn't have a global reputation. The CEO said of the switch, "It is crucial to our future to reinforce our corporate voice and present a single clear, cohesive, seamless integrated presence. . . .We have adopted the belief that large companies—including ours—must globalize or die.[10]

[8]"Corporate Name and Identity Changes Surge," *Graphic Design: USA,* August 1994, p. 1.
[9]"Uncertainty Slows Pace of Corporate Naming," *Atlanta Journal,* June 29, 1993, p. B7.
[10]"Bates Pitches Global Identity (for Itself)," *Graphic Design: USA,* May 1994, p. 1.

The Process for Developing Memorable Names

There probably isn't a single procedure everyone accepts for selecting names. Keeping this in mind, let's look at a fairly typical process you might use in selecting a new product name. First, specific image objectives are set. Then you would develop a list of 200 to 1,000 names, which you would match against the objectives. A basic legal search would be made of each name to see if someone else owns the rights to it. This process reduces the possibilities by about 80 percent. You again analyze the remaining names against the objective and reduce them to a list of about a dozen or so. At this point, you would probably perform a linguistic analysis to determine what happens when the name is translated into foreign languages. Then you might test the names on consumers. You get the idea. Correctly done, the result is a memorable name that is adapted to a number of advertising formats (see Exhibit 21.10). Now let's look at the specific steps:

First, pull together the basic information:

- **Describe what you are naming.** Include in your description key features and characteristics, competitive advantages, and anything else that differentiates your company, product, or service from the rest of the field.

- **Summarize what you want your name to do.** Should it suggest an important product characteristic (example, "Blokrot" for treated lumber) or convey

EXHIBIT
21.10

....

The name and symbol design must not only work in an ad, but on all promotional items—letterheads, trucks, signs—and has to be distinctive.

Why you'll never find a Williams tool in the same place as one of these.

Some places sell frozen treats. And some places sell industrial tools. We just happen to believe that no place can do a good job of selling both. After all, how good could a hand tool be if it's one aisle over from lawn chairs, garbage cans or pantyhose? Good enough for you to risk your reputation on? We don't think so.

That's why, at Williams, we only sell our hand tools through a select group of industrial distributors. Not like some tool lines that show up in big mall stores, your neighborhood hardware store – even the discount chains.

So when you're a Williams distributor, you know we're backing your business with all the resources at our disposal. And thanks to the added support of Snap-on, our new parent company, that's saying a lot.

If you want to hear more, call Jim Emilio at 706-563-9590. And treat your distributorship to something really sweet.

WILLIAMS

A Snap-on Company.

©1994 J.H. Williams Company. 8969 Jamesson Road, Columbus, GA 31909

(Courtesy: Sawyer Riley Compton.)

a particular image (example, "Pandora's Secrets" for an expensive perfume)? Write down the characteristics and images you want your name to convey.

■ **Describe whom you are targeting with the name.** Identify your targets and their demographic/lifestyle characteristics. Would they react more positively to a traditional, conservative name or to a liberal, flashy one? List the name qualities you think would appeal to them (name length, sound, and image).

■ **List names that you like and dislike.** Try to come up with a few dozen current names in both categories (include your competitors' names). Note words and roots that might work for your new name and jot them down.

■ **Build a list of new name ideas.** Start with the list of names that you like and add to it by pulling ideas from a good thesaurus (example, *The Synonym Finder* by Jerome Rodale), a book of names (example, *The Trademark Register of the United States*), relevant trade journals, a book of root words (example, *Dictionary of English Word Roots* by Robert Smith), and other sources.

■ **Combine name parts and words.** Take words, syllables, and existing name parts and recombine them to form new names.

■ **Pick your favorites.** Select several names that meet all your criteria (just in case your top choice is unavailable or tests poorly).

Next verify the name's availability and test your favorites:

■ **Conduct a trademark search.** Check to make sure your names are not already in use. Thomson & Thomson in Boston or Compu-Mark in Washington are two companies that can help check state and U.S. patent and trademark records.

Coca-Cola ran into a controversy over its New Age soft drink Fruitopia's name. In 1991, students at Miami (Ohio) University came up with a total marketing plan, which included a product name, for a sparkling water and juice drink in development for the Minute Maid brand at Coca-Cola Foods Canada. When presented to Coca-Cola, they thought the name Fruitopia was very *iffy*. The product rolled out in the United States in 1994 with the Fruitopia name; although there was no question about the legal rights of ownership—Coca-Cola had paid the university a fee for all of the students' work—there was a question of who developed the name. Coca-Cola said that a marketing group, working independently with Chiat/Day advertising, came up with the name. This is a reason most companies don't take unsolicited proposals for new products, ads, or product names. If Coca-Cola had not paid for the rights of the students' work, there could have been a legal battle for the name Fruitopia.

■ **Test your name before using it.** Regardless of how fond you are of the new name, others may have a different opinion. Solicit reactions to your name from prospective consumers, stockholders, and industry experts.

Name Assistance. The naming of products may be developed by the advertiser or the advertising agency, each working independently or together. There are companies and consultants that specialize in helping companies and agencies develop memorable names. The Namestormers use software to help develop product and company names like Auto Source, the Sensible Chef, Pandora's Secrets, Visual Edge, and SatisFAXtion. Namelab, another company that develops names, used constructional linguistics to create the names Acura, Compaq, Geo, Lumina, and Zapmail.

Protect the Usage of Corporate Symbol

Earlier we indicated companies should control how the trademark is used in writing, ads, etc. Many companies provide departments and units with written guidelines instructing the use of trademarks. For example, Kodak has a 10-page document for the proper use of trademarks and examples of incorrect usage of trademarks. This includes trademark printing instruction for black-and-white and color usage. Exhibit 21.11 is the Healthtex logo sheet and color specifications for external and general use.

Blockbuster Corporation warns its employees to "Always use the exact registration or trademark form"; never change the word or design; never change the upper-and lowercase letters; never change the colors; never change the plural or singular form; never add the word *the* to the word or design; never add a design to the word, or vice versa; and never make the mark a possessive noun.

PACKAGING

In the modern world of self-service marketing, the product package is much more than a container. The package must be designed to take several factors into account. First, it must protect the package contents; every other consideration is secondary to the function of the package as a utilitarian container. Second, the package must meet reasonable cost standards. Because the product package is a major expense for most firms, steps must be taken to hold down costs as much as possible.

Once these two requirements of package protection and cost are satisfactorily met, we move to the marketing issues involved in packaging. These include adopting a package that is conduci–ve to getting shelf space at the retail level. A unique package with strange dimensions or protruding extensions or nonflat surfaces is going to be rejected by many retailers. A package must

EXHIBIT
21.11

Healthtex™

(Courtesy: Healthtex.™)

be easy to handle, store, and stack. It should not take up more shelf room than any other product in that section, as might a pyramid-shape bottle. Odd shapes are suspect: Will they break easily? Tall packages are suspect: Will they keep falling over? The package should be soil-resistant. Does it have ample and convenient space for marking? The product should come in the full range of sizes and packaging common to the field.

For products bought upon inspection, such as men's shirts, the package needs transparent facing. The package can make the difference in whether a store stocks the item.

Small items are expected to be mounted on cards under plastic domes, called *blister cards,* to provide ease of handling and to prevent pilferage. Often these cards are mounted on a large card that can be hung on a wall, making profitable use of that space. Remember, the buyer working for the store judges how a product display will help the store, not the manufacturer.

Once we have considered the requirements of the retail trade, we can turn our attention to designing a container that is both practical and eye-catching. The package is, after all, the last chance to sell the consumer and the most practical form of point-of-purchasing advertising. Therefore, it should be designed to achieve maximum impact on the store shelf. Striving for distinctiveness is particularly critical in retail establishments such as grocery stores, where the consumer is choosing from hundreds of competing brands.

Changing Package Design and Marketing Strategies

Design firms redesign packages to suit changing market strategies for existing consumer products and develop new packaging concepts for product introductions. Several trends in package design can be cited. One is the increasing tendency to use packaging to shore up store brands. Another is the use of sophisticated design approaches or unique packaging to establish a high quality for upscale, private-label brands. There has also been a shift from packaging that suits the convenience of the manufacturer to packaging that is "consumer-friendly" in terms of opening and use, reclosing, and portions. In short, package design is responding to a more sophisticated, discerning consumer.

Today's package design firms do more than provide renderings for clients. They often act as adjunct marketing consultants, providing information on the retail environment and marketing trends, as well as expertise on the roles of positioning, timing, and brand equity in the success or failure of a product.

Packaging and Color Influence

High-quality imagery is changing. In the past, black or deep, vibrant colors communicated premium imagery. Today designs for upscale brands use lighter, softer, pastel colors. White, once associated with generic brands, is make a comeback as an upscale communicator.[11]

Today, color is a significant consideration in any new product label or packaging. Exhibit 21.12 shows the importance of color considerations.

---

[11]Herbert M. Meyers, "Forecast: Design and Production," *Graphic Design USA,* January 1989, p. 30.

Color packaging considerations are extremely important for shelf, advertising, and promotion appeal.

Advertisers are very much aware that colors work on people's subconscious and that each color produces a psychological reaction. Reactions to color can be pleasant or unpleasant. Color can inform consumers about the type of product inside the package and influence their perceptions of quality, value, and purity. Thus, color in packaging is an important tool in marketing communications.

What kind of consumer perceptions would you encounter if you brewed the same coffee in a blue coffeepot, a yellow pot, a brown pot, and a red pot? Would the perceptions of the coffee be the same? Probably not. Studies indicate that coffee from the blue pot would be perceived as having a mild aroma, coffee from the yellow pot would be thought a weaker blend, the brown pot's coffee would be judged too strong, and the red pot's coffee would be perceived as rich and full-bodied.

Color has recently come to the forefront. The same contemporary colors that you can find in Saks Fifth Avenue can be found in the health and beauty aisles of the local supermarket or drug chain. In the past, packaged goods used to lag years behind the color trends. Today, marketers are more willing to experiment with such colors as teal or purple than in the past.

Packaging and Marketing

Until this century, the role of product packages was generally confined to protecting the product. Only the package label was linked with promotional activities. The Uneeda Biscuit package introduced in 1899 is generally considered to be the first that was utilized for promotion. However, few companies followed Uneeda's lead.

It was during the depression of the 1930s that the role of packaging as a promotional tool changed dramatically. Most companies had limited advertising funds during this period, so they resorted to using the package as an in-store means of promotion. So successful were their efforts that the role of packaging in the marketing mix became routinely accepted by manufacturers.

The package design for most products is developed in much the same way as an advertising campaign. Although each package is developed, designed, and promoted in a unique fashion, there are some common approaches to the successful use of a package as a marketing tool:

1. *The type of product and function of the package.* Is the product extremely fragile? Do consumers use the product directly from the package? Are there special storage or shipping problems associated with the product?

2. *The type of marketing channels to be used for the product.* If the product is sold in a variety of outlets, will this require some special packaging considerations? Will the package be displayed in some special way at the retail level? Are there special point-of-purchase opportunities for the product?

3. *The prime prospects for the product.* Are adults, children, upper-income families, or young singles most likely to buy the product? What package style would be most appealing to the target market?

4. *Promotion and advertising for the product and its package.* Will the package be used to complement other promotional efforts? Are on-pack coupons or premiums being considered? Can standard package-design ideas be adapted to any special promotional efforts being considered? The Holidays brand chocolates package is suitable to holiday promotions (see Exhibit 21.13).

5. *The relationship to other packages in a product line.* Will the product be sold in different sizes? Is the product part of a product line that is promoted together? Does the product line use the same brand name and packaging style?

EXHIBIT 21.13

Holidays brand chocolates are packaged plain, peanuts, and almonds. The packages lend themselves to in-store promotions.

(Courtesy: Actmedia.)

6. *The typical consumer use of the product.* Will the package be stored for long periods in the home? Does the product require refrigeration or freezing? Are only portions of the product used from the package?

Obviously, the answers to these and other questions can be obtained only through careful research. The package designer must strive for a balance between creativity and function.

Package Research

Today, effective packaging is a vital part of marketing a product. The only absolute in testing a package design is to sell it in a test market setting. There are several aspects of assessing a package design, including recognition, imagery, structure, and behavior.

- **Recognition.** A package must attract attention to itself so that the consumer can easily identify it in the retail environment. The recognition properties of a package can be measured. Research can determine how long it takes a consumer to recognize the package and what elements are most memorable.

- **Imagery.** The package must be easily recognized, but it must project a brand image compatible with the corporate brand-imagery objectives. A package can reinforce advertising, or it can negate it.

- **Structure.** The objective is to determine any structural problems consumers pinpoint that may inhibit repeat purchases. Is the package easy to open? Is it easy to close? Is it easy to handle? Is it easy to use?

- **Behavior.** This can be the most expensive means of researching packages. Often, this approach presents simulated shelf settings to groups of people and monitors whether they pick up or purchase a product.

Package Differentiation

Twelve suburban women sit around a focus group table, psyching themselves up to talk about cat food for two hours. Through the course of the evening, only two things really perk them up: the chance to describe their cats and a vacuum-packed foil bag of cat food.

Even before they've examined the nuggets of cat food, most of the women said they would buy it, intrigued by the high-tech, brick-like bag they've come to expect to see in the coffee aisle, certainly, but never spotted before among the cans, boxes, and bags of pet food.

It's a point increasingly driven home to marketers of food, health, and beauty product lines and over-the-counter drugs: The package is the brand.

Marketers are paying more attention to package design because products are so much more at parity these days. When differentiation through taste, color, and other product elements has reached parity, packaging makes a critical difference.[12] A case in point is Pepsi-Cola's reaction to making its plasticization of the famous curved bottle. It couldn't duplicate the curved bottle, but it did create a stable of designs with monikers like "Fast Break" or "Big

---

[12]Betsy Spethmann, "The Mystique of the Brand: Jarred, Bagged, Boxed, Canned," *Brandweek,* June 27, 1994, p. 25.

EXHIBIT

21.14

· · · · · · · · · · · · · · · · · ·

Wrigley's has built
strong brand identity
and equity through
years of using strong
packaging design with
its arrow symbol.

(Courtesy: Actmedia.)

Slam." It found that the bottles are a way to build excitement without changing the formula.

Unique Designs Cement Brand Image

Packaged goods marketers are paying special attention these days to delivery systems. A unique delivery system, like Mentadent toothpaste's double pump, can cement a brand's image. And designs based on consumers' use of a package make consumers feel like the manufacturer cares about them.

Brand Identity

Brand identity is a specific combination of visual and verbal elements that help achieve the following attributes of a successful brand: create recognition, provide differentiation, shape the brand's imagery, link all brand communications to the brand, and—very importantly—be the proprietary, legal property of the company that owns the brand.

There are a surprisingly short number of components that make up a brand identity. These include names logos, which are the designed version of a name; symbols and other graphic devices; color; package configuration (the physical structure of a package); and permanent support messages—slogans and jingles.[13] See Exhibit 21.14.

Restaging Brand Identity: An Example

Spurred by the growth of Home Depot and other stores targeting do-it-yourselfers, Price Pfister has restaged its line of faucets, hoping to strengthen brand identity with new packaging and a $6 million TV campaign.

The new packaging emphasizes the brand name by making it larger and by keeping the front of the box free of other copy. The goal was for Price Pfister to *become a brand instead of a manufacturer.*[14]

---

[13]Anita K. Hersh and John Lister, "Brand identity," *The Advertiser,* Spring 1993, pp. 66–71.
[14]"Price Pfister Repositions," *Brandweek,* August 5, 1994, p.13.

Cotrends and Packaging

Cobranding, coadvertising, and copackaging are trends that enable companies with strong brand equities to team together to gain more market share at a lower cost. For example, Betty Crocker cobrands with Reeses Candy, Sunkist with Kraft, and Stayfree with Arm & Hammer. The challenge is to present the brand identities and brand communications in such a way that both brand names are strengthened by the visual association, while marketing costs are shared.

Package Design

A product's package is more than a necessary production expense. Therefore, much care needs to be given to the role of packaging in the integrated marketing, relationship marketing with its emphasis on quality, and interactive media and the information superhighway. In its promotion function, the package does everything a medium should. At the point-of-purchase, it alone reminds, informs, attracts, and reminds the consumer. At the point-of-use it reinforces the purchase decision. Quality and value are viewed as relatively new marketing concepts, yet some 15 years ago the Design and Market Research Laboratory showed that quality perception was one of the key criteria for packaging assessment. But quality and value have always been part of the marketing and packaging equation.

Since packaging is such an important weapon in the marketing arsenal, it should be approached as other marketing elements with marketing research, specifically user research with target consumers.

Frank Tobolski, president of JTF Marketing/Studios, says research techniques measure the communication strengths and weaknesses of package graphics. They answer such questions as: Do the graphics communicate well? Do the graphics reinforce and enhance the image positioning? Do the products and package sell? He reports on a case where a toy company developed new packaging for a line of products. Perceptual and imagery evaluation in a diagnostic laboratory test was performed, indicating some problems and potential negative sales effects. To obtain behavioral sales data, test quantities of packages were produced for a balanced store test. For six weeks during the Christmas season, 18 stores stocked the new test design and 18 stocked the existing control design. Toy specialty, discount, department store, and mass-merchandiser stores were used for the matched store pairings. The bottom line after six weeks found the existing control packages sold 63 percent more units than the test packages. Even after adjusting the test stores, the new designs sold 35 percent less.[15] A major loss in sales was diverted by testing. Imagine the loss if there had been a full new package rollout.

Today's packaged-goods marketing managers constantly face the critical task of justifying expenditures in terms of the potential return on investment (ROI). Although most can instantly give you current sales figures, few know the yield on their latest shelf media or, specifically, packaging design.

Why? There is growing evidence that packaging design has a much stronger impact on sales than is realized.

---

[15]Frank Tobolski, "Package Design Requires Research," *Marketing News,* June 6, 1994, p. 4.

Two examples, redesigns of the popular Rice-a-Roni and Del Monte tomato product lines, illustrate how packaging design contributes to gains in market share and provides a significant ROI.

A packaging revitalization focused on the true personality of the product, unified the line, and added a dimension of quality and appetite appeal. When a freshened and updated Rice-a-Roni package hit the shelves, the brand experienced a 20 percent increase in sales compared with the previous year. The new design gave Rice-a-Roni considerably stronger shelf impact and clearly contributed to the strong sales increase.[16]

As any brand manager will tell you, packaging represents a substantial portion of brand equity. When the word *Coke* is uttered, it's more than likely that an image of the trademarked, hourglass-shaped bottle comes to mind.

The PackageValue survey suggests that marketers should benchmark new packaging proposals against their own brand equity.

The study interviewed a total of 251 men and women, all primary grocery shoppers. Those polled were shown a card with a brand name printed on it and asked to rate the brand on a scale of 1 (agree strongly) to 5 (disagree strongly).

Using "top box" methodology, only respondents who said they "agreed strongly" with all statements were included in the final results.

The subjects were then shown photos of actual packaging. The difference between the scores recorded when people were supplied with a brand name and when they were influenced by actual packaging is what makes the study intriguing. For example, when asked to rate the quality of Procter & Gamble's Tide, both the brand name and the packaging got scores of 61.[17]

Legal Aspects of Packaging

There are both federal and state laws that regulate packaging and labeling. The Fair Packaging and Labeling Act of 1966 says:

> Informed consumers are essential to the fair and efficient functioning of a free economy. Packages and their labels should enable consumers to obtain accurate information as to the quality of the contents and should facilitate value comparisons. Therefore it is hereby declared to be the policy of the Congress to assist consumers and manufacturers in reaching these goals in the marketing of goods.

This is the most far-reaching law affecting packaging and labeling. For example, all food packages must display the ingredients prominently (a loaf of bread lists all the ingredients in descending order of quantity used); over-the-counter drug products follow the same rule; and drug products must prominently display instructions for use, precautions, and instructions in case of accidental overdose. The Food and Drug Administration is responsible for enforcing the law as it affects food, drugs, cosmetics, and health devices. The Federal Trade Commission has jurisdiction over "other consumer commodities."

---

[16]Michael Prone, "Package Design Has Stronger ROI Potential Than Many Believe," *Marketing News,* October 11, 1993, p. 13.
[17]Terry Lofton, "If Your Brand's Number Two, Get with the Package Program," *BrandWeek,* June 27, 1994, p. 26.

The Food-Labeling Mandate

Nutrient content and health claims are generally prohibited unless authorized by the regulations.

Strict standards remain for use of the descriptive terms *free, low, less, light* or *lite, reduced, more, high, good source, lean, extra,* and *fresh.* The regulations also include a veritable laundry list of approved synonyms for these terms.

Product brand names are also affected by the labeling regulations. The regulations apply to brand names that contain express or implied nutrient content claims unless that name was in use before October 25, 1989, and is not misleading.

Some claims may still be made without qualifications. A claim that a food has added value (for instance, "made with real butter") is permitted. The same is true with so-called avoidance claims such as "made without milk" or "contains no pork" that are made for religious or other nonnutritive purposes. A different qualifying criterion applies to foods whose single-serving size is under 30 grams, like cereal.

Under these regulations, a nutrient content claim may be in type two times larger than the statement identifying the food. The proposed regulations did not allow a nutrient content claim to exceed the size of the statement of the product's identity. There are specific requirements to qualify for using the terms *reduced* or *less.* Both now require at least a 25 percent reduction of a nutrient or calories to be used in labeling. *Reduced* is qualitatively the same as *less.* That does not mean the terms can be used interchangeably, however. *Reduced* refers to comparisons made with the regular product: For instance, reduced-calorie cupcakes have 33-1/3 fewer calories than regular cupcakes.

The FDA has defined the term *healthy.* That term may be used only when a product can be considered low in fat and does not contain too much cholesterol or sodium.[18]

Design Firms

There are many design firms that specialize in packaging and brand identity programs for corporations. These work with the agency or the corporation or both in developing packaging and may be involved with the total design concept of a corporation or brand. For example, when you think of the McDonald's Corporation—the hamburger people—what comes to mind? Golden Arches? Employee uniforms? Employees? Cup designs? Paper or box designs? Logo? Paper bags? Premiums? Letterheads? Publications? There are many elements that help identify McDonald's—every element has its name or logo for starters. The corporate design people help the marketer and sometimes the agency develop strong corporate visual communications. Exhibits 21.15 and 21.16 are examples of design basics—the letterhead, envelope, mailing labels, business cards, etc., for a restaurant company and the design firm's own logo. Exhibit 21.17 shows Longwater's visual communication designs all of which are building the Port of Savannah (obviously they don't have product packages) identity—from ads to brochures.

---

[18]Maxine S. Lans, "Labeling Right May Be More Difficult Than Eating Right," *Marketing News,* March 29, 1992, p. 16.

EXHIBIT

21.15

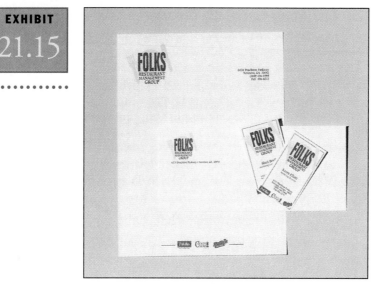

(Courtesy: Sterrett Dymond Advertising.)

Among the large packaging design firms are Landor Associates (San Francisco), Gertsman+Meyers (New York) Peterson & Blyth (New York), and the Schechter Group (New York) (see Exhibit 21.18).

SUMMARY

Today packaging is a very important part of the brand equity equation. It has been labeled as the only true method of international branding.

A product trademark is like a person's name. It gives a product an identity and allows customers to be sure they are getting the same quality for each purchase. In addition, the trademark makes advertising and promotion ac-

EXHIBIT

21.16

EXHIBIT
21.17

• • • • • • • • • • • • • • •

Brochure, ads, and visual communication pieces that build brand identity.

(Courtesy: Longwater.)

EXHIBIT
21.18

• • • • • • • • • • • • • • • •

(Courtesy: Ralf Colonna, Colonna, Farrell: Design.)

tivities possible. For established products, the trademark is one of the company's most valuable assets. It would be very difficult to estimate the value of trademarks such as Coca-Cola, Pepsi-Cola, IBM, or Mercedes. That is why companies take such pains to protect their trademarks.

The trademark can take the form of a word, design, or a combination of both. Its format can include letters, numbers, slogans, geometric shapes, color combinations, etc. When a trademark is a picture or other design, it is called a logotype. The same principle of trademark protection that applies to brand names also applies to logos. A successful trademark may take many forms; however, it should be easy to pronounce, have something in common with the product, and lend itself to a variety of advertising and design formats.

The package design is developed in much the same way as an advertising campaign. Package research can help in assessing a number of factors including recognition, imagery, structure, and behavior. Packaging is an important marketing tool and should be researched with target groups. Cobranding, coadvertising, and copackaging enable are current trends to gain market share at lower cost. Brand identity continues to be an important issue.

Questions

1. What is a trademark?
2. What is the difference between trademark and trade name?
3. Name several considerations for selecting brand names.
4. Briefly, give some general trademark rules.
5. What is a house mark?

The **Complete**
Campaign

CHAPTER 22

CHAPTER OBJECTIVES

As we indicated earlier, we generally don't create ads—we create advertising campaigns that fit into the total integrated marketing communication program. After reading this chapter you will understand:

- **Situation analysis**
- **Creative objectives and strategy**
- **Media objectives**
- **The sales promotion plan**
- **The research relationship**

As we have said earlier, we are truly in the midst of a marketing revolution fueled by new data sources and technology. The need to build brand equity is more important than ever before. As Larry Light, chairman of the Colition for Brand Equity put it, "Brand Loyalty marketing is the way to build enduring, profitable growth for brands and companies." **And every marketing plan** should contain four

EXHIBIT

22.1

· · · · · · · · · · · · · · · · · · · ·

The Link planning
process for building
strong brand equity in
advertising campaigns.

(Courtesy: Lintas: Worldwide.)

elements: What are we doing to *identify, attract, defend,* and *strengthen* brand loyalty?[1]

The Link strategy system discussed in Chapter 3 focuses on the premise that a brand is a living entity that is created through communication. It carries a history, which represents its accumulated capital, but it must continue to build new communication by asserting its presence, its sovereignty, and its territory. In doing so, however, the brand must maintain a consistent identity. The link system's four components are synthesized into an action plan for developing all communications for a brand (integrated marketing), including advertising, sales promotion, public relations, packaging design, and direct marketing (see Exhibit 22.1 as a refresher).

We have specifically talked about important components of the advertising process—development of strategy, media, research, print ads, and broadcast—all of which are extremely important. The truth is we don't generally think in terms of individual ads because most brand advertising depends on a series of ads run over a period of time—in other words, a campaign. The ad campaign also doesn't work alone; it is integrated into the sales and marketing program.

As a general rule, campaigns are designed to run over a longer period of time than an individual ad, although there are exceptions. The average length of a regional or national campaign is about 17 months, although it is not uncommon for a campaign to last three or four years, and a few campaigns have lasted much longer. For example, in 1929 DuPont started using the campaign theme "Better Things for Better Living Through Chemistry." Fifty-five years later it was changed—"through chemistry" was dropped. That is building a lot of brand equity. Basically, the messages remained true to its original campaign premise.

Positioning

Segmenting a market by creating a product to meet the needs of a select group or by using a distinctive advertising appeal to meet the needs of a specialized group, without making changes in the physical product.

---

[1]Larry Light, "Brand Loyalty Marketing Key to Enduring Growth," *Advertising Age,* October 3, 1994, p. 20.

On the other hand, some campaigns need to change. "Pardon me, would you have any Grey Poupon?" worked too well. The strategy of making Grey Poupon a *premium* brand worked a little too well: Consumers tended to reserve it for only special occasions and not for everyday eating. To change consumer habits meant going another direction and resulted in another campaign to get consumers to use it at ordinary meals. The commercials, in which stuffy aristocrats pass the Grey Poupon through their Rolls-Royce windows, lasted a long time because of their appeal to both affluent and working-class consumers alike. The campaign said everybody could live the good life of the affluent, when it comes to mustard. The simpler lifestyles of the mid-1990s diluted the impact and called for a broader approach to the product. The new direction asked consumers to "Poupon the potato salad" and "class up the cold cuts."

There is no reason to change an advertising campaign for the sake of change. There is never a guarantee that the next campaign will be as strong, let alone stronger. And some companies grope for a better campaign with little success. For example, in the mid-1970s, Burger King had maybe its most famous campaign, "Have it your way," but decided it was time to change. So it followed with the following:

> *America loves burgers, and we're America's Burger King. (Nov. 77–Feb. 78)*
> *Who's got the best darn burger? (Feb. 78–Jan. 80)*
> *Make it special. Make it Burger King. (Jan. 80–Jan. 82)*
> *Aren't you hungry for Burger King now? (Jan. 82–Sept. 82)*
> *Battle of the burgers. (Sept. 82–March 83)*
> *Broiling vs frying. (March 83–Sept. 83)*
> *The big switch. (Sept. 83–Nov. 85)*
> *Search for Herb. (Nov. 95–June 1986)*
> *This is a Burger King town. (June 86–Jan. 87)*
> *We do it like you do it. (April 88–May 89)*
> *Sometimes you gotta break the rules. (Oct. 89–April 91)*
> *Your way. Right away. (April 91–Oct. 92)*
> *BK Tee Vee: I love this place. (Oct. 92–94)*

Any campaign needs to bring together all of the advertising elements we have discussed into a unified campaign. This calls for an advertising plan. As we have emphasized, good advertising starts with a clear understanding of marketing goals, both short and long term. These goals are often expressed as sales or share-of-market objectives to be accomplished for a given budget and over a specific time period.

With our marketing goals in mind, we begin to build the advertising plan with a situation analysis.

SITUATION ANALYSIS

In order to plan and create future advertising, we need to establish a current benchmark or starting point—this is the role of the situation analysis. It has two time orientations: the past and the present. In other words, it asks two basic questions: Where are we today, and how did we get here? The rest of the advertising plan asks the third basic question: Where are we going?

Situation analysis
The part of the advertising plan that answers the questions: Where are we today and how did we get here? It deals with the past and present.

The Product

Successful advertising and marketing begin with a good product. At this point, we need to analyze our product's strengths and weaknesses objectively. Most product failures stem from an overly optimistic appraisal of a product. Among the questions usually asked are:

1. What are the unique consumer benefits the product will deliver?

2. What is the value of the product relative to the proposed price?

3. Are adequate distribution channels available?

4. Can quality control be maintained?

Prime-Prospect Identification

The next step is to identify our prime prospects and determine if there are enough of them to market the product profitably. As we discussed in Chapter 4, there are a number of ways to identify the primary consumer of our product.

Competitive Atmosphere and Marketing Climate

We carefully review every aspect of the competition including direct and indirect competitors. Which specific brand and products compete with your brand, and in what product categories or subcategories do they belong? Is Mountain Dew's competition 7-Up or Sprite, Mellow-Yellow or Crush, or does it extend to colas, iced tea, and milk? If so, to what extent in each case?

What does Neon directly compete with? Indirectly? Neon's competitive subcompact set includes Honda Civic, Ford Escort, Saturn, Nissan Sentra, Toyota Tercel, Toyota Corolla, Chevrolet Cavalier, Geo Prism, Plymouth Sundance, Dodge Shadow. When we examine the demographic competitive set: The typical subcompact buyers are 50–55 percent female, over half are married, they tend to be 35–40 years of age, and less than half have a college degree. Honda Civic and Saturn models attract the most distinguishable buyer profiles—typically better educated, earning more income, and younger. Pyschographic—competitive set. The greatest fluctuations in psychographic profiles for this set exists between import and domestic buyers. Domestic buyers tend to be motivated by style over engineering, prefer roomier cars and greater performance. Import buyers prefer engineering over style, like compact cars and believe imports offer higher quality overall. Now we're beginning to scratch the surface. As you can see there are numerous factors.

CREATIVE OBJECTIVES AND STRATEGY

At this point, we begin to select those advertising themes and selling appeals that are most likely to move our prime prospects to action. As we discussed in Chapter 16, advertising motivates people by appealing to their problems, desires, and goals—it is not creative if it does not sell. Once we establish the overall objectives of the copy, we are ready to implement the copy strategy by outlining how this creative plan will contribute to accomplishing our predetermined marketing goals:

1. Determine the specific claim that will be used in advertising copy. If there is more than one, the claims should be listed in order of priority.

2. Consider various advertising executions. Review the PAPA discussion in Chapter 16 with an eye toward finding the best approach to convince consumers that your product will solve their problem better than any alternative.

3. In the final stage of the creative process, develop the copy and production of advertising.

Creative Criteria for Campaigns

Ken Roman and Jane Mass in *The New How to Advertise* stress how essential *similarity* between one advertisement and another is in developing successful advertising campaigns. Another term, *continuity*, is used to describe the relationship of one ad to another ad throughout a campaign. This similarity or continuity may be visual, verbal, aural, or attitudinal.[2]

Visual Similarity. All print ads use the same typeface or virtually the same layout format so that consumers will learn to recognize the advertiser just by glancing at the ads. This may entail making illustrations about the same size in ad after ad and/or the headline about the same length in each ad. We've shown you a number of ads in campaigns throughout the book: Lowe's, Healthtex, Andersen Windows, MOL, Port of Savannah, Egg Beaters, etc. The illustrations in the Lowe's ads are the same size, heads are visually treated in the same manner, the left column of body copy is in italics, and there is an illustration at the top of each photo (see Exhibit 22.2). For a different kind of client and reader, Mitsui O.S.K. Lines uses similar treatment in this campaign about its containers (see Exhibit 22.3). You have the same visual feel from ad to ad, although the headline treatment isn't exactly the same and the body copy varies in length. Again, we're saying visual continuity—not sameness. These examples are print, but the look could easily be carried over to television or direct marketing. Another device is for all ads in a campaign to use the same spokesperson or continuing character in ad after ad. Still another way to achieve visual continuity is to use the same demonstration in ad after ad from one medium to the other.

Verbal Similarity. It is not unusual for a campaign to use certain words or phrases in each ad to sum up the product's benefits. It is more than a catchy phrase. The proper objective is a set of words that illuminates the advertising, encapsulates the promise, and can be associated with one brand only.

Here are a few campaign phrases that have worked:

You expect more from a leader.	*(AMOCO)*
Make yourself comfortable.	*(Lane furniture)*
Better care makes better cats.	*(Purina Cat Chow)*
Helping add value to your home.	*(Lowe's)*
You'll love the way we fly.	*(Delta Air Lines)*
The sign of a great cook.	*(Jenn-Air)*
It's everywhere you want to be.	*(Visa)*

---

[2]Kenneth Roman and Jane Maas, *The New How to Advertise*, (New York: St. Martin's Press, 1992), pp. 71–78.

EXHIBIT

22.2

The Lowe's ads in this
text have a similar
look, feel and copy
tone.

(Courtesy: Lowe's Corp. as seen in Southern Living Magazine.)

Tailor-made for your hang-ups.

If textile and clothing products are your style, then Mitsui O.S.K. Lines could be a perfect fit. Don't feel hemmed in by the usual shipping delays and frustrations. Let MOL show you a little something in your size...

Whether you're importing hanging garments or flat packs from the expanding Asian markets, you will find that our containers and transit times are tailor-made to suit you.

Our seamless, fixed-day, fixed hour transpacific shipping schedule, combined with a trendsetting cargo tracking system, guarantees delivery of your fashions while they're still chic.

Because in this business, there's no such thing as fashionably late.

So don't let your hang-ups get hung up where they shouldn't be. Call the intermodal experts at MOL today. Because, no matter where you're shipping, Mitsui O.S.K. Lines can make it an address for success!

For more information, call the MOLAM office nearest you: Corporate Headquarters 201/200-5200; Atlanta 404/763-0111; Chicago 312/683-7300; Long Beach 310/437-8251; Seattle 206/464-3930.

MOL

Shoes us

If the shoe fits, chances are it was handled by Mitsui O.S.K. Lines, which has developed a specialized transportation logistics system that's right in step with the unique requirements of today's competitive footwear trade.

MOL enables well-heeled customers to outpace the competition by providing reliable fixed-day, fixed-hour intermodal service via four transpacific liner routes linking China, Korea, and other South Asian markets with distribution centers throughout the U.S. And frequent sailings help footwear shippers toe the bottom line by planning their inventories more effectively.

But more than that, MOL's 40' and 45' high cube containers are a perfect fit for footwear shipments, while our NAVI-GATOR system and customer service specialists make shippers feel as comfortable with us as a favorite pair of shoes. And that's our sole concern.

Because regardless of what you ship, great service laced with personal attention can help you keep a step ahead of the competition. So if you're ready to put your best foot forward, call the global logistics specialists at Mitsui O.S.K. Lines today and let them show you how to shoes a winner!

For more information, call the MOLAM office nearest you: Corporate Headquarters 201/200-5200 or 800/ OK-GATOR; Atlanta 404/763-0111; Boston 617/330-9295; Chicago 312/683-7300; Kansas City 816/842-4842; Long Beach 310/437-8251; Memphis 901/681-4260; Seattle 206/464-3930; Toronto 416/629-5900.

MOL

(Courtesy: Longwater, Inc.)

EXHIBIT

22.3

· · · · · · · · · · · · · · · · · · ·

These Mitsui O.S.K. Lines ads are clearly different but have a similar look.

"You're in the Pepsi Generation." These words helped position Pepsi among a younger audience and made Coca-Cola appear to be an old-fashioned brand. But it didn't limit all the up-beat, self-assuring benefits of membership of being part of the Pepsi generation to people between 13 and 24 years old; it opened it up to everybody—everybody wanted to be in the Pepsi Generation. It wasn't a point in *time* of years; it was a point of *view*. No matter what your age, you could be part of the Pepsi Generation. Great words and great strategy make great campaigns. Here are a few other words and classic campaign strategies:

> *Aren't you glad you use Dial?*
> *Don't you wish everybody did?*
>
> *You're in good hands with Allstate.*
>
> *American Express. Don't leave home without it.*
>
> *Have it your way at Burger King.*
>
> *Is it true blondes have more fun?*
> *Be a Lady Clairol blonde and see!*
>
> *You deserve a break today, at McDonald's.*

Repeating the benefits, theme, and key copy points in ad after ad bestows continuity across all media and helps build brand personality.

We have shown a number of award-winning Healthtex ads throughout this text to give you a real taste of its campaign. These ads use visual, verbal, and attitude similarity. And we didn't include all the great ones: "When you're bald and toothless, you'd better wear cute clothes," for example. Joe Alexander, the copywriter on this campaign, comments on its success: "The best advertising is always personal. It relates to me or to something happening in my life. We understood what moms and dads wanted to know. We wanted to show kids as they really are." It just happens that three of the four members of the Healthtex creative team (a copywriter and two art directors) have children. The fourth (a copywriter) has numerous nieces and nephews.

The Healthtex campaign is really about smart marketing. They do a lot of account planning. And conceptually, this enabled the agency to speak in a language that talks to Mom. The campaign budget was $5 million and ran in parenting magazines. Over a two-year period, sales increased 42 percent and advertising awareness is up 35 percent, and the awards have rolled in. According to Alexander, Healthtex positioned itself in a leadership position in a me-too market. This has been a great campaign. (see Exhibits 22.4, and 22.5).

Aural Similarity. In broadcast, you may use the same music or jingle. Using the same announcer's voice in each ad also helps build continuity. The same sound effect can make a campaign very distinctive. Avon used the sound of a doorbell for many years in its "Avon calling" advertising. And Maxwell House used the perking sound for its Master Blend commercial, giving an audible campaign signal.

Attitudinal Similarity. Each ad expresses a consistent attitude toward the product and the people using it. The commercial's attitude is an expression

EXHIBIT

22.4

(Courtesy: Healthtex™ and The Martin Agency.)

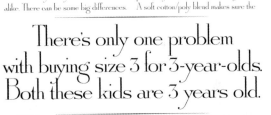

(Courtesy: Healthtex™ and The Martin Agency.)

of brand personality. The Pepsi Generation campaign was more than words. It communicated an attitude to younger consumers and older consumers. And, of course, the Nike shoe campaign which said, "Just do it."

These guidelines for building effective advertising campaigns can be used in numerous combinations. Most effective campaigns will use at least one of these techniques to build continuity in ad after ad.

MEDIA OBJECTIVES

Although we have chosen to discuss creative strategy before media objectives, both functions are considered simultaneously in an advertising campaign. In fact, creative and media planning have the same foundations—marketing strategy and prospect identification—and cannot be isolated from each other. The media plan involves three primary areas.

Media Strategy

At the initial stages of media planning, the general approach and role of media in the finished campaign are determined:

1. *Prospect identification.* The prime prospect is of major importance in both the media and the creative strategy. However, the media planner has the additional burden of identifying prospects. The media strategy must match prospects for a product with users of specific media. This requires that prospects be identified in terms that are compatible with traditional media audience breakdowns. You will recall that this need for standardization has resulted in the 4A's standard demographic categories discussed in Chapter 4.

2. *Timing.* All media, with the possible exception of direct mail, operate on their own schedule, not that of advertisers. The media planner must consider many aspects of timing, including media closing dates, production time required for ads and commercials, campaign length, and the number of exposures desired during the product-purchase cycle.

3. *Creative considerations.* The media and creative teams must accommodate each other. They must compromise between using those media that allow the most creative execution and those that are most efficient in reaching prospects.

Media Tactics

At this point, the media planner decides on media vehicles and the advertising weight each is to receive. The reach-versus-frequency question must be addressed and appropriate budget allocations made.

Media Scheduling

Finally, an actual media schedule and justification are developed, as described in the example in Chapter 7.

The Sales Promotion Plan

As with any integrated communications planning, the sales-promotion plan for consumers is discussed very early, and its relationship to the advertising plan (and other communications activities) is determined. Sales-promotion activities may involve dealer displays, in-store promotions, premiums, cooperative advertising, and/or couponing offers. In the case of services, like health care, promotion may be different. Harris Regional Hospital invites people to look into their operation in Exhibit 22.6. In Exhibit 22.7 you are invited to their fish hook promotion celebrating their name change. And Exhibit 22.8 shows several creative invitations.

Once a theme for communications has been established, creative work is begun on the sales-promotion material, which is presented along with the consumer advertising material for final approval. Naturally, advertising and sales-promotion materials would reinforce each other. Once the sales-promotion

C.J. Harris Community changed its name to Harris Regional Hospital. It invites consumers to take a look at its benefits.

(Courtesy: Sterrett Dymond Advertising.)

EXHIBIT

22.7

· · · · · · · · · · · · · · · · · ·

This direct mail piece
uses a real fish hook
to hook the reader.

material is approved, the production is carefully planned so that all of the sales-promotion material will be ready before the consumer advertising breaks.

GETTING THE CAMPAIGN APPROVED

We now have a complete campaign: the ads, the media schedule, sales-promotion material, and costs for everything spelled out, ready for management's final approval. For that approval, it is wise to present a statement of the company's marketing goals. The objectives may be to launch a new product, to increase sales by x percent, to raise the firm's share of the market by z percent, or to promote a specific service of a firm. Next, the philosophy and strategy of the advertising are described, together with the reasons for believing that the proposed plan will help attain those objectives. Not until then are the ads or the commercials presented, along with the media proposal and the plans for coordinating the entire effort with that of the sales department.

What are the reasons for each recommendation in the program? On what basis were these dollar figures arrived at? On what research were any decisions based? What were the results of preliminary tests, if any? What is the competition doing? What alternatives were considered? What is the total cost? Finally, how may the entire program contribute to the company's return on its investment? Those people who control the corporate purse strings like to have definite answers to such questions before they approve a total advertising program.

RESEARCH—POSTTESTS

The final part of the campaign entails testing its success. Posttesting falls into two related stages. In the first, the expected results are defined in specific and measurable terms. What do you expect the advertising campaign to accomplish? Typical goals of a campaign are to increase brand awareness by 10 percent or improve advertising recall by 25 percent.

Eating fish like this could send you to the hospital.

And we hope it does.

To celebrate our new name change, we're having an old-fashioned fish fry, complete with rainbow trout and all the trimmings. So come out to Harris Regional Hospital on the afternoon of June 5th between 12:30 and 2:30. And join us for the catch of the day.

Harris Regional Hospital Fish Fry, June 5.

This free lunch invitation comes with a catch.

To celebrate our new name change, we're having an old-fashioned fish fry, complete with all the trimmings. So come on out to Harris Regional Hospital on the afternoon of June 5th between 12:30 and 2:30. And join us for the catch of the day.

Harris Regional Hospital Fish Fry, June 5.

(Courtesy: Sterrett Dymond Advertising.)

EXHIBIT

22.8

· · · · · · · · · · · · · · · · · · · ·

In the second stage, the actual research is conducted to see if these goals were met. Regardless of what research technique is used (for example, test markets, consumer panels), the problem is separating the results of the advertising campaign from consumer behavior that would have occurred in any case. That is, if we find that 20 percent of the population recognizes our brand at the end of a campaign, the question is what would the recognition level have been if no advertising took place. In order to answer this question, a research design is often used as a pretest. The pretest is intended not only to provide a benchmark for the campaign, but also to determine reasonable goals for future advertising.

Case History

MARKETING SITUATION

In today's market, the race for color television supremacy is run in the Very Large Screen segment (VLS = 30" and above). Success in VLS is critical because it is the fastest growing segment in the category, allows the highest profit margins, and most importantly, provides image leadership for flanker lines in the brand.

For these reasons, it was essential that RCA establish a presence in the segment. Major obstacles, however, stood in their path. Two factors define success in VLS: product performance and brand name panache. Consumers believed RCA lacked both.

In the last 20 years, performance has been the domain of the innovative Japanese, not RCA. This perception was reinforced by the conventional wisdom that associated high price with high performance. Sagging sales through the 1980's had forced RCA to cut price. Once cut, the Trade bristled at every attempt to raise prices, so RCA was increasingly perceived as being a "value brand."

Moreover, imagery surrounding the RCA name —once synonymous with the invention of TV—had decayed to a mournful collection of adjectives like "stodgy,""old fashioned," and "backward." Very little brand name panache there.

Perhaps the greatest obstacle facing RCA was the overwhelming strength of the competition—especially Mitsubishi, who literally invented VLS. In 1979 Mitsubishi introduced the world's first one-piece projection television and in 1986 they launched the first direct view 35" screen (the flagship screen size in the direct view segment).

Fully exploiting their advantage as first mover into VLS, Mitsubishi had dominated market share in both projection and VLS direct view since 1986. Even Sony—the perceived gold standard in every other segment of the consumer electronics category—hovers between 8 and 15 share points *behind* Mitsubishi in VLS.

Fueling Mitsubishi's dominance are two factors not available to RCA:

1. An obvious association with "Japan Inc.," the perennial innovators of the consumer electronics market, and,
2. Mitsubishi trademark advertising (behind automobiles, etc.) that, outpaced RCA's total consumer electronics spending by a *factor of 10*.

Thus, the race for success in the VLS market pitted the juggernaut Mitsubishi against RCA—a mid-priced television whose outdated brand imagery belied its state-of-the-art features and performance. Since RCA could not credibly face Mitsubishi by positioning itself on the cutting edge of innovation, advertising would have to focus on big picture and

sound. This, however, was the central benefit of all VLS televisions and the main copy point in virtually all competitive advertising. To separate itself from the competition, RCA (with Nipper and Chipper's help) decided to bring big picture and big sound to life in a warm, accessible way and thereby make the end benefit *home entertainment* rather than just the output from a cold, impersonal box of technology.

CAMPAIGN OBJECTIVES

Given the growing sense that they were playing David to Mitsubishi's Goliath, RCA had great expectations of the new Home Theatre campaign:

1. Try to erode Mitsubishi's share lead—
   RCA trailed Mitsubishi by more than ten share points.
2. Unit sales should keep pace with VLS category growth—
   No small feat since the young category had been growing at approximately 30% per year.
3. Primary message must be heard and the commercials must be liked—
   * Playback the Big Picture/Big Sound message should meet RCA norms.
   * Likeability measures should be high to support strategic positioning.

TARGET AUDIENCE

MALES 35–54: Tend to dominate consumer electronics purchases.

HH INCOME: $40.000+ VLS televisions retail between $1,800 and $5,000

"VIDEOPHILES": Highly involved, discerning electronics consumers.

CREATIVE STRATEGY

In order to establish its credentials in the VLS market, RCA chose to focus on the basics: big picture and big sound. These benefits would be communicated on two levels:

* To give the Home Theatre line credibility and reason for being, big picture and big sound would have to be brought to life in a vivid and expressive way.
* To separate the brand from the "techno-box" competition, advertising would have to be warm, likable and accessible.

Nipper, the symbol of RCA in its glory, and Chipper, the puppy who embodies RCA's promise for the future, would again help recall the brand's proud heritage while at the same time helping RCA reverse their old-fashioned, low-tech imagery.

MEDIA STRATEGY

The Media plan was 70% Television/30% Print and was concentrated in the 1st and 4th Quarters to correspond with national purchase trends.

70% of the budget was dedicated to Television because the Big Picture/Sound story can only truly come to life in a fluid medium. Print reinforced the television presence by offering increased frequency and allowing more space for deeper explanation of selected product features.

RCA's approximate SOV of Color TV advertising was 13%, behind Magnavox at 40%, Sony at 20% and Mitsubishi at 15%. As mentioned earlier, Mitsubishi's total trademark spending exceeded RCA's by a factor of 10.

OTHER MARKETING PROGRAMS

RCA implemented no other programs in conjunction with this campaign.

(Courtesy: Ammirati & Puris)

EVIDENCE OF RESULTS

Objective #1: Erode Mitsubishi's share lead

RCA has achieved the unimaginable. For the first time in the history of the category, Mitsubishi has fallen to second place and *RCA is #1*. RCA's share of the VLS category leaped 7.9 points and, in the latest reporting period (August-September), leads Mitsubishi by .4 points.

Objective #2: Keep pace with category growth

RCA's unit sales grew an astounding *3.25 times faster* than the category. While the category grew at a strong *34.3%*, RCA's unit sales exploded by 111.5%. Share data would suggest that much of this volume came at Mitsubishi's expense.

Objective #3: Primary message must be heard and the commercials must be liked

The Home Theatre campaign communicated outstanding sound and/or picture quality at almost *double* the level of any previous RCA commercial and achieved some of the highest likeability scores in RCA history:

Execution	Primary Message	Playback	Likeability
Sunrise	Picture Quality	95%	85%
Looks Like, Feels Like	Sound Quality	80%	83%
Bulldozer	Home Theatre System	74%	84%

OVERALL

Despite the state-of-the-art product line, RCA and the Home Theatre campaign attacked the VLS segment from a position of weakness. Lacking both a perception of performance and brand name panache, RCA was forced to build a big screen story from the gound up. What emerged was a campaign that vividly brought Picture and Sound to life in a warm, accessible way.

As a result, RCA is the unlikely VLS market share leader and the vanquished Mitsubishi is scrambling to counterattack with yet another product innovation: the world's first 40″ direct view television. Ladies and gentlemen, start your engines.

A 10-year study by Information Resources Inc.'s BehaviorScan showed that advertising produces long-term growth even after a campaign ends. The study emphasized TV campaigns and concluded the following:

■ **Increased ad weight alone will not boost sales.**

■ **Typically, advertising for new brands, line extensions, or little-known brands produced the best incremental sales results.**

■ **Campaigns in which the "message in the copy is new" or the media strategy had changed also produced good sales results.**

■ **Results of copy recall and persuasion tests were unlikely to predict sales reliably.**

The study also suggested that discounting results in "training customers to buy only on a deal," and the trade promotion actually worked against TV advertising. However, couponing often helped a brand message and spurred a sale.

The test was conducted in 10 markets with household panels of 3,000 respondents in each market. The commercials were transmitted to two equal groups of homes. This study compared purchase information obtained through scanners and a card encoded with demographic and other information that was presented at supermarket checkout stands.[3]

---

[3]Gary Levin, "Tracing Ads' Impact," *Advertising Age,* November 4, 1991, p. 49.

Case History

MARKETING SITUATION

America is in the midst of a much-publicized health-care crisis. As health-care costs and associated insurance premiums have escalated, many working Americans have been faced with a net loss of health insurance coverage. For employers and their employees to receive adequate coverage at an affordable price, cost-saving measures have been introduced in the form of copayments and deductibles, which expose the consumer financially. *Supplemental* health insurance, as a category, is playing an increasingly vital role in providing adequate and affordable protection to millions of Americans.

The supplemental insurance category is extremely competitive and has traditionally been crowded with smaller companies, each with a niche within the broad supplemental field. Now, larger, well-established companies like Prudential, Aetna, and others are entering the supplemental category with broad product offerings. In an industry where reputation and credibility are important purchase criteria, AFLAC had only 14 months earlier changed its name from American Family Life Assurance Company. As a "new" entity it was absolutely vital for AFLAC to build its awareness and establish an image.

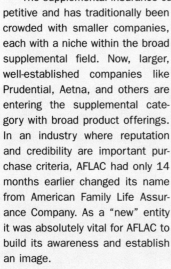

CAMPAIGN OBJECTIVES

AFLAC'S objectives were:

- To build awareness for the AFLAC name, and AFLAC as a supplemental insurer
- To build credibility for AFLAC as judged by five specific attributes (see Results section)
- To enhance sales force recruitment efforts

TARGET AUDIENCE

There were two primary audiences: (1) Key decision makers in the benefits process at mid-sized companies: CEO, president, DFO, controller, human resources manager, and personnel manager. This target is largely male, well educated, and upper income. (2) Consumers: Adults age 35 plus with household income of $30K+. There was one secondary audience: employees of mid-sized companies. And there was one tertiary audience: AFLAC employees.

CREATIVE STRATEGY

To position AFLAC as the leader in the *supplemental* health insurance field: AFLAC provides innovative solutions to com-

(Courtesy: McCann-Erickson, Inc. and AFLAC.)

plex insurance problems so that employers, their employees, and consumers alike can have peace of mind.

AFLAC's creative executions purposely avoided the heavy "gloom and doom" normally associated with insurance advertising. Advertising portrayed real-life companies and people struggling with significant health insurance problems from a sensitive and caring point of view.

MEDIA STRATEGY

The strategy was to purchase media that reach its defined target audiences efficiently and effectively, *and* to do so in high-profile, high-visibility opportunities that imply a leadership position. It was also important to establish awareness for the AFLAC name quickly, especially in the southeastern United States, where sales potential was highest and a majority of AFLAC policies were already in force.

AFLAC purchased Network News, NBC Summer Olympics, Braves baseball, ABC college basketball, and CNN news programming. Additionally, programming with implied "ownership" was negotiated wherever possible.

Print vehicles included the *Wall Street Journal, Fortune, Forbes, CFO Magazine, Chief Executive Magazine, Financial World, Newsweek,* and *Time.* Premium positions were negotiated wherever possible.

EVIDENCE OF RESULTS

On-going quantitative research measurers awareness and image attributes among several targets.

Data highlights that can be revealed are as follows:

Measure	Latest Measure (4/92)	Growth vs. Benchmark (10/90)
Awareness among all consumers	21%	+162%
Awareness among consumers $50K+	29%	+290%
Awareness among employed consumers	25%	+179%
Advertising awareness— all consumers	53%	+120%

Image Measurement Scores (7-point scale)

AFLAC as:		
	Trustworthy	5.63
	Reputable	5.80
	Responsive	5.63
	Financially Stable	5.55

Additionally, surveys among AFLAC's sales force and employees indicated enthusiastic support for the advertising. The sales force has experienced improved reception and assumed credibility from sales prospects.

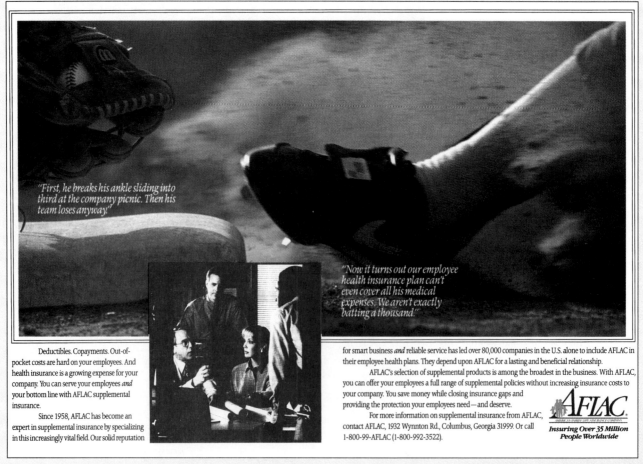

(Courtesy: McGann-Erickson, Inc. and AFLAC.)

SUMMARY

The steps in preparing a national campaign for a consumer product may be enumerated as follows:

1. Situation analysis
    a. Product analysis
    b. Prime-prospect identification.
    c. Prime-prospect problem analysis
    d. Competitive atmosphere and market climate

2. Creative objectives and strategy
    a. Determine specific copy claims
    b. Consider various advertising executions
    c. Begin creation of ads, commercials

3. Media objectives
    a. Media strategy—includes prospect identification, timing, and creative considerations
    b. Media tactics
    c. Media scheduling

4. The sales-promotion plan

5. Getting the campaign approved

6. Research posttests

Questions

1. What is an advertising campaign?
2. How long does an advertising campaign run?
3. Name the creative criteria for developing campaigns.

MARKETING SITUATION

The 1993 Dodge Intrepid was launched as the first in a series of new and innovative products as the foundation to reposition Dodge as a contemporary, forward-thinking company that builds quality products for the twenty-first century. It was important for the long-term success of Dodge for the company to win over skeptical, upscale buyers outside its current customers. Intrepid advertising had to provide evidence that the Dodge brand is changing, convert import car buyers, overcome negative quality perceptions of Dodge, and compete with other automotive brands attempting similar strategies. Dodge Intrepid sought to compete in the volatile mid-size market which accounted for 23.8 percent of total car sales at the time of launch.

CAMPAIGN OBJECTIVES

The Intrepid launch had several primary objectives:

1. To establish name awareness among at least 40 percent of the target market 12 months after launch
2. To generate consideration in excess of 5 percent of the target market at the end of the year
3. To begin shifting the demographic profile upscale by appealing to younger, more affluent prospects, including import prospects
4. To build the perception of complete quality through improved customer service by providing purchase information through an aggressively promoted 800 number program
5. To support retail sales objectives of 39,500 units

TARGET AUDIENCE

Intrepid strategy targeted first-time Dodge buyers who were younger (35–50 years old) and more upscale ($40–60,000 household income) than traditional Dodge buyers. This target market buys on the basis of reliability/durability and prefers to buy American automobiles, but remains skeptical about domestic car quality.

CREATIVE STRATEGY

The creative strategy was to convince the target audience that Dodge Intrepid is an automobile that would meet or exceed its definition of quality. Intrepid was positioned as a

INTREPID ◆ THE NEW DODGE

high-quality product equal to or superior to its competition. Because of the target audience's "information orientation" and its need for explicit proof of quality, the advertising had to be dramatically different in content and tone from past Dodge commercials. Creative execution emphasized:

1. Avoiding traditional superiority product claims (best-in-class claims, world-class references)
2. Avoiding specific labels (family sedan, sports sedan)
3. Leading with the product and minimizing use of the Dodge name to prevent consumers from rejecting Intrepid outright
4. Focusing on design and attention to detail
5. A tone that conveys an atmosphere of confidence, intelligence, and above all honesty
6. Show, rather then tell consumers how good Intrepid is, by offering the car itself as proof

Intrepid involved some 25,000 florists through FTD in a nationwide sweepstakes program that garnered more than 185,000 entries. Polaroid joined with Dodge to offer a One Film Camera Kit for test-driving Intrepid. Finally, *Motor Trend* magazine produced a special 96-page "In-Depth Guide to the 1993 Dodge Intrepid" for distribution to 800 number callers and at auto shows.

MEDIA STRATEGY

Network TV election coverage offered properties to reach the target audience. Media were purchased in two-week flights or bursts that maximized impact and created a strong presence for the Intrepid name. Prime prospects were reached through geodemographic editions of major news weeklies. An 8-page gatefold was purchased in *USA Today*. Prior to its launch outdoor was used to introduce the Intrepid theme "We're Changing Everything."

EVIDENCE OF RESULTS

Dodge met or exceeded all of its campaign objectives. The Chrysler Monitor Study is the standard for measuring new car intentions in the automotive market. Based on the second quarter monthly telephone survey of 4,529 new car intenders (six months after launch), Intrepid scores were extremely high both overall and relative to import intenders.

Video Case

CONVERSE BASKETBALL

MARKETING SITUATION

Converse was once the dominant leader in the basketball footwear market. As it reviewed its position as third behind Nike and Reebok in the mid-1990s, it determined a strategy to recapture part of the lost market. What it found was dynamic changes in the market place since its domination. In the 1980s the market experienced tremendous growth. Basketball footwear sales from 1982 to 1992 grew from less than $500 million to over $1.7 billion, as Nike and Reebok burst onto the scene and the category became very market driven. Nike, with its star endorser Michael Jordan and aggressive marketing, had captured 35 percent share by 1991, compared to Converse's 9 percent. At the same time, Reebok used product innovation and strong advertising to capture a 20 percent share.

By 1992, the growth of the athletic shoe and basketball market slowed. Dollar sales in the basketball category were flat, while the number of pairs purchased declined; however, Nike had its share rise to 44 percent, Reebok grew to 18 percent, and Converse had its share continue to decline to 8 percent.

The mid-1990s saw a decline in basketball footwear sales for the first time since the early 1980s. Consumers had shifted away from high-performance footwear to more casual footwear. All three top basketball footwear companies suffered sales decreases.

Major brands in the category have traditionally positioned themselves around NBA endorsers. Nike built its business around the highest-profile players in the NBA: Michael Jordan, Charles Barkley, and David Robinson. Reebok signed Shaquille O'Neal and Shawn Kemp. Converse, however, watched its major endorsers, Larry Bird and Magic Johnson, retire from the game. In 1991, Converse signed rookie Larry Johnson and Kevin Johnson and began to reposition itself around the power and speed of these new young endorsers.

CAMPAIGN OBJECTIVES

The Converse long-term mission in basketball is to regain its position as the market leader. Mid-1990s objectives were:
1. To increase top-of-mind (unaided) awareness
2. To increase positive brand associations
3. To increase purchase intent/interest
4. To build awareness of Converse premier endorsers
5. To see new technology and react
6. To introduce/create awareness for new shoes—Run 'N' Slam and Aerojam

TARGET AUDIENCE

Converse targeted male teenagers. Its basketball shoes average $65 in cost and Run 'N' Slam and Aerojam cost $85 and $110, respectively. Male teenagers tend to purchase multiple pairs and spend more dollars per pair. The target was segmented to focus on African American male teens as the core Converse audience. This segment buys more multiple pairs and are more likely to purchase high-priced shoes.

CREATIVE AND MEDIA STRATEGY

The campaign creative strategy was built around the Converse NBA endorsers. It had a three-part strategy:
1. Sell NBA endorsers, Kevin Johnson and Larry Johnson
2. Create two distinctive positionings, *power* and *speed*
3. Introduce Converse's two new premier products, selling their unique performance attributes.

Television was the medium of choice. Yankelovich research has shown that television has the greatest impact on male teenagers. Converse's own tracking studies and focus groups found it is the one medium that kids talk about.

EVIDENCE OF RESULTS

The Converse basketball campaign was the most successful in the history of the company and positioned Converse as an emerging player in the basketball market.
Sales Results
- Basketball market share increased from 8 to 10 percent, from September to September.
- Converse basketball sales up 30 percent, while market is down 3 percent. (Converse estimates)
- For the back-to-school season Converse replaced Reebok as the number 2 company in basketball sales.
- The Converse Run 'N' Slam was the best-selling basketball shoe in the back-to-school season.
- Run 'N' Slam was the most successful Converse basketball shoe introduction ever (Converse estimates).

Communication Results. The advertising had tremendous impact in building positive brand perceptions and desirability of Converse. It changed the way the target market views basketball shoes from Converse.

The Converse A & U September Tracking Study confirmed the market perceptions:
- Brand awareness (unaided) increased.
- Purchase intent increased.
- Positive brand opinion increased.
- Unaided awareness of performance shoe technologies showed that REACT had the highest awareness of any shoe technology.
- Retailers rated the Converse Run 'N' Slam advertising as the most effective of the back-to-school season.

Other Environments of Advertising

As we have

seen throughout this text, advertising does not function in a void. It is profoundly affected by the economy, cultural conventions, society's acceptance of various products and their presentations, and the formal legal and regulatory environment designed to protect consumers. In this section we will discuss some of the specialized areas of advertising and the way in which advertisers adapt to specialized advertising and marketing problems.

Chapter 23 begins with a discussion of retail advertising, where results are measured in next-day sales. In Chapter 24 we turn from the local retailer to the multinational giants of advertising and marketing. These advertisers must develop marketing and advertising plans that will successfully overcome barriers of language, culture, product distribution and usage, and insufficient audience research data to sell products on a global basis.

Finally, in Chapters 25 and 26 we conclude the text with an examination of the legal, regulatory, and ethical constraints on advertisers. In the last 20 years the public has increased its expectations of advertising. Today, most customers expect that advertising be socially responsible as well as literally truthful. In many respects, advertising has higher visibility than any other business enterprise. Consequently, advertising must strive to avoid even the appearance of unethical conduct. Certainly, in the last 50 years the advertising industry has developed both a formal system of self-regulation through the Council of Better Business Bureaus and, more importantly, a sense of responsibility largely unknown to the advertisers of the 19th century.

Retail
Advertising

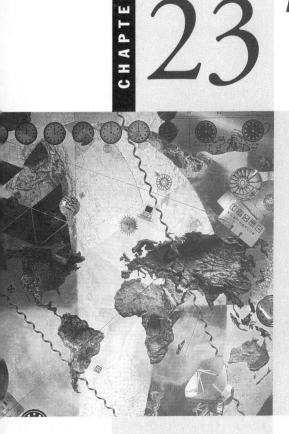

CHAPTER 23

CHAPTER OBJECTIVES

Both retailers and consumers have changed and are changing the way they do business and shop. The local media have responded to these changes. After reading this chapter you will understand:

- **Retail trends**
- **Changes in retailing**
- **Differences in national and retail advertising**
- **Media in retailing**
- **Use of cooperative advertising**

You're not surprised to be told retailing has recently gone through significant changes. **Consumers have new kinds of retail outlets**—category killers, internet, CD-ROM catalogs, interactive television in a battle with department stores, specialty, and mom-and-pop stores. Yet JCPenney's catalog division is selling products on interactive shopping channels. **Then there is** the growth of brand-name retailers like Warner Bros. and Nike Town, which are selling retail as entertainment. Printed catalogs are growing rapidly as consumers are finding they are pressed for time. It seems like retailing is schizophrenic.

Despite the strength of discounters like Wal-Mart and category killers (for example, Home Depot, Office Depot, Toys "R" Us), there hasn't been any sign of the demise of the small retailer, especially in such categories as consumer electronics, cameras, and home furnishings, which account for significant employment and growth.

National retail companies have refocused themselves to become more competitive and profitable. Over recent years, Sears has reinvented itself and spends over $300 million on advertising. And, at the same time, many smaller retailers have gotten smarter in how to compete.

Retail advertising
Advertising by a merchant who sells directly to the consumer.

If we mention JCPenney or Lord & Taylor ads, you think of typical department store advertising—especially in print—despite these two companies having distinctively different approaches. Retail advertising takes on all forms and involves all media—Exhibit 23.1, 23.2, and 23.3 illustrate three different approaches: County Seats Cafe is pushing a New York's Finest strip steak for only $10.95. Wolf Camera is telling the world that it uses Kodak Royal Paper. The retail travel ads promote price for Venezuela packages.

Before we discuss the advertising, let's take a look at retail trends and the nature and scope of the business.

EXHIBIT
23.1

This newspaper ad focuses on product and price.

(Courtesy: Folks, Inc.)

Wolf camera focuses
on the quality of their
products in this co-op
ad with Kodak.

(Courtesy: Leigh Kain Advertising.)

This travel ad features
vacation value.

(Courtesy: Promotion Solutions and Viasa Airways.)

RETAIL TRENDS

Marketing research indicates continued change in the supermarket, discount department stores, traditional department stores, megastores, specialty apparel, and shopping centers:[1]

Supermarkets are the most shopped type of retail store, with 85 percent of respondents indicating they had shopped a supermarket in the past 30 days. Despite more than $275 billion in sales each year, supermarkets are beset with two main competitive alternatives: discount supercenters (such as Super Kmart, Super Wal-Mart) and warehouses (such as Sam's Club). Without more efficient operating procedures, supermarkets might be overtaken in the low-margin grocery business by wholesale clubs and supercenters.

Discount department stores continue to attract more shoppers every year as they have for 20 years. Elements that will contribute to their continued growth in the next decade include operating efficiencies due to extensive use of technologies, emphasis on low prices, wide selections, and service.

Traditional department stores have experienced a 24 percent decline in shopping frequency since 1974. The recent recession and leveraged buyouts have left most department stores weakened financially.

Wholesale clubs attracted 18 percent of shoppers in 1993. To compete with the emerging strength of expanded format supermarkets and combination superstores, warehouse clubs are moving away from their original concepts by adding bakeries and perishables. Saturation of clubs is predicted soon as growth falters.

Big-box destination retailers, or mega warehouses are booming in almost every category: computers, office supplies, children's toys, building materials, pet supplies, sporting goods, baby supplies, books, crafts, etc. In each category we'll see a rush for expansion and market share, followed by consolidation to establish format dominance.

Specialty apparel retailers have been losing customers for the past 20 years as demographics and shopping habits have changed. The result has been a 14 percent decline in shopping frequency over these years. The future will bring closings and consolidation as competition for normal apparel specialists in outlet centers and power strip centers intensifies.

Shopping centers have seen sales per square foot decline from $174 to $160 since 1974. Customer visits to shopping centers have also declined since 1980, and the number of stores visited per trip also declined. Trips to regional malls are declining almost as rapidly as visits to downtown areas. The future is bright only for those with superior regional access, densely populated trade areas, and economically strong anchors.

Continued Retailing Changes

Retailing should continue to undergo massive structure changes, according to Roper research, especially as consumers increasingly demand reasonable prices. The rise of off-price and warehouse clubs and superstores (or *category killers*) has changed the way people shop. Many traditional retailers can expect to wither away if they do not learn to adapt to the new environment.

---

[1] Howard L. Green, "New Consumer Realities for Retailers," *Marketing News,* April 25, 1994, p. 4.

Let's examine a few trends in retailing:[2]

- **Grocery stores.** The future of local grocery and chains may well depend on their ability to create individual store personalities, making geodemographic targeting essential.

- **Traditional retailers.** Smaller stores and retailers will feel intensifying pressure from high-volume deep-discount competitors. Many will not be able to compete on price, but they can build their reputations in specific areas—as JCPenney did with quality, value-priced goods. Traditional retailers should consider adopting new strategies that combine traditional retail business with mail-order or transactional TV components. The direct-response option should inspire more interest in the retailer.

- **Restaurants.** The trend points to a continuing boom in *ethnic* chains and broader menus. Established chains from Pizza Hut to Taco Bell evidence the successful *Americanization* of Italian and Mexican fare. Current growth areas include Chinese and possibly Thai or Indian.

- **Home shopping.** Television continues to be a promising arena for home shopping. The home shopping networks on cable television will continue to see sales climb. And as programming becomes more interactive, TV shopping by category or department is a likely scenario. Videotext and computer shopping should finally take off as shopping outlets.

- **Fashion.** Rather than fitting themselves into the latest styles, Americans will demand that clothing fit their style and lifestyle. Office wear will be more functional and less formal. Evening wear will err on the side of simplicity and flexibility. This shift does not mean an abandonment of high style. But it will take less ornamentation to impress. Vanity will give way to value: A dress that goes to work should also be adaptable for dinner—at home or on the town. The trend will favor clothing with lasting, go-anywhere, flexible, interchangeable lines, but distinction will not disappear. Highly expressive accessories, from scarves to suspenders, will enable consumers to produce one-of-a-kind fashions for special occasions.

- **Entertainment and freedom products.** The boom in home entertainment products is only beginning—especially audio formats like the digital audio tape player, digital compact cassette player, and the mini–disc player. The *electronic hearth* will be the center of fun and family recreation for the baby-boom generation. The 1990s has brought *nomadic* products—the first of which was the Walkman—allowing consumers to bring their inside world to the outside, and vice versa. The video telephone, for example, will allow business travelers to keep children and loved ones in close view. The convenience these products give is their greatest selling point. They can be used anywhere, from poolside to airplane. Ultimately, nomadic products empower consumers—or at least executives and professionals—by granting them control of the use of their time.

Nontraditional Buying Trends Predicted

Curt Salmon Associates, a consulting company, predicts that by the year 2010, at least 55 percent of all shopping will be done through nontraditional methods such as home TV shopping, interactive shopping, computer shopping,

[2]"25 Major Trends Shaping the Future of American Business," *The Public Pulse*, 8, no. 5.

and old-fashioned ordering by phone. Technological advances and consumers' increasing time pressure will be the catalysts.

It is predicted that factories will customize mass-produced goods, and 60 percent of the merchandise will be shipped directly to consumers. Salmon Associates predicts stores will become pseudo-theaters that display new merchandising ideas.[3]

CONSUMER ATTITUDES

The *Curt Salmon Associates Retail Pulse,* a survey of 1,060 women nationwide, found that 95 percent of the respondents questioned the credibility of prices at traditional malls, department stores, and specialty stores. Also, 53 percent said they shopped at discount department stores more often than they did two years ago.

When asked which aspects of store and display design they would like to see improved, 23 percent said crowded merchandise; 22 percent mentioned price tags and markings on merchandise; 17 percent said amenities (rest rooms, parking, etc.); 10 percent said organization of departments and merchandise; and 10 percent mentioned directional signs in stores.[4]

Skepticism of Retail and Sales Ads

The Better Business Bureau study found a high degree of skepticism about truthfulness of local retail and sale ads. (Exhibit 23.4). Only 6.6 percent of respondents from midwestern cities said retail ads were truthful; only about 13 percent thought sale ads were very truthful.

EXHIBIT 23.4

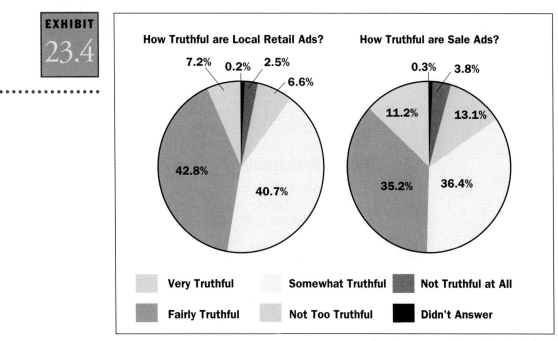

How Truthful are Local Retail Ads?
7.2% 0.2% 2.5%
6.6%
42.8%
40.7%

How Truthful are Sale Ads?
0.3% 3.8%
11.2% 13.1%
35.2% 36.4%

| Very Truthful | Somewhat Truthful | Not Truthful at All |
| Fairly Truthful | Not Too Truthful | Didn't Answer |

(Source: Advertising Age, *November 19, 1991)*

[3]"Is Technology Making Stores Obsolete?" *Atlanta Journal/Constitution,* February 26, 1994, p. E2.
[4]"Do Malls Still Have it All?" *POPAI Insider,* April 1993, p. 1.

Among consumers' objections:

- **Insults to one's intelligence**
- **False and exaggerated savings claims**
- **False and exaggerated product claims**

Consumers found, and you won't be surprised, car dealerships, appliance retailers, furniture dealers, and discount stores among those thought most guilty.

A Marketing Emphasis

Retailers are increasingly turning to marketing and marketing research to compete in this new retail environment. The National Retail Merchants Association points out the importance of an organized marketing strategy for retailers:

> Because customers are motivated in their purchases by lifestyle as well as value/price considerations, this has resulted in the segmentation of shoppers according to attitudes, forcing retailers to make clearer distinctions between such segments in their assortments, point-of-sale presentation, and advertising.

Retailers expect the local media vehicles to aid retailers' marketing efforts by defining their audiences. Newspapers are particularly aware of the need to provide in-depth readership data. They also recognize the importance of relating this readership data to the local retail community. In the future we will definitely see a much greater use of media-generated marketing research in making retail advertising decisions.

Perhaps the most used and potentially most beneficial retail research device is the Universal Product Code (UPC). The UPC, developed by IBM and in use since 1974, is on virtually every packaged goods product and is expanding into other product categories at a rapid pace. Originally intended to speed up the check-out of customers and to aid in inventory control, it has become an important research tool over the past decade or so. The scanner can determine exactly when and where products are bought. Sometimes consumer panels are used in conjunction with the scanner so that product purchases can be correlated with consumer demographics and media usage.

Retail Satisfaction Profiles

Frequency Marketing Inc., identifies the household member who does the most department store shopping by demographics, values and attitudes, and shopping behavior. There are five classifications for women:[5]

Fashion Statements. The most affluent and educated women's group. Because of their household incomes ($73,400), they have a high index of planned purchases and like being on the cutting edge of fashion. They account for 13.2 percent of primary department store shoppers.

Wanna-Buys. Have some of the same attitudes as Fashion Statements, but don't have as much money ($40,600). They account for 18.6 percent of shoppers and buy on impulse.

---

[5]Susan Krafft, "How Shoppers Get Satisfaction," *American Demographics,* October 1993, pp. 13–16.

Family Values. This group accounts for one in six shoppers and a large percentage have children living at home. Half have college degrees, and 9 in 10 are professionals. They are most likely to be planning to buy children's clothing, sporting goods, or a new washer or dryer.

Down To Basics. They have more children than other groups (about 60 percent have children), a median age of 34, and a household income of $32,600. Only 3 percent graduated from college. Despite having less money, they have similar attitudes as those in Family Values. They are careful spenders and buy little on credit. They check for sales and buy little other than for children. They account for roughly 16 percent of primary shoppers.

Matriarchs. These are older women often living in retired households and are the most conservative group. Their favorite place to shop is in department stores; however, they have fewer planned purchases and feel *things change too fast these days.*

Men fall into three classifications:

Patricians. Just one in five are married, have the most money ($57,500) and are good targets for men's clothing, electronics, and sporting goods.

Practicals. Have an income of $39,500, and are likely to be single. They prefer to pay with cash and are more likely to shop in discount stores. They are good targets for men's clothing, and even better targets for electronics and sporting goods.

Patriarchs. Lowest educated and have the lowest household incomes of male clusters. They are the oldest of the male clusters and buy primarily to replace worn-out items; however, they replace them with the top-of-the-line items.

Success Is More Than Advertising

Haggar Apparel Co. and Farrah Manufacturing soaked up sales in the wrinkle-free men's pants business, while Levi's Dockers were slow to make decisions entering this market, which resulted in an estimated $200 million loss in sales. Levi's is slow in terms of customer support for merchants. Levi's might take 25 to 30 days to replenish a standard lot of pants; Haggar or Farrah do it in 10, says JCPenney's top merchandiser.[6] So advertising isn't the only factor in the success or failure of a company to make merchants and consumers happy—you can't buy it if the store can't get the right styles or products.

Integrated Marketing Includes P-O-P

Today's emphasis on integrated marketing and consistency of message means more involvement of point-of-purchase at the early stages of creative planning. A Point-of-Purchase Advertising Institute study of brand management found that 40 percent of all in-store media is purchased from or developed by sales promotion and advertising agencies. Ad agencies were responsible for recommending 36.8 percent of temporary p-o-p and 27.8 percent of permanent in-store programs.

---

[6]"Managing by Values," *Business Week,* August 1, 1994, p. 49.

EXHIBIT
23.5

Old El Paso features a
line of product in this
point-of-purchase.

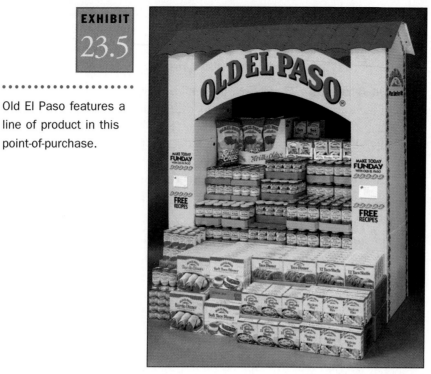

(Courtesy: Henschel-Steinau.)

A Kmart study found that p-o-p merchandising increased sales of coffee by 567 percent, paper towels by 773 percent, and toothpaste by 119 percent. Exhibit 23.5 shows a massive Old El Paso display.

A&P, like most retailers, is very selective about the p-o-p it uses. P-o-p policies are incorporated in its store decor, signage, and shelf positioning to raise total category sales, not just individual brand sales. P-o-p advertising is adapting to interactive electronic and high-tech displays, whether stand-alone kiosks or on-shelf units, they all grab attention.

RETAILING IN THE 1990S

Frequency Marketing's director of customer relations research says, "Retailing in the 1990s is all about understanding customers and catering to their specific needs regarding merchandise, quality, value, and customer service."

The growth of discount retailing illustrates the changing value systems of shoppers today. Shoppers can no longer be identified by a single-value concept. They display multiple values. For example, consumers still prefer traditional department stores for adult fashions, but even the most upscale shoppers look to discount stores for children's clothing.[7]

National Retailers Seek Niche

Answering the consumer call for convenience and value, apparel marketer the Gap opened Old Navy Clothing pricing apparel basics at about 20 to 25 percent below Gap's prices, and offers clothing for the entire family. Located

---

[7]"Dayton's Is Top Retailer in Customer Satisfaction Survey," *Marketing News,* June 6, 1994, p. 8.

mainly in strip malls, Old Navy is targeting the mass middle market of households with incomes in the $20,000 to $50,000 range that accounts for almost half of the apparel market. Initial advertising has been local print and outdoor ads.

The bottom line at Old Navy is value, underscored by inexpensive items, more synthetic fabrics and less detailed stitching and workmanship than traditional Gap merchandise. About 80 percent of the merchandise sells for less than $22. It also stocks non-apparel products and gifts. Of course, there is a danger that the Gap could cannibalize itself.

Victoria's Secret is intended to be "every woman's fantasy of what a lingerie store should be. Someplace small, intimate, a store that is probably English, or French, or Viennese." Leslie Wexner of The Limited originally thought that such a store needed only soft lighting and classical music. He did not research the concept. He did not survey women or look at lingerie sales figures. Instead, over a 10-year period, Wexner probably spent 60 to 80 days walking around looking at stores throughout the world, photographing what he liked, and later studying all his photos. The inspiration for Victoria's Secret surfaced in the early 1980s after he visited a small lingerie shop in England called Courtney's. He later bought an unsuccessful lingerie company called Victoria's Secrets. He then molded the company into his image of what it should be—using Cybill Shepard as his model customer: "Would Cybill buy it? Would Cybill shop in a place like this?". After answering all the questions, he opened 250 Victoria's Secret stores in three years.[8] Then came its successful mail-order catalogs featuring provocative items. The company knew that sexy pictures sell more products, but it was always concerned that if the ads got too provocative, they would lose sales because their products would be labeled as erotica. The company always has to be concerned about the perception of its ads—which are designed to sell the fantasy.

NATIONAL AND RETAIL ADVERTISING

National advertising

Advertising by a marketer of a trademarked product or service sold through different outlets, in contrast to *local advertising*.

National advertising is chiefly done by a marketer to get people to buy the marketer's branded goods wherever they are sold. *Retail advertising* is done by local merchants or service organizations to attract customers—in person, by mail, or by telephone—to buy the goods and services they have to offer.

The primary difference between consumer product advertising and retail advertising is that product advertising is generally feature and benefit oriented, while much of retail advertising is price and availability oriented. Occasionally, a retailer will run *image* advertising to develop the public's perceptions about the store(s) (see Exhibit 23.6), but the bulk of retail advertising features a number of products promoting price. In national advertising, the advertising says, *Buy this brand or product at any store.* In retail advertising, the ad says, *Buy this product here. Better come early.*

In national advertising, it is difficult to trace the sales effect of a single insertion of an ad. Even tracing the effect of a series of ads takes time and is hard unless the series runs exclusively in one medium. In retail advertising, on the other hand, an advertiser can usually tell by noon of the day after the ad appeared how effective it is.

---

[8]Paul B. Brown, *Marketing Masters* (New York: Harper & Row Publishers, 1988).

TYPES OF RETAIL ADVERTISING

Retail advertising is as diverse as the establishments that use it. However, there are certain patterns of retail advertising that reflect the character and goals of various retailers. The Newspaper Advertising Bureau has suggested six categories of retail advertising:[9]

1. *Promotional.* Here the emphasis is on sales and high sale volume at a reduced price. Discount stores such as Kmart are the primary users of this type of advertising.

2. *Semipromotional.* In this type of advertising, sale offerings are interspersed with many regular-priced items. Most department stores and supermarkets use this advertising strategy.

3. *Nonpromotional.* Many small shops and specialty stores adopt a no-sale advertising strategy. Their advertising plays down price and emphasizes dignified appeals featuring the quality of the merchandise and the expertise of their sales staffs (Exhibit 23.6).

4. *Assortment ads.* The intent of these ads is to show the large variety of products. The ads have an institutional aspect in that they promote the store as a place for one-stop shopping.

5. *Omnibus ads.* Though similar to assortment ads, omnibus ads are usually more clearly sales oriented. These ads may feature related items or a variety of nonrelated items for several departments.

6. *Institutional ads.* Many stores use advertising that emphasizes their unique character. Institutional ads must be careful to tell a story of importance to a store's customers.

Institutional advertising
Advertising done by an organization speaking of its work, views, and problems as a whole, to gain public goodwill and support rather than to sell a specific product. Sometimes called *public-relations advertising*.

Retailer's Business Cycles

Retailer's don't sell the same amount of merchandise every month. These selling cycles vary according to the product or service category. Exhibit 23.7 shows that August is the best month for restaurants, followed by July and June; new domestic auto dealers' best months are May and August; Novem-

EXHIBIT 23.6

Creating awareness for this new company with this image ad.

(Courtesy: Sterrett Dymond Advertising.)

---

[9] *The I-Wonder-How-to-Set-Up-an-Advertising-Program-and-How-Much-to-Budget Book,* Newspaper Advertising Bureau.

	JAN	FEB	MAR	APR	MAY	JUN	JUL	AUG	SEP	OCT	NOV	DEC
ALL STORES AND SERVICES (%)	7.2	7.0	**8.2**	**8.1**	8.7	**8.5**	**8.4**	8.8	**8.2**	**8.3**	8.6	10.0
Appliance Stores	7.2	6.6	7.7	7.7	8.6	8.7	8.9	8.5	7.7	8.3	9.1	10.9
Auto Dealers (New Domestic)	7.5	7.4	8.8	8.6	9.2	9.1	8.9	9.2	8.5	8.2	7.6	7.1
Auto Dealers (New Import)	7.4	7.2	9.0	8.6	9.3	9.1	8.8	9.6	8.1	8.2	7.4	7.3
Beer	7.7	7.3	8.4	8.2	9.2	9.3	9.4	9.6	8.1	8.3	7.6	7.0
Book Stores	9.4	6.4	6.5	6.4	6.9	6.9	6.9	10.0	10.1	7.9	8.6	14.0
Bridal Market	5.0	5.8	6.4	7.6	9.8	11.4	9.3	10.5	9.6	9.0	7.7	8.0
Department Stores	5.5	5.9	7.8	7.6	7.9	7.6	7.1	8.5	7.6	8.2	10.4	16.0
Discount Stores	5.8	5.9	7.6	7.7	8.2	8.1	7.6	8.4	7.6	8.2	10.2	14.7
Drug Stores	7.8	7.5	8.2	7.9	8.3	8.1	8.0	8.4	8.0	8.4	8.5	11.0
Fabric & Sewing Stores	7.5	7.2	8.3	7.7	7.7	7.2	7.9	8.5	8.2	10.0	10.6	9.2
Fast Food	7.3	7.2	8.3	8.2	8.6	8.9	9.1	9.2	8.3	8.4	8.1	8.4
Jewelry Stores	5.6	6.7	6.5	6.6	8.5	7.4	6.9	7.3	6.6	7.1	9.2	21.5
Restaurants	7.5	7.3	8.2	8.3	8.7	8.8	8.9	9.2	8.3	8.5	8.1	8.2
Shoe Stores	6.4	6.1	8.8	8.5	8.5	8.1	7.6	9.9	8.4	7.9	8.6	11.2
Women's Wear Stores	6.3	6.1	8.1	8.1	8.5	7.8	7.7	8.5	8.0	8.3	9.4	13.1

(Courtesy: Radio Advertising Bureau.)

EXHIBIT 23.7

· · · · · · · · · · · · · · · · · ·

Advertisers' seasonal business cycles.

ber is the month for carpets; December sales are double any other month for jewelry stores; November is tops for fabric and sewing stores; and May tops hardware store sales. Retailers use this information in planning their advertising and promotional efforts.

Special Promotion Times

It's no surprise if we say there are special promotions for Christmas, Mother's Day, President's Day, Memorial Day, and Father's Day (see Exhibit 23.8), but

EXHIBIT 23.8

· · · · · · · · · · · · · · · · · ·

Mother's Day is PoFolks best day of the year. This special promotion features Father's Day another major opportunity.

(Courtesy: Folks, Inc.)

there are many, many more opportunities including Boss's Day, National Singles Week, Pancake Day, Man Watcher's Compliment Week, National Library Week, Girl's Club Week, Jewish Heritage Month, Senior Citizens Month, National Pet Week, Comedy Celebration Day, National Pie Day, Better Sleep Month, National Decorating Month, National Barbecue Month, Nurse's Day, International Pickle Week, and National Anti-Boredom Month—you get the idea, lot's of advertising and promotional opportunities.

THE RETAIL ADVERTISING MIX

Like other styles of advertising, retail advertising must (1) determine overall goals and objectives to the marketing and advertising programs, (2) identify target markets, and (3) develop a copy and media strategy to reach these targets. But the way in which retail advertising strategy is carried out differs markedly from that in which national advertising (which we discussed earlier) is carried out.

A retail advertising campaign usually includes media other than newspapers. Radio advertising is used frequently with great success because it is reasonable in cost and easy to produce and can be changed within hours if necessary. Television is also used more frequently now, although not as often as radio. And many successful campaigns use brochures and catalogs. Frequently, the catalogs are distributed with Sunday newspapers. (See outdoor ads for McDonald's, Exhibit 23.9.)

Selecting local media is a "How best to . . . ?" problem: how best to use newspapers, radio, television, direct mail—the chief media—alone or in combination to sell merchandise and attract store traffic.

Newspapers in Retailing

Newspapers are the primary local advertising vehicle, although they don't have the dominance among retailers they once enjoyed. Research indicates

EXHIBIT 23.9

McDonald's uses local market outdoor to promote special prices and products.

(Courtesy: Robinson & Associates.)

that both consumers and retailers regard newspapers as the prime medium for local advertising. In 1994, local newspaper advertising expenditures reached $33.7 billion.

Today's newspapers offer a retailer more than just retail advertising space. Exhibit 23.10 is a promotion piece telling retailers the newspaper is more than a newspaper and offers a wide variety of advertising options. For example, the *Atlanta Journal and Constitution's* (AJC) services are typical of metro newspapers:

Preprinted Inserts. A *Zoned Area Preprints* program offers select or total market coverage. Advertising preprints are inserted directly into the newspaper and are distributed to subscribers and single-copy purchasers.

Direct Mail. The *ZIP* program allows advertisers to reach nonsubscribers by mailing their preprint to selected zip codes (see Exhibit 23.11). This program enables advertisers to take advantage of less expensive newspaper distribution to reach subscribers while using direct mail for nonsubscribers. Shared mail, solo mail, and a variety of targeting options are also available.

Extra Editions. Some seven extra community editions with 11 advertising zones cover the metro area enabling advertisers to target primary market areas.

EXHIBIT
23.10

· · · · · · · · · · · · · · · · · · ·

This newspaper promotion touts the many advertising options offered retailers beyond simple ad space.

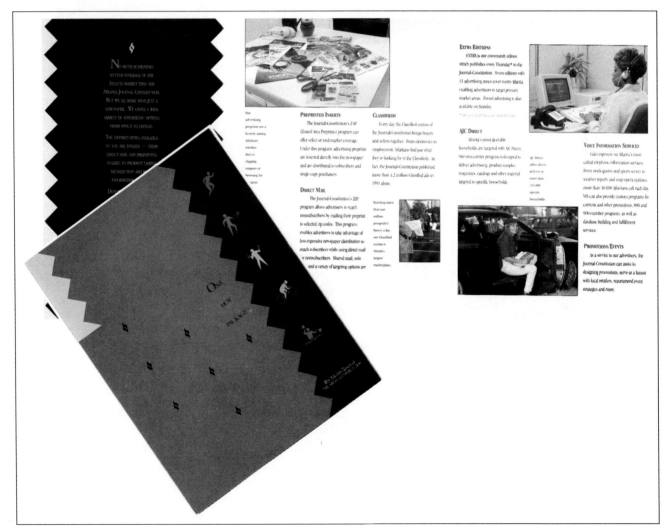

(Courtesy: The Atlanta Journal/The Atlanta Constitution.*)*

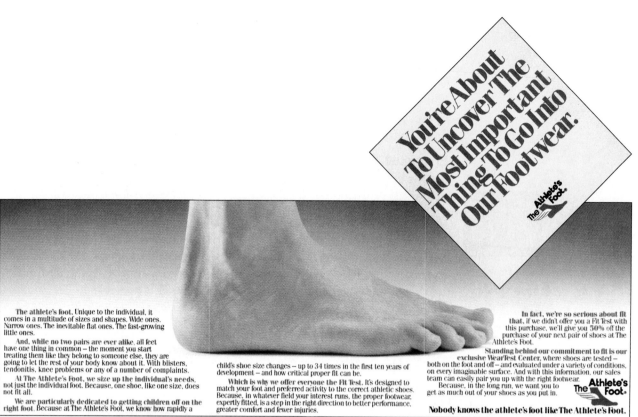

The athlete's foot. Unique to the individual, it comes in a multitude of sizes and shapes. Wide ones. Narrow ones. The inevitable flat ones. The fast-growing little ones.

And, while no two pairs are ever alike, all feet have one thing in common – the moment you start treating them like they belong to someone else, they are going to let the rest of your body know about it. With blisters, tendonitis, knee problems or any of a number of complaints.

At The Athlete's Foot, we size up the individual's needs, not just the individual foot. Because, one shoe, like one size, does not fit all.

We are particularly dedicated to getting children off on the right foot. Because at The Athlete's Foot, we know how rapidly a child's shoe size changes – up to 34 times in the first ten years of development – and how critical proper fit can be.

Which is why we offer everyone the Fit Test. It's designed to match your foot and preferred activity to the correct athletic shoes. Because, in whatever field your interest runs, the proper footwear, expertly fitted, is a step in the right direction to better performance, greater comfort and fewer injuries.

In fact, we're so serious about fit that, if we didn't offer you a Fit Test with this purchase, we'll give you 50% off the purchase of your next pair of shoes at The Athlete's Foot.

Standing behind our commitment to fit is our exclusive WearTest Center, where shoes are tested – both on the foot and off – and evaluated under a variety of conditions, on every imaginable surface. And with this information, our sales team can easily pair you up with the right footwear.

Because, in the long run, we want you to get as much out of your shoes as you put in.

Nobody knows the athlete's foot like The Athlete's Foot.

(Courtesy: The Athlete's Foot and Leigh Kain Advertising.)

EXHIBIT
23.11

....

This brochure could use the newspaper's direct mail service.

Ajc Direct. The most desirable households are targeted with their own carrier program to deliver advertising, product samples, magazines, catalogs, and other material targeted to some 350,000 upscale households. The paper can also merge the advertiser's customer names/credit card list with the newspaper's subscriber list and eliminate any duplication.

As you can see, these newspaper services can be tailored to the advertiser's needs.

Retail is also more than just shops, discount stores, and department stores. Fast-food, restaurants, and other service organizations have objectives of getting customers into their establishments. The Charlotte Checkers hockey team needs to sell season tickets in Exhibit 23.12.

Radio in Retailing

Local radio advertising dominates the radio market with 7.9 billion in sales in 1994, out of a total radio expenditure of some $9.9 billion.

Prego restaurant was one of the hottest San Francisco eateries in the 1980s. The 1990s, however, gave birth to a new crop of trendy restaurants competing for the same customer. Research indicated that the restaurant still had favor with potential customers, but they sought to try many of the newer eateries. It created on-air promotions and commercials that were funny, imaginative, and offbeat and that satirized the trendy restaurant scene while still maintaining Prego's allure and conveying the promise of a good time. The tag was:

EXHIBIT
23.12

A creative effort by Charlotte hockey team to sell seats.

(Courtesy: Charlotte Checkers and Sterrett Dymond Advertising.)

"See. Be Seen. Be seen eating." Excerpts from their offbeat commercials follow:

> Announcer: Paola has just enjoyed his fabulous meal of Capolini' Pomedoro at Prego the restaurant. He pays the bill and makes his way toward the bar. Everyone admires him—or so it seems to Paolo. He is on the prowl, Paola is a cat—a panther—he is . . . Paolo! Does he care that his fly is down? No! He doesn't care, he doesn't know so why should he care? . . . he believes he has made an impression on a lady brunette perched at the end of the bar. What is it she sees? Is it the blueness of his eyes? . . . No! It is the spinach caught between his teeth . . . it has been there for hours—Prego (location) See. Be seen. Be seen eating.

Television in Retailing

Television became a major force in retailing during the 1980s. Currently, some $9 billion of TV revenue is local. Much of the retail advertising dollars have been a result of the growth of independent TV station and cable outlets with relatively low advertising rates. Spots on both independent stations and cable may be as low as $20 to $50.

Most major markets have more than one cable system, which means an advertiser with stores on one side of town can simply target prospects by buying only the cable system(s) that reach their prospective customers. At the same time, there are companies that will allow an advertiser to make one buy and reach multiple cable systems. Advertisers can buy cable networks such as CNN, ESPN, USA, CNN's Headline News, the Weather Channel, MTV,

VH-1, etc., because of the availability of time for local advertisers, usually at rates significantly lower than stations in the same market. The audience is probably significantly smaller at any given time on a specific cable network than the number of households hooked to cable, which means a high cost per thousand, but the cost is within the budgets of the smallest retail advertiser.

Database Marketing

Of the 96 plus households in the United States, 74 percent have a Sears relationship, and Sears is trying to make the most of it. In 1995, Sears started a program to make better use of its customer database—typical of most major retailers. Sears sends out some 16 million mailings per month to a selection of the database. Building customer loyalty—through retention and upgrading of *most-valued customers*—is a major item.

Measured marketing, a term used by supermarkets that issue plastic cards to their customers so they can build a database, permits the stores to identify their best customers and treat them differently. Customers in the top 10 percent group make 1.8 visits per week and spend $3,674 per year—double what the next best decile spend. The top 30 percent of the cardholders account for roughly 75 percent of the store's total sales.[10]

Cooperative Advertising

Cooperative advertising
(1) Joint promotion of a national advertiser (manufacturer) and local retail outlet on behalf of the manufacturer's product on sale in the retail store. (2) Joint promotion through a trade association for firms in a single industry. (3) Advertising venture jointly conducted by two or more advertisers.

The simplest definition of cooperative advertising is a joint promotion of a national advertiser (manufacturer) and a local retailer on behalf of the manufacturer's product or service in the retail store. The Kodak ad in Exhibit 23.13 is prepared by Kodak and is available for the local merchant to advertise and have Kodak pay as much as 50 percent of the advertising cost. A retailer that uses a lot of cooperative advertising could double its advertising budget.

Chief advantages:

- **Cooperative advertising helps the buyer stretch his or her advertising capability.**

- **It may provide good artwork of the product advertised, with good copy—which is especially important to the small store (Exhibit 23.13.)**

- **It helps the store earn a better volume discount for all its advertising.**

Cooperative advertising works best when the line is highly regarded and is either a style or some other kind of leader in its field.

Chief disadvantages:

- **Although the store pays only 50 percent of the cost, that sum may be disproportionate for the amount of sales and profit the store realizes.**

- **Most manufacturers' ads emphasize the brand name at the expense of the store name.**

---

[10]Arthur Middleton Hughes, "The Real Truth about Supermarkets—and Customers," *DM News,* October 3, 1994, p. 40.

(Courtesy: Leigh Kain Advertising.)

Manufacturers' ads cannot have the community flavor and style of store ads. To localize co-op advertising, some retailers, instead of accepting manufacturer-produced ads, incorporate manufacturer-supplied product information into an ad that conforms to their own advertising style.

Co-op requires a lot of paperwork. Most newspapers and some radio stations have co-op advertising departments that help retailers seek co-op allowances from manufacturers, and supply affidavits and other documentation required by a manufacturer. Many small advertisers find the paperwork prohibitive, and the media try to make it easier in hope of getting their share of the advertising. In some cases, the retailer may have a business department inside its advertising department to make sure the store collects all the money due it.

SUMMARY

The media mix has expanded for retailers over recent years. While newspapers still account for the majority of retail advertising, retailers use virtually every medium to promote their stores, products, and services. As with business in general, the retail business has and is significantly changing. Many of the changes are driven by the way consumers shop—from supermarkets, discount department stores, wholesale clubs, shopping centers, and malls, to big-box category killers. Shopping patterns have changed.

These changes has given rise to sophisticated segmentation and niche marketers. Retail advertising is done by local merchants or service organizations to attract customers. Retailers use business-cycle information to decide when to advertise. Cooperative advertising offers retailers allowances from manufactures that can actually double the advertising budgets.

As retailers get more sophisticated marketing information, the media have responded with services. For example, newspapers offer many extra services (direct mail, zones, direct mail opportunities, research, and other services) to compete with the broadcast media and direct mail.

Case History

FOLKS, INC.:
Restaurant Case

BACKGROUND

Folks. Inc., a restaurant management group, is the largest franchise of PoFolks, Inc., headquartered in Atlanta. PoFolks specializes in hearty homestyle cooking and is in the family restaurant category. Folks operates about 20 restaurants in Atlanta, and it also has stores in other markets like Gainesville and Rome.

Originally PoFolks was known for its great fried foods. As consumer attitudes and health concerns changed, so did PoFolks menu, although some consumers still think of it serving only fried foods.

Folks has won many awards for its PoFolks fried chicken but created a quarterly promotion featuring "grilled, baked, and fried" foods (see Exhibit 23.C1) to inform consumers it offered food other than fried foods. After fried chicken, vegetable plates are consistently a major seller.

Folks also operates other restaurant concepts. It has an in-house advertising agency consisting of a marketing director, Karen Elliott, who also functions as creative director, media planner, and buyer; Sheri Bevil, who functions as head of field marketing, in-store promotions, public relations, etc. It uses an outside design firm, Leigh Kain Advertising, to execute its ideas and consult on creative—including product photography. It uses a media buying consultant to review its radio packages and buy television.

POFOLKS COMPETITION

The Atlanta market is one of the most competitive restaurant markets in the country. New national competition opens weekly. Among Folks competitors in Atlanta are family and casual restaurants like Shoney's, Black Eyed Pea, and Cracker Barrel; cafeterias like Morrison's and Piccadilly; and grazing restaurants like Ryan's.

TARGET

Each store pulls a different mix of consumers—some a little older, a little better educated, more ethnic, etc. Basically, it attracts families—from young families to grandparents—in the middle-income range. It attracts slightly more males than females, and more blue collar than white collar; however, the clientele is a mix.

MEDIA

PoFolks develops its advertising and promotion on a quarterly basis. Primarily it uses radio to segment to the many user groups: country (males and females), top 40 (women), classic rock and roll (males), talk radio (older and empty nesters), etc. It uses limited magazines and newspapers. It usually uses a quarterly FSI drop. It occasionally uses television, outdoor advertising, and direct mail (it also targets direct mail for customers of specific stores).

POSITIONING

It is positioned as a hearty homestyle family restaurant featuring good food and value.

Questions

1. What is retail advertising?
2. What is national advertising?
3. Contrast the trends of discount department stores and traditional department stores.
4. What is the future for non-traditional shopping?
5. What are consumer's objections to local ads?

International Advertising

CHAPTER OBJECTIVES

Advertising is a global form of communication.
Multinational companies compete on a worldwide basis
with advertising as a primary tool to gain brand awareness
in both developed and emerging countries. After reading
this chapter you will understand:

- **Advertising practices in a global economy**
- **The concept of global marketing**
- **The relationship among economics, politics, and culture**
- **Agency organization in a global economy**
- **Unique advertising practices country by country**

A Beijing FM station blasts the sound of hoof-
beats as a male voice beckons its listeners to
"Come to Marlboro Country!" and advertising
touting air conditioners, beer, and lonely
hearts have become a regular part of the
everyday routine of millions of Chinese. **In
Moscow,** Russian citizens wrestle with runaway inflation as they deal with the first steps

toward a free economy by buying Chinese sneakers, American candy bars, and Polish vodka from shabby street kiosks.[1]

The international marketing revolution is very much in evidence throughout the world, including the United States. In 1993, Canon, the Japanese maker of cameras, optical supplies, and business equipment, ranked first in the number of patent registrations in the United States. Canon filed more patents (1,106) than General Electric, IBM, Eastman Kodak, General Motors, or any other American firm.[2] In China's Guangdong province, Avon cosmetics has a direct selling workforce of 17,000 and total sales in China of $20 million. These sales were achieved since 1990 when Avon came to China.[3] If there was ever any doubt that we are in a global economy, it was removed on the evening of April 19, 1994, when the Siberian steel maker, NOSTA, became the first Russian company to advertise on an American TV network when it ran a commercial on CBS News.

A global economy, once only the subject of theoretical speculation, is now a reality. Even medium-sized companies find that they must have some international expertise in order to survive. Perhaps the most significant change in this global order is the shift of the United States from an exporter of goods and expertise to that of an importer/exporter. In a survey of American-based companies, executives saw modest growth for their firms in the United States, but great potential in selected foreign markets (see Exhibit 24.1).

Not only are American companies faced with competition from foreign companies, but these international firms have the financial resources to rival the giants of American industry. For example, of the *Fortune* 500 largest industrial corporations, 161 are American companies. Japan is second with 128, followed by Great Britain (40), Germany (32), and France (30). The sales of these large companies are directly attributable to their success in moving into international markets. For example, foreign subsidiaries of both Ford and

EXHIBIT
24.1

· · · · · · · · · · · · · · · · ·

The future for most companies is in a global market.

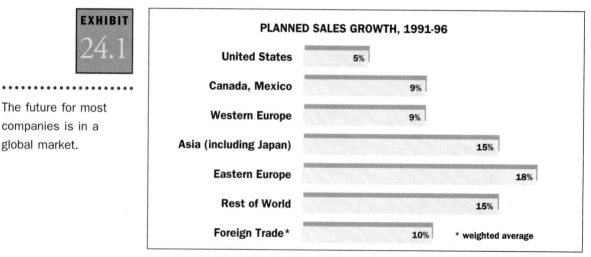

PLANNED SALES GROWTH, 1991-96

United States	5%
Canada, Mexico	9%
Western Europe	9%
Asia (including Japan)	15%
Eastern Europe	18%
Rest of World	15%
Foreign Trade*	10% * weighted average

*(Source: "The Good News Is, They're Trying the Bad News," Adweek, June 28, 1993. p. 20.
© 1993 Adweek, L.P. Used with permission from Adweek.)*

[1]"Marketing Revolution Hits Staid Giants," *Advertising Age,* July 19, 1993, p. 18.
[2]Profile of Fujio Mitarai, *Fortune,* August 9, 1993, p. S-25.
[3]Andrew Geddes, "Avon Products," *Advertising Age,* August 16, 1993, p. I-6.

General Motors have experienced high levels of profitability during years when both companies lost money in this country.

American companies engaged in international sales will find many differences compared to domestic marketing. However, the common dominator of successful entry into foreign countries is market availability. A study conducted by the Arthur D. Little Company asked foreign companies for the major reasons for investing in Germany and countries of Eastern Europe. The three leading investment factors were:

1. Availability of markets   37 percent

2. Adequate labor force   13

3. Government subsidies   12

Obviously, companies, even those contemplating manufacturing ventures, look first to the presence of a market for their goods.[4]

American companies cannot exploit the potential of international sales by luck or accident. It will require product development, research, and market planning that is quite different from what U.S. companies are accustomed to in domestic sales. However, advertising is a key to introducing American products in many markets, especially those with emerging free (or freer) economies. As we have discussed in earlier chapters, a primary role of advertising is to introduce products and establish brand equity.

In mature markets such as the United States, the majority of companies and brands are well known to most consumers. In established markets, we are much more likely to see competition based on price and value-added promotions, with advertising playing a lesser role. However, in many foreign markets, U.S. products are largely unknown and even the product category may be unfamiliar to most consumers. In this introductory phase, advertising is often the most important part of the marketing plan. In fact, sometimes products that are available only in limited supplies are heavily advertised to create awareness in anticipation of later distribution.

While companies selling in developing nations may regard advertising as an investment in future profits, the cost of advertising is a distinct advantage in establishing a foothold in many countries. For example, major corporations operating in Russia find that sales volume for most consumer products is very low compared to the population. However, the average CPM for Russian TV advertising is approximately 6 cents as compared to approximately $6 on U.S. prime-time television.[5]

On a worldwide basis advertising expenditures are estimated at $308 billion. The United States accounted for less than half of this total, or about $149 billion. If, as expected, China and Eastern Europe continue to move toward some form of capitalism, the share of U.S. advertising expenditures as a total of worldwide advertising will continue to decrease.

---

[4]"Investment Conditions for Foreign Companies in Eastern Germany," *Deutschland,* November/December 1993, p. 9.

[5]Celestine Bohlen, "Crash Russian Course for Procter & Gamble," *New York Times,* December 19, 1993, p. 5.

THE NEW WORLD ECONOMIC ORDER

Nowhere has the global economy been more apparent than in advertising and marketing. Until the 1970s, American advertising expertise was unchallenged. For the most part this position was true of virtually every industry where "American-made" denoted quality and superiority. In many respects, the United States was unprepared for the ascension of international trade and marketing. "[I]ts [a global economy] recent surge caught America napping, or at least coasting on illusions that our historic advantages would last forever: unparalleled abundance of raw materials, land, labor and capital at favorable ratios, and access to an internal national market on a continental scale. Then came our emergence from World War II, which had devastated our natural competitors, with an industrial preeminence that for a generation allowed illusions of supremacy to obscure needs of new investment, new operating procedures, and new public policies."[6]

The same illusion of superiority that led to America's losing dominance in a number of industries also affected advertising. Currently, 5 of the world's 10 largest agency groups are foreign controlled. These five companies generate worldwide income of over $8 billion, almost half of total estimated agency income. Accompanying these income figures is the fact that many of the oldest and most established American agencies have been bought by foreign-based agency groups during the past decade. For example, J. Walter Thompson and Ogilvy & Mather Worldwide, the second and seventh largest U.S. agencies, respectively, are both owned by London's WPP Group. Not only do American companies fight daily with foreign competitors, but American agencies struggle to keep their accounts out of the hands of international agencies. At the same time, U.S. agencies see a growing percentage of their billings coming from advertising in foreign countries.

The shift to international business has brought fundamental changes in the way advertising is conducted. The advertising agency is changing, and these changes have not come without stress. First, clients demanded that agencies become conversant with a menu of marketing and promotional techniques beyond the traditional expertise of many organizations. At the same time, agencies were asked to work efficiently in new and totally unfamiliar markets and situations.

In the remainder of this chapter, we will discuss the complex world of international marketing and advertising. The changing environment of multinational marketing is uncertain. However, it is safe to predict that the advertising agency of the future will fall into two categories: (1) giant, full-service multinational agencies with offices and clients throughout the world, and (2) small agencies and boutiques serving primarily local firms. The medium-sized agency is caught in the middle with little prospect for growth or future success.

GLOBAL MARKETING AND ADVERTISING

One of the catch phrases of multinational selling is *global marketing*. The term, attributed to Theodore Levitt of Harvard University, suggests that companies can develop worldwide advertising and marketing strategies for their

Multinational advertising

The coordination and execution of advertising campaigns that are directed to a number of countries.

Global marketing

Term that denotes the use of advertising and marketing strategies on an international basis.

---

[6]John E. Sawyer, "The President's Report," Williams College, 1992, p. 4.

products. At the heart of the concept is the assumption that consumers are basically alike all over the world and will respond to similar appeals regardless of their apparent differences.

In fact, depending on specific products and management philosophies, there are several strategies that companies adopt to enter the international marketing arena:

1. *Export both the product and the advertising to other countries.* This is the strictest interpretation of global marketing. In this situation, the product (including brand name and logo) and marketing strategy would be identical in every country. The advantages in efficiency and cost savings to such a strategy are obvious. Some form of global marketing is the model that every firm seeks and rarely finds. Coca-Cola is probably the closest to the ideal global product. However, even Coca-Cola has a number of brands unique to various parts of the world (see Exhibit 24.2).

2. *Adapt a product and marketing plan exclusively for the international market.* Some products do well in the United States but fail in other countries. For example, diet soft drinks comprise 26 percent of U.S. volume as contrasted to only 4 percent in the rest of the world. Pepsi decided to buck this trend and take advantage of worldwide concern with a healthy diet by introducing a newly formulated diet drink in Italy and Great Britain. However, because diet soft drinks have not been particularly successful in the past,

EXHIBIT
24.2

Coca-Cola markets a number of brands throughout the world such as Krest ginger ale in South Africa.

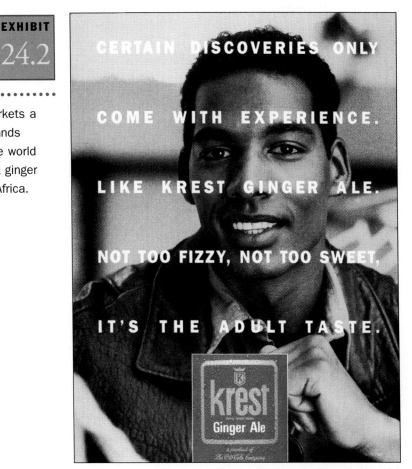

(Courtesy: Bernstein Loxton, Golding and Klein (PTY), Ltd. & New York Festivals International Advertising Awards.)

Pepsi chose to market the product under the name Max.[7] Pepsi also developed a separate international advertising plan to overcome the past aversion to diet drinks.

3. *Export the product, but change the name.* When Campbell Soup Company began European distribution of its Pepperidge Farm cookies, it did so under the Biscuits Maison de Delacre brand. The product was introduced with the same name, pricing, and advertising throughout Europe. Prior to the introduction of Biscuits Maison, Campbell sold cookies on a country-by-country basis with different brands and packages. The new strategy saved substantial dollars and increased sales compared to the earlier segmented strategy.[8]

4. *Keep the brand name and advertising strategy, but adapt the product country by country.* Jacob's Creek Wines of Australia has entered countries in Asia, Europe, and North America with a strategy of affordable, high-quality wines all sold under the Jacob's Creek label. However, the company's success has depended on its ability to judge the diverse tastes of wine drinkers in the various countries to which it exports.

5. *Keep the brand name and product, but adapt the advertising to each country.* Ironically, as high-profile brands have come under growing competitive pressure in this country, they have attained unprecedented popularity abroad. Major American companies have an image of producing high-quality products. As American movies and TV networks such as CNN make international communication commonplace, consumers, even in remote parts of the world, are familiar with American brands. More importantly, these American brands often command premium prices. Johnson & Johnson baby shampoo and Band-Aid adhesive strips sell for 500 percent above domestic brands in China, and Gillette charges double the price of local competition for its disposable razors and has steadily increased its Chinese market share.

There are numerous variations on each of these international strategies. The important point is that no plan will work for every brand or product category in every country. Even ideas that would seem to be universal, demonstrate wide variations of adoption and acceptability from one country to another. For example, companies that want to take commercial advantage of current environmental concerns should be prepared to modify their messages in multinational marketing.

One study sought to determine how various countries and cultures reacted to environmental marketing messages. Focus groups conducted in a number of countries found vast differences in levels of consumer information about the environment, who consumers held responsible for the problem, and consumer expectations for companies to deal with the issues. Companies that expect to gain significant advantage with an environmental advertising theme will be sorely disappointed in many parts of the world (see Exhibit 24.3).

Multinational marketers and their agencies must be prepared to deal with prevailing social and economic conditions in each of the countries and re-

---

[7] "Eurofizz," *Fortune*, March 22, 1993, p. 15.
[8] Elena Bowes, "Campbell Biscuits Europe," *Advertising Age*, August 16, 1993, p. I-8.

EXHIBIT
24.3

Even issues such as the environment demonstrate major cultural differences.

Five degrees of environmentalism

Spectators:	India, Brazil, Chile, Nigeria
Passive Environmentalists:	South Africa, Colombia, Uruguay
Lip-Service Environmentalists:	Spain, Italy, Australia, Greece, Argentina
Negotiators:	France, Belgium, Japan, UK, New Zealand
Anxious Experts:	U.S., Canada, Germany, Netherlands, Norway

(Source: Gary Levin,"Too Green for Their Own Good." Advertising Age, April 12, 1993, p. 29.)

gions they wish to enter. For example, Exhibit 24.4 shows the wide variance in the popularity and acceptance of advertising in a number of countries. Too often, marketers focus only on their products and ignore the more general questions of economic stability, inflation, government attitudes and regula-

EXHIBIT
24.4

Advertising is not equally accepted from country to country.

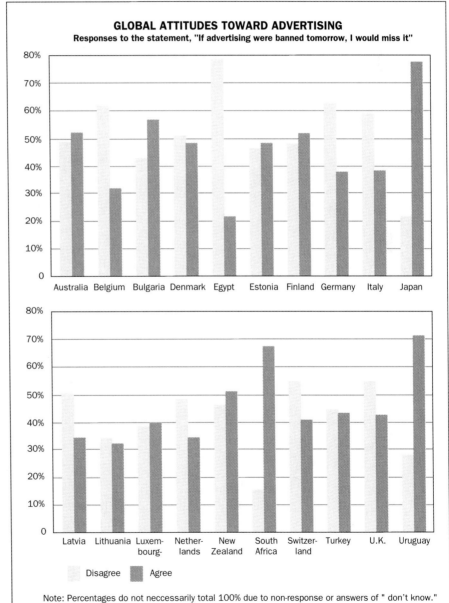

GLOBAL ATTITUDES TOWARD ADVERTISING
Responses to the statement, "If advertising were banned tomorrow, I would miss it"

Note: Percentages do not neccessarily total 100% due to non-response or answers of " don't know."

(Source: Gallup International, Advertising Age International, October 11, 1993 p. I-21)

**EXHIBIT
24.5**

••••••••••••••••••

Multinational firms usually develop marketing plans that represent a compromise between the needs of consumers and the firm.

Continuum of Marketing/Advertising Strategy	
Company Oriented	Consumer Oriented
Global Marketing	Marketing Concept
One strategy One execution	Different strategy Different execution

tions toward foreign investment, availability of media advertising, audience information, and cultural and language problems unique to each country.

With a few exceptions, it is unlikely that true global marketing will be available to multinational marketers. However, the general concept and its many variations become more practical each year. Satellite transmission and the popularity of television have permitted regional TV networks on every continent. At a minimum, these satellite systems permit multinational advertisers to gain a cost-effective foothold in every region of the world. "While it is not conceivable that pan regional media opportunities will take the place of individual market activities, in some cases the pan regional 'medium' does offer marketers efficiencies, in some cases an alternative. It is certainly an opportunity to complement local media buys."[9]

Technology is available to make the *idea* of international advertising and global marketing a reality. However, it is impossible to accommodate all the cultural and national differences in any single marketing strategy. "In the new, more unified global marketplace, persistent differences in language, culture and perception make it a delicate balancing act to establish a unified global presence which also reflects local nuances. Less formally stated, this principle says that, even in the global village, the biggest building is still the Tower of Babel."[10]

Global marketing is such an appealing concept from a cost and efficiency standpoint that companies are tempted to adopt it even when it has obvious pitfalls. It can be argued that the misapplication of global marketing places the well-being of the firm ahead of the consumer. Exhibit 24.5 demonstrates the continuum of a one-strategy, one-execution global marketing approach versus a consumer-oriented marketing concept with a different-strategy, different-execution in each country approach.

As we saw in earlier examples of international marketing plans, the idea of a continuum of strategies is more common than an either/or notion of choosing between a strict interpretation of global marketing and the consumer orientation of the marketing concept. In most cases, companies develop a broad marketing and advertising plan. From this plan they then make necessary adaptations that consider the special cultural, economic, and language differences present in each country they enter.

---

[9]Mark Buckman, "With a Consumer Base of 268 Million, Latin America's Potential Is Serious," *Mediaweek,* July 5, 1993, p. 9.

[10]Ron K. Glover, "Establishing a Presence around the Globe," speech to the Conference Board, January 26, 1993, p. 1.

Country-of-origin (CO) promotion

A marketing strategy that attempts to create a positive image for a product by emphasizing the county in which it was produced.

International advertising also has created a heightened awareness of the advisability of promoting products on a *country-of-origin* (CO) basis. CO refers to the image of a product when it is associated with a particular country. The CO image of a product can relate positively or negatively to the economic, political, and cultural characteristics of a country. Many customers resist buying products manufactured in the Republic of China because they think it is wrong to support that country's political structure.

In other cases, CO may create an image for all products produced in a particular country. Some customers regard Germany as a country that is known for precision and quality of workmanship. To some customers, "German made" is a sign of quality regardless of the product. In some cases, CO factors may relate to product-specific attributes. For example, French perfume and wine are acknowledged as among the best in the world.[11]

Despite the importance of CO image for some products, we must keep in mind that consumers, by and large, purchase brands without regard to a product's country of origin. The average consumer would be unlikely to know or care whether Nestlé is headquartered in Geneva or Omaha. Therefore, we must realize that most of the benefits of global marketing accrue to the companies using it, not to their customers. All of this is not to lessen the importance of a multinational approach to marketing and advertising problems. However, it is mandatory that the marketing concept, with its consumer orientation, be kept in mind in developing international advertising plans just as in domestic advertising.

POLITICAL AND ECONOMIC MOVEMENTS TOWARD A WORLD ECONOMY

At no time in recent history has there been such a concerted effort on so many fronts to foster international trade. Steps toward removing artificial barriers to commerce are in place or at the discussion stage throughout the world. When President Clinton dropped U.S. trade barriers with Vietnam in 1994, it offered yet another dramatic example of the movement to a world economy. We will briefly discuss three of the most important agreements.

The North American Free Trade Agreement

North American Free Trade Agreement (NAFTA)

A treaty designed to eliminate trade barriers among the U.S., Mexico, and Canada.

In November, 1993 Congress ratified the North American Free Trade Agreement (NAFTA), which will eliminate all trade barriers among the United States, Canada, and Mexico over the next 15 years. It is estimated that the agreement will create a market of 360 million people and goods totaling $6.7 *trillion*. Experts predict that NAFTA will have a larger impact on Mexico than the more developed economy of Canada. However, since Mexico is the third largest market for U.S. exports (after Canada and Japan), NAFTA, when fully implemented, offers a major source of international expansion to American firms.[12]

---

[11]Ravi Parameswaran and R. Mohan Pisharodi, "Facets of Country of Origin Image: An Empirical Assessment," *Journal of Advertising*, March 1994, p. 45.

[12]Geoffrey Brewer, "New World Orders," *Sales & Marketing Management*, January 1994, p. 60.

The General Agreement on Tariffs and Trade

The most far-reaching trade agreement is the General Agreement on Tariffs and Trade (GATT) accords signed by some 117 nations in 1993. While not as all-inclusive as the NAFTA agreement, it takes a number of steps to reduce tariffs and import duties among countries that are party to the agreement. It is estimated that GATT has the potential of adding $270 million to the world economy.

A major drawback to GATT is the number of countries and diverse cultures that are party to the agreement. While price reductions will be a primary benefit to consumers in these countries, GATT will not overcome cultural, language, and product usage differences among these countries. As one international marketing executive pointed out, "The cost of the product is not the most important issue for a . . . marketer, but rather the cost of customer."[13] New customer development is difficult enough in domestic markets, much less dealing with customers throughout the world.

The Economic Unification of Europe

While it is too soon to judge the full implications of NAFTA and GATT, we can learn from the experiences of European nations in developing an environment for free trade. Since 1992, Europe has moved slowly toward a unified market consisting of most of the developed countries of the region. Called the European Community (EC), it represents the largest and most important experiment in bringing the concept of a global market to fruition. The idea of the EC is to eliminate most of the physical, fiscal, and technical barriers to trade among the 12 nations of Western Europe.[14]

The proponents of the EC claim that when fully implemented, it will provide a common trade area with 345 million people and a total value of $5 trillion. It will be 50 percent larger than the United States in population and 20 percent greater in sales potential. If all goes as planned, it will be the first demonstration that global marketing will work.

Obviously, an undertaking of this magnitude is a tremendous task. Countries that have been political and economic rivals for centuries are being asked to set aside their differences and make significant compromises for the common good. Let's look at a few areas that demonstrate the issues, large and small, that must be dealt with in creating this single market:[15]

- **Customs regulations.** Goods move freely across borders resulting in the elimination of 60 million documents.

- **Environmental standards.** Common standards for industries throughout the EC have been agreed upon, but target dates have not been reached.

- **Prices.** They vary widely. Cameras cost 40 percent more in Portugal than in France.

Margin notes

General Agreement on Tariffs (GATT)

A treaty designed to lower trade barriers among 117 nations.

European Community (EC)

The developing economic integration of Europe. Potentially a single market of some 300 million consumers in 1991.

---

[13]Matthew Rose, "GATT Hailed by Some—But Not All—DMers," *DM News,* December 27, 1993, p. 26.
[14]The EC consists of Germany, Italy, Great Britain, France, Spain, the Netherlands, Belgium, Portugal, Greece, Denmark, Ireland, Luxembourg.
[15]"A Business Guide to the New Europe," *New York Times,* January 2, 1993, p. 13.

716   PART SIX   *Other Environments of Advertising*

- **Company statutes.** EC-wide companies cannot be established because of disagreement on provisions from country to country about worker participation in management.

- **Television.** A major breakthrough is the fact that there are no restrictions on broadcasting across borders

- **Cheese.** After a long fight, the EC members allowed France to sell its cheese made from nonpasteurized milk throughout the EC.

- **Pasta.** Italy was blocked from blocking the import of soft-wheat pasta from other EC countries. The case went all the way to the European Court of Justice.

These, and a thousand other details, are still being negotiated. From purity standards for beer to major concessions concerning currency exchange and taxes, the EC faces a formidable job of bringing the loose ends together. The detractors of the EC plan say that it will never happen because, in fact, there is no common European community. According to critics, it is impractical to assume that geographic proximity can lead to economic cooperation on a scale suggested by the EC.

Like global marketing itself, the EC concept will probably find its final place somewhere between its strongest supporters and its harshest critics. Evidence points up the fact that nationalism among the EC countries will not be swept away overnight. For example, what brand of car EC residents buy is strongly influenced by whether the car is made in their country (see Exhibit 24.6). While automobiles are more closely identified with a country than most consumer products, these data do indicate the nationalistic influence that the EC must overcome.

EXHIBIT 24.6

....

Countries where marketers have greatest and least penetration.

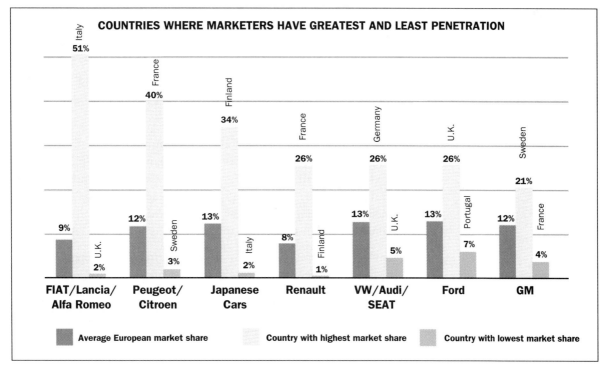

COUNTRIES WHERE MARKETERS HAVE GREATEST AND LEAST PENETRATION

FIAT/Lancia/Alfa Romeo — Average European market share 9%, Italy (highest) 51%, U.K. (lowest) 2%

Peugeot/Citroen — Average European market share 12%, France (highest) 40%, Sweden (lowest) 3%

Japanese Cars — Average European market share 13%, Finland (highest) 34%, Italy (lowest) 2%

Renault — Average European market share 8%, France (highest) 26%, Finland (lowest) 1%

VW/Audi/SEAT — Average European market share 13%, Germany (highest) 26%, U.K. (lowest) 5%

Ford — Average European market share 13%, U.K. (highest) 26%, Portugal (lowest) 7%

GM — Average European market share 12%, Sweden (highest) 21%, France (lowest) 4%

- Average European market share
- Country with highest market share
- Country with lowest market share

(Source: "Japanese Autos Hold Strong Appeal in Europe," Advertising Age, April 19, 1993, p. I-14.)

Many companies that are involved in the EC and other multinational marketing find that they must immerse themselves in the total culture of a country to be successful. "It is not enough to translate from one language to another. We must accurately convey the thought. Even beyond that, we must fit the culture of the country, the way they manage, the way they make buying decisions, the way they think about business."[16]

The full implementation of the EC is many years in the future. However, it offers an excellent laboratory for multinational marketing. If developed countries such as the ones that comprise the EC are having the difficulties they are encountering, one can only image the problems implicit in the development of a true worldwide marketing program. However, it is the world, with all its inherent challenges, that offers the best prospects for most American companies.

THE MULTINATIONAL ADVERTISING AGENCY

As marketing has become a multinational enterprise, advertising has had to follow. In the 1940s and 1950s, when McCann-Erickson and J. Walter Thompson led American agencies into the international arena, they started foreign branches on a country-by-country basis. These branch agencies would be responsible for a few large clients in a limited number of countries.

This approach to international advertising was extremely expensive and did not guarantee that the American imported agencies would adequately serve the international needs of their clients. During the 1970s, U.S. agencies adopted some form of joint venture or minority ownership of existing foreign agencies. This plan overcame the long start-up time involved in beginning a new agency and provided advertising plans that reflected local business practices and culture. Joint ventures also recognized the growing expertise of local advertising talent and the fact that around the world new, young agencies were catching up with their older partners.

Today, international advertising is most often characterized by centralization of management. For example, Procter & Gamble recently announced that it would reduce its worldwide agencies to three for some of its major brands. Related to this trend toward reorganization is the move toward centralization of brand responsibility.

Worldwide brands are so large and their multinational advertising so complex that it has become a full-time job to handle a single account. This has resulted in a class of "super account executives" with authority to run global accounts that are as large as mid-sized agencies. When J. Walter Thompson assigned its president of JWT-Italy to worldwide responsibility for its Unilever account, the account had the same billings as the entire Italian office.[17]

Agency organizations, especially in the international arena, reflect those of their clients. Remember, agencies are first and foremost service companies. As corporations restructure with an eye toward greater centralization, agencies must follow suit. If brand decisions worldwide are being made by a mar-

---

[16]Sawyer, Riley, Compton Inc., "Alert" newsletter.
[17]Laurel Wentz, "Marketers' Global Goals Breed New Agency Exec," *Advertising Age*, January 18, 1993, p. I-8.

keting vice president in London, then agencies need to have a counterpart in London to develop advertising. When clients went into countries one by one after World War II, this dictated a decentralized approach with agency branches in each country.

Nike's agency, Wieden & Kennedy, recently opened a branch office in Amsterdam. It was no coincidence that Nike had opened an international headquarters in Holland in 1992. The manager of the Dutch branch said, "Our move was a natural evolution of the relationship we had with our main client. We have been managing Nike's European account from our Portland office for quite some time, but the volume of its business in Europe was such that it [Nike] was putting more of its decision-makers at its European headquarters."[18]

Agencies face two major problems in developing organizations that will meet the demands of clients. First, they are always following the leader. An agency with several multinational accounts often finds that the specific needs for account management will differ from one client to the other. In effect, some agencies find that they need different management organizations for each client.

When Reebok International, a major manufacturer of athletic shoes, moved its account from Chiat/Day to Leo Burnett Co., it cited Burnett's greater ability to deal with Reebok's global needs. Reebok's vice president for marketing services said, "Chiat did not have the resources and we made the decision . . . that it was an opportunity to take another look at the kind of resources we needed."[19]

The second major problem faced by multinational agencies is how to manage centrally and communicate locally. The adage "Think globally, act locally" is a dilemma for every agency. Agencies must translate broad company marketing strategy to the level of the individual customer in each country they serve. Despite the pitfalls of centralized advertising management, there is little doubt that the trend will only be more prevalent in the future. The major advantages of centralized management are the following:

1. Coordination offers cost savings in terms of client time and personnel and, to some extent, production costs.

2. It facilitates the sharing of experience: Lessons learned in one market can readily be applied in another.

3. It enables the effective control of the overall advertising budget so that funds are spent where and at the level they are needed.

4. The international importance of the account will ensure that it gets the benefit of the agency's top resources locally, regardless of the size of the budget for any particular market.

5. Most important, consistency of approach means that a positioning and image for a product can be built over time and across territory, a consideration of growing importance as internationally received media become more commonplace. Instead of being written off as a short-term tactical cost,

---

[18]"In Hot Pursuit," *Media International,* May 1993, p. 36.
[19]Pat Sloan, "Why Reebok Fired Chiat, Once and for All," *Advertising Age,* September 20, 1993, p. 58.

advertising becomes an investment in an increasingly valuable international asset.

The Advertising Function In International Advertising

It is very difficult to discuss common denominators of international advertising. Not only is the execution of advertising vastly different from country to country, but the objectives and basic goals also demonstrate extraordinary diversity. As firms introduce products on a worldwide basis, their problems range from something as familiar as product category competition to the much more difficult problem of convincing buyers to change established habits or even reject previously held cultural taboos.

Regardless of the objective of a particular international campaign, there are three problem areas that face most multinational advertisers: creative, media, and cultural considerations.

Creative Considerations

Effective advertising often depends on humor, puns, twists on familiar words, and an insider's knowledge of a culture and society. It is very difficult for an outsider to address these issues, and even more difficult to do so as advertising crosses international boundaries. The most common mistakes in advertising creativity are the simple mistranslations of slogans or idioms.

Some of the misunderstandings of translation are legendary such as "Body by Fisher" becoming "Corpse by Fisher" or the Thai translation of "Come alive, you're in the Pepsi Generation," which read, "Pepsi brings your ancestors back from the dead." However, these blunders are largely a thing of the past as both advertisers and foreign consumers become more sophisticated about the language of advertising. Sometimes problems arise because of too much communication rather than too little. Several years ago, the British division of McDonald's was damaged by persistent rumors that it supported the Irish Republican Army. After a good deal of research it was discovered that CNN had reported that management had encouraged McDonald's employees to invest in IRAs. Since individual retirement accounts meant nothing to most British viewers, they assumed that the company had entered the political arena.[20]

It is easy to run afoul of local convention even in countries with common heritages and language (see Exhibit 24.7). In the United States, commercial television is the norm, since advertising and television evolved together. However, in Great Britain, where TV advertising was not permitted for the first 20 years after the medium's introduction, there is a consumer suspicion of commercials. British viewers also prefer soft-sell, humorous commercials and are generally turned off by the hard sell of many American messages.[21]

As we have discussed, the cost efficiencies of common creative themes, especially lower advertising production costs, make it important to try to develop creative campaigns that are exportable. More and more international campaigns seek to highlight similar consumer motivations and develop messages that emphasize the Big Idea rather than local differences among consumers.

---

[20]Glover, "Establishing a Presence around the Globe," p. 14.
[21]Terence Nevett, "Differences between American and British Television Advertising: Explanations and Implications," *Journal of Advertising,* December 1992, p. 64.

EXHIBIT

24.7

Factors Responsible for Differences in American and British Television Advertising—Summary of Findings

Factors	U.S. Effect	U.K. Effect
SOCIO-CULTURAL CONTEXTS		
Historical Evolution	Advertising and television evolved together	Advertising not permitted until 20 years after introduction of television
Effects of Culture	Hard sell	Soft sell, idiosyncratic
Emphasis on Entertainment	Generally less	Generally more
Influence of Opinion Leaders	——	Historical dislike of advertising–Advertisers made more sensitive to criticism
ADVERTISING INDUSTRY ENVIRONMENTS		
Substantiation Requirements	Rigorous	Rigorous
Local/National Advertising	Higher proportion of local	Higher proportion of national
Clutter	Viewer may be exposed to more than 27% non program material	Limit of average of 6 minutes advertising/hour restrictions on positioning of commercials in programs
PHILOSOPHY AND EXECUTION		
Management Views and Philosophies	Possibly greater acceptance of hierarchies-of-effect	Apparent rejection of hierarchies-of-effects
Pretesting	Largely quantitative– Tends to be based on hierarchies-of-effects proposition	Largely qualitative– Tends to be based on need to understand creative proposition
Commercial Length	Tends to be short	Tends to be longer

(Source: Journal of Advertising *December 1992, p. 64.)*

There are several approaches to making multinational advertising more effective:

1. *Aim to create an international campaign from the outset.* Approach the advertising problem as an international one rather than attempting to translate an idea after the fact.

2. *Develop a creative strategy with a general consumer perspective rather than a nationalistic view.*

3. *Emphasize the central theme, not the execution.* The best international advertising tends to be for products with an easily understood product benefit. Levi-Strauss jeans and Haagen-Dazs ice cream have had great success with cross-country advertising.

4. *Admit that some products need unique advertising campaigns in each country.* As one advertising executive declared, "Too many clients get so concerned about producing ads that everyone can understand, they end up with ads that no one notices."[22]

MEDIA PLANNING: A GLOBAL PERSPECTIVE

Increasingly, media planning will involve a multinational perspective as firms move across borders to add market share and profits and to reflect growing competition from abroad. During the past two decades, the international media buying function has changed dramatically. One by one, automobiles, consumer electronics, and textile manufacturers moved to foreign countries, and American companies found themselves in a truly competitive international marketplace.

In this new environment, the media planner must have extensive knowledge of foreign competition as well as information concerning the local conditions in a number of other countries. Marketing and advertising executives for companies such as Coca-Cola and Procter & Gamble routinely sell their products in approximately 200 countries. At the same time, they must have the expertise to compete effectively with foreign giants such as Lever Brothers and Nestlé which market dozens of brands in this country.

As the EC reaches maturity and countries of the Middle East and Asia present selling opportunities to American companies, the media buyer of the future will face a number of problems and opportunities. Global media planning involves a number of complex problems not encountered in the typical domestic advertising campaign.

The media function must, at a minimum, consider three primary areas in developing an international plan:

1. A market audit for each of the countries being considered.

2. The methods that will be used to market the product in the international arena. This process is sometimes called the *translation* of the marketing plan.

3. The specific methods that will be used to gain entry into each market. Some of these will be dictated by the legal or regulatory climate of an individual country.

The Market Audit

In many respects the marketing audit conducted for an international client is similar to one for a domestic client. However, the complexity and range of differences in most international environments make an international audit more difficult. Obviously, each audit must be unique to the country or countries and products being examined. However, there are a number of areas that would be considered in such a study.

The first step in such an audit would be to view the economic development of the potential new market. What is the stage of economic development? Is there a market for the product of a size to warrant introduction? Is there a distribution system adequate for the product, or could one be economically

---

[22]"Can Advertising Cross Boundaries?" *Media International,* July 1993, p. 16.

put in place? An examination of the basic economy of a country is usually the starting point of an audit because if the basic characteristics of a developed market are absent, it probably will be extremely difficult to introduce a product.

The second step in such an audit would be a review of the present competition. Are other multinational companies marketing similar products in the country? What is their success, and is there demand for more brands? Can you differentiate your product in a meaningful way from those of brands already established in the country?

Finally, the audit must look at the culture of a country to see if the product and the marketing techniques can be successfully used in this country. In some cases, a cultural audit may find that some product characteristics must be emphasized in a unique manner, or the product might have to be specially adapted to another culture. A thorough review of marketing methods, product uses, and advertising messages can prevent major foreign disasters.

The Translation Process

Marketing translation
The process of adapting a general marketing plan to a multinational environments.

Once the audit is completed, the process of executing marketing plans begins. The translation of marketing plans from one country to another is perhaps the most difficult stage of international marketing and one that will be increasingly important for the media planner in developing a global perspective. The three primary areas of international translation are language, media, and consumption patterns.

Because of cost efficiencies, there is a great temptation to make the translation as simple as possible. In many product fields there is a similarity of usage and motivation from country to country and it is very possible, indeed, cost-efficient, to generate uniform advertising. Other products, such as food and beer, are less suited to this approach. In these areas, the variation in consumption patterns and product styles from country to country is very great and to attempt to impose uniformity would be counterproductive.

Methods of Implementing the Media Function

Advertising media planning is a tremendous challenge to the multinational advertiser. There are two major problems faced by agencies as they service clients on an international basis:

■ **Variance of media usage levels from country to country**

■ **Methods of media buying and availability of audience data**

American advertisers find that media preferences, advertising availability, and costs of time and space differ markedly in international advertising from those in the United States. For example, in the Netherlands people read newspapers before going to work. However, in virtually every other European country radio is the preferred morning medium and morning television is rare. On the other hand, most newspaper reading is done before lunch at work. If there is a constant, it is that television is clearly the fastest growing source of advertising revenue.

Many advertising executives view television as the most efficient means of achieving high audience penetration levels on a global basis. We think of the

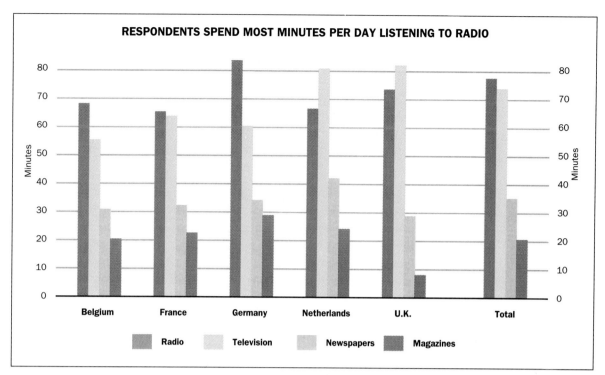

RESPONDENTS SPEND MOST MINUTES PER DAY LISTENING TO RADIO

(Source: "Data Watch," Advertising Age, October 26, 1992, p. J-10.)

EXHIBIT
24.8

• • • • • • • • • • • • • • • • • •

Media usage in Europe differs markedly among various countries.

United States as the leader in TV viewing. However, we trail Japan in household viewing hours, and five nations presently have a higher percentage of cable households than the United States. In fact, Belgium and the Netherlands each have close to 90 percent cable households compared to just over 60 percent in America.[23]

Despite the potential benefits for international television, in most of the world, TV viewing is very low compared to the American obsession with the medium. In Europe, Great Britain and the Netherlands report the highest viewing levels. However, in both countries only 31 percent of viewers watch more than two hours a day. Exhibit 24.8 shows media preferences and average daily minutes of usage of media in selected countries.

In some respects, international media usage mirrors trends in the United States. Television is growing in popularity in virtually every country in the world. Likewise, this growth seems to be at the expense of print media, especially newspapers. In most of the world, television is the primary advertising medium, held back only by advertising restrictions in several countries. Advertising executives predict that as television continues to expand through satellite and cable, it will emerge as the major international medium in much the same manner as in the United States. What is troubling to newspapers is that they are losing advertising revenue shares in spite of significant cost efficiencies compared to television (see Exhibit 24.9).

The emergence of television in Asia, South America, and Africa will create even more competition for newspapers in the future. For example, advertising on STAR-TV, a Hong Kong–based satellite service, grew 500 percent in eight months and now has 12 million viewers. In Bombay, satellites have

---

[23]"Who Has Cable," *Target Marketing,* February 1994, p. 43.

EXHIBIT
24.9

Ad costs vary by medium and country

Country	CPMs for adults 15 and older			
	TV peak time	Radio peak time	Newspapers	Magazines
France	$9.49	$7.00	$21.63	$5.33
Germany	$13.31	$2.20	$7.41	$6.91
Italy	$11.62	$3.24	$5.80	$4.89
Japan	$4.91	N/A	$2.25	$4.08
Netherlands	$11.68	N/A	$4.84	$5.04
Spain	$7.99	$5.39	$6.63	$4.14
Switzerland	$23.72	$15.46	$9.28	$18.64
U.K.	$6.82	N/A	$4.16	$4.88
U.S.	$6.66	$1.53	$11.26	$4.91

(Source: Jeff Jensen, "TV is Advertisers' Big Pick in Europe." Advertising Age, June 21, 1993, p. I-19.)

made possible some 2,000 cable *networks*.[24] Satellites, carrying both radio and TV programming, have brought the most remote parts of the world instant communications. In areas where distribution of print media is impossible and low literacy rates make them of limited use, a satellite links people to the rest of the world. A review of newspaper circulation shows that newspaper sales are flat or decreasing in most countries (see Exhibit 24.10).

Perhaps the best indication of the growing value of TV advertising in international marketing is the demand for audience ratings. In 1993, TV people meters were installed in Bahrain, Kuwait, Saudi Arabia, Lebanon, and Egypt.[25] TV audience measurements are found in large Latin American and Asian markets and soon will enter other African countries. However, since widespread commercial television is so new in many countries, planners must buy spots more on faith than on reliable data.

In addition to the differences in use of traditional media in various countries, media planners also must deal with nontraditional media, which are very important in some areas of the world. For example, cinema advertising, regarded as a very minor medium in America, is a primary vehicle in Asia. Out-of-home advertising is also extremely important in many countries.

One of the fastest-growing forms of advertising throughout the world is direct response. There are a number of advantages to international direct response. Direct mail can be translated into appropriate languages to reach segments within a multilingual country. It also can be targeted to take into account special cultural or product usage patterns. The problem with direct response is finding adequate information. In most Latin American countries, reliable mailing lists are very scarce, and in most of Asia there are severe restrictions on the use of proprietary information about consumers, which makes building databases difficult.

Regardless of the media strategy adopted, advertisers must deal with the problems of buying and executing the plan. The media function is so complex for large multinational buys that the media buying function is increasingly concentrated in buying combines or brokers that buy for a number of agencies. Two of the largest of these media brokers are Carat and The Media Partner-

---

[24]Walt Potter, "News of the World," *presstime,* July 1993, p. 67.
[25]"Keeping Track of TV's Footprints," *Media International,* January 1993, p. 35.

EXHIBIT

24.10

NEWSPAPER SALES AROUND THE WORLD

The U.S. trails many countries in newspaper readership.

Daily newspapers sold per 1,000 inhabitants

	1988	1991	1992
Norway	550	600	619
Japan	580	591	584
Sweden	519	518	522
Finland	550	539	521
Germany	336*	311	335
Switzerland	432	416	415
Austria	357	337	409
Czech Republic	—	—	396
United Kingdom	391	367	362
Singapore	281	329	348
Denmark	355	327	340
Luxemburg	—	320	333
Netherlands	313	317	317
New Zealand	—	301	264
USA	255	251	244
Russia	337	210	222
Canada	221	218	214
Australia	—	220	199
Estonia	430	409	195
Slovak Republic	246	187	179
Ireland	176	183	177
Belgium	182	173	173
Israel	135	158	—
France	157	157	—
Poland	—	—	126
Italy	117	113	115
Malaysia	—	112	—
Cyprus	102	96	91
Greece	127	92	83
Spain	79	81	81
Argentina	—	—	79
Turkey	55	69	56
South Africa	41	43	44
Philippines	—	43	—
Portugal	—	39	39
Uruguay	—	—	35
Tunisia	—	—	30
India	21	23	24
Brazil	12	15	15

*1988 Figure refers to West Germany only

(Source: Walt Potter, "News of the World," presstime, July, 1993, p. 66.)

ship Europe (TMP). TMP is a joint effort of four agencies and has media billings of $5 billion.[26]

These combines can afford to hire highly trained personnel, conduct multinational audience research, and establish databases that would be beyond the financial reach of any single agency. The combines also can gain significant media discounts by buying as a group instead of on the basis of single agencies or brands. U.S. media generally give media discounts based on corporate media placement. However, in many parts of the world, media allow

---

[26]"Good Relations," *Media International*, February 1993, p. 23.

agencies to combine media placement for all their clients to establish discounts. Discounts based on total agency placement means that the larger the broker, the greater the financial advantage to its clients.

The major problem faced by the multi-agency media brokers is satisfying competing agencies all vying for the best placement of their advertising. However, the financial advantages of these brokers are worth the potential hazards of client conflicts invited by multinational media brokers. As American agencies become more comfortable with media brokers, it would not be surprising to find that similar systems are adopted in this country. Competitive pressures on media might move them to offer agency (as opposed to corporate discounts) and thereby speed up the process.

One problem with these multinational media brokers is their success. Some have grown so large and control such a significant percentage of advertising dollars that local government agencies are reviewing their operations. Regulators fear that there is a potential danger that brokers might influence the editorial content of media by controlling such a large share of advertising expenditures to media.

CULTURAL CONSIDERATIONS

One of the most difficult aspects of international advertising is determining how to assimilate societal norms into messages. Advertising is not confined to carrying information about products. Rather, it communicates and persuades within a context of culture and values unique to each country. Even in developed countries such as the United States, advertisers find that localization of advertising is often needed to take into account the many local customs of product usage, values, terminology, and distribution.

Even most experienced international companies are not immune from the pitfalls of cross-cultural selling. For example, when Procter & Gamble introduced Pampers disposable diapers in Japan during the 1970s it found that Japanese mothers did not like the bulk of the American diapers. The company had failed to note that Japanese women change diapers approximately 14 times a day—more than twice as often as American mothers. Procter & Gamble began to market a thinner diaper in Japan and quickly captured over 20 percent of the market.[27] Despite its belated success, Procter & Gamble paid a price for failing to know the culture of its market before introducing a product.

International marketers must be sociologists. They must understand the manner in which individuals are socialized into adopting certain attitudes, beliefs, and values. Product consumption is a primary manner in which people communicate their social role. Each person has a status within a community and a culture. Advertisers that are ignorant or insensitive to the social environment of their prospects are doomed to fail.

Despite the important differences from country to country, worldwide communication is giving a common "look" to advertising. American advertising pioneered in reason-why copy, family vignettes, and product comparisons (see Exhibit 24.11 for a Spanish version of a tried-and-true strategy for hosiery advertising). Now these creative approaches are seen throughout the world.

---

[27]Alecia Swasy, "Don't Sell Thick Diapers in Tokyo," *New York Times,* October 3, 1993, p. F-9.

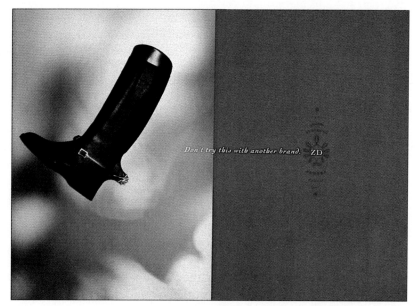

Don't try this with another brand. ZD

(Source: Paco Segarva—Creative Director, Jordi Alumni—Art Director
& New York Festivals International Advertising Awards.)

LEGAL AND REGULATORY PROHIBITIONS

In Chapter 25, we will discuss the complex legal and regulatory environment of American advertising. However, on a worldwide scale, the regulation of media and advertising constitutes a crazy quilt of rules, legal opinions, laws, and constitutional prohibitions that often affect advertisers and the media they use. Media ownership and importation of foreign programming are restricted in a number of countries. In the United Kingdom, individuals must have permission from the Department of Trade and Industry to own a newspaper with more than 500,000 circulation. In Italy a network TV owner may not own a newspaper.[28]

Many countries, including the United States, have enacted a number of regulations concerning advertising and promotion. For example, France prohibits the display of cigarette logos on racing cars. France also prohibits cigarette and alcohol advertising on television but allows alcohol ads in magazines. The international advertiser must exercise great care in developing media plans and creative themes or risk running afoul of the many local regulations pertaining to advertising.

ADVERTISING DIVERSITY IN THE UNITED STATES

To most of us, multinational advertising means American companies going abroad. However, domestic advertisers in this country are not immune to the demands of an increasingly diversified society. A company that ignores the significant changes in American society does so at its own risk.

The U. S. Census Bureau reported that 31 million people (14 percent of the population) speak a language other than English at home. Spanish is the most popular non-English language, followed by French and German. However, the fastest-growing non-English language segment of the population are Asian

---

[28]Anton Lensen, "Concentration in the Media Industry," Annenberg Washington Program, 1992, p. 16.

Language barrier

The number of some foreign-language households is exploding

Language	(in thousands) 1980	1990	Change
Spanish	11,549	17,339	+50.1%
Chinese	632	1,249	+97.7%
Korean	275	626	+127.2%
Vietnamese	203	507	+149.5%
Arabic	226	355	+57.4%
Hindi	130	331	+155.1%
Russian	175	242	+38.5%
Hebrew	99	144	+45.5%
. . .while others are declining			
German	1,607	1,547	− 3.7%
Italian	1,633	1,309	−19.9%
Polish	826	723	−12.4%

Figures for 1990 measure population age 5 and over; 1980 figures measure population 3 and older. An average 2.5% decrease in 1990 is attributed to the change in age groups.

(Source: Gary Levin, "Marketers Learning New Languages for Ads," Advertising Age, May 10, 1993, p. 33.)

Americans. Statistics show increases of over 100 percent in Korean and Vietnamese speakers in the United States since 1980 (see Exhibit 24.12).

More important than the size of this market is its potential buying power. For example, Asian households have total buying power of $110 billion. During the last census period these households also showed the largest increase in median income to $36,800.[29] Hispanic Americans represent an even larger U.S. market, with total purchasing power of $206 billion and average household income of almost $29,000. It is projected that by the year 2010 Hispanic Americans will constitute America's largest minority group.[30]

Major metropolitan media, just as their advertising counterparts, are facing the growing number of immigrants in a number of ways. For example, the *Boston Globe* published a newcomers guide to Boston in 8 languages (see Exhibit 24.13). The special section, published in English, Chinese, Haitian, Cambodian, Portuguese, Russian, Spanish, and Vietnamese, reflects the diverse ethnic and cultural mix of contemporary America.

Reaching this multicultural U.S. market presents many of the same problems faced by multinational advertisers. A major problem is that these markets are not homogeneous. That is, Hispanic Americans and other ethnic subgroups demonstrate the same level of differences as any other culture. A problem faced by advertisers is determining the degree of assimilation of these groups into American culture. Advertisers must walk a fine line between communicating to these groups as "non-Americans" on the one hand, or ignoring their heritage for which they are justifiably proud on the other.

There are a number of challenges and opportunities in reaching emerging U.S. markets. "These millions of potential consumers can be reached through their respective ethnic media. But for each individual culture, the voice must

[29]Chau Lam, "National Advertising Now Targeting Growing Group of Asian Americans," *Athens Daily News,* January 25, 1993. p. 6A.
[30]Christy Fisher, "Hispanic Media See Siesta Ending," *Advertising Age,* January 24, 1994, p. S-1.

EXHIBIT
24.13

An example of a mainline medium's attempt to reach a culturally diverse population.

(Courtesy: The Boston Globe.)

be authentic, not simply a strategic overlay translated, without thought or insight, into as many languages as needed. Marketers must start from scratch in the language of each target market, work within the context of the original culture and formulate copy and design rooted in—rather than transplanted to—the culture itself. And if you end up with 10 different campaigns, so be it."[31]

The key to success in these markets is to talk to them with a blend of the old and new. The more an advertiser is able to show a real understanding and insight for these cultures, the easier it is to build trust and consumer loyalty. Conversely, if advertisers commit major communication blunders, they would be better off sticking to "Americanized" advertising. The importance of the multicultural market is apparent in the growing number of foreign-language promotional messages seen across the United States in recent years (see Exhibit 24.14).

EXHIBIT
24.14

An example of a foreign-language ad intended to reach a growing multicultural population.

(Courtesy: ESOAA)

---

[31]Yuri Radzievsky, "Untapped Markets: Ethnics in the U.S.," *Advertising Age,* June 21, 1993, p. 26.

SUMMARY

International advertising might better be described as *multicultural* advertising because it has long ago transcended geographic boundaries. To one degree or another, the world has become the marketplace for most large corporations. However, the complexities of dealing in a global economy are testing the planning, research, and managerial abilities of both companies and their agencies. The difficulties experienced by the European Community, a developed region with one of the highest standards of living in the world, reinforce the problems companies face as they introduce their products in the emerging nations.

Still, whether or not to develop an international position is no longer a subject of debate for most companies. The mature economies of the United States and Europe no longer offer the level of growth and expansion needed by large firms. In addition, sales in major developed countries are largely made at the expense of brand switching rather than resulting from real growth. The potential for foreign success offers rewards that will motivate companies to take significant risks.

Advertising will play a much larger role in most international markets compared to the United States. The most successful brands will be those that establish the first beach head in emerging markets. For example, both Pepsi and Coke have made major investments in bottling companies in China. Yet, for the present, the average Chinese citizen drinks a little more cola in a year than the typical American drinks in a day.[32] The common criteria for U.S. advertising, CPMs, cost-per-point, audited circulation, verified ratings, etc., are simply not applicable in many foreign markets. Instead, experience and judgment must be used to deal with the intricacies of international marketing.

Even those agencies that do not participate in multinational advertising will be faced with the challenges of ethnic diversity in this country. The growth of Hispanic, Asian, and other cultures within American society will increasingly require the creative use of media, promotion, and sales messages to reach this evolving market. Not just marketing expertise but a sensitivity to the culture, language, and values of other peoples will be a requirement in this new marketplace. However, for those willing to devote the time to learn how to operate in this diverse environment, the rewards will be great.

Clearly, multicultural advertising will continue to undergo a period of dramatic change throughout this decade. Many of these changes are unpredictable, but a number of future trends are apparent:

- **Overseas advertising growth will continue to increase at a greater rate than U.S. advertising investment. Non-U.S. advertising will increase as the largely untapped markets of Latin America and Asia are opened and commercial satellite television becomes more available in Europe.**

- **Multinational advertising opportunities will continue to increase. The availability and demand for media are prompting governments to loosen current restrictions on commercial media, creating additional advertising opportunities.**

---

[32]Vynthia Mitchell, "Pepsi, Coca-Cola Wage War in China," *Atlanta Journal,* August 20, 1993, p. F5.

EXHIBIT

24.15

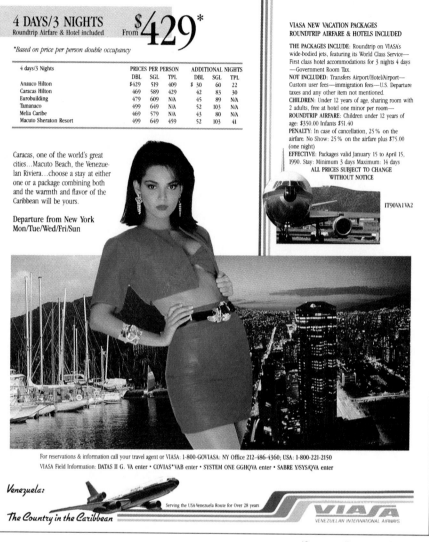

(Courtesy: Promotion Solutions.)

■ **U.S. companies will increasingly find domestic competition stemming from international corporations operating in this country. In some cases these competitors will compete in areas once dominated by American companies (see Exhibit 24.15).**

■ **The number of multinational and global brands will continue to expand. As American, European, and Asian products seek expanded sales, the world will become their marketplace with resulting fierce competition in a number of countries.**

We should not leave our discussion of international advertising without emphasizing that while many countries are showing percentage increases far in excess of those in the United States, America remains the largest advertiser by a wide margin. For example, advertising spending in the United States is in excess of $130 billion, approximately $100 billion greater than runner-up Japan and more than seven times greater than third-place Germany. Granted, many of these dollars are spent by international advertisers selling in the

United States. Nevertheless, America remains the world's major consumer market for both sales and advertising.

Questions

1. What is global marketing?
2. What are the primary advantages and disadvantages of the implementation of global marketing?
3. Why is the term *multicultural* more appropriate than international advertising?
4. Why is television the fastest-growing international medium?
5. Why is multinational marketing becoming more centralized?
6. How does the media function differ between the United States and most international markets?

Legal and Other Restraints on Advertising

CHAPTER OBJECTIVES

Advertising operates in an environment of increasing regulation and public scrutiny. Major advertisers know that ethical practices also are good business in the long run. After reading this chapter you will understand:

- **Advertising regulation and the public interest**
- **The role of the FTC and other regulators**
- **Advertising and First Amendment protections**
- **Professional services advertising**
- **The role of individual states in advertising regulation**
- **Advertising self-regulation**

Throughout this text we have discussed the fact that advertising does not operate in a vacuum. Nowhere is this more apparent than in the regulatory and legal environment in which advertising currently operates. **In addition** to the formal governmental organizations that review both local and national advertising, there are a number of public-interest and self-regulatory bodies that ex-

EXHIBIT

25.1

Many complaints about advertising are ill founded.

amine the content and practices of advertising. There are few business functions that come under the continuing scrutiny reserved for advertising, and this trend has become more prevalent in recent years.

As we discussed in Chapter 1, the turn of the century marked a much-needed examination and housecleaning of flagrant advertising abuses. Today, most advertisers agree that those companies that create illegal or unethical advertising should be dealt with harshly. Not only is misleading advertising wrong; it is bad business. As Leonard Matthews, former president of the 4A's observed, "The vast majority of advertisers and agencies consider truthful advertising to be in their own best interest. Untruthful advertising is a false promise for a product or service. Then what you've got is a dissatisfied customer. No business can survive by accumulating unhappy customers."[1]

However, many advertisers see in the current environment a troubling move to target advertising for a great deal of unwarranted criticism. Many advertising executives view some criticism as not only unfair but totally unrealistic and ignorant of the role of advertising. For example, a number of groups have attacked outdoor advertising on the basis of their personal dislike for the medium. Even those signs in industrial or urban zoned areas promoting the most benign products run the risk of coming under attack (see Exhibit 25.1). As one leading advertiser points out:

> It is now politically correct and politically expedient to blame the advertising industry for many of America's socioeconomic problems. It's advertising's fault that some kids skip school and rob other kids for those expensive sneakers endorsed by famous athletes. Obesity results from the advertising of food rather than from genetics or a lack of discipline and exercise. There are even those who blame our business for America's deteriorating infrastructure, claiming that money "wasted" on advertising could be better used if only the federal government would limit the amount of advertising in our marketplace. It's easier

---

[1]"What Every Account Executive Should Know about the Law and Advertising," American Association of Advertising Agencies, 1990, p. 7.

EXHIBIT

25.2

• • • • • • • • • • • • • • • • •

Advertising agencies
take their responsibility
for truthful advertising
seriously.

Creative Code of the
American Association of Advertising Agencies

ADOPTED APRIL 26, 1962

The members of the American Association of Advertising Agencies recognize:

1. That advertising bears a dual responsibility in the American economic system and way of life.

To the public it is a primary way of knowing about the goods and services that are the products of American free enterprise—goods and services that can be freely chosen to suit the desires and needs of the individual. The public is entitled to expect that advertising will be reliable in content and honest in presentation.

To the advertiser it is a primary way of persuading people to buy his goods or services, within the framework of a highly competitive economic system. He is entitled to regard advertising as a dynamic means of building his business and his profits.

2. That advertising enjoys a particularly intimate relationship to the American family.

It enters the home as an integral part of television and radio programs, to speak to the individual and often to the entire family. It shares the pages of favorite newspapers and magazines. It presents itself to travelers and to readers of the daily mails. In all these forms, it bears a special responsibility to respect the tastes and self-interest of the public.

3. That advertising is directed to sizable groups or to the public at large, which is made up of many interests and many tastes.

As is the case with all public enterprises, ranging from sports to education and even to religion, it is almost impossible to speak without finding someone in disagreement. Nonetheless, advertising people recognize their obligation to operate within the traditional American limitations: to serve the interests of the majority and to respect the rights of the minority.

Therefore we, the members of the American Association of Advertising Agencies, in addition to supporting and obeying the laws and legal regulations pertaining to advertising, undertake to extend and broaden the application of high ethical standards. Specifically, we will not knowingly produce advertising that contains:

    a. False or misleading statements or exaggerations, visual or verbal.

    b. Testimonials that do not reflect the real choice of a competent witness.

    c. Price claims that are misleading.

    d. Comparisons that unfairly disparage a competitive product or service.

    e. Claims insufficiently supported, or which distort the true meaning or practicable application of statements made by professional or scientific authority.

    f. Statements, suggestions, or pictures offensive to public decency.

We recognize that there are areas subject to honestly different interpretations and judgment. Taste is subjective and may even vary from time to time as well as from individual to individual. Frequency of seeing or hearing advertising messages will necessarily vary greatly from person to person.

However, we agree not to recommend to an advertiser and to discourage the use of advertising that is in poor or questionable taste or is deliberately irritating through content, presentation, or excessive repetition.

Clear and willful violations of this Code shall be referred to the Board of Directors of the American Association of Advertising Agencies for appropriate action, including possible annulment of membership as provided in Article IV, Section 5, of the Constitution and By-Laws.

Conscientious adherence to the letter and the spirit of this Code will strengthen advertising and the free enterprise system of which it is a part.

(Courtesy: American Association of Advertising Agencies.)

and more fashionable to blame—and punish—advertising for our problems than it is to get to the root cause.[2]

Regardless of whether advertisers think that current criticism is unfair is largely immaterial; the fact is that they must deal with the reality of an atmosphere that is often hostile. In this highly charged and controversial arena, it is imperative that advertisers avoid even the appearance of impropriety or deception. Advertisers must be extremely careful not to run afoul of the various laws and regulations applied to advertising messages.

There are three primary constraints on advertising:

1. Laws and regulations of legally constituted bodies such as Congress and the Federal Trade Commission

2. Control by the media through advertising acceptability guidelines

3. Self-regulation by advertisers and agencies through various trade practice recommendations and codes of conduct (see Exhibit 25.2)

You will notice that two of the three types of constraints are basically self-imposed. The typical advertiser is as concerned about misleading, false, or in-

---

[2]Charles D. Peebler, Jr., "What, Me Worry?" *American Advertising,* Winter 1992–93, p. 22.

appropriate advertising as any regulatory body. Advertising is not only a means of communicating with the public but also determines how the public perceives the companies, products, and services that advertise. Anything that damages the overall image of advertising hurts the efforts of each advertiser.

Prior to the twentieth century, commerce operated under the libertarian notion of *caveat emptor,* "Let the buyer beware." This concept was based on the classical economic perception of a free marketplace of goods and ideas and perfect knowledge on the part of the participants in that marketplace. That is, buyers and sellers were presumed to have equal information, and it was assumed that both groups, being rational, would make correct economic choices without government interference into business transactions.

In this century, the complexities of the marketplace have led to the rejection of the principle of *caveat emptor.* It has been replaced by the idea that consumers cannot hope to have perfect knowledge of the marketplace and must be protected by legal guarantees of the authenticity of advertising claims. To shield the public from false and misleading advertising, numerous laws have been passed. Chief among these is the Federal Trade Commission Act, which we discuss first.

THE FEDERAL TRADE COMMISSION

The most visible and effective governmental agency controlling advertising is the Federal Trade Commission. The original intent of the Federal Trade Commission Act, passed in 1914, was that "unfair methods of competition are hereby declared unlawful." During this period, it was thought that protecting one business from another, especially local retailers from large chains, was a major role of government regulation.

The FTC did not take action against a business unless it could be shown that competitors were being harmed by illegal trade practices. Business practices that injured only the public were not considered within its jurisdiction. It was not until 1922, in *FTC* v. *Winsted Hosiery Company,* that the Supreme Court held that false advertising was an unfair trade practice. However, the FTC continued to function as a means of protecting one business from another.

Then in 1938, passage of the Wheeler-Lea amendments broadened this interpretation to include the principle that the FTC could protect consumers from deceptive advertising. This law also gave the FTC specific authority over false advertising in the fields of food, drugs, therapeutic devices, and cosmetics. Today, the FTC has sweeping power over the advertising of all products sold or advertised across state lines.

The Role of the FTC

The FTC's role in regulating advertising is to ensure that consumers make product choices on the basis of complete, truthful, and nondeceptive advertising, according to Commissioner Janet Steiger in testimony before a congressional committee. In order to accomplish this goal, the FTC tends to concentrate on those areas of concern deemed most important to the commission at any particular time. According to Steiger, "We [FTC] continue to focus our consumer protection resources on three principal areas—telemarketing

---

Caveat emptor

Latin for "Let the buyer beware." Represents the notion that there should be no government interference in the marketplace.

Federal Trade Commission (FTC)

The agency of the federal government empowered to prevent unfair competition and to prevent fraudulent, misleading, or deceptive advertising in interstate commerce.

Winsted Hosiery Company

The case of *FTC v. Winsted Hosiery Company* established the precedent that false advertising was an unfair trade practice.

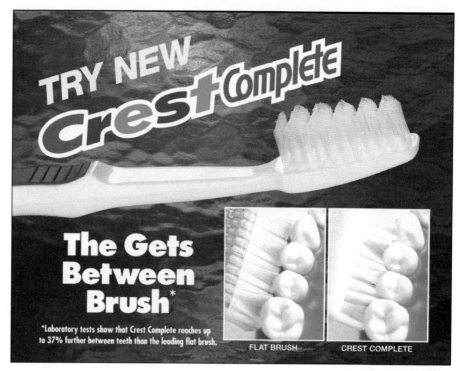

(Courtesy: Actmedia.)

and credit fraud, deceptive advertising, and enforcement of our rules and special statutes."[3]

Deceptive Advertising

According to the FTC, "deception occurs when there is a representation or omission that is likely to mislead consumers, acting reasonably under the circumstances, to the consumers' detriment."[4] The key to FTC enforcement is the notion of substantiation of advertising claims. Advertisers must be prepared to prove, with objective and generally accepted evidence including scientific studies, that their claims are true. Often advertisers note in their advertising copy that some type of substantiation has taken place (see Exhibit 25.3). Deceptive advertising has not been specifically defined by Congress, so the FTC operates through a series of guidelines developed over the years. The judgment in ruling an ad or claim deceptive hinges on whether or not it will cause a customer to take some action that would not have been taken if the ad had not been deceptive. In fact, general rules of deception are difficult to draft and must be considered on an ad-by-ad basis.

Currently, the FTC uses a three-part test to determine if an advertisement is deceptive or untruthful:

1. *There must be a representation, omission, or practice that is likely to mislead the consumer.* A statement does not have to be untrue to be deceptive. Sometimes advertisers will make a claim that is literally true, but the total impression of the ad is misleading. One of the most difficult areas of deceptive advertising is the omission of information. When does the omission of information in an otherwise truthful ad make the message mis-

---
[3]"Advertising Topics," Council of Better Business Bureaus, April/May 1993, p. 2.
[4]"Advertising Topics," Council of Better Business Bureaus, September/October 1993, p. 2.

leading or deceptive? In one case, a soup ad claimed that because the product was low in fat and cholesterol it could reduce the risk of heart disease. However, the soup was also high in sodium, a fact omitted in the ad. Since sodium may be harmful to those with heart disease, the FTC ruled the omission made the other claims in the ad deceptive.

2. *The act or practice must be considered from the perspective of a consumer who is acting reasonably.* The advertiser is not responsible for every possible interpretation, no matter how far-fetched or unreasonable, that might be made by a consumer. However, ads directed to specific audiences such as children will be judged on the basis of how that audience might interpret the advertisement.

3. *The representation, omission, or practice must be material.* The claim, even if it is not true, must be judged to have had some influence over a consumer's decision. For example, the courts have ruled that using plastic ice cubes in a soft drink commercial is not deceptive because no claims are being made about the ice cubes. Sometimes advertisers are tempted to substitute items in commercial demonstrations because the time and hot lights of television may change the perception of a product. When this is done, the consumer should be told, or the advertiser should be certain that the changes will not be regarded as material to the message of the commercial.[5] When the FTC decides that deception has indeed taken place, it can move quickly to stop the practice or advertising and severely penalize the company found guilty of the deception.

Methods of FTC Enforcement

The enforcement process of the FTC works in concert with the courts. In the ideal situation, the FTC will work with advertisers to validate a claim or to have advertisers end deceptive practices. However, if an advertiser refuses to stop running advertising that has been ruled deceptive, there is recourse in the courts for both parties:

1. The first step in the process is to file a claim of deceptive practices with the FTC. The complaint can come from consumers, competitors, or the FTC staff.

2. The FTC then begins its investigation. Normally, the investigation starts with a request for substantiation from the advertiser.

3. If the commission finds the practice to be unsubstantiated and therefore deceptive, a complaint is issued. At this point, the advertiser is asked to sign a *consent decree* in which the firm agrees to end the deceptive practice or advertising. Most complaints are settled in this way. An advertiser that continues the practice after signing a consent decree is liable for a fine of $10,000 per day.

4. If an advertiser refuses to sign a consent decree, the commission issues a *cease and desist* order. Before such an order can become final, a hearing is held before an administrative law judge. The judge can dismiss the case and negate the cease and desist order. If it is upheld, the company may appeal the decision to the full commission.

Substantiation
The key to FTC enforcement is that advertisers must be able to prove the claims made in their advertising.

Consent decree
Issued by the FTC. An advertiser signs the decree, stops the practice under investigation, but admits no guilt.

Cease and desist orders
If an advertiser refuses to sign a consent decree, the FTC may issue a cease and desist order that can carry a $10,000-per-day fine.

---

[5]Don R. Pember, *Mass Media Law* (Dubuque, Ia.: Wm. C. Brown, 1990), pp. 488–491.

Corrective advertising

To counteract the past residual effect of previous deceptive advertising, the FTC may require the advertiser to devote future space and time to disclosure of previous deception. Began around the late 1960s.

5. Even if an advertiser agrees to abide by a cease and desist order, the commission may find that simply stopping a particular practice does not repair past damage to consumers. To counteract the residual effects of the deceptive advertising, the FTC may require the firm to run *corrective advertisements*. They are designed to "dissipate the effects of that deception." The FTC often stipulates several requirements for corrective advertising such as content, format, frequency, and even the media schedule. The commission normally requires corrective advertising when major advertising themes are the basis for consumers' choices. In one of the first cases of corrective advertising, Listerine was ordered to insert messages in $10 million worth of advertising that Listerine did not cure colds or lessen their severity, which had been a long-running theme of its advertising.

6. If a company cannot reach an agreement with the commission, its next recourse is the federal courts. First, to the federal Court of Appeals and finally to the Supreme Court. It is extremely rare that a case goes beyond the cease and desist order. From a practical standpoint most advertising campaigns have run their course by the time an advertiser would go to court. Equally important is the fact that few firms want the adverse publicity that surrounds a protracted court battle. However, in one case the FTC won a judgment against Geritol, 11 years after the original cease and desist order was issued.

Some Basic Rules of the Courts and the FTC

As we noted earlier, deception is largely determined on a case-by-case basis. However, agencies and clients can consider precedents from past commission rulings in developing advertising claims. Some recent examples of FTC actions that might provide guidance for advertisers are:

1. A national telemarketer of coins allegedly made false statements to consumers concerning the value and investment potential of these coins. The FTC required the company to refund more than $800,000 to customers.

2. A professional organization was cited for prohibiting members to engage in truthful advertising that referred to the quality of their services. Under a consent decree the organization agreed to discontinue the practice.

3. A franchiser agreed to settle FTC claims that it misrepresented the earning potential of its franchisees. The company was required to repay $100,000.

4. A used-car company was cited for failing to post required warranty information and agreed to do so in the future.

5. A funeral home agreed to settle an FTC charge that it failed to provide pricing and other required information to customers.

As you can see from these sample cases, the responsibility of the FTC covers numerous business practices involving a variety of products and services. Over the years, the FTC has developed a number of industry-specific guidelines or FTC rules that outline in some detail exactly what a business can and cannot do in terms of business practices. Examples of such FTC guidelines are:

- **Used Car Rule**

- **Funeral Rule**

- **Franchise Rule**

- **R-Value Rule (for home insulation products)**

The FTC has a number of other rules that are being modified or added to as circumstances warrant.

Unfortunately, many of these cases involved companies that may have knowingly violated FTC regulations. However, in most cases advertisers run afoul of these regulations simply through ignorance or misunderstanding. In the following section we will show some of the problems most often faced by advertisers and how the FTC views them.

Advertising as a Contract. One of the many gray areas of advertising is the degree to which an ad constitutes a binding contractual agreement with the consumer. For the most part, the courts and the FTC have ruled that it is unreasonable to expect an advertisement or commercial to contain all the details of a formal contract. The commission expects that such a contract will be part of the final sales negotiation, whereas advertising is normally the first step in the process of selling a product. By the same token, the courts have been lenient on pricing errors in ads where no deception is intended.

However, under certain circumstances advertisements have been regarded as constituting binding offers. For example, when there is some language or commitment, no error in the ad, and the defendant has some control over potential liability, a court may find an obligation to provide a good or service at an advertised price. Since the issue is somewhat ill defined, cautious advertisers would be well advised to treat every advertisement as if it were potentially a contract.

Fact versus Puffery. Where do we draw the line between legitimate expression of positive (and biased) information by an advertiser and untrue and misleading material? Perhaps no area of advertising is more controversial than puffery. An extreme position taken by some critics would categorize any statement that is not literally true as deceptive. Most consumers, however, accept the fact that attention-getting, creative advertising will take some liberties with reality but not necessarily mislead consumers. The legal definition of puffery is that it is "an exaggeration or overstatement expressed in broad, vague, and commendatory language, and is *distinguishable* from misdescriptions or false representations of specific characteristics of a product and, as such, is not actionable."

Most regulatory agencies, courts, consumers, and even advertisers are very wary of pushing the boundaries of puffery too far. It is easy to cross the line between humorous or creative messages and misleading claims. The late Sid Bernstein summed up puffery for many advertisers: "I don't want anybody to monkey with the truth in advertising or promotions, or create false implications. But I certainly don't want the Supreme Court to have to decide whether there is really a Pepsi generation or whether the *New York Times* actually contains 'all the news that's fit to print.'"[6]

Testimonials. At one time testimonial advertising, especially celebrity endorsements, were viewed very liberally by regulators. It really didn't matter if

[6]Sid Bernstein, "Con-SID-erations," *Advertising Age,* October 23, 1972, p. 18.

celebrities used the product they endorsed or not. However, in recent years, the commission has taken the position that consumers can reasonably expect celebrities to be satisfied users of the products they endorse. To put teeth into this opinion, the courts have consistently held that endorsers who willfully engage in deception can be held liable for damages along with the advertiser. This ruling gives many would-be endorsers pause before they jump into a commercial.

Related to personal endorsements is the practice of placing products in movies. Companies hope to gain an implied endorsement and/or visibility for a product by having it appear in a hit movie. Many companies pay a fee to producers for such placement. The most famous example of such a placement was Reese's Pieces candy in the movie *ET.* When the movie came to the screen, sales of the product experienced unprecedented increases and encouraged many other companies to follow suit.

In 1992, a number of individuals and organizations petitioned the FTC, asking the commission to order motion picture companies to stop using undisclosed product placements and require that all paid placements be disclosed at the beginning of the film. The commission responded to the request, "Due to the apparent lack of a pervasive pattern of deception and substantial consumer injury attributable to product placements, the commission has determined that an industry-wide rulemaking is inappropriate at this time. If particular instances of product placement arise where there is significant evidence of consumer injury, the commission will consider these matters on a case-by-case basis."[7]

Lotteries.   Lotteries are schemes for the distribution of prizes won by chance. In most states, lotteries, except state-operated ones, are illegal if a person has to pay to enter them. Promotional sweepstakes are lotteries, but since they don't require an entry fee, they are not illegal. Both the United States Postal Service and the FTC will move against lotteries that either use the mail or are advertised across state lines. In recent years, a number of states have started their own lotteries to augment tax revenues.

Even in the case of state-run lotteries, the courts have ruled that interstate promotion of lotteries is under federal jurisdiction. For example, the courts have ruled that states that do not have lotteries may prohibit lottery advertising from being imported from lottery states. This prohibition will cost some broadcasters significant revenues by banning such advertising even if only a small portion of their audience resides in a nonlottery state.

THE ROBINSON-PATMAN ACT AND COOPERATIVE ADVERTISING

The FTC, through its antitrust division, has responsibility for enforcing another law affecting marketing and advertising, the Robinson-Patman Act. The Robinson-Patman Act is part of a three-law "package" that evolved over a period of almost 50 years. These laws and their purposes are as follows:

1. *1890 Federal Sherman Antitrust Act.* This act was designed to prevent alliances of firms formed to restrict competition.

---

[7]"Advertising Topics," January/February 1993, Council of Better Business Bureaus.

2. *1914 Clayton Antitrust Act.* This act amended the Sherman Act. It eliminated preferential price treatment when manufacturers sold merchandise to retailers.

Robinson-Patman Act
A federal law, enforced by the FTC. Requires a manufacturer to give proportionate discounts and advertising allowances to all competing dealers in a market. Purpose: to protect smaller merchants from unfair competition of larger buyers.

3. *1936 Robinson-Patman Act.* In turn, this law amended the Clayton Act. It prevents manufacturers from providing a "promotional allowance" to one customer unless it is also offered to competitors on a proportionally equal basis. Prior to Robinson-Patman, some manufacturers were using a loophole in the Clayton Act. They seemed to be charging all their customers equitable prices, but were actually giving money back to their bigger customers in the form of promotional allowances. For example, large retailers might be given co-op advertising allowances that were unavailable to small retailers and, in effect, lowered the price of the goods sold to these large retailers. Thus, the promotional allowance was a device for under-the-table rebates.

The regulation of co-op allowances has evolved as the media environment has become more complex and the relationships between retailers and manufacturers have changed. At the time Robinson-Patman was passed, the vast majority of retail advertising dollars were placed in newspapers. Today, with the growth of alternative retail advertising vehicles, the FTC requires that functional alternative promotions must be offered in co-op programs. For example, a manufacturer may not limit co-op dollars to television, knowing that many retailers do not use television in a particular market. Such an offer is known as an *improperly structured program.*

The FTC also interprets Robinson-Patman as requiring manufacturers to assume the responsibility of developing equitable co-op programs even for retailers with whom they deal indirectly through independent distributors. "This [indirect responsibility] has posed some very real problems for many manufacturers in that they don't always know all the customers a distributor has. Nonetheless, they have had to put forth a legitimate effort at informing all customers. Some manufacturers have used trade advertising...and even gone as far as printing the [co-op] program on cartons to insure that it reaches everyone."[8] After almost 60 years, Robinson-Patman is still a strong deterrent to antitrust practices at the retail level.

THE FEDERAL FOOD, DRUG, AND COSMETIC ACT

Closely tied to the Federal Trade Commission Act is the Federal Food, Drug, and Cosmetic Act, passed in 1938, giving the Food and Drug Administration (FDA) broad power over the labeling and branding—as contrasted with the advertising—of foods, drugs, therapeutic devices, and cosmetics. It is under this law that food and drug manufacturers must put their ingredients on the labels.

The jurisdiction of the FDA to control and regulate labeling was enhanced with congressional passage of the Nutritional Labeling and Education Act of 1990. The act provided for two major changes in FDA regulatory guidelines. First, it gave the FDA jurisdiction over food labeling, which preempted any contrary state laws. National manufacturers had pushed for this change in or-

---

[8]Richard Bogash and Tom McGoldrick, "What Every Account Executive Should Know about Co-op Advertising," American Association of Advertising Agencies, 1990, p. 11.

der to deal with one set of guidelines rather than having to negotiate with each state. The policy of giving priority to the FDA and other federal regulations is called *federal preemption.*

The second part of the legislation requires that food marketers provide label information on calories, salt, cholesterol, fats, fiber, vitamins, and minerals. Further, food manufacturers must work with the FDA to establish definitions for terms such as *light, low fat,* and *low salt.*[9] After July 1994, the FDA also required that makers of dietary supplements and vitamins provide proof of any health claims and no later than 1995 list all nutrients contained in these supplements.

The primary areas of FDA enforcement are labels that carry misleading information such as "fresh" when the product has been frozen or reconstituted, foods such as cereal, which may carry a health claim on their labels, and cosmetics labeled as "cures." Such product claims require extensive substantiation and product testing before they can be used. Those products that carry health claims on their labels can expect even more stringent enforcement by the agency in the future.

The Nutritional Labeling and Education Act provides four basic guidelines under which the FDA reviews food products:

1. The product is to be nutritionally labeled.

2. The claim is not misleading.

3. The claim is supported by valid scientific evidence.

4 The claim is consistent with generally, recognized principles for a healthy, well-balanced diet.

While the FDA does not have direct responsibility for advertising, there is a cooperative relationship between its activities and those of the FTC. For example, based on actions of the FDA, the FTC announced, "Our goal is to help ensure that the messages consumers get from food advertising are consistent with those they see in food labeling today and in the future, given the new FDA labeling guidelines."[10]

OTHER FEDERAL CONTROLS OF ADVERTISING
Bureau of Alcohol, Tobacco, and Firearms (BATF) Division of the Treasury Department

The liquor industry's advertising must conform to the basic regulatory and legal rules of all advertising. However, in addition, the industry is required to adhere to unique requirements administrated by the Treasury Department through the BATF, generally referred to as ATF. For an interesting historical reason, the federal laws are under the jurisdiction of the Treasury Department. The first American excise tax was levied on alcoholic beverages under Secretary of the Treasury Alexander Hamilton. Enforcement of labeling, advertising, and other alcohol-related regulations are still under that department.

---

[9]Julie Liesse and Steven W. Colford, "Marketers Like New Label Law," *Advertising Age,* October 29, 1990.
[10]"Food Advertising and Labeling," *Advertising Topics,* Council of Better Bureaus, April/May 1994, p. 1.

Like the FTC, ATF enforces basic legislation through a number of guidelines and interpretations of the law. For example, ATF ruled that the term *Russian* on labels of alcoholic beverages requires that the product come from the Russian Federation. Likewise, ATF ruled that terms such as *Russian type* or *Russian style* would not be permitted.[11]

Securities and Exchange Commission

The SEC is the government agency that controls all advertising of public offerings of stocks or bonds. It insists on full disclosure of facts relevant to the company and the stock to be sold so that the prospective investor can form an opinion.

Its insistence on the facts that must be published—including a statement of negative elements affecting the investment—is firm and thorough. The SEC never recommends or refuses to recommend a security; its concern is with the disclosure of full information.

United States Postal Service

The postal service has the authority to stop the delivery of mail to all firms guilty of using the mails to defraud—which is enough to put any firm out of business. It deals mainly with mail-order frauds.

ADVERTISING AND THE FIRST AMENDMENT

One of the philosophical bulwarks of American society is the First Amendment. Many would argue that the First Amendment is what makes our society unique. A primary historical attribute of the First Amendment is that it creates an open "marketplace of ideas" where differing opinions compete and the strongest ideas win the support of the majority. Advertisers have long argued that a commercial marketplace of ideas is required to provide consumers with information about new products, competitive promotions, even ideas and opinions expressed by corporations. Yet advertising has never been afforded full protection under the First Amendment. Whereas noncommercial speech is offered the widest possible protection, advertising is held to a much stricter standard. In addition, the specific limits that can be placed on commercial speech is a constantly changing process open to continuing interpretation by the courts.

Various organizations, advertisers, and individuals have called upon the courts to judge advertising by the same standards as other types of speech. They argue that there is no compelling reason to view commercial speech as different from any other form of discourse and, in fact, to do so is damaging to both advertisers and the public. "[T]he only legitimate role in the regulation of commercial advertising in a pluralistic society is to assist consumers in receiving truthful, nonmisleading information to aid in their making informed choices about lawful products and services. To utilize advertising speech regulation as a back door method of manipulating consumer decisions is to exceed that proper role, and is inconsistent with the Court's teachings under the First Amendment."[12]

---

[11]*Advertising Topics,* April/May 1993, Council of Better Business Bureaus.
[12]*Advertising Topics,* February/March 1993, Council of Better Business Bureaus.

Many advertisers take the position that they are fighting for rights that they already possess. These proponents of advertising argue that, in fact, the original writers of the Constitution made no distinction as to what type of speech would be granted constitutional protection.

Regardless of one's position, the courts have consistently ruled that advertising does not enjoy full protection of the First Amendment. There has long been a willingness by the courts to tolerate a degree of restraint that would be totally unacceptable for any other form of speech.

In the past 50 years, commercial speech has been afforded some First Amendment protection. However, the problem for advertisers is that judicial opinions supporting commercial speech have been uneven and contradictory with a consistent doctrine of commercial speech yet to be enunciated by the courts. Each time advertisers think they have made a significant breakthrough in establishing commercial speech as in equal partner with other forms of expression, the Court seems to take a backward step in one of its decisions.

The Development of the First Amendment and Advertising

While lacking full First Amendment protection, advertising has made progress in achieving a greater status for these rights than in the past. In order to examine this issue, we need to take a brief look at the development of the status of advertising and the historical protection of commercial speech by the courts.[13]

1942. The Supreme Court ruled that advertising was not entitled to First Amendment protection. The Court ruled that there were *no* restraints on government's right to prohibit commercial speech.

1964. The Court decided that an advertisement that expressed an opinion on a *public issue* was protected by the First Amendment, but only because it did not contain commercial speech.

1975. The Court gave advertising its first constitutional protection when it overturned a Virginia law making it a criminal offense to advertise out-of-state abortion clinics in Virginia newspapers. However, the ruling left open the question of protection for purely commercial speech that did not deal with opinion or some controversial public issue.

1976. In what many advertisers regard as a breakthrough, the Court held in the case of *Virginia State Board of Pharmacy* v. *Virginia Citizens Consumer Council* that the state of Virginia could not prohibit the advertising of prescription drug prices. It said, in effect, that society benefits from a free flow of commercial information just as it benefits from a free exchange of political ideas.

1979. Advertisers' optimism that they had finally achieved full constitutional protection was short-lived. In the case of *Friedman* v. *Rogers* the Court upheld the right of the state of Texas to prevent an optometrist from using an "assumed name, corporate name, trade name or any other than the name under which he is licensed to practice optometry in Texas." In its decision,

---

[13]Stephen R. Bergerson, "Supreme Court Strikes a Blow for Commercial Speech," *American Advertising,* Summer 1993, p. 24.

the Court said that First Amendment protection for commercial speech is not absolute and that regulation of commercial speech can be allowed even when the restrictions would be unconstitutional "in the realm of noncommercial expression."

1980. Until this year, the Court seemingly ruled on each case involving commercial speech on a purely ad hoc basis. Advertisers were left with little if any guidance or precedent as to how the next case would be settled. However, in 1980 the Court enunciated a set of general guidelines concerning the limits of constitutional protection that would be afforded commercial speech. These guidelines were set forth in the case of *Central Hudson Gas & Electric* v. *Public Service Commission of New York.*

Central Hudson four-part test
Supreme Court test to determine if specific commercial speech is protected under the Constitution.

This case concerned a prohibition by the New York Public Service Commission of all promotional advertising by utilities. The state's rationale was that the ban was compatible with public concerns over energy conservation. In overturning the prohibition, the Court established a four-part test to determine when commercial speech is constitutionally protected and when regulation is permissible. These guidelines known as the *Central Hudson Four-Part Test* are:

1. *Is the commercial expression eligible for First Amendment protection?* That is, is it neither deceptive nor promoting an illegal activity? Obviously, no constitutional protection can be provided for commercial speech that fails this test.

2. *Is the government interest asserted in regulating the expression substantial?* This test requires that the stated reason for regulating the advertisement must be of primary interest to the state rather than of a trivial, arbitrary, or capricious nature.

3. *If the first two tests are met,* the Court then considers if the regulation of advertising imposed advances the cause of the governmental interest asserted. That is, if we assume that an activity is of legitimate government concern, will the prohibition of commercial speech further the government's goals?

4. *If the first three tests are met,* the Court must finally decide if the regulation is more extensive than necessary to serve the government's interest.

In the *Central Hudson* case, the Court ruled that the case met the first three guidelines, but that a total prohibition of utility advertising was more extensive than necessary. Thus, it failed the fourth part of the test and was ruled unconstitutional.

1986. Most advertisers thought that *Central Hudson* had provided significant protection in limiting the right of states to ban legitimate advertising. However, in the case of *Posada de Puerto Rico Associates* v. *Tourism Company of Puerto Rico,* the Court seemed to once again liberalize the ability of states to ban advertising. This case involved a Puerto Rican law banning advertising of gambling casinos to residents of Puerto Rico even though casino gambling is legal there. In a 5–4 decision, the Court ruled that the ban met all four standards of the Central Hudson test.

1988. Many legal scholars see 1994 as marking a significant change in the Court's attitude toward advertising and, just as importantly, a change in its interpretation of Central Hudson. *Board of Trustees of the State University* of *New York* v. *Fox* dealt with a college regulation that restricted "private commercial enterprises" on campus. Students challenged the regulation, arguing that at events such as "Tupperware parties" noncommercial subjects were discussed. Since the regulation had the effect of prohibiting both noncommercial and commercial speech, it was too broad and, therefore, did not meet the fourth part of the Central Hudson test.

In upholding the regulation, the Court ruled that regulations must be "narrowly tailored," but not necessarily the "least restrictive" option available. Critics of the decision point out that "narrowly tailored" is vague and may eliminate the protections of *Central Hudson*.

1993. Two cases in this year seemed to demonstrated the difficulty of predicting how the Court will rule in commercial speech cases. In the first case, *City of Cincinnati* v. *Discovery Network,* the Court seemed to offer a clear victory for proponents of First Amendment protection of commercial speech. In a 6–3 decision the Court held that the Cincinnati City Council violated the First Amendment by banning newsracks for free promotional publications, but allowing them for traditional newspapers. The Court ruled that since the ban was based solely on the content of the publications in the racks, it did not meet the "narrowly tailored" test. The case was widely seen as a victory for commercial speech.

The euphoria among advertisers did not last long. Later in the year, the Court again upheld the right of a state to ban advertising for a legal activity. In the case of Edge Broadcasting Co. v. USA & Federal Communications Commission, the Court upheld federal regulations prohibiting broadcasters in states that forbid lottery advertising from airing spots for lotteries in other states. The case involved an FCC rule that prohibited a North Carolina radio station from broadcasting commercials for the Virginia lottery. Some experts see an irony in the *Edge* and *Posadas* cases. In *Posadas* the Court allowed gambling ads in other states, but permitted Puerto Rico to ban them locally. In *Edge,* the Court allowed the FCC to ban gambling commercials in states that prohibit gambling, but to permit them in states that have a lottery. The ban was upheld even though it is perfectly legal for a North Carolina resident to go to Virginia and play the lottery.

Clearly, these cases, and the history of advertising and the First Amendment in general, create an inconsistent patchwork of decisions. Advertisers argue that the modifications in *Central Hudson* leave them in a quandary as to how the next cases to come before the Court may be settled. Proponents of First Amendment protection for advertising still want full protection for commercial speech. If advertising fails to achieve equal status with noncommercial speech, they insist that, at a minimum, the courts develop a consistent pattern of decisions and guidelines for advertising.

Corporate Speech and Advertising

In recent years, we have seen a tremendous growth in corporate advertising espousing some idea or corporate philosophy as contrasted to selling a product or service. Like all other forms of commercial speech, corporate advertising falls into a gray area. Similar to commercial speech, the Court has ruled that corporate advertising is protected under certain circumstances. In *First*

National Bank of Boston v. *Bellotti* the Court overturned a state law that prohibited national banks from using corporate funds to advocate voting against a state constitutional amendment that would allow the legislature to impose a graduated income tax.

Over the years the Court has delineated several legal principles concerning corporate speech:

1. Spending money to speak does not, in itself, result in the loss of First Amendment rights.

2. Speaking on commercial subjects does not entail loss of First Amendment rights.

3. Speaking for economic interests does not entail loss of First Amendment rights.[14]

We should note that the Court is saying that a commercial aspect to speech does not *necessarily* remove that speech from the rights granted by the First Amendment. However, the converse of this view does not automatically grant these rights to either advertising or corporate speech. In the next section, we will discuss some of the guidelines used by the Court in allowing limitations to commercial speech.

Advertising and the Right of Publicity

A private individual is protected by right of privacy from having his or her likeness used in an advertisement without permission. Courts have ruled that public figures have far less protection than the general public in terms of their right of privacy. However, in recent years the courts have held that public figures may be protected from commercial use of their name or likeness by a doctrine of the right of publicity.

The courts generally hold that public figures have a commercial value attached to their names. Whether or not they want to exploit that value is up to them. However, when an advertiser, without permission, uses a public figure to promote a product, the company has probably run afoul of the person's right of publicity. This usage is pretty clear cut, and only the most unsophisticated advertiser would use a public figure in such a manner.

However, the problem is more complex when the personality is deceased or an advertiser uses an impersonator for a celebrity's likeness or voice. Even if an impersonator is identified so that the public is not misled, the courts still may hold that the celebrity's commercial value has been exploited without compensation.

Several states have recognized the right of a celebrity's estate to control his or her commercial use after the person dies. For example, in California a person's heir can control commercial use of a deceased celebrity for 50 years. "[S]tatutory recognition of the right of publicity strengthened in recent years, so there is little opportunity to circumvent the laws. For this reason no one should continue any effort to exploit the fame of a public figure without first securing sound legal advice."[15]

---

[14]Candiss Baksa Vibbert, "Freedom of Speech and Corporations: Supreme Court Strategies for the Extension of the First Amendment," *Communications* 12 (1990): 26.
[15]Bernard R. Gans, "Stars' Exert Right of Publicity," *American Advertising*, Spring 1993, pp. 26–27.

ADVERTISING OF PROFESSIONAL SERVICES

One of the most controversial areas of commercial speech involves advertising by professionals, especially attorneys. State laws and bar associations restricted legal advertising for most of this century. Critics of restrictions on legal advertising claim that one of the overriding concerns was to limit competition for established law firms rather than to provide any public benefit.

Due in part to reaction to this criticism, the absolute prohibition of attorney advertising was lifted in 1977 in the case of *Bates* v. *State Bar of Arizona*. The Supreme Court ruled that state laws forbidding advertising by attorneys were unconstitutional on First Amendment grounds. The fourth test of the *Central Hudson* case seems to reinforce the Bates decision. That is, most legal scholars think that the total prohibition of a class of advertising will generally not meet the fourth test, since any such total ban will be considered broader than necessary. Bar associations and other professional groups still have regulatory powers over the accuracy and scope of their members' advertising, but they cannot prohibit their members from advertising.

In 1988, the Supreme Court extended the right of attorneys to advertise professional services. A Kentucky lawyer, Richard Shapero, was cited for violating a Kentucky law prohibiting targeted mail solicitations to people who were in need of legal services because of some special circumstance. In this case Shapero had mailed an advertisement to homeowners facing foreclosure.

The Court ruled that although personal contact by an attorney could be prohibited, a letter posed no threat of undue influence to consumers who are under threat of legal action. In addition, the Court reasoned that a written proposal to a potential client could be more carefully regulated than a personal contact. The Shapero case had the immediate effect of lifting the ban on targeted letters in the 25 states that prohibited them.

In 1993, the Court made an interesting distinction among various types of professional solicitations. The Florida Board of Accountancy banned personal solicitations for clients, either in person or by telephone. In *Edenfield* v. *Fane* the Court overturned the ban and, in doing so, made a clear distinction between lawyers and accountants. The Court held that, unlike lawyers, CPAs are not trained in the art of persuasion, are dealing with clients who probably have had a previous professional relationship with an accountant, and the client of a CPA is probably not under the stress that a lawyer's potential client might be. The Court found that it was unlikely that the potential clients of CPAs would be subject to "uninformed acquiescenc," which might be the case in a lawyer's client.

These recent court rulings are related in many respects to the issue of advertising and First Amendment protection. While the Court has eliminated sweeping bans against professional advertising, it has not given such promotion the status of other form of speech. Furthermore, *Edenfield* v. *Fane* demonstrates again the difficulty of anticipating how the Court may rule in any particular case involving commercial expression.

State and Local Laws Relating to Advertising

The first explicit attempt to formalize the regulation of state and local advertising was the *Printers' Ink* Model Statute, proposed in 1911. It sought to

---

Printers' Ink Model Statutes (1911)

The act directed at fraudulent advertising, prepared and sponsored by *Printers' Ink*, which was the pioneer advertising magazine.

EXHIBIT
25.4

Printers' Ink was a
leader in the fight for
truthful advertising.

THE *PRINTERS' INK* MODEL STATUTE FOR STATE
LEGISLATION AGAINST FRAUDULENT ADVERTISING

Any person, firm, corporation, or association, who with intent to sell or in any
wise dispose of merchandise, securities, service, or anything offered by such person, firm, corporation, or association, directly or indirectly, to the public for sale
or distribution, or with intent to increase the consumption thereof, or to induce
the public in any manner to enter into any obligation relating thereto, or to ac-
quire title thereto, or an interest therein, makes, publishes, disseminates, circulates,
or places before the public, or causes, directly or indirectly, to be made, published,
disseminated, circulated, or placed before the public, in this state, in a newspaper
or other publication, or in the form of a book, notice, handbill, poster, bill, circular, pamphlet, or letter, or in any other way, an advertisement of any sort regarding merchandise, securities, service, or anything so offered to the public, which
advertisement contains assertions, representation, or statement of fact which is untrue, deceptive, or misleading shall be guilty of a misdemeanor.

regulate "untrue, deceptive, or misleading" local advertising. *Printers Ink* magazine, the pioneer trade paper of advertising, has died; but its model statute,
in its original or modified form, has influenced local advertising in virtually
every state (see Exhibit 25.4).

Until recently, the roles of states and federal jurisdictions in advertising regulation were clearly separated. At the national level the FTC had primary responsibility for regulating advertising in interstate commerce, while individual states were involved in local consumer protection legislation. These state
actions usually dealt with retailers and smaller companies operating locally.

Currently, advertisers see a shift toward more local control or, even worse,
laws that are moving toward allowing states to go beyond federal legislation.
National advertisers argue that the cost of developing different campaigns,
advertising appeals, and creative executions for each state would make national advertising impossible. They are joined in their complaints by the national media. Advertisers ask that whatever limitations are placed on advertising should be consistent across states and, in general, administered by the
FTC. Advertisers are seeking a broad federal preemption policy similar to that
we discussed in the section on FDA regulations.

Regardless of complaints by advertisers, the trend is toward greater control
of advertising by local agencies. The National Association of Attorneys General (NAAG) has been at the forefront of local advertising regulation. The
organization and the attorneys general in several states have moved aggressively against a number of advertisers, even those that operate nationally. For
example, car rental agreements have been a favorite target of this group.

There is some question about the extent that states will be allowed to develop
guidelines for national companies. Advertisers are somewhat optimistic, since
the federal courts ruled that the NAAG cannot regulate airline price ads.
However, advertisers worry that they will have to go through lengthy court
proceedings for every category of product that local jurisdictions might want
to regulate.

There is some hope that under the Clinton administration, there will be at
least a general agreement about the proper role of states versus federal ad-

vertising regulation. All but the most ardent critics of advertising recognize that both advertisers and the media would be thrown into chaos if each state, much less cities, was allowed to impose its own regulations over national advertisers. If such a situation existed on a widespread basis, it would immediately eliminate national magazines and broadcast networks. At this point, most reasonable observers think that reason will prevail, and some federal guidelines will be established to review national advertising.

COMPARISON ADVERTISING

Comparison advertising

Used interchangeably with the term *comparative advertising,* it directly contrasts an advertiser's product with other named or identified products.

Comparison advertising compares competing products, usually by name. Comparative advertising is not new; in 1930, J. Sterling Getchell, head of the agency bearing his name, introduced the Chrysler car, never on the market before, by inviting customers to "try all three." For many years afterward, car advertisers compared a feature or the track record of their cars to other named brands. However, the conventional wisdom of the advertising trade was that if you mentioned a competitor's name, you were giving away free advertising. However, when properly executed, comparative advertising is still an effective sales tool in competitive markets.

The push for comparative advertising came in 1972, when the FTC urged ABC and CBS to allow commercials that named competitors. Until then, only NBC had permitted such messages, whereas ABC and CBS would allow nothing but "Brand X" comparisons. Since then, comparative advertising has become a popular, although extremely controversial, advertising technique. A major category of competitor-initiated complaints directed to major regulatory bodies involve comparative advertising.

Using Comparative Advertising

In recent years, it appears that the number of comparative advertisements and commercials has increased. Critics also claim that the tone of many of these messages has grown more shrill and negative. However, many advertisers view this trend toward "attack" comparison advertising with caution. "The apparent success of negative advertising in the political arena has led to a noticeable increase in its use in the marketing of goods and services. . . . prior to using negative advertising with confidence in the marketing of goods and services, a better understanding of the factors influencing its effectiveness must first be achieved."[16]

Comparative advertising that portrays a competitor, especially one that is named, in a negative light can backfire. If consumers perceive that such advertising is malicious or vicious, or whose primary goal is to belittle a competitor they may regard the advertising as violating fundamental principles of fair play and either disregard it or even develop a sympathy for the brand that is being attacked. Exhibit 25.5 shows some of the major reasons cited for not using comparative advertising.

Beyond problems with public perception of comparative advertising, both advertisers and their agencies may have legal problems if their advertising is

---

[16]Karen E. James and Paul J. Hensel, "Negative Advertising: The Malicious Strain of Comparative Advertising," *Journal of Advertising,* June 1991, p. 66.

EXHIBIT
25.5
· · · · · · · · · · · · · · · ·
Comparative advertising carries a number of risks to those companies using it.

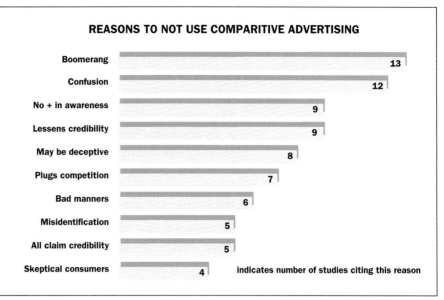

REASONS TO NOT USE COMPARITIVE ADVERTISING

Boomerang	13
Confusion	12
No + in awareness	9
Lessens credibility	9
May be deceptive	8
Plugs competition	7
Bad manners	6
Misidentification	5
All claim credibility	5
Skeptical consumers	4

indicates number of studies citing this reason

(Source: Thomas E. Barry, "Comparative Advertising: What Have We Learned in Two Decades?" Journal of Advertising Research, March/April 1993, p. 23.)

ruled deceptive. The primary legal recourse open to companies are several provisions of the Lanham Act. As amended in 1988, the Lanham Act allows an advertiser to sue if a competitor "misrepresents the nature, characteristics, qualities, or geographic origin of his or her or another person's goods, services, or commercial activities." Prior to this amendment, Company A could sue only if an ad for Company B made false statements about its own (that is, Company B) products. Under the amended act, companies may sue to stop ads in which false claims are made either about the defendant's products or about the plaintiff's. Naming competitors, either directly or by insinuation, is not without risk to both the agency and client. If a competitor can show damages (such as a decrease in market share) resulting from a dishonest or unfair comparison, it may collect multi-million-dollar settlements under the act.

Courts have ruled that a competitor may sue if claims made in an ad were false or if the overall perception of a literally true ad was designed to create consumer confusion. For example, if your advertising claims that your product meets all tests for quality (which is true), but leaves the impression that competing products do not, then the advertising may be actionable.

By the same token, the courts have ruled that if an advertisement refers to some specific and measurable standard of product performance (that is, a motor oil leads to longer engine life), this is not acceptable puffery but must be substantiated in tests with other motor oil. Generally, the courts have taken a dim view of claims that advertising misstatements were acceptable because the "public knows that the message is simply advertising exaggeration."

Furthermore, advertisers are not protected from action under the Lanham Act just because a competitor is not named. In some cases, the courts have held that a company may have damaged a number of other firms by claiming some product superiority that is not unique to that brand even when no competing brand is named. In other cases, successful suits have been brought by companies claiming that any intelligent consumer would have been expected to know which unnamed brand was the topic of unfair comparison.

In summary, there are three primary standards against which unfair competition is measured:

1. *Confusion.* The most common form of unfair competition that the law recognizes as wrongful is the marketing of products or services in a way that may confuse buyers about identity, source, or sponsorship.

2. *Disparagement.* The disparagement of competitors is recognized by courts as an actionable wrong, but carries with it the onerous requirement that resulting lost business be proved. Although many advertising professionals think that any form of competitive disparagement is unprofessional, the Lanham Act is concerned only with disparaging statements that are factually untrue and injure a competitor's business in a demonstrable fashion.

3. *Misrepresentation.* Misrepresentation of the qualities of the advertised product or service, whether or not derogatory of competitive offerings, may afford the basis for a lawsuit by competitors that can show that the misrepresentation has diverted or may divert business from them through deception of the public.[17]

Negative comparative advertising is viewed by critics, advertisers, and many consumers as inappropriate. Despite the many legal remedies available to companies wronged by such advertising, it is the public perception of such messages that may do the most damage to those using it. However, many advertising executives think that the damage of such advertising goes far beyond just the agencies and clients who engage in such promotion. Their fear is that it demeans the entire industry. Certainly, there is a place for measured, provable product comparisons. However, the tone of such advertising and the temptation to name competitors should be carefully considered before engaging in comparative campaigns.

The concern of the advertising industry for the use of comparative advertising is reflected in the "Creative Code of the American Association of Advertising Agencies" (see Exhibit 25.2). You will note that the subject of comparative advertising is specifically addressed in number 3.

THE ADVERTISING CLEARANCE PROCESS

Advertising clearance process

The internal process of clearing ads for publication and broadcast, conducted primarily by ad agencies and clients.

To this point, we have emphasized the legal and regulatory environment in which contemporary advertising must function. However, it would be a mistake to assume that most companies and agencies produce honest advertising only to avoid legal penalties or that there is little interest in truthful advertising beyond what meets the minimum legal standards. In fact, the vast majority of advertisers not only want to produce truthful advertising, but are equally interested in making sure that their peers do likewise. When consumers are misled by untruthful advertising, all advertisers pay a price.

The initial stage of the clearance process is advertising agencies and/or media (see Exhibit 25.6). In the past, advertising agencies were rarely held accountable for false advertising as long as they could show that they were not aware that client claims were untrue. This is not to suggest that agencies did not have an ethical and practical responsibility for the advertising they cre-

---

[17]"What Every Account Executive Should Know about the Law and Advertising," American Association of Advertising Agencies, 1990, p. 20.

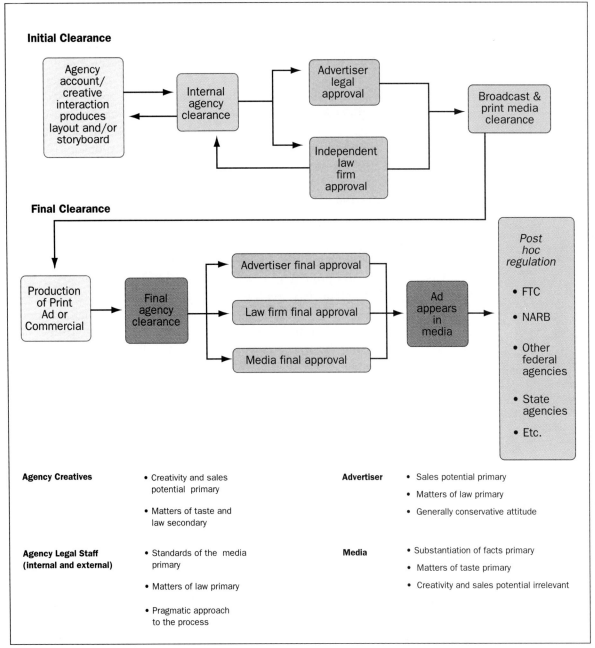

Initial Clearance

Agency account/creative interaction produces layout and/or storyboard → Internal agency clearance → Advertiser legal approval / Independent law firm approval → Broadcast & print media clearance

Final Clearance

Production of Print Ad or Commercial → Final agency clearance → Advertiser final approval / Law firm final approval / Media final approval → Ad appears in media → Post hoc regulation

Post hoc regulation
- FTC
- NARB
- Other federal agencies
- State agencies
- Etc.

Agency Creatives	• Creativity and sales potential primary • Matters of taste and law secondary
Agency Legal Staff (internal and external)	• Standards of the media primary • Matters of law primary • Pragmatic approach to the process
Advertiser	• Sales potential primary • Matters of law primary • Generally conservative attitude
Media	• Substantiation of facts primary • Matters of taste primary • Creativity and sales potential irrelevant

(Courtesy: Eric Zanot, "Unseen but Effective Advertising Regulation: The Clearance Process," Journal of Advertising 14, November 4, 1985:p. 46–47.

EXHIBIT

25.6

· · · · · · · · · · · · · · · · · ·

The advertising clearance process.

ated. Obviously, it is not good business to be associated with deceptive advertising regardless of the legal consequences.

However, recent rulings have placed much greater legal liability on agencies for the work they produce. In one case, the FTC cited both Hasbro and its agency, Griffin Bacal, for falsely representing the performance of certain toys in the G.I. Joe line. The allegations stemmed from a TV commercial that appeared to show a toy helicopter that could "hover and fly in a sustained manner" when it cannot. Both Hasbro and its agency agreed in consent decrees not to engage in any further deceptive toy advertising as cited by the FTC.[18]

---

[18]"Toy Manufacturer, Ad Agency Settle FTC False Representation Charges," *Advertising Topics,* April/May 1993, Council of Better Business Bureaus.

Recent court decisions have been equally harsh in holding agencies to the same standards as their clients. New York U.S. District Court Judge Kimba Wood ruled that a Wilkenson Sword razor advertisement was "false and damaging to Gillette Co." The judge held both Wilkenson and its agency, Friedman Franklin, to be "jointly and severally liable" for damages. What is particularly troublesome about the decision is that it appears that the judge was suggesting that agencies be liable even when they have no reason to question a client's research.[19] In the case of small agencies that lack the resources to validate client research, this ruling is a significant problem. Currently, agencies find themselves in the position of taking a much more active role in ensuring that any advertising they produce is based on substantiated claims. Clearly, the public would probably view this as a minimal responsibility on their part.

The Media's Role in the Clearance Process

The second primary gatekeepers for the advertising clearance process are the media. The media's role is particularly important for local advertising, much of which is placed directly by retailers rather than through an agency. Newspapers, as the primary local medium, have long had guidelines concerning advertising they will accept. At the national level, TV networks have a very formalized system of advertising clearance.

Recent cases have placed the media in potential joint liability for the advertising they accept. If a statement in an advertisement or commercial is false or defamatory, the media can be sued along with the advertiser. One of the most publicized cases of media liability involved *Soldier of Fortune* magazine. The publication carried an advertisement that resulted in the hiring of a man to carry out a murder for hire. The family of the man who was killed sued the publication for damages. The suit resulted in a multimillion dollar judgment against *Soldier of Fortune*.

In a decision on an appeal of the ruling, a lower court ruled that the First Amendment does not prohibit a state from imposing liability upon a publisher for negligently publishing a commercial advertisement that, on its face, and without the need for investigation, makes it apparent that there is a substantial danger of harm to the public.[20] The Supreme Court refused to review the case. The decision stood.

While the *Soldier of Fortune* case may give some pause to other media, as a practical matter, the advertisement was so unusual that media have little to fear from the decision. A more practical concern of media is the loss of goodwill with their audiences if a deceptive ad is cleared for publication or broadcast. No responsible agency or medium would argue that deceptive advertising should be created or run.

A question that falls into a much more gray area is whether or not to accept truthful advertising that is controversial to the point that it might cause financial harm to the medium. For example, the *Des Moines Register* accepted an advertisement from the People for the Ethical Treatment of Animals [PETA]. The advertisement compared serial killer Jeffry Dahmer's mutilation

---

[19]"A Court Verdict That Stings," *Advertising Age,* September 7, 1992, p. 16.
[20]Rene Milam, Analysing the Effect of Braun vs Soldier of Fortune, *Classified Update,* April 1993, p.5.

killings in Milwaukee to livestock slaughter. The ad appeared only a month after Dahmer was arrested.

The ensuing public outcry cost the newspaper more than $1 million in lost advertising and circulation revenues. The newspaper's advertising director took the position that the advertisement should not be censored. She said, "While the pictures it [the ad] painted were graphic, it wasn't posing anything illegal. We thought it had a place and that people should decide for themselves, instead of the paper deciding for them, about the [PETA] organization. So we went for no censorship."[21]

Whether the question is one of taste, deception, or controversy, the media will increasingly be faced with hard decisions about the advertising they accept. However, the joint liability aspect of these questions increases the potential risk to both agencies and media.

It is too early to predict the long term ramifications of this greater potential liability for all parties in the advertising process. For certain, the clearance process by advertisers, agencies, and media will take on a more legalistic tone in the future. No longer will the clearance process be solely interested in protecting the consumer in a responsible manner. Now the process will be concerned with the major legal liability that might ensue from accepting the wrong ad.

SELF-REGULATION BY INDUSTRYWIDE GROUPS

In addition, to the efforts of individual agencies and media to ensure that advertising is truthful, there are similar efforts by industrywide groups to review advertising on both a national and local basis. These efforts offer the public, competitors, and other interested parties a voluntary forum for negotiation without resorting to a formal legal or regulatory body for the adjudication of disagreements.

Industry self-regulation serves two important purposes beyond ensuring more informative and truthful advertising. First, it partially overcomes the relatively poor public perception of advertising by showing that there is a concerted attempt to foster responsible advertising. Second, strong self-regulation may ward off even stricter government control.

One of the ways in which the industry promotes better advertising is through various guidelines and codes of practice both from advertising agencies and media as well as trade associations and professional organizations. One of the leading advertising groups promoting truthful and ethical advertising is the American Advertising Federation. The AAF advocates truthful and fair advertising through local advertising clubs (see Exhibit 25.7).

Despite the best efforts of federal regulatory agencies, the media, and individual advertisers, the perception persists among a large group of consumers that advertising is either basically deceptive or does not provide sufficient information. Given the investment that companies are making in advertising, this perception is a major problem and one that needs to be addressed with a united front by all honest businesses. As we will see in this section, the ad-

---

[21]Mary Hardie, "Careful Evaluation of Ads: It's Crucial" *Gannetteer,* February 1993, p. 15.

CHAPTER 25 *Legal and Other Restraints on Advertising* 757

EXHIBIT
25.7

....
The American Advertis-
ing Federation is a ma-
jor advocate of fair and
truthful advertising.

Can't say something nice?
Don't advertise.

WE'RE JUST PARAPHRASING what Mom used to tell us. Sure that sounds a little silly, but the point is that advertising which unfairly slams its competition is not representative of the high standards the advertising industry has established for itself.

Some advertising just needs to grow up.

According to the American Advertising Federation's Advertising Principles of American Business, "Advertising shall offer merchandise or service on its merits, and refrain from attacking competitors unfairly or disparaging their products, services or methods of doing business."

You have a right to speak out.

Contact your local Ad Club or Federation anytime you find advertising that is misleading, irresponsible or simply not to your liking. We'll show you a way to make your voice heard where it counts. And we'll send you a copy of the AAF's Advertising Principles of American Business.

No kidding.

Advertising Is Worth Doing Right.

AAF A PUBLIC SERVICE OF THIS PUBLICATION
AND THE OKLAHOMA CITY AD CLUB, PO BOX 20408, OKLAHOMA CITY, OK 73156

(Courtesy: Oklahoma City Advertising Club.)

Better Business Bureau
An organization
launched by advertisers
that now has wide busi-
ness support, formed
to protect the public
against deceptive adver-
tising and fraudulent
business methods.
Works widely at local
levels. Also identified
with the National Adver-
tising Review Board.

vertising industry is making substantial investments in moving against deceptive advertising.

Better Business Bureaus[22]

One of the best-known, aggressive, and successful organization, in the fight for honest and truthful advertising is the national network of Better Business Bureaus coordinated by the Council of Better Business Bureaus (CBBB). The forerunners of the modern BBBs date to 1905, when various local advertising clubs formed a national association that today is known as the National Advertising Federation. In 1911, this association launched a campaign for truth in advertising coordinated by local vigilance committees. In 1916, these local committees adopted the name Better Business Bureaus, and they became autonomous in 1926. Today, there are approximately 180 local bureaus in the United States and Canada.

[22]Information concerning the Better Business Bureaus and the National Advertising Review Council is supplied courtesy of the Council of Better Business Bureaus.

Although the BBBs have no legal authority, they are a major influence on truth and accuracy in advertising. The BBBs are able to exert both the force of public opinion and peer pressure to set up voluntary efforts to solve advertising trouble spots.

The NAD/NARB Self-Regulation Program

National Advertising Division (NAD)

The policy-making arm of the National Advertising Review Board.

In 1971, in response to the many different consumer groups complaining about deceptive advertising, the major advertising organizations—the American Advertising Federation, the American Association of Advertising Agencies, and the Association of National Advertisers—joined with the CBBB to form the National Advertising Review Council (NARC). NARC's primary purpose was to "develop a structure which would effectively apply the persuasive capacities of peers to seek the voluntary elimination of national advertising which professionals would consider deceptive." Its objective was to sustain high standards of truth and accuracy in national advertising.

NARC established a comprehensive two-tier program for advertising self-regulation. The first tier, the active investigative unit, is the National Advertising Division (NAD) of the Council of Better Business Bureaus. The second tier, the National Advertising Review Board (NARB), provides an advertiser with a jury of peers if it chooses to appeal an NAD decision.

The NAD is staffed by full-time lawyers who respond to complaints from competitors and consumers and referrals from local BBBs. They also monitor national advertising. The greatest number of inquiries are initiated by competitors. This source of challenge has remained number one over the years.

After a complaint is received, the NAD determines the issues, collects and evaluates data, and makes an initial decision on whether the claims are substantiated. If the NAD finds that substantiation is satisfactory, it announces that fact. If the NAD finds that the substantiation is not adequate, it will recommend that the advertiser modify or discontinue the offending claims. If the advertiser does not agree, it may appeal to the NARB. NAD decisions are released to the press and also are published in its monthly publication *NAD Case Reports.*

The NARB is composed of 70 members—40 representing advertisers, 20 representing advertising agencies, and 10 from the public sector. Five members in the same proportion are assigned to hear an appeal. If the panel thinks the NAD's decision is justified, but the advertiser still refuses to correct the deceptive element, the NARB may refer the advertising to the appropriate government agency. Exhibit 25.8 outlines the entire process.

A summary of recent cases investigated by the NAD shows that only 2 percent of cases are referred to a governmental agency, while more than 90 percent of claims are modified or discontinued (see Exhibit 25.9). In addition, NAB figures show that more than half of total cases are initiated by competitors (see Exhibit 25.9). To give you an idea of the manner in which an NARB appeal of Microsoft BallPoint Mouse (see Exhibit 25.10).

In over 20 years of operation, no advertiser that participated in the complete process has declined to abide by an NARB decision, necessitating a referral to the FTC.

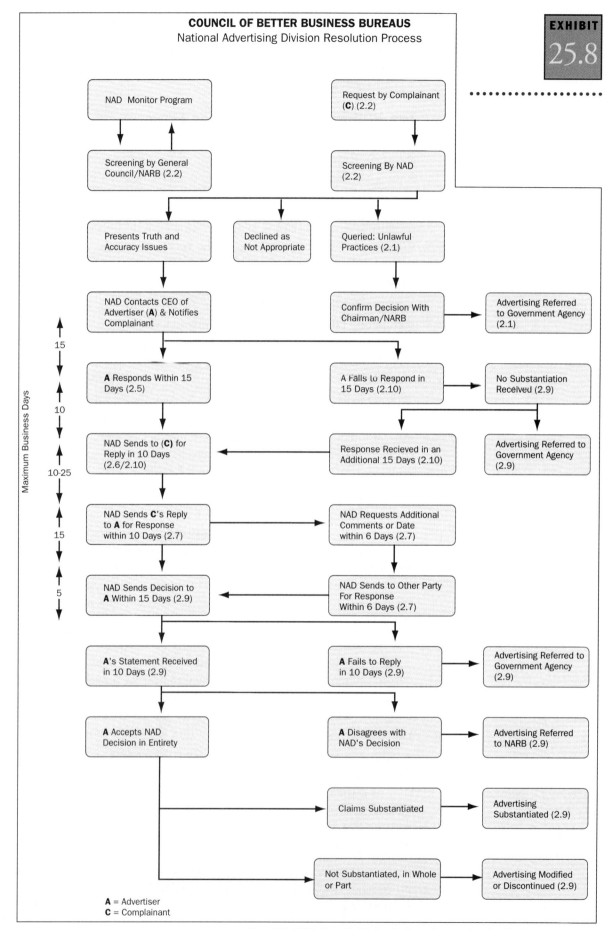

COUNCIL OF BETTER BUSINESS BUREAUS
National Advertising Division Resolution Process

EXHIBIT
25.8

NAD Monitor Program

Request by Complainant (**C**) (2.2)

Screening by General Council/NARB (2.2)

Screening By NAD (2.2)

Presents Truth and Accuracy Issues

Declined as Not Appropriate

Queried: Unlawful Practices (2.1)

NAD Contacts CEO of Advertiser (**A**) & Notifies Complainant

Confirm Decision With Chairman/NARB

Advertising Referred to Government Agency (2.1)

A Responds Within 15 Days (2.5)

A Fails to Respond in 15 Days (2.10)

No Substantiation Received (2.9)

NAD Sends to (**C**) for Reply in 10 Days (2.6/2.10)

Response Recieved in an Additional 15 Days (2.10)

Advertising Referred to Government Agency (2.9)

NAD Sends **C**'s Reply to **A** for Response within 10 Days (2.7)

NAD Requests Additional Comments or Date within 6 Days (2.7)

NAD Sends Decision to **A** Within 15 Days (2.9)

NAD Sends to Other Party For Response Within 6 Days (2.7)

A's Statement Received in 10 Days (2.9)

A Fails to Reply in 10 Days (2.9)

Advertising Referred to Government Agency (2.9)

A Accepts NAD Decision in Entirety

A Disagrees with NAD's Decision

Advertising Referred to NARB (2.9)

Claims Substantiated

Advertising Substantiated (2.9)

Not Substantiated, in Whole or Part

Advertising Modified or Discontinued (2.9)

Maximum Business Days

15

10

10-25

15

5

A = Advertiser
C = Complainant

(Copyright, 1994, Council of Better Business Bureaus, Inc. Reprinted with permission.)

In our examination of the NAD/NARB process, we should understand that it cannot

- **Order an advertiser to stop an ad**

- **Impose a fine**

- **Bar anyone from advertising**

- **Boycott an advertiser or a product**

What it can do is bring to bear the judgment of an advertiser's peers that the company has produced advertising that is not truthful and is harmful to the industry, to the public, and to the offender. This judgment has great moral weight. It is reinforced by the knowledge that, if the result of an appeal to the NARB are not accepted, the whole matter will be referred to the appropriate government agency and at the same time will be released to the public. This step, unique in business self-regulation machinery, avoids any problem of violating antitrust laws, presents the entire matter to public view, and still leaves the advertiser subject to an FTC ruling on the advertising.

The Children's Advertising Unit of the NAD

Children's Advertising Review Unit (CARU)
The CARU functions much as the NAD to review complaints about advertising to children.

In the past decade, more and more advertisers are targeting children as prime prospects for their products. It has been estimated that children constitute a $60 billion annual market. Not only have companies targeted advertising to children, but they also have developed a number of products and services especially for them. Fast-food restaurants provide special children's meals in unique packages, airlines have established kids clubs for frequent travelers, and banks have set up savings programs for children.[23]

Identification of children as a discrete market has raised questions among a number of groups about advertising directed to this unsophisticated audience. Advertising claims that would be perfectly suitable for adults might be unacceptable for children, especially younger ones. Because of this concern with children's advertising, the NAD along with the children's advertising community, founded the Children's Advertising Review Unit (CARU) in

**EXHIBIT
25.9**

Voluntary Self-Regulation of National Advertising
Analysis of 1993 Closings

Decisions	1993		1992		Sources	1993		1992	
	#	%	#	%		#	%	#	%
Substantiated	31	36	14	22	NAD Monitoring	21	24	8	12
Modified/Discontinued	50	57	47	72	Competitor Challenges	47	54	47	72
Referred to Govt. (1)	2	2	4	6	Local BBBs	3	3	2	3
No Subst. Received (1)	4	5	0	0	Consumer Complaints	12	14	7	11
Total	87	100%	65	100%	Other	4	5	1	2
					Total	87	100%	65	100%

Note: (1) Two headings—Referred to Government Agency and No Substantiation Received —were introduced in 1991. A total of four cases were initially reported under the "No Substantiation Received" heading during 1993; in 1992, one.

(Copyright, 1994, Council of Better Business Bureaus, Inc. Reprinted with permission.)

---

[23]Carrie Teegardin, "Target Marketing Takes Aim at Kids," *Atlanta Journal,* June 7, 1993, p. E8.

NARB National Advertising Review Board

845 Third Avenue, New York, N.Y. 10022

REPORT OF NARB PANEL 81

DISPOSITION OF ADVERTISING REFERRED TO NARB REGARDING
ADVERTISING FOR MICROSOFT BALLPOINT MOUSE

The Panel met in New York City on Wednesday June 1, 1994 at 9:30 a.m., to consider disposition of the above appeal.

Panel Members

Christopher Hoppin, Chairman
John Crowley
Leo Greenland
Ronald Kos
David Robertson

Also present at the hearing were:

Representing the National Advertising Review Board

Eric D. Haueter, *Executive Director*
Steven J. Cole, Esq., *General Counsel*

Representing the National Advertising Division

Debra Goldstein, Esq., *Acting Director*
Mark Levine, Esq., *Ad Review Specialist*

Representing Microsoft Corporation

Annette Wilson Skinner, Esquire
Ronald E. Cox, Esquire, Preston Gates & Ellis

Background

The advertiser, Microsoft Corporation, requested NARB adjudication of a determination by the National Advertising Division (NAD) of the Council of Better Business Bureaus that an advertising claim concerning the superior performance of the Microsoft BallPoint Mouse pointing device be modified.

The NAD case (#3099Mpol) resulted from NAD's ongoing monitoring program.

The issue on appeal stems from the following claim:

"And which is why, in independent tests, people worked 35% faster with the BallPoint mouse than with other leading portable and built-in pointing devices."

The advertiser maintained that the totality of the advertisement emphasizes the superior control the Microsoft BallPoint mouse offers, and that there was no basis to single out an individual claim for criticism. In support of the speed claim against "other leading competitors" the advertiser submitted the results of independent tests of both simple and complex functions performed by persons using the Microsoft BallPoint mouse and various other competing devices.

The NAD held that the challenged claim was "that the Microsoft mouse performed better than all of the 'other leading portable and built-in pointing devices' " [emphasis in NAD's original decision]. In the test results, however, the Microsoft BallPoint mouse operated 35% faster than five, but not all, of the six leading competitors tested.

In its advertiser's statement appended to the NAD decision, the advertiser argued that NAD had challenged a claim that Microsoft never made, i.e. that its BallPoint mouse performed better than all of the other leading portable and built-in pointing devices. It stressed that the word "all" was neither contained in the challenged advertisement nor implied by a fair reading of the plain English text.

Findings and Conclusions

The advertiser makes two principal contentions on appeal. First, that the NAD decision should be reversed

because the advertiser had discontinued the advertising in question before the NAD decision, thereby eliminating the need for the decision.[1] Second, that the decision was incorrect because NAD, without consumer evidence supporting its position, wrongly interpreted the advertising claim as "necessarily" implying that the claim would be interpreted by consumers as one against "all" leading devices.

The panel disagrees with the advertiser's position on both of these points, and finds the NAD's recommendation to have been appropriate as a matter of procedure and on the merits.

Under the NAD/NARB rules, advertising that has been "permanently withdrawn from use prior to the filing of the complaint" will not be subjected to NAD's "formal investigation." Rule 2.2 B (i). This rule has two salutary purposes.

First, it conserves advertiser and NAD resources for cases with continuing impact. Here, because the claim had not been permanently withdrawn prior to the case opening, NAD (and the advertiser) expended time and resources on the case. In fact, as noted, all of the casework and decision-writing had been completed before the advertiser raised the question of the discontinuance of the claim. It would have been wasteful were NAD to have declined to publish its decision, intended for the benefit of the entire advertising community, after all the work had been concluded. It is just such waste and lost opportunity that the rules are intended to avoid.

Second, the rule precludes the possibility that an advertiser, who may not have adequate substantiation, may intentionally "moot" a case "once caught" in order to avoid a public decision and acknowledgment that the unsubstantiated claim will not be reinstated at a future date. While the panel is not saying this was the advertiser's motive in this case, the rule recognizes this possibility. It provides for continuation of the NAD/NARB process to its conclusion, regardless of the advertiser's motive, if the dispute is a live one when the case is opened.

Because the NAD properly decided the case, this panel

[1]In fact, NAD was not informed that the advertising was discontinued until after it had provided its final decision to the advertiser to allow the addition of the advertiser's statement to the decision. The advertiser thus was willing to have the case proceed to decision, and only raised the discontinuance issue after it was apprised of the NAD recommendation.

also has the responsibility under the rules, again for the benefit of the entire industry, to decide if the substantiation provided by the advertiser was sufficient to support its claim. Frankly, given the existence of NAD's published decision, the panel would expect an advertiser to want the opportunity to have the NAD recommendation reviewed on its merits, and corrected by the NARB if necessary.

Turning to the substantiation for the claim, the panel is in full agreement with the NAD disposition.

Initially, the advertiser argued to the NAD and to this panel that the claim regarding speed should not be taken out of context, that it is part of an advertisement that predominantly describes the greater control afforded by the product, and that in that larger context it is not appropriate to single out one sentence for criticism because the advertising as a whole is not deceptive.

While the advertiser is certainly correct that any claim must be reviewed in the totality of an entire advertisement, the fact is that a specific, verifiable claim such as the one under review here must be substantiated. The advertiser points to nothing about the context of the advertisement that should affect consumer interpretation of the specific comparative speed claim made by the advertiser. If anything, the context demonstrates the importance of substantiation for the speed claim, because the speed claim reinforces the control claims, by providing an objective, identifiable basis for such greater control.

With regard to the specific claim, the advertiser mistakenly assumes that NAD had the obligation to establish, through scientific consumer perception evidence, precisely what consumers understood the words "other leading devices" to mean. The NAD and NARB have both consistently interpreted their mandate from the advertising industry as requiring them to use their own expert, professional judgments about the likely consumer interpretation of a claim in the absence of evidence submitted by the advertiser or any challenger. Were this practice not followed, the self-regulation system would find it difficult, if not impossible, to protect consumers from unsubstantiated implied claims or claims susceptible to multiple interpretations, whenever the advertiser failed to produce a study.

The panel also agrees with NAD's judgment as to likely consumer perception. While some consumers will surely

interpret the claim as a comparison against "some" leading competitor mouse devices, it is equally true that many other reasonable consumers will interpret the claim as a comparison against "all" leading devices.

As NAD observed at the hearing, it is "black letter law" that an advertiser must be prepared to substantiate all reasonable interpretations. Thus, the advertiser's criticism that NAD interpreted the ad as "necessarily" implying that the claim was against "all" devices misses the mark. Substantiation for the comparative claim against all leading competitors is needed not because it is the only interpretation, but because it is a reasonable one.

Of course, as the advertiser has conceded, its pointing device is not 35% faster than "all" leading competitors. Accordingly, the claim is not substantiated.[2]

Recommendation

The panel recommends that, if reinstated by the advertiser in the future based on existing research, the claim that the Microsoft BallPoint mouse is 35% faster than other devices be modified to clarify that the product is not 35% faster than all leading competitors.

Advertiser's Statement

Future advertising, if any, will be modified to be not inconsistent with the recommendation of the National Advertising Review Board.

[2]There was much discussion at the hearing of the relevant market and how the leading competitors and their shares of that market should be calculated. For example, the record shows that Compaq, the competitor against whose device the claim could not be substantiated, had approximately 20% of the trackball (built in) market, but the record did not show its percentage share of the combined built-in and portable device market, which the advertiser contended was the market to which the claim applied. Moreover, in addressing Compaq's market share, however defined, it appears that the advertiser included one of its other pointing devices as part of the universe to which the advertiser's product was being compared, notwithstanding the fact that the claim was for its"new" "redesigned" mouse. This led the panel to speculate whether Compaq was not only "a" leading competitor, but perhaps "the " leading competitor in the market to which the advertiser directed the consumer's attention. If so, its exclusion from the reference to "other leading competitors" would have been even more problematic. In light of the advertiser's concession that Compaq is a "leading competitor" and given absence of pertinent data in the record on these points, the panel did not believe a resolution of these issues was warranted or necessary.

(Courtesy: National Advertising Review Board and the Council of Better Business Bureaus.)

1974. The mission of the CARU is "to promote truthful, accurate advertising to children which is sensitive to the special nature of its audience."[24] CARU takes the position that children's view and understanding of the world are different from adults', and that their experience in the marketplace is limited.

The primary activity of CARU involves the review and evaluation of advertising directed to children under the age of 12. CARU systematically monitors broadcast, cable, print, and other advertising directed to children. In addition, local Better Business Bureaus, consumer groups, governmental agencies, and other advertisers refer questions to the CARU. The CARU has extensive guidelines that help advertisers deal sensitively and honestly with children. Many advertisers submit storyboards or videotapes of proposed advertising to CARU for assessment. This prescreening does not constitute approval of the final advertising but can overcome obvious problems before the final advertising is produced.

In recent years, three areas of children's advertising have constituted the most frequently raised concerns:

1. *Product presentation.* Children look at, listen to, and remember many different elements in advertising. Therefore, advertisers need to examine the total advertising message, viewed from a child's perspective, to avoid misleading or misinforming children. In particular, CARU is concerned that a product is demonstrated in a manner than can be duplicated by the child and that it is shown in a safe environment.

2. *Adequacy of disclosures.* Children have a more limited vocabulary and less-developed language skills than adolescents and adults. They read less well, if at all, and rely more on information presented pictorially than verbally. Studies have shown that simplified wording such as "you have to put it together" instead of "assembly required" significantly increases comprehension.

   Advertisers should include all essential information in their advertising. For example, are batteries required, or must some of the items shown in the ad be purchased separately? All product disclaimers and disclosures should be clearly worded, legible, and prominent. In TV advertising, both audio and video disclosures are encouraged.

3. *Sales pressure.* Children are not as prepared as adults to make judicious, independent purchase decisions. Therefore, advertisers should avoid using extreme sales pressure in advertising presentations to children. In particular, children should not be encouraged to ask parents to buy a product. Certainly, there should be no suggestion that a parent who buys a product for a child is better, more intelligent, or more generous than one who does not. Finally, advertising should not suggest that children who possess some product will be more accepted by their peers than those who do not.

It is obvious from these guidelines that television is the most important focus for CARU. This interest is dictated by the share of children's advertising that appears on television. Exhibit 25.11 shows that over 65 percent of all

---

[24]Information in this section is provided by the Children's Advertising Review Unit.

EXHIBIT

25.11

Children's Advertising and Promotion Budgets
Share of Spending

	% Share 1992	Projected 1993 % Share	Net Percent Change
Network TV	21.7	26.9	+23.9%
Spot TV	9.4	7.9	+15.9
Cable TV	14.9	13.5	−09.3
Consumer & Mass Market Magazines	8.5	9.7	+14.1
Co-op Advertising	3.7	3.6	−02.7
Syndicated TV	13.6	11.7	−13.9
Cable Spot TV	3.9	5.9	+51.2
Consumer Promotions/Event Sponsorship	6.3	6.8	+7.9
Newspapers	.8	.8	0.0
Retail Promotions Allowances	2.9	2.8	−03.4
Network Radio	5.6	1.0	−82.1
Point-of-Purchase Displays	2.7	2.2	−18.5
Business Publications	1.7	1.7	0.0
Direct Mail/Telemarketing	2.0	1.8	−10.0
Trade Shows	1.0	1.0	0.0
Other	1.2	1.7	+41.6

(Source: Mediaweek, July 5, 1993, p. 18.)

children's advertising is on television. By comparison, the second-place medium, consumer magazines, account for less than 10 percent.

Current legislative and regulatory attitudes indicate that advertisers will not be allowed the latitude in advertising to children that they have with adults. Beginning October 1, 1991, the FTC mandated limits on children program advertising to 10 1/2 minutes an hour on weekdays and 12 minutes on weekends. The action of the commission underscores the fact that children's television, both programming and advertising, is considered a separate category from that directed to general audiences.

In the area of children's advertising, there are no right answers. Many critics think that no advertising should be directed to children. To these people only a total ban will be satisfactory. However, given the economic support of the media through advertising, it is unlikely that any such ban will ever be permitted. It is imperative that all parties involved (media, advertisers, parents, special interest groups) work to ensure that children's advertising is appropriate for the audience to which it is intended. With public opinion running against them, advertisers must be extremely cautious about the content of all advertising messages directed to children.

SUMMARY

It is clear from this chapter that the legal and regulatory environment in which advertising operates is extremely complex and shows no indication of being less so in the future. Even the most ethical and careful advertiser is at risk of running afoul of the many rules guiding the advertising function. In addition to the formal rules directing advertising, companies also find that public opinion must be carefully considered before engaging in promotions.

Among major advertisers, there is little disagreement that advertising should be fair, truthful and follow both the letter and the spirit of the law. In fact, honest advertisers are among the most aggressive groups in weeding out the charlatans who make it difficult for all advertisers by eroding public confidence in the process. For the foreseeable future, it is clear that advertisers will have to contend with the numerous, sometimes conflicting, and constantly changing advertising regulations.

Questions

1. What is the primary national governmental regulatory body for advertising?
2. What is the key element that the FTC requires in determining whether advertising is deceptive?
3. What is the concept of the "rational or reasonable consumer" in FTC enforcement?
4. What is meant by puffery?
5. What is the intent of the Central Hudson Four-Part Test?
6. What is the legal status of professional advertising?
7. What is corrective advertising?
8. What is a company's primary legal recourse when it has been harmed by deceptive comparison advertising?
9. What is the advertising clearance process?
10. What is the primary source of industry-wide advertising self-regulation?

Economic and Social Effects of Advertising

26

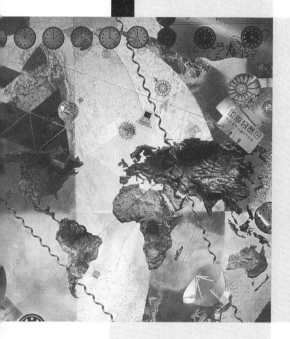

CHAPTER OBJECTIVES

Advertising functions in both an economic and a social context. By portraying people in certain settings and engaging in certain occupations, it contributes to stereotyping groups in our society. After reading this chapter you will understand:

- **The economic role of advertising**
- **Advertising and overtly social communication**
- **The inadvertent social role of advertising**
- **The Advertising Council as a social institution**
- **Growing sensitivity of advertisers**

Throughout most of this book, we have discussed the techniques and business practices associated with the advertising industry. **As we come to the end** of our discussion of the many facets of advertising, it is appropriate that we reflect on advertising as both a social and economic institution. **As we have seen,** advertising is the highest-profile segment of marketing communications and, as a result, is often the target of unfair criticism that should more correctly be directed at other aspects of marketing or business.

Advertising, like most business functions, is simply a tool. It may be used for the best or worse motives and practiced by those of high moral standards or charlatans. Advertising should be judged by how it is practiced, not in some abstract sense. Effective advertising provides efficient and profitable communication for the firms that utilize it and reaches prospects with information that will aid them in making beneficial purchase decisions. However, to the extent that advertising has an important social component, advertisers have a special responsibility to the public.

The dual role of balancing economic efficiency and social responsibility is not always an easy one. However, most advertising practitioners are sensitive to the dilemma and work hard to fulfill both of these responsibilities. In the remainder of this chapter, we will seek to discover how advertising seeks to find a balance between economic efficiency for sellers and social benefits for buyers.

The first step is to understand that the social and economic elements of advertising are not mutually exclusive. For example, businesses are part of society and benefit from attention to environmental issues, better education, and other relevant societal issues that are brought to the public's attention through advertising. By the same token, to the extent that advertising can contribute to ending economic recession and expanding the economy, the public will gain by higher employment.

John O'Toole, past president of the American Association of Advertising Agencies, points out that "advertising produces sales in the most economical way thus far conceived, that more advertising is better than less, and that the road out of a recession is paved with advertising. More advertising produces more sales which, in turn, produce more jobs and more profit. And those are sure cures for a recession."[1] In this chapter, we will examine two major roles of advertising. First we will discuss advertising's contribution to economic efficiency. That is, does advertising provide market information in a manner that could not be more efficiently accomplished by other means? The second area of discussion is advertising's role in the social process. Here we recognize that advertising has broad, noneconomic effects on society.

THE ECONOMIC ROLE OF ADVERTISING

One of the most controversial areas of advertising is the specific role it plays as part of the economy. To some it is a vital and extremely efficient means of introducing and maintaining product visibility. Numerous studies have indicated that a strong positive relationship exists between high brand awareness and market dominance.

For example, Landor Associates conducted a global study that reviewed the relationship among level of advertising, share-of-mind, and esteem of products in a number of countries. Landor identified Coca-Cola, Campbell's Soup, Hallmark, Kellogg, Pepsi, Kodak, and Levi as some of the most powerful brands in the United States and abroad. In each case, these "power brands"

---

[1]John E. O'Toole, "What the Country Needs Is More Advertising," *Link,* October 1992, p. 72.

were both the leader in sales and the leader in advertising for their product category. Landor concluded that is was not coincidental that those products that were the most esteemed and that sell the most were also those that advertised the most.[2]

We would, of course, be seriously mistaken to ascribe all of the success of these brands to advertising. However, it is clear that most of the major brands and companies in the world have put a great deal of faith in the power of advertising. They demonstrate their conviction by the expenditure of billions of dollars on advertising each year. While we should be realistic about the role of advertising in the marketing mix, we should not be too quick to dismiss its role as too many of its critics do.

One of the most difficult aspects of determining the economic contributions of advertising is our inability to precisely identify the role that advertising plays in moving consumers to purchases and its contributions to company profits. It is extremely difficult to separate the value of advertising in the intricate matrix of consumer behavior. For example, why did you buy the shoes, belt, or T-shirt you are wearing? To what degree did advertising, promotion, public relations, or personal selling enter into the steps that led to your purchase? For that matter, to what degree did marketing communication functions play a role in buying your last car or other high-ticket item?

Added value

The assumption that advertising adds value to a product in the same way that manufacturing and distribution do.

Most of us would be hard-pressed to identify a particular role that advertising played in any particular decision. Obviously, if we are unsure about the role of advertising in our own purchase behavior, it is even more difficult for companies to determine its role in their overall sales. Despite the difficulty of determining the exact relationship between advertising and purchase behavior, evidence does indicate that favorable product perception is important for sales success. "Taken together, product/service design, quality control, advertising, and comparisons by consumers determine a business's relative perceived quality in the marketplace. Relative quality and relative advertising expenditures are two of the five key factors that drive relative price. Relative perceived quality and relative price determine customer-perceived relative value."[3]

Simply put, effective advertising enhances the consumer's image of a product, which in turn increases the likelihood that the product will be purchased. Advertising's contribution to product enhancement will often lead to a significantly higher profit margin compared to products with lower customer esteem.

Exhibit 26.1 demonstrates that advertising can be positioned in a manner to increase a number of attitudinal dimensions of a company or product. In the case highlighted here, an instrument manufacturer sought to enhance awareness among engineering and corporate managers who were increasingly involved in corporate purchasing decisions. The advertising goals were to establish the company as a "safe buy" by enhancing its reputation for accuracy and reliability.

---

[2]Bernard Ryan, Jr., *It Works!* (New York: American Association of Advertising Agencies, 1991), p. 8.
[3] *The Impact of Advertising Expenditures on Profits for Consumer Businesses,* Ogilvy Center for Research and Development, June 1988, p. 3.

EXHIBIT

26.1

An instrument manufacturer increased the perception of its corporate reputation for product reliability by 35% among purchase influencers using nine single-theme corporate positioning ads over one year.

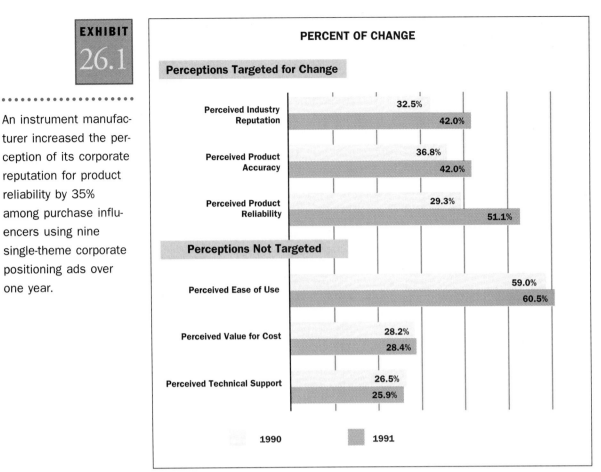

(Courtesy: Cahners Publishing Company.)

The company ran ads nine times over an 11-month period in a leading business publication. Research showed sellers noted significant changes in featured benefits among potential buyers while nontargeted features such as technical support showed no significant differences in audience perception.

Advertising's Contributions to the Economy

When examining the economic role of advertising, we must look at several facets of advertising's contribution to economic well-being.

Communication Efficiency of Advertising. There is no question that advertising is the least expensive form of marketing communication. However, communication, no matter how effective, will not ensure sales. Advertising works within an extremely complex matrix of variables that ultimately determine our purchase behavior. Product price, availability, service, and quality all play a role in making advertising effective and in turn are affected by advertising. Basically, advertising operates on two levels. Exhibit 26.2 shows how advertising moves the consumer vertically (generic demand) and horizontally (brand demand). However, it generally channels existing wants and needs rather than creating demand.

Generic demand

The demand demonstrated for a product class rather than a specific brand.

In recent years, companies have begun to place even more importance on the value of high brand visibility and company reputation. As we discussed in Chapter 14, firms realize the potential long-term damage to brand equity brought about by an overreliance on sales promotion, price cutting, and other

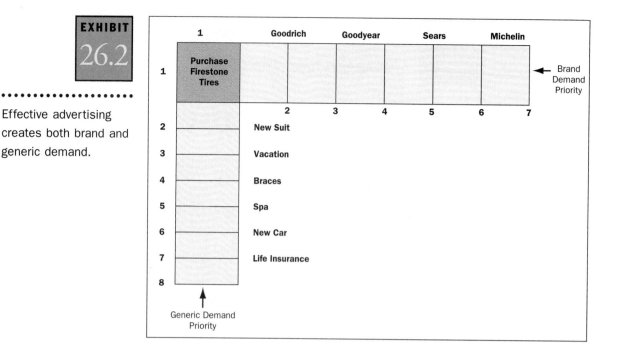

"quick fixes." They have also found that strong brands can simultaneously work at both generic and brand demand levels, whereas most sales promotion is directed solely at brand demand.

A number of advertising executives predict a return to the importance of brand awareness and advertising as a means of achieving meaningful product differentiation. Exhibit 26.3 demonstrates the importance of brand-name reputation. Perhaps the most important finding of this study is that 82 percent of respondents thought that "buying an unfamiliar brand is often risky." Since consumers rarely want to take a risk, this single finding is reason enough for companies to invest heavily in advertising.

Effect of Advertising on Corporate Profits.   The obvious answer to this question is that businesses would not spend over $140 billion on advertising if it did not contribute to corporate profitability. However, the prudent advertiser knows that advertising is only a contributing factor to overall profits.

Once we acknowledge the supplementary role of advertising in creating sales, we can make a more reasoned judgment of its value. As we discussed in Chapter 2, advertising can accomplish a number of goals and occupies a greater or lesser place in the marketing mix depending on the specific objectives of a firm. However, few products can be successfully introduced and marketed without advertising. The requirements of a self-service economy and the economies of scale achieved by mass production demand high levels of product awareness only feasible through advertising.

A leading promotion executive, Larry Light, points out that profitability and a company's continued success are based on three factors:

1. *Reliability.* You must start with a reliable product or service. But above all, you must make product and service promises that people can rely on. Reliability isn't something that happens inside the product; reliability is something that happens inside the customer's mind.

2. *Reputation.* Reputation is the result of every contact with the customer.

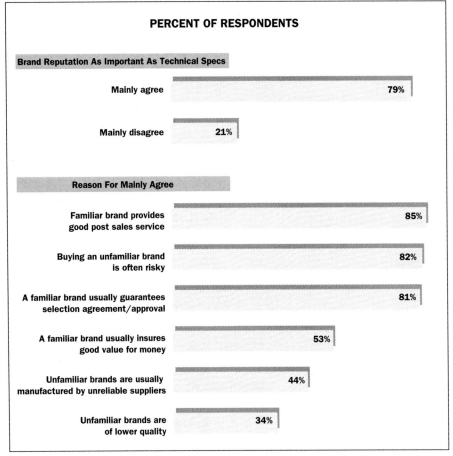

PERCENT OF RESPONDENTS

Brand Reputation As Important As Technical Specs

Mainly agree — 79%

Mainly disagree — 21%

Reason For Mainly Agree

Familiar brand provides good post sales service — 85%

Buying an unfamiliar brand is often risky — 82%

A familiar brand usually guarantees selection agreement/approval — 81%

A familiar brand usually insures good value for money — 53%

Unfamiliar brands are usually manufactured by unreliable suppliers — 44%

Unfamiliar brands are of lower quality — 34%

(Source: Cahners-Simmons Affinity Index)

3. *Rank.* In business as in life, how you rate is interesting, how you rank is everything. . . . Be a leader in every market in which you choose to compete. . . . Remember this law. We call it the Law of Dominance. One is wonderful, two is terrific, three is threatened, four is fatal.[4]

Profitability depends on a good, reliable product that is perceived in that way, a reputation that is built by strong equity-oriented advertising, and a market rank that is built by advertising and enhanced by promotion. It is clear that profits are based on brand reputation, and reputation is determined in large measure by a combination of marketing communication techniques.

Exhibit 26.4 shows that those companies with the highest market share are also likely to spend the most on media advertising as a share of market sales. Clearly, companies regard traditional advertising as a critical element in maintaining market share, and those companies that are most dominant are both able and willing to invest the most dollars to maintain their high share levels. These data also demonstrate that advertising is not only important in achieving initial success but is utilized to continue dominance by leading firms in various product categories.

Even the harshest critics of advertising acknowledge its place in modern selling. Increasingly, criticism of advertising is directed toward its form and execution rather than arguments concerning whether it should exist. The value

---

[4]Larry Light, "At the Center of It All Is the Brand," *Advertising Age,* March 29, 1993, p. 22.

EXHIBIT

26.4

· · · · · · · · · · · · · · · · · · ·

The higher a company's market share, the more it typically spends on media advertising.

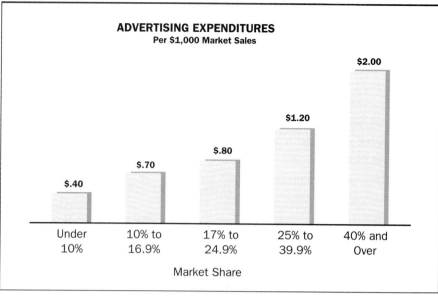

ADVERTISING EXPENDITURES
Per $1,000 Market Sales

$2.00

$1.20

$.80

$.70

$.40

| Under 10% | 10% to 16.9% | 17% to 24.9% | 25% to 39.9% | 40% and Over |

Market Share

(Courtesy: Cahners Publishing Company)

of advertising is best demonstrated by the dependency on advertising as a primary sales tool of so many firms.

Contributions of Advertising to the Overall Welfare of the Economy. Economic productivity must be viewed from the perspective of both the individual firm and the total economy. Clearly, single corporations must advertise to prevent brand-share erosion even in the absence of overall sales increases in a particular industry or in total gross national product (GNP). However, most economists are interested in advertising from a macroeconomic perspective. That is, what does advertising contribute to the overall economic system rather than to a specific firm? Does it efficiently introduce new products and create jobs?

Currently, American advertising accounts for approximately 2.5 percent of the national GNP. While this figure is less than a comparable investment 50 years ago, it still represents a tremendous expenditure. Economists view advertising's contribution to the economy as falling into one of four categories:

1. *Counterproductive.* That is, advertising is counterproductive when it raises prices or in some other way creates dissatisfaction with products that still have utility, thus causing unnecessary consumption.

2. *Unproductive.* Unproductive advertising that does not increase generic demand but causes no harm. Advertising designed to create brand switching among present consumers would fall into this category.

3. *Somewhat productive.* Advertising in this category creates an increase in overall demand, but at a level lower than some other technique or at an unreasonably high cost.

4. *Most productive.* The most productive advertising produces the greatest economic well-being at the lowest cost. The implication of this category is that both buyer and seller benefit equally.

It is difficult to deal in generalities when evaluating the economic value of advertising. Advertising's contribution to product sales is dependent on a host

EXHIBIT

26.5

Advertising investments can contribute to lower consumer prices for many products.

WITHOUT ADVERTISING, THE PRICE OF A JAR OF HONEY COULD REALLY STING YOU.

It's basic economics. The more people who know about a product, the more people are likely to buy it. The more product you sell, the less you have to charge for it. Advertising is the medium that brings the message to millions. It helps increase the volume of sales and decrease the cost. So whether it's a jar of honey or a jar of pickles, advertising helps keep a lid on the price.

Advertising. That's the way it works.

INTERNATIONAL ADVERTISING ASSOCATION

The global partnership of advertisers, agencies and media

(Courtesy: International Advertising Association.)

of circumstances unique to each product. The utility of advertising in a market for a relatively new product such as home computers is much different from advertising for the beer or cigarette industries, which are characterized by flat sales and brand switching among present users. However, it is obvious that overall advertising does contribute to profitability or companies would not use it (see Exhibit 26.5).

THE SOCIAL ROLE OF ADVERTISING

There is little disagreement, even among advertising's harshest critics, that it serves a useful role in informing customers of new products, location, prices, and distribution outlets. These are the economic functions of the institution of advertising. What is less clear, and the topic of growing discussion in a number of quarters, is the social role of advertising.

While there is significant controversy as to the positive social benefits that advertising contributes to society, there is general agreement that the advertising functions in two distinctive ways as a social force. First is the so-called *inadvertent* social role of advertising. Some people claim that the manner in which advertising portrays various segments of society—the elderly, minority groups, the young, etc.—determines in some measure how these people will be treated by others.

Dear Santa,
I want
1) A PONY
2) A Racecar
3) Daddy to stop hitting me

"All I want for Christmas is my two front teeth that dad knocked out."

Safety shouldn't be a child's wish;
it should be his right.
If you or anyone you know is a
victim of child abuse we can help!

Please write to us at:
National Committee for
Prevention of Child Abuse
P.O. Box 2866 K
Chicago, IL 60690

(Courtesy: Newspaper Association of America Foundation and Jeff Graham.)

EXHIBIT

26.6

· · · · · · · · · · · · · · · · · · ·

Increasingly, advertising is used to address serious social issues.

The second social role of advertising is *overt*. When advertising champions the fight against child abuse, forest fires, or drugs, or promotes adult literacy or higher levels of voter turnout, it is being used in a social activist role. Exhibit 26.6 is an example of advertising used for an overtly social purpose. In the past decade, we have seen a significant growth in this type of advertising as more and more special-interest groups have seen the value and efficiency of advertising in getting their messages before the public.

A review of contemporary advertising criticism vividly points out the important role that social issues play in debate concerning the value and propriety of modern advertising. Most criticism falls into one or more of the following four categories:

The Content of Advertising

The most widespread criticism of advertising concerns the execution of specific ads and commercials. The use of sexual themes, debasement of language by using misspelled words and incorrect grammar, the creation of stereotypes, and the pandering to children are among the most often heard criticisms. As we saw in Chapter 25, the advertising industry is attempting to address the problem of children's advertising through the Children's Advertising Review Unit of the NARB.

Criticism of advertising content focuses on two primary issues. The first is the portrayal of some group in an unflattering or unrealistic manner. In recent years, the advertising industry has taken positive steps to correct this situation. For example, companies including Saturn automobiles, BellSouth, and Reebok have featured women as the centerpiece of their advertising in recent years. In the future, we will see an even more realistic view of society in contemporary advertising. While these changes are the ethical and proper thing for companies to do for their own sake, it is also good business.

It is estimated that by the year 2000, 60 percent of women will be earning money outside the home, an increase from 10 percent in 1950. More importantly, women are the primary decision makers for many major purchases. Today, women buy 50 percent of automobiles and life insurance, make 45 percent of car rentals, and own 42 percent of all stock. When companies create realistic advertising it is a recognition of both their social responsibility and the realities of the marketplace.[5]

Not only women, but minority groups also have received more favorable treatment in advertising in recent years. While we do see African American and Hispanic families as the focus of more commercials, there is still significant disagreement as to whether or not advertising has done enough to properly portray various groups in a realistic fashion. Simply including a person in a commercial is not the same as placing that person in a proper social context.

For example, even among advertising industry executives, there is wide disagreement as to whether enough is being done to realistically show African Americans in ads and commercials. In an *Advertising Age* survey of advertising practitioners, 40.8 percent of respondents thought there are "enough black people in print ads," while 54.8 percent thought there were too few. TV com-

---

[5]Jeffry Scott, "Women & Advertising," *Atlanta Journal*, July 6, 1993, p. C1.

mercials received similar results, with 52.4 percent thinking there were too few blacks in commercials and 42.3 thinking the number was "about right."

African Americans are particularly sensitive to the problem of inclusion without consideration of the portrayals of blacks. Valerie Graves, a senior advertising executive, points out that, "Most smart advertisers have some African American representation in their commercials, but that's a far cry from having our culture and concerns as the focus of the action. You see an African American there but he's not doing anything, not making any contribution, and that might contribute to a second-class citizen mentality."[6]

A second content-oriented criticism focuses on factors such as exaggeration and excessive puffery in advertising. Many critics charge that advertising is likely to provide misinformation that barely skirts basic legal requirements with negative appeals or, in some cases, outright falsehoods. As we discussed in Chapter 25, there is no business enterprise that undergoes more governmental and regulatory scrutiny than advertising. But apart from these formal constraints, advertisers know that it is bad business to mislead consumers. While false or misleading advertising may influence a consumer to make an initial purchase, rarely will a dissatisfied consumer return. Putting aside the question of whether or not advertising is inherently less ethical than other business practices, we should at least give its practitioners credit for common sense.

The Product Being Advertised

This criticism is probably the most frustrating to advertisers. They argue that it is unfair to single out particular products for censure simply because some segment of the population doesn't feel comfortable or is personally opposed to them. In recent years, the most vocal public opposition has been against tobacco and alcoholic beverage advertising. Of course, critics have been successful in eliminating at least certain types of these ads, particularly on broadcast media. Even when there is no legal or regulatory ban on advertising for a product category, public opinion plays a major role in advertising decisions. In June 1993, the *Seattle Times* announced that it would no longer accept cigarette advertising. In making the announcement, the *Times* publisher cited concerns for readers' health. The decision was criticized by tobacco industry groups as impeding freedom of speech.[7]

Due to the potential health hazards associated with both tobacco and alcohol, critics have gained widespread public support and even grudging acknowledgment of the problem in some advertising circles. However, it is much more difficult for advertising to deal with those who want to ban advertising for condoms, personal hygiene items, and other controversial products. Advertisers argue that public criticism of this type of advertising is unrealistic and tries to prevent society from gaining useful information about legitimate products.

Excessive Advertising Exposure

Another commonly heard criticism of advertising is that there is simply too much of it and that it is often intrusive. Most of the criticism in this cate-

---

[6]Adrienne Ward, "What Role Do Ads Play in Racial Tension?" *Advertising Age*, August 10, 1992, p. 35.
[7]"Seattle Times to ban cigarette ads," *Atlanta Journal*, June 15, 1993, p. F3.

gory is directed toward television, since print ads are easily ignored by simply turning the page. As we indicated in Chapter 13, both direct mail and telemarketing are fighting a constant battle against those who wish to place legal restrictions against the use of these promotional techniques.

While we are some years away from the general introduction of the new technology discussed in Chapter 8, the fragmentation and interactive nature of future media vehicles will no doubt curtail a major portion of this criticism. Obviously, when interactive media allow consumers to seek out programming, advertising, or infomercials, there is little likelihood that advertising will be regarded as intrusive.

Advertising's Unwanted Influences on Society

Much of the criticisms in this category are more urban legend than scientific fact. But like all legends, they have taken on a life of their own, and no amount of argument will dissuade those who view advertising as the devil incarnate.

Charges that advertising *makes* people buy things they don't want or need, lowers morals, and generally exploits the most susceptible segments of society are among the most common in this category of criticism. Most research shows that mass communication, especially overtly persuasive communication such as advertising, has a very difficult time making even small changes in behavioral intentions or attitudes. The idea that we see an ad and are compelled against our wishes to purchase a product is preposterous. Like any mass communication, there are going to be times when some reader or listener behaves in a manner totally contrary to the intent of the sender of the message. It is interesting that the overwhelming criticism in this fourth category is designed to protect other people, not the critics themselves. That is, most critics take the view that while a particular advertising element will not fool them, they are duty bound to help those less intelligent who may be misled by some advertising ploy.

A brief review of the history of advertising and its critics demonstrates that both have changed markedly over the past 130 years. Clearly, advertisers are asked to meet different standards than those of earlier years. The public view of advertising has changed over three major periods:

1. *The Era of Exaggerated Claims, 1865–1900.* During this period most people accepted advertising as "buyer beware" communication, where virtually any claim for a product was allowed. Some advertising claims, especially for patent medicine, were so outlandish that one wonders how anyone could have believed them.

2. *The Era of Public Awareness, 1900–1965.* By the turn of the century, legislation such as the Pure Food and Drug Act of 1906 demonstrated a recognition that the public was demanding a truthful portrayal of products and services. Many responsible advertisers feared for the very existence of the industry as deceptive advertising became more and more prevalent during the closing years of the nineteenth century.

3. *The Era of Social Responsibility, 1965–present.* During the past 25 years, advertisers have come to realize that literal truth is not sufficient to meet the demands of many consumers. Advertisers know that they must meet a stan-

Social responsibility
The demand that advertising be aware of its responsibility to the public. It should not only sell goods and services.

dard of social responsibility in addition to providing truthful advertising. The consumer movement of the 1960s, concerns with environmental safety, and a heightened awareness of social issues are reflected in modern advertising.

You will recall in Chapter 25 that we discussed the formal regulatory constraints on advertising. In addition to these organizations, there are a number of consumer and public policy groups that seek to constrain deceptive or misleading advertising through publicity. Among the many groups that publicize advertising that they think fails to meet adequate standards of serving consumers are the following:

1. *The Center for Science in the Public Interest* presents the annual Harlan Page Hubbard Memorial Award to those advertisers who have failed to serve the public interest. The award "honors" the nineteenth-century ad man who touted such products as Lydia Pinkham's Vegetable Compound, which promised cures for ailments from cancer to impotence.

2. *The Center for Auto Safety* presents "lemons" to automotive related advertising that it thinks is misleading or incomplete.

3. *Kids against Junk Food* publicizes advertising claims that it thinks may encourage children to choose junk food over items that are more nutritious.

4. *The Safe Energy Communications Council* monitors energy companies and publicizes their advertising if it thinks it is giving incomplete or misleading information.[8]

These and dozens of other consumer advocacy groups have no official or legal authority. They do have the ability to muster negative public opinion and provide national scrutiny for dubious product advertising. No reputable company wants to receive this type of notoriety and will usually respond to these consumer organizations in a positive manner if they think the criticism is justified.

INADVERTENT SOCIAL IMPLICATIONS OF ADVERTISING

Inadvertent role of advertising

Advertising sometimes communicates social messages unintended by the advertiser. Stereotyping and less-than-flattering portrayals of individuals and ethnic or social audience segments can lead to negative perceptions of advertising.

As we have seen in our discussion of common criticisms of advertising, most of the criticism of advertising comes from the social aspects of advertising that are not necessarily intended by its sponsor. For example, *Advertising Age* columnist Bob Garfield took General Tire Company to task for what he regarded as ethnic stereotyping in its commercial for Hydro 2000 tires, which portrayed an Indian family oblivious to a torrential rainstorm. To the extent that the commercial projected racial stereotypes, this was certainly not the intent of General Tire. However, as Garfield pointed out, the standards of "good" advertising go beyond factual product information and involve elements such as the sensitive depiction of cultures.

Some argue that American society is too ready to jump on any misstep, no matter how innocuous, in the name of political correctness. Others view a healthy trend where advertisers are becoming more sensitive to the potential harm they may cause my using humor at the expense of others. The reality of the situation was summed up by one advertising executive who said, "The

---

[8]"Lemon Awards," *Athens Daily News,* January 28, 1994, p. 6B.

problem is there are so many sensitivities that it's a question of walking through a mine field. The real lesson learned is that before you get into anything with any ethnic or social overtones you have to be sure that the return is worth the risk."

Garfield summed up his criticism of the General Tire spot, "a TV commercial is not a TV show, and it is no place for dancing on the border of social satire and mean-spirited ridicule. What advertising *is* a place for is selling."[9] In addition to the issue of sensitivity, the recent debate has brought to the forefront the matter of advertising's social role. This awareness of a dimension long ignored by most advertisers is perhaps the most positive element to come out of these recent controversies.

OVERT USE OF ADVERTISING FOR SOCIAL CAUSES

In the preceding section we discussed components of advertising that may be construed as inadvertently contributing to some social action. In this section, we will discuss a much more important use of advertising in a social context —that is, the overt use of advertising to further some social agenda or nonprofit organization. For example, the Kentucky Literacy Commission uses advertising to promote adult literacy in the state (see Exhibit 26.7).

The same characteristics that make advertising such a beneficial tool in marketing products and services are also used to move people to adopt various social causes and support for nonprofit organizations. For some time, advertising has been used to promote these organizations. However, in the past decade both the amount and quality of such advertising have increased markedly (see Exhibit 26.8).

In recent years a number of civic, religious, and public policy organizations have increasingly used advertising to disseminate their messages to the widest possible audience. For example, college and universities throughout the nation find themselves under severe budget pressure. At one time, college fundraising solicitations were confined to alumni magazines and telemarketing and direct-mail campaigns targeted to alumni. Now we are seeing more general appeals to both alumni and the general public (see Exhibit 26.9).

The most organized effort of social advocacy is the Advertising Council, which we mentioned briefly in Chapter 1.

The Advertising Council[10]

From its inception in 1943 as the War Advertising Council to the present, the council has contributed billions of dollars of advertising space and creative talent to solving a number of social ills. The War Advertising Council campaigns had the strident tone of war (see Exhibit 26.10), but the success of the council during World War II showed that advertising could be a powerful tool for unifying the public and for effecting change in attitudes toward less clearly defined goals in peacetime.

During the early years of the council, a variety of topics were promoted. Some such as wearing seat belts or getting chest X-rays were noncontroversial and

---

[9]Bob Garfield, "Ethnic Jokes and Tires a Bad Mix for Reiman," *Advertising Age,* May 24, 1993, p. 50.
[10]Information in this section was provided by the Advertising Council.

EXHIBIT
26.7

A creative approach to
a serious problem.

THE CATCHER
IN THE RYE

J. D. SALINGER

Why ban it when 3 out of 10 adult Kentuckians can't read it?

Some people in our state have worked hard to rid libraries of books they deem offensive. Soon, they may not have to work as hard to censor these books – few people will be able to read them.

There are 400,000 adult non-readers in Kentucky and the number is growing. Let's concentrate our hard work on teaching these people the skills they need to read and write. If you know any adult non-readers, help them enroll in a Kentucky Literacy Commission reading program.

We can teach them to read at their own pace in private sessions. The instruction is free. To find out more, call 1-800-928-7323.

Kentucky Literacy Commission
Teaching adult Kentuckians to read.

An Agency of Workforce Development Cabinet

(Courtesy: Doe-Anderson Advertising Agency.)

readily understood by the public. Other issues were much more complex, such as racial tolerance, equal rights, and opportunities for education, jobs, and housing.

Advertising Council
A non-profit network of agencies, media, and advertisers dedicated to promoting social programs through advertising.

The Advertising Council continues to select, define, and address some of the nation's most pressing problems, but only those problems that a public informed through advertising could help solve. Familiar figures have become synonymous with its work, Smokey the Bear, the Crying Indian who wept for a land once beautiful (see Exhibit 26.11), and McGruff, the spokesdog for crime prevention (see Exhibit 26.12), among others. The Advertising Council pioneered in bringing issues like child abuse, understanding mental illness, and AIDS to the public's attention, and in advocating actions people can take to prevent inhumanity, discrimination, and the spread of disease. Council programs will result in the donation of over $1.5 billion worth of time and space in 1994.

In the past, a major problem facing the council was a lack of provable results. While product advertising can point to sales or other objective criteria to show its value, it is much harder to trace the value of a public-service cam-

(Courtesy: Evans Group.)

EXHIBIT

26.8

Advertising is used by a number of social service agencies to promote their organizations.

paign. However, recently the council sponsored a research study to determine the value of a campaign to encourage people to have regular checks for colon cancer. Results were extremely positive, with awareness of the value of colon cancer checkups going from 11 percent prior to the advertising to 40 percent after one year. More importantly, the campaign resulted in a 28.6 percent increase in people consulting their doctor about colon cancer checkups.

Due in large measure to the efforts of the Advertising Council, the use of advertising to communicate social issues has been taken up by a number of other companies and organizations. Social institutions such as churches have turned to advertising, and advocacy advertising has also been used by corporations that believe that media presentations of certain issues have been unfair and want to get their side of a story to the public. While some people have reservations about the role of advertising in promoting certain social institutions and issues, proponents argue that there is no more effective or inexpensive means of getting their messages to the public.

In the future, we can expect this type of advertising to increase as people accept the legitimate role of the mass media as a forum for public debate as well as product information. The availability of media with narrowly defined audiences, such as cable and specialized publications, will lead to even more, and perhaps franker, discussions of a host of nonproduct and sometimes controversial topics.

As the use of advocacy advertising has grown in recent years, so has the reluctance of some media to carry these ads. Media outlets sometimes think that

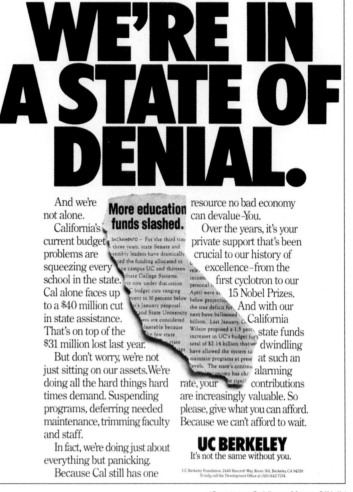

(Courtesy: Goldberg Moser O'Neil.)

carrying a particularly controversial ad will imply an endorsement of the position. In other cases, media have been reluctant to carry ads that attack major advertisers, fearing a loss of advertising revenue. The 4A's has urged media to protect the flow of ideas by allowing wide latitude in accepting advocacy advertising. As it rightfully points out, advertising clearly identifies the sponsor of a message and therefore diminishes the chances of confusion between the views of the sponsor and those of the media carrying the message.

Advertising and Cause-Related Marketing

Cause-related marketing

Marketing strategies that attempt to link a company to some social or charitable cause.

It would be a mistake to consider socially responsible advertising and marketing as being in some fundamental conflict with good business practice. To the contrary, responsible behavior is rarely an impediment to profit and can often be the focus of promotions to consumers.

In recent years we have seen a number of advertisers that linked their sales message with some worthy cause. American Express is credited with introducing *cause-related* marketing in 1983 when it promised to make a donation to the renovation of the Statue of Liberty each time someone used its card. Cause-related marketing allows both companies and their customers to help some organization, while the company increases sales. A poll by Roper and Cone Communications in Boston indicated that "66 percent of con-

The War Advertising
Council was a partner
in the war effort during
World War II.

(Courtesy: The Advertising Council.)

sumers will choose a product with a relationship with a cause or charitable organization over others in its category if it's also competitive in price and quality."[11]

Like any marketing execution, cause-related marketing should have a clear objective. Some examples of the ways cause-related marketing has been used by some firms include the following:

1. *Global marketing.* Avon advocates different issues in each of its markets. For example, in the United States, it's breast cancer research; in Malaysia, violence against women; in China, child nourishment; and in Thailand, AIDS prevention.

2. *Short-term promotion.* In 1993, American Express offered to donate two cents per transaction to Share Our Strength, an antihunger organization.

3. *Image building.* Coors Brewing pledged $40 million over five years to literacy organizations and public service advertising for literacy.

4. *Marketing to women.* Midas issues certificates for Midas service to anyone buying a Century 1000 STE car seat for children.[12]

---

[11]Nancy Arnott, "Marketing with a Passion," *Sales & Marketing Management,* January 1994, p. 65.
[12]Geoffrey Smith and Ron Stodghill, "Are Good Causes Good Marketing?" *Business Week,* March 21, 1994, p. 64.

EXHIBIT
26.11

One of the Ad Council's
most famous
campaigns.

(Courtesy: Keep America Beautiful, Inc.)

Environment Marketing

In recent years, environmental concerns have become so important that they have become an important part of the marketing plans of many companies. The environment has not only provided marketers with opportunities to promote environmentally sound practices but, in many cases, has been mandated by consumers. This so-called green marketing movement was once thought to be a passing fad of the 1980s. However, environmental concerns related to packaging, product development, and other marketing issues have only grown stronger in the 1990s.

The move toward environmentally responsible purchasing has become more formalized with the introduction of the *Green Seal*. A voluntary organization, "Green Seal will make it easier for consumers to translate attitudes into action. After two years of development, the first Green Seal goes to an American bathroom and facial tissue company, which complies with all requirements, including 100 percent recovered material, a high percentage of post-consumer material, and no chlorine bleach."[13] Eventually, Green Seal hopes to have 31 product categories, each with its own compliance standards, eligible for the seal.

In an *Advertising Age* study, 85 percent of respondents thought that American business should be doing more to become environmentally responsible.

---

[13]S. K. List, "The Green Seal of Eco-Approval," *American Demographics*, January 1993, p. 9.

The Ad Council made America safer with its crime awareness campaign.

(Courtesy: The Advertising Council.)

More importantly, the same study indicated that 73 percent of consumers purchased products as a result of environmental claims (see Exhibit 26.13). Given the importance of environmental issues on purchase behavior, it is obvious that a number of product categories fall short of consumer expectations (see Exhibit 26.14).

Unfortunately, a number of companies have tried to take advantage of the green marketing movement with claims that cannot be substantiated. One problem is that there are no federal government guidelines for many terms such as *recyclable, biodegradable, compostable,* etc. This lack of standards is not only confusing to companies, but also allows wide discretion in the use of the terms. In addition, where state standards have been developed they are often different, making it impossible for a national firm to comply.

In July 1992, the FTC issued the first national guidelines for environmental marketing claims. The guidelines are voluntary but offer guidance that, if adhered to, will prevent a firm from being subject to federal regulatory action. The commission is especially interested in unqualified general claims of environmental benefits such as "biodegradable or compostable." Below are two examples of the FTC guidelines:

1. An ad touting a package as "50 percent more recycled content than before" could be misleading if the recycled content had increased from 2 percent to 3 percent.

EXHIBIT

26.13

Advertising must consider environmental issues in their promotional messages.

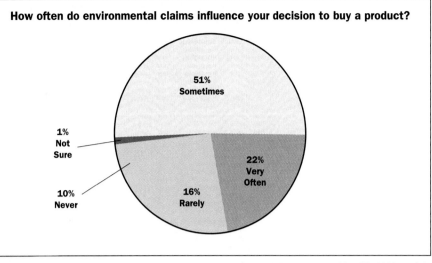

How often do environmental claims influence your decision to buy a product?

51%
Sometimes

1%
Not
Sure

22%
Very
Often

10%
Never

16%
Rarely

(Source: Advertising Age, May 29, 1992, p. S-4.)

2. An ad touting a shampoo bottle as containing "20 percent more recycled content" would be considered misleading if it didn't say whether the product is being compared with a rival or the product's previous container.[14]

Advertisers must realize that they are dealing with committed, sophisticated consumers who are deadly serious about environmental issues. A study by the Roper Organization showed that the number of serious environmental consumers (which they call True-Blue Greens) increased over 80 percent from 1990 to 1992.[15]

EXHIBIT

26.14

Many product categories have significant problems with environmentally aware consumers.

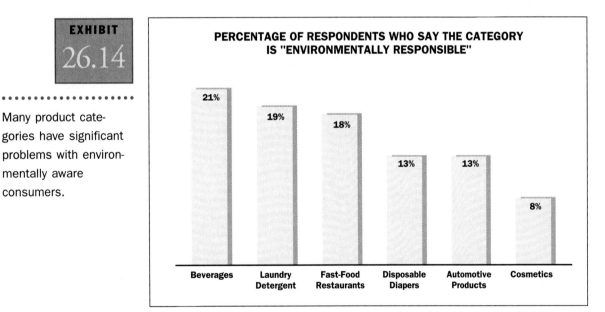

PERCENTAGE OF RESPONDENTS WHO SAY THE CATEGORY IS "ENVIRONMENTALLY RESPONSIBLE"

Beverages	Laundry Detergent	Fast-Food Restaurants	Disposable Diapers	Automotive Products	Cosmetics
21%	19%	18%	13%	13%	8%

(Source: Advertising Age, May 29, 1992, p. S-4.)

[14]Steven W. Colford, "FTC Green Guidelines May Spark Ad Efforts," *Advertising Age,* August 3, 1992, p. 29.
[15]List, "Green Seal of Eco-Approval," p. 9.

Marketers are finding that an environmental initiative is not an option. Consumers are increasingly demanding that some evidence of environmental responsibility be evident in a company's products, or they will buy alternatives. However, paying lip service to the problem is not enough; words must be backed up with actions.

In a study conducted by the Peter Hart Organization, results showed that consumers do boycott products for environmental and political concerns (for example, made in China). However, the study indicated that fewer than 1 percent of consumers would boycott on the basis of morality or violence. According to these results, a company runs a much greater risk of consumer backlash if it is identified as an environmental polluter than if it runs advertising on an adult TV show such as *NYPD Blue*."[16] It is clear that environmental marketing is an area that companies must deal with on a serious basis.

Another approach to environmental marketing is demonstrated when companies join with an environmental organization to raise money for their causes and promote the company at the same time. For example, Miller Brewing Company made a $1 million contribution to Nature Conservancy and backed it with a heavy TV and print campaign, and Glidden Co. sponsored a promotional campaign called "Clean Air for Kids," which included a $60,000 donation to the National Audubon Society.

However, companies cannot simply give money to some environmental cause and become a member in good standing of the green community. When companies that have a less than stellar record of environmental responsibility start giving money to various projects and promoting these donations heavily, environmentalists accuse them of "green washing." Activists regard this cynical approach to the environmental issue as worse than doing nothing.[17]

ADVERTISING AND ETHICAL CONSIDERATIONS

It is not surprising that advertising, with its high visibility and overtly persuasive intent, is the target of both criticism and charges of unethical conduct. To this point we have discussed a number of the major types of advertising criticism from both an economic and social perspective. In this section, we are going to examine two specific ethical questions that both advertisers and media face from time to time.

Advertising Interference in the Editorial Process

In the summer of 1993, Mercedes-Benz announced that it would bar any American magazine from carrying Mercedes-Benz advertising if the publication placed Mercedes ads adjacent to negative articles about the carmaker or Germany itself. The company quickly scuttled this idea in the face of critical industry and press reaction.[18] However, the incident pointed up the continuing criticism that advertisers sometimes influences, or attempts to influence, the editorial content of media. Obviously, this is a serious charge, since one of the positive features of an advertising-supported press system is that

[16]Jenny Pfalzgraf, "Boycott Phobia, " *American Advertising*, Summer 1994, p. 18.
[17]Jeffery D. Zbar, "Environmental Marketing, " *Advertising Age*, June 28, 1993, p. S-2.
[18]Eugene Secunda, "Ad-Editorial Wall Crumbling," *Advertising Age*, October 4, 1993, p. 34.

it allows the media to function without the constraints of either government or special-interest groups.

The dilemma of separating advertising and editorial functions is not a new problem. It may have begun when the first advertiser met the first publisher. In 1911, the famous publisher and newspaper owner E. W. Scripps summed up the uneasy relationship with advertising, "The big advertiser is the mortal foe of honest journalism. I would rather go through a dark alley with a thug than to couple up, in a business way, as a young newspaperman, with a big advertising patron." Scripps' views have been echoed by both broadcasters and print journalists throughout this century.

Most advertising executives, like their editorial counterparts, see the demands for editorial control by advertisers as both unethical and bad business. By the same token, they argue that it makes no sense to buy advertising in media that are critical of their products or companies. You will recall that in Chapter 11 we discussed the importance of the qualitative aspects of advertising's association with media. Many media offer a higher degree of credibility to advertisers simply because the public regards a particular magazine, newspaper, or broadcast vehicle as being honest and responsible. If this media credibility is tainted by a public perception that the editorial content is "for sale," it can only be to the detriment of both the medium and the advertising it carries.

A second point made by advertisers is that if a medium is for sale to one advertiser, it stands to reason that it is for sale to others. How much value is there in having you and your competitors buying time and space in a medium that will soon be regarded as nothing more than a public relations vehicle for any business or special-interest group with enough advertising dollars to put pressure on its owner?

There are no good reasons, ethical, moral, or economic, to have advertisers pressure the media to change or delete stories or commentary. That is why recent indications of advertising pressure being applied to media, especially newspapers, is so depressing.

A survey of daily newspaper editors indicated that 71 percent said they were pressured to kill stories; 93 percent said advertisers threatened to withdraw advertising because of content disputes; and 89 percent said advertisers had carried through on the threats. Even more distressing is the fact that 37 percent of these editors reported that advertisers succeeded in influencing news and features. More than half, 55 percent, said there was pressure from *within* the newspaper to write or tailor stories to please advertisers.

The study also found that while large and small newspapers were equally likely to be approached by advertisers, smaller, and presumably less financially strong, newspapers were more likely to cave in to these demands.[19] While this particular study dealt only with newspapers, there have also been reports in recent years of major national advertisers applying the same tactics to TV networks and magazines. Regardless of how often it happens, and once is one too many, it is a practice that the advertising community and public should strongly condemn, and the media should make it clear that any approach by an advertiser will be reported as a news story.

---

[19]"Ad Pressure Still Prevails," *Presstime,* February 1993, p. 9.

The Advertorial

A second ethical concern of many media executives is the growing use of the advertorial and especially advertorial sections, often sponsored by a single company or organization. The origin of the advertorial is simple enough. A company, special-interest group, or other organization would place an ad to promote an idea rather than a product. The term *advertorial* suggests that the advertiser is placing a clearly identified message (or editorial) to bring some topic to the attention of readers or listeners. In principle, the idea is worthwhile and some would argue in the finest traditions of a free press.

Since the early 1980s, the use of the advertorial has changed dramatically, and its critics would say for the worst. Today, many advertorials are in the form of special sections that look very much like the editorial matter of a newspaper or magazine. These special sections are devoted to topics such as lawn care or the purchase of automobiles. Some sections are sponsored by foreign countries such as Turkey or Saudi Arabia and include lengthy pieces on economic and cultural issues. Sometimes the sections are liberally sprinkled with advertisements for a single sponsor or a number of related companies.

The difference between these advertorial sections and the rest of the publication is that rather than being written by the editorial staff, they are produced by advertising copywriters or public relations specialists. The "editorial" matter is an extension of the advertising and is totally dictated by the sponsor of the section.

Both newspaper and magazine editors view the trend toward advertorials as an uneasy alliance. It is estimated that magazine advertorials (also called *feature advertising*) bring in over $230 million in revenues. While many editors accept the financial inevitability of the continued use of the advertorial, Ruth Whitney, editor-in-chief of *Glamour*, summed up the feelings of many editors, "The only thing that's bad about them is the effort to deceive the reader, which was really their purpose in the beginning, to convince the reader that this was editorial material. It's imitation editorial."

It is obvious that the advertorial or feature advertising section is a permanent addition to the print landscape. In broadcasting, many would compare some of the talk-show format infomercials, discussed in Chapter 8, to the print advertorial. In order to protect the public from being misled by advertorials, both the American Society of Magazine Editors and individual newspapers have developed guidelines for their use. Some common rules for advertorial use are as follows:

1. Advertising supplements should not use the standard body type or headline type used by the news department.

2. The supplement's cover should carry clear identification that it is a sponsored piece, preferably above or below the nameplate.

3. The identification of the sponsor and who prepared the copy should be placed in a dominant position toward the front of the supplement.

4. Each page should be marked "Paid Advertising Supplement."

Of course, each publication will adopt its own guidelines for its advertisers. However, it is important that the reader is completely aware of the advertising nature of the piece. Studies indicate that readers are willing to accept advertorials, but only if they know immediately that what they are reading is a paid advertisement. If readers think they have been misled, both the advertiser and the publication risk a serious loss of credibility with their readers.[20]

SUMMARY

As we conclude our discussion of the diverse field of advertising, it is fitting that we examine the ethical, social, and economic contributions of advertising. As we have seen, there are no easy answers to many of the questions raised by both critics and proponents of advertising. Advertisers, their agencies, and the media constantly wrestle with ethical problems of content, presentation, and the acceptability of a host of product categories, claims, and advertising practices. These problems do not have easy solutions and must be handled on a case-by-case basis.

While advertising cannot ignore questions of taste, sexual portrayals, treatment of ethnic groups and women, and other social issues, it cannot be held captive to every criticism. In the end, advertisers will have to follow the advice of one industry executive who said that they must carefully consider all criticism but follow their own conscience and sense of values.

Advertising industry leaders are increasingly concerned about the attacks made on legal and truthful advertising by critics who fail to see the economic and social value of unencumbered communication. As Howard Bell, past CEO of the American Advertising Federation, pointed out, "The value-of-advertising message needs to be targeted to public opinion leaders . . . The message needs to emphasize that constitutional protection of commercial speech must be preserved, not for the benefit of the industry but because it benefits the people in a democratic society founded on the principle of free choice."[21]

The future of advertising will indeed be one of change and adaptation. The public interest will become an increasingly important part of the modern advertiser's agenda. It is very clear that advertising has reached a point of maturity where untruthful, misleading, and deceptive advertising is the great exception, practiced only by the short-termers and fast-buck artists. Contemporary advertising must incorporate the idea of social responsibility as routinely as it depends on a well thought out marketing plan for its success.

The future will be one of even more critical issues for the advertising industry. Technology will present advertisers with special problems and opportunities that are only now becoming apparent. For example, the issues of consumer privacy must be considered as our ability to gather more precise information about various target segments becomes more sophisticated. What is our responsibility in selling to children? Does advertising have a moral responsibility to refuse to sell products that are of little if any social benefit, even if these products are legal? Where is the line between acceptable product puffery and creative selling and exploitation? All questions with no easy answers.

---

[20]Rebecca Ross Albers, "When Is News Not News?" *Presstime,* April 1993, p. 52.
[21]Howard Bell, "Threat to Advertising's Freedom Is Real," *Advertising Age,* December 13, 1993, p. 20.

Questions

1. What is the primary economic advantage of advertising?
2. Why is it so difficult to trace the effects of advertising?
3. How is market share related to advertising?
4. What is the role of brand switching from a macro-advertising perspective?
5. What is meant by inadvertent social consequences of advertising?
6. Why do most advertisers oppose unethical advertising?
7. What were the three major periods of advertising from a social perspective?
8. Discuss the role of the Advertising Council.

Video Case

MARKETING SITUATION

The Edward J. DeBartolo Corporation is the nation's largest mall developer with about 70 properties. Sales and promotion participation levels had been stagnant in the mid-1990s. Retail space in the 1990s has consistently outpaced population growth. It has been difficult to create a competitive advantage. In many markets, regional malls share the same store mix, similar interior and exterior look, similar pricing, and retail promotion offers/events.

There have been declines in shopping frequency at malls in recent years. From 1988 to 1992, shoppers frequenting the mall at least once a month dropped from 52 percent to 41 percent.

CAMPAIGN OBJECTIVES

This Back-to-School promotion had five main objectives:

1. Generate mall traffic and purchasing. The goal was a 5–8 percent average sales increase per mall.
2. Encourage teenagers to spend *more* money in *more* stores.
3. Achieve a minimum of 50 percent retailer/tenant participation at all 68 participating malls.
4. Motivate mall personnel and encourage them to develop, low-cost campaign *add-ons* and stretch the media dollars for each mall. The goal was to achieve $300,000 in incremental media support.
5. Target and secure a *national* partner to reinforce image of the campaign and to offset promotion costs.

TARGET AUDIENCE

The audience for the Back-to-School campaign was:
Primary. Male and female teenagers 13–19 shopping for back-to-school needs.
Secondary. Mothers shopping for young school children.

CREATIVE STRATEGY

To develop an in-mall creative package that would:

1. Be entertaining for the high-energy teenage audience.
2. Position DeBartolo Malls as the place for back-to-school by communicating what makes them different.
3. Showcase purchase incentive that rewards shoppers for higher-than-normal spending and reinforces the image critical to teens.

4. Highlight the Back-to-School Savings Card, designed to encourage multiple-store visits.
5. Leverage of our promotional partner, Pepsi.
6. Create a sense of mallwide fun and excitement.

INTEGRATED PROGRAMS

1. Designed CD premium with Billboard Entertainment featuring established artists and emerging acts. It was offered free to shoppers who spent $100 during the period.
2. A Crystal Pepsi Cool Zone was constructed in each mall. Teenagers could stop for a free Crystal Pepsi, register for the Back-to-School Sweepstakes, and pick up their Back-to-Cool Savings Card.
3. DeBartolo Malls offered a $10,000 Shopping Spree as a grand prize in the Sweepstakes.

MEDIA STRATEGY

Television, radio, and newspaper ads were used to drive traffic into malls. A complete in-mall POP package was created to *drive* traffic through the malls. Scheduling, such as front loading, road blocking, sponsorships, and multiple spotting were used and value-added exposure opportunities were negotiated with key teen radio stations to extend the base buys.

EVIDENCE OF RESULTS

The results of the DeBartolo campaign included:

1. Mall traffic and retailer sales were impacted as 70,000 CD premiums were awarded during the first 14 days of the promotion, representing $10 million in mall sales. Sales were increased 10 percent over the previous season.
2. The expenditure during a mall visit is $70. During this promotion, the average rose to $100.
3. The retailer/tenant participation rate was 75 percent, exceeding the 50 percent objective.
4. Pepsi's TV tags for Crystal Pepsi added $500,000 to the schedule of TV flights. Over $1 million of Crystal Pepsi was distributed and over $100,000 in Pepsi prizes for the in-mall sweepstakes was awarded.
5. Two million Back-to-School Savings Cards were distributed, driving sales at the tenant level. And there were over 30,000 entries per mall in the sweepstakes.

Video Case

MARKETING SITUATION

PSE&G conducted research that determined that energy conservation was regarded as a major sacrifice with little savings in energy costs. Few customers thought there was a relationship between energy conservation and environmental concerns. A barrier to conservation is that it has a low awareness and importance level. Many of the factors that led to energy conservation in the 1970s were no longer apparent to the average customer.

Research found that if a linkage between energy conversation and environmental protection was communicated, consumers would be likely to adopt conservation measures. Research findings indicated that the public expected businesses to take a leadership role in energy conservation. PSE&G had to convince audiences of the importance of energy conservation programs.

CAMPAIGN OBJECTIVES

The primary public objectives of the campaign were to:
1. Reach 100 percent of PSE&G's customer base
2. Generate response and participation in PSE&G's Power Moves campaign
3. Show that energy conservation will help the environment
4. Position PSE&G as an innovative leader in New Jersey
5. Measure responses and begin to target audience segments

The primary business objectives of the campaign were to:
1. Save six million therms (gas) annually (two million from residential customers and four million from business customers)
2. Save 150 megawatts (electric) annually

TARGET AUDIENCE

There were four audience that the campaign sought to reach: residential customers (2.8 million), industrial, PSE&G employees, and legislators, regulators, shareholders.

CREATIVE STRATEGY

The Power Moves campaign strategy had a number of goals. It sought to establish a program name and to create awareness of Power Moves as a PSE&G program. It wanted to convince all audiences that Power Moves are an easy way to help the environment, and introduce a spokesperson who was credible. The first step in the campaign was the naming and testing of the Power Moves concept.

The rollout consisted of three segments: The introductory phase was designed to announce Power Moves. The commercial phase began two weeks into the introductory

period to get business participation and to show residential customers that businesses were making the effort to conserve. The residential campaign began shortly thereafter and gave customers Power Moves actions. P. J. Carlesimo, who was at that time basketball coach at Seton Hall University was signed as spokesman.

OTHER COMMUNICATION PROGRAMS

The campaign featured Energy Edition radio, a daily 90-second program providing customers with conservation tips. Brochures using a standardized graphic design were developed for the residential and business Power Moves programs. Employee programs were introduced consisting of a video and posters explaining Power Moves.

MEDIA STRATEGY

The objectives of the media strategy were to create awareness of the benefits of energy conservation and how PSE&G's program could benefit both the customer and the environment. Spot television and radio accounted for 71.6 percent of the budget, while 28.4 percent was allocated to print. Print advertising was designed to offer more detailed information than broadcast media.

The introductory phase ran for six weeks and included full-page newspaper ads, spot television, cable television, and spot radio. The industrial and commercial campaign ran in newspapers, spot radio, consumer business publications, and trade publications. The residential campaign ran in newspapers, consumer magazines, spot television, cable television, and radio.

EVIDENCE OF RESULTS

Responses to PSE&G's conservation center increased by 50 percent, or an additional 500 calls daily. Research showed:
1. Awareness of energy conservation increased from 29 to 39 percent.
2. Aided awareness of PSE&G's energy conservation programs increased from 49 to 64 percent.
3. Percentage of residential customers who feel that environmental issues do not get enough attention declined from 60 to 49.
4. Customers believing that helping the environment is related to energy conservation increased from 48 to 56 percent.
5. Advertising awareness for PSE&G increased 12 percentage points.
6. Aided awareness of Power Moves associated with PSE&G was 40 percent.

Glossary

A

Account planner. An outgrowth of British agency structure where a planner initiates and reviews research and participates in the creative process. In some agencies, the planner is considered a spokesperson for the consumer.

Ad banking. Practice of some magazines of clustering ads at the front and back of their publications.

Ad hoc network. Television networks consisting of affiliates that come together only for a special program such as a sporting event.

Added value. The assumption that advertising adds value to a product in the same way that manufacturing and distribution do.

Advertising clearance process. The internal process of clearing ads for publication and broadcast, conducted primarily by ad agencies and clients.

Advertising Council. A non-profit network of agencies, media, and advertisers dedicated to promoting social programs through advertising.

Advertising goals. The communication objectives designed to accomplish certain tasks within the total marketing program.

Advertising objectives. Those specific outcomes that are to be accomplished through advertising.

American Association of Advertising Agencies (AAAA, 4 As). The national organization of advertising agencies.

American Society of Newspaper Editors (ASNE). An organization primarily concerned with matters of editorial content and readership of newspapers.

Amplitude modulation (AM). The method of transmitting electromagnetic signals by varying the *amplitude* (size) of the electromagnetic wave, in contrast to varying its *frequency* (FM). Quality is not as good as FM but can be heard farther, especially at night. *See* Frequency modulation (FM).

Animation (TV). Making inanimate objects appear alive and moving by setting them before an animation camera and filming one frame at a time.

Appeal. The motive to which an ad is directed, it is designed to stir a person toward a goal the advertiser has set.

Arbitron Ratings Company. Syndicated radio and TV ratings company. Dominant in local radio ratings.

Audience fragmentation. The segmenting of mass-media audiences into smaller groups because of diversity of media outlets.

Audit Bureau of Circulations (ABC). The organization sponsored by publishers, agencies, and advertisers for securing accurate circulation statements.

Automatic dialing recorded message programs (ADRMP). Computerized telemarketing system that automatically dials random numbers in an area code.

Average quarter-hour estimates (AQHE). Manner in which radio ratings are presented. Estimates include average number of people listening, rating, and metro share of audience.

B

Barter syndication. Station obtains a program at no charge. The program has presold national commercials and time is available for local station spots.

Barter. Acquisition of broadcast time by an advertiser or an agency in exchange for operating capital or merchandise. No cash is involved.

Better Business Bureau. An organization launched by advertisers that now has wide business support, formed to protect the public against deceptive advertising and fraudulent business methods. Works widely at local levels. Also identified with the National Advertising Review Board.

Bleed. Printed matter that runs over the edges of an outdoor board or of a page, leaving no margin.

Bounce-back circular. An enclosure in the package of a product that has been ordered by mail. It offers other products of the same company and is effective in getting more business.

Brand Development Index (BDI). A method of allocating advertising budgets to those geographic areas that have the greatest sales potential.

Brand equity. The value of how such people as consumers, distributors, and salespeople think and feel about a brand relative to its competition over a period of time.

Brand loyalty. Degree to which a consumer purchases a certain brand without considering alternatives.

Brand name. The written or spoken part of a trademark, in contrast to the pictorial mark; a trademark word.

Brand Positioning. Consumers' perceptions of specific brands relative to the various brands of goods or services currently available to them.

Brand. A name, term, sign, design, or a unifying combination of them, intended to identify and distinguish the product or service from competing products or services.

Business-to-business advertising. Advertising that promotes goods through trade and industrial journals that are used in the manufacturing, distributing, or marketing of goods to the public.

C

Cable networks. Networks available only to cable subscribers. They are transmitted via satellite to local cable operators for redistribution either as part of basic service or at an extra cost charged to subscribers.

Cable television. TV signals that are carried to households by cable. Programs originate with cable operators through high antennas, satellite disks, or operator-initiated programming.

Category manager. A relatively new corporate position. This manager is responsible for all aspects of the brands in a specific product category for a company including research, manufacturing, sales, and advertising. Each product's advertising manager reports to the category manager. Example: Procter & Gamble's Tide and Cheer detergent report to a single Category Manager.

Cause-related marketing. Marketing strategies that attempt to link a company to some social or charitable cause.

Caveat emptor. Latin for "Let the buyer beware." Represents the notion that there should be no government interference in the marketplace.

Cease and desist orders. If an advertiser refuses to sign a consent decree, the FTC may issue a cease and desist order that can carry a $10,000-per-day fine.

Central Hudson four-part test. Supreme Court test to determine if specific commercial speech is protected under the Constitution.

Checkerboarding. When a station runs a different syndicated show in the same time slot each day.

Children's Advertising Review Unit (CARU). The CARU functions much as the NAD to review complaints about advertising to children.

Classified advertising. Found in columns so labeled, published in sections of a newspaper or magazine set aside for certain classes of goods or services—for example, Help Wanted, Positions Wanted, Houses for Sale, Cars for Sale. The ads are limited in size and generally are without illustration.

Clutter. Refers to a proliferation of commercials (in a medium) that reduces the impact of any single message.

Coined word. An original and arbitrary combination of syllables forming a word. Extensively used for trademarks, such as PoFolks, Mazola, Gro-Pup, Zerone. (Opposite of a dictionary word.)

Committee on Nationwide Television Audience Measurement (CONTAM). Industry-wide organization to improve the accuracy and reliability of television ratings.

Communications component (media plan). That portion of the media plan that considers the effectiveness of message delivery as contrasted to the efficiency of audience delivery.

Comparison advertising. Used interchangeably with the term *comparative advertising*, it directly contrasts an advertiser's product with other named or identified products.

Compensation. The payment of clearance fees by a TV network to local stations carrying its shows.

Competitive stage. The advertising stage a product reaches when its general usefulness is recognized but its superiority over similar brands has to be established in order to gain preference. (*Compare* Pioneering stage; Retentive stage.)

Computer generated imagery (CGI). Technology allowing computer operators to create multitudes of electronic effects for TV—to squash, stretch, or squeeze objects— much more quickly than earlier tools could. It can add layers of visuals simultaneously.

Concept testing. The target audience evaluation of (alternative) creative strategy. Testing attempts to separate good and bad ideas and provide insight into factors motivating acceptance or rejection.

Consent decree. Issued by the FTC. An advertiser signs the decree, stops the practice under investigation, but admits no guilt.

Consumer advertising. Directed to people who will use the product themselves, in contrast to trade advertising, industrial advertising, or professional advertising.

Consumer Price Index. Comparative index that charts what an urban family pays for a select group of goods including housing and transportation.

Contest. A promotion in which consumers compete for prizes and the winners are selected strictly on the basis of skill. *See Sweepstakes.*

Continuity. A TV or radio script. Also refers to the length of time given media schedule runs.

Continuous tone. An unscreened photographic picture or image, on paper or film, that contains all gradations of tonal values from white to black.

Controlled-circulation publications. Sent without cost to people responsible for making buying decisions. To get on such lists, people must state their positions in companies; to stay on it, they must request it annually. Also known as *qualified- circulation publications.*

Cooperative advertising. (1) Joint promotion of a national advertiser (manufacturer) and local retail outlet on behalf of the manufacturer's product on sale in the retail store. (2) Joint promotion through a trade association for firms in a single industry. (3) Advertising venture jointly conducted by two or more advertisers.

Cooperative advertising. Joint promotion of a national advertiser (manufacturer) and local retail outlet on behalf of the manufacturer's product on sale in the retail store.

Copy approach. The method of opening the text of an ad. Chief forms: factual approach, emotional approach.

Copy testing. Measuring the effectiveness of ads.

Corrective advertising. To counteract the past residual effect of previous deceptive advertising, the FTC may require the advertiser to devote future space and time to disclosure of previous deception. Began around the late 1960s.

Cost per rating point (CCP). The cost per rating point is used to estimate the cost of TV advertising on several shows.

Cost per thousand (CPM). A method of comparing the cost for media of different circulations. Also weighted or demographic cost per thousand calculates the CPM using only that portion of a medium's audience falling into a prime-prospect category.

Country-of-origin (CO) promotion. A marketing strategy that attempts to create a positive image for a product by emphasizing the county in which it was produced.

Coupon. Most popular type of sales-promotion technique.

Cross-media buys. Several media or vehicles within one medium package themselves to be sold to advertisers to gain a synergistic communication effect and efficiencies in purchasing time or space.

D

Data base marketing. A process of continually updating information about individual consumers. Popular techniques with direct-response sellers.

Digital artist. A computer specialist that works as an art director or with an art director depending on the agency structure.

Direct houses. In specialty advertising, firms that combine the functions of supplier and distributor.

Direct Market Association (DMA). Organization to promote direct-mail and direct-response advertising.

Direct marketing. Selling goods and services without the aid of wholesaler or retailer. Includes direct-response advertising and advertising for leads for sales people. Also direct door-to-door selling. Uses many media: direct mail, publications, TV, radio.

Direct premium. A sales incentive given to customers at the time of purchase.

Direct-response advertising. Any form of advertising done in direct marketing. Uses all types of media: direct mail, TV, magazines, newspapers, radio. Term replaces *mail-order advertising. See Direct marketing.*

Drive time (radio). A term used to designate the time of day when people are going to, or coming from, work. Usually 6 A.M. to 10 A.M. and 3 P.M. to 7 P.M., but this varies from one community to another. The most costly time on the rate card.

E

Effective reach. The percentage of an audience that is exposed to a certain number of messages or has achieved a specific level of awareness.

Eight-sheet poster. Outdoor poster used in urban areas, about one-fourth the size of the standard 30-sheet poster. Also called *junior poster.*

80/20 rule. Rule of thumb that says a minority of consumers (20%) will purchase a large portion (80%) of specific goods or services.

Ethnic niches. Specifically targeting marketing efforts toward narrow ethnic groups or subgroups. For instance, Hispanic: Puerto Ricans, Cubans, Mexicans, etc.; blacks, Asians, and so on.

European Community (EC). The developing economic integration of Europe. Potentially a single market of some 300 million consumers in 1991.

Event marketing. A promotion sponsored in connection with some special event such as a sports contest or musical concert.

Everyday low pricing (EDLP). A marketing strategy that uses permanent price reductions instead of occasional sales promotion incentives.

Exclusionary zones (outdoor). Industry code of conduct that prohibits the advertising of products within 500 feet of churches, schools, or hospitals of any products that cannot be used legally by children.

F

Family life cycle. Concept that demonstrates changing purchasing behavior as a person or a family matures.

Fast close. Some magazines offer short-notice ad deadlines such as a premium cost.

Federal Communications Commission (FCC). The federal authority empowered to license radio and TV stations and to assign wavelengths to stations "in the public interest."

Federal preemption. The policy of giving federal jurisdiction priority over state and local laws and regulation.

Federal Trade Commission (FTC). The agency of the federal government empowered to prevent unfair competition and to prevent fraudulent, misleading, or deceptive advertising in interstate commerce.

Flat rate. A uniform charge for space in a medium, without regard to the amount of space used or the frequency of insertion. When flat rates do not prevail, *time discounts* or *quantity discounts* are offered.

Flight. The length of time a broadcaster's campaign runs. Can be days, weeks, or months—but does not refer to a year. A flighting sche-dule alternates periods of activity with periods of inactivity.

Focus group. A qualitative research interviewing method using indepth interviews with a group rather than with an individual.

Four-color process. The process for reproducing color illustrations by a set of plates, one which prints all the yellows, another the blues, a third the reds, and the fourth the blacks (sequence variable). The plates are referred to as *process plates.*

Fragmentation. In advertising a term that refers to the increasing selectivity of media vehicles and the segmenting of the audience that results.

Free-standing inserts. Preprinted inserts distributed to newspapers, where they are inserted and delivered within the paper.

Frequency discounts. Discounts based on total time or space bought, usually within a year. Also called *bulk discounts.*

Frequency modulation (FM). A radio transmission wave that transmits by the variation in the frequency of its wave, rather than its size (as in AM modulation). An FM wave is twenty times the width of an AM wave, which is the source of its fine tone. To transmit such a wave, it has to be placed high on the electromagnetic spectrum, far from AM waves with their interference and static. Hence its outstanding tone.

Frequency. (1) The number of waves per second that a transmitter radiates, measured in kilohertz (kHz) and megahertz (MHz). The FCC assigns to each TV and radio station the frequency on which it may operate, to prevent interference with other stations. (2) Of media exposure the number of times an individual or household is exposed to a medium within a given period of time. (3) In statistics the number of times each element appears in each step of a distribution scale.

Fulfillment firm. Company that handles the couponing process including receiving, verification and payment. It also handles contests and sweepstake responses.

Full-service agency. One that handles planning, creation, production, and placement of advertising for advertising clients. May also handle sales promotion and other related services as needed by client.

G

General Agreement on Tariffs (GATT). A treaty designed to lower trade barriers among 117 nations.

Generic demand. The demand demonstrated for a product class rather than a specific brand.

Global marketing. Term that denotes the use of advertising and marketing strategies on an international basis.

Gross rating points (GRP). Each rating point represents 1 percent of the universe being measured for the market. In TV it is 1 percent of the households having TV sets in that area.

H

Harris Donovan Model (outdoor). Computerized system of measuring the audience exposed to an outdoor showing.

Highway Beautification Act of 1965. Federal law that controls outdoor signs in noncommercial, nonindustrial areas.

Hoarding. First printed outdoor signs—the forerunner of modern outdoor advertising.

House mark. A primary mark of a business concern, usually used with the trademark of its products. *General Mills* is a house mark; *Betty Crocker* is a trademark; *DuPont* is a house mark; *Teflon II* is a trademark.

I

Idea (nonproduct) advertising. Advertising used to promote an idea or cause rather than to sell a product or service.

Illuminated posters. 75 to 80% of all outdoor posters are illuminated for 24-hour exposure.

Imagery transfer research. A technique that measures the ability of radio listeners to correctly describe the primary visual elements of related television commercials.

In-house agency. An arrangement whereby the advertiser handles the total agency function by buying individually, on a fee basis, the needed services (for example, creative, media services, and placement) under the direction of an assigned advertising director.

Inadvertent role of advertising. Advertising sometimes communicates social messages unintended by the advertiser. Stereotyping and less-than-flattering portrayals of individuals and ethnic or social audience segments can lead to negative perceptions of advertising.

Incentives. Sales promotion directed at wholesalers, retailers, or a company's sales force.

Independent delivery companies. Private companies that contract with magazine publishers to deliver their publications.

Industrial advertising. Addressed to manufacturers who buy machinery, equipment, raw materials, and the components needed to produce goods they sell.

Inner brand. That tangible asset that no other brand owns.

Institutional advertising. Advertising done by an organization speaking of its work, views, and problems as a whole, to gain public goodwill and support rather than to sell a specific product. Sometimes called *public-relations advertising.*

Integrated marketing. The joint planning, execution, and coordination of all areas of marketing communication.

Interior transit signs. Signs carried inside mass transit vehicles.

J

Jingle. A commercial set to music, usually carrying the slogan or theme line of a campaign. May make a brand name and slogan more easily remembered.

Johann Gutenberg. Began the era of mass communication in 1438 with the invention of movable type.

L

Leading. (also called line spacing). Insertion of extra spacing between lines of type usually in points of space.

Letter shop. A firm that not only addresses the mailing envelope but also is mechanically equipped to insert material, seal and stamp envelopes, and deliver them to the post office according to mailing requirements.

Letterpress. Printing from a relief, or raised, surface. The raised surface is inked and comes in direct contact with the paper, like a rubber stamp. *See Offset, Rotogravure.*

Lifestyle segmentation. Identifying consumers by combining several demographics and lifestyles.

Line drawing. A drawing made with a brush, pen, pencil, or crayon, with shading produced by variations in size and spacing of lines, not by tone.

List broker. In direct-mail advertising an agent who rents the prospect lists of one advertiser to another advertiser. The broker receives a commission from the seller for this service.

List manager. Promotes client's lists to potential renters and buyers.

Lithography. A printing process by which originally an image was formed on special stone by a greasy material, the design then being transferred to the printing paper. Today the more frequently used process is *offset* lithography, in which a thin and flexible metal sheet replaces the stone. In this process the design is "offset" from the metal sheet to a rubber blanket, which then transfers the image to the printing paper.

Logotype, or logo. A trademark or trade name embodied in the form of a distinctive lettering or design. Famous example: Coca-Cola.

M

Magazine networks. Groups of magazines that can be purchased together using one insertion order and paying a single invoice.

Marcon manager. In integrated marketing communication organizations adapting the business-to-business structure where all the communication activities

is centralized under one person or office.

Market profile. A demographic and psychographic description of the people or the households of a product's market. It may also include economic and retailing information about a territory.

Market segmentation. The division of an entire market of consumers into groups whose similarity makes them a market for products serving their special needs.

Market. A group of people who can be identified by some common characteristic, interest, or problem; use a certain product to advantage; afford to buy it; and be reached through some medium.

Marketing communication. The communication components of marketing, which include public relations, advertising, personal selling, and sales promotion, are referred to as marketing communication.

Marketing concept. A management orientation that views the needs of consumers as primary to the success of a firm.

Marketing goals. The overall objectives that a company wishes to accomplish through its marketing program.

Marketing mix. Combination of marketing functions, including advertising, used to sell a product.

Marketing translation. The process of adapting a general marketing plan to a multinational environments.

Match print. A high-quality color proof used for approvals prior to printing. Similar to a Signature print.

Media buyers. Media buyers execute and monitor the media schedule developed by media planners.

Media imperatives. Based on research by Simmons Media Studies, showed the importance of using both TV and magazines for full market coverage.

Media plan. The complete analysis and execution of the media component of a campaign.

Media planners. Media planners are responsible for the overall strategy of the media component of an advertising campaign.

Media schedule. The detailed plan or calendar showing when ads and commercials will be distributed and in what media vehicles they will appear.

Media strategy. Planning of ad media buys, including identification of audience, selection of media vehicles, and determination of timing of a media schedule.

Merge/purge (merge & purge). A system used to eliminate duplication by direct-response advertisers who use different mailing lists for the same mailing. Mailing lists are sent to a central merge/purge office that electronically picks out duplicate names. Saves mailing costs, especially important to firms that send out a million pieces in one mailing. Also avoids damage to the goodwill of the public.

Mergenthaler Linotype. Ottmar Mergenthaler invented the linotype, which replaced hand-set type by automatically setting and distributing metal type.

Message management. Utilizes database information to offer different message to various consumer categories.

Morphing. An electronic technique that allows you to transform one object into another object.

Multinational advertising. The coordination and execution of advertising campaigns that are directed to a number of countries.

N

National Advertising Division (NAD). The policy-making arm of the National Advertising Review Board.

National advertising. Advertising by a marketer of a trademarked product or service sold through different outlets, in contrast to *local advertising.*

Negative-option direct response. Technique used by record and book clubs whereby a customer receives merchandise unless the seller is notified not to send it.

Network. (1) Interconnecting stations for the simultaneous transmission of TV or radio broadcasts. (2) Any group of media sold as a single unit.

Newspaper networks. Groups of newspapers that allow advertisers to buy several papers simultaneously with one insertion order and one invoice.

Niche marketing. A combination of product and target market strategy. It is a flanking strategy that focuses on niches or comparatively narrow windows of opportunity within a broad product market or industry. Its guiding principle is to pit your strength against their weakness.

Nonwired networks. Groups of radio and TV stations whose advertising is sold simultaneously by station representatives.

North American Free Trade Agreement (NAFTA). A treaty designed to eliminate trade barriers among the U.S., Mexico, and Canada.

O

Off-network syndication. Syndicated programs that previously have been aired by a major network.

On-line services. Refers to computer-accessed data bases and information services for business and home use.

Open rate. In print, the highest advertising rate at which all discounts are placed. It is also called Basic rate, Transient rate, or One-time rate.

Opticals. Visual effects that are put on a TV film in a laboratory, in contrast to those that are included as part of the original photography.

Out-of-home media. Outdoor advertising; transportation advertising.

Outbound telemarketing. A technique that involves a seller calling prospects.

Outside Producer. The production company person who is hired by the agency to create the commercial according to agency specifications.

P

Partial run editions. When magazines offer less than their entire circulation to advertisers. Partial runs include demographic, geographic, and split-run editions.

Pass-along readership. Readers who receive a publication from a primary buyer. In consumer publications, pass-along readers are considered inferior to the primary audience, but this is usually not the case with business publications.

Passive meters. Unobtrusive device that measures individual viewing habits through sensors keyed to household members.

People meter. Device that measures TV set usage by individuals rather than by households.

Per inquiry (PI). Advertising time or space where medium is paid on a per response received basis.

Personal Drive Analysis (PDA). A technique used to uncover a consumer's individual psychological drives.

Photoplatemaking. Making plates (and the films preceding the plates) for any printing process by camera, in color or black and white.

Pica, pica em. The unit for measuring width in printing. There are 6 picas to an inch. A page of type 24 picas wide is 4 inches wide.

Pioneering stage. The advertising stage of a product in which the need for such product is not recognized and must be established or in which the need has been established but the success of a commodity in filling those requirements has to be established. *See Competitive stage, Retentive stage.*

Plant operator. In outdoor advertising the local company who arranges to lease,

erect, and maintain the outdoor sign and to sell the advertising space on it.

Point (pt). The unit of measurement of type, about 1/72 inch in depth. Type is specified by its point size, as 8 pt., 12 pt., 24 pt., 48 pt. The unit for measuring thickness of paper, 0.001 inch.

Point-of-purchase advertising. Displays prepared by the manufacturer for use where the product is sold.

Positioning. Segmenting a market by creating a product to meet the needs of a select group or by using a distinctive advertising appeal to meet the needs of a specialized group, without making changes in the physical product.

Poster panel. A standard surface on which outdoor posters are placed. The posting surface is of sheet metal. An ornamental molding of standard green forms the frame. The standard poster panel is 12 feet high and 25 feet long (outside dimensions).

Preference. When all marketing conditions are equal, a consumer will choose a preferred brand over another.

Premarketing Era. The period from prehistoric times to the 18th century. During this time, buyers and sellers communicated in very primitive ways.

Premium. An item, other than the product itself, given to purchasers of a product as an inducement to buy. Can be free with a purchase (for example, on the package, in the package, or the container itself) or available upon proof of purchase and a payment (self-liquidating premium).

Printers' Ink Model Statutes (1911). The act directed at fraudulent advertising, prepared and sponsored by *Printers' Ink,* which was the pioneer advertising magazine.

PRIZM (Potential Rating Index by ZIP Market). A method of audience segmentation developed by the Claritas Corporation.

Product differentiation. Unique product attributes that set off one brand from another.

Product manager. In package goods, the person responsible for the profitability of a product (brand) or product line, including advertising decisions. Also called a brand manager.

Product timing. The correct gauging of market demand that assures successful product introduction.

Product-user segmentation. Identifying consumers by the amount of product usage.

Professional advertising. Directed at those in professions such as medicine, law, or architecture, who are in a position to recommend the use of a particular product or service to their clients.

Psychographics. A description of a market based on factors such as attitudes, opinions, interests, perceptions, and lifestyles of consumers comprising that market. *See Demographic characteristics.*

Public relations. Communication with various internal and external publics to create an image for a product or corporation.

Puffery. Advertiser's opinion of a product that is considered a legitimate expression of biased opinion.

Q

Qualitative research. This involves finding out what people say they think or feel. It is usually exploratory or diagnostic in nature.

R

Radio Advertising Bureau (RAB). Association to promote the use of radio as an advertising medium.

Radio All Dimension Audience Research (RADAR). Service of Statistical Research, Inc., major source of network radio ratings.

Rate differential. The controversial practice of newspapers charging significantly higher rates to national advertisers as compared to local accounts.

Rating point (TV). (1) The percentage of TV households in a market a TV station reaches with a program. The percentage varies with the time of day. A station may have a 10 rating between 6:00 and 6:30 P.M., and a 20 rating between 9:00 and 9:30.

Reach. The total audience a medium actually covers.

Rebate. The amount owed to an advertiser by a medium when circulation falls below some guaranteed level or the advertiser qualifies for a higher *space* or *time discount.*

Relationship marketing. A strategy that develops marketing plans from a consumer perspective.

Remnant space. Unsold advertising space in geographic or demographic editions. It is offered to advertisers at a significant discount.

Representative (rep). An individual or organization representing a medium selling time or space outside the city or origin.

Residual. A sum paid to certain talent on a TV or radio commercial every time the commercial is run after 13 weeks, for the life of the commercial.

Retail advertising. Advertising by a merchant who sells directly to the consumer.

Retentive stage. The third advertising stage of a product, reached when its general usefulness is widely known, its individual qualities are thoroughly appreciated, and it is satisfied to retain its patronage merely on the strength of its past reputation. *See Pioneering state, competitive stage.*

Reverse time table. Used in direct mail to schedule a job. The schedule starts with the date it is to reach customers and works backward to a starting date.

Ride-alongs. Direct-mail pieces that are sent with other mailings, such as bills.

Riding the boards. Inspecting an outdoor showing after posting.

Roadblocking. Simultaneously airing the same commercial on a number of stations.

Robinson-Patman Act. A federal law, enforced by the FTC. Requires a manufacturer to give proportionate discounts and advertising allowances to all competing dealers in a market. Purpose: to protect smaller merchants from unfair competition of larger buyers.

Rotary bulletins (outdoor). Movable painted bulletins that are moved from one fixed location to another one in the market at regular intervals. The locations are viewed and approved in advance by the advertiser.

Rotogravure. The method of intaglio printing in which the impression is produced by chemically etched cylinders and run on a rotary press; useful in long runs of pictorial effects.

S

Sales promotion. (1) Sales activities that supplement both personal selling and marketing, coordinate the two, and help to make them effective. For example, displays are sales promotions. (2) More loosely, the combination of personal selling, advertising, and all supplementary selling activities.

Sampling. The method of introducing and promoting merchandise by distributing a miniature or full-size trial package of the product free or at a reduced price.

Scatter plan (TV). The use of announcements, over a variety of network programs and stations, to reach as many people as possible in a market.

Screen Printing. A simple printing process that uses a stencil. It is economical but is limited in reproduction quality.

Secondary Research. Research or data that is already gathered by someone else for another purpose.

Selective binding. Binding different material directed to various reader segments in a single issue of a magazine.

Self-liquidating premium. A premium offered to consumers for a fee that covers its cost plus handling.

Service advertising. Advertising that promotes a service rather than a product.

Service mark. A word or name used in the sale of services, to identify the services of a firm and distinguish them from those of others, for example, Hertz Drive Yourself Service, Weight Watchers Diet Course. Comparable to trademarks for products.

Share of audience. The percentage of households using TV tuned to a particular program.

Short rate. The balance advertisers have to pay if they estimated that they would run more ads in a year than they did and entered a contract to pay at a favorable rate. The short rate is figured at the end of the year or sooner if advertisers fall behind schedule. It is calculated at a higher rate for the fewer insertions.

Showing. Outdoor posters are bought by groups, referred to as *showings.* The size of a showing is referred to as a 100-GRP showing or a 75- or 50-GRP showing, depending on the gross rating points of the individual boards selected.

Simmons Market Research Bureau, Inc. (SMRB). Firm that provides audience data for several media. Best known for magazine research.

Siquis. Handwritten posters in sixteenth- and seventeenth-century England—forerunners of modern advertising.

Situation analysis. The part of the advertising plan that answers the questions: Where are we today and how did we get here? It deals with the past and present.

Social responsibility. The demand that advertising be aware of its responsibility to the public. It should not only sell goods and services.

Specialty advertising. A gift given to a consumer to encourage a purchase.

Spectacular. An outdoor sign built to order, designed to be conspicuous for its location, size, lights, motion, or action. The costliest form of outdoor advertising.

Spot TV. Purchase of time from a local station, in contrast to purchasing from a network.

SRDS. Standard Rate and Data Service (SRDS) publishes a number of directories (including print production data) giving media and production information.

Standard Advertising Unit (SAU). Allows national advertisers to purchase newspaper advertising in standard units from one paper to another.

Standard Industrial Classification (SIC). The Bureau of the Budget's division of all industry into detailed standard classifications identified by code numbers. Useful in making marketing plans.

Stock music. Existing recorded music that may be purchased for use in a TV or radio commercial.

Storyboard. Series of drawings used to present a proposed commercial. Consists of illustrations of key action (video), accompanied by the audio part. Used for getting advertiser approval and as a production guide.

Substantiation. The key to FTC enforcement is that advertisers must be able to prove the claims made in their advertising.

Sweepstakes. A promotion in which prize winners are determined on the basis of chance alone. Not legal if purchaser must risk money to enter. See Contest.

Syndicated TV program. A program that is sold or distributed to more than one local station by an independent organization outside the national network structure. Includes reruns of former network entries as well as first-run programs produced specifically for the syndication market.

Synergistic effect. In media buying, combining a number of complementary media that create adverting awareness greater than the sum of each.

T

Target audience. That group that composes the present and potential prospects for a product or service.

Target marketing. Identifying and communicating with groups of prime prospects.

Telemarketing. Major area of direct marketing.

The Mass Communication Era. From the 1700s to the early decades of this century, advertisers were able to reach large segments of the population through the mass media.

The Newspaper Association of America (NAA). The major trade association of daily and Sunday newspaper publishers.

The Research Era. In recent years advertisers increasingly have been able to identify narrowly defined audience segments through sophisticated research methods.

The War Advertising Council. Forerunner of Advertising Council. Agency and media members provided free advertising to support the war effort during WWII.

Theater of the mind. In radio, a writer paints pictures in the mind of the listener through the use of sound.

Time-shift viewing. Recording programs on a VCR for viewing at a later time.

Total market coverage (TMC). Where newspapers augment their circulation with direct mail or shoppers to deliver all households in a market.

Trade advertising. Advertising directed to the wholesale or retail merchants or sales agencies through whom the product is sold.

Trade name. A name that applies to a business as a whole, not to an individual product.

Trade paper. A business publication directed to those who buy products for resale (wholesalers, jobbers, retailers).

Trademark. Any device or word that identifies the origin of a product, telling who made it or who sold it. Not to be confused with *trade name*.

Traffic Audit Bureau for Media Measurement (TAB). An organization designed to investigate how many people pass and may see a given outdoor sign, to establish a method of evaluating traffic measuring a market.

Traffic building premium. A sales incentive to encourage customers to come to a store where a sale can be closed.

TV Director. The person who casts and rehearses a commercial and is the key person in the shooting of the commercial.

TvQ. A service of Marketing Evaluations that measures the popularity (opinion of audience rather than size of audience) of shows and personalities.

Typography. The art of using type effectively.

U

Up-front buys. Purchase of network TV time by national advertisers during the first offering by networks. Most expensive network advertising.

Upselling. A telemarketing technique designed to sell additional merchandise to callers.

V

Value. The subjective worth that a consumer places on a product.

Values and lifestyles system (VALS). Developed by SRI International to cluster consumers according to several variables in order to predict consumer behavior.

Vendor program. Special form of co-op advertising where a retailer designs the program and approaches advertisers for support.

Vertical publications. Business publications dealing with the problems of a specific industry: for example, *Chain Store Age, National Petroleum News, Textile World. See also Horizontal publications.*

Videologs. Catalogs produced on video cassettes, intended for specialized audiences.

W

Wheeler-Lea Amendments. Broadened the scope of the FTC to include consumer advertising.

Winsted Hosiery Company. The case of *FTC v. Winsted Hosiery Company* established the precedent that false advertising was an unfair trade practice.

Z

Zoning. Newspaper practice of offering advertisers partial coverage of a market, often accomplished with weekly inserts distributed to certain sections of that market.

Index

M

McCabe & Company, 501
McCann-Erickson, Inc., 146, 148, 149, 497, 679, 680, 718
Machine finish paper, 438
Macintosh computer, 82, 608, 629
Magazine(s), 23. *See also* Business press and business-to-business advertising; Consumer magazine(s)
  as advertising medium, 329–33
  complementary use of TV and, 329, 330
  dates for, 332–33, 348
  direct-response advertising and, 416–17
  elements of, 337–43
  features of advertising in, 333–37
  forerunners of, 11
  19th century, 11–12, 13
  pros and cons of, 196–97
  psychographic research and, 336–37
  selectivity of audiences, 417, 418
Magazine Publishers of America (MPA), 136, 324, 328, 338*n*
  1994–1995 Magazine Handbook, 325
Magazine rate structure, 345–46
Magazine supplements, 316–17, 329
Mailing house, selecting, 440
Mailing list, 431–34
  ML/USA's List Usage Guidelines, 434–35
  pretesting, 429–30
Mailing List Users and Suppliers Association, 434
Mail order. *See* Direct marketing
Mail-order advertising. *See* Direct-response advertising
Mail-production program, 438–40
Majority fallacy, 105
Make-goods, 232
Makers (consumers), 494
Management and finance department in agency, 143
Management philosophy of advertising, 50
Management publications, 365
Managers
  brand, 160
  category, 160, 162, 174
  communications, 164
  marcon, 163, 164
Manual effects, 617
Manufacturer to wholesaler co-op, 469
MARC, 144
Marcon manager, 163, 164
Margeotes/Fertitta & Weiss, 547
Market, 105
  profile of, 115–16
Market audit for international client, 722–23
Market context, 88–89
Marketing, 28
  global, 710–15, 782
  integrated, 31–36
  packaging and, 652, 653–55
Marketing approach to visualization, 536
Marketing climate, analyzing, 666
Marketing communication, 28, 29. *See also* Integrated marketing communication
Marketing concept, 102–6
Marketing environment, 170–74, 496
Marketing evaluations, 254
Marketing goals, 28, 178
Marketing mix, 31–32, 51

Marketing plan, 28–29, 40
Marketing problem, analyzing, 139
Marketing process, 50–63
  business and professional advertising and, 54–57
  consumer advertising and, 52–53
  nonproduct advertising and, 57–59
  stages of, 29–31
Marketing research. *See* Upfront (marketing) research
Marketing revolution, 97
Marketing services department in agency, 142–43
Marketing-services system, 159–60, 161
Marketing translation, 722, 723
Market profile, 115–16
Market research, 499–500
Market segmentation, 106–10. *See also* Niche marketing; Positioning
  benefits and attitude segmentation, 110
  by brand loyalty, 103–5
  geographic segmentation, 107–8
  lifestyle segmentation, 109–10
  product differentiation and, 47
  product-user segmentation, 108–9
  risks in, 110
Market Segment Research, 99
Market segregation, PRIZM system, 200–201, 202
Market share, 30, 74, 115
Markups, 153
Married couples, 101
Martin Agency, 73, 133, 134, 148, 511, 512, 670, 671
Mass appeal strategy, 290, 294
Mass Communication Era, 5
Mass production, 13–14
Master brands, 93
Match print, 583
Matriarchs, 693
Matte, 599
Mature couples, 101
Maxi Marketing, 87
Max Plan, 214
Measured marketing, 702
Mechanicals, 543–44, 569–83
Media
  advertising from 1870–1900 and, 11–12
  clearance process and, 756–57
  estimated advertising expenditures in major (1994), 193
  interactive, 187, 204, 415
  out-of-home, 373
  targeting of, 188
  usage levels from country to country, 723–25
Media alliances, 155–56
Media brokers, 725–26, 727
Media buyers, 143, 190
Media buying combines, 725, 726–27
Media-buying services, 151–52
Media commissions, 152–53
Media competition, 297, 327
Media departments, 187–93
  media buying department, 190–93
  media planning department, 188
  media research department, 189
Media director, 143, 152
Media diversity, 190–91
Media equity segments, 332

Media imperatives, 327, 328
Media negotiation, 191–92
Media Networks, 349
Media Nielsen Research, 219
Media objectives, 672–74
Media plan. *See under* Media strategy
Media planners, 190, 297
Media services, unbundling of, 192–93
Media strategy, 186–216, 672. *See also specific media*
  agency media departments and, 187–93
  budget, 213, 233
  competition and, pressure of, 210–13
  cross-media concept and, 213–14
  defined, 188
  media characteristics and, 193–98
  media plan, 140, 187, 198–208; communication requirements and creative elements, 201–4; defined, 191; efficiency/effectiveness balance, 205–8; geography and, 204–5; international advertising and, 722–27; target audience and, 198–201
  media schedule, 209–10
Media synergism, 245, 329, 357–58
Mega-agencies, 148–49
Megabrands, 93
Mega-Brands survey, 86
Mega warehouses, 689
Men, classifications of, 693
Merchandising (value-added) programs, 310, 343–45
Mergenthaler linotype, 10
Merge/purge (merge & purge), 432
Mergers, ad agency, 133, 147
Message
  creative message development, 406
  direct-response, testing, 430
  targeting of, 188
Message management, 425, 427
Message research, advertising, 500–502
Metered audience measurement, 253
Metro rating area, 235
Metro survey area (MSA), 281
Mezzotint line conversion, 575
MGI Education Network System, 431
Micromarketing, 122
MIDI (musical instrument digital interface), 629
Milline rate, 311
Minority groups. *See also* African Americans; Hispanics
  changes in, 99–101
  treatment in advertising, 774–75
Misrepresentation of competition, 754
ML/USA List and Data Usage Guidelines, 434–35
Model Statute, *Printers' Ink*, 16
Moderation, 171
Mood imagery, 592
Morphing, 609
Morris & Fellows, 623
Mortise, 573, 575
Motel 6, 622
Motivation, 491
Motivational research, 514
Movement, music for, 601
Movies, placing products in, 742
MPA, 330, 331, 334, 338, 340
MRI Business-to-Business, 126

Out-of-home advertising, 372–96, 725
   outdoor advertising, 6–7, 8, 197–98, 373–89; advantages/disadvantages of, 198, 375–76; audience measurement, 388; buying, 386–87; Consumer Outdoor Recognition Study (CORS), 507; designing, 384–86; forms of, 380–84; image of, 377–78, 389; outdoor networks, 387; overview of industry, 373–80; plan, 379–80; trends in, 388–89; verifying, 387
   shelter advertising, 392, 394
   transit advertising, 389–91, 393
Out-of-home media, 373
Outside producer, 603, 605
Overlay proofs, 583
Overt social role of advertising, 774, 778–86

P

Package inserts, 436
Package plans, radio, 278
Package rates, 238
PackageValue, 658
Packaging, 634–35, 651–60
   brand identity and, 656
   color influence and, 651–53
   cotrends and, 657
   design firms for, 659–60, 661
   food-labeling mandate, 659
   legal aspects of, 658
   marketing and, 652, 653–55
   package design, 652, 657–58
   package differentiation, 655–56
   package research, 655
   unique designs for brand image, 656
PACT (Position Advertising Copy Testing), 179–80, 502–3
Paid circulation, 350
Painted bulletins, 388
Pampers disposable diapers, 30, 42, 727
Panning, 591
Pantone Color Imaging Guide, 577
Pantone Color Institute, 542
Pantone Matching System (PMS), 570
Paper for direct-mail advertising, selecting, 438–39
Parity performance, 170
Partial-run magazine editions, 330, 333–36
Pass-along readership, 350, 351, 365
Passive people meter, 253
Patent applications, 10
Patent-medicine advertising, 12, 13
Patriarchs (shopper group), 693
Patricians (shopper group), 693
Payout plan, 168–69
Penny newspapers, 11
People for the Ethical Treatment of Animals (PETA), 756–57
People meters, 253, 277
Peopletalk, 486
Percentage of sales method of budgeting, 167–68
Perception, consumer, 44, 46, 47, 69–70
Performance fee, 153
Performance Reporting and Auditing System (PRAS), 388
Performer Q, 254
Per-inquiry (PI) advertising, 416–17
Permanent decoys, 434

Personal computers, 79–80
Personal Drive Analysis (PDA), 495–96
Personality types, matching media with, 331, 332
Personal medium, radio as, 260
Personal message, direct response as, 398–99
Personal names as trademarks, 639–40
Personal responsibility, 172
Personal selling, 32, 426–27
Peterson & Blyth, 660
Peterson Magazine Network, 349
Peterson Publishing Company, 349
Petrina Trace Show Training System, 471
Photoengraving, 558
Photography, 547–48
   sources of, 548–51
Photomatics, 504
Photoplatemaking (prepress), 569–74
   offset and gravure, 583–84
Photoshop, 546
Pica, pica em, 566
Pick-up rates, 310
Pictorial trademarks, 641
Pioneering advertising stage, 67–72, 75–77
   newer and newest, 79–81
Pixel, 544
Place-based media planning, 200
Plan, media. *See under* Media strategy
Planning, 64–95
   advertising stages of product and, 67–83; advertising spiral, 74–75, 80, 81–83; competitive stage, 72–74, 75–76; new pioneering stage, 79–82, 84; pioneering stage, 67–72, 75–77; retentive stage, 74, 75, 77; after retentive stage, 77–79
   of direct-mail piece, 436–38
   Lintas:Link and, 88–94, 485, 530, 664
   outdoor advertising, 379–80
   print production, 555–58
   TV commercial, 594–96
Plant operator, 380
Pocket people meter, 253
Point-of-purchase advertising, 447–49
Point-of-Purchase Advertising Institute, 693
Point-of-purchase merchandising, 693–94
Point (pt), 566
Politics, television and, 22
Pollack Levitt Chalet, 224, 545, 546
Polyfax, 358
POPAI Supermarket Buying Habits Study, 448, 449
Popularity seekers (shopper group), 497
Popular magazines, 12
Population
   growth from 1870–1900, advertising and, 9–10
   by region, 206
   shifts, newspapers and, 23
   trends in, 97–98
Portable people meter, 277
Posada De Puerto Rico Associates v. *Tourism Company of Puerto Rico*, 747
Position Advertising Copy Testing (PACT), 179–80, 502–3
Positioning, 112–15
   brand, 90
   defined, 664
   to expand brand share, 113–14
   how to approach problem of, 114–15
   technological leader, 612

Position of advertising in consumer magazines, 337–38
Post-buy inspection, 380, 387
Poster panels, 380–81
Poster test, 503
Posttests of advertising campaign, 674–80
Postproduction process for TV commercial, 602, 606–9
Potential Rating Index by Zip Code (PRIZM) system, 126, 200–201, 202, 283, 337
Power consumption, 11
Practicals (shopper group), 693
Pragmatists (shopper group), 496
Predictive dialing, 410–11
Preemptible with two weeks' notice, 237, 238
Preemption, federal, 744
Preemption rate, 237–38
Preference, brand, 29–30
Preferred-position rates, 309
Premarketing Era, 5
Premiums, 449–53, 457
Preprinted newspaper inserts, 699
Preproduction for TV commercial, 602, 603
Prerecorded radio commercial, 630
Presses, sheet-fed versus web-fed, 560
Press proofs, 582–83
Presstek/Heidelberg GTo-DI, 586
Prestige of magazines, 416
Pretesting, 497, 498, 675
Pretest research, 501–2
Price, 47–49
   advertising level and, 61
   everyday low pricing (EDLP), 457–58
   as strategic marketing tool, 48
Price/McNabb Advertising, 594, 630
Prime prospects, 97, 666
Primetime Access Rule, 240
Principle-oriented consumers, 493–94
Printer, selecting a, 439–40
Printer controllers, 584
Printers' Ink Model Statutes (1911), 750–51
Printing buyers, 553–54
Print producers, 553
Print production, 552–87
   computer production, 555–58
   duplicate material, making, 584–85
   functions in, 553–54
   mechanical and artwork, 569–83; color proofing, 577–82; desktop color, 574–77; halftones, 12, 570–74; line plates, 569–70; press proofs, 582–83
   new technology, 585–86
   offset and gravure photoplatemaking, 583–84
   planning and scheduling, 555–58
   printing process, selecting, 558–61
   production data, 554–55
   typography, 561–69; measurement of type, 566–67; reading and, 561–63; typefaces, 563, 565; type fonts and families, 563–65; typesetting methods, 567–69
Print testing example, 505
Privacy, invasion of, 338, 402
Private-label deal segment, 104
Private-label loyal segment, 104
Private-label switcher, 104
PRIZM system, 126, 200–201, 202, 283, 337
Problems, outlining of, 28
Problem solution technique, 592
Producer, TV commercial, 603–5

Wheeler-Lea Act (1938), 19, 737
White space, 543
Wholesale clubs, 689
Wholesalers, space, 135
Wieden & Kennedy, 511, 719
Wipe, 599–600
Women
  in ads and commercials, 774–75
  classificaitons for, 692–93
  marketing to, 782
  newspaper reading by, 295
Women's Home Companion, 23
Wool Bureau, 646
Words for radio commercials, 617
Work plan, creative, 530
Works Progress Administration (WPA), 19

World economic order, new, 710, 715–18
World War I, advertising in, 17
World War II, advertising in, 19–22
Writing stocks, 438
WSL Marketing, 99, 100

X

Xerox, 528, 639

Y

Yankelovich Clancy Shulman, 112
Young adults, newspaper reading by, 295
Young & Rubicam, 486, 530

Z

Zimmerman Agency, 123, 166, 539, 568, 572, 642
ZIP codes, penetration by, 298–99
ZIP program, 699
Zoned editions, 298–99
Zones Area Preprint (ZAP) Program, 299, 699
Zoning, 298

1986

9th edition

The emergence of new technology opened significant markets for advertising. It also required a level of communication and creativity unique in advertising history.

N C R

1988

10th edition

The segmented market of the 1980s required substantial changes in companies' approaches to product development, marketing, and advertising.

S W A T C H

K E L L O G G ' S

1983

8th edition

The 1980s marked the beginning of a widespread consumer movement where advertising was held accountable for nutritional, environmental, and other socially beneficial information.

Roses are forever